GUNSLINGER GIRL

OMNIBUS COLLECTION 1

Vol. 1-3

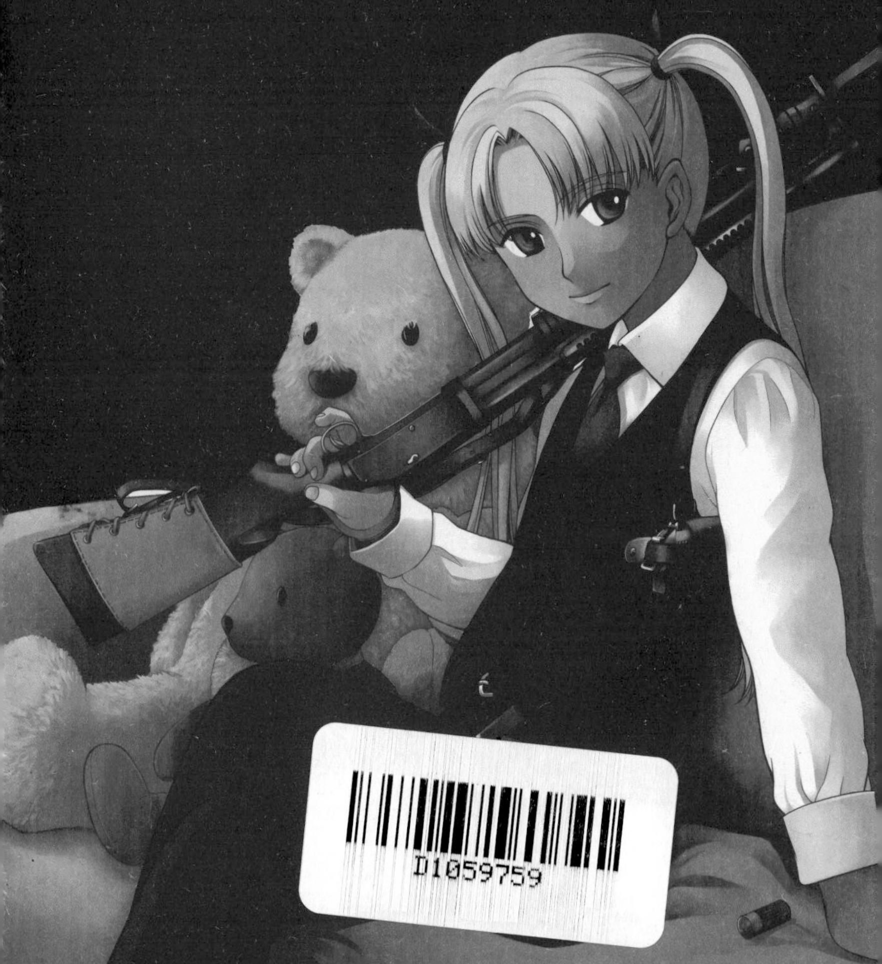

STORY & ART BY

YU AIDA

GUNSLINGERGIRL

OMNIBUS COLLECTION 1

Vol. 1-3

STORY & ART BY
YU AIDA

STAFF CREDITS

translation	Adrienne Beck
adaptation	Janet Houck
retouch & lettering	Roland Amago
cover design	Nicky Lim
layout	Bambi Eloriaga-Amago
copy editor	Shanti Whitesides
editor	Adam Arnold

publisher	Jason DeAngelis
	Seven Seas Entertainment

GUNSLINGER GIRL OMNIBUS COLLECTION 1
Content originally published as Gunslinger Girl Vol. 1-3.
Copyright © Yu Aida 2002-2004
First published in 2002-2004 by Media Works Inc., Tokyo, Japan.
English translation rights arranged with ASCII MEDIA WORKS.

Visit us online at www.gomanga.com.

ISBN: 978-1-934876-92-3

Printed in Canada

First Printing: February 2011

10 9 8 7 6 5 4 3

CONTENTS

Vol. 1-3

Chapter 1:   Astronomical Observations   005

Chapter 2:   Love Thy Neighbor   043

Chapter 3:   The Snow White   077

Chapter 4:   The Death of Elsa de Sica, Part 1   111

Chapter 5:   The Death of Elsa de Sica, Part 2   143

Chapter 6:   A Kitchen Garden   181

Chapter 7:   Gelato in Piazza di Spagna   215

Chapter 8:   Ode to Joy   241

Chapter 9:   How Beautiful My Florence Is!   259

Chapter 10: The Prince of the Kingdom of Pasta, Part 1   291

Chapter 11: The Prince of the Kingdom of Pasta, Part 2   315

Chapter 12: Kaleidoscope   349

Chapter 13: Pinocchio (1)   366

Chapter 14: Pinocchio (2)   399

Chapter 15: Pinocchio (3)   421

Chapter 16: Sever the Chains of Retaliation   454

Chapter 17: Retiring Tibetan Terrier   489

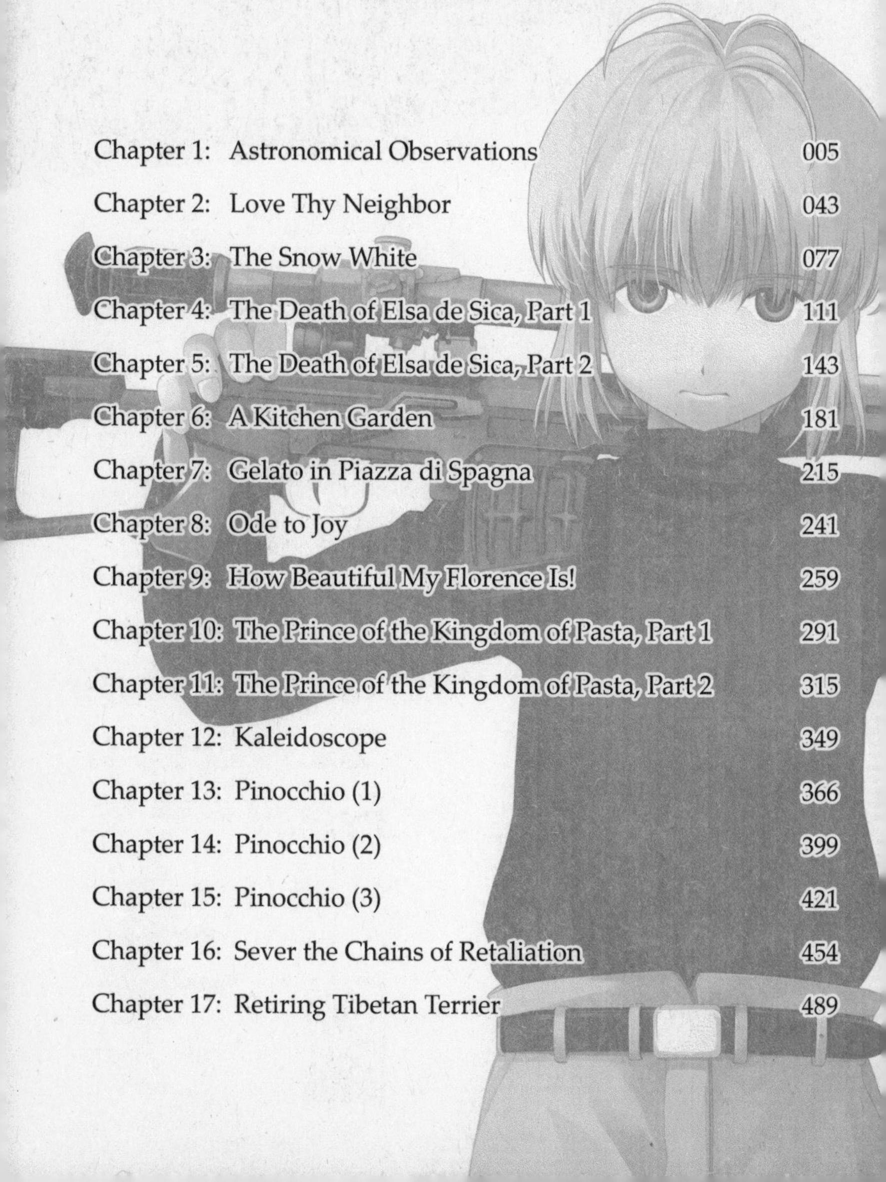

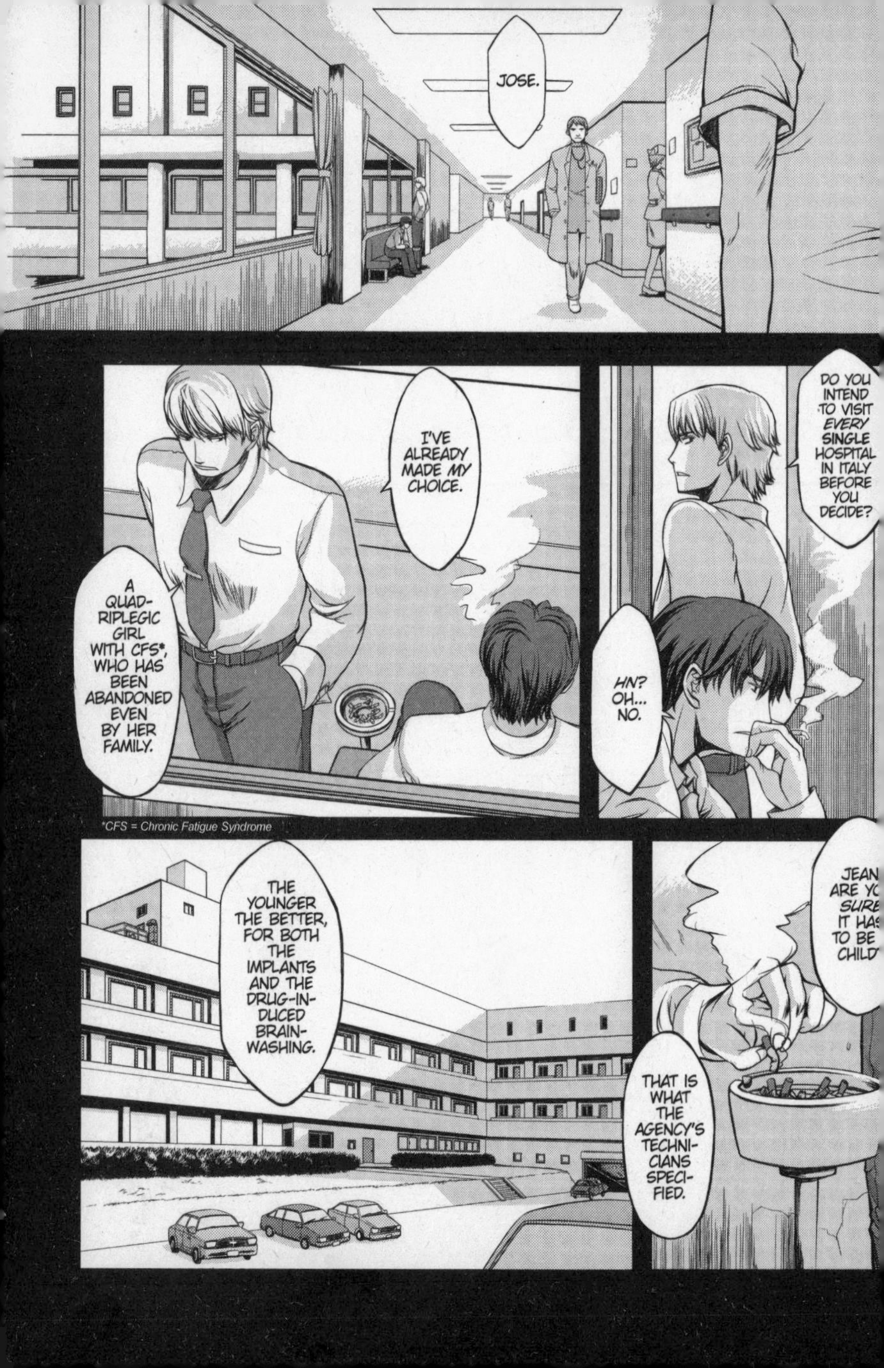
JOSE.
DO YOU INTEND TO VISIT *EVERY* SINGLE HOSPITAL IN ITALY BEFORE YOU DECIDE?
HN? OH... NO.
I'VE ALREADY MADE *MY* CHOICE.
A QUAD-RIPLEGIC GIRL WITH CFS*, WHO HAS BEEN ABANDONED EVEN BY HER FAMILY.
JEAN ARE YO *SURE* IT HA TO BE CHILD
THAT IS WHAT THE AGENCY'S TECHNI-CIANS SPECI-FIED.
THE YOUNGER THE BETTER, FOR BOTH THE IMPLANTS AND THE DRUG-IN-DUCED BRAIN-WASHING.

*CFS = Chronic Fatigue Syndrome

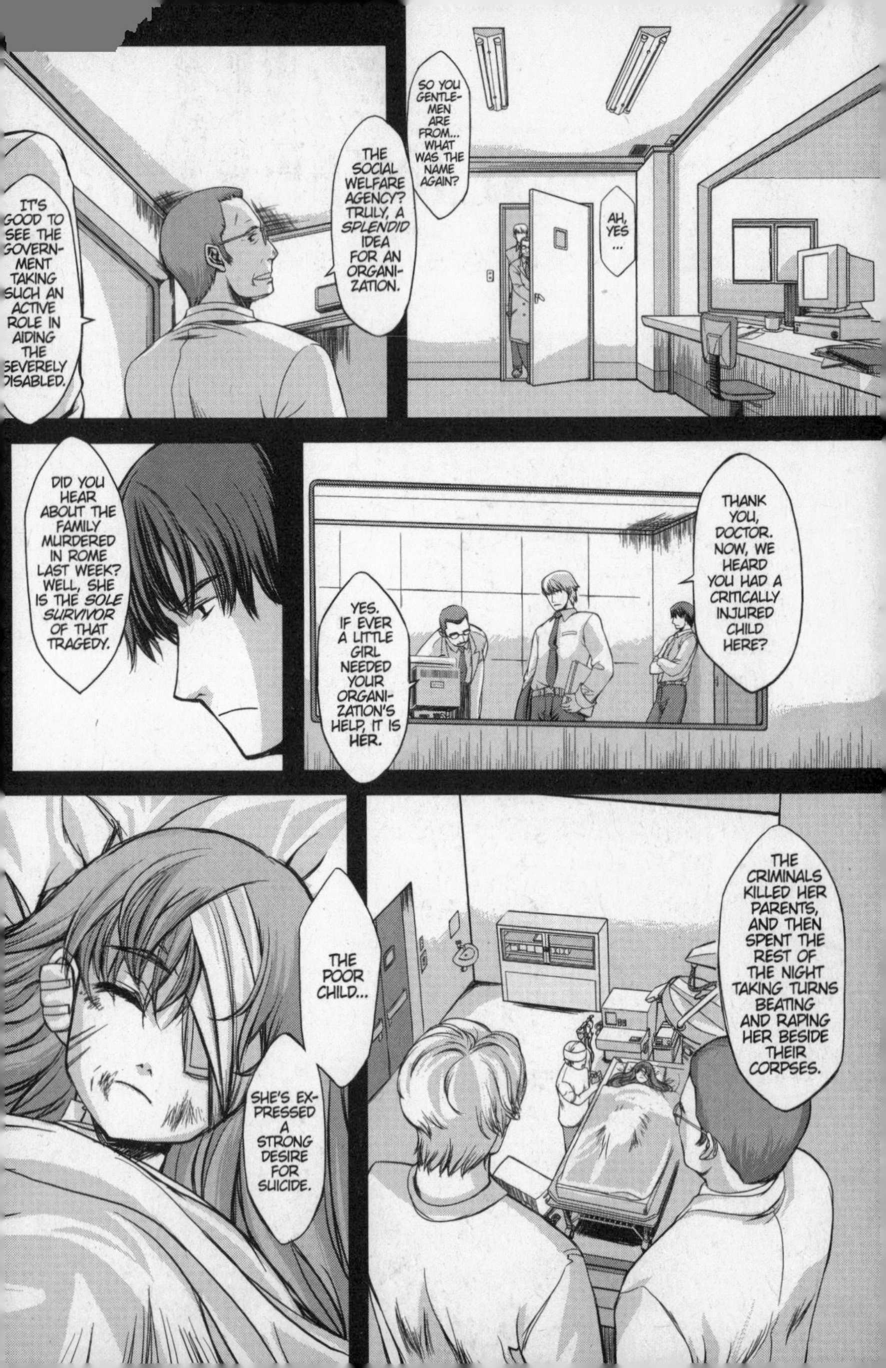
SO YOU GENTLEMEN ARE FROM... WHAT WAS THE NAME AGAIN?
AH, YES ...
THE SOCIAL WELFARE AGENCY? TRULY, A *SPLENDID* IDEA FOR AN ORGANIZATION.
IT'S GOOD TO SEE THE GOVERNMENT TAKING SUCH AN ACTIVE ROLE IN AIDING THE SEVERELY DISABLED.
THANK YOU, DOCTOR. NOW, WE HEARD YOU HAD A CRITICALLY INJURED CHILD HERE?
YES. IF EVER A LITTLE GIRL NEEDED YOUR ORGANIZATION'S HELP, IT IS HER.
DID YOU HEAR ABOUT THE FAMILY MURDERED IN ROME LAST WEEK? WELL, SHE IS THE *SOLE SURVIVOR* OF THAT TRAGEDY.
THE CRIMINALS KILLED HER PARENTS, AND THEN SPENT THE REST OF THE NIGHT TAKING TURNS BEATING AND RAPING HER BESIDE THEIR CORPSES.
THE POOR CHILD...
SHE'S EXPRESSED A STRONG DESIRE FOR SUICIDE.

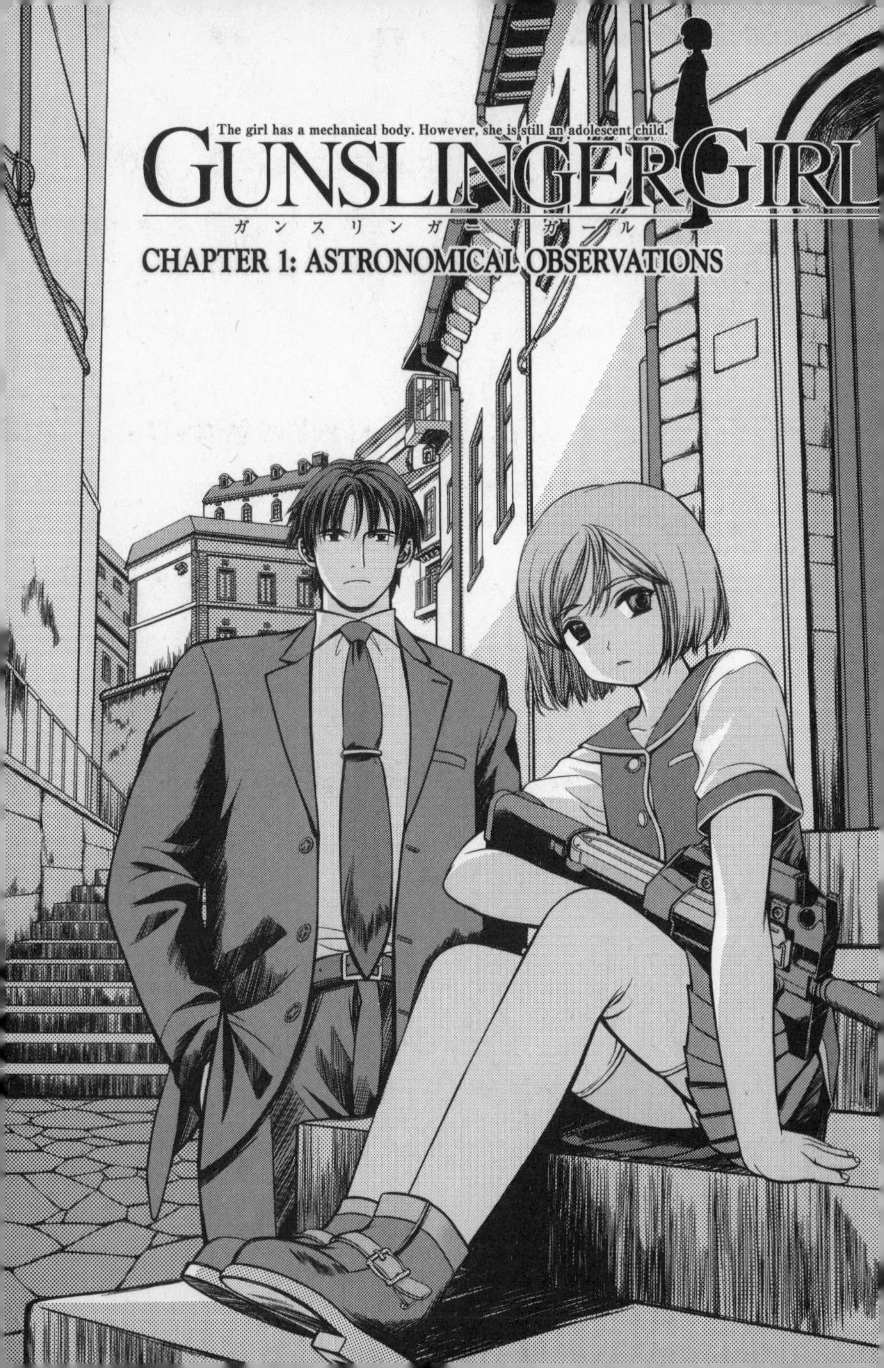
The girl has a mechanical body. However, she is still an adolescent child.
GUNSLINGER GIRL
ガンスリンガー ガール
CHAPTER 1: ASTRONOMICAL OBSERVATIONS

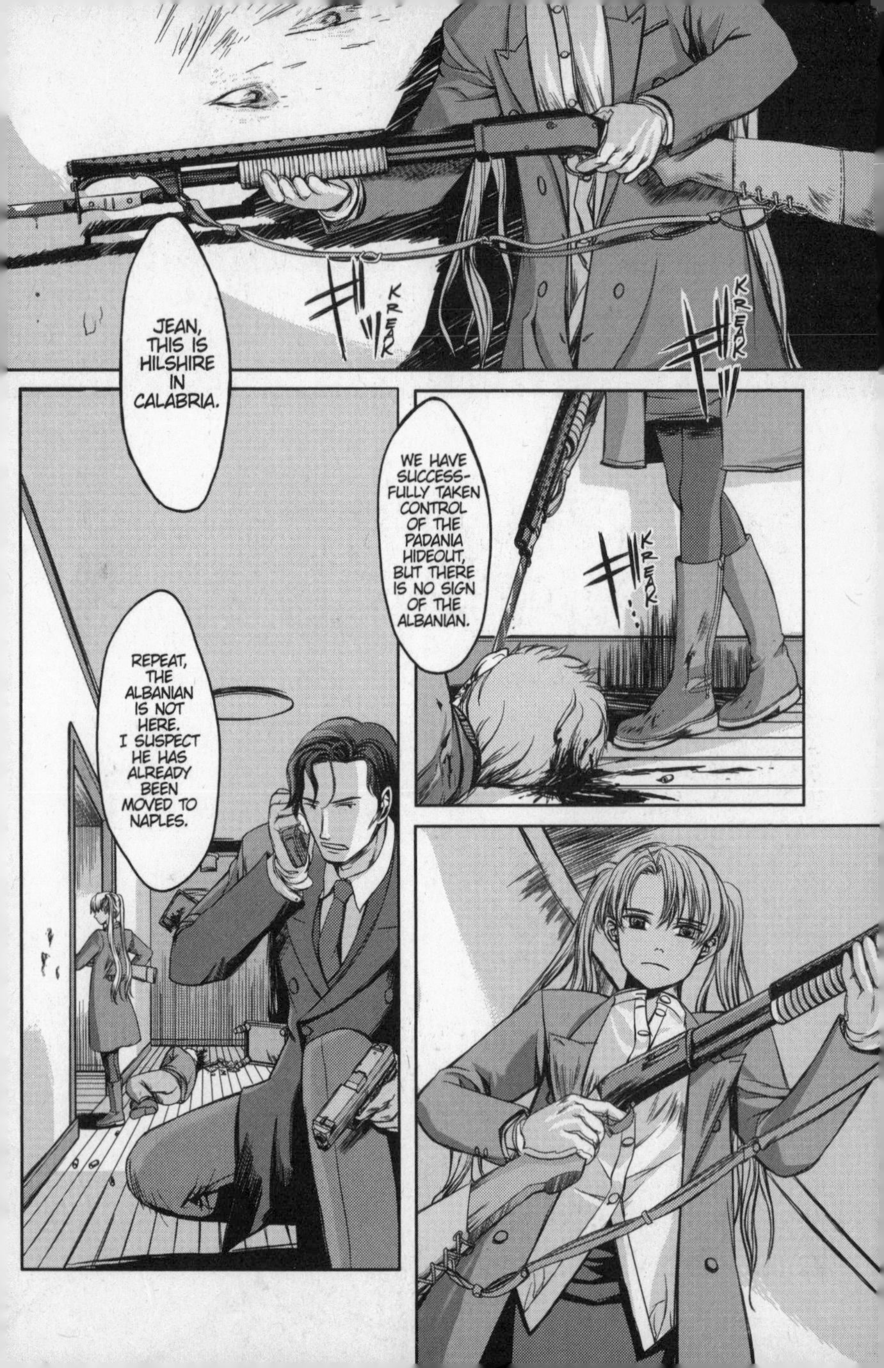
KREAK
KREAK
JEAN, THIS IS HILSHIRE IN CALABRIA.
WE HAVE SUCCESS-FULLY TAKEN CONTROL OF THE PADANIA HIDEOUT, BUT THERE IS NO SIGN OF THE ALBANIAN.
KREAK
REPEAT, THE ALBANIAN IS NOT HERE. I SUSPECT HE HAS ALREADY BEEN MOVED TO NAPLES.

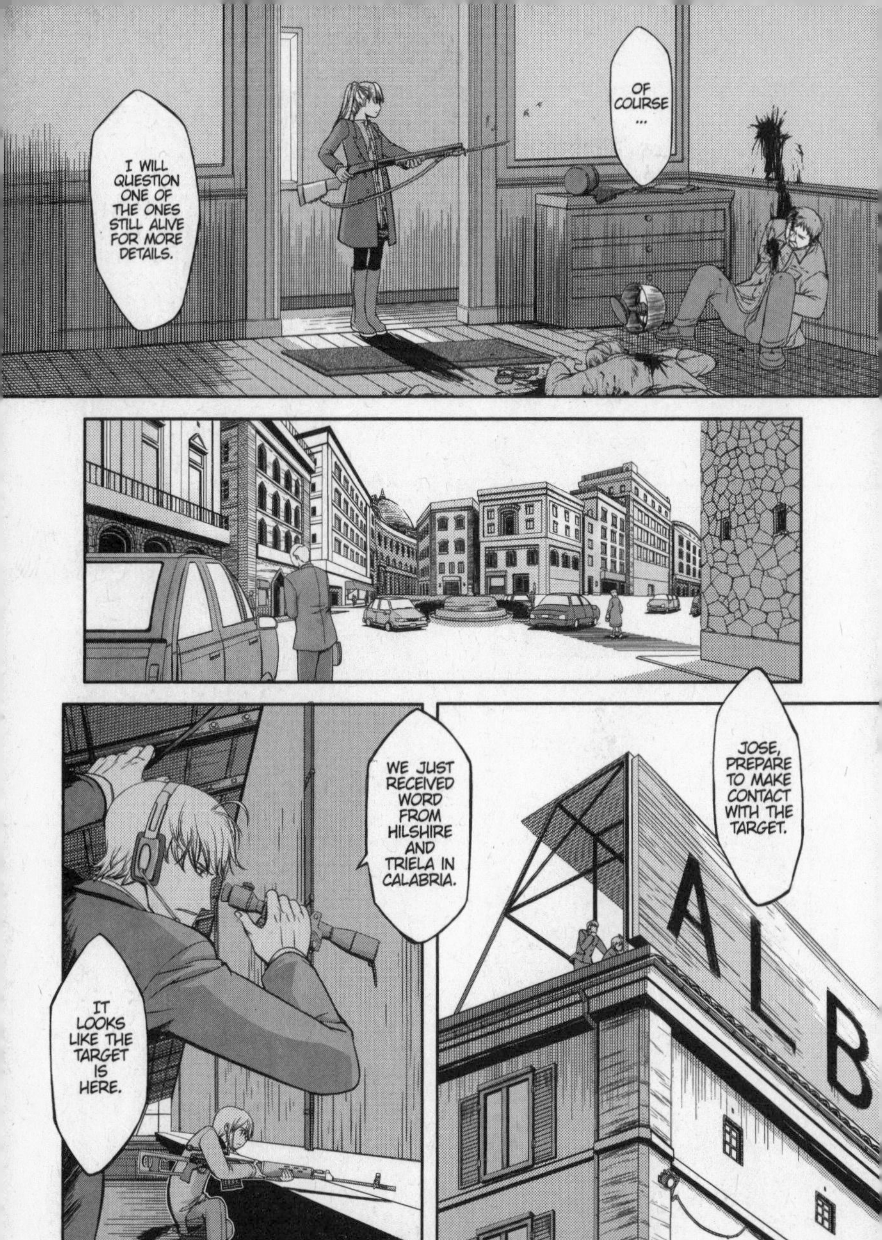
OF COURSE ...
I WILL QUESTION ONE OF THE ONES STILL ALIVE FOR MORE DETAILS.
JOSE, PREPARE TO MAKE CONTACT WITH THE TARGET.
ALB
WE JUST RECEIVED WORD FROM HILSHIRE AND TRIELA IN CALABRIA.
IT LOOKS LIKE THE TARGET IS HERE.

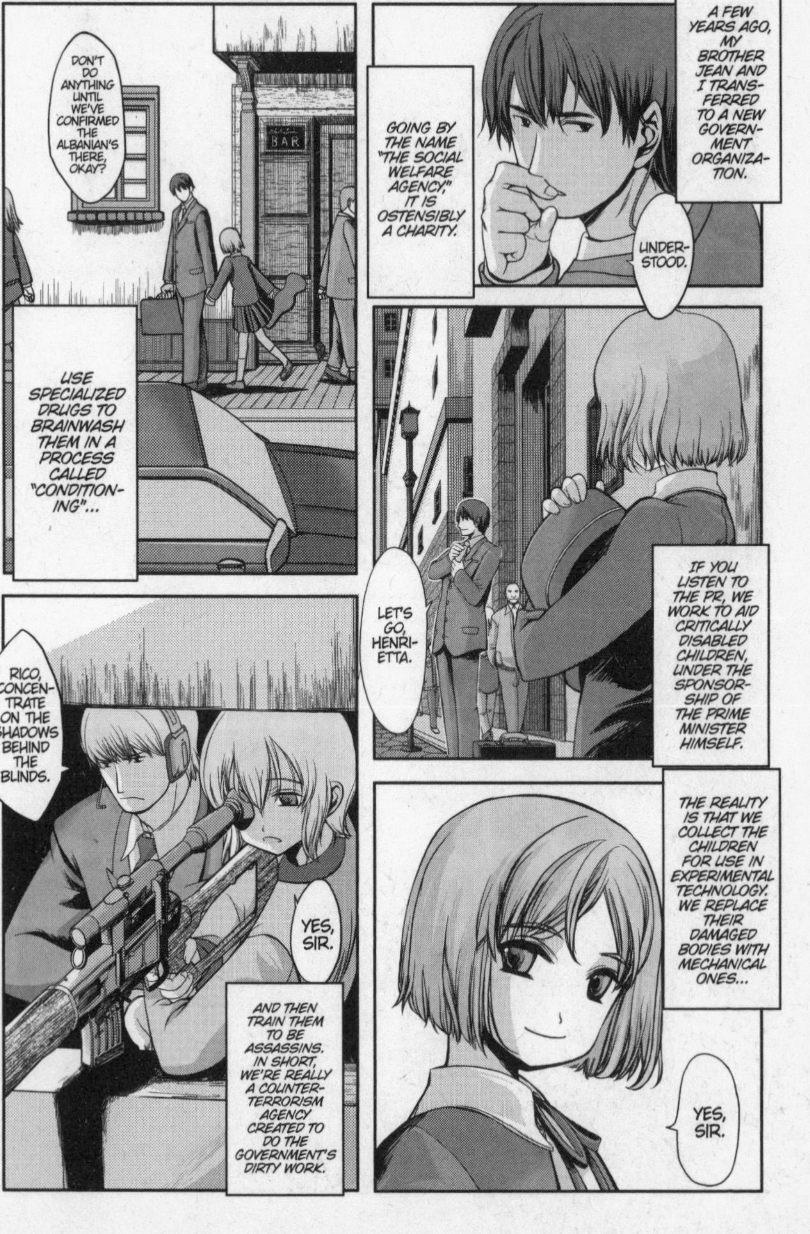

A FEW YEARS AGO, MY BROTHER JEAN AND I TRANSFERRED TO A NEW GOVERNMENT ORGANIZATION.
GOING BY THE NAME "THE SOCIAL WELFARE AGENCY," IT IS OSTENSIBLY A CHARITY.
UNDERSTOOD.
IF YOU LISTEN TO THE PR, WE WORK TO AID CRITICALLY DISABLED CHILDREN, UNDER THE SPONSORSHIP OF THE PRIME MINISTER HIMSELF.
LET'S GO, HENRIETTA.
THE REALITY IS THAT WE COLLECT THE CHILDREN FOR USE IN EXPERIMENTAL TECHNOLOGY. WE REPLACE THEIR DAMAGED BODIES WITH MECHANICAL ONES...
YES, SIR.
DON'T DO ANYTHING UNTIL WE'VE CONFIRMED THE ALBANIAN'S THERE, OKAY?
BAR
USE SPECIALIZED DRUGS TO BRAINWASH THEM IN A PROCESS CALLED "CONDITIONING"...
RICO, CONCENTRATE ON THE SHADOWS BEHIND THE BLINDS.
YES, SIR.
AND THEN TRAIN THEM TO BE ASSASSINS. IN SHORT, WE'RE REALLY A COUNTER-TERRORISM AGENCY CREATED TO DO THE GOVERNMENT'S DIRTY WORK.

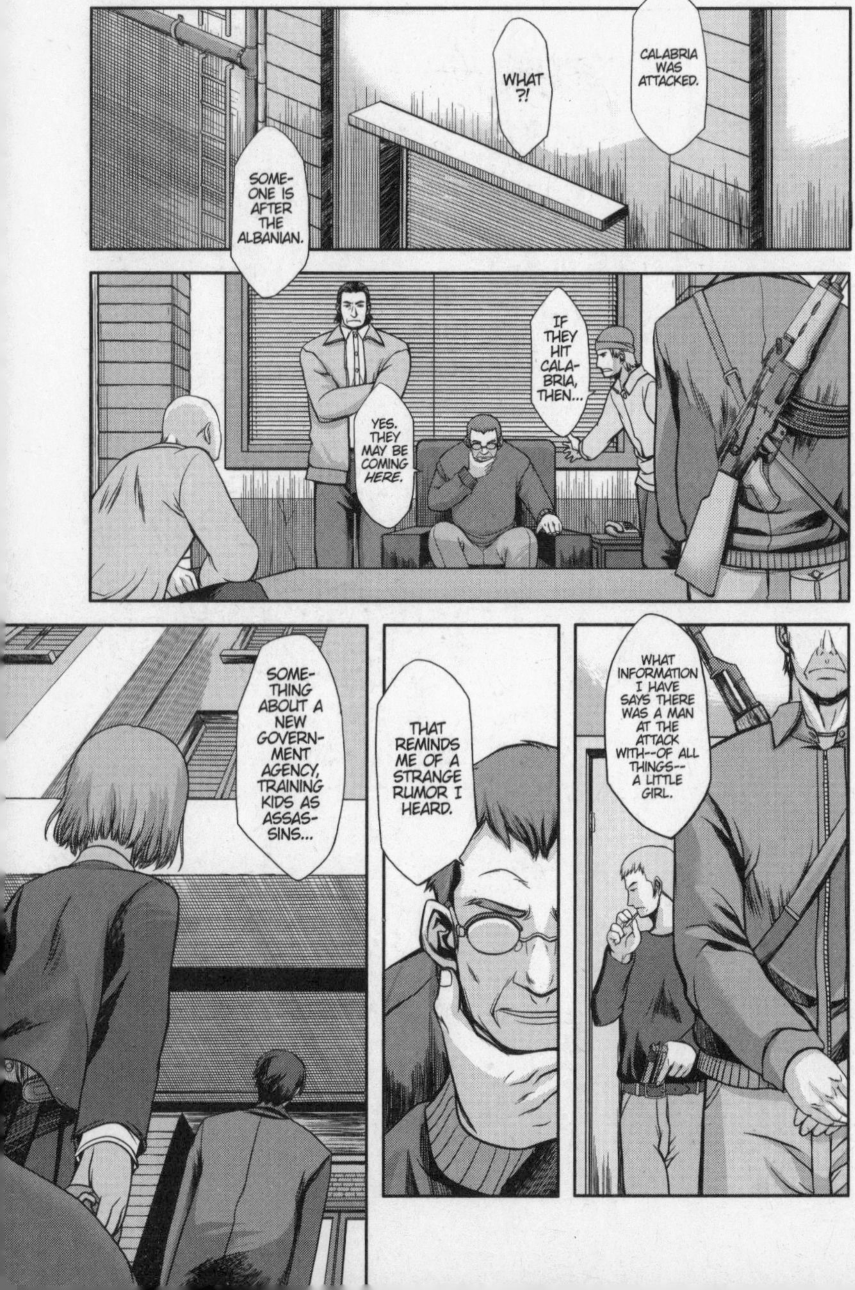
CALABRIA WAS ATTACKED.
WHAT ?!
SOMEONE IS AFTER THE ALBANIAN.
IF THEY HIT CALABRIA, THEN...
YES. THEY MAY BE COMING HERE.
WHAT INFORMATION I HAVE SAYS THERE WAS A MAN AT THE ATTACK WITH--OF ALL THINGS--A LITTLE GIRL.
THAT REMINDS ME OF A STRANGE RUMOR I HEARD.
SOMETHING ABOUT A NEW GOVERNMENT AGENCY, TRAINING KIDS AS ASSASSINS...

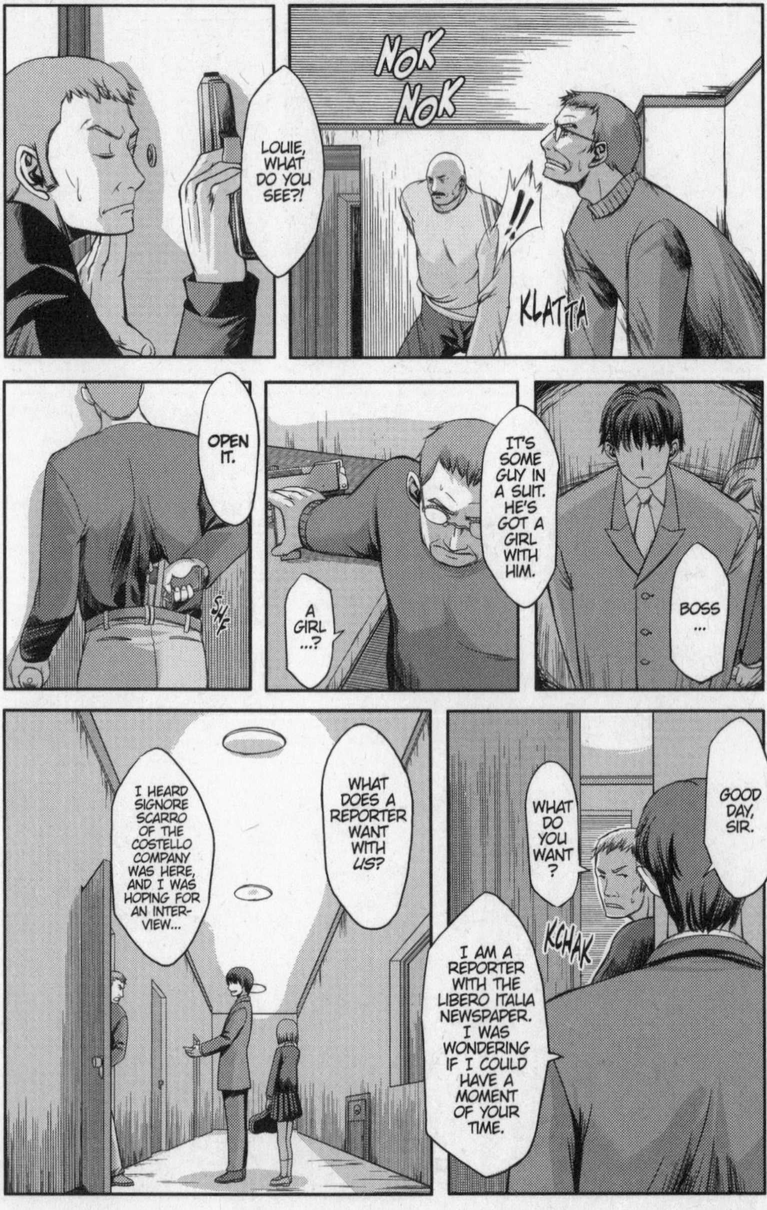
NOK NOK
KLATTA
LOUIE, WHAT DO YOU SEE?!
BOSS ...
IT'S SOME GUY IN A SUIT. HE'S GOT A GIRL WITH HIM.
A GIRL ...?
OPEN IT.
SHF
GOOD DAY, SIR.
WHAT DO YOU WANT ?
KCHAK
I AM A REPORTER WITH THE LIBERO ITALIA NEWSPAPER. I WAS WONDERING IF I COULD HAVE A MOMENT OF YOUR TIME.
WHAT DOES A REPORTER WANT WITH US?
I HEARD SIGNORE SCARRO OF THE COSTELLO COMPANY WAS HERE, AND I WAS HOPING FOR AN INTER-VIEW...

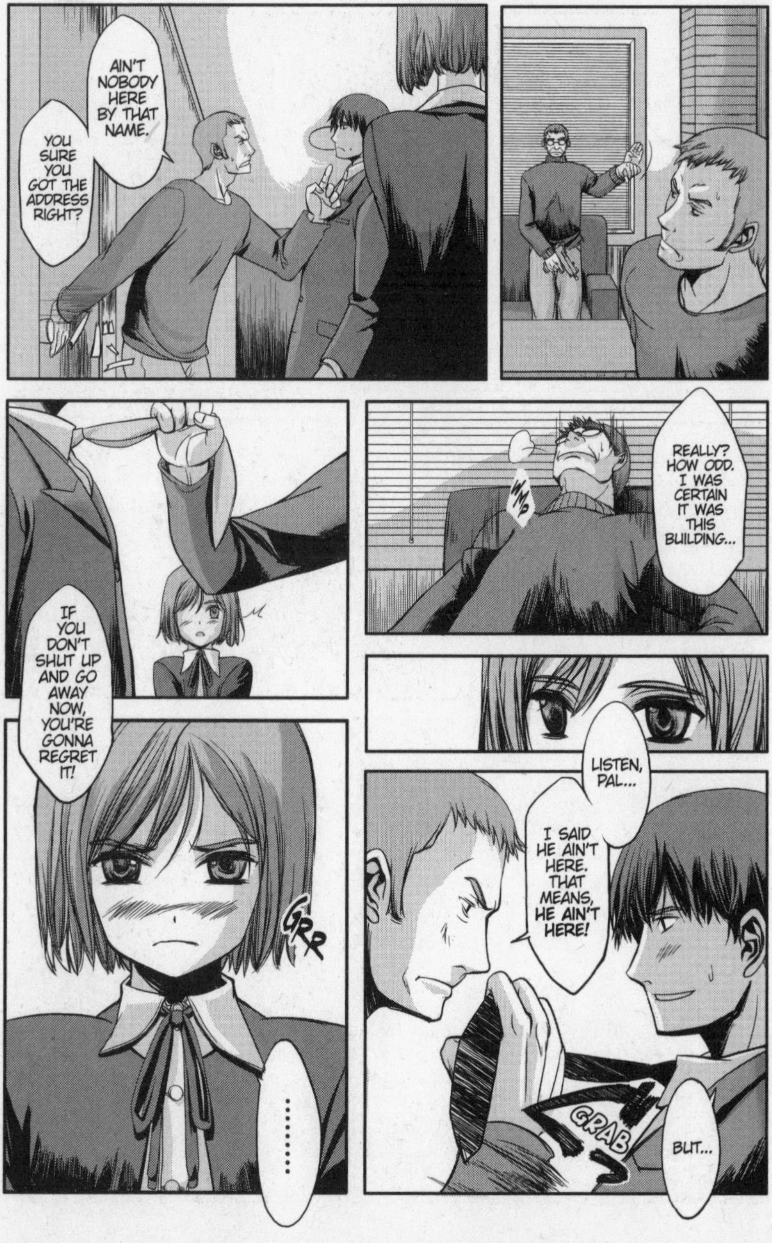
AIN'T NOBODY HERE BY THAT NAME.
YOU SURE YOU GOT THE ADDRESS RIGHT?
REALLY? HOW ODD. I WAS CERTAIN IT WAS THIS BUILDING...
WMP
IF YOU DON'T SHUT UP AND GO AWAY NOW, YOU'RE GONNA REGRET IT!
GRR
......
LISTEN, PAL...
I SAID HE AIN'T HERE. THAT MEANS, HE AIN'T HERE!
GRAB
BUT...

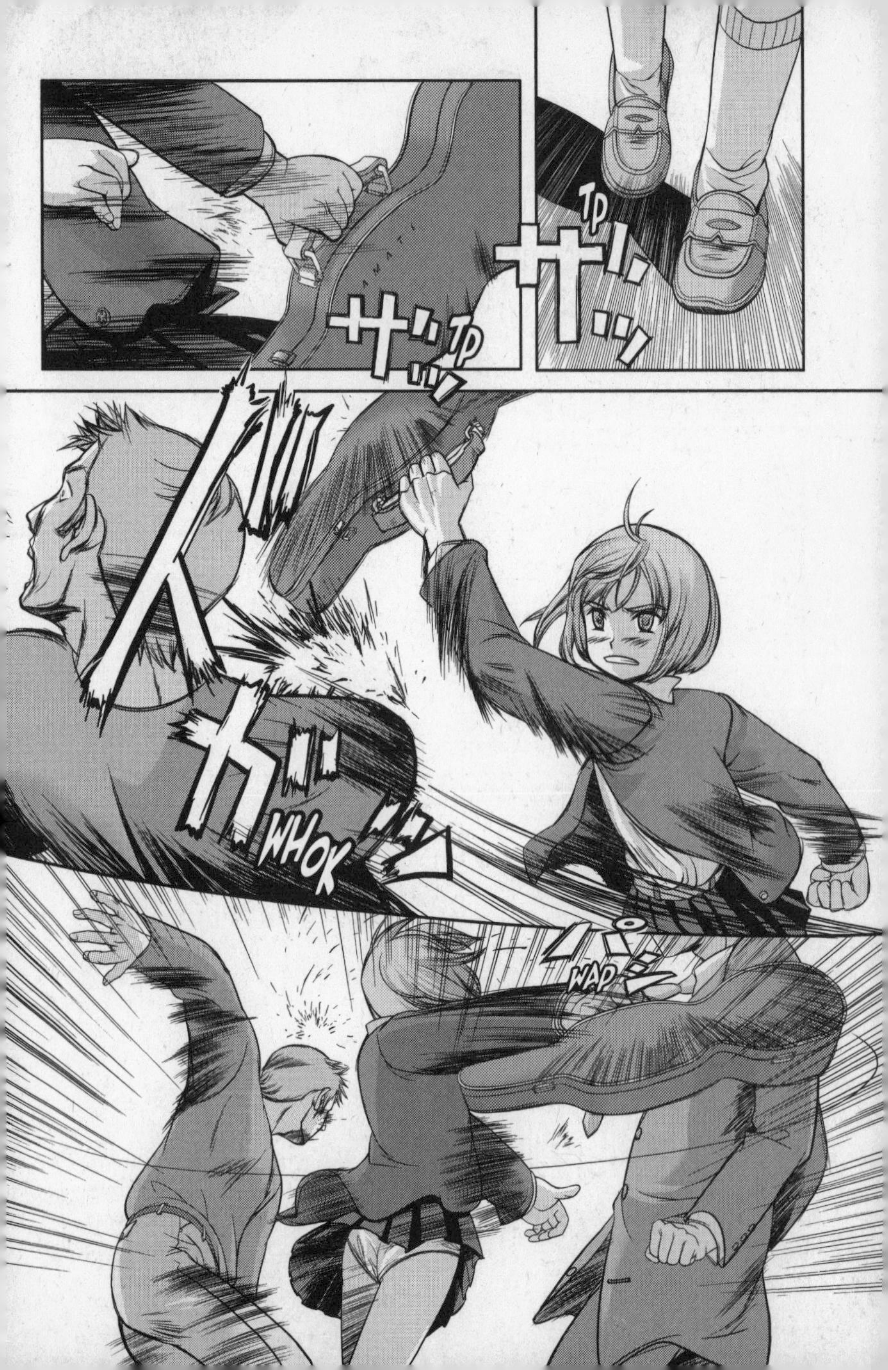
TP
TP
WHOK
WAP

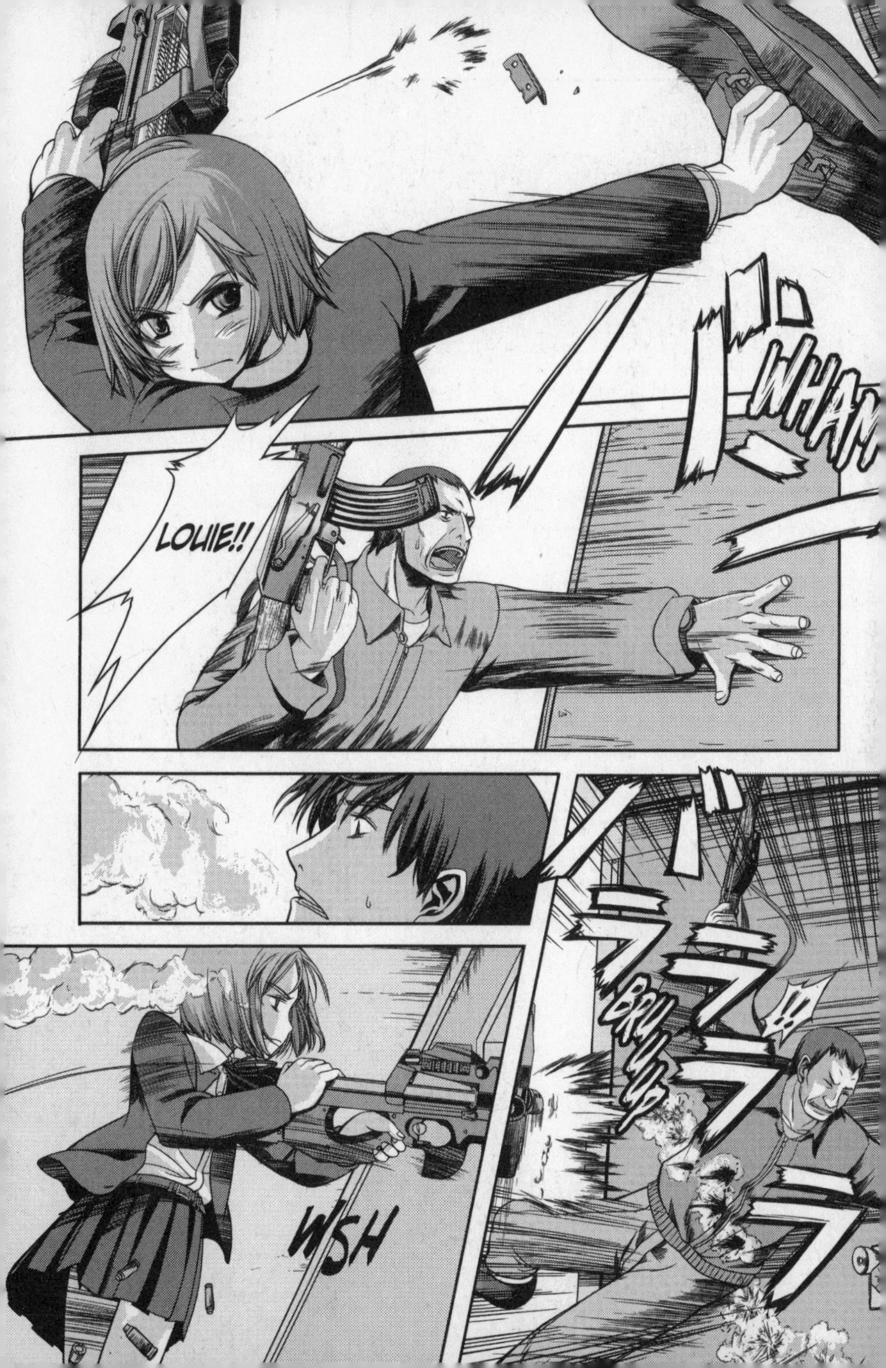
WHAM
LOUIE!!
BRUUUP
!!
WSH

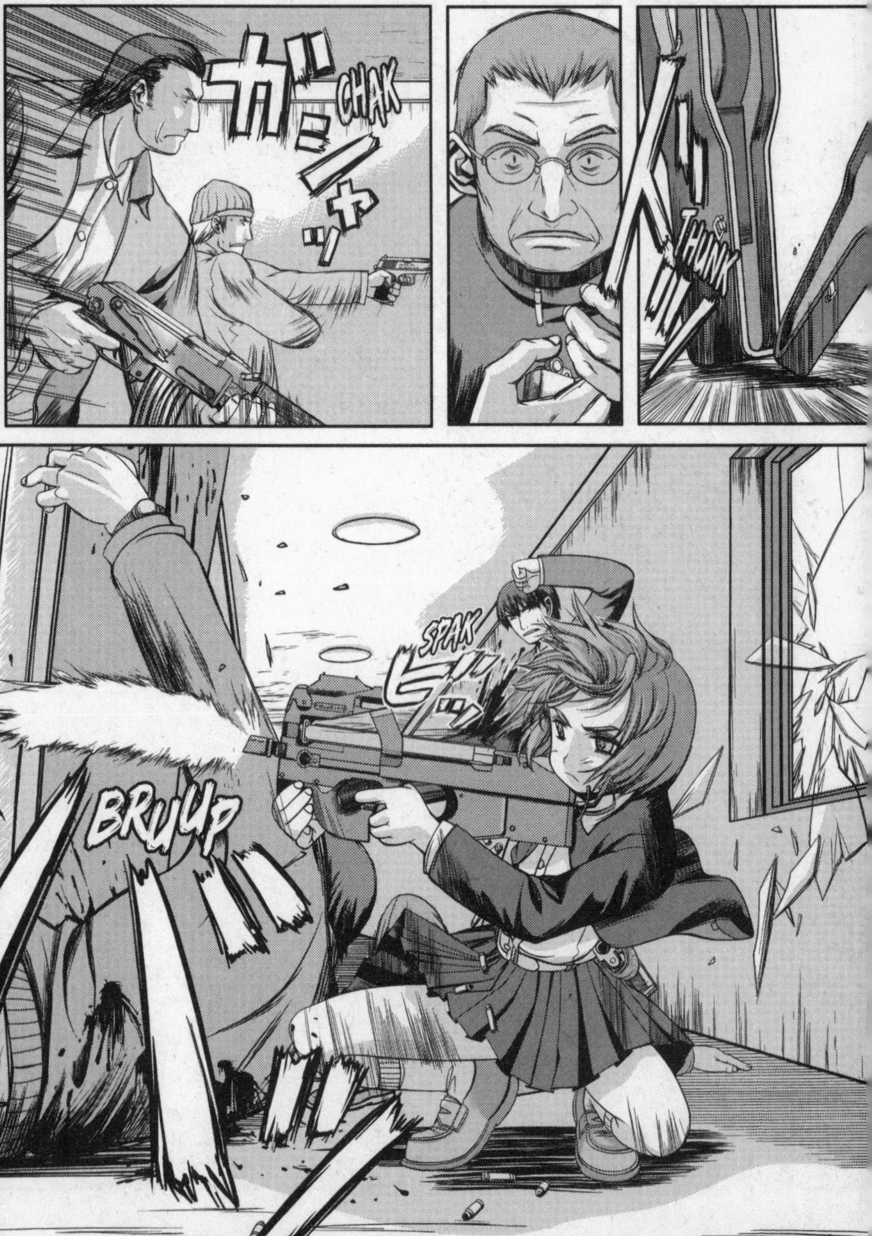
THUNK
CHAK
SPAK
BRUUP

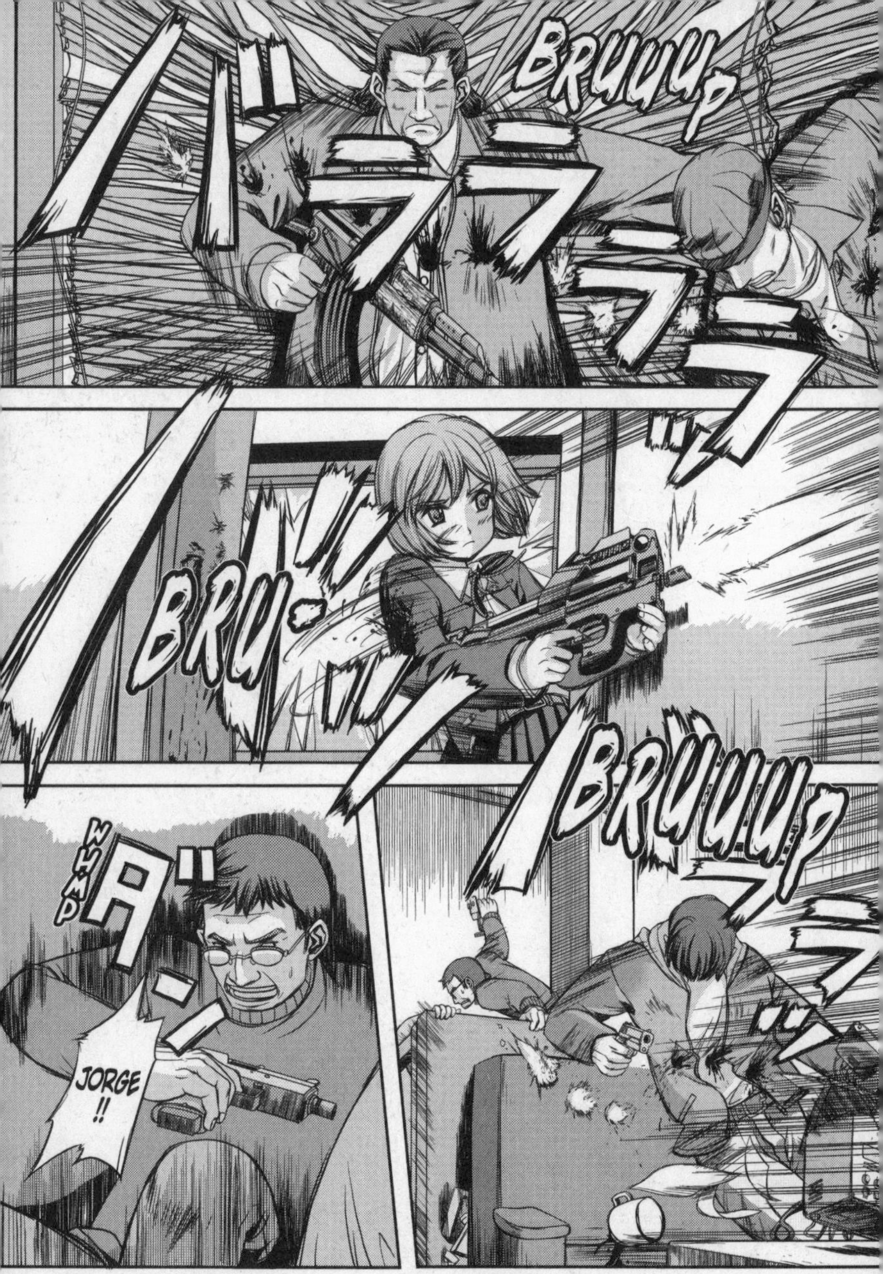
BRUUUP
BRU-
BRUUUP
WHMP
JORGE !!

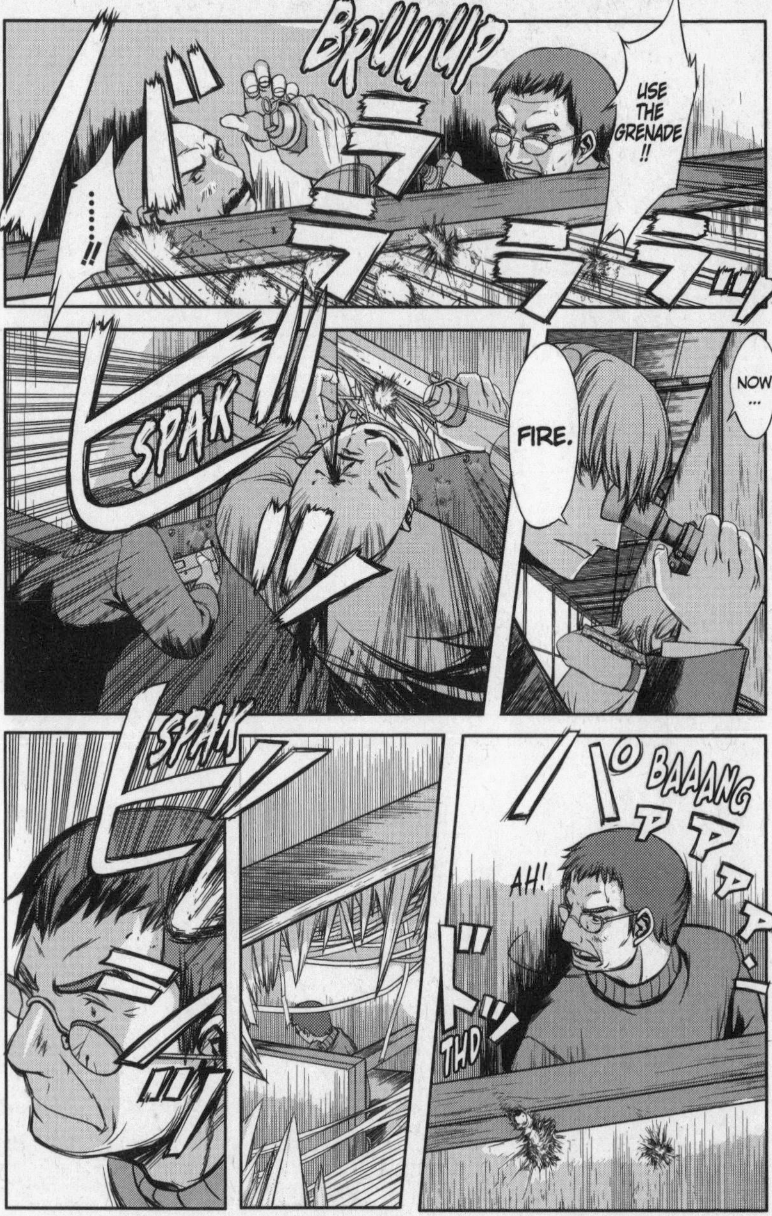
BRUUUP
USE THE GRENADE !!
......!!
NOW ...
FIRE.
SPAK
BAAANG
AH!
THD
SPAK

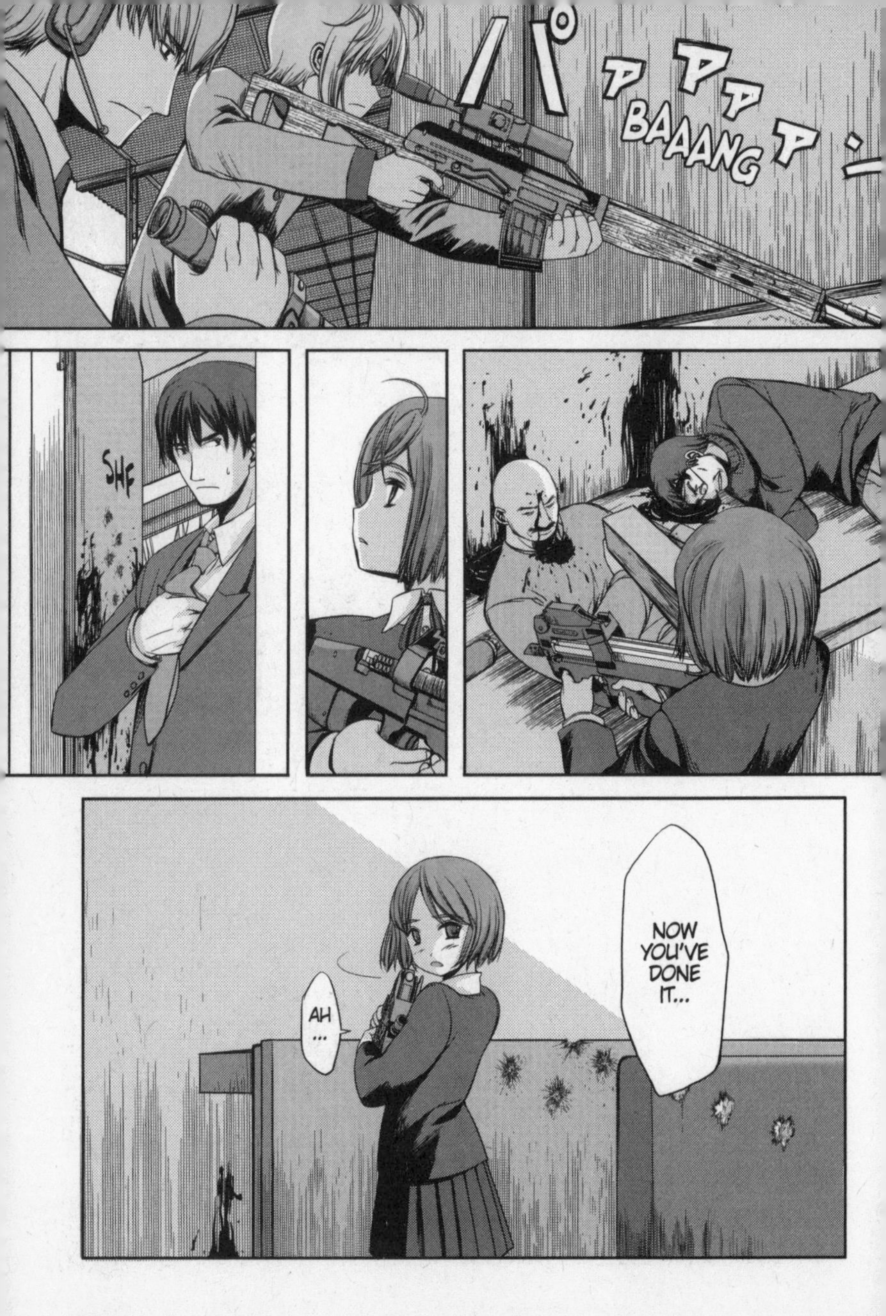
パァァァァ
BAAANG
SHF
NOW YOU'VE DONE IT...
AH ...

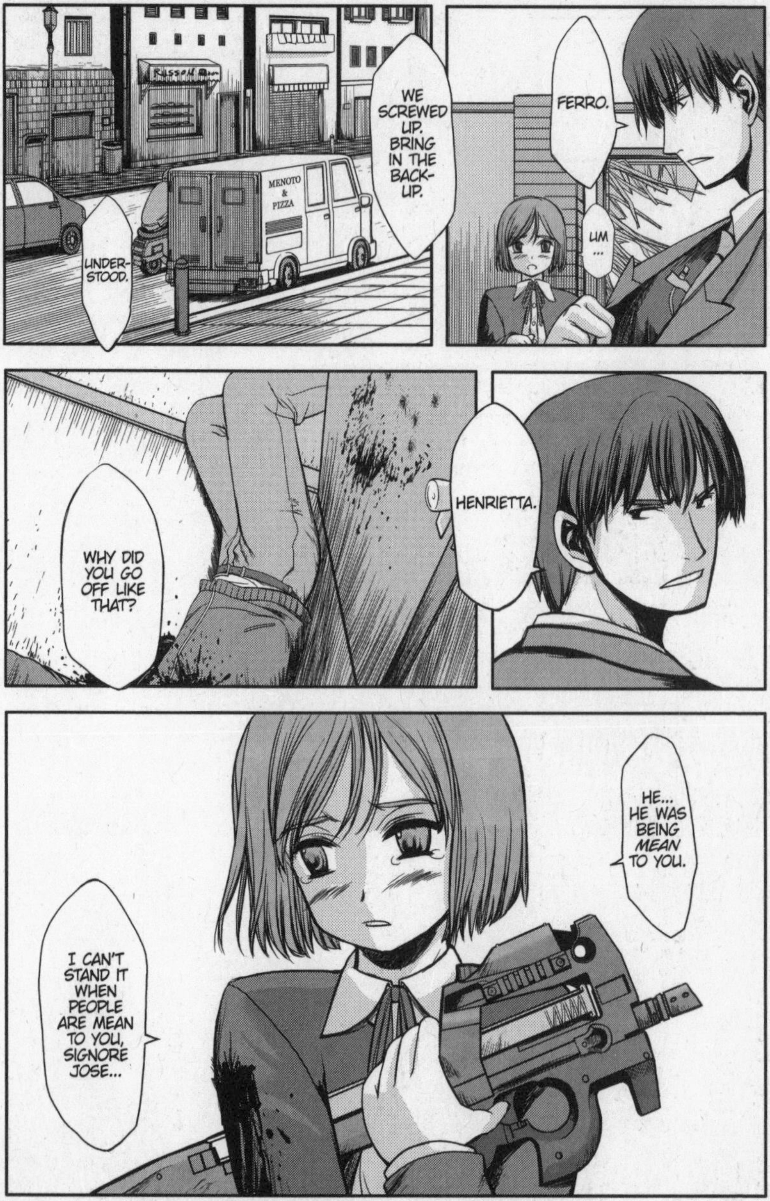
FERRO.
UM ...
WE SCREWED UP. BRING IN THE BACK-UP.
MENOTO & PIZZA
UNDER-STOOD.
HENRIETTA.
WHY DID YOU GO OFF LIKE THAT?
HE... HE WAS BEING *MEAN* TO YOU.
I CAN'T STAND IT WHEN PEOPLE ARE MEAN TO YOU, SIGNORE JOSE...

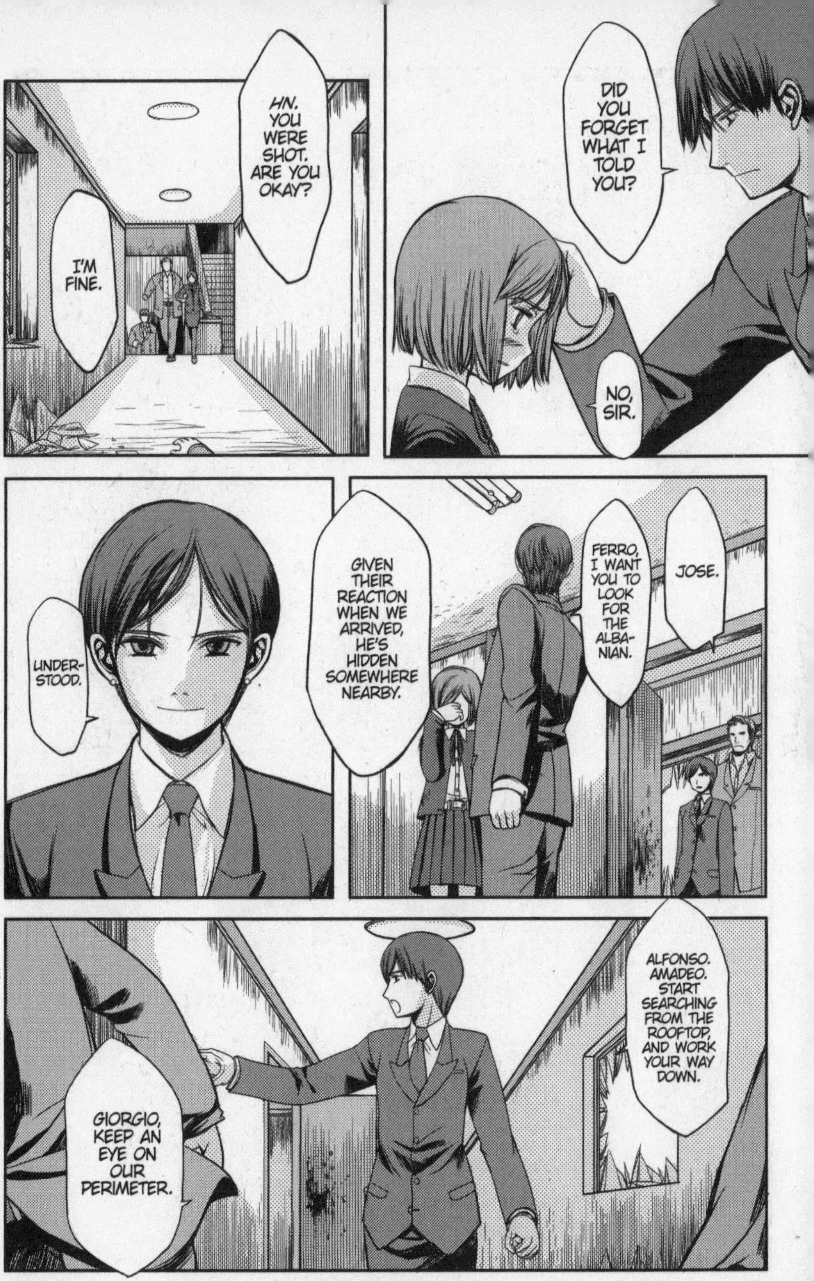
DID YOU FORGET WHAT I TOLD YOU?
NO, SIR.
HN. YOU WERE SHOT. ARE YOU OKAY?
I'M FINE.
JOSE.
FERRO, I WANT YOU TO LOOK FOR THE ALBA-NIAN.
GIVEN THEIR REACTION WHEN WE ARRIVED, HE'S HIDDEN SOMEWHERE NEARBY.
UNDER-STOOD.
ALFONSO. AMADEO. START SEARCHING FROM THE ROOFTOP, AND WORK YOUR WAY DOWN.
GIORGIO, KEEP AN EYE ON OUR PERIMETER.

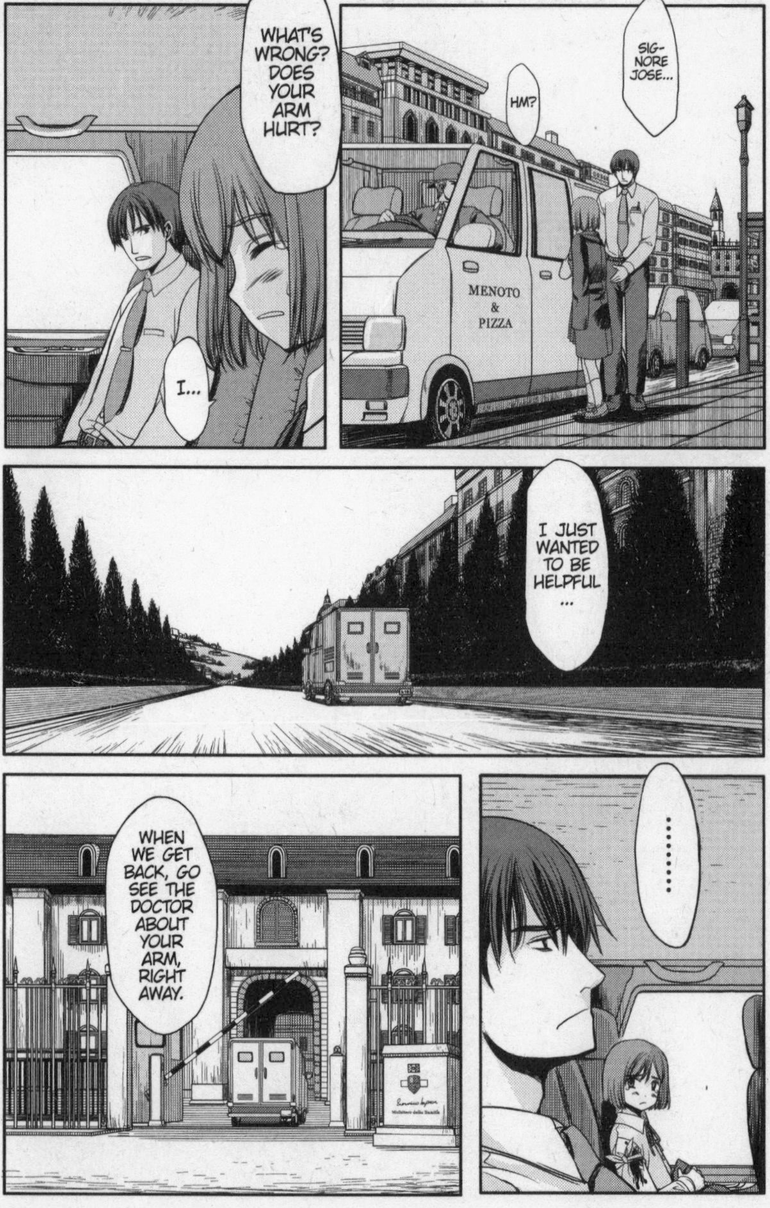
SIG-NORE JOSE...
HM?
MENOTO & PIZZA
WHAT'S WRONG? DOES YOUR ARM HURT?
I...
I JUST WANTED TO BE HELPFUL ...
....
WHEN WE GET BACK, GO SEE THE DOCTOR ABOUT YOUR ARM, RIGHT AWAY.

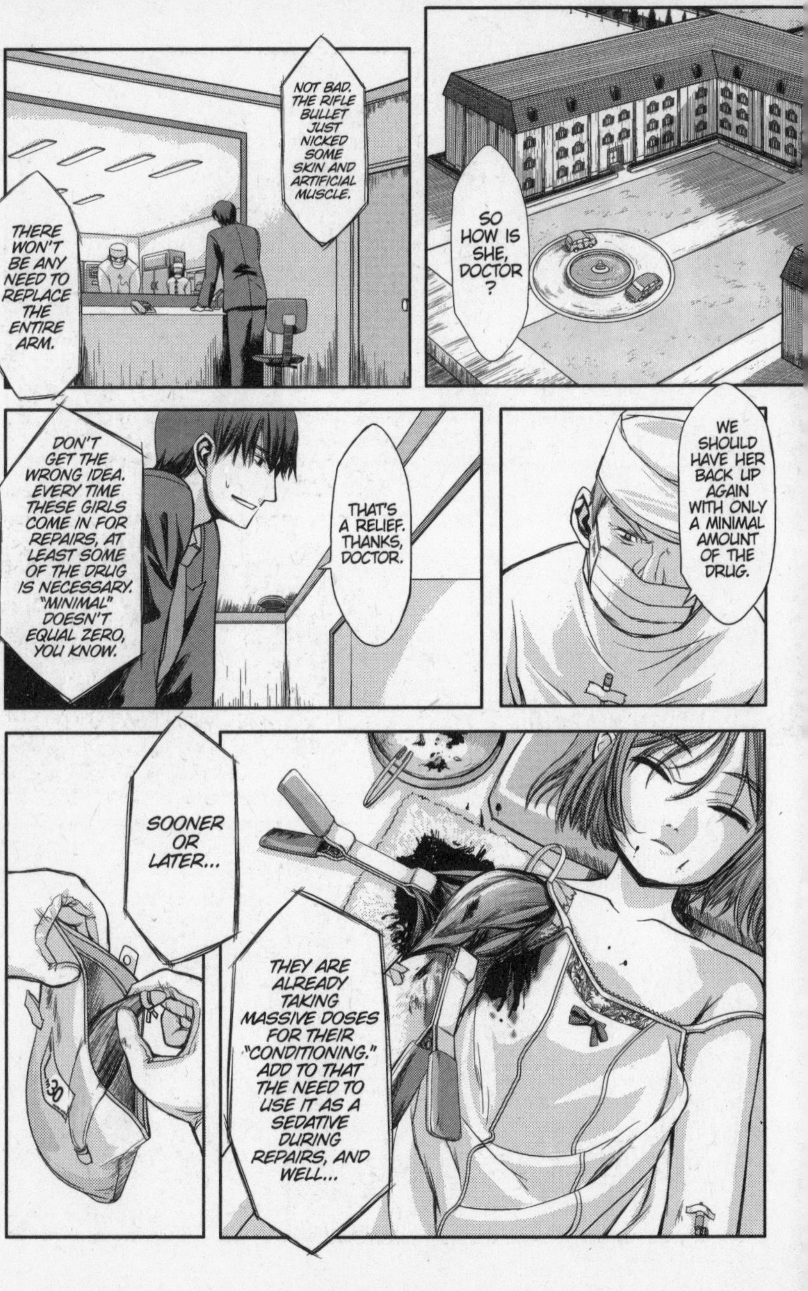
SO HOW IS SHE, DOCTOR?
NOT BAD. THE RIFLE BULLET JUST NICKED SOME SKIN AND ARTIFICIAL MUSCLE.
THERE WON'T BE ANY NEED TO REPLACE THE ENTIRE ARM.
WE SHOULD HAVE HER BACK UP AGAIN WITH ONLY A MINIMAL AMOUNT OF THE DRUG.
THAT'S A RELIEF. THANKS, DOCTOR.
DON'T GET THE WRONG IDEA. EVERY TIME THESE GIRLS COME IN FOR REPAIRS, AT LEAST SOME OF THE DRUG IS NECESSARY. "MINIMAL" DOESN'T EQUAL ZERO, YOU KNOW.
THEY ARE ALREADY TAKING MASSIVE DOSES FOR THEIR "CONDITIONING." ADD TO THAT THE NEED TO USE IT AS A SEDATIVE DURING REPAIRS, AND WELL...
SOONER OR LATER...

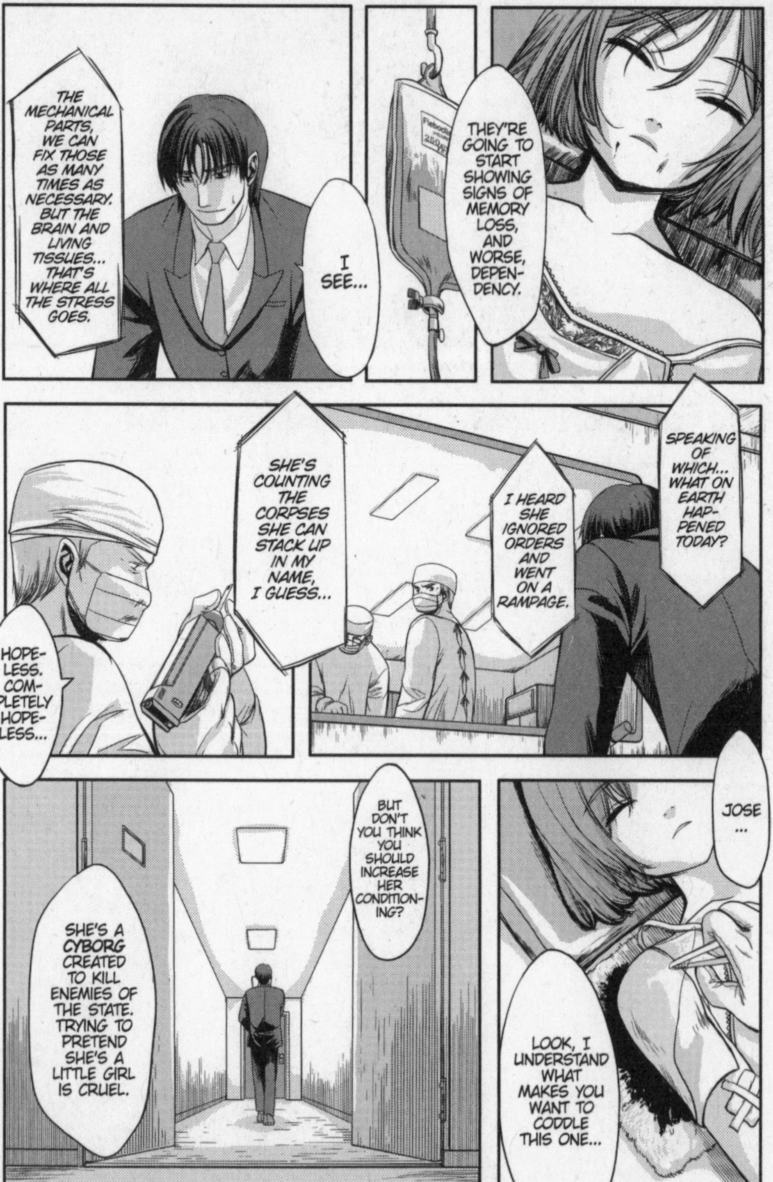
THEY'RE GOING TO START SHOWING SIGNS OF MEMORY LOSS, AND WORSE, DEPENDENCY.
I SEE...
THE MECHANICAL PARTS, WE CAN FIX THOSE AS MANY TIMES AS NECESSARY. BUT THE BRAIN AND LIVING TISSUES... THAT'S WHERE ALL THE STRESS GOES.
SPEAKING OF WHICH... WHAT ON EARTH HAPPENED TODAY?
I HEARD SHE IGNORED ORDERS AND WENT ON A RAMPAGE.
SHE'S COUNTING THE CORPSES SHE CAN STACK UP IN MY NAME, I GUESS...
HOPELESS. COMPLETELY HOPELESS...
JOSE ...
LOOK, I UNDERSTAND WHAT MAKES YOU WANT TO CODDLE THIS ONE...
BUT DON'T YOU THINK YOU SHOULD INCREASE HER CONDITIONING?
SHE'S A **CYBORG** CREATED TO KILL ENEMIES OF THE STATE. TRYING TO PRETEND SHE'S A LITTLE GIRL IS CRUEL.

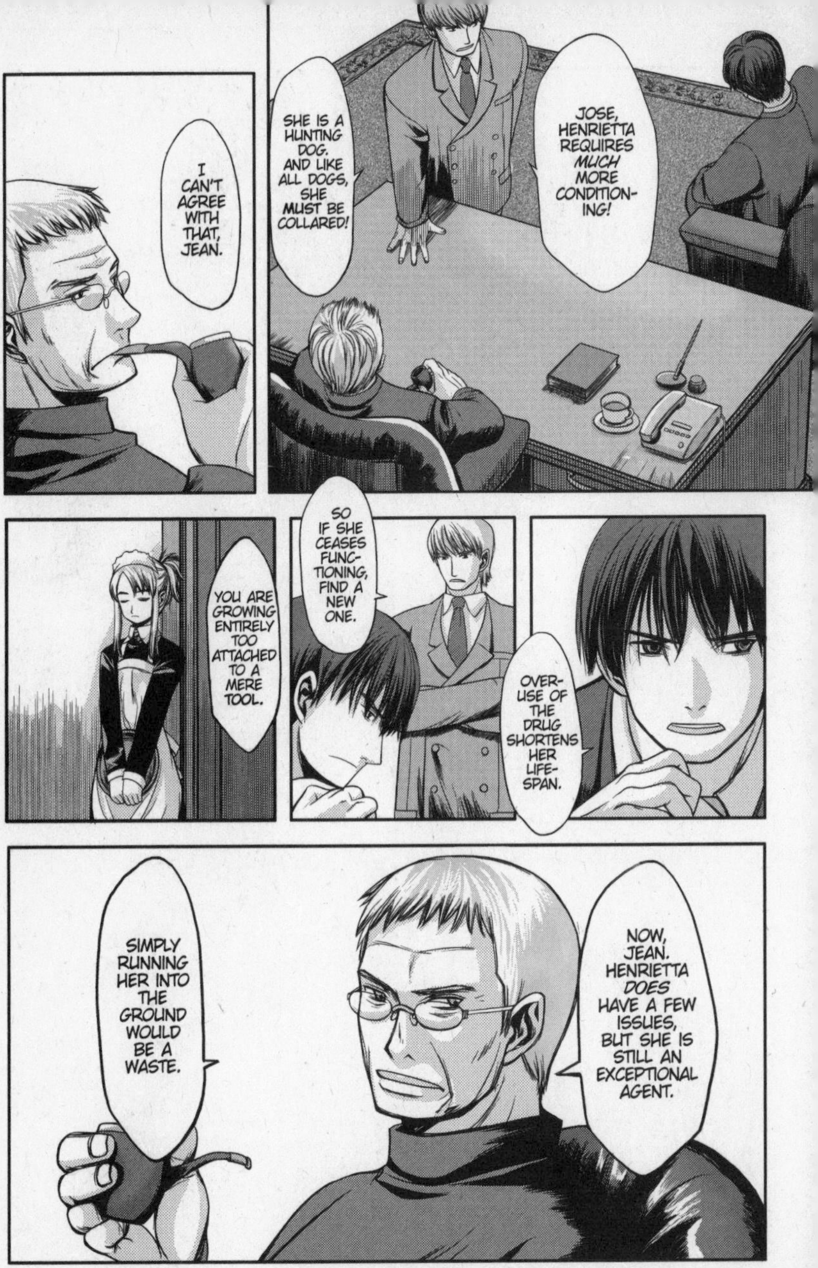

JOSE, HENRIETTA REQUIRES *MUCH* MORE CONDITIONING!
SHE IS A HUNTING DOG. AND LIKE ALL DOGS, SHE *MUST* BE COLLARED!
I CAN'T AGREE WITH THAT, JEAN.
OVER-USE OF THE DRUG SHORTENS HER LIFE-SPAN.
SO IF SHE CEASES FUNCTIONING, FIND A NEW ONE.
YOU ARE GROWING ENTIRELY TOO ATTACHED TO A MERE TOOL.
NOW, JEAN. HENRIETTA *DOES* HAVE A FEW ISSUES, BUT SHE IS STILL AN EXCEPTIONAL AGENT.
SIMPLY RUNNING HER INTO THE GROUND WOULD BE A WASTE.

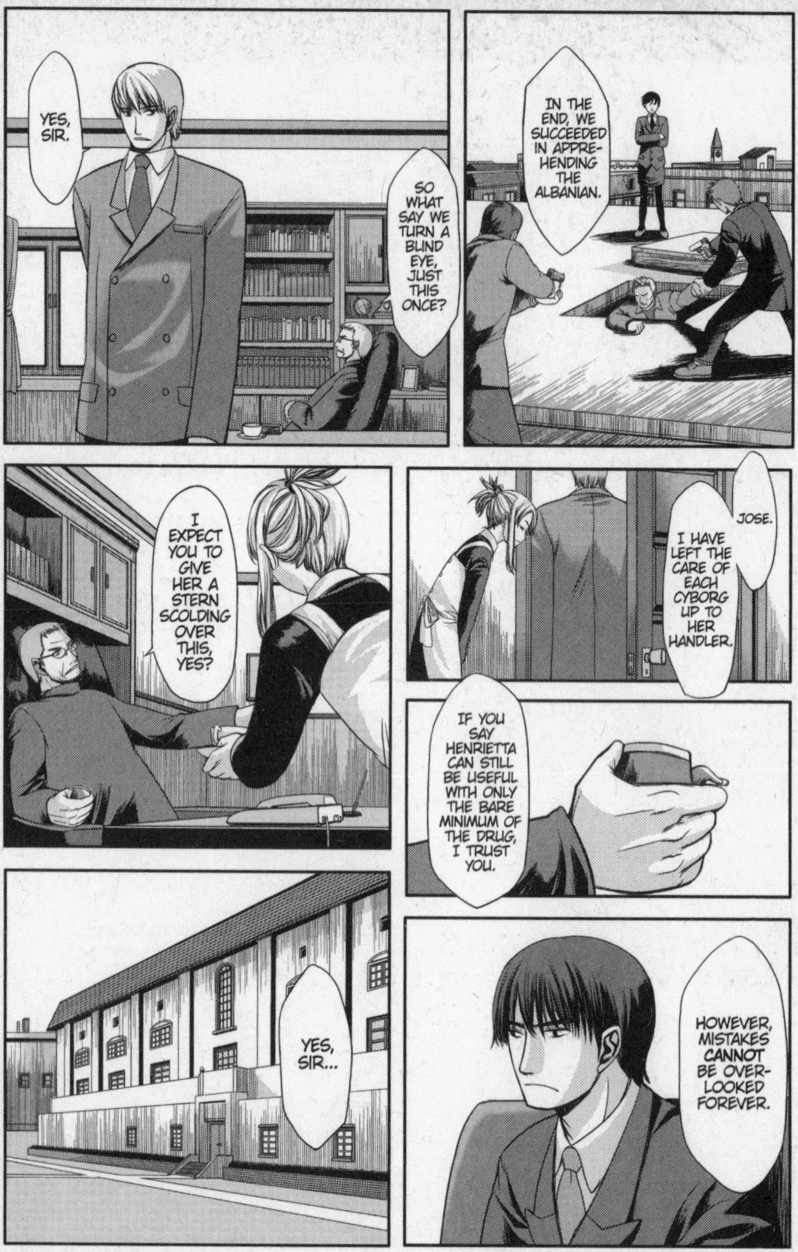
IN THE END, WE SUCCEEDED IN APPREHENDING THE ALBANIAN.
SO WHAT SAY WE TURN A BLIND EYE, JUST THIS ONCE?
YES, SIR.
JOSE.
I HAVE LEFT THE CARE OF EACH CYBORG UP TO HER HANDLER.
IF YOU SAY HENRIETTA CAN STILL BE USEFUL WITH ONLY THE BARE MINIMUM OF THE DRUG, I TRUST YOU.
I EXPECT YOU TO GIVE HER A STERN SCOLDING OVER THIS, YES?
HOWEVER, MISTAKES CANNOT BE OVER-LOOKED FOREVER.
YES, SIR...

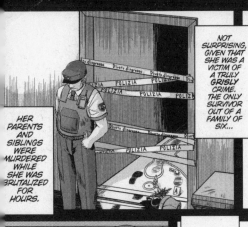

WHEN HENRIETTA WAS FIRST BROUGHT TO THE AGENCY, SHE WAS A VERY QUIET CHILD.

NOT SURPRISING, GIVEN THAT SHE WAS A VICTIM OF A TRULY GRISLY CRIME. THE ONLY SURVIVOR OUT OF A FAMILY OF SIX...

HER PARENTS AND SIBLINGS WERE MURDERED WHILE SHE WAS BRUTALIZED FOR HOURS.

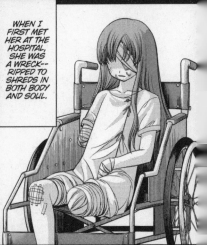

WHEN I FIRST MET HER AT THE HOSPITAL, SHE WAS A WRECK-- RIPPED TO SHREDS IN BOTH BODY AND SOUL.

SO I CHOSE HER AS MY PARTNER.

ALL I DO KNOW IS THAT I WANTED TO SAVE HER.

MAYBE I WAS FEELING CHARITABLE. MAYBE I WAS FEELING SYMPATHETIC. I DON'T KNOW...

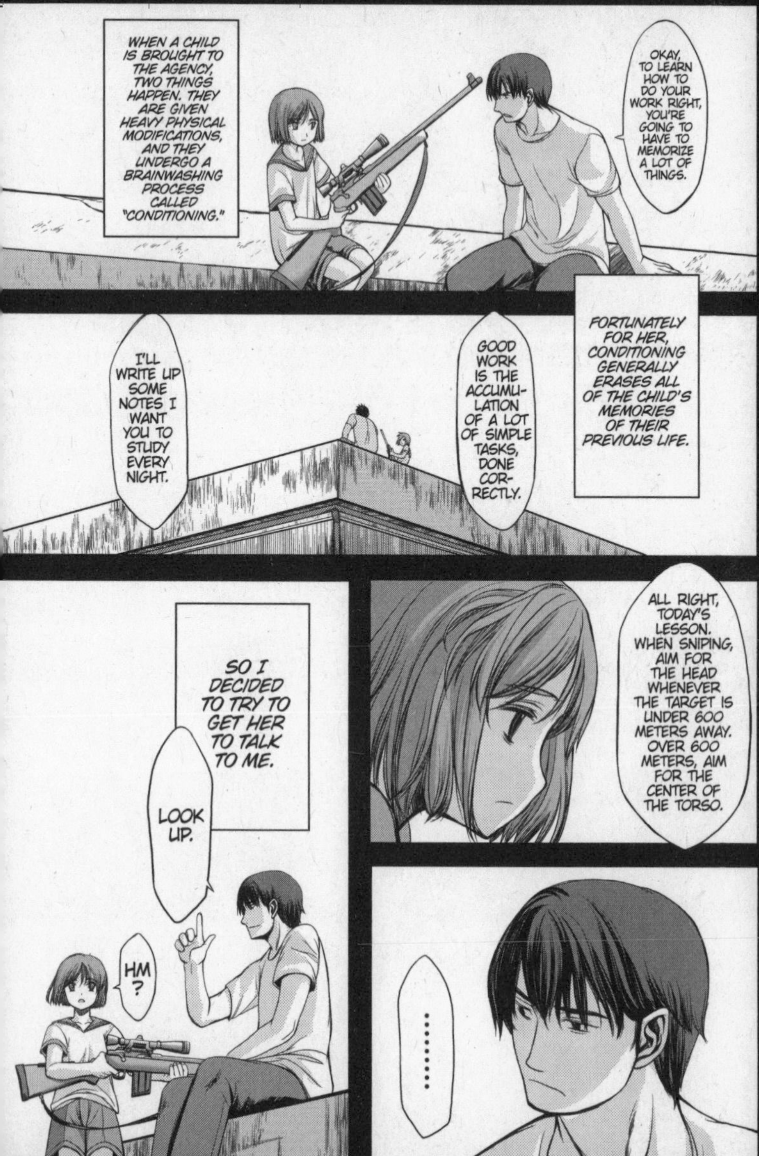
OKAY, TO LEARN HOW TO DO YOUR WORK RIGHT, YOU'RE GOING TO HAVE TO MEMORIZE A LOT OF THINGS.
WHEN A CHILD IS BROUGHT TO THE AGENCY, TWO THINGS HAPPEN. THEY ARE GIVEN HEAVY PHYSICAL MODIFICATIONS, AND THEY UNDERGO A BRAINWASHING PROCESS CALLED "CONDITIONING."
FORTUNATELY FOR HER, CONDITIONING GENERALLY ERASES ALL OF THE CHILD'S MEMORIES OF THEIR PREVIOUS LIFE.
GOOD WORK IS THE ACCUMULATION OF A LOT OF SIMPLE TASKS, DONE CORRECTLY.
I'LL WRITE UP SOME NOTES I WANT YOU TO STUDY EVERY NIGHT.
ALL RIGHT, TODAY'S LESSON. WHEN SNIPING, AIM FOR THE HEAD WHENEVER THE TARGET IS UNDER 600 METERS AWAY. OVER 600 METERS, AIM FOR THE CENTER OF THE TORSO.
....
SO I DECIDED TO TRY TO GET HER TO TALK TO ME.
LOOK UP.
HM?

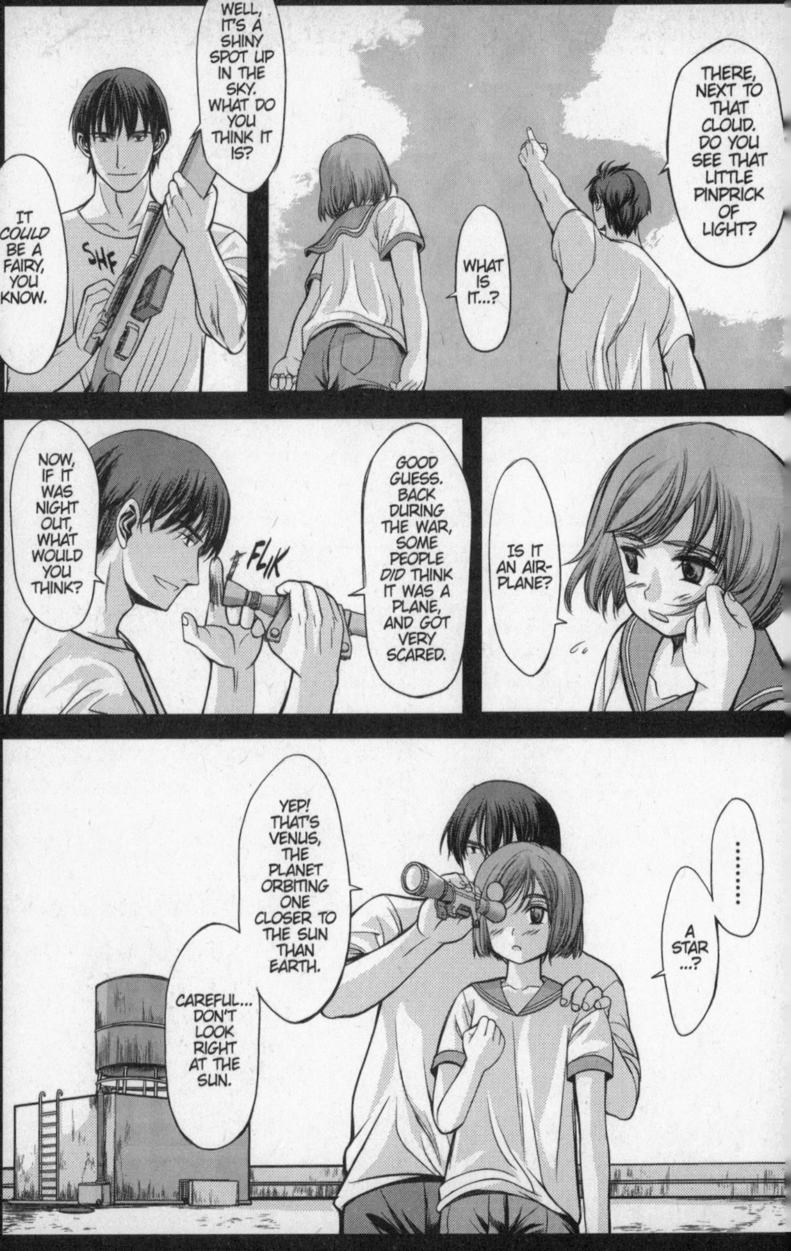
THERE, NEXT TO THAT CLOUD. DO YOU SEE THAT LITTLE PINPRICK OF LIGHT?
WHAT IS IT...?
WELL, IT'S A SHINY SPOT UP IN THE SKY. WHAT DO YOU THINK IT IS?
IT COULD BE A FAIRY, YOU KNOW.
SHF
IS IT AN AIR-PLANE?
GOOD GUESS. BACK DURING THE WAR, SOME PEOPLE *DID* THINK IT WAS A PLANE, AND GOT VERY SCARED.
FLIK
NOW, IF IT WAS NIGHT OUT, WHAT WOULD YOU THINK?
....
A STAR ...?
YEP! THAT'S VENUS, THE PLANET ORBITING ONE CLOSER TO THE SUN THAN EARTH.
CAREFUL... DON'T LOOK RIGHT AT THE SUN.

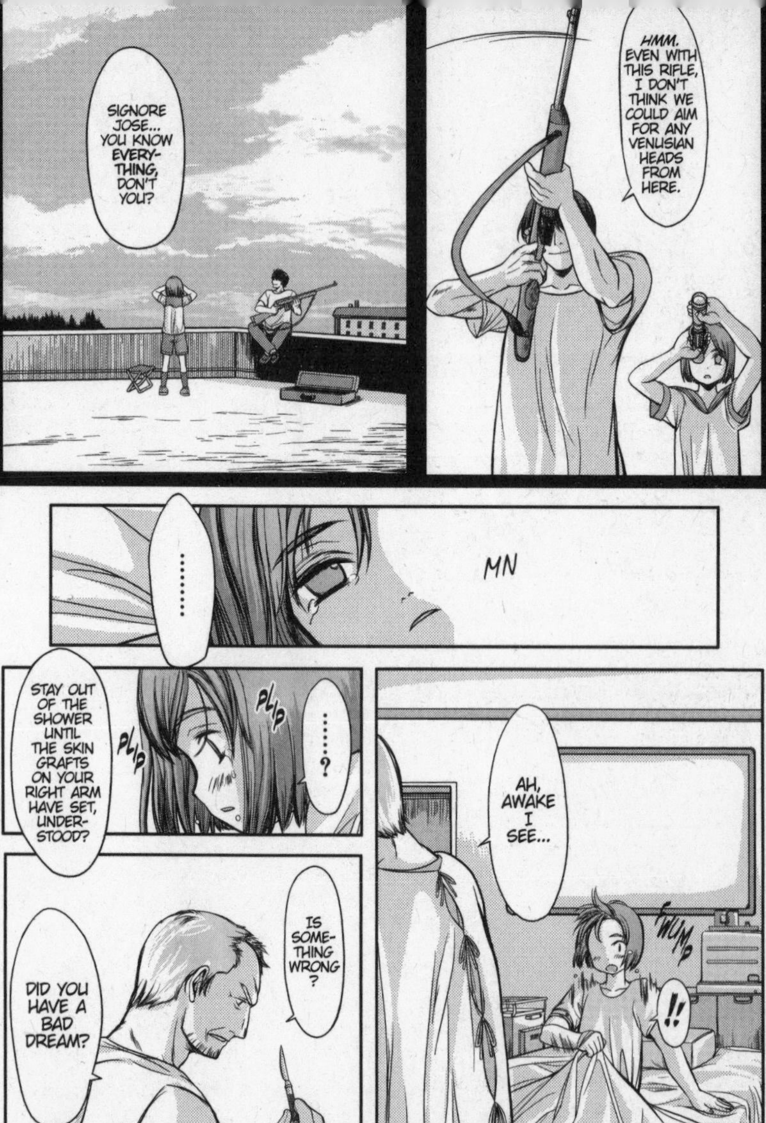
HMM. EVEN WITH THIS RIFLE, I DON'T THINK WE COULD AIM FOR ANY VENUSIAN HEADS FROM HERE.
SIGNORE JOSE... YOU KNOW EVERY-THING, DON'T YOU?
....
MN
AH, AWAKE I SEE...
FWUMP
!!
......?
PLIP
PLIP
STAY OUT OF THE SHOWER UNTIL THE SKIN GRAFTS ON YOUR RIGHT ARM HAVE SET, UNDER-STOOD?
IS SOME-THING WRONG?
DID YOU HAVE A BAD DREAM?

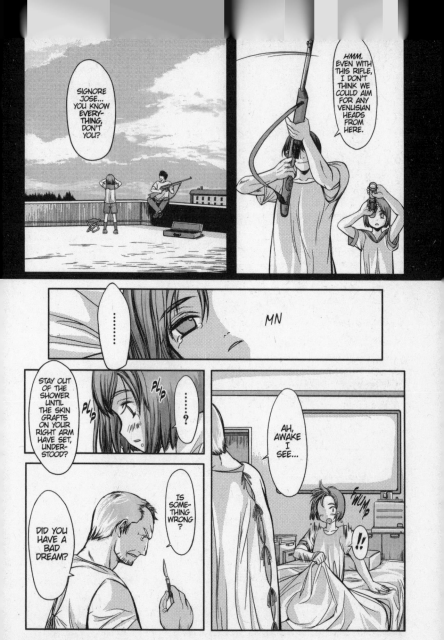

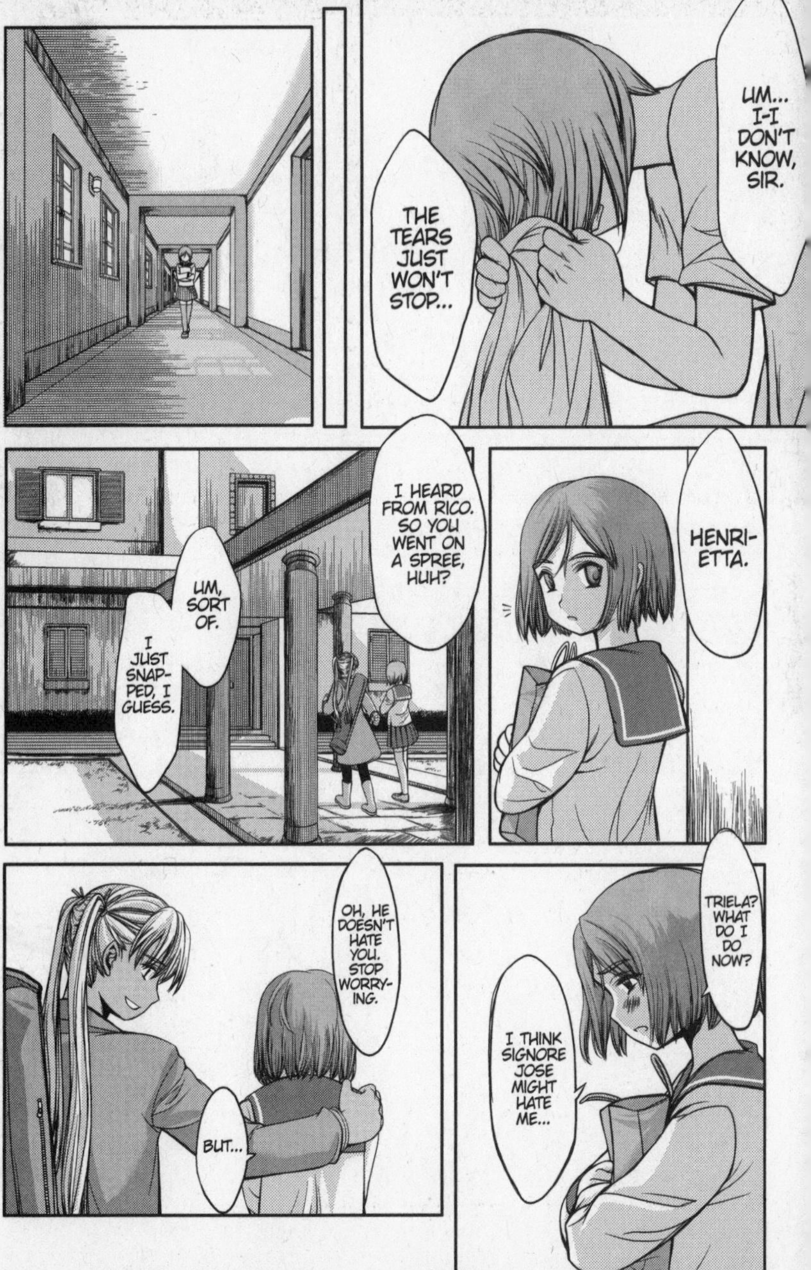
UM... I-I DON'T KNOW, SIR.
THE TEARS JUST WON'T STOP...
HENRI-ETTA.
I HEARD FROM RICO. SO YOU WENT ON A SPREE, HUH?
UM, SORT OF.
I JUST SNAP-PED, I GUESS.
TRIELA? WHAT DO I DO NOW?
I THINK SIGNORE JOSE MIGHT HATE ME...
OH, HE DOESN'T HATE YOU. STOP WORRY-ING.
BUT...

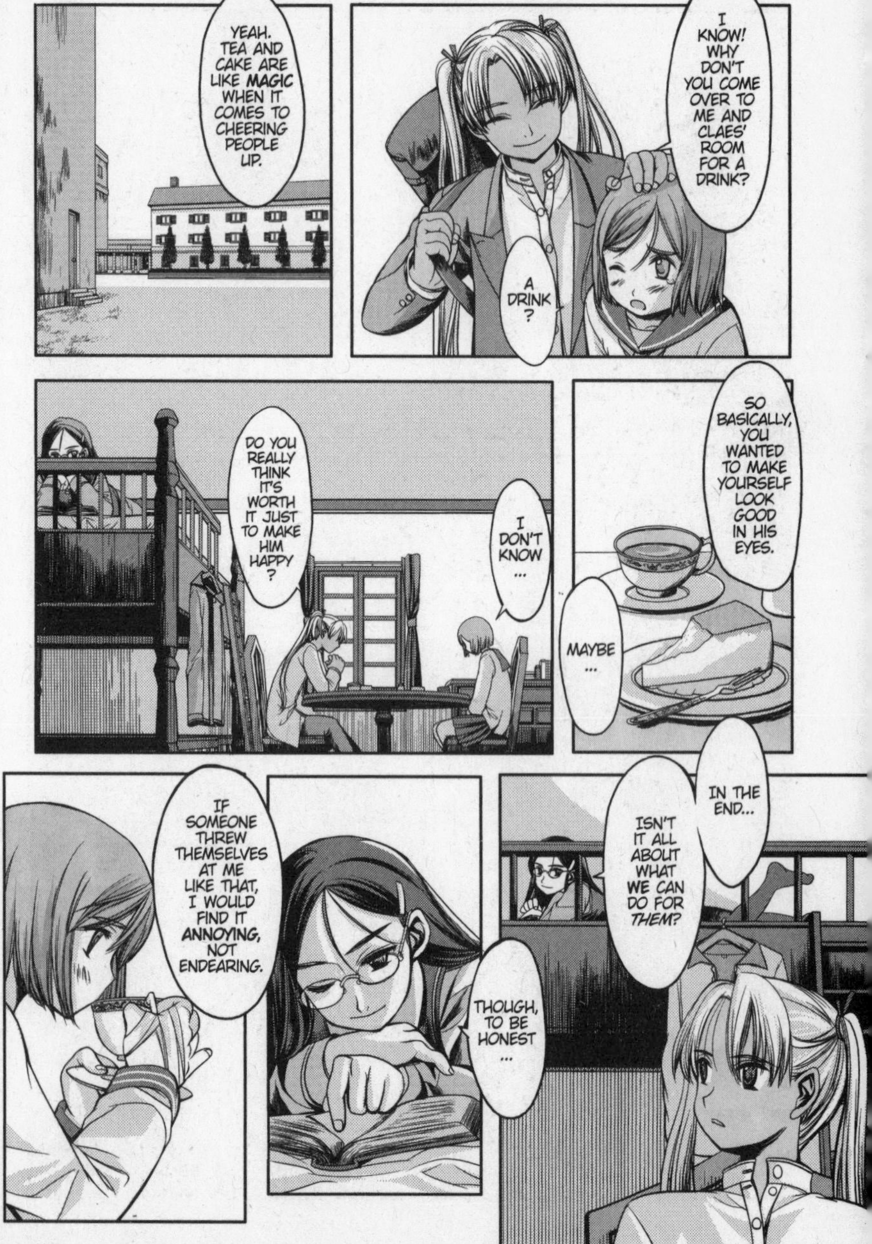
I KNOW! WHY DON'T YOU COME OVER TO ME AND CLAES' ROOM FOR A DRINK?
A DRINK?
YEAH. TEA AND CAKE ARE LIKE **MAGIC** WHEN IT COMES TO CHEERING PEOPLE UP.
SO BASICALLY, YOU WANTED TO MAKE YOURSELF LOOK GOOD IN HIS EYES.
MAYBE...
DO YOU REALLY THINK IT'S WORTH IT JUST TO MAKE HIM HAPPY?
I DON'T KNOW...
IN THE END...
ISN'T IT ALL ABOUT WHAT WE CAN DO FOR *THEM*?
THOUGH, TO BE HONEST...
IF SOMEONE THREW THEMSELVES AT ME LIKE THAT, I WOULD FIND IT **ANNOYING**, NOT ENDEARING.

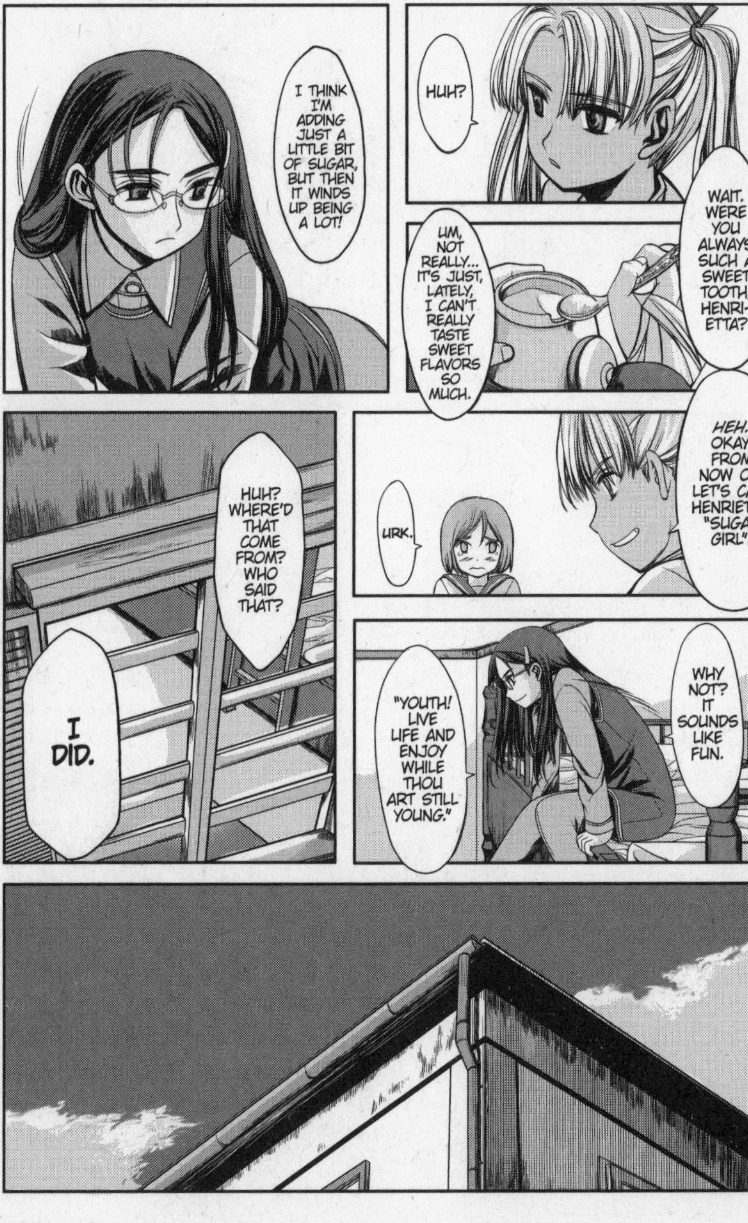
HUH?
WAIT. WERE YOU ALWAYS SUCH A SWEET TOOTH, HENRIETTA?
UM, NOT REALLY... IT'S JUST, LATELY, I CAN'T REALLY TASTE SWEET FLAVORS SO MUCH.
I THINK I'M ADDING JUST A LITTLE BIT OF SUGAR, BUT THEN IT WINDS UP BEING A LOT!
HEH. OKAY, FROM NOW ON, LET'S CALL HENRIETTA, "SUGAR GIRL"!
URK.
WHY NOT? IT SOUNDS LIKE FUN.
"YOUTH! LIVE LIFE AND ENJOY WHILE THOU ART STILL YOUNG."
HUH? WHERE'D THAT COME FROM? WHO SAID THAT?
I DID.

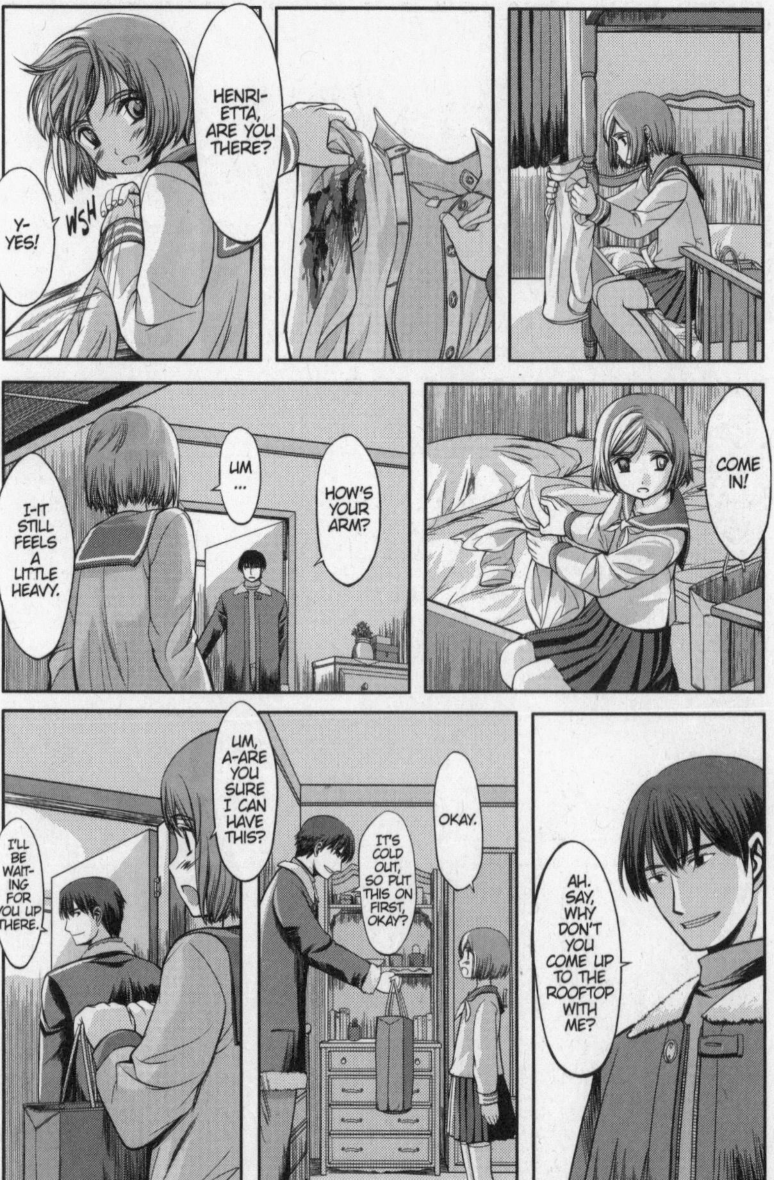
HENRI-ETTA, ARE YOU THERE?
Y-YES!
WSH
COME IN!
HOW'S YOUR ARM?
UM ...
I-IT STILL FEELS A LITTLE HEAVY.
AH. SAY, WHY DON'T YOU COME UP TO THE ROOFTOP WITH ME?
OKAY.
IT'S COLD OUT, SO PUT THIS ON FIRST, OKAY?
UM, A-ARE YOU SURE I CAN HAVE THIS?
I'LL BE WAITING FOR YOU UP THERE.

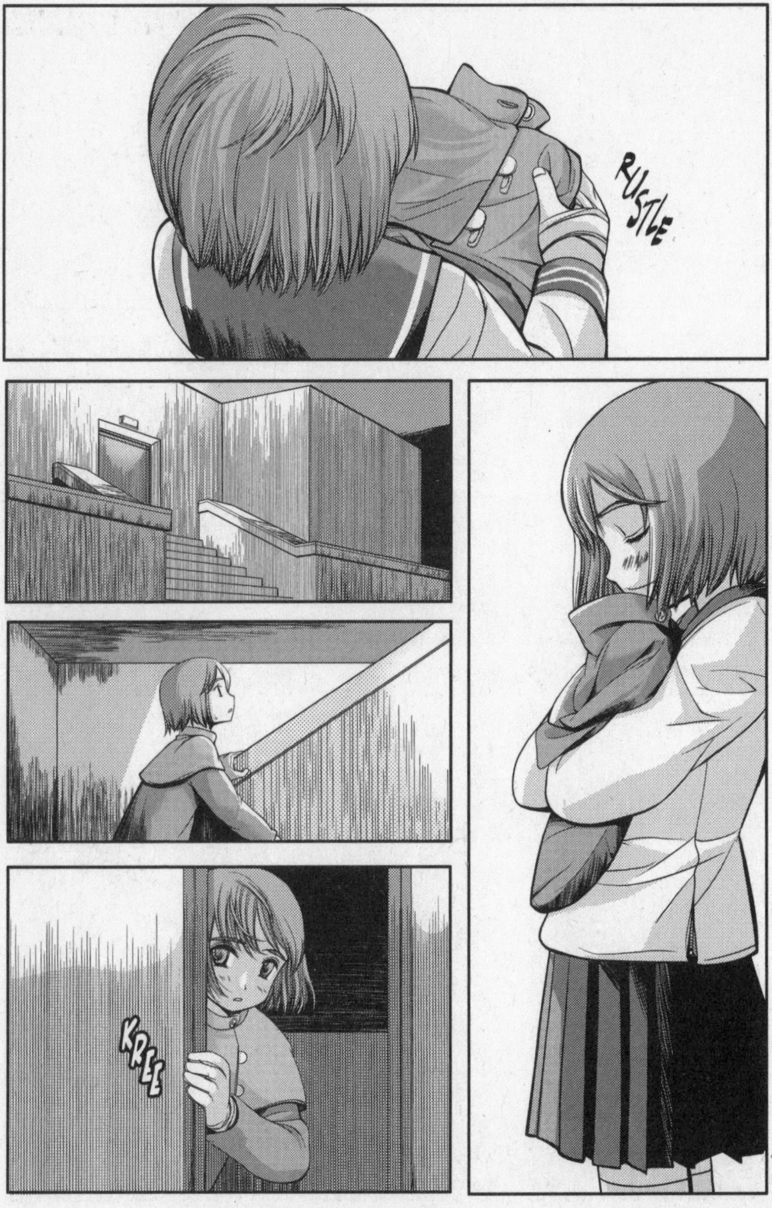
RUSTLE
KREE

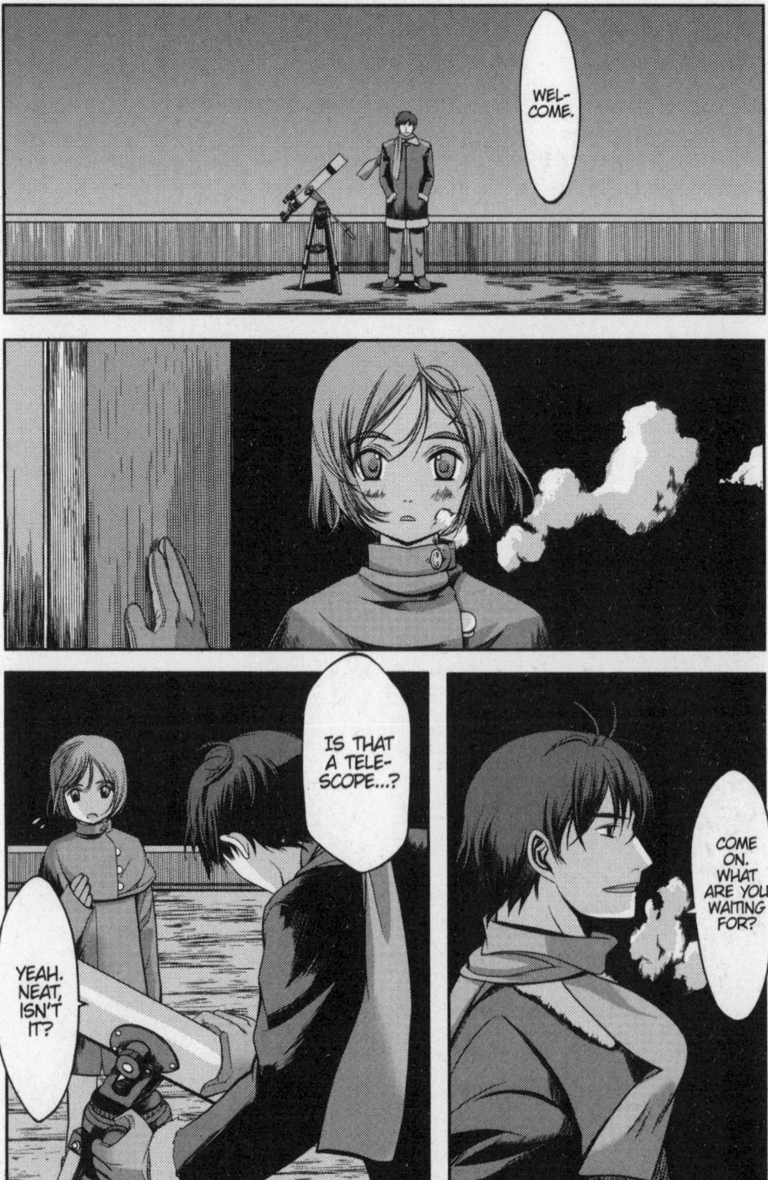
WEL-COME.
COME ON. WHAT ARE YOU WAITING FOR?
IS THAT A TELE-SCOPE...?
YEAH. NEAT, ISN'T IT?

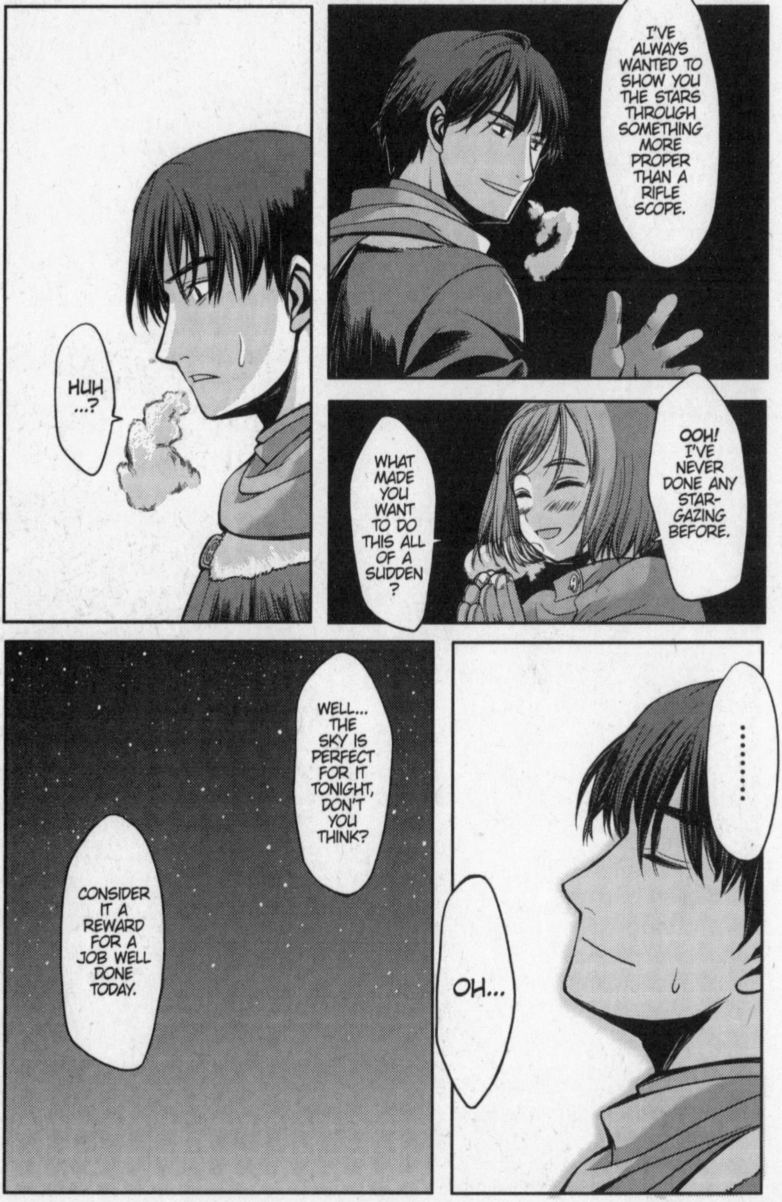
I'VE ALWAYS WANTED TO SHOW YOU THE STARS THROUGH SOMETHING MORE PROPER THAN A RIFLE SCOPE.
OOH! I'VE NEVER DONE ANY STAR-GAZING BEFORE.
WHAT MADE YOU WANT TO DO THIS ALL OF A SUDDEN?
HUH ...?
....
OH...
WELL... THE SKY IS PERFECT FOR IT TONIGHT, DON'T YOU THINK?
CONSIDER IT A REWARD FOR A JOB WELL DONE TODAY.

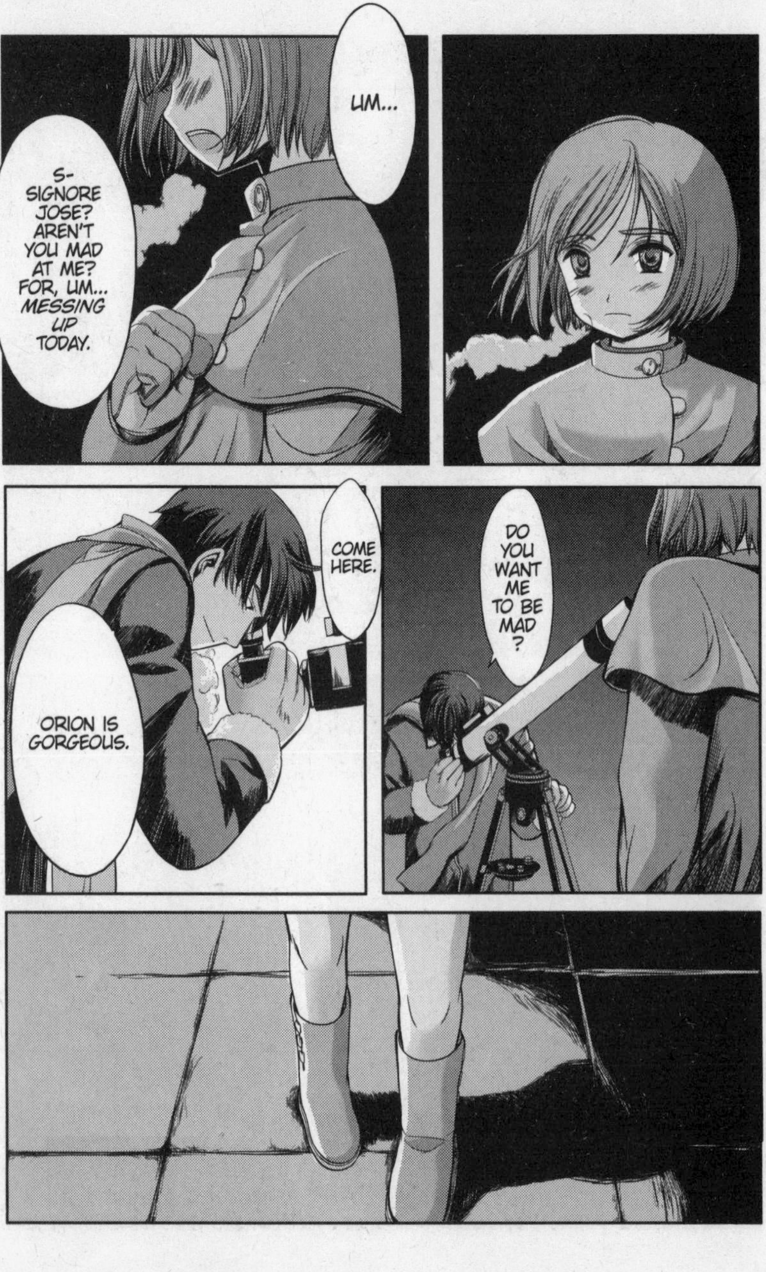
UM...
S-SIGNORE JOSE? AREN'T YOU MAD AT ME? FOR, UM... MESSING UP TODAY.
DO YOU WANT ME TO BE MAD?
COME HERE.
ORION IS GORGEOUS.

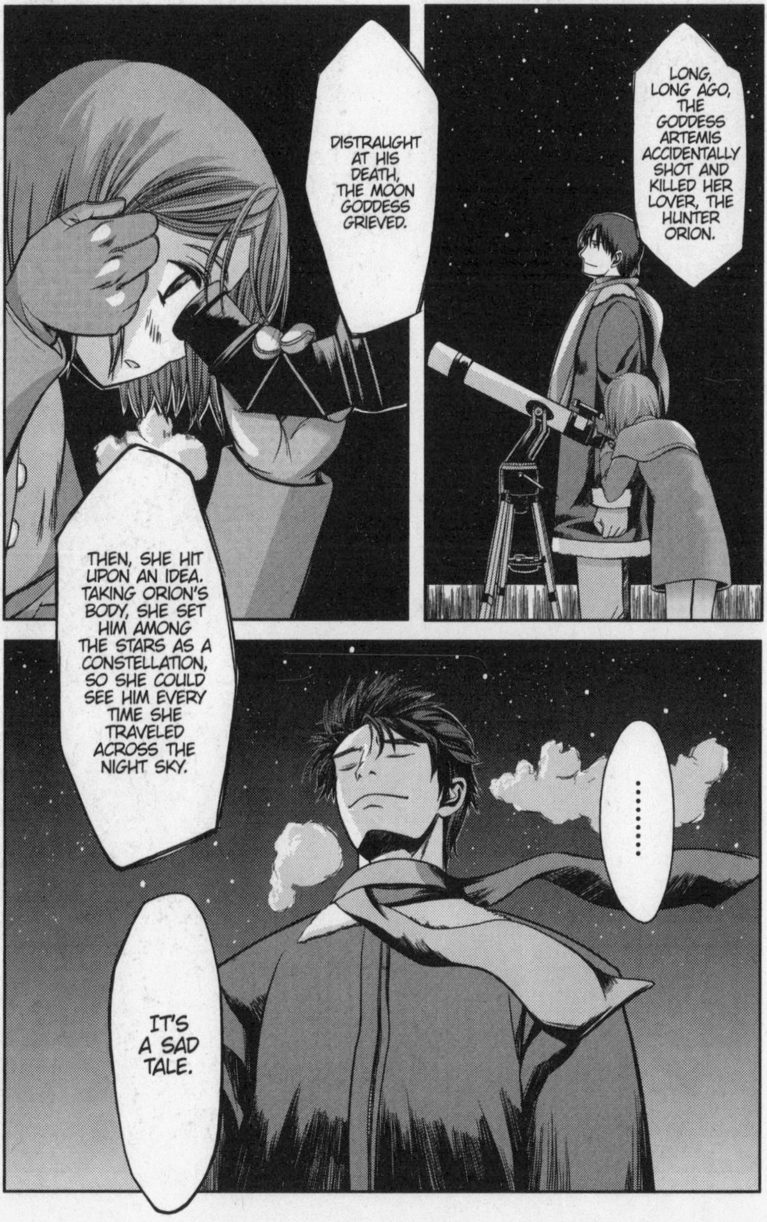
LONG, LONG AGO, THE GODDESS ARTEMIS ACCIDENTALLY SHOT AND KILLED HER LOVER, THE HUNTER ORION.
DISTRAUGHT AT HIS DEATH, THE MOON GODDESS GRIEVED.
THEN, SHE HIT UPON AN IDEA. TAKING ORION'S BODY, SHE SET HIM AMONG THE STARS AS A CONSTELLATION, SO SHE COULD SEE HIM EVERY TIME SHE TRAVELED ACROSS THE NIGHT SKY.
......
IT'S A SAD TALE.

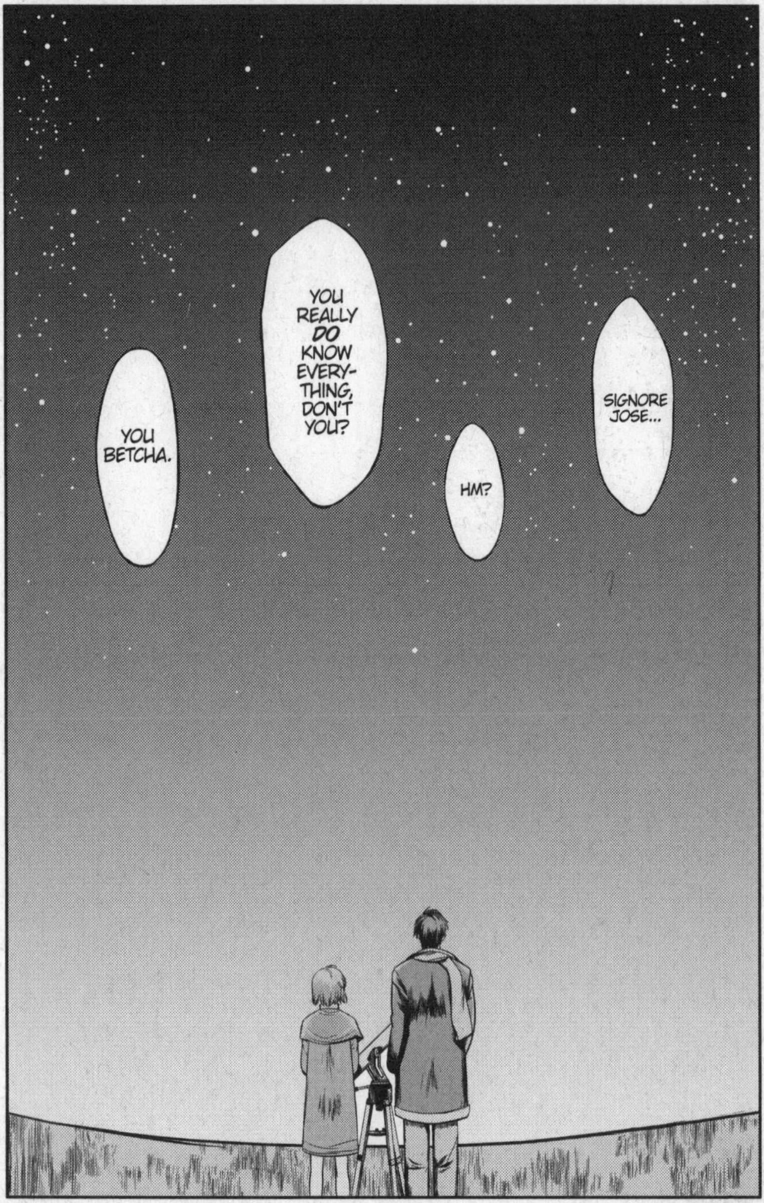
SIGNORE JOSE...
HM?
YOU REALLY *DO* KNOW EVERY-THING, DON'T YOU?
YOU BETCHA.

GUNSLINGERGIRL.

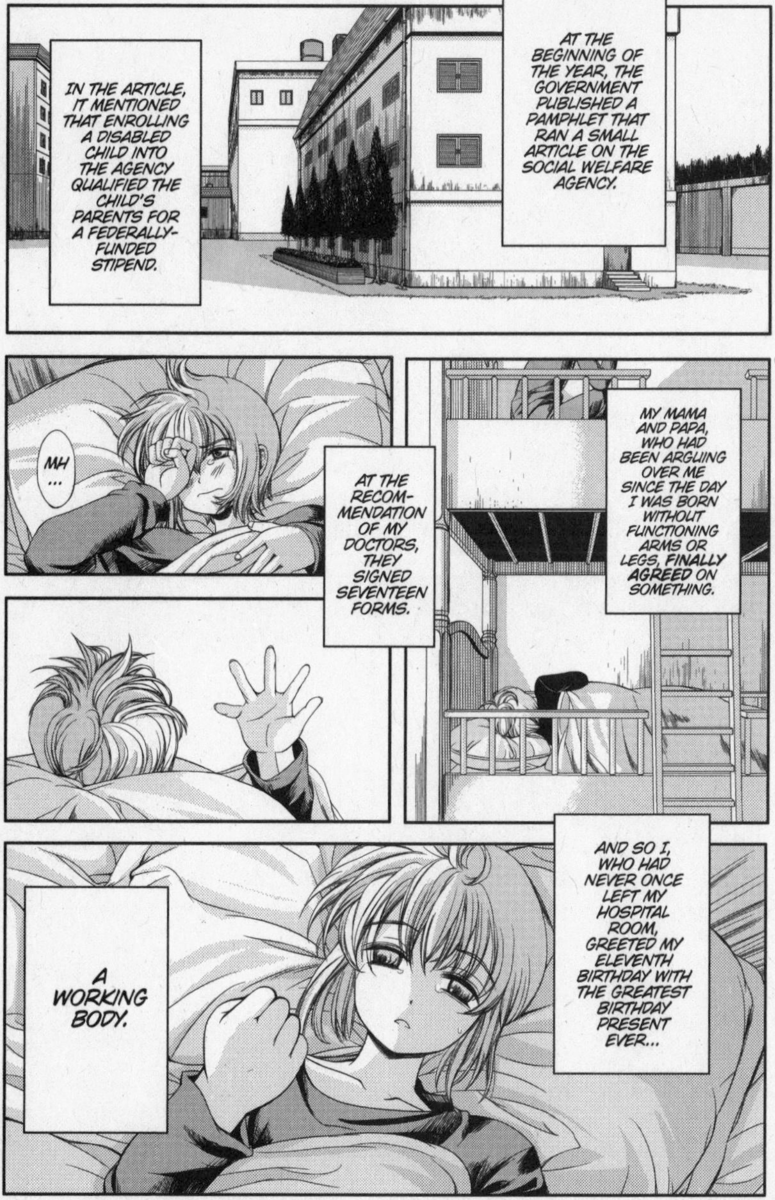
AT THE BEGINNING OF THE YEAR, THE GOVERNMENT PUBLISHED A PAMPHLET THAT RAN A SMALL ARTICLE ON THE SOCIAL WELFARE AGENCY.
IN THE ARTICLE, IT MENTIONED THAT ENROLLING A DISABLED CHILD INTO THE AGENCY QUALIFIED THE CHILD'S PARENTS FOR A FEDERALLY-FUNDED STIPEND.
MY MAMA AND PAPA, WHO HAD BEEN ARGUING OVER ME SINCE THE DAY I WAS BORN WITHOUT FUNCTIONING ARMS OR LEGS, FINALLY AGREED ON SOMETHING.
AT THE RECOMMENDATION OF MY DOCTORS, THEY SIGNED SEVENTEEN FORMS.
MH ...
AND SO I, WHO HAD NEVER ONCE LEFT MY HOSPITAL ROOM, GREETED MY ELEVENTH BIRTHDAY WITH THE GREATEST BIRTHDAY PRESENT EVER...
A WORKING BODY.

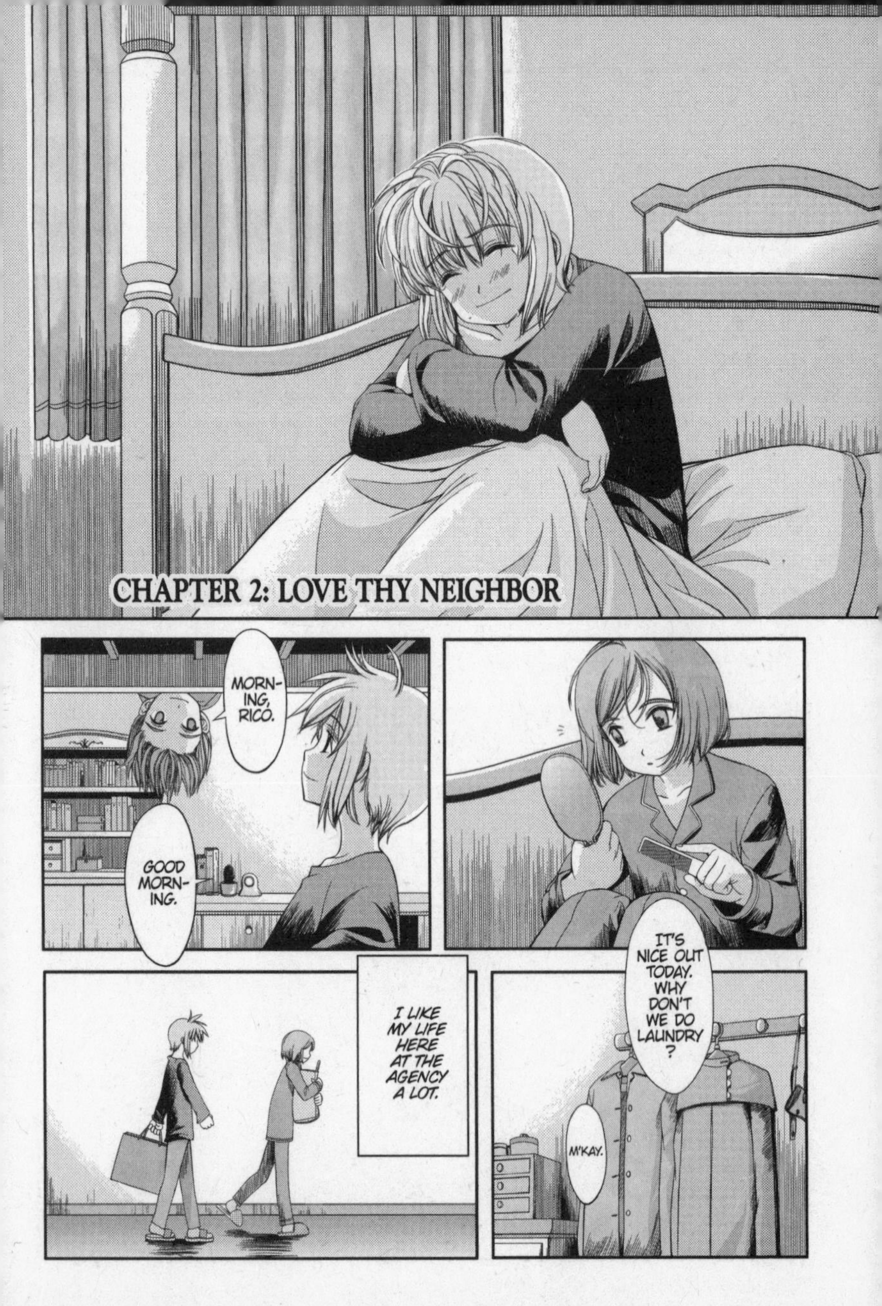
CHAPTER 2: LOVE THY NEIGHBOR
MORNING, RICO.
GOOD MORNING.
IT'S NICE OUT TODAY. WHY DON'T WE DO LAUNDRY?
M'KAY.
I LIKE MY LIFE HERE AT THE AGENCY A LOT.

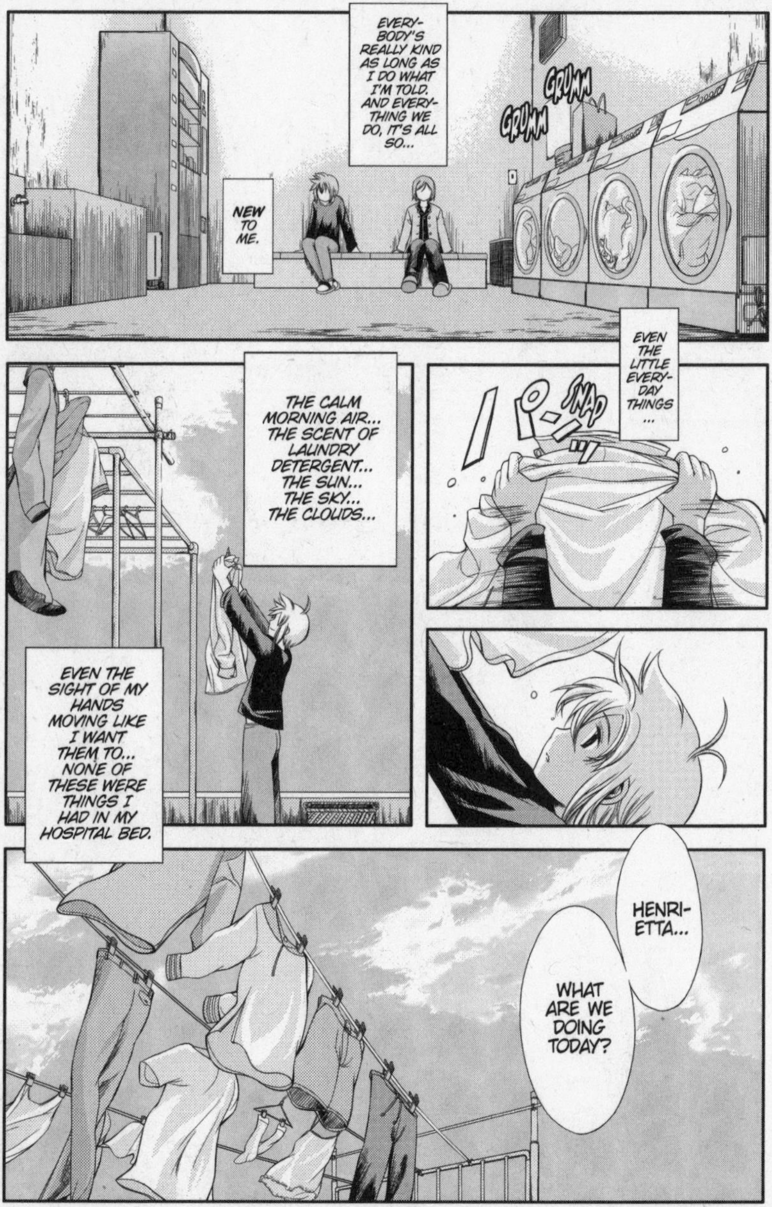
EVERY-BODY'S REALLY KIND AS LONG AS I DO WHAT I'M TOLD. AND EVERY-THING WE DO, IT'S ALL SO...
GRUMM
GRUMM
NEW TO ME.
EVEN THE LITTLE EVERY-DAY THINGS ...
SNAP
THE CALM MORNING AIR... THE SCENT OF LAUNDRY DETERGENT... THE SUN... THE SKY... THE CLOUDS...
EVEN THE SIGHT OF MY HANDS MOVING LIKE I WANT THEM TO... NONE OF THESE WERE THINGS I HAD IN MY HOSPITAL BED.
HENRI-ETTA...
WHAT ARE WE DOING TODAY?

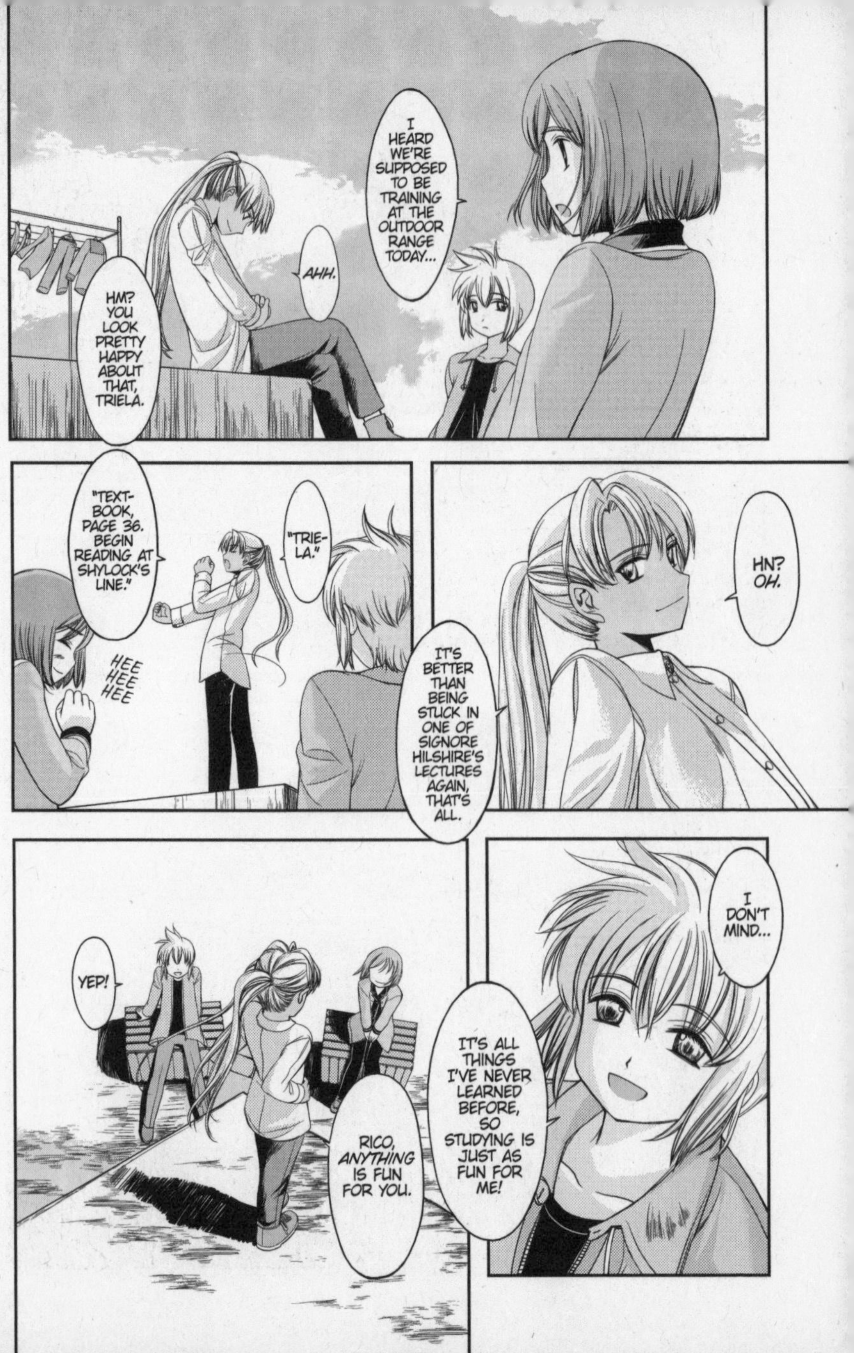
I HEARD WE'RE SUPPOSED TO BE TRAINING AT THE OUTDOOR RANGE TODAY...
AHH.
HM? YOU LOOK PRETTY HAPPY ABOUT THAT, TRIELA.
HN? OH.
IT'S BETTER THAN BEING STUCK IN ONE OF SIGNORE HILSHIRE'S LECTURES AGAIN, THAT'S ALL.
"TRIE-LA."
"TEXT-BOOK, PAGE 36. BEGIN READING AT SHYLOCK'S LINE."
HEE HEE HEE
I DON'T MIND...
IT'S ALL THINGS I'VE NEVER LEARNED BEFORE, SO STUDYING IS JUST AS FUN FOR ME!
RICO, *ANYTHING* IS FUN FOR YOU.
YEP!

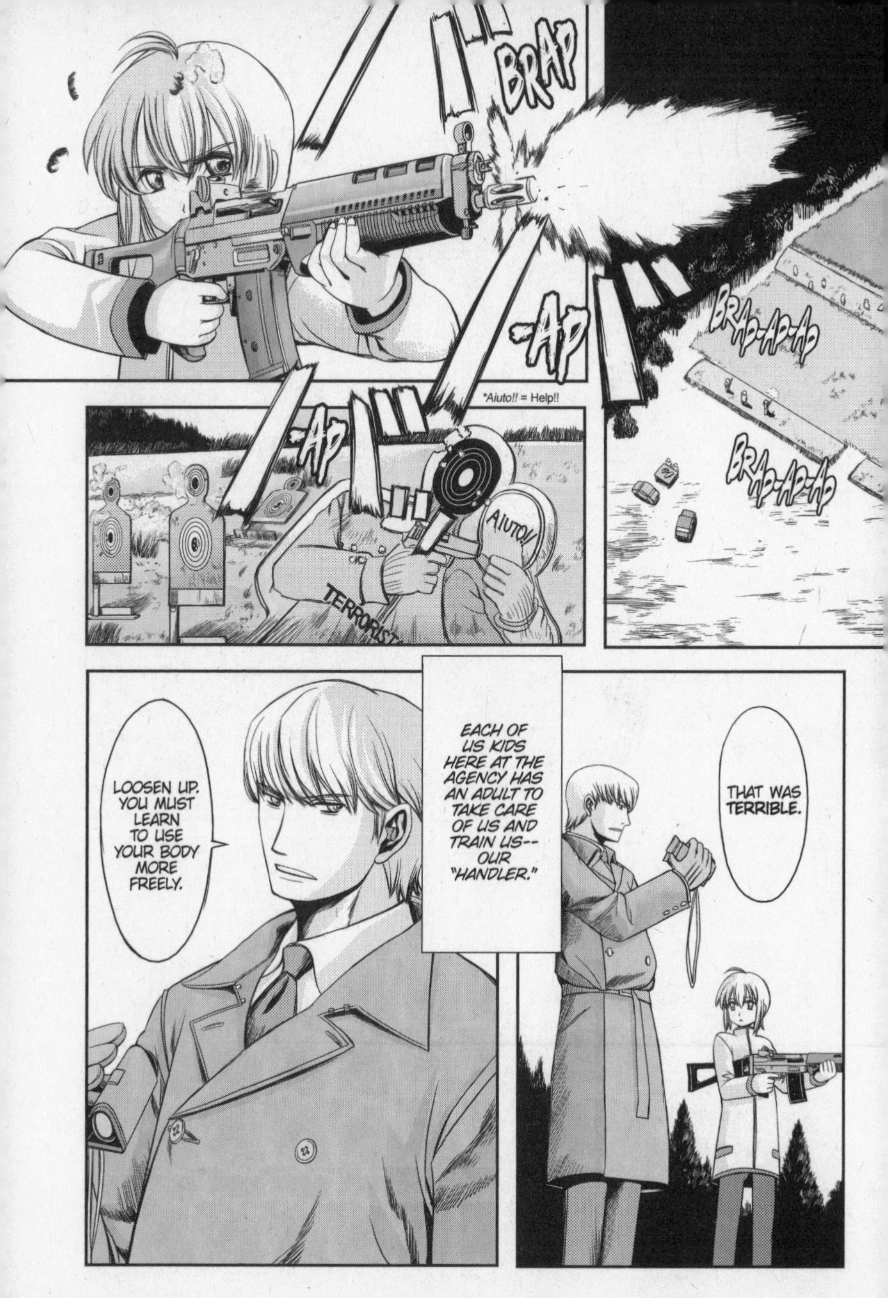
BRAP
-AP
-AP
BRAP-AP-AP
BRAP-AP-AP
*Aiuto!! = Help!!
AIUTO!!
TERRORIST
THAT WAS TERRIBLE.
EACH OF US KIDS HERE AT THE AGENCY HAS AN ADULT TO TAKE CARE OF US AND TRAIN US-- OUR "HANDLER."
LOOSEN UP. YOU MUST LEARN TO USE YOUR BODY MORE FREELY.

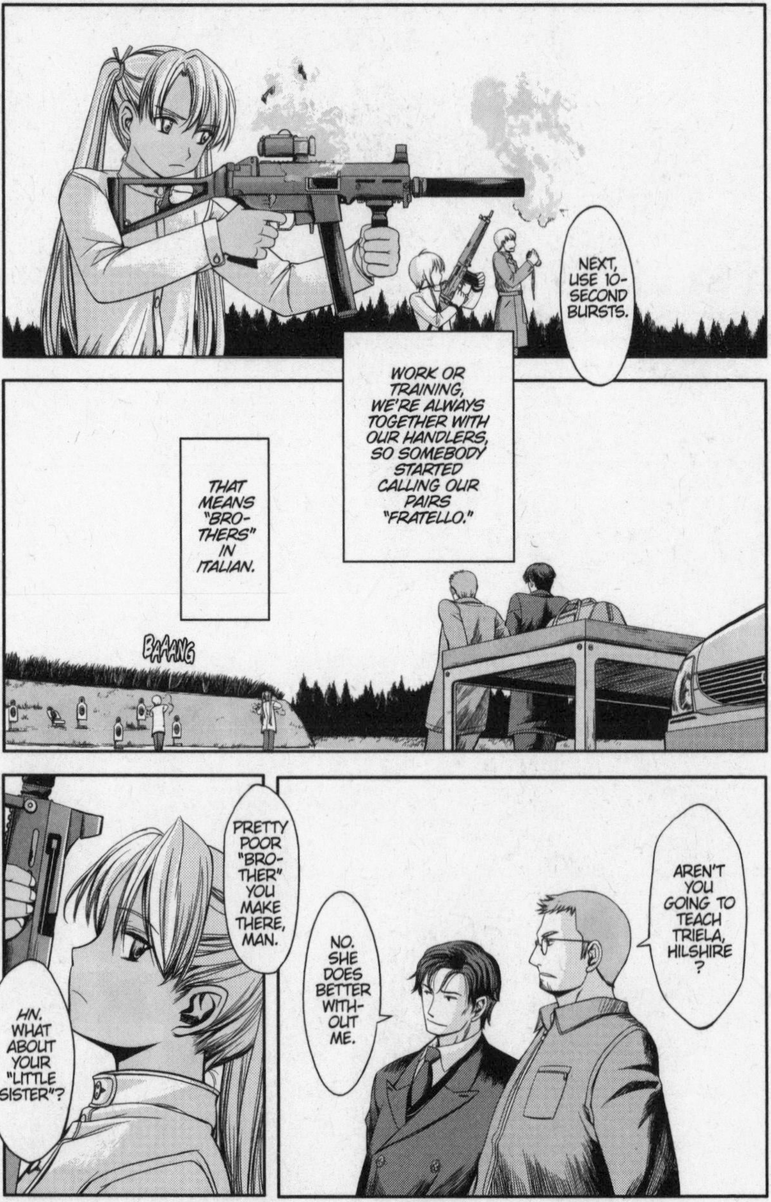

NEXT, USE 10-SECOND BURSTS.
WORK OR TRAINING, WE'RE ALWAYS TOGETHER WITH OUR HANDLERS, SO SOMEBODY STARTED CALLING OUR PAIRS "FRATELLO."
THAT MEANS "BROTHERS" IN ITALIAN.
BAAANG
AREN'T YOU GOING TO TEACH TRIELA, HILSHIRE?
NO. SHE DOES BETTER WITHOUT ME.
PRETTY POOR "BROTHER" YOU MAKE THERE, MAN.
HN. WHAT ABOUT YOUR "LITTLE SISTER"?

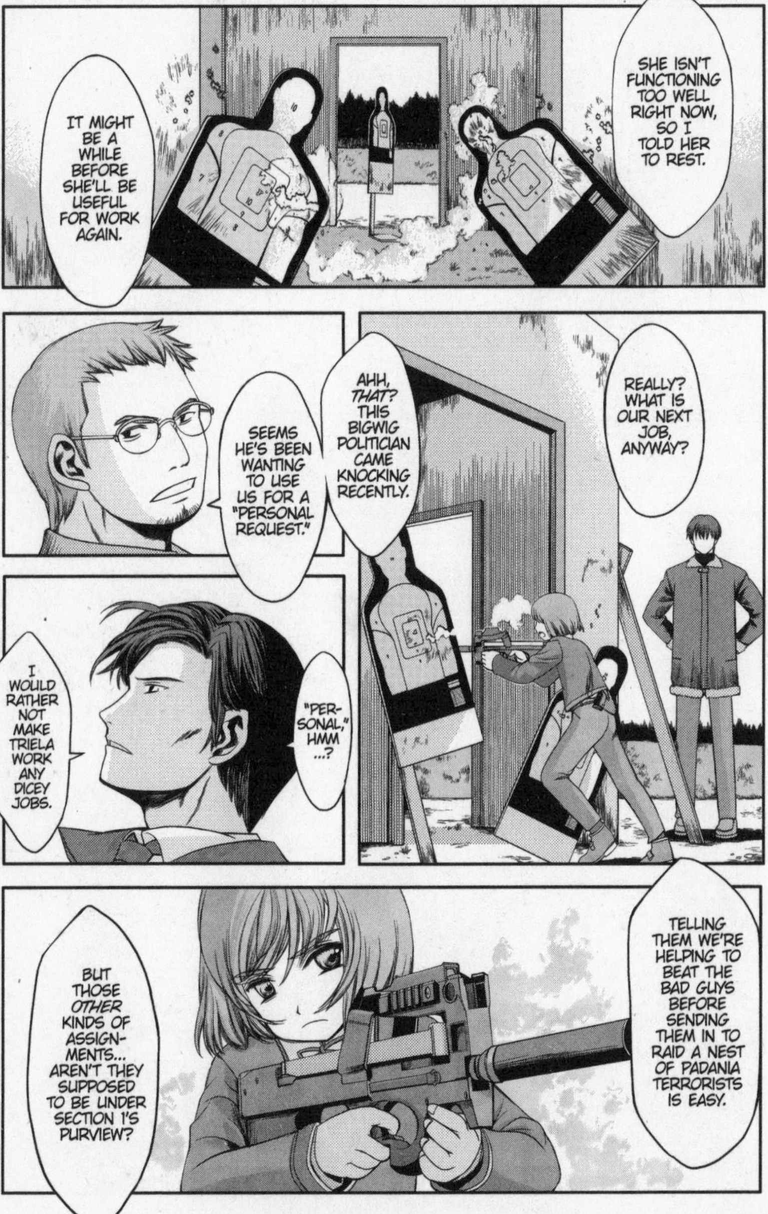
SHE ISN'T FUNCTIONING TOO WELL RIGHT NOW, SO I TOLD HER TO REST.
IT MIGHT BE A WHILE BEFORE SHE'LL BE USEFUL FOR WORK AGAIN.
REALLY? WHAT IS OUR NEXT JOB, ANYWAY?
AHH, *THAT*? THIS BIGWIG POLITICIAN CAME KNOCKING RECENTLY.
SEEMS HE'S BEEN WANTING TO USE US FOR A "PERSONAL REQUEST."
"PERSONAL," HMM ...?
I WOULD RATHER NOT MAKE TRIELA WORK ANY DICEY JOBS.
TELLING THEM WE'RE HELPING TO BEAT THE BAD GUYS BEFORE SENDING THEM IN TO RAID A NEST OF PADANIA TERRORISTS IS EASY.
BUT THOSE *OTHER* KINDS OF ASSIGNMENTS... AREN'T THEY SUPPOSED TO BE UNDER SECTION 1'S PURVIEW?

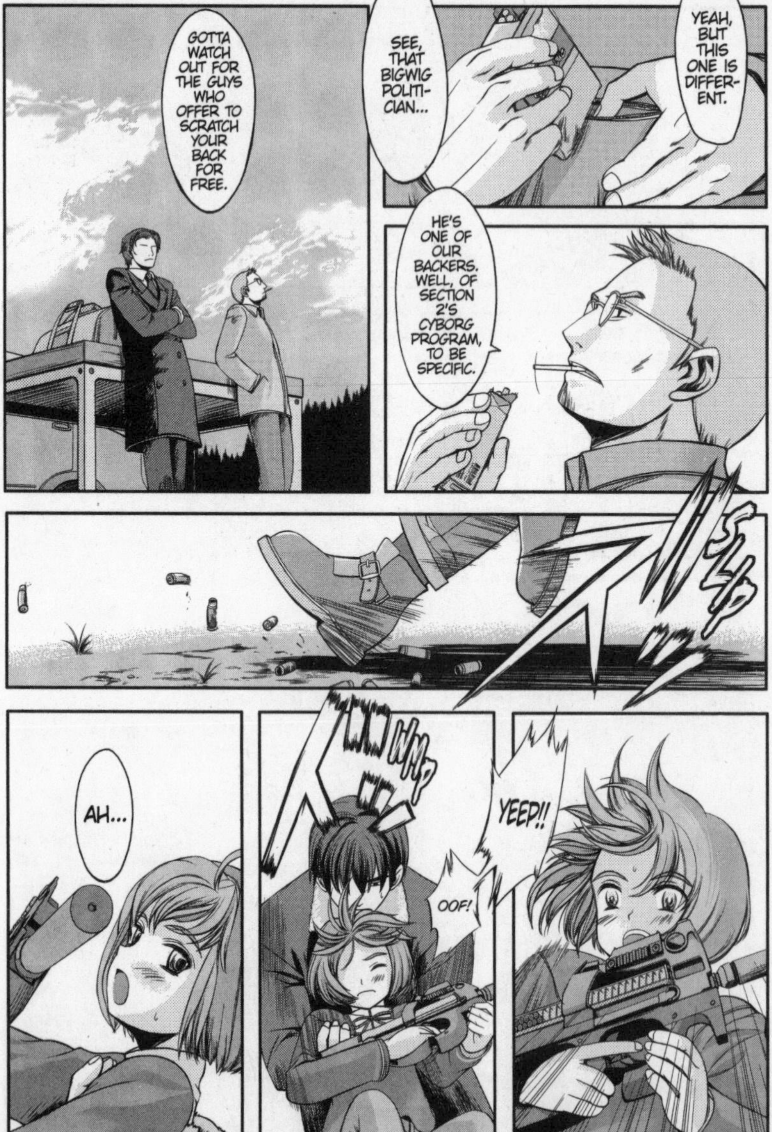
YEAH, BUT THIS ONE IS DIFFER-ENT.
SEE, THAT BIGWIG POLITI-CIAN...
HE'S ONE OF OUR BACKERS. WELL, OF SECTION 2'S CYBORG PROGRAM, TO BE SPECIFIC.
GOTTA WATCH OUT FOR THE GUYS WHO OFFER TO SCRATCH YOUR BACK FOR FREE.
YEEP!!
OOF!
AH...

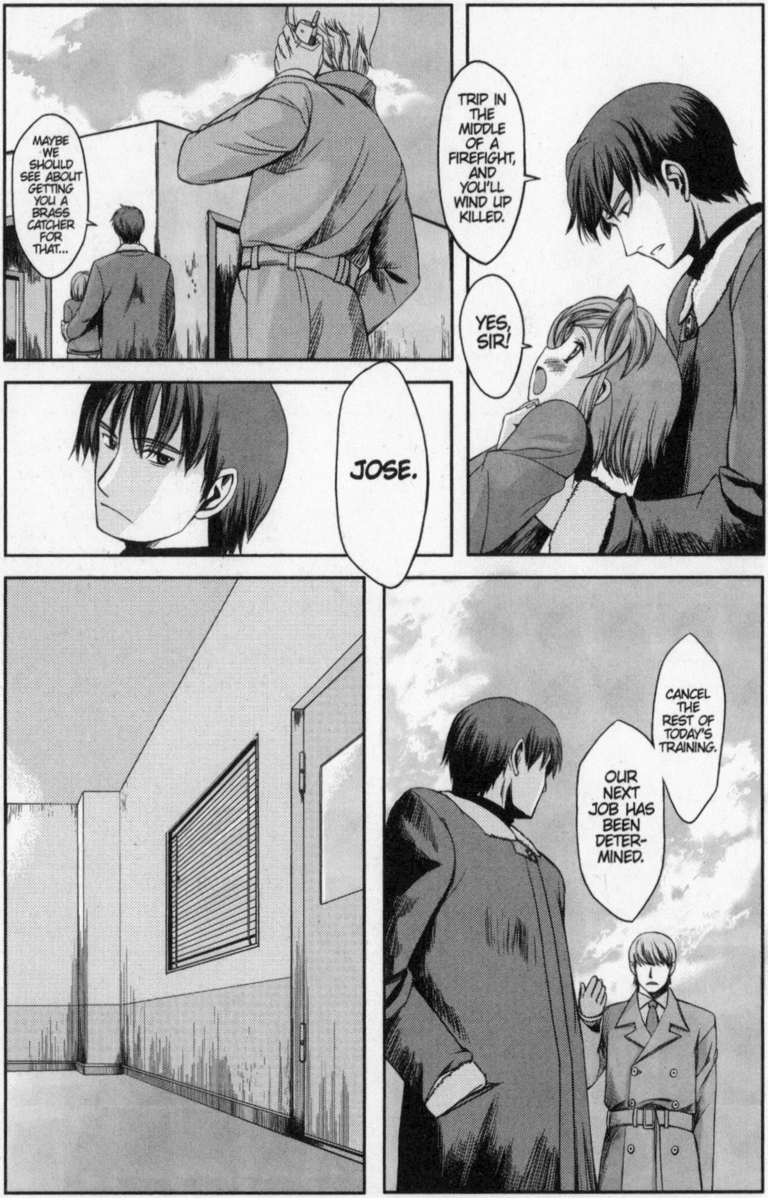
TRIP IN THE MIDDLE OF A FIREFIGHT, AND YOU'LL WIND UP KILLED.
YES, SIR!
MAYBE WE SHOULD SEE ABOUT GETTING YOU A BRASS CATCHER FOR THAT...
JOSE.
CANCEL THE REST OF TODAY'S TRAINING.
OUR NEXT JOB HAS BEEN DETER-MINED.

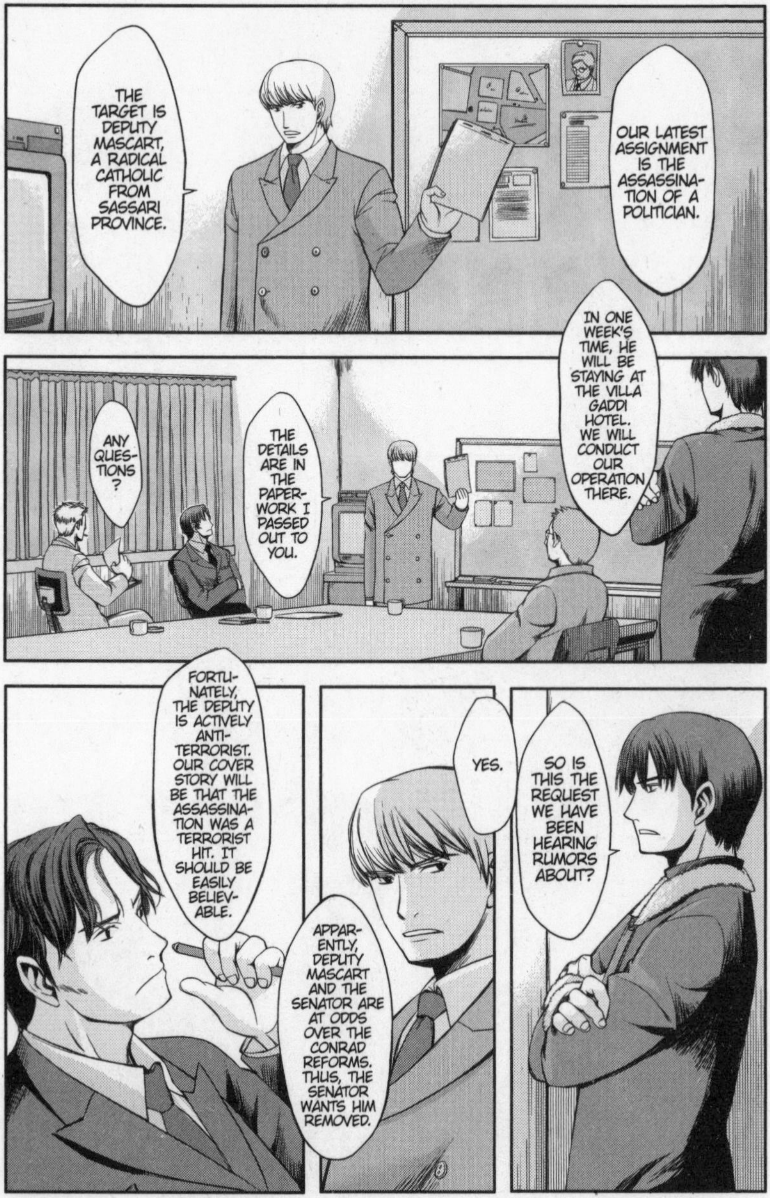
OUR LATEST ASSIGNMENT IS THE ASSASSINATION OF A POLITICIAN.
THE TARGET IS DEPUTY MASCART, A RADICAL CATHOLIC FROM SASSARI PROVINCE.
IN ONE WEEK'S TIME, HE WILL BE STAYING AT THE VILLA GADDI HOTEL. WE WILL CONDUCT OUR OPERATION THERE.
THE DETAILS ARE IN THE PAPERWORK I PASSED OUT TO YOU.
ANY QUESTIONS?
SO IS THIS THE REQUEST WE HAVE BEEN HEARING RUMORS ABOUT?
YES.
APPARENTLY, DEPUTY MASCART AND THE SENATOR ARE AT ODDS OVER THE CONRAD REFORMS. THUS, THE SENATOR WANTS HIM REMOVED.
FORTUNATELY, THE DEPUTY IS ACTIVELY ANTI-TERRORIST. OUR COVER STORY WILL BE THAT THE ASSASSINATION WAS A TERRORIST HIT. IT SHOULD BE EASILY BELIEVABLE.

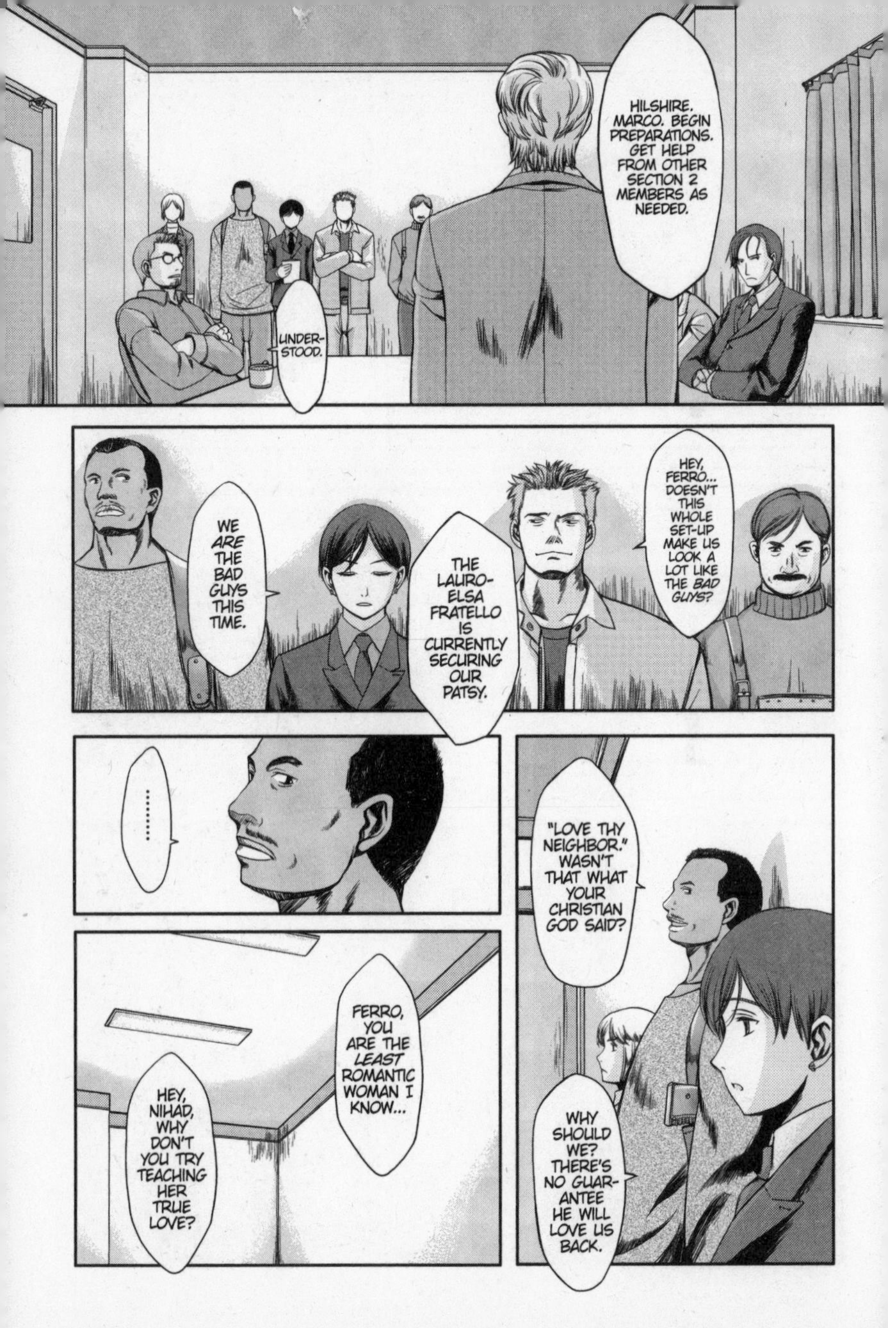
HILSHIRE. MARCO. BEGIN PREPARATIONS. GET HELP FROM OTHER SECTION 2 MEMBERS AS NEEDED.
UNDER-STOOD.
HEY, FERRO... DOESN'T THIS WHOLE SET-UP MAKE US LOOK A LOT LIKE THE *BAD GUYS*?
THE LAURO-ELSA FRATELLO IS CURRENTLY SECURING OUR PATSY.
WE *ARE* THE BAD GUYS THIS TIME.
"LOVE THY NEIGHBOR." WASN'T THAT WHAT YOUR CHRISTIAN GOD SAID?
WHY SHOULD WE? THERE'S NO GUAR-ANTEE HE WILL LOVE US BACK.
......
FERRO, YOU ARE THE *LEAST* ROMANTIC WOMAN I KNOW...
HEY, NIHAD, WHY DON'T YOU TRY TEACHING HER TRUE LOVE?

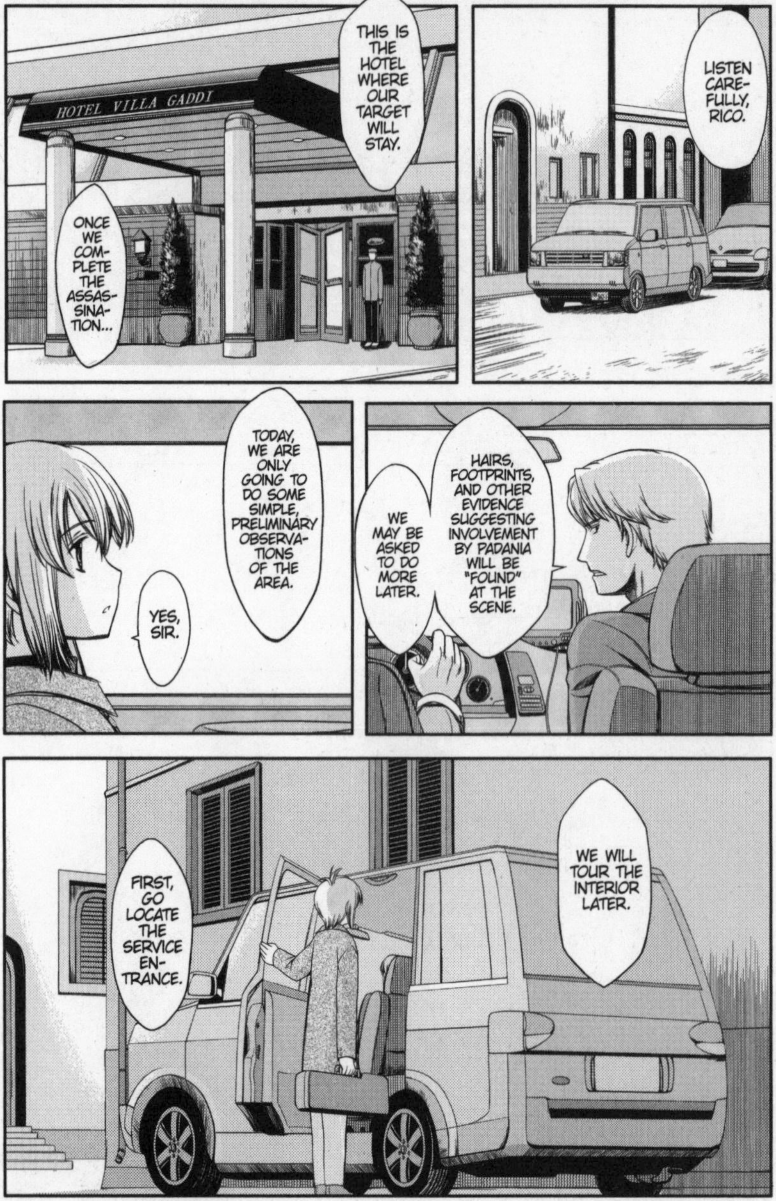
LISTEN CARE-FULLY, RICO.
HOTEL VILLA GADDI
THIS IS THE HOTEL WHERE OUR TARGET WILL STAY.
ONCE WE COM-PLETE THE ASSAS-SINA-TION...
HAIRS, FOOTPRINTS, AND OTHER EVIDENCE SUGGESTING INVOLVEMENT BY PADANIA WILL BE "FOUND" AT THE SCENE.
WE MAY BE ASKED TO DO MORE LATER.
TODAY, WE ARE ONLY GOING TO DO SOME SIMPLE, PRELIMINARY OBSERVA-TIONS OF THE AREA.
YES, SIR.
WE WILL TOUR THE INTERIOR LATER.
FIRST, GO LOCATE THE SERVICE EN-TRANCE.

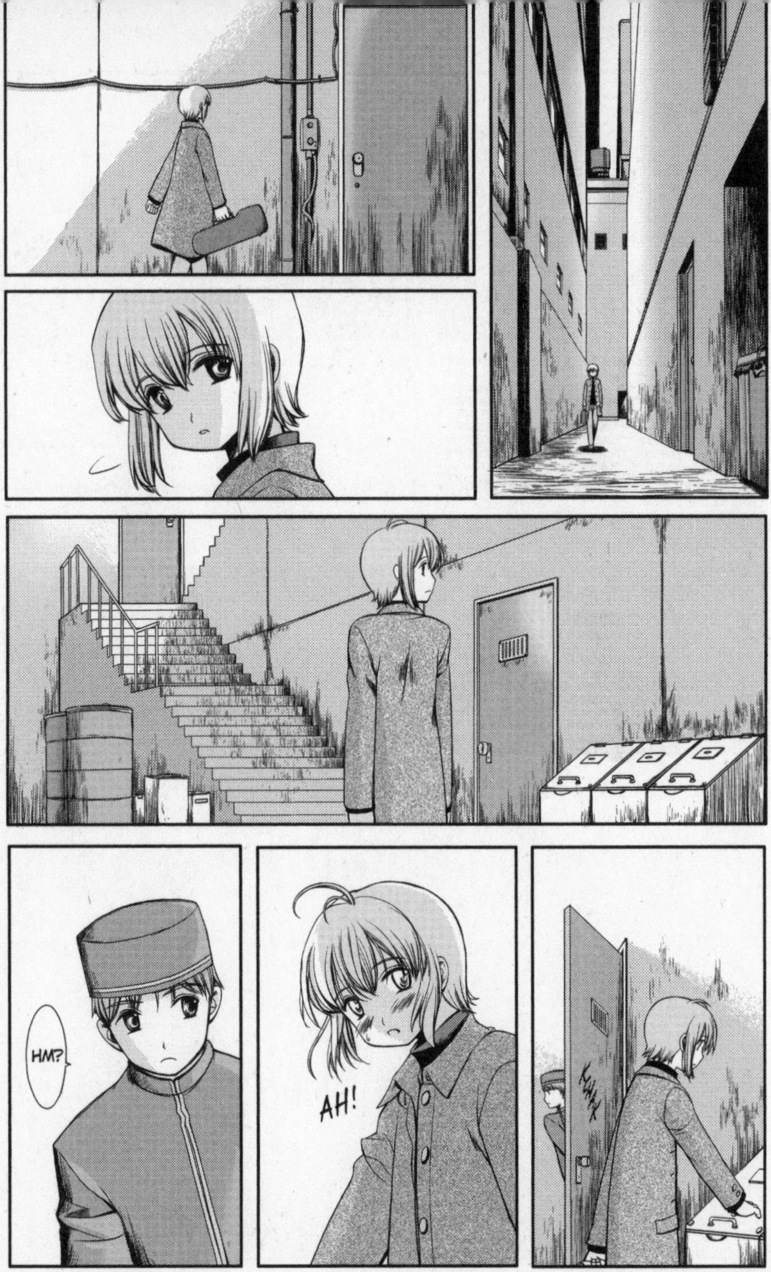
AH!
HM?

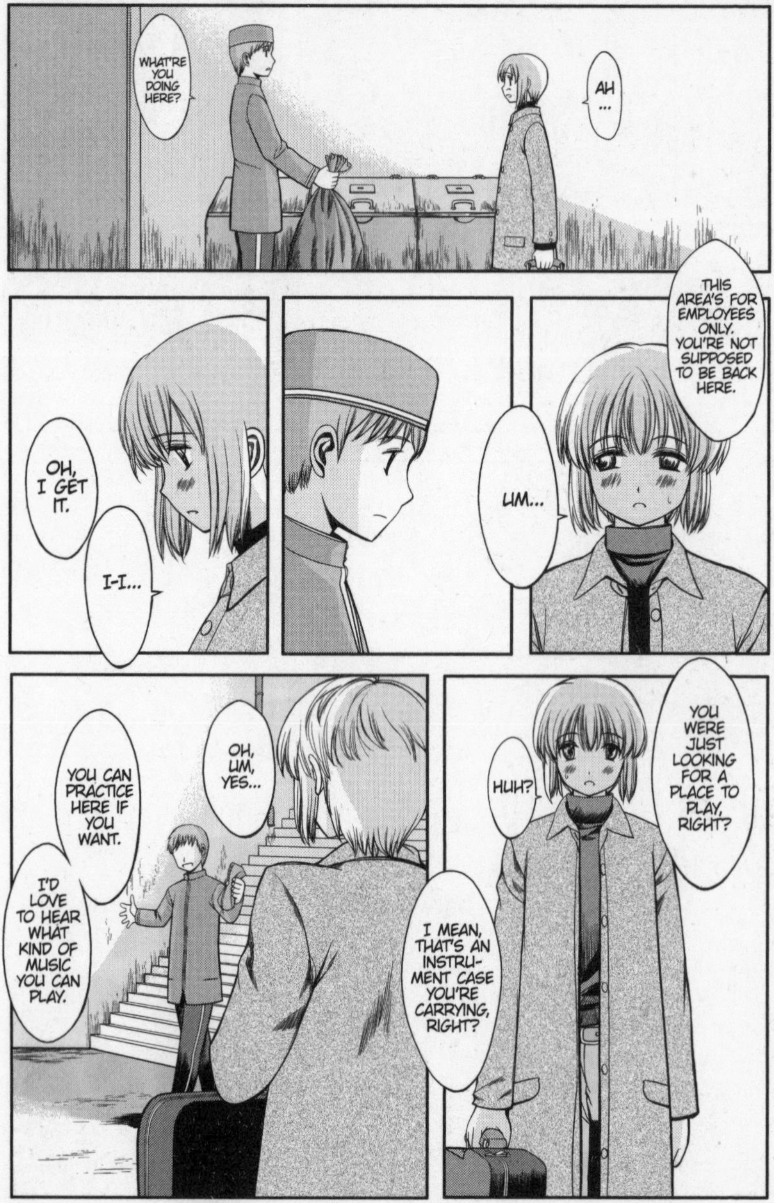
AH ...
WHAT'RE YOU DOING HERE?
THIS AREA'S FOR EMPLOYEES ONLY. YOU'RE NOT SUPPOSED TO BE BACK HERE.
UM...
OH, I GET IT.
I-I...
YOU WERE JUST LOOKING FOR A PLACE TO PLAY, RIGHT?
HUH?
I MEAN, THAT'S AN INSTRU-MENT CASE YOU'RE CARRYING, RIGHT?
OH, UM, YES...
YOU CAN PRACTICE HERE IF YOU WANT.
I'D LOVE TO HEAR WHAT KIND OF MUSIC YOU CAN PLAY.

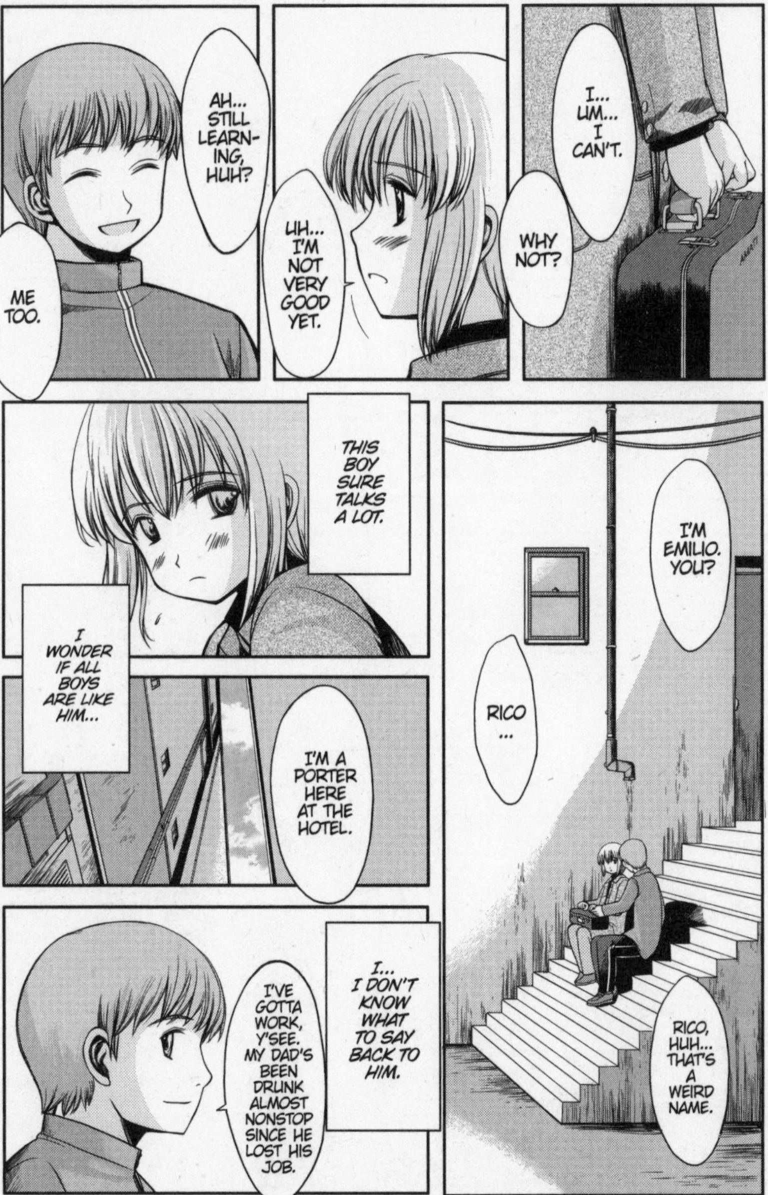
I... UM... I CAN'T.
WHY NOT?
UH... I'M NOT VERY GOOD YET.
AH... STILL LEARNING, HUH?
ME TOO.
I'M EMILIO. YOU?
RICO...
RICO, HUH... THAT'S A WEIRD NAME.
THIS BOY SURE TALKS A LOT.
I WONDER IF ALL BOYS ARE LIKE HIM...
I'M A PORTER HERE AT THE HOTEL.
I... I DON'T KNOW WHAT TO SAY BACK TO HIM.
I'VE GOTTA WORK, Y'SEE. MY DAD'S BEEN DRUNK ALMOST NONSTOP SINCE HE LOST HIS JOB.

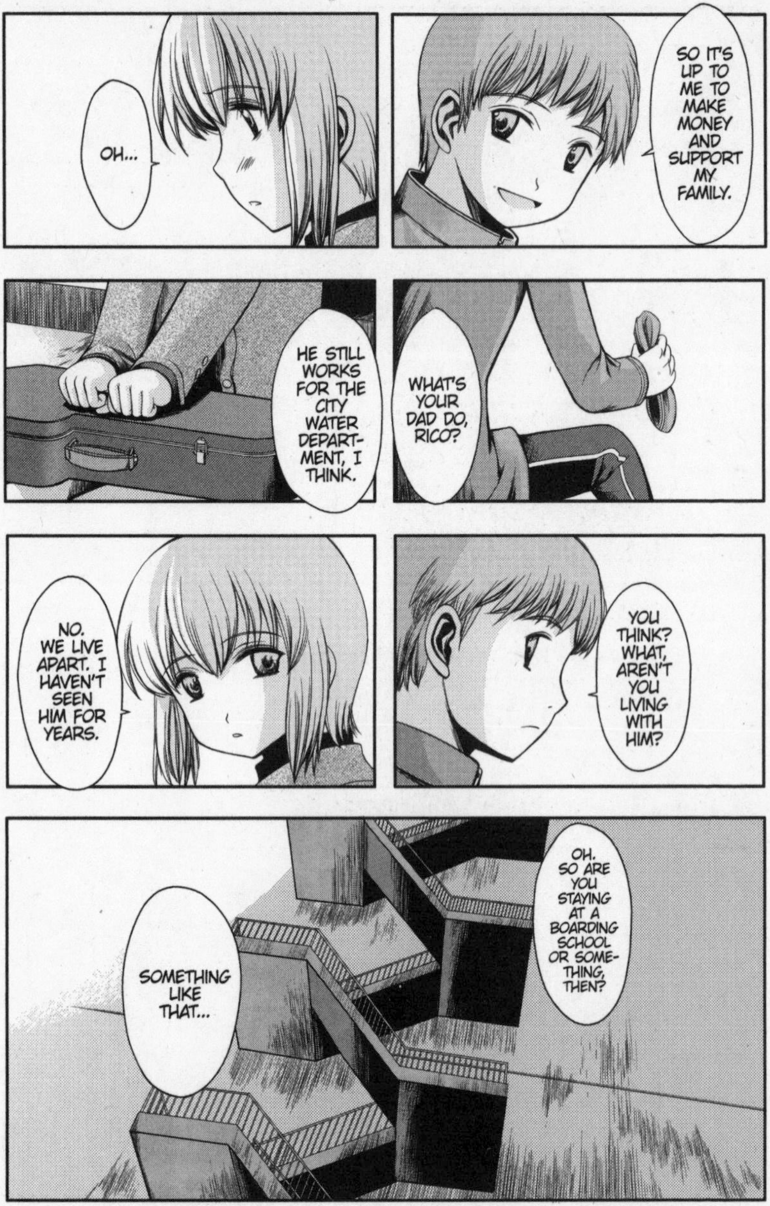
SO IT'S UP TO ME TO MAKE MONEY AND SUPPORT MY FAMILY.
OH...
WHAT'S YOUR DAD DO, RICO?
HE STILL WORKS FOR THE CITY WATER DEPARTMENT, I THINK.
YOU THINK? WHAT, AREN'T YOU LIVING WITH HIM?
NO. WE LIVE APART. I HAVEN'T SEEN HIM FOR YEARS.
OH. SO ARE YOU STAYING AT A BOARDING SCHOOL OR SOMETHING, THEN?
SOMETHING LIKE THAT...

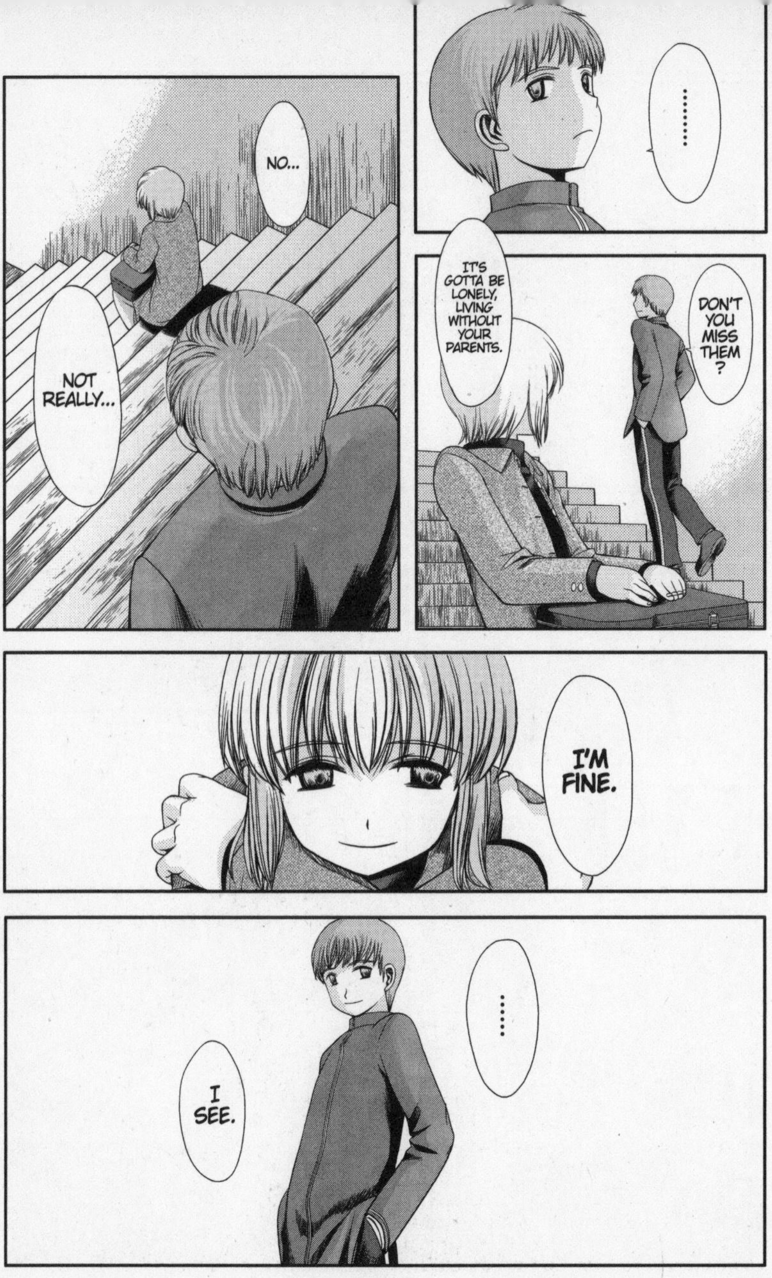
......
DON'T YOU MISS THEM?
IT'S GOTTA BE LONELY, LIVING WITHOUT YOUR PARENTS.
NO...
NOT REALLY...
I'M FINE.
......
I SEE.

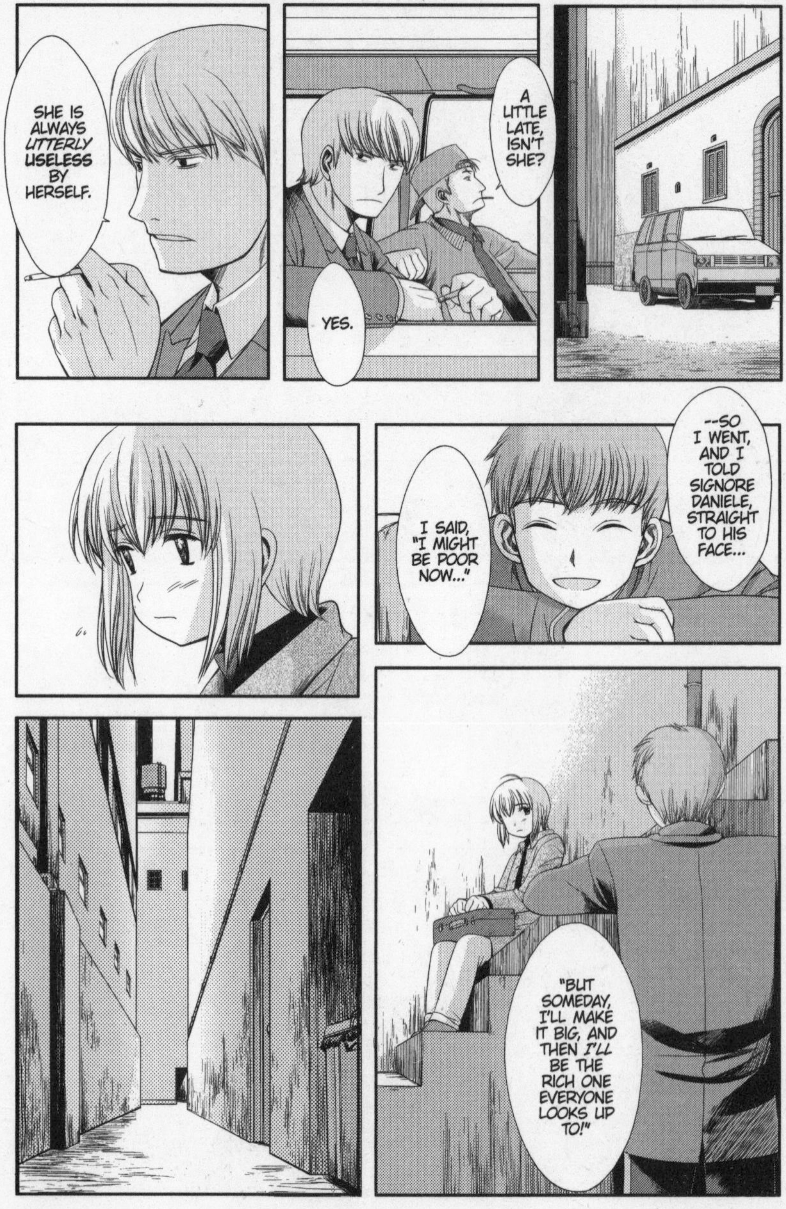
A LITTLE LATE, ISN'T SHE?
YES.
SHE IS ALWAYS *UTTERLY* USELESS BY HERSELF.
--SO I WENT, AND I TOLD SIGNORE DANIELE, STRAIGHT TO HIS FACE...
I SAID, "I MIGHT BE POOR NOW..."
"BUT SOMEDAY, I'LL MAKE IT BIG, AND THEN *I'LL* BE THE RICH ONE EVERYONE LOOKS UP TO!"

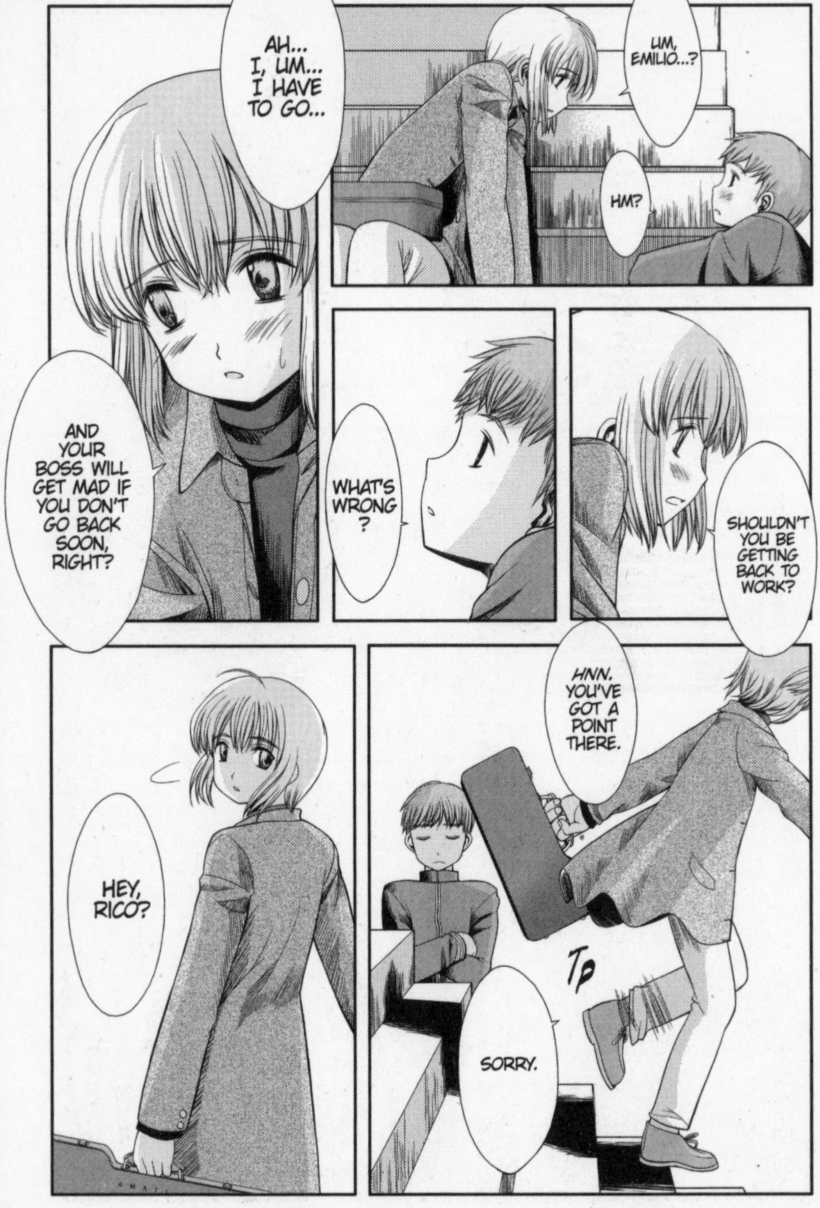
UM, EMILIO...?
HM?
SHOULDN'T YOU BE GETTING BACK TO WORK?
WHAT'S WRONG?
AH... I, UM... I HAVE TO GO...
AND YOUR BOSS WILL GET MAD IF YOU DON'T GO BACK SOON, RIGHT?
HNN. YOU'VE GOT A POINT THERE.
TP
SORRY.
HEY, RICO?

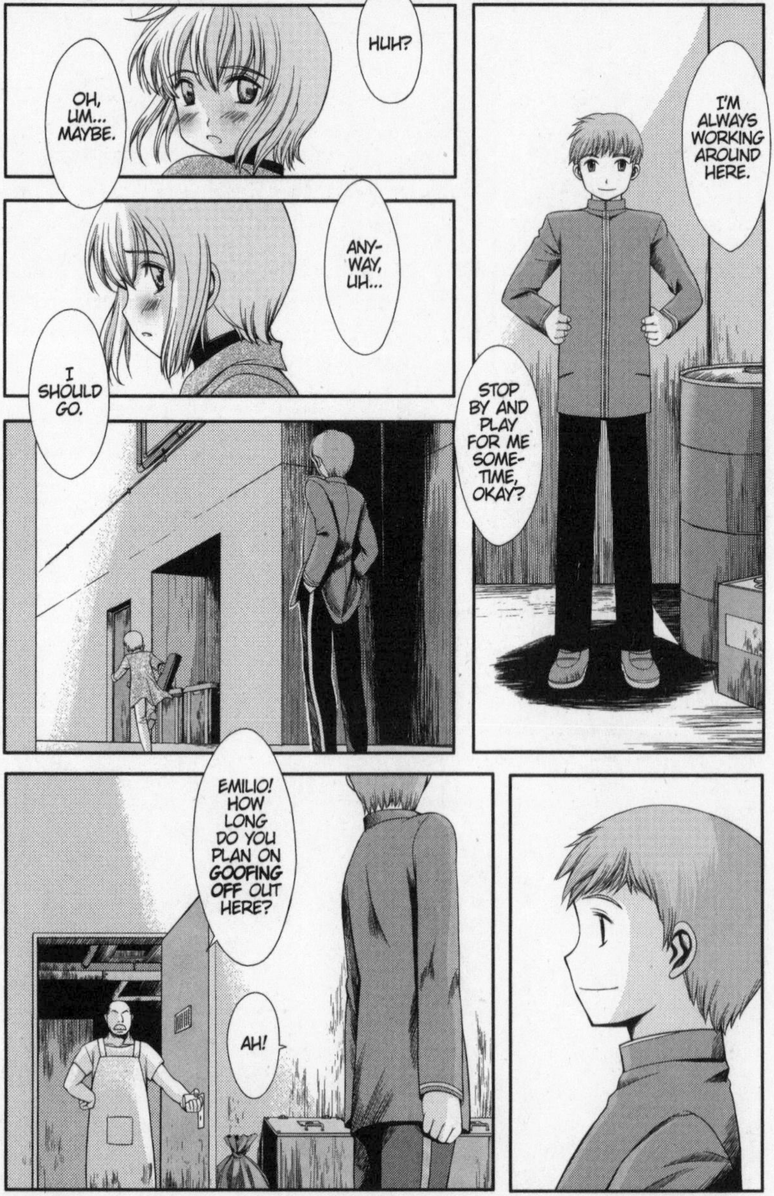
I'M ALWAYS WORKING AROUND HERE.
STOP BY AND PLAY FOR ME SOME-TIME, OKAY?
HUH?
OH, UM... MAYBE.
ANY-WAY, UH...
I SHOULD GO.
EMILIO! HOW LONG DO YOU PLAN ON GOOFING OFF OUT HERE?
AH!

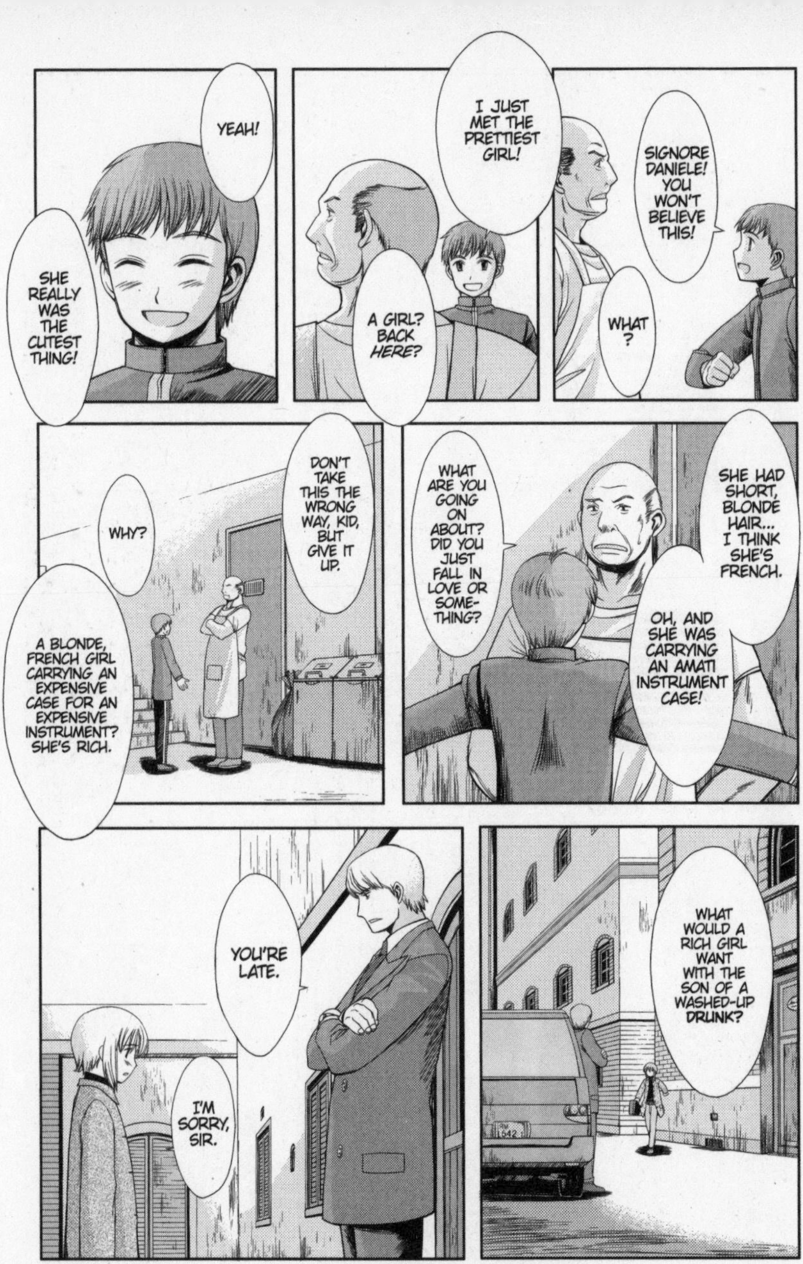
SIGNORE DANIELE! YOU WON'T BELIEVE THIS!
WHAT?
I JUST MET THE PRETTIEST GIRL!
A GIRL? BACK HERE?
YEAH!
SHE REALLY WAS THE CUTEST THING!
SHE HAD SHORT, BLONDE HAIR... I THINK SHE'S FRENCH.
OH, AND SHE WAS CARRYING AN AMATI INSTRUMENT CASE!
WHAT ARE YOU GOING ON ABOUT? DID YOU JUST FALL IN LOVE OR SOME-THING?
DON'T TAKE THIS THE WRONG WAY, KID, BUT GIVE IT UP.
WHY?
A BLONDE, FRENCH GIRL CARRYING AN EXPENSIVE CASE FOR AN EXPENSIVE INSTRUMENT? SHE'S RICH.
WHAT WOULD A RICH GIRL WANT WITH THE SON OF A WASHED-UP DRUNK?
YOU'RE LATE.
I'M SORRY, SIR.

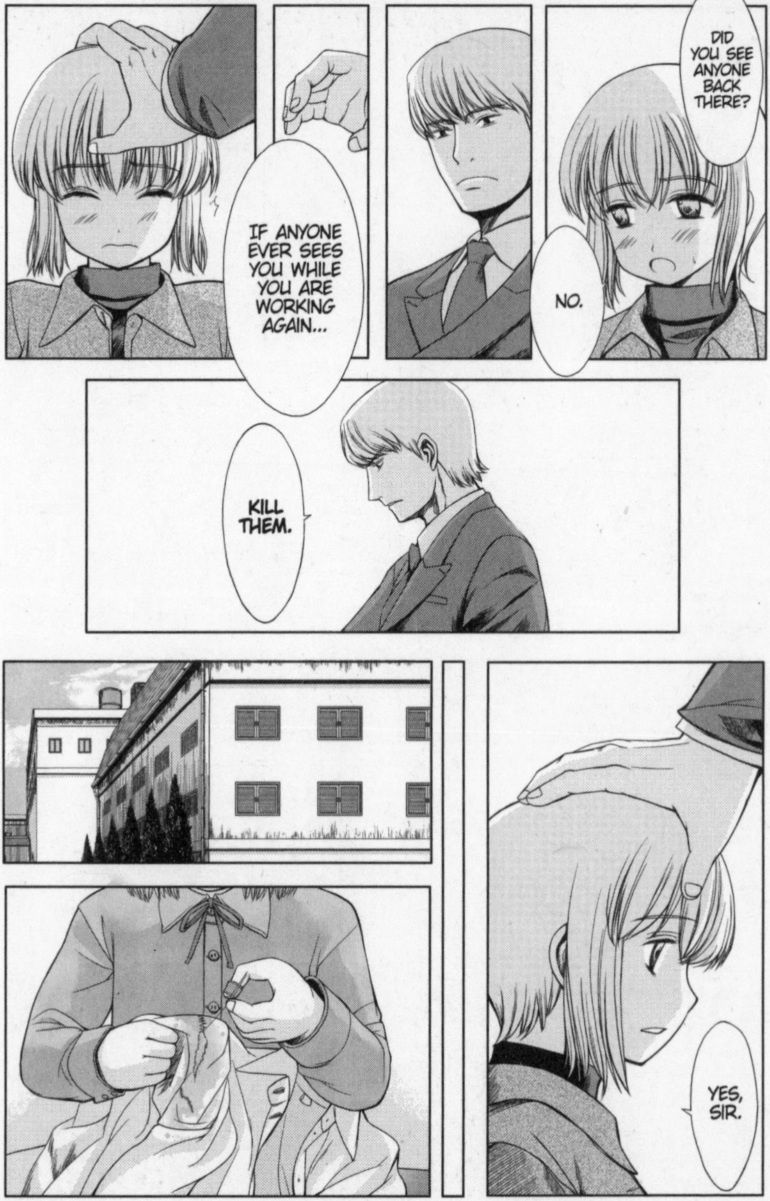
DID YOU SEE ANYONE BACK THERE?
NO.
IF ANYONE EVER SEES YOU WHILE YOU ARE WORKING AGAIN...
KILL THEM.
YES, SIR.

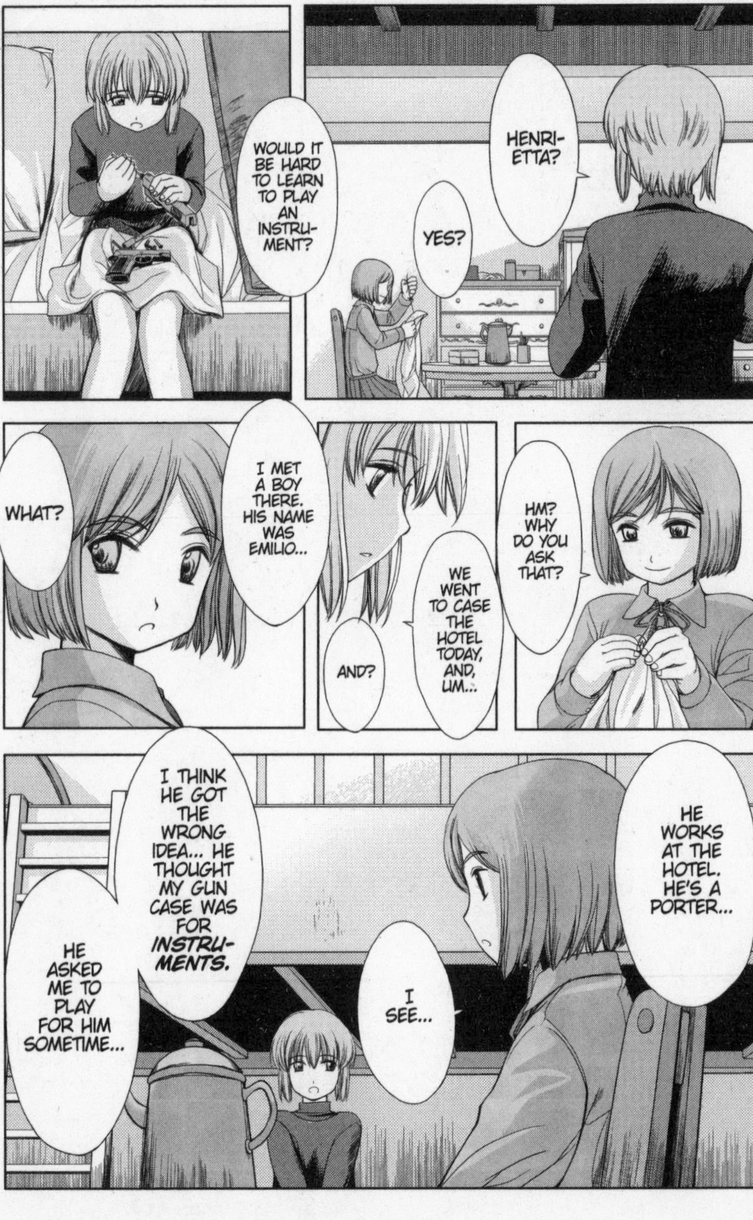
HENRI-ETTA?
YES?
WOULD IT BE HARD TO LEARN TO PLAY AN INSTRU-MENT?
HM? WHY DO YOU ASK THAT?
WE WENT TO CASE THE HOTEL TODAY, AND, UM...
AND?
I MET A BOY THERE. HIS NAME WAS EMILIO...
WHAT?
HE WORKS AT THE HOTEL. HE'S A PORTER...
I SEE...
I THINK HE GOT THE WRONG IDEA... HE THOUGHT MY GUN CASE WAS FOR *INSTRU-MENTS.*
HE ASKED ME TO PLAY FOR HIM SOMETIME...

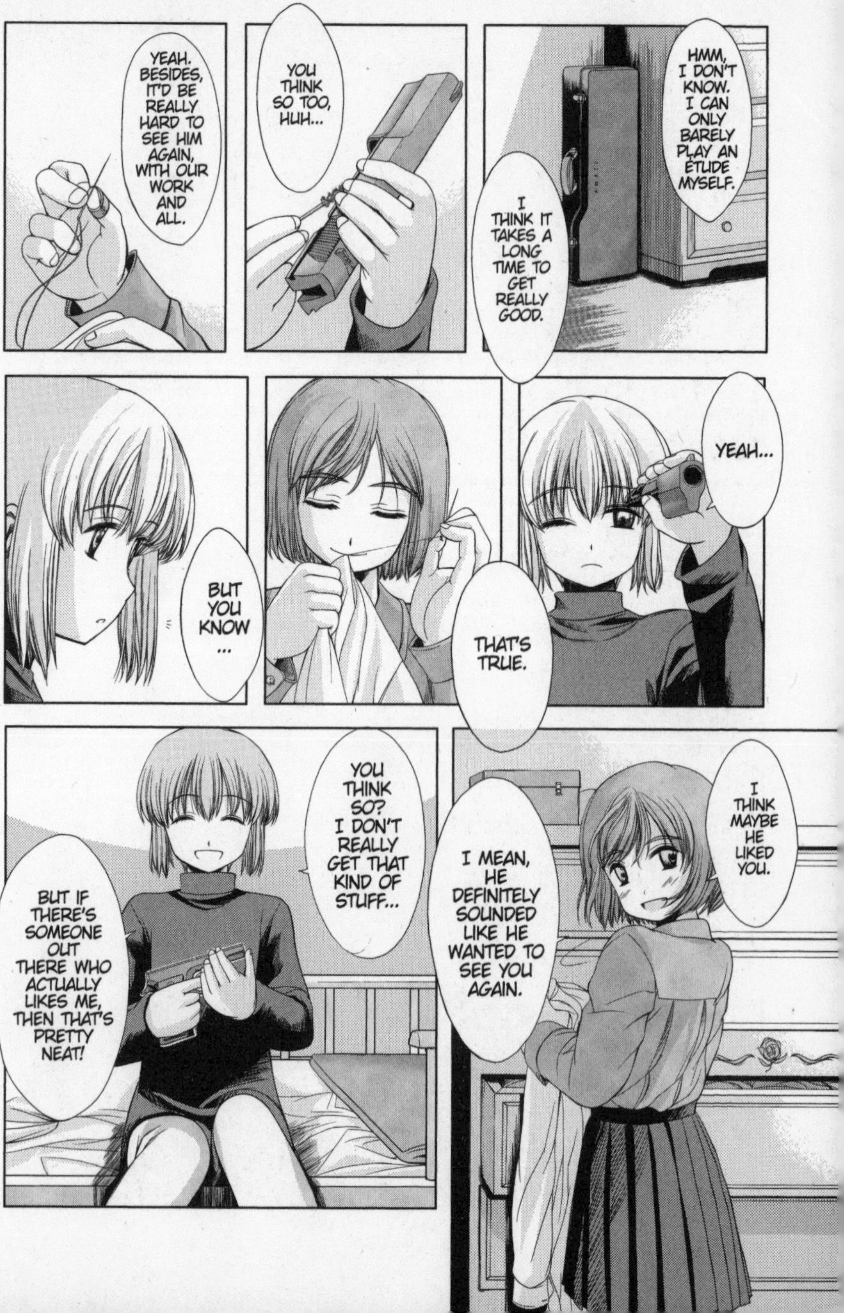
HMM, I DON'T KNOW. I CAN ONLY BARELY PLAY AN ÉTUDE MYSELF.
I THINK IT TAKES A LONG TIME TO GET REALLY GOOD.
YOU THINK SO TOO, HUH...
YEAH. BESIDES, IT'D BE REALLY HARD TO SEE HIM AGAIN, WITH OUR WORK AND ALL.
YEAH...
THAT'S TRUE.
BUT YOU KNOW ...
I THINK MAYBE HE LIKED YOU.
I MEAN, HE DEFINITELY SOUNDED LIKE HE WANTED TO SEE YOU AGAIN.
YOU THINK SO? I DON'T REALLY GET THAT KIND OF STUFF...
BUT IF THERE'S SOMEONE OUT THERE WHO ACTUALLY LIKES ME, THEN THAT'S PRETTY NEAT!

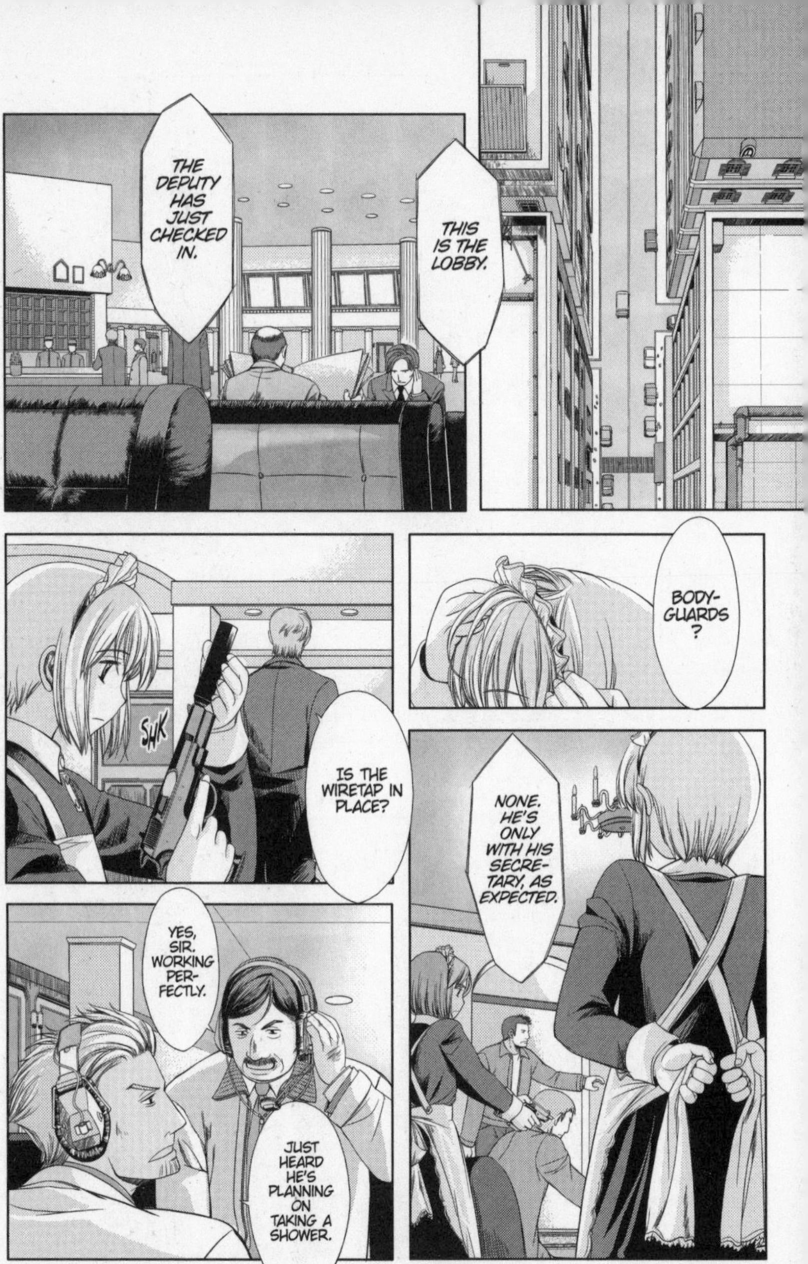
THIS IS THE LOBBY.
THE DEPUTY HAS JUST CHECKED IN.
BODY-GUARDS?
NONE. HE'S ONLY WITH HIS SECRETARY, AS EXPECTED.
SHK
IS THE WIRETAP IN PLACE?
YES, SIR. WORKING PERFECTLY.
JUST HEARD HE'S PLANNING ON TAKING A SHOWER.

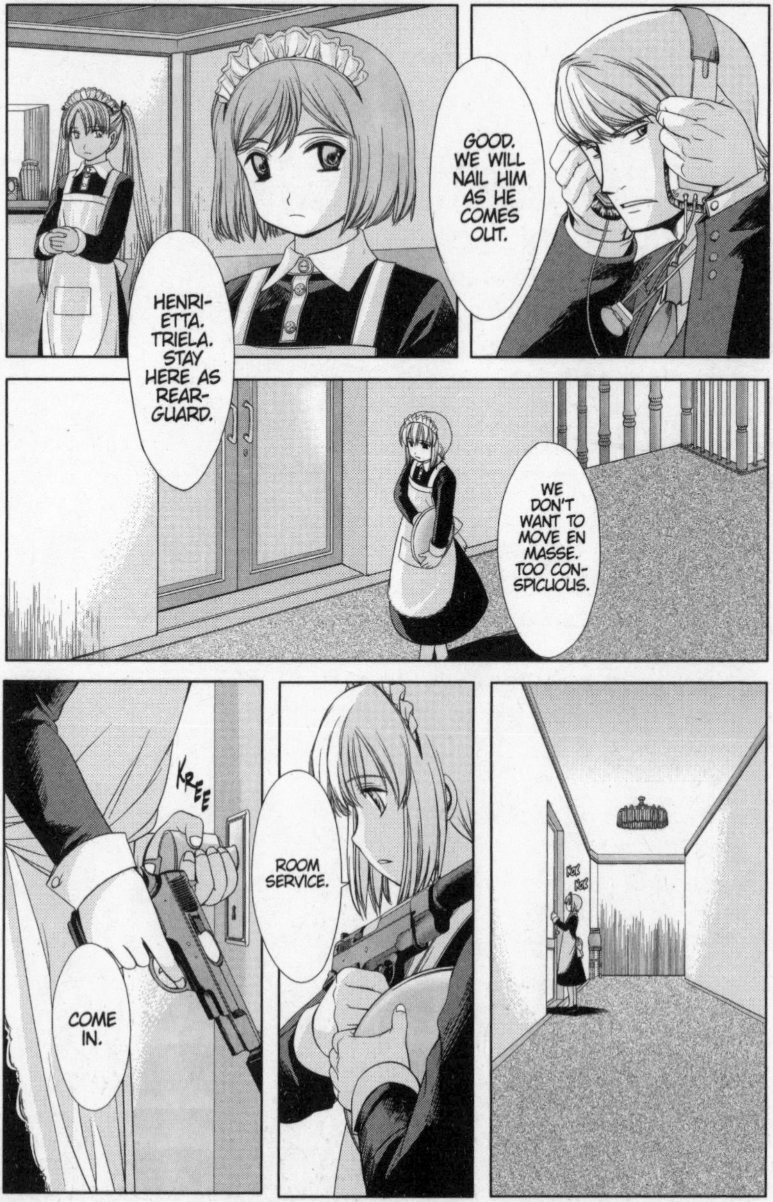
GOOD. WE WILL NAIL HIM AS HE COMES OUT.
HENRIETTA. TRIELA. STAY HERE AS REARGUARD.
WE DON'T WANT TO MOVE EN MASSE. TOO CONSPICUOUS.
NOK NOK
ROOM SERVICE.
KREE
COME IN.

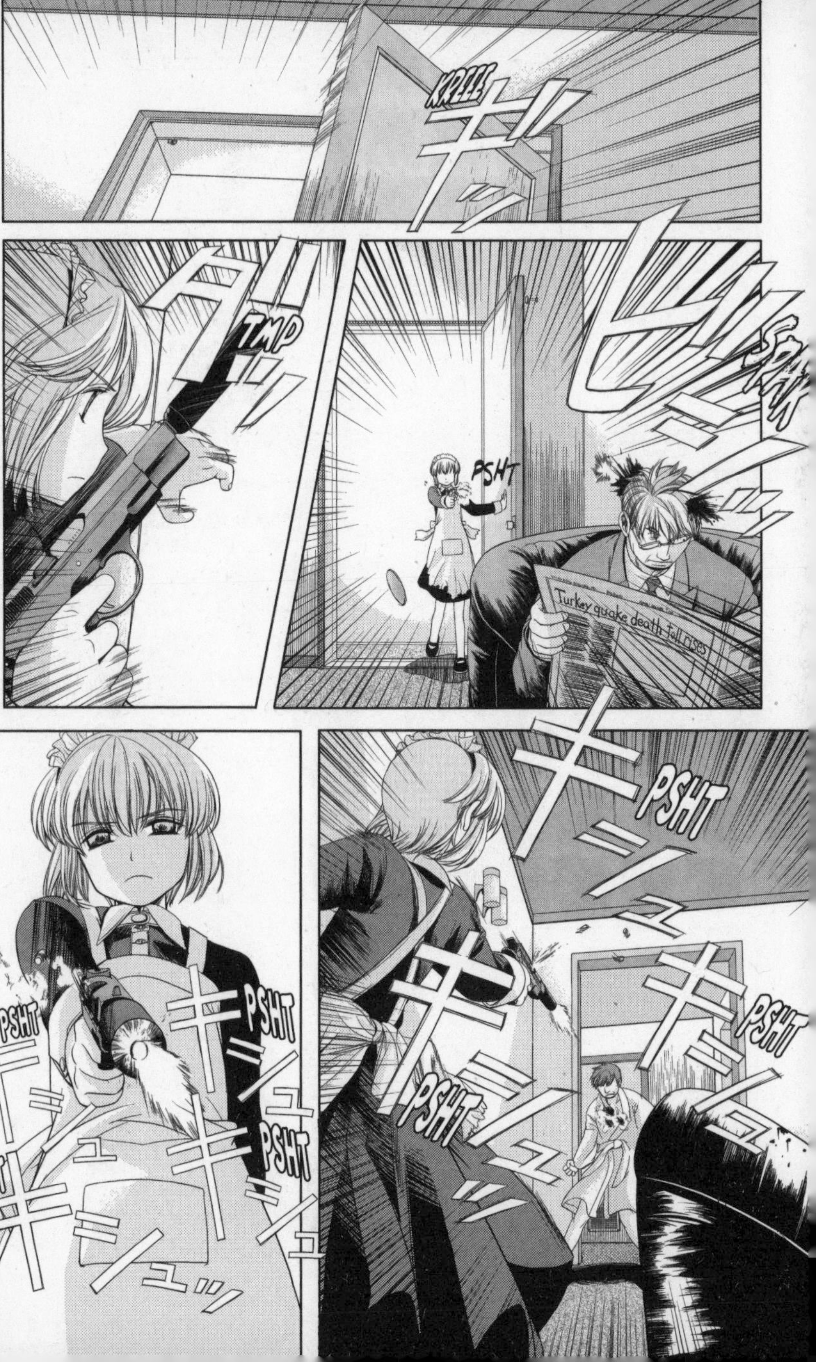
KREEE
SPAK
PSHT
Turkey quake death toll rises
TMP
PSHT
PSHT
PSHT
PSHT
PSHT
PSHT
PSHT

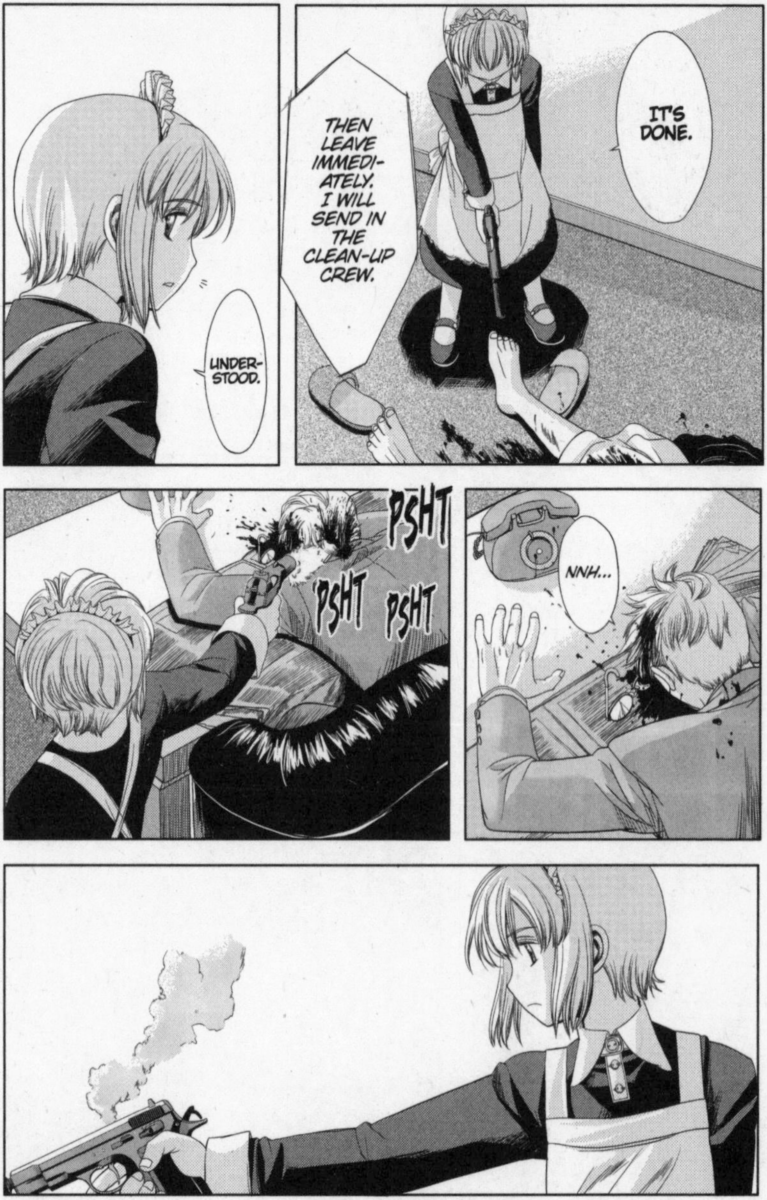

IT'S DONE.
THEN LEAVE IMMEDI-ATELY. I WILL SEND IN THE CLEAN-UP CREW.
UNDER-STOOD.
NNH...
PSHT
PSHT
PSHT

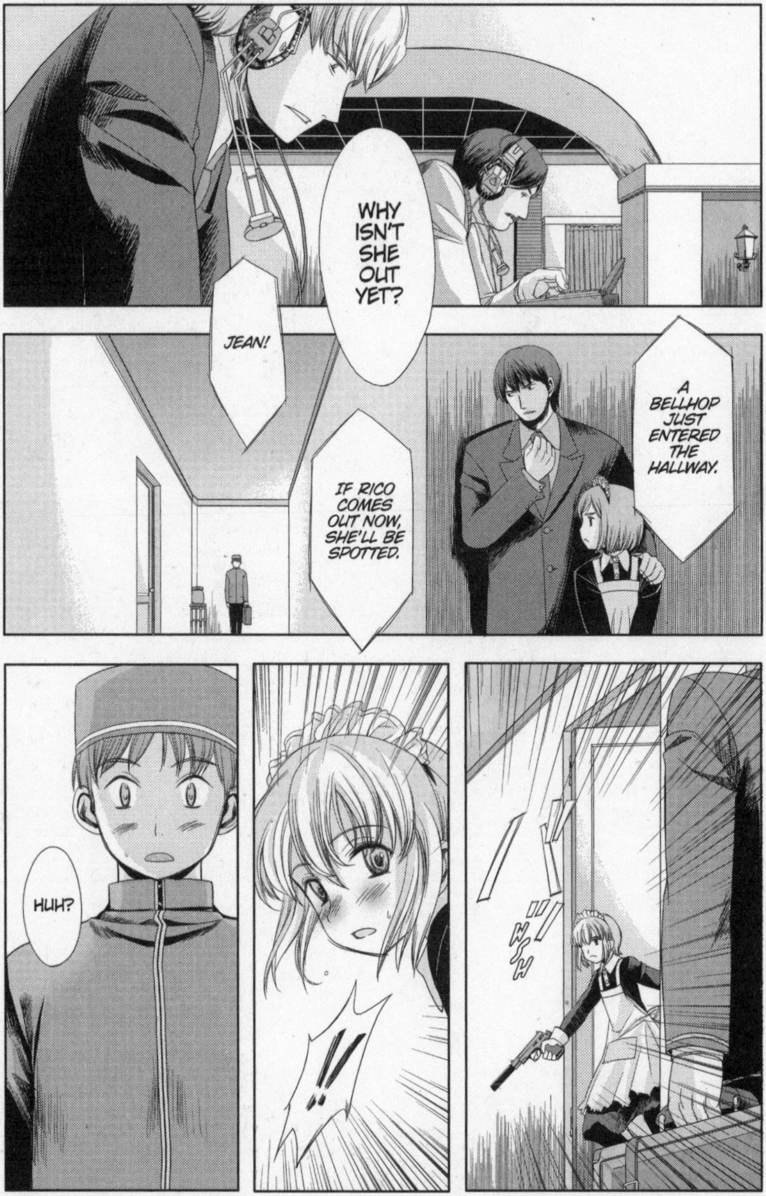
WHY ISN'T SHE OUT YET?
JEAN!
A BELLHOP JUST ENTERED THE HALLWAY.
IF RICO COMES OUT NOW, SHE'LL BE SPOTTED.
!!
HUH?

WHAT ARE YOU DOING HERE?

RICO...?

AND WHAT ARE YOU DOING, WEARING A MAID UNIFORM?

I COMPLETELY FORGOT WHAT I'M SUPPOSED TO SAY AT TIMES LIKE THIS...

UM...

OH NO...!

OH, I REMEMBER NOW!

RICO...

I'M SORRY.

HUH
?

GUNSLINGERGIRL.

Chapter 3: The Snow White

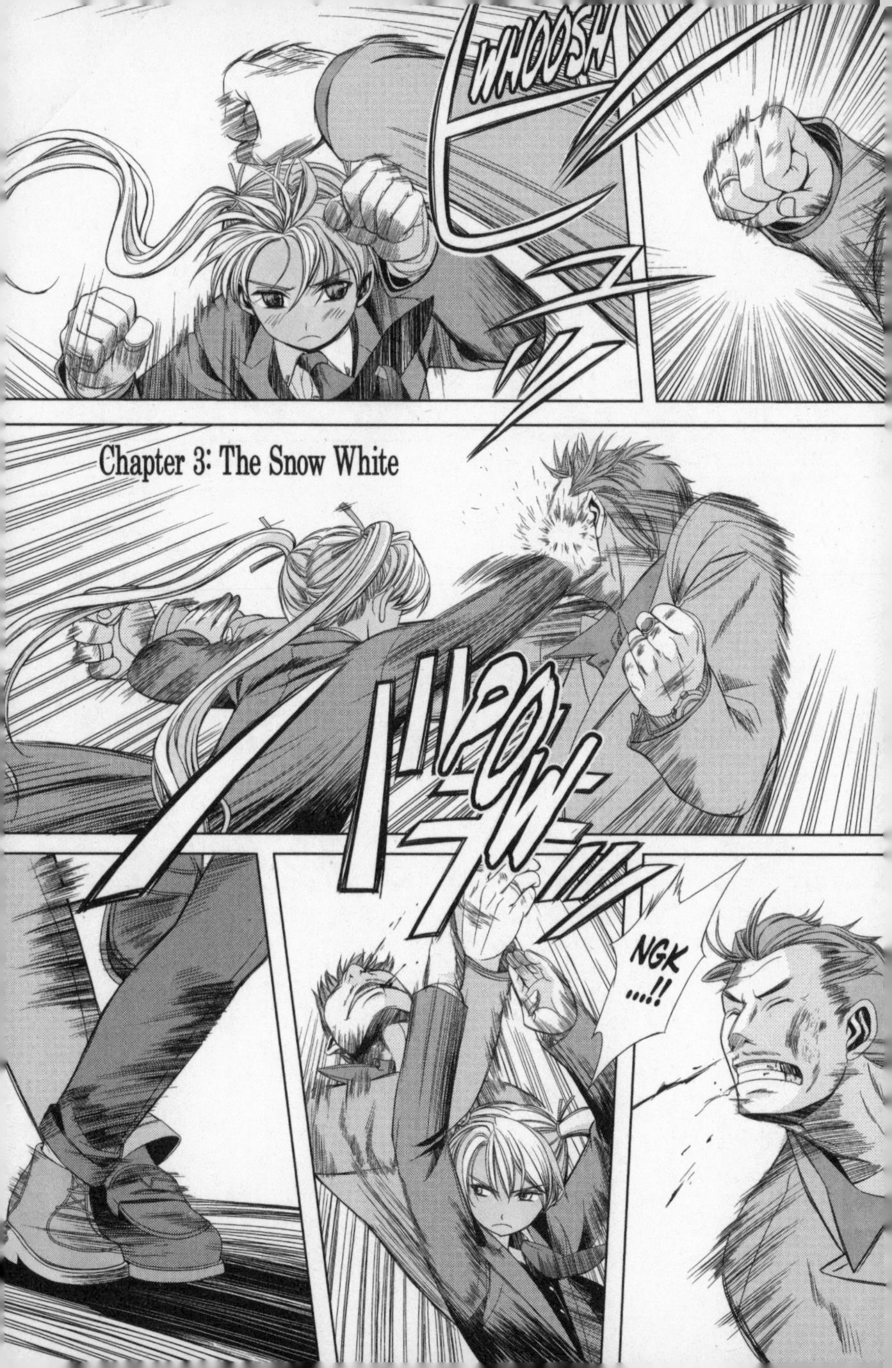
WHOOSH
POW
NGK ...!!

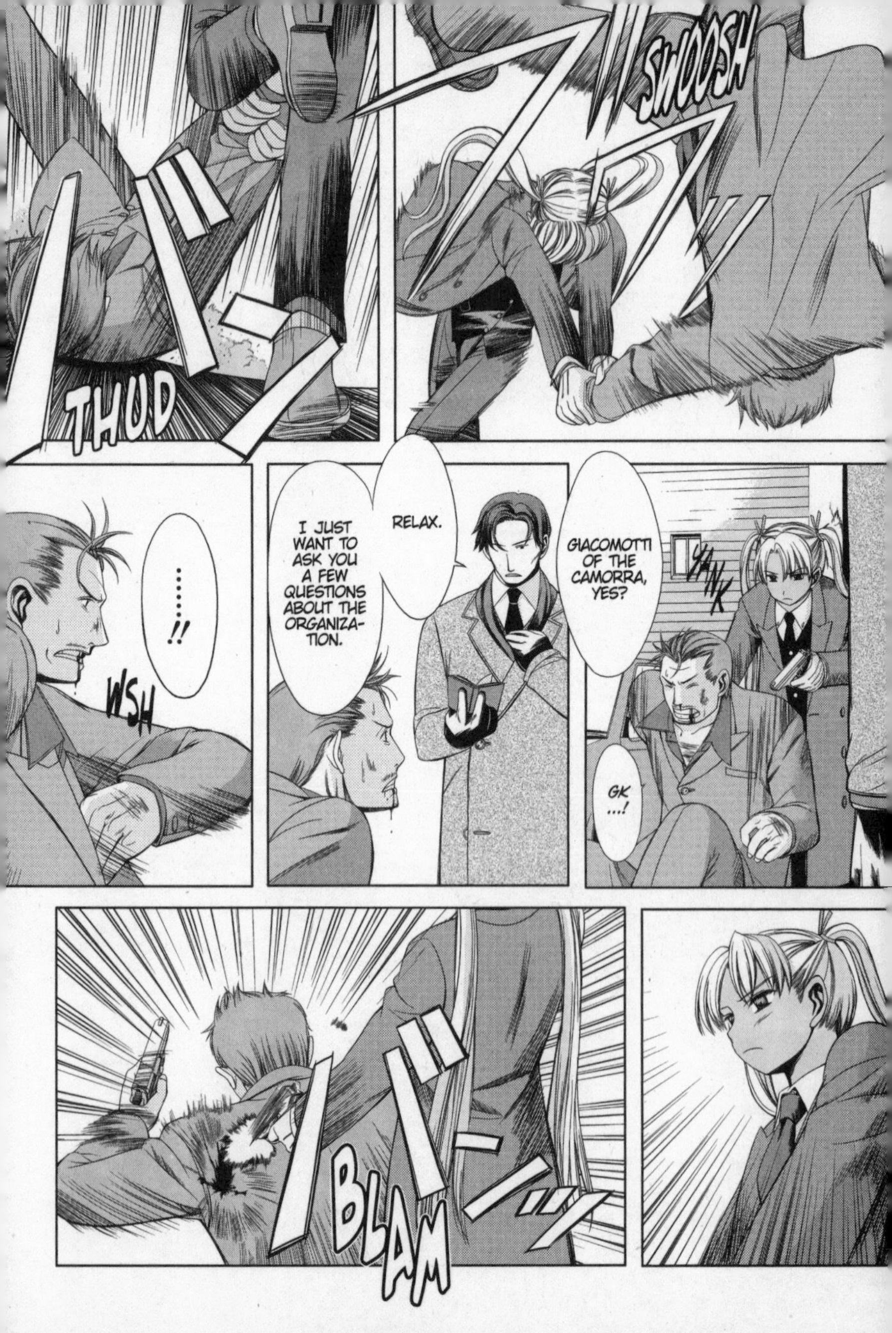
SWOOSH
THUD
GIACOMOTTI OF THE CAMORRA, YES?
YANK
GK ...!
RELAX.
I JUST WANT TO ASK YOU A FEW QUESTIONS ABOUT THE ORGANIZATION.
......!!
WSH
BLAM

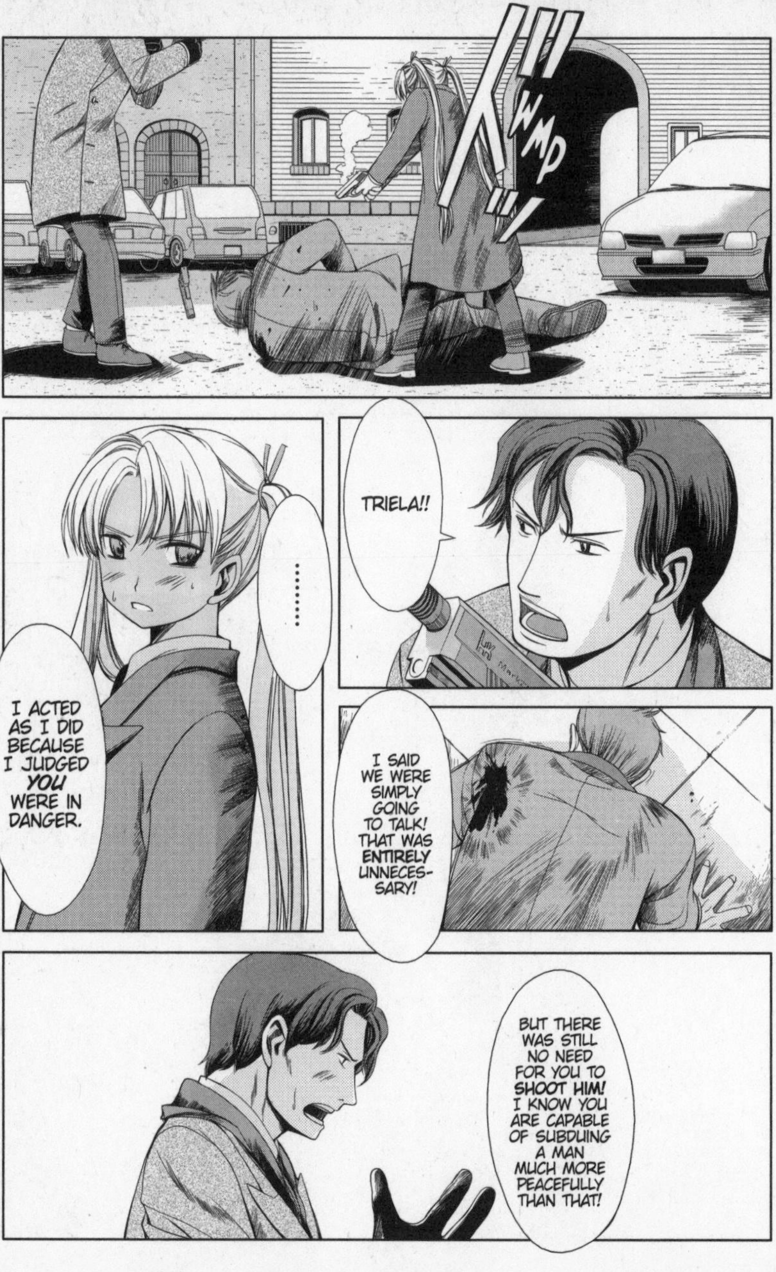
KWMP!!
TRIELA!!
I SAID WE WERE SIMPLY GOING TO TALK! THAT WAS ENTIRELY UNNECESSARY!
......
I ACTED AS I DID BECAUSE I JUDGED YOU WERE IN DANGER.
BUT THERE WAS STILL NO NEED FOR YOU TO SHOOT HIM! I KNOW YOU ARE CAPABLE OF SUBDUING A MAN MUCH MORE PEACEFULLY THAN THAT!

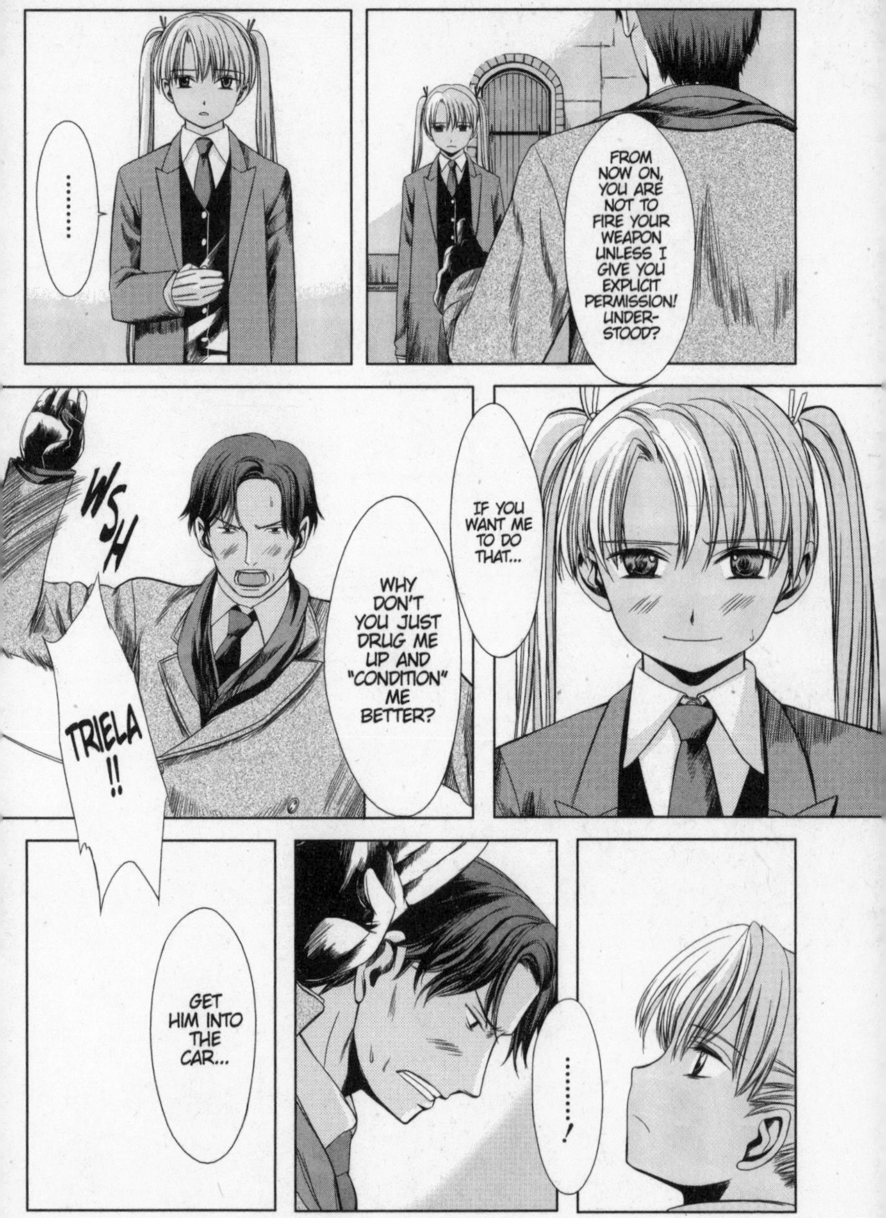
FROM NOW ON, YOU ARE NOT TO FIRE YOUR WEAPON UNLESS I GIVE YOU EXPLICIT PERMISSION! UNDER-STOOD?
......
IF YOU WANT ME TO DO THAT...
WHY DON'T YOU JUST DRUG ME UP AND "CONDITION" ME BETTER?
WSH
TRIELA!!
......!
GET HIM INTO THE CAR...

CHAPTER 3: THE SNOW WHITE

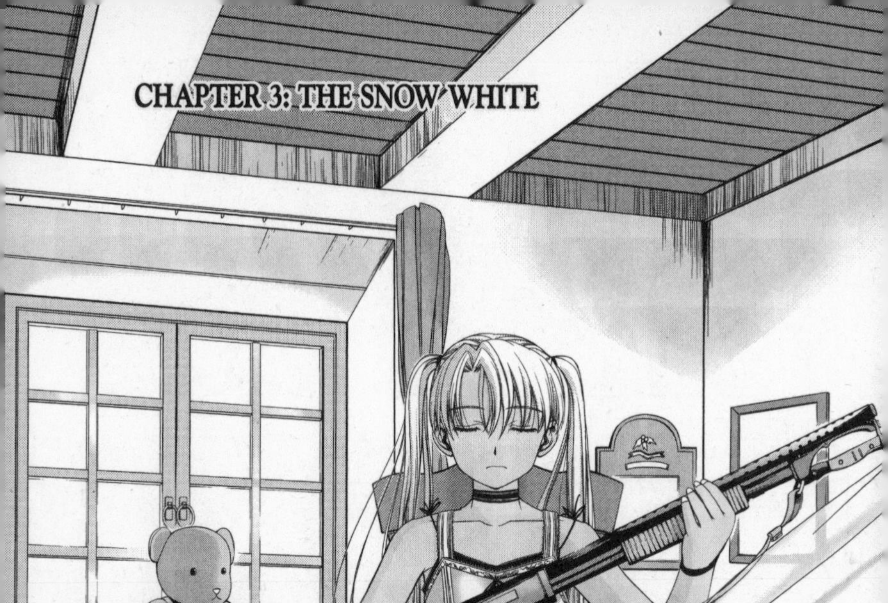

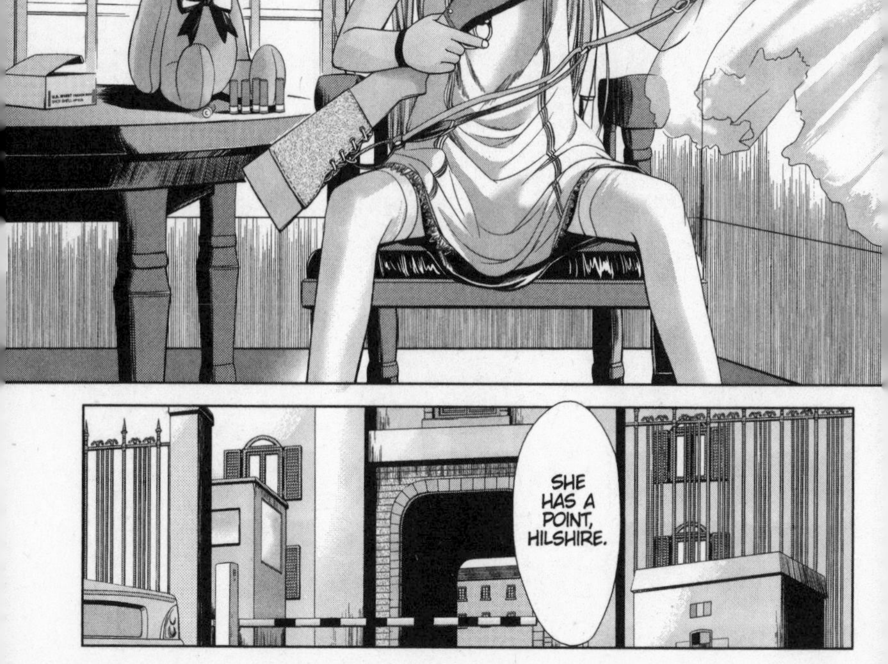
SHE HAS A POINT, HILSHIRE.

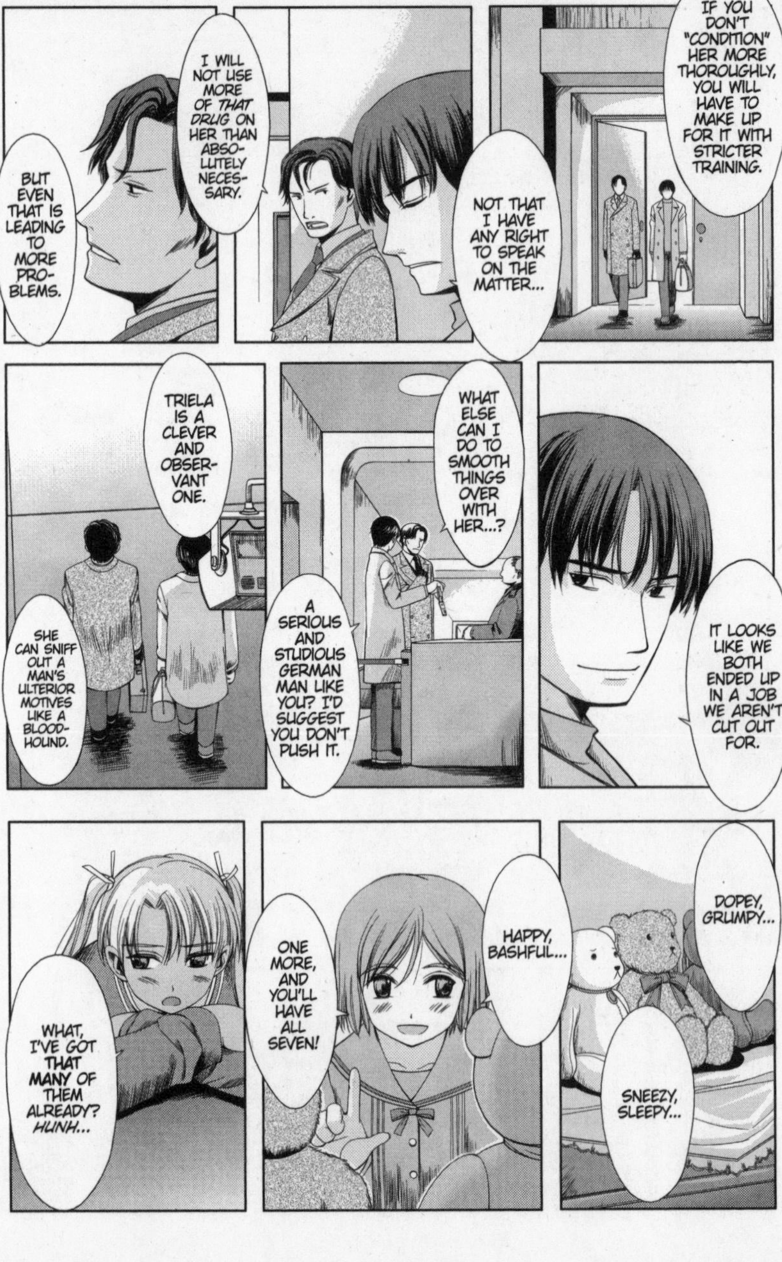
IF YOU DON'T "CONDITION" HER MORE THOROUGHLY, YOU WILL HAVE TO MAKE UP FOR IT WITH STRICTER TRAINING.
NOT THAT I HAVE ANY RIGHT TO SPEAK ON THE MATTER...
I WILL NOT USE MORE OF *THAT DRUG* ON HER THAN ABSOLUTELY NECESSARY.
BUT EVEN THAT IS LEADING TO MORE PROBLEMS.
IT LOOKS LIKE WE BOTH ENDED UP IN A JOB WE AREN'T CUT OUT FOR.
WHAT ELSE CAN I DO TO SMOOTH THINGS OVER WITH HER...?
A SERIOUS AND STUDIOUS GERMAN MAN LIKE YOU? I'D SUGGEST YOU DON'T PUSH IT.
TRIELA IS A CLEVER AND OBSERVANT ONE.
SHE CAN SNIFF OUT A MAN'S ULTERIOR MOTIVES LIKE A BLOODHOUND.
DOPEY, GRUMPY...
SNEEZY, SLEEPY...
HAPPY, BASHFUL...
ONE MORE, AND YOU'LL HAVE ALL SEVEN!
WHAT, I'VE GOT THAT **MANY** OF THEM ALREADY? *HUNH...*

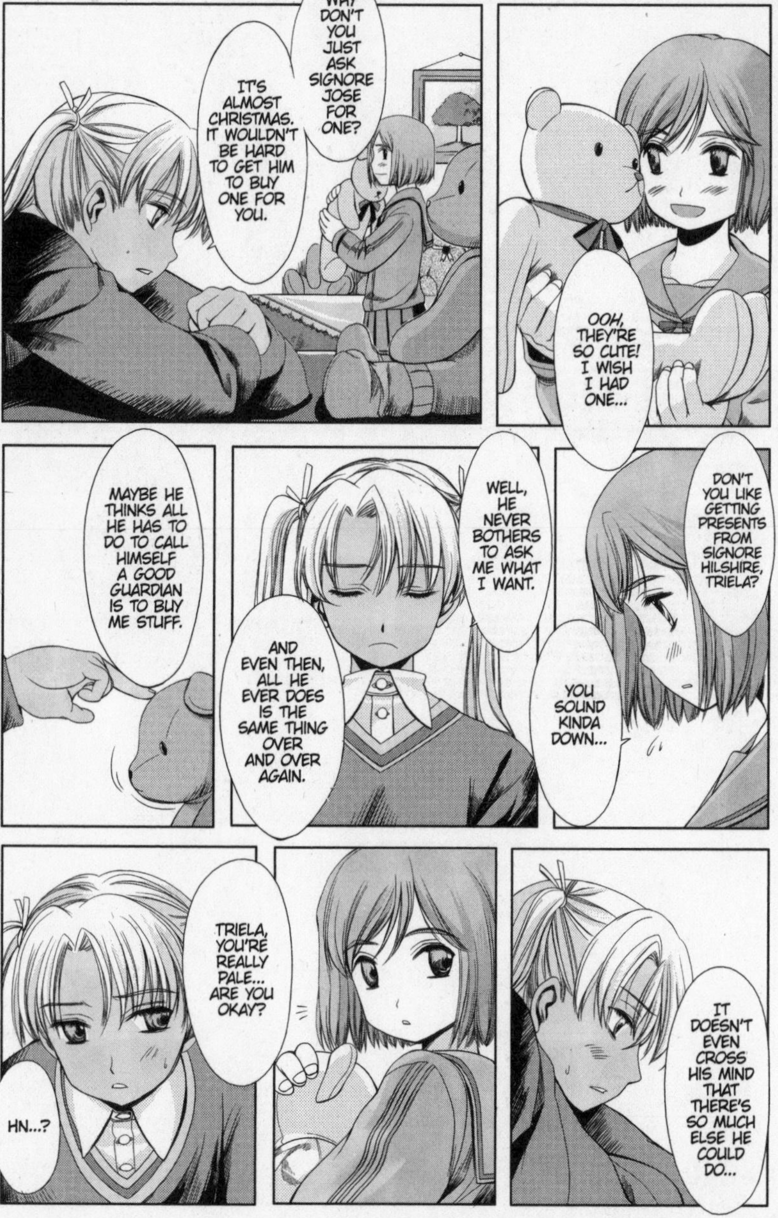
OOH, THEY'RE SO CUTE! I WISH I HAD ONE...
WHY DON'T YOU JUST ASK SIGNORE JOSE FOR ONE?
IT'S ALMOST CHRISTMAS. IT WOULDN'T BE HARD TO GET HIM TO BUY ONE FOR YOU.
DON'T YOU LIKE GETTING PRESENTS FROM SIGNORE HILSHIRE, TRIELA?
YOU SOUND KINDA DOWN...
WELL, HE NEVER BOTHERS TO ASK ME WHAT I WANT.
AND EVEN THEN, ALL HE EVER DOES IS THE SAME THING OVER AND OVER AGAIN.
MAYBE HE THINKS ALL HE HAS TO DO TO CALL HIMSELF A GOOD GUARDIAN IS TO BUY ME STUFF.
IT DOESN'T EVEN CROSS HIS MIND THAT THERE'S SO MUCH ELSE HE COULD DO...
TRIELA, YOU'RE REALLY PALE... ARE YOU OKAY?
HN...?

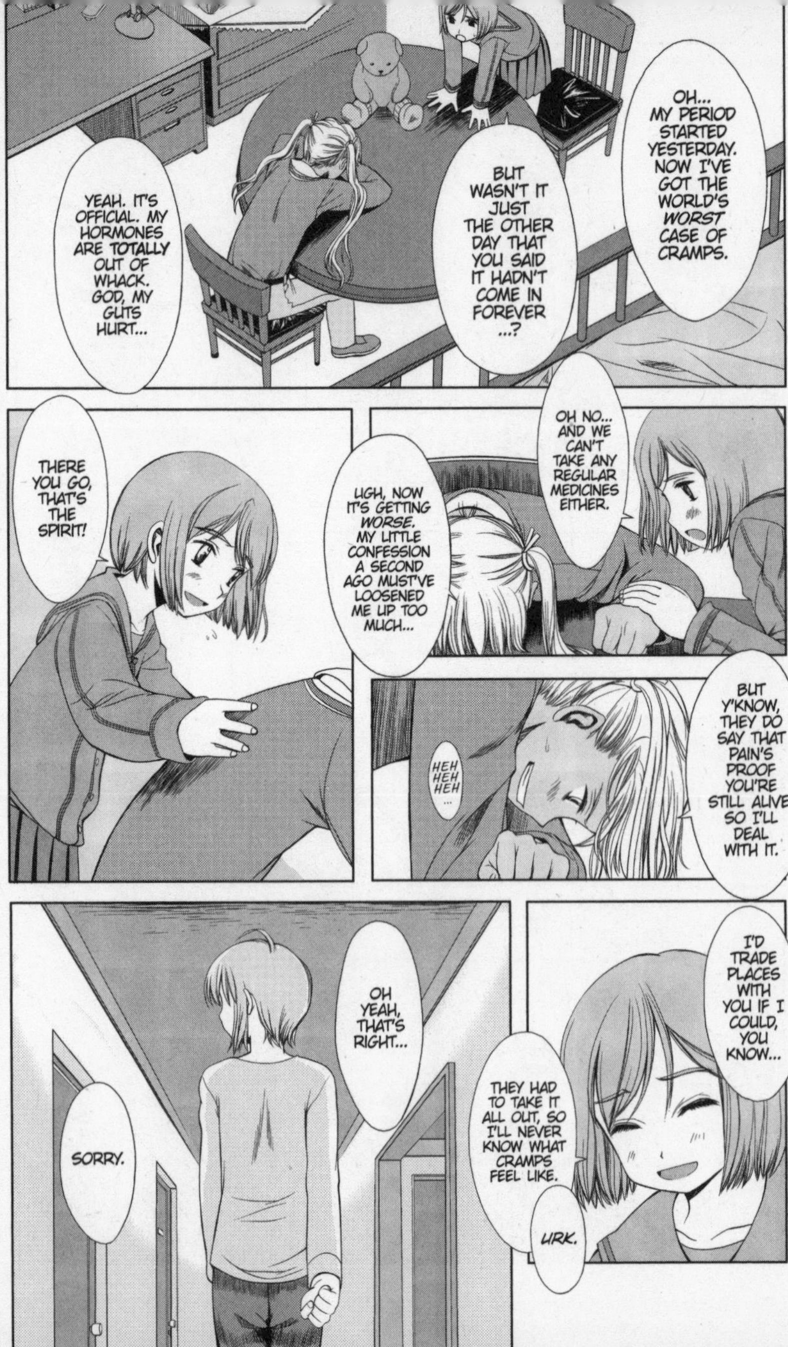
OH... MY PERIOD STARTED YESTERDAY. NOW I'VE GOT THE WORLD'S *WORST* CASE OF CRAMPS.
BUT WASN'T IT JUST THE OTHER DAY THAT YOU SAID IT HADN'T COME IN FOREVER ...?
YEAH. IT'S OFFICIAL. MY HORMONES ARE TOTALLY OUT OF WHACK. GOD, MY GUTS HURT...
OH NO... AND WE CAN'T TAKE ANY REGULAR MEDICINES EITHER.
UGH, NOW IT'S GETTING *WORSE.* MY LITTLE CONFESSION A SECOND AGO MUST'VE LOOSENED ME UP TOO MUCH...
BUT Y'KNOW, THEY DO SAY THAT PAIN'S PROOF YOU'RE STILL ALIVE. SO I'LL DEAL WITH IT.
HEH HEH HEH ...
THERE YOU GO, THAT'S THE SPIRIT!
I'D TRADE PLACES WITH YOU IF I COULD, YOU KNOW...
THEY HAD TO TAKE IT ALL OUT, SO I'LL NEVER KNOW WHAT CRAMPS FEEL LIKE.
URK.
OH YEAH, THAT'S RIGHT...
SORRY.

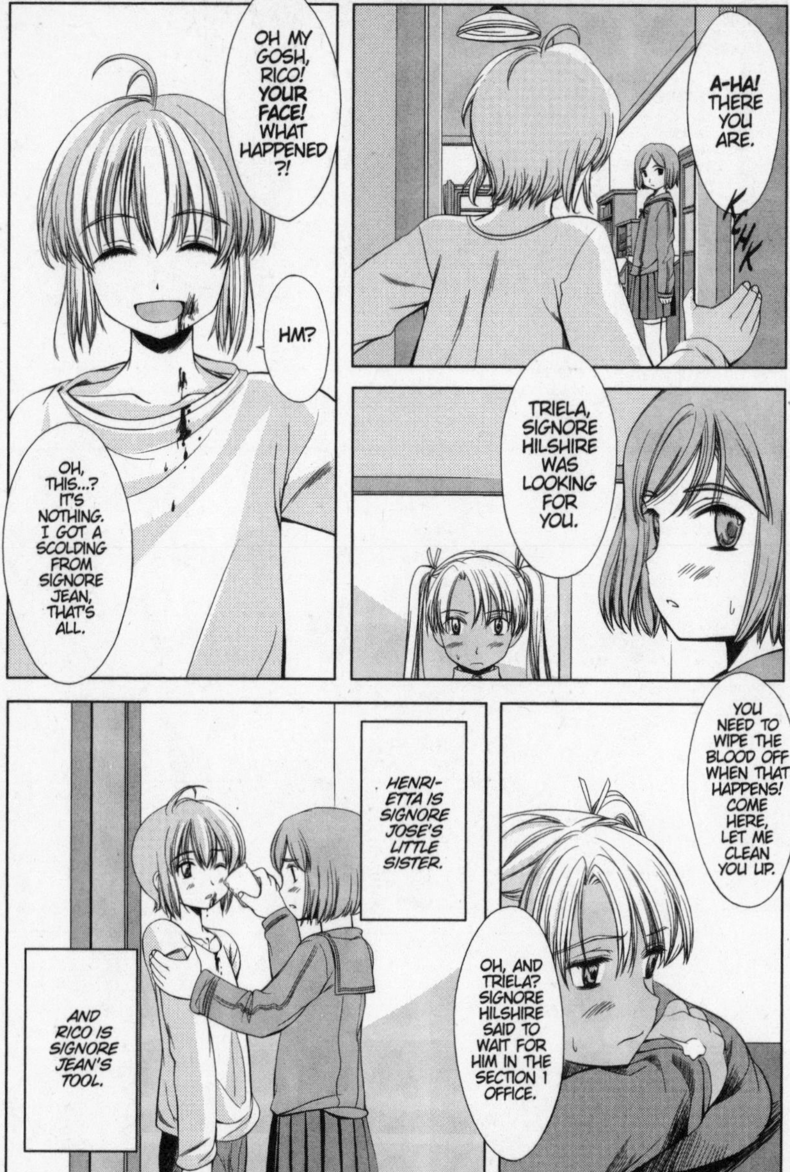
A-HA! THERE YOU ARE.
KCHK
TRIELA, SIGNORE HILSHIRE WAS LOOKING FOR YOU.
OH MY GOSH, RICO! YOUR FACE! WHAT HAPPENED?!
HM?
OH, THIS...? IT'S NOTHING. I GOT A SCOLDING FROM SIGNORE JEAN, THAT'S ALL.
YOU NEED TO WIPE THE BLOOD OFF WHEN THAT HAPPENS! COME HERE, LET ME CLEAN YOU UP.
OH, AND TRIELA? SIGNORE HILSHIRE SAID TO WAIT FOR HIM IN THE SECTION 1 OFFICE.
HENRIETTA IS SIGNORE JOSE'S LITTLE SISTER.
AND RICO IS SIGNORE JEAN'S TOOL.

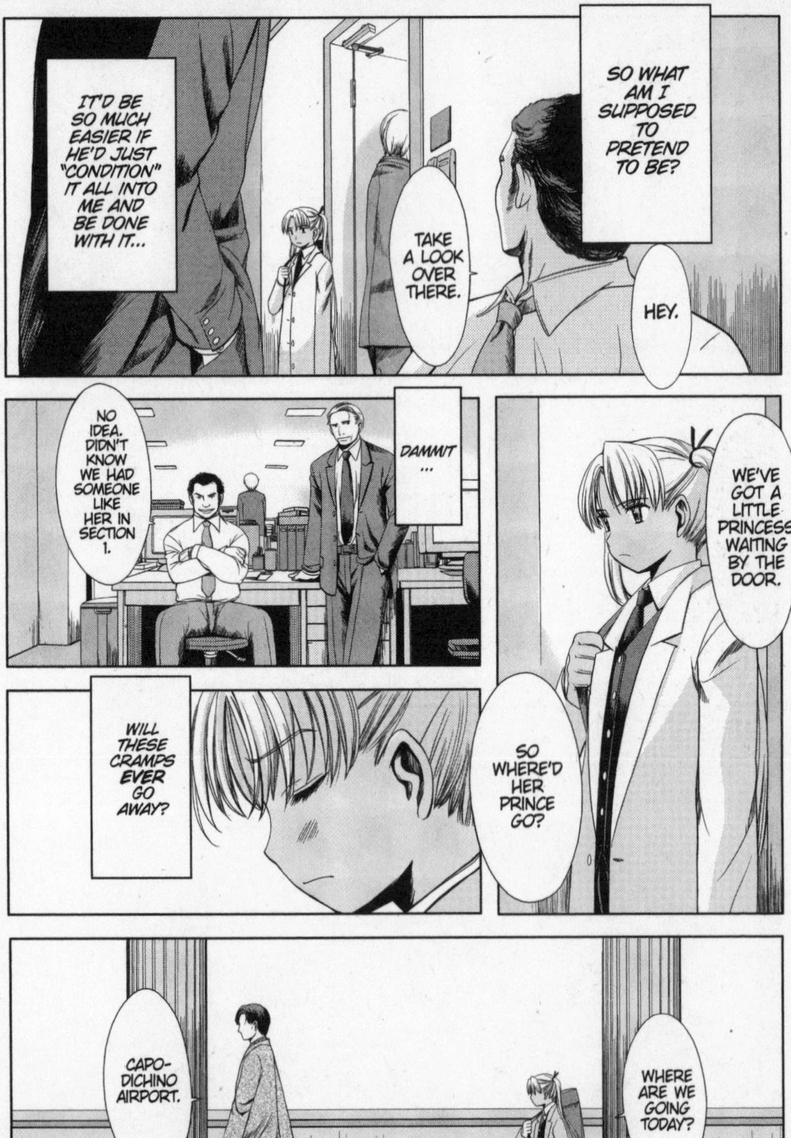
SO WHAT AM I SUPPOSED TO PRETEND TO BE?
HEY.
TAKE A LOOK OVER THERE.
IT'D BE SO MUCH EASIER IF HE'D JUST "CONDITION" IT ALL INTO ME AND BE DONE WITH IT...
WE'VE GOT A LITTLE PRINCESS WAITING BY THE DOOR.
SO WHERE'D HER PRINCE GO?
DAMMIT...
NO IDEA. DIDN'T KNOW WE HAD SOMEONE LIKE HER IN SECTION 1.
WILL THESE CRAMPS **EVER** GO AWAY?
WHERE ARE WE GOING TODAY?
CAPO-DICHINO AIRPORT.

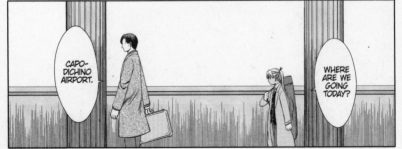

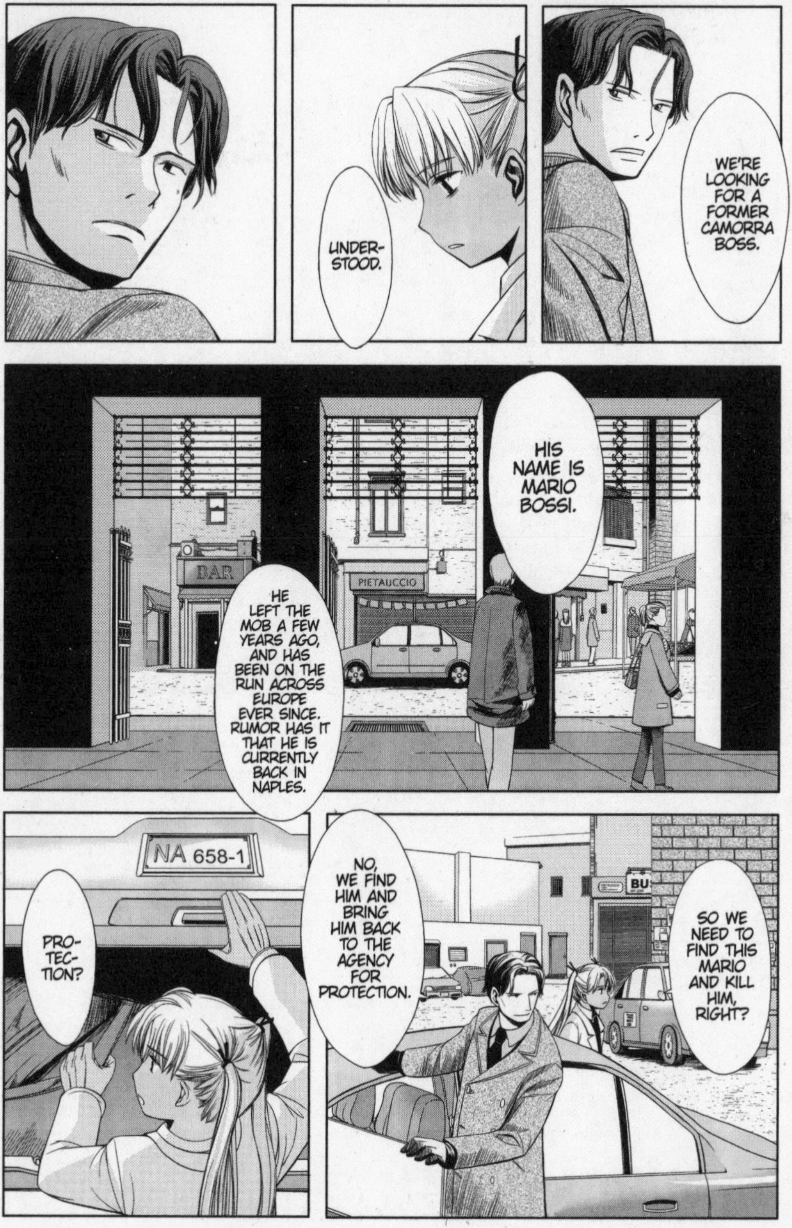
WE'RE LOOKING FOR A FORMER CAMORRA BOSS.
UNDER-STOOD.
HIS NAME IS MARIO BOSSI.
HE LEFT THE MOB A FEW YEARS AGO, AND HAS BEEN ON THE RUN ACROSS EUROPE EVER SINCE. RUMOR HAS IT THAT HE IS CURRENTLY BACK IN NAPLES.
BAR
PIETAUCCIO
SO WE NEED TO FIND THIS MARIO AND KILL HIM, RIGHT?
NO, WE FIND HIM AND BRING HIM BACK TO THE AGENCY FOR PROTECTION.
NA 658-1
PRO-TEC-TION?

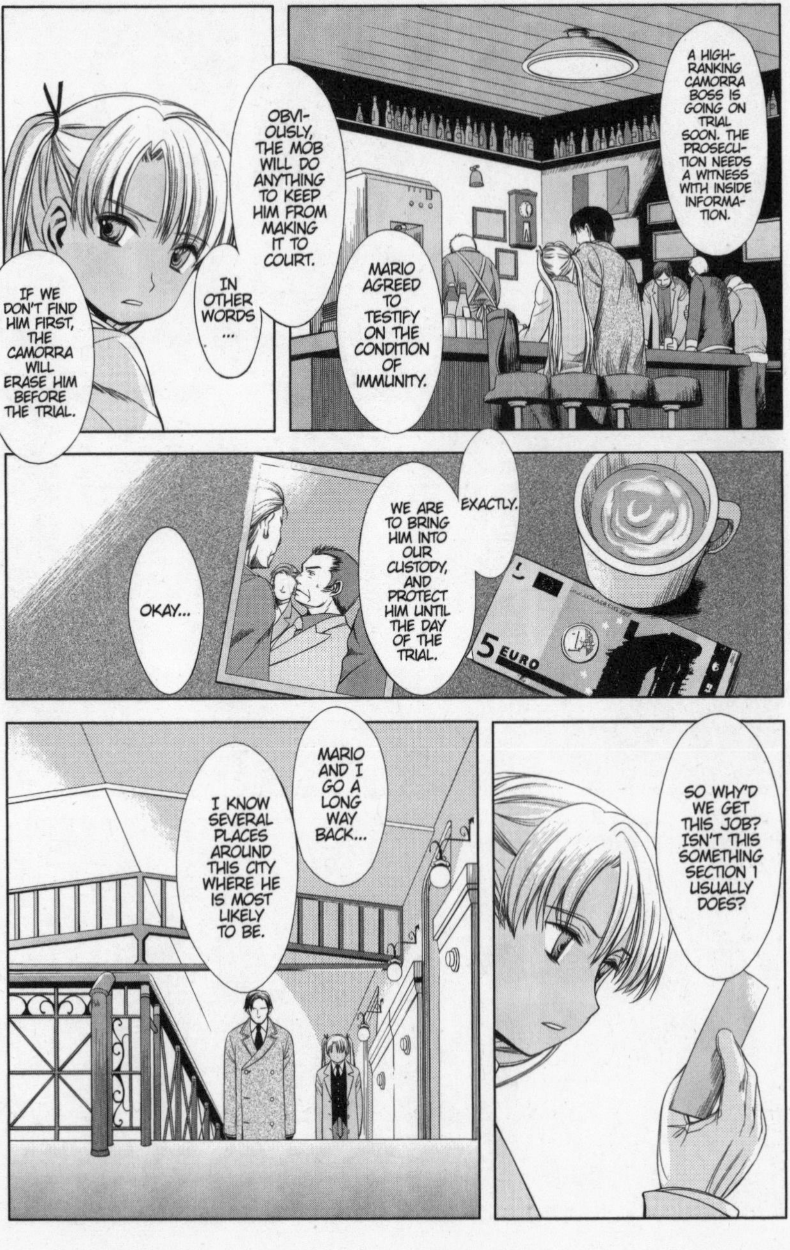
A HIGH-RANKING CAMORRA BOSS IS GOING ON TRIAL SOON. THE PROSECUTION NEEDS A WITNESS WITH INSIDE INFORMATION.
MARIO AGREED TO TESTIFY ON THE CONDITION OF IMMUNITY.
OBVIOUSLY, THE MOB WILL DO ANYTHING TO KEEP HIM FROM MAKING IT TO COURT.
IN OTHER WORDS ...
IF WE DON'T FIND HIM FIRST, THE CAMORRA WILL ERASE HIM BEFORE THE TRIAL.
EXACTLY.
WE ARE TO BRING HIM INTO OUR CUSTODY, AND PROTECT HIM UNTIL THE DAY OF THE TRIAL.
OKAY...
5 EURO
SO WHY'D WE GET THIS JOB? ISN'T THIS SOMETHING SECTION 1 USUALLY DOES?
MARIO AND I GO A LONG WAY BACK...
I KNOW SEVERAL PLACES AROUND THIS CITY WHERE HE IS MOST LIKELY TO BE.

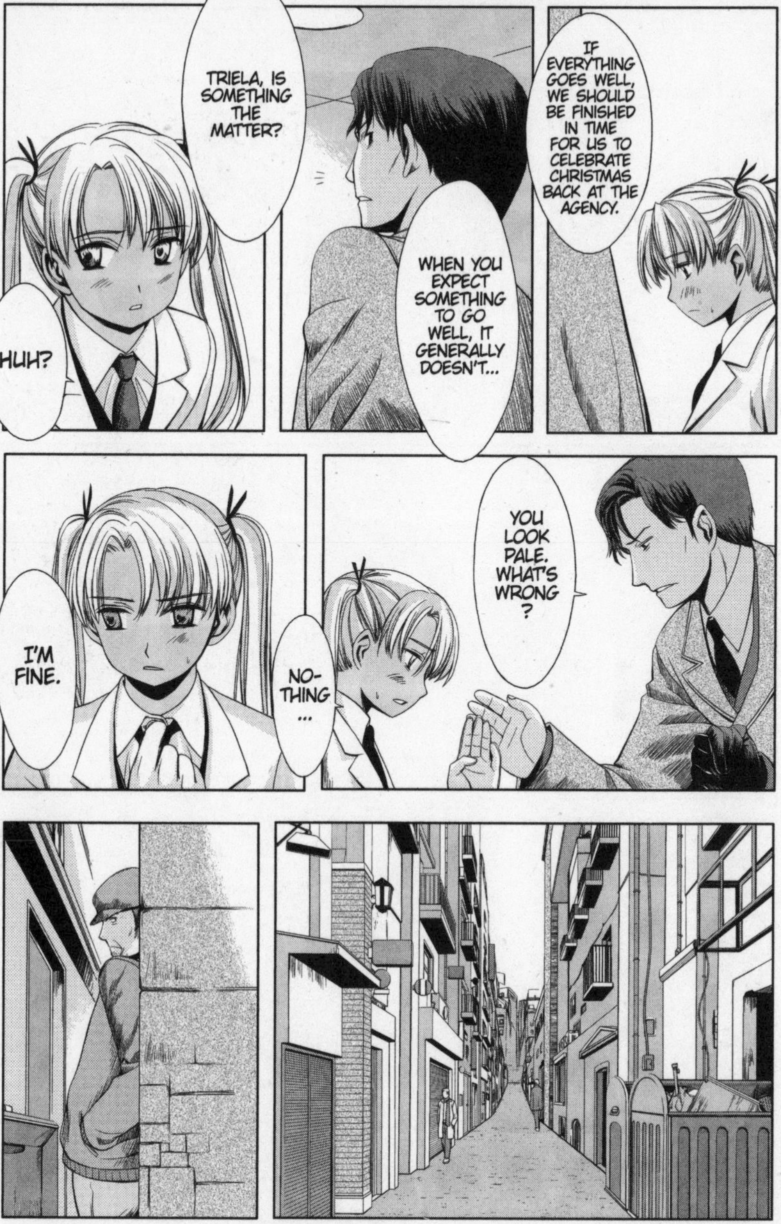
IF EVERYTHING GOES WELL, WE SHOULD BE FINISHED IN TIME FOR US TO CELEBRATE CHRISTMAS BACK AT THE AGENCY.
WHEN YOU EXPECT SOMETHING TO GO WELL, IT GENERALLY DOESN'T...
TRIELA, IS SOMETHING THE MATTER?
HUH?
YOU LOOK PALE. WHAT'S WRONG?
NO-THING...
I'M FINE.

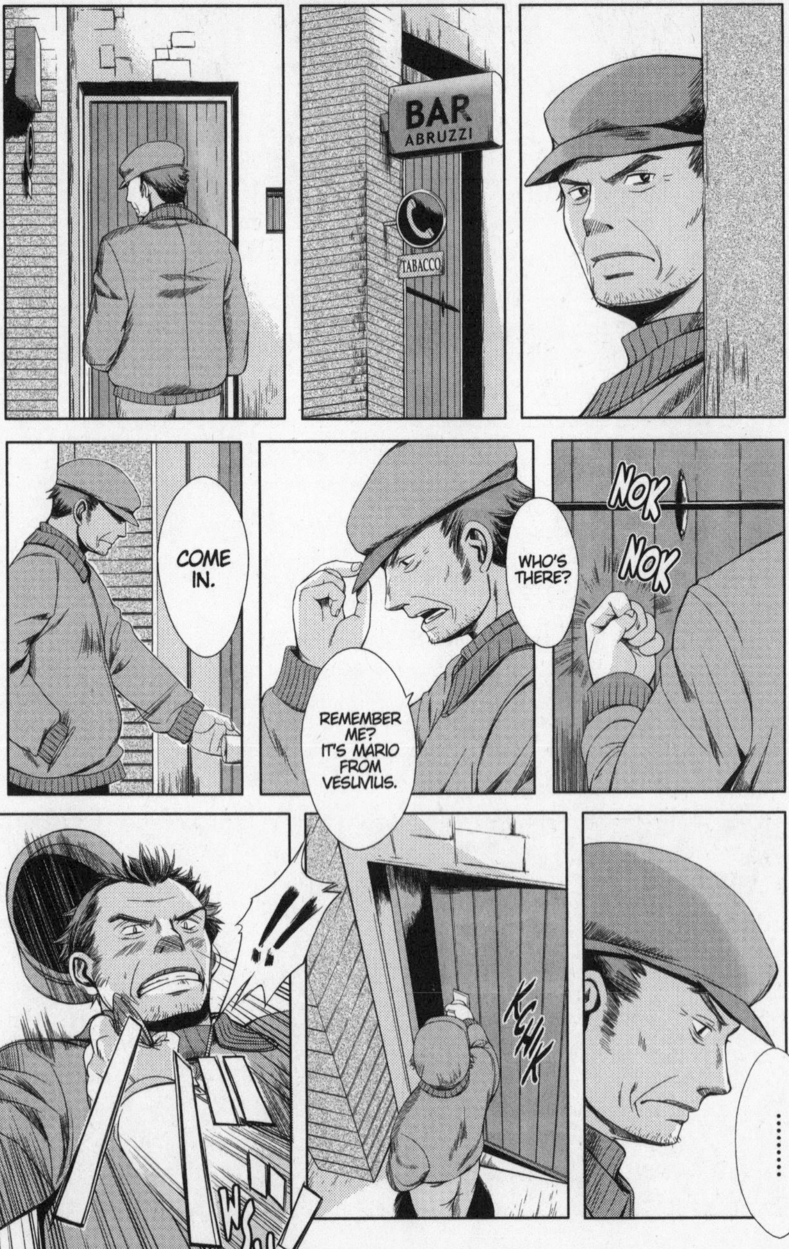
BAR
ABRUZZI
TABACCO
NOK
NOK
WHO'S THERE?
REMEMBER ME? IT'S MARIO FROM VESUVIUS.
COME IN.
......
KCHIK
!!
WSH

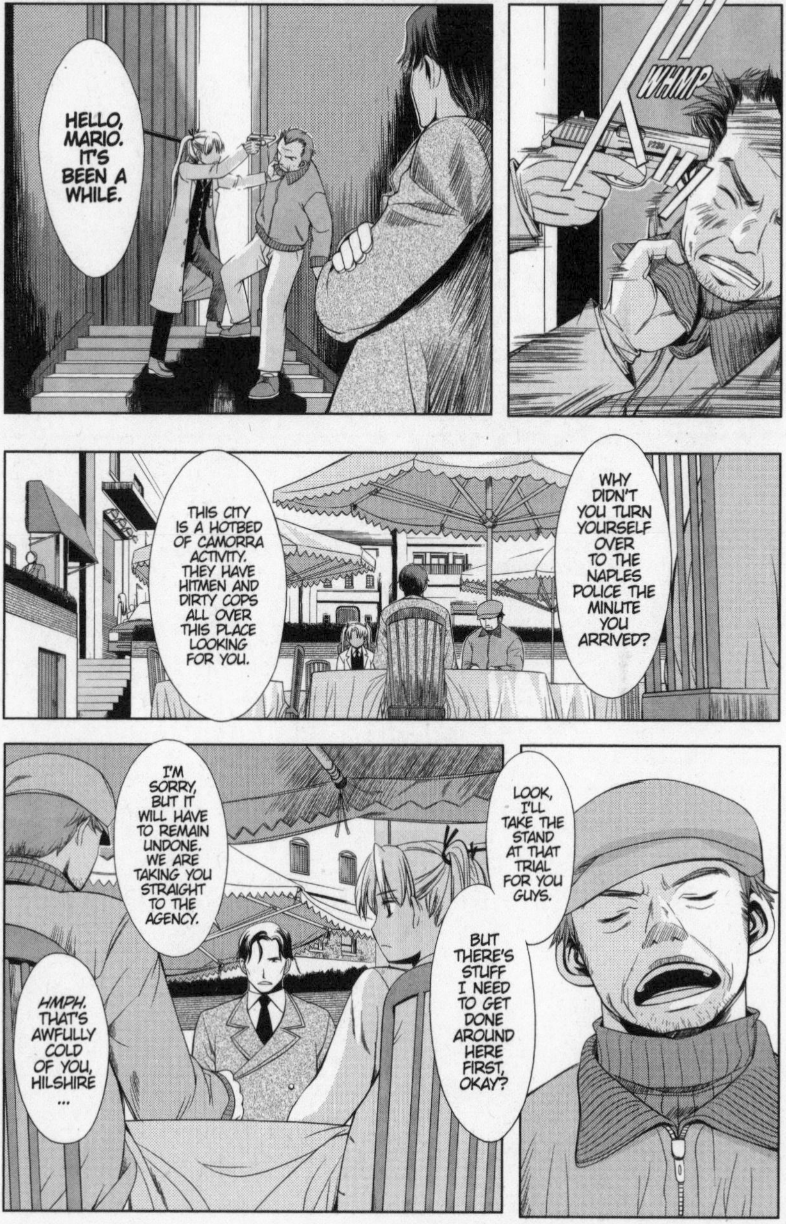
WHMP
HELLO, MARIO. IT'S BEEN A WHILE.
WHY DIDN'T YOU TURN YOURSELF OVER TO THE NAPLES POLICE THE MINUTE YOU ARRIVED?
THIS CITY IS A HOTBED OF CAMORRA ACTIVITY. THEY HAVE HITMEN AND DIRTY COPS ALL OVER THIS PLACE LOOKING FOR YOU.
LOOK, I'LL TAKE THE STAND AT THAT TRIAL FOR YOU GUYS.
BUT THERE'S STUFF I NEED TO GET DONE AROUND HERE FIRST, OKAY?
I'M SORRY, BUT IT WILL HAVE TO REMAIN UNDONE. WE ARE TAKING YOU STRAIGHT TO THE AGENCY.
HMPH. THAT'S AWFULLY COLD OF YOU, HILSHIRE ...

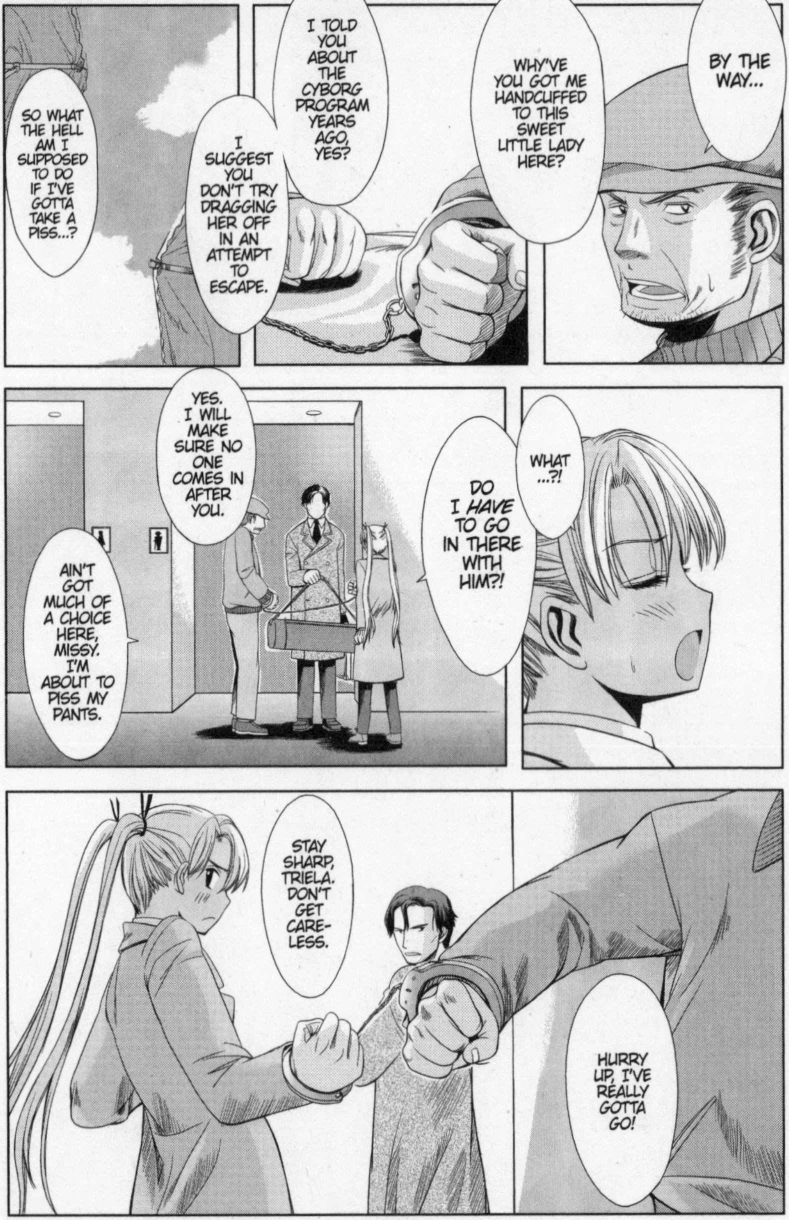
BY THE WAY...
WHY'VE YOU GOT ME HANDCUFFED TO THIS SWEET LITTLE LADY HERE?
I TOLD YOU ABOUT THE CYBORG PROGRAM YEARS AGO, YES?
I SUGGEST YOU DON'T TRY DRAGGING HER OFF IN AN ATTEMPT TO ESCAPE.
SO WHAT THE HELL AM I SUPPOSED TO DO IF I'VE GOTTA TAKE A PISS...?
WHAT ...?!
DO I *HAVE* TO GO IN THERE WITH HIM?!
YES. I WILL MAKE SURE NO ONE COMES IN AFTER YOU.
AIN'T GOT MUCH OF A CHOICE HERE, MISSY. I'M ABOUT TO PISS MY PANTS.
HURRY UP, I'VE REALLY GOTTA GO!
STAY SHARP, TRIELA. DON'T GET CARE-LESS.

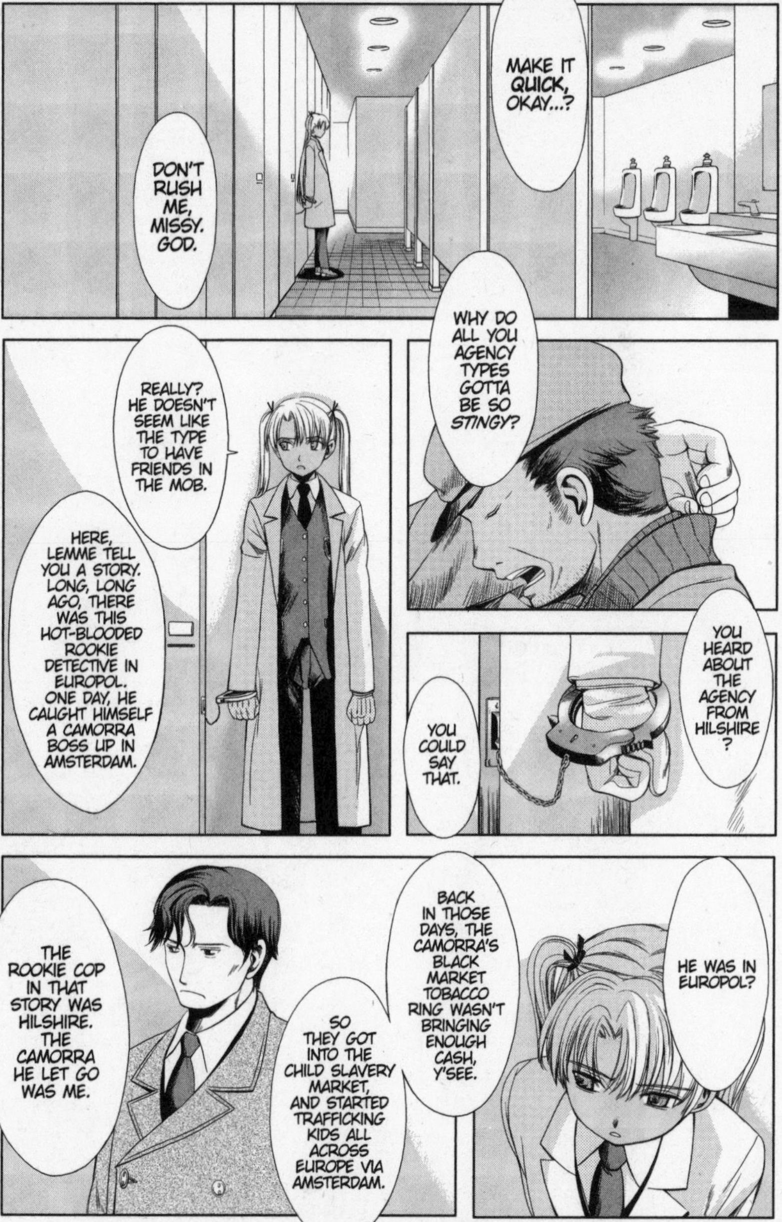
MAKE IT QUICK, OKAY...?
DON'T RUSH ME, MISSY. GOD.
WHY DO ALL YOU AGENCY TYPES GOTTA BE SO STINGY?
YOU HEARD ABOUT THE AGENCY FROM HILSHIRE?
YOU COULD SAY THAT.
REALLY? HE DOESN'T SEEM LIKE THE TYPE TO HAVE FRIENDS IN THE MOB.
HERE, LEMME TELL YOU A STORY. LONG, LONG AGO, THERE WAS THIS HOT-BLOODED ROOKIE DETECTIVE IN EUROPOL. ONE DAY, HE CAUGHT HIMSELF A CAMORRA BOSS UP IN AMSTERDAM.
HE WAS IN EUROPOL?
BACK IN THOSE DAYS, THE CAMORRA'S BLACK MARKET TOBACCO RING WASN'T BRINGING ENOUGH CASH, Y'SEE.
SO THEY GOT INTO THE CHILD SLAVERY MARKET, AND STARTED TRAFFICKING KIDS ALL ACROSS EUROPE VIA AMSTERDAM.
THE ROOKIE COP IN THAT STORY WAS HILSHIRE. THE CAMORRA HE LET GO WAS ME.

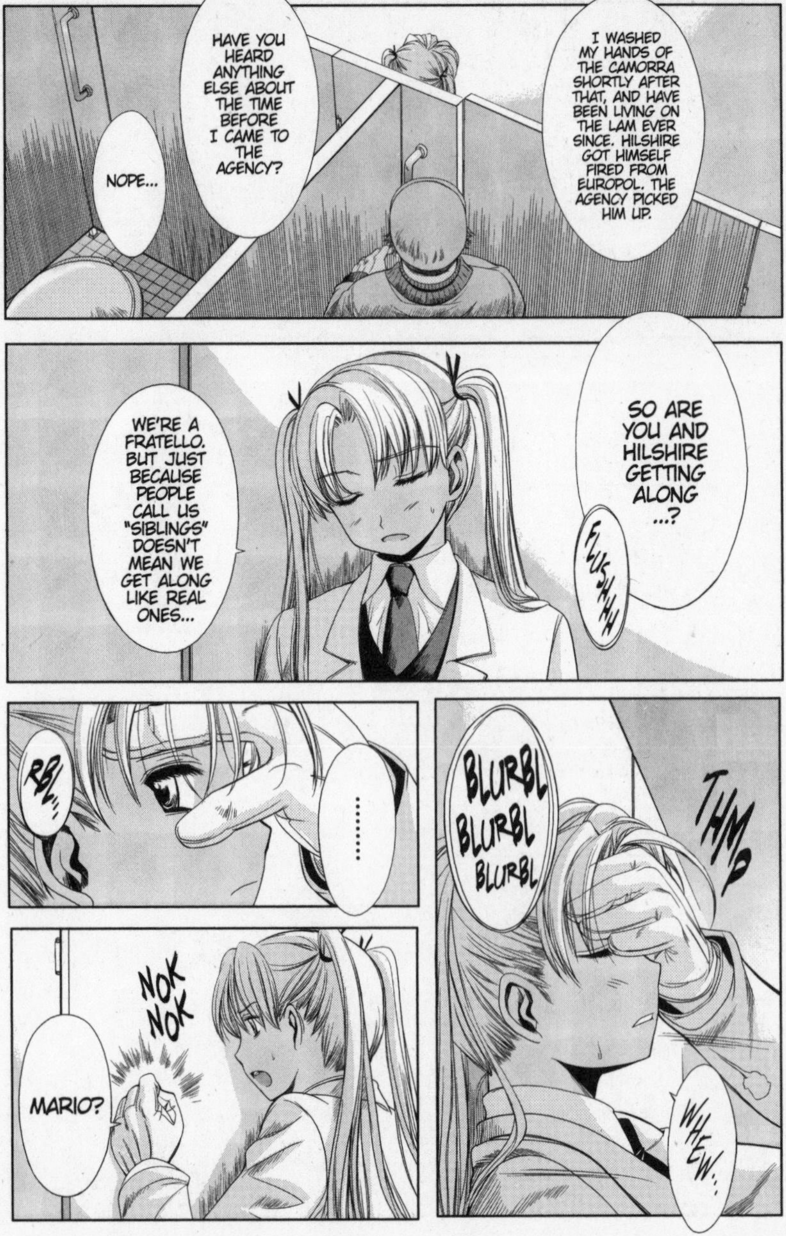
I WASHED MY HANDS OF THE CAMORRA SHORTLY AFTER THAT, AND HAVE BEEN LIVING ON THE LAM EVER SINCE. HILSHIRE GOT HIMSELF FIRED FROM EUROPOL. THE AGENCY PICKED HIM UP.
HAVE YOU HEARD ANYTHING ELSE ABOUT THE TIME BEFORE I CAME TO THE AGENCY?
NOPE...
SO ARE YOU AND HILSHIRE GETTING ALONG ...?
FLUSHHH
WE'RE A FRATELLO. BUT JUST BECAUSE PEOPLE CALL US "SIBLINGS" DOESN'T MEAN WE GET ALONG LIKE REAL ONES...
THMP
BLURBL
BLURBL
BLURBL
WHEW...
....
RBL...
NOK NOK
MARIO?

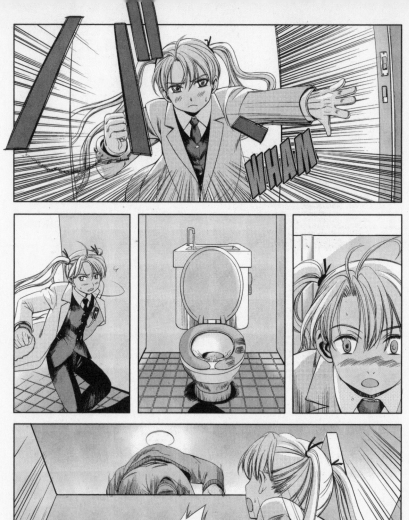

WHAM

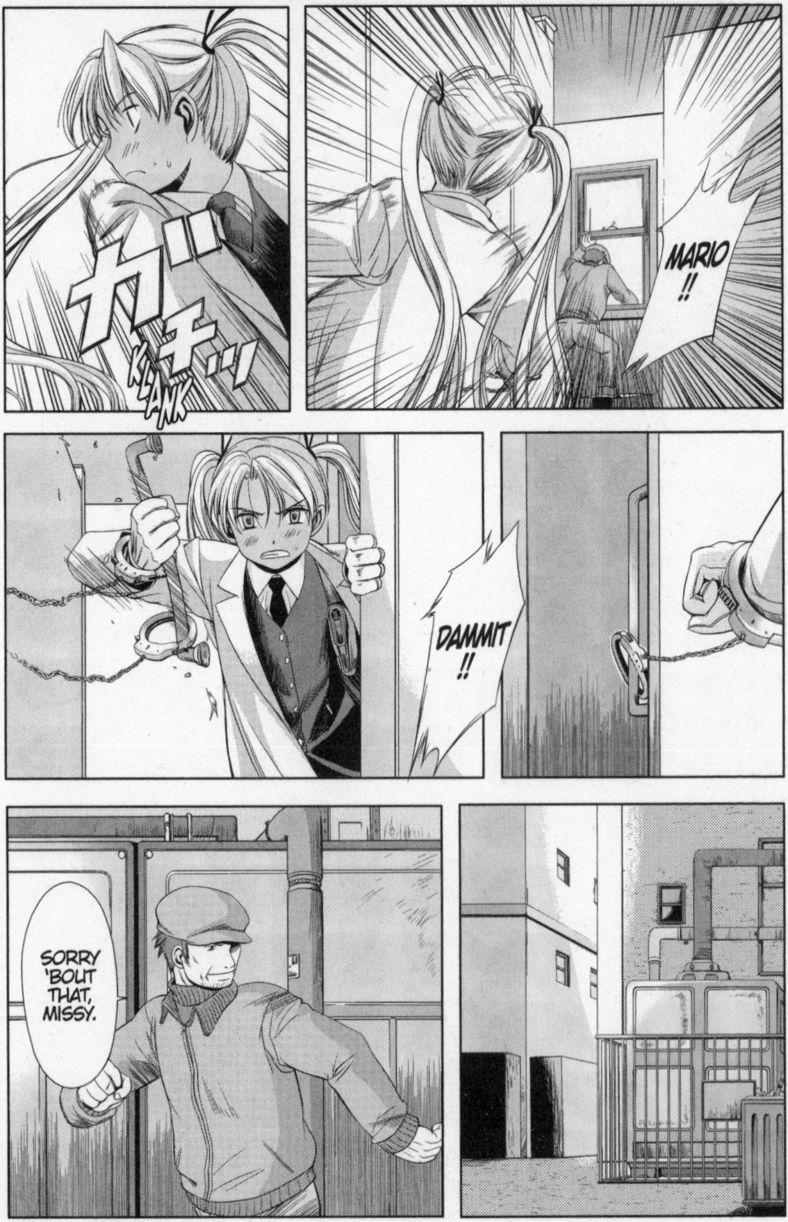
MARIO !!
ガチッ
KLANK
DAMMIT !!
SORRY 'BOUT THAT, MISSY.

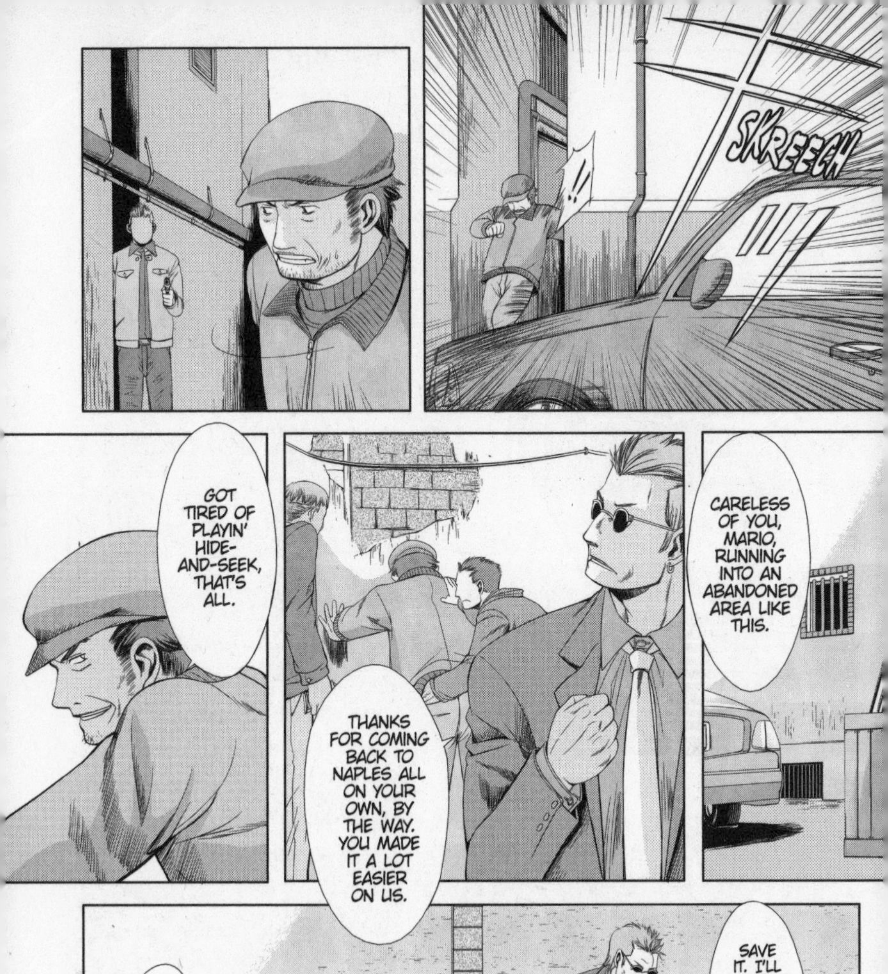
SKREECH
!!
CARELESS OF YOU, MARIO, RUNNING INTO AN ABANDONED AREA LIKE THIS.
THANKS FOR COMING BACK TO NAPLES ALL ON YOUR OWN, BY THE WAY. YOU MADE IT A LOT EASIER ON US.
GOT TIRED OF PLAYIN' HIDE-AND-SEEK, THAT'S ALL.
SAVE IT. I'LL LISTEN TO WHAT YOU HAVE TO SAY LATER.
IF YOU GUYS ARE GONNA TAKE ME SOME-WHERE, YOU'D BEST BE QUICK ABOUT IT.
BECAUSE IF YOU AREN'T...

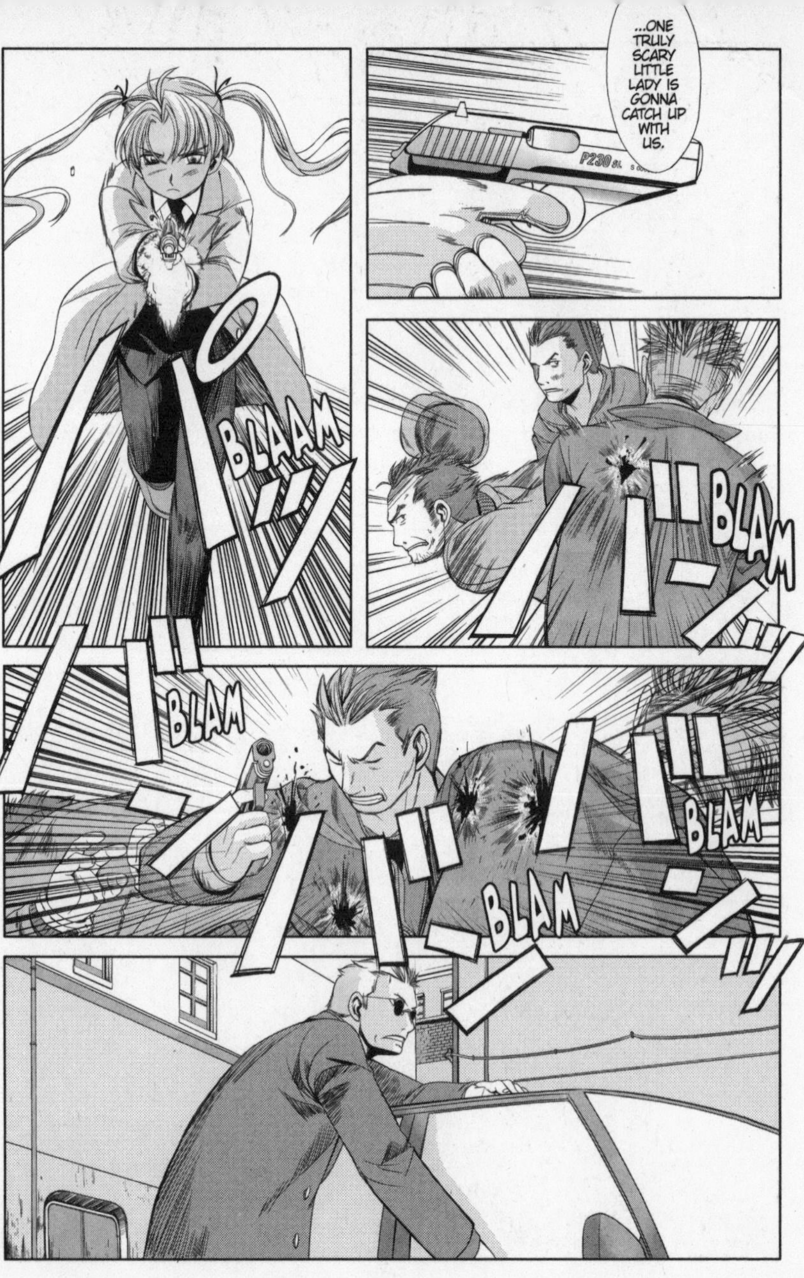
...ONE TRULY SCARY LITTLE LADY IS GONNA CATCH UP WITH US.
P230 SL
BLAM
BLAAM
BLAM
BLAM
BLAM

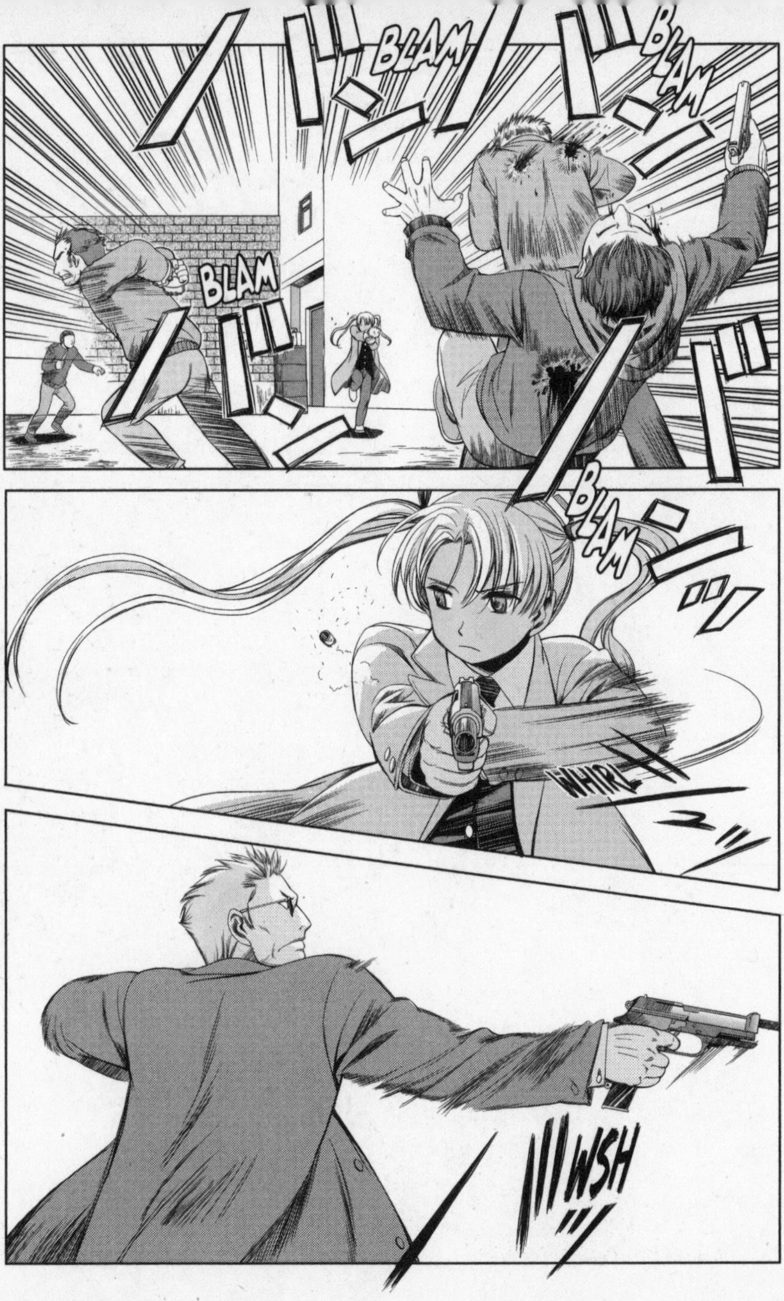
BLAM
BLAM
BLAM
BLAM
WHIRL
WSH

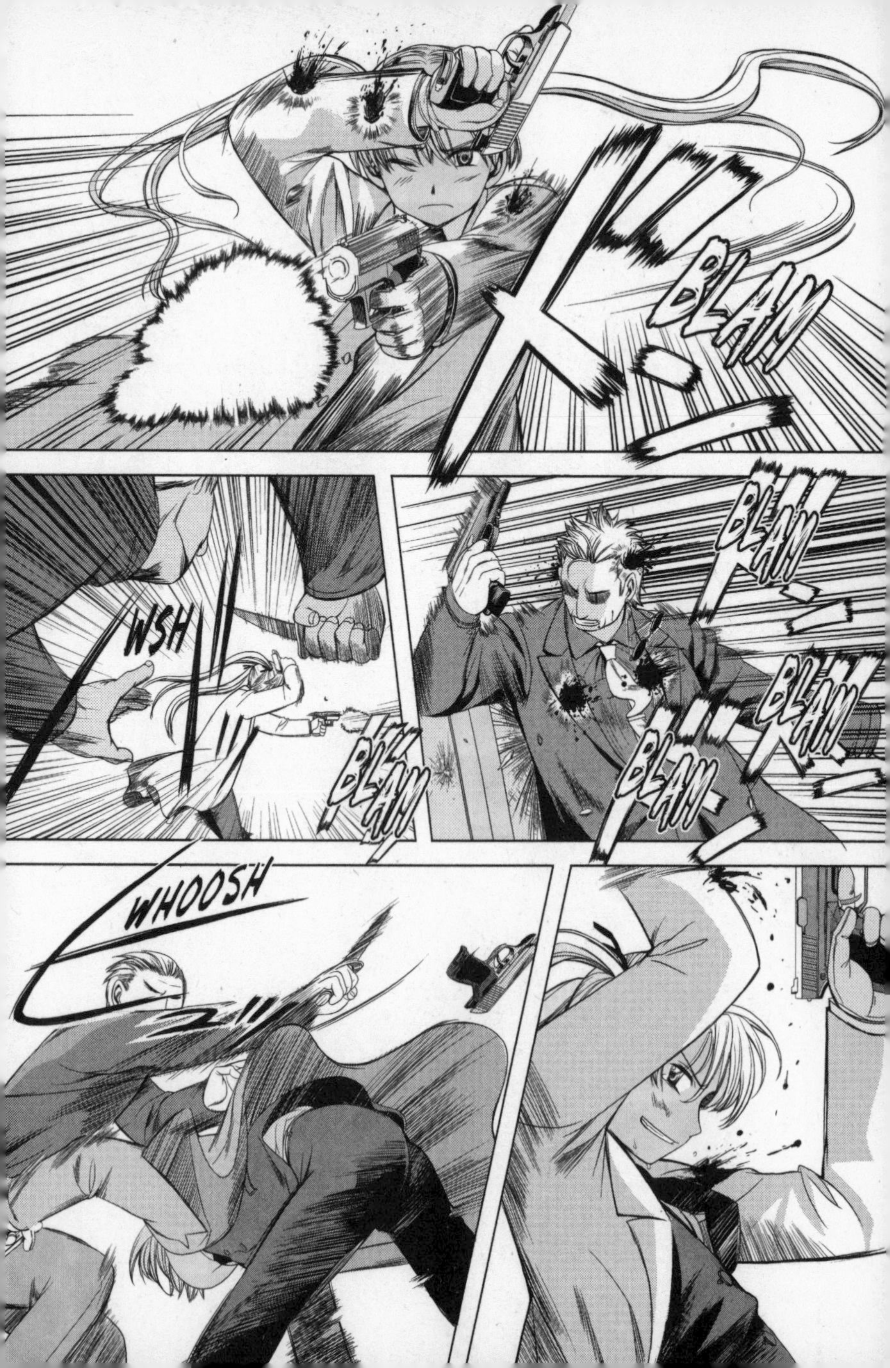
BLAM
BLAM
BLAM
BLAM
WSH
BLAM
WHOOSH

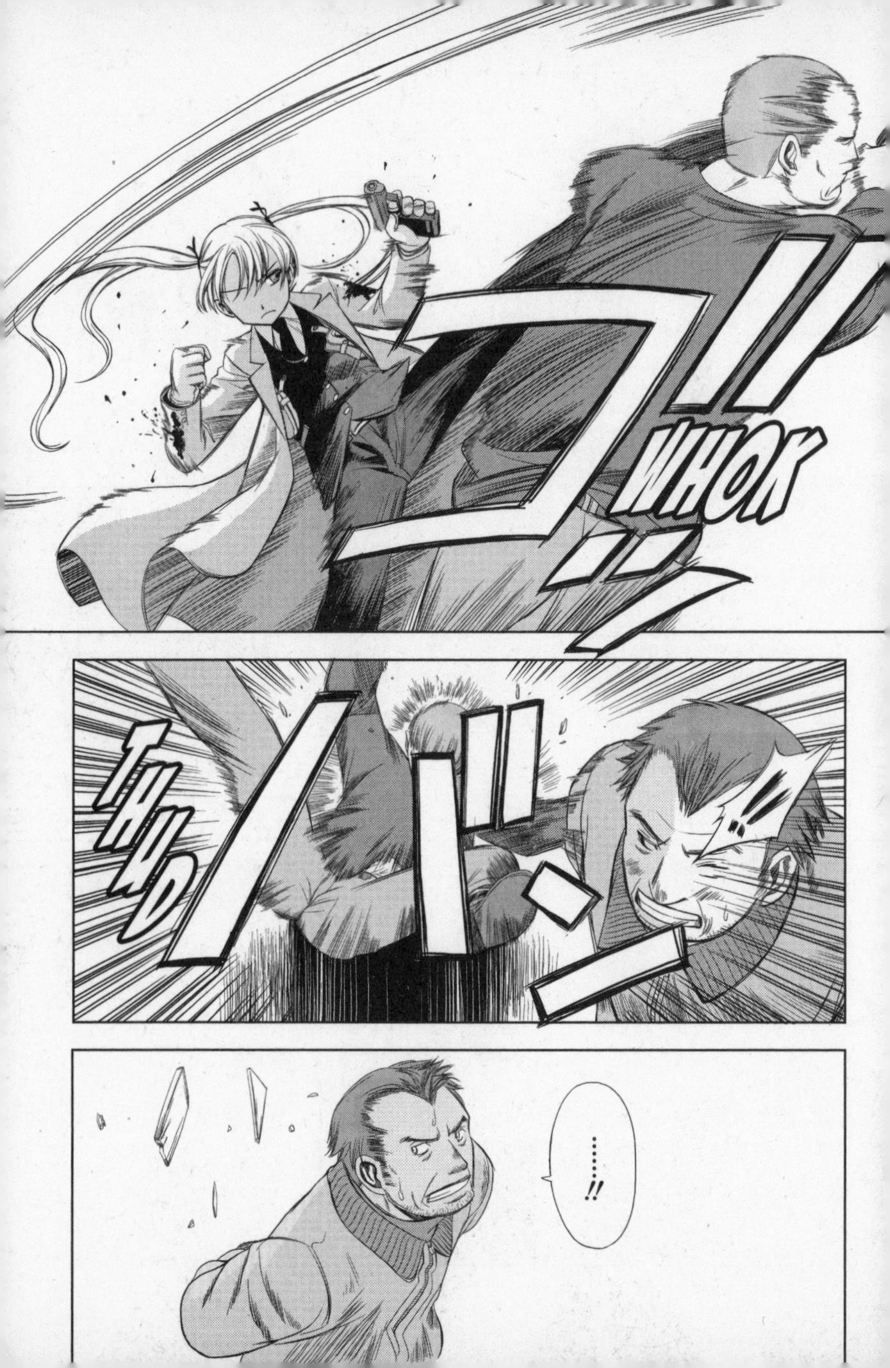
WHOK
THUD
......!!

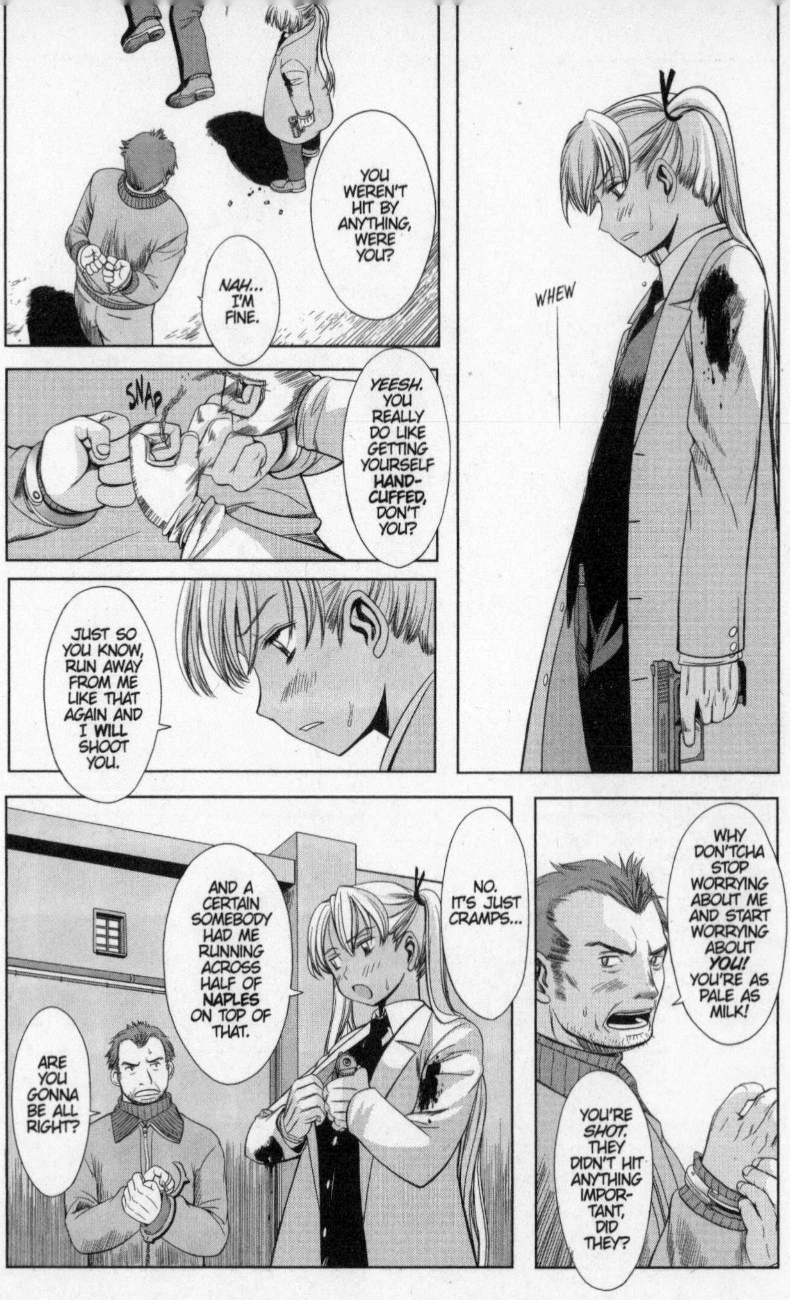
WHEW
YOU WEREN'T HIT BY ANYTHING, WERE YOU?
NAH... I'M FINE.
SNAP
YEESH. YOU REALLY DO LIKE GETTING YOURSELF HAND-CUFFED, DON'T YOU?
JUST SO YOU KNOW, RUN AWAY FROM ME LIKE THAT AGAIN AND I WILL SHOOT YOU.
WHY DON'TCHA STOP WORRYING ABOUT ME AND START WORRYING ABOUT YOU! YOU'RE AS PALE AS MILK!
YOU'RE SHOT. THEY DIDN'T HIT ANYTHING IMPOR-TANT, DID THEY?
NO. IT'S JUST CRAMPS...
AND A CERTAIN SOMEBODY HAD ME RUNNING ACROSS HALF OF NAPLES ON TOP OF THAT.
ARE YOU GONNA BE ALL RIGHT?

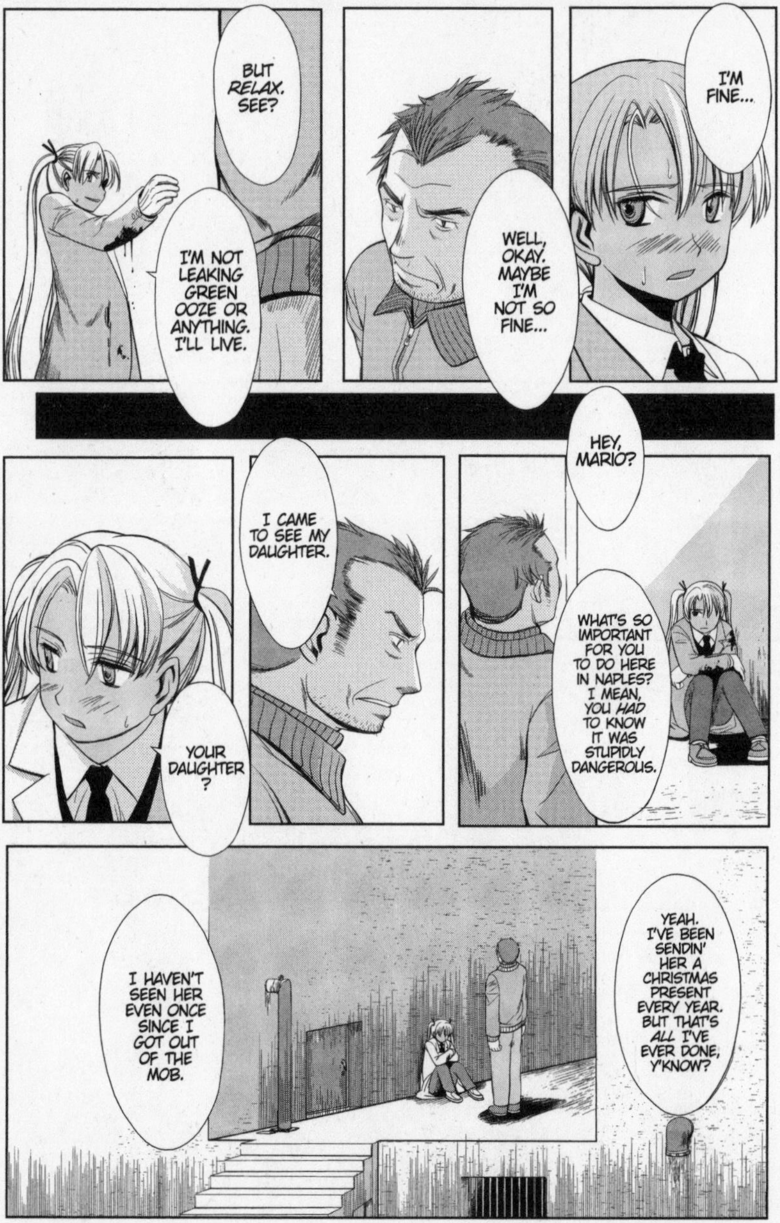
I'M FINE...
WELL, OKAY. MAYBE I'M NOT SO FINE...
BUT *RELAX.* SEE?
I'M NOT LEAKING GREEN OOZE OR ANYTHING. I'LL LIVE.
HEY, MARIO?
WHAT'S SO IMPORTANT FOR YOU TO DO HERE IN NAPLES? I MEAN, YOU *HAD* TO KNOW IT WAS STUPIDLY DANGEROUS.
I CAME TO SEE MY DAUGHTER.
YOUR DAUGHTER?
YEAH. I'VE BEEN SENDIN' HER A CHRISTMAS PRESENT EVERY YEAR. BUT THAT'S *ALL* I'VE EVER DONE, Y'KNOW?
I HAVEN'T SEEN HER EVEN ONCE SINCE I GOT OUT OF THE MOB.

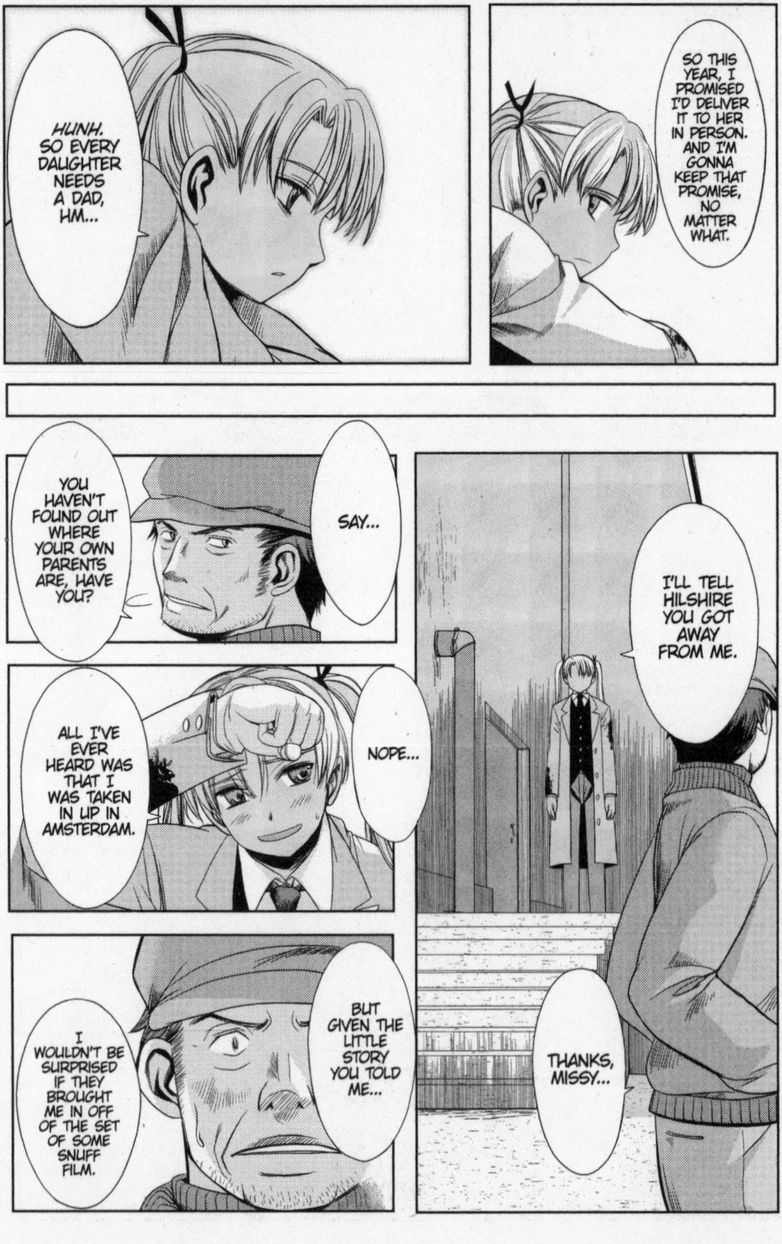
SO THIS YEAR, I PROMISED I'D DELIVER IT TO HER IN PERSON. AND I'M GONNA KEEP THAT PROMISE, NO MATTER WHAT.
HUNH. SO EVERY DAUGHTER NEEDS A DAD, HM...
I'LL TELL HILSHIRE YOU GOT AWAY FROM ME.
THANKS, MISSY...
SAY...
YOU HAVEN'T FOUND OUT WHERE YOUR OWN PARENTS ARE, HAVE YOU?
NOPE...
ALL I'VE EVER HEARD WAS THAT I WAS TAKEN IN UP IN AMSTERDAM.
BUT GIVEN THE LITTLE STORY YOU TOLD ME...
I WOULDN'T BE SURPRISED IF THEY BROUGHT ME IN OFF OF THE SET OF SOME SNUFF FILM.

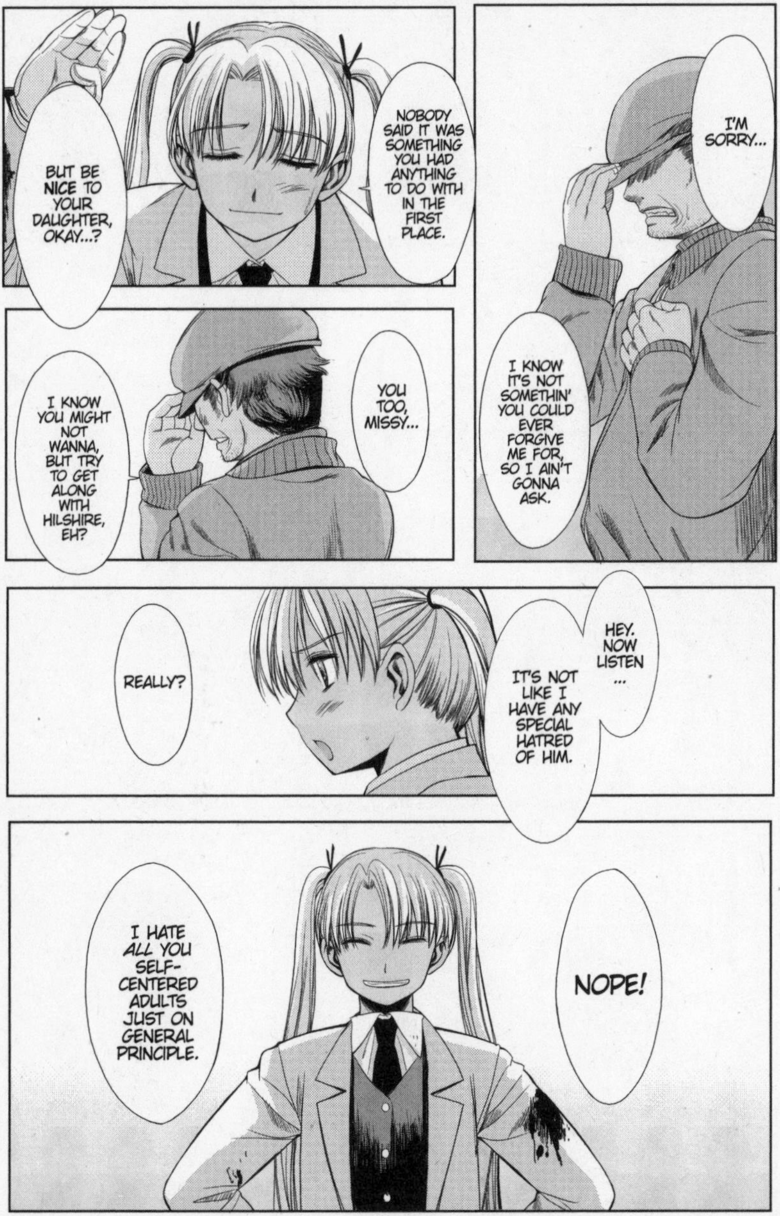
I'M SORRY...
I KNOW IT'S NOT SOMETHIN' YOU COULD EVER FORGIVE ME FOR, SO I AIN'T GONNA ASK.
NOBODY SAID IT WAS SOMETHING YOU HAD ANYTHING TO DO WITH IN THE FIRST PLACE.
BUT BE NICE TO YOUR DAUGHTER, OKAY...?
YOU TOO, MISSY...
I KNOW YOU MIGHT NOT WANNA, BUT TRY TO GET ALONG WITH HILSHIRE, EH?
HEY. NOW LISTEN ...
IT'S NOT LIKE I HAVE ANY SPECIAL HATRED OF HIM.
REALLY?
NOPE!
I HATE ALL YOU SELF-CENTERED ADULTS JUST ON GENERAL PRINCIPLE.

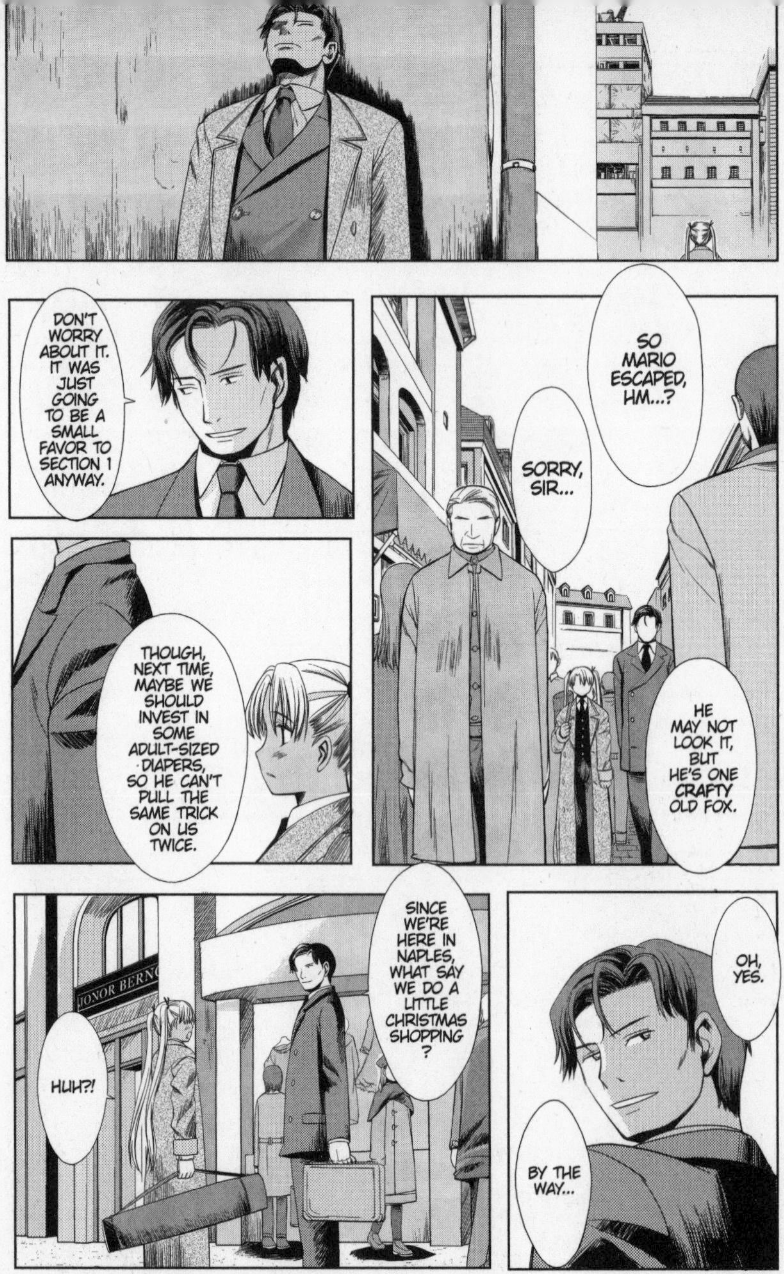
SO MARIO ESCAPED, HM...?
SORRY, SIR...
HE MAY NOT LOOK IT, BUT HE'S ONE CRAFTY OLD FOX.
DON'T WORRY ABOUT IT. IT WAS JUST GOING TO BE A SMALL FAVOR TO SECTION 1 ANYWAY.
THOUGH, NEXT TIME, MAYBE WE SHOULD INVEST IN SOME ADULT-SIZED DIAPERS, SO HE CAN'T PULL THE SAME TRICK ON US TWICE.
OH, YES.
BY THE WAY...
SINCE WE'RE HERE IN NAPLES, WHAT SAY WE DO A LITTLE CHRISTMAS SHOPPING ?
HUH?!

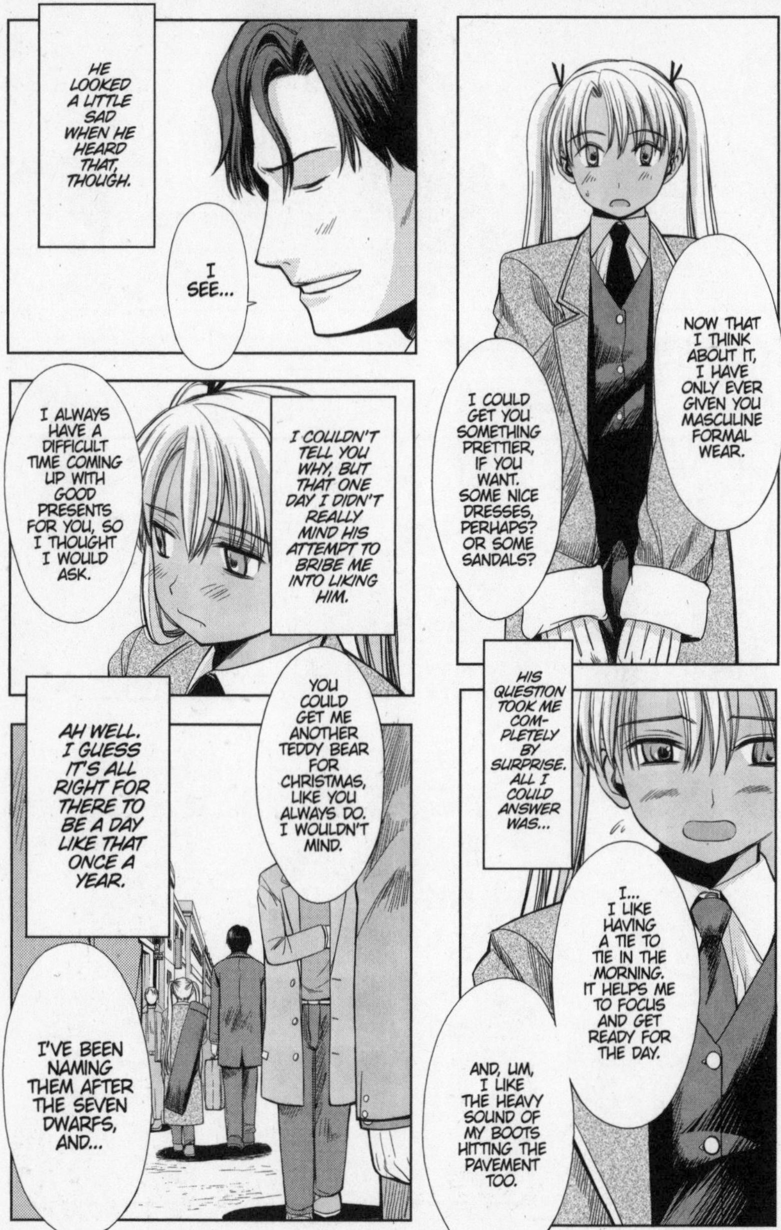
NOW THAT I THINK ABOUT IT, I HAVE ONLY EVER GIVEN YOU MASCULINE FORMAL WEAR.
I COULD GET YOU SOMETHING PRETTIER, IF YOU WANT. SOME NICE DRESSES, PERHAPS? OR SOME SANDALS?
HIS QUESTION TOOK ME COM-PLETELY BY SURPRISE. ALL I COULD ANSWER WAS...
I... I LIKE HAVING A TIE TO TIE IN THE MORNING. IT HELPS ME TO FOCUS AND GET READY FOR THE DAY.
AND, UM, I LIKE THE HEAVY SOUND OF MY BOOTS HITTING THE PAVEMENT TOO.
HE LOOKED A LITTLE SAD WHEN HE HEARD THAT, THOUGH.
I SEE...
I ALWAYS HAVE A DIFFICULT TIME COMING UP WITH GOOD PRESENTS FOR YOU, SO I THOUGHT I WOULD ASK.
I COULDN'T TELL YOU WHY, BUT THAT ONE DAY I DIDN'T REALLY MIND HIS ATTEMPT TO BRIBE ME INTO LIKING HIM.
YOU COULD GET ME ANOTHER TEDDY BEAR FOR CHRISTMAS, LIKE YOU ALWAYS DO. I WOULDN'T MIND.
AH WELL. I GUESS IT'S ALL RIGHT FOR THERE TO BE A DAY LIKE THAT ONCE A YEAR.
I'VE BEEN NAMING THEM AFTER THE SEVEN DWARFS, AND...

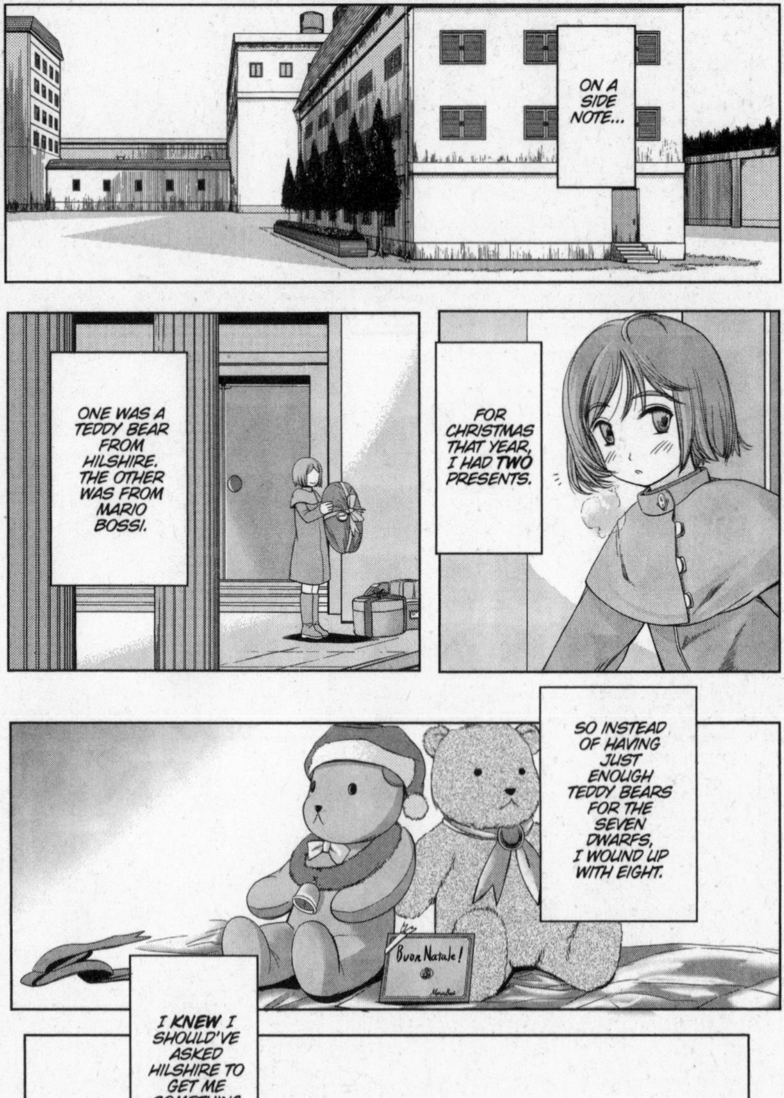

ON A SIDE NOTE...
FOR CHRISTMAS THAT YEAR, I HAD **TWO** PRESENTS.
ONE WAS A TEDDY BEAR FROM HILSHIRE. THE OTHER WAS FROM MARIO BOSSI.
SO INSTEAD OF HAVING JUST ENOUGH TEDDY BEARS FOR THE SEVEN DWARFS, I WOUND UP WITH EIGHT.
Buon Natale!
I **KNEW** I SHOULD'VE ASKED HILSHIRE TO GET ME SOMETHING DIFFERENT.

GUNSLINGERGIRL.

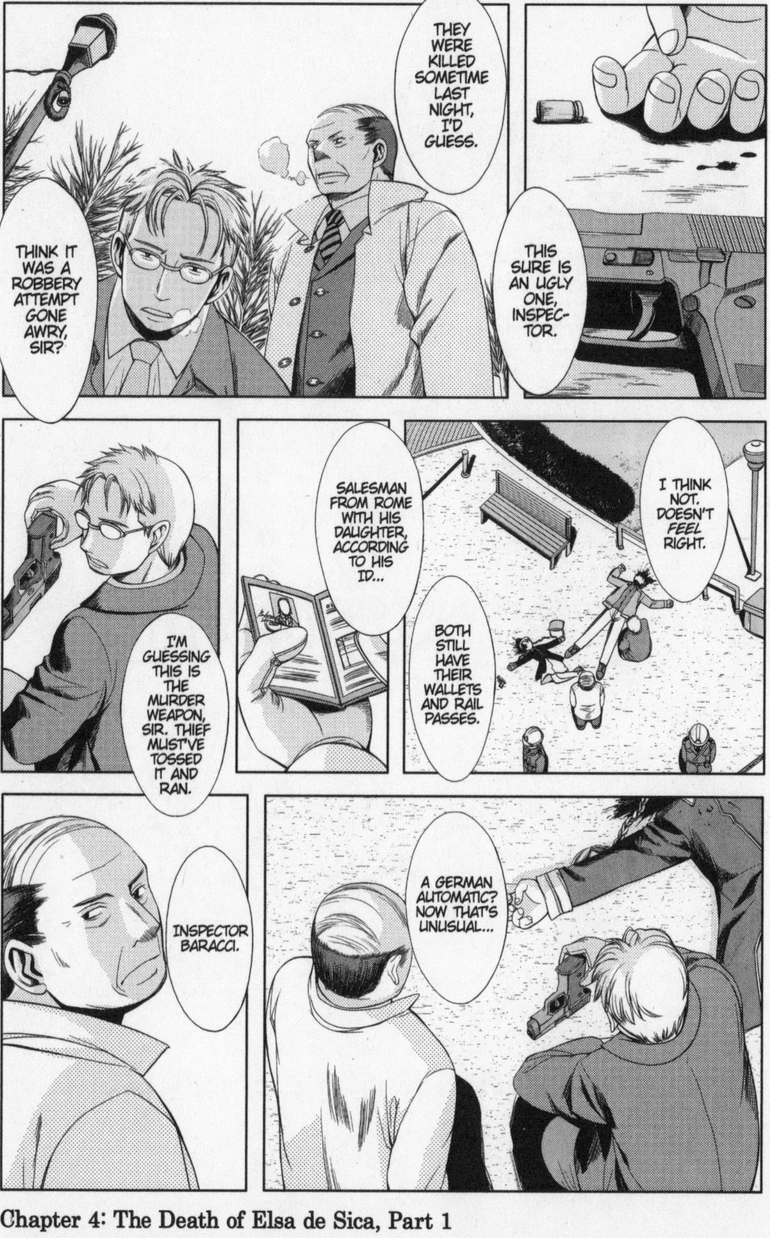
THIS SURE IS AN UGLY ONE, INSPECTOR.
THEY WERE KILLED SOMETIME LAST NIGHT, I'D GUESS.
THINK IT WAS A ROBBERY ATTEMPT GONE AWRY, SIR?
I THINK NOT. DOESN'T FEEL RIGHT.
BOTH STILL HAVE THEIR WALLETS AND RAIL PASSES.
SALESMAN FROM ROME WITH HIS DAUGHTER, ACCORDING TO HIS ID...
I'M GUESSING THIS IS THE MURDER WEAPON, SIR. THIEF MUST'VE TOSSED IT AND RAN.
A GERMAN AUTOMATIC? NOW THAT'S UNUSUAL...
INSPECTOR BARACCI.

Chapter 4: The Death of Elsa de Sica, Part 1

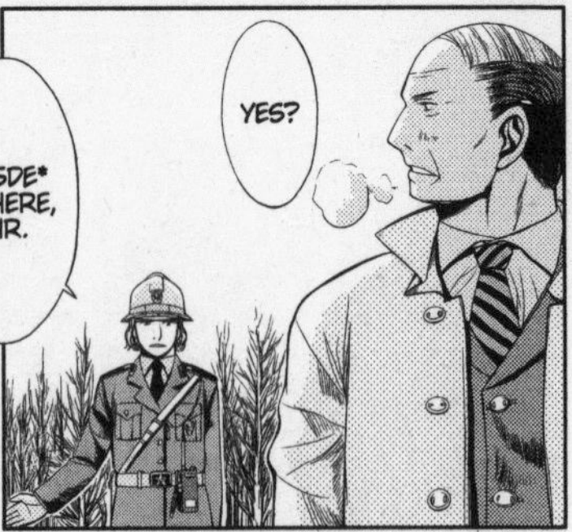
YES?
SISDE* IS HERE, SIR.

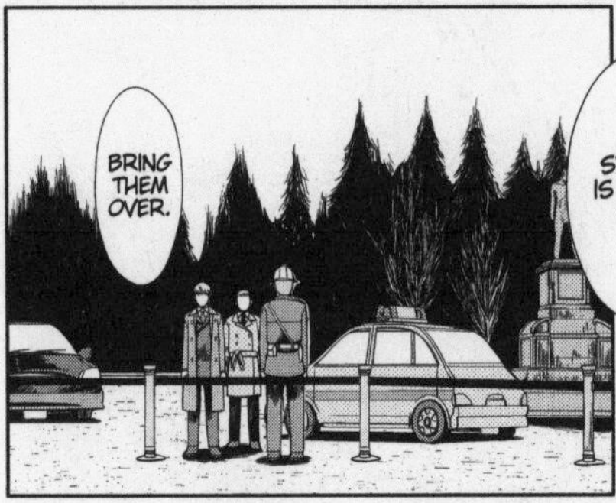
BRING THEM OVER.

*SISDE = Servizio per le Informazioni e la Sicurezza Democratica

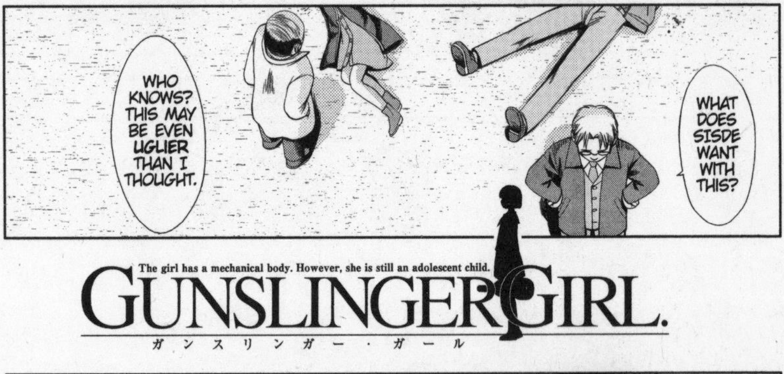
WHAT DOES SISDE WANT WITH THIS?
WHO KNOWS? THIS MAY BE EVEN UGLIER THAN I THOUGHT.

The girl has a mechanical body. However, she is still an adolescent child.

GUNSLINGER GIRL.

ガンスリンガー・ガール

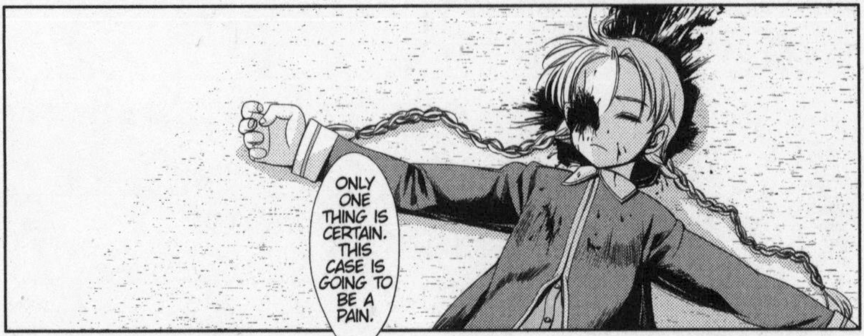
ONLY ONE THING IS CERTAIN. THIS CASE IS GOING TO BE A PAIN.

CHAPTER 4: THE DEATH OF ELSA DE SICA, PART 1

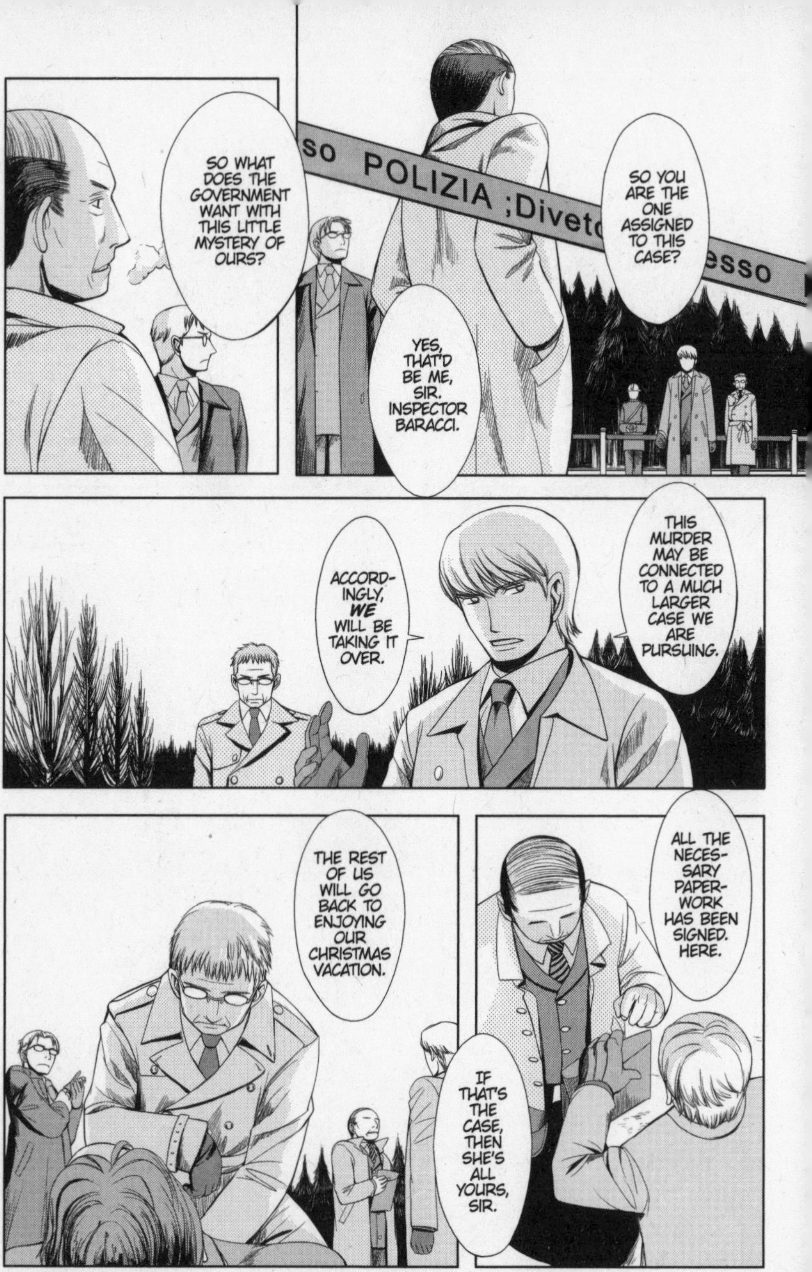
so POLIZIA ;Diveto
esso
SO YOU ARE THE ONE ASSIGNED TO THIS CASE?
YES, THAT'D BE ME, SIR. INSPECTOR BARACCI.
SO WHAT DOES THE GOVERNMENT WANT WITH THIS LITTLE MYSTERY OF OURS?
THIS MURDER MAY BE CONNECTED TO A MUCH LARGER CASE WE ARE PURSUING.
ACCORDINGLY, **WE** WILL BE TAKING IT OVER.
ALL THE NECES-SARY PAPER-WORK HAS BEEN SIGNED. HERE.
IF THAT'S THE CASE, THEN SHE'S ALL YOURS, SIR.
THE REST OF US WILL GO BACK TO ENJOYING OUR CHRISTMAS VACATION.

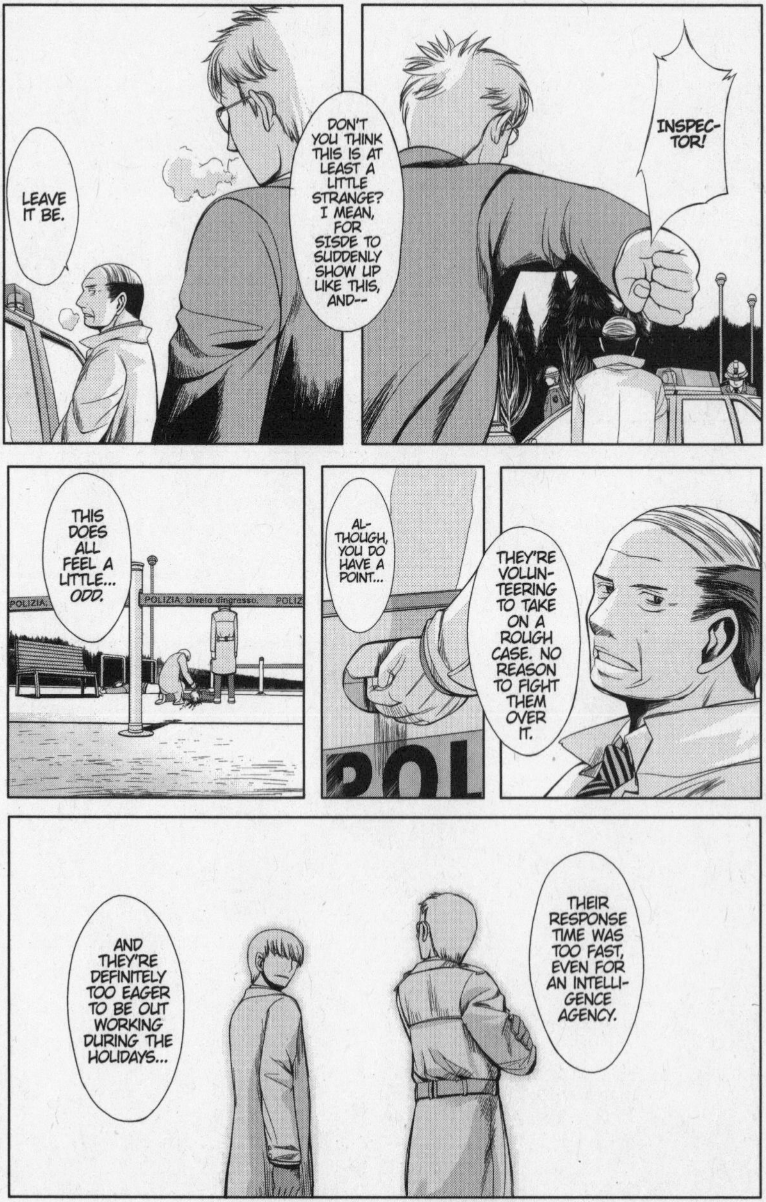
INSPECTOR!
DON'T YOU THINK THIS IS AT LEAST A LITTLE STRANGE? I MEAN, FOR SISDE TO SUDDENLY SHOW UP LIKE THIS, AND--
LEAVE IT BE.
THEY'RE VOLUNTEERING TO TAKE ON A ROUGH CASE. NO REASON TO FIGHT THEM OVER IT.
ALTHOUGH, YOU DO HAVE A POINT...
POL
THIS DOES ALL FEEL A LITTLE... *ODD.*
POLIZIA. Diveto dingresso.
THEIR RESPONSE TIME WAS TOO FAST, EVEN FOR AN INTELLIGENCE AGENCY.
AND THEY'RE DEFINITELY TOO EAGER TO BE OUT WORKING DURING THE HOLIDAYS...

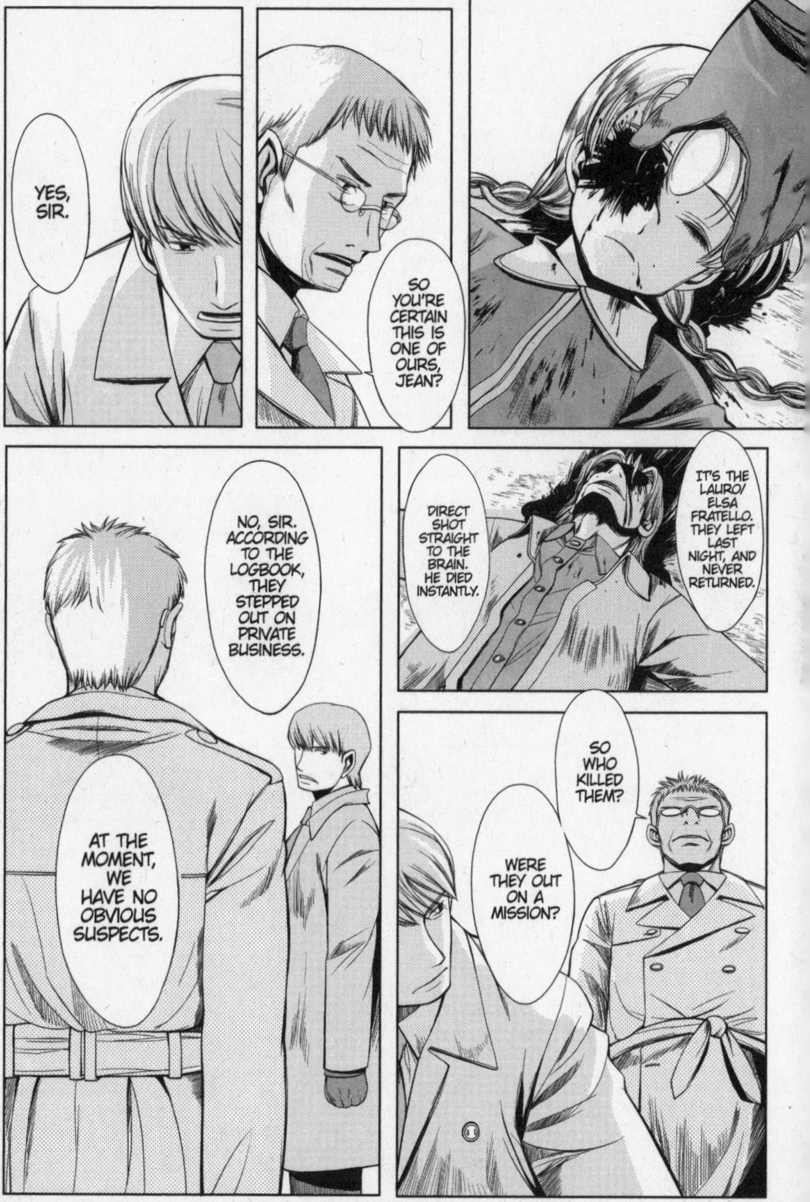
SO YOU'RE CERTAIN THIS IS ONE OF OURS, JEAN?
YES, SIR.
IT'S THE LAURO/ ELSA FRATELLO. THEY LEFT LAST NIGHT, AND NEVER RETURNED.
DIRECT SHOT STRAIGHT TO THE BRAIN. HE DIED INSTANTLY.
SO WHO KILLED THEM?
WERE THEY OUT ON A MISSION?
NO, SIR. ACCORDING TO THE LOGBOOK, THEY STEPPED OUT ON PRIVATE BUSINESS.
AT THE MOMENT, WE HAVE NO OBVIOUS SUSPECTS.

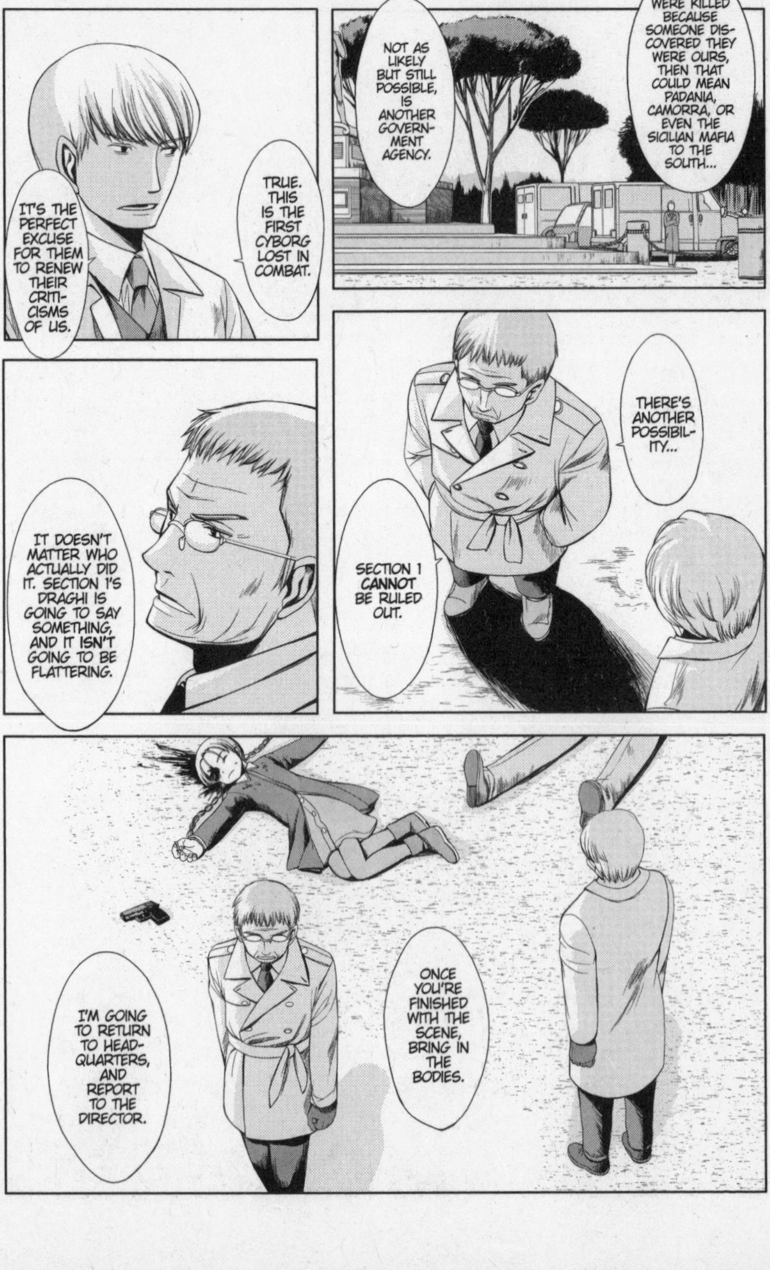
IF THEY WERE KILLED BECAUSE SOMEONE DIS-COVERED THEY WERE OURS, THEN THAT COULD MEAN PADANIA, CAMORRA, OR EVEN THE SICILIAN MAFIA TO THE SOUTH...
NOT AS LIKELY BUT STILL POSSIBLE, IS ANOTHER GOVERN-MENT AGENCY.
TRUE. THIS IS THE FIRST CYBORG LOST IN COMBAT.
IT'S THE PERFECT EXCUSE FOR THEM TO RENEW THEIR CRITI-CISMS OF US.
THERE'S ANOTHER POSSIBIL-ITY...
SECTION 1 CANNOT BE RULED OUT.
IT DOESN'T MATTER WHO ACTUALLY DID IT. SECTION 1'S DRAGHI IS GOING TO SAY SOMETHING, AND IT ISN'T GOING TO BE FLATTERING.
ONCE YOU'RE FINISHED WITH THE SCENE, BRING IN THE BODIES.
I'M GOING TO RETURN TO HEAD-QUARTERS, AND REPORT TO THE DIRECTOR.

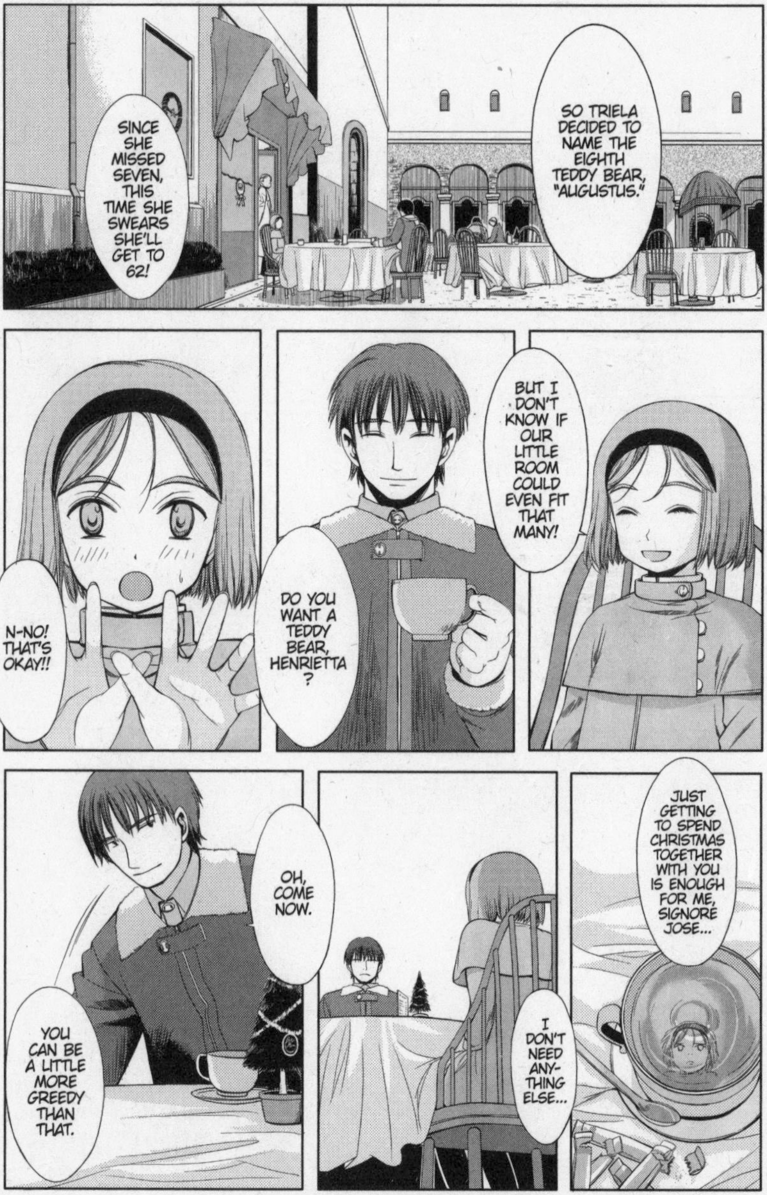
SO TRIELA DECIDED TO NAME THE EIGHTH TEDDY BEAR, "AUGUSTUS."
SINCE SHE MISSED SEVEN, THIS TIME SHE SWEARS SHE'LL GET TO 62!
BUT I DON'T KNOW IF OUR LITTLE ROOM COULD EVEN FIT THAT MANY!
DO YOU WANT A TEDDY BEAR, HENRIETTA?
N-NO! THAT'S OKAY!!
JUST GETTING TO SPEND CHRISTMAS TOGETHER WITH YOU IS ENOUGH FOR ME, SIGNORE JOSE...
I DON'T NEED ANY-THING ELSE...
OH, COME NOW.
YOU CAN BE A LITTLE MORE GREEDY THAN THAT.

HERE.

THESE MAY NOT BE AS CUTE AS A TEDDY BEAR, BUT I THOUGHT YOU MIGHT LIKE THEM.

UM...

I'LL OPEN THEM NOW, IF YOU DON'T MIND.

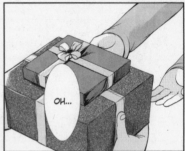

OH...

YOU'RE BEING AWFULLY CAREFUL ABOUT THAT.

THANK YOU!

YES. I LIKE IRONING THE WRAPPING PAPER FLAT AND KEEPING IT.

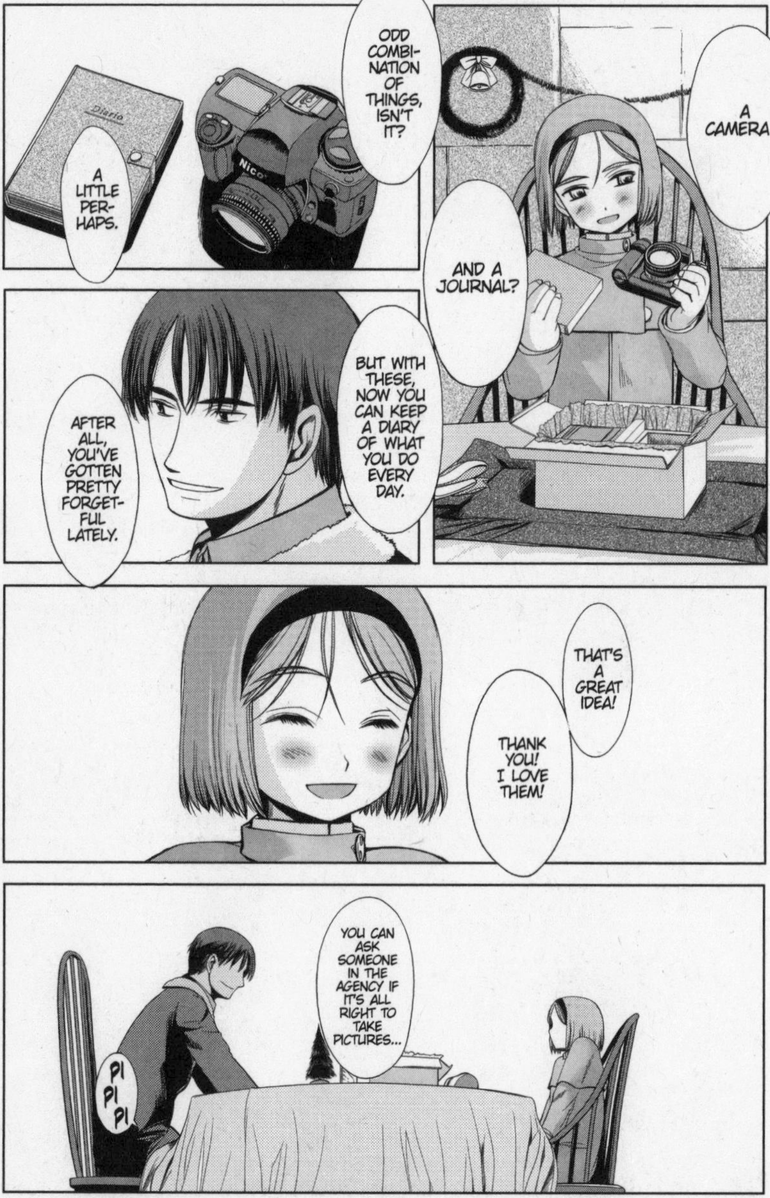
A CAMERA...
AND A JOURNAL?
ODD COMBINATION OF THINGS, ISN'T IT?
Diario
A LITTLE PERHAPS.
BUT WITH THESE, NOW YOU CAN KEEP A DIARY OF WHAT YOU DO EVERY DAY.
AFTER ALL, YOU'VE GOTTEN PRETTY FORGETFUL LATELY.
THAT'S A GREAT IDEA!
THANK YOU! I LOVE THEM!
YOU CAN ASK SOMEONE IN THE AGENCY IF IT'S ALL RIGHT TO TAKE PICTURES...
PI PI PI

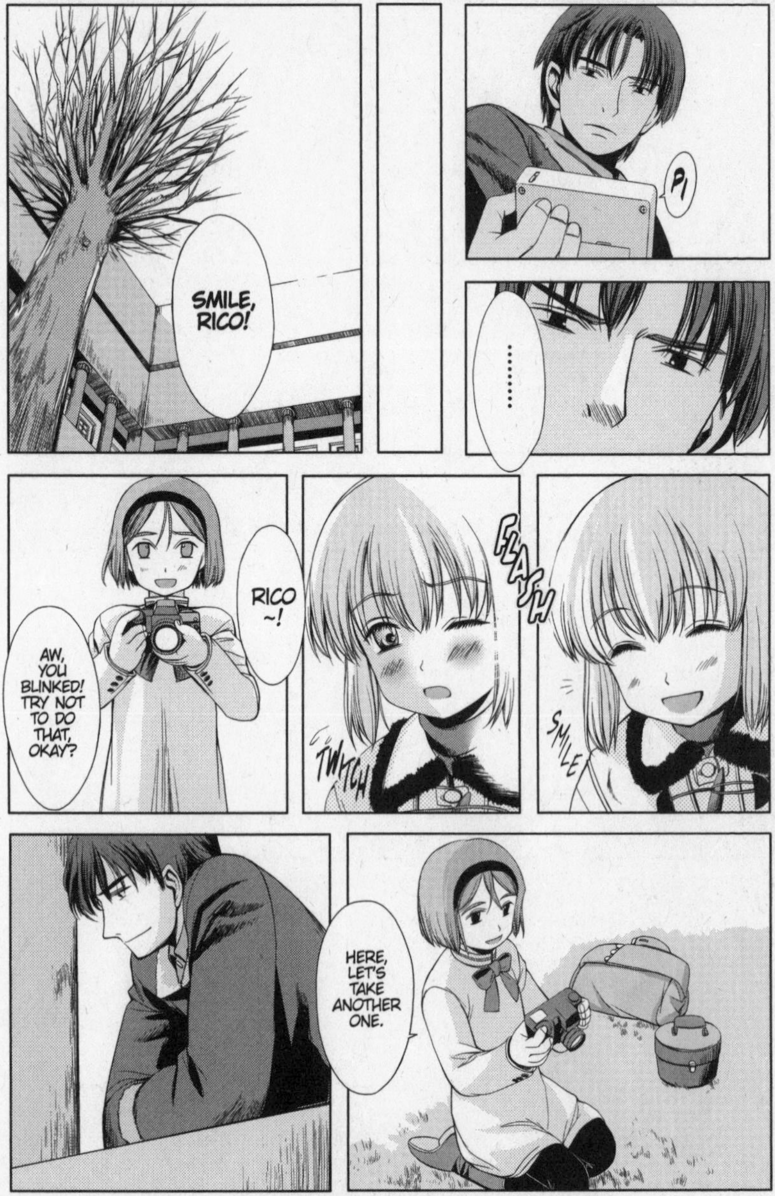
PI
....
SMILE, RICO!
FLASH
SMILE
TWITCH
RICO ~!
AW, YOU BLINKED! TRY NOT TO DO THAT, OKAY?
HERE, LET'S TAKE ANOTHER ONE.

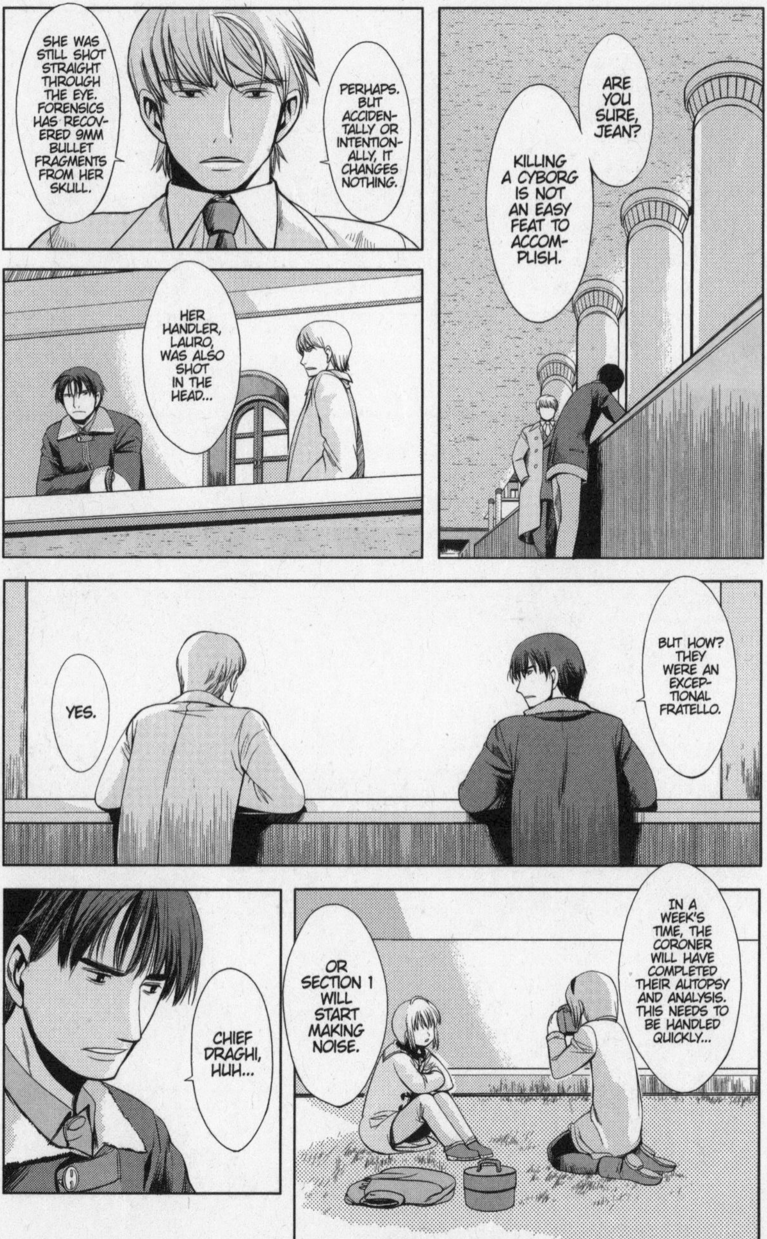
ARE YOU SURE, JEAN?
KILLING A CYBORG IS NOT AN EASY FEAT TO ACCOMPLISH.
PERHAPS. BUT ACCIDENTALLY OR INTENTIONALLY, IT CHANGES NOTHING.
SHE WAS STILL SHOT STRAIGHT THROUGH THE EYE. FORENSICS HAS RECOVERED 9MM BULLET FRAGMENTS FROM HER SKULL.
HER HANDLER, LAURO, WAS ALSO SHOT IN THE HEAD...
BUT HOW? THEY WERE AN EXCEPTIONAL FRATELLO.
YES.
IN A WEEK'S TIME, THE CORONER WILL HAVE COMPLETED THEIR AUTOPSY AND ANALYSIS. THIS NEEDS TO BE HANDLED QUICKLY...
OR SECTION 1 WILL START MAKING NOISE.
CHIEF DRAGHI, HUH...

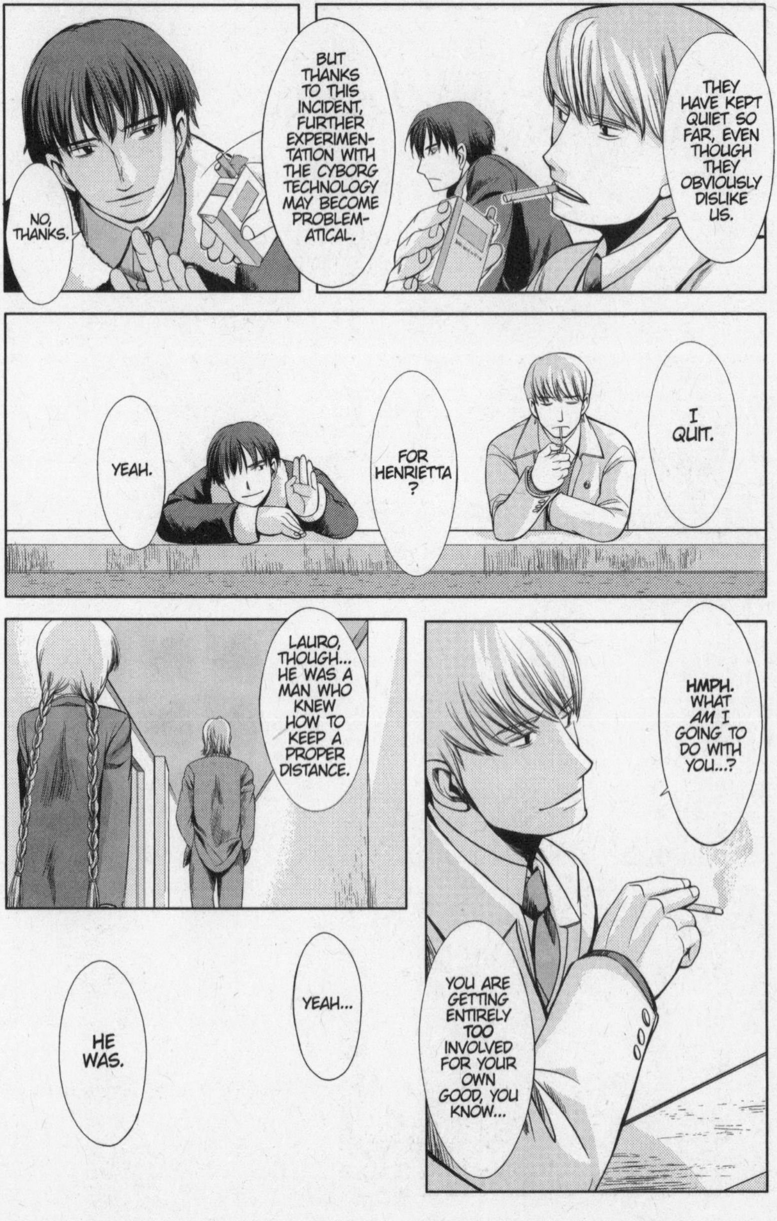
THEY HAVE KEPT QUIET SO FAR, EVEN THOUGH THEY OBVIOUSLY DISLIKE US.
BUT THANKS TO THIS INCIDENT, FURTHER EXPERIMENTATION WITH THE CYBORG TECHNOLOGY MAY BECOME PROBLEMATICAL.
NO, THANKS.
I QUIT.
FOR HENRIETTA?
YEAH.
HMPH. WHAT *AM* I GOING TO DO WITH YOU...?
YOU ARE GETTING ENTIRELY TOO INVOLVED FOR YOUR OWN GOOD, YOU KNOW...
LAURO, THOUGH... HE WAS A MAN WHO KNEW HOW TO KEEP A PROPER DISTANCE.
YEAH...
HE WAS.

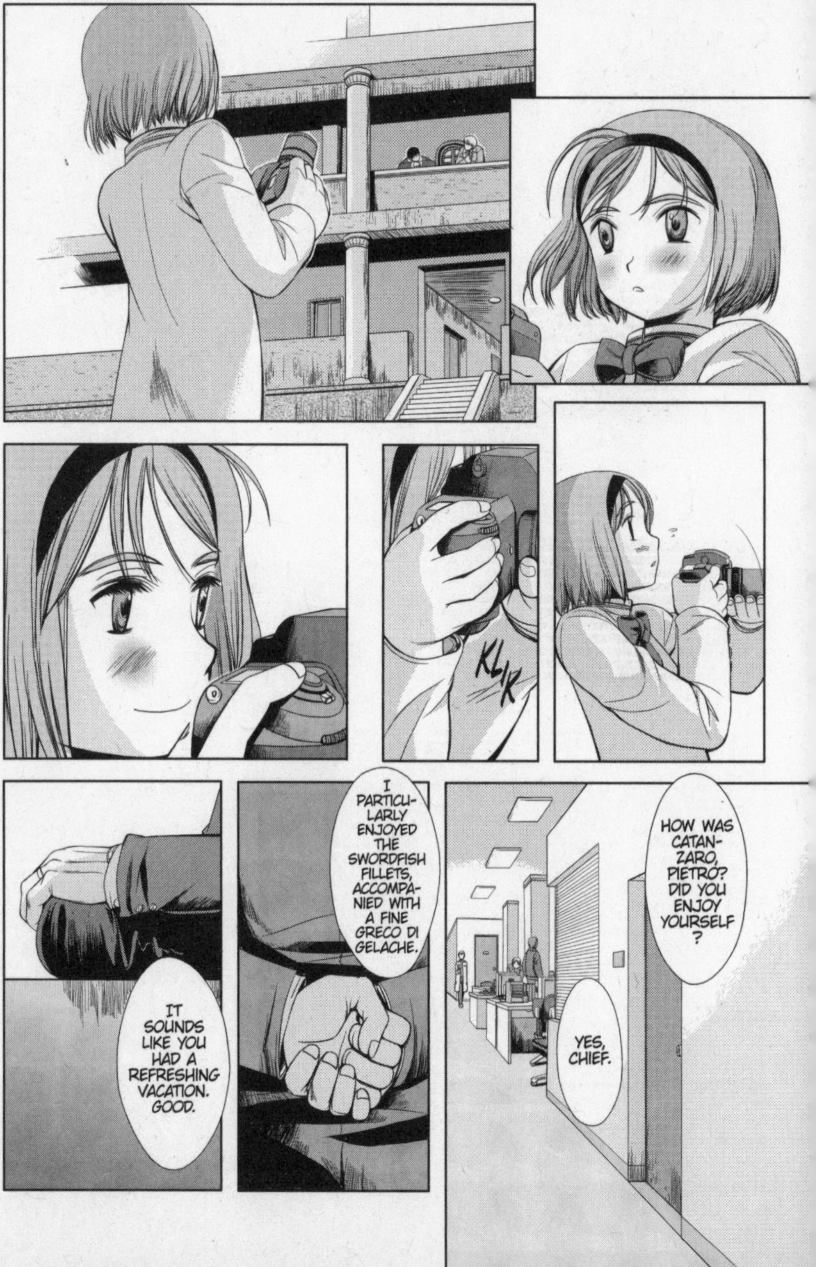
KLIK
HOW WAS CATANZARO, PIETRO? DID YOU ENJOY YOURSELF?
YES, CHIEF.
I PARTICULARLY ENJOYED THE SWORDFISH FILLETS, ACCOMPANIED WITH A FINE GRECO DI GELACHE.
IT SOUNDS LIKE YOU HAD A REFRESHING VACATION. GOOD.

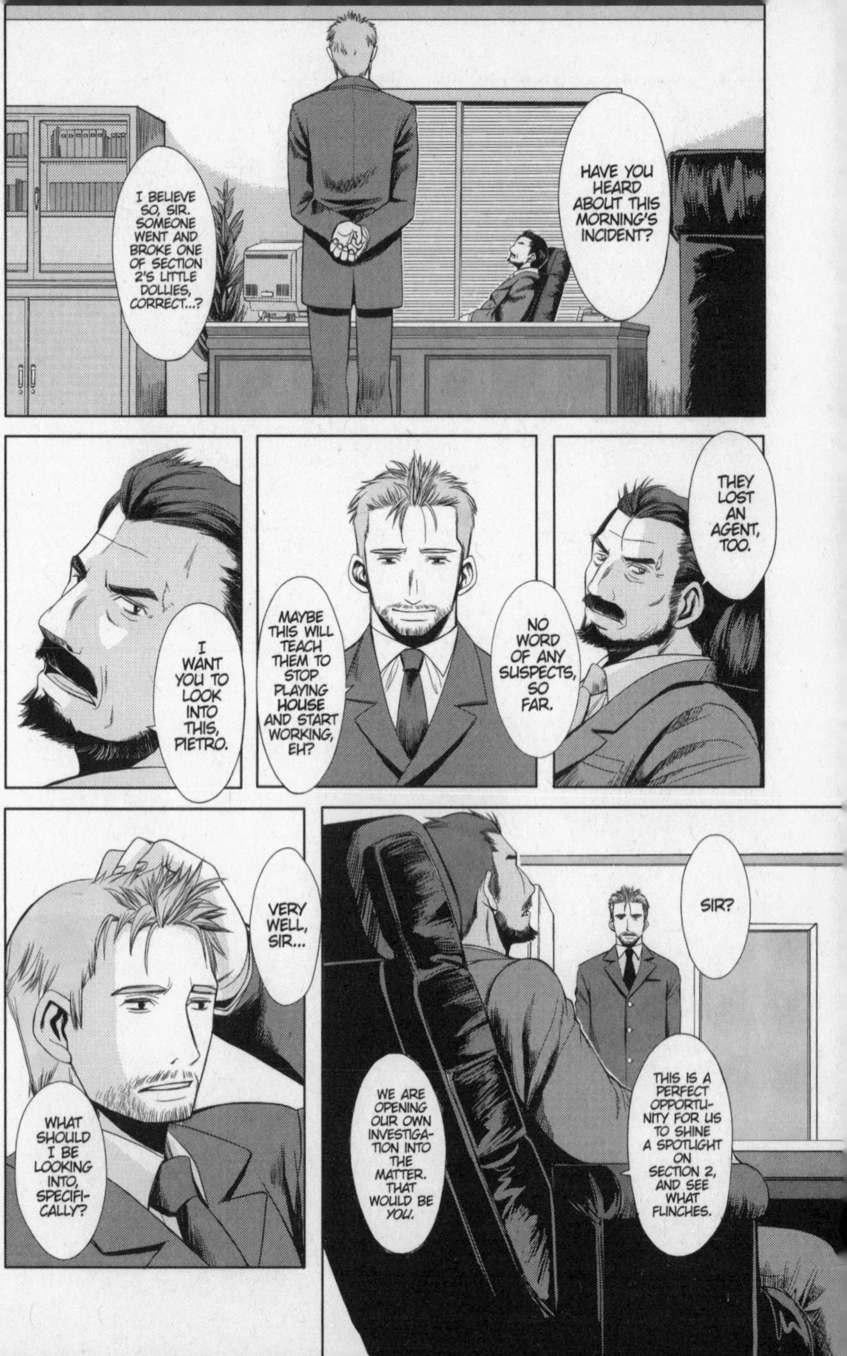
HAVE YOU HEARD ABOUT THIS MORNING'S INCIDENT?
I BELIEVE SO, SIR. SOMEONE WENT AND BROKE ONE OF SECTION 2'S LITTLE DOLLIES, CORRECT...?
THEY LOST AN AGENT, TOO.
NO WORD OF ANY SUSPECTS, SO FAR.
MAYBE THIS WILL TEACH THEM TO STOP PLAYING HOUSE AND START WORKING, EH?
I WANT YOU TO LOOK INTO THIS, PIETRO.
SIR?
THIS IS A PERFECT OPPORTUNITY FOR US TO SHINE A SPOTLIGHT ON SECTION 2, AND SEE WHAT FLINCHES.
WE ARE OPENING OUR OWN INVESTIGATION INTO THE MATTER. THAT WOULD BE *YOU*.
VERY WELL, SIR...
WHAT SHOULD I BE LOOKING INTO, SPECIFICALLY?

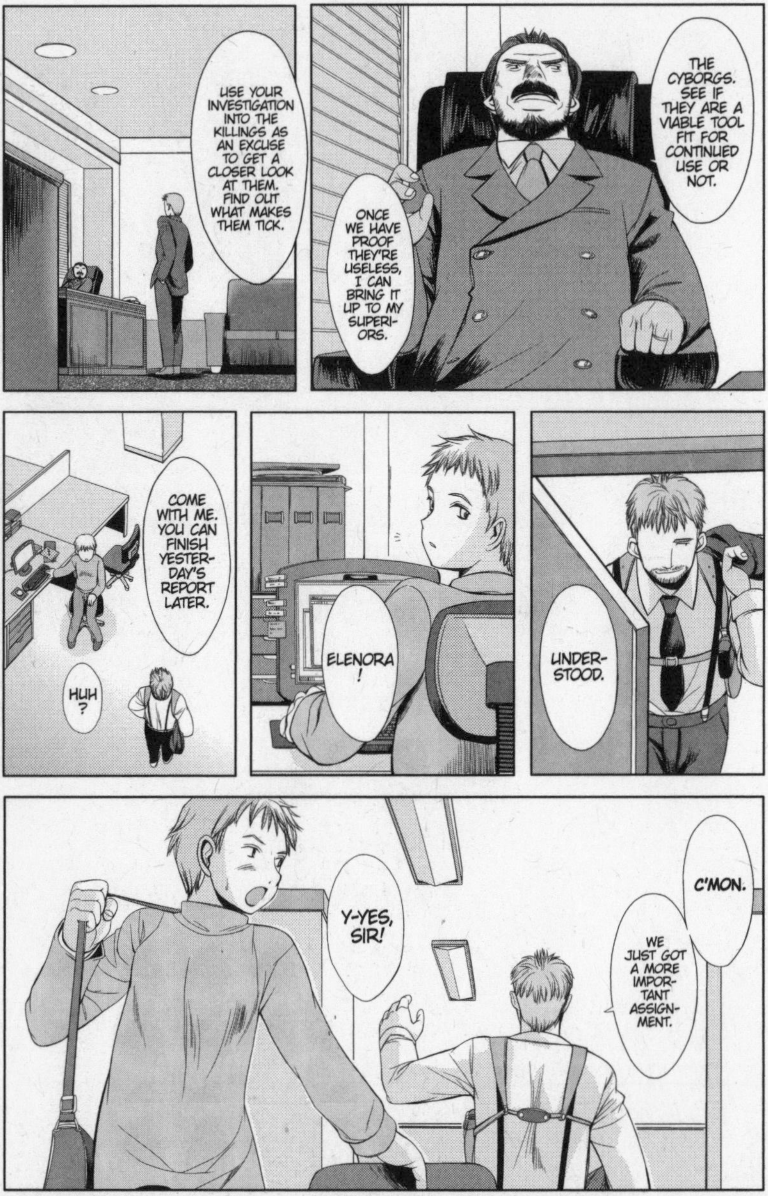
THE CYBORGS. SEE IF THEY ARE A VIABLE TOOL FIT FOR CONTINUED USE OR NOT.
ONCE WE HAVE PROOF THEY'RE USELESS, I CAN BRING IT UP TO MY SUPERIORS.
USE YOUR INVESTIGATION INTO THE KILLINGS AS AN EXCUSE TO GET A CLOSER LOOK AT THEM. FIND OUT WHAT MAKES THEM TICK.
UNDERSTOOD.
ELENORA!
COME WITH ME. YOU CAN FINISH YESTERDAY'S REPORT LATER.
HUH?
C'MON.
WE JUST GOT A MORE IMPORTANT ASSIGNMENT.
Y-YES, SIR!

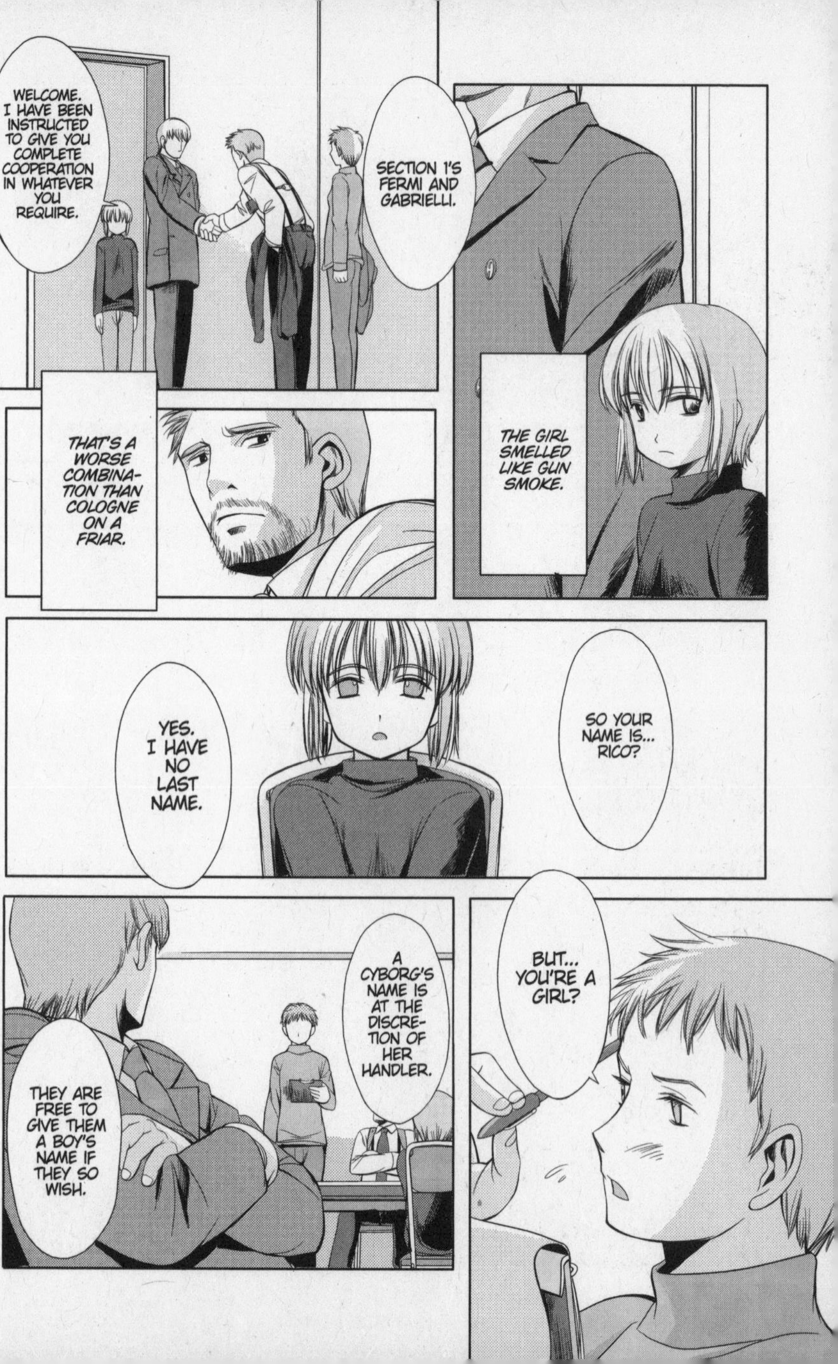
THE GIRL SMELLED LIKE GUN SMOKE.
SECTION 1'S FERMI AND GABRIELLI.
WELCOME. I HAVE BEEN INSTRUCTED TO GIVE YOU COMPLETE COOPERATION IN WHATEVER YOU REQUIRE.
THAT'S A WORSE COMBINATION THAN COLOGNE ON A FRIAR.
SO YOUR NAME IS... RICO?
YES. I HAVE NO LAST NAME.
BUT... YOU'RE A GIRL?
A CYBORG'S NAME IS AT THE DISCRETION OF HER HANDLER.
THEY ARE FREE TO GIVE THEM A BOY'S NAME IF THEY SO WISH.

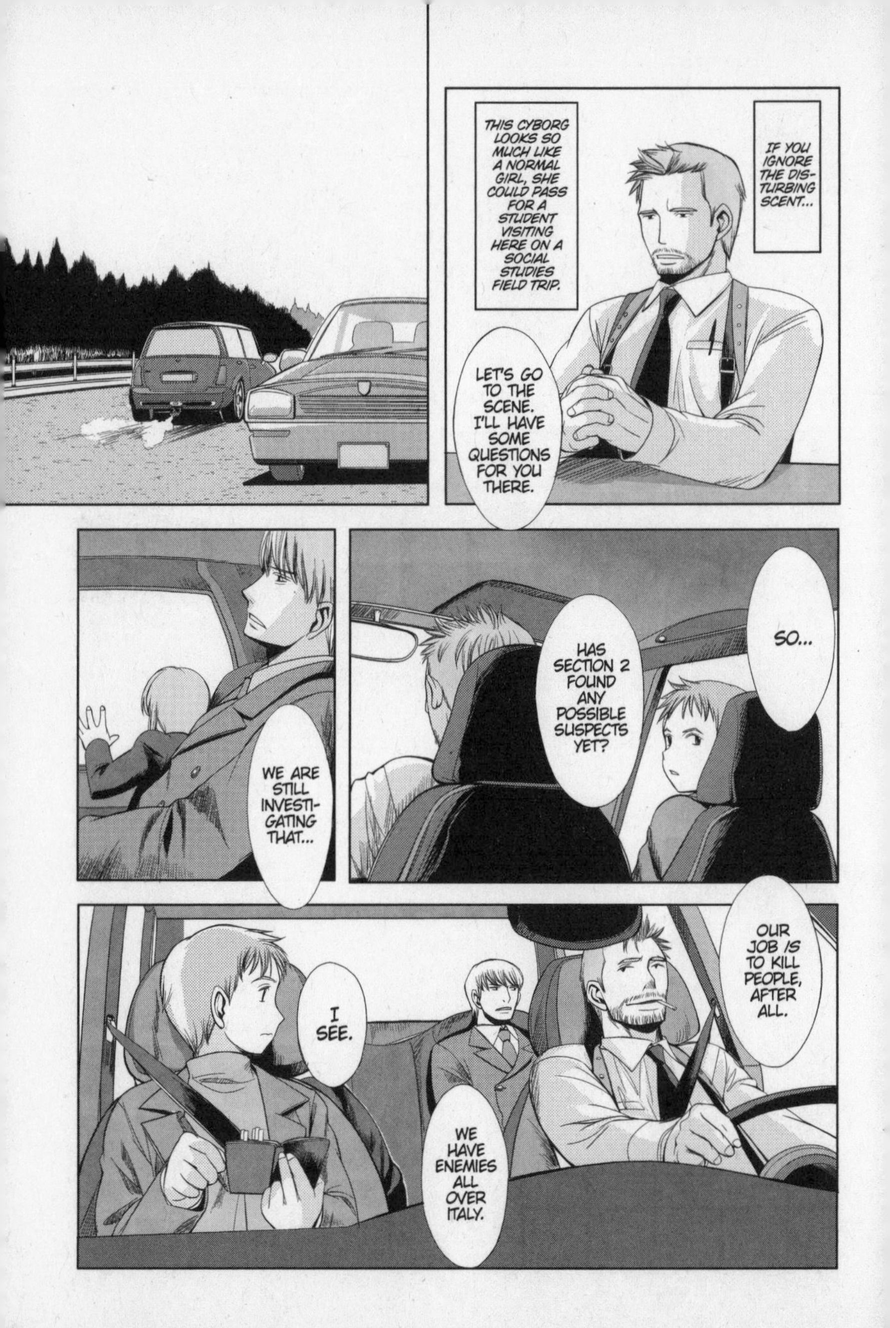
IF YOU IGNORE THE DISTURBING SCENT...
THIS CYBORG LOOKS SO MUCH LIKE A NORMAL GIRL, SHE COULD PASS FOR A STUDENT VISITING HERE ON A SOCIAL STUDIES FIELD TRIP.
LET'S GO TO THE SCENE. I'LL HAVE SOME QUESTIONS FOR YOU THERE.
SO...
HAS SECTION 2 FOUND ANY POSSIBLE SUSPECTS YET?
WE ARE STILL INVESTIGATING THAT...
OUR JOB IS TO KILL PEOPLE, AFTER ALL.
WE HAVE ENEMIES ALL OVER ITALY.
I SEE.

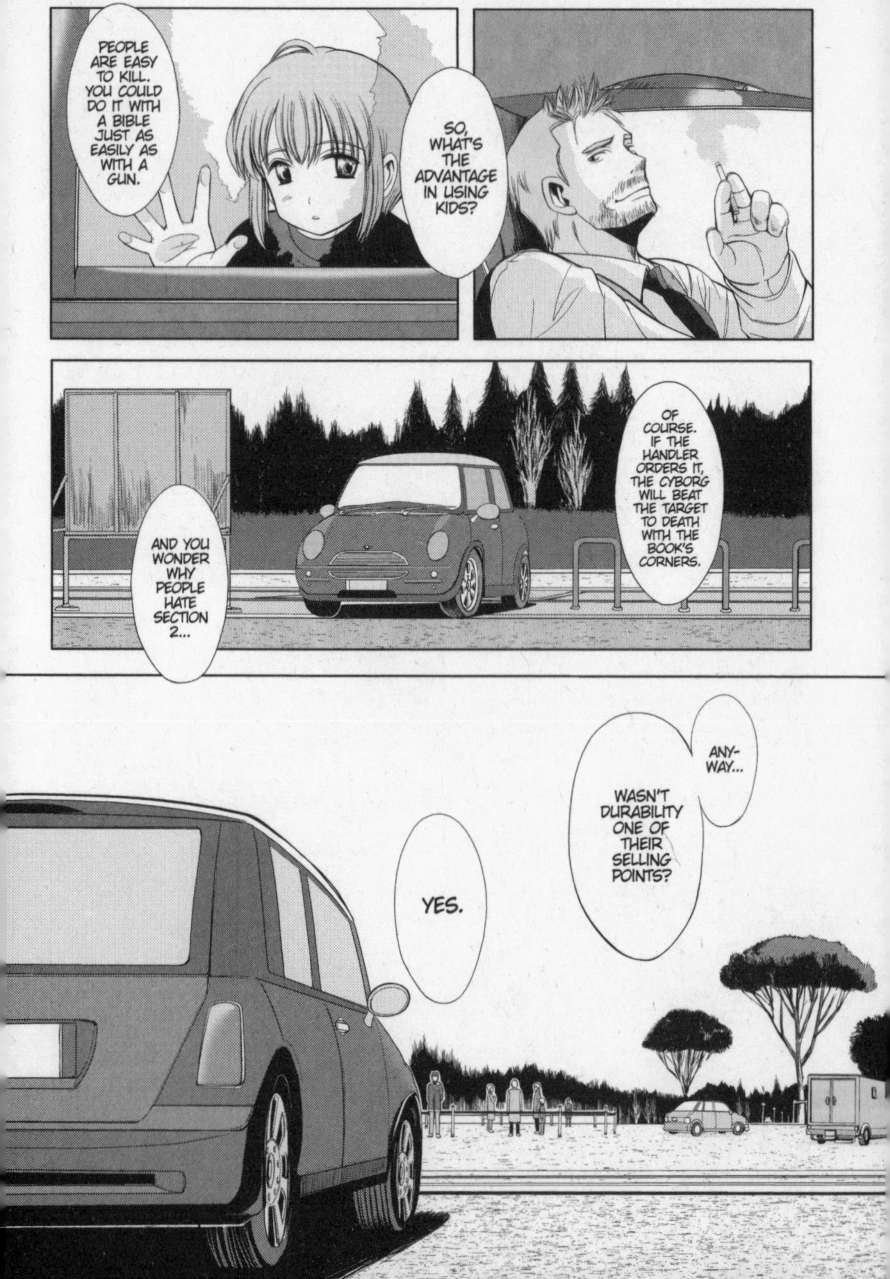
SO, WHAT'S THE ADVANTAGE IN USING KIDS?
PEOPLE ARE EASY TO KILL. YOU COULD DO IT WITH A BIBLE JUST AS EASILY AS WITH A GUN.
OF COURSE. IF THE HANDLER ORDERS IT, THE CYBORG WILL BEAT THE TARGET TO DEATH WITH THE BOOK'S CORNERS.
AND YOU WONDER WHY PEOPLE HATE SECTION 2...
ANY-WAY...
WASN'T DURABILITY ONE OF THEIR SELLING POINTS?
YES.

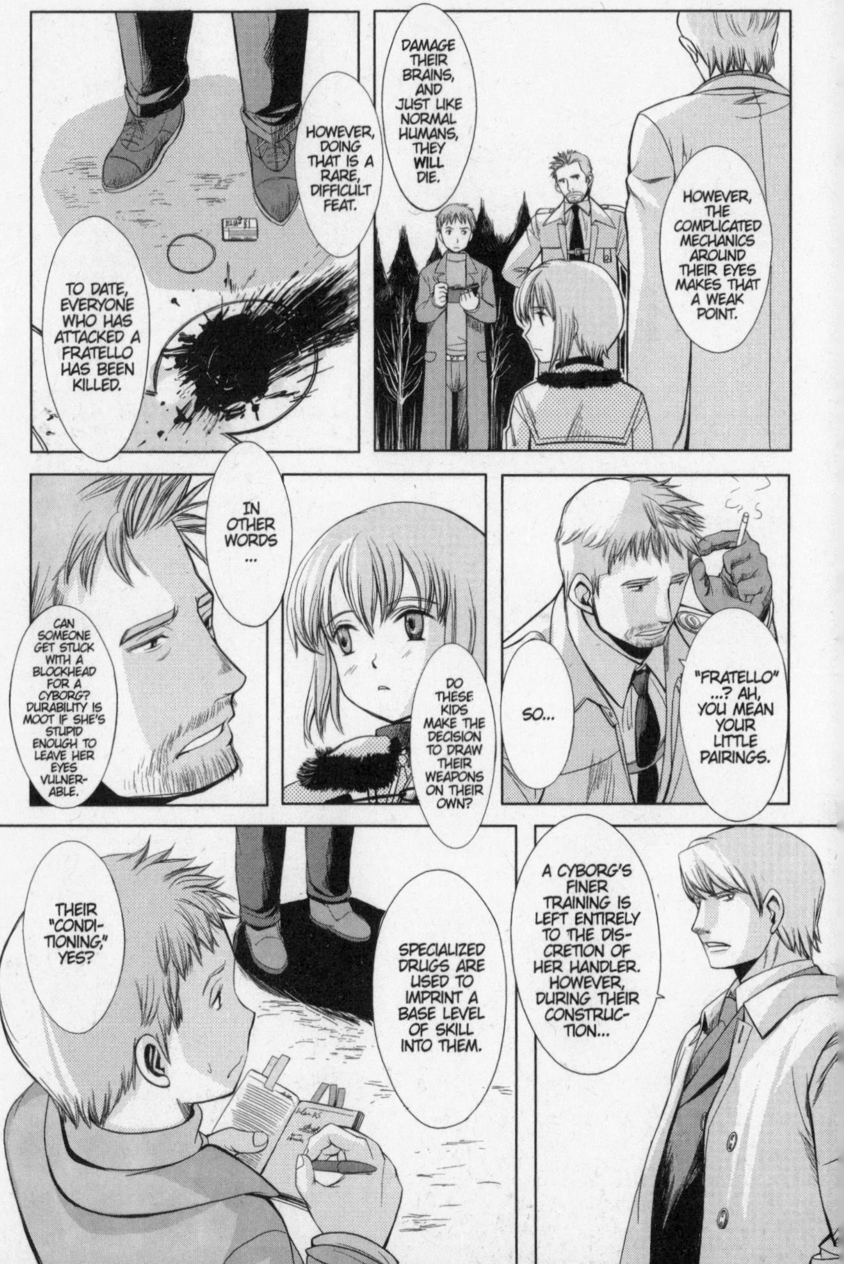
HOWEVER, THE COMPLICATED MECHANICS AROUND THEIR EYES MAKES THAT A WEAK POINT.
DAMAGE THEIR BRAINS, AND JUST LIKE NORMAL HUMANS, THEY WILL DIE.
HOWEVER, DOING THAT IS A RARE, DIFFICULT FEAT.
TO DATE, EVERYONE WHO HAS ATTACKED A FRATELLO HAS BEEN KILLED.
"FRATELLO" ...? AH, YOU MEAN YOUR LITTLE PAIRINGS.
SO...
IN OTHER WORDS ...
DO THESE KIDS MAKE THE DECISION TO DRAW THEIR WEAPONS ON THEIR OWN?
CAN SOMEONE GET STUCK WITH A BLOCKHEAD FOR A CYBORG? DURABILITY IS MOOT IF SHE'S STUPID ENOUGH TO LEAVE HER EYES VULNER-ABLE.
A CYBORG'S FINER TRAINING IS LEFT ENTIRELY TO THE DIS-CRETION OF HER HANDLER. HOWEVER, DURING THEIR CONSTRUC-TION...
SPECIALIZED DRUGS ARE USED TO IMPRINT A BASE LEVEL OF SKILL INTO THEM.
THEIR "CONDI-TIONING," YES?

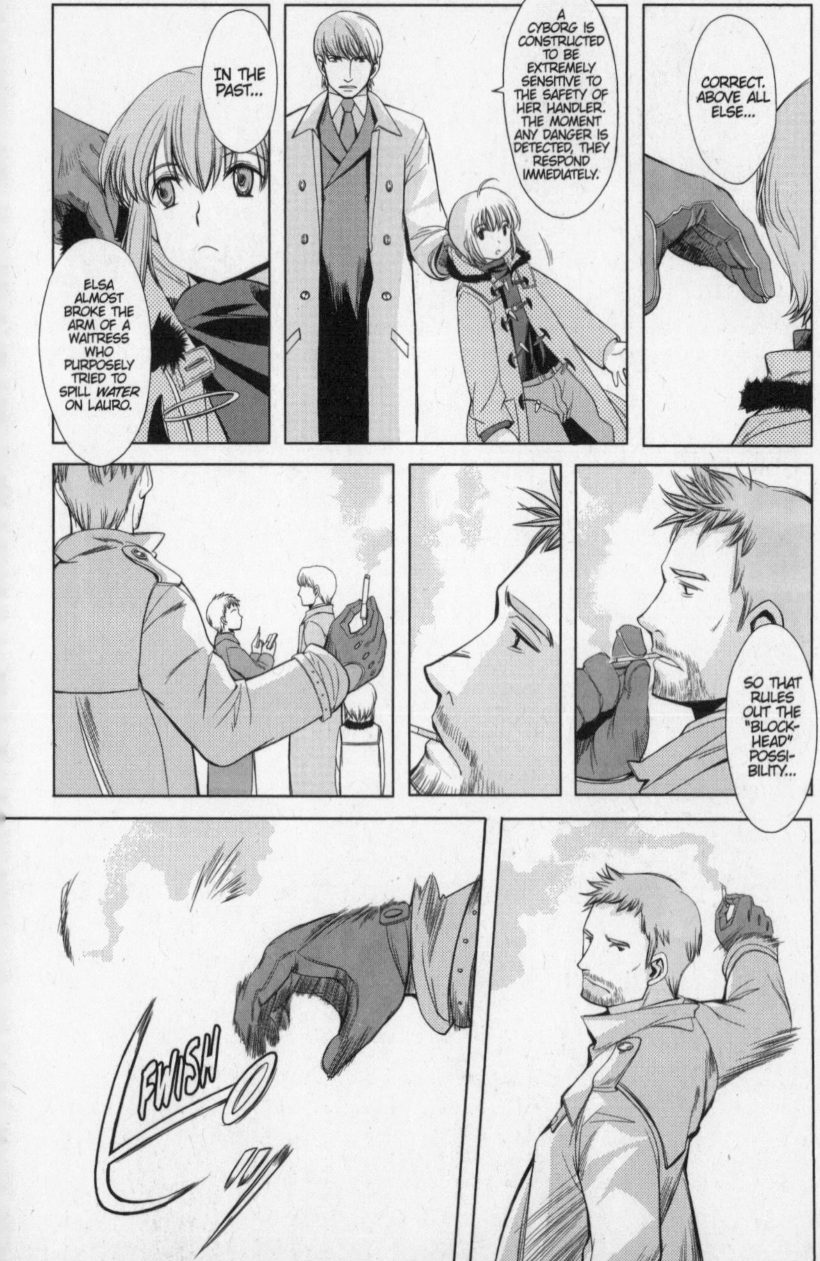
CORRECT. ABOVE ALL ELSE...
A CYBORG IS CONSTRUCTED TO BE EXTREMELY SENSITIVE TO THE SAFETY OF HER HANDLER. THE MOMENT ANY DANGER IS DETECTED, THEY RESPOND IMMEDIATELY.
IN THE PAST...
ELSA ALMOST BROKE THE ARM OF A WAITRESS WHO PURPOSELY TRIED TO SPILL *WATER* ON LAURO.
SO THAT RULES OUT THE "BLOCK-HEAD" POSSI-BILITY...
FWISH

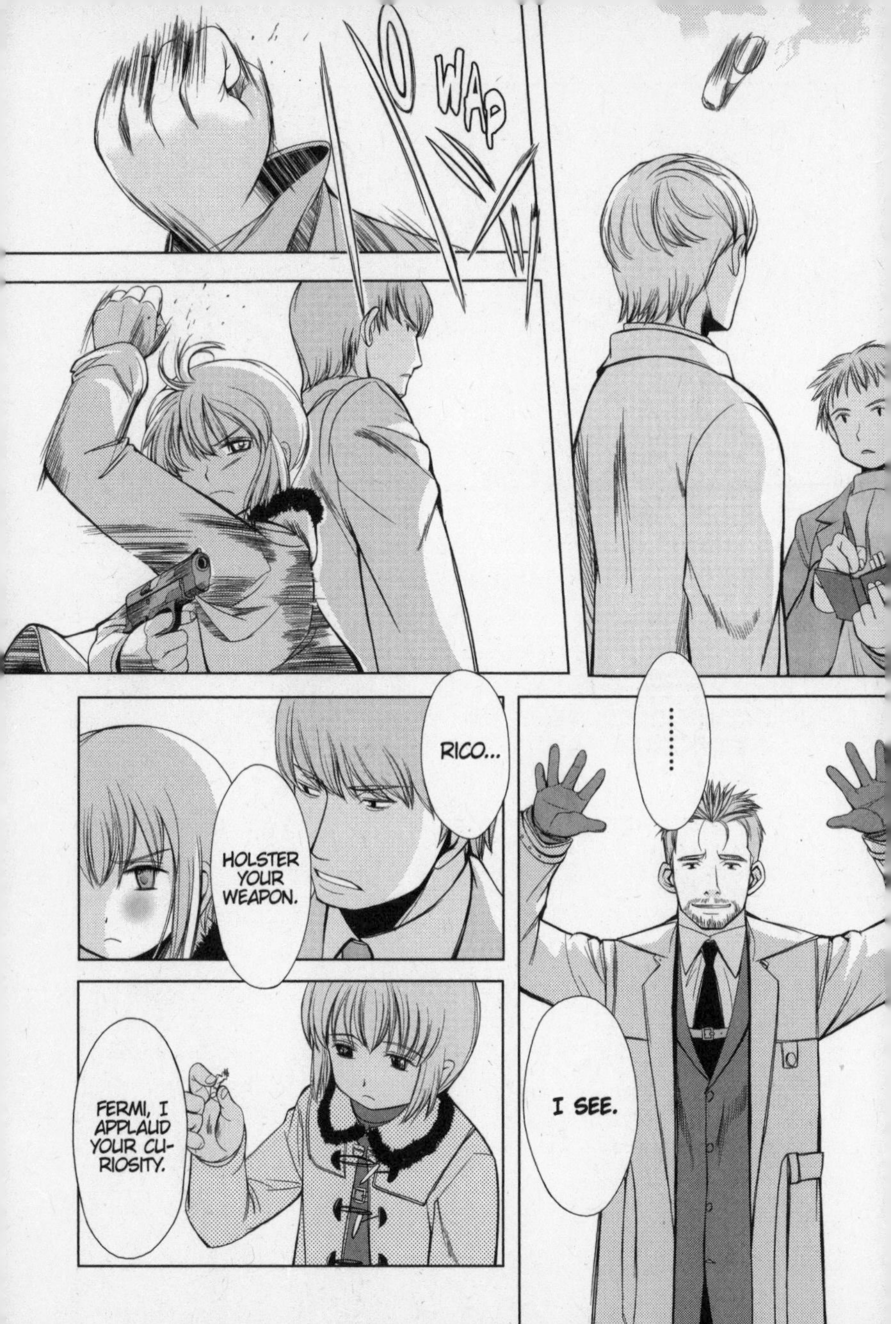
WAP
......
I SEE.
RICO...
HOLSTER YOUR WEAPON.
FERMI, I APPLAUD YOUR CURIOSITY.

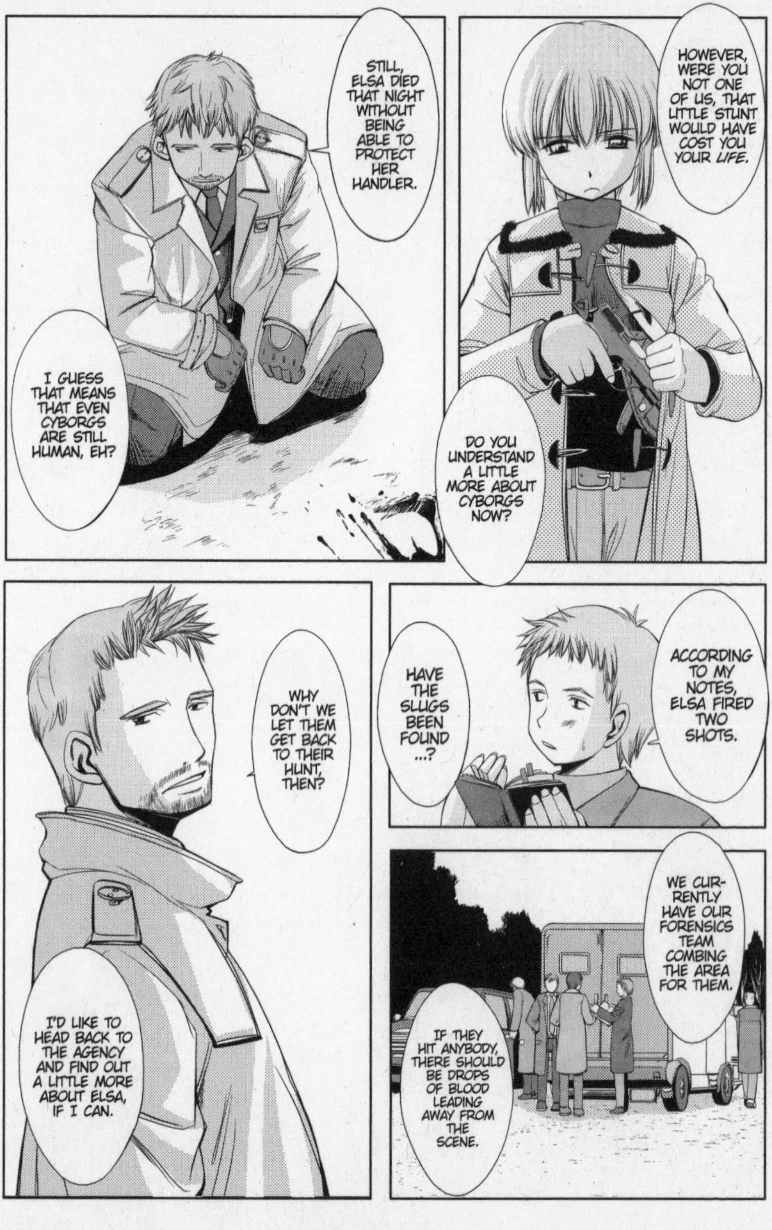
HOWEVER, WERE YOU NOT ONE OF US, THAT LITTLE STUNT WOULD HAVE COST YOU YOUR LIFE.
DO YOU UNDERSTAND A LITTLE MORE ABOUT CYBORGS NOW?
STILL, ELSA DIED THAT NIGHT WITHOUT BEING ABLE TO PROTECT HER HANDLER.
I GUESS THAT MEANS THAT EVEN CYBORGS ARE STILL HUMAN, EH?
ACCORDING TO MY NOTES, ELSA FIRED TWO SHOTS.
HAVE THE SLUGS BEEN FOUND ...?
WE CUR-RENTLY HAVE OUR FORENSICS TEAM COMBING THE AREA FOR THEM.
IF THEY HIT ANYBODY, THERE SHOULD BE DROPS OF BLOOD LEADING AWAY FROM THE SCENE.
WHY DON'T WE LET THEM GET BACK TO THEIR HUNT, THEN?
I'D LIKE TO HEAD BACK TO THE AGENCY AND FIND OUT A LITTLE MORE ABOUT ELSA, IF I CAN.

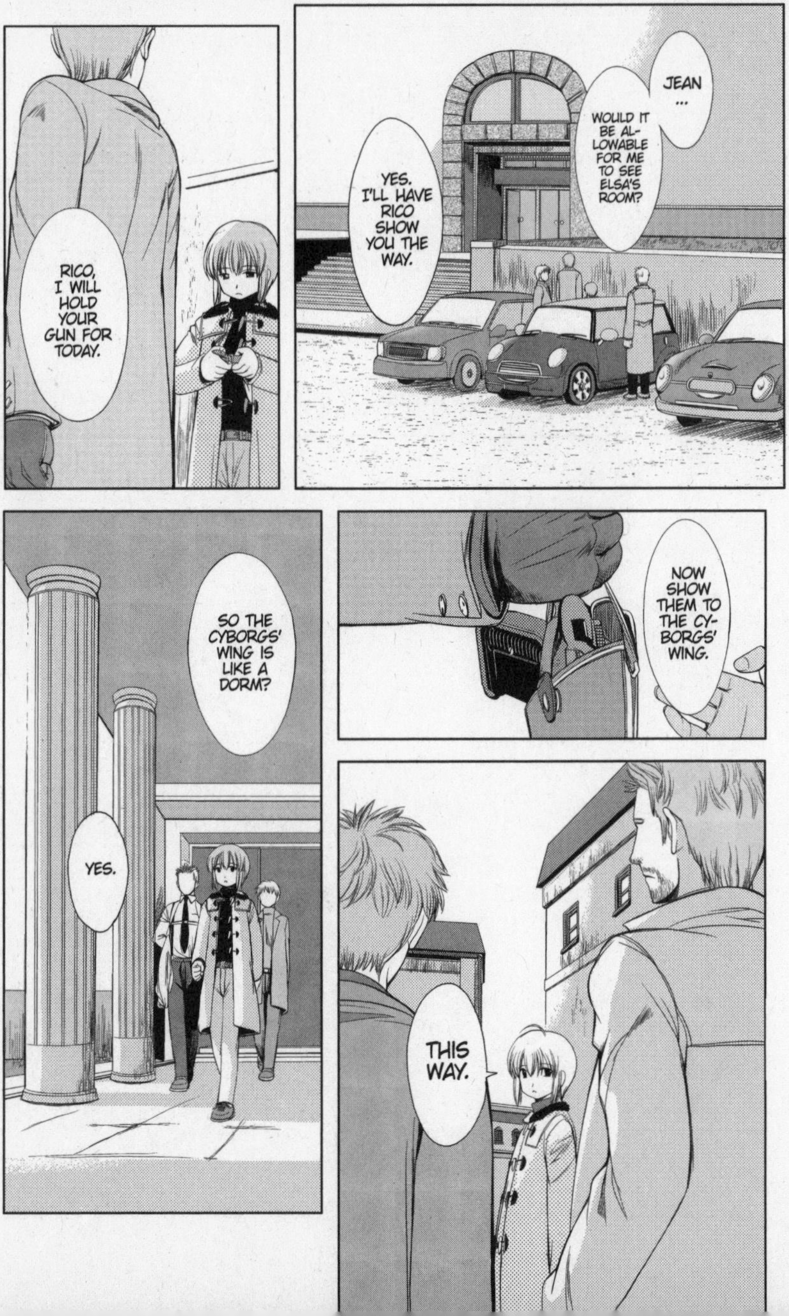
JEAN ...
WOULD IT BE ALLOWABLE FOR ME TO SEE ELSA'S ROOM?
YES. I'LL HAVE RICO SHOW YOU THE WAY.
RICO, I WILL HOLD YOUR GUN FOR TODAY.
NOW SHOW THEM TO THE CYBORGS' WING.
THIS WAY.
SO THE CYBORGS' WING IS LIKE A DORM?
YES.

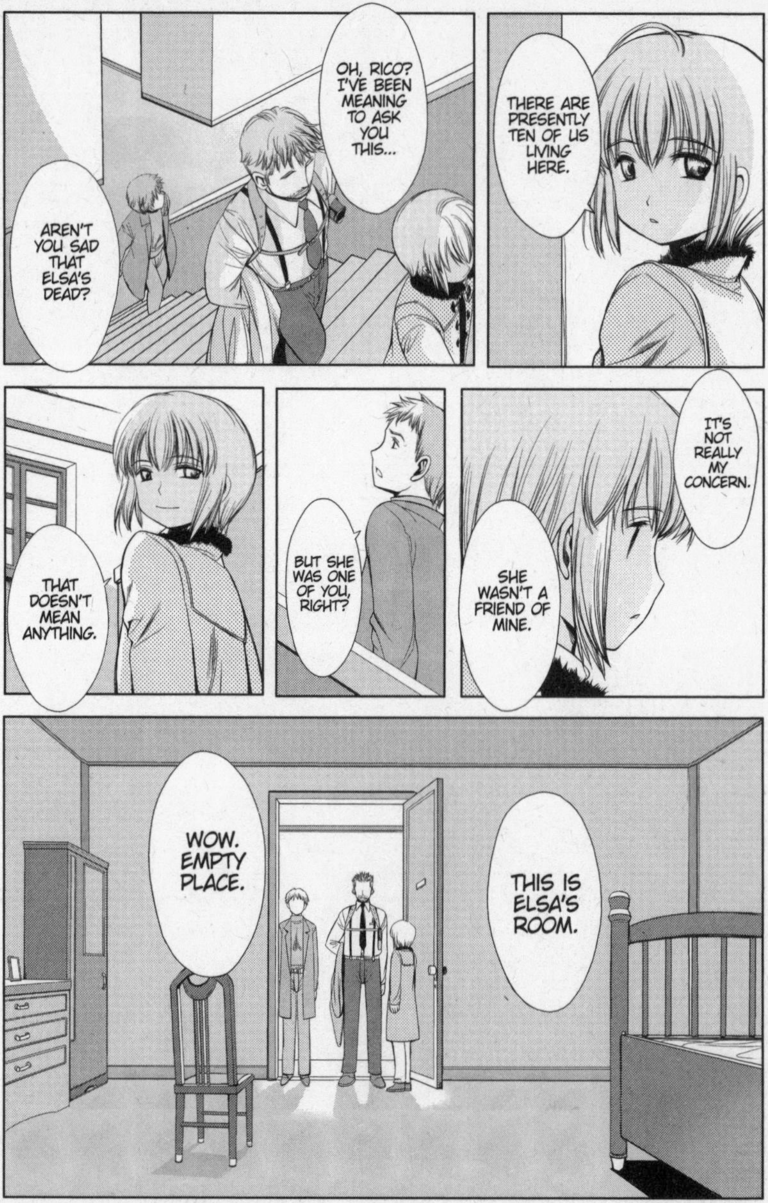
THERE ARE PRESENTLY TEN OF US LIVING HERE.
OH, RICO? I'VE BEEN MEANING TO ASK YOU THIS...
AREN'T YOU SAD THAT ELSA'S DEAD?
IT'S NOT REALLY MY CONCERN.
SHE WASN'T A FRIEND OF MINE.
BUT SHE WAS ONE OF YOU, RIGHT?
THAT DOESN'T MEAN ANYTHING.
THIS IS ELSA'S ROOM.
WOW. EMPTY PLACE.

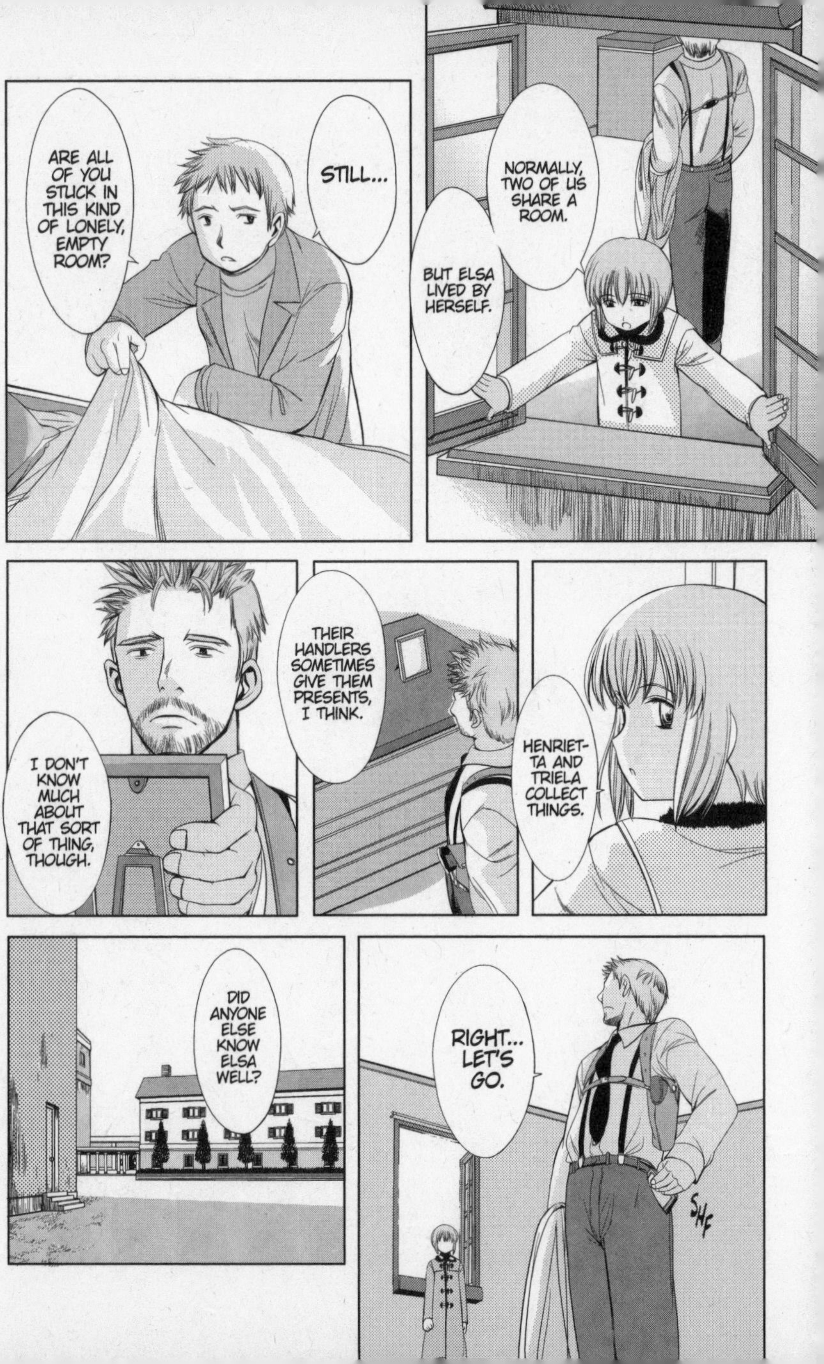
NORMALLY, TWO OF US SHARE A ROOM.
BUT ELSA LIVED BY HERSELF.
STILL...
ARE ALL OF YOU STUCK IN THIS KIND OF LONELY, EMPTY ROOM?
HENRIET-TA AND TRIELA COLLECT THINGS.
THEIR HANDLERS SOMETIMES GIVE THEM PRESENTS, I THINK.
I DON'T KNOW MUCH ABOUT THAT SORT OF THING, THOUGH.
RIGHT... LET'S GO.
SHF
DID ANYONE ELSE KNOW ELSA WELL?

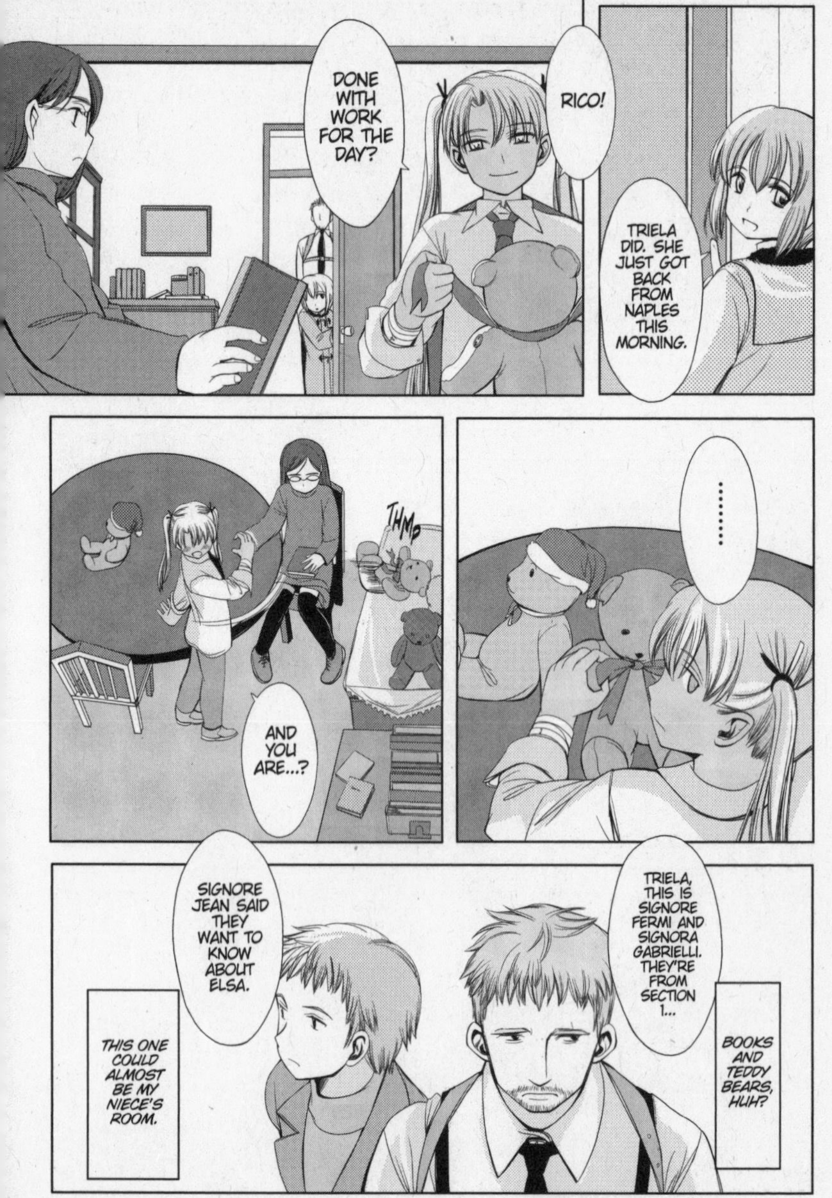
TRIELA DID. SHE JUST GOT BACK FROM NAPLES THIS MORNING.
RICO!
DONE WITH WORK FOR THE DAY?
......
THMP
AND YOU ARE...?
TRIELA, THIS IS SIGNORE FERMI AND SIGNORA GABRIELLI. THEY'RE FROM SECTION 1...
BOOKS AND TEDDY BEARS, HUH?
SIGNORE JEAN SAID THEY WANT TO KNOW ABOUT ELSA.
THIS ONE COULD ALMOST BE MY NIECE'S ROOM.

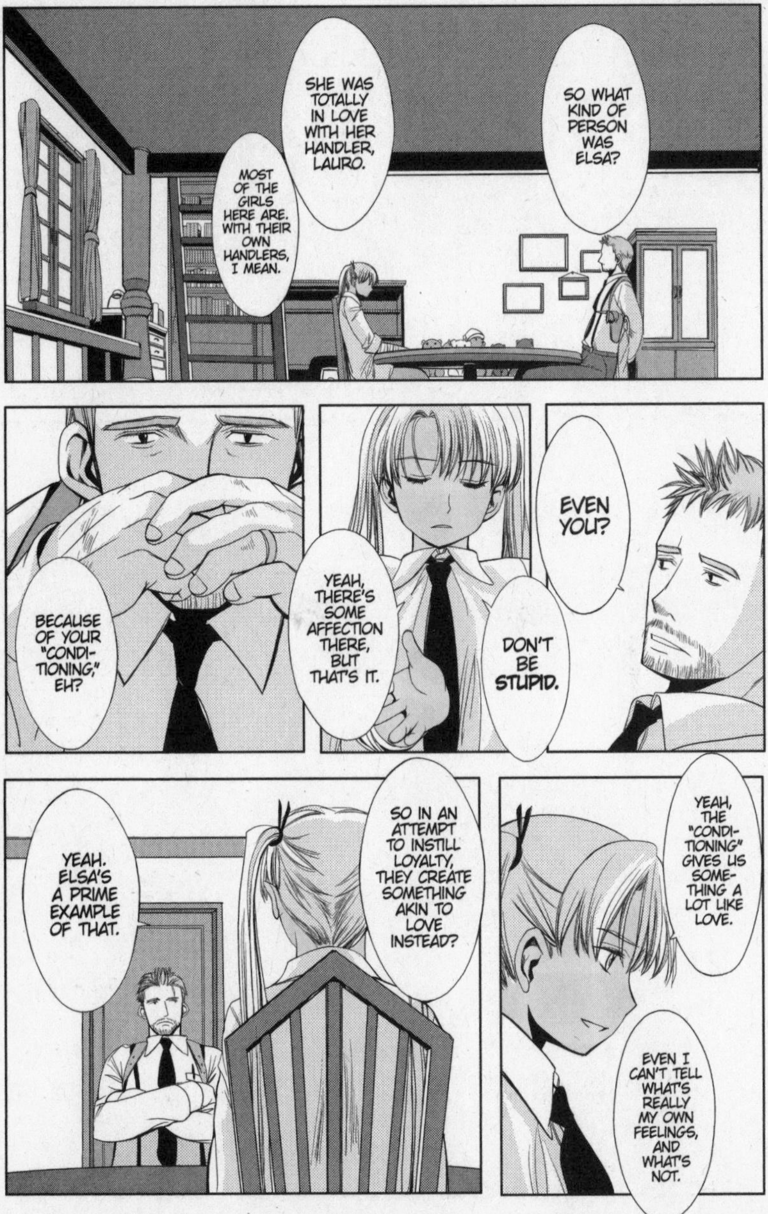
SO WHAT KIND OF PERSON WAS ELSA?
SHE WAS TOTALLY IN LOVE WITH HER HANDLER, LAURO.
MOST OF THE GIRLS HERE ARE. WITH THEIR OWN HANDLERS, I MEAN.
EVEN YOU?
DON'T BE STUPID.
YEAH, THERE'S SOME AFFECTION THERE, BUT THAT'S IT.
BECAUSE OF YOUR "CONDITIONING," EH?
YEAH, THE "CONDITIONING" GIVES US SOMETHING A LOT LIKE LOVE.
EVEN I CAN'T TELL WHAT'S REALLY MY OWN FEELINGS, AND WHAT'S NOT.
SO IN AN ATTEMPT TO INSTILL LOYALTY, THEY CREATE SOMETHING AKIN TO LOVE INSTEAD?
YEAH. ELSA'S A PRIME EXAMPLE OF THAT.

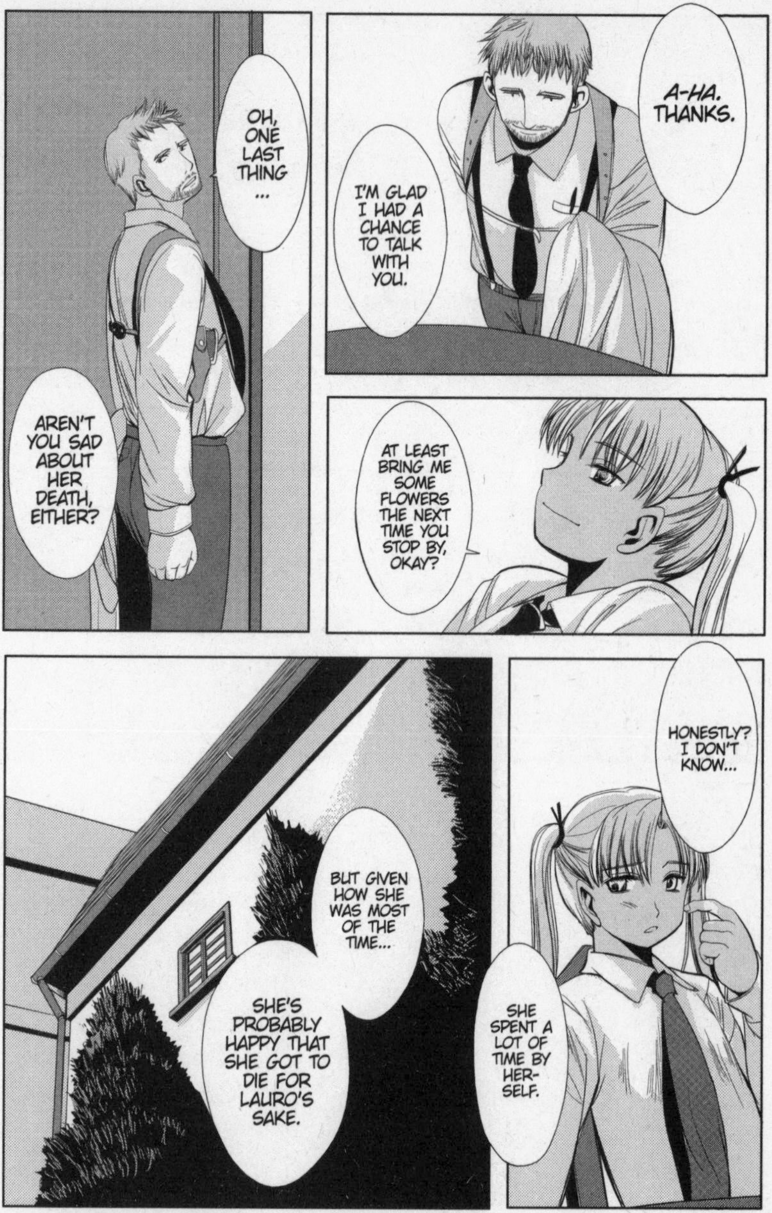
A-HA. THANKS.
I'M GLAD I HAD A CHANCE TO TALK WITH YOU.
AT LEAST BRING ME SOME FLOWERS THE NEXT TIME YOU STOP BY, OKAY?
OH, ONE LAST THING ...
AREN'T YOU SAD ABOUT HER DEATH, EITHER?
HONESTLY? I DON'T KNOW...
SHE SPENT A LOT OF TIME BY HER-SELF.
BUT GIVEN HOW SHE WAS MOST OF THE TIME...
SHE'S PROBABLY HAPPY THAT SHE GOT TO DIE FOR LAURO'S SAKE.

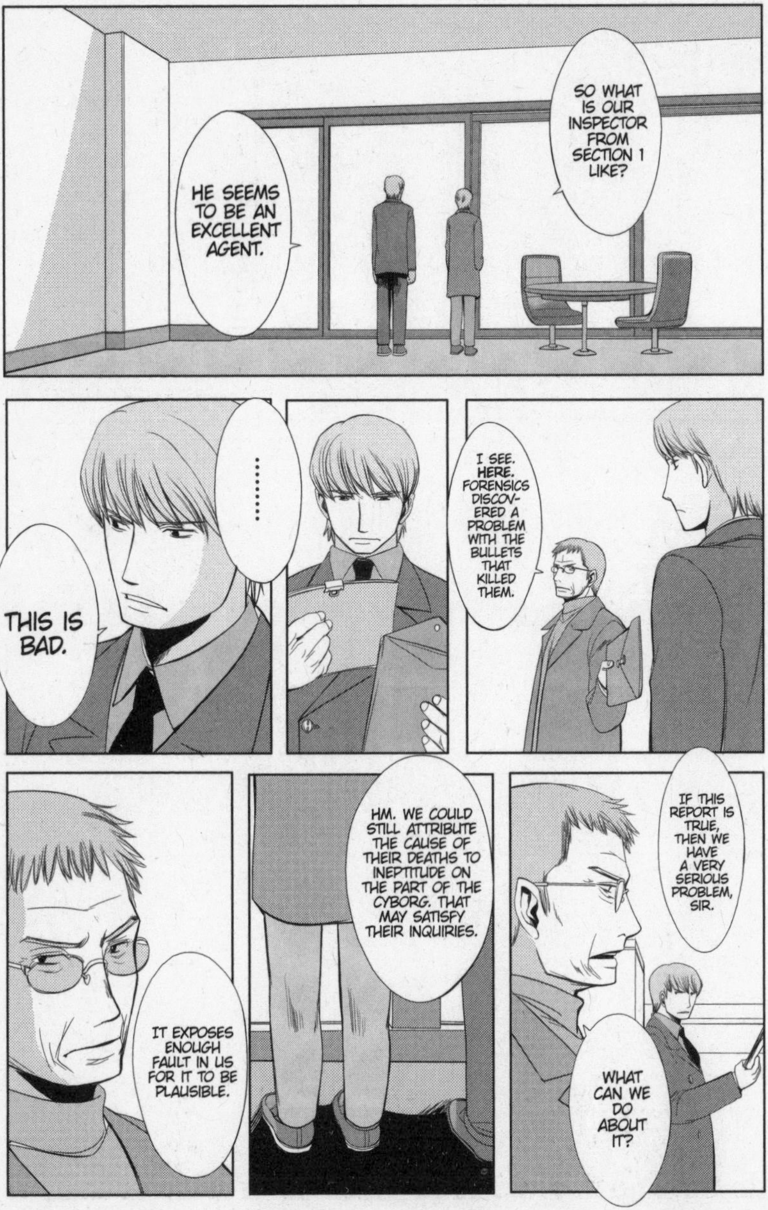
SO WHAT IS OUR INSPECTOR FROM SECTION 1 LIKE?
HE SEEMS TO BE AN EXCELLENT AGENT.
I SEE. HERE. FORENSICS DISCOVERED A PROBLEM WITH THE BULLETS THAT KILLED THEM.
......
THIS IS BAD.
IF THIS REPORT IS TRUE, THEN WE HAVE A VERY SERIOUS PROBLEM, SIR.
WHAT CAN WE DO ABOUT IT?
HM. WE COULD STILL ATTRIBUTE THE CAUSE OF THEIR DEATHS TO INEPTITUDE ON THE PART OF THE CYBORG. THAT MAY SATISFY THEIR INQUIRIES.
IT EXPOSES ENOUGH FAULT IN US FOR IT TO BE PLAUSIBLE.

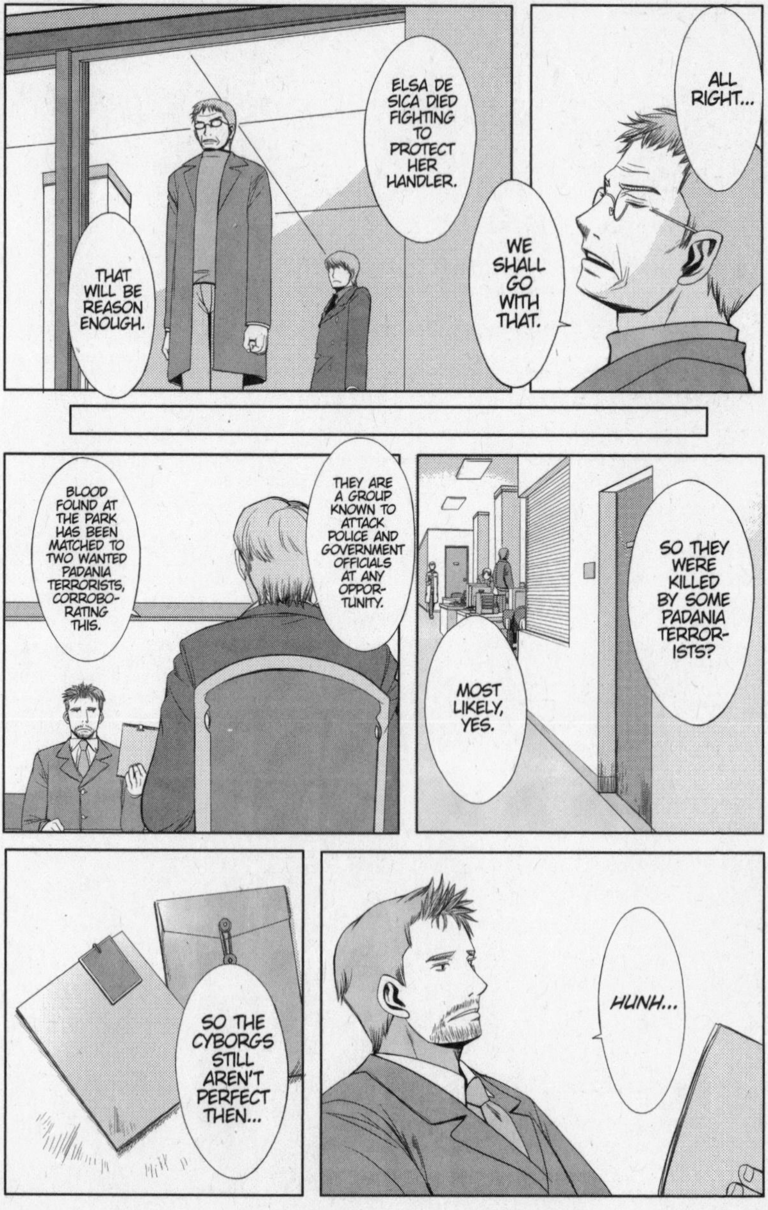
ALL RIGHT...
WE SHALL GO WITH THAT.
ELSA DE SICA DIED FIGHTING TO PROTECT HER HANDLER.
THAT WILL BE REASON ENOUGH.
SO THEY WERE KILLED BY SOME PADANIA TERRORISTS?
MOST LIKELY, YES.
THEY ARE A GROUP KNOWN TO ATTACK POLICE AND GOVERNMENT OFFICIALS AT ANY OPPORTUNITY.
BLOOD FOUND AT THE PARK HAS BEEN MATCHED TO TWO WANTED PADANIA TERRORISTS, CORROBORATING THIS.
HUNH...
SO THE CYBORGS STILL AREN'T PERFECT THEN...

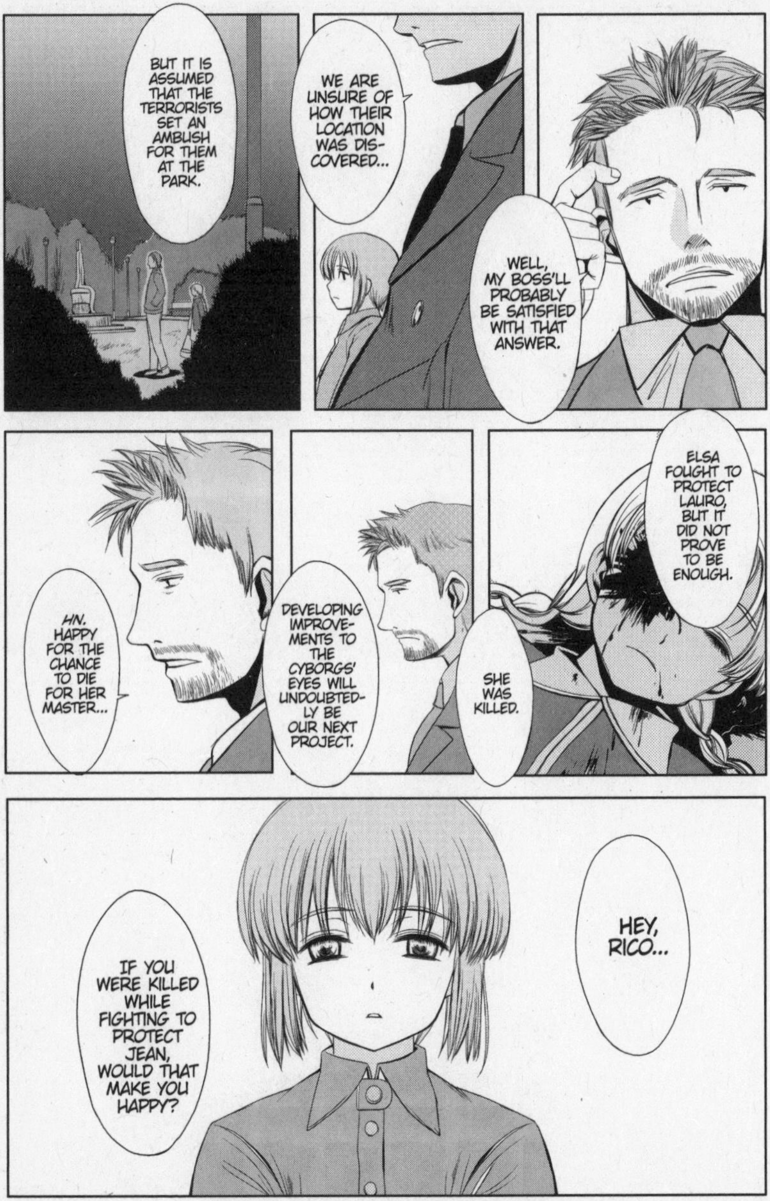
WELL, MY BOSS'LL PROBABLY BE SATISFIED WITH THAT ANSWER.
WE ARE UNSURE OF HOW THEIR LOCATION WAS DISCOVERED...
BUT IT IS ASSUMED THAT THE TERRORISTS SET AN AMBUSH FOR THEM AT THE PARK.
ELSA FOUGHT TO PROTECT LAURO, BUT IT DID NOT PROVE TO BE ENOUGH.
SHE WAS KILLED.
DEVELOPING IMPROVE-MENTS TO THE CYBORGS' EYES WILL UNDOUBTED-LY BE OUR NEXT PROJECT.
HN. HAPPY FOR THE CHANCE TO DIE FOR HER MASTER...
HEY, RICO...
IF YOU WERE KILLED WHILE FIGHTING TO PROTECT JEAN, WOULD THAT MAKE YOU HAPPY?

UM... I...
I THINK I'D RATHER NOT DIE IN THE FIRST PLACE.
BUT...
A CYBORG EXISTS FOR THE SAKE OF HER HANDLER.
DYING TO PROTECT HIM IS A MATTER OF COURSE.
RICO...?
IF SIGNORE JEAN SAYS SO...
THEN IT MUST BE TRUE.

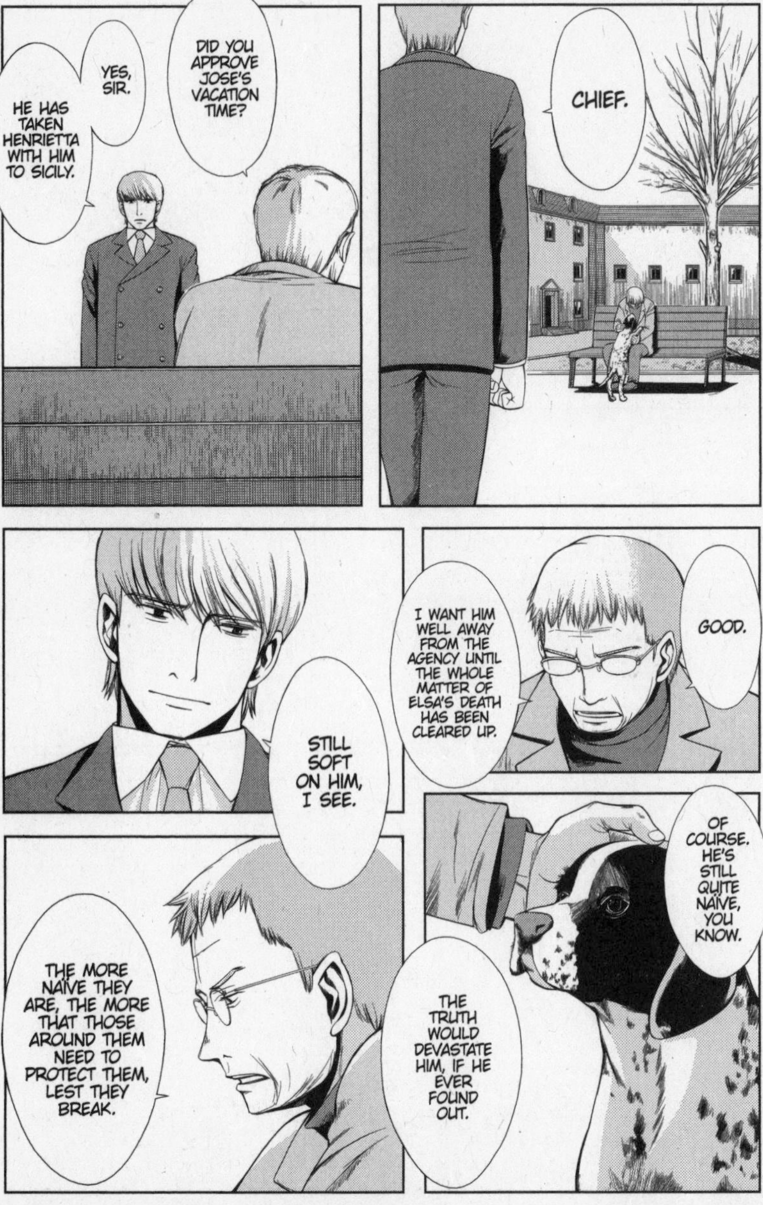
CHIEF.
DID YOU APPROVE JOSE'S VACATION TIME?
YES, SIR.
HE HAS TAKEN HENRIETTA WITH HIM TO SICILY.
GOOD.
I WANT HIM WELL AWAY FROM THE AGENCY UNTIL THE WHOLE MATTER OF ELSA'S DEATH HAS BEEN CLEARED UP.
STILL SOFT ON HIM, I SEE.
OF COURSE. HE'S STILL QUITE NAÏVE, YOU KNOW.
THE TRUTH WOULD DEVASTATE HIM, IF HE EVER FOUND OUT.
THE MORE NAÏVE THEY ARE, THE MORE THAT THOSE AROUND THEM NEED TO PROTECT THEM, LEST THEY BREAK.

Chapter 5: The Death of Elsa de Sica, Part 2

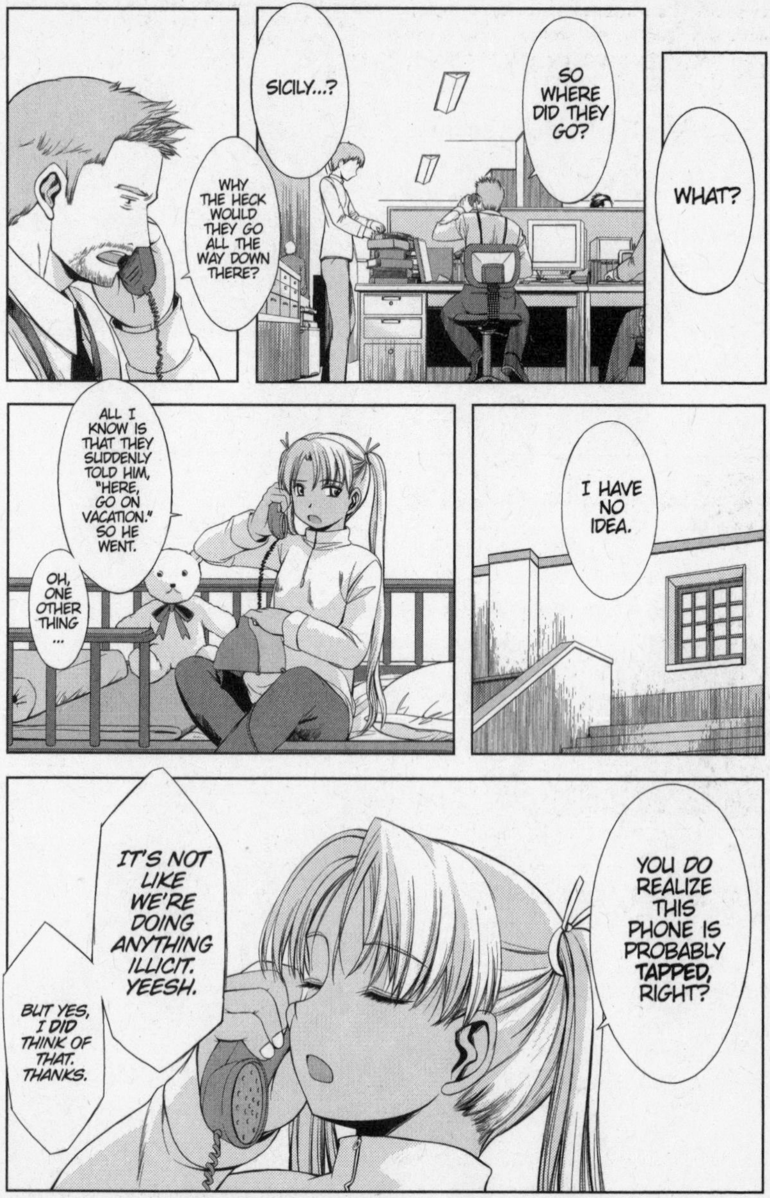
WHAT?
SO WHERE DID THEY GO?
SICILY...?
WHY THE HECK WOULD THEY GO ALL THE WAY DOWN THERE?
I HAVE NO IDEA.
ALL I KNOW IS THAT THEY SUDDENLY TOLD HIM, "HERE, GO ON VACATION." SO HE WENT.
OH, ONE OTHER THING ...
YOU DO REALIZE THIS PHONE IS PROBABLY TAPPED, RIGHT?
IT'S NOT LIKE WE'RE DOING ANYTHING ILLICIT. YEESH.
BUT YES, I DID THINK OF THAT. THANKS.

CHAPTER 5: THE DEATH OF ELSA DE SICA, PART 2

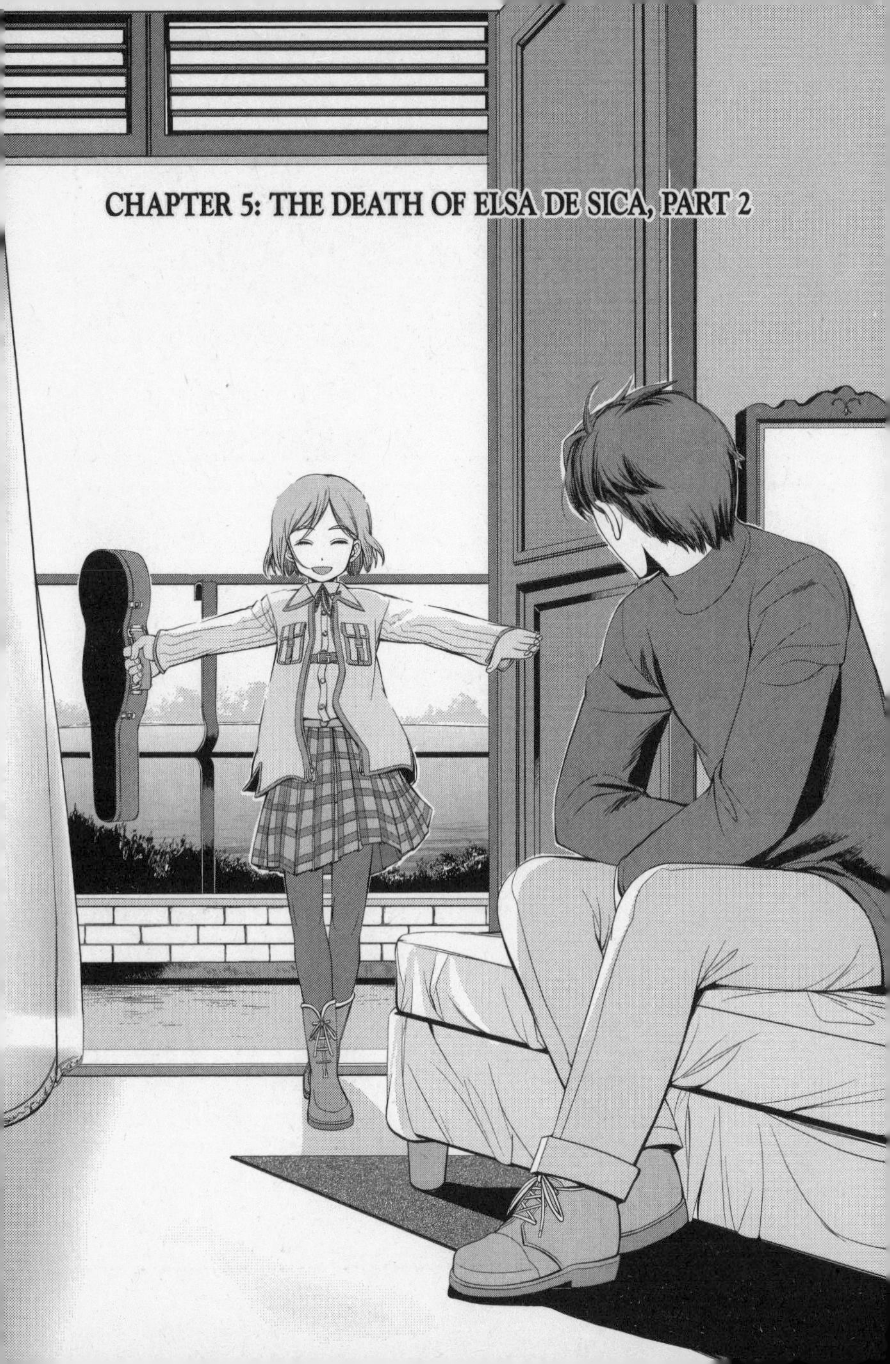

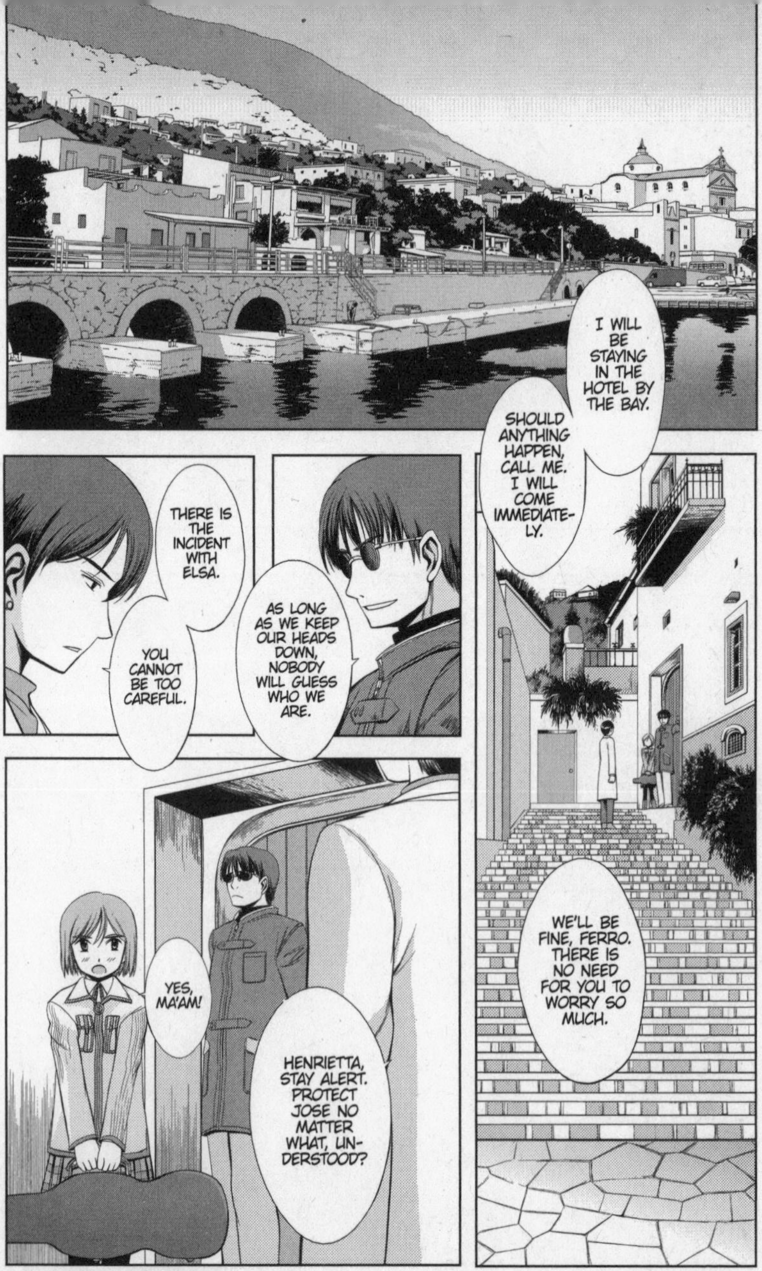
I WILL BE STAYING IN THE HOTEL BY THE BAY.
SHOULD ANYTHING HAPPEN, CALL ME. I WILL COME IMMEDIATE-LY.
WE'LL BE FINE, FERRO. THERE IS NO NEED FOR YOU TO WORRY SO MUCH.
AS LONG AS WE KEEP OUR HEADS DOWN, NOBODY WILL GUESS WHO WE ARE.
THERE IS THE INCIDENT WITH ELSA.
YOU CANNOT BE TOO CAREFUL.
HENRIETTA, STAY ALERT. PROTECT JOSE NO MATTER WHAT, UN-DERSTOOD?
YES, MA'AM!

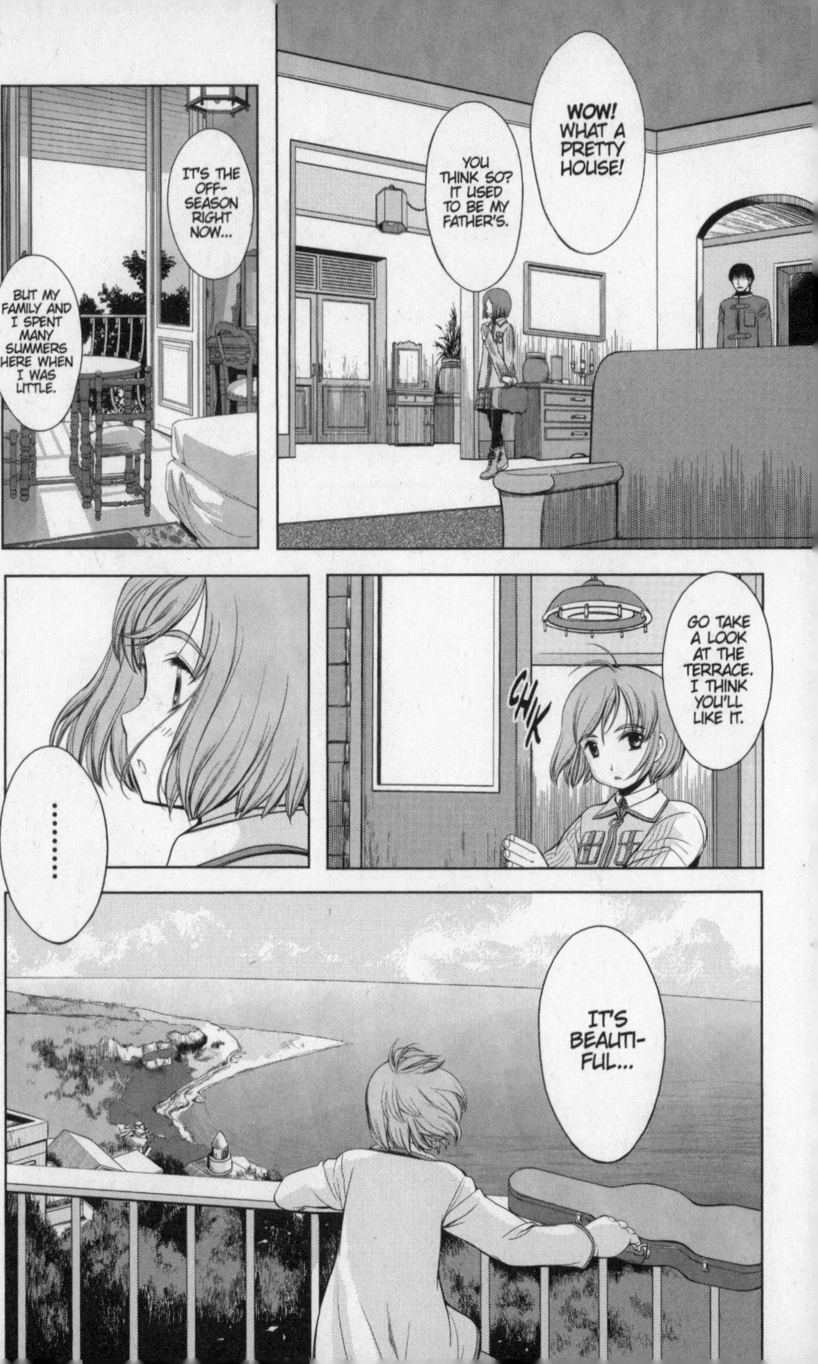
WOW! WHAT A PRETTY HOUSE!
YOU THINK SO? IT USED TO BE MY FATHER'S.
IT'S THE OFF-SEASON RIGHT NOW...
BUT MY FAMILY AND I SPENT MANY SUMMERS HERE WHEN I WAS LITTLE.
GO TAKE A LOOK AT THE TERRACE. I THINK YOU'LL LIKE IT.
CHIK
....
IT'S BEAUTI-FUL...

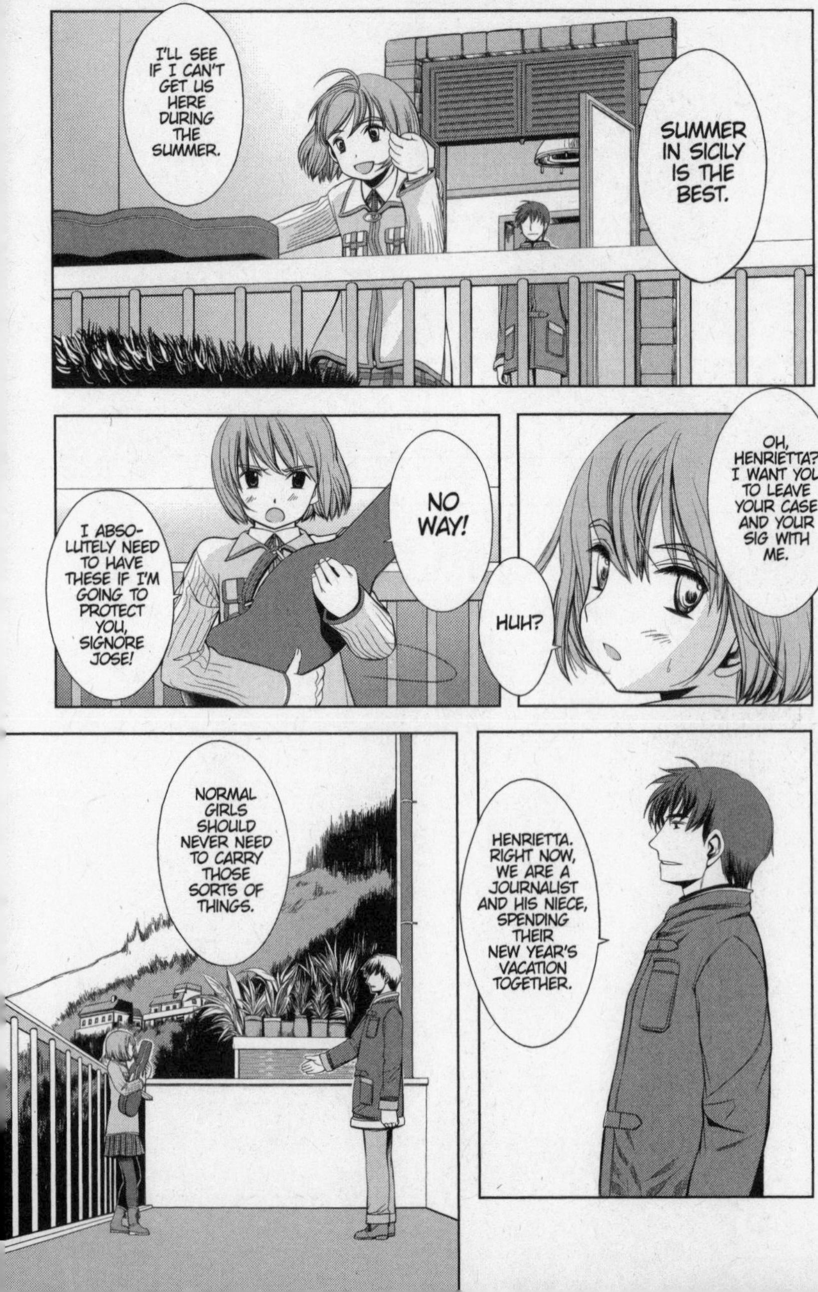
SUMMER IN SICILY IS THE BEST.
I'LL SEE IF I CAN'T GET US HERE DURING THE SUMMER.
OH, HENRIETTA? I WANT YOU TO LEAVE YOUR CASE AND YOUR SIG WITH ME.
HUH?
NO WAY!
I ABSOLUTELY NEED TO HAVE THESE IF I'M GOING TO PROTECT YOU, SIGNORE JOSE!
HENRIETTA. RIGHT NOW, WE ARE A JOURNALIST AND HIS NIECE, SPENDING THEIR NEW YEAR'S VACATION TOGETHER.
NORMAL GIRLS SHOULD NEVER NEED TO CARRY THOSE SORTS OF THINGS.

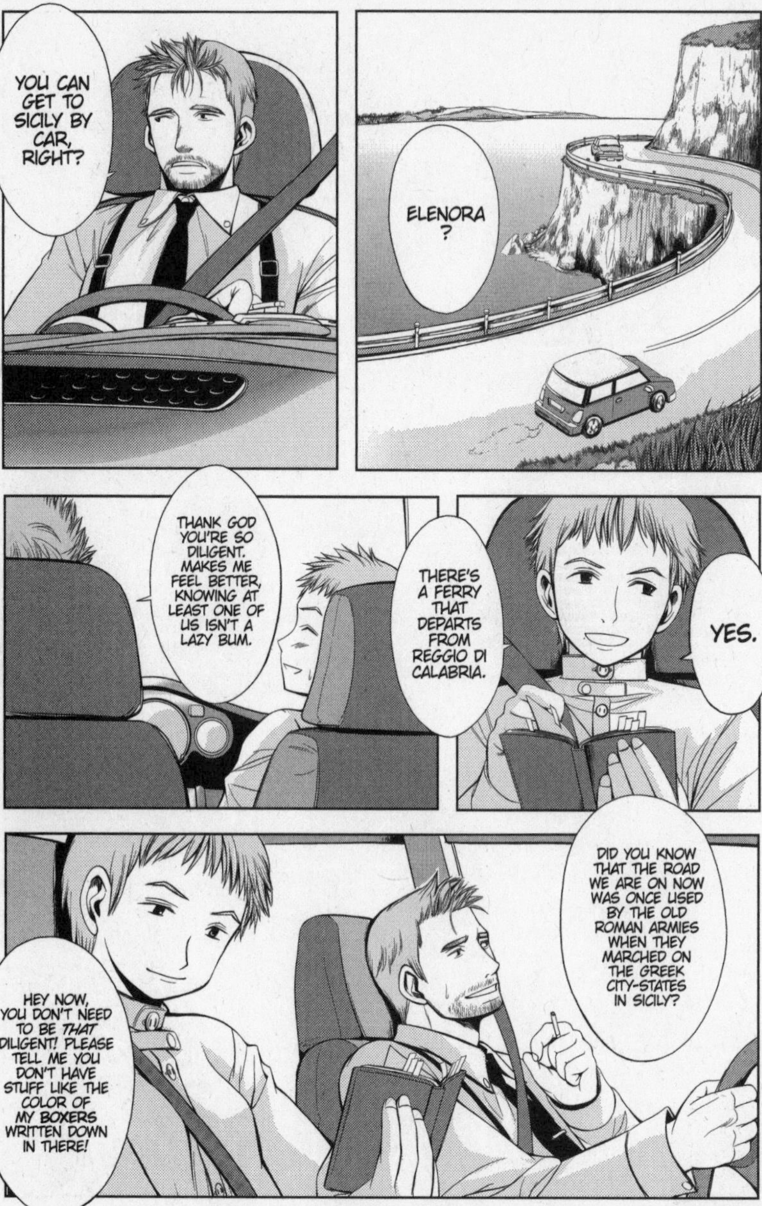
ELENORA?
YOU CAN GET TO SICILY BY CAR, RIGHT?
YES.
THERE'S A FERRY THAT DEPARTS FROM REGGIO DI CALABRIA.
THANK GOD YOU'RE SO DILIGENT. MAKES ME FEEL BETTER, KNOWING AT LEAST ONE OF US ISN'T A LAZY BUM.
DID YOU KNOW THAT THE ROAD WE ARE ON NOW WAS ONCE USED BY THE OLD ROMAN ARMIES WHEN THEY MARCHED ON THE GREEK CITY-STATES IN SICILY?
HEY NOW, YOU DON'T NEED TO BE *THAT* DILIGENT! PLEASE TELL ME YOU DON'T HAVE STUFF LIKE THE COLOR OF MY BOXERS WRITTEN DOWN IN THERE!

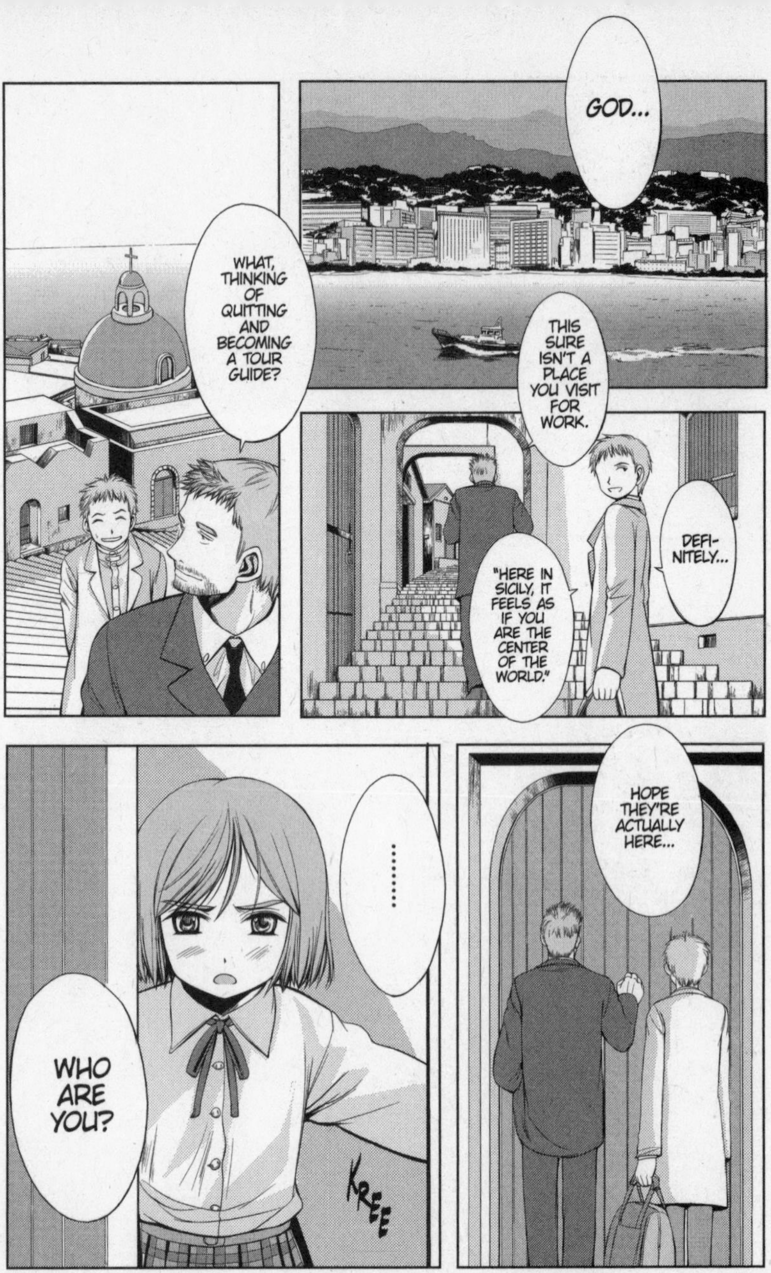
GOD...
THIS SURE ISN'T A PLACE YOU VISIT FOR WORK.
DEFI-NITELY...
"HERE IN SICILY, IT FEELS AS IF YOU ARE THE CENTER OF THE WORLD."
WHAT, THINKING OF QUITTING AND BECOMING A TOUR GUIDE?
HOPE THEY'RE ACTUALLY HERE...
....
KREE
WHO ARE YOU?

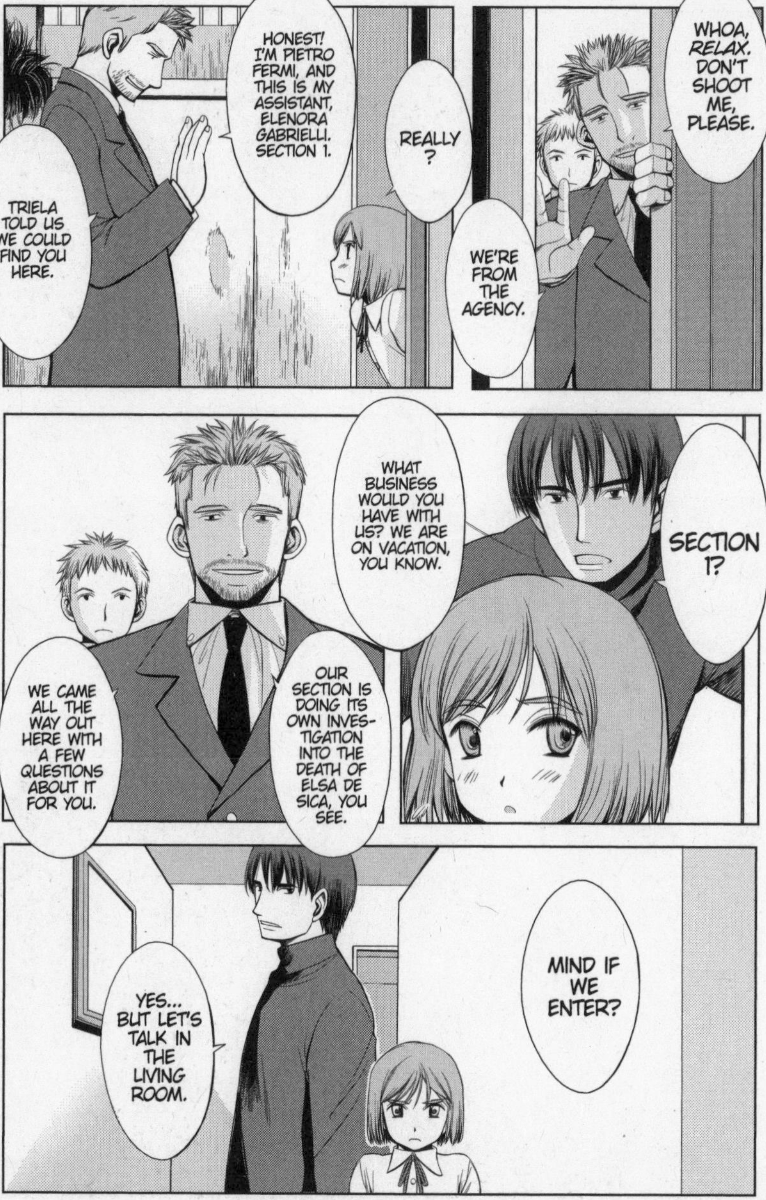
WHOA, RELAX. DON'T SHOOT ME, PLEASE.
WE'RE FROM THE AGENCY.
REALLY?
HONEST! I'M PIETRO FERMI, AND THIS IS MY ASSISTANT, ELENORA GABRIELLI. SECTION 1.
TRIELA TOLD US WE COULD FIND YOU HERE.
SECTION 1?
WHAT BUSINESS WOULD YOU HAVE WITH US? WE ARE ON VACATION, YOU KNOW.
OUR SECTION IS DOING ITS OWN INVESTIGATION INTO THE DEATH OF ELSA DE SICA, YOU SEE.
WE CAME ALL THE WAY OUT HERE WITH A FEW QUESTIONS ABOUT IT FOR YOU.
MIND IF WE ENTER?
YES... BUT LET'S TALK IN THE LIVING ROOM.

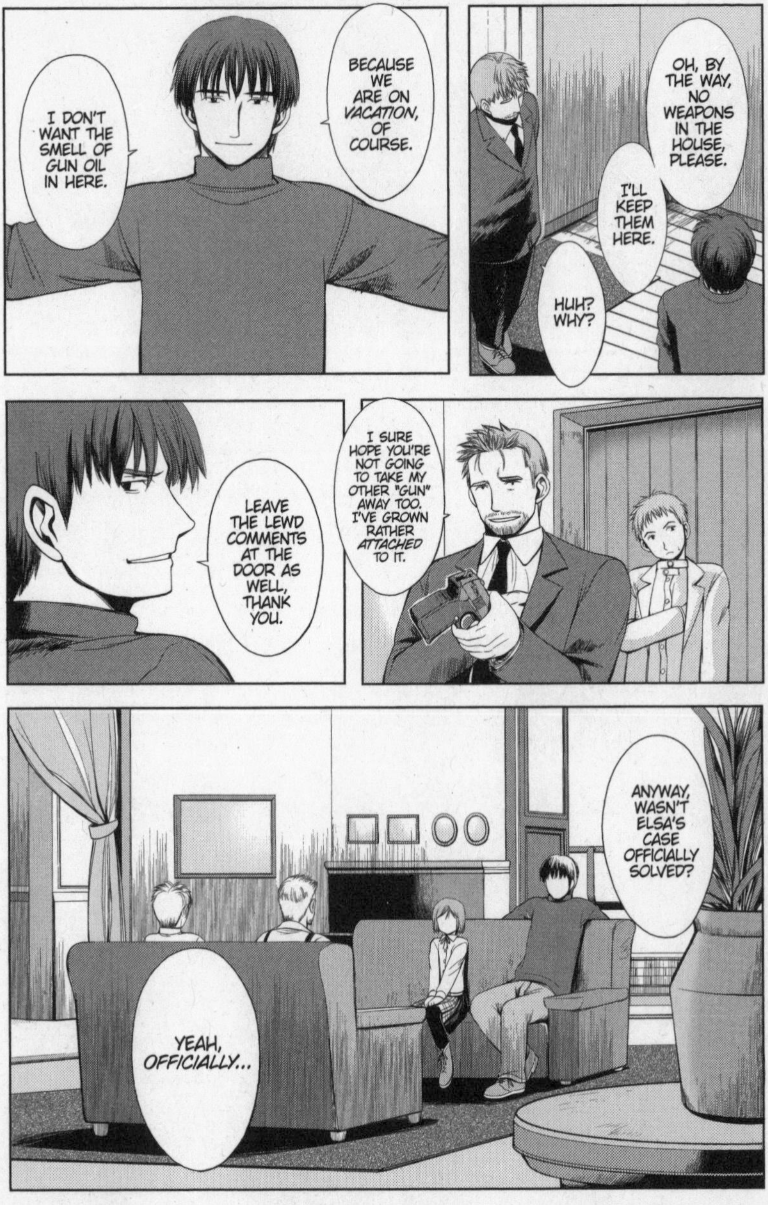
OH, BY THE WAY, NO WEAPONS IN THE HOUSE, PLEASE.
I'LL KEEP THEM HERE.
HUH? WHY?
BECAUSE WE ARE ON *VACATION*, OF COURSE.
I DON'T WANT THE SMELL OF GUN OIL IN HERE.
I SURE HOPE YOU'RE NOT GOING TO TAKE MY OTHER "GUN" AWAY TOO. I'VE GROWN RATHER *ATTACHED* TO IT.
LEAVE THE LEWD COMMENTS AT THE DOOR AS WELL, THANK YOU.
ANYWAY, WASN'T ELSA'S CASE OFFICIALLY SOLVED?
YEAH, *OFFICIALLY...*

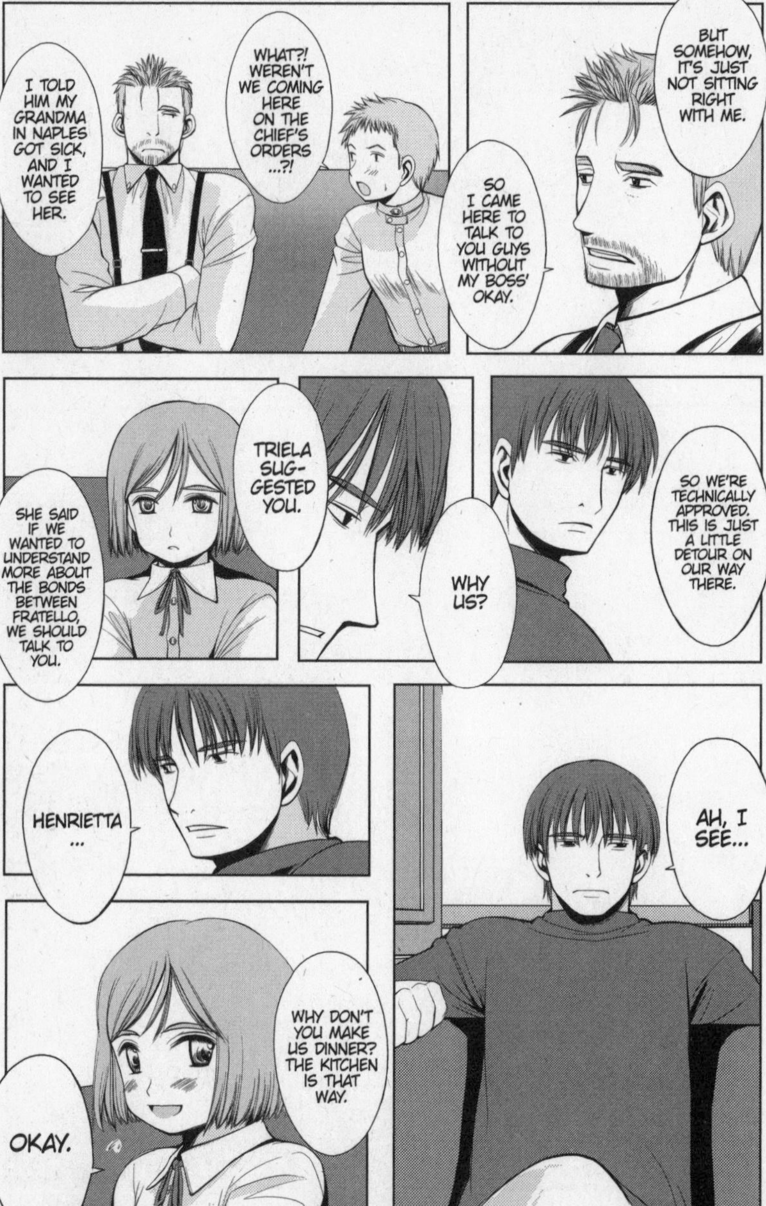
BUT SOMEHOW, IT'S JUST NOT SITTING RIGHT WITH ME.
SO I CAME HERE TO TALK TO YOU GUYS WITHOUT MY BOSS' OKAY.
WHAT?! WEREN'T WE COMING HERE ON THE CHIEF'S ORDERS ...?!
I TOLD HIM MY GRANDMA IN NAPLES GOT SICK, AND I WANTED TO SEE HER.
SO WE'RE TECHNICALLY APPROVED. THIS IS JUST A LITTLE DETOUR ON OUR WAY THERE.
WHY US?
TRIELA SUG-GESTED YOU.
SHE SAID IF WE WANTED TO UNDERSTAND MORE ABOUT THE BONDS BETWEEN FRATELLO, WE SHOULD TALK TO YOU.
AH, I SEE...
HENRIETTA ...
WHY DON'T YOU MAKE US DINNER? THE KITCHEN IS THAT WAY.
OKAY.

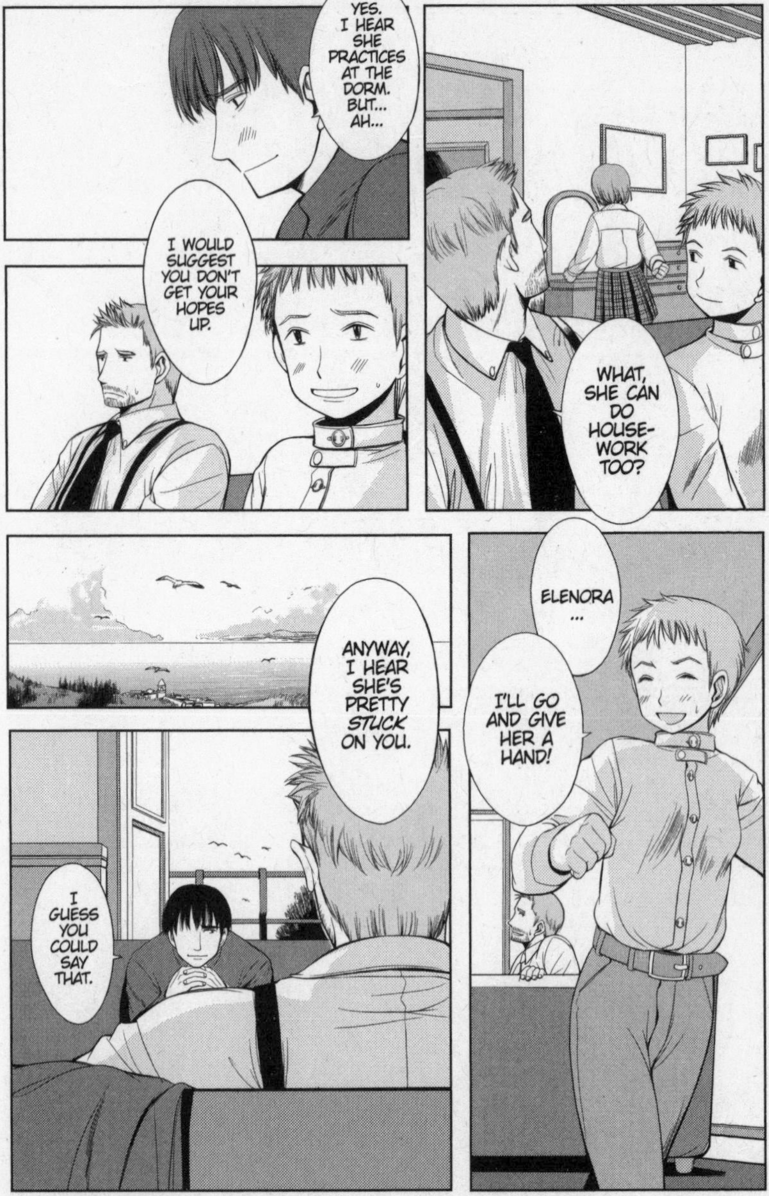
WHAT, SHE CAN DO HOUSE-WORK TOO?
YES. I HEAR SHE PRACTICES AT THE DORM. BUT... AH...
I WOULD SUGGEST YOU DON'T GET YOUR HOPES UP.
ELENORA...
I'LL GO AND GIVE HER A HAND!
ANYWAY, I HEAR SHE'S PRETTY *STUCK* ON YOU.
I GUESS YOU COULD SAY THAT.

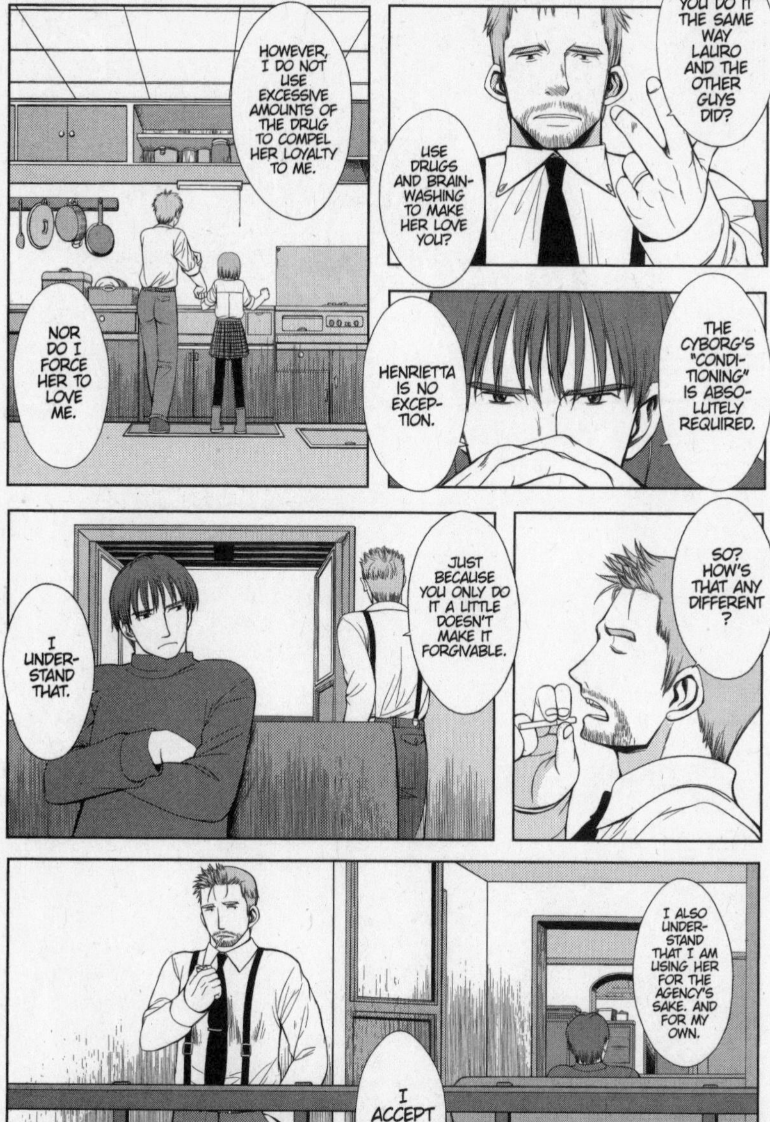
SO DID YOU DO IT THE SAME WAY LAURO AND THE OTHER GUYS DID?
USE DRUGS AND BRAIN-WASHING TO MAKE HER LOVE YOU?
THE CYBORG'S "CONDI-TIONING" IS ABSO-LUTELY REQUIRED.
HENRIETTA IS NO EXCEP-TION.
HOWEVER, I DO NOT USE EXCESSIVE AMOUNTS OF THE DRUG TO COMPEL HER LOYALTY TO ME.
NOR DO I FORCE HER TO LOVE ME.
SO? HOW'S THAT ANY DIFFERENT?
JUST BECAUSE YOU ONLY DO IT A LITTLE DOESN'T MAKE IT FORGIVABLE.
I UNDER-STAND THAT.
I ALSO UNDER-STAND THAT I AM USING HER FOR THE AGENCY'S SAKE. AND FOR MY OWN.
I ACCEPT THIS...

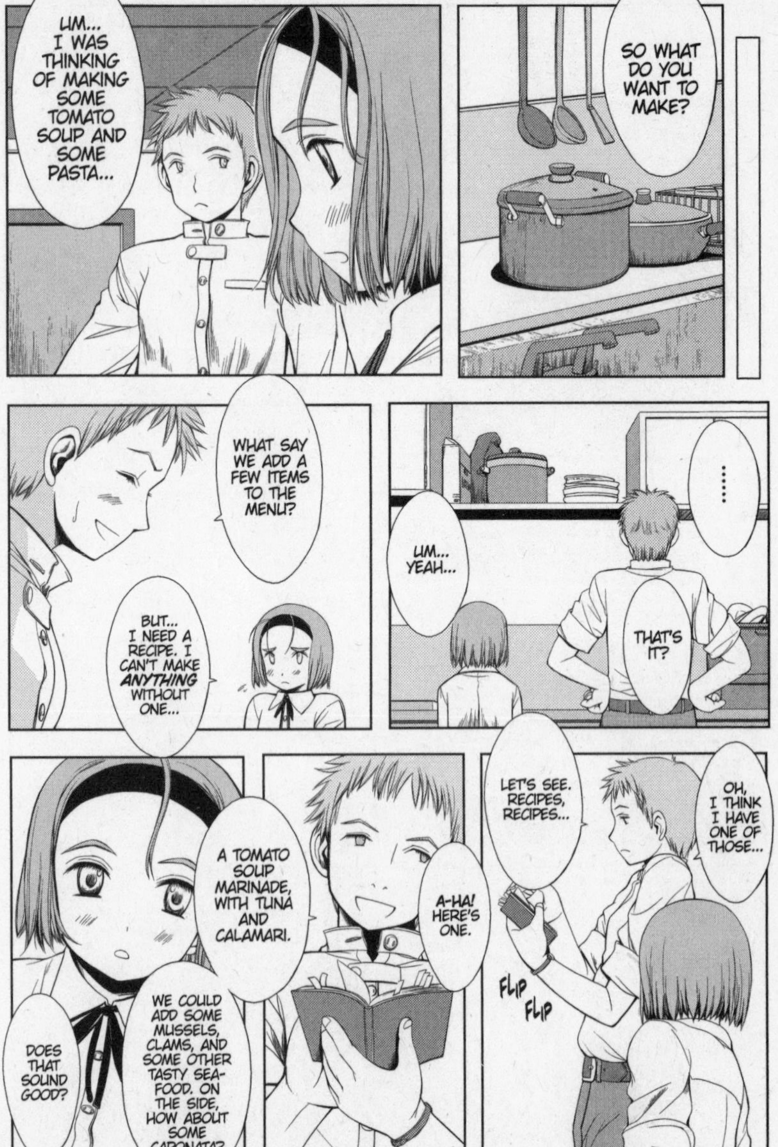
SO WHAT DO YOU WANT TO MAKE?
UM... I WAS THINKING OF MAKING SOME TOMATO SOUP AND SOME PASTA...
......
THAT'S IT?
UM... YEAH...
WHAT SAY WE ADD A FEW ITEMS TO THE MENU?
BUT... I NEED A RECIPE. I CAN'T MAKE *ANYTHING* WITHOUT ONE...
OH, I THINK I HAVE ONE OF THOSE...
LET'S SEE. RECIPES, RECIPES...
FLIP FLIP
A-HA! HERE'S ONE.
A TOMATO SOUP MARINADE, WITH TUNA AND CALAMARI.
WE COULD ADD SOME MUSSELS, CLAMS, AND SOME OTHER TASTY SEA-FOOD. ON THE SIDE, HOW ABOUT SOME CAPONATA?
DOES THAT SOUND GOOD?

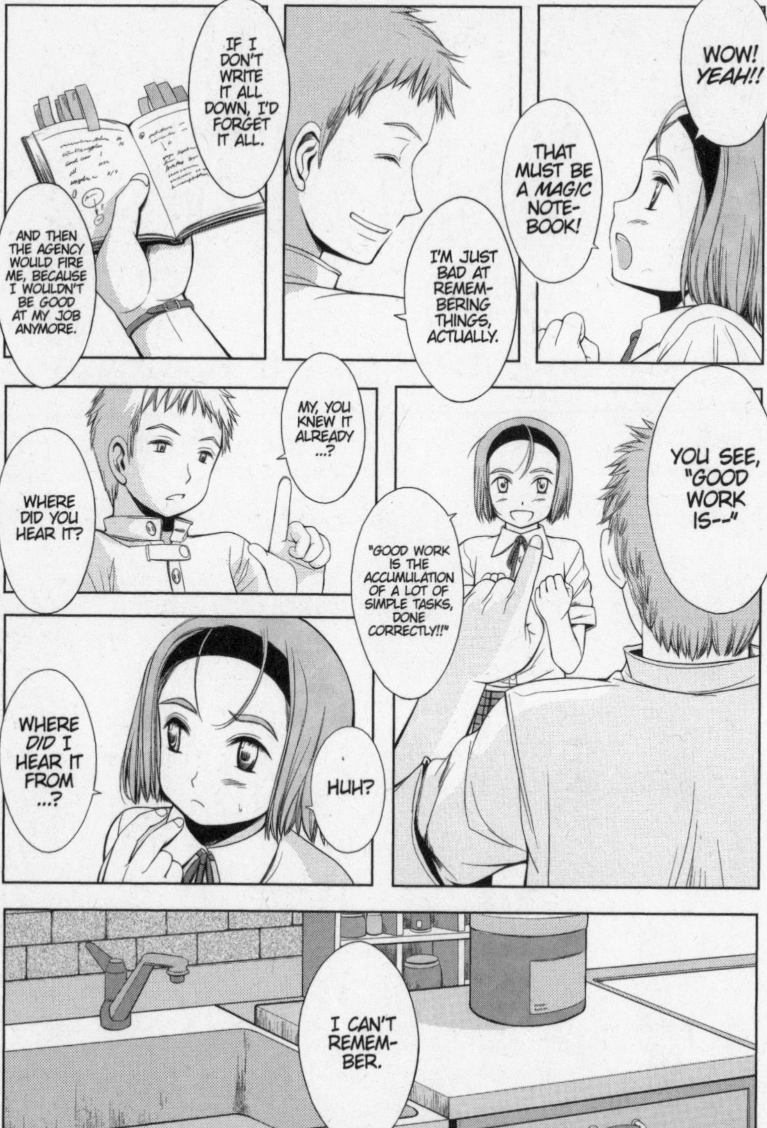
WOW! YEAH!!
THAT MUST BE A *MAGIC* NOTE-BOOK!
I'M JUST BAD AT REMEM-BERING THINGS, ACTUALLY.
IF I DON'T WRITE IT ALL DOWN, I'D FORGET IT ALL.
AND THEN THE AGENCY WOULD FIRE ME, BECAUSE I WOULDN'T BE GOOD AT MY JOB ANYMORE.
YOU SEE, "GOOD WORK IS--"
"GOOD WORK IS THE ACCUMULATION OF A LOT OF SIMPLE TASKS, DONE CORRECTLY!!"
MY, YOU KNEW IT ALREADY ...?
WHERE DID YOU HEAR IT?
HUH?
WHERE *DID* I HEAR IT FROM ...?
I CAN'T REMEM-BER.

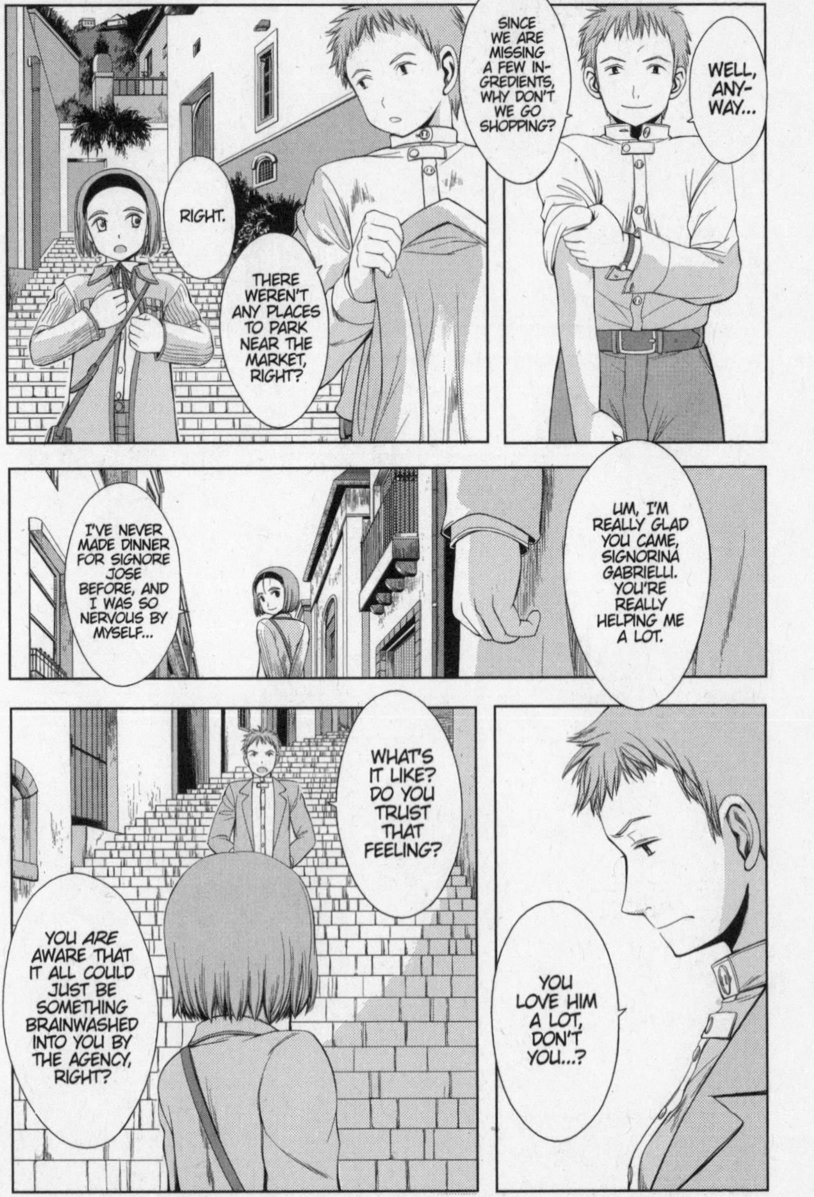
WELL, ANYWAY...
SINCE WE ARE MISSING A FEW INGREDIENTS, WHY DON'T WE GO SHOPPING?
THERE WEREN'T ANY PLACES TO PARK NEAR THE MARKET, RIGHT?
RIGHT.
UM, I'M REALLY GLAD YOU CAME, SIGNORINA GABRIELLI. YOU'RE REALLY HELPING ME A LOT.
I'VE NEVER MADE DINNER FOR SIGNORE JOSE BEFORE, AND I WAS SO NERVOUS BY MYSELF...
YOU LOVE HIM A LOT, DON'T YOU...?
WHAT'S IT LIKE? DO YOU TRUST THAT FEELING?
YOU *ARE* AWARE THAT IT ALL COULD JUST BE SOMETHING BRAINWASHED INTO YOU BY THE AGENCY, RIGHT?

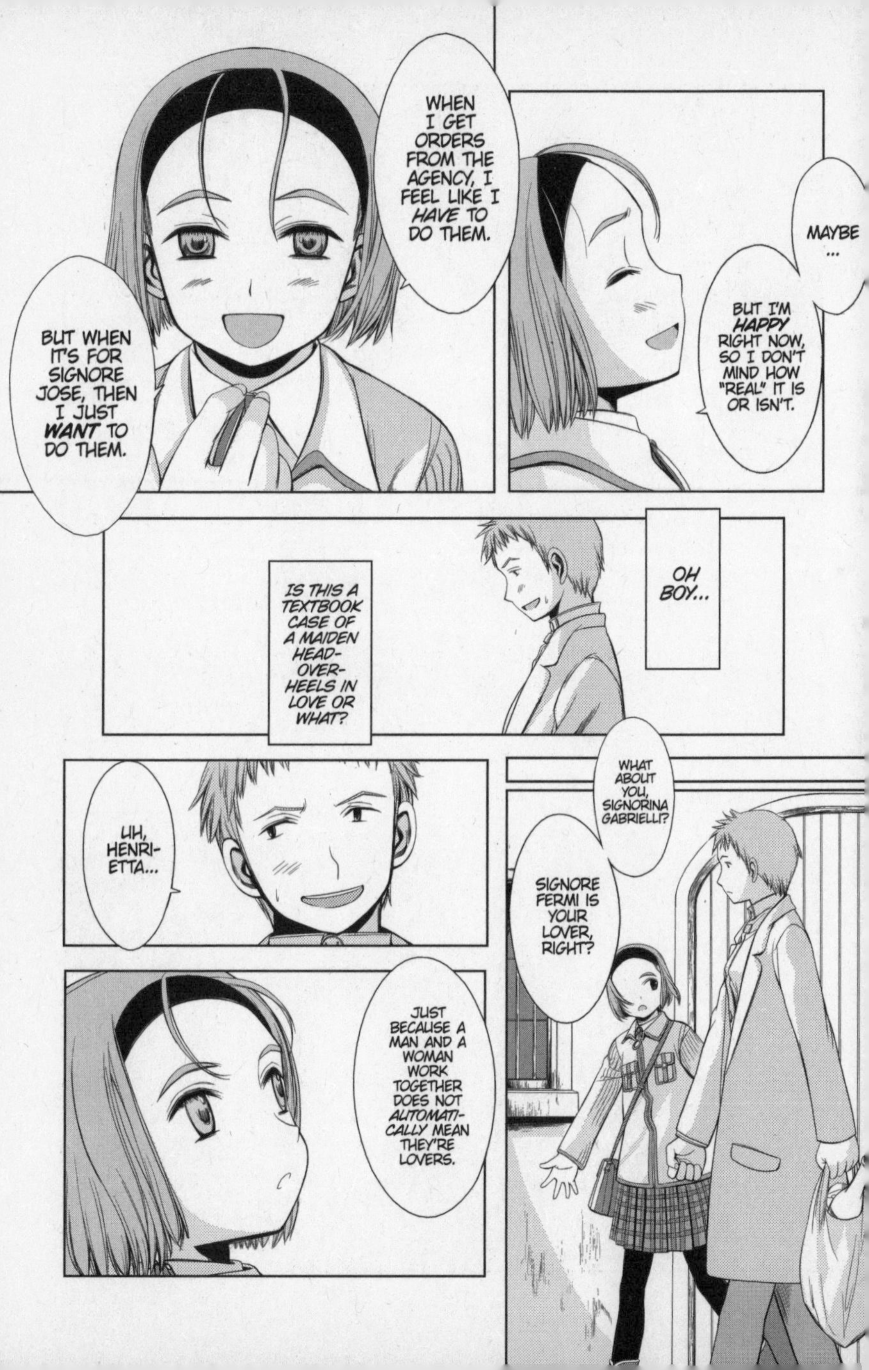
MAYBE ...
BUT I'M *HAPPY* RIGHT NOW, SO I DON'T MIND HOW "REAL" IT IS OR ISN'T.
WHEN I GET ORDERS FROM THE AGENCY, I FEEL LIKE I *HAVE* TO DO THEM.
BUT WHEN IT'S FOR SIGNORE JOSE, THEN I JUST ***WANT*** TO DO THEM.
OH BOY...
IS THIS A TEXTBOOK CASE OF A MAIDEN HEAD-OVER-HEELS IN LOVE OR WHAT?
WHAT ABOUT YOU, SIGNORINA GABRIELLI?
SIGNORE FERMI IS YOUR LOVER, RIGHT?
UH, HENRI-ETTA...
JUST BECAUSE A MAN AND A WOMAN WORK TOGETHER DOES NOT *AUTOMATI-CALLY* MEAN THEY'RE LOVERS.

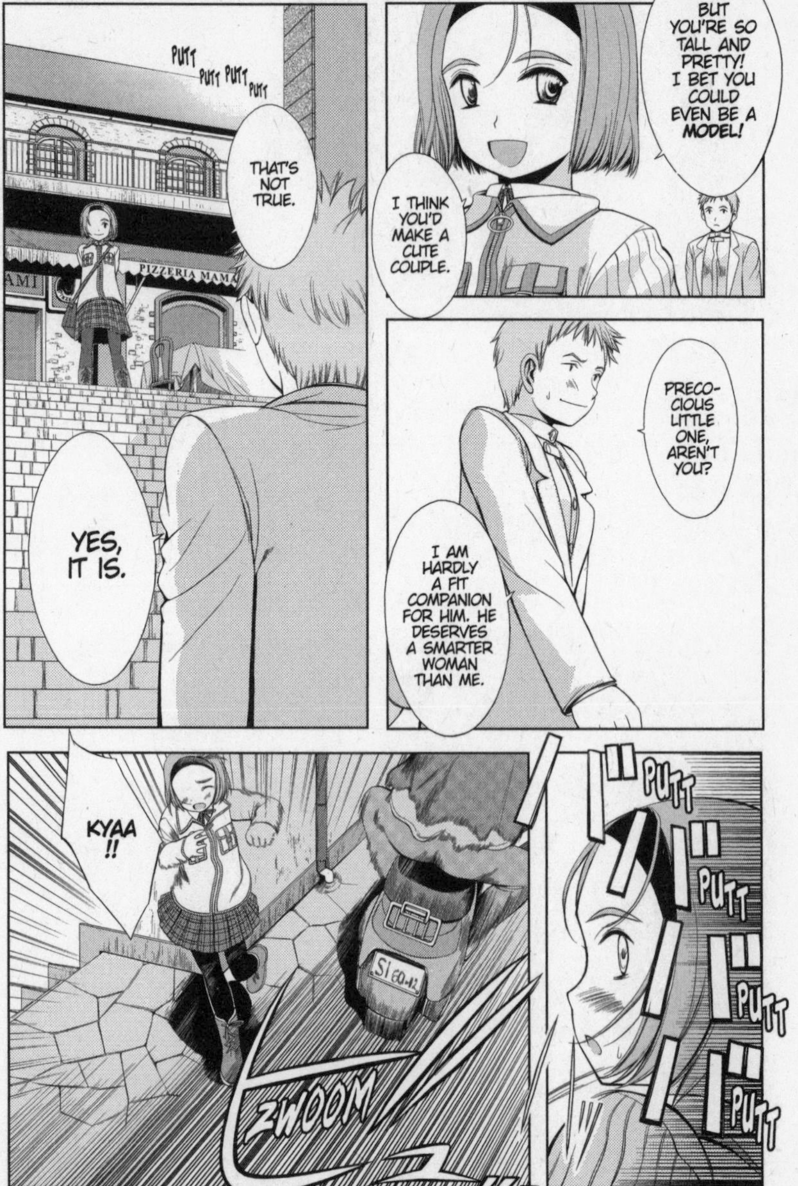
BUT YOU'RE SO TALL AND PRETTY! I BET YOU COULD EVEN BE A MODEL!
I THINK YOU'D MAKE A CUTE COUPLE.
PRECOCIOUS LITTLE ONE, AREN'T YOU?
I AM HARDLY A FIT COMPANION FOR HIM. HE DESERVES A SMARTER WOMAN THAN ME.
PUTT PUTT PUTT PUTT
PIZZERIA MAMA
THAT'S NOT TRUE.
YES, IT IS.
PUTT
PUTT
PUTT
PUTT
KYAA!!
ZWOOM

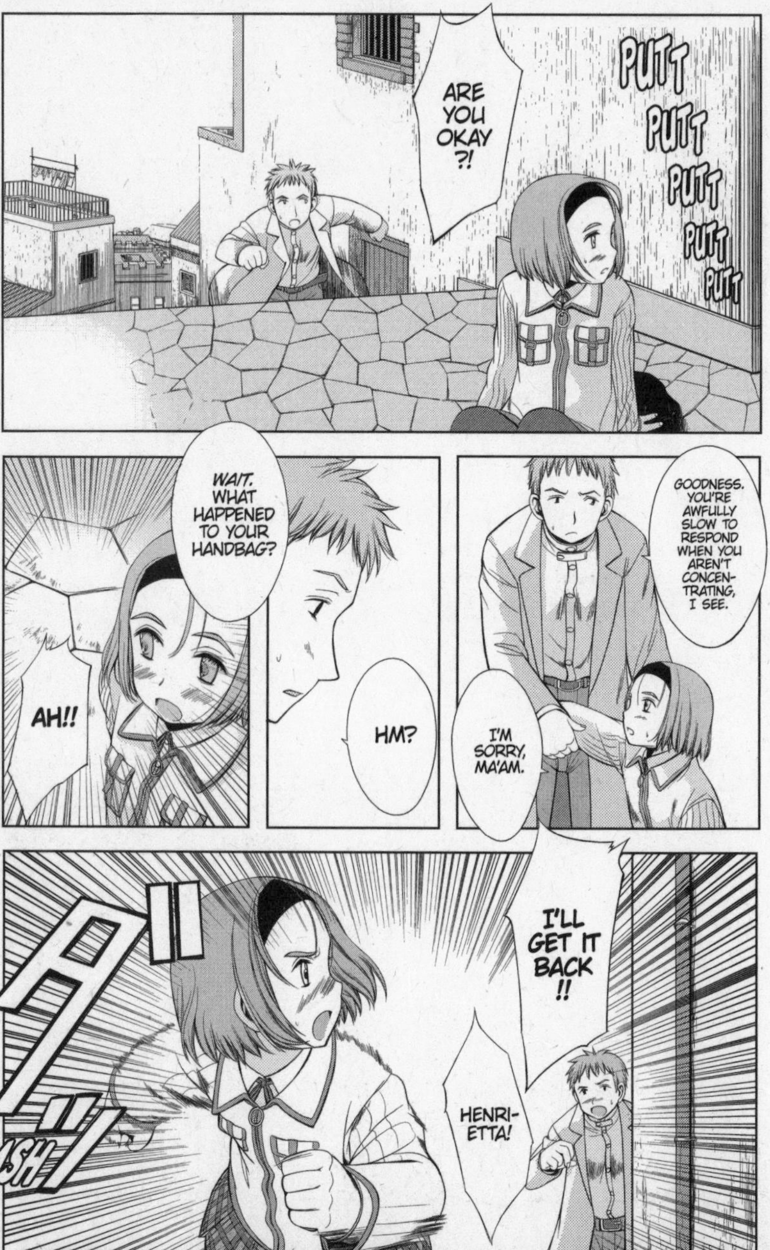
PUTT PUTT PUTT PUTT PUTT
ARE YOU OKAY?!
GOODNESS. YOU'RE AWFULLY SLOW TO RESPOND WHEN YOU AREN'T CONCENTRATING, I SEE.
I'M SORRY, MA'AM.
WAIT. WHAT HAPPENED TO YOUR HANDBAG?
HM?
AH!!
I'LL GET IT BACK!!
HENRIETTA!
DASH

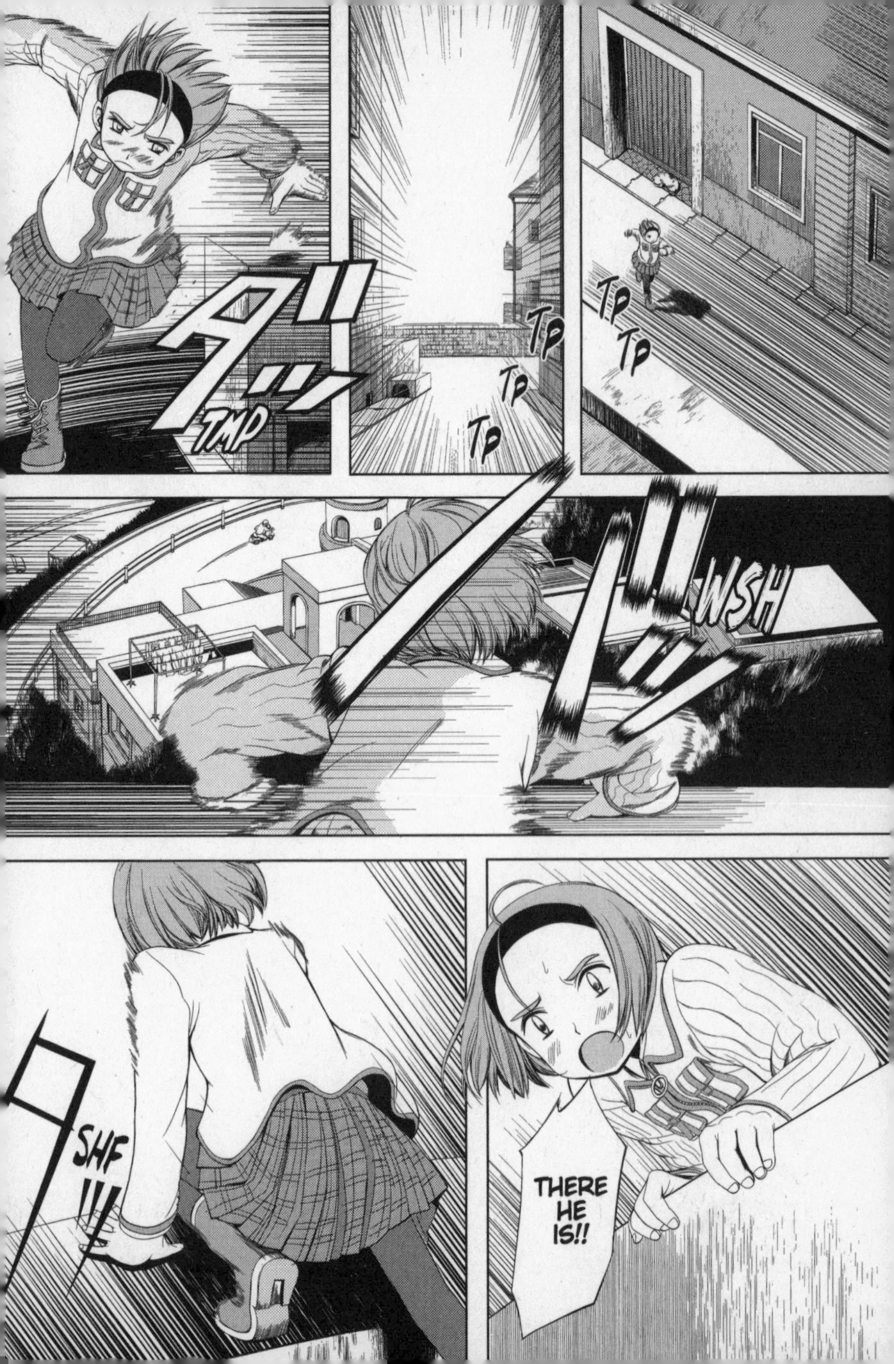
Tp
Tp
Tp
Tp
Tp
Tp
TMP
WSH
THERE HE IS!!
SHF

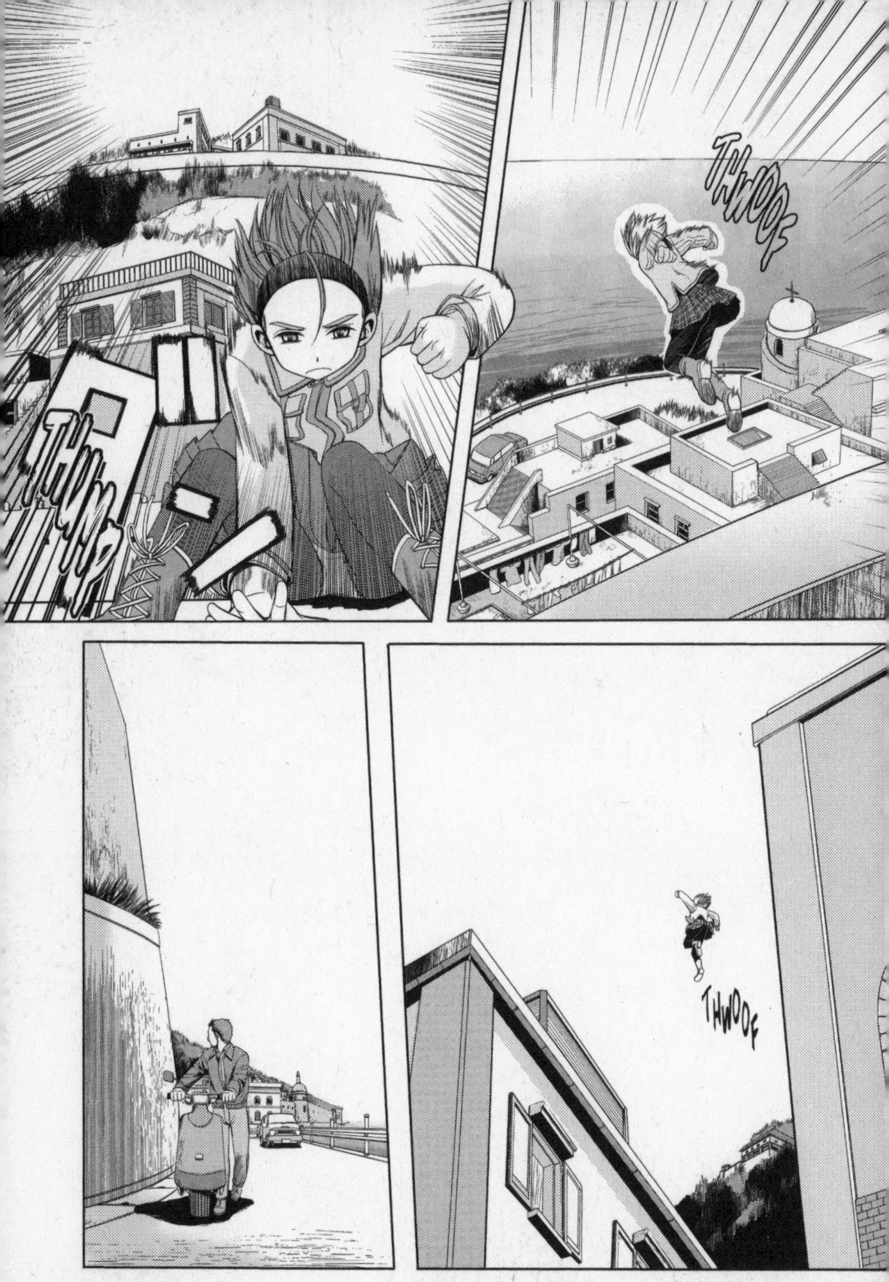
THWOOF
THUMP
THWOOF

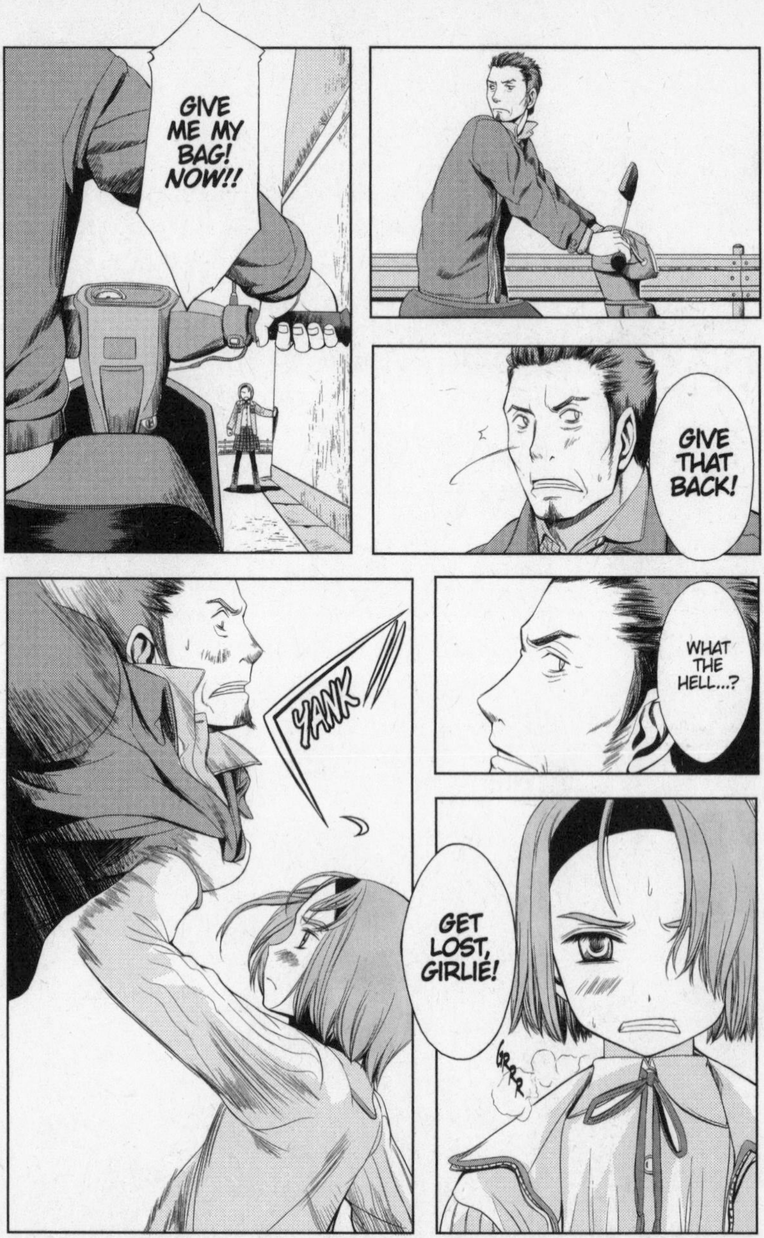
GIVE THAT BACK!
GIVE ME MY BAG! NOW!!
WHAT THE HELL...?
GET LOST, GIRLIE!
GRRR
YANK

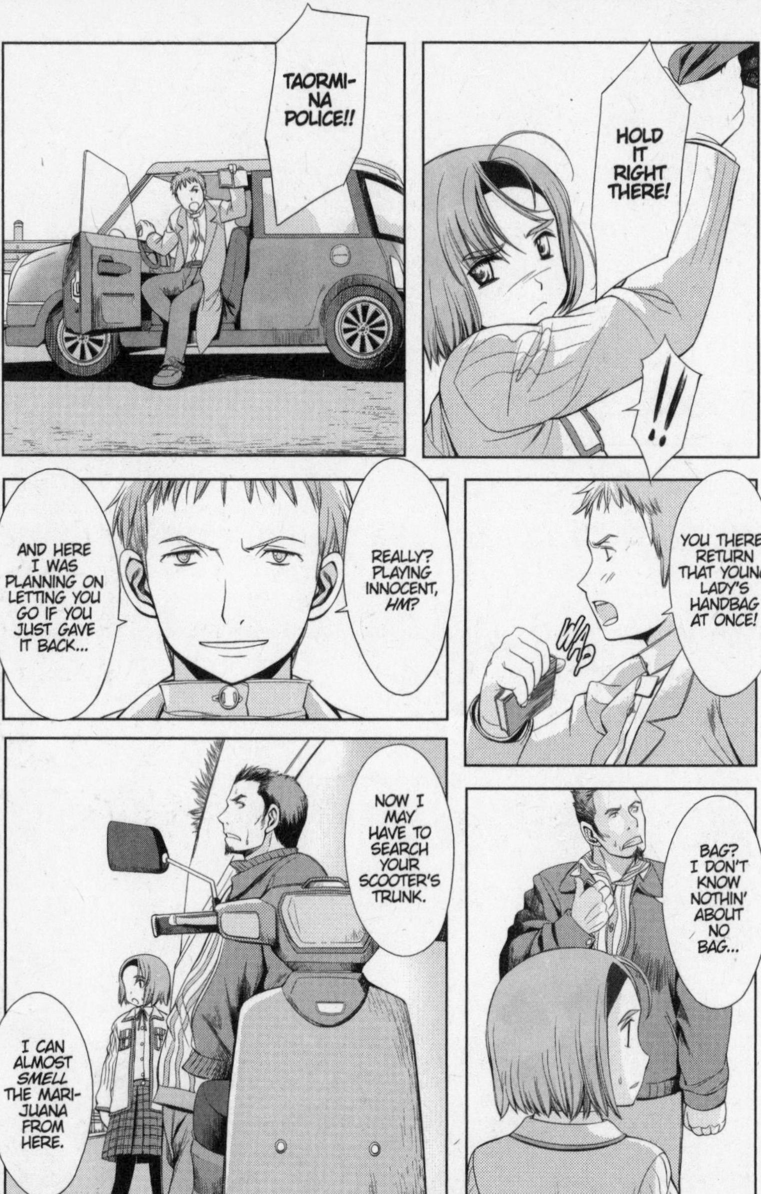
HOLD IT RIGHT THERE!
!!
TAORMI-NA POLICE!!
YOU THERE! RETURN THAT YOUNG LADY'S HANDBAG AT ONCE!
WAP
BAG? I DON'T KNOW NOTHIN' ABOUT NO BAG...
REALLY? PLAYING INNOCENT, *HM?*
AND HERE I WAS PLANNING ON LETTING YOU GO IF YOU JUST GAVE IT BACK...
NOW I MAY HAVE TO SEARCH YOUR SCOOTER'S TRUNK.
I CAN ALMOST *SMELL* THE MARI-JUANA FROM HERE.

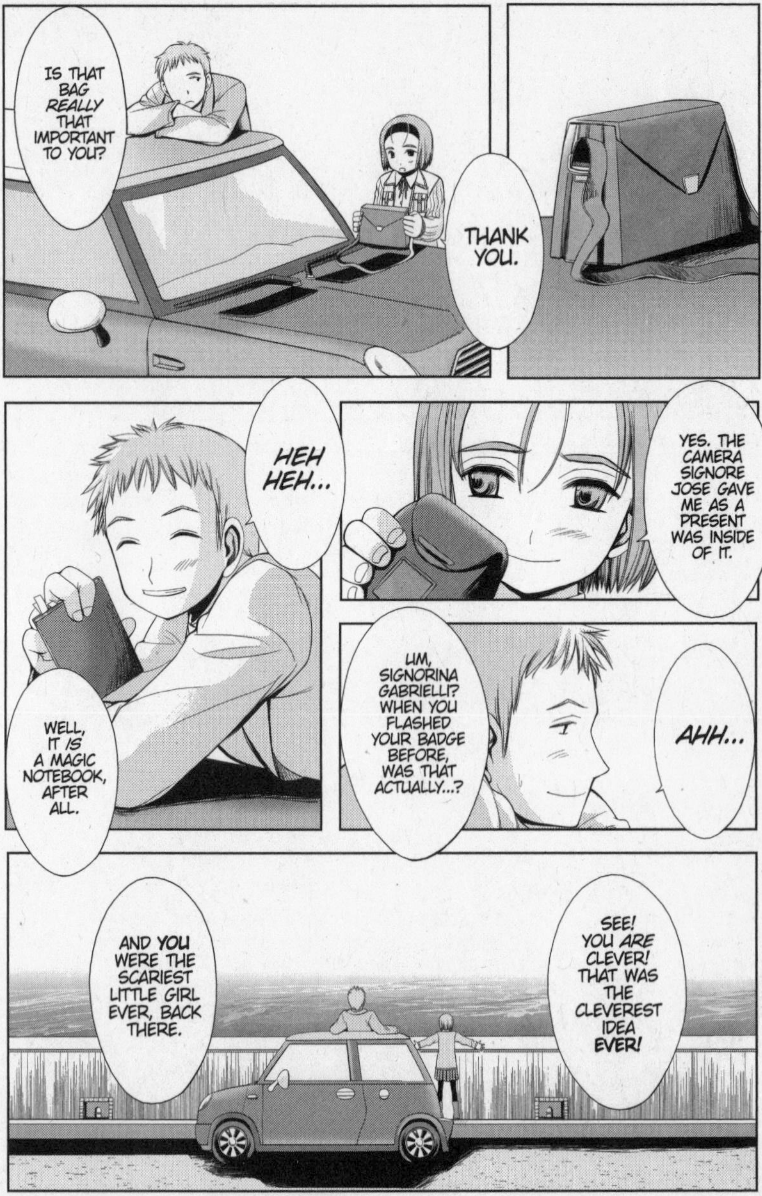
THANK YOU.
IS THAT BAG *REALLY* THAT IMPORTANT TO YOU?
YES. THE CAMERA SIGNORE JOSE GAVE ME AS A PRESENT WAS INSIDE OF IT.
AHH...
UM, SIGNORINA GABRIELLI? WHEN YOU FLASHED YOUR BADGE BEFORE, WAS THAT ACTUALLY...?
HEH HEH...
WELL, IT *IS* A MAGIC NOTEBOOK, AFTER ALL.
SEE! YOU *ARE* CLEVER! THAT WAS THE CLEVEREST IDEA **EVER**!
AND **YOU** WERE THE SCARIEST LITTLE GIRL EVER, BACK THERE.

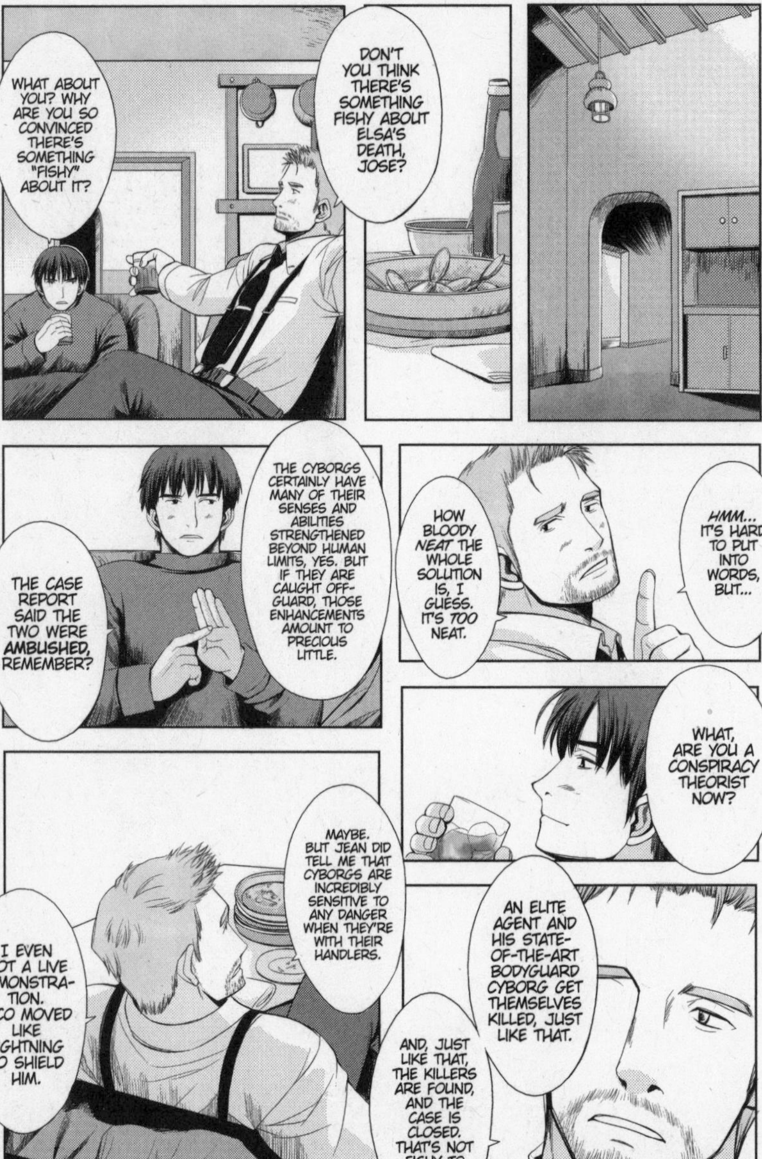
DON'T YOU THINK THERE'S SOMETHING FISHY ABOUT ELSA'S DEATH, JOSE?
WHAT ABOUT YOU? WHY ARE YOU SO CONVINCED THERE'S SOMETHING "FISHY" ABOUT IT?
HMM... IT'S HARD TO PUT INTO WORDS, BUT...
HOW BLOODY *NEAT* THE WHOLE SOLUTION IS, I GUESS. IT'S *TOO* NEAT.
THE CYBORGS CERTAINLY HAVE MANY OF THEIR SENSES AND ABILITIES STRENGTHENED BEYOND HUMAN LIMITS, YES. BUT IF THEY ARE CAUGHT OFF-GUARD, THOSE ENHANCEMENTS AMOUNT TO PRECIOUS LITTLE.
THE CASE REPORT SAID THE TWO WERE **AMBUSHED**, REMEMBER?
WHAT, ARE YOU A CONSPIRACY THEORIST NOW?
AN ELITE AGENT AND HIS STATE-OF-THE-ART BODYGUARD CYBORG GET THEMSELVES KILLED, JUST LIKE THAT.
AND, JUST LIKE THAT, THE KILLERS ARE FOUND, AND THE CASE IS CLOSED. THAT'S NOT FISHY TO YOU...?
MAYBE. BUT JEAN DID TELL ME THAT CYBORGS ARE INCREDIBLY SENSITIVE TO ANY DANGER WHEN THEY'RE WITH THEIR HANDLERS.
I EVEN GOT A LIVE DEMONSTRA-TION. RICO MOVED LIKE LIGHTNING TO SHIELD HIM.

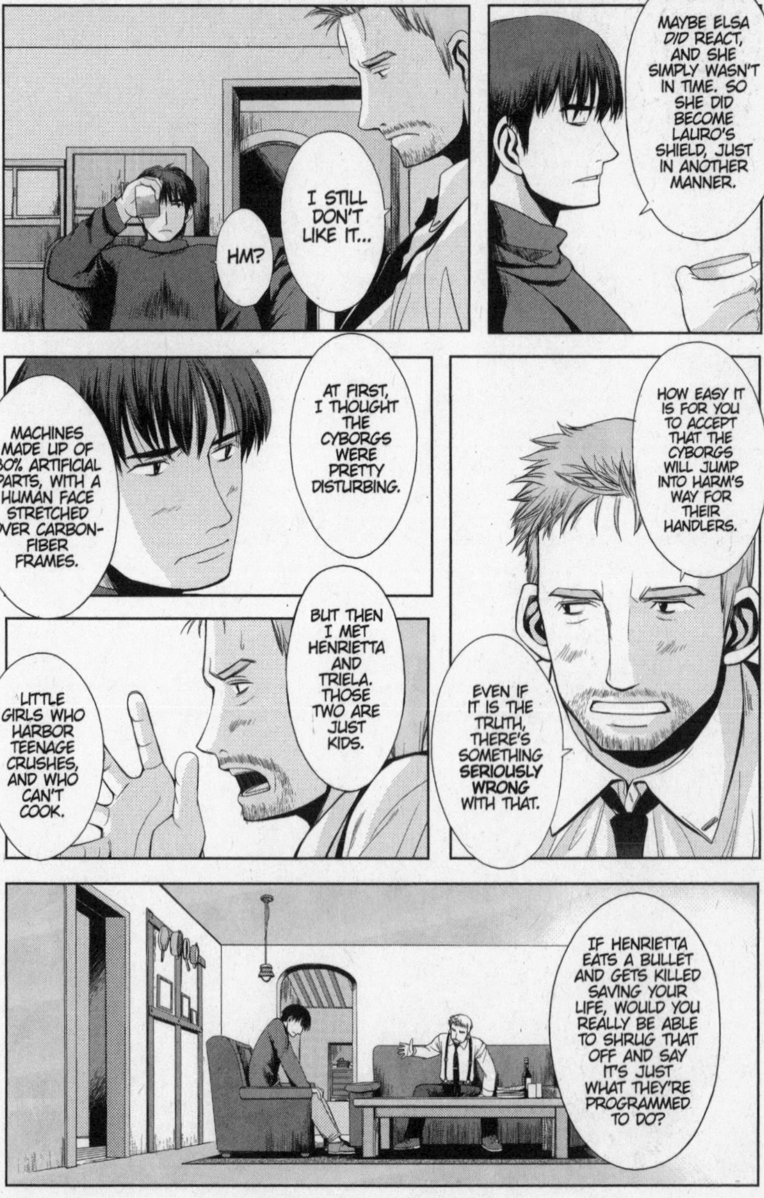
MAYBE ELSA *DID* REACT, AND SHE SIMPLY WASN'T IN TIME. SO SHE DID BECOME LAURO'S SHIELD, JUST IN ANOTHER MANNER.
I STILL DON'T LIKE IT...
HM?
HOW EASY IT IS FOR YOU TO ACCEPT THAT THE CYBORGS WILL JUMP INTO HARM'S WAY FOR THEIR HANDLERS.
EVEN IF IT IS THE TRUTH, THERE'S SOMETHING **SERIOUSLY WRONG** WITH THAT.
AT FIRST, I THOUGHT THE CYBORGS WERE PRETTY DISTURBING.
MACHINES MADE UP OF 80% ARTIFICIAL PARTS, WITH A HUMAN FACE STRETCHED OVER CARBON-FIBER FRAMES.
BUT THEN I MET HENRIETTA AND TRIELA. THOSE TWO ARE JUST KIDS.
LITTLE GIRLS WHO HARBOR TEENAGE CRUSHES, AND WHO CAN'T COOK.
IF HENRIETTA EATS A BULLET AND GETS KILLED SAVING YOUR LIFE, WOULD YOU REALLY BE ABLE TO SHRUG THAT OFF AND SAY IT'S JUST WHAT THEY'RE PROGRAMMED TO DO?

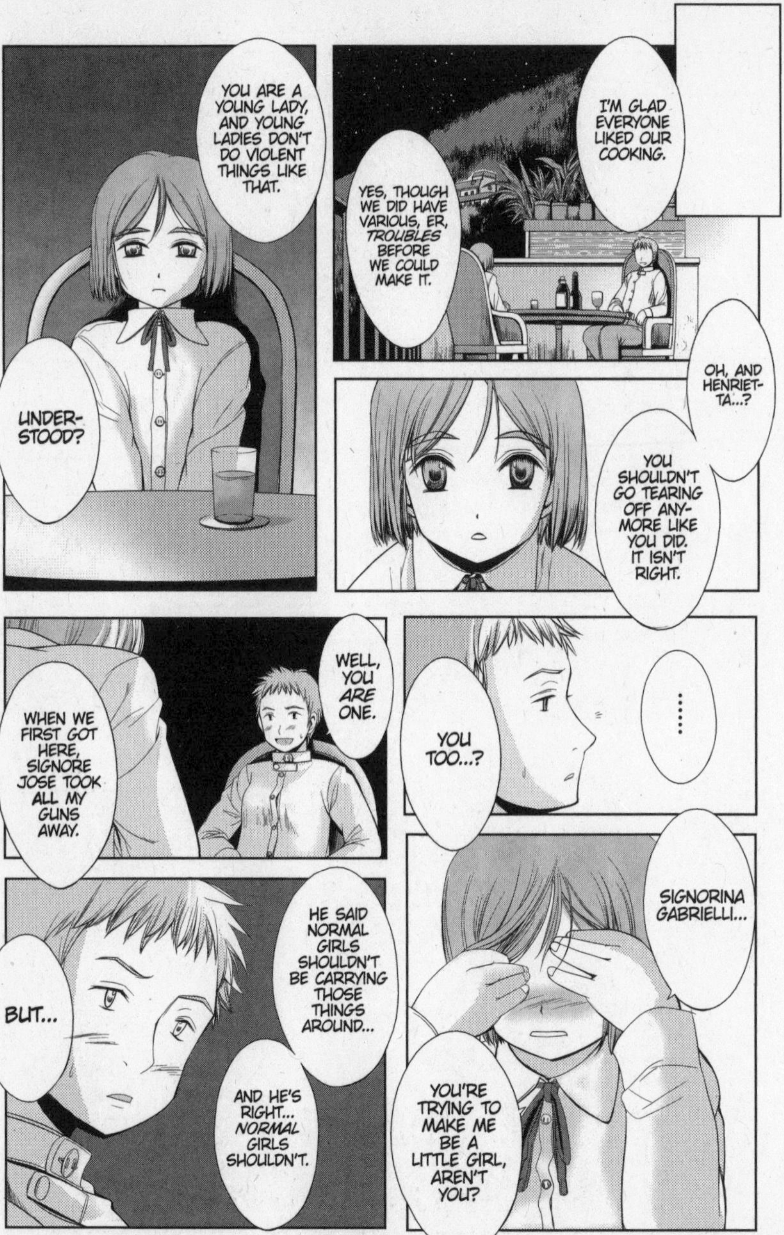
I'M GLAD EVERYONE LIKED OUR COOKING.
YES, THOUGH WE DID HAVE VARIOUS, ER, *TROUBLES* BEFORE WE COULD MAKE IT.
OH, AND HENRIETTA...?
YOU SHOULDN'T GO TEARING OFF ANYMORE LIKE YOU DID. IT ISN'T RIGHT.
YOU ARE A YOUNG LADY, AND YOUNG LADIES DON'T DO VIOLENT THINGS LIKE THAT.
UNDERSTOOD?
......
YOU TOO...?
WELL, YOU *ARE* ONE.
WHEN WE FIRST GOT HERE, SIGNORE JOSE TOOK ALL MY GUNS AWAY.
SIGNORINA GABRIELLI...
YOU'RE TRYING TO MAKE ME BE A LITTLE GIRL, AREN'T YOU?
HE SAID NORMAL GIRLS SHOULDN'T BE CARRYING THOSE THINGS AROUND...
BUT...
AND HE'S RIGHT... *NORMAL* GIRLS SHOULDN'T.

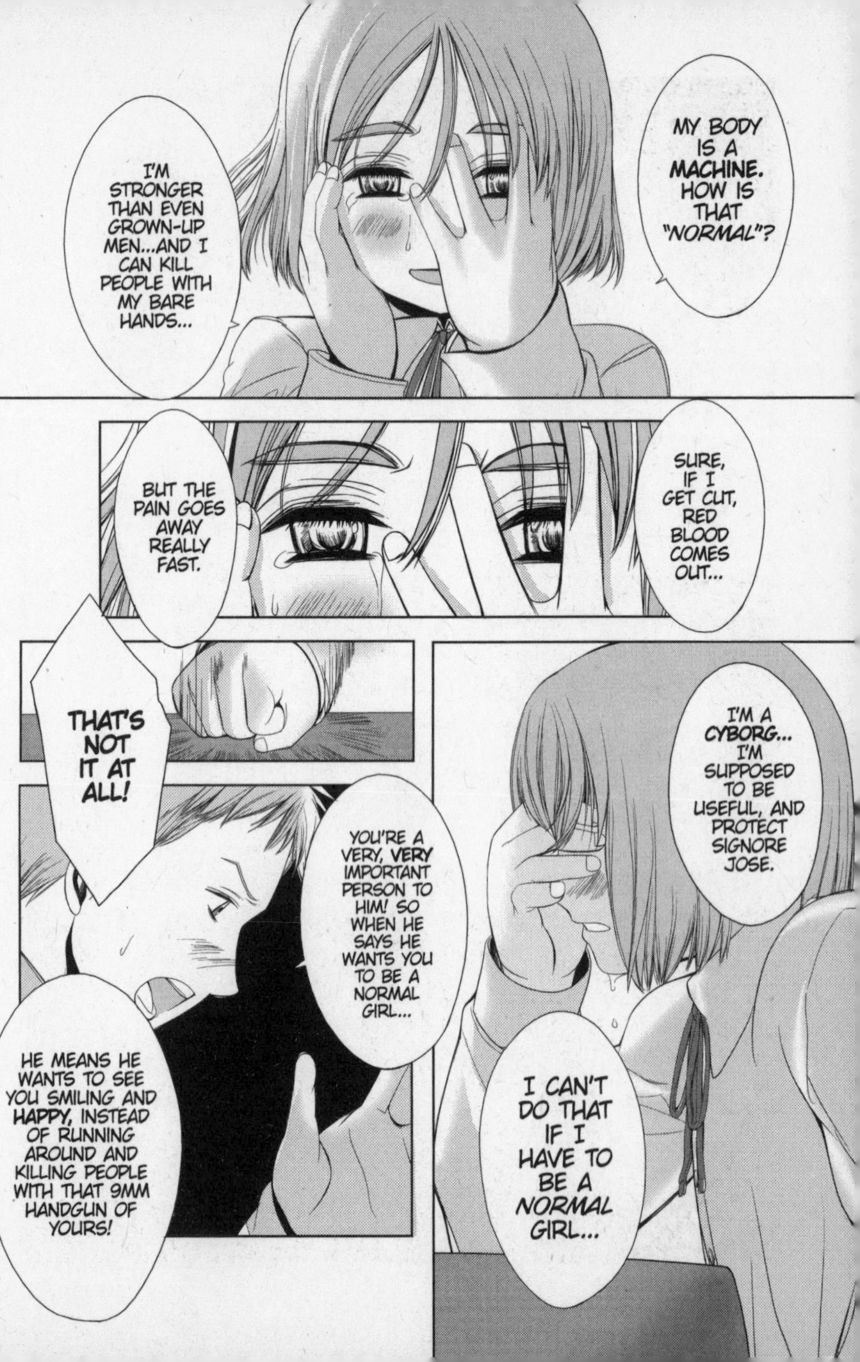
MY BODY IS A MACHINE. HOW IS THAT "NORMAL"?
I'M STRONGER THAN EVEN GROWN-UP MEN...AND I CAN KILL PEOPLE WITH MY BARE HANDS...
SURE, IF I GET CUT, RED BLOOD COMES OUT...
BUT THE PAIN GOES AWAY REALLY FAST.
I'M A CYBORG... I'M SUPPOSED TO BE USEFUL, AND PROTECT SIGNORE JOSE.
I CAN'T DO THAT IF I HAVE TO BE A NORMAL GIRL...
THAT'S NOT IT AT ALL!
YOU'RE A VERY, VERY IMPORTANT PERSON TO HIM! SO WHEN HE SAYS HE WANTS YOU TO BE A NORMAL GIRL...
HE MEANS HE WANTS TO SEE YOU SMILING AND HAPPY, INSTEAD OF RUNNING AROUND AND KILLING PEOPLE WITH THAT 9MM HANDGUN OF YOURS!

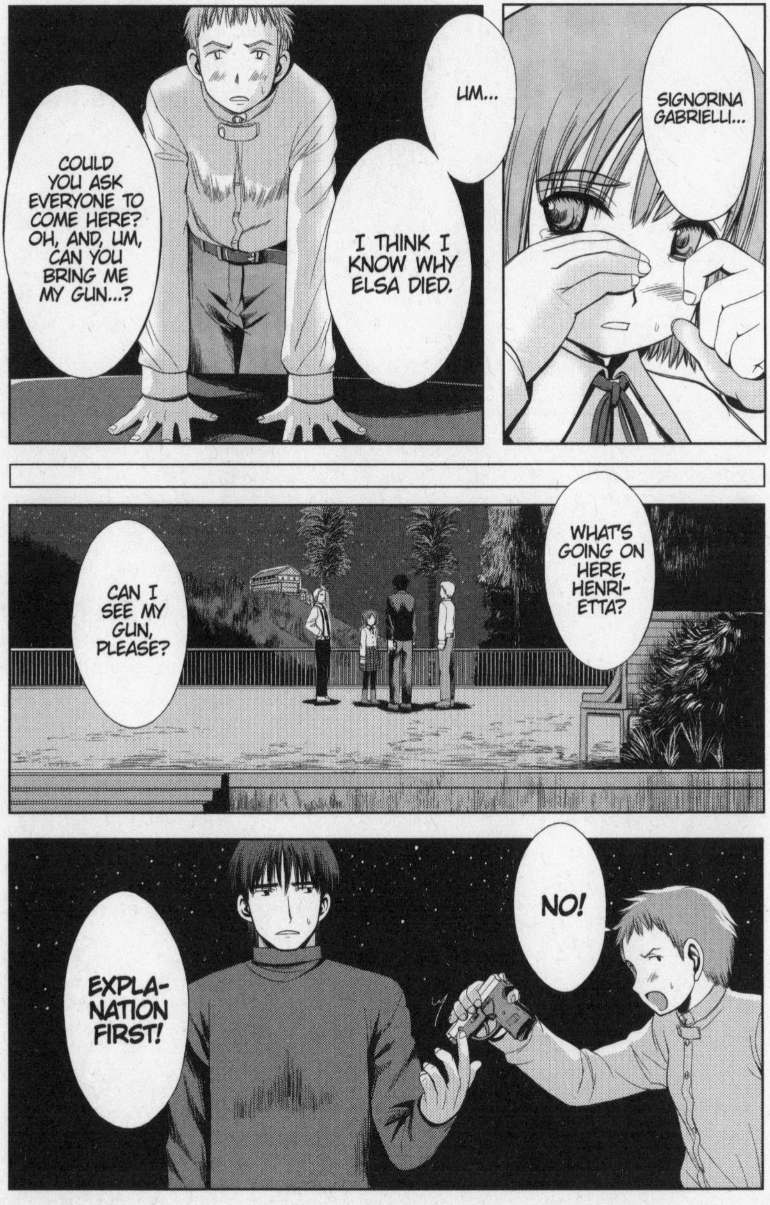
SIGNORINA GABRIELLI...
UM...
I THINK I KNOW WHY ELSA DIED.
COULD YOU ASK EVERYONE TO COME HERE? OH, AND, UM, CAN YOU BRING ME MY GUN...?
WHAT'S GOING ON HERE, HENRI-ETTA?
CAN I SEE MY GUN, PLEASE?
NO!
EXPLA-NATION FIRST!

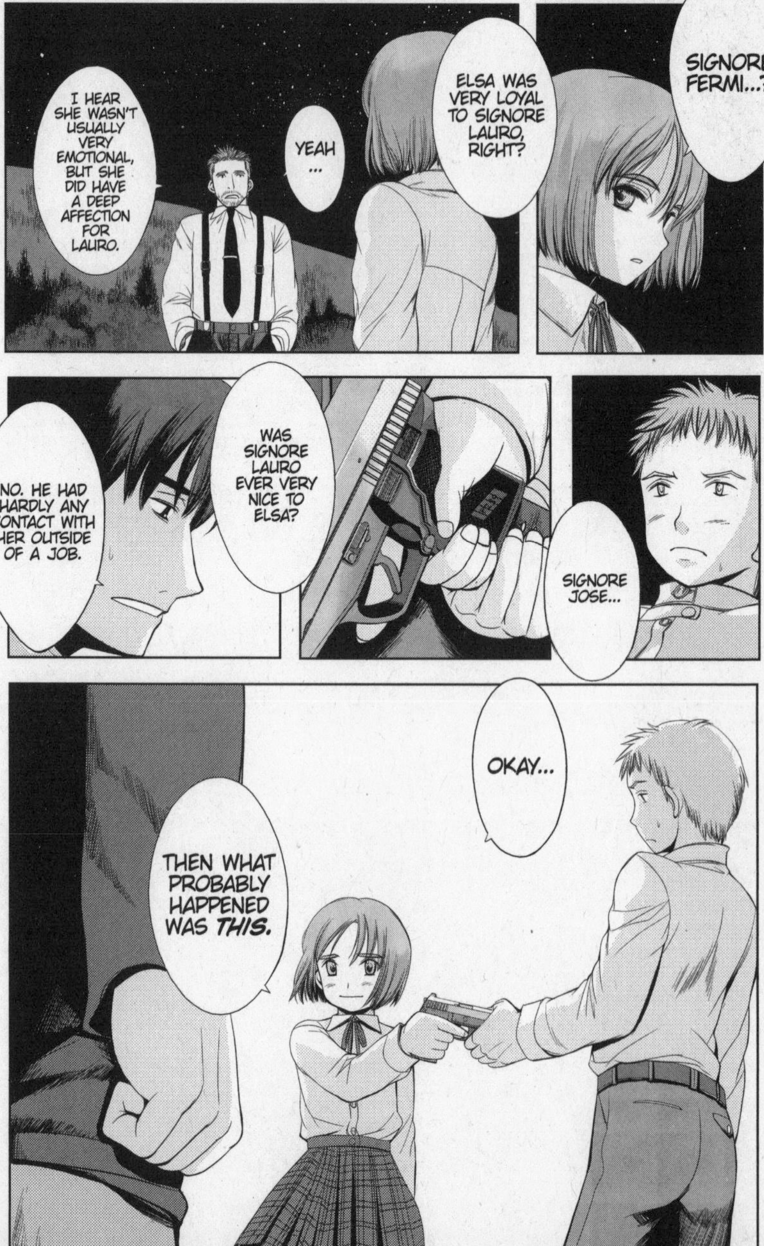
SIGNORE FERMI...?
ELSA WAS VERY LOYAL TO SIGNORE LAURO, RIGHT?
YEAH ...
I HEAR SHE WASN'T USUALLY VERY EMOTIONAL, BUT SHE DID HAVE A DEEP AFFECTION FOR LAURO.
SIGNORE JOSE...
WAS SIGNORE LAURO EVER VERY NICE TO ELSA?
NO. HE HAD HARDLY ANY CONTACT WITH HER OUTSIDE OF A JOB.
OKAY...
THEN WHAT PROBABLY HAPPENED WAS *THIS.*

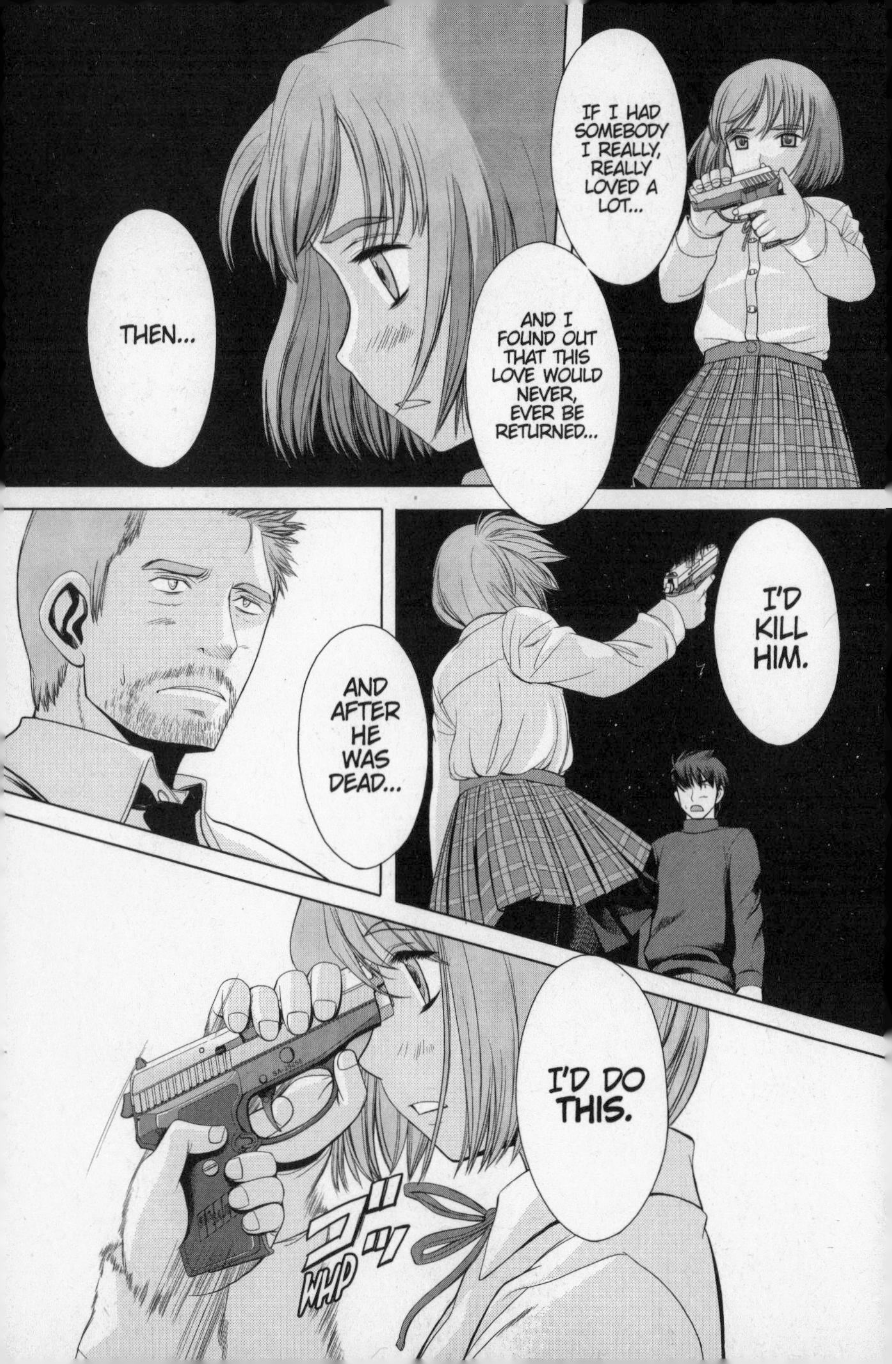
IF I HAD SOMEBODY I REALLY, REALLY LOVED A LOT...
AND I FOUND OUT THAT THIS LOVE WOULD NEVER, EVER BE RETURNED...
THEN...
I'D KILL HIM.
AND AFTER HE WAS DEAD...
I'D DO THIS.
WHP

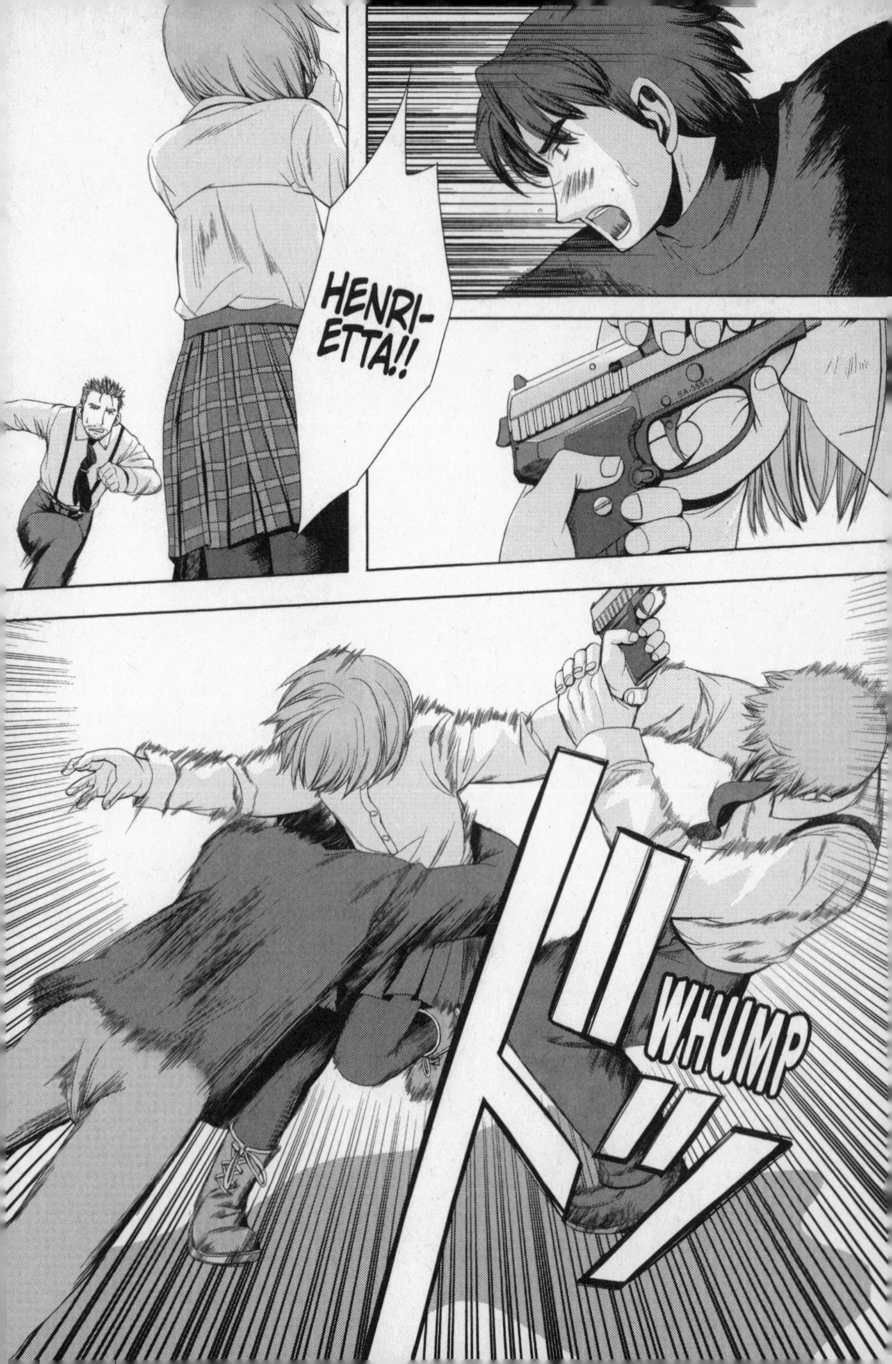
HENRI-
ETTA!!
WHUMP

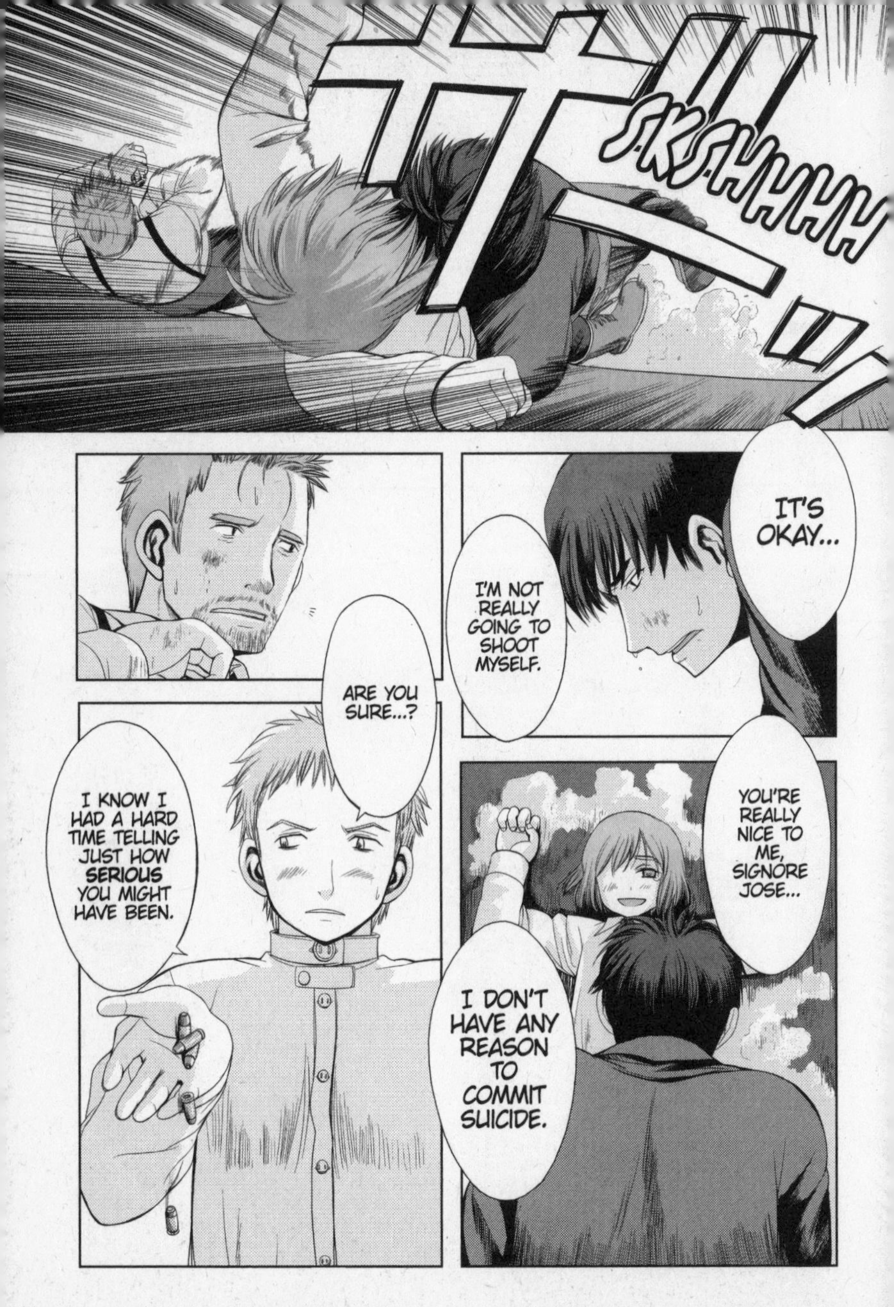
SKSHHHH
IT'S OKAY...
I'M NOT REALLY GOING TO SHOOT MYSELF.
YOU'RE REALLY NICE TO ME, SIGNORE JOSE...
I DON'T HAVE ANY REASON TO COMMIT SUICIDE.
ARE YOU SURE...?
I KNOW I HAD A HARD TIME TELLING JUST HOW SERIOUS YOU MIGHT HAVE BEEN.

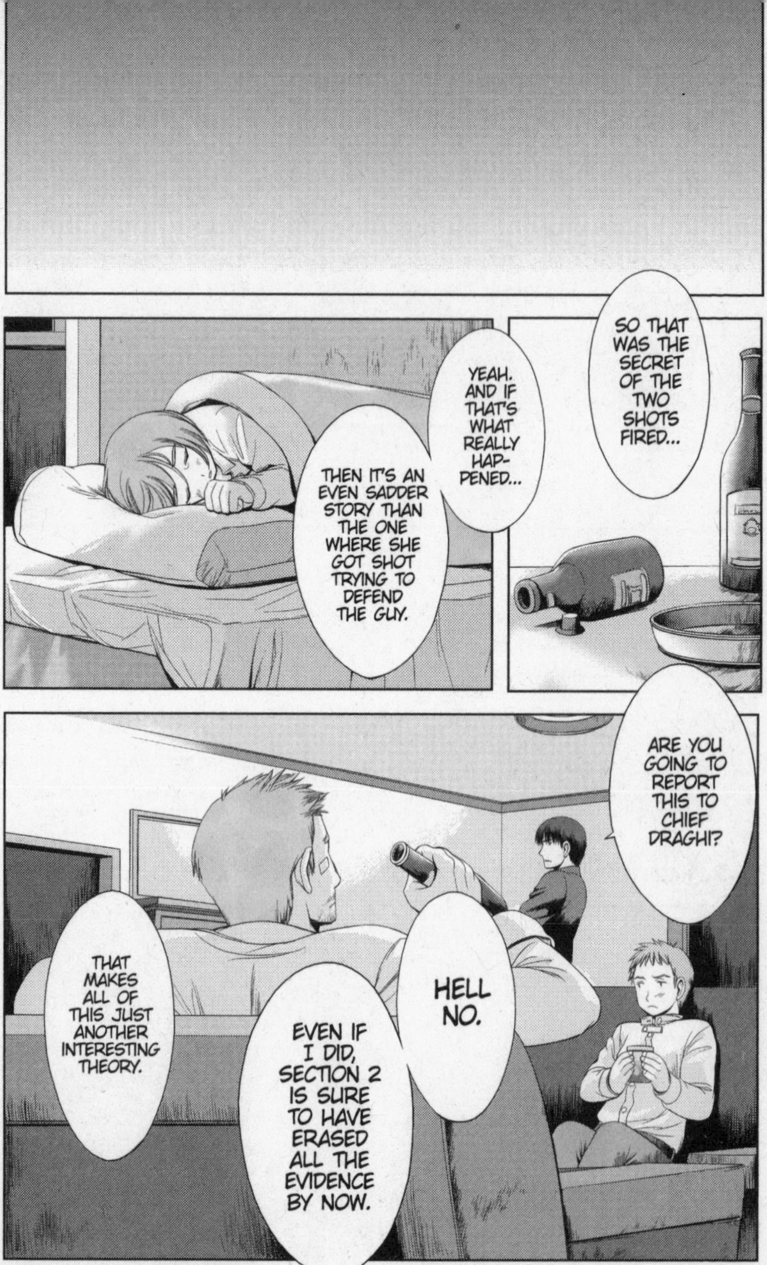
SO THAT WAS THE SECRET OF THE TWO SHOTS FIRED...
YEAH. AND IF THAT'S WHAT REALLY HAP-PENED...
THEN IT'S AN EVEN SADDER STORY THAN THE ONE WHERE SHE GOT SHOT TRYING TO DEFEND THE GUY.
ARE YOU GOING TO REPORT THIS TO CHIEF DRAGHI?
HELL NO.
EVEN IF I DID, SECTION 2 IS SURE TO HAVE ERASED ALL THE EVIDENCE BY NOW.
THAT MAKES ALL OF THIS JUST ANOTHER INTERESTING THEORY.

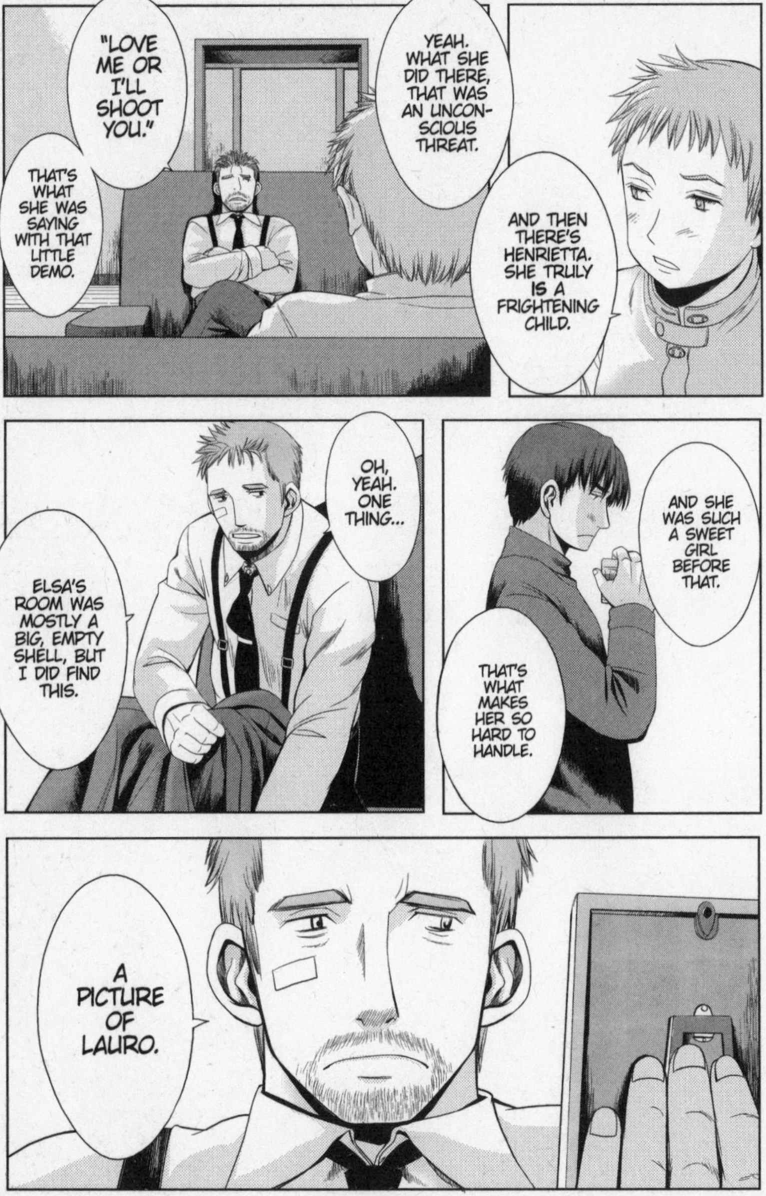
AND THEN THERE'S HENRIETTA. SHE TRULY IS A FRIGHTENING CHILD.
YEAH. WHAT SHE DID THERE, THAT WAS AN UNCON-SCIOUS THREAT.
"LOVE ME OR I'LL SHOOT YOU."
THAT'S WHAT SHE WAS SAYING WITH THAT LITTLE DEMO.
AND SHE WAS SUCH A SWEET GIRL BEFORE THAT.
THAT'S WHAT MAKES HER SO HARD TO HANDLE.
OH, YEAH. ONE THING...
ELSA'S ROOM WAS MOSTLY A BIG, EMPTY SHELL, BUT I DID FIND THIS.
A PICTURE OF LAURO.

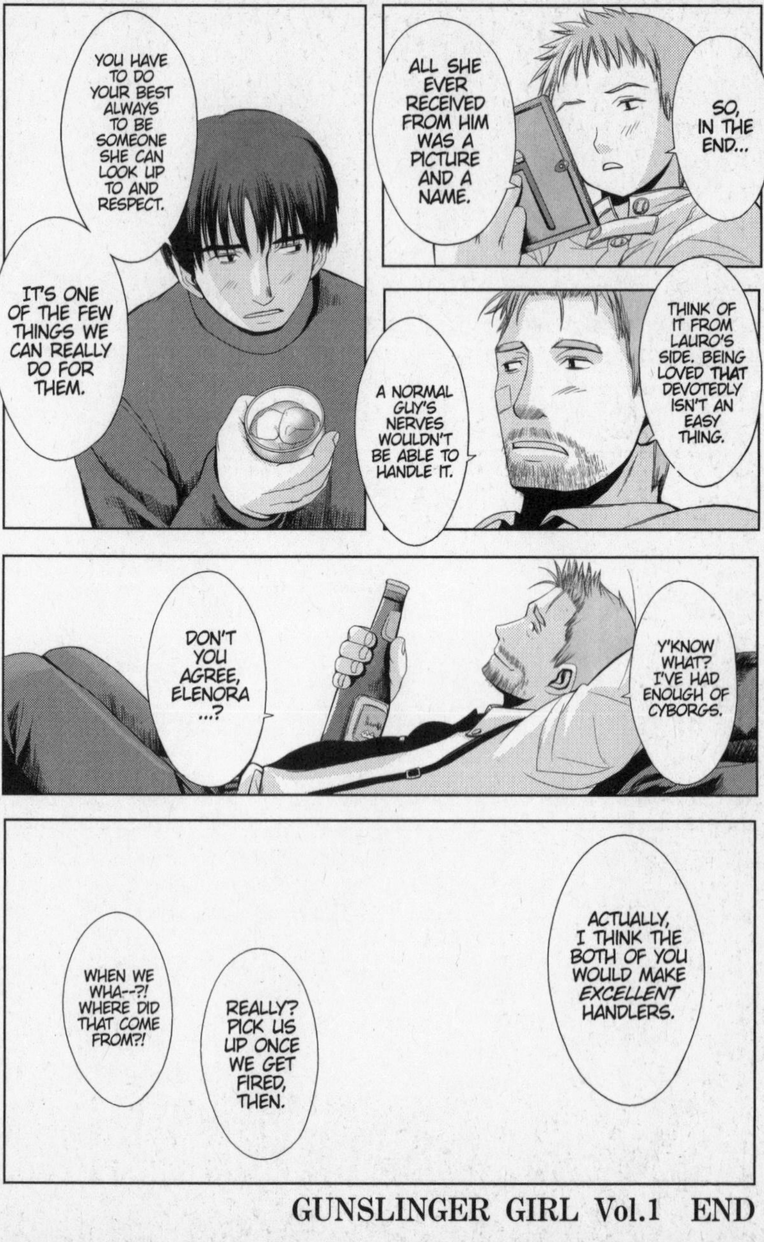
SO, IN THE END...
ALL SHE EVER RECEIVED FROM HIM WAS A PICTURE AND A NAME.
THINK OF IT FROM LAURO'S SIDE. BEING LOVED THAT DEVOTEDLY ISN'T AN EASY THING.
A NORMAL GUY'S NERVES WOULDN'T BE ABLE TO HANDLE IT.
YOU HAVE TO DO YOUR BEST ALWAYS TO BE SOMEONE SHE CAN LOOK UP TO AND RESPECT.
IT'S ONE OF THE FEW THINGS WE CAN REALLY DO FOR THEM.
Y'KNOW WHAT? I'VE HAD ENOUGH OF CYBORGS.
DON'T YOU AGREE, ELENORA ...?
ACTUALLY, I THINK THE BOTH OF YOU WOULD MAKE *EXCELLENT* HANDLERS.
REALLY? PICK US UP ONCE WE GET FIRED, THEN.
WHEN WE WHA--?! WHERE DID THAT COME FROM?!

GUNSLINGER GIRL Vol.1 END

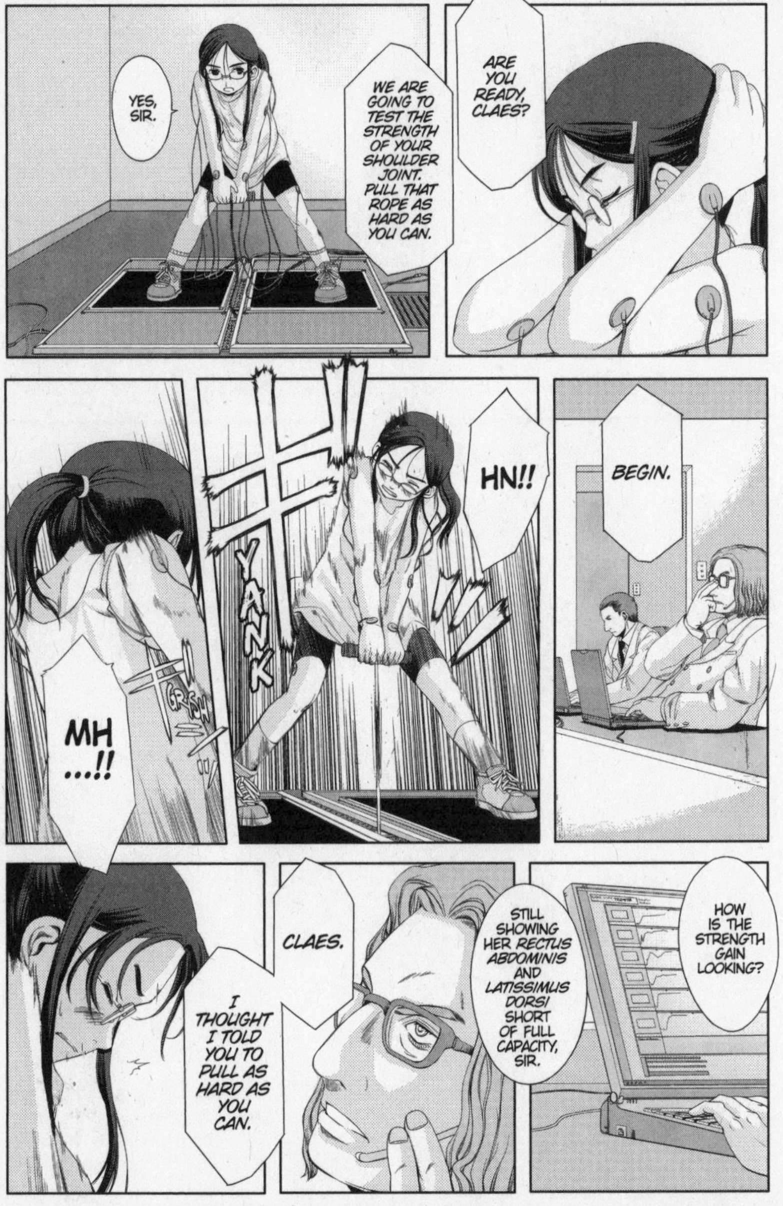
ARE YOU READY, CLAES?
WE ARE GOING TO TEST THE STRENGTH OF YOUR SHOULDER JOINT. PULL THAT ROPE AS HARD AS YOU CAN.
YES, SIR.
BEGIN.
HN!!
YANK
MH ...!!
HOW IS THE STRENGTH GAIN LOOKING?
STILL SHOWING HER RECTUS ABDOMINIS AND LATISSIMUS DORSI SHORT OF FULL CAPACITY, SIR.
CLAES.
I THOUGHT I TOLD YOU TO PULL AS HARD AS YOU CAN.

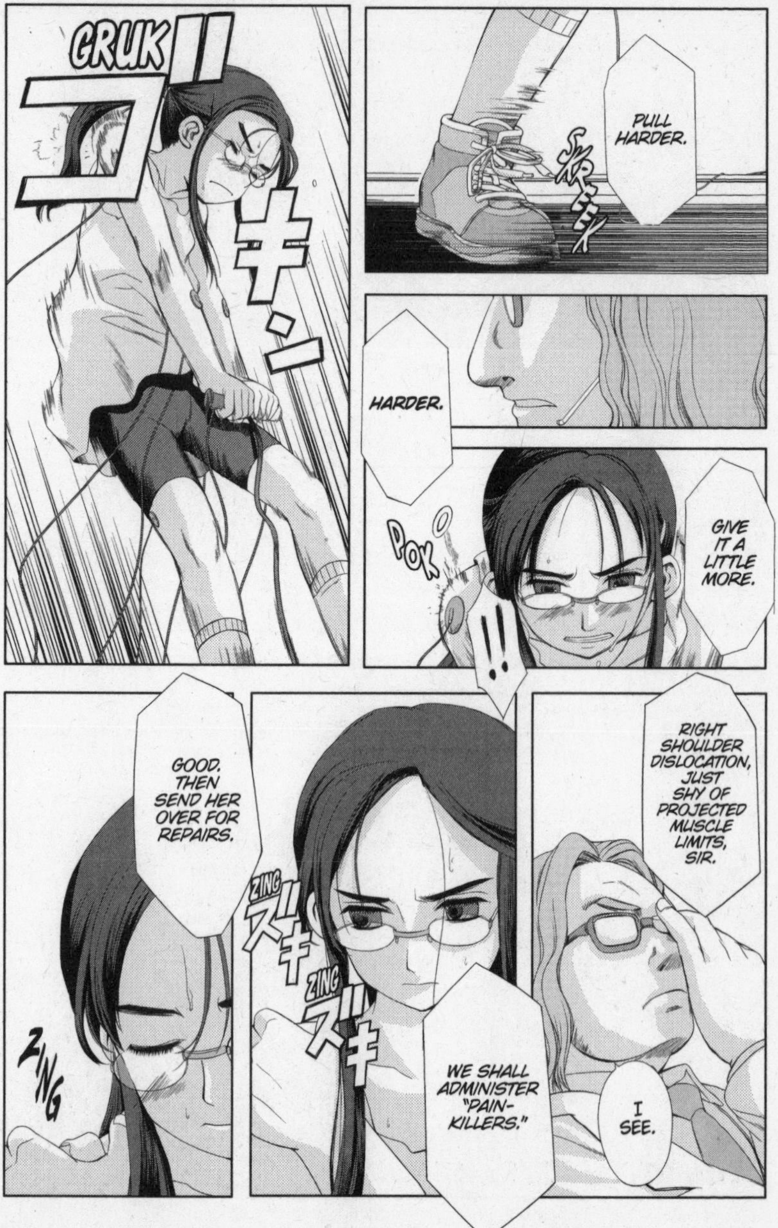
PULL HARDER.
SKREEK
HARDER.
GIVE IT A LITTLE MORE.
POK
!!
GRUK
RIGHT SHOULDER DISLOCATION, JUST SHY OF PROJECTED MUSCLE LIMITS, SIR.
I SEE.
ZING
ZING
WE SHALL ADMINISTER "PAIN-KILLERS."
GOOD. THEN SEND HER OVER FOR REPAIRS.
ZING

The girl has a mechanical body. However, she is still an adolescent child.

GUNSLINGER GIRL.

ガンスリンガー・ガール

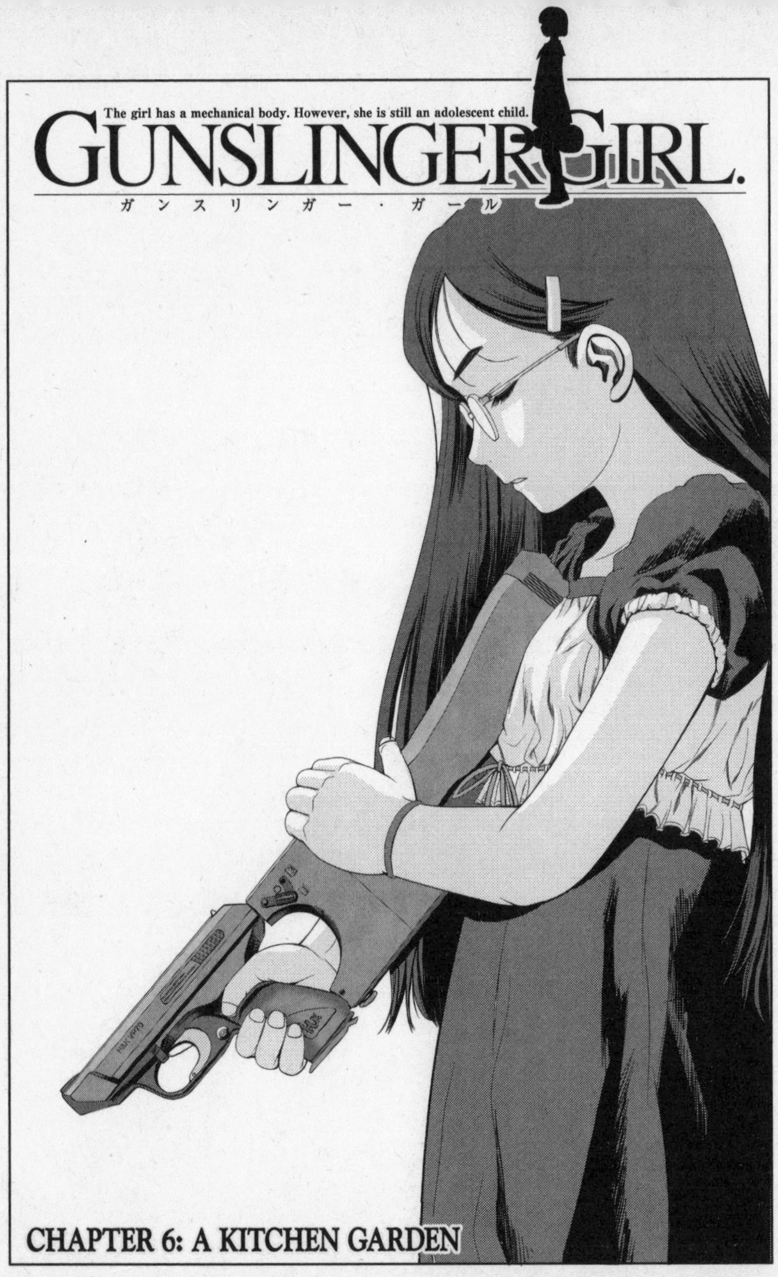

CHAPTER 6: A KITCHEN GARDEN

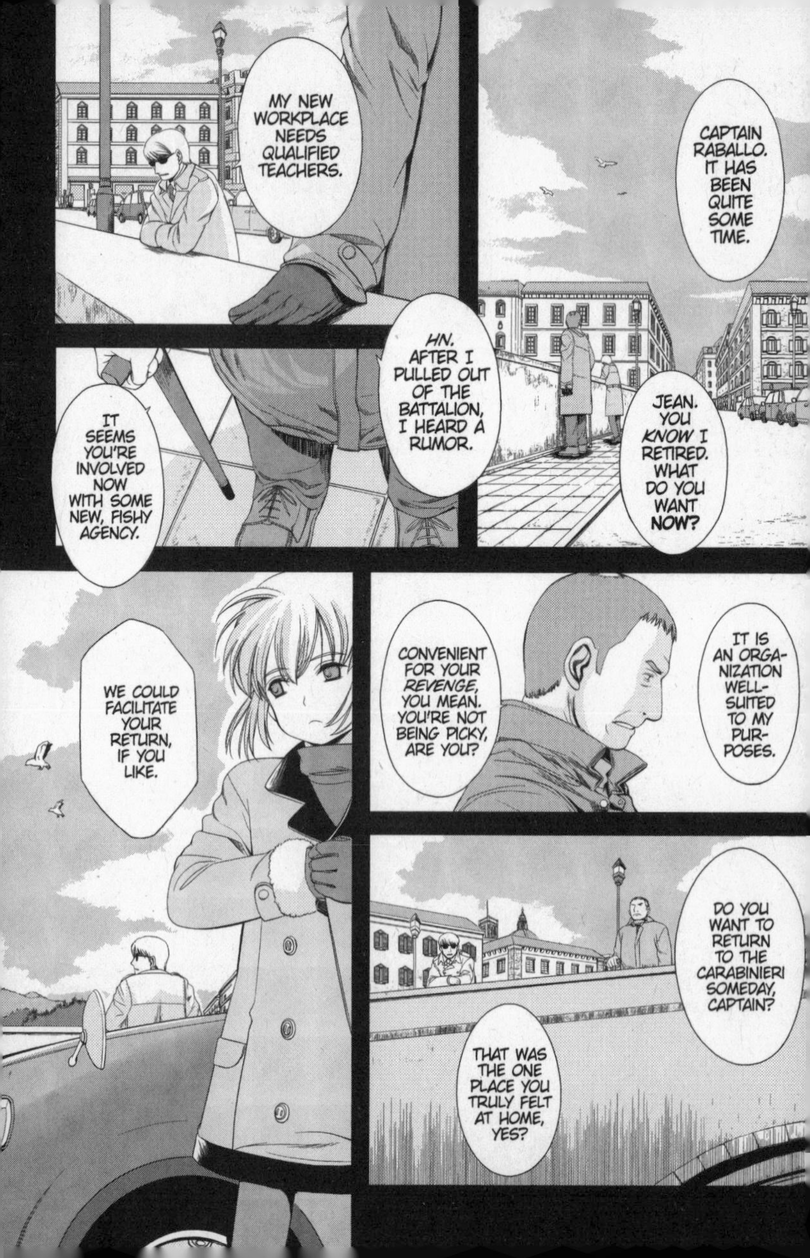
CAPTAIN RABALLO. IT HAS BEEN QUITE SOME TIME.
JEAN. YOU *KNOW* I RETIRED. WHAT DO YOU WANT **NOW?**
MY NEW WORKPLACE NEEDS QUALIFIED TEACHERS.
HN. AFTER I PULLED OUT OF THE BATTALION, I HEARD A RUMOR.
IT SEEMS YOU'RE INVOLVED NOW WITH SOME NEW, FISHY AGENCY.
IT IS AN ORGA-NIZATION WELL-SUITED TO MY PUR-POSES.
CONVENIENT FOR YOUR *REVENGE*, YOU MEAN. YOU'RE NOT BEING PICKY, ARE YOU?
DO YOU WANT TO RETURN TO THE CARABINIERI SOMEDAY, CAPTAIN?
THAT WAS THE ONE PLACE YOU TRULY FELT AT HOME, YES?
WE COULD FACILITATE YOUR RETURN, IF YOU LIKE.

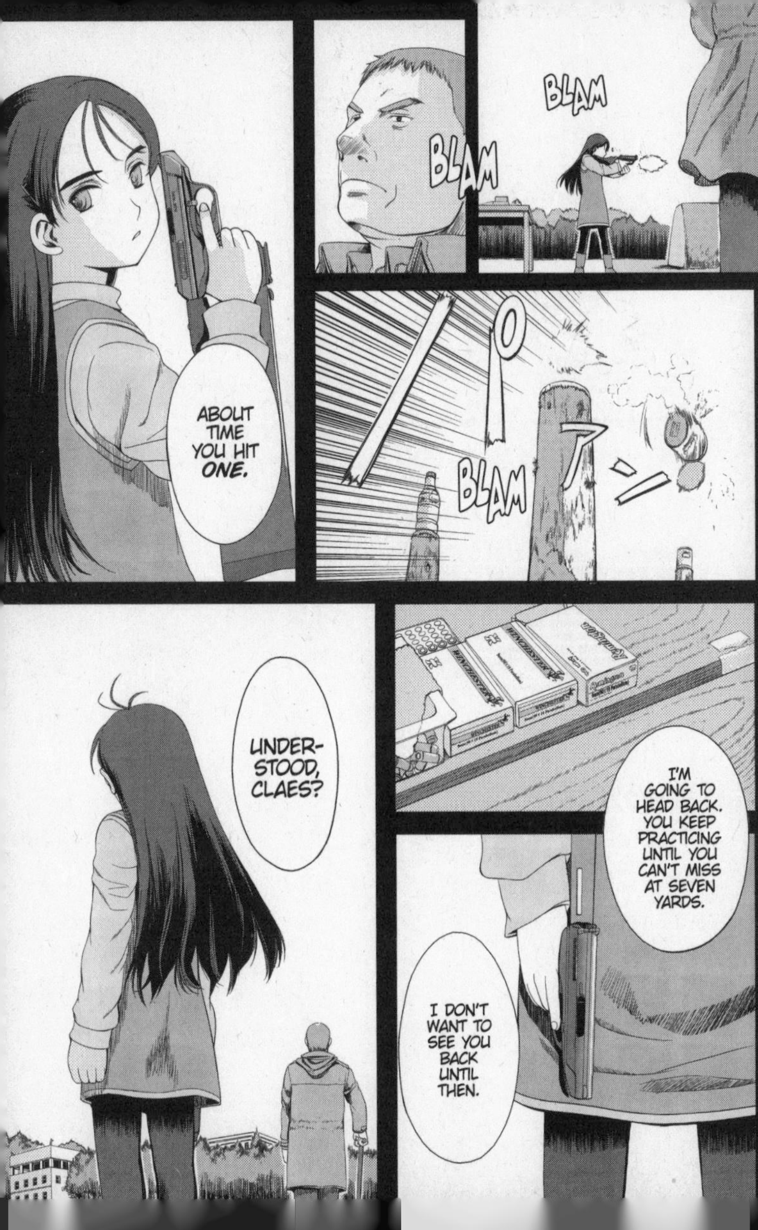
BLAM
BLAM
BLAM
ABOUT TIME YOU HIT ONE.
I'M GOING TO HEAD BACK. YOU KEEP PRACTICING UNTIL YOU CAN'T MISS AT SEVEN YARDS.
I DON'T WANT TO SEE YOU BACK UNTIL THEN.
UNDER-STOOD, CLAES?

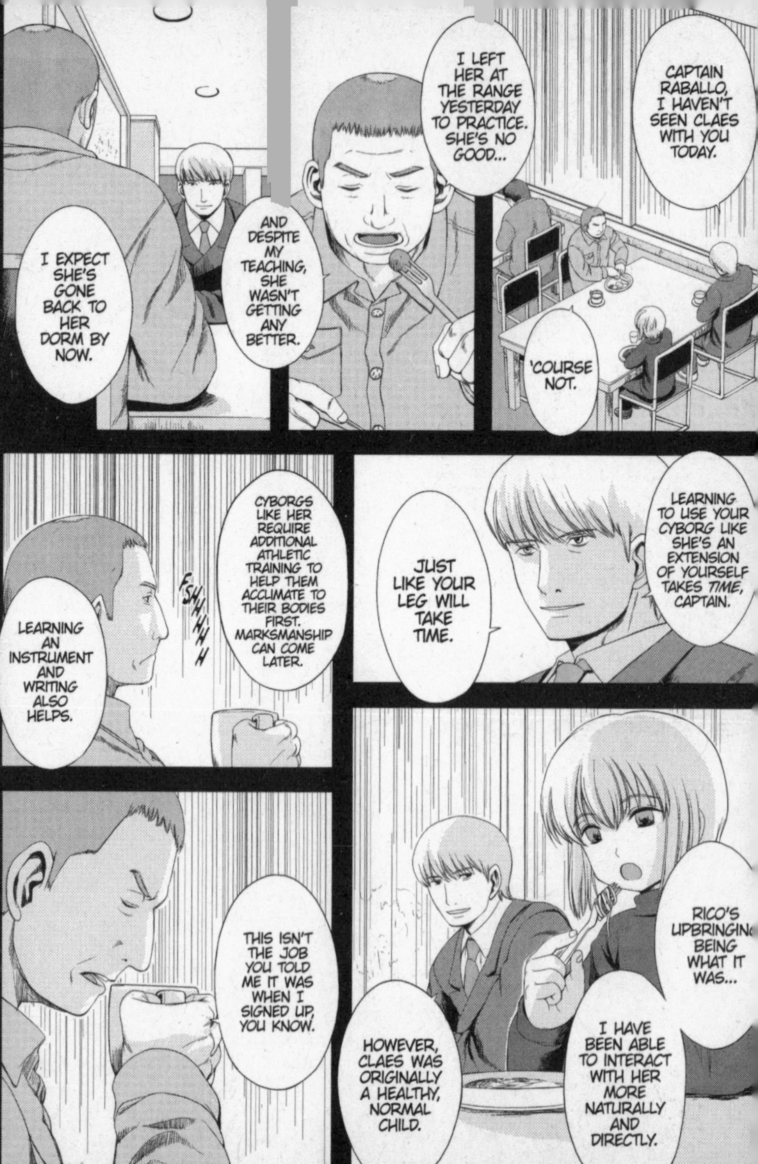
CAPTAIN RABALLO, I HAVEN'T SEEN CLAES WITH YOU TODAY.
'COURSE NOT.
I LEFT HER AT THE RANGE YESTERDAY TO PRACTICE. SHE'S NO GOOD...
AND DESPITE MY TEACHING, SHE WASN'T GETTING ANY BETTER.
I EXPECT SHE'S GONE BACK TO HER DORM BY NOW.
LEARNING TO USE YOUR CYBORG LIKE SHE'S AN EXTENSION OF YOURSELF TAKES *TIME*, CAPTAIN.
JUST LIKE YOUR LEG WILL TAKE TIME.
CYBORGS LIKE HER REQUIRE ADDITIONAL ATHLETIC TRAINING TO HELP THEM ACCLIMATE TO THEIR BODIES FIRST. MARKSMANSHIP CAN COME LATER.
FSHHHHH
LEARNING AN INSTRUMENT AND WRITING ALSO HELPS.
RICO'S UPBRINGIN BEING WHAT IT WAS...
I HAVE BEEN ABLE TO INTERACT WITH HER MORE NATURALLY AND DIRECTLY.
HOWEVER, CLAES WAS ORIGINALLY A HEALTHY, NORMAL CHILD.
THIS ISN'T THE JOB YOU TOLD ME IT WAS WHEN I SIGNED UP, YOU KNOW.

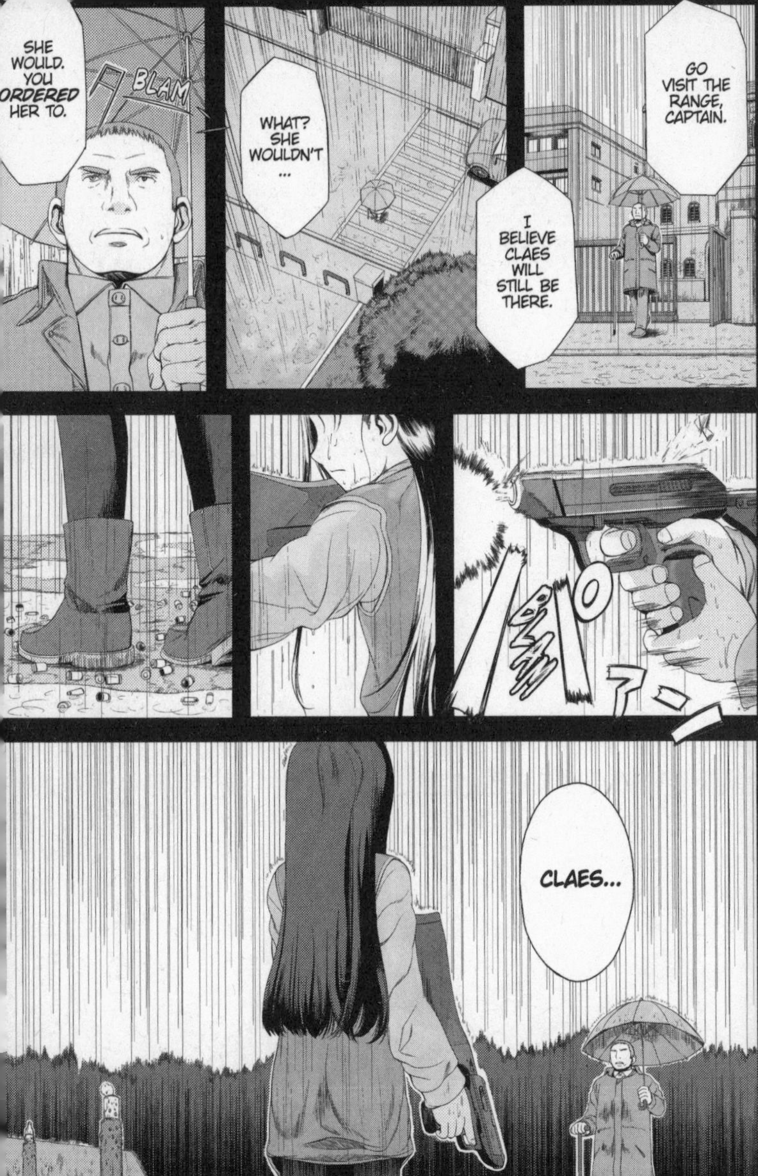
GO VISIT THE RANGE, CAPTAIN.
I BELIEVE CLAES WILL STILL BE THERE.
WHAT? SHE WOULDN'T ...
BLAM
SHE WOULD. YOU ORDERED HER TO.
BLAM
CLAES...

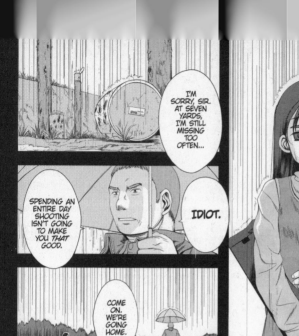

SIGNORE RABALLO...
I'M SORRY, SIR. AT SEVEN YARDS, I'M STILL MISSING TOO OFTEN...
IDIOT.
SPENDING AN ENTIRE DAY SHOOTING ISN'T GOING TO MAKE YOU *THAT* GOOD.
COME ON. WE'RE GOING HOME.
Fleda-Claes-Johansson 10 anni

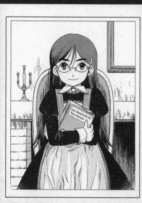

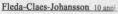

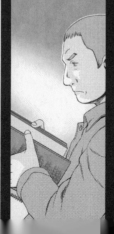

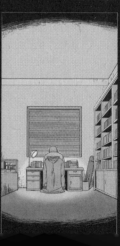

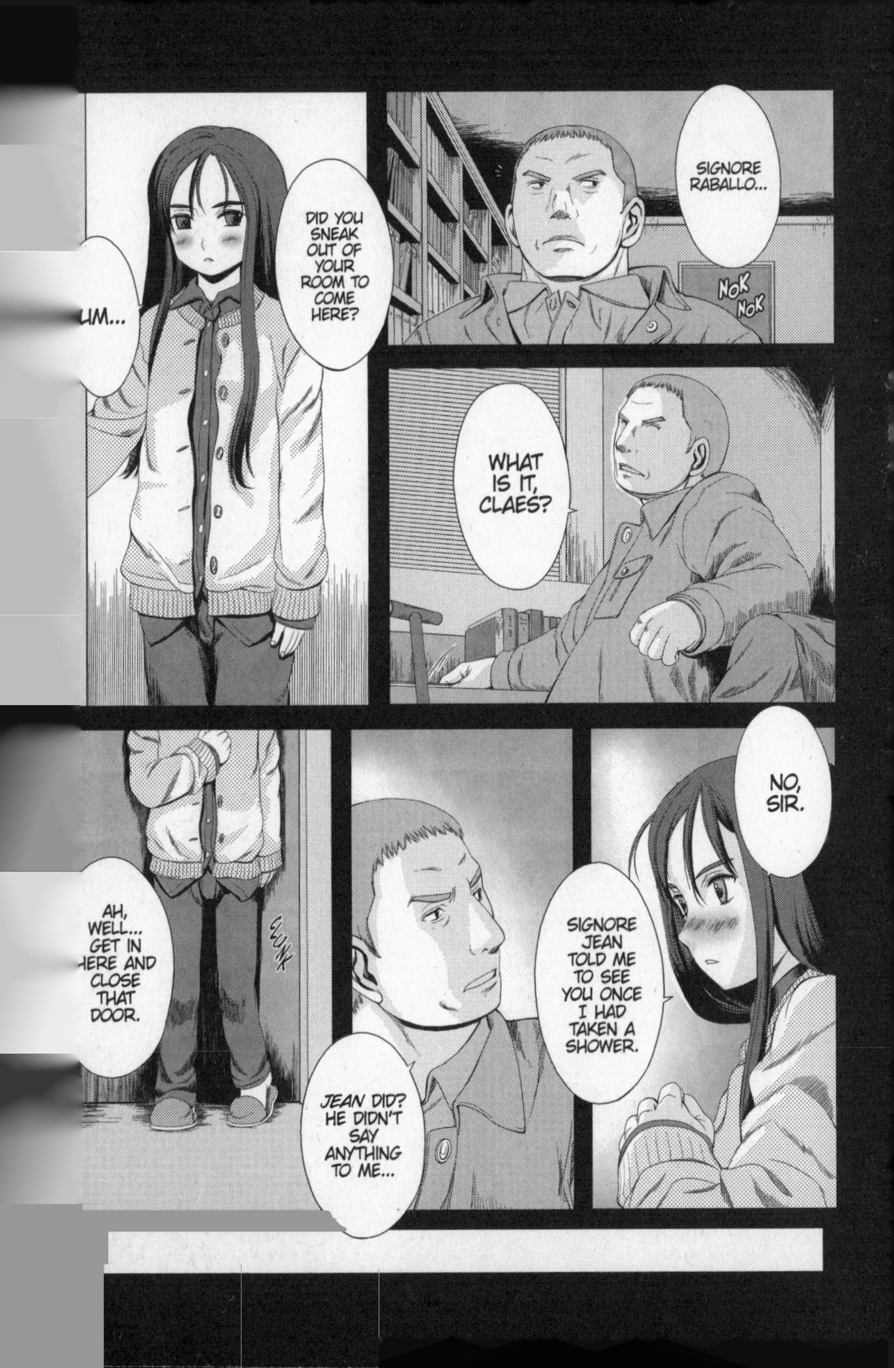
SIGNORE RABALLO...
NOK NOK
WHAT IS IT, CLAES?
DID YOU SNEAK OUT OF YOUR ROOM TO COME HERE?
UM...
NO, SIR.
SIGNORE JEAN TOLD ME TO SEE YOU ONCE I HAD TAKEN A SHOWER.
JEAN DID? HE DIDN'T SAY ANYTHING TO ME...
AH, WELL... GET IN HERE AND CLOSE THAT DOOR.
CLUNK

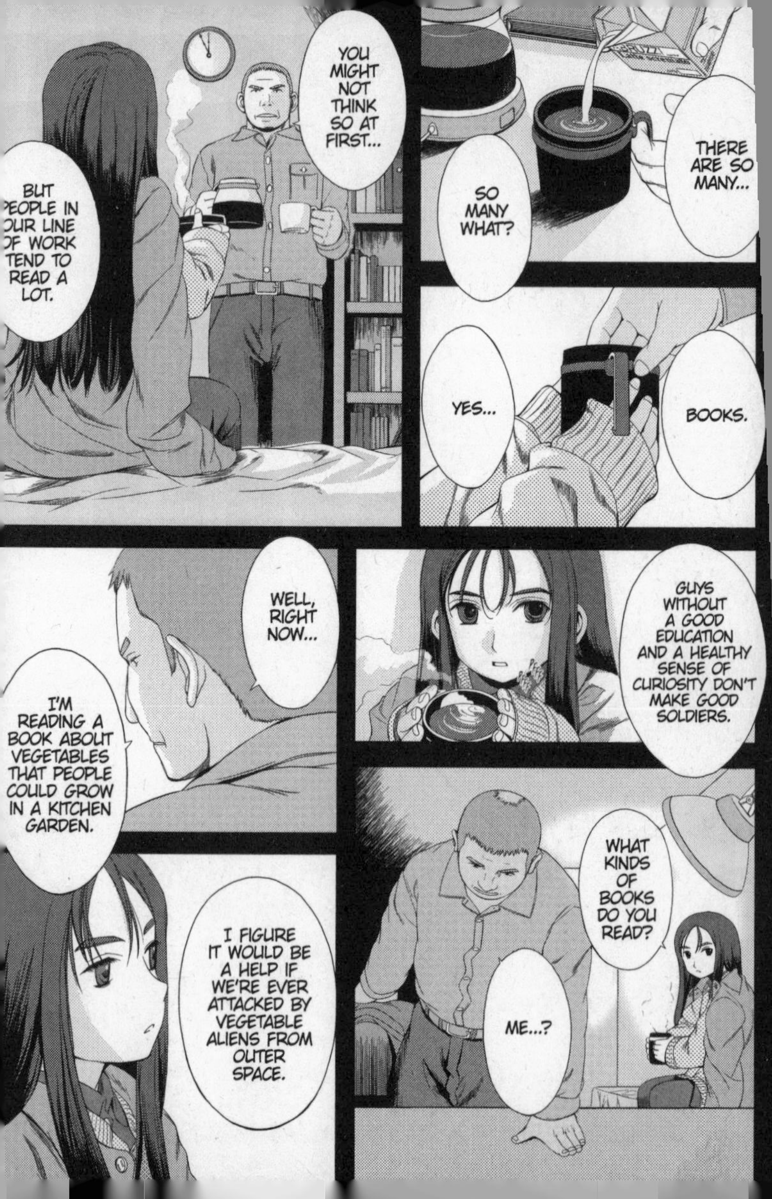
THERE ARE SO MANY...
SO MANY WHAT?
BOOKS.
YES...
YOU MIGHT NOT THINK SO AT FIRST...
BUT PEOPLE IN OUR LINE OF WORK TEND TO READ A LOT.
GUYS WITHOUT A GOOD EDUCATION AND A HEALTHY SENSE OF CURIOSITY DON'T MAKE GOOD SOLDIERS.
WHAT KINDS OF BOOKS DO YOU READ?
ME...?
WELL, RIGHT NOW...
I'M READING A BOOK ABOUT VEGETABLES THAT PEOPLE COULD GROW IN A KITCHEN GARDEN.
I FIGURE IT WOULD BE A HELP IF WE'RE EVER ATTACKED BY VEGETABLE ALIENS FROM OUTER SPACE.

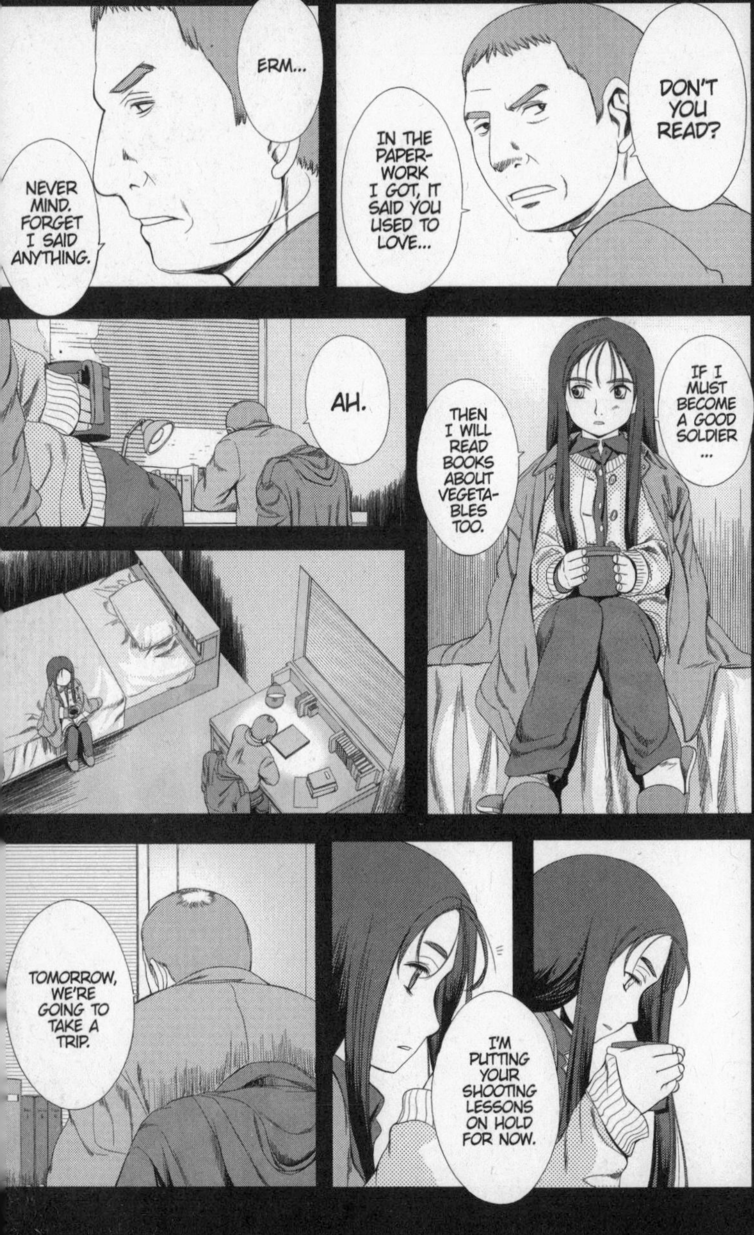
DON'T YOU READ?
IN THE PAPER-WORK I GOT, IT SAID YOU USED TO LOVE...
ERM...
NEVER MIND. FORGET I SAID ANYTHING.
IF I MUST BECOME A GOOD SOLDIER ...
THEN I WILL READ BOOKS ABOUT VEGETA-BLES TOO.
AH.
I'M PUTTING YOUR SHOOTING LESSONS ON HOLD FOR NOW.
TOMORROW, WE'RE GOING TO TAKE A TRIP.

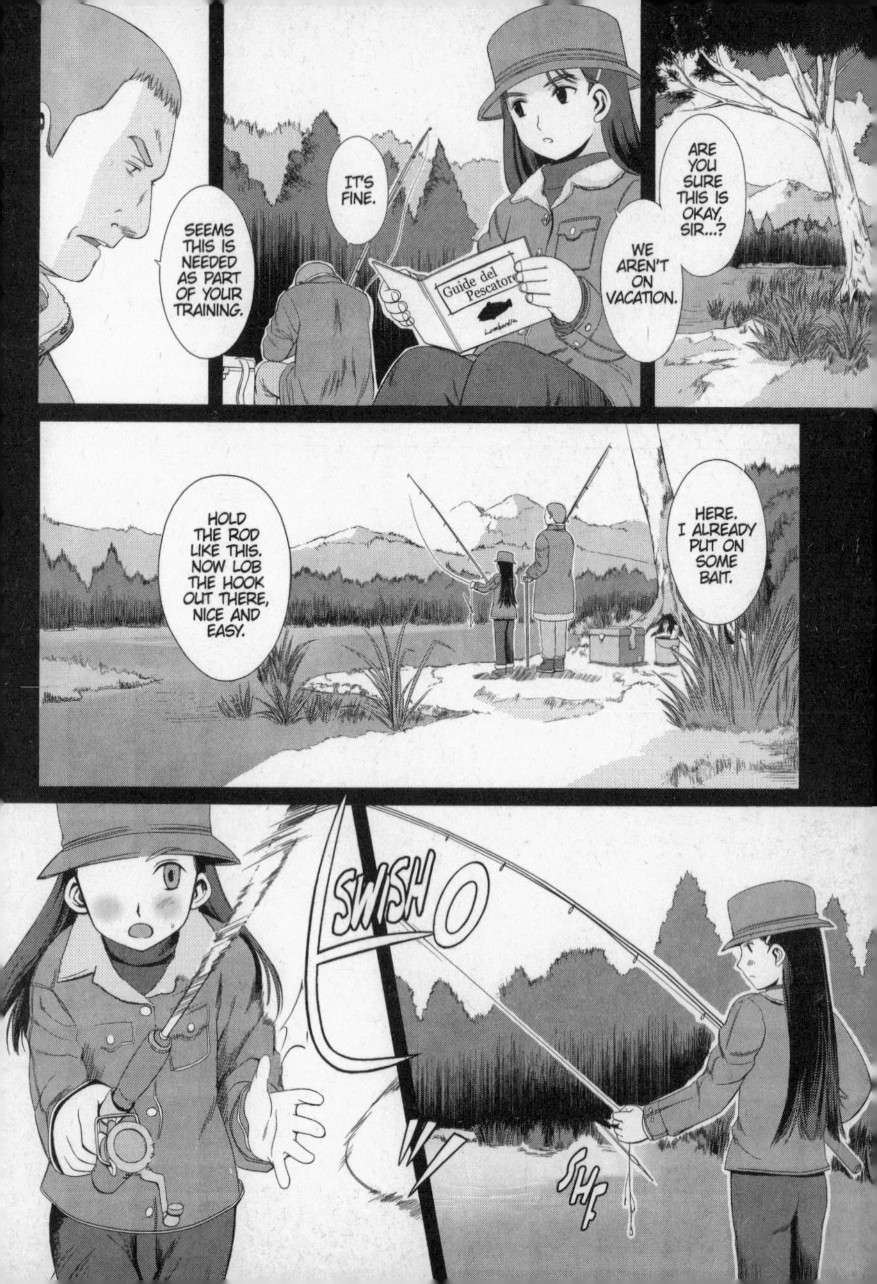
ARE YOU SURE THIS IS OKAY, SIR...?
WE AREN'T ON VACATION.
IT'S FINE.
Guide del Pescator
SEEMS THIS IS NEEDED AS PART OF YOUR TRAINING.
HERE. I ALREADY PUT ON SOME BAIT.
HOLD THE ROD LIKE THIS. NOW LOB THE HOOK OUT THERE, NICE AND EASY.
SWISH
SHF

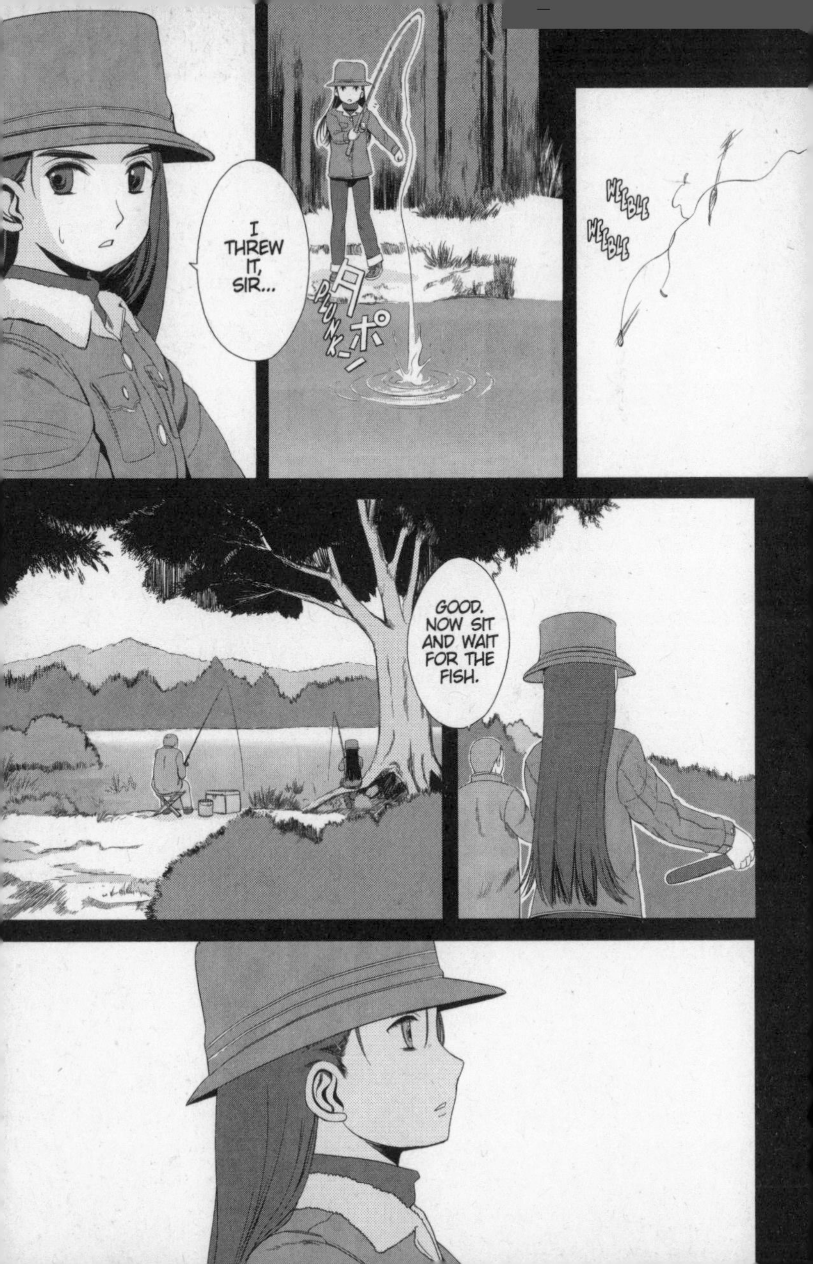
WEEBLE
WEEBLE
PLUNK
I THREW IT, SIR...
GOOD. NOW SIT AND WAIT FOR THE FISH.

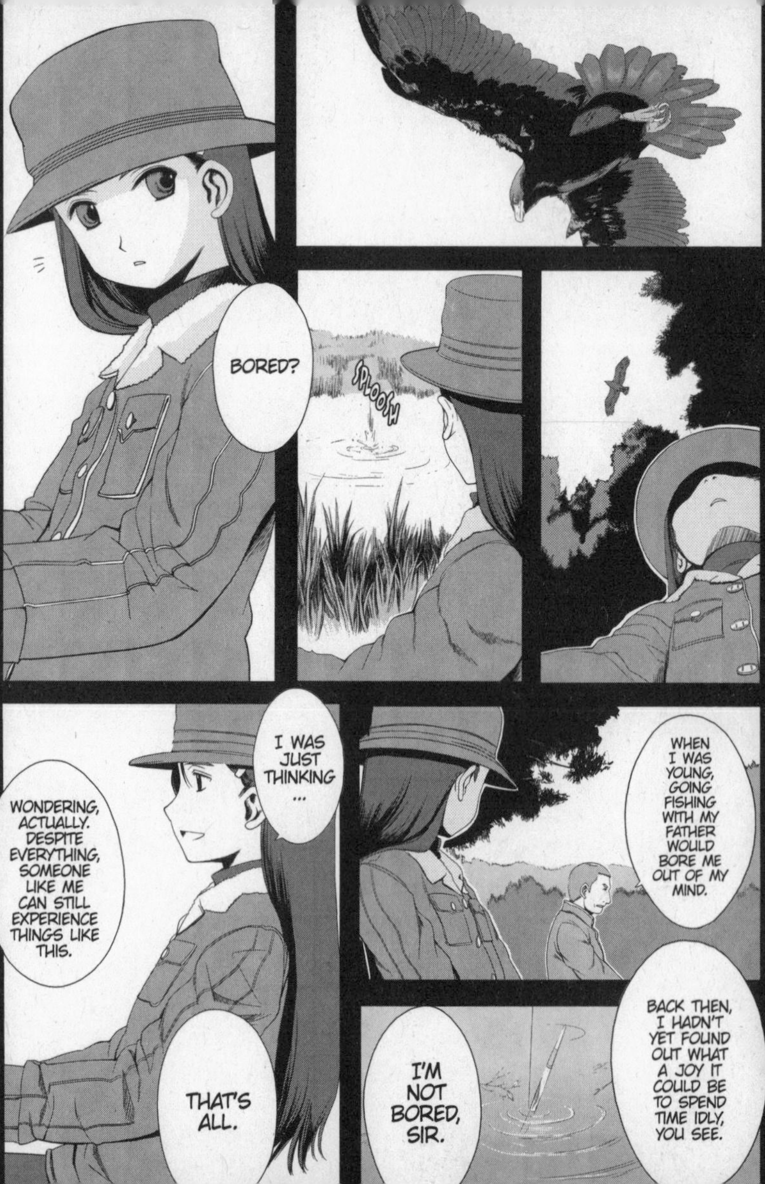
SPLOOSH
BORED?
WHEN I WAS YOUNG, GOING FISHING WITH MY FATHER WOULD BORE ME OUT OF MY MIND.
BACK THEN, I HADN'T YET FOUND OUT WHAT A JOY IT COULD BE TO SPEND TIME IDLY, YOU SEE.
I'M NOT BORED, SIR.
I WAS JUST THINKING ...
WONDERING, ACTUALLY. DESPITE EVERYTHING, SOMEONE LIKE ME CAN STILL EXPERIENCE THINGS LIKE THIS.
THAT'S ALL.

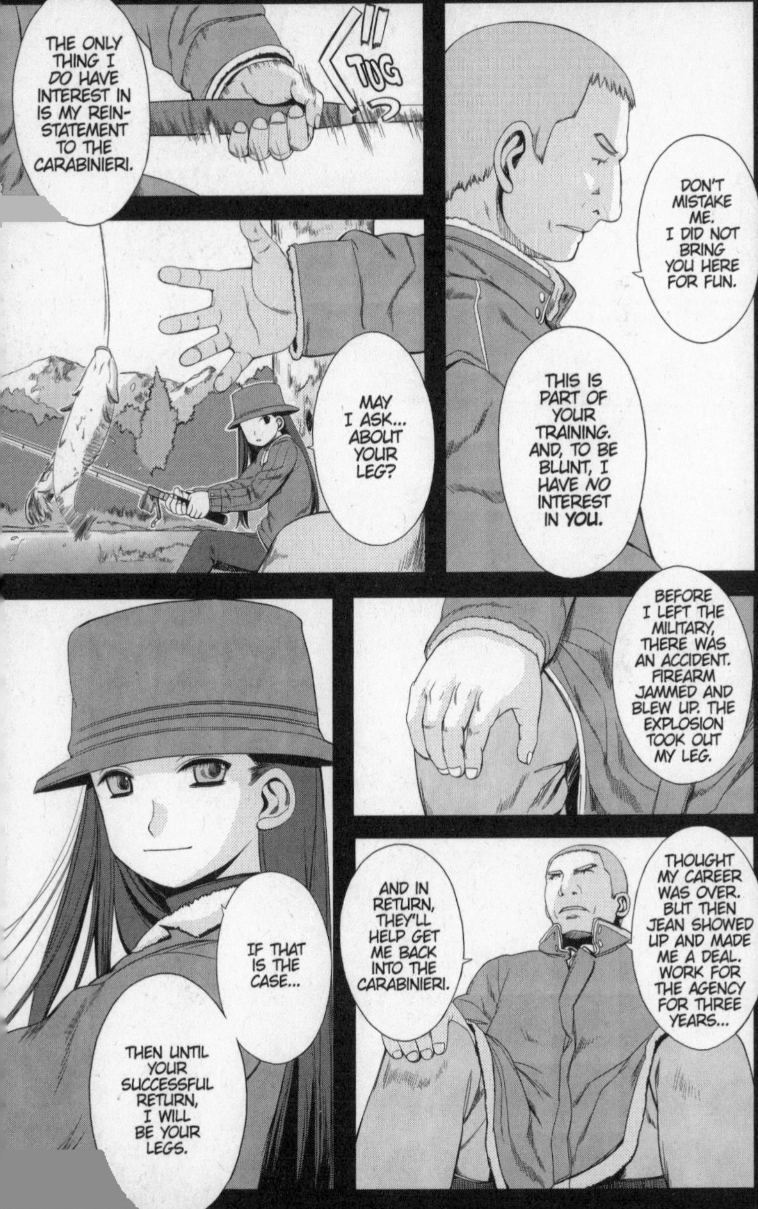
DON'T MISTAKE ME. I DID NOT BRING YOU HERE FOR FUN.
THIS IS PART OF YOUR TRAINING. AND, TO BE BLUNT, I HAVE *NO* INTEREST IN **YOU.**
TUG
THE ONLY THING I *DO* HAVE INTEREST IN IS MY REIN-STATEMENT TO THE CARABINIERI.
MAY I ASK... ABOUT YOUR LEG?
BEFORE I LEFT THE MILITARY, THERE WAS AN ACCIDENT. FIREARM JAMMED AND BLEW UP. THE EXPLOSION TOOK OUT MY LEG.
THOUGHT MY CAREER WAS OVER. BUT THEN JEAN SHOWED UP AND MADE ME A DEAL. WORK FOR THE AGENCY FOR THREE YEARS...
AND IN RETURN, THEY'LL HELP GET ME BACK INTO THE CARABINIERI.
IF THAT IS THE CASE...
THEN UNTIL YOUR SUCCESSFUL RETURN, I WILL BE YOUR LEGS.

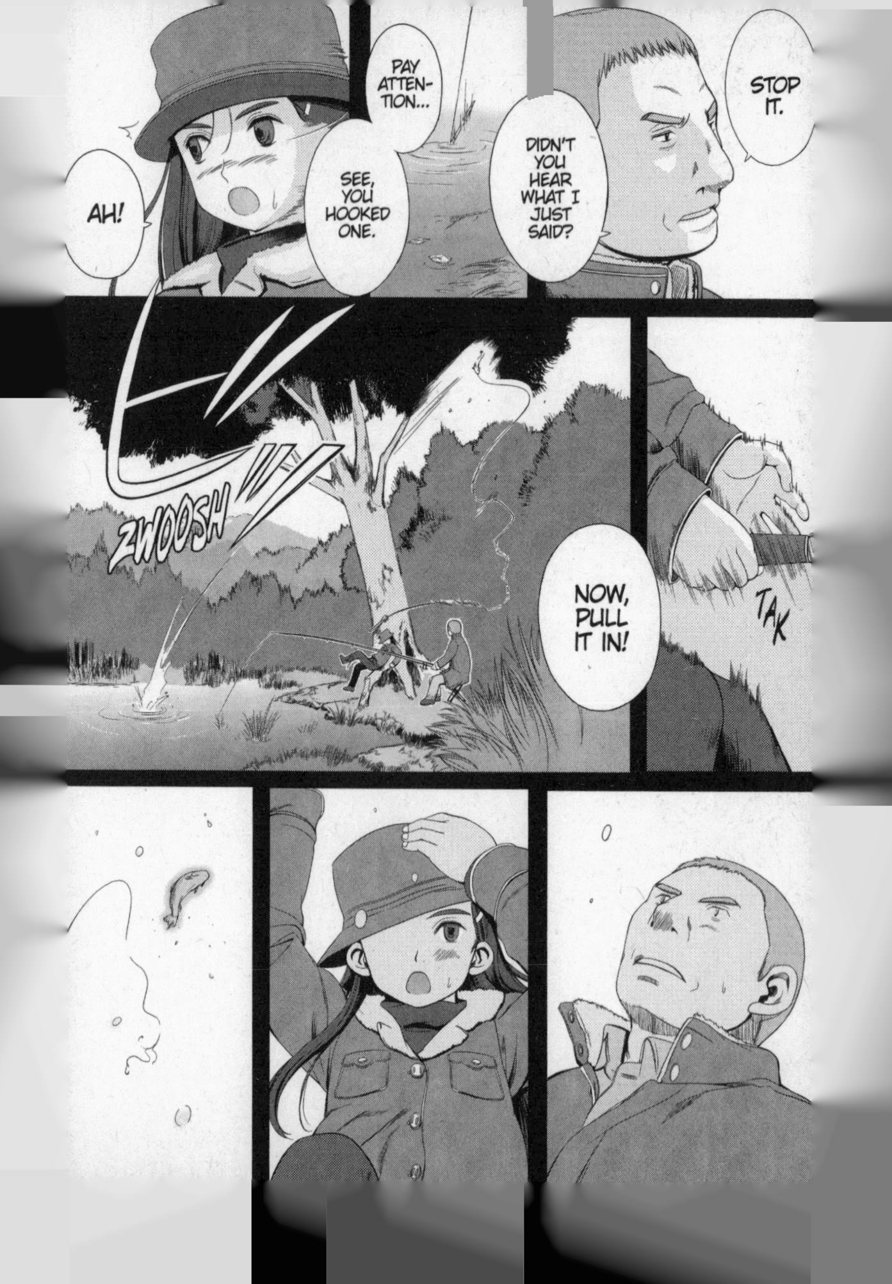
STOP IT.
DIDN'T YOU HEAR WHAT I JUST SAID?
PAY ATTEN-TION...
SEE, YOU HOOKED ONE.
AH!
NOW, PULL IT IN!
TAK
ZWOOSH

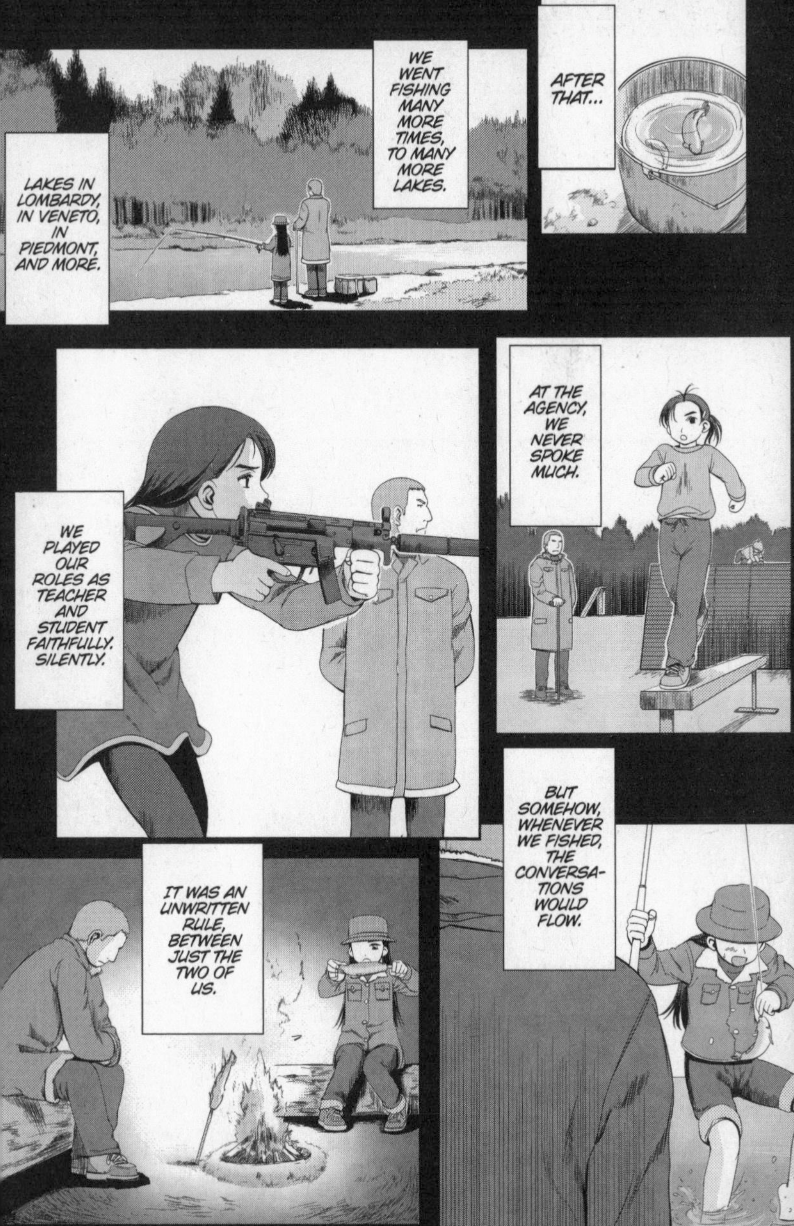
AFTER THAT...
WE WENT FISHING MANY MORE TIMES, TO MANY MORE LAKES.
LAKES IN LOMBARDY, IN VENETO, IN PIEDMONT, AND MORE.
AT THE AGENCY, WE NEVER SPOKE MUCH.
WE PLAYED OUR ROLES AS TEACHER AND STUDENT FAITHFULLY. SILENTLY.
BUT SOMEHOW, WHENEVER WE FISHED, THE CONVERSA-TIONS WOULD FLOW.
IT WAS AN UNWRITTEN RULE, BETWEEN JUST THE TWO OF US.

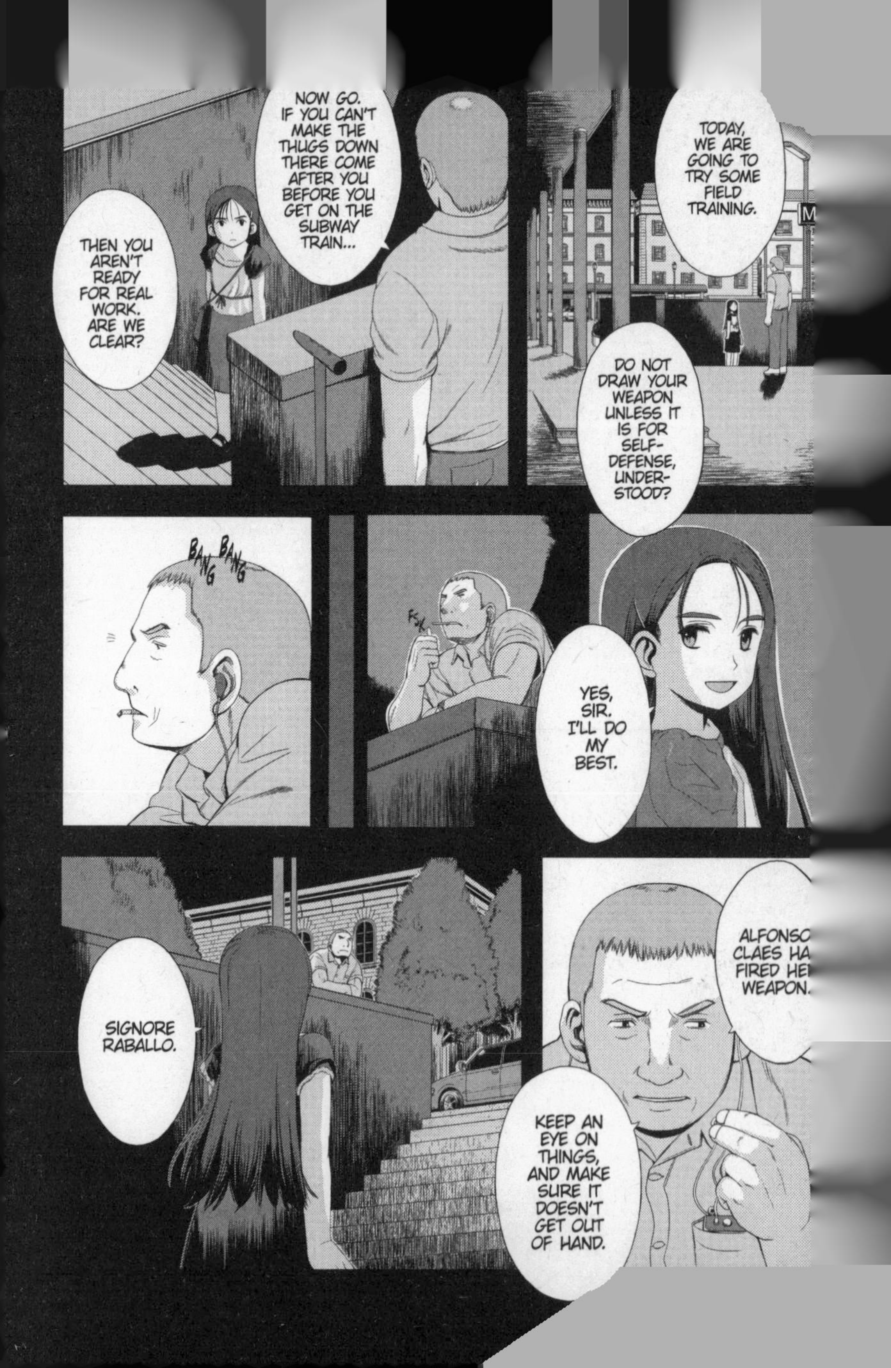
TODAY, WE ARE GOING TO TRY SOME FIELD TRAINING.
DO NOT DRAW YOUR WEAPON UNLESS IT IS FOR SELF-DEFENSE, UNDERSTOOD?
NOW GO. IF YOU CAN'T MAKE THE THUGS DOWN THERE COME AFTER YOU BEFORE YOU GET ON THE SUBWAY TRAIN...
THEN YOU AREN'T READY FOR REAL WORK. ARE WE CLEAR?
YES, SIR. I'LL DO MY BEST.
FSK
BANG BANG
ALFONSO CLAES HA FIRED HE WEAPON.
KEEP AN EYE ON THINGS, AND MAKE SURE IT DOESN'T GET OUT OF HAND.
SIGNORE RABALLO.

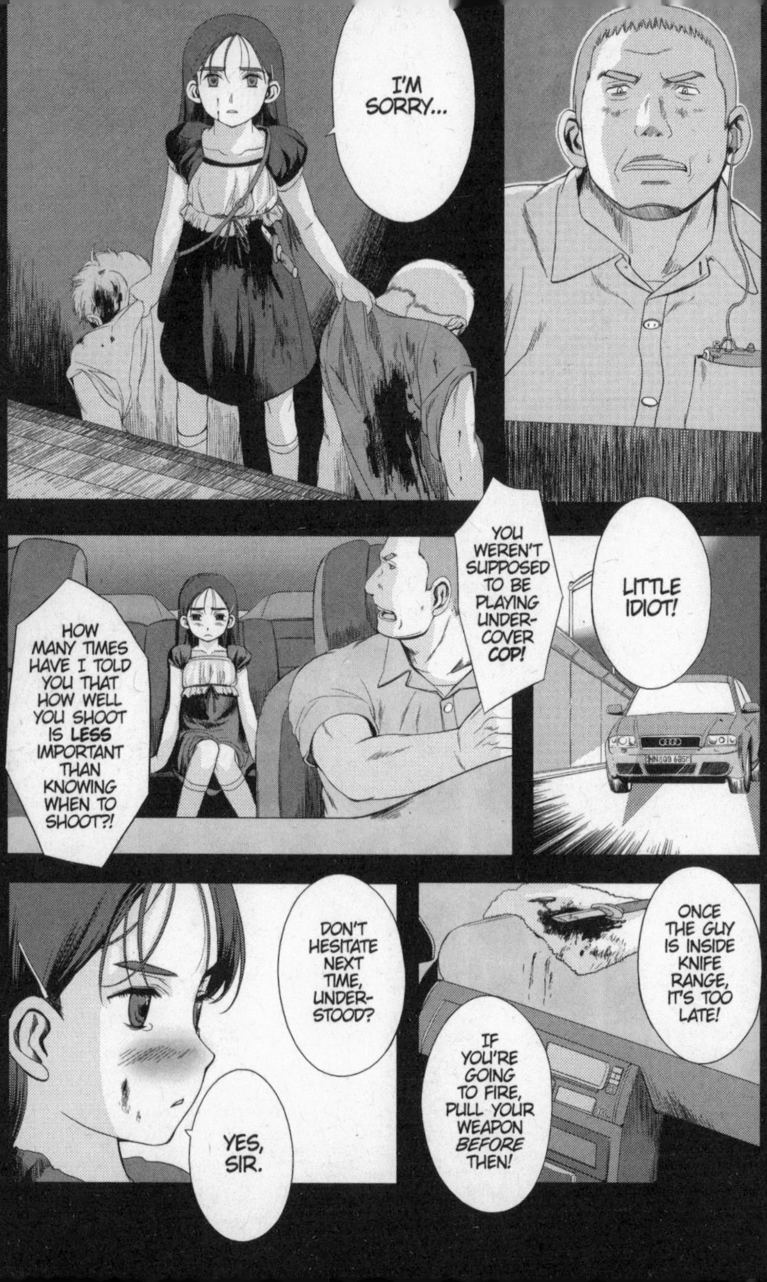
I'M SORRY...
LITTLE IDIOT!
YOU WEREN'T SUPPOSED TO BE PLAYING UNDER-COVER COP!
HOW MANY TIMES HAVE I TOLD YOU THAT HOW WELL YOU SHOOT IS LESS IMPORTANT THAN KNOWING WHEN TO SHOOT?!
ONCE THE GUY IS INSIDE KNIFE RANGE, IT'S TOO LATE!
IF YOU'RE GOING TO FIRE, PULL YOUR WEAPON *BEFORE* THEN!
DON'T HESITATE NEXT TIME, UNDER-STOOD?
YES, SIR.

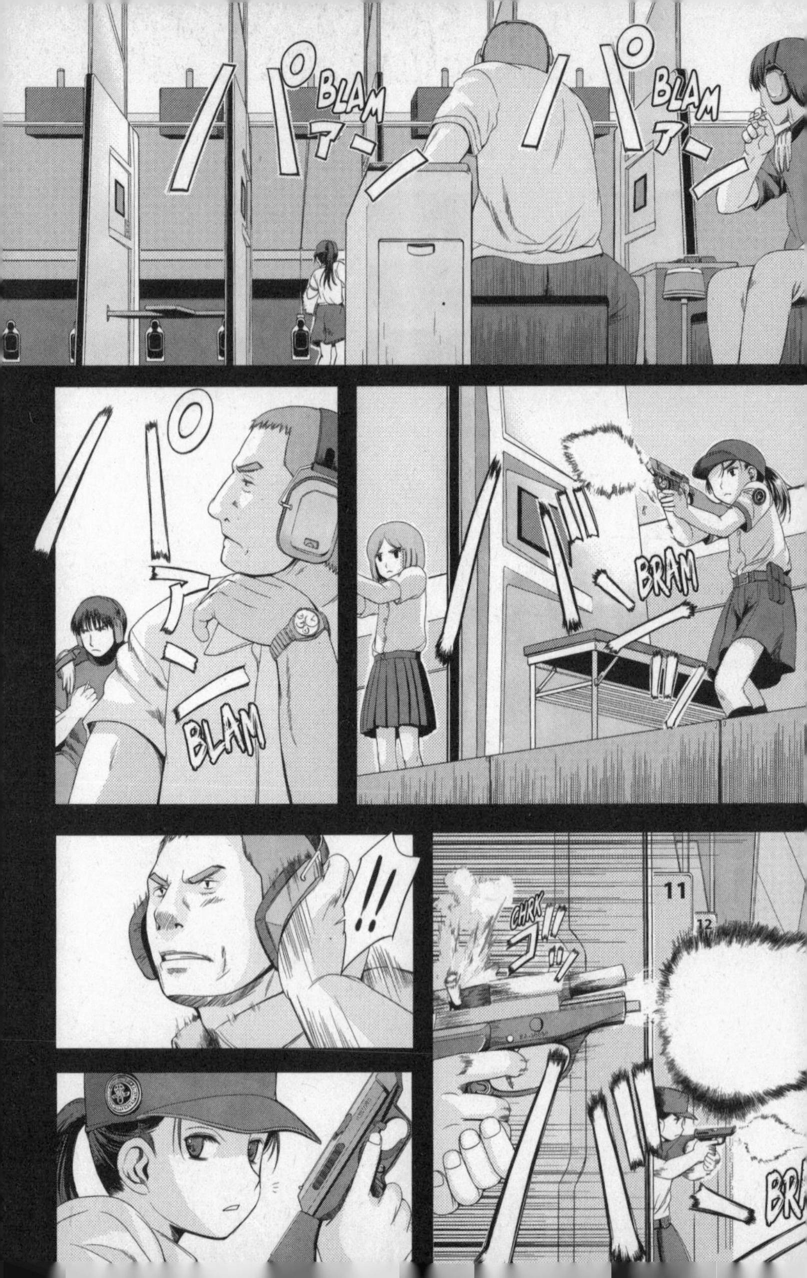
BLAM
BLAM
BRAM
BLAM
11
12
CHRK
!!

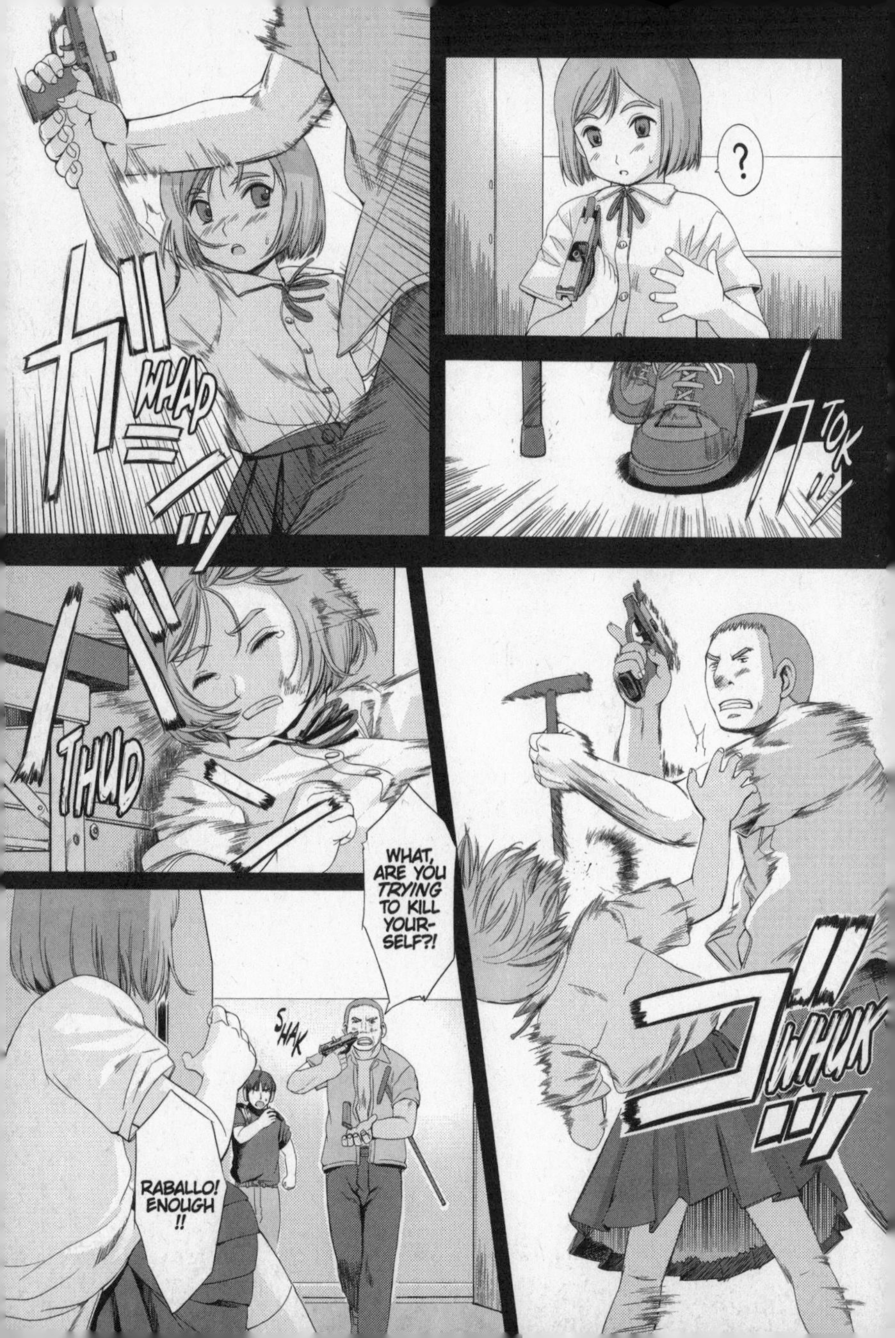
?
TOK
WHAP
WHUK
THUD
WHAT, ARE YOU TRYING TO KILL YOURSELF?!
SHAK
RABALLO! ENOUGH!!

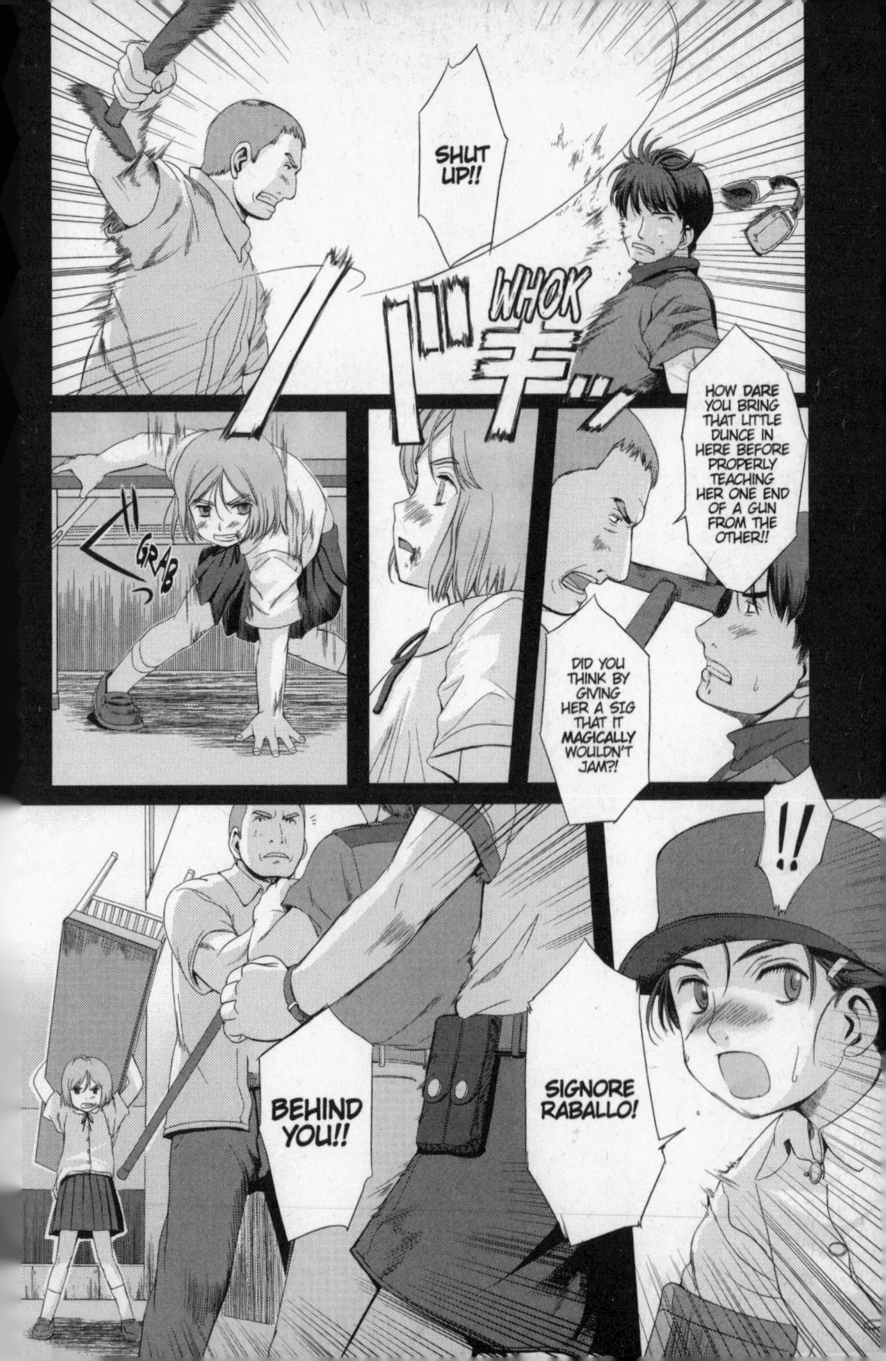
SHUT UP!!
WHOK
HOW DARE YOU BRING THAT LITTLE DUNCE IN HERE BEFORE PROPERLY TEACHING HER ONE END OF A GUN FROM THE OTHER!!
DID YOU THINK BY GIVING HER A SIG THAT IT MAGICALLY WOULDN'T JAM?!
GRAB
!!
SIGNORE RABALLO!
BEHIND YOU!!

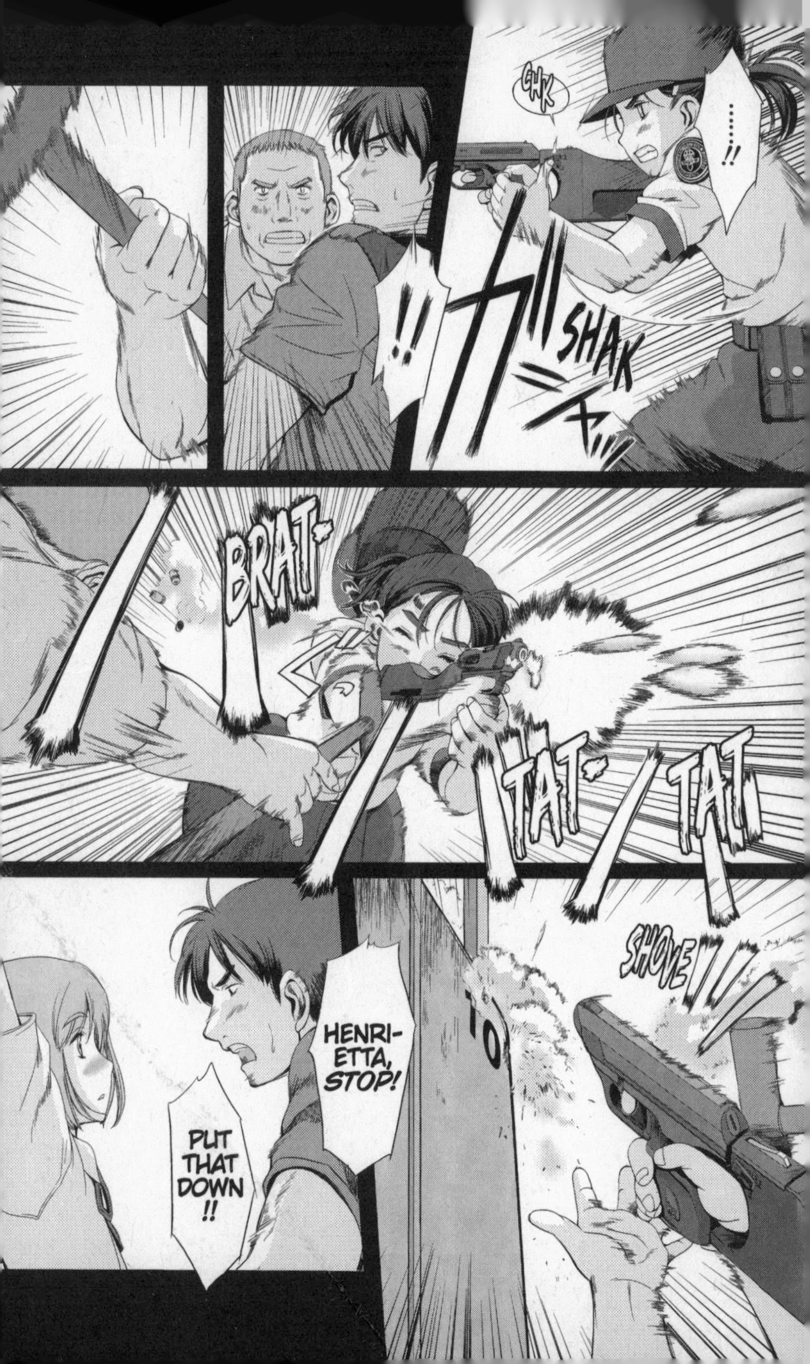
GHK
......!!
SHAK
!!
BRAT-
TAT-
TAT
SHOVE
HENRI-ETTA, STOP!
PUT THAT DOWN !!

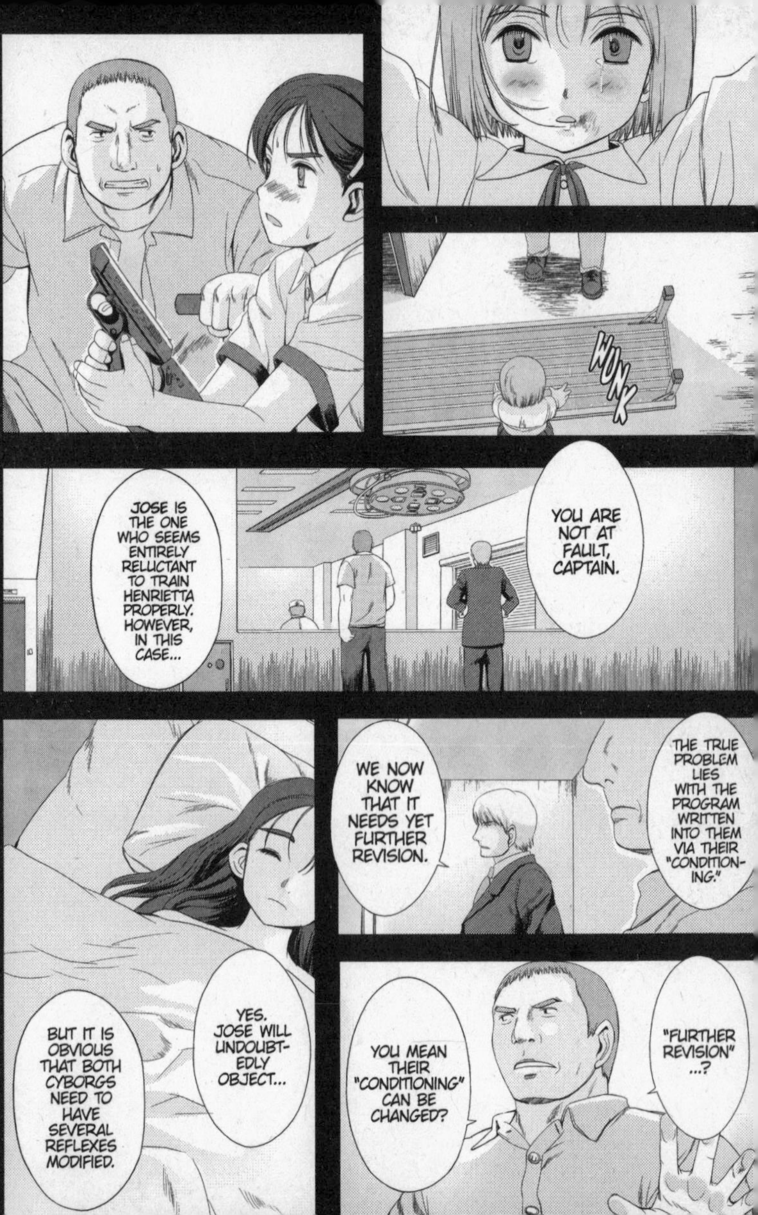
WUNK
YOU ARE NOT AT FAULT, CAPTAIN.
JOSE IS THE ONE WHO SEEMS ENTIRELY RELUCTANT TO TRAIN HENRIETTA PROPERLY. HOWEVER, IN THIS CASE...
THE TRUE PROBLEM LIES WITH THE PROGRAM WRITTEN INTO THEM VIA THEIR "CONDITIONING."
WE NOW KNOW THAT IT NEEDS YET FURTHER REVISION.
"FURTHER REVISION" ...?
YOU MEAN THEIR "CONDITIONING" CAN BE CHANGED?
YES. JOSE WILL UNDOUBTEDLY OBJECT...
BUT IT IS OBVIOUS THAT BOTH CYBORGS NEED TO HAVE SEVERAL REFLEXES MODIFIED.

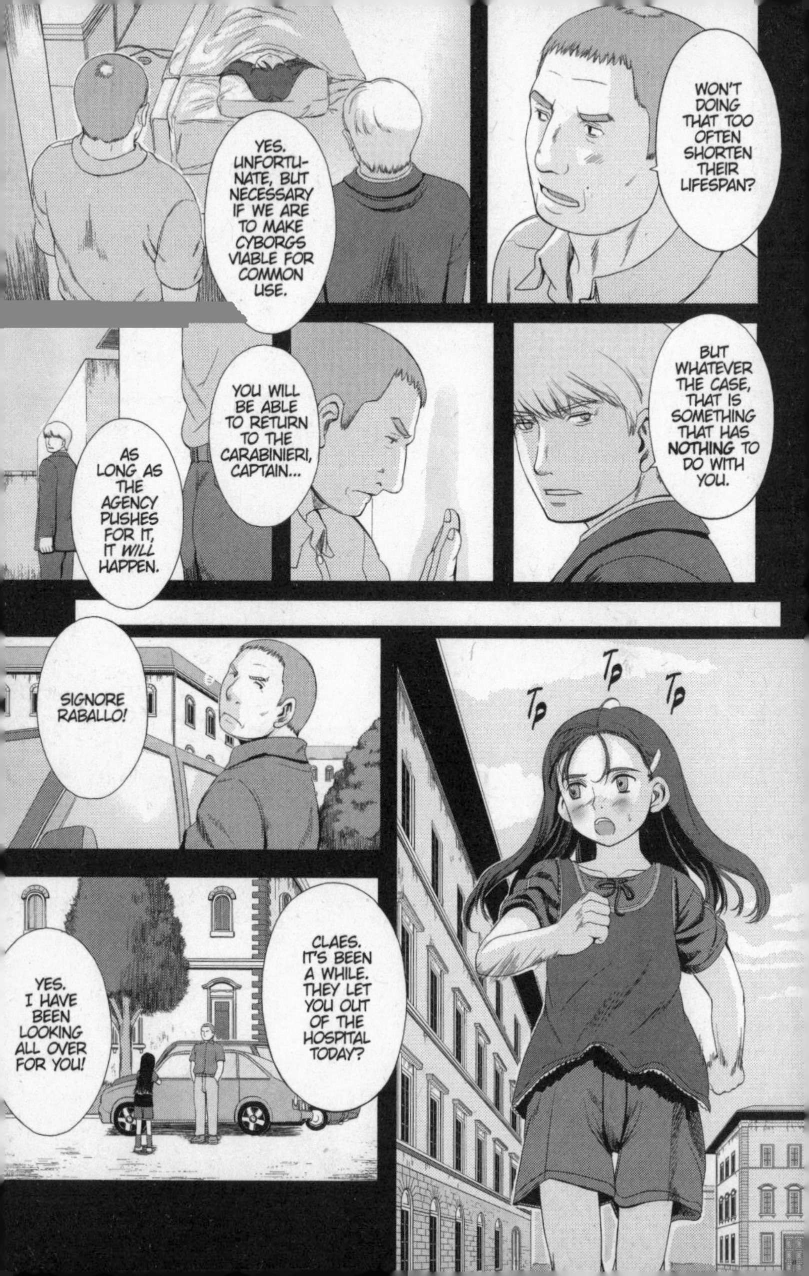
WON'T DOING THAT TOO OFTEN SHORTEN THEIR LIFESPAN?
YES. UNFORTUNATE, BUT NECESSARY IF WE ARE TO MAKE CYBORGS VIABLE FOR COMMON USE.
BUT WHATEVER THE CASE, THAT IS SOMETHING THAT HAS **NOTHING** TO DO WITH YOU.
YOU WILL BE ABLE TO RETURN TO THE CARABINIERI, CAPTAIN...
AS LONG AS THE AGENCY PUSHES FOR IT, IT *WILL* HAPPEN.
Tp
Tp
Tp
SIGNORE RABALLO!
CLAES. IT'S BEEN A WHILE. THEY LET YOU OUT OF THE HOSPITAL TODAY?
YES. I HAVE BEEN LOOKING ALL OVER FOR YOU!

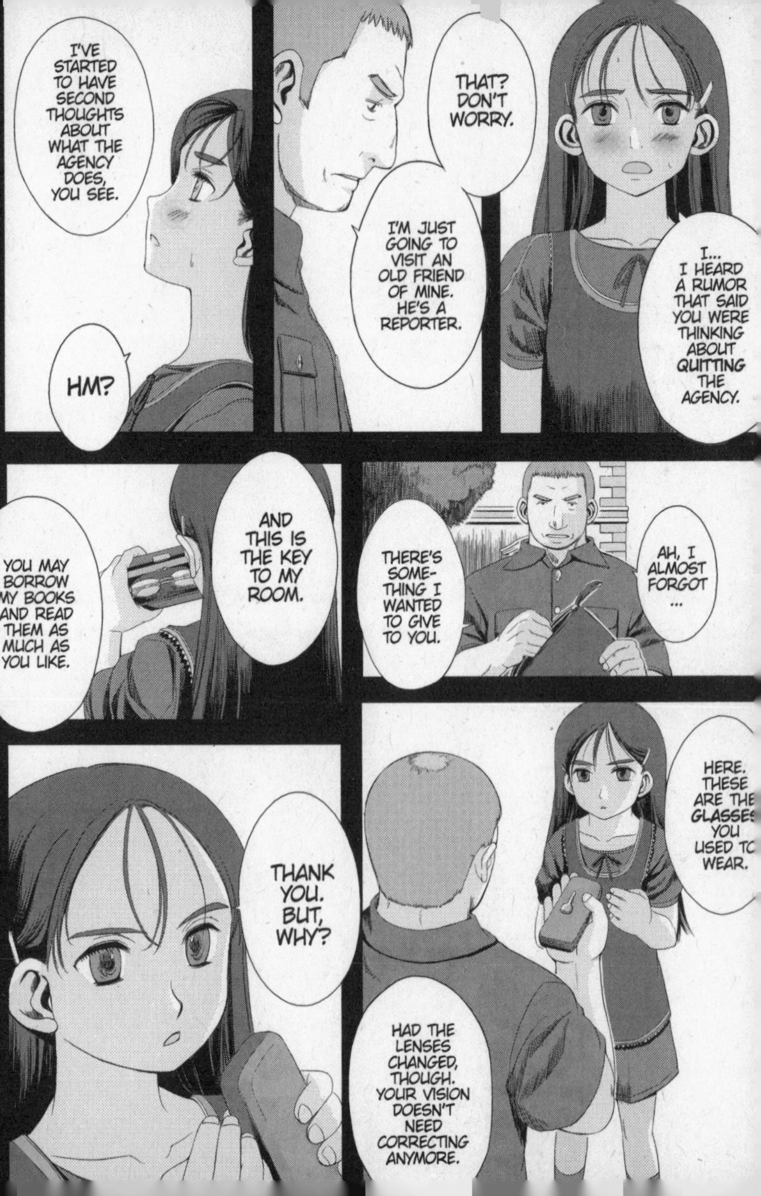
I... I HEARD A RUMOR THAT SAID YOU WERE THINKING ABOUT QUITTING THE AGENCY.
THAT? DON'T WORRY.
I'M JUST GOING TO VISIT AN OLD FRIEND OF MINE. HE'S A REPORTER.
I'VE STARTED TO HAVE SECOND THOUGHTS ABOUT WHAT THE AGENCY DOES, YOU SEE.
HM?
AH, I ALMOST FORGOT ...
THERE'S SOME-THING I WANTED TO GIVE TO YOU.
AND THIS IS THE KEY TO MY ROOM.
YOU MAY BORROW MY BOOKS AND READ THEM AS MUCH AS YOU LIKE.
HERE. THESE ARE THE GLASSES YOU USED TO WEAR.
HAD THE LENSES CHANGED, THOUGH. YOUR VISION DOESN'T NEED CORRECTING ANYMORE.
THANK YOU. BUT, WHY?

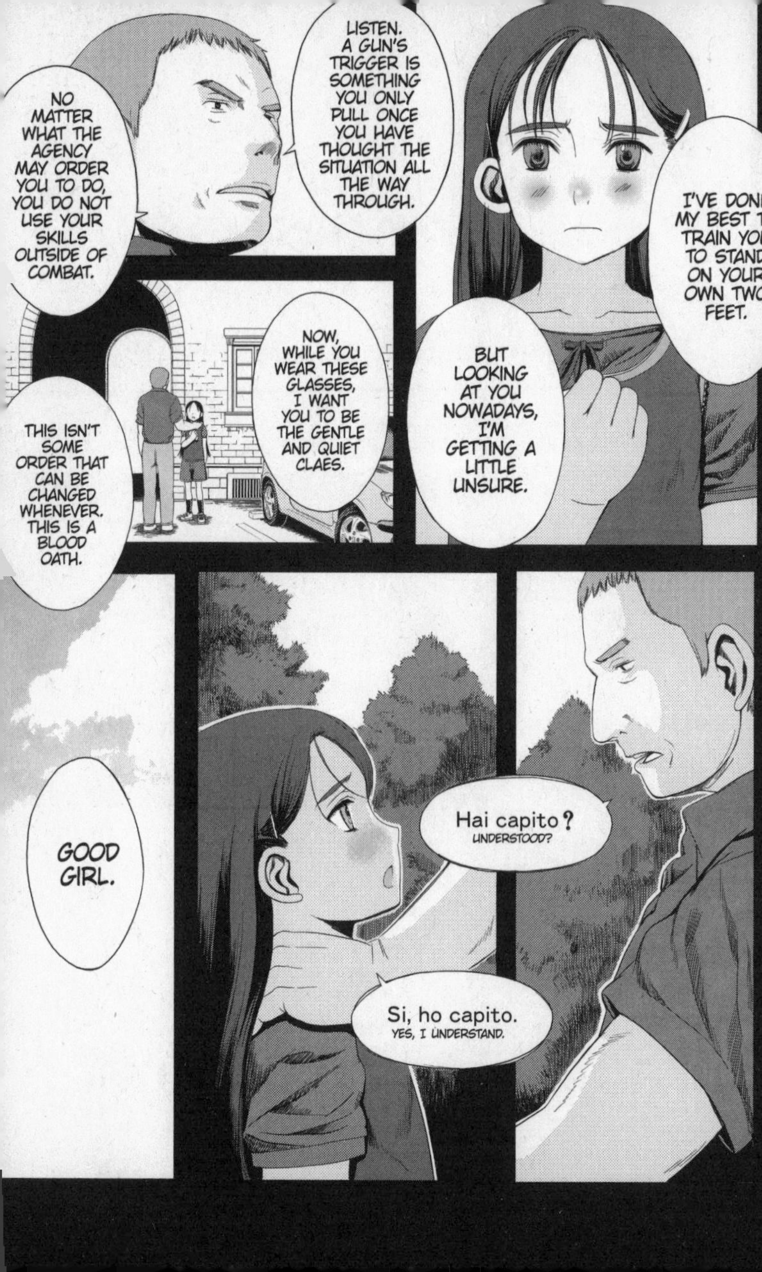
I'VE DONE MY BEST TO TRAIN YOU TO STAND ON YOUR OWN TWO FEET.
BUT LOOKING AT YOU NOWADAYS, I'M GETTING A LITTLE UNSURE.
LISTEN. A GUN'S TRIGGER IS SOMETHING YOU ONLY PULL ONCE YOU HAVE THOUGHT THE SITUATION ALL THE WAY THROUGH.
NO MATTER WHAT THE AGENCY MAY ORDER YOU TO DO, YOU DO NOT USE YOUR SKILLS OUTSIDE OF COMBAT.
NOW, WHILE YOU WEAR THESE GLASSES, I WANT YOU TO BE THE GENTLE AND QUIET CLAES.
THIS ISN'T SOME ORDER THAT CAN BE CHANGED WHENEVER. THIS IS A BLOOD OATH.
Hai capito?
UNDERSTOOD?
Si, ho capito.
YES, I UNDERSTAND.
GOOD GIRL.

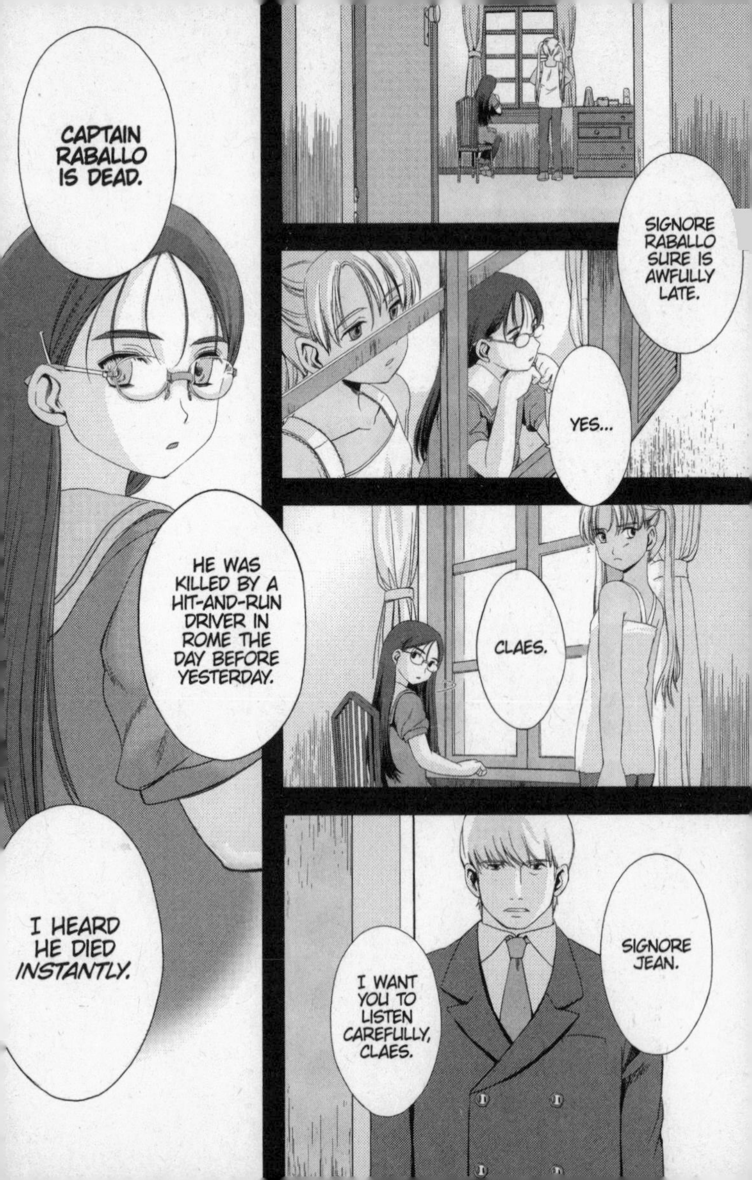
SIGNORE RABALLO SURE IS AWFULLY LATE.
YES...
CLAES.
SIGNORE JEAN.
I WANT YOU TO LISTEN CAREFULLY, CLAES.
CAPTAIN RABALLO IS DEAD.
HE WAS KILLED BY A HIT-AND-RUN DRIVER IN ROME THE DAY BEFORE YESTERDAY.
I HEARD HE DIED *INSTANTLY.*

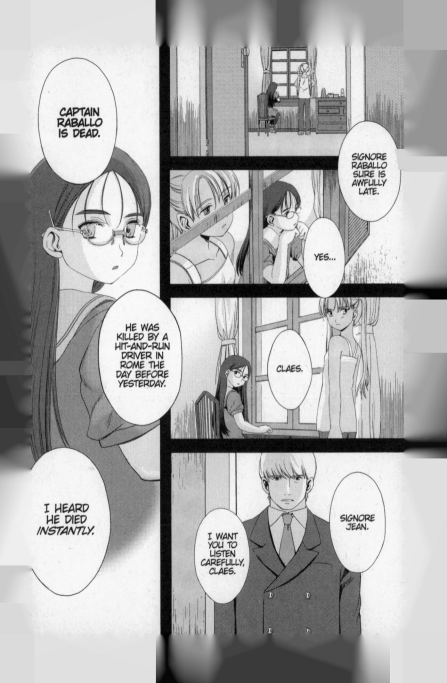

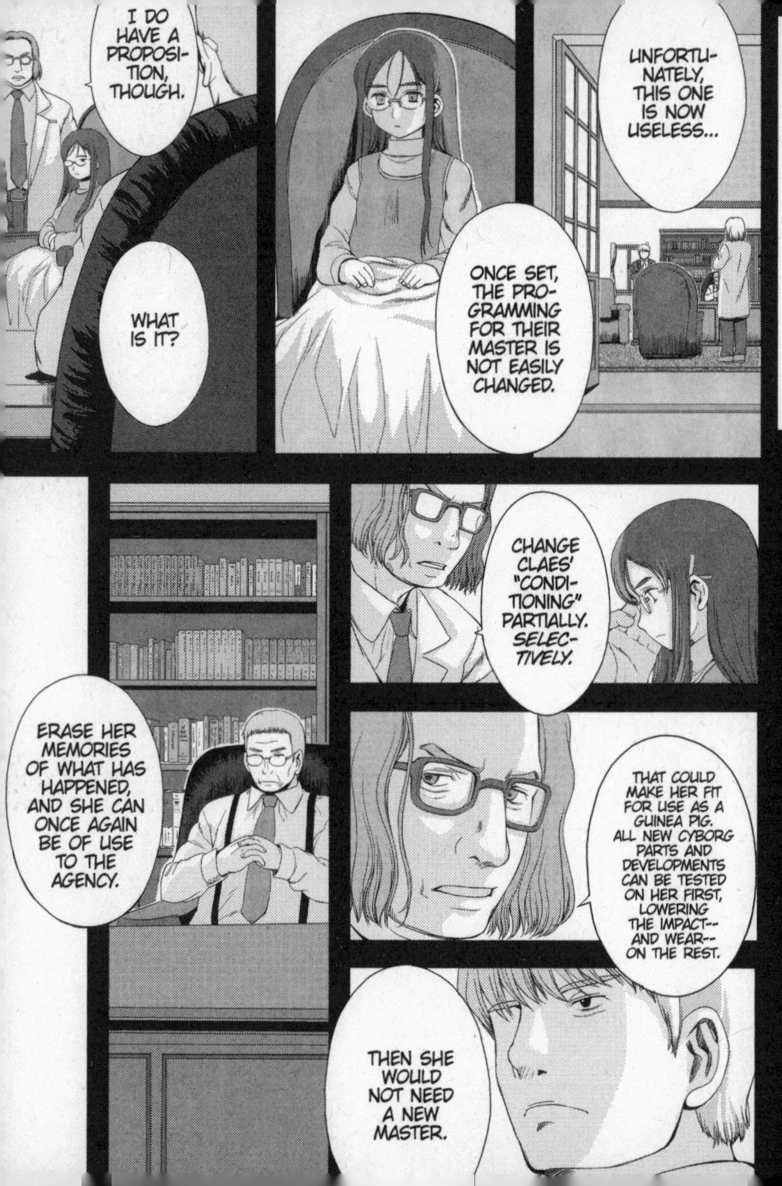
UNFORTUNATELY, THIS ONE IS NOW USELESS...
ONCE SET, THE PROGRAMMING FOR THEIR MASTER IS NOT EASILY CHANGED.
I DO HAVE A PROPOSITION, THOUGH.
WHAT IS IT?
CHANGE CLAES' "CONDITIONING" PARTIALLY. SELECTIVELY.
THAT COULD MAKE HER FIT FOR USE AS A GUINEA PIG. ALL NEW CYBORG PARTS AND DEVELOPMENTS CAN BE TESTED ON HER FIRST, LOWERING THE IMPACT--AND WEAR--ON THE REST.
THEN SHE WOULD NOT NEED A NEW MASTER.
ERASE HER MEMORIES OF WHAT HAS HAPPENED, AND SHE CAN ONCE AGAIN BE OF USE TO THE AGENCY.

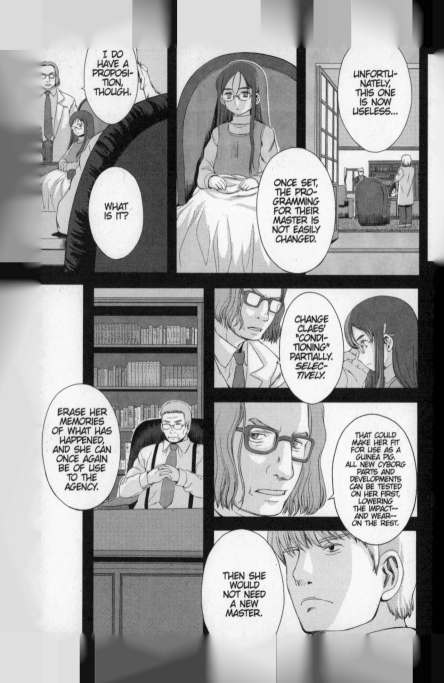

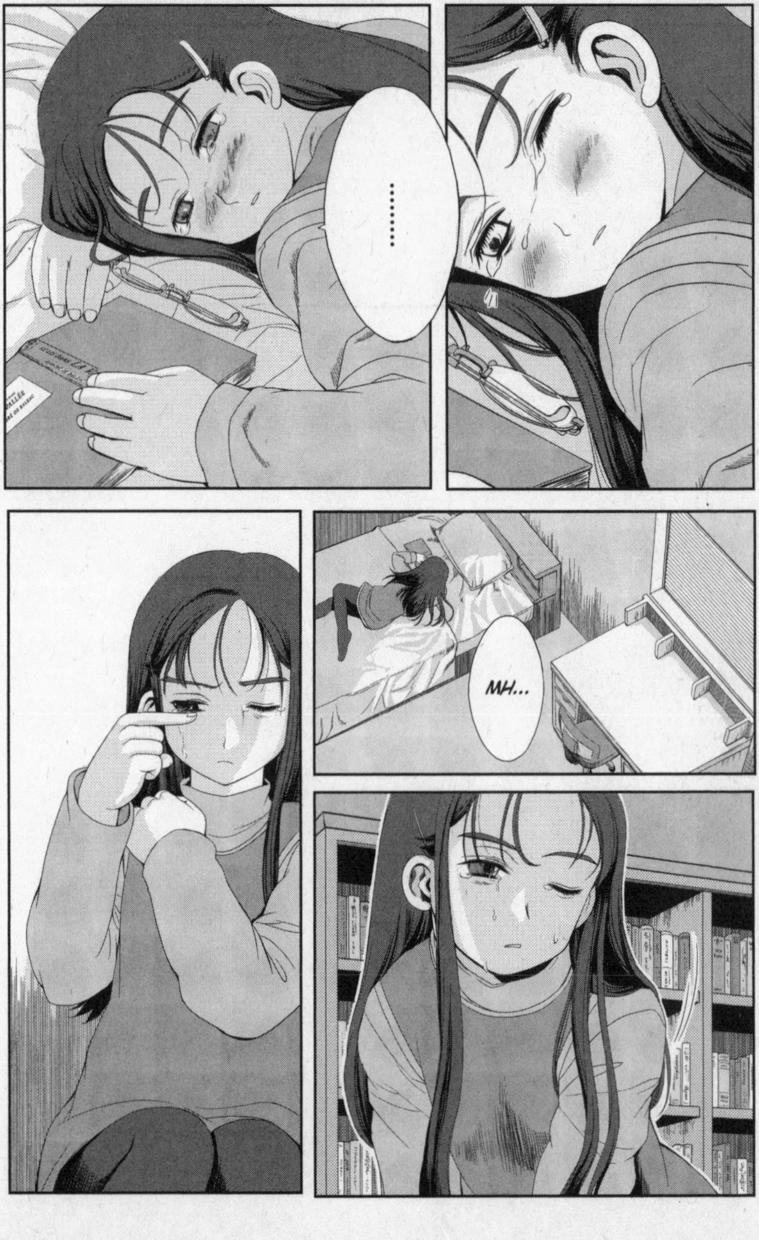
......
MH...

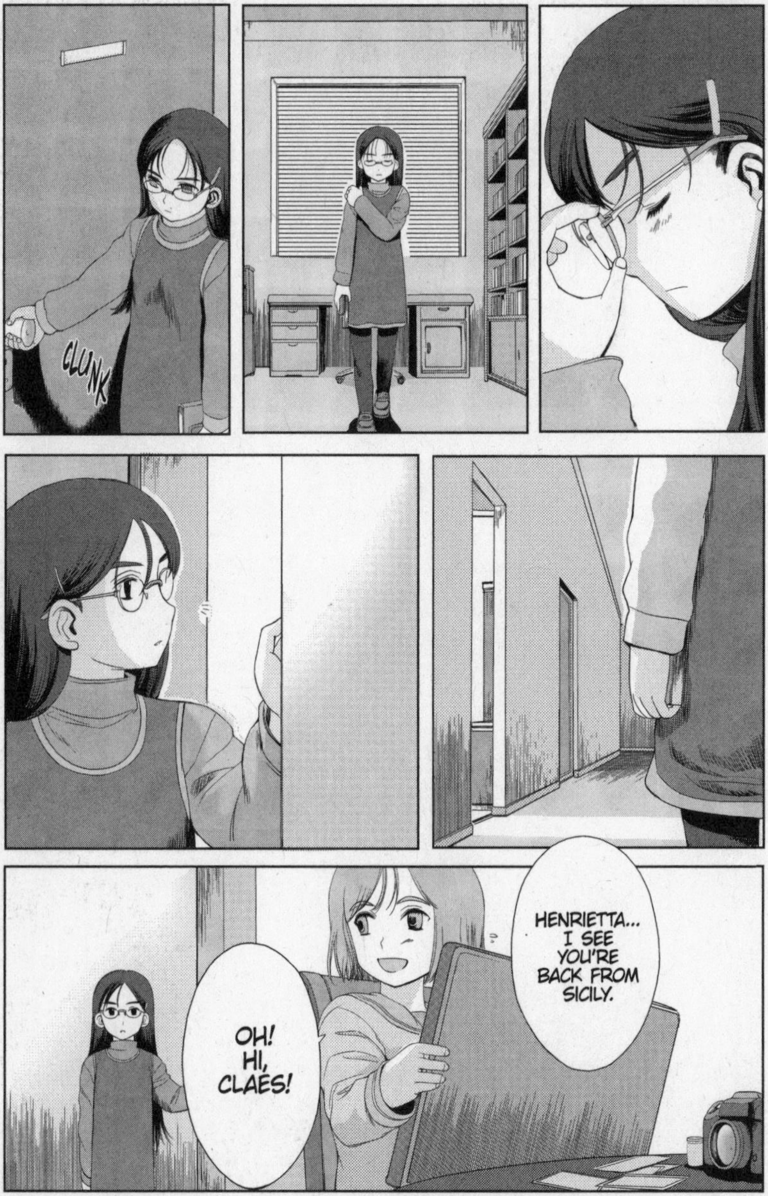
CLUNK
HENRIETTA... I SEE YOU'RE BACK FROM SICILY.
OH! HI, CLAES!

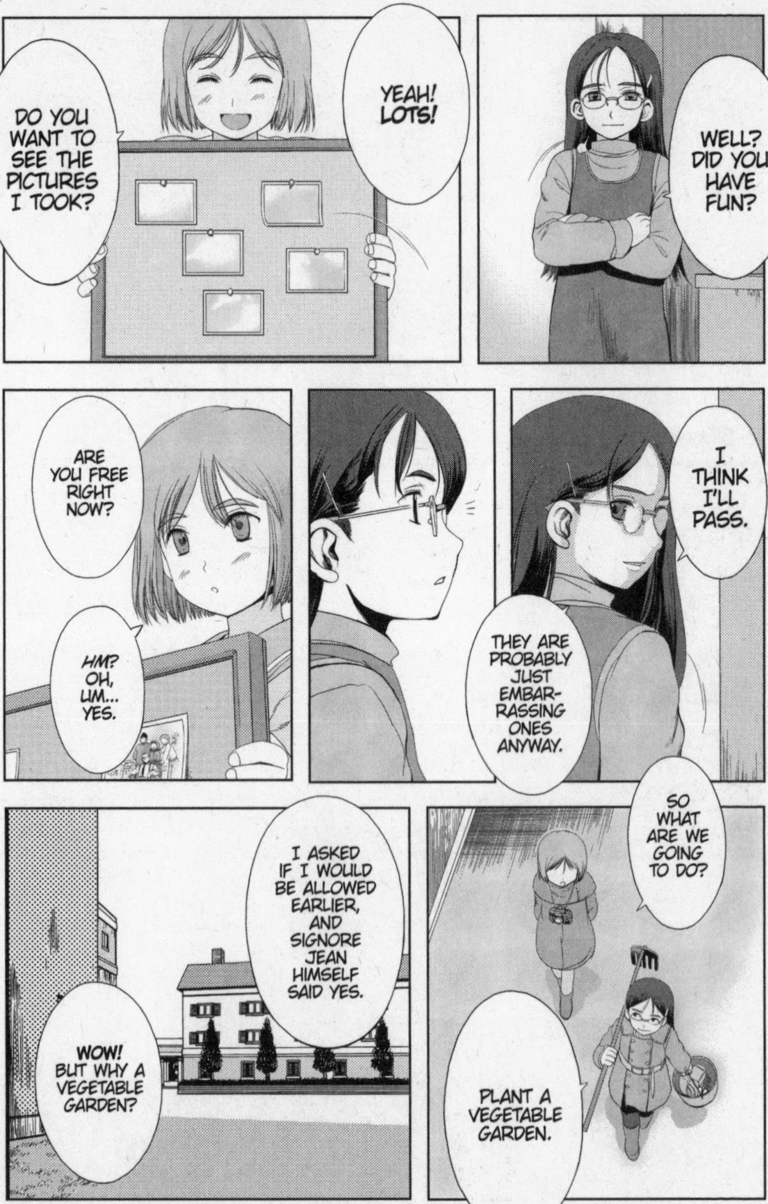
WELL? DID YOU HAVE FUN?
YEAH! LOTS!
DO YOU WANT TO SEE THE PICTURES I TOOK?
I THINK I'LL PASS.
THEY ARE PROBABLY JUST EMBARRASSING ONES ANYWAY.
ARE YOU FREE RIGHT NOW?
HM? OH, UM... YES.
SO WHAT ARE WE GOING TO DO?
PLANT A VEGETABLE GARDEN.
I ASKED IF I WOULD BE ALLOWED EARLIER, AND SIGNORE JEAN HIMSELF SAID YES.
WOW! BUT WHY A VEGETABLE GARDEN?

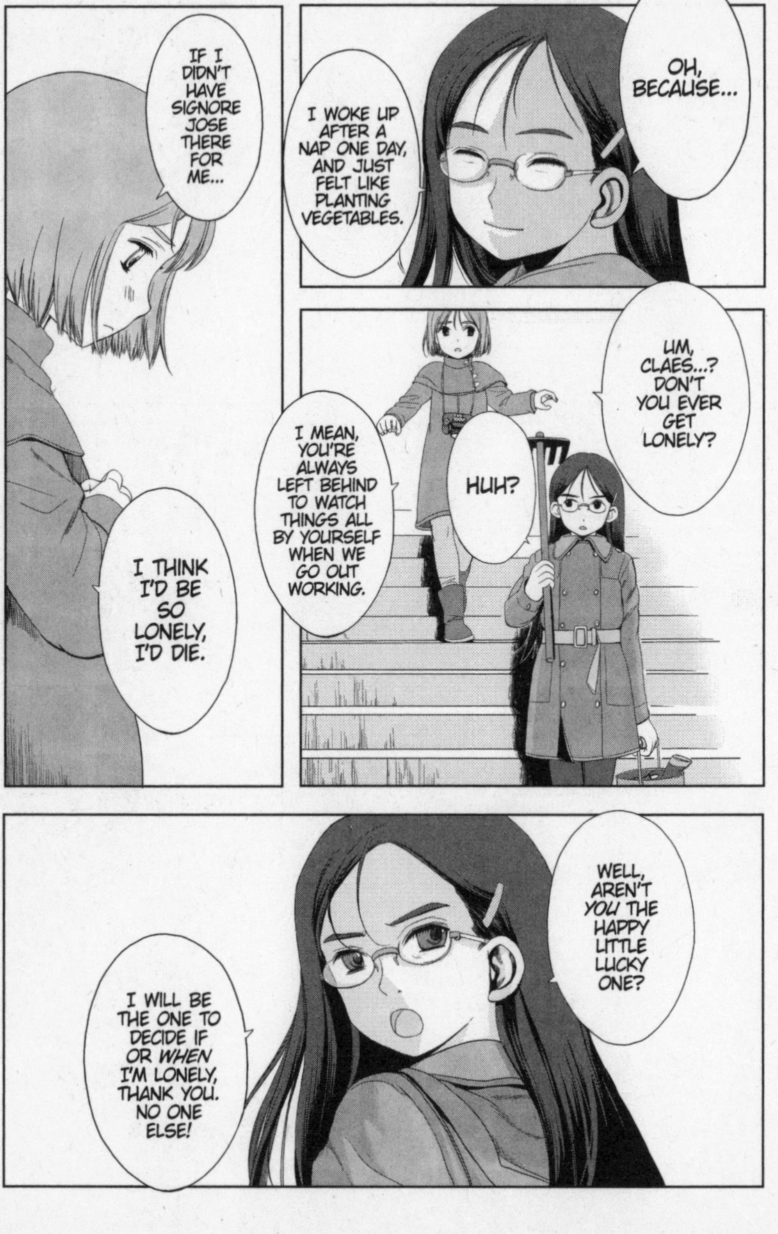
OH, BECAUSE...
I WOKE UP AFTER A NAP ONE DAY, AND JUST FELT LIKE PLANTING VEGETABLES.
UM, CLAES...? DON'T YOU EVER GET LONELY?
HUH?
I MEAN, YOU'RE ALWAYS LEFT BEHIND TO WATCH THINGS ALL BY YOURSELF WHEN WE GO OUT WORKING.
IF I DIDN'T HAVE SIGNORE JOSE THERE FOR ME...
I THINK I'D BE SO LONELY, I'D DIE.
WELL, AREN'T *YOU* THE HAPPY LITTLE LUCKY ONE?
I WILL BE THE ONE TO DECIDE IF OR *WHEN* I'M LONELY, THANK YOU. NO ONE ELSE!

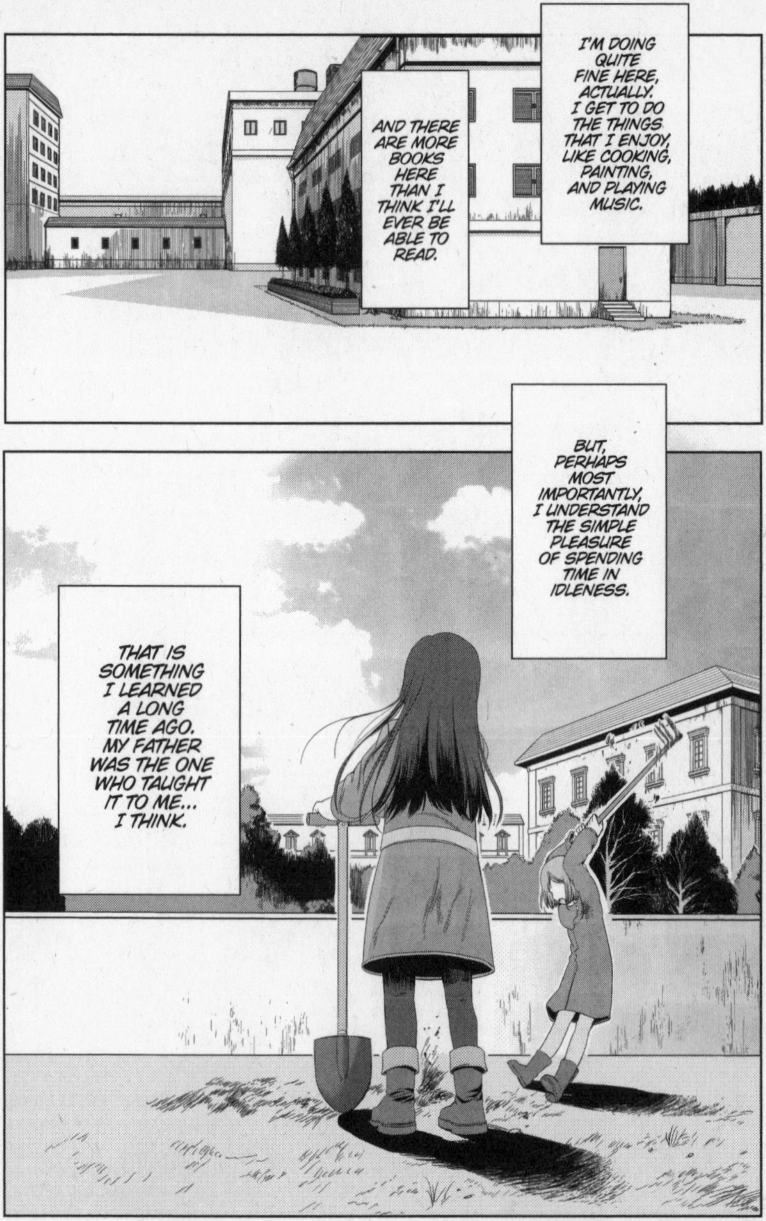
I'M DOING QUITE FINE HERE, ACTUALLY. I GET TO DO THE THINGS THAT I ENJOY, LIKE COOKING, PAINTING, AND PLAYING MUSIC.
AND THERE ARE MORE BOOKS HERE THAN I THINK I'LL EVER BE ABLE TO READ.
BUT, PERHAPS MOST IMPORTANTLY, I UNDERSTAND THE SIMPLE PLEASURE OF SPENDING TIME IN IDLENESS.
THAT IS SOMETHING I LEARNED A LONG TIME AGO. MY FATHER WAS THE ONE WHO TAUGHT IT TO ME... I THINK.

Chapter 6 / END

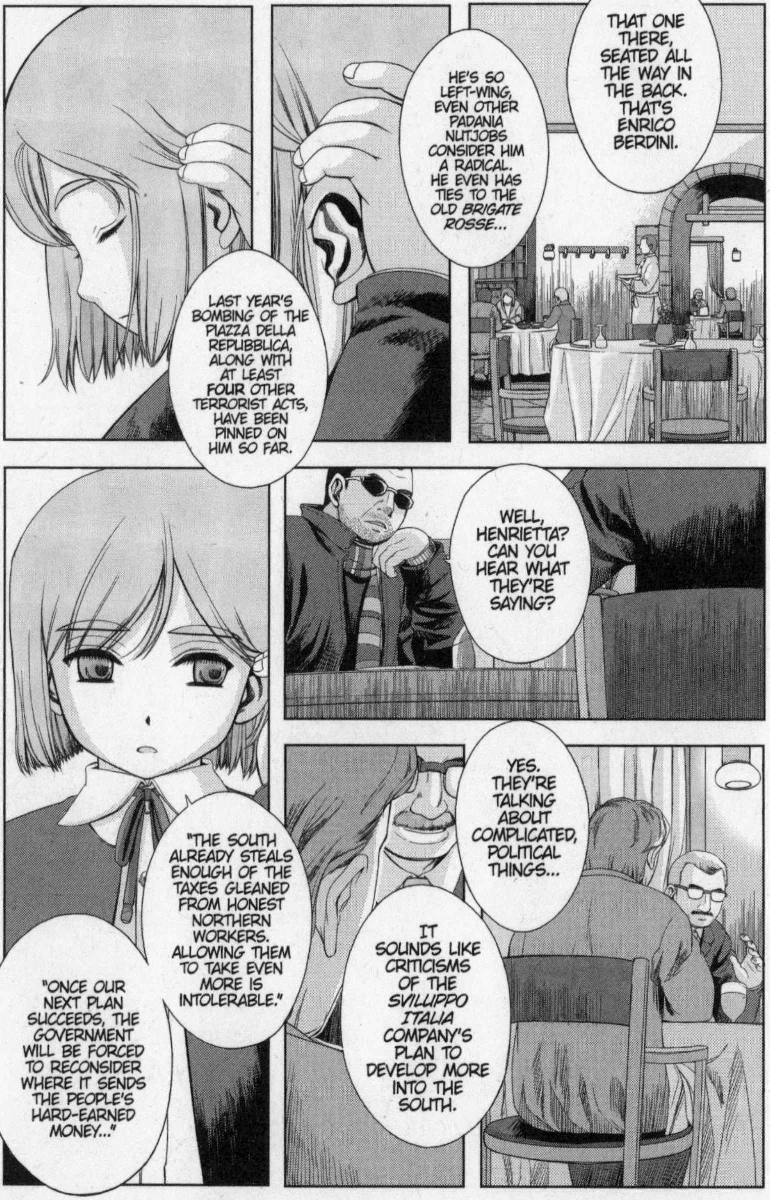
THAT ONE THERE, SEATED ALL THE WAY IN THE BACK. THAT'S ENRICO BERDINI.
HE'S SO LEFT-WING, EVEN OTHER PADANIA NUTJOBS CONSIDER HIM A RADICAL. HE EVEN HAS TIES TO THE OLD *BRIGATE ROSSE*...
LAST YEAR'S BOMBING OF THE PIAZZA DELLA REPUBBLICA, ALONG WITH AT LEAST **FOUR** OTHER TERRORIST ACTS, HAVE BEEN PINNED ON HIM SO FAR.
WELL, HENRIETTA? CAN YOU HEAR WHAT THEY'RE SAYING?
YES. THEY'RE TALKING ABOUT COMPLICATED, POLITICAL THINGS...
IT SOUNDS LIKE CRITICISMS OF THE *SVILUPPO ITALIA* COMPANY'S PLAN TO DEVELOP MORE INTO THE SOUTH.
"THE SOUTH ALREADY STEALS ENOUGH OF THE TAXES GLEANED FROM HONEST NORTHERN WORKERS. ALLOWING THEM TO TAKE EVEN MORE IS INTOLERABLE."
"ONCE OUR NEXT PLAN SUCCEEDS, THE GOVERNMENT WILL BE FORCED TO RECONSIDER WHERE IT SENDS THE PEOPLE'S HARD-EARNED MONEY..."

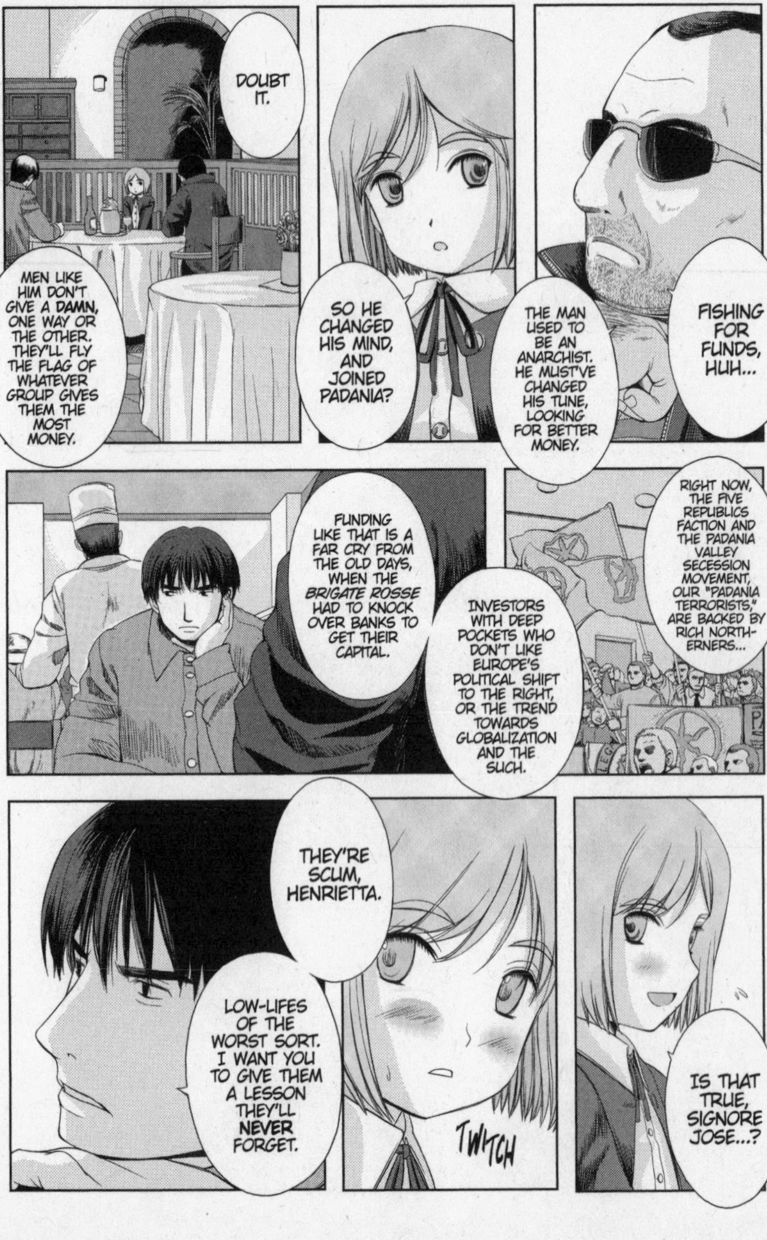
FISHING FOR FUNDS, HUH...
THE MAN USED TO BE AN ANARCHIST. HE MUST'VE CHANGED HIS TUNE, LOOKING FOR BETTER MONEY.
SO HE CHANGED HIS MIND, AND JOINED PADANIA?
DOUBT IT.
MEN LIKE HIM DON'T GIVE A DAMN, ONE WAY OR THE OTHER. THEY'LL FLY THE FLAG OF WHATEVER GROUP GIVES THEM THE MOST MONEY.
RIGHT NOW, THE FIVE REPUBLICS FACTION AND THE PADANIA VALLEY SECESSION MOVEMENT, OUR "PADANIA TERRORISTS," ARE BACKED BY RICH NORTHERNERS...
INVESTORS WITH DEEP POCKETS WHO DON'T LIKE EUROPE'S POLITICAL SHIFT TO THE RIGHT, OR THE TREND TOWARDS GLOBALIZATION AND THE SUCH.
FUNDING LIKE THAT IS A FAR CRY FROM THE OLD DAYS, WHEN THE *BRIGATE ROSSE* HAD TO KNOCK OVER BANKS TO GET THEIR CAPITAL.
IS THAT TRUE, SIGNORE JOSE...?
THEY'RE SCUM, HENRIETTA.
LOW-LIFES OF THE WORST SORT. I WANT YOU TO GIVE THEM A LESSON THEY'LL NEVER FORGET.
TWITCH

CHAPTER 7: GELATO IN PIAZZA DI SPAGNA

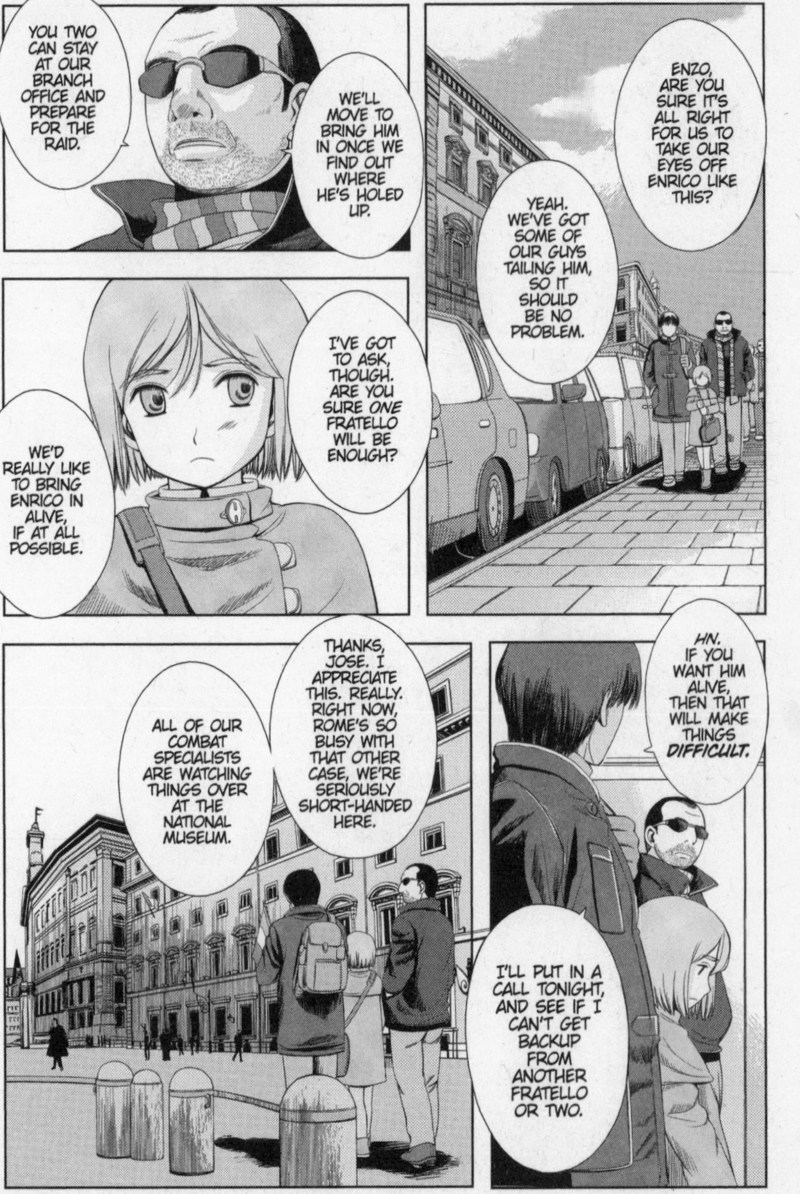
ENZO, ARE YOU SURE IT'S ALL RIGHT FOR US TO TAKE OUR EYES OFF ENRICO LIKE THIS?
YEAH. WE'VE GOT SOME OF OUR GUYS TAILING HIM, SO IT SHOULD BE NO PROBLEM.
YOU TWO CAN STAY AT OUR BRANCH OFFICE AND PREPARE FOR THE RAID.
WE'LL MOVE TO BRING HIM IN ONCE WE FIND OUT WHERE HE'S HOLED UP.
I'VE GOT TO ASK, THOUGH. ARE YOU SURE *ONE* FRATELLO WILL BE ENOUGH?
WE'D REALLY LIKE TO BRING ENRICO IN ALIVE, IF AT ALL POSSIBLE.
HN. IF YOU WANT HIM ALIVE, THEN THAT WILL MAKE THINGS ***DIFFICULT.***
I'LL PUT IN A CALL TONIGHT, AND SEE IF I CAN'T GET BACKUP FROM ANOTHER FRATELLO OR TWO.
THANKS, JOSE. I APPRECIATE THIS. REALLY. RIGHT NOW, ROME'S SO BUSY WITH THAT OTHER CASE, WE'RE SERIOUSLY SHORT-HANDED HERE.
ALL OF OUR COMBAT SPECIALISTS ARE WATCHING THINGS OVER AT THE NATIONAL MUSEUM.

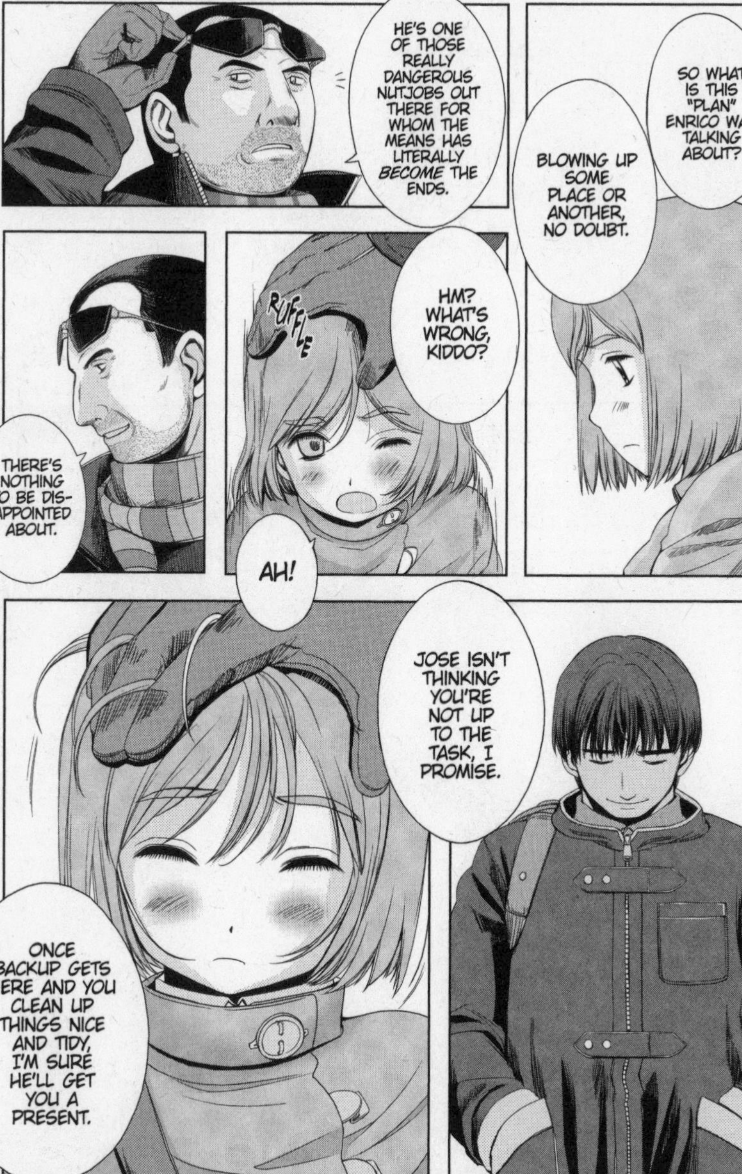
SO WHAT IS THIS "PLAN" ENRICO WAS TALKING ABOUT?
BLOWING UP SOME PLACE OR ANOTHER, NO DOUBT.
HE'S ONE OF THOSE REALLY DANGEROUS NUTJOBS OUT THERE FOR WHOM THE MEANS HAS LITERALLY *BECOME* THE ENDS.
HM? WHAT'S WRONG, KIDDO?
RUFFLE
AH!
THERE'S NOTHING TO BE DIS-APPOINTED ABOUT.
JOSE ISN'T THINKING YOU'RE NOT UP TO THE TASK, I PROMISE.
ONCE BACKUP GETS HERE AND YOU CLEAN UP THINGS NICE AND TIDY, I'M SURE HE'LL GET YOU A PRESENT.

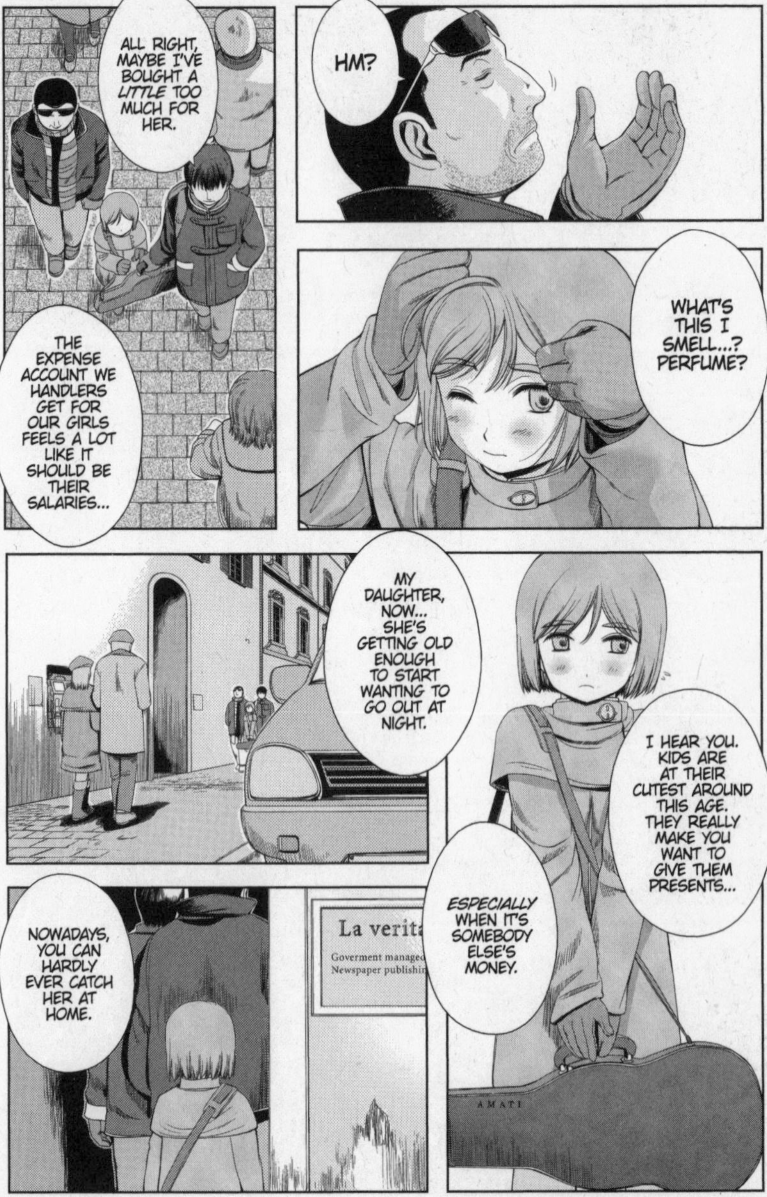
ALL RIGHT, MAYBE I'VE BOUGHT A *LITTLE* TOO MUCH FOR HER.
THE EXPENSE ACCOUNT WE HANDLERS GET FOR OUR GIRLS FEELS A LOT LIKE IT SHOULD BE THEIR SALARIES...
HM?
WHAT'S THIS I SMELL...? PERFUME?
MY DAUGHTER, NOW... SHE'S GETTING OLD ENOUGH TO START WANTING TO GO OUT AT NIGHT.
NOWADAYS, YOU CAN HARDLY EVER CATCH HER AT HOME.
La verita
Goverment managed
Newspaper publishin
I HEAR YOU. KIDS ARE AT THEIR CUTEST AROUND THIS AGE. THEY REALLY MAKE YOU WANT TO GIVE THEM PRESENTS...
ESPECIALLY WHEN IT'S SOMEBODY ELSE'S MONEY.
AMATI

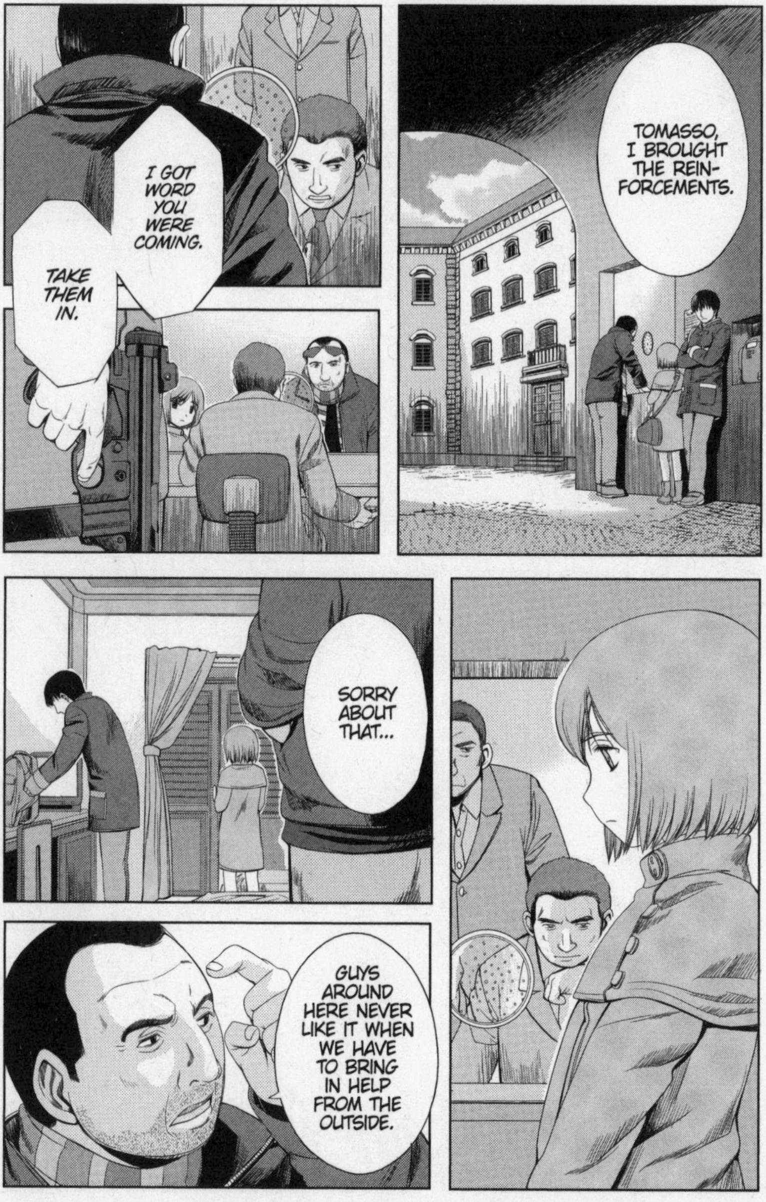
TOMASSO, I BROUGHT THE REIN-FORCEMENTS.
I GOT WORD YOU WERE COMING.
TAKE THEM IN.
SORRY ABOUT THAT...
GUYS AROUND HERE NEVER LIKE IT WHEN WE HAVE TO BRING IN HELP FROM THE OUTSIDE.

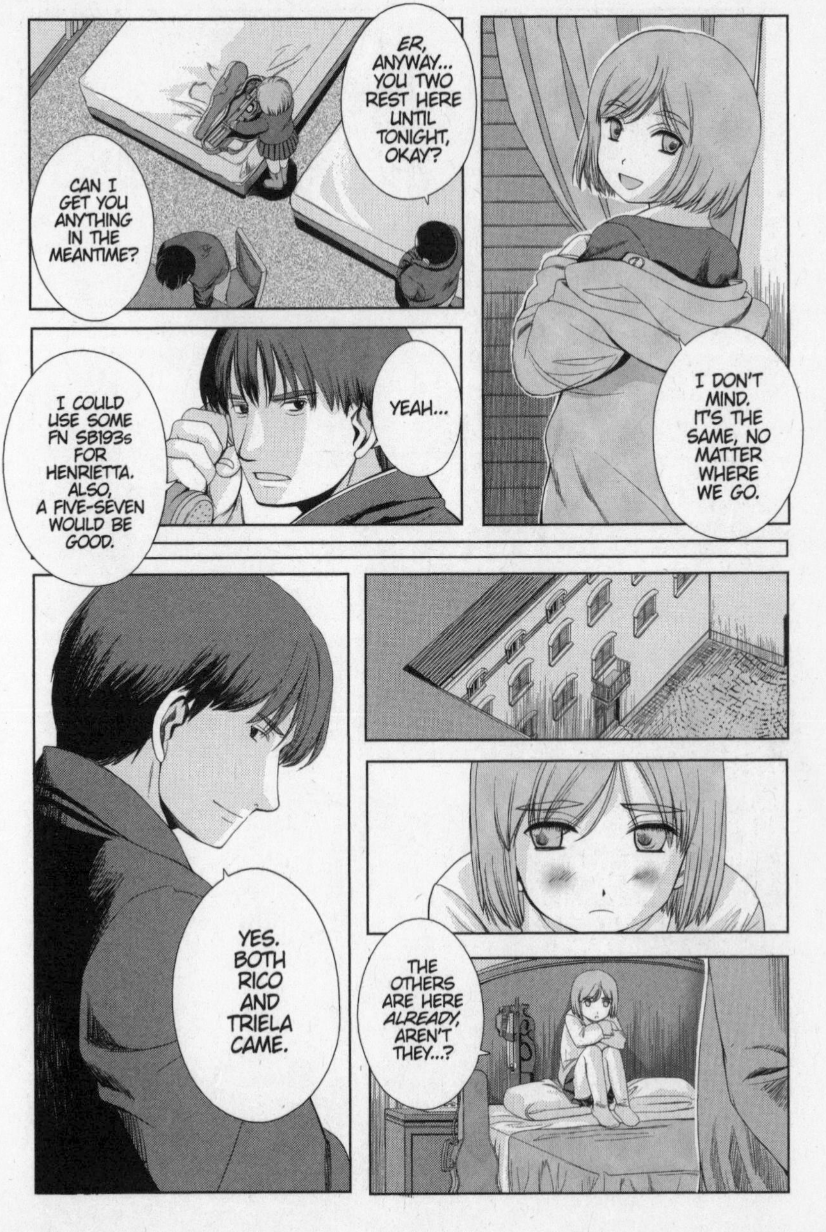
I DON'T MIND. IT'S THE SAME, NO MATTER WHERE WE GO.
ER, ANYWAY... YOU TWO REST HERE UNTIL TONIGHT, OKAY?
CAN I GET YOU ANYTHING IN THE MEANTIME?
YEAH...
I COULD USE SOME FN SB193s FOR HENRIETTA. ALSO, A FIVE-SEVEN WOULD BE GOOD.
THE OTHERS ARE HERE ALREADY, AREN'T THEY...?
YES. BOTH RICO AND TRIELA CAME.

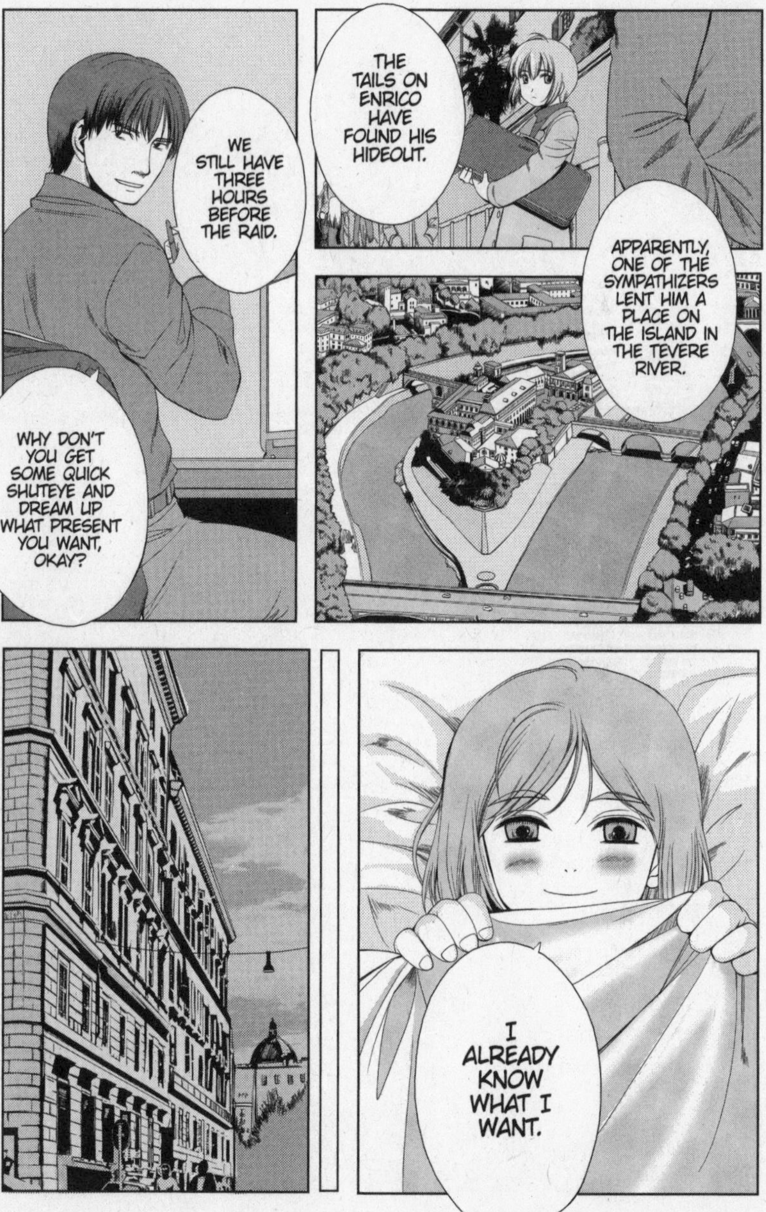
THE TAILS ON ENRICO HAVE FOUND HIS HIDEOUT.
APPARENTLY, ONE OF THE SYMPATHIZERS LENT HIM A PLACE ON THE ISLAND IN THE TEVERE RIVER.
WE STILL HAVE THREE HOURS BEFORE THE RAID.
WHY DON'T YOU GET SOME QUICK SHUTEYE AND DREAM UP WHAT PRESENT YOU WANT, OKAY?
I ALREADY KNOW WHAT I WANT.

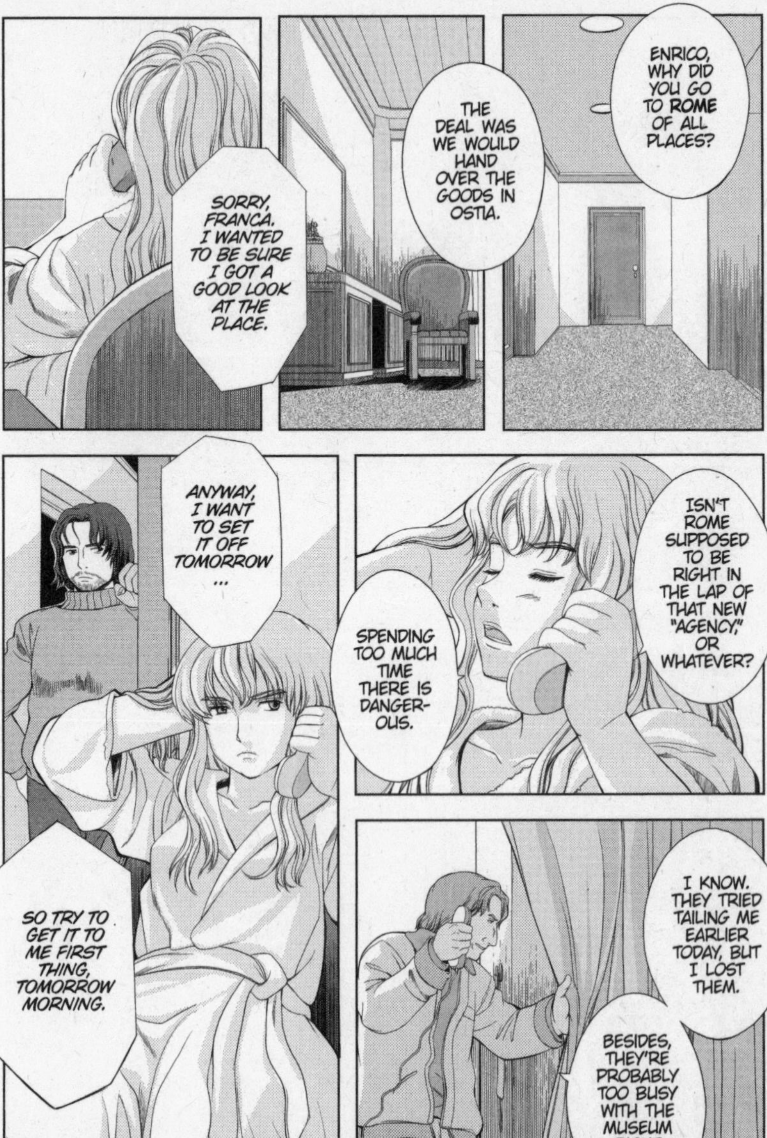
ENRICO, WHY DID YOU GO TO ROME OF ALL PLACES?
THE DEAL WAS WE WOULD HAND OVER THE GOODS IN OSTIA.
SORRY, FRANCA. I WANTED TO BE SURE I GOT A GOOD LOOK AT THE PLACE.
ISN'T ROME SUPPOSED TO BE RIGHT IN THE LAP OF THAT NEW "AGENCY," OR WHATEVER?
SPENDING TOO MUCH TIME THERE IS DANGER-OUS.
I KNOW. THEY TRIED TAILING ME EARLIER TODAY, BUT I LOST THEM.
BESIDES, THEY'RE PROBABLY TOO BUSY WITH THE MUSEUM RIGHT NOW.
ANYWAY, I WANT TO SET IT OFF TOMORROW ...
SO TRY TO GET IT TO ME FIRST THING, TOMORROW MORNING.

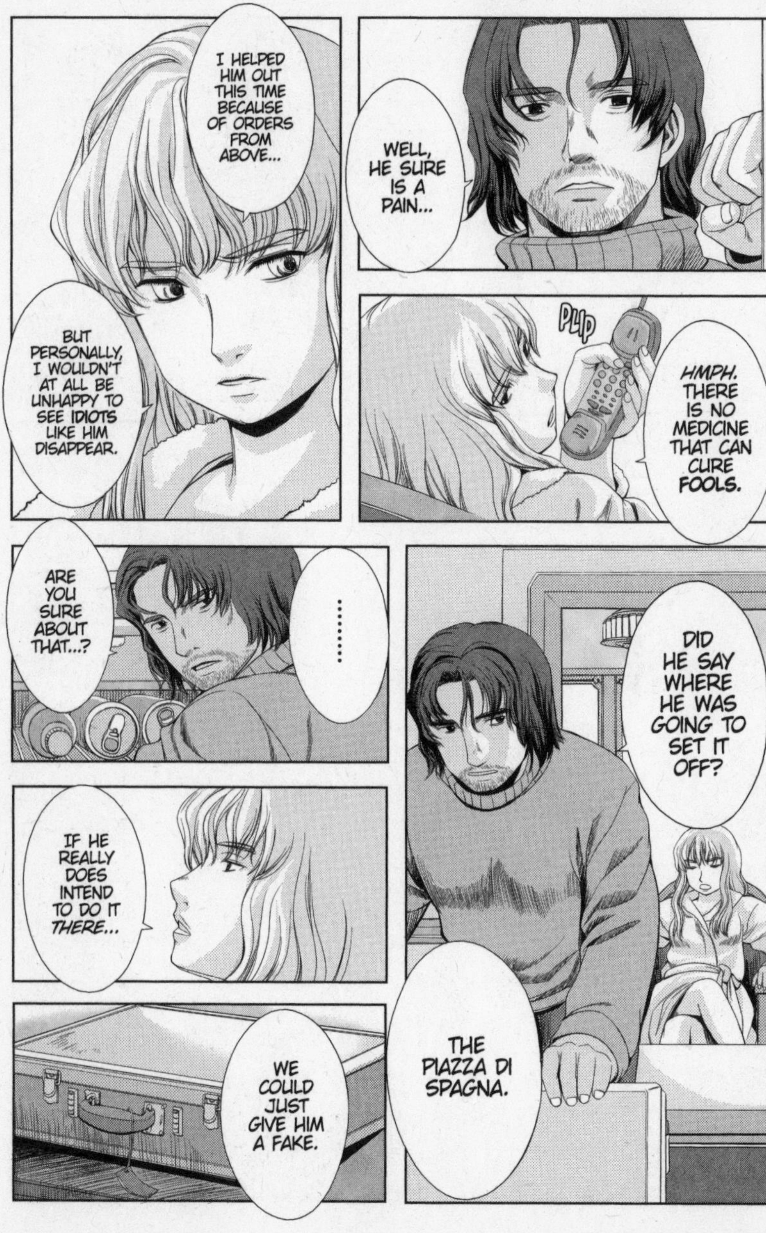
WELL, HE SURE IS A PAIN...
PLIP
HMPH. THERE IS NO MEDICINE THAT CAN CURE FOOLS.
I HELPED HIM OUT THIS TIME BECAUSE OF ORDERS FROM ABOVE...
BUT PERSONALLY, I WOULDN'T AT ALL BE UNHAPPY TO SEE IDIOTS LIKE HIM DISAPPEAR.
DID HE SAY WHERE HE WAS GOING TO SET IT OFF?
THE PIAZZA DI SPAGNA.
......
ARE YOU SURE ABOUT THAT...?
IF HE REALLY DOES INTEND TO DO IT *THERE*...
WE COULD JUST GIVE HIM A FAKE.

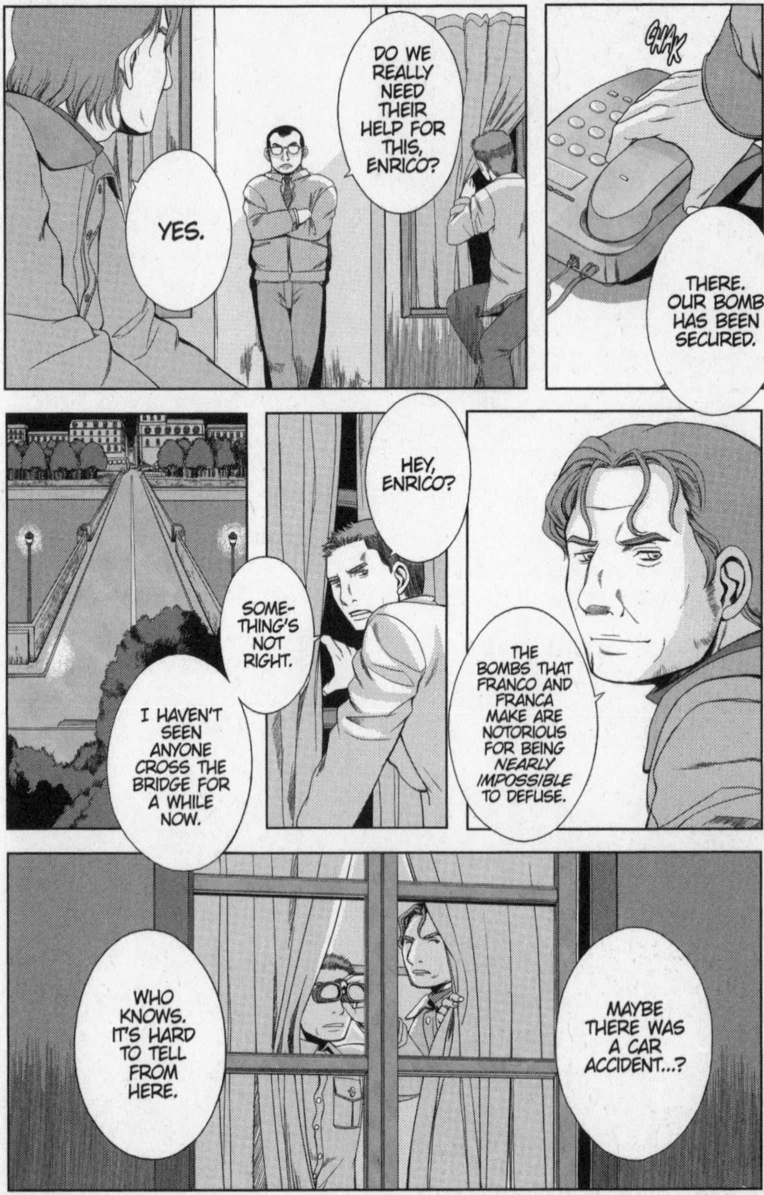
CHAK
THERE. OUR BOMB HAS BEEN SECURED.
DO WE REALLY NEED THEIR HELP FOR THIS, ENRICO?
YES.
THE BOMBS THAT FRANCO AND FRANCA MAKE ARE NOTORIOUS FOR BEING *NEARLY IMPOSSIBLE* TO DEFUSE.
HEY, ENRICO?
SOME-THING'S NOT RIGHT.
I HAVEN'T SEEN ANYONE CROSS THE BRIDGE FOR A WHILE NOW.
MAYBE THERE WAS A CAR ACCIDENT...?
WHO KNOWS. IT'S HARD TO TELL FROM HERE.

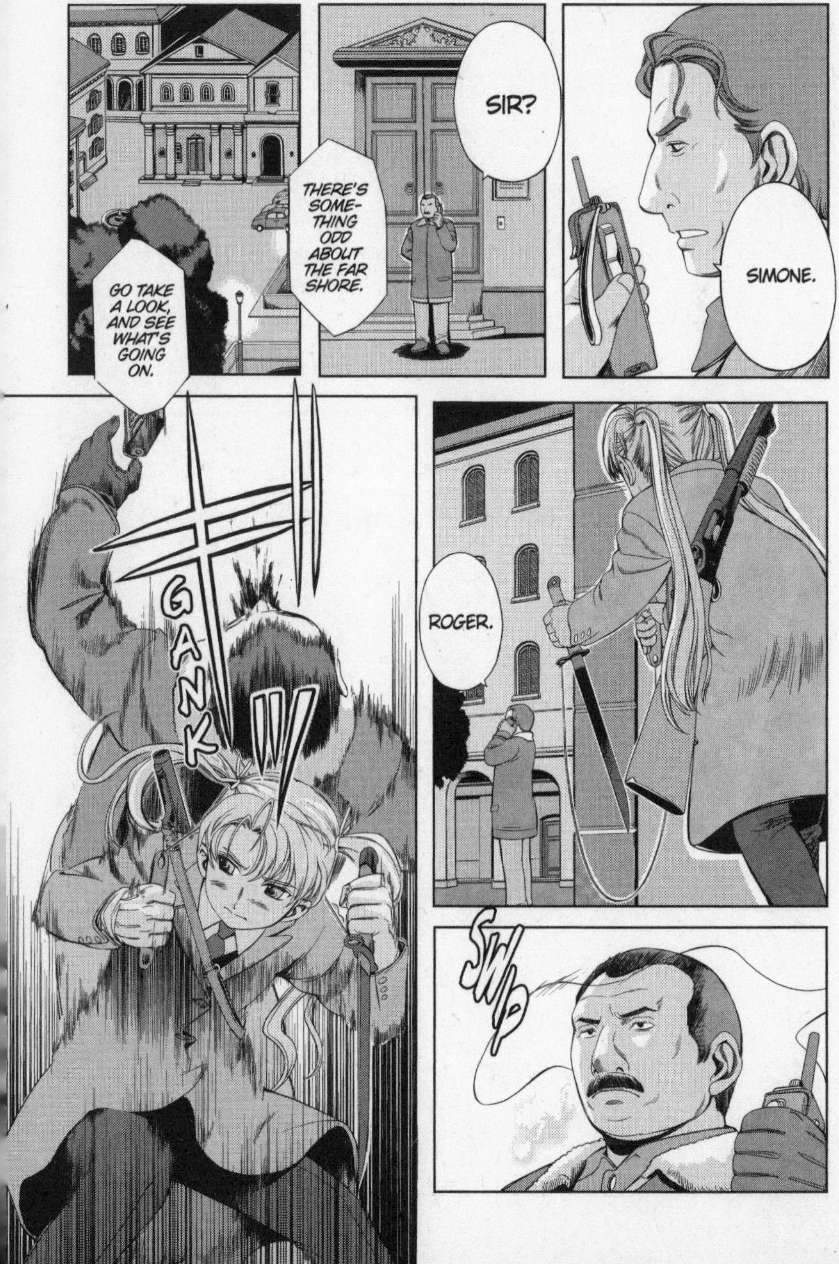
SIMONE.
SIR?
THERE'S SOME-THING ODD ABOUT THE FAR SHORE.
GO TAKE A LOOK, AND SEE WHAT'S GOING ON.
ROGER.
SWIP
GANK

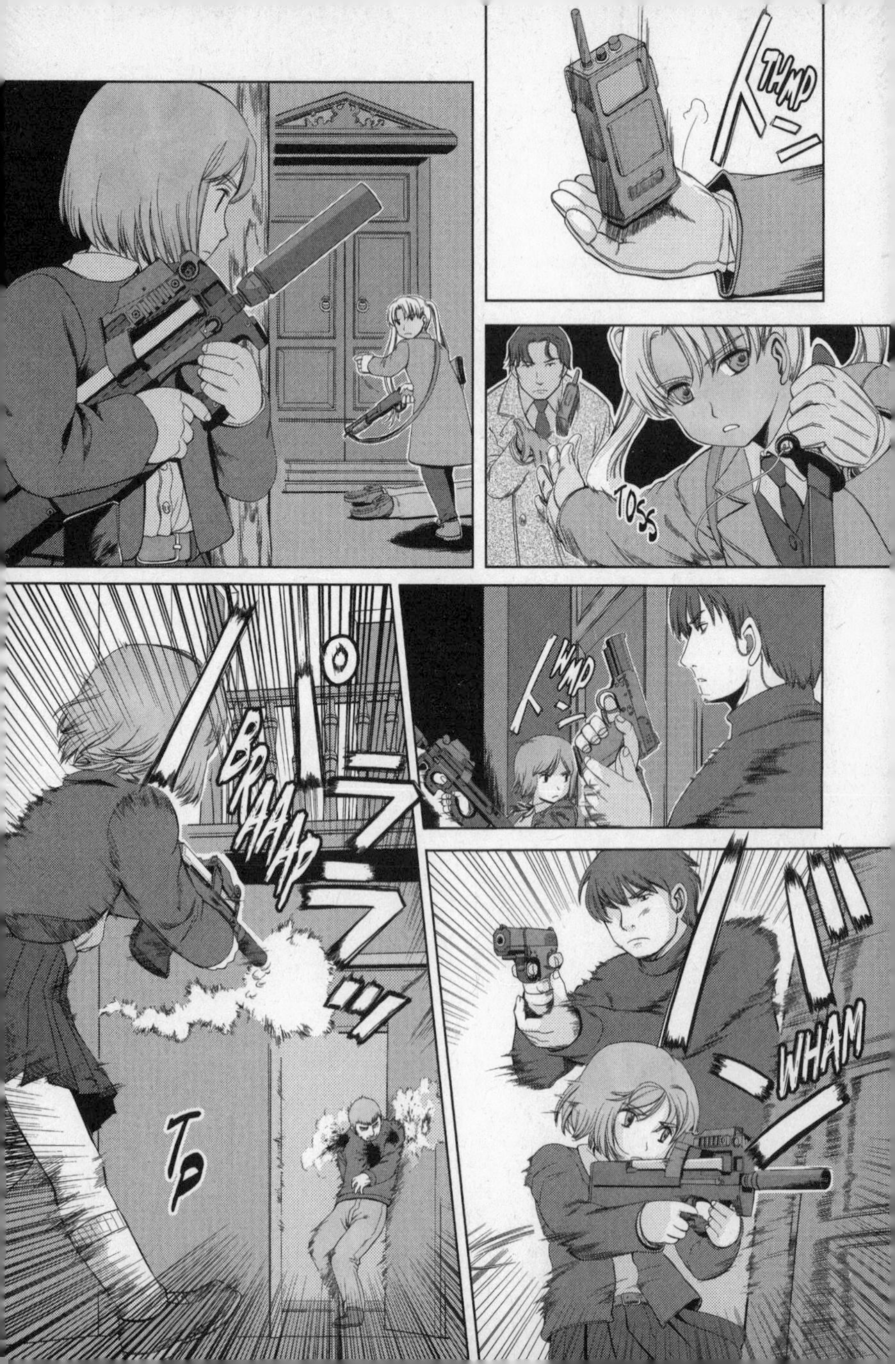
THMP
TOSS
WMP
WHAM
BRAAAP
Tp

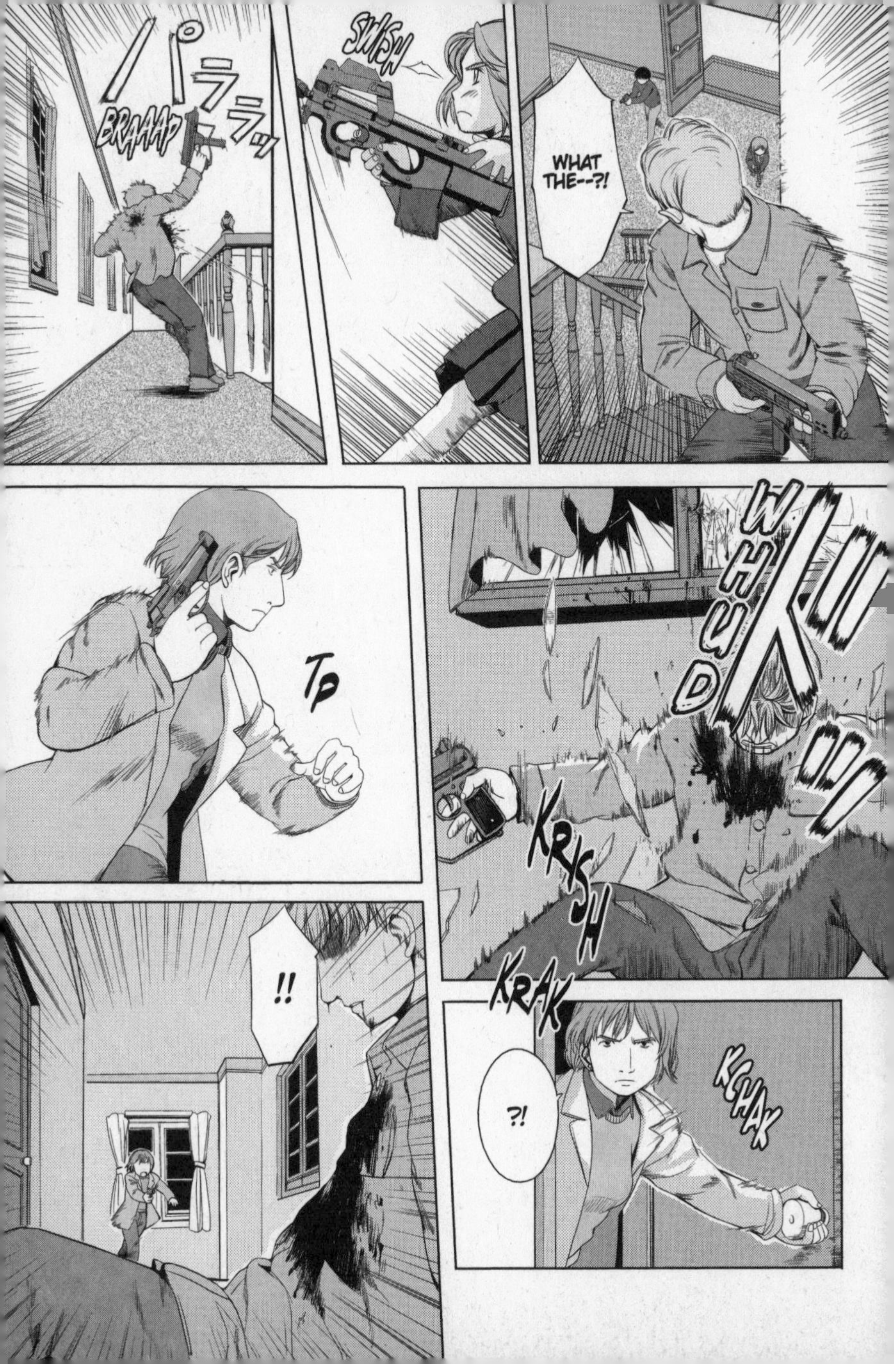

WHAT THE--?!
SWISH
パララッ
BRAAAP
WHUD
KRISH
Tp
KRAK
?!
KCHAK
!!

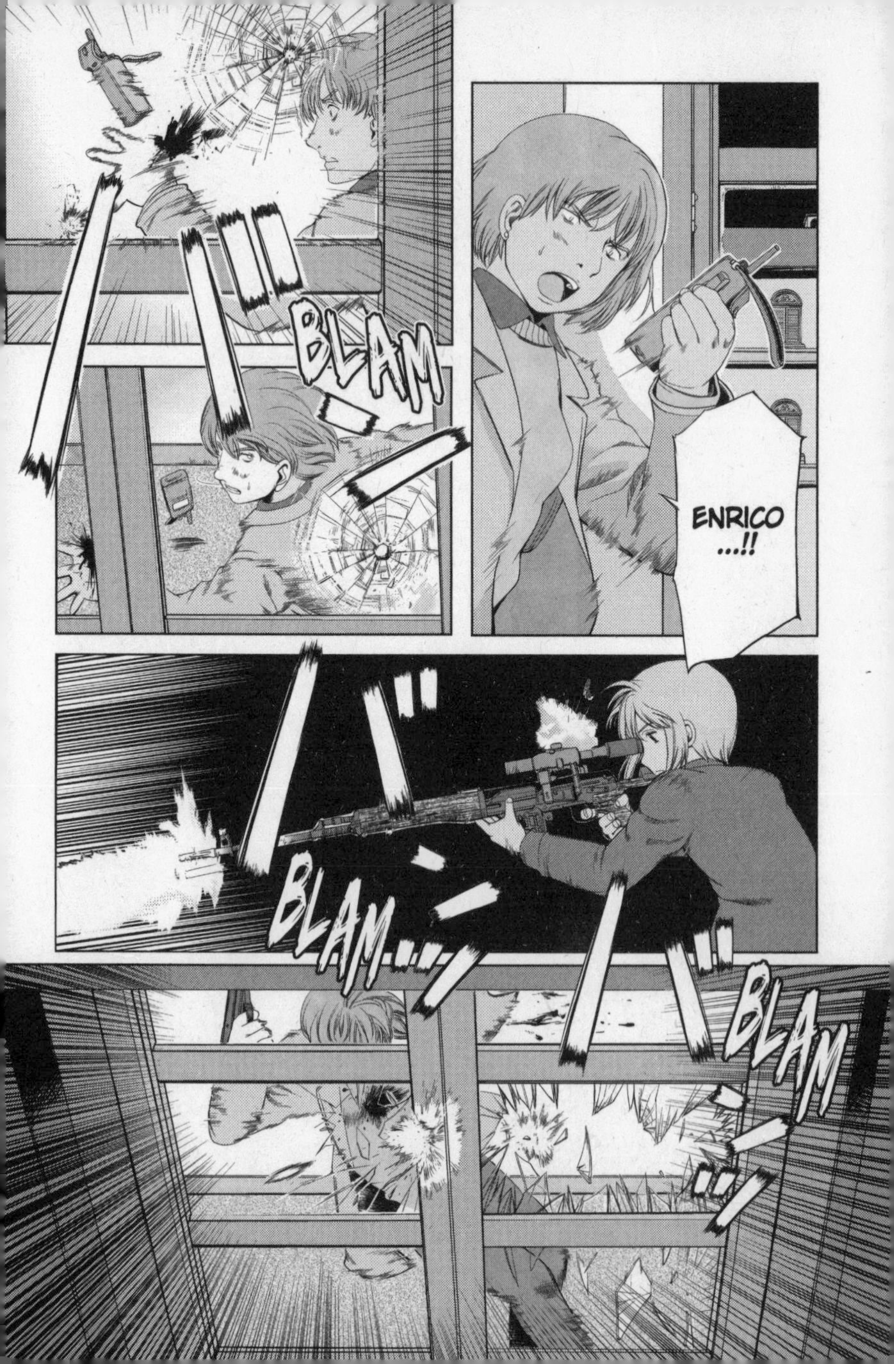
ENRICO ...!!
BLAM
BLAM...
BLAM

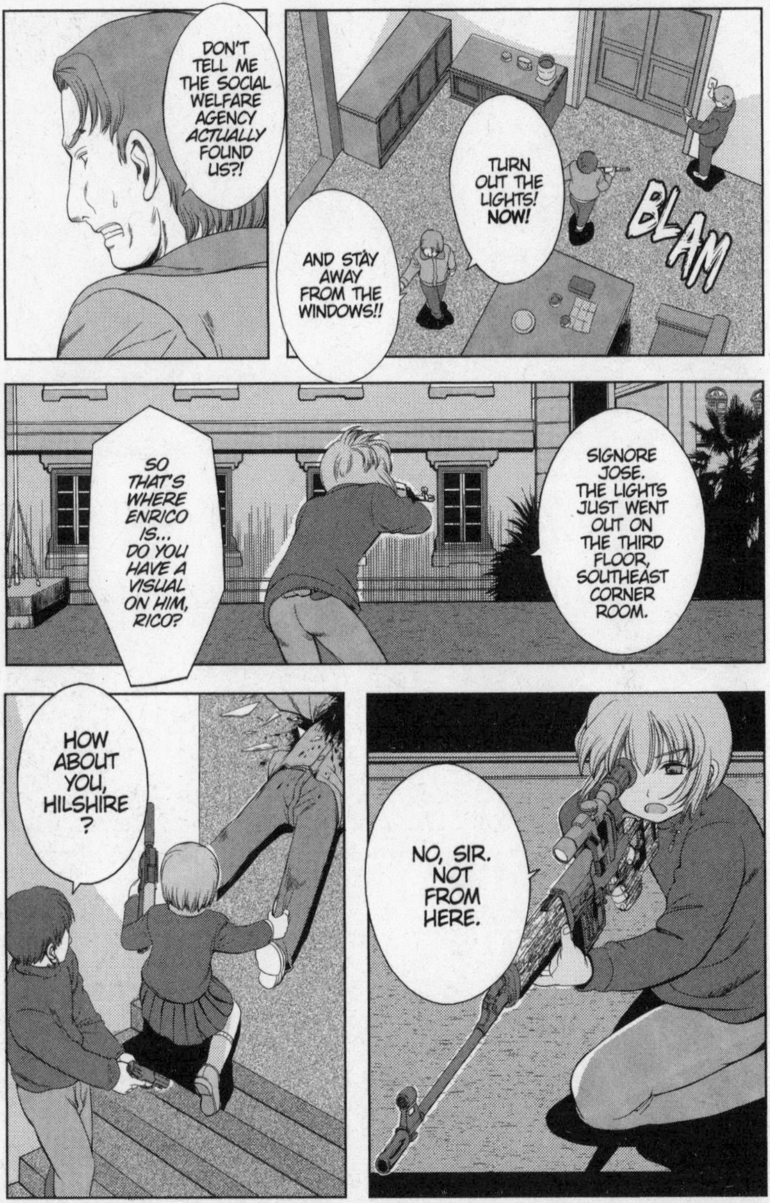
TURN OUT THE LIGHTS! NOW!
BLAM
AND STAY AWAY FROM THE WINDOWS!!
DON'T TELL ME THE SOCIAL WELFARE AGENCY ACTUALLY FOUND US?!
SIGNORE JOSE. THE LIGHTS JUST WENT OUT ON THE THIRD FLOOR, SOUTHEAST CORNER ROOM.
SO THAT'S WHERE ENRICO IS... DO YOU HAVE A VISUAL ON HIM, RICO?
NO, SIR. NOT FROM HERE.
HOW ABOUT YOU, HILSHIRE?

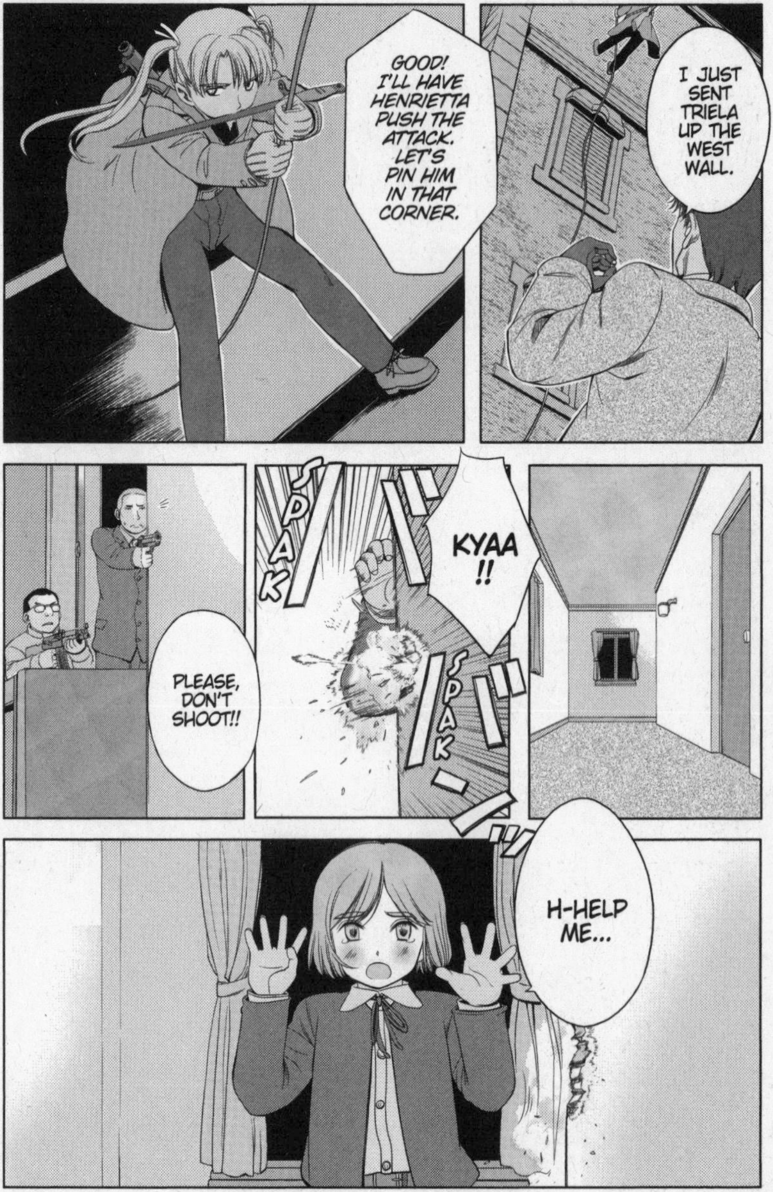
I JUST SENT TRIELA UP THE WEST WALL.
GOOD! I'LL HAVE HENRIETTA PUSH THE ATTACK. LET'S PIN HIM IN THAT CORNER.
KYAA !!
SPAK
SPAK
PLEASE, DON'T SHOOT!!
H-HELP ME...

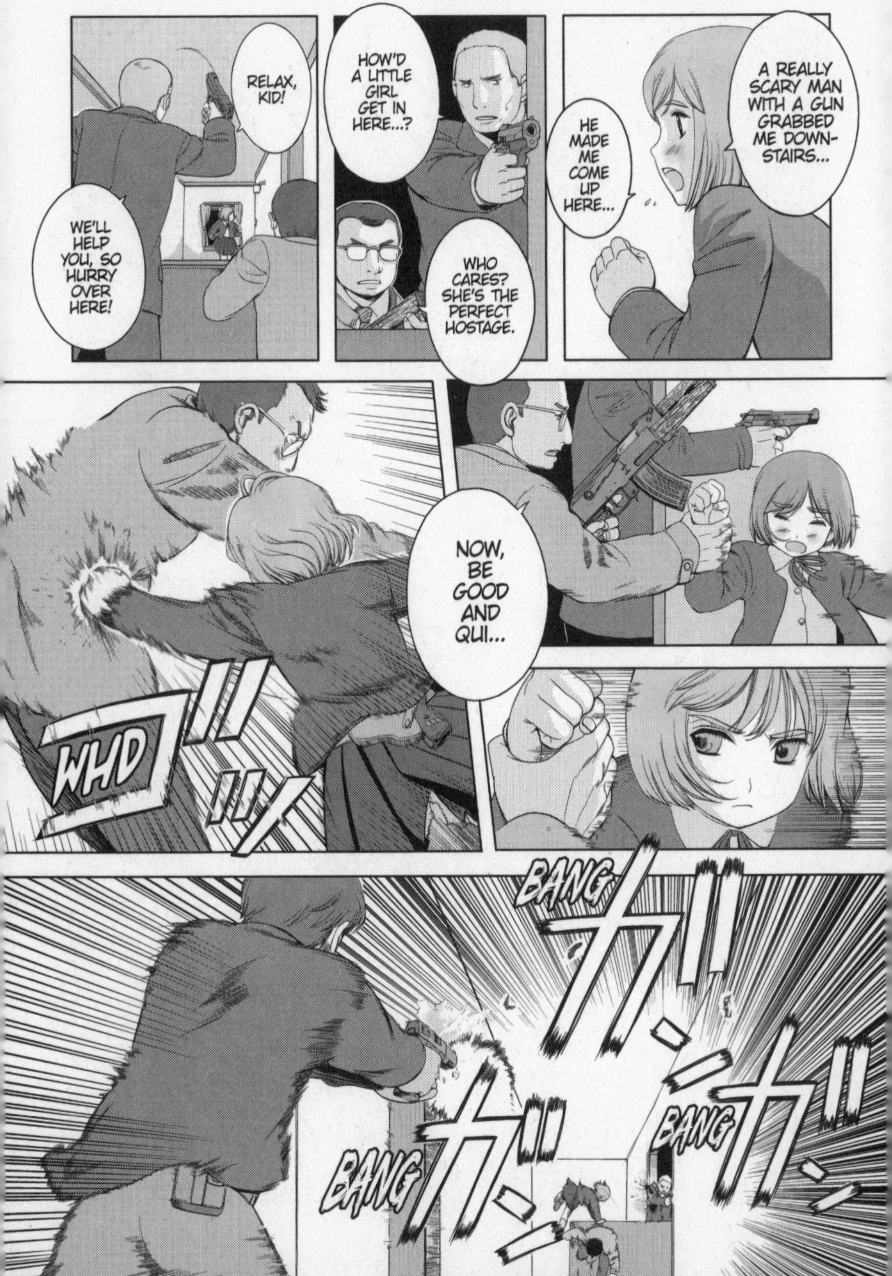
A REALLY SCARY MAN WITH A GUN GRABBED ME DOWN-STAIRS...
HE MADE ME COME UP HERE...
HOW'D A LITTLE GIRL GET IN HERE...?
WHO CARES? SHE'S THE PERFECT HOSTAGE.
RELAX, KID!
WE'LL HELP YOU, SO HURRY OVER HERE!
NOW, BE GOOD AND QUI...
WHD
BANG
BANG
BANG

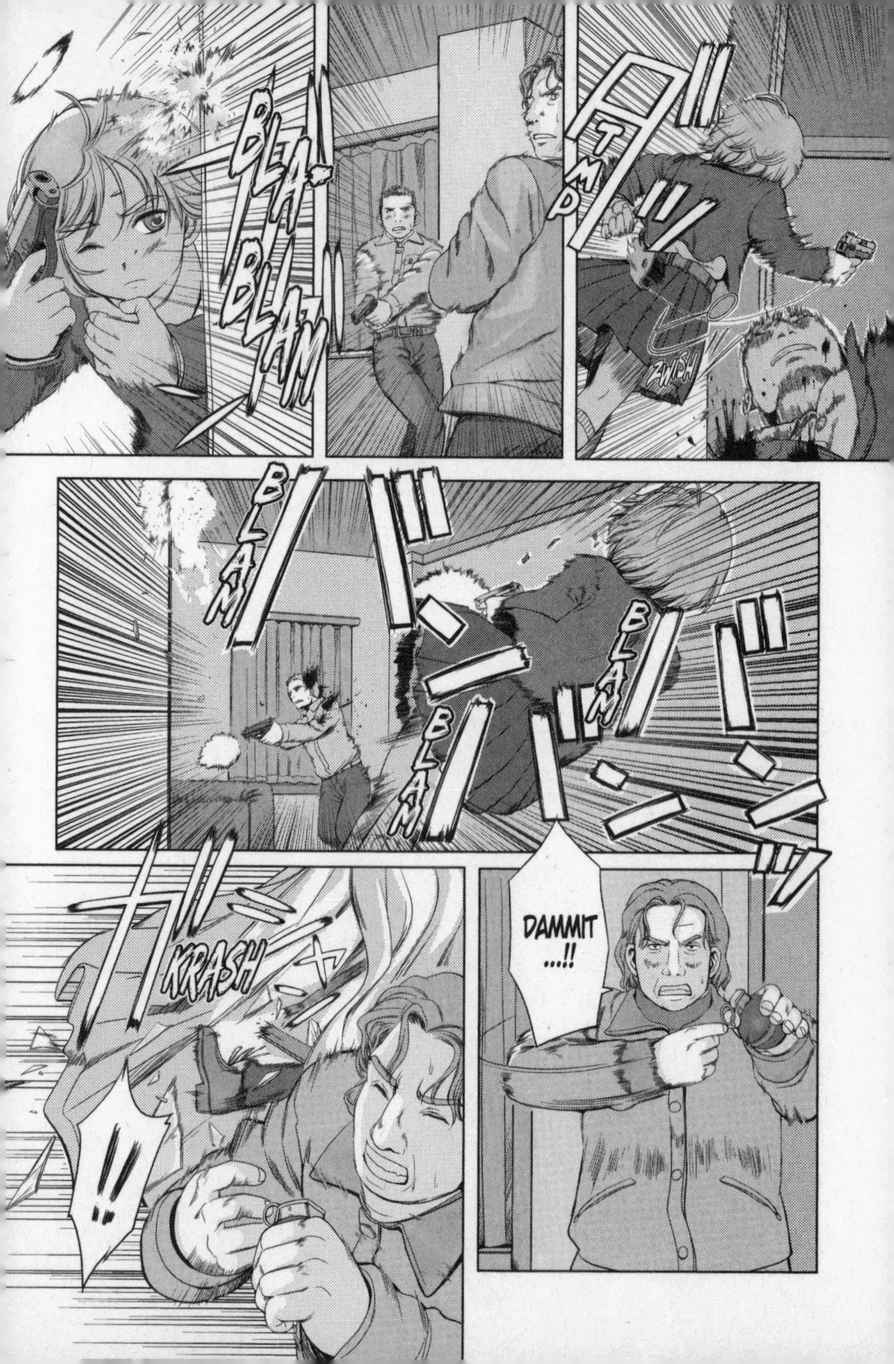
TMP
ZWISH
BLA-BLAM
BLAM
BLAM
BLAM
BLAM
DAMMIT ...!!
KRASH
!!

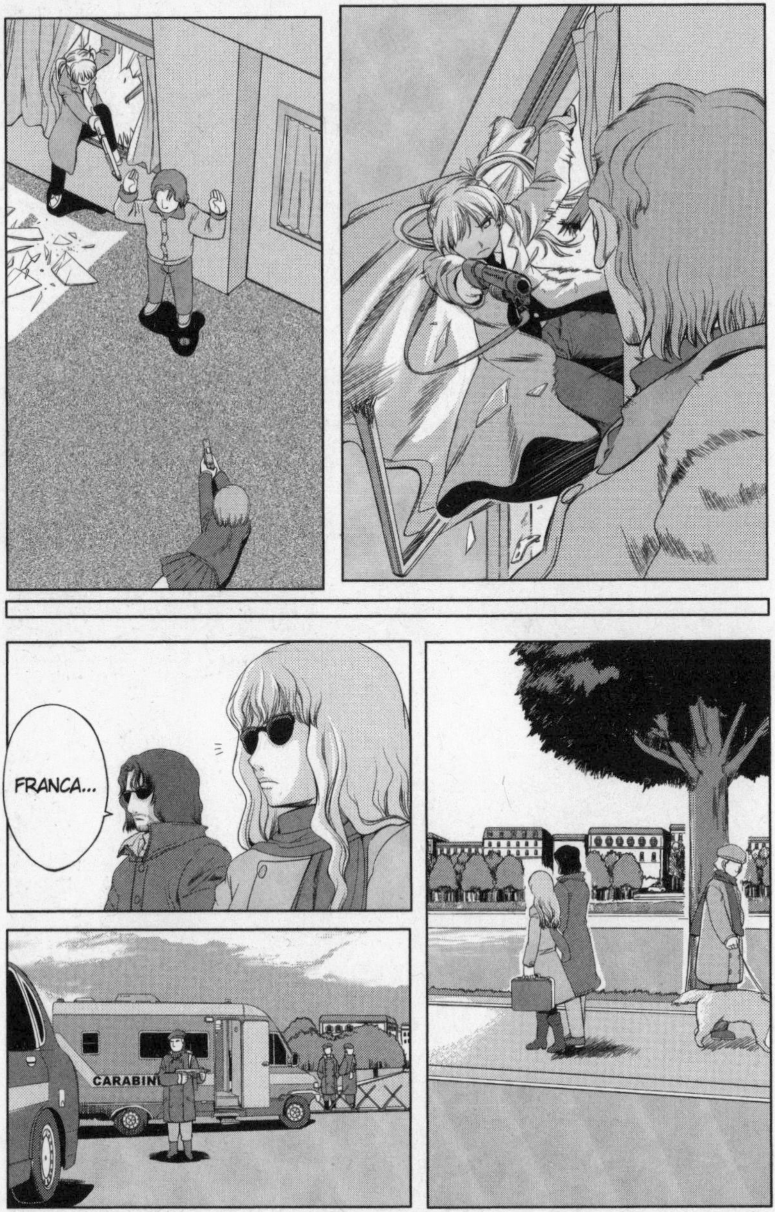
FRANCA...
CARABINI

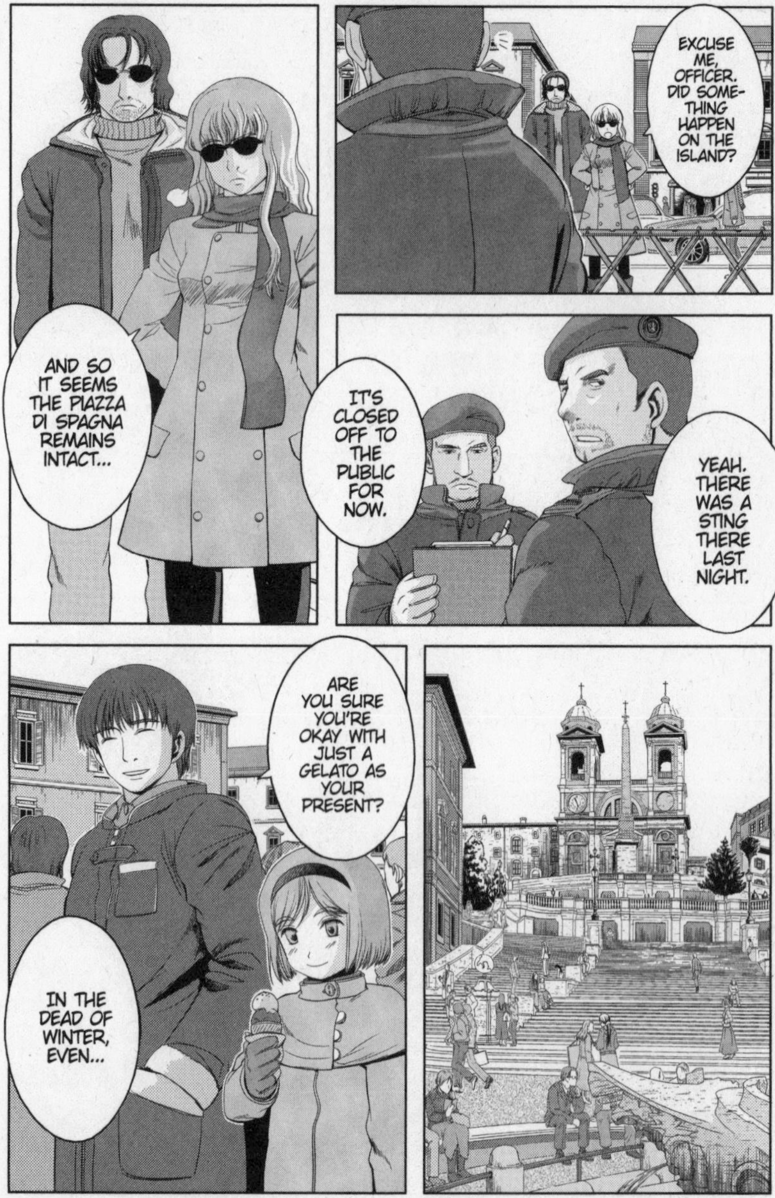
EXCUSE ME, OFFICER. DID SOMETHING HAPPEN ON THE ISLAND?
YEAH. THERE WAS A STING THERE LAST NIGHT.
IT'S CLOSED OFF TO THE PUBLIC FOR NOW.
AND SO IT SEEMS THE PIAZZA DI SPAGNA REMAINS INTACT...
ARE YOU SURE YOU'RE OKAY WITH JUST A GELATO AS YOUR PRESENT?
IN THE DEAD OF WINTER, EVEN...

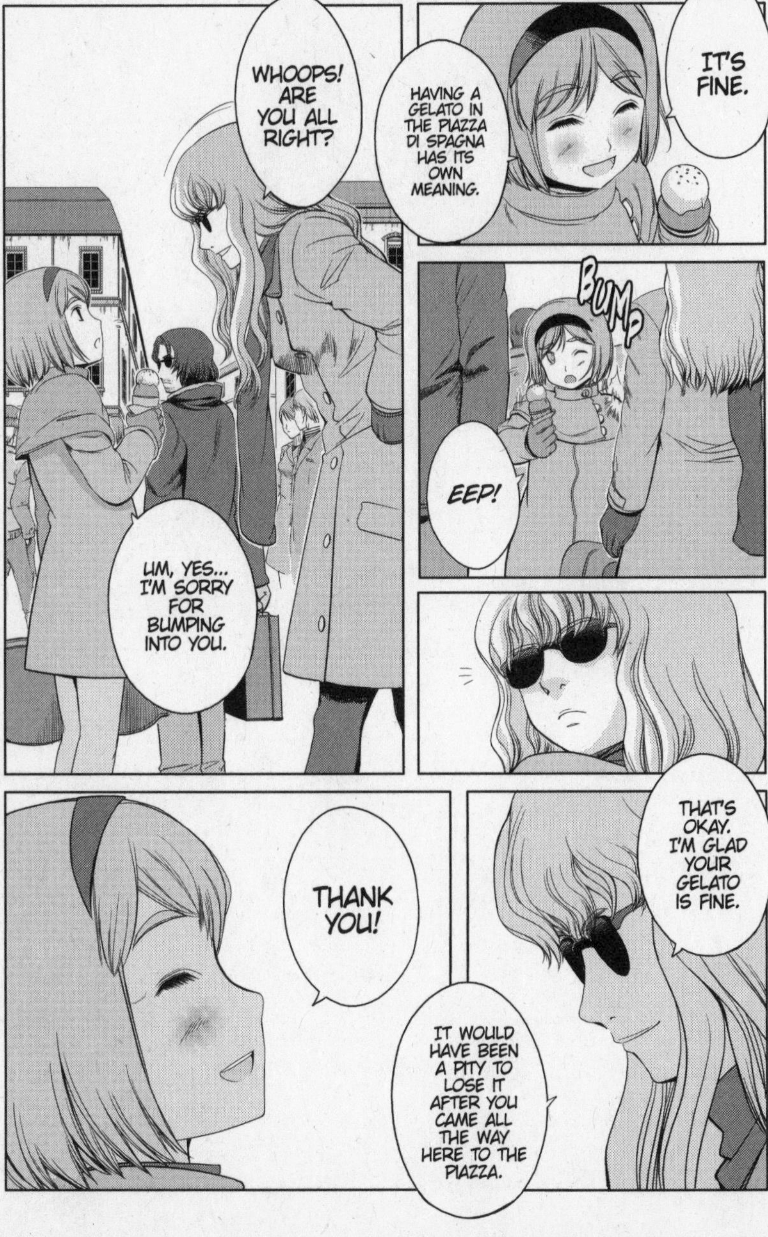

IT'S FINE.
HAVING A GELATO IN THE PIAZZA DI SPAGNA HAS ITS OWN MEANING.
BUMP
EEP!
WHOOPS! ARE YOU ALL RIGHT?
UM, YES... I'M SORRY FOR BUMPING INTO YOU.
THAT'S OKAY. I'M GLAD YOUR GELATO IS FINE.
IT WOULD HAVE BEEN A PITY TO LOSE IT AFTER YOU CAME ALL THE WAY HERE TO THE PIAZZA.
THANK YOU!

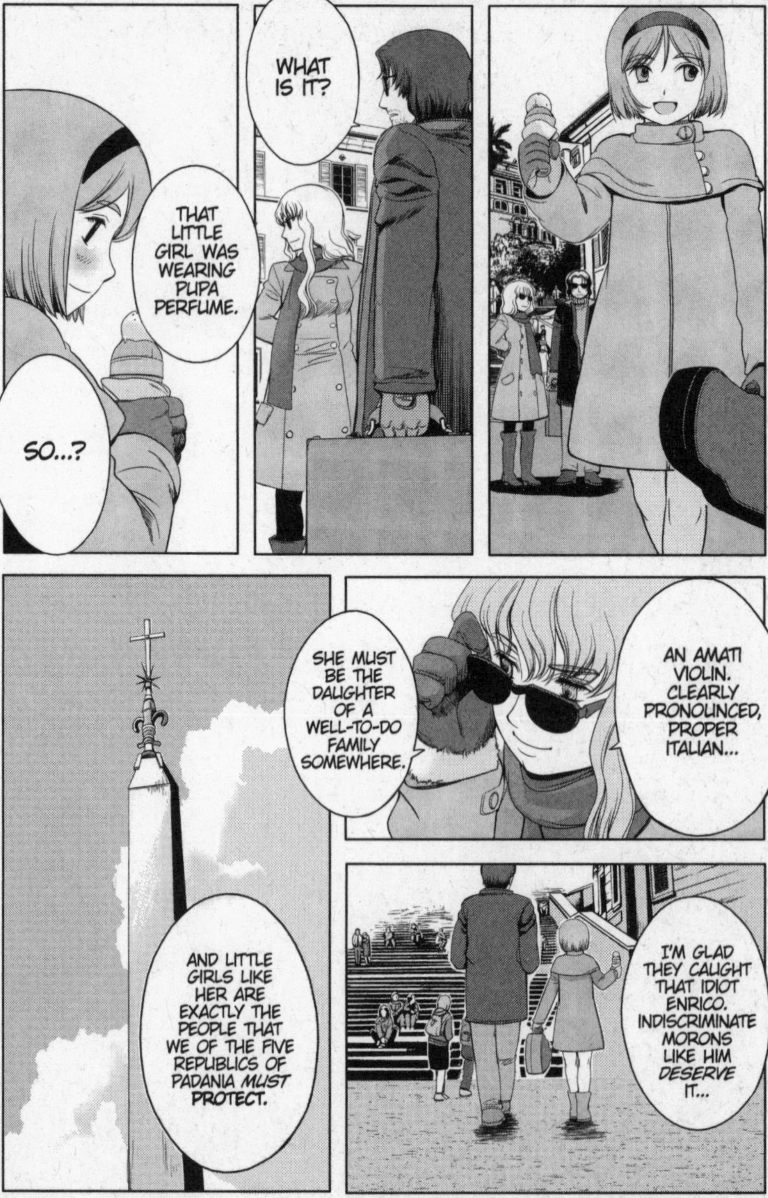
WHAT IS IT?
THAT LITTLE GIRL WAS WEARING PUPA PERFUME.
SO...?
AN AMATI VIOLIN. CLEARLY PRONOUNCED, PROPER ITALIAN...
SHE MUST BE THE DAUGHTER OF A WELL-TO-DO FAMILY SOMEWHERE.
I'M GLAD THEY CAUGHT THAT IDIOT ENRICO. INDISCRIMINATE MORONS LIKE HIM *DESERVE* IT...
AND LITTLE GIRLS LIKE HER ARE EXACTLY THE PEOPLE THAT WE OF THE FIVE REPUBLICS OF PADANIA *MUST* PROTECT.

Chapter 7 / END

GUNSLINGERGIRL.

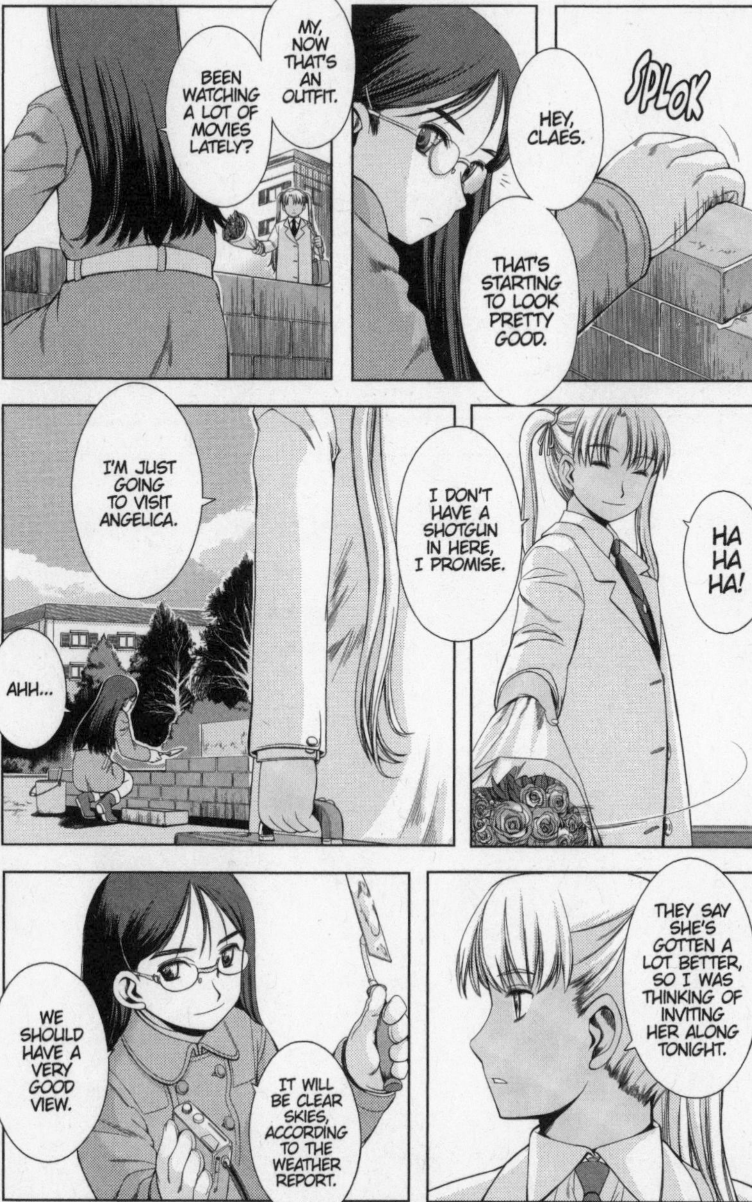
SPLOK
HEY, CLAES.
THAT'S STARTING TO LOOK PRETTY GOOD.
MY, NOW THAT'S AN OUTFIT.
BEEN WATCHING A LOT OF MOVIES LATELY?
HA HA HA!
I DON'T HAVE A SHOTGUN IN HERE, I PROMISE.
I'M JUST GOING TO VISIT ANGELICA.
AHH...
THEY SAY SHE'S GOTTEN A LOT BETTER, SO I WAS THINKING OF INVITING HER ALONG TONIGHT.
IT WILL BE CLEAR SKIES, ACCORDING TO THE WEATHER REPORT.
WE SHOULD HAVE A VERY GOOD VIEW.

Chapter 8: Ode to Joy

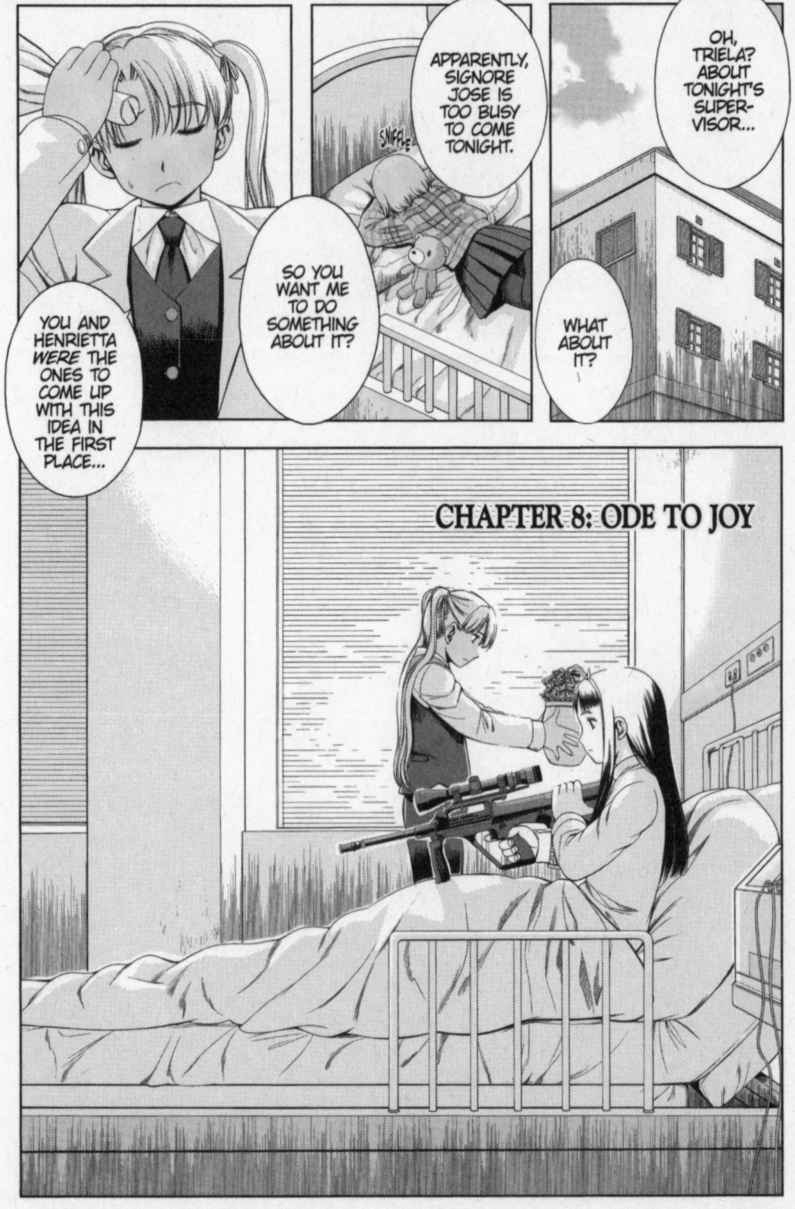
OH, TRIELA? ABOUT TONIGHT'S SUPER-VISOR...
WHAT ABOUT IT?
APPARENTLY, SIGNORE JOSE IS TOO BUSY TO COME TONIGHT.
SNIFFLE
SO YOU WANT ME TO DO SOMETHING ABOUT IT?
YOU AND HENRIETTA *WERE* THE ONES TO COME UP WITH THIS IDEA IN THE FIRST PLACE...
CHAPTER 8: ODE TO JOY

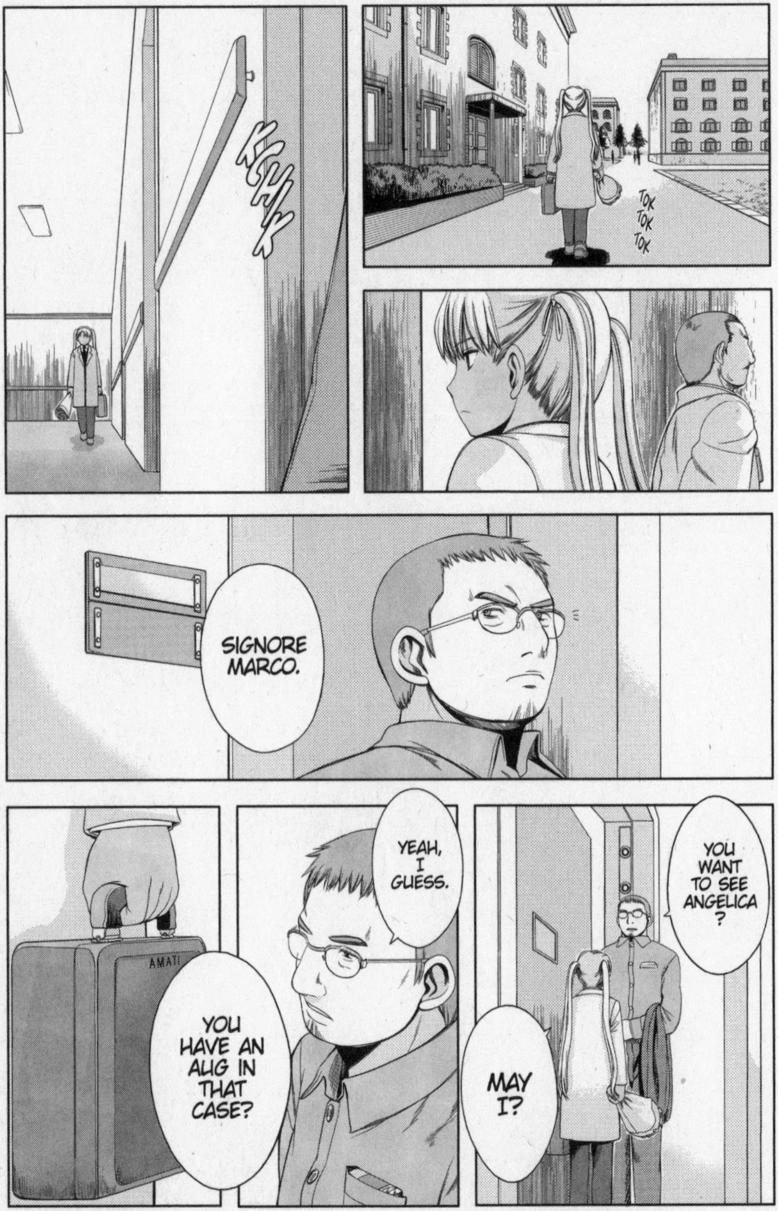
TOK TOK TOK
KCHK
SIGNORE MARCO.
YOU WANT TO SEE ANGELICA?
MAY I?
YEAH, I GUESS.
YOU HAVE AN AUG IN THAT CASE?
AMATI

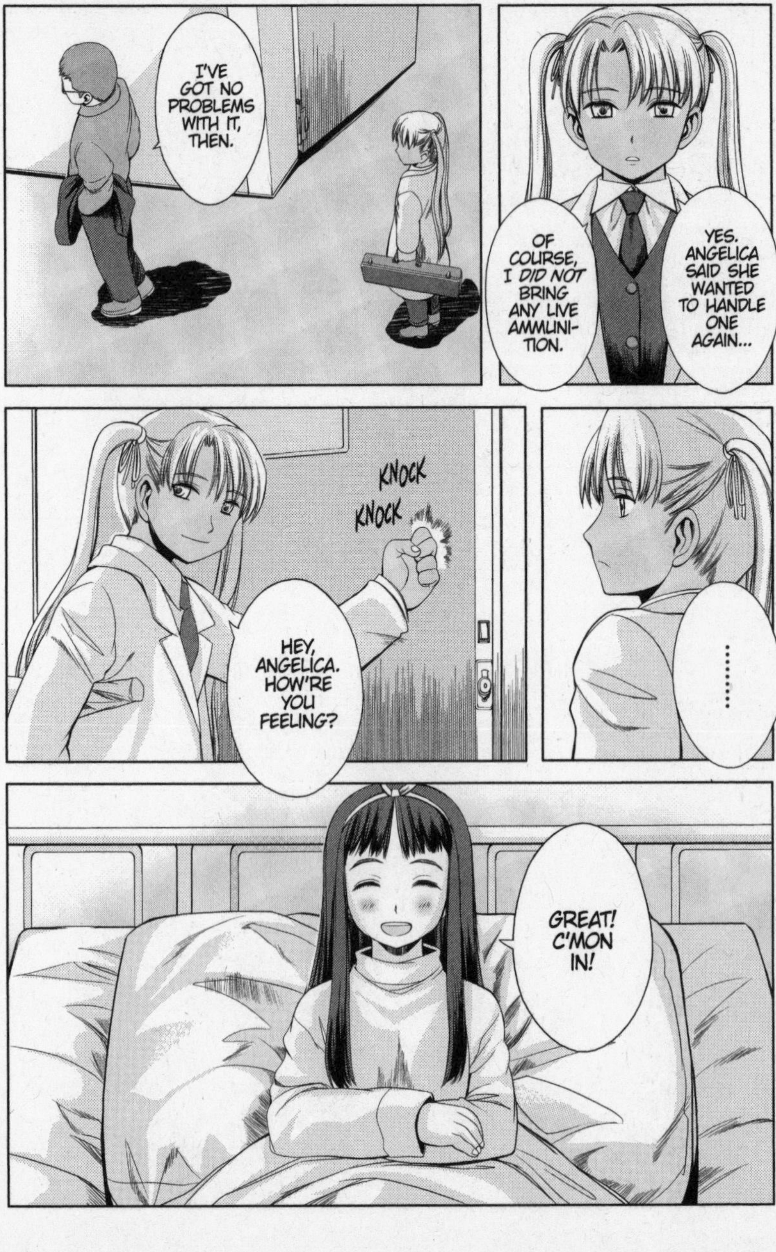
YES. ANGELICA SAID SHE WANTED TO HANDLE ONE AGAIN...
OF COURSE, I *DID NOT* BRING ANY LIVE AMMUNI-TION.
I'VE GOT NO PROBLEMS WITH IT, THEN.
......
KNOCK
KNOCK
HEY, ANGELICA. HOW'RE YOU FEELING?
GREAT! C'MON IN!

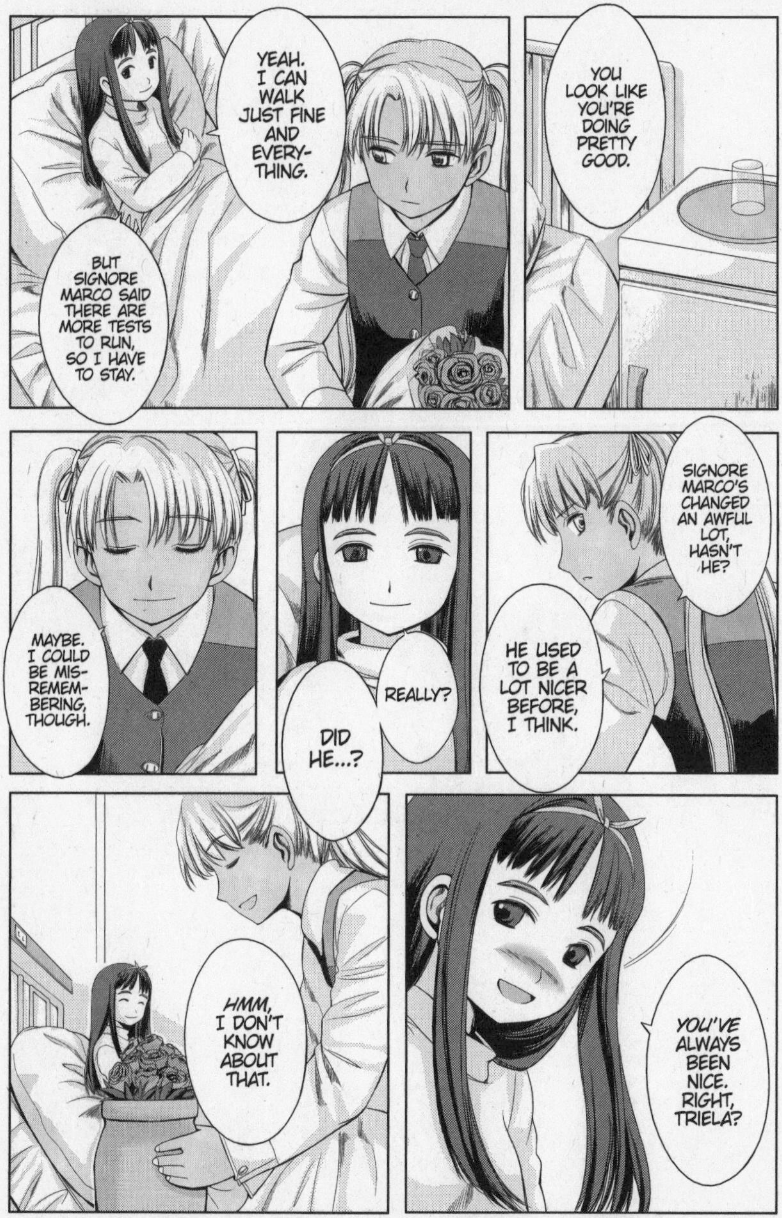
YOU LOOK LIKE YOU'RE DOING PRETTY GOOD.
YEAH. I CAN WALK JUST FINE AND EVERY-THING.
BUT SIGNORE MARCO SAID THERE ARE MORE TESTS TO RUN, SO I HAVE TO STAY.
SIGNORE MARCO'S CHANGED AN AWFUL LOT, HASN'T HE?
HE USED TO BE A LOT NICER BEFORE, I THINK.
REALLY?
DID HE...?
MAYBE. I COULD BE MIS-REMEMBERING, THOUGH.
YOU'VE ALWAYS BEEN NICE. RIGHT, TRIELA?
HMM, I DON'T KNOW ABOUT THAT.

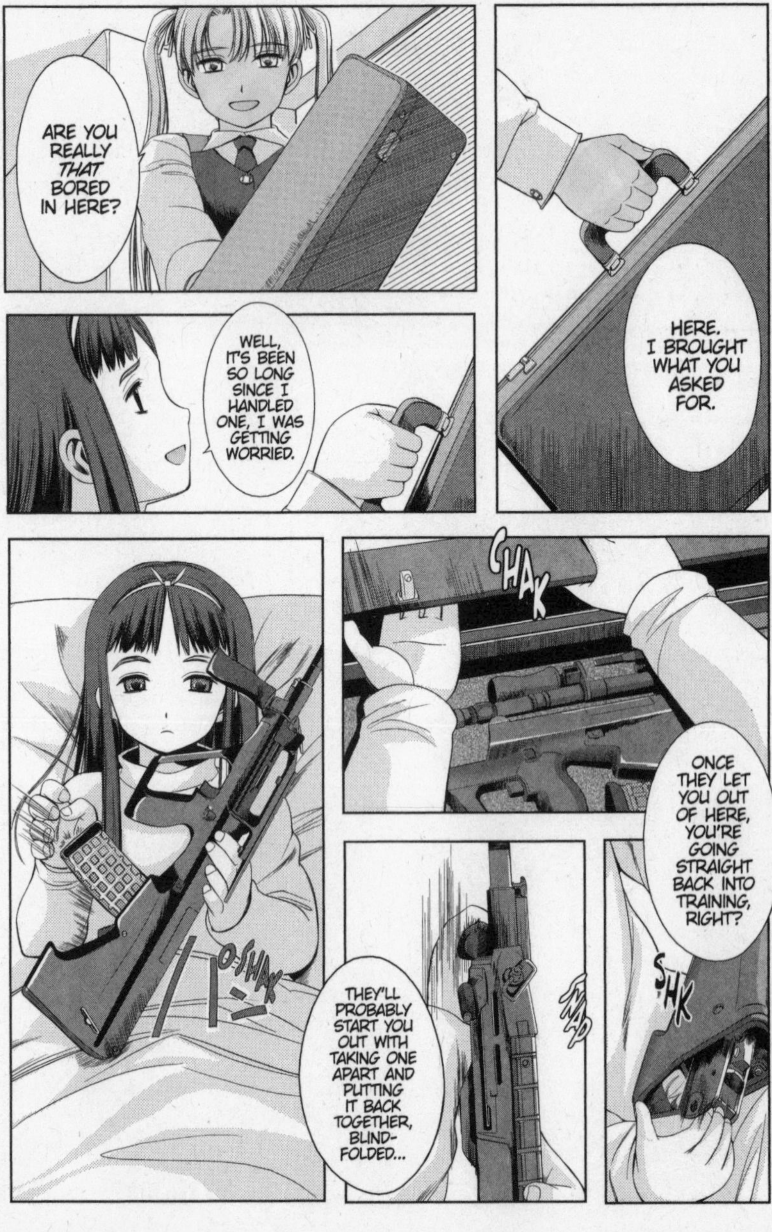
HERE. I BROUGHT WHAT YOU ASKED FOR.
ARE YOU REALLY *THAT* BORED IN HERE?
WELL, IT'S BEEN SO LONG SINCE I HANDLED ONE, I WAS GETTING WORRIED.
CHAK
ONCE THEY LET YOU OUT OF HERE, YOU'RE GOING STRAIGHT BACK INTO TRAINING, RIGHT?
SHK
THEY'LL PROBABLY START YOU OUT WITH TAKING ONE APART AND PUTTING IT BACK TOGETHER, BLIND-FOLDED...
SNAP
O-SHAK

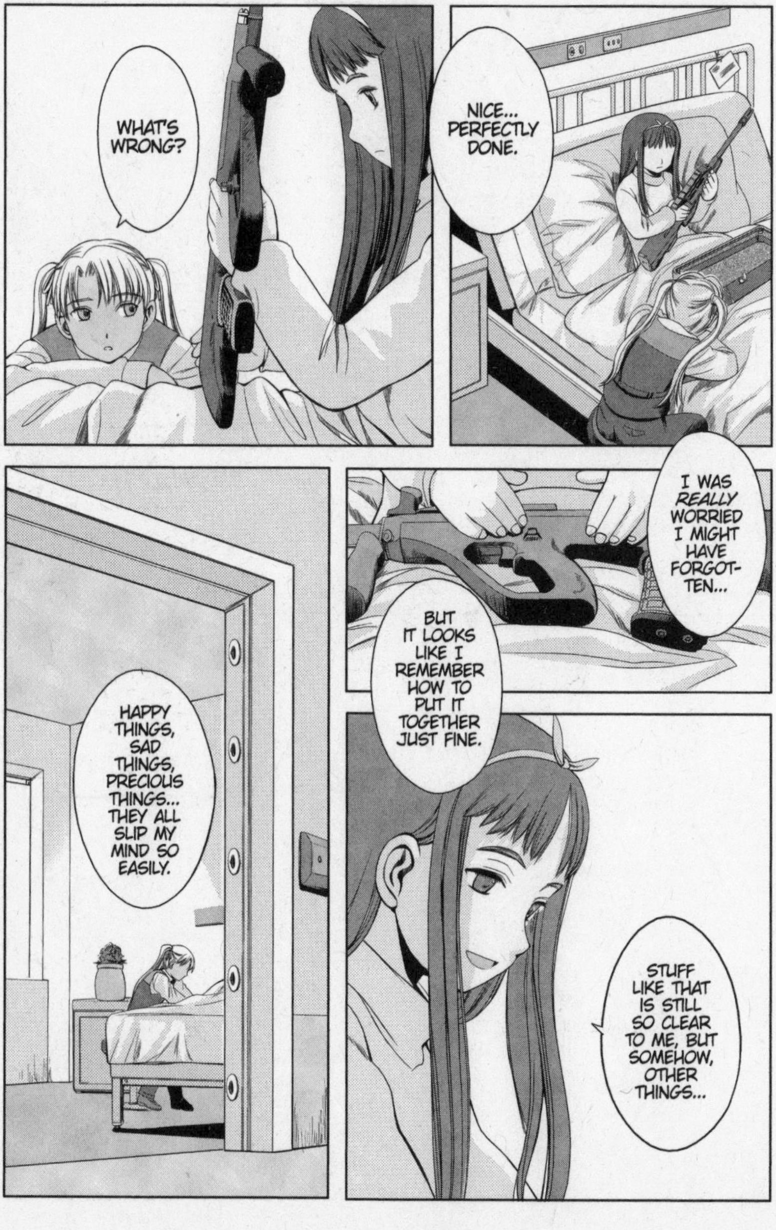
NICE... PERFECTLY DONE.
WHAT'S WRONG?
I WAS *REALLY* WORRIED I MIGHT HAVE FORGOT-TEN...
BUT IT LOOKS LIKE I REMEMBER HOW TO PUT IT TOGETHER JUST FINE.
STUFF LIKE THAT IS STILL SO CLEAR TO ME, BUT SOMEHOW, OTHER THINGS...
HAPPY THINGS, SAD THINGS, PRECIOUS THINGS... THEY ALL SLIP MY MIND SO EASILY.

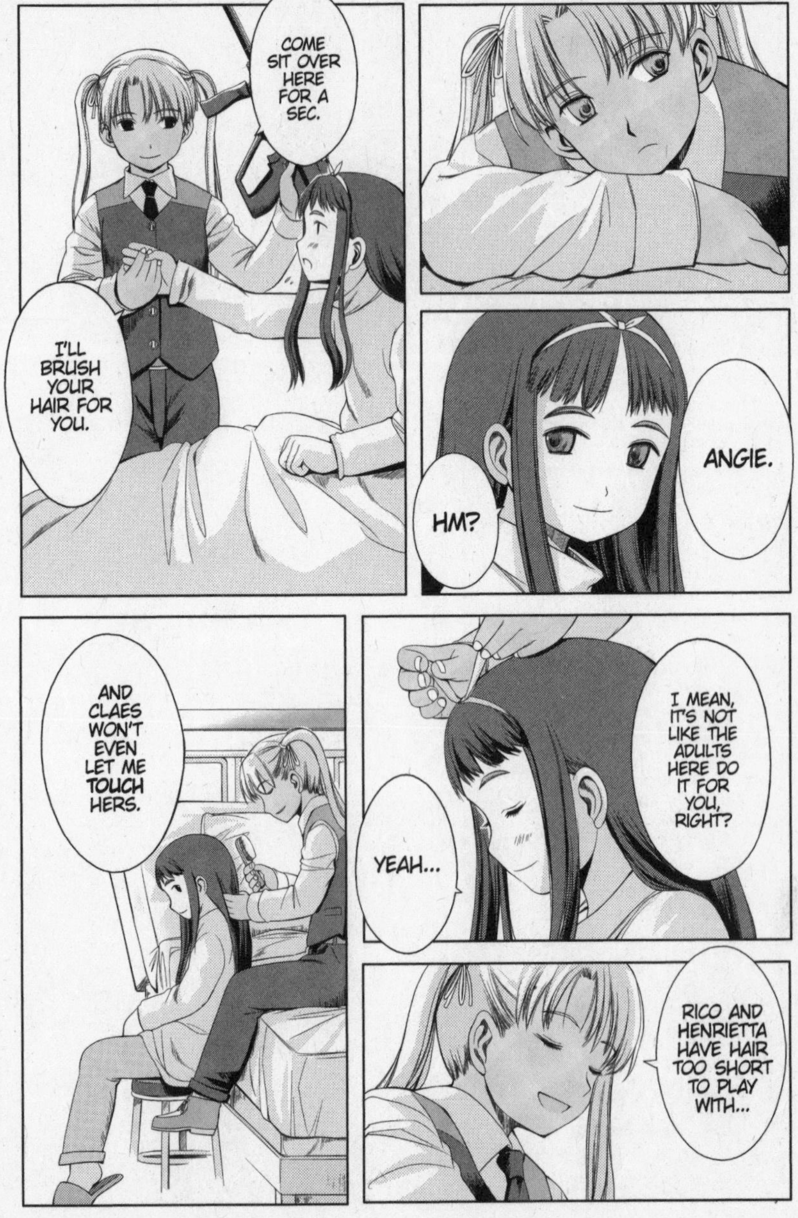
ANGIE.
HM?
COME SIT OVER HERE FOR A SEC.
I'LL BRUSH YOUR HAIR FOR YOU.
I MEAN, IT'S NOT LIKE THE ADULTS HERE DO IT FOR YOU, RIGHT?
YEAH...
RICO AND HENRIETTA HAVE HAIR TOO SHORT TO PLAY WITH...
AND CLAES WON'T EVEN LET ME TOUCH HERS.

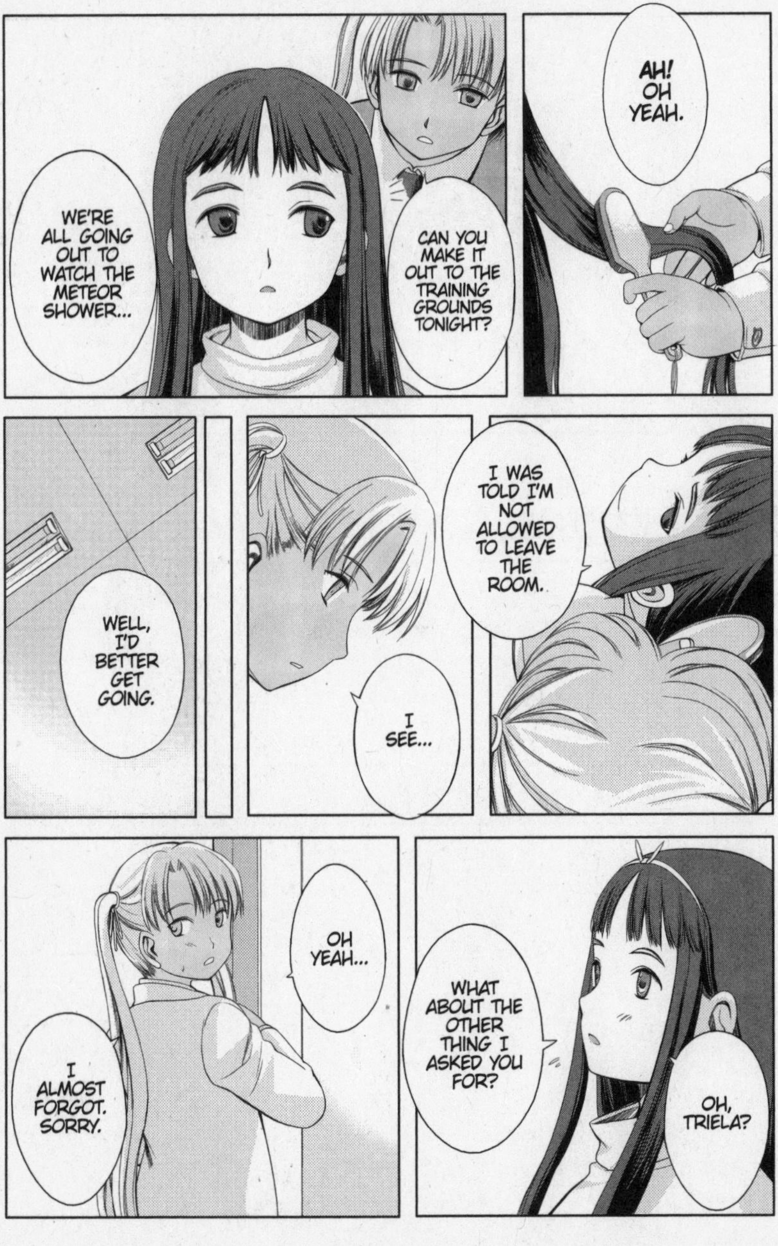
AH! OH YEAH.
CAN YOU MAKE IT OUT TO THE TRAINING GROUNDS TONIGHT?
WE'RE ALL GOING OUT TO WATCH THE METEOR SHOWER...
I WAS TOLD I'M NOT ALLOWED TO LEAVE THE ROOM.
I SEE...
WELL, I'D BETTER GET GOING.
OH, TRIELA?
WHAT ABOUT THE OTHER THING I ASKED YOU FOR?
OH YEAH...
I ALMOST FORGOT. SORRY.

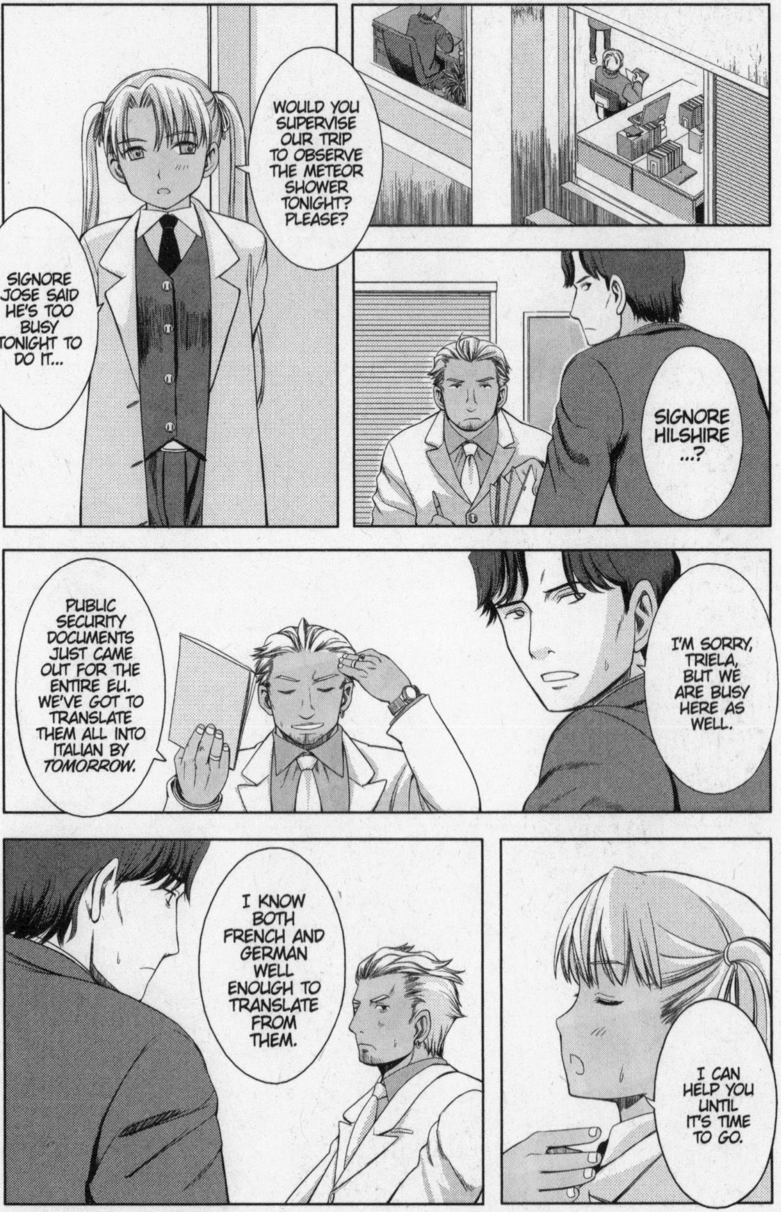
SIGNORE HILSHIRE ...?
WOULD YOU SUPERVISE OUR TRIP TO OBSERVE THE METEOR SHOWER TONIGHT? PLEASE?
SIGNORE JOSE SAID HE'S TOO BUSY TONIGHT TO DO IT...
I'M SORRY, TRIELA, BUT WE ARE BUSY HERE AS WELL.
PUBLIC SECURITY DOCUMENTS JUST CAME OUT FOR THE ENTIRE EU. WE'VE GOT TO TRANSLATE THEM ALL INTO ITALIAN BY *TOMORROW.*
I CAN HELP YOU UNTIL IT'S TIME TO GO.
I KNOW BOTH FRENCH AND GERMAN WELL ENOUGH TO TRANSLATE FROM THEM.

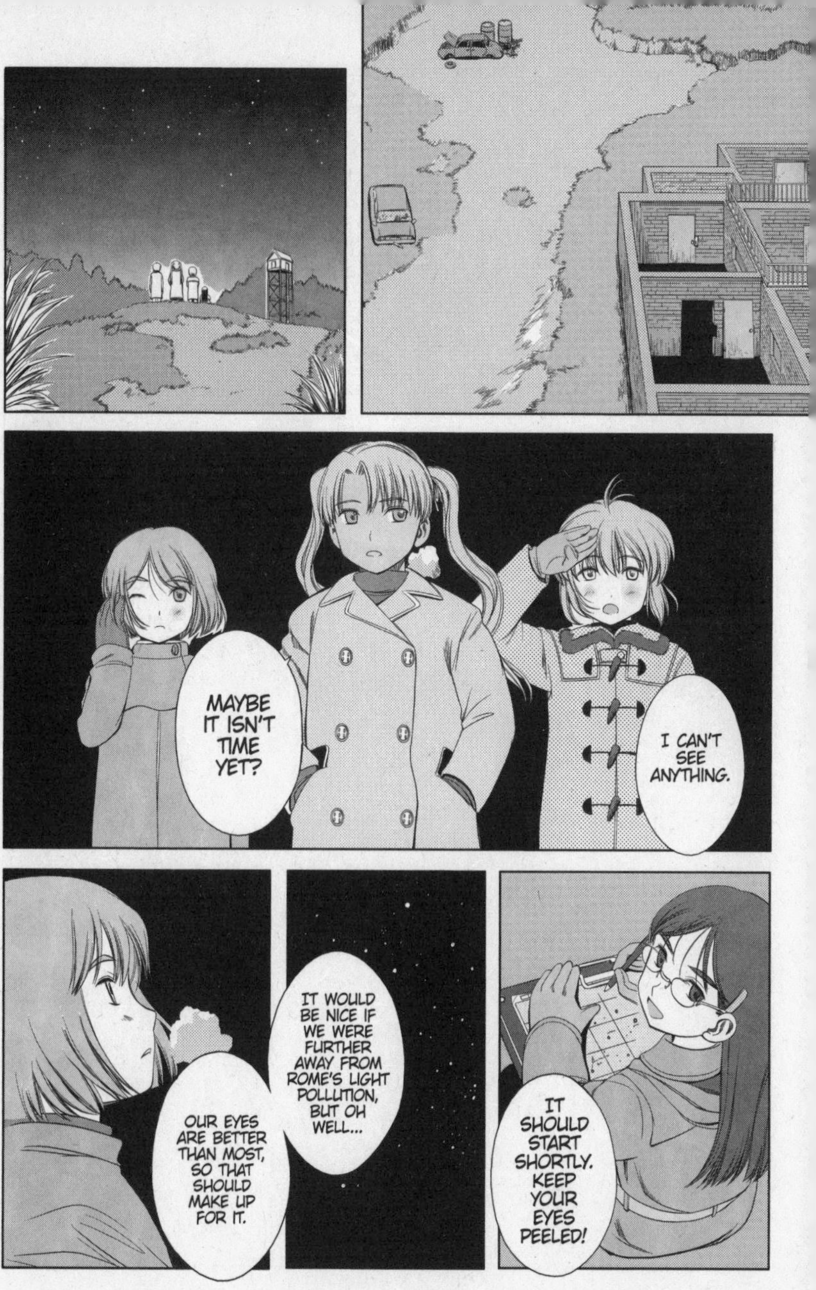
I CAN'T SEE ANYTHING.
MAYBE IT ISN'T TIME YET?
IT SHOULD START SHORTLY. KEEP YOUR EYES PEELED!
IT WOULD BE NICE IF WE WERE FURTHER AWAY FROM ROME'S LIGHT POLLUTION, BUT OH WELL...
OUR EYES ARE BETTER THAN MOST, SO THAT SHOULD MAKE UP FOR IT.

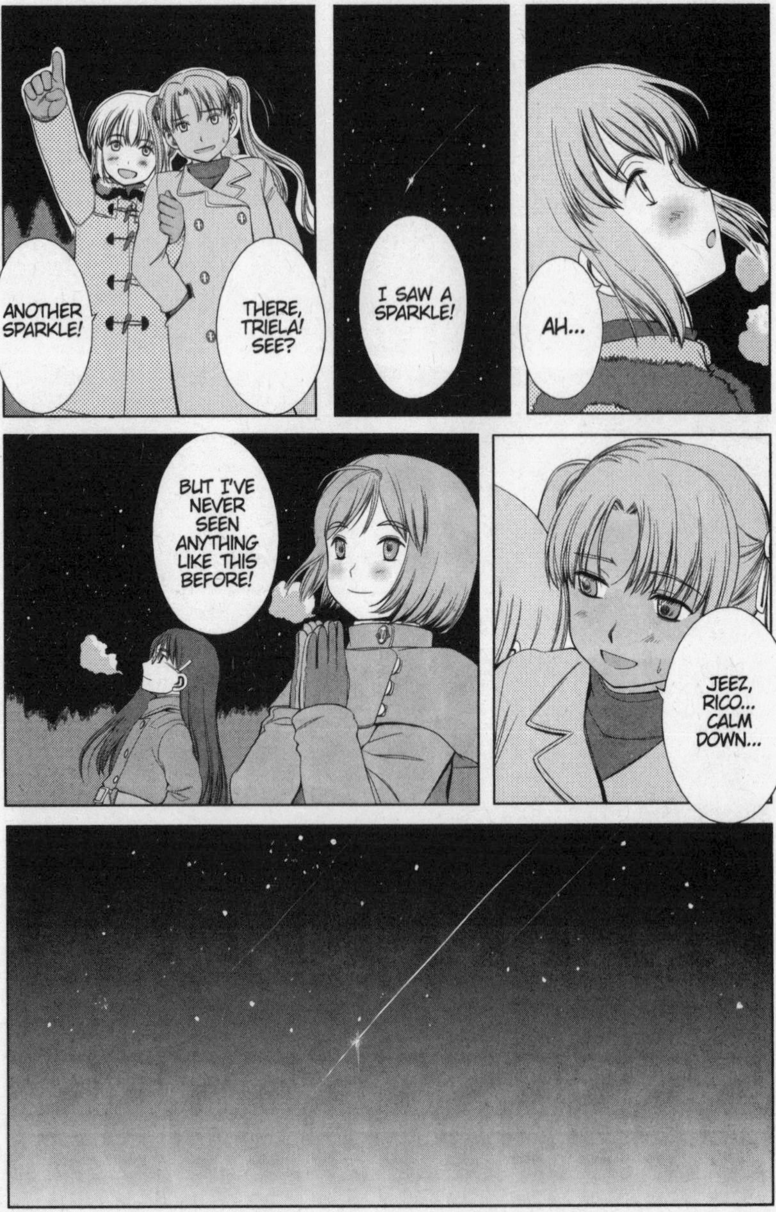
AH...
I SAW A SPARKLE!
THERE, TRIELA! SEE?
ANOTHER SPARKLE!
JEEZ, RICO... CALM DOWN...
BUT I'VE NEVER SEEN ANYTHING LIKE THIS BEFORE!

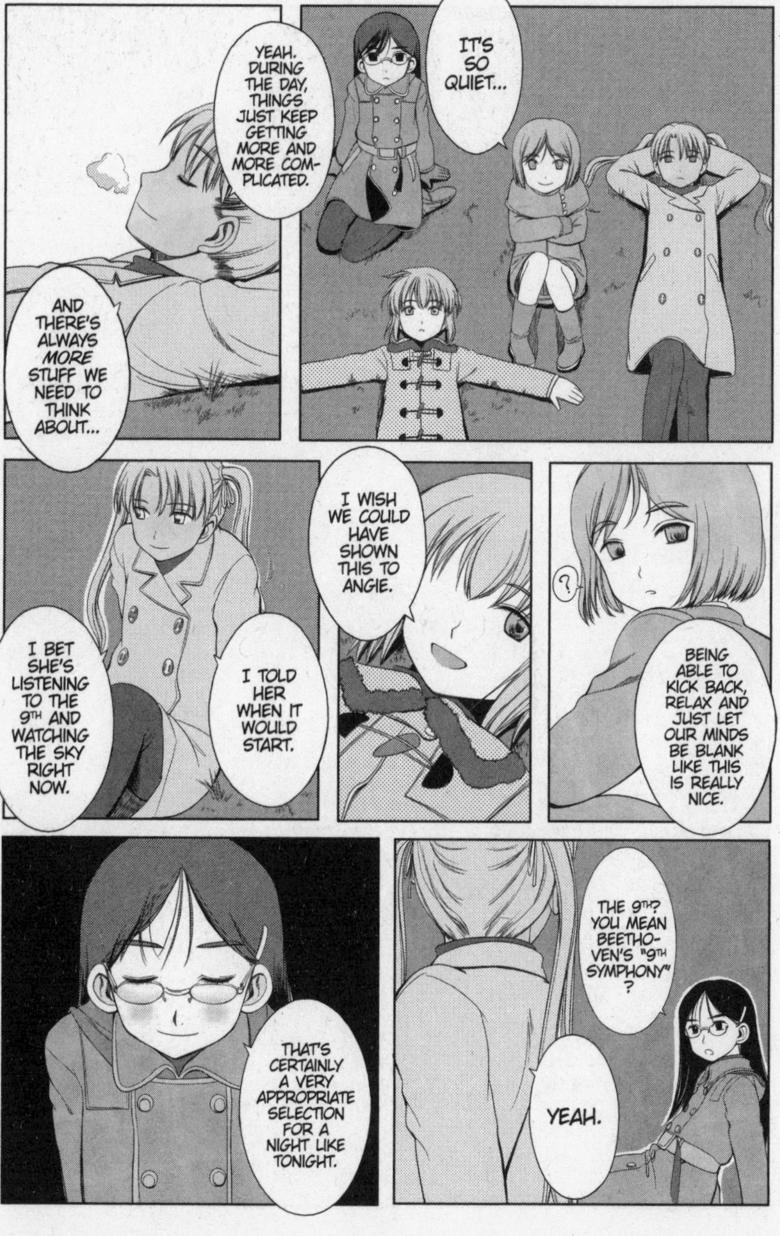

IT'S SO QUIET...
YEAH. DURING THE DAY, THINGS JUST KEEP GETTING MORE AND MORE COMPLICATED.
AND THERE'S ALWAYS *MORE* STUFF WE NEED TO THINK ABOUT...
?
BEING ABLE TO KICK BACK, RELAX AND JUST LET OUR MINDS BE BLANK LIKE THIS IS REALLY NICE.
I WISH WE COULD HAVE SHOWN THIS TO ANGIE.
I TOLD HER WHEN IT WOULD START.
I BET SHE'S LISTENING TO THE 9TH AND WATCHING THE SKY RIGHT NOW.
THE 9TH? YOU MEAN BEETHOVEN'S "9TH SYMPHONY"?
YEAH.
THAT'S CERTAINLY A VERY APPROPRIATE SELECTION FOR A NIGHT LIKE TONIGHT.

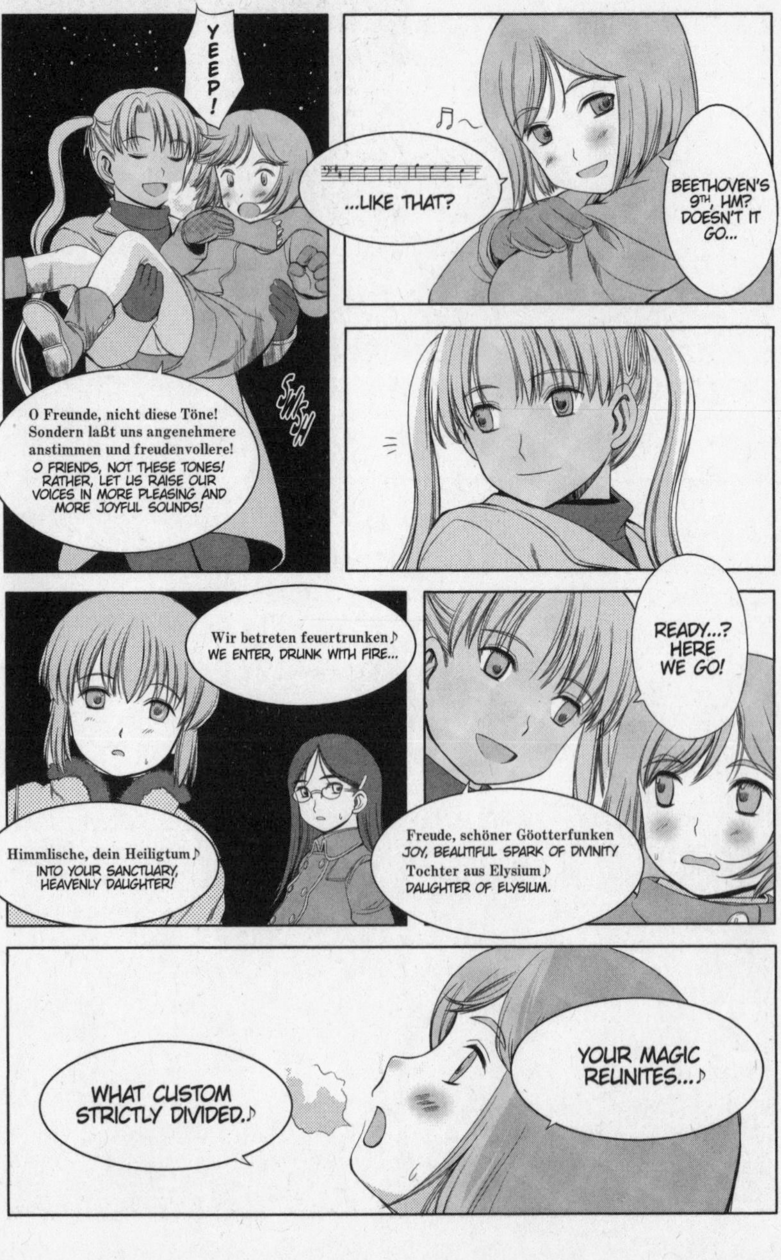
BEETHOVEN'S 9TH, HM? DOESN'T IT GO...
...LIKE THAT?
YEEEP!
O Freunde, nicht diese Töne! Sondern laßt uns angenehmere anstimmen und freudenvollere!
O FRIENDS, NOT THESE TONES! RATHER, LET US RAISE OUR VOICES IN MORE PLEASING AND MORE JOYFUL SOUNDS!
READY...? HERE WE GO!
Freude, schöner Göotterfunken
JOY, BEAUTIFUL SPARK OF DIVINITY
Tochter aus Elysium♪
DAUGHTER OF ELYSIUM.
Wir betreten feuertrunken♪
WE ENTER, DRUNK WITH FIRE...
Himmlische, dein Heiligtum♪
INTO YOUR SANCTUARY, HEAVENLY DAUGHTER!
YOUR MAGIC REUNITES...♪
WHAT CUSTOM STRICTLY DIVIDED.♪

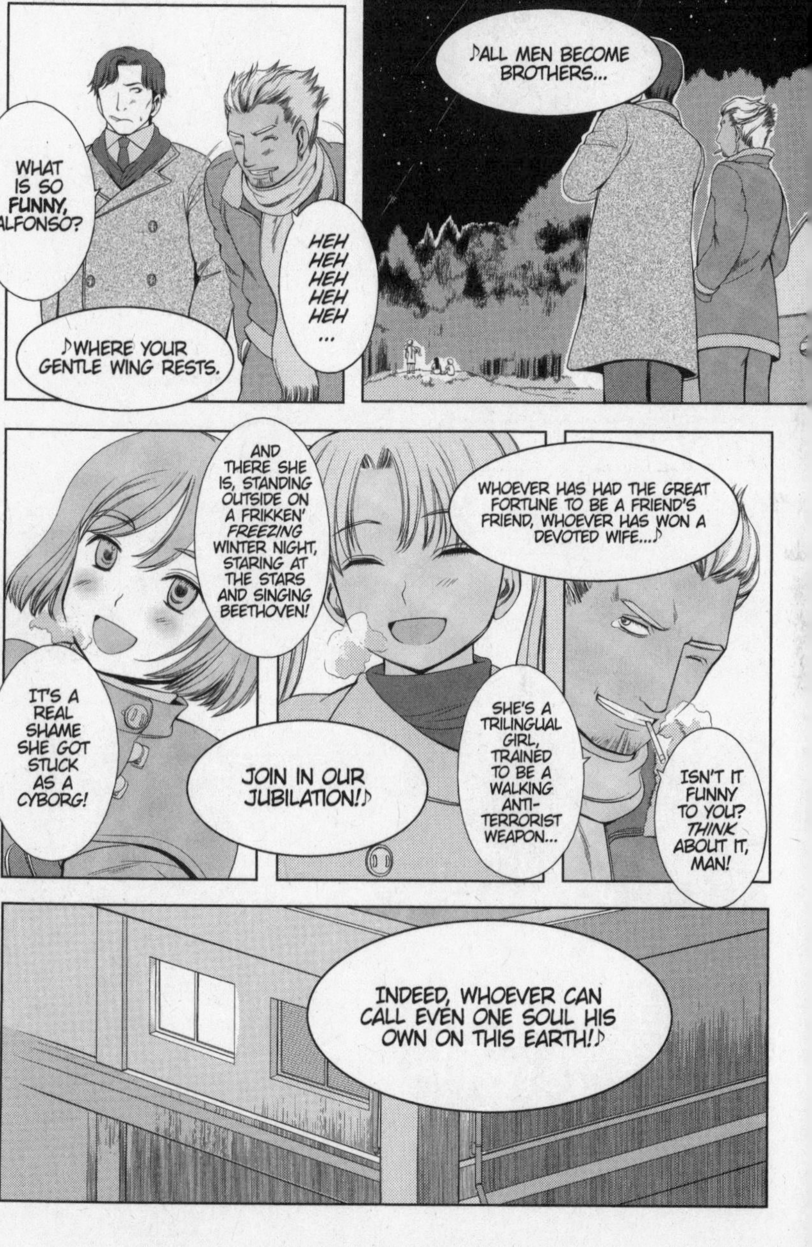
♪ALL MEN BECOME BROTHERS...
HEH HEH HEH HEH HEH ...
WHAT IS SO FUNNY, ALFONSO?
♪WHERE YOUR GENTLE WING RESTS.
WHOEVER HAS HAD THE GREAT FORTUNE TO BE A FRIEND'S FRIEND, WHOEVER HAS WON A DEVOTED WIFE...♪
AND THERE SHE IS, STANDING OUTSIDE ON A FRIKKEN' *FREEZING* WINTER NIGHT, STARING AT THE STARS AND SINGING BEETHOVEN!
SHE'S A TRILINGUAL GIRL, TRAINED TO BE A WALKING ANTI-TERRORIST WEAPON...
JOIN IN OUR JUBILATION!♪
IT'S A REAL SHAME SHE GOT STUCK AS A CYBORG!
ISN'T IT FUNNY TO YOU? *THINK* ABOUT IT, MAN!
INDEED, WHOEVER CAN CALL EVEN ONE SOUL HIS OWN ON THIS EARTH!♪

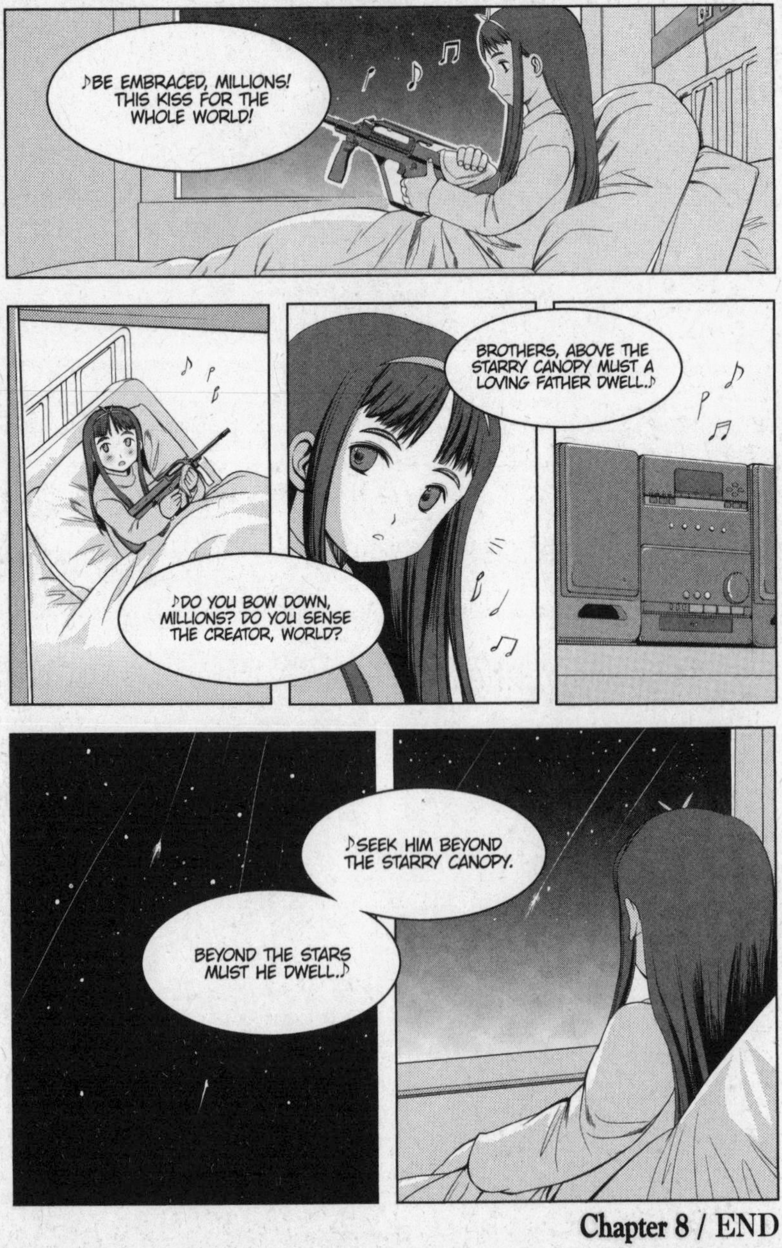
♪BE EMBRACED, MILLIONS! THIS KISS FOR THE WHOLE WORLD!
BROTHERS, ABOVE THE STARRY CANOPY MUST A LOVING FATHER DWELL.♪
♪DO YOU BOW DOWN, MILLIONS? DO YOU SENSE THE CREATOR, WORLD?
♪SEEK HIM BEYOND THE STARRY CANOPY.
BEYOND THE STARS MUST HE DWELL.♪

Chapter 8 / END

GUNSLINGERGIRL.

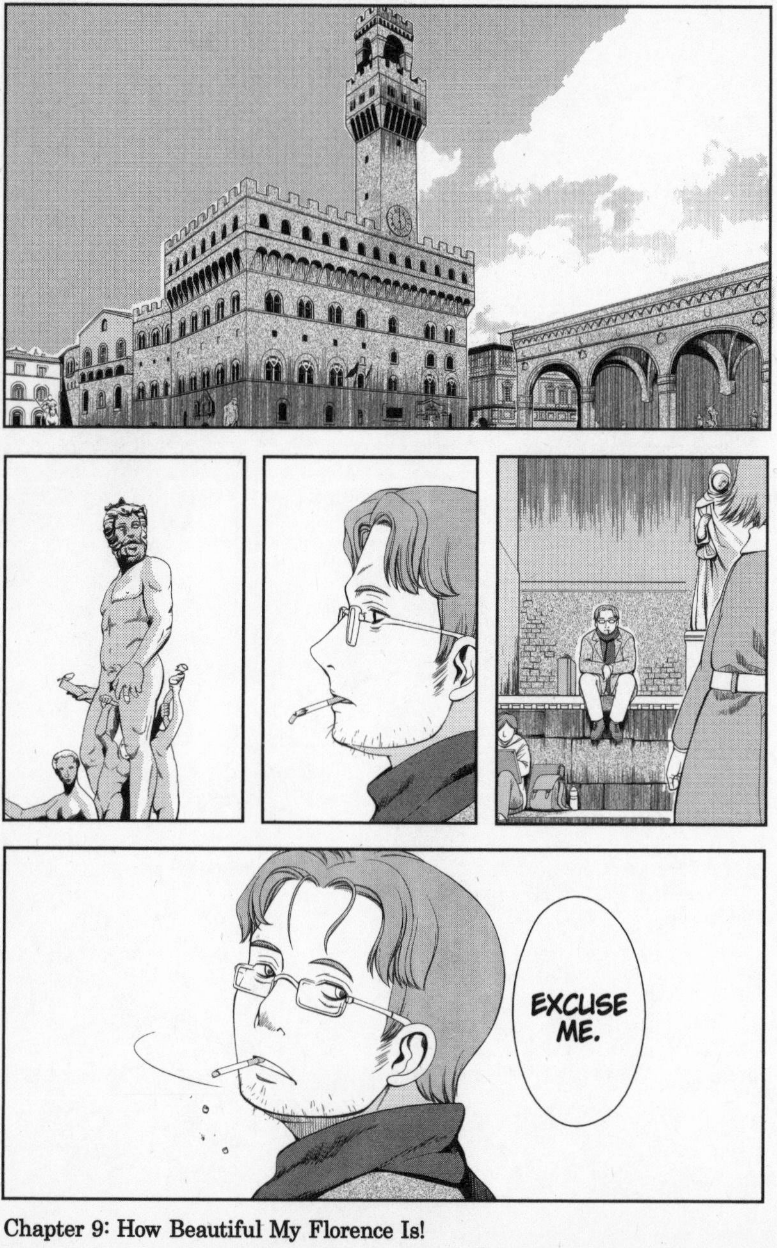
EXCUSE ME.

Chapter 9: How Beautiful My Florence Is!

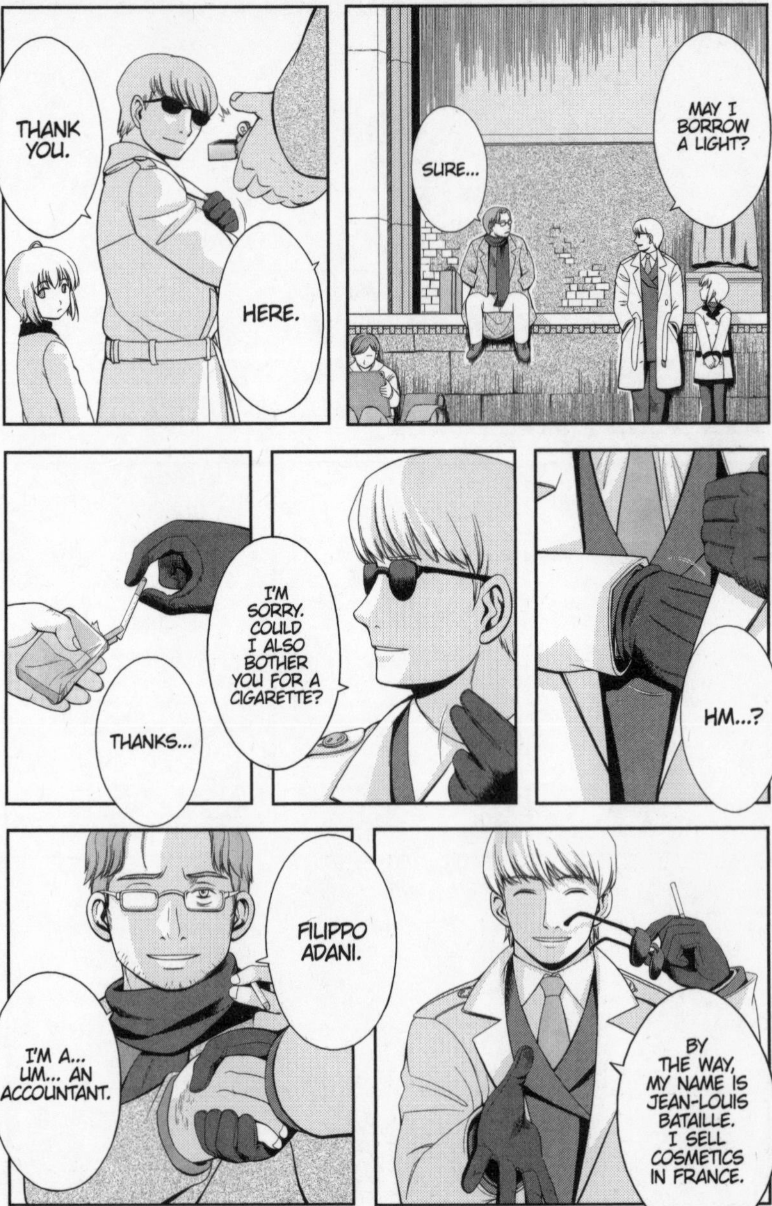
MAY I BORROW A LIGHT?
SURE...
HERE.
THANK YOU.
HM...?
I'M SORRY. COULD I ALSO BOTHER YOU FOR A CIGARETTE?
THANKS...
BY THE WAY, MY NAME IS JEAN-LOUIS BATAILLE. I SELL COSMETICS IN FRANCE.
FILIPPO ADANI.
I'M A... UM... AN ACCOUNTANT.

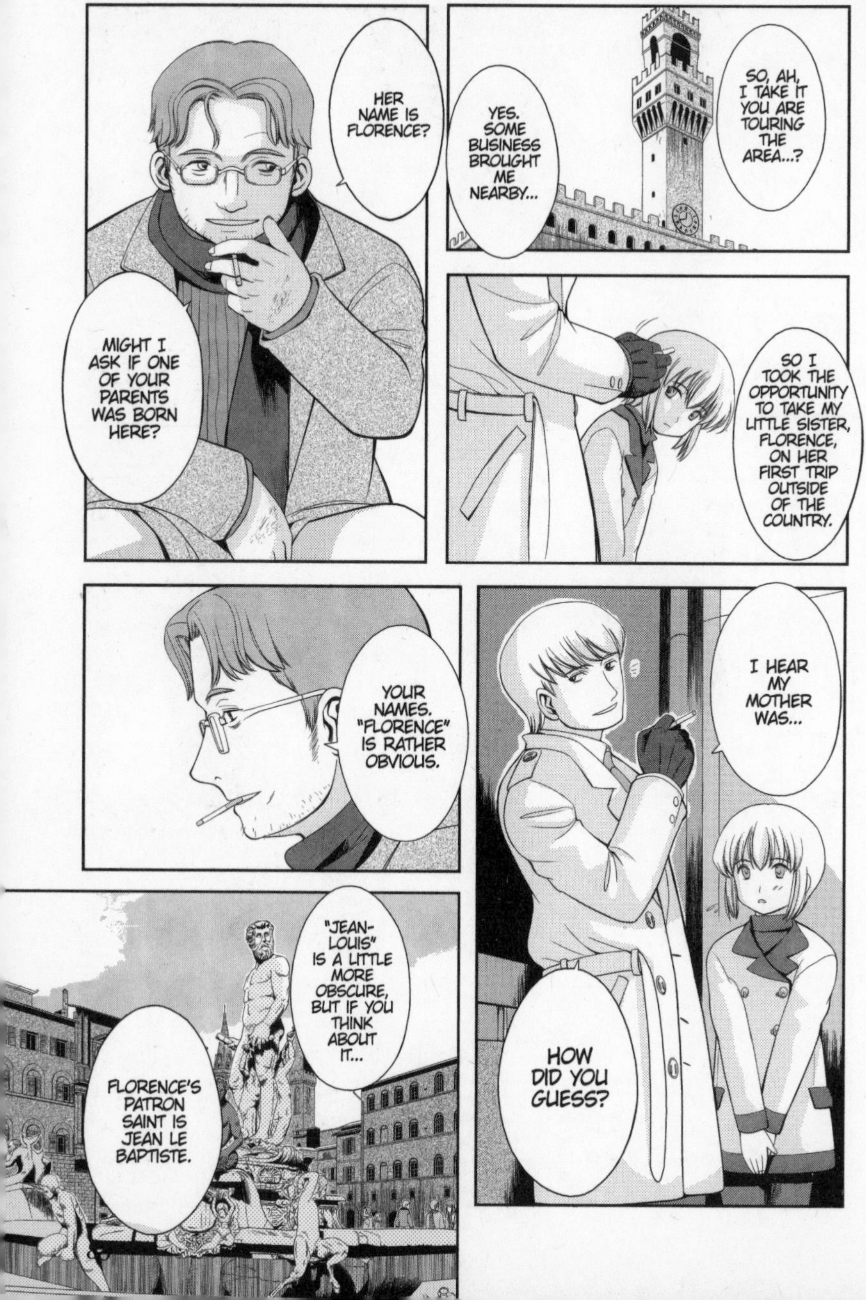
SO, AH, I TAKE IT YOU ARE TOURING THE AREA...?
YES. SOME BUSINESS BROUGHT ME NEARBY...
SO I TOOK THE OPPORTUNITY TO TAKE MY LITTLE SISTER, FLORENCE, ON HER FIRST TRIP OUTSIDE OF THE COUNTRY.
HER NAME IS FLORENCE?
MIGHT I ASK IF ONE OF YOUR PARENTS WAS BORN HERE?
I HEAR MY MOTHER WAS...
HOW DID YOU GUESS?
YOUR NAMES. "FLORENCE" IS RATHER OBVIOUS.
"JEAN-LOUIS" IS A LITTLE MORE OBSCURE, BUT IF YOU THINK ABOUT IT...
FLORENCE'S PATRON SAINT IS JEAN LE BAPTISTE.

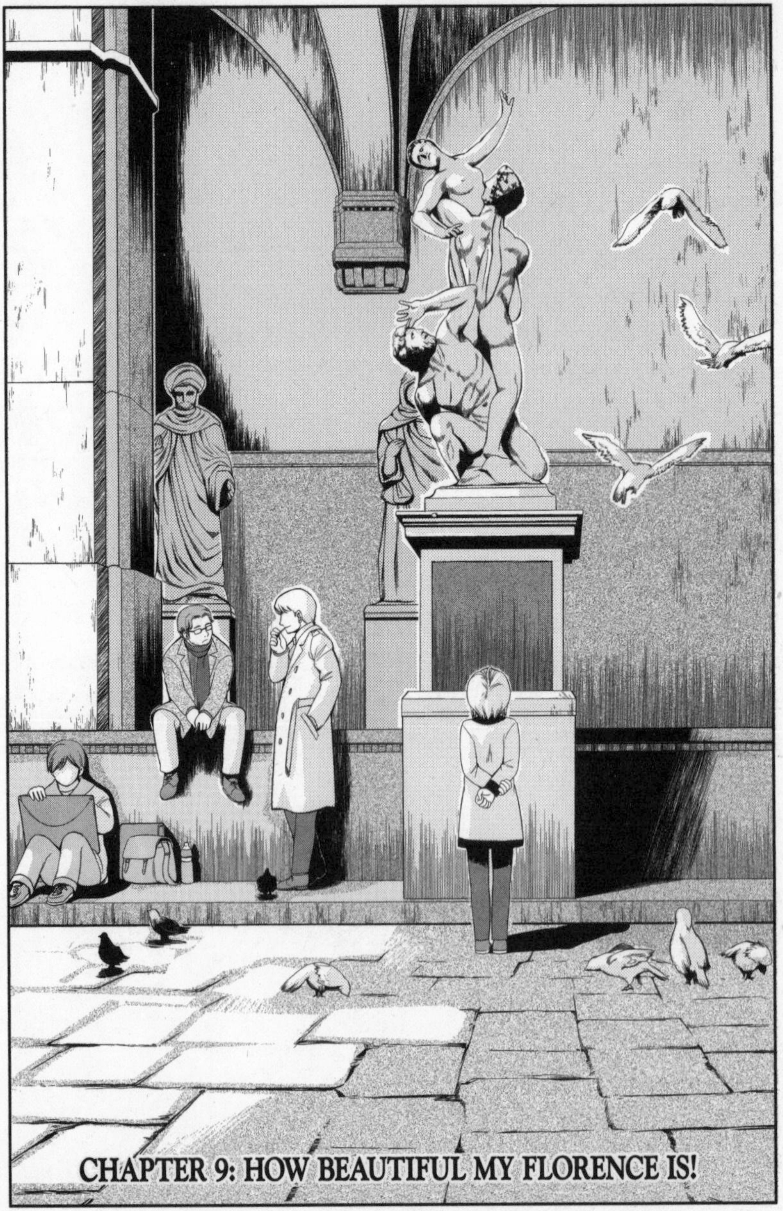
CHAPTER 9: HOW BEAUTIFUL MY FLORENCE IS!

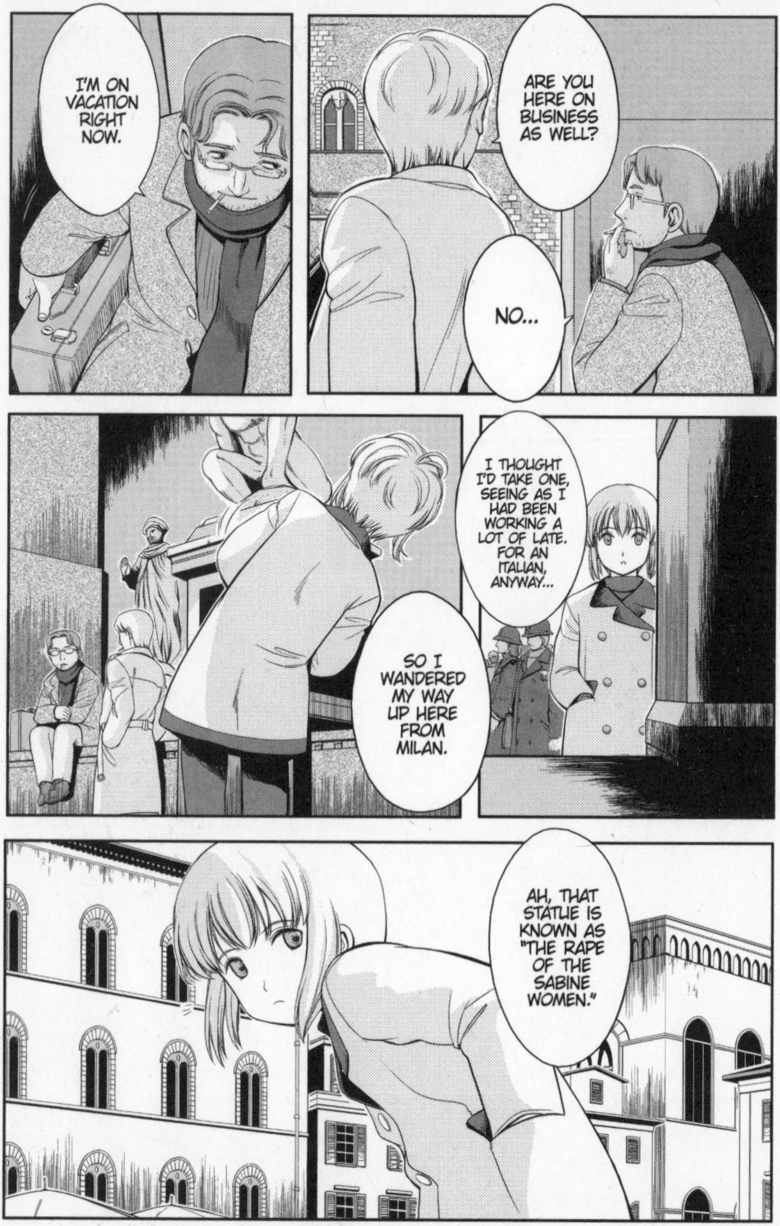
ARE YOU HERE ON BUSINESS AS WELL?
NO...
I'M ON VACATION RIGHT NOW.
I THOUGHT I'D TAKE ONE, SEEING AS I HAD BEEN WORKING A LOT OF LATE. FOR AN ITALIAN, ANYWAY...
SO I WANDERED MY WAY UP HERE FROM MILAN.
AH, THAT STATUE IS KNOWN AS "THE RAPE OF THE SABINE WOMEN."

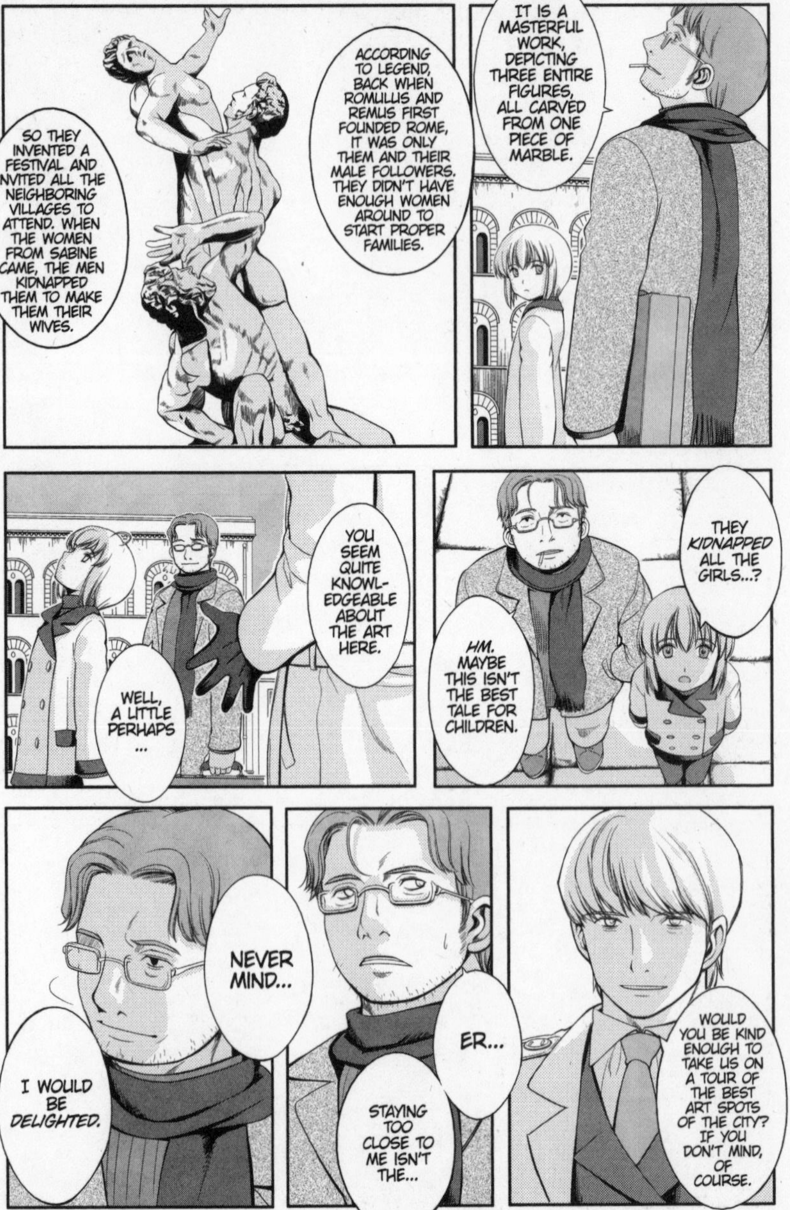
IT IS A MASTERFUL WORK, DEPICTING THREE ENTIRE FIGURES, ALL CARVED FROM ONE PIECE OF MARBLE.
ACCORDING TO LEGEND, BACK WHEN ROMULUS AND REMUS FIRST FOUNDED ROME, IT WAS ONLY THEM AND THEIR MALE FOLLOWERS. THEY DIDN'T HAVE ENOUGH WOMEN AROUND TO START PROPER FAMILIES.
SO THEY INVENTED A FESTIVAL AND INVITED ALL THE NEIGHBORING VILLAGES TO ATTEND. WHEN THE WOMEN FROM SABINE CAME, THE MEN KIDNAPPED THEM TO MAKE THEM THEIR WIVES.
THEY *KIDNAPPED* ALL THE GIRLS...?
HM. MAYBE THIS ISN'T THE BEST TALE FOR CHILDREN.
YOU SEEM QUITE KNOWL-EDGEABLE ABOUT THE ART HERE.
WELL, A LITTLE PERHAPS ...
WOULD YOU BE KIND ENOUGH TO TAKE US ON A TOUR OF THE BEST ART SPOTS OF THE CITY? IF YOU DON'T MIND, OF COURSE.
ER...
STAYING TOO CLOSE TO ME ISN'T THE...
NEVER MIND...
I WOULD BE *DELIGHTED.*

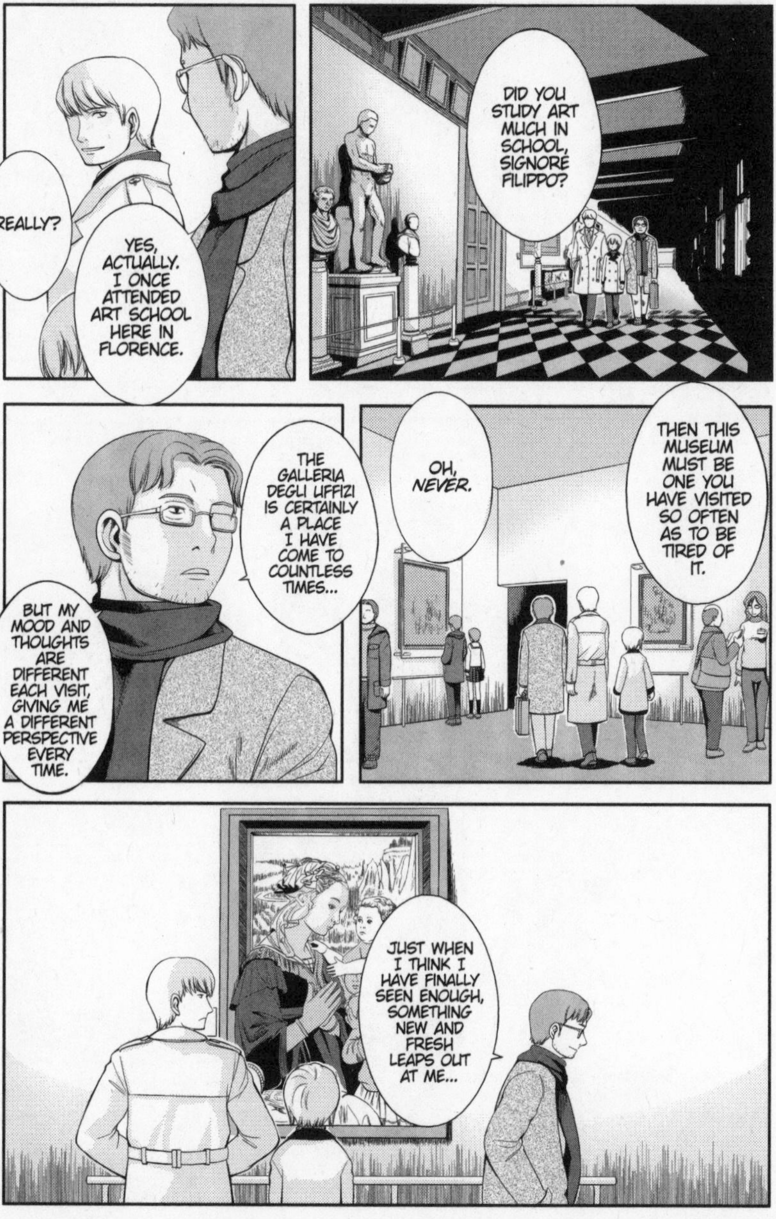
DID YOU STUDY ART MUCH IN SCHOOL, SIGNORE FILIPPO?
YES, ACTUALLY. I ONCE ATTENDED ART SCHOOL HERE IN FLORENCE.
REALLY?
THEN THIS MUSEUM MUST BE ONE YOU HAVE VISITED SO OFTEN AS TO BE TIRED OF IT.
OH, *NEVER.*
THE GALLERIA DEGLI UFFIZI IS CERTAINLY A PLACE I HAVE COME TO COUNTLESS TIMES...
BUT MY MOOD AND THOUGHTS ARE DIFFERENT EACH VISIT, GIVING ME A DIFFERENT PERSPECTIVE EVERY TIME.
JUST WHEN I THINK I HAVE FINALLY SEEN ENOUGH, SOMETHING NEW AND FRESH LEAPS OUT AT ME...

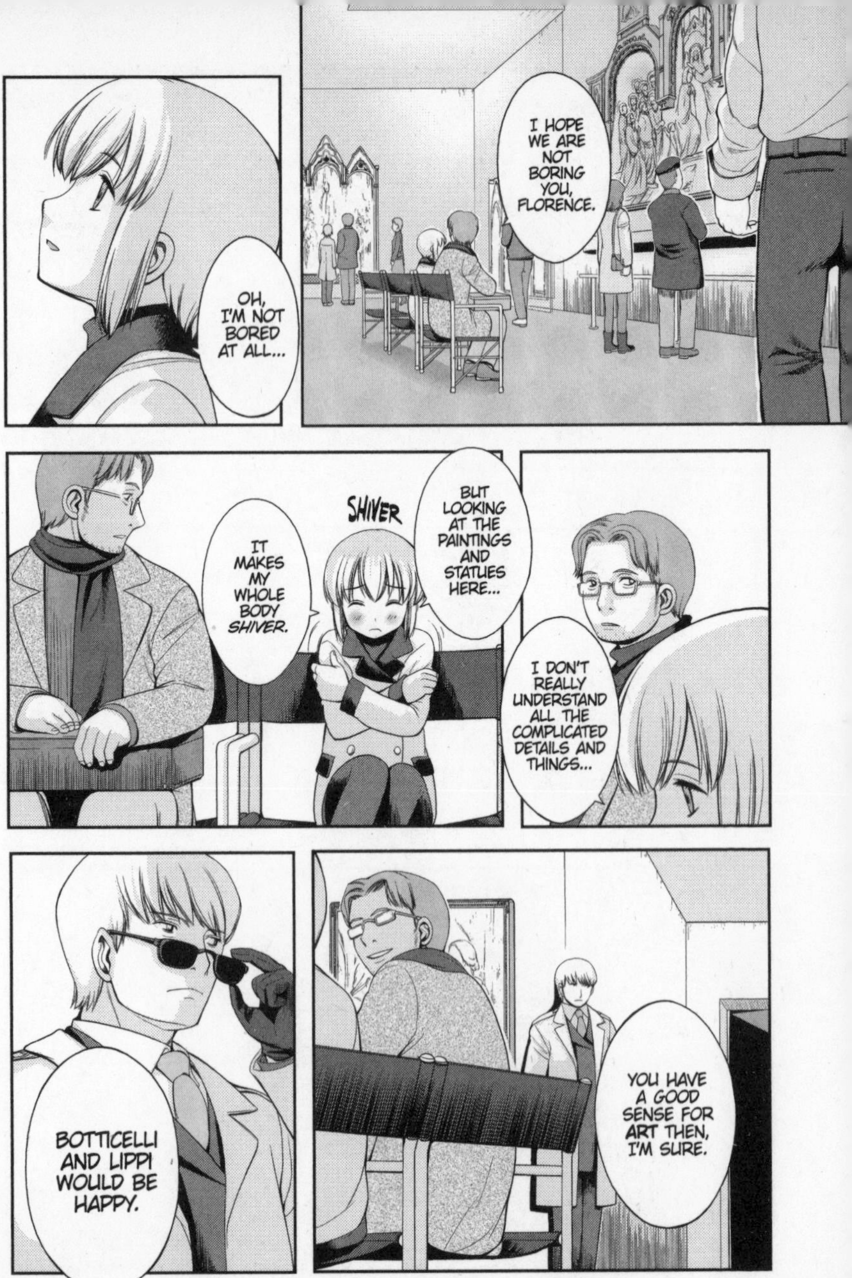
I HOPE WE ARE NOT BORING YOU, FLORENCE.
OH, I'M NOT BORED AT ALL...
I DON'T REALLY UNDERSTAND ALL THE COMPLICATED DETAILS AND THINGS...
BUT LOOKING AT THE PAINTINGS AND STATUES HERE...
SHIVER
IT MAKES MY WHOLE BODY *SHIVER.*
YOU HAVE A GOOD SENSE FOR ART THEN, I'M SURE.
BOTTICELLI AND LIPPI WOULD BE HAPPY.

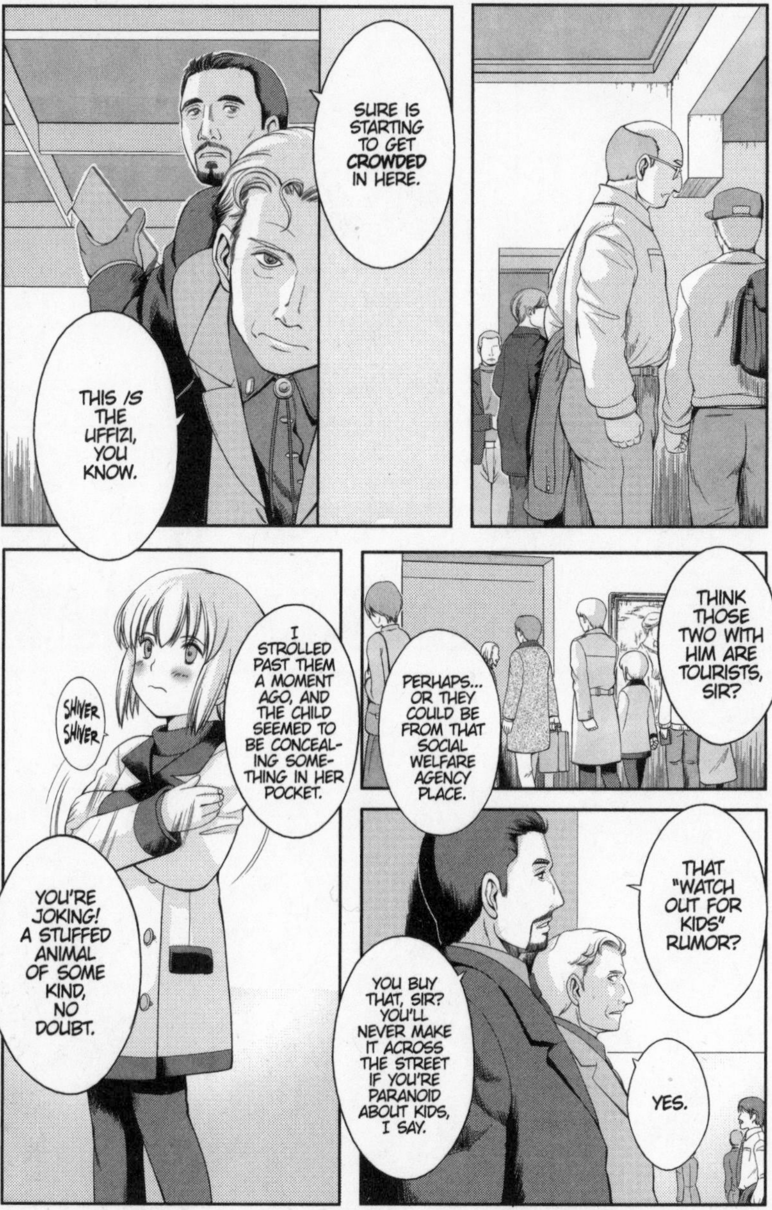
SURE IS STARTING TO GET CROWDED IN HERE.
THIS IS THE UFFIZI, YOU KNOW.
THINK THOSE TWO WITH HIM ARE TOURISTS, SIR?
PERHAPS... OR THEY COULD BE FROM THAT SOCIAL WELFARE AGENCY PLACE.
THAT "WATCH OUT FOR KIDS" RUMOR?
YES.
YOU BUY THAT, SIR? YOU'LL NEVER MAKE IT ACROSS THE STREET IF YOU'RE PARANOID ABOUT KIDS, I SAY.
I STROLLED PAST THEM A MOMENT AGO, AND THE CHILD SEEMED TO BE CONCEALING SOMETHING IN HER POCKET.
SHIVER SHIVER
YOU'RE JOKING! A STUFFED ANIMAL OF SOME KIND, NO DOUBT.

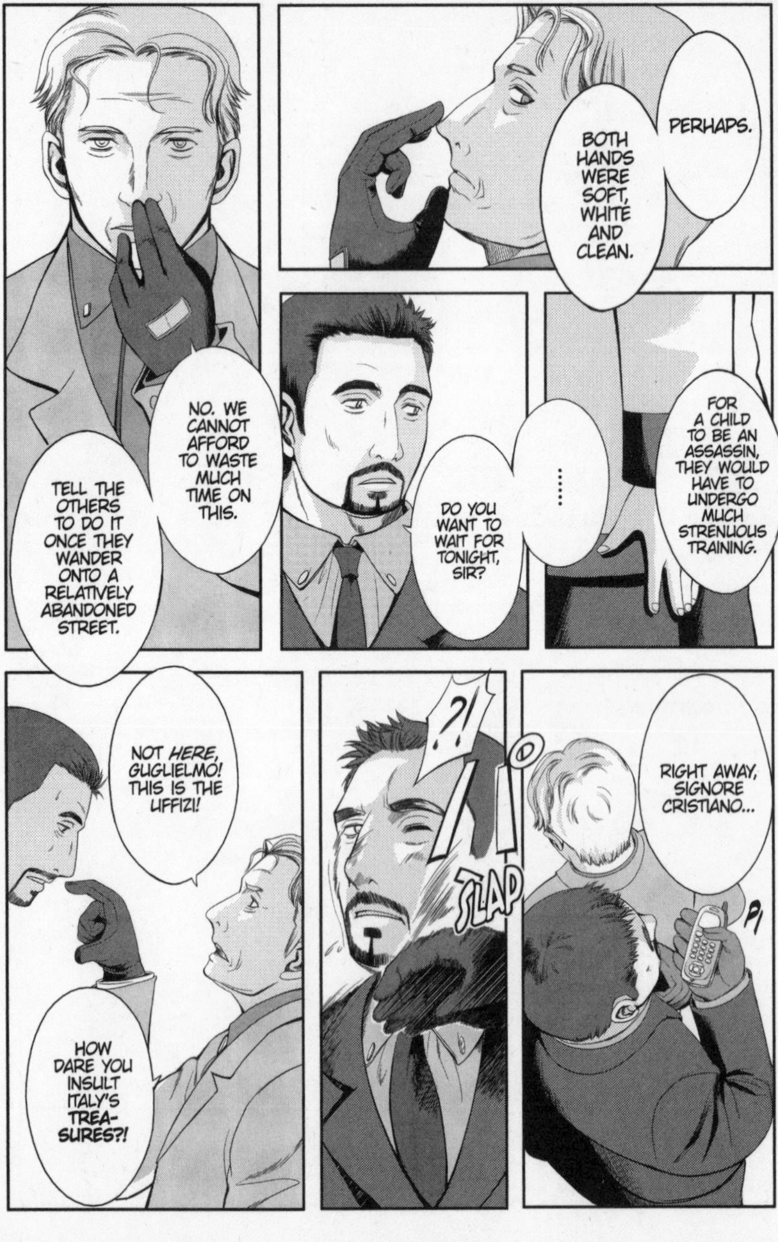
PERHAPS.
BOTH HANDS WERE SOFT, WHITE AND CLEAN.
FOR A CHILD TO BE AN ASSASSIN, THEY WOULD HAVE TO UNDERGO MUCH STRENUOUS TRAINING.
......
DO YOU WANT TO WAIT FOR TONIGHT, SIR?
NO. WE CANNOT AFFORD TO WASTE MUCH TIME ON THIS.
TELL THE OTHERS TO DO IT ONCE THEY WANDER ONTO A RELATIVELY ABANDONED STREET.
RIGHT AWAY, SIGNORE CRISTIANO...
PI
?!
SLAP
NOT *HERE*, GUGLIELMO! THIS IS THE UFFIZI!
HOW DARE YOU INSULT ITALY'S **TREA-SURES**?!

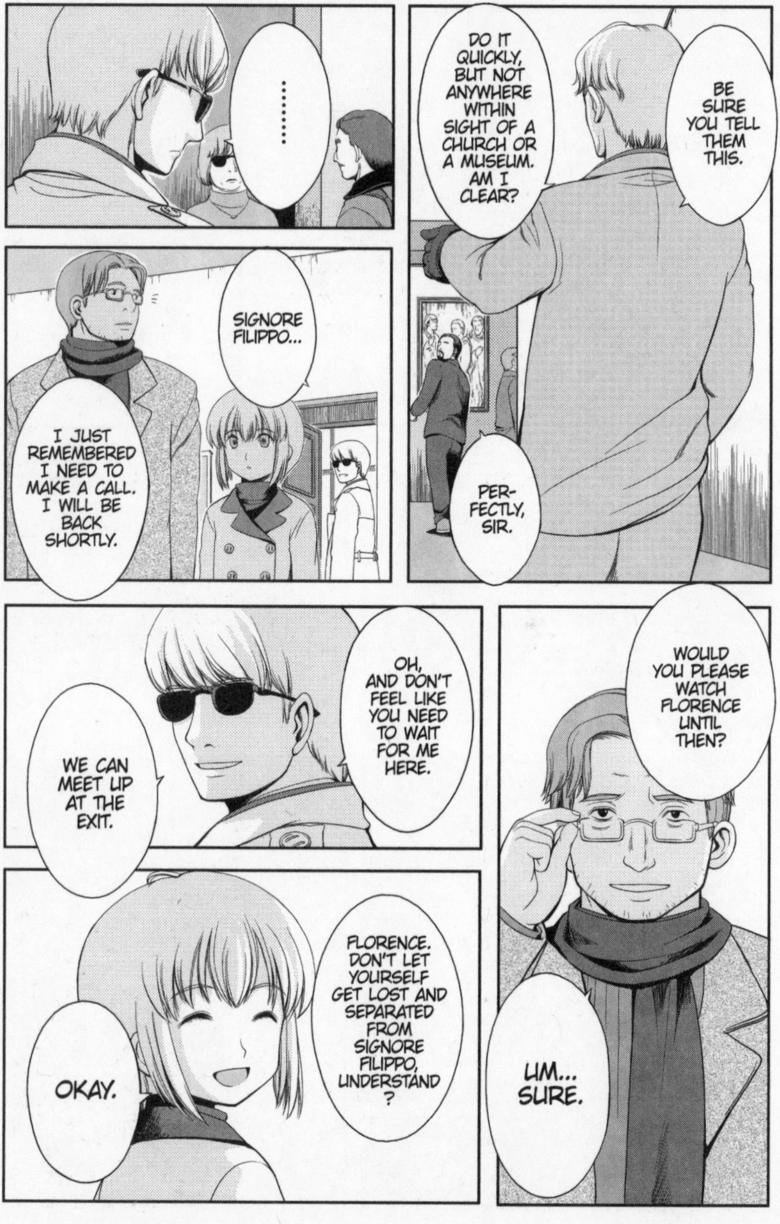
BE SURE YOU TELL THEM THIS.
DO IT QUICKLY, BUT NOT ANYWHERE WITHIN SIGHT OF A CHURCH OR A MUSEUM. AM I CLEAR?
PER- FECTLY, SIR.
....
SIGNORE FILIPPO...
I JUST REMEMBERED I NEED TO MAKE A CALL. I WILL BE BACK SHORTLY.
WOULD YOU PLEASE WATCH FLORENCE UNTIL THEN?
UM... SURE.
OH, AND DON'T FEEL LIKE YOU NEED TO WAIT FOR ME HERE.
WE CAN MEET UP AT THE EXIT.
FLORENCE. DON'T LET YOURSELF GET LOST AND SEPARATED FROM SIGNORE FILIPPO, UNDERSTAND ?
OKAY.

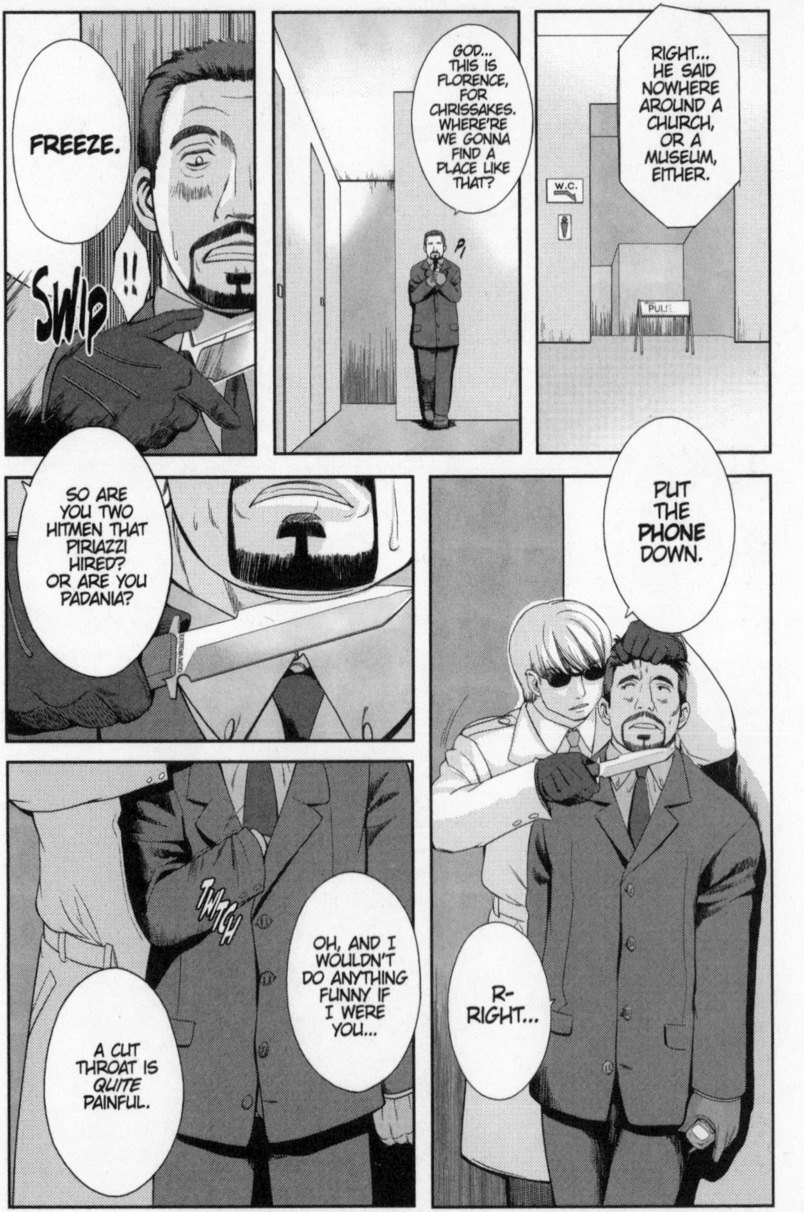
RIGHT... HE SAID NOWHERE AROUND A CHURCH, OR A MUSEUM, EITHER.
W.C.
PULL
GOD... THIS IS FLORENCE, FOR CHRISSAKES. WHERE'RE WE GONNA FIND A PLACE LIKE THAT?
PI
FREEZE.
!!
SWIP
PUT THE PHONE DOWN.
R-RIGHT...
SO ARE YOU TWO HITMEN THAT PIRIAZZI HIRED? OR ARE YOU PADANIA?
TWITCH
OH, AND I WOULDN'T DO ANYTHING FUNNY IF I WERE YOU...
A CUT THROAT IS *QUITE* PAINFUL.

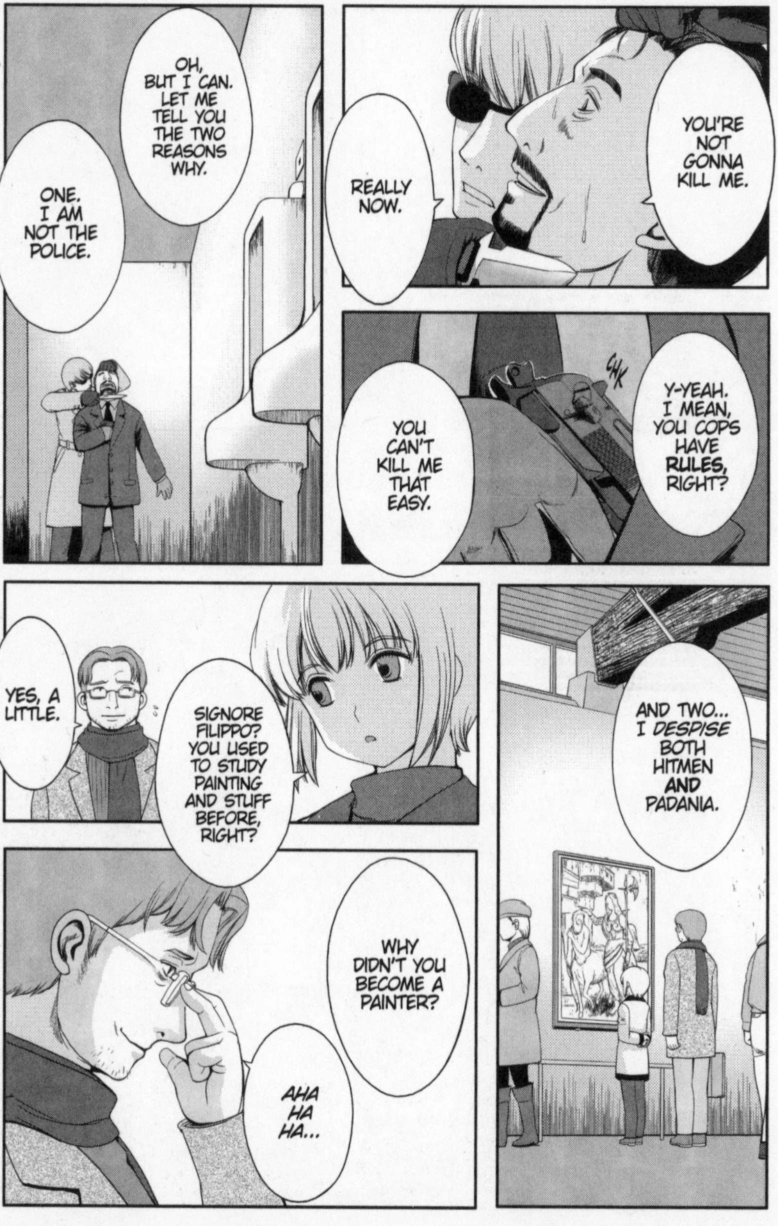
YOU'RE NOT GONNA KILL ME.
REALLY NOW.
Y-YEAH. I MEAN, YOU COPS HAVE RULES, RIGHT?
CHK
YOU CAN'T KILL ME THAT EASY.
OH, BUT I CAN. LET ME TELL YOU THE TWO REASONS WHY.
ONE. I AM NOT THE POLICE.
AND TWO... I DESPISE BOTH HITMEN AND PADANIA.
SIGNORE FILIPPO? YOU USED TO STUDY PAINTING AND STUFF BEFORE, RIGHT?
YES, A LITTLE.
WHY DIDN'T YOU BECOME A PAINTER?
AHA HA HA...

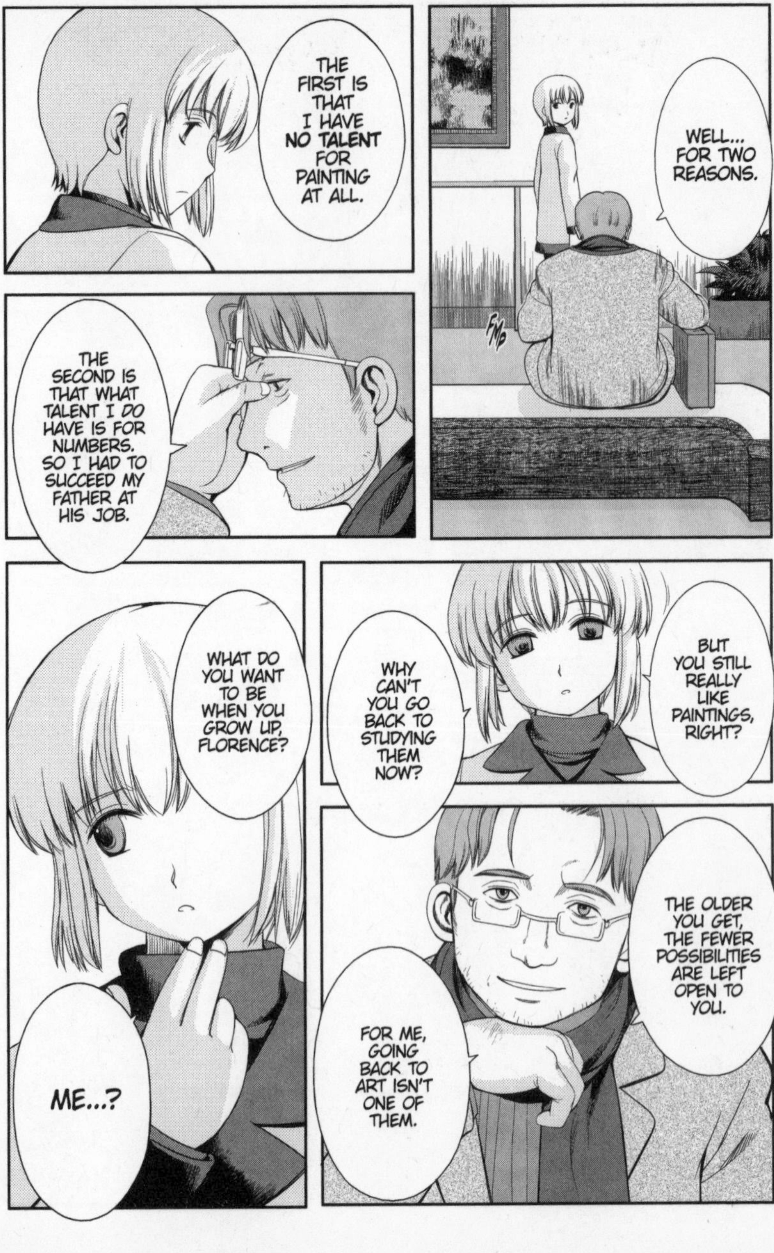
WELL... FOR TWO REASONS.
FMP
THE FIRST IS THAT I HAVE NO TALENT FOR PAINTING AT ALL.
THE SECOND IS THAT WHAT TALENT I *DO* HAVE IS FOR NUMBERS. SO I HAD TO SUCCEED MY FATHER AT HIS JOB.
BUT YOU STILL REALLY LIKE PAINTINGS, RIGHT?
WHY CAN'T YOU GO BACK TO STUDYING THEM NOW?
THE OLDER YOU GET, THE FEWER POSSIBILITIES ARE LEFT OPEN TO YOU.
FOR ME, GOING BACK TO ART ISN'T ONE OF THEM.
WHAT DO YOU WANT TO BE WHEN YOU GROW UP, FLORENCE?
ME...?

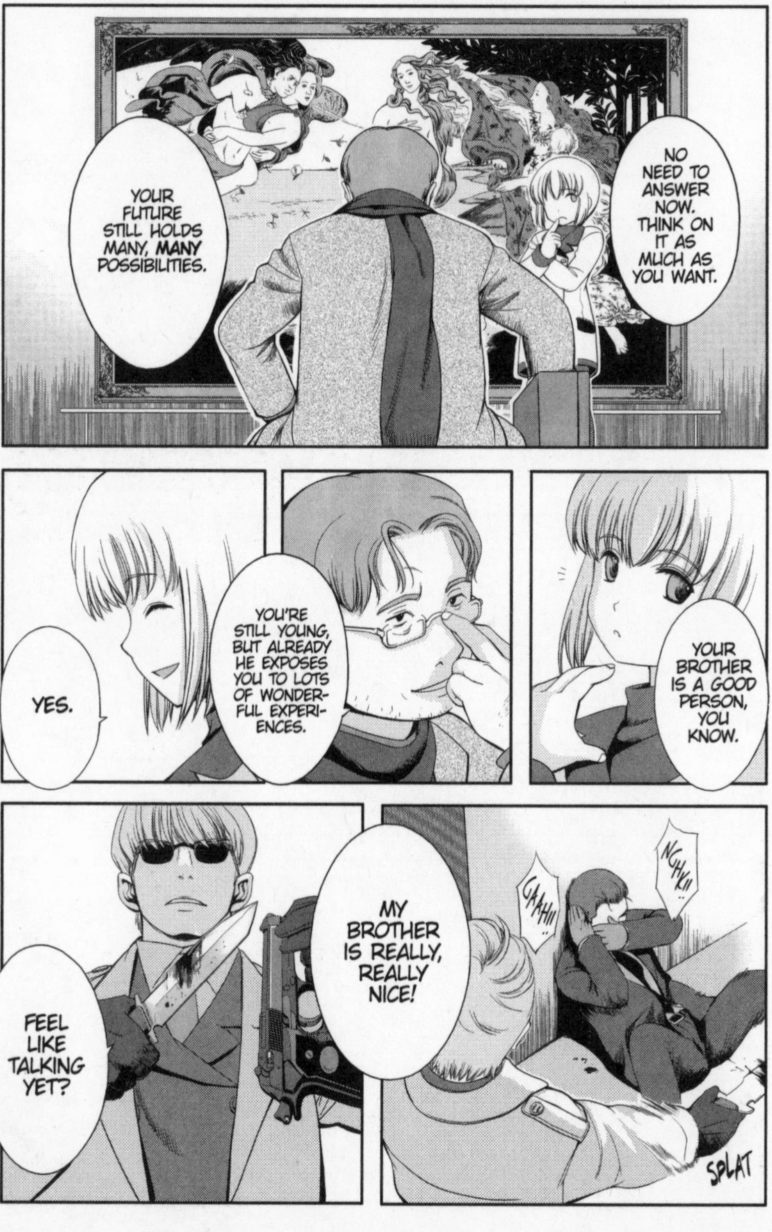
NO NEED TO ANSWER NOW. THINK ON IT AS MUCH AS YOU WANT.
YOUR FUTURE STILL HOLDS MANY, **MANY** POSSIBILITIES.
YOUR BROTHER IS A GOOD PERSON, YOU KNOW.
YOU'RE STILL YOUNG, BUT ALREADY HE EXPOSES YOU TO LOTS OF WONDERFUL EXPERIENCES.
YES.
NGHK!!
GAAH!!
MY BROTHER IS REALLY, REALLY NICE!
SPLAT
FEEL LIKE TALKING YET?

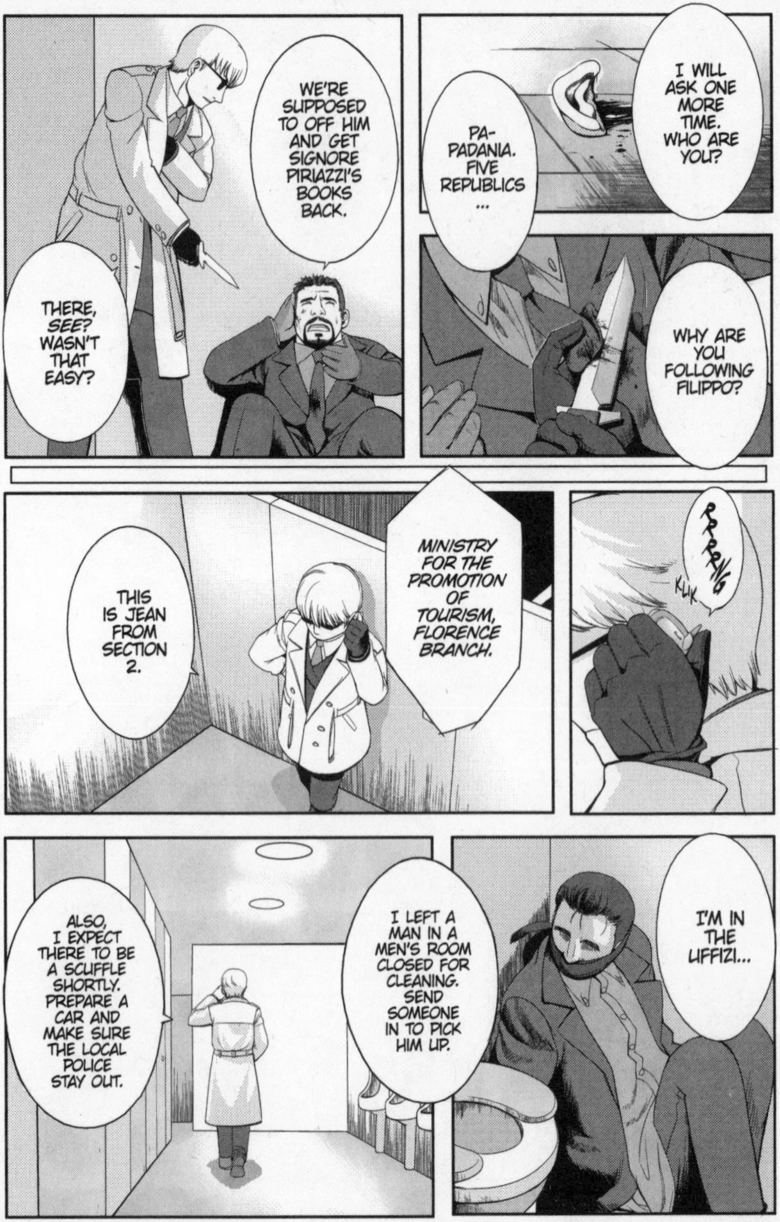

I WILL ASK ONE MORE TIME. WHO ARE YOU?
PA-PADANIA. FIVE REPUBLICS ...
WHY ARE YOU FOLLOWING FILIPPO?
WE'RE SUPPOSED TO OFF HIM AND GET SIGNORE PIRIAZZI'S BOOKS BACK.
THERE, *SEE?* WASN'T THAT EASY?
RRRRING
KLIK
MINISTRY FOR THE PROMOTION OF TOURISM, FLORENCE BRANCH.
THIS IS JEAN FROM SECTION 2.
I'M IN THE UFFIZI...
I LEFT A MAN IN A MEN'S ROOM CLOSED FOR CLEANING. SEND SOMEONE IN TO PICK HIM UP.
ALSO, I EXPECT THERE TO BE A SCUFFLE SHORTLY. PREPARE A CAR AND MAKE SURE THE LOCAL POLICE STAY OUT.

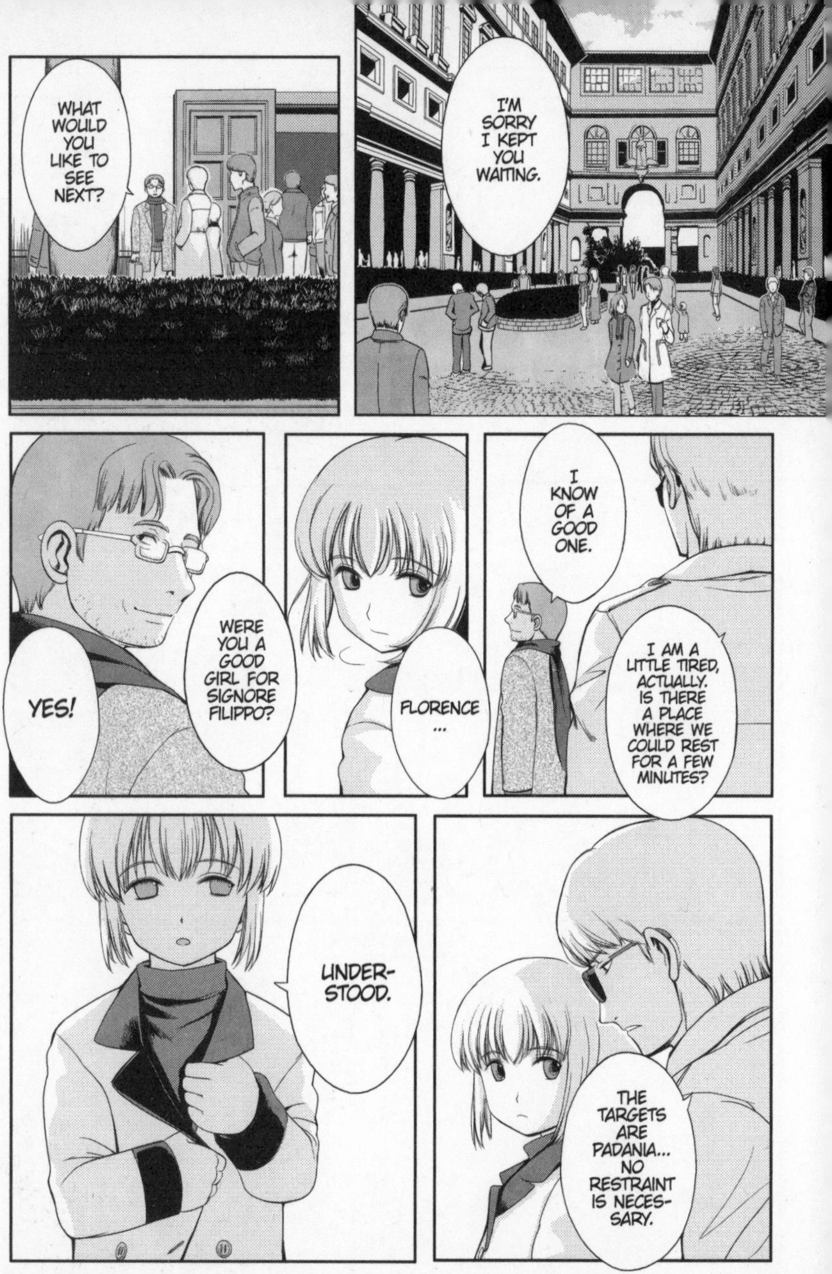
I'M SORRY I KEPT YOU WAITING.
WHAT WOULD YOU LIKE TO SEE NEXT?
I AM A LITTLE TIRED, ACTUALLY. IS THERE A PLACE WHERE WE COULD REST FOR A FEW MINUTES?
I KNOW OF A GOOD ONE.
FLORENCE ...
WERE YOU A GOOD GIRL FOR SIGNORE FILIPPO?
YES!
THE TARGETS ARE PADANIA... NO RESTRAINT IS NECES-SARY.
UNDER-STOOD.

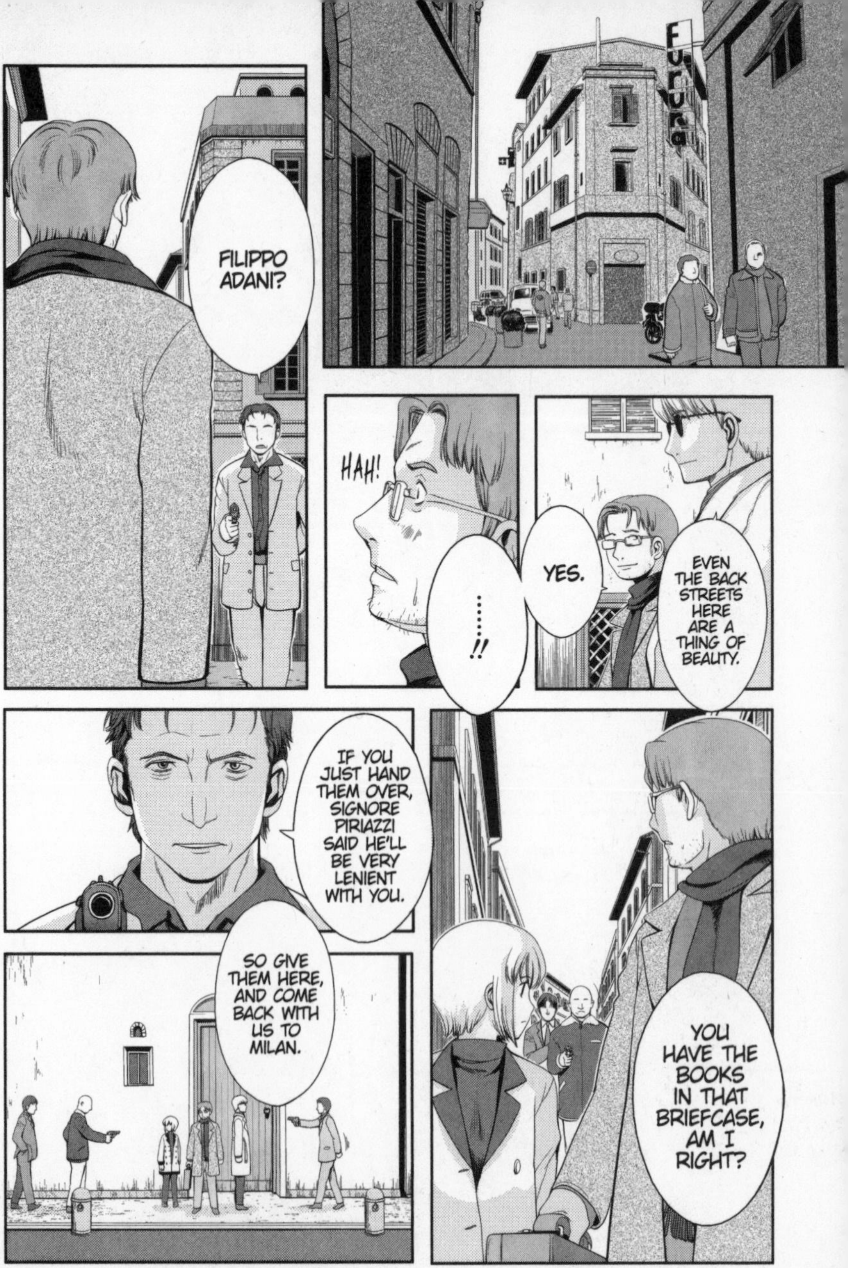
EVEN THE BACK STREETS HERE ARE A THING OF BEAUTY.
YES.
HAH!
......!!
FILIPPO ADANI?
YOU HAVE THE BOOKS IN THAT BRIEFCASE, AM I RIGHT?
IF YOU JUST HAND THEM OVER, SIGNORE PIRIAZZI SAID HE'LL BE VERY LENIENT WITH YOU.
SO GIVE THEM HERE, AND COME BACK WITH US TO MILAN.

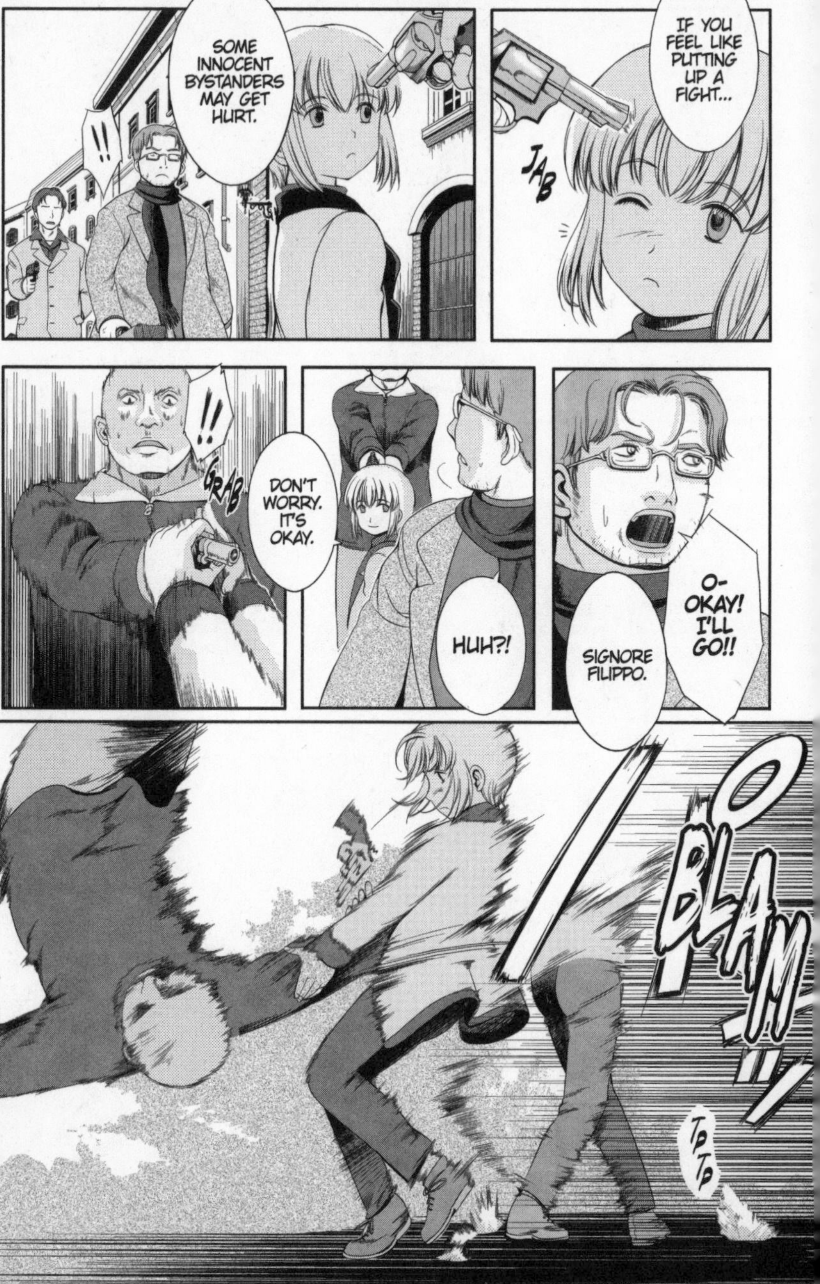
IF YOU FEEL LIKE PUTTING UP A FIGHT...
JAB
SOME INNOCENT BYSTANDERS MAY GET HURT.
!!
O-OKAY! I'LL GO!!
SIGNORE FILIPPO.
HUH?!
DON'T WORRY. IT'S OKAY.
!!
GRAB
BLAM
TPTP

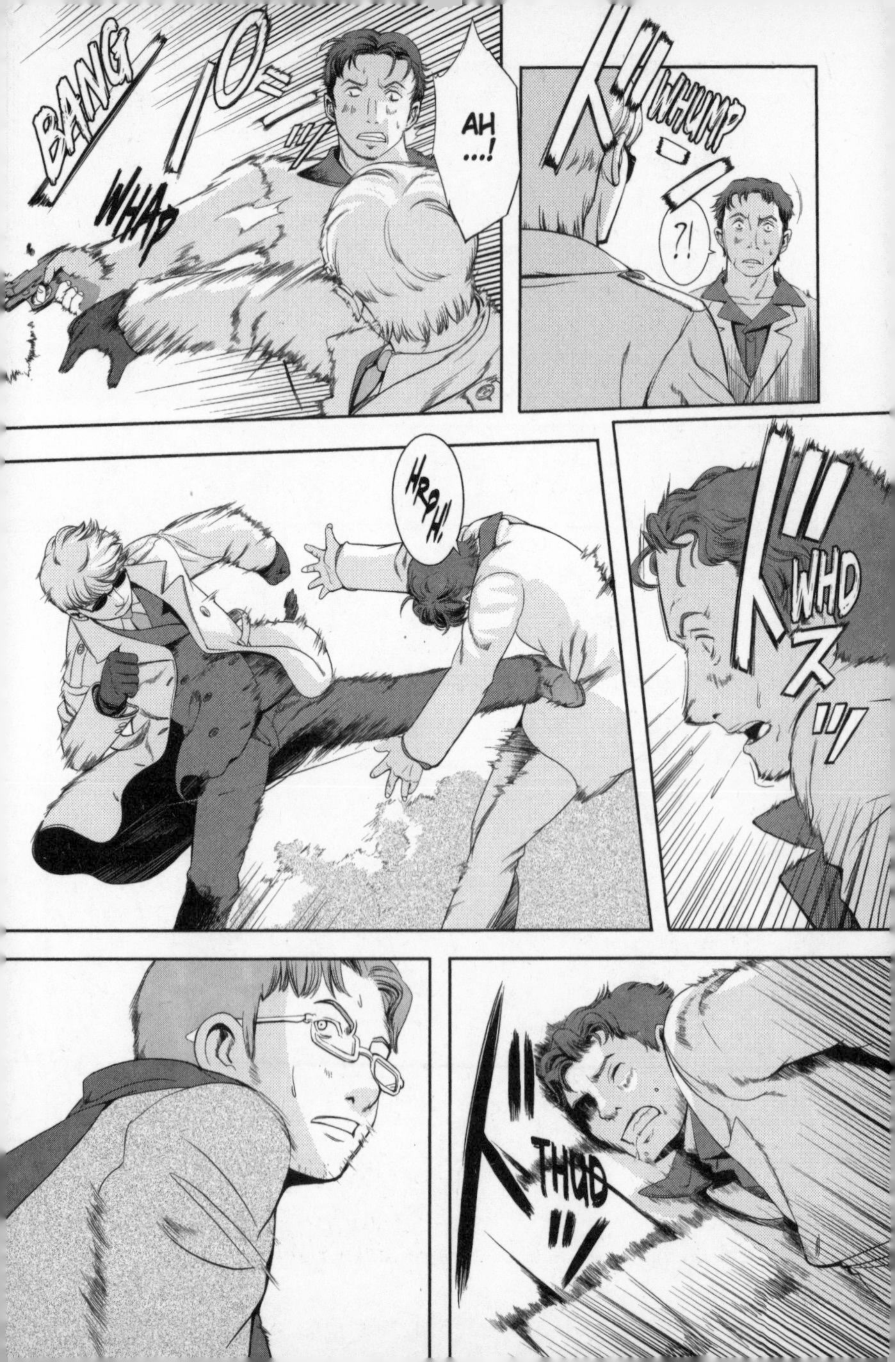
WHUMP
?!
AH ...!
BANG
WHAP
WHD
HRGH!
THUD

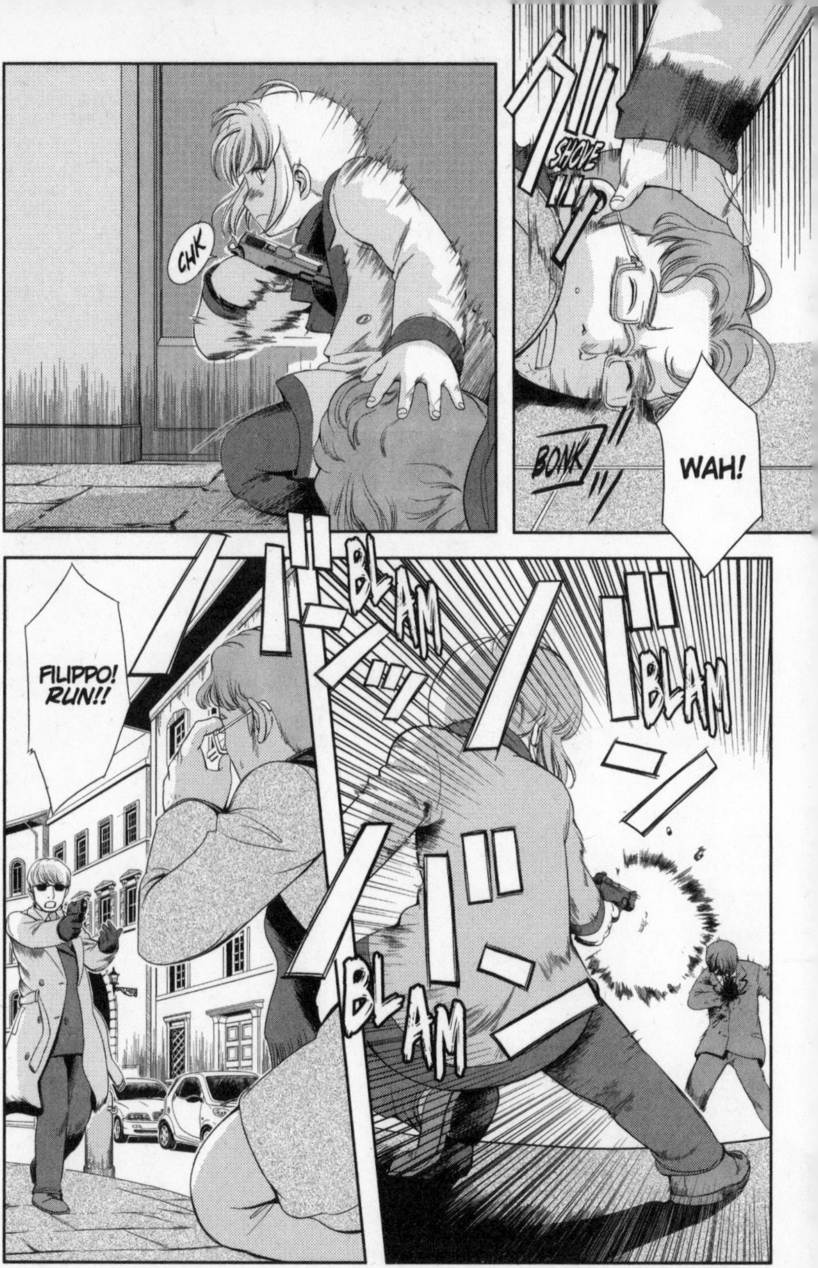
SHOVE
BONK
WAH!
CHK
BLAM
BLAM
FILIPPO! RUN!!
BLAM

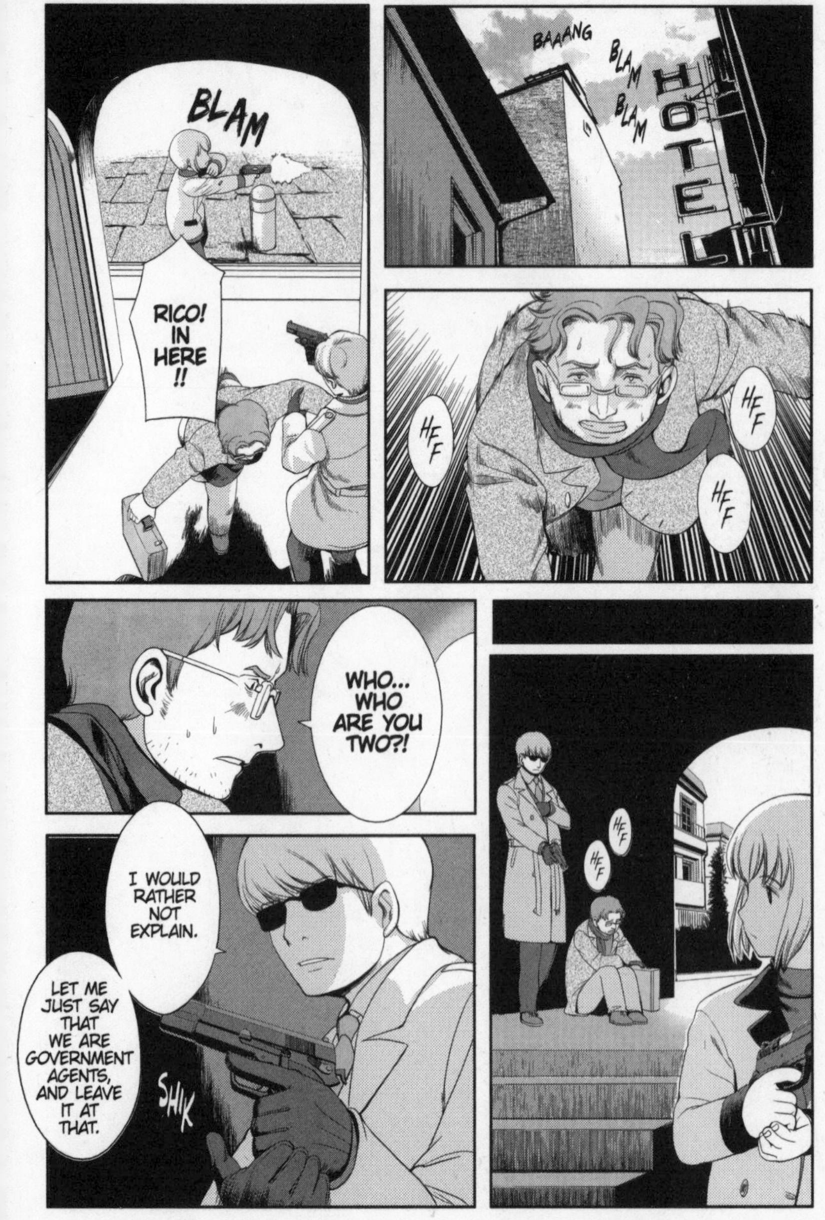
BAAAANG
BLAM
BLAM
BLAM
HOTEL
HEF
HEF
HEF
BLAM
RICO! IN HERE!!
HEF
HEF
WHO... WHO ARE YOU TWO?!
I WOULD RATHER NOT EXPLAIN.
LET ME JUST SAY THAT WE ARE GOVERNMENT AGENTS, AND LEAVE IT AT THAT.
SHIK

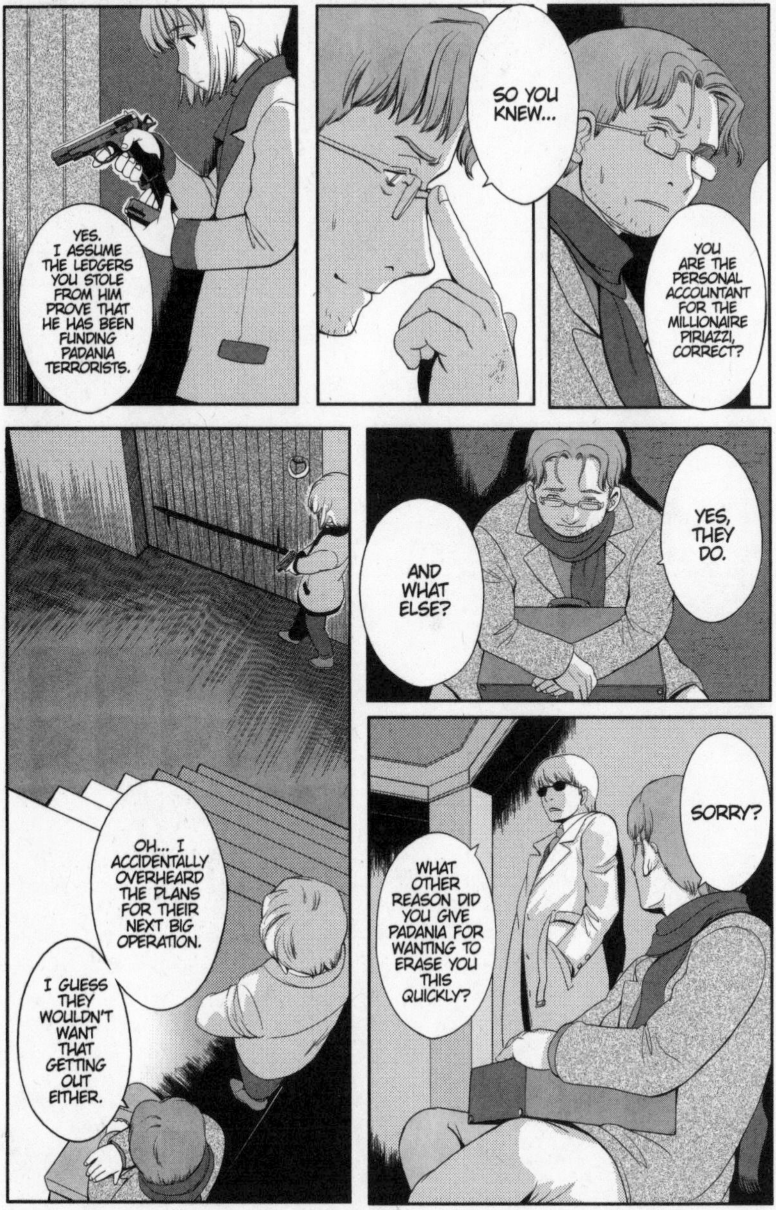
YOU ARE THE PERSONAL ACCOUNTANT FOR THE MILLIONAIRE PIRIAZZI, CORRECT?
SO YOU KNEW...
YES. I ASSUME THE LEDGERS YOU STOLE FROM HIM PROVE THAT HE HAS BEEN FUNDING PADANIA TERRORISTS.
YES, THEY DO.
AND WHAT ELSE?
SORRY?
WHAT OTHER REASON DID YOU GIVE PADANIA FOR WANTING TO ERASE YOU THIS QUICKLY?
OH... I ACCIDENTALLY OVERHEARD THE PLANS FOR THEIR NEXT BIG OPERATION.
I GUESS THEY WOULDN'T WANT THAT GETTING OUT EITHER.

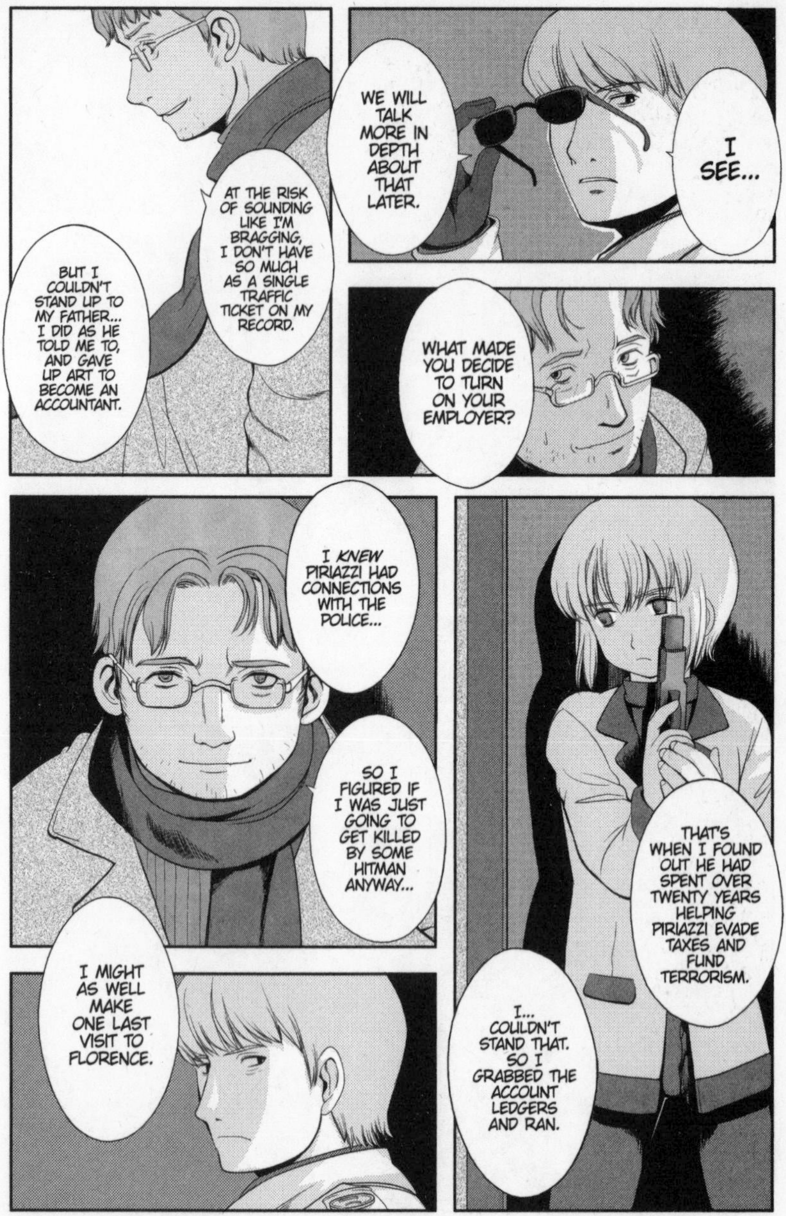
I SEE...
WE WILL TALK MORE IN DEPTH ABOUT THAT LATER.
WHAT MADE YOU DECIDE TO TURN ON YOUR EMPLOYER?
AT THE RISK OF SOUNDING LIKE I'M BRAGGING, I DON'T HAVE SO MUCH AS A SINGLE TRAFFIC TICKET ON MY RECORD.
BUT I COULDN'T STAND UP TO MY FATHER... I DID AS HE TOLD ME TO, AND GAVE UP ART TO BECOME AN ACCOUNTANT.
THAT'S WHEN I FOUND OUT HE HAD SPENT OVER TWENTY YEARS HELPING PIRIAZZI EVADE TAXES AND FUND TERRORISM.
I... COULDN'T STAND THAT. SO I GRABBED THE ACCOUNT LEDGERS AND RAN.
I *KNEW* PIRIAZZI HAD CONNECTIONS WITH THE POLICE...
SO I FIGURED IF I WAS JUST GOING TO GET KILLED BY SOME HITMAN ANYWAY...
I MIGHT AS WELL MAKE ONE LAST VISIT TO FLORENCE.

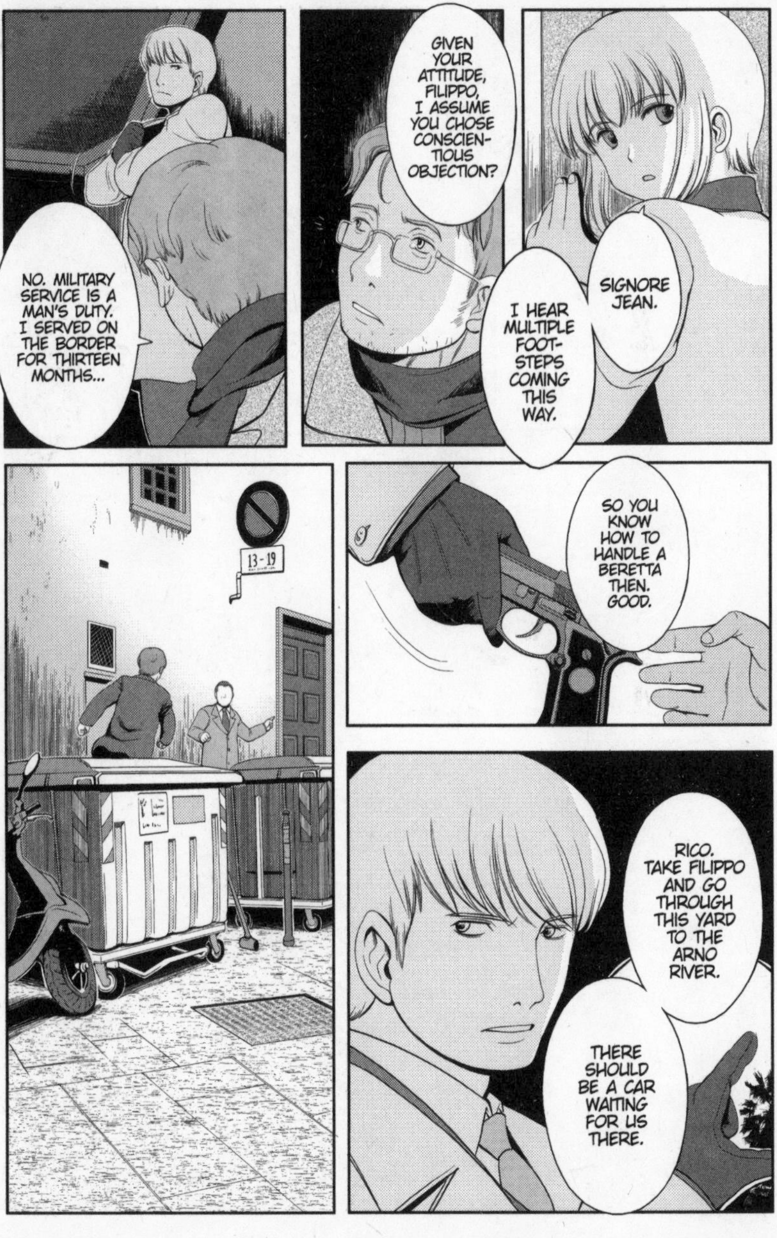
SIGNORE JEAN.
I HEAR MULTIPLE FOOT-STEPS COMING THIS WAY.
GIVEN YOUR ATTITUDE, FILIPPO, I ASSUME YOU CHOSE CONSCIEN-TIOUS OBJECTION?
NO. MILITARY SERVICE IS A MAN'S DUTY. I SERVED ON THE BORDER FOR THIRTEEN MONTHS...
SO YOU KNOW HOW TO HANDLE A BERETTA THEN. GOOD.
RICO. TAKE FILIPPO AND GO THROUGH THIS YARD TO THE ARNO RIVER.
THERE SHOULD BE A CAR WAITING FOR US THERE.
13 - 19

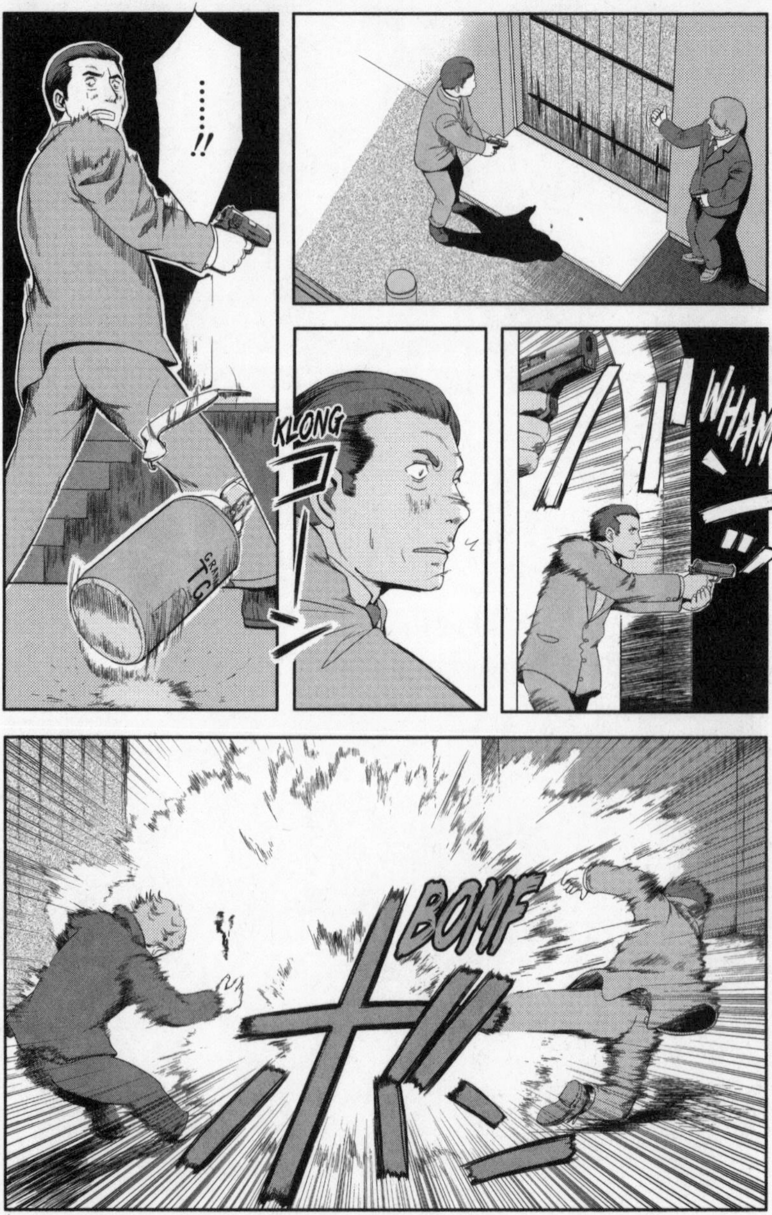
WHAM
KLONG
......!!
BOMF

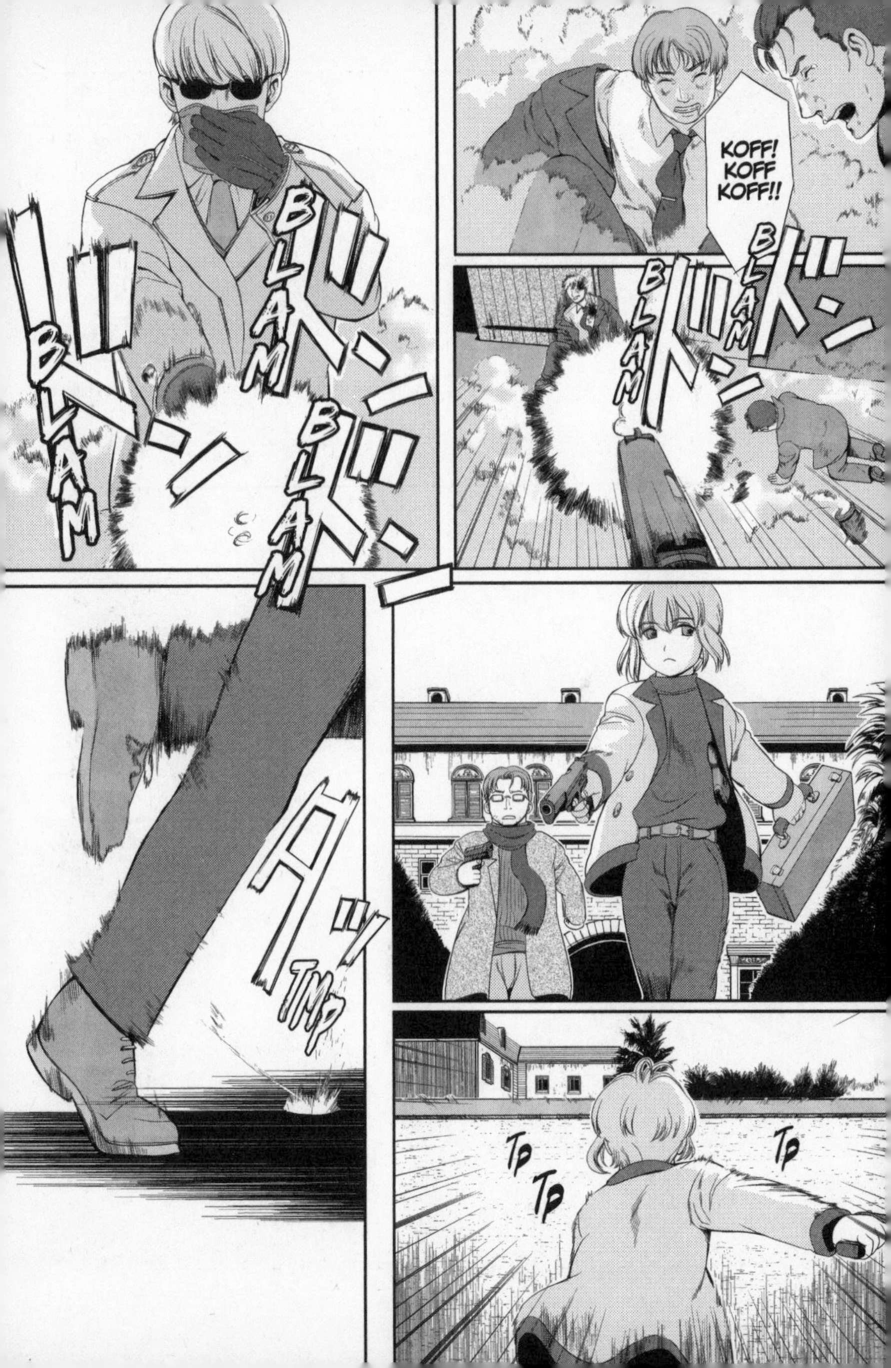
KOFF! KOFF KOFF!!
BLAM
BLAM
BLAM
BLAM
BLAM
Tp
Tp
Tp
TMP

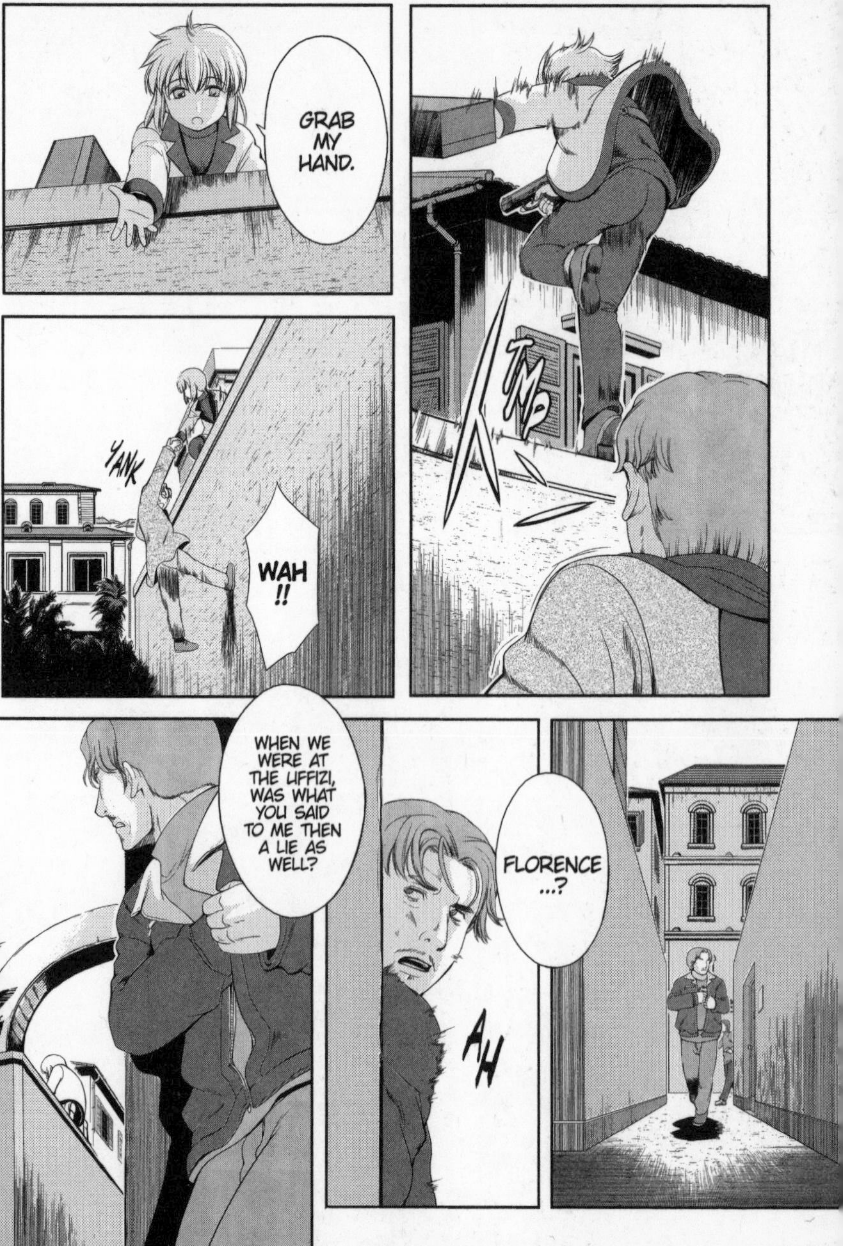
TMP
GRAB MY HAND.
YANK
WAH!!
FLORENCE ...?
AH
WHEN WE WERE AT THE UFFIZI, WAS WHAT YOU SAID TO ME THEN A LIE AS WELL?

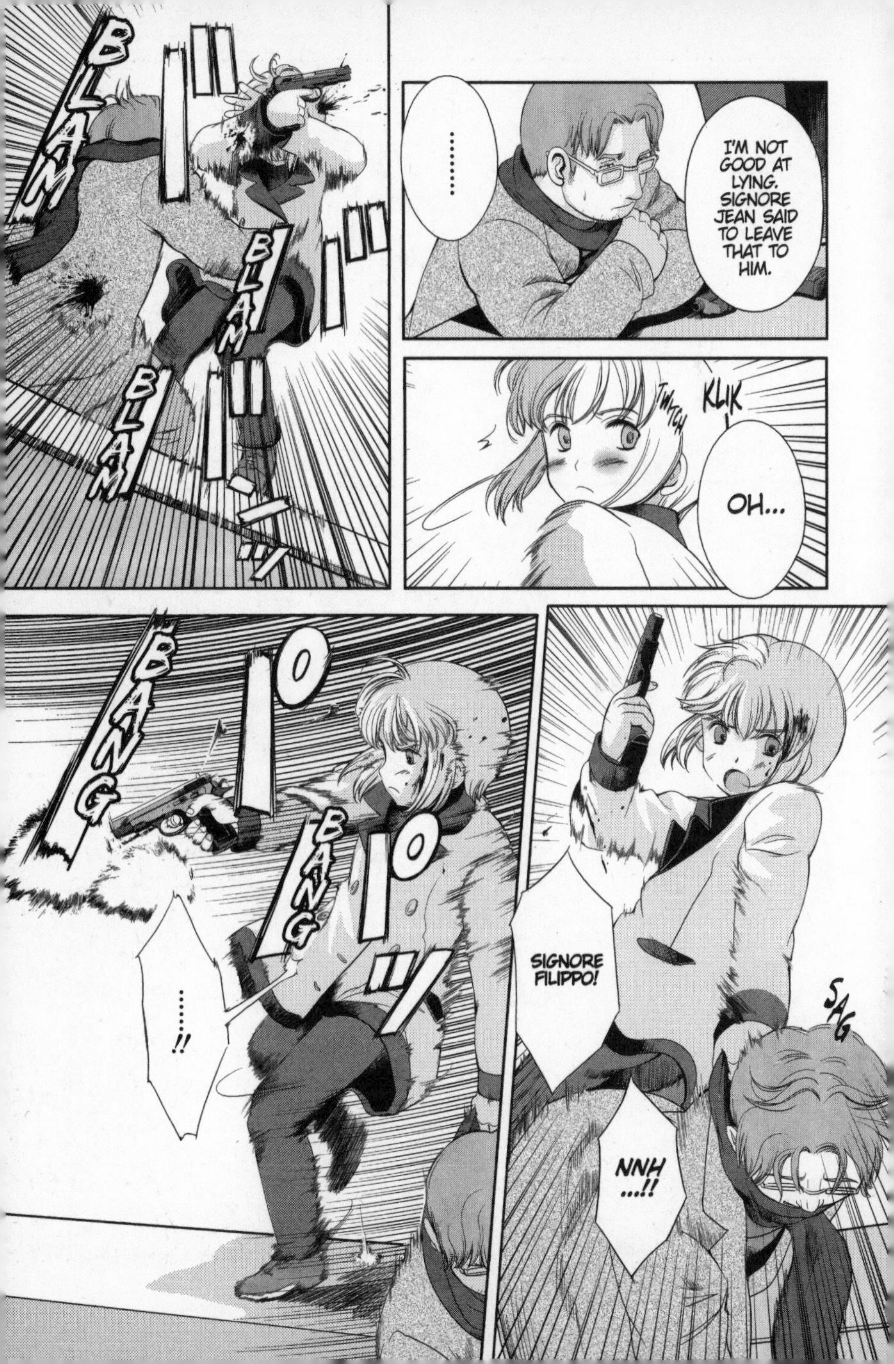
I'M NOT GOOD AT LYING. SIGNORE JEAN SAID TO LEAVE THAT TO HIM.
......
KLIK
TWITCH
OH...
BLAM
BLAM
BLAM
SIGNORE FILIPPO!
SAG
NNH ...!!
BANG
BANG
......!!

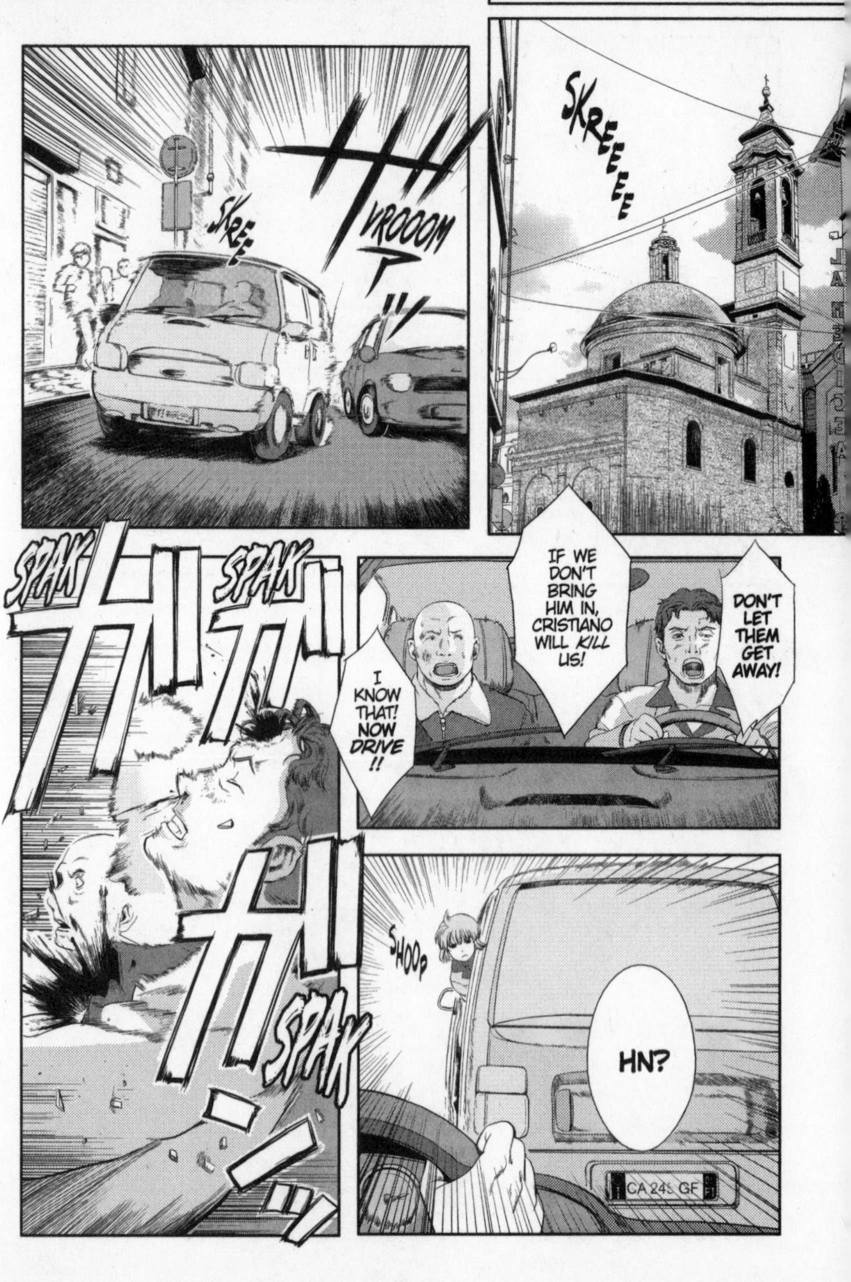
SKREEEEE
SKREE
VROOOM
DON'T LET THEM GET AWAY!
IF WE DON'T BRING HIM IN, CRISTIANO WILL KILL US!
I KNOW THAT! NOW DRIVE!!
SHOOP
HN?
SPAK
SPAK
SPAK

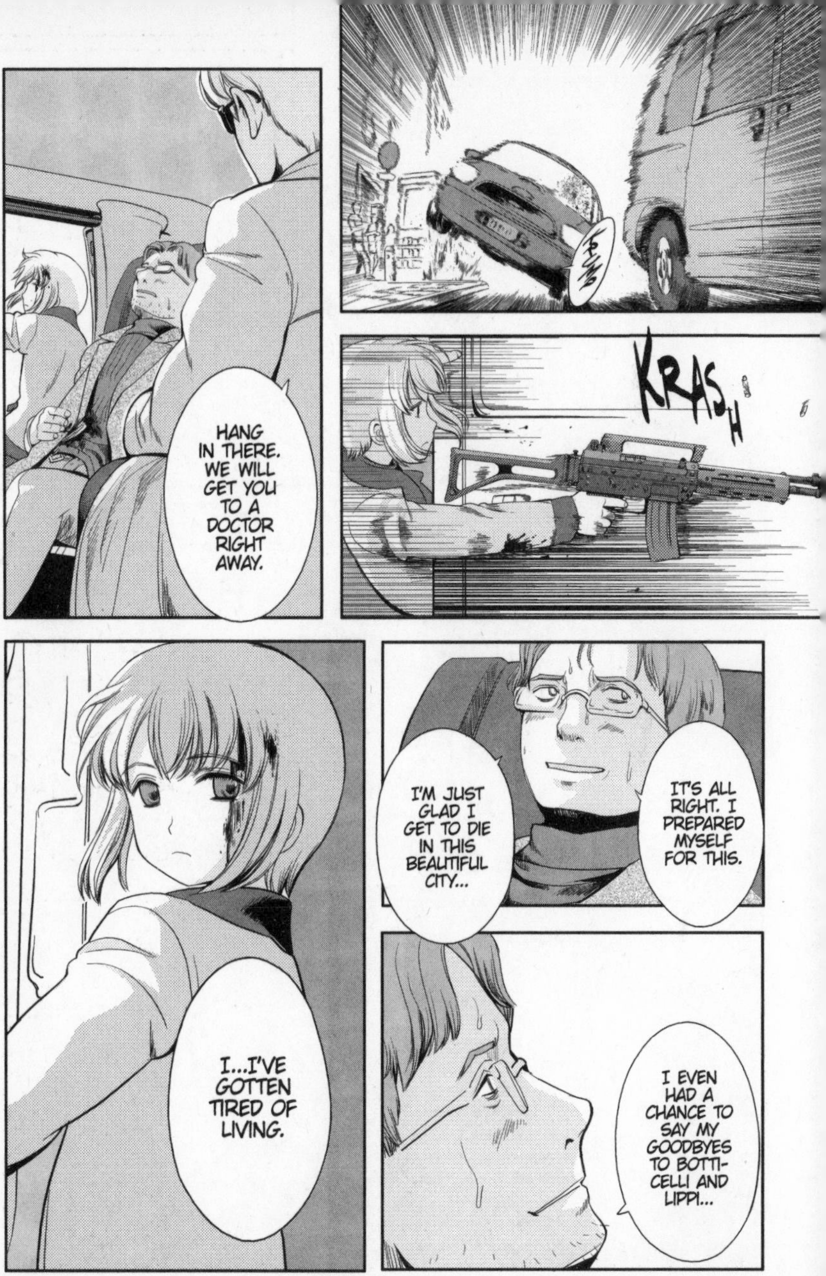
KRASH
HANG IN THERE. WE WILL GET YOU TO A DOCTOR RIGHT AWAY.
IT'S ALL RIGHT. I PREPARED MYSELF FOR THIS.
I'M JUST GLAD I GET TO DIE IN THIS BEAUTIFUL CITY...
I EVEN HAD A CHANCE TO SAY MY GOODBYES TO BOTTI-CELLI AND LIPPI...
I...I'VE GOTTEN TIRED OF LIVING.

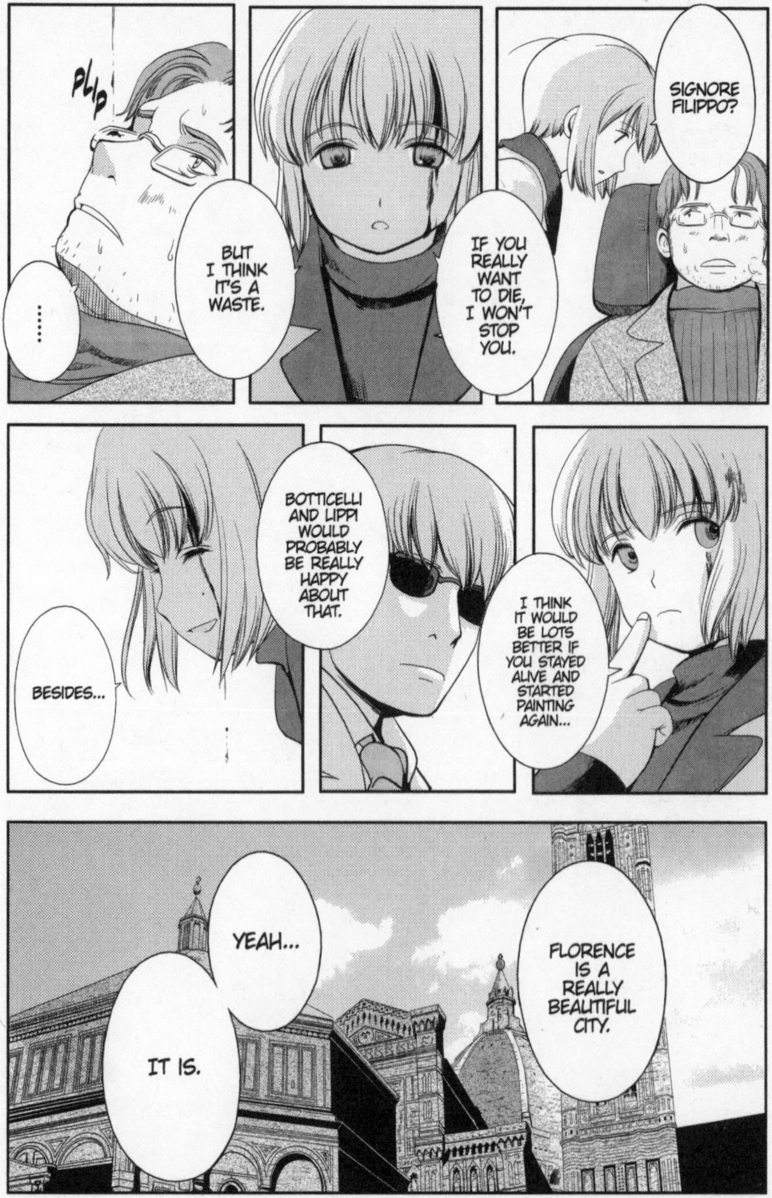
SIGNORE FILIPPO?
IF YOU REALLY WANT TO DIE, I WON'T STOP YOU.
BUT I THINK IT'S A WASTE.
PLIP
......
I THINK IT WOULD BE LOTS BETTER IF YOU STAYED ALIVE AND STARTED PAINTING AGAIN...
BOTTICELLI AND LIPPI WOULD PROBABLY BE REALLY HAPPY ABOUT THAT.
BESIDES...
FLORENCE IS A REALLY BEAUTIFUL CITY.
YEAH...
IT IS.

Chapter 9 / END

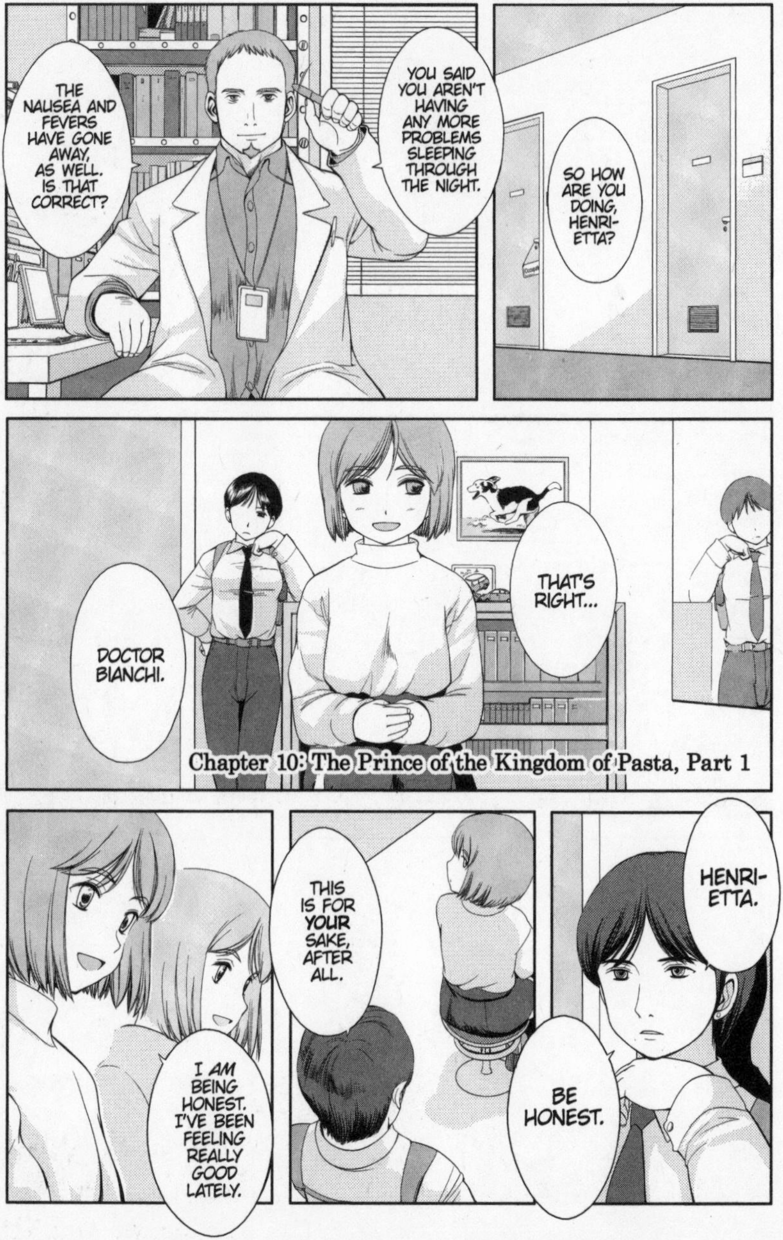
SO HOW ARE YOU DOING, HENRI-ETTA?
YOU SAID YOU AREN'T HAVING ANY MORE PROBLEMS SLEEPING THROUGH THE NIGHT.
THE NAUSEA AND FEVERS HAVE GONE AWAY, AS WELL. IS THAT CORRECT?
THAT'S RIGHT...
DOCTOR BIANCHI.
HENRI-ETTA.
BE HONEST.
THIS IS FOR YOUR SAKE, AFTER ALL.
I AM BEING HONEST. I'VE BEEN FEELING REALLY GOOD LATELY.

Chapter 10: The Prince of the Kingdom of Pasta, Part 1

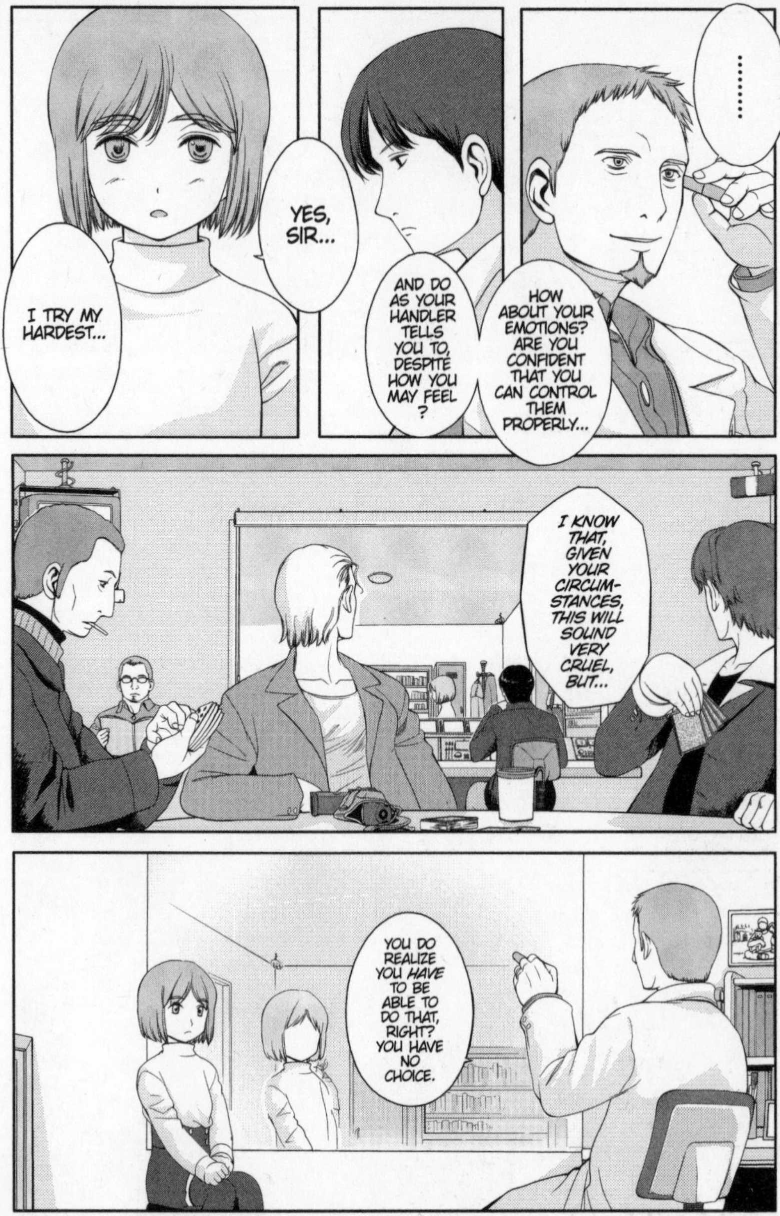
......
HOW ABOUT YOUR EMOTIONS? ARE YOU CONFIDENT THAT YOU CAN CONTROL THEM PROPERLY...
AND DO AS YOUR HANDLER TELLS YOU TO, DESPITE HOW YOU MAY FEEL?
YES, SIR...
I TRY MY HARDEST...
I KNOW THAT, GIVEN YOUR CIRCUMSTANCES, THIS WILL SOUND VERY CRUEL, BUT...
YOU DO REALIZE YOU *HAVE* TO BE ABLE TO DO THAT, RIGHT? YOU HAVE NO CHOICE.

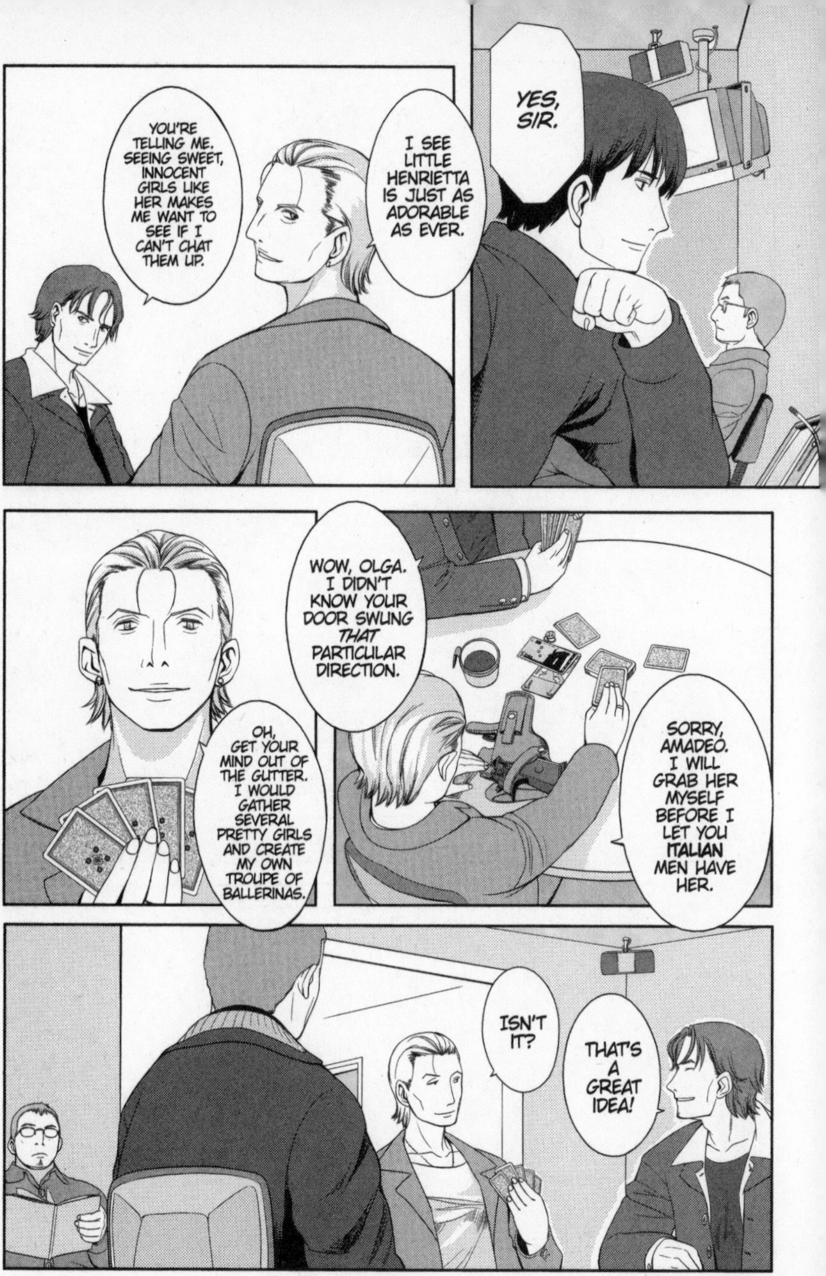
YES, SIR.
I SEE LITTLE HENRIETTA IS JUST AS ADORABLE AS EVER.
YOU'RE TELLING ME. SEEING SWEET, INNOCENT GIRLS LIKE HER MAKES ME WANT TO SEE IF I CAN'T CHAT THEM UP.
WOW, OLGA. I DIDN'T KNOW YOUR DOOR SWUNG *THAT* PARTICULAR DIRECTION.
SORRY, AMADEO. I WILL GRAB HER MYSELF BEFORE I LET YOU **ITALIAN** MEN HAVE HER.
OH, GET YOUR MIND OUT OF THE GUTTER. I WOULD GATHER SEVERAL PRETTY GIRLS AND CREATE MY OWN TROUPE OF BALLERINAS.
THAT'S A GREAT IDEA!
ISN'T IT?

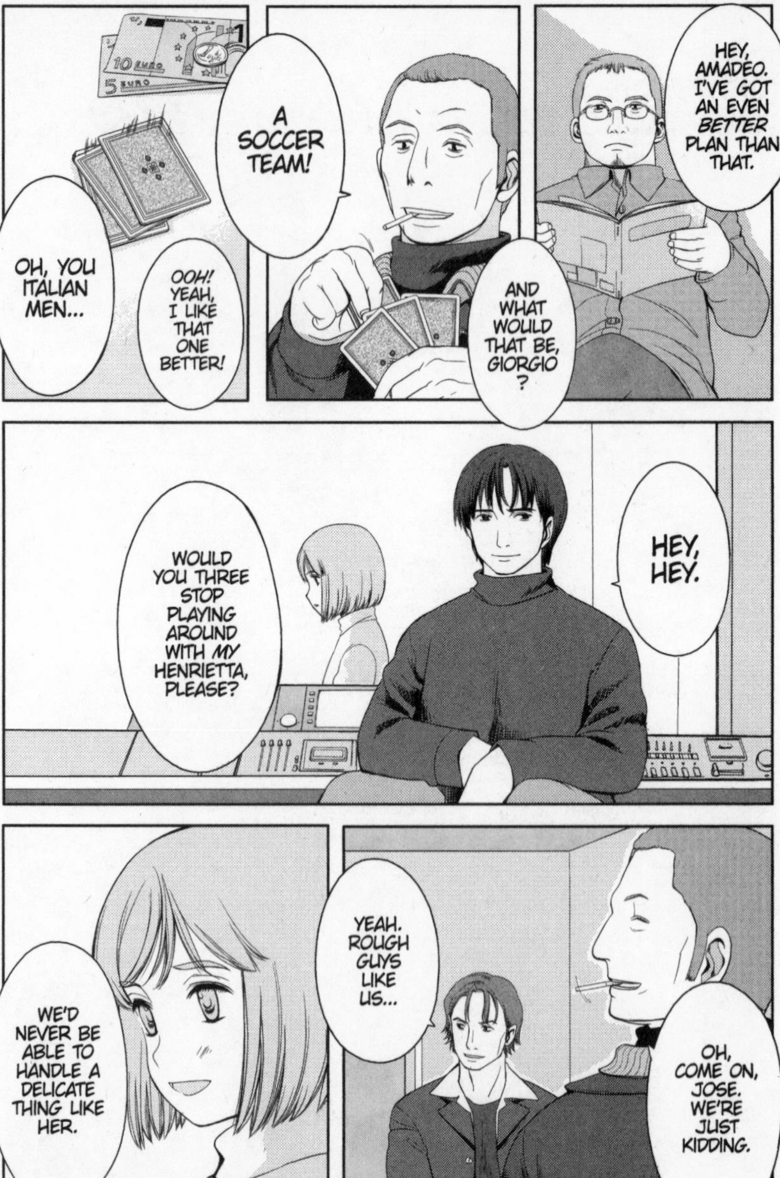
HEY, AMADEO. I'VE GOT AN EVEN *BETTER* PLAN THAN THAT.
AND WHAT WOULD THAT BE, GIORGIO?
A SOCCER TEAM!
OOH! YEAH, I LIKE THAT ONE BETTER!
OH, YOU ITALIAN MEN...
HEY, HEY.
WOULD YOU THREE STOP PLAYING AROUND WITH *MY* HENRIETTA, PLEASE?
OH, COME ON, JOSE. WE'RE JUST KIDDING.
YEAH. ROUGH GUYS LIKE US...
WE'D NEVER BE ABLE TO HANDLE A DELICATE THING LIKE HER.

CHAPTER 10:
THE PRINCE OF THE KINGDOM OF PASTA, PART 1

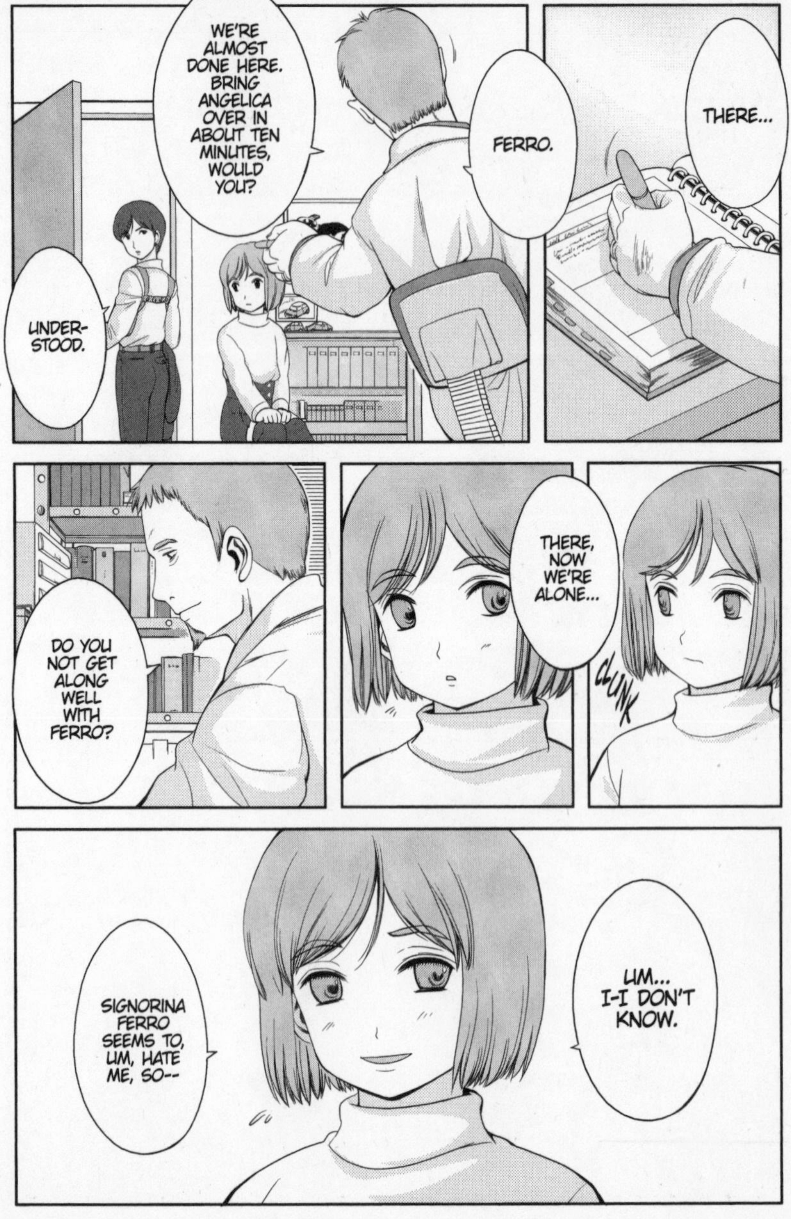
THERE...
FERRO.
WE'RE ALMOST DONE HERE. BRING ANGELICA OVER IN ABOUT TEN MINUTES, WOULD YOU?
UNDER-STOOD.
CLUNK
THERE, NOW WE'RE ALONE...
DO YOU NOT GET ALONG WELL WITH FERRO?
UM... I-I DON'T KNOW.
SIGNORINA FERRO SEEMS TO, UM, HATE ME, SO--

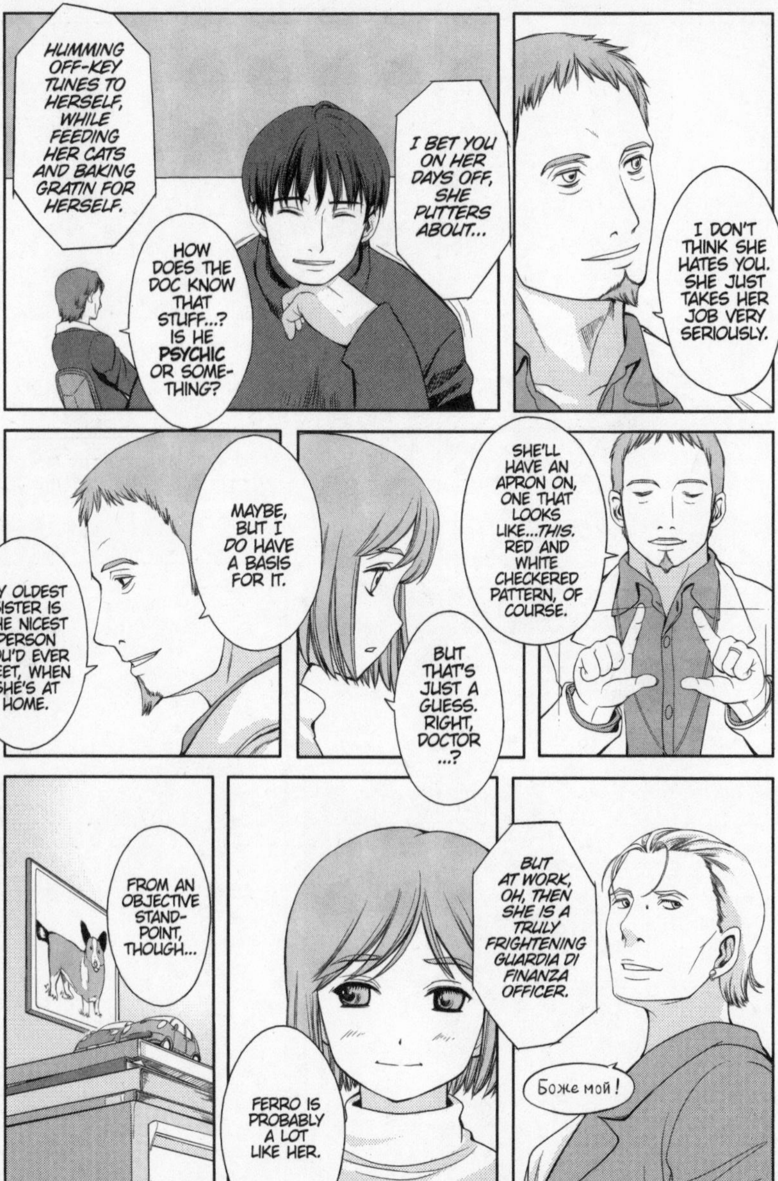

I DON'T THINK SHE HATES YOU. SHE JUST TAKES HER JOB VERY SERIOUSLY.
I BET YOU ON HER DAYS OFF, SHE PUTTERS ABOUT...
HUMMING OFF-KEY TUNES TO HERSELF, WHILE FEEDING HER CATS AND BAKING GRATIN FOR HERSELF.
HOW DOES THE DOC KNOW THAT STUFF...? IS HE PSYCHIC OR SOMETHING?
SHE'LL HAVE AN APRON ON, ONE THAT LOOKS LIKE...THIS. RED AND WHITE CHECKERED PATTERN, OF COURSE.
BUT THAT'S JUST A GUESS. RIGHT, DOCTOR ...?
MAYBE, BUT I DO HAVE A BASIS FOR IT.
MY OLDEST SISTER IS THE NICEST PERSON YOU'D EVER MEET, WHEN SHE'S AT HOME.
BUT AT WORK, OH, THEN SHE IS A TRULY FRIGHTENING GUARDIA DI FINANZA OFFICER.
Боже мой!
FERRO IS PROBABLY A LOT LIKE HER.
FROM AN OBJECTIVE STANDPOINT, THOUGH...

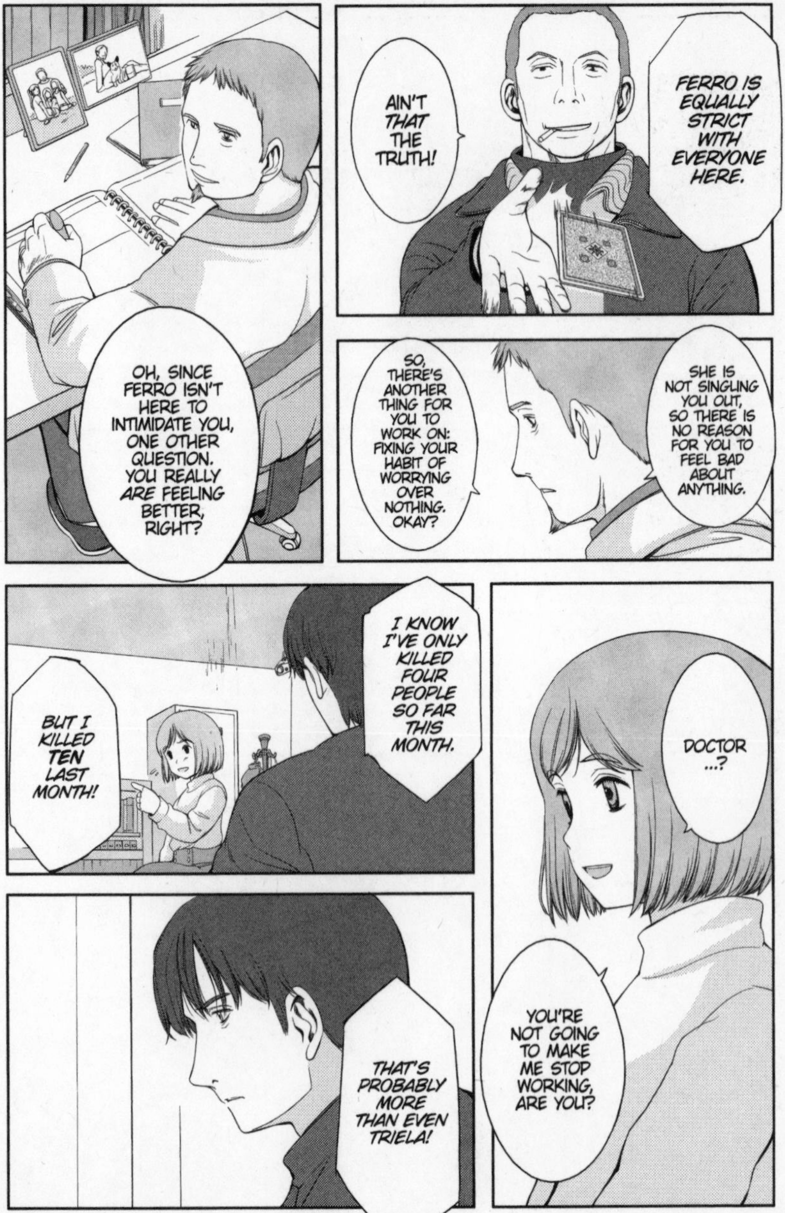

FERRO IS EQUALLY STRICT WITH EVERYONE HERE.
AIN'T *THAT* THE TRUTH!
SHE IS NOT SINGLING YOU OUT, SO THERE IS NO REASON FOR YOU TO FEEL BAD ABOUT ANYTHING.
SO, THERE'S ANOTHER THING FOR YOU TO WORK ON: FIXING YOUR HABIT OF WORRYING OVER NOTHING. OKAY?
OH, SINCE FERRO ISN'T HERE TO INTIMIDATE YOU, ONE OTHER QUESTION. YOU REALLY *ARE* FEELING BETTER, RIGHT?
DOCTOR ...?
YOU'RE NOT GOING TO MAKE ME STOP WORKING, ARE YOU?
I KNOW I'VE ONLY KILLED FOUR PEOPLE SO FAR THIS MONTH.
BUT I KILLED TEN LAST MONTH!
THAT'S PROBABLY MORE THAN EVEN TRIELA!

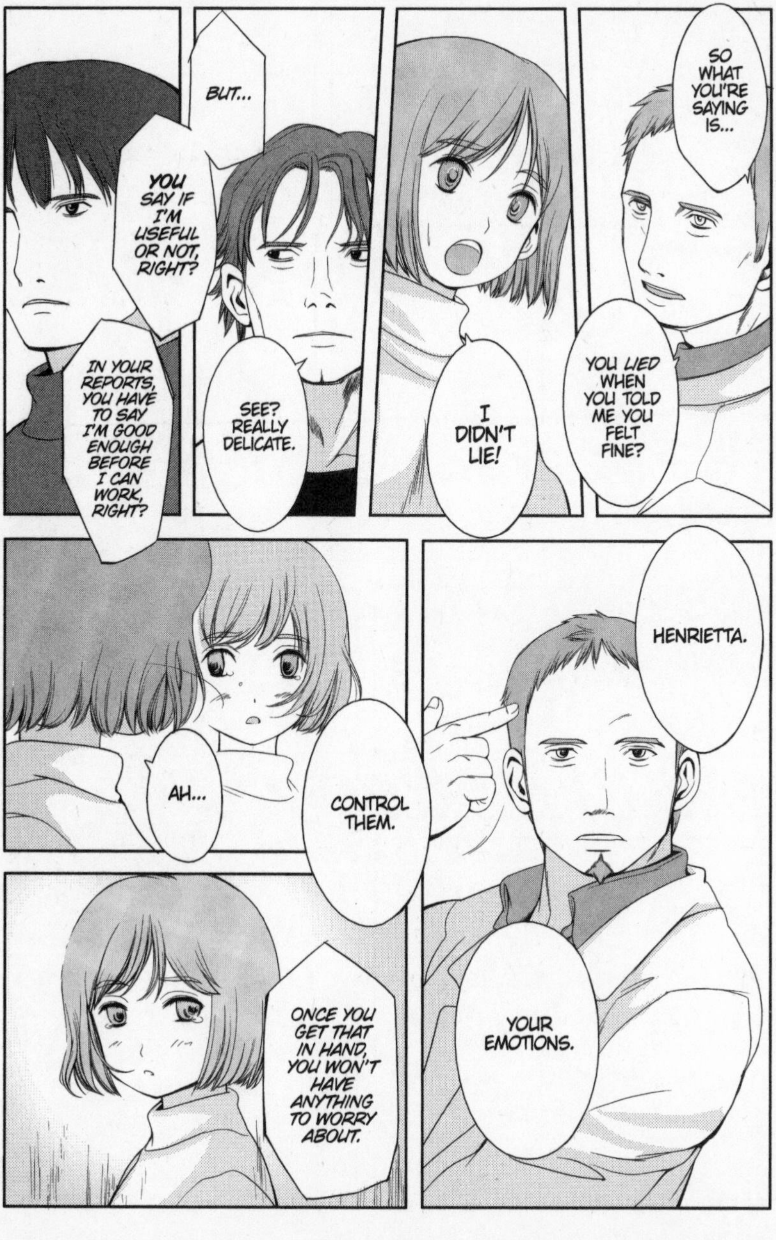
SO WHAT YOU'RE SAYING IS...
YOU *LIED* WHEN YOU TOLD ME YOU FELT FINE?
I DIDN'T LIE!
BUT...
YOU SAY IF I'M USEFUL OR NOT, RIGHT?
IN YOUR REPORTS, YOU HAVE TO SAY I'M GOOD ENOUGH BEFORE I CAN WORK, RIGHT?
SEE? REALLY DELICATE.
HENRIETTA.
AH...
CONTROL THEM.
YOUR EMOTIONS.
ONCE YOU GET THAT IN HAND, YOU WON'T HAVE ANYTHING TO WORRY ABOUT.

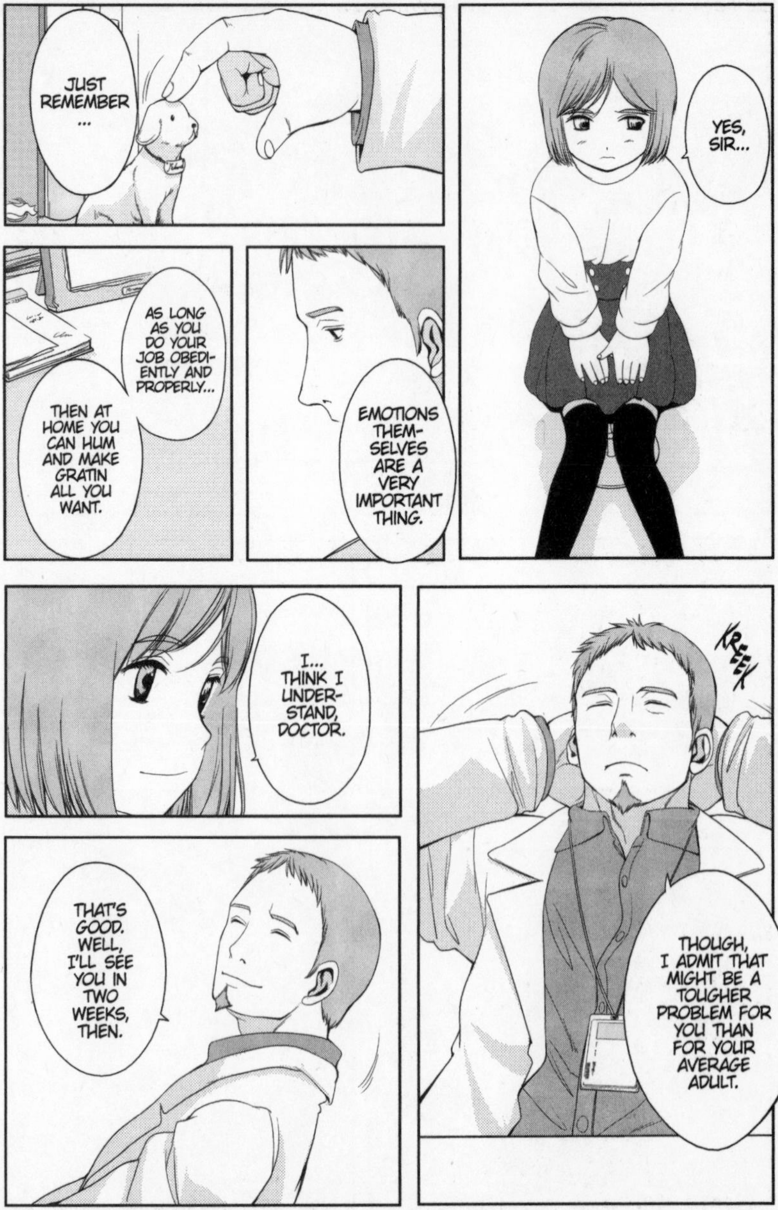
YES, SIR...
JUST REMEMBER ...
EMOTIONS THEM-SELVES ARE A VERY IMPORTANT THING.
AS LONG AS YOU DO YOUR JOB OBEDI-ENTLY AND PROPERLY...
THEN AT HOME YOU CAN HUM AND MAKE GRATIN ALL YOU WANT.
KREEK
THOUGH, I ADMIT THAT MIGHT BE A TOUGHER PROBLEM FOR YOU THAN FOR YOUR AVERAGE ADULT.
I... THINK I UNDER-STAND, DOCTOR.
THAT'S GOOD. WELL, I'LL SEE YOU IN TWO WEEKS, THEN.

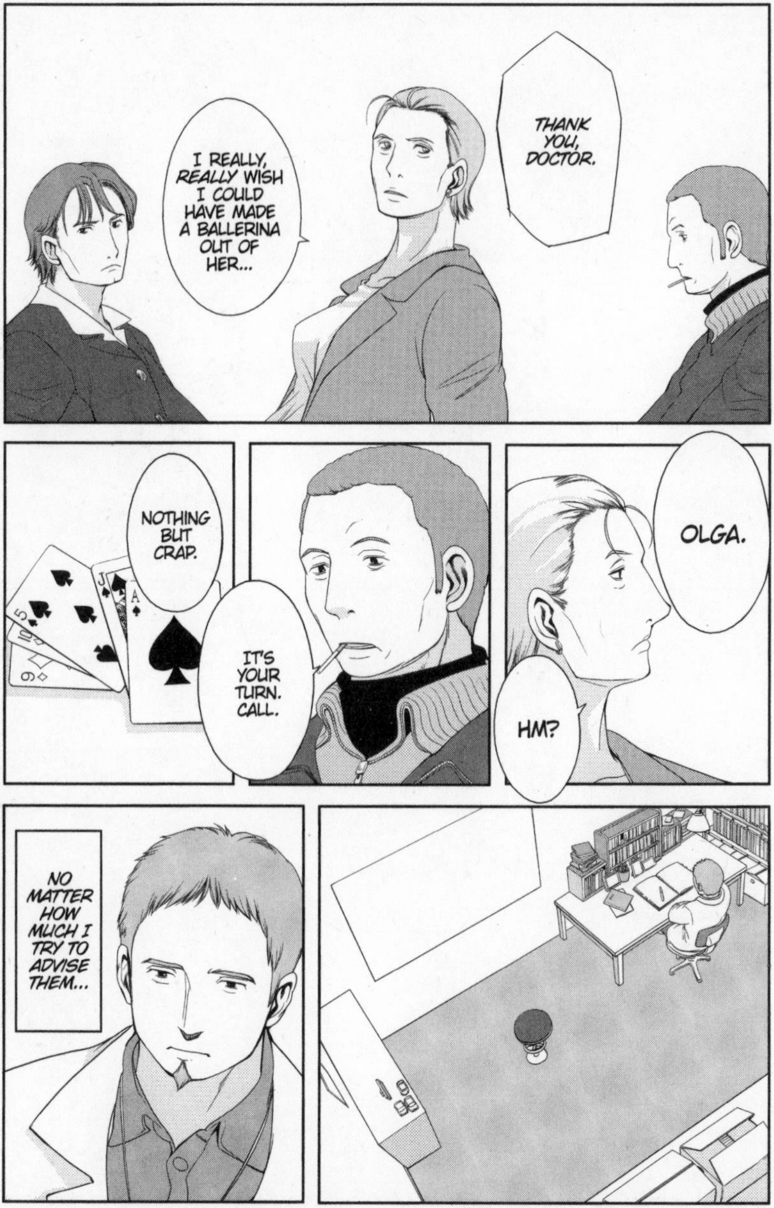
THANK YOU, DOCTOR.
I REALLY, REALLY WISH I COULD HAVE MADE A BALLERINA OUT OF HER...
OLGA.
HM?
IT'S YOUR TURN. CALL.
NOTHING BUT CRAP.
NO MATTER HOW MUCH I TRY TO ADVISE THEM...

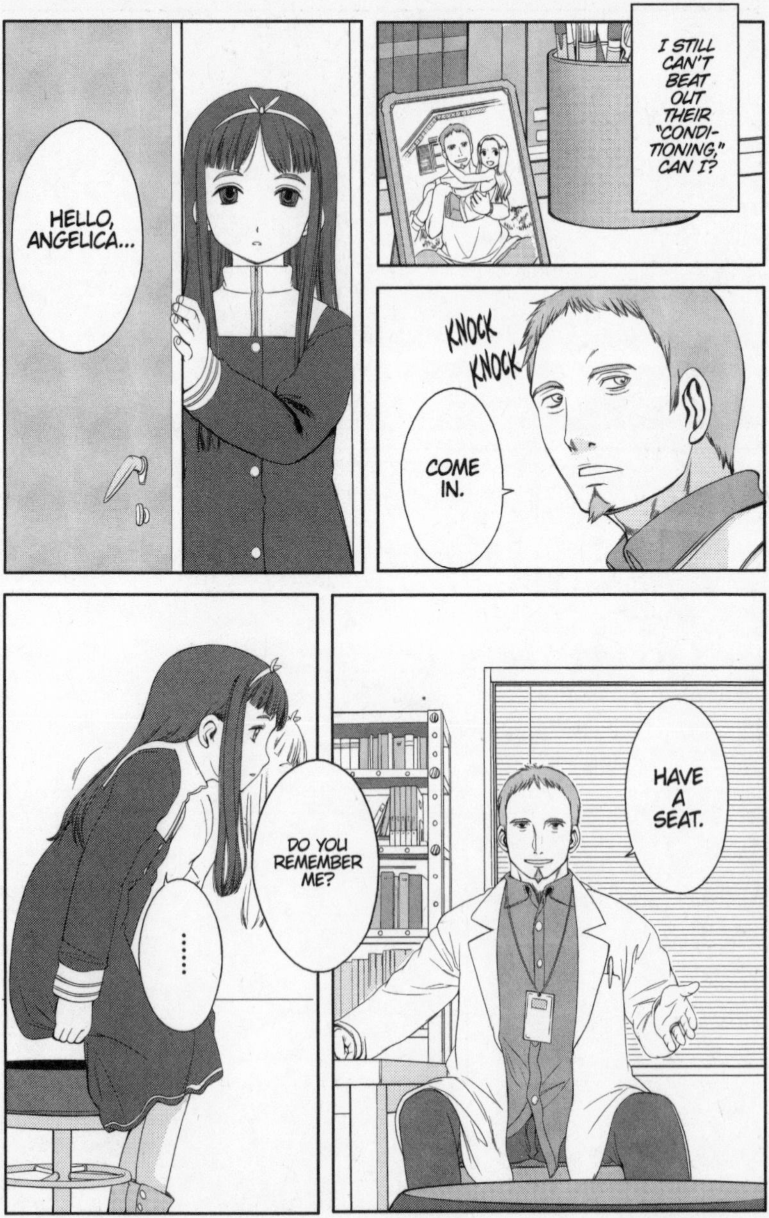
I STILL CAN'T BEAT OUT THEIR "CONDITIONING," CAN I?
KNOCK KNOCK
COME IN.
HELLO, ANGELICA...
HAVE A SEAT.
DO YOU REMEMBER ME?
......

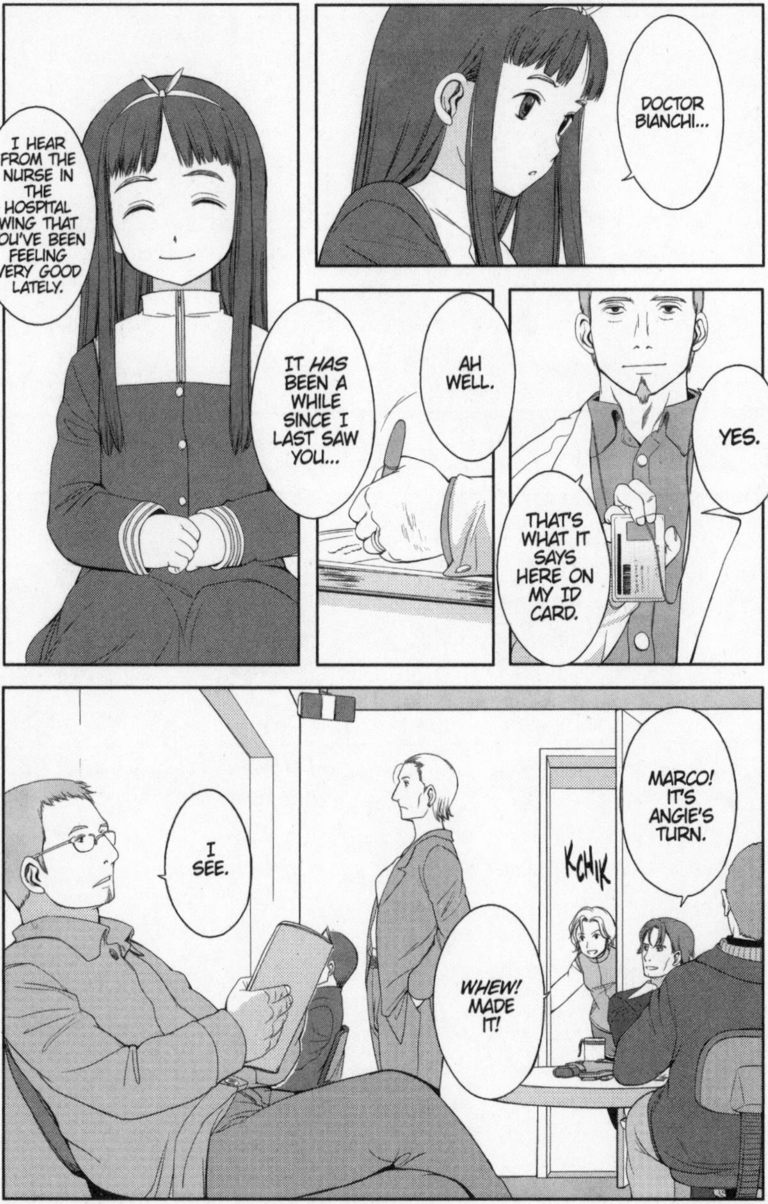
DOCTOR BIANCHI...
YES.
THAT'S WHAT IT SAYS HERE ON MY ID CARD.
AH WELL.
IT *HAS* BEEN A WHILE SINCE I LAST SAW YOU...
I HEAR FROM THE NURSE IN THE HOSPITAL WING THAT YOU'VE BEEN FEELING VERY GOOD LATELY.
MARCO! IT'S ANGIE'S TURN.
K-CHIK
WHEW! MADE IT!
I SEE.

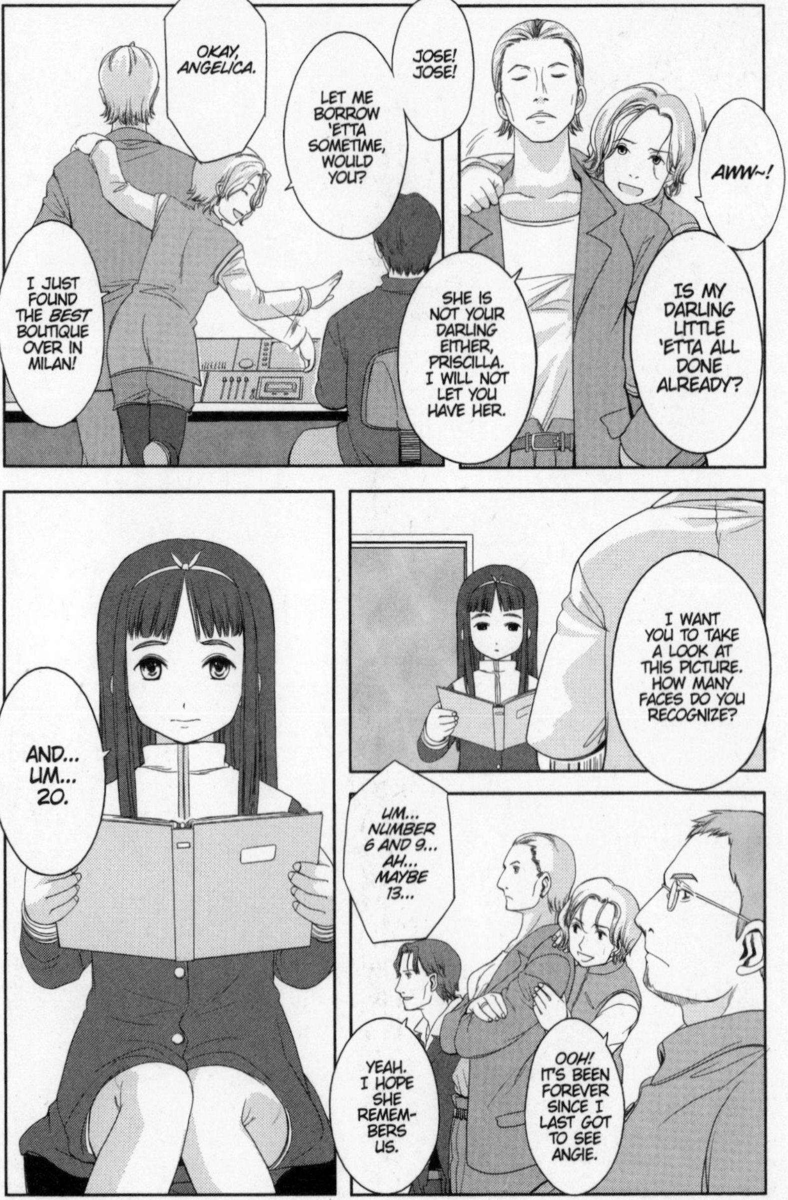
AWW~!
IS MY DARLING LITTLE 'ETTA ALL DONE ALREADY?
SHE IS NOT YOUR DARLING EITHER, PRISCILLA. I WILL NOT LET YOU HAVE HER.
JOSE! JOSE!
LET ME BORROW 'ETTA SOMETIME, WOULD YOU?
OKAY, ANGELICA.
I JUST FOUND THE *BEST* BOUTIQUE OVER IN MILAN!
I WANT YOU TO TAKE A LOOK AT THIS PICTURE. HOW MANY FACES DO YOU RECOGNIZE?
UM... NUMBER 6 AND 9... AH... MAYBE 13...
OOH! IT'S BEEN FOREVER SINCE I LAST GOT TO SEE ANGIE.
YEAH. I HOPE SHE REMEM-BERS US.
AND... UM... 20.

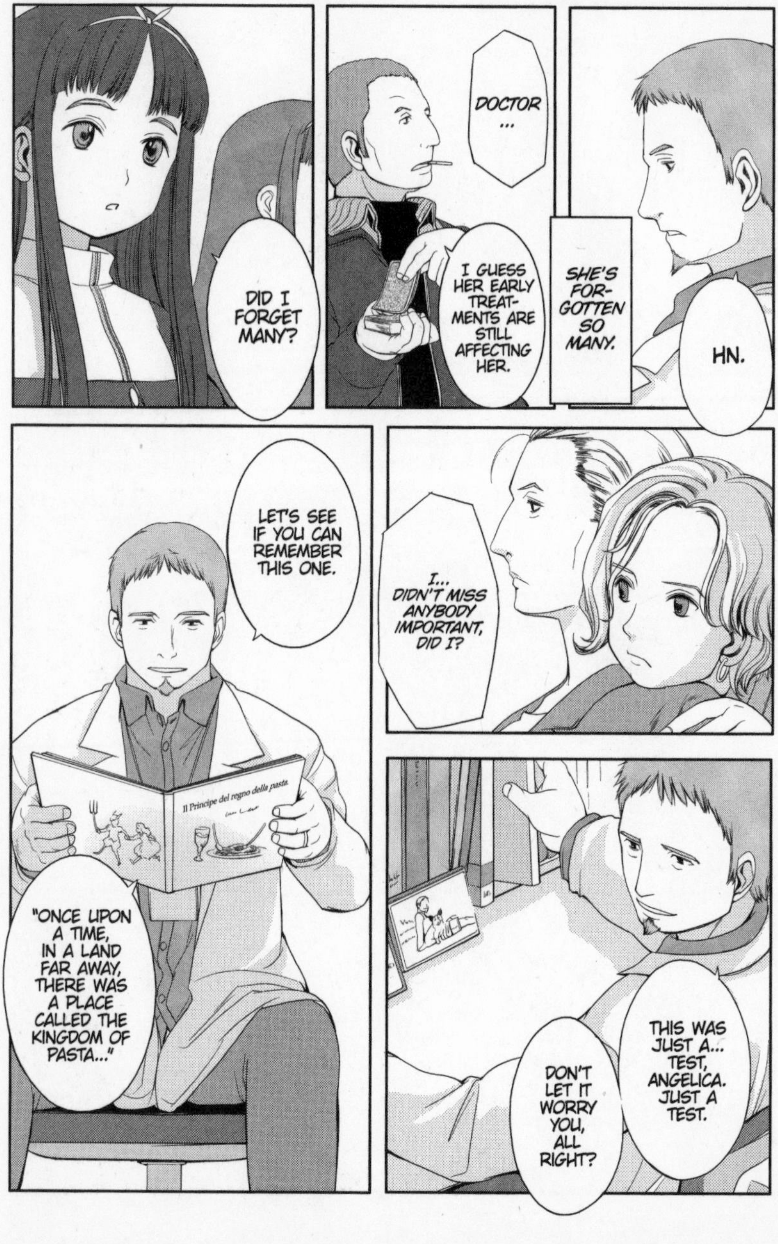
SHE'S FOR-GOTTEN SO MANY.
HN.
DOCTOR ...
I GUESS HER EARLY TREAT-MENTS ARE STILL AFFECTING HER.
DID I FORGET MANY?
I... DIDN'T MISS ANYBODY IMPORTANT, DID I?
THIS WAS JUST A... TEST, ANGELICA. JUST A TEST.
DON'T LET IT WORRY YOU, ALL RIGHT?
LET'S SEE IF YOU CAN REMEMBER THIS ONE.
Il Principe del regno della pasta.
"ONCE UPON A TIME, IN A LAND FAR AWAY, THERE WAS A PLACE CALLED THE KINGDOM OF PASTA..."

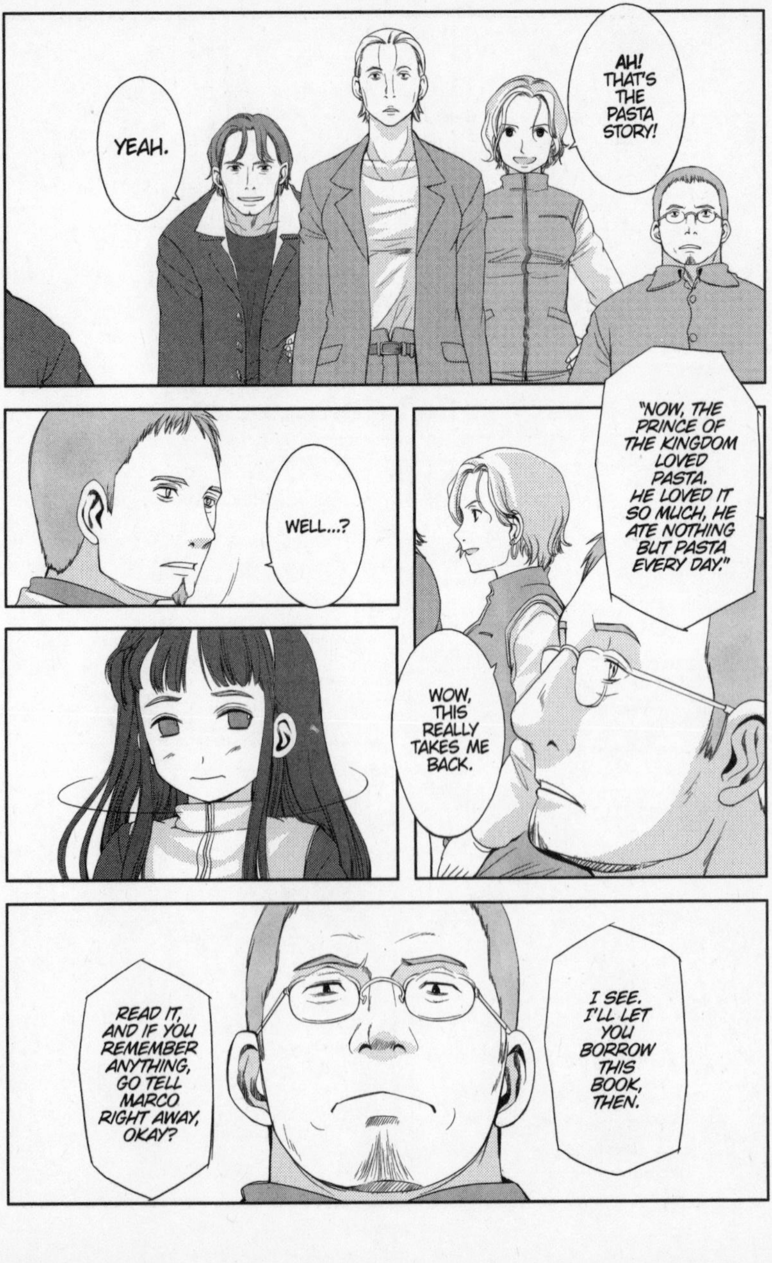
AH! THAT'S THE PASTA STORY!
YEAH.
"NOW, THE PRINCE OF THE KINGDOM LOVED PASTA. HE LOVED IT SO MUCH, HE ATE NOTHING BUT PASTA EVERY DAY."
WOW, THIS REALLY TAKES ME BACK.
WELL...?
I SEE. I'LL LET YOU BORROW THIS BOOK, THEN.
READ IT, AND IF YOU REMEMBER ANYTHING, GO TELL MARCO RIGHT AWAY, OKAY?

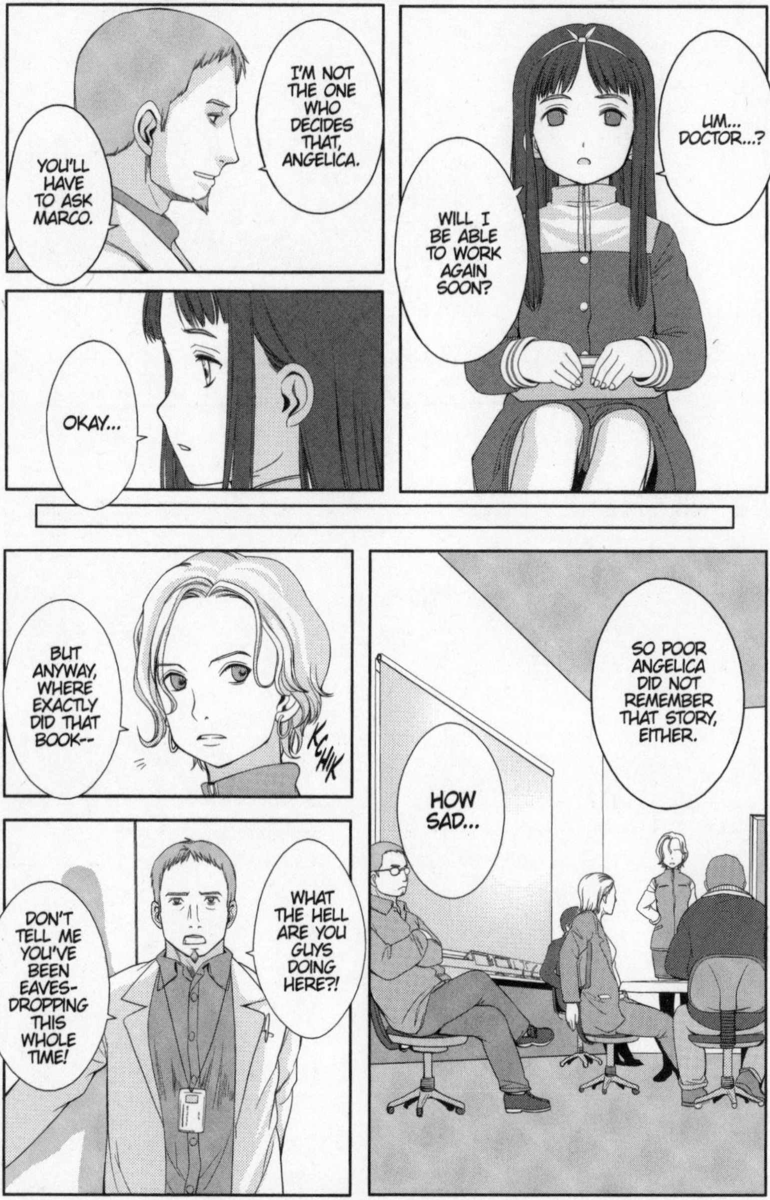
UM... DOCTOR...?
WILL I BE ABLE TO WORK AGAIN SOON?
I'M NOT THE ONE WHO DECIDES THAT, ANGELICA.
YOU'LL HAVE TO ASK MARCO.
OKAY...
SO POOR ANGELICA DID NOT REMEMBER THAT STORY, EITHER.
HOW SAD...
BUT ANYWAY, WHERE EXACTLY DID THAT BOOK--
KCHIK
WHAT THE HELL ARE YOU GUYS DOING HERE?!
DON'T TELL ME YOU'VE BEEN EAVES-DROPPING THIS WHOLE TIME!

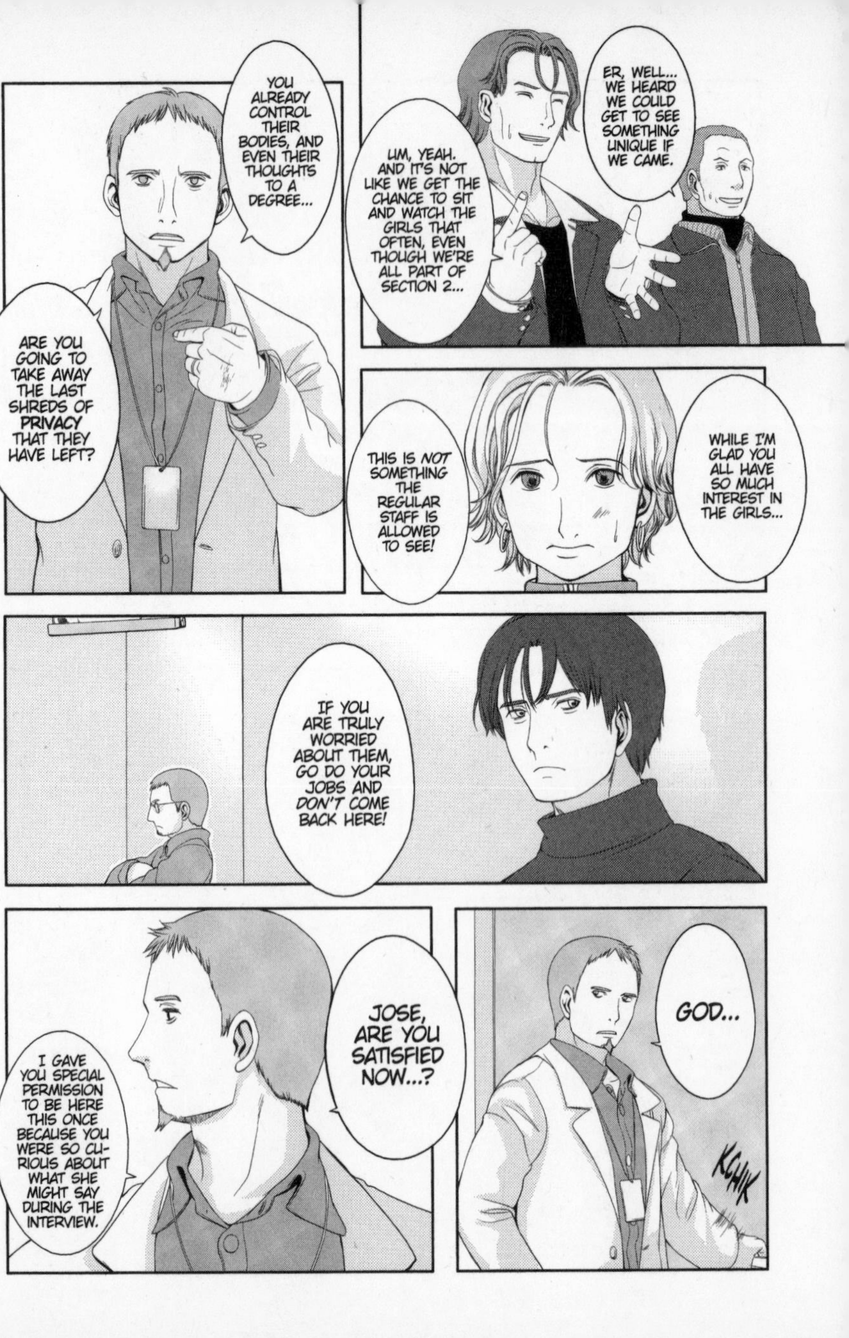
ER, WELL... WE HEARD WE COULD GET TO SEE SOMETHING UNIQUE IF WE CAME.
UM, YEAH. AND IT'S NOT LIKE WE GET THE CHANCE TO SIT AND WATCH THE GIRLS THAT OFTEN, EVEN THOUGH WE'RE ALL PART OF SECTION 2...
WHILE I'M GLAD YOU ALL HAVE SO MUCH INTEREST IN THE GIRLS...
THIS IS *NOT* SOMETHING THE REGULAR STAFF IS ALLOWED TO SEE!
YOU ALREADY CONTROL THEIR BODIES, AND EVEN THEIR THOUGHTS TO A DEGREE...
ARE YOU GOING TO TAKE AWAY THE LAST SHREDS OF **PRIVACY** THAT THEY HAVE LEFT?
IF YOU ARE TRULY WORRIED ABOUT THEM, GO DO YOUR JOBS AND *DON'T* COME BACK HERE!
GOD...
KCHIK
JOSE, ARE YOU SATISFIED NOW...?
I GAVE YOU SPECIAL PERMISSION TO BE HERE THIS ONCE BECAUSE YOU WERE SO CU-RIOUS ABOUT WHAT SHE MIGHT SAY DURING THE INTERVIEW.

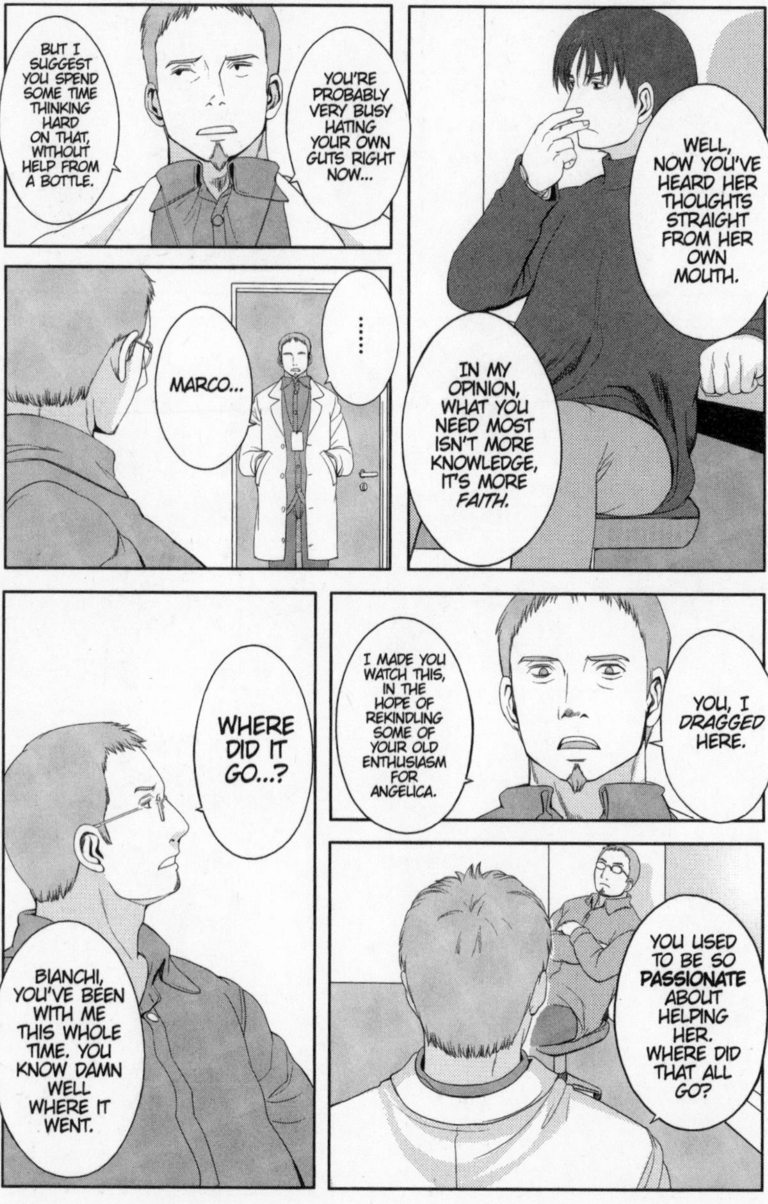
WELL, NOW YOU'VE HEARD HER THOUGHTS STRAIGHT FROM HER OWN MOUTH.
IN MY OPINION, WHAT YOU NEED MOST ISN'T MORE KNOWLEDGE, IT'S MORE *FAITH.*
YOU'RE PROBABLY VERY BUSY HATING YOUR OWN GUTS RIGHT NOW...
BUT I SUGGEST YOU SPEND SOME TIME THINKING HARD ON THAT, WITHOUT HELP FROM A BOTTLE.
......
MARCO...
YOU, I *DRAGGED* HERE.
I MADE YOU WATCH THIS, IN THE HOPE OF REKINDLING SOME OF YOUR OLD ENTHUSIASM FOR ANGELICA.
YOU USED TO BE SO **PASSIONATE** ABOUT HELPING HER. WHERE DID THAT ALL GO?
WHERE DID IT GO...?
BIANCHI, YOU'VE BEEN WITH ME THIS WHOLE TIME. YOU KNOW DAMN WELL WHERE IT WENT.

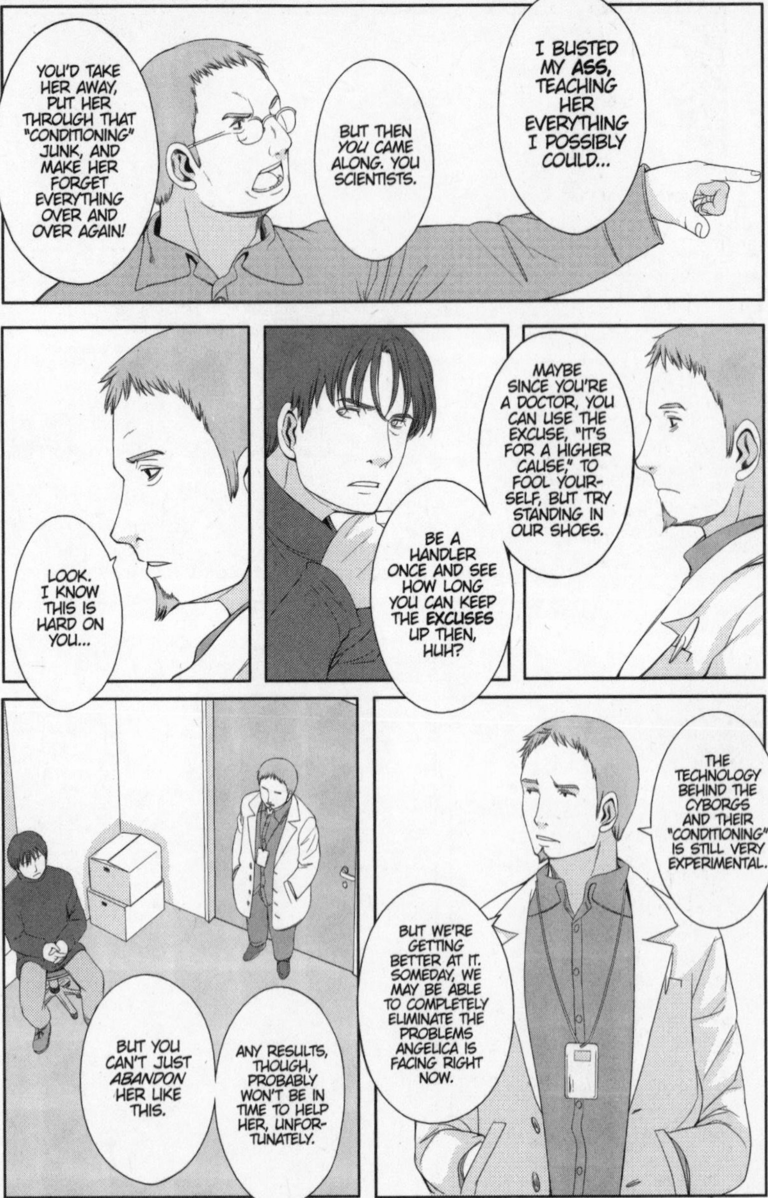
I BUSTED MY ASS, TEACHING HER EVERYTHING I POSSIBLY COULD...
BUT THEN YOU CAME ALONG. YOU SCIENTISTS.
YOU'D TAKE HER AWAY, PUT HER THROUGH THAT "CONDITIONING" JUNK, AND MAKE HER FORGET EVERYTHING OVER AND OVER AGAIN!
MAYBE SINCE YOU'RE A DOCTOR, YOU CAN USE THE EXCUSE, "IT'S FOR A HIGHER CAUSE," TO FOOL YOURSELF, BUT TRY STANDING IN OUR SHOES.
BE A HANDLER ONCE AND SEE HOW LONG YOU CAN KEEP THE EXCUSES UP THEN, HUH?
LOOK. I KNOW THIS IS HARD ON YOU...
THE TECHNOLOGY BEHIND THE CYBORGS AND THEIR "CONDITIONING" IS STILL VERY EXPERIMENTAL.
BUT WE'RE GETTING BETTER AT IT. SOMEDAY, WE MAY BE ABLE TO COMPLETELY ELIMINATE THE PROBLEMS ANGELICA IS FACING RIGHT NOW.
ANY RESULTS, THOUGH, PROBABLY WON'T BE IN TIME TO HELP HER, UNFORTUNATELY.
BUT YOU CAN'T JUST ABANDON HER LIKE THIS.

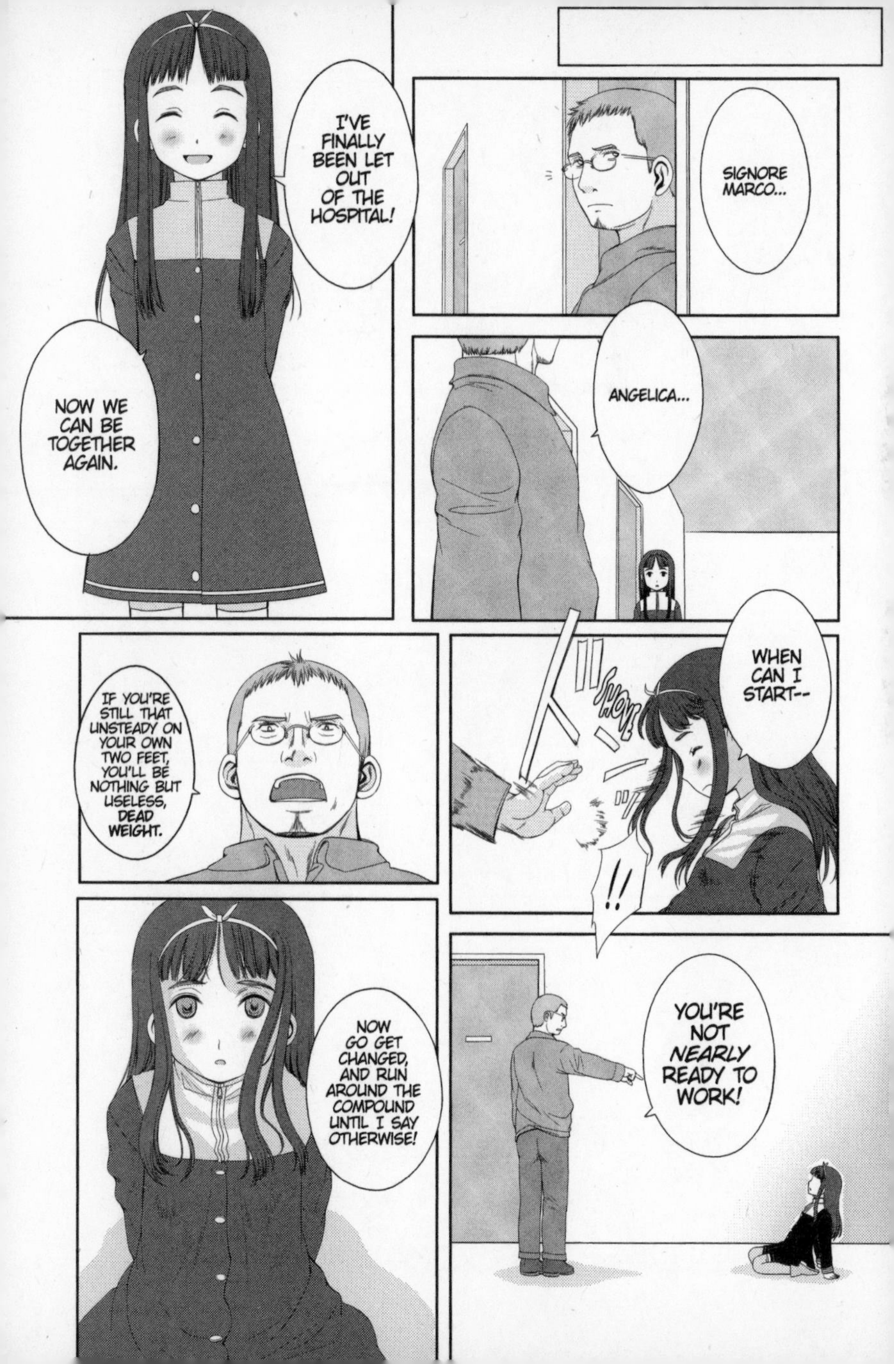
SIGNORE MARCO...
ANGELICA...
I'VE FINALLY BEEN LET OUT OF THE HOSPITAL!
NOW WE CAN BE TOGETHER AGAIN.
WHEN CAN I START--
SHOVE
!!
IF YOU'RE STILL THAT UNSTEADY ON YOUR OWN TWO FEET, YOU'LL BE NOTHING BUT USELESS, DEAD WEIGHT.
YOU'RE NOT *NEARLY* READY TO WORK!
NOW GO GET CHANGED, AND RUN AROUND THE COMPOUND UNTIL I SAY OTHERWISE!

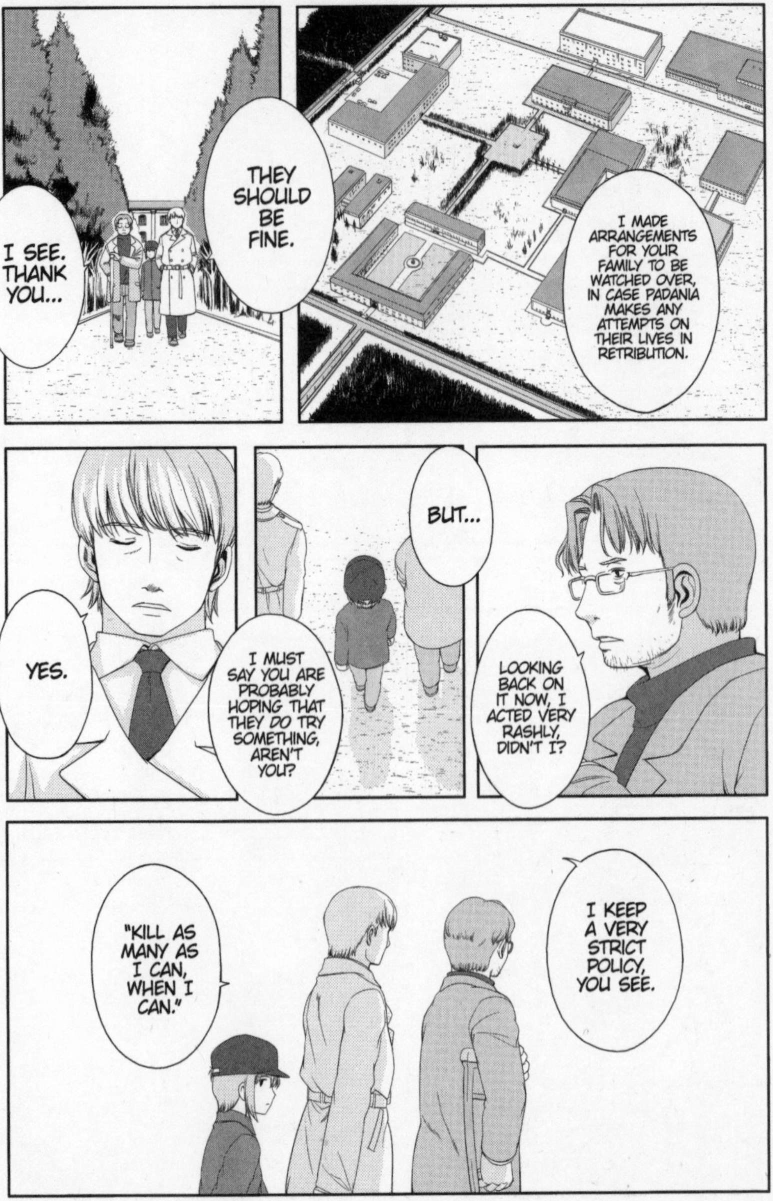
I MADE ARRANGEMENTS FOR YOUR FAMILY TO BE WATCHED OVER, IN CASE PADANIA MAKES ANY ATTEMPTS ON THEIR LIVES IN RETRIBUTION.
THEY SHOULD BE FINE.
I SEE. THANK YOU...
LOOKING BACK ON IT NOW, I ACTED VERY RASHLY, DIDN'T I?
BUT...
I MUST SAY YOU ARE PROBABLY HOPING THAT THEY *DO* TRY SOMETHING, AREN'T YOU?
YES.
I KEEP A VERY STRICT POLICY, YOU SEE.
"KILL AS MANY AS I CAN, WHEN I CAN."

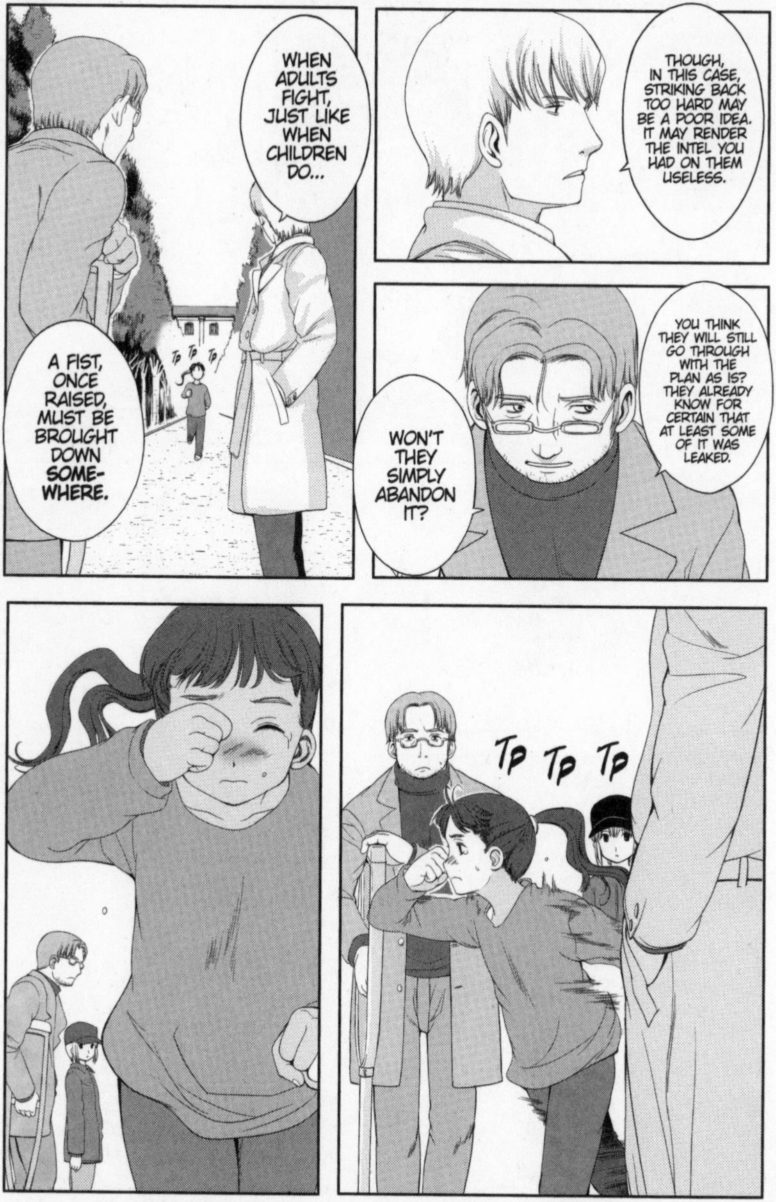
THOUGH, IN THIS CASE, STRIKING BACK TOO HARD MAY BE A POOR IDEA. IT MAY RENDER THE INTEL YOU HAD ON THEM USELESS.
YOU THINK THEY WILL STILL GO THROUGH WITH THE PLAN AS IS? THEY ALREADY KNOW FOR CERTAIN THAT AT LEAST SOME OF IT WAS LEAKED.
WON'T THEY SIMPLY ABANDON IT?
WHEN ADULTS FIGHT, JUST LIKE WHEN CHILDREN DO...
Tp Tp Tp
A FIST, ONCE RAISED, MUST BE BROUGHT DOWN SOME-WHERE.
Tp Tp Tp

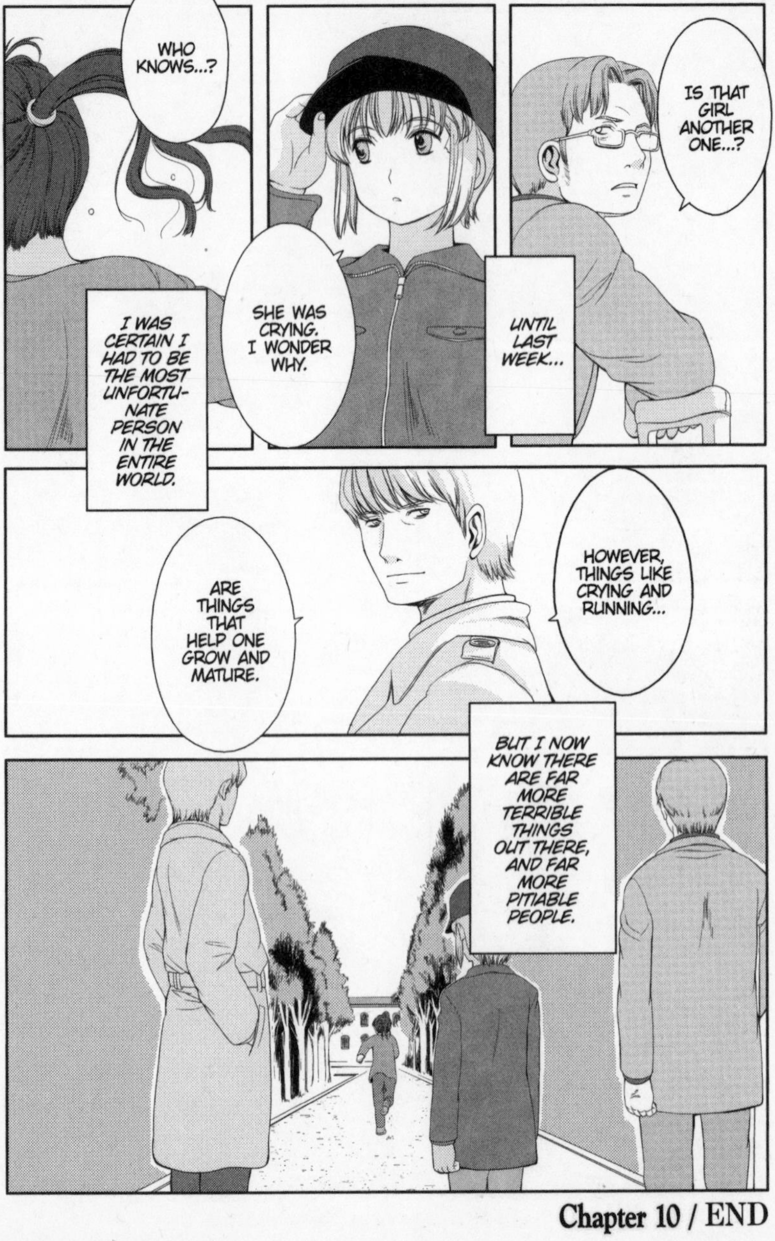
IS THAT GIRL ANOTHER ONE...?
UNTIL LAST WEEK...
SHE WAS CRYING. I WONDER WHY.
WHO KNOWS...?
I WAS CERTAIN I HAD TO BE THE MOST UNFORTUNATE PERSON IN THE ENTIRE WORLD.
HOWEVER, THINGS LIKE CRYING AND RUNNING...
ARE THINGS THAT HELP ONE GROW AND MATURE.
BUT I NOW KNOW THERE ARE FAR MORE TERRIBLE THINGS OUT THERE, AND FAR MORE PITIABLE PEOPLE.

Chapter 10 / END

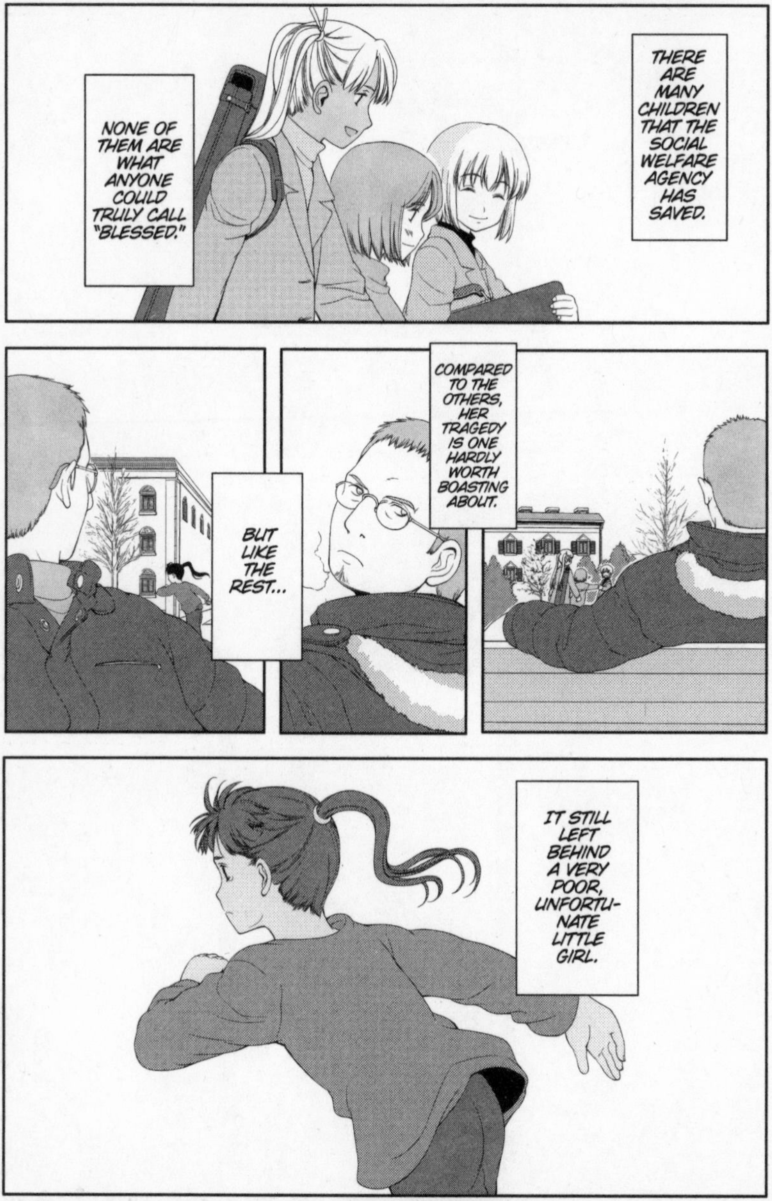
THERE ARE MANY CHILDREN THAT THE SOCIAL WELFARE AGENCY HAS SAVED.
NONE OF THEM ARE WHAT ANYONE COULD TRULY CALL "BLESSED."
COMPARED TO THE OTHERS, HER TRAGEDY IS ONE HARDLY WORTH BOASTING ABOUT.
BUT LIKE THE REST...
IT STILL LEFT BEHIND A VERY POOR, UNFORTU-NATE LITTLE GIRL.

Chapter 11: The Prince of the Kingdom of Pasta, Part 2

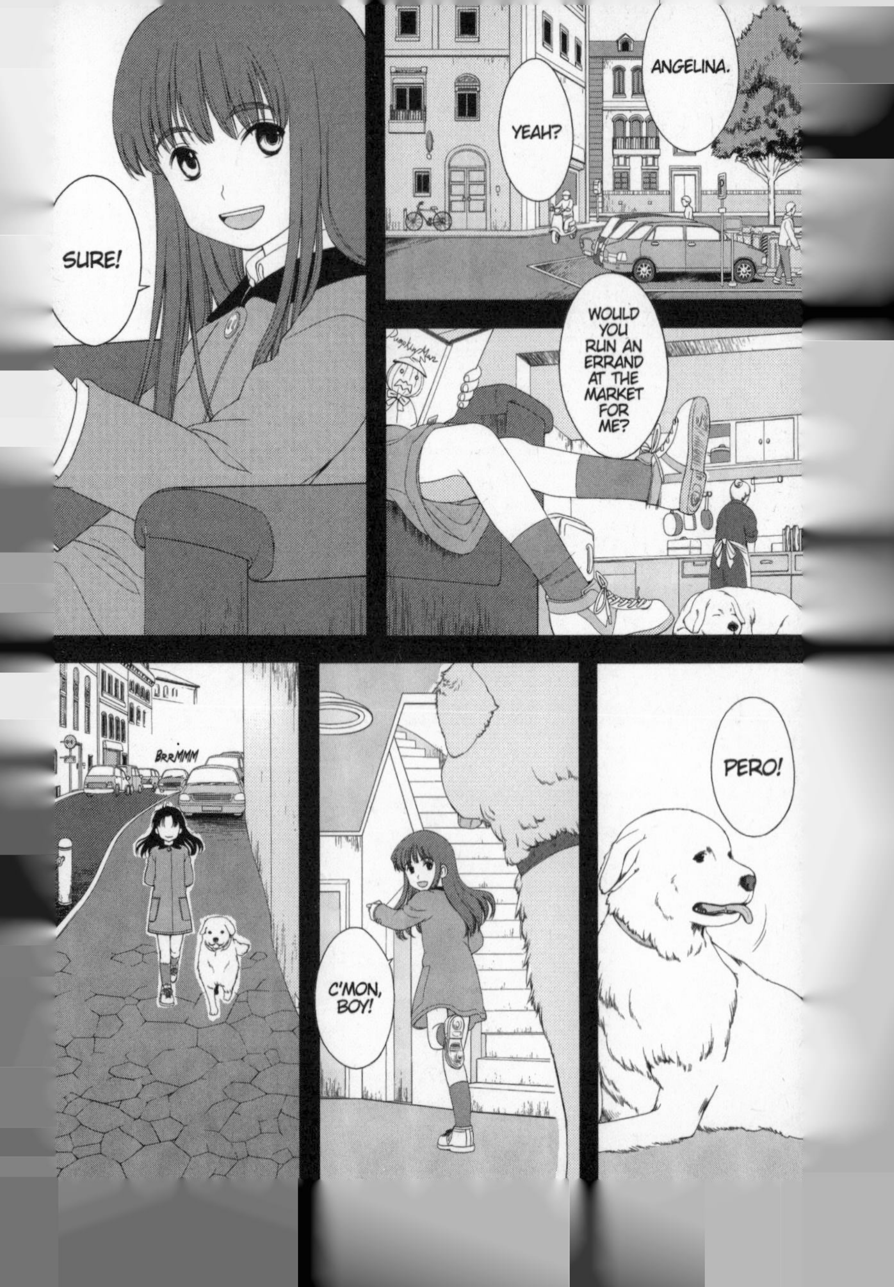
ANGELINA.
YEAH?
WOULD YOU RUN AN ERRAND AT THE MARKET FOR ME?
SURE!
PERO!
C'MON, BOY!
BRRMMM

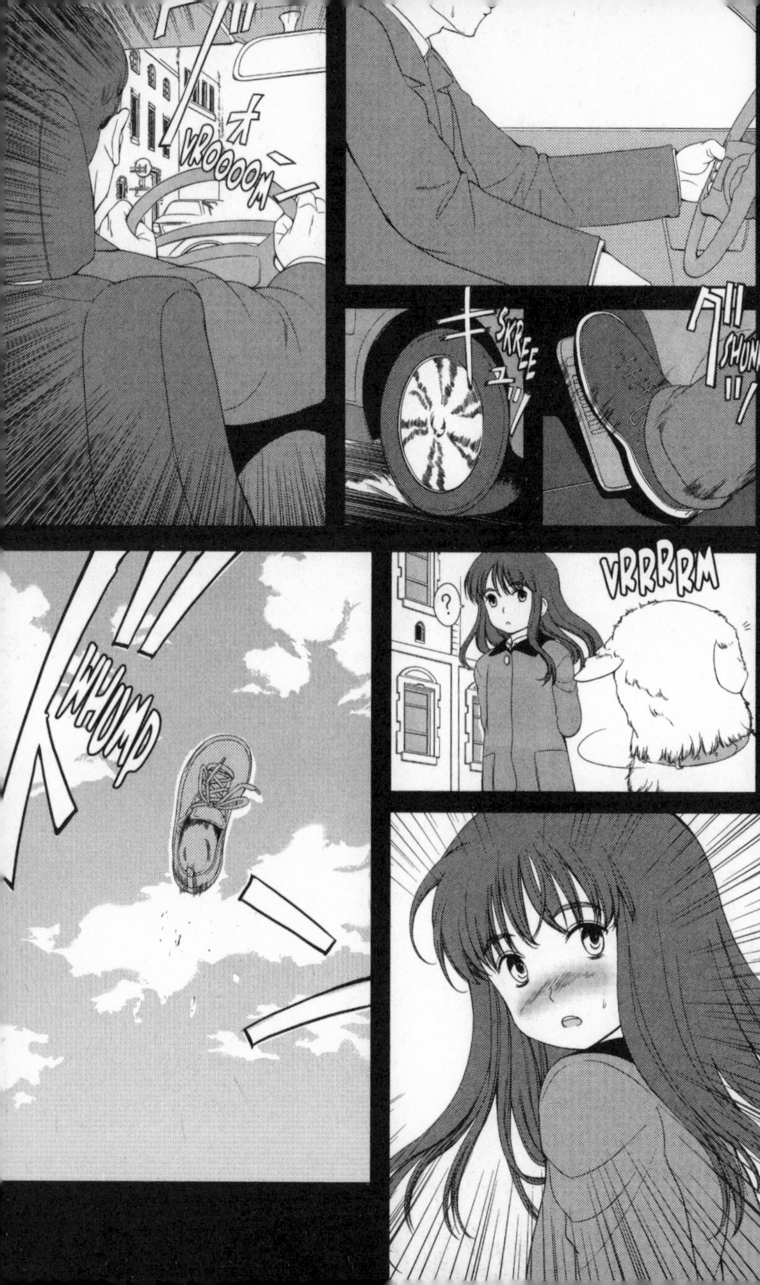
SHUNK
SKREEE
VROOOOOM
VRRRRM
?
WHUMP

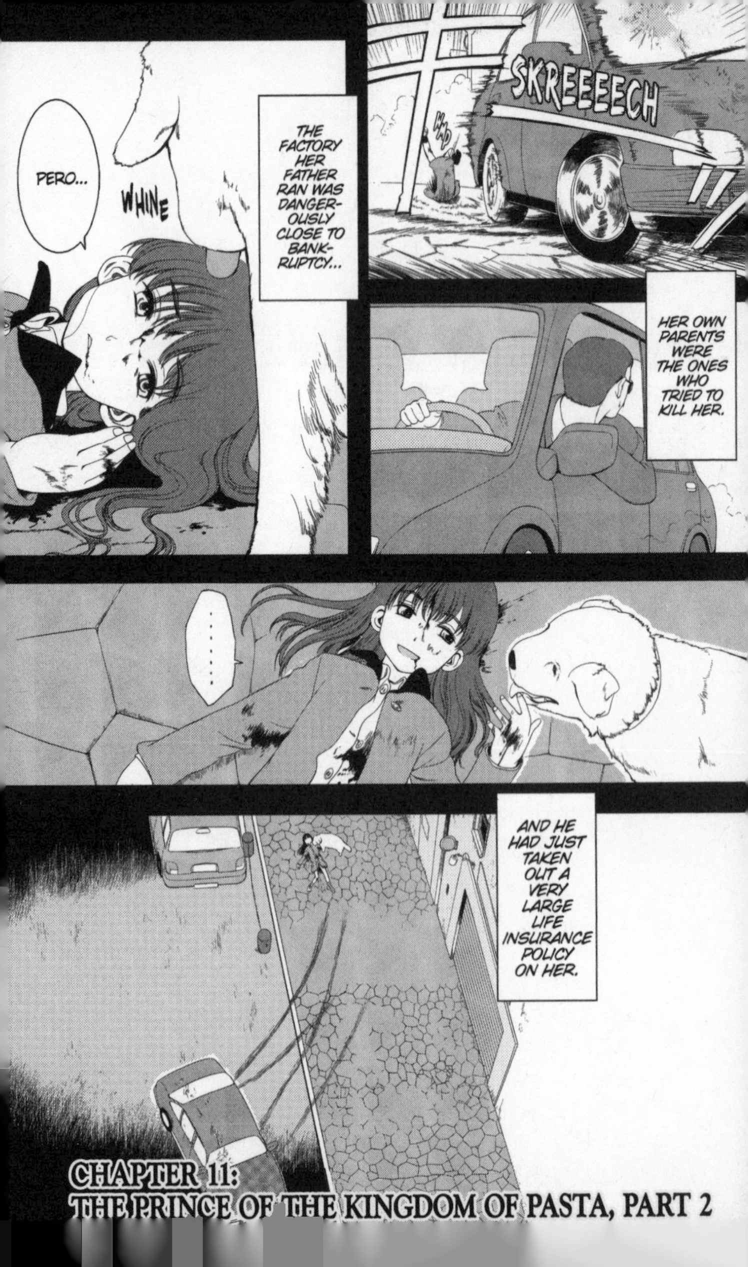
SKREEEECH
HER OWN PARENTS WERE THE ONES WHO TRIED TO KILL HER.
THE FACTORY HER FATHER RAN WAS DANGER-OUSLY CLOSE TO BANK-RUPTCY...
PERO...
WHINE
......
AND HE HAD JUST TAKEN OUT A VERY LARGE LIFE INSURANCE POLICY ON HER.

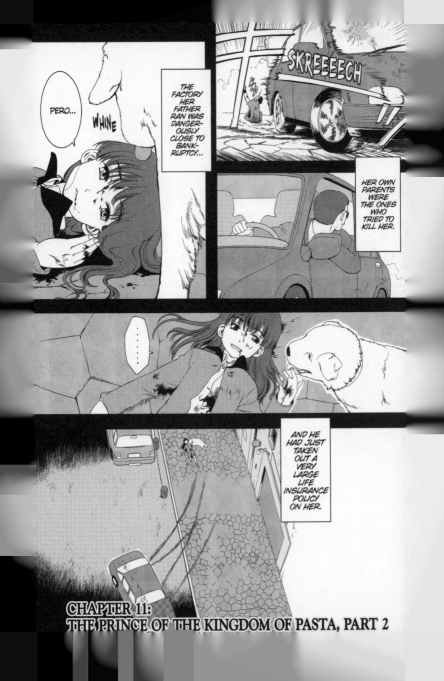

CHAPTER 11:
THE PRINCE OF THE KINGDOM OF PASTA, PART 2

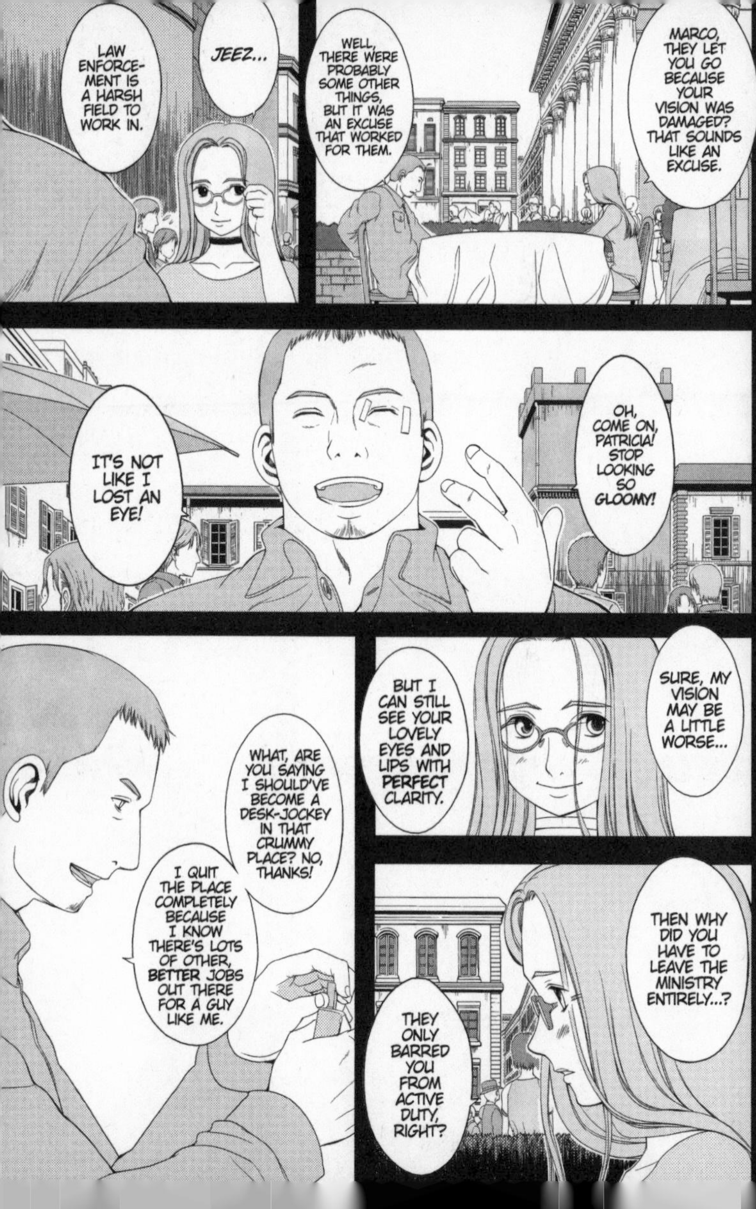
MARCO, THEY LET YOU GO BECAUSE YOUR VISION WAS DAMAGED? THAT SOUNDS LIKE AN EXCUSE.
WELL, THERE WERE PROBABLY SOME OTHER THINGS, BUT IT WAS AN EXCUSE THAT WORKED FOR THEM.
JEEZ...
LAW ENFORCEMENT IS A HARSH FIELD TO WORK IN.
OH, COME ON, PATRICIA! STOP LOOKING SO GLOOMY!
IT'S NOT LIKE I LOST AN EYE!
SURE, MY VISION MAY BE A LITTLE WORSE...
BUT I CAN STILL SEE YOUR LOVELY EYES AND LIPS WITH PERFECT CLARITY.
THEN WHY DID YOU HAVE TO LEAVE THE MINISTRY ENTIRELY...?
THEY ONLY BARRED YOU FROM ACTIVE DUTY, RIGHT?
WHAT, ARE YOU SAYING I SHOULD'VE BECOME A DESK-JOCKEY IN THAT CRUMMY PLACE? NO, THANKS!
I QUIT THE PLACE COMPLETELY BECAUSE I KNOW THERE'S LOTS OF OTHER, BETTER JOBS OUT THERE FOR A GUY LIKE ME.

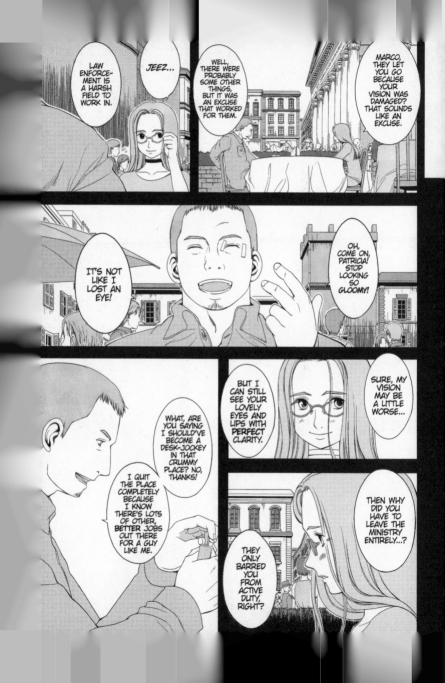

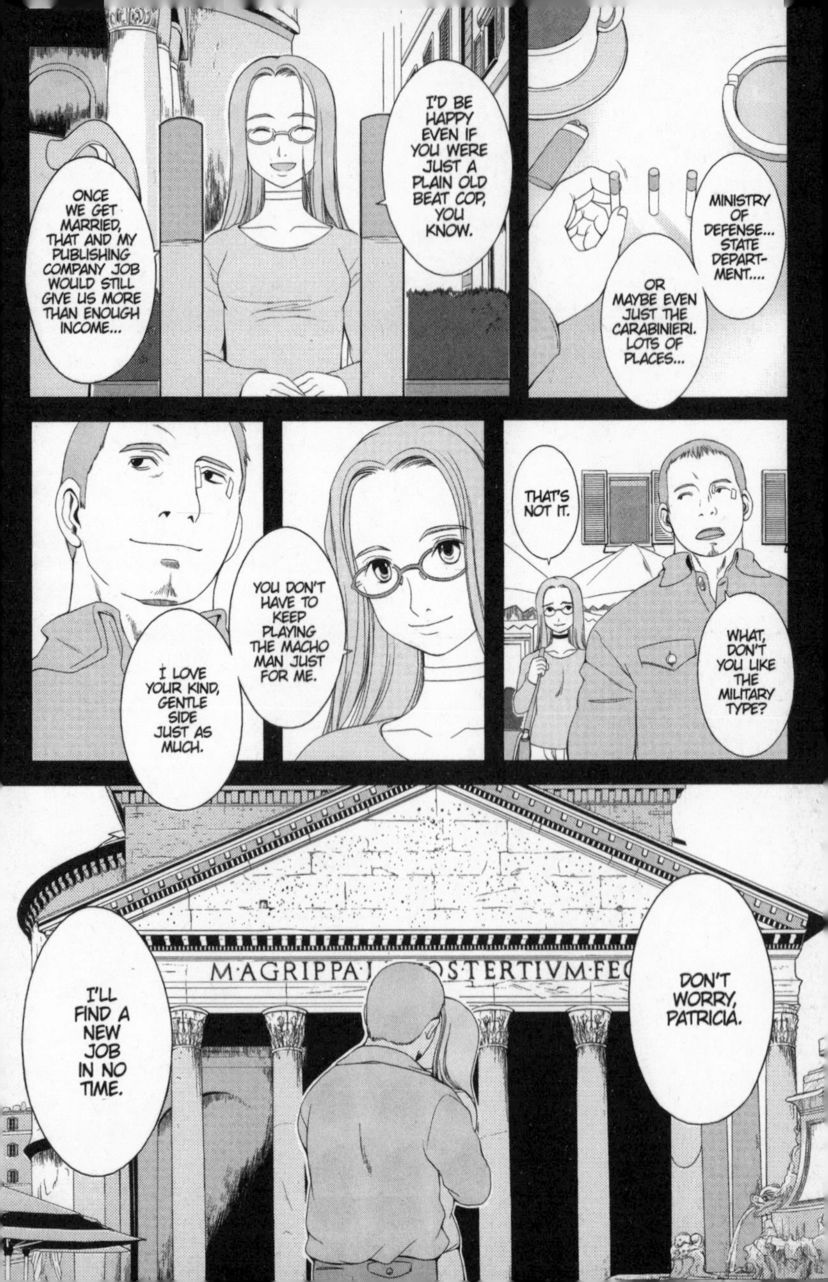
MINISTRY OF DEFENSE... STATE DEPART-MENT....
OR MAYBE EVEN JUST THE CARABINIERI. LOTS OF PLACES...
I'D BE HAPPY EVEN IF YOU WERE JUST A PLAIN OLD BEAT COP, YOU KNOW.
ONCE WE GET MARRIED, THAT AND MY PUBLISHING COMPANY JOB WOULD STILL GIVE US MORE THAN ENOUGH INCOME...
WHAT, DON'T YOU LIKE THE MILITARY TYPE?
THAT'S NOT IT.
YOU DON'T HAVE TO KEEP PLAYING THE MACHO MAN JUST FOR ME.
I LOVE YOUR KIND, GENTLE SIDE JUST AS MUCH.
DON'T WORRY, PATRICIA.
I'LL FIND A NEW JOB IN NO TIME.

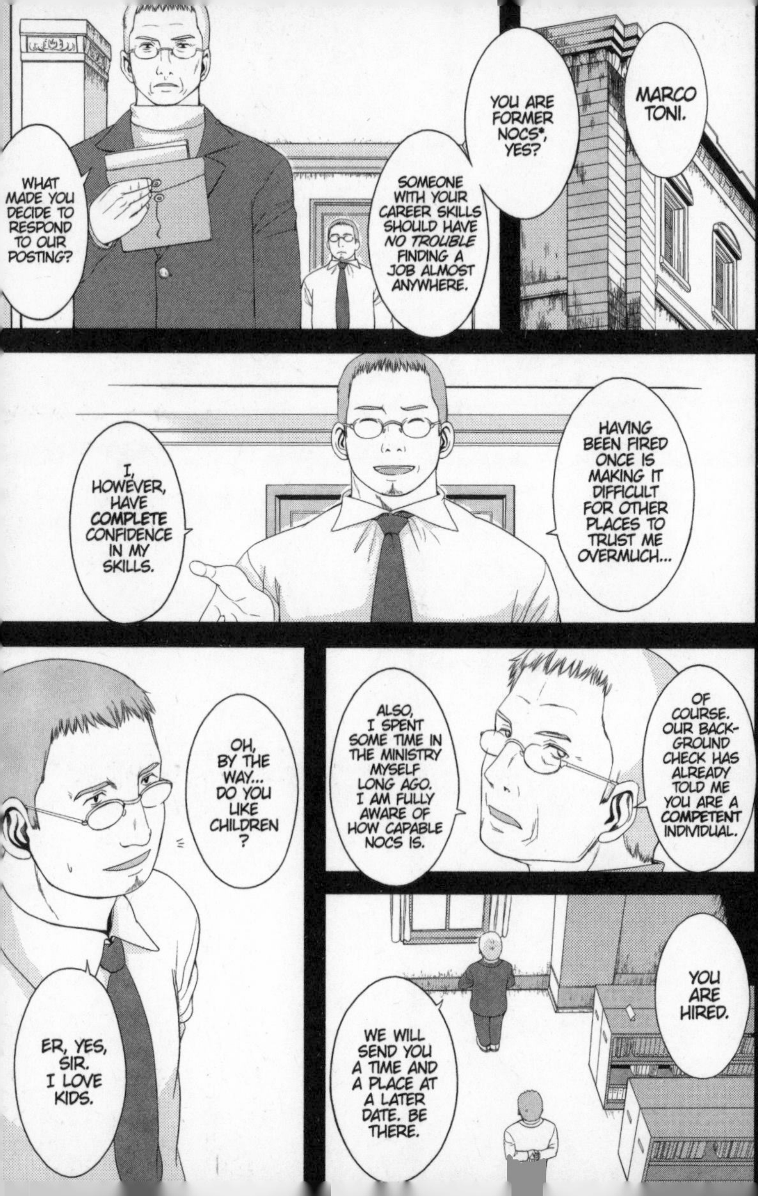
MARCO TONI.
YOU ARE FORMER NOCS*, YES?
SOMEONE WITH YOUR CAREER SKILLS SHOULD HAVE *NO TROUBLE* FINDING A JOB ALMOST ANYWHERE.
WHAT MADE YOU DECIDE TO RESPOND TO OUR POSTING?
HAVING BEEN FIRED ONCE IS MAKING IT DIFFICULT FOR OTHER PLACES TO TRUST ME OVERMUCH...
I, HOWEVER, HAVE **COMPLETE** CONFIDENCE IN MY SKILLS.
OF COURSE. OUR BACKGROUND CHECK HAS ALREADY TOLD ME YOU ARE A **COMPETENT** INDIVIDUAL.
ALSO, I SPENT SOME TIME IN THE MINISTRY MYSELF LONG AGO. I AM FULLY AWARE OF HOW CAPABLE NOCS IS.
YOU ARE HIRED.
WE WILL SEND YOU A TIME AND A PLACE AT A LATER DATE. BE THERE.
OH, BY THE WAY... DO YOU LIKE CHILDREN?
ER, YES, SIR. I LOVE KIDS.

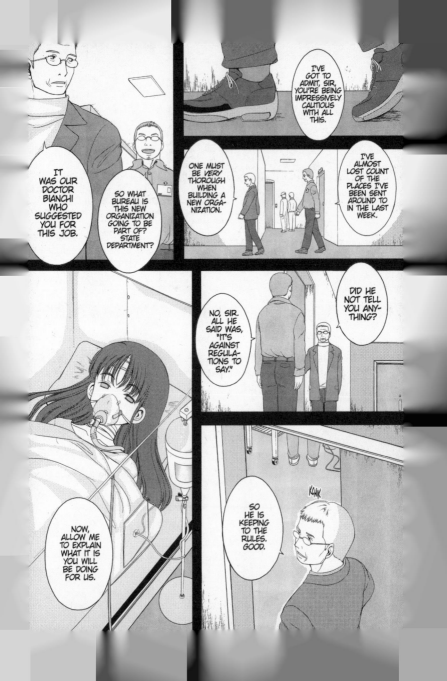

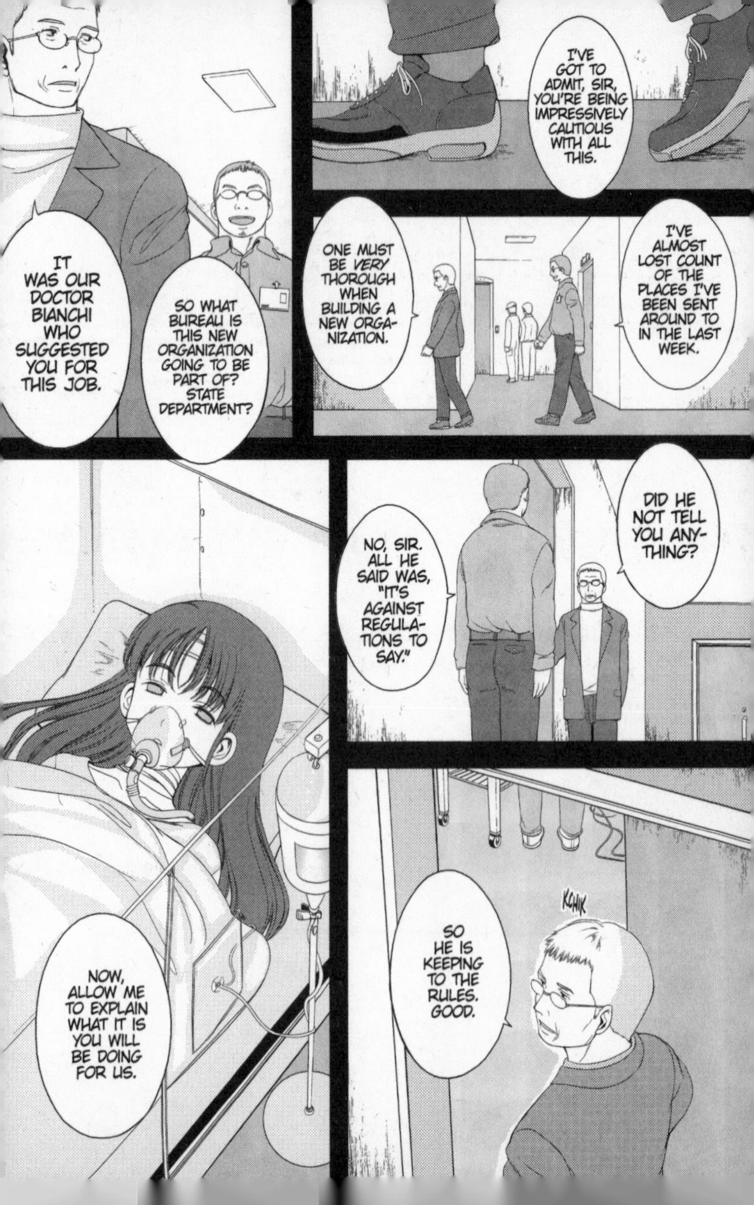
I'VE GOT TO ADMIT, SIR, YOU'RE BEING IMPRESSIVELY CAUTIOUS WITH ALL THIS.
I'VE ALMOST LOST COUNT OF THE PLACES I'VE BEEN SENT AROUND TO IN THE LAST WEEK.
ONE MUST BE *VERY* THOROUGH WHEN BUILDING A NEW ORGANIZATION.
SO WHAT BUREAU IS THIS NEW ORGANIZATION GOING TO BE PART OF? STATE DEPARTMENT?
IT WAS OUR DOCTOR BIANCHI WHO SUGGESTED YOU FOR THIS JOB.
DID HE NOT TELL YOU ANYTHING?
NO, SIR. ALL HE SAID WAS, "IT'S AGAINST REGULATIONS TO SAY."
KCHIK
SO HE IS KEEPING TO THE RULES. GOOD.
NOW, ALLOW ME TO EXPLAIN WHAT IT IS YOU WILL BE DOING FOR US.

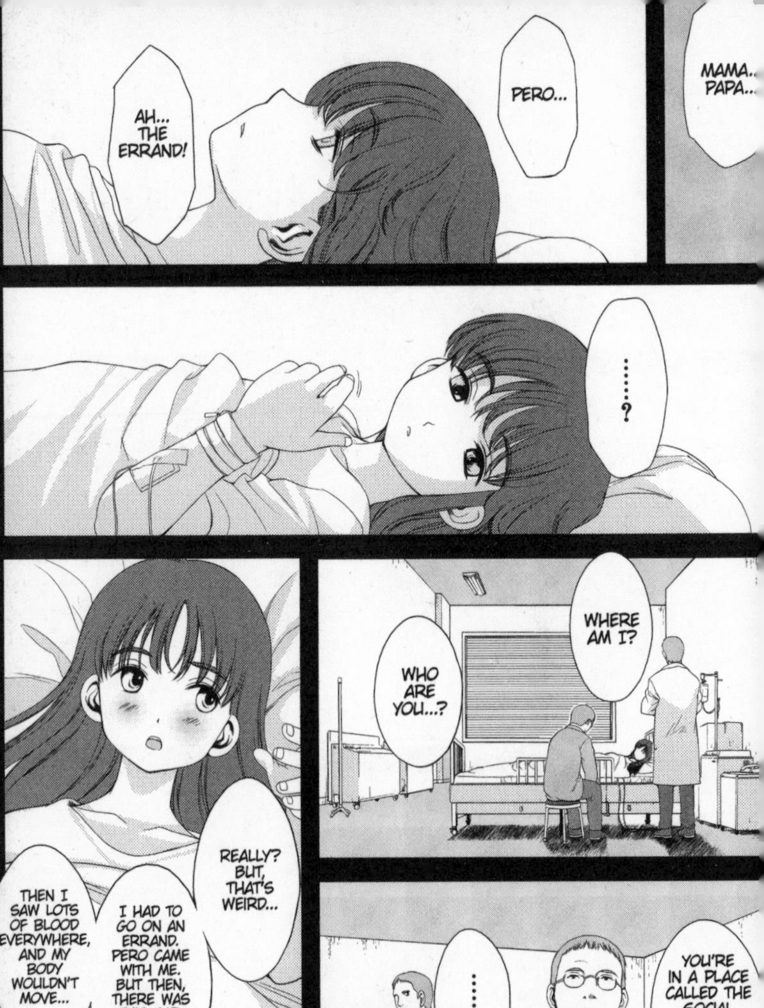
MAMA.. PAPA...
PERO...
AH... THE ERRAND!
......?
WHERE AM I?
WHO ARE YOU...?
YOU'RE IN A PLACE CALLED THE SOCIAL WELFARE AGENCY. IT'S LIKE A HOSPITAL.
......
REALLY? BUT, THAT'S WEIRD...
I HAD TO GO ON AN ERRAND. PERO CAME WITH ME. BUT THEN, THERE WAS THIS CAR, AND A LOUD THUMP.
THEN I SAW LOTS OF BLOOD EVERYWHERE, AND MY BODY WOULDN'T MOVE...

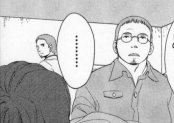

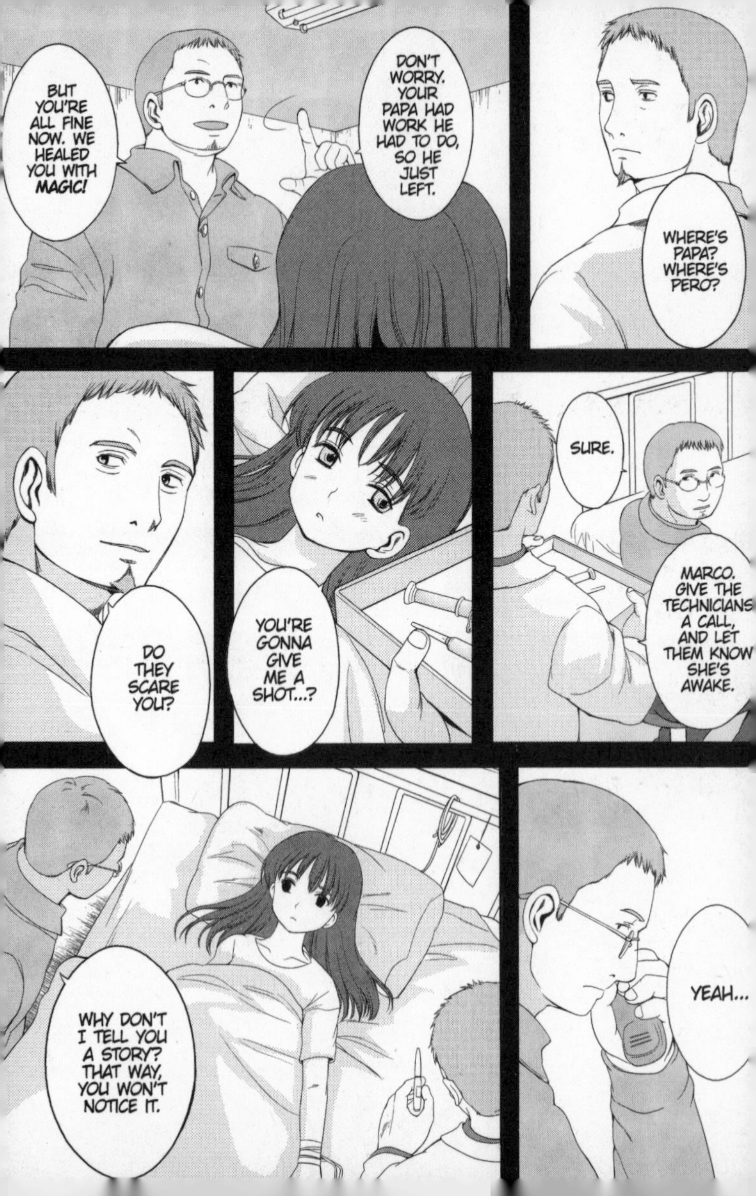
WHERE'S PAPA? WHERE'S PERO?
DON'T WORRY. YOUR PAPA HAD WORK HE HAD TO DO, SO HE JUST LEFT.
BUT YOU'RE ALL FINE NOW. WE HEALED YOU WITH MAGIC!
MARCO. GIVE THE TECHNICIANS A CALL, AND LET THEM KNOW SHE'S AWAKE.
SURE.
YOU'RE GONNA GIVE ME A SHOT...?
DO THEY SCARE YOU?
YEAH...
WHY DON'T I TELL YOU A STORY? THAT WAY, YOU WON'T NOTICE IT.

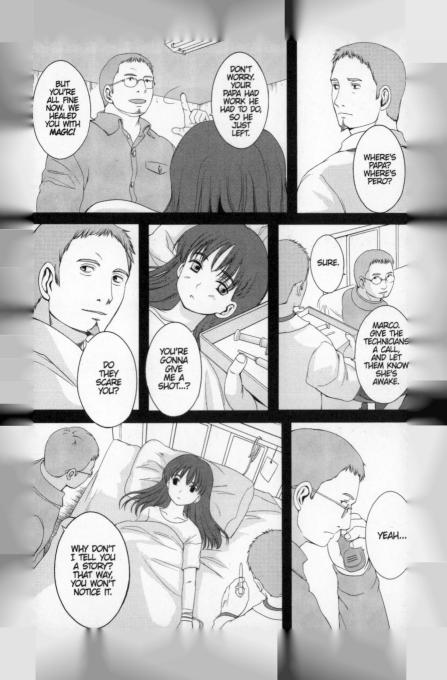

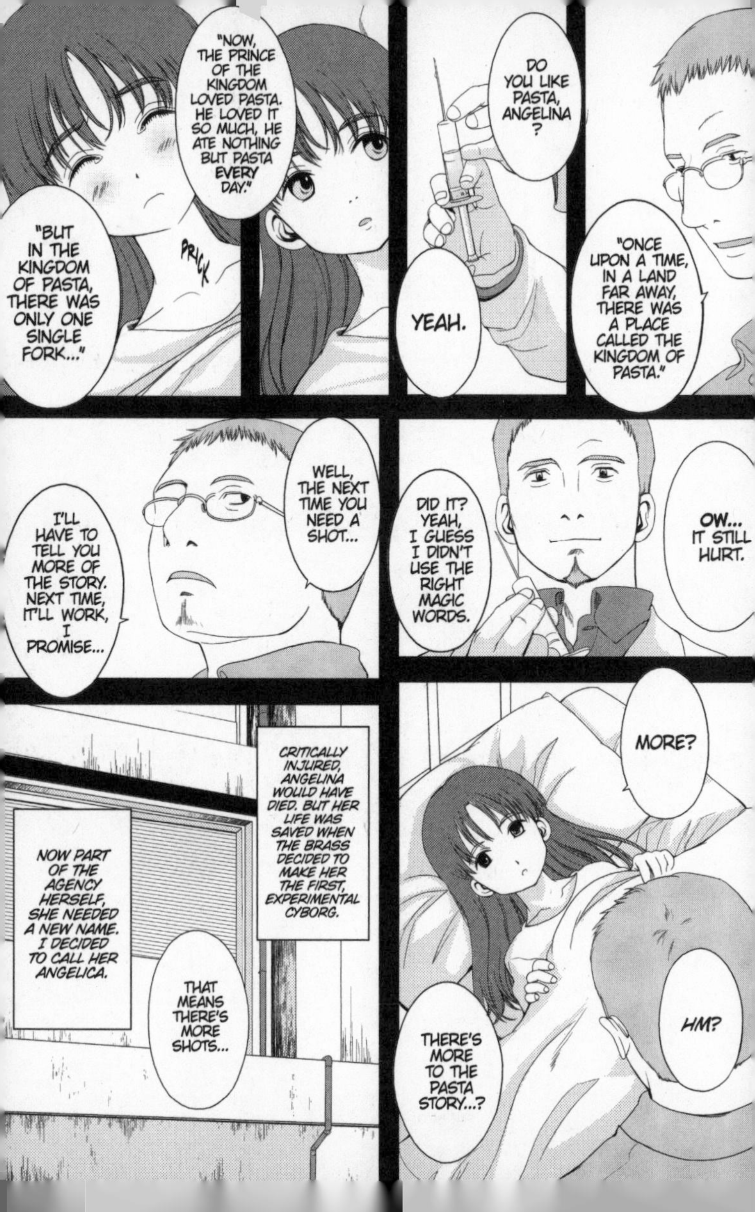
"ONCE UPON A TIME, IN A LAND FAR AWAY, THERE WAS A PLACE CALLED THE KINGDOM OF PASTA."
DO YOU LIKE PASTA, ANGELINA?
YEAH.
"NOW, THE PRINCE OF THE KINGDOM LOVED PASTA. HE LOVED IT SO MUCH, HE ATE NOTHING BUT PASTA EVERY DAY."
PRICK
"BUT IN THE KINGDOM OF PASTA, THERE WAS ONLY ONE SINGLE FORK..."
OW... IT STILL HURT.
DID IT? YEAH, I GUESS I DIDN'T USE THE RIGHT MAGIC WORDS.
WELL, THE NEXT TIME YOU NEED A SHOT...
I'LL HAVE TO TELL YOU MORE OF THE STORY. NEXT TIME, IT'LL WORK, I PROMISE...
MORE?
HM?
THERE'S MORE TO THE PASTA STORY...?
CRITICALLY INJURED, ANGELINA WOULD HAVE DIED. BUT HER LIFE WAS SAVED WHEN THE BRASS DECIDED TO MAKE HER THE FIRST, EXPERIMENTAL CYBORG.
NOW PART OF THE AGENCY HERSELF, SHE NEEDED A NEW NAME. I DECIDED TO CALL HER ANGELICA.
THAT MEANS THERE'S MORE SHOTS...

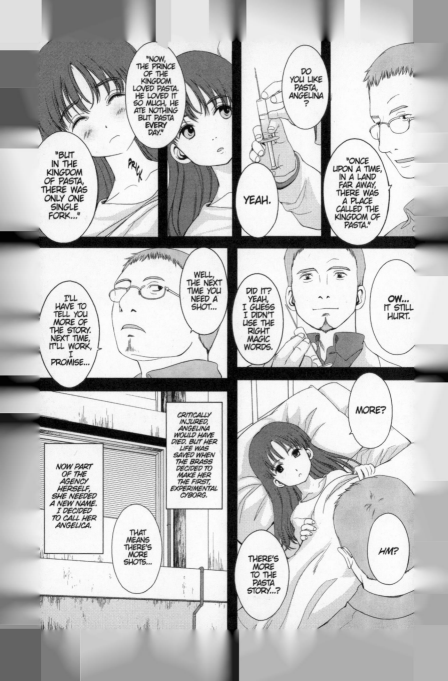

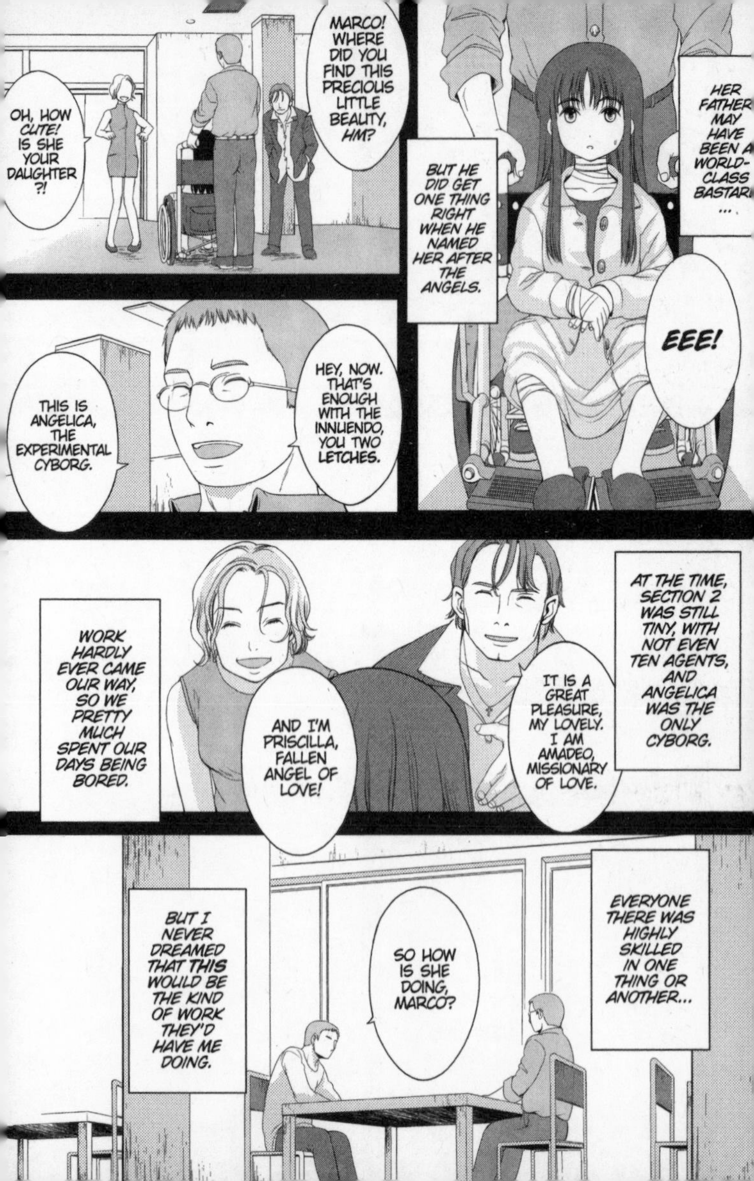

HER FATHER MAY HAVE BEEN A WORLD-CLASS BASTAR…
BUT HE DID GET ONE THING RIGHT WHEN HE NAMED HER AFTER THE ANGELS.
EEE!
MARCO! WHERE DID YOU FIND THIS PRECIOUS LITTLE BEAUTY, HM?
OH, HOW CUTE! IS SHE YOUR DAUGHTER?!
HEY, NOW. THAT'S ENOUGH WITH THE INNUENDO, YOU TWO LETCHES.
THIS IS ANGELICA, THE EXPERIMENTAL CYBORG.
AT THE TIME, SECTION 2 WAS STILL TINY, WITH NOT EVEN TEN AGENTS, AND ANGELICA WAS THE ONLY CYBORG.
IT IS A GREAT PLEASURE, MY LOVELY. I AM AMADEO, MISSIONARY OF LOVE.
AND I'M PRISCILLA, FALLEN ANGEL OF LOVE!
WORK HARDLY EVER CAME OUR WAY, SO WE PRETTY MUCH SPENT OUR DAYS BEING BORED.
EVERYONE THERE WAS HIGHLY SKILLED IN ONE THING OR ANOTHER…
SO HOW IS SHE DOING, MARCO?
BUT I NEVER DREAMED THAT THIS WOULD BE THE KIND OF WORK THEY'D HAVE ME DOING.

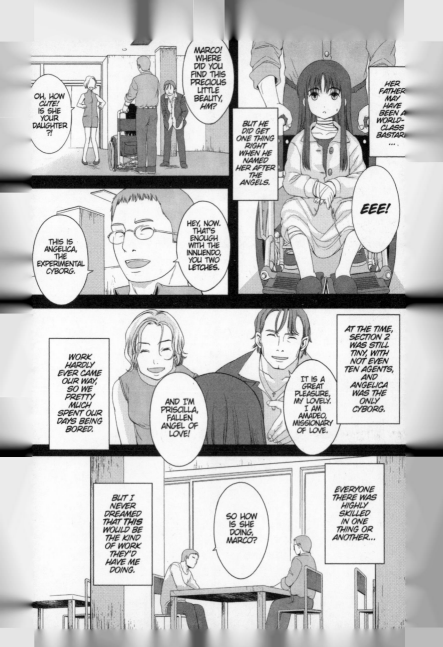

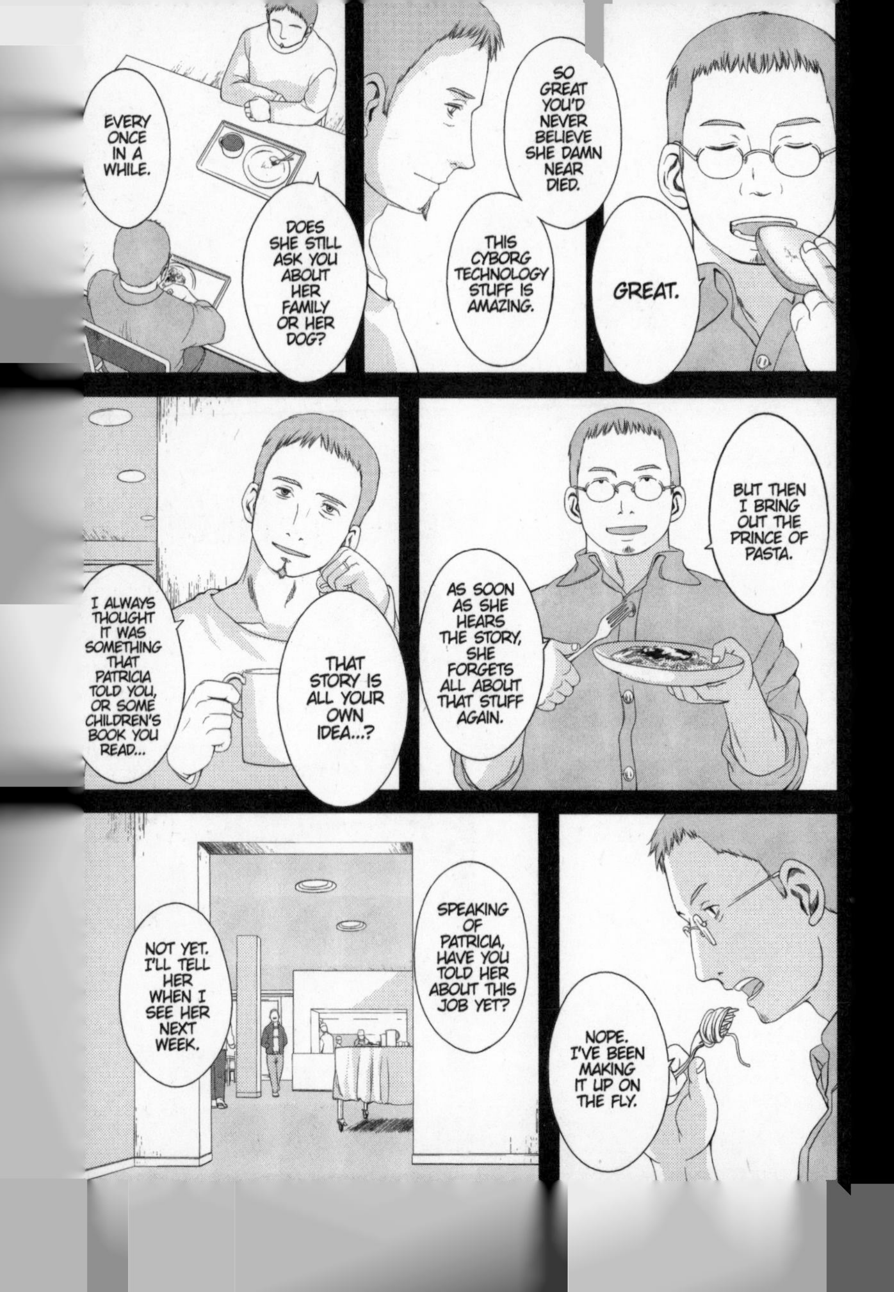
GREAT.
SO GREAT YOU'D NEVER BELIEVE SHE DAMN NEAR DIED.
THIS CYBORG TECHNOLOGY STUFF IS AMAZING.
DOES SHE STILL ASK YOU ABOUT HER FAMILY OR HER DOG?
EVERY ONCE IN A WHILE.
BUT THEN I BRING OUT THE PRINCE OF PASTA.
AS SOON AS SHE HEARS THE STORY, SHE FORGETS ALL ABOUT THAT STUFF AGAIN.
THAT STORY IS ALL YOUR OWN IDEA...?
I ALWAYS THOUGHT IT WAS SOMETHING THAT PATRICIA TOLD YOU, OR SOME CHILDREN'S BOOK YOU READ...
NOPE. I'VE BEEN MAKING IT UP ON THE FLY.
SPEAKING OF PATRICIA, HAVE YOU TOLD HER ABOUT THIS JOB YET?
NOT YET. I'LL TELL HER WHEN I SEE HER NEXT WEEK.

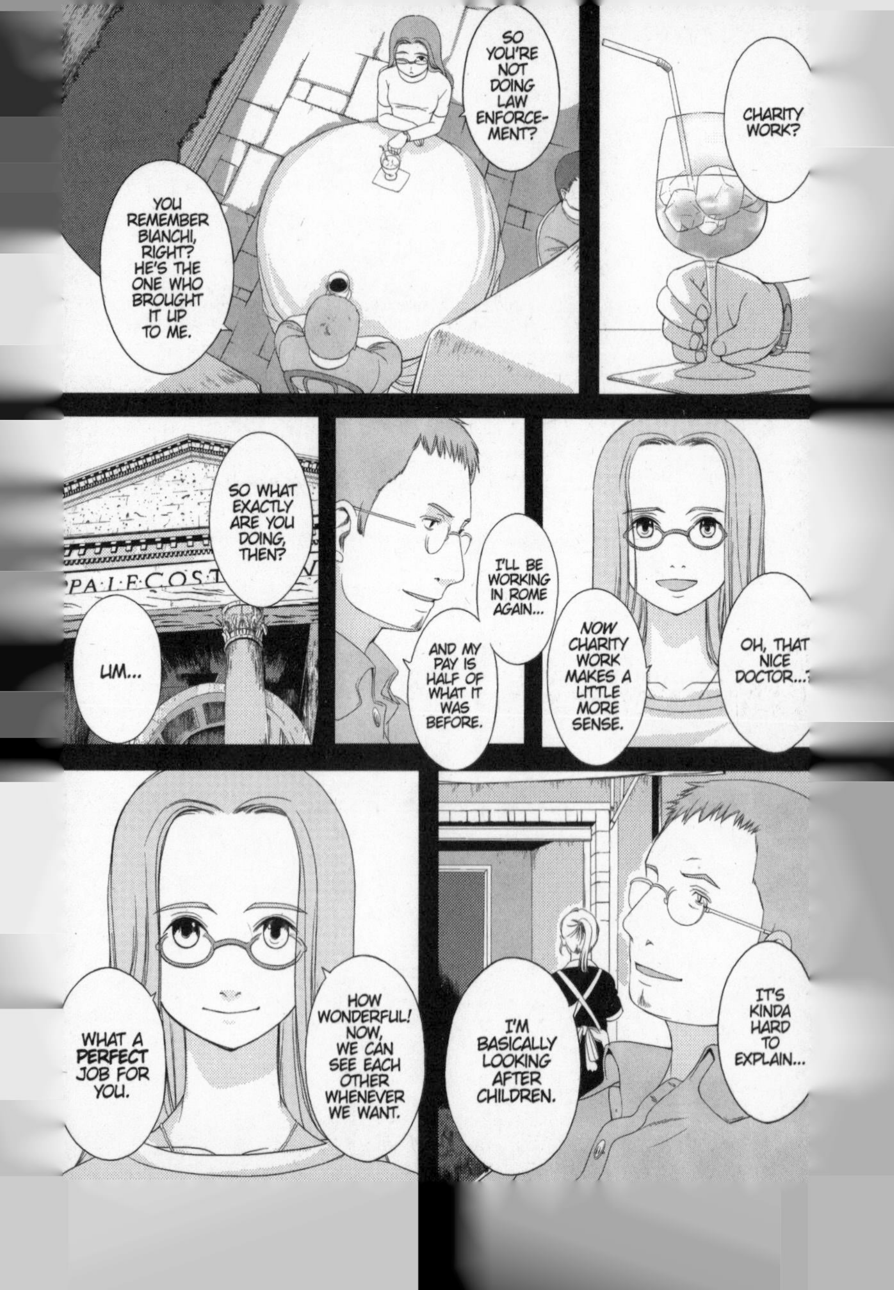
CHARITY WORK?
SO YOU'RE NOT DOING LAW ENFORCEMENT?
YOU REMEMBER BIANCHI, RIGHT? HE'S THE ONE WHO BROUGHT IT UP TO ME.
OH, THAT NICE DOCTOR...?
NOW CHARITY WORK MAKES A LITTLE MORE SENSE.
I'LL BE WORKING IN ROME AGAIN...
AND MY PAY IS HALF OF WHAT IT WAS BEFORE.
SO WHAT EXACTLY ARE YOU DOING, THEN?
UM...
IT'S KINDA HARD TO EXPLAIN...
I'M BASICALLY LOOKING AFTER CHILDREN.
HOW WONDERFUL! NOW, WE CAN SEE EACH OTHER WHENEVER WE WANT.
WHAT A **PERFECT** JOB FOR YOU.

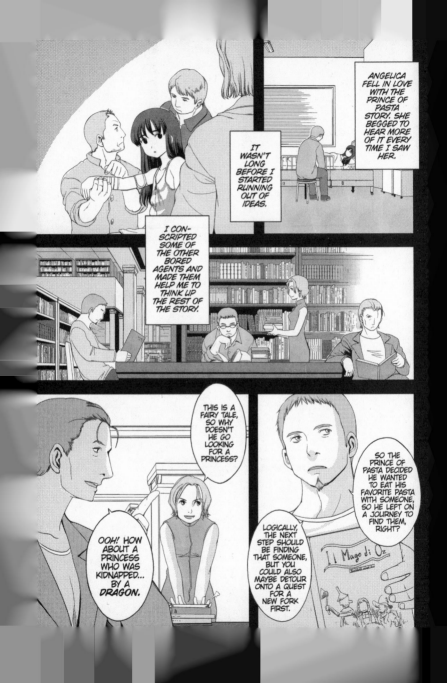

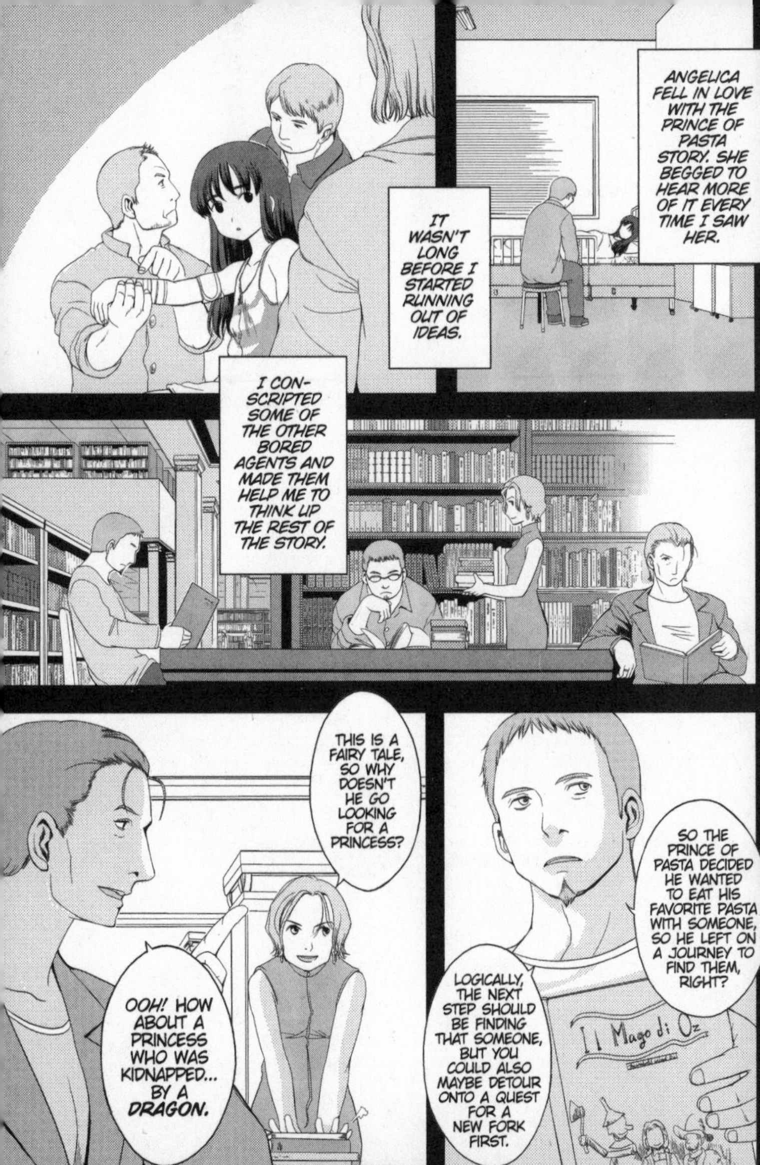
ANGELICA FELL IN LOVE WITH THE PRINCE OF PASTA STORY. SHE BEGGED TO HEAR MORE OF IT EVERY TIME I SAW HER.
IT WASN'T LONG BEFORE I STARTED RUNNING OUT OF IDEAS.
I CON-SCRIPTED SOME OF THE OTHER BORED AGENTS AND MADE THEM HELP ME TO THINK UP THE REST OF THE STORY.
SO THE PRINCE OF PASTA DECIDED HE WANTED TO EAT HIS FAVORITE PASTA WITH SOMEONE, SO HE LEFT ON A JOURNEY TO FIND THEM, RIGHT?
LOGICALLY, THE NEXT STEP SHOULD BE FINDING THAT SOMEONE, BUT YOU COULD ALSO MAYBE DETOUR ONTO A QUEST FOR A NEW FORK FIRST.
Il Mago di Oz
THIS IS A FAIRY TALE, SO WHY DOESN'T HE GO LOOKING FOR A PRINCESS?
OOH! HOW ABOUT A PRINCESS WHO WAS KIDNAPPED... BY A DRAGON.

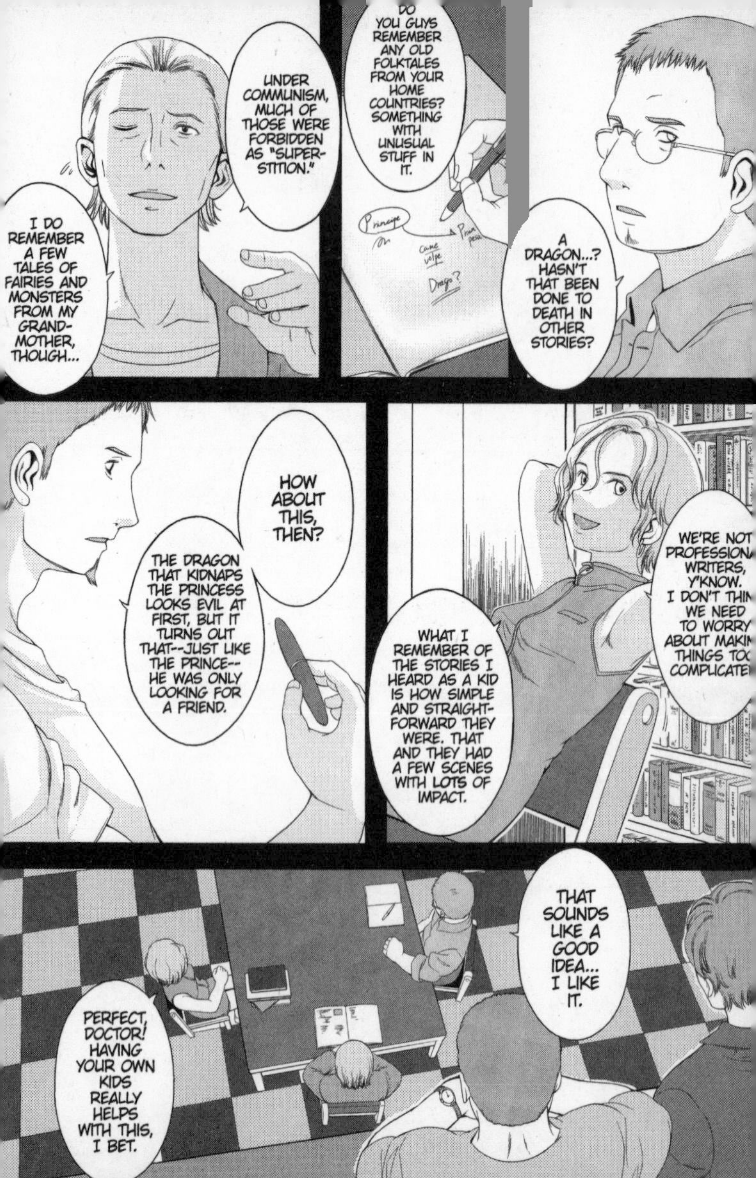
A DRAGON...? HASN'T THAT BEEN DONE TO DEATH IN OTHER STORIES?
DO YOU GUYS REMEMBER ANY OLD FOLKTALES FROM YOUR HOME COUNTRIES? SOMETHING WITH UNUSUAL STUFF IN IT.
UNDER COMMUNISM, MUCH OF THOSE WERE FORBIDDEN AS "SUPER-STITION."
I DO REMEMBER A FEW TALES OF FAIRIES AND MONSTERS FROM MY GRAND-MOTHER, THOUGH...
WE'RE NOT PROFESSIONA WRITERS, Y'KNOW. I DON'T THIN WE NEED TO WORRY ABOUT MAKIN THINGS TOO COMPLICATE
WHAT I REMEMBER OF THE STORIES I HEARD AS A KID IS HOW SIMPLE AND STRAIGHT-FORWARD THEY WERE. THAT AND THEY HAD A FEW SCENES WITH LOTS OF IMPACT.
HOW ABOUT THIS, THEN?
THE DRAGON THAT KIDNAPS THE PRINCESS LOOKS EVIL AT FIRST, BUT IT TURNS OUT THAT--JUST LIKE THE PRINCE--HE WAS ONLY LOOKING FOR A FRIEND.
THAT SOUNDS LIKE A GOOD IDEA... I LIKE IT.
PERFECT, DOCTOR! HAVING YOUR OWN KIDS REALLY HELPS WITH THIS, I BET.

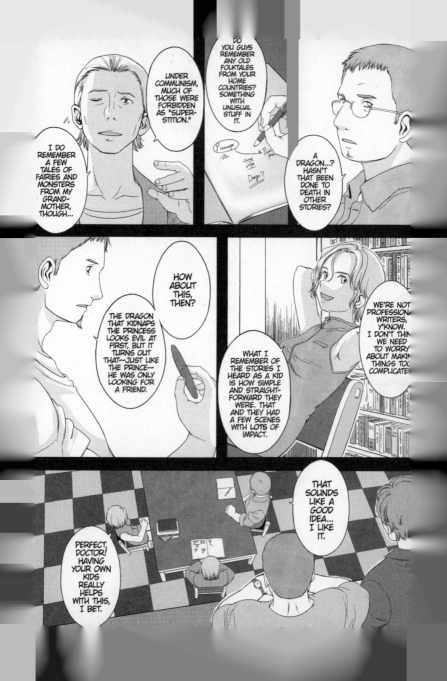

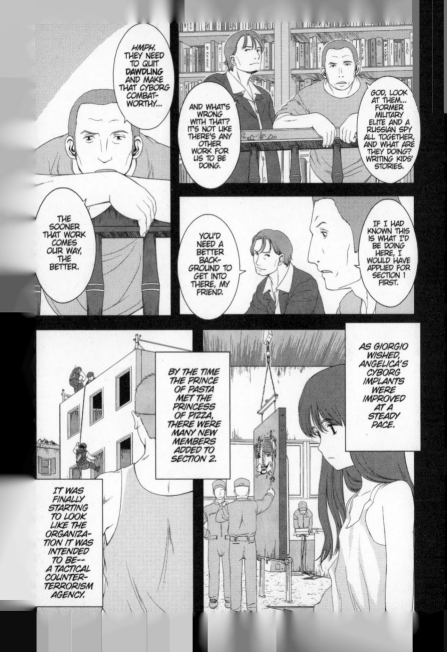

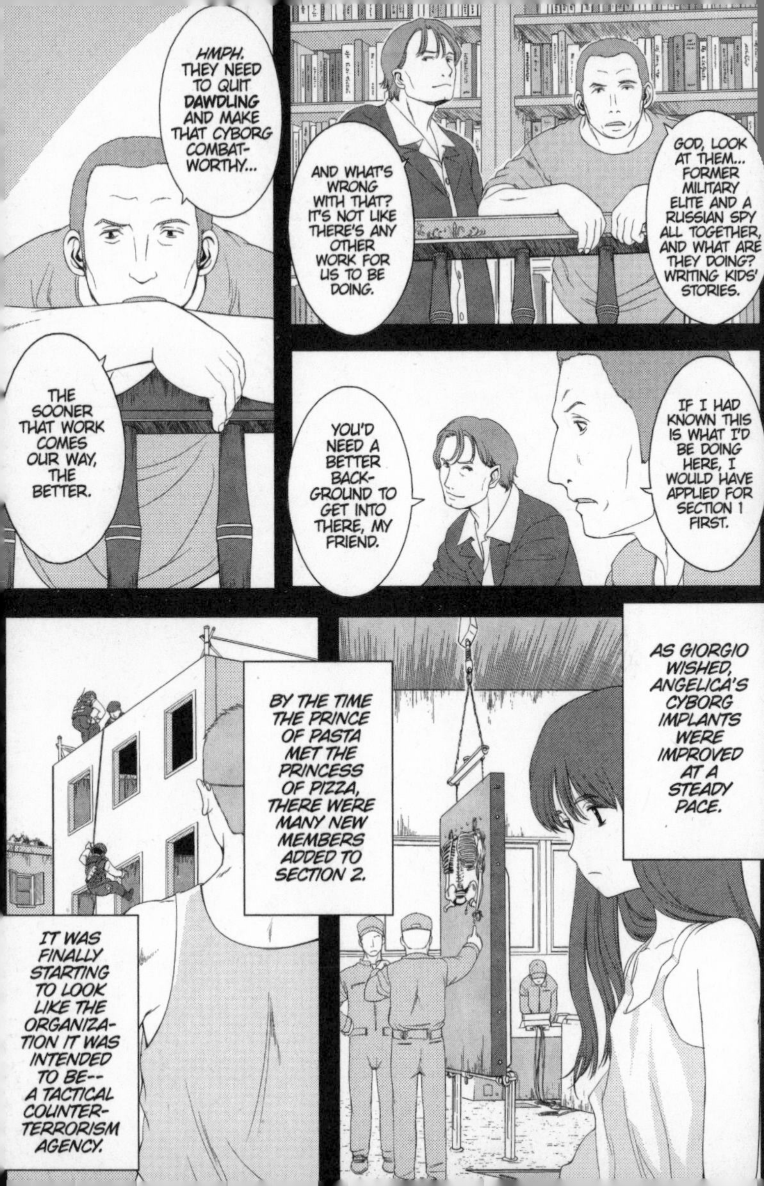
GOD, LOOK AT THEM... FORMER MILITARY ELITE AND A RUSSIAN SPY ALL TOGETHER, AND WHAT ARE THEY DOING? WRITING KIDS' STORIES.
AND WHAT'S WRONG WITH THAT? IT'S NOT LIKE THERE'S ANY OTHER WORK FOR US TO BE DOING.
IF I HAD KNOWN THIS IS WHAT I'D BE DOING HERE, I WOULD HAVE APPLIED FOR SECTION 1 FIRST.
YOU'D NEED A BETTER BACK-GROUND TO GET INTO THERE, MY FRIEND.
HMPH. THEY NEED TO QUIT DAWDLING AND MAKE THAT CYBORG COMBAT-WORTHY...
THE SOONER THAT WORK COMES OUR WAY, THE BETTER.
AS GIORGIO WISHED, ANGELICA'S CYBORG IMPLANTS WERE IMPROVED AT A STEADY PACE.
BY THE TIME THE PRINCE OF PASTA MET THE PRINCESS OF PIZZA, THERE WERE MANY NEW MEMBERS ADDED TO SECTION 2.
IT WAS FINALLY STARTING TO LOOK LIKE THE ORGANIZA-TION IT WAS INTENDED TO BE-- A TACTICAL COUNTER-TERRORISM AGENCY.

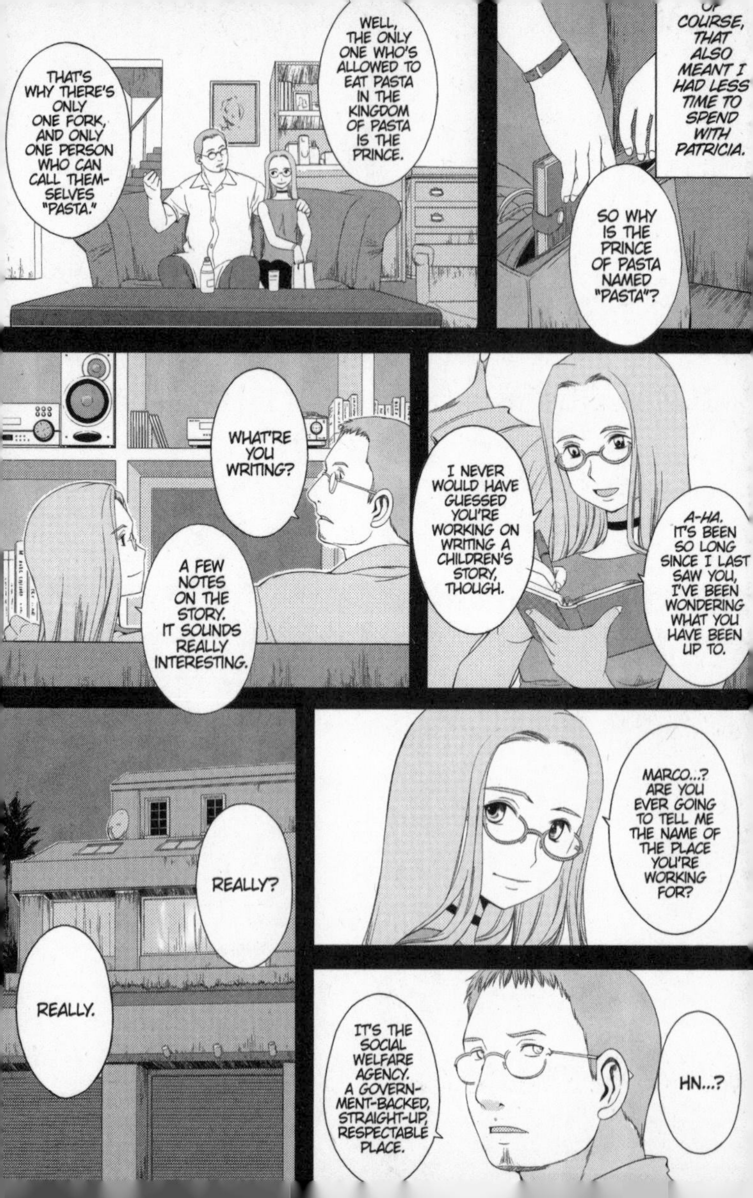
OF COURSE, THAT ALSO MEANT I HAD LESS TIME TO SPEND WITH PATRICIA.
SO WHY IS THE PRINCE OF PASTA NAMED "PASTA"?
WELL, THE ONLY ONE WHO'S ALLOWED TO EAT PASTA IN THE KINGDOM OF PASTA IS THE PRINCE.
THAT'S WHY THERE'S ONLY ONE FORK, AND ONLY ONE PERSON WHO CAN CALL THEM-SELVES "PASTA."
A-HA. IT'S BEEN SO LONG SINCE I LAST SAW YOU, I'VE BEEN WONDERING WHAT YOU HAVE BEEN UP TO.
I NEVER WOULD HAVE GUESSED YOU'RE WORKING ON WRITING A CHILDREN'S STORY, THOUGH.
WHAT'RE YOU WRITING?
A FEW NOTES ON THE STORY. IT SOUNDS REALLY INTERESTING.
MARCO...? ARE YOU EVER GOING TO TELL ME THE NAME OF THE PLACE YOU'RE WORKING FOR?
HN...?
IT'S THE SOCIAL WELFARE AGENCY. A GOVERN-MENT-BACKED, STRAIGHT-UP, RESPECTABLE PLACE.
REALLY?
REALLY.

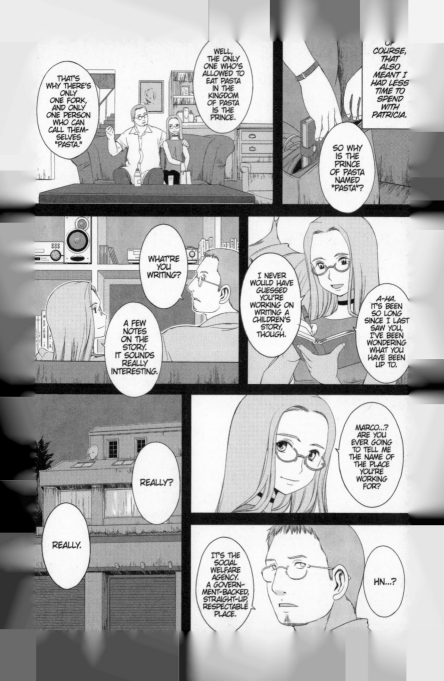

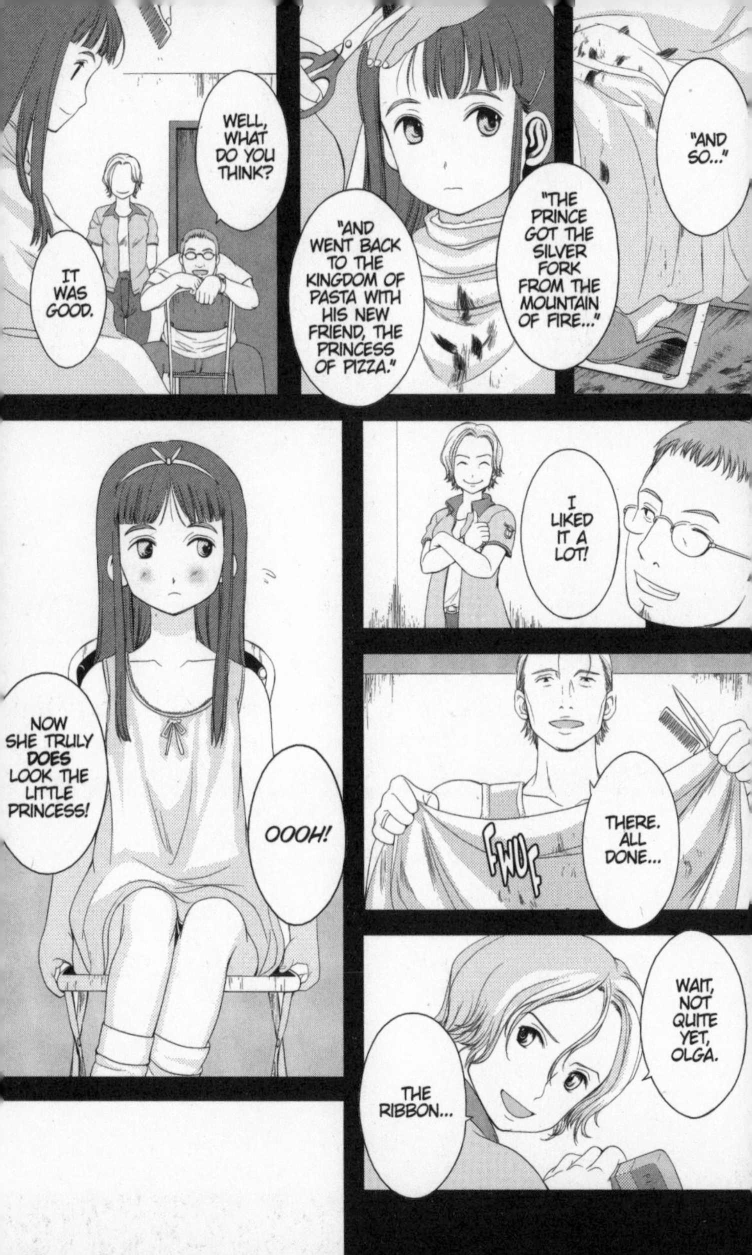
"AND SO..."
"THE PRINCE GOT THE SILVER FORK FROM THE MOUNTAIN OF FIRE..."
"AND WENT BACK TO THE KINGDOM OF PASTA WITH HIS NEW FRIEND, THE PRINCESS OF PIZZA."
WELL, WHAT DO YOU THINK?
IT WAS GOOD.
I LIKED IT A LOT!
FWUF
THERE. ALL DONE...
WAIT, NOT QUITE YET, OLGA.
THE RIBBON...
OOOH!
NOW SHE TRULY DOES LOOK THE LITTLE PRINCESS!

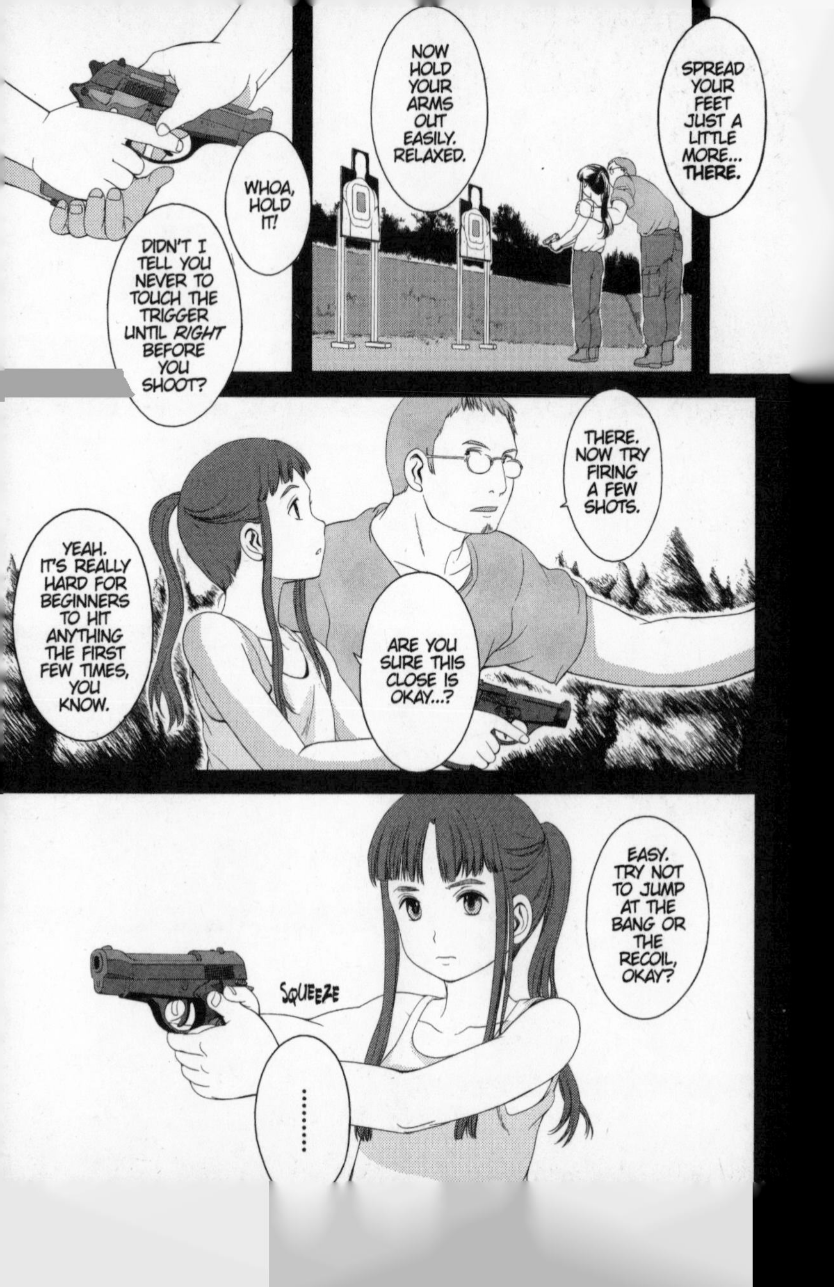
SPREAD YOUR FEET JUST A LITTLE MORE... THERE.
NOW HOLD YOUR ARMS OUT EASILY. RELAXED.
WHOA, HOLD IT!
DIDN'T I TELL YOU NEVER TO TOUCH THE TRIGGER UNTIL *RIGHT* BEFORE YOU SHOOT?
THERE. NOW TRY FIRING A FEW SHOTS.
ARE YOU SURE THIS CLOSE IS OKAY...?
YEAH. IT'S REALLY HARD FOR BEGINNERS TO HIT ANYTHING THE FIRST FEW TIMES, YOU KNOW.
EASY. TRY NOT TO JUMP AT THE BANG OR THE RECOIL, OKAY?
SQUEEZE
....

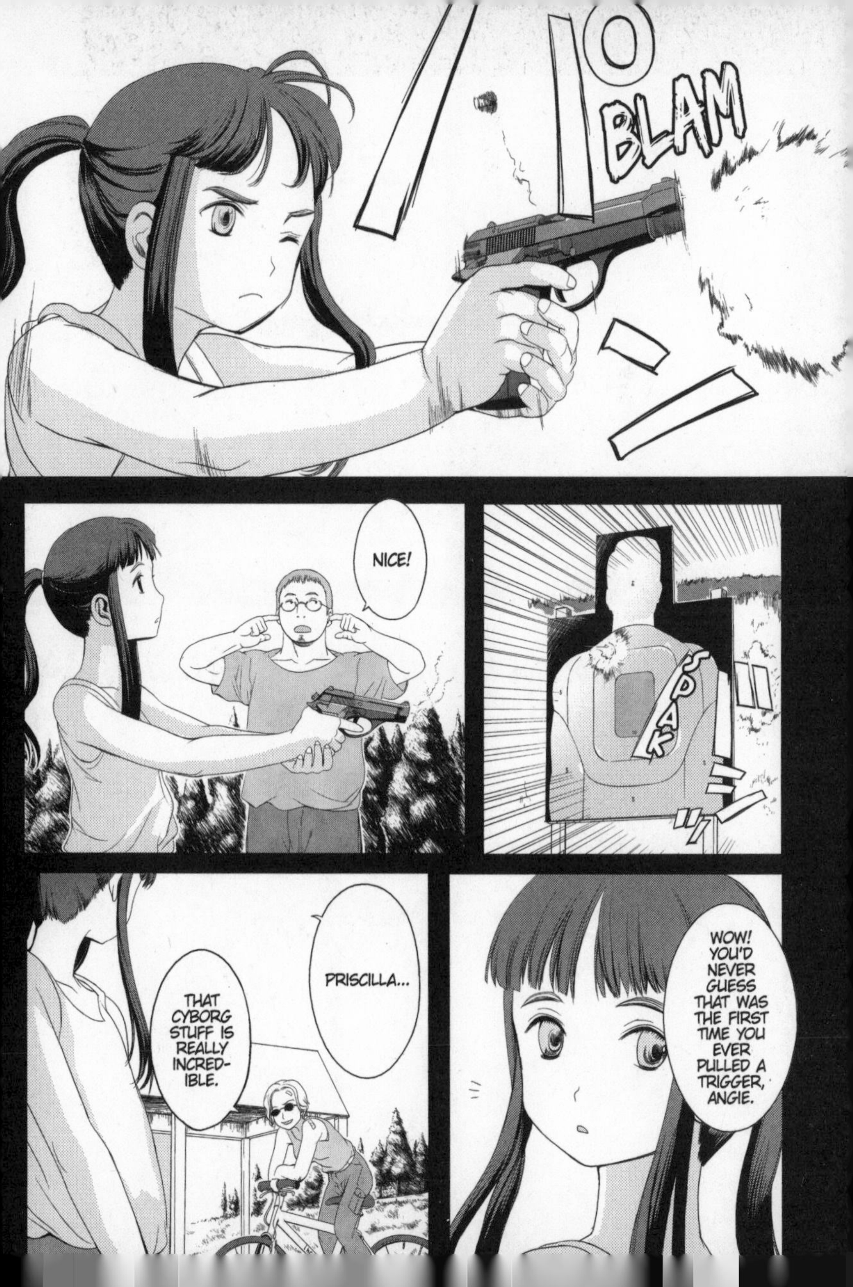
BLAM
SPAK
NICE!
WOW! YOU'D NEVER GUESS THAT WAS THE FIRST TIME YOU EVER PULLED A TRIGGER, ANGIE.
PRISCILLA...
THAT CYBORG STUFF IS REALLY INCRED-IBLE.

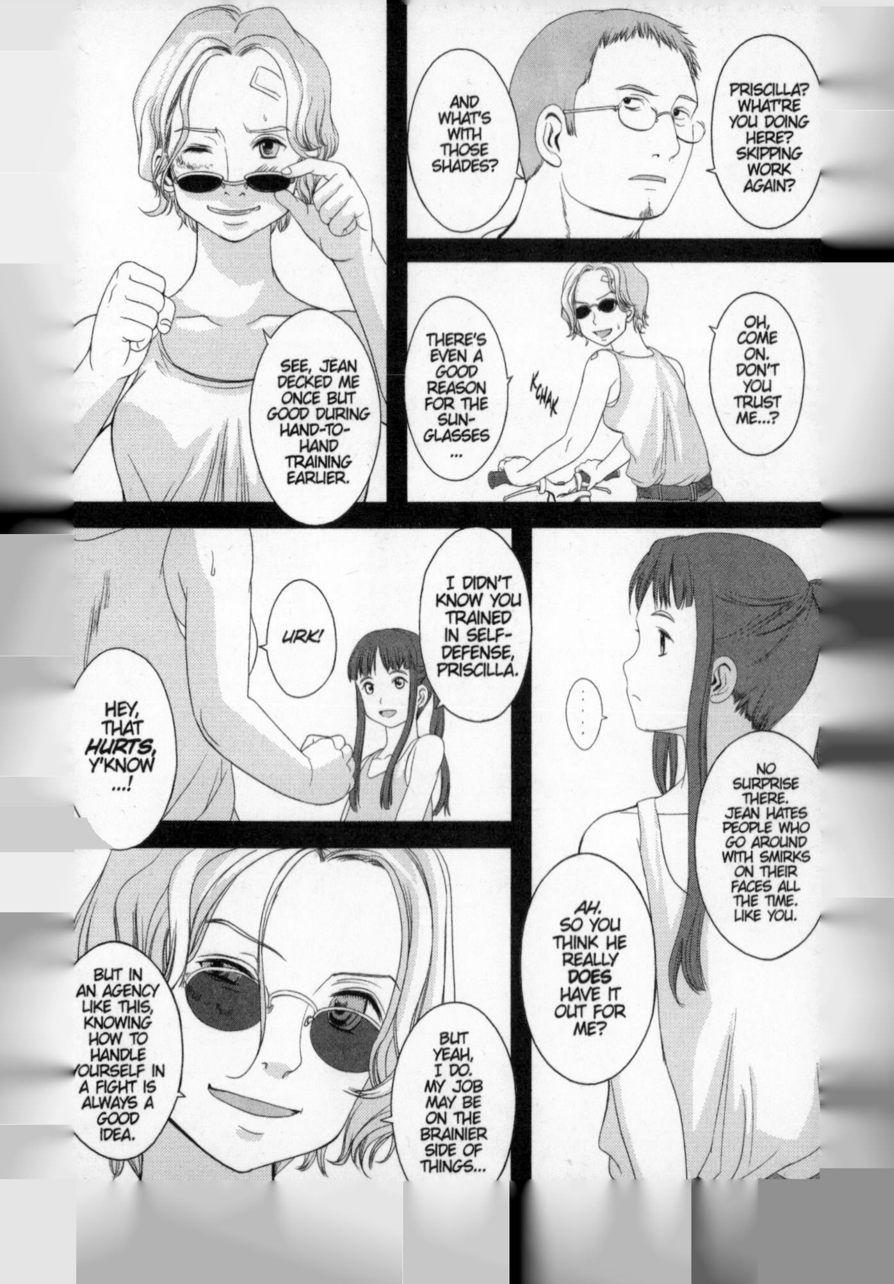
PRISCILLA? WHAT'RE YOU DOING HERE? SKIPPING WORK AGAIN?
AND WHAT'S WITH THOSE SHADES?
OH, COME ON. DON'T YOU TRUST ME...?
K'CHAK
THERE'S EVEN A GOOD REASON FOR THE SUN-GLASSES ...
SEE, JEAN DECKED ME ONCE BUT GOOD DURING HAND-TO-HAND TRAINING EARLIER.
. . . . .
NO SURPRISE THERE. JEAN HATES PEOPLE WHO GO AROUND WITH SMIRKS ON THEIR FACES ALL THE TIME. LIKE YOU.
AH. SO YOU THINK HE REALLY DOES HAVE IT OUT FOR ME?
I DIDN'T KNOW YOU TRAINED IN SELF-DEFENSE, PRISCILLA.
URK!
HEY, THAT HURTS, Y'KNOW ...!
BUT YEAH, I DO. MY JOB MAY BE ON THE BRAINIER SIDE OF THINGS...
BUT IN AN AGENCY LIKE THIS, KNOWING HOW TO HANDLE YOURSELF IN A FIGHT IS ALWAYS A GOOD IDEA.

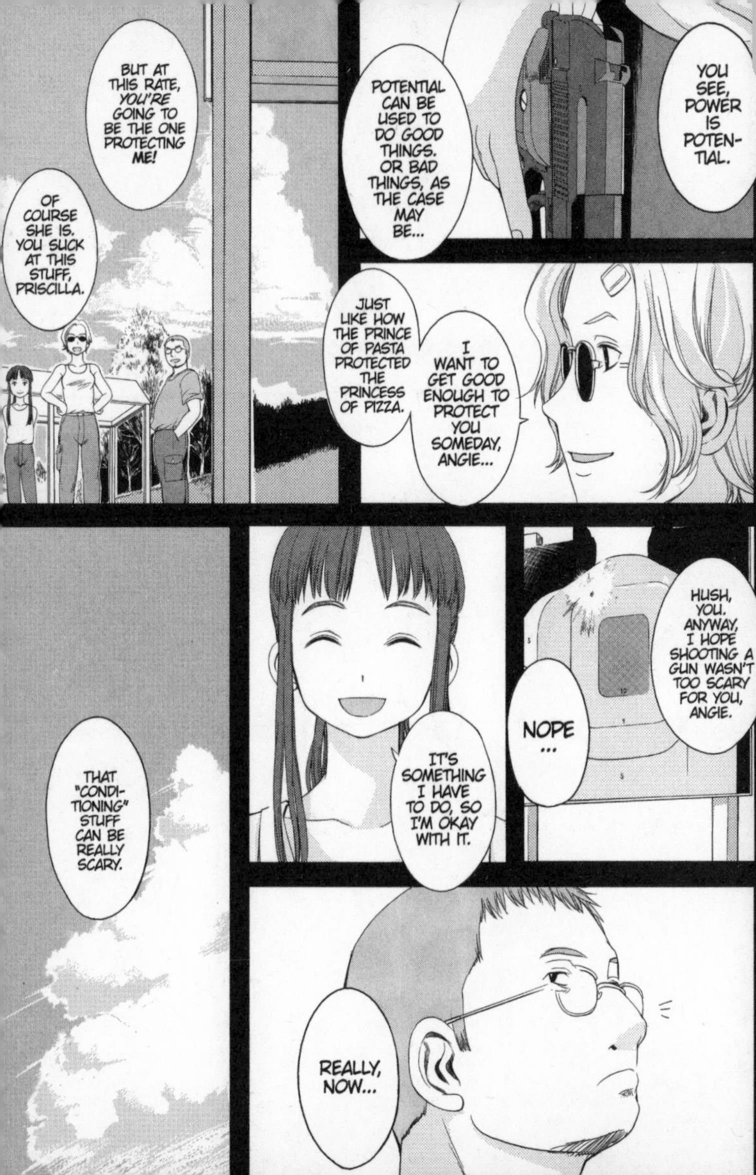
YOU SEE, POWER IS POTEN-TIAL.
POTENTIAL CAN BE USED TO DO GOOD THINGS. OR BAD THINGS, AS THE CASE MAY BE...
I WANT TO GET GOOD ENOUGH TO PROTECT YOU SOMEDAY, ANGIE...
JUST LIKE HOW THE PRINCE OF PASTA PROTECTED THE PRINCESS OF PIZZA.
BUT AT THIS RATE, *YOU'RE* GOING TO BE THE ONE PROTECTING ME!
OF COURSE SHE IS. YOU SUCK AT THIS STUFF, PRISCILLA.
HUSH, YOU. ANYWAY, I HOPE SHOOTING A GUN WASN'T TOO SCARY FOR YOU, ANGIE.
NOPE...
IT'S SOMETHING I HAVE TO DO, SO I'M OKAY WITH IT.
REALLY, NOW...
THAT "CONDI-TIONING" STUFF CAN BE REALLY SCARY.

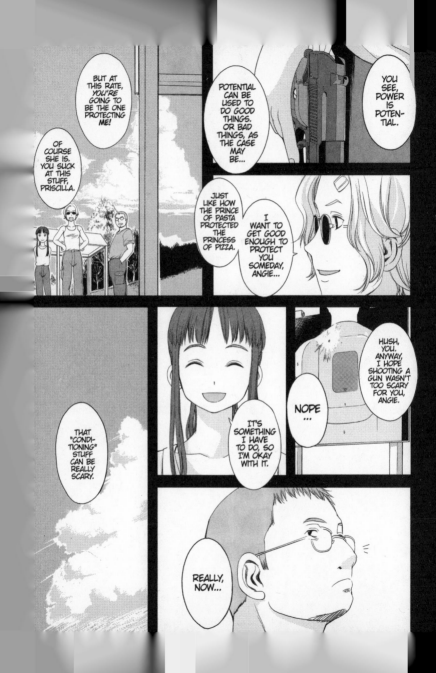

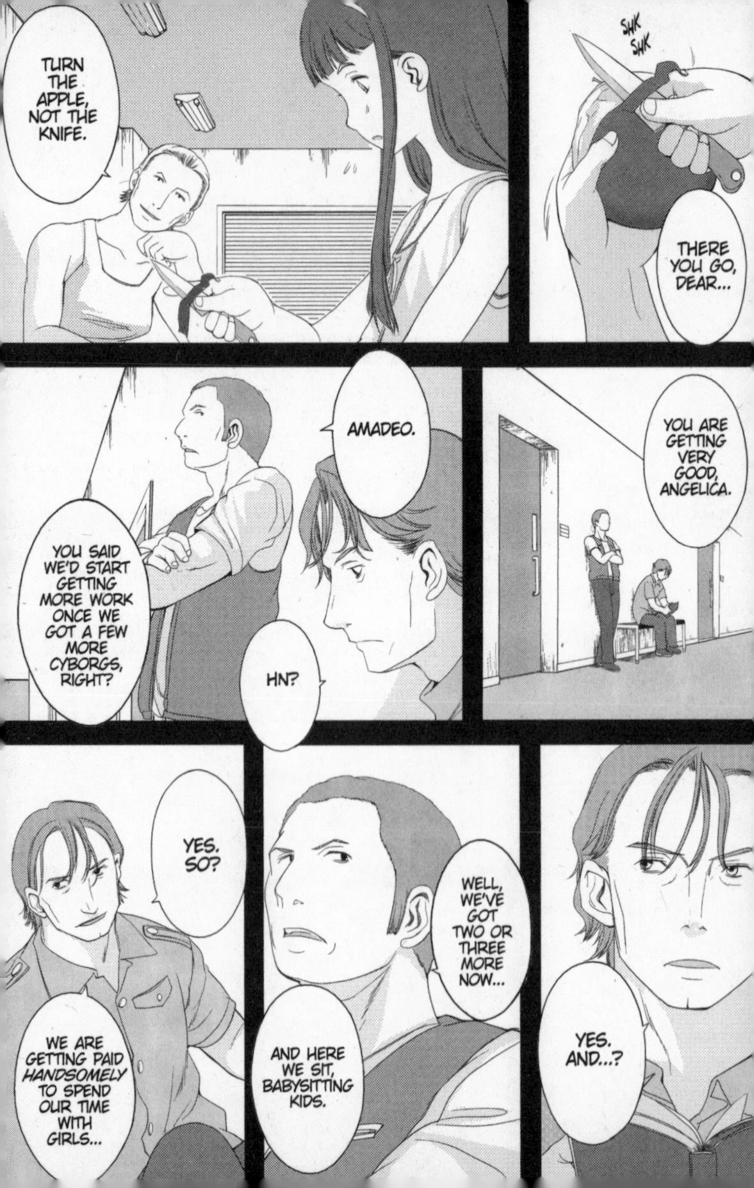
TURN THE APPLE, NOT THE KNIFE.
SHK SHK
THERE YOU GO, DEAR...
AMADEO.
HN?
YOU SAID WE'D START GETTING MORE WORK ONCE WE GOT A FEW MORE CYBORGS, RIGHT?
YOU ARE GETTING VERY GOOD, ANGELICA.
YES. SO?
WE ARE GETTING PAID *HANDSOMELY* TO SPEND OUR TIME WITH GIRLS...
WELL, WE'VE GOT TWO OR THREE MORE NOW...
AND HERE WE SIT, BABYSITTING KIDS.
YES. AND...?

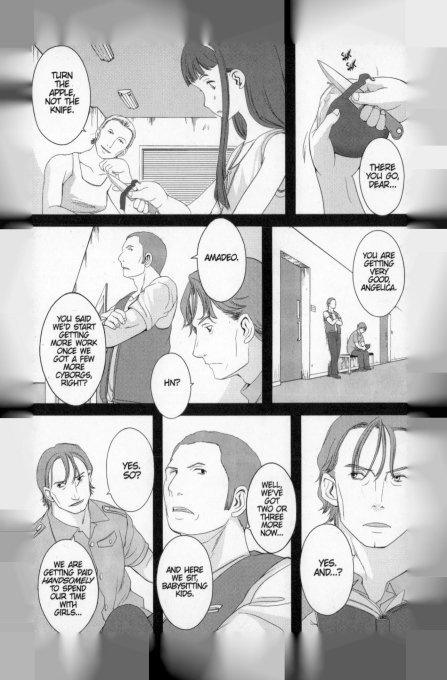

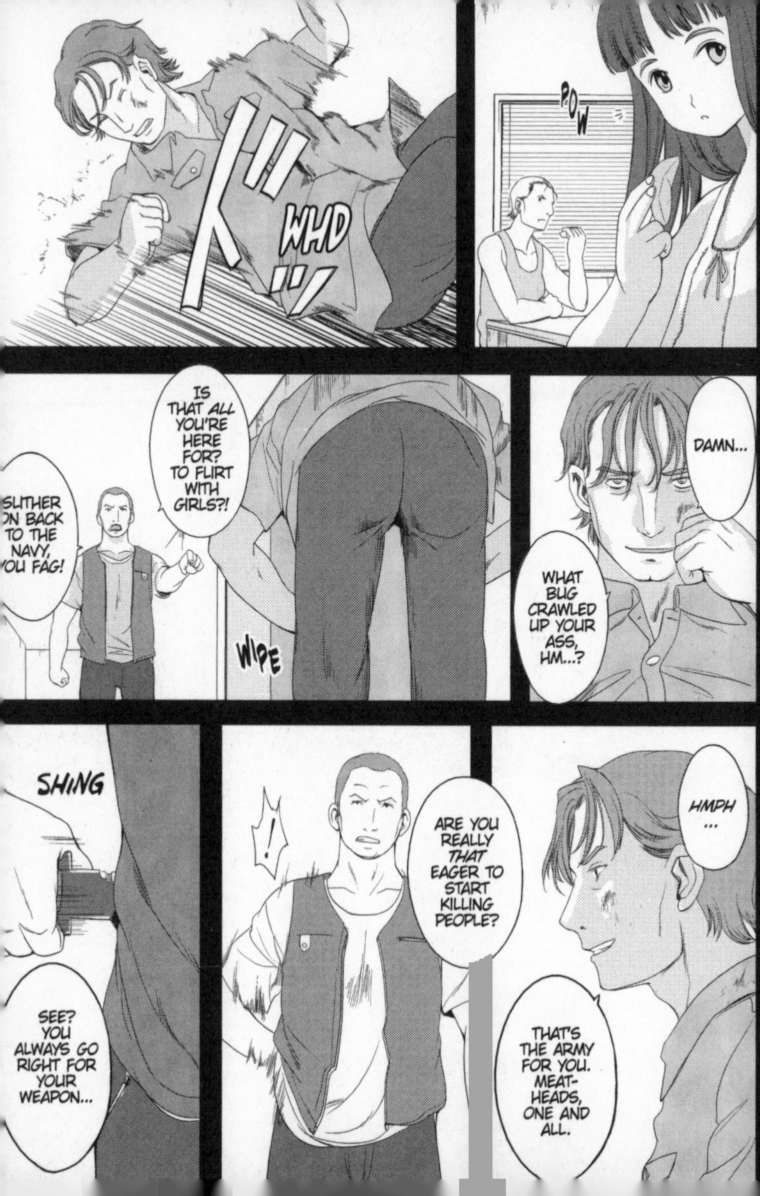
POW
WHD
DAMN...
WHAT BUG CRAWLED UP YOUR ASS, HM...?
WIPE
IS THAT ALL YOU'RE HERE FOR? TO FLIRT WITH GIRLS?!
SLITHER ON BACK TO THE NAVY, YOU FAG!
HMPH ...
THAT'S THE ARMY FOR YOU. MEAT-HEADS, ONE AND ALL.
ARE YOU REALLY THAT EAGER TO START KILLING PEOPLE?
!
SHING
SEE? YOU ALWAYS GO RIGHT FOR YOUR WEAPON...

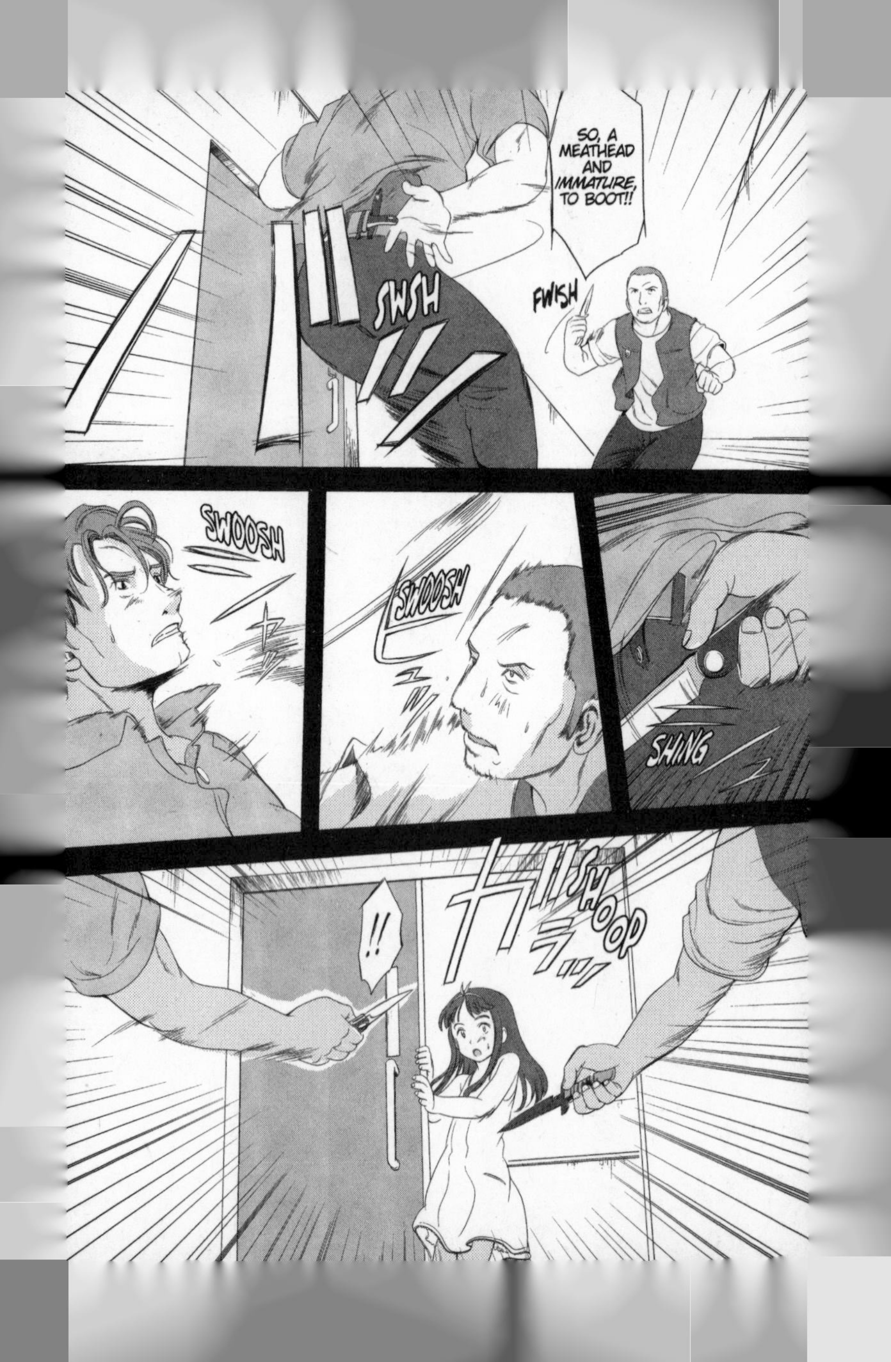
SO, A MEATHEAD AND IMMATURE, TO BOOT!!
FWISH
SWSH
SHING
SWOOSH
SWOOSH
FWSHOOP
!!

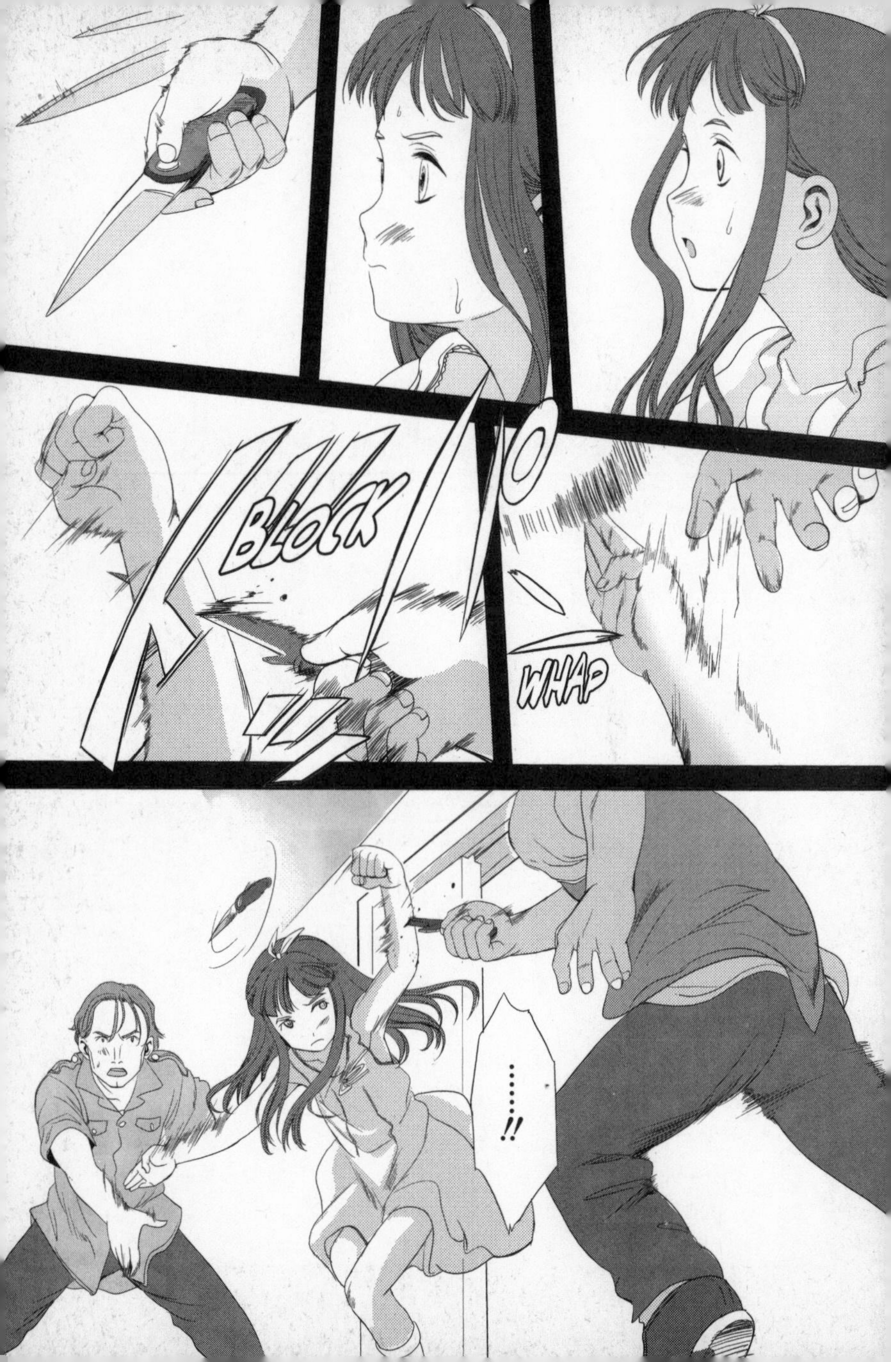
BLOCK
WHAP
......!!

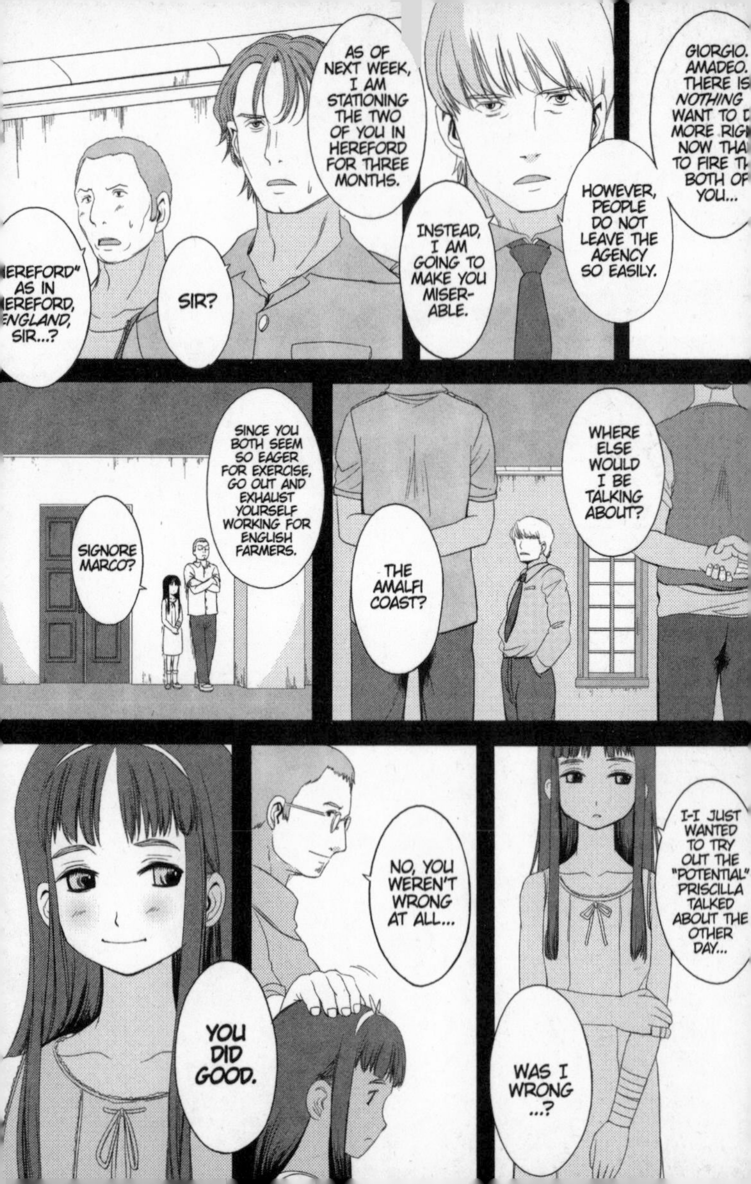
GIORGIO. AMADEO. THERE IS *NOTHING* WANT TO D MORE RIGH NOW THA TO FIRE TH BOTH OF YOU...
HOWEVER, PEOPLE DO NOT LEAVE THE AGENCY SO EASILY.
INSTEAD, I AM GOING TO MAKE YOU MISER-ABLE.
AS OF NEXT WEEK, I AM STATIONING THE TWO OF YOU IN HEREFORD FOR THREE MONTHS.
SIR?
EREFORD" AS IN EREFORD, NGLAND, SIR...?
WHERE ELSE WOULD I BE TALKING ABOUT?
THE AMALFI COAST?
SINCE YOU BOTH SEEM SO EAGER FOR EXERCISE, GO OUT AND EXHAUST YOURSELF WORKING FOR ENGLISH FARMERS.
SIGNORE MARCO?
I-I JUST WANTED TO TRY OUT THE "POTENTIAL" PRISCILLA TALKED ABOUT THE OTHER DAY...
WAS I WRONG ...?
NO, YOU WEREN'T WRONG AT ALL...
YOU DID GOOD.

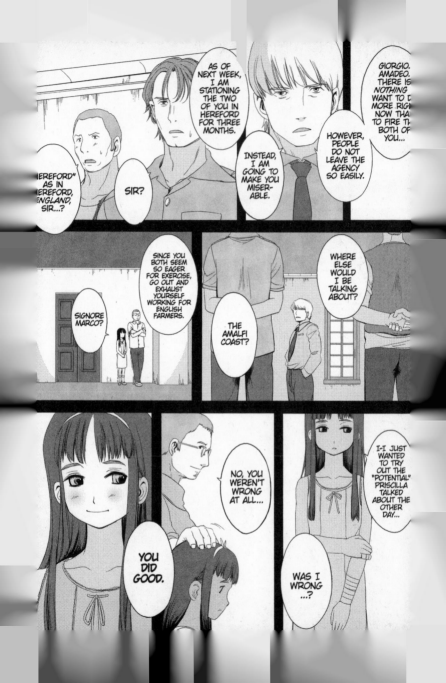

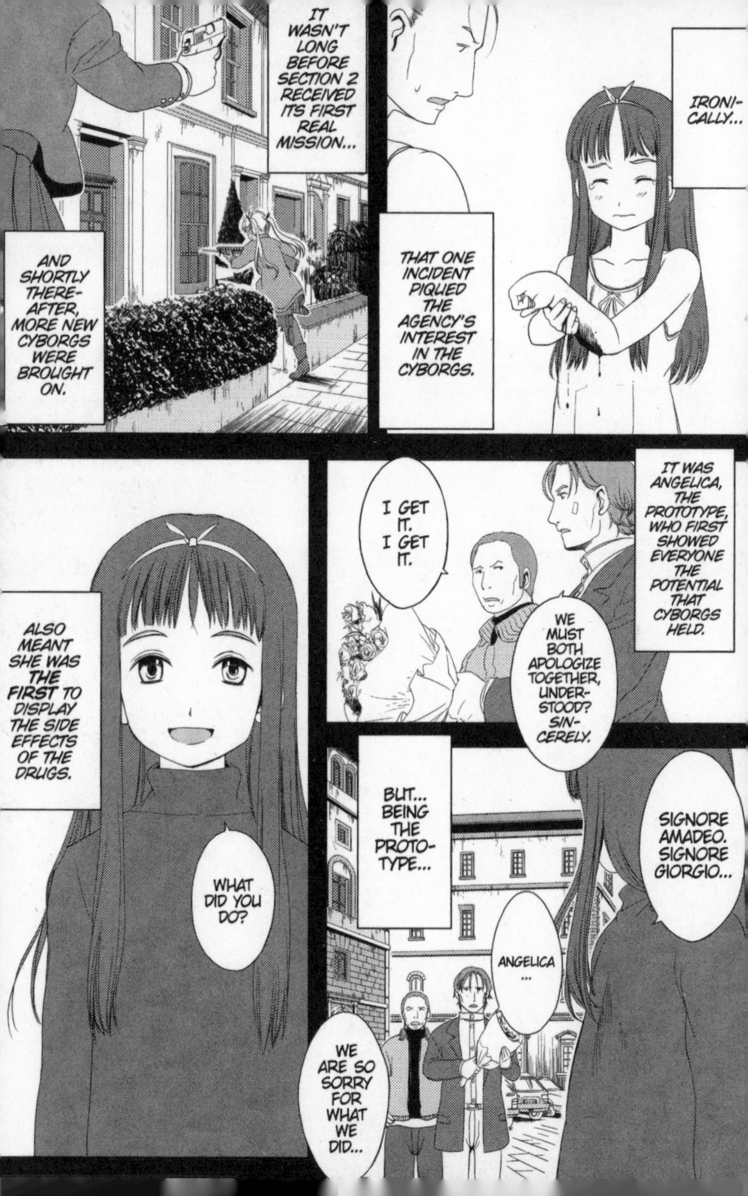
IRONICALLY...
THAT ONE INCIDENT PIQUED THE AGENCY'S INTEREST IN THE CYBORGS.
IT WASN'T LONG BEFORE SECTION 2 RECEIVED ITS FIRST REAL MISSION...
AND SHORTLY THEREAFTER, MORE NEW CYBORGS WERE BROUGHT ON.
IT WAS ANGELICA, THE PROTOTYPE, WHO FIRST SHOWED EVERYONE THE POTENTIAL THAT CYBORGS HELD.
WE MUST BOTH APOLOGIZE TOGETHER, UNDERSTOOD? SINCERELY.
I GET IT. I GET IT.
SIGNORE AMADEO. SIGNORE GIORGIO...
ANGELICA...
WE ARE SO SORRY FOR WHAT WE DID...
BUT... BEING THE PROTOTYPE...
ALSO MEANT SHE WAS **THE FIRST** TO DISPLAY THE SIDE EFFECTS OF THE DRUGS.
WHAT DID YOU DO?

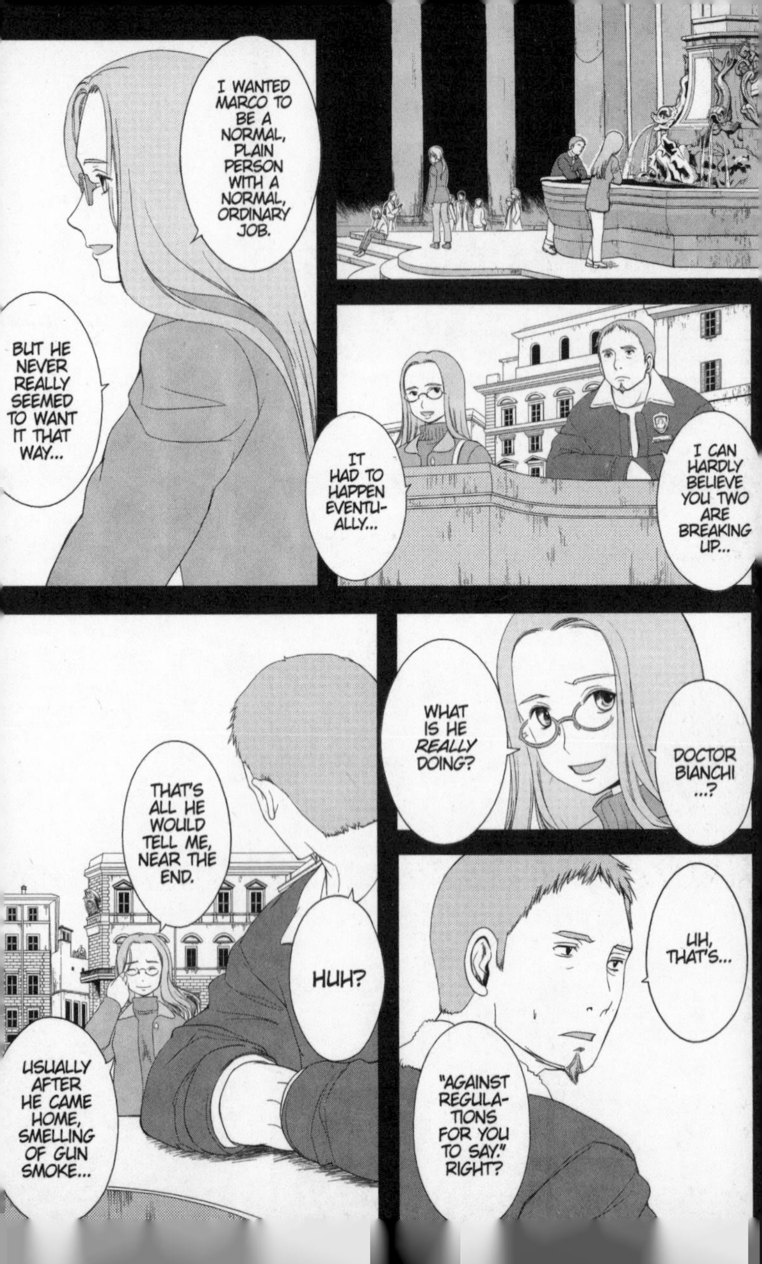
I CAN HARDLY BELIEVE YOU TWO ARE BREAKING UP...
IT HAD TO HAPPEN EVENTUALLY...
I WANTED MARCO TO BE A NORMAL, PLAIN PERSON WITH A NORMAL, ORDINARY JOB.
BUT HE NEVER REALLY SEEMED TO WANT IT THAT WAY...
DOCTOR BIANCHI ...?
WHAT IS HE *REALLY* DOING?
UH, THAT'S...
"AGAINST REGULATIONS FOR YOU TO SAY." RIGHT?
HUH?
THAT'S ALL HE WOULD TELL ME, NEAR THE END.
USUALLY AFTER HE CAME HOME, SMELLING OF GUN SMOKE...

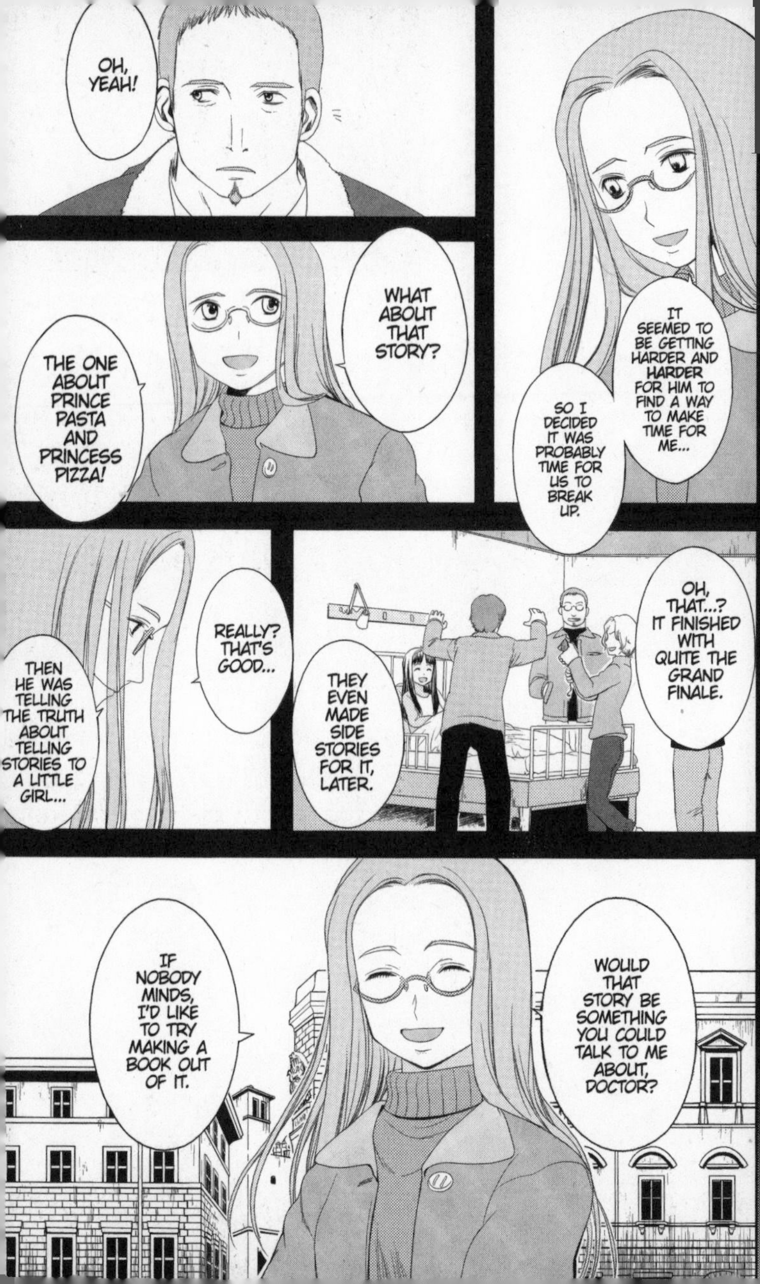
IT SEEMED TO BE GETTING HARDER AND HARDER FOR HIM TO FIND A WAY TO MAKE TIME FOR ME...
SO I DECIDED IT WAS PROBABLY TIME FOR US TO BREAK UP.
OH, YEAH!
WHAT ABOUT THAT STORY?
THE ONE ABOUT PRINCE PASTA AND PRINCESS PIZZA!
OH, THAT...? IT FINISHED WITH QUITE THE GRAND FINALE.
THEY EVEN MADE SIDE STORIES FOR IT, LATER.
REALLY? THAT'S GOOD...
THEN HE WAS TELLING THE TRUTH ABOUT TELLING STORIES TO A LITTLE GIRL...
WOULD THAT STORY BE SOMETHING YOU COULD TALK TO ME ABOUT, DOCTOR?
IF NOBODY MINDS, I'D LIKE TO TRY MAKING A BOOK OUT OF IT.

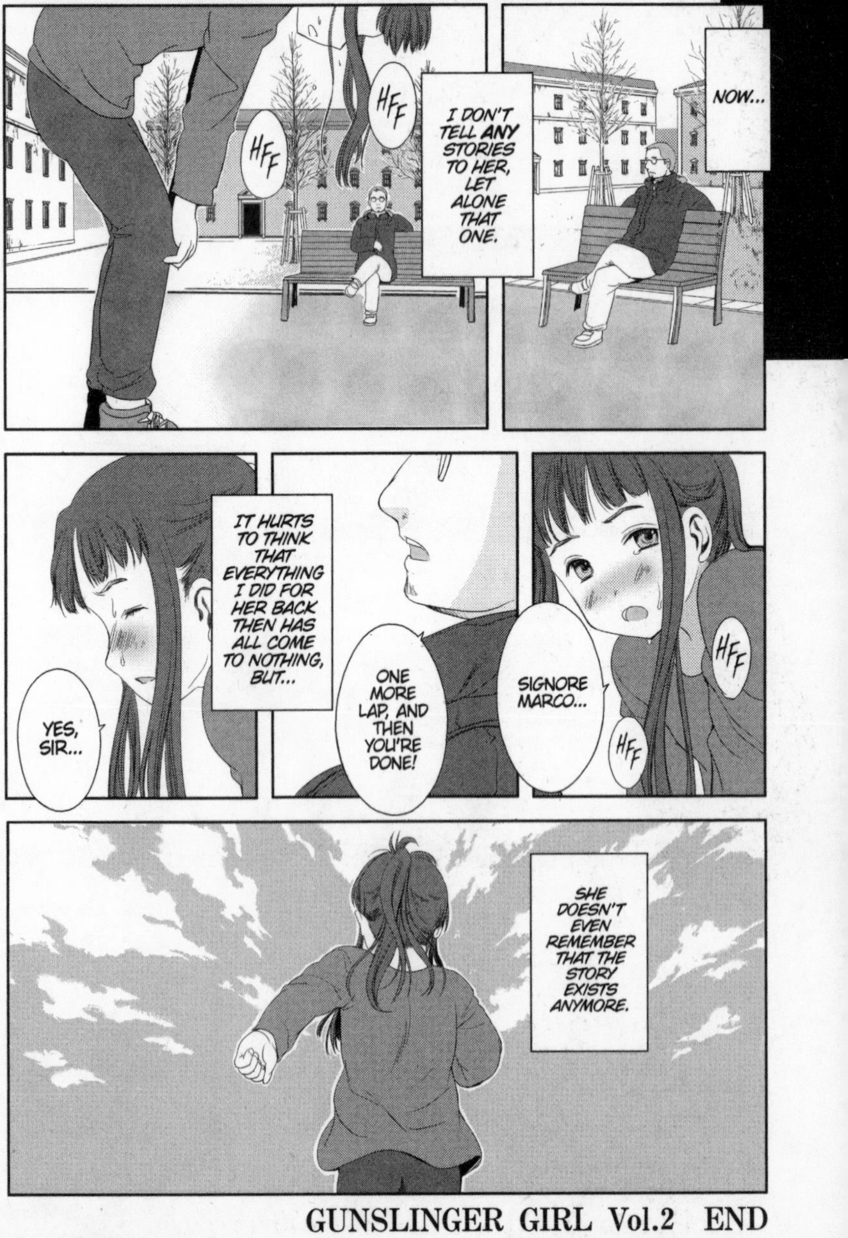
NOW...
I DON'T TELL ANY STORIES TO HER, LET ALONE THAT ONE.
HFF
HFF
HFF
SIGNORE MARCO...
HFF
ONE MORE LAP, AND THEN YOU'RE DONE!
IT HURTS TO THINK THAT EVERYTHING I DID FOR HER BACK THEN HAS ALL COME TO NOTHING, BUT...
YES, SIR...
SHE DOESN'T EVEN REMEMBER THAT THE STORY EXISTS ANYMORE.

GUNSLINGER GIRL Vol.2 END

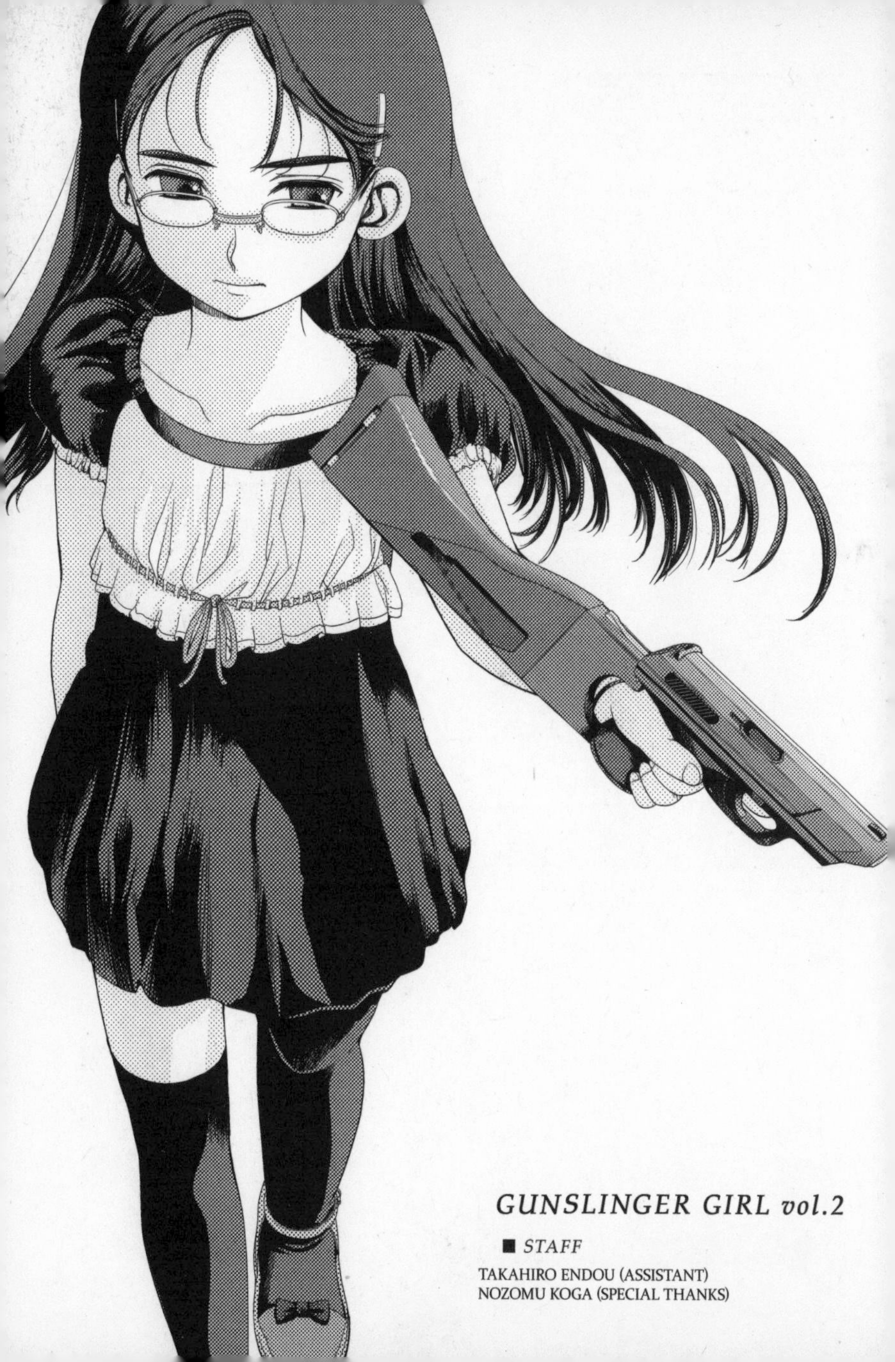

GUNSLINGER GIRL vol.2

■ STAFF

TAKAHIRO ENDOU (ASSISTANT)
NOZOMU KOGA (SPECIAL THANKS)

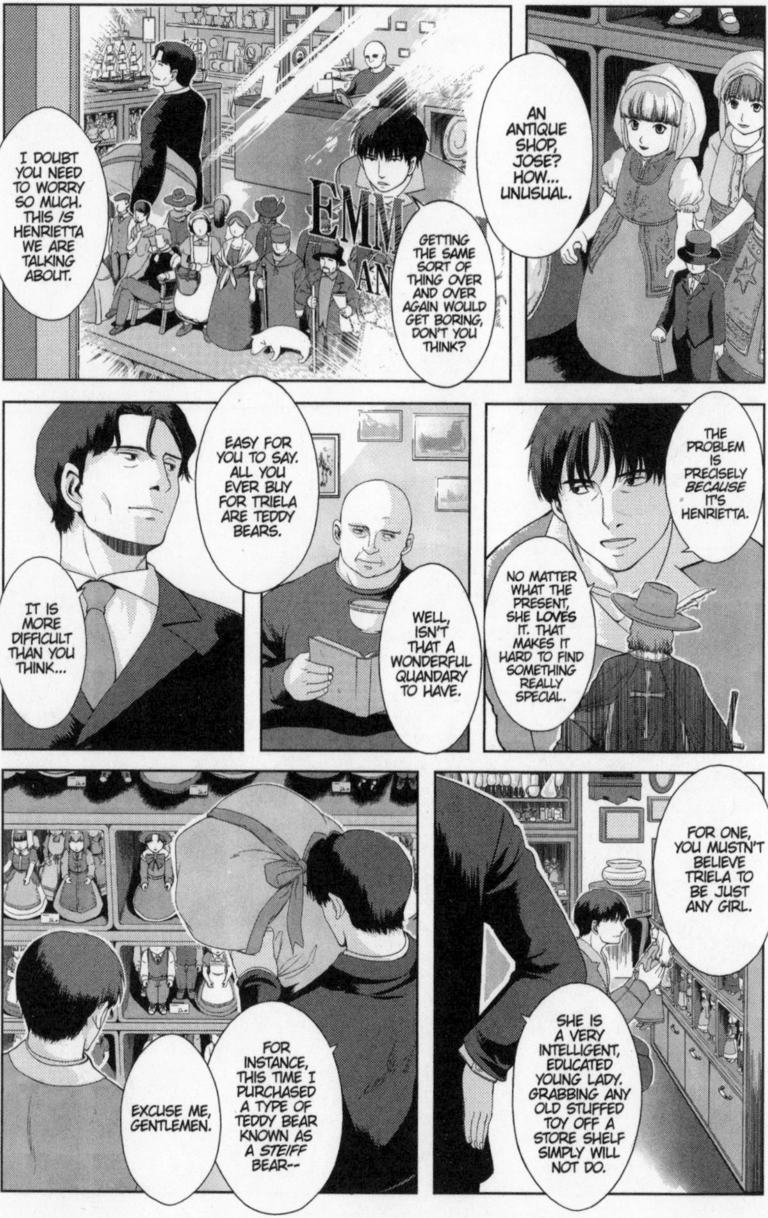
AN ANTIQUE SHOP, JOSE? HOW... UNUSUAL.
GETTING THE SAME SORT OF THING OVER AND OVER AGAIN WOULD GET BORING, DON'T YOU THINK?
I DOUBT YOU NEED TO WORRY SO MUCH. THIS *IS* HENRIETTA WE ARE TALKING ABOUT.
THE PROBLEM IS PRECISELY *BECAUSE* IT'S HENRIETTA.
NO MATTER WHAT THE PRESENT, SHE **LOVES** IT. THAT MAKES IT HARD TO FIND SOMETHING REALLY SPECIAL.
EASY FOR YOU TO SAY. ALL YOU EVER BUY FOR TRIELA ARE TEDDY BEARS.
WELL, ISN'T THAT A WONDERFUL QUANDARY TO HAVE.
IT IS MORE DIFFICULT THAN YOU THINK...
FOR ONE, YOU MUSTN'T BELIEVE TRIELA TO BE JUST ANY GIRL.
SHE IS A VERY INTELLIGENT, EDUCATED YOUNG LADY. GRABBING ANY OLD STUFFED TOY OFF A STORE SHELF SIMPLY WILL NOT DO.
FOR INSTANCE, THIS TIME I PURCHASED A TYPE OF TEDDY BEAR KNOWN AS A *STEIFF* BEAR--
EXCUSE ME, GENTLEMEN.

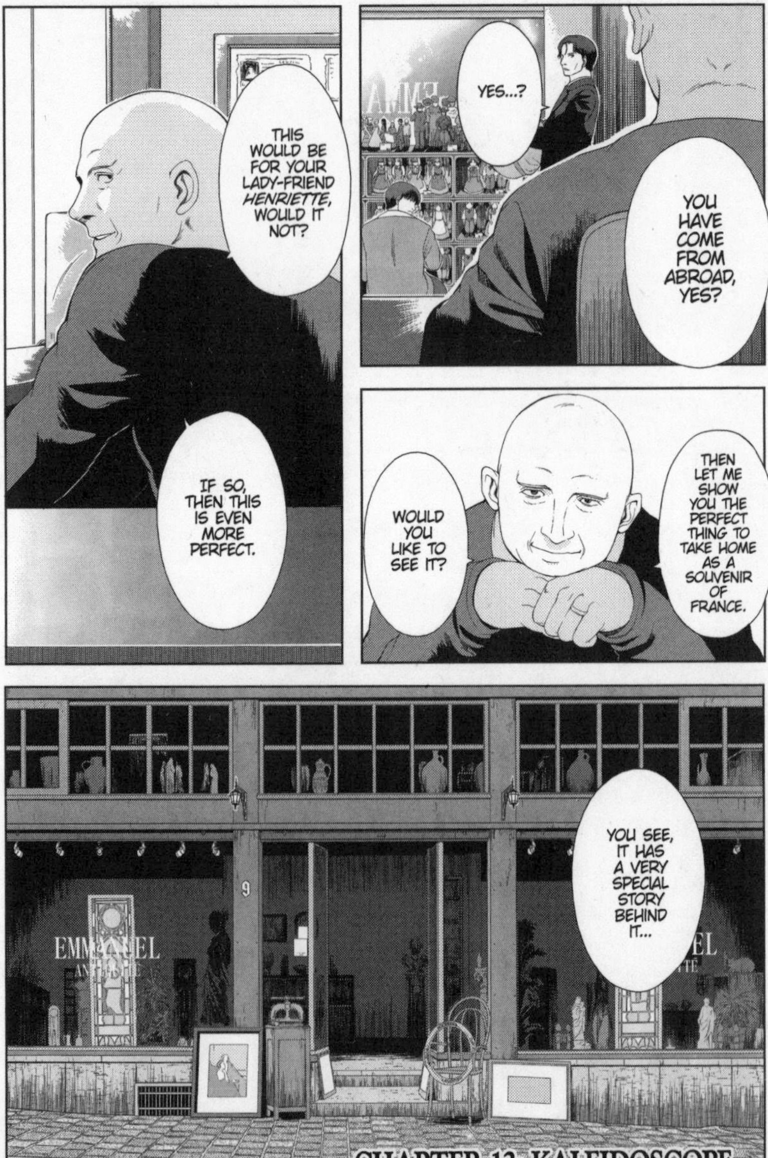
YOU HAVE COME FROM ABROAD, YES?
YES...?
THEN LET ME SHOW YOU THE PERFECT THING TO TAKE HOME AS A SOUVENIR OF FRANCE.
WOULD YOU LIKE TO SEE IT?
THIS WOULD BE FOR YOUR LADY-FRIEND *HENRIETTE*, WOULD IT NOT?
IF SO, THEN THIS IS EVEN MORE PERFECT.
YOU SEE, IT HAS A VERY SPECIAL STORY BEHIND IT...
EMMANUEL
CHAPTER 12: KALEIDOSCOPE

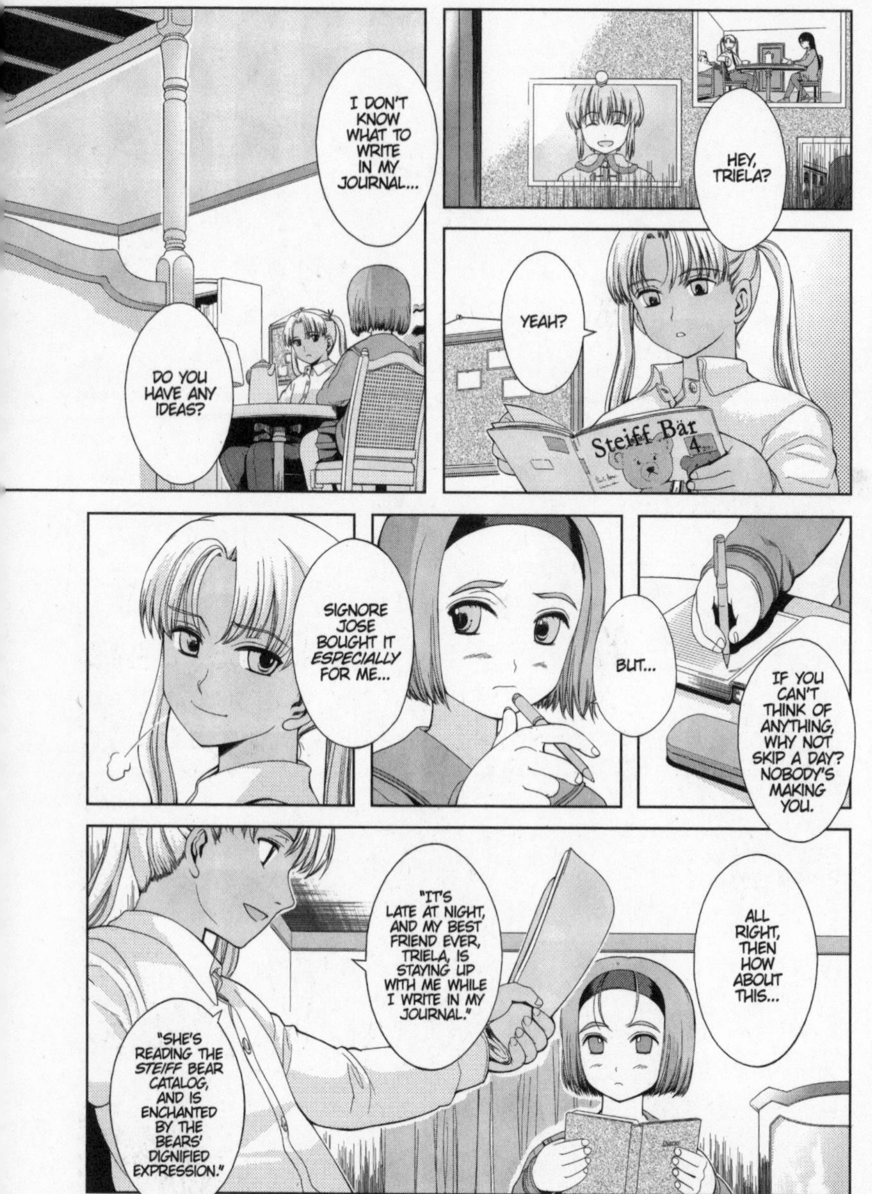
HEY, TRIELA?
YEAH?
I DON'T KNOW WHAT TO WRITE IN MY JOURNAL...
DO YOU HAVE ANY IDEAS?
Steiff Bär
IF YOU CAN'T THINK OF ANYTHING, WHY NOT SKIP A DAY? NOBODY'S MAKING YOU.
BUT...
SIGNORE JOSE BOUGHT IT *ESPECIALLY* FOR ME...
ALL RIGHT, THEN HOW ABOUT THIS...
"IT'S LATE AT NIGHT, AND MY BEST FRIEND EVER, TRIELA, IS STAYING UP WITH ME WHILE I WRITE IN MY JOURNAL."
"SHE'S READING THE *STEIFF* BEAR CATALOG, AND IS ENCHANTED BY THE BEARS' DIGNIFIED EXPRESSION."

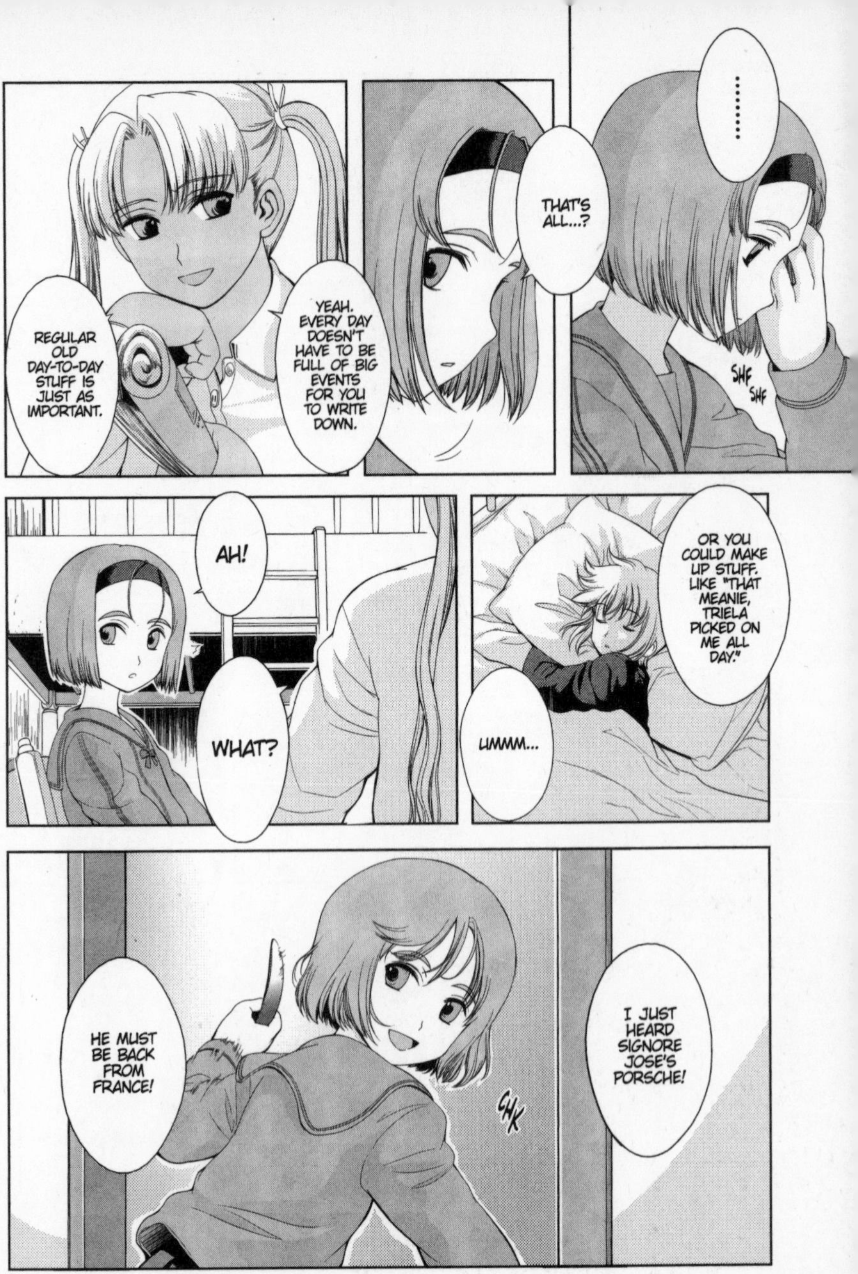
……
SHF SHF
THAT'S ALL...?
YEAH. EVERY DAY DOESN'T HAVE TO BE FULL OF BIG EVENTS FOR YOU TO WRITE DOWN.
REGULAR OLD DAY-TO-DAY STUFF IS JUST AS IMPORTANT.
OR YOU COULD MAKE UP STUFF. LIKE "THAT MEANIE, TRIELA PICKED ON ME ALL DAY."
UMMM...
AH!
WHAT?
I JUST HEARD SIGNORE JOSE'S PORSCHE!
CHK
HE MUST BE BACK FROM FRANCE!

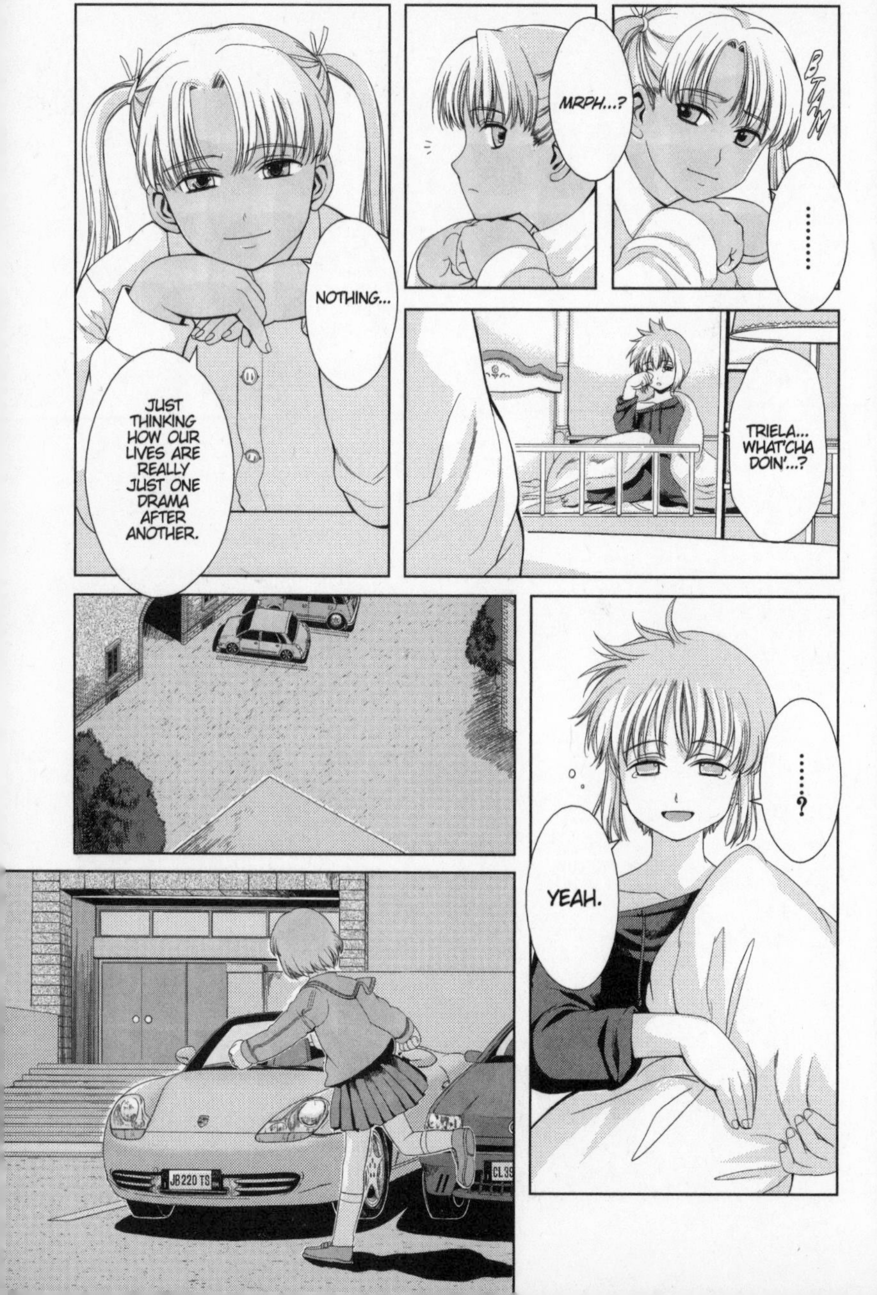
BTAM
......
MRPH...?
TRIELA... WHAT'CHA DOIN'...?
NOTHING...
JUST THINKING HOW OUR LIVES ARE REALLY JUST ONE DRAMA AFTER ANOTHER.
......?
YEAH.

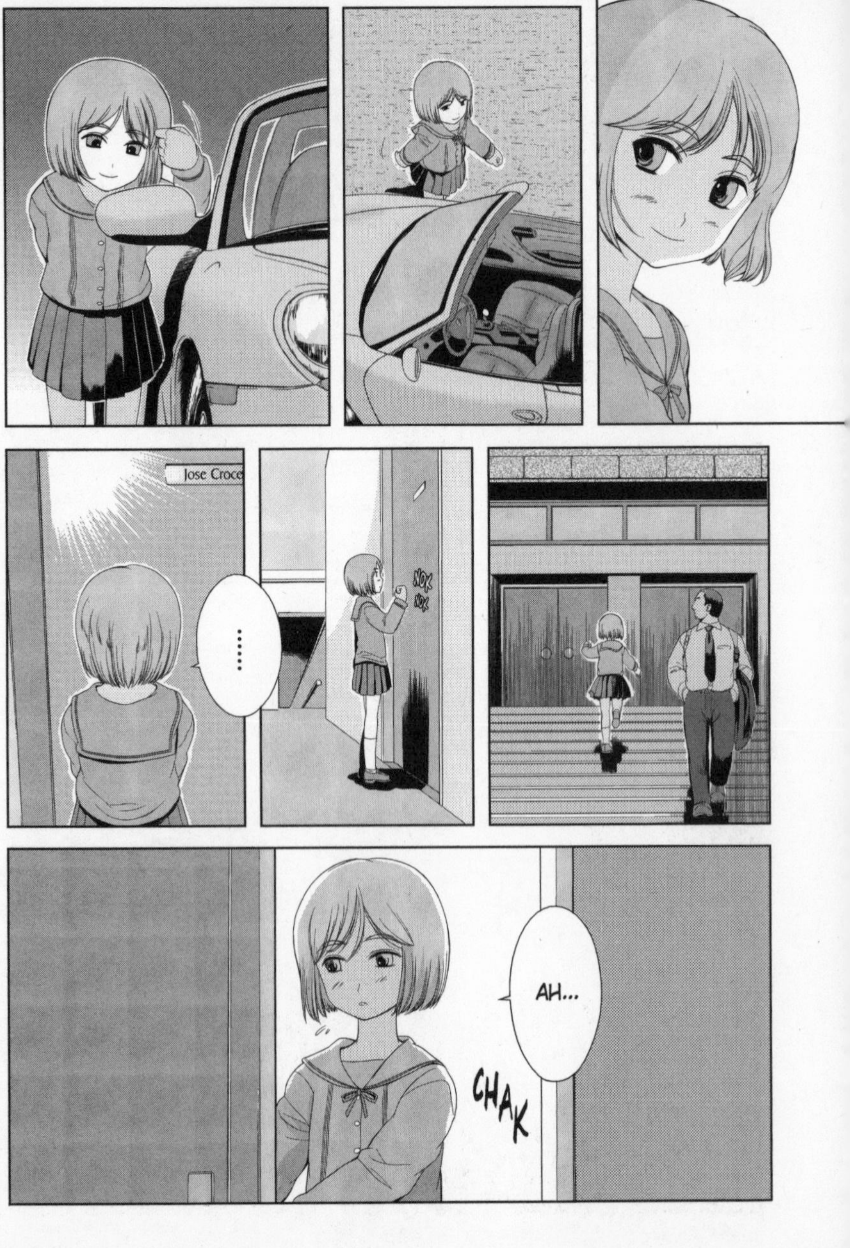
NOK
NOK
Jose Croce
......
AH...
CHAK

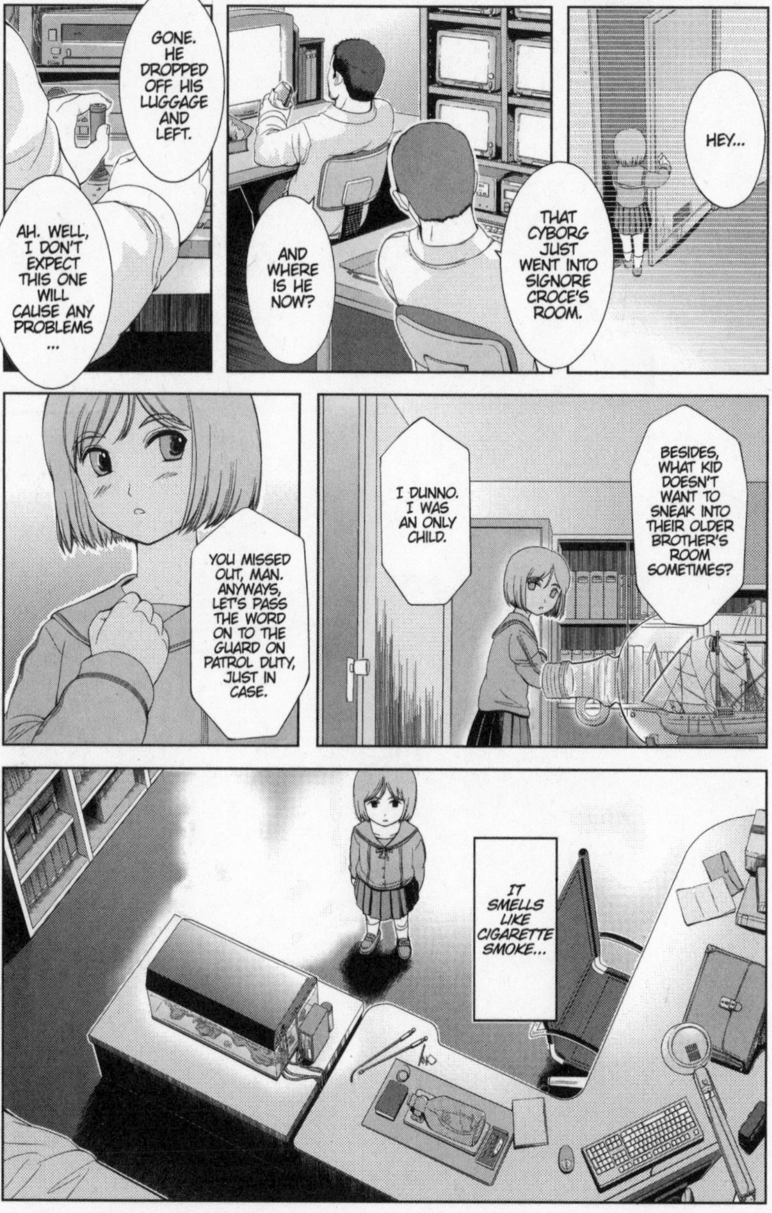
HEY...
THAT CYBORG JUST WENT INTO SIGNORE CROCE'S ROOM.
AND WHERE IS HE NOW?
GONE. HE DROPPED OFF HIS LUGGAGE AND LEFT.
AH. WELL, I DON'T EXPECT THIS ONE WILL CAUSE ANY PROBLEMS ...
BESIDES, WHAT KID DOESN'T WANT TO SNEAK INTO THEIR OLDER BROTHER'S ROOM SOMETIMES?
I DUNNO. I WAS AN ONLY CHILD.
YOU MISSED OUT, MAN. ANYWAYS, LET'S PASS THE WORD ON TO THE GUARD ON PATROL DUTY, JUST IN CASE.
IT SMELLS LIKE CIGARETTE SMOKE...

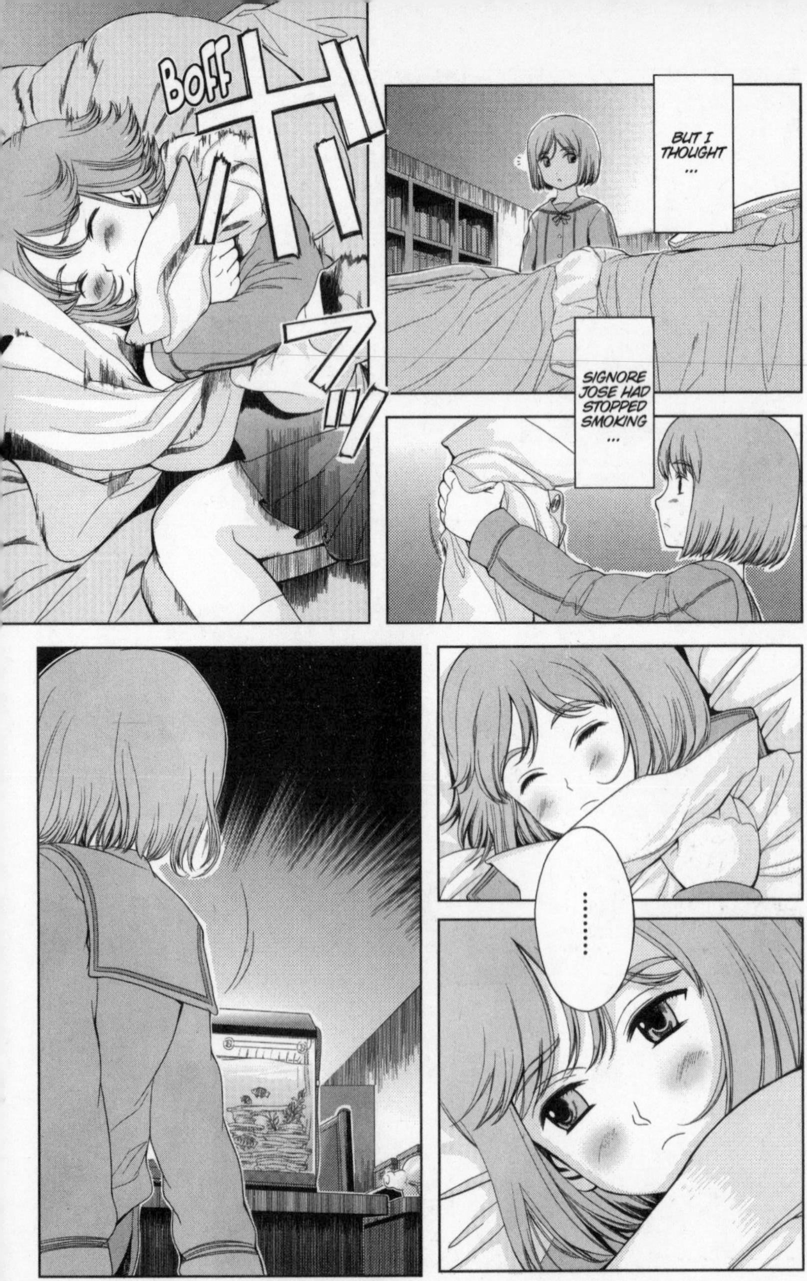
BUT I THOUGHT ...
SIGNORE JOSE HAD STOPPED SMOKING ...
BOFF
......

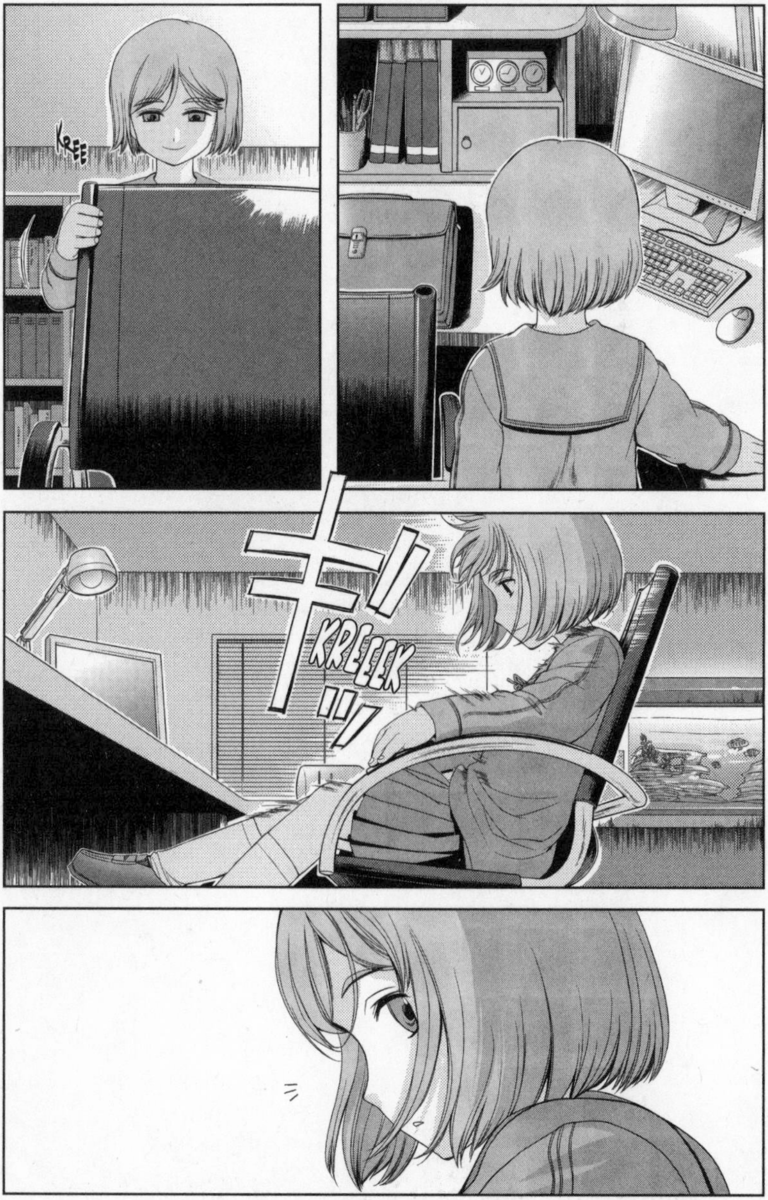
KREE
キ
KREEEK

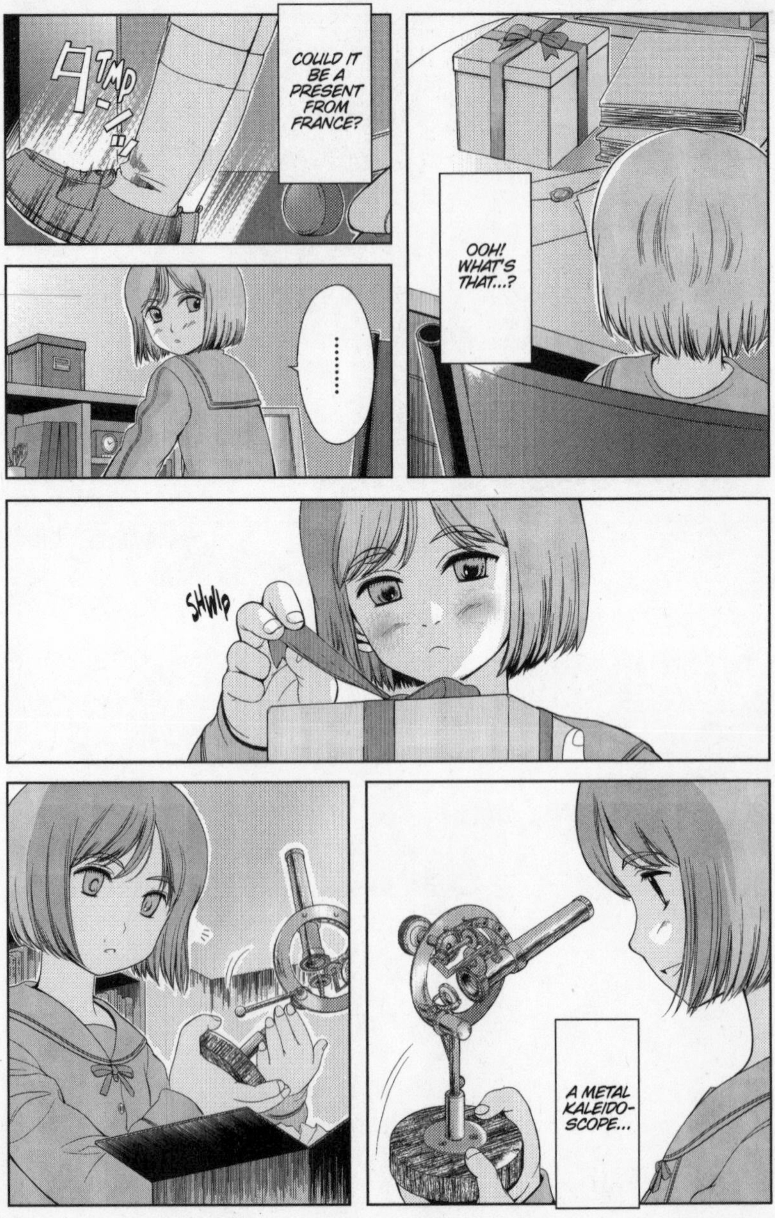
OOH! WHAT'S THAT...?
COULD IT BE A PRESENT FROM FRANCE?
TMP
....
SHWIP
A METAL KALEIDO-SCOPE...

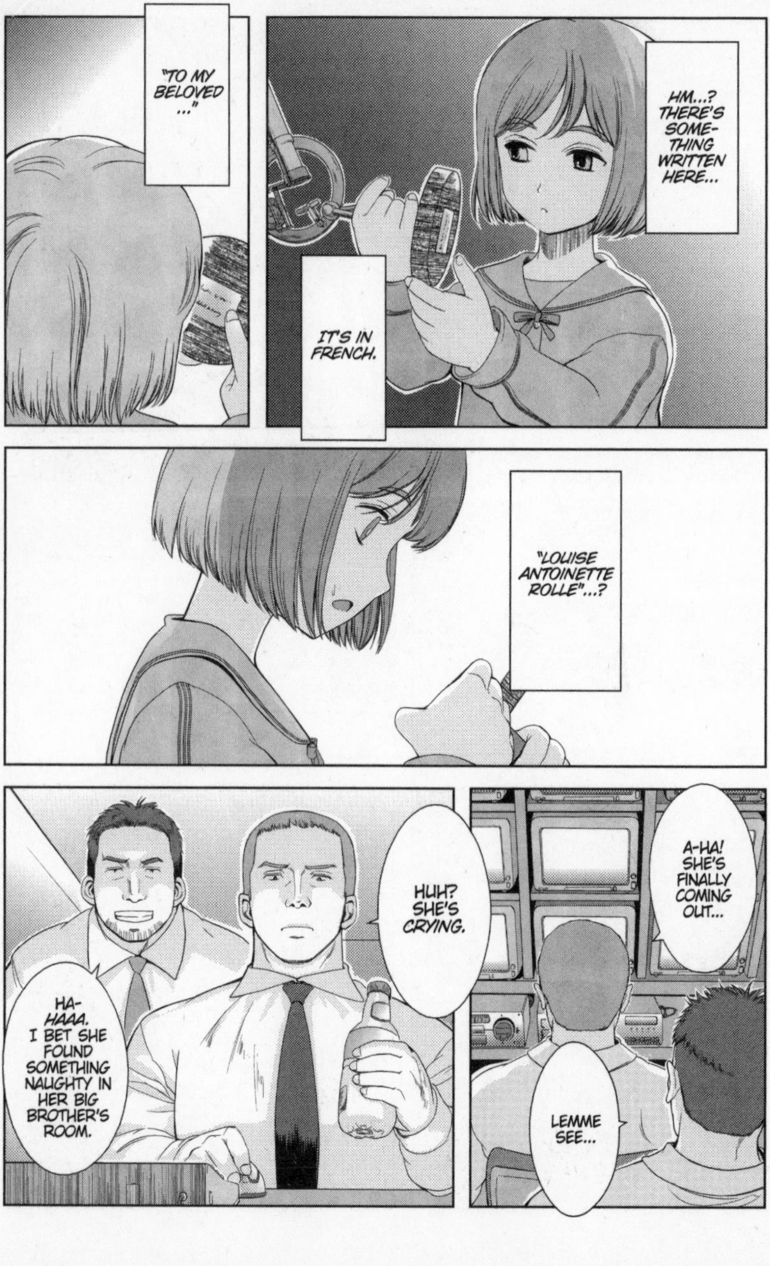
HM...? THERE'S SOME-THING WRITTEN HERE...
IT'S IN FRENCH.
"TO MY BELOVED ..."
"LOUISE ANTOINETTE ROLLE"...?
A-HA! SHE'S FINALLY COMING OUT...
LEMME SEE...
HUH? SHE'S CRYING.
HA-HAAA. I BET SHE FOUND SOMETHING NAUGHTY IN HER BIG BROTHER'S ROOM.

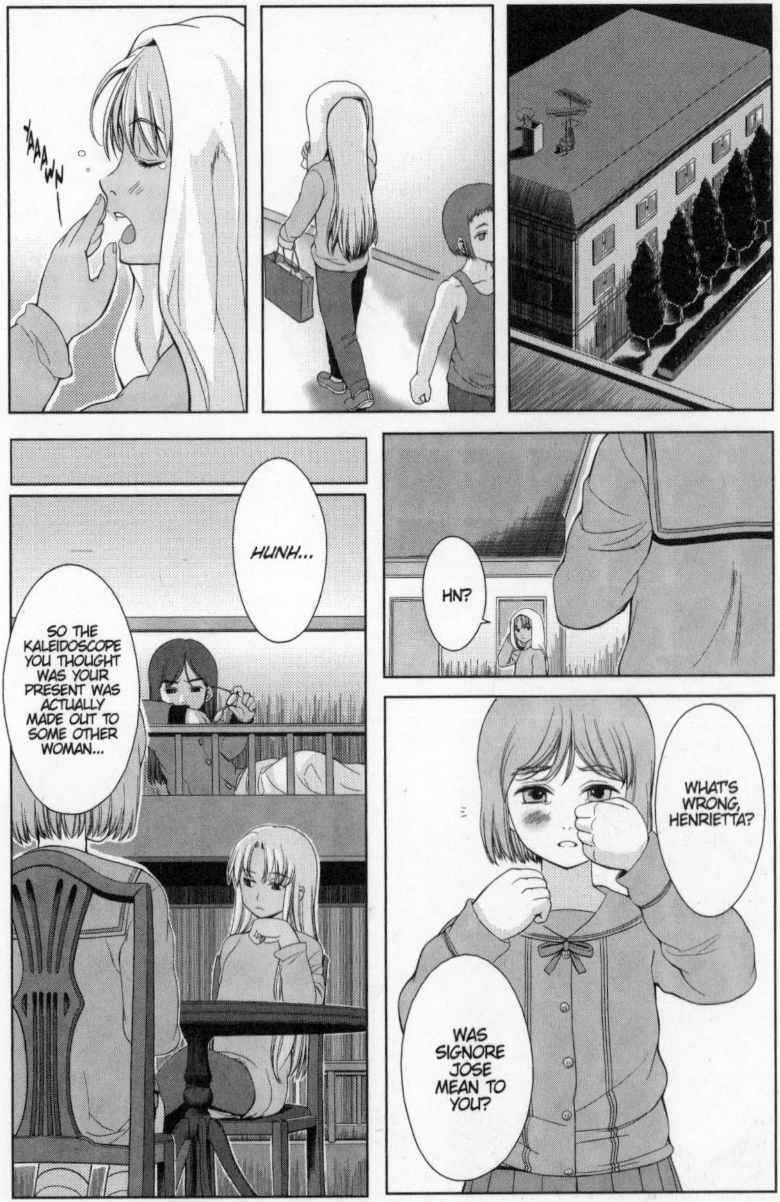

YAAAAWN
HN?
WHAT'S WRONG, HENRIETTA?
WAS SIGNORE JOSE MEAN TO YOU?
HUNH...
SO THE KALEIDOSCOPE YOU THOUGHT WAS YOUR PRESENT WAS ACTUALLY MADE OUT TO SOME OTHER WOMAN...

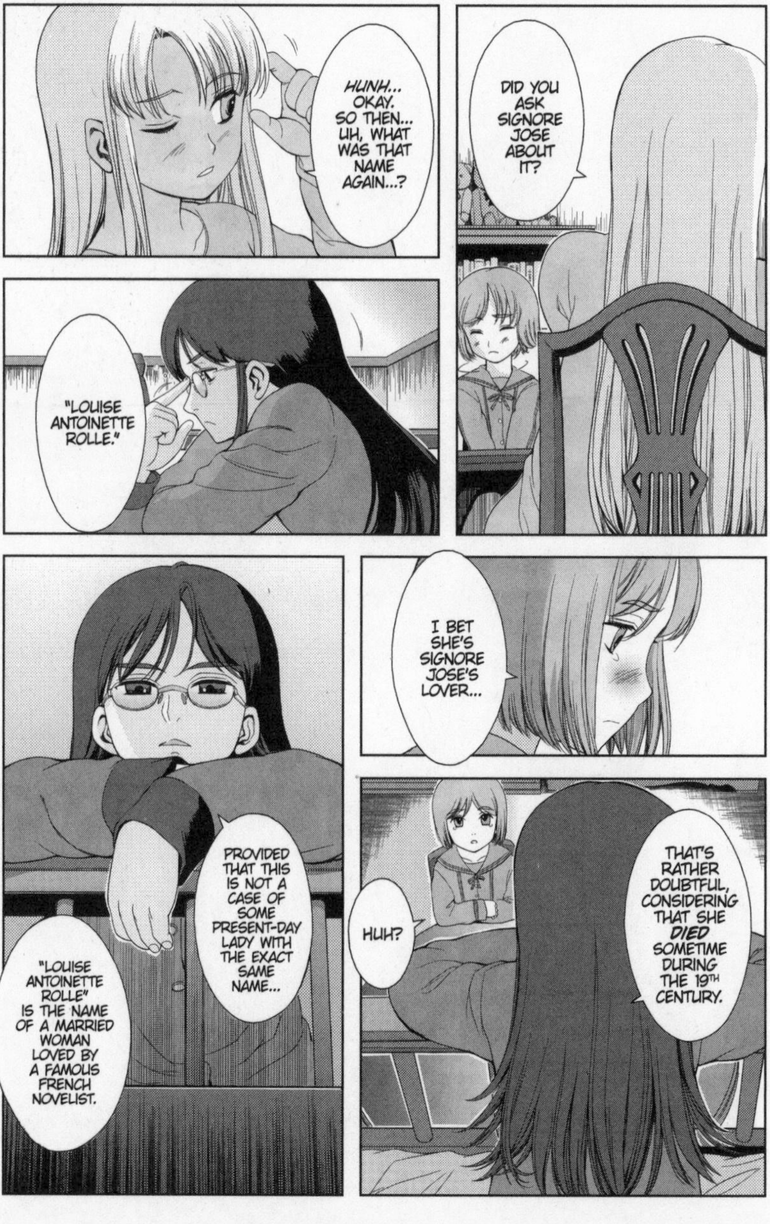
DID YOU ASK SIGNORE JOSE ABOUT IT?
HUNH... OKAY. SO THEN... UH, WHAT WAS THAT NAME AGAIN...?
"LOUISE ANTOINETTE ROLLE."
I BET SHE'S SIGNORE JOSE'S LOVER...
THAT'S RATHER DOUBTFUL, CONSIDERING THAT SHE *DIED* SOMETIME DURING THE 19TH CENTURY.
HUH?
PROVIDED THAT THIS IS NOT A CASE OF SOME PRESENT-DAY LADY WITH THE EXACT SAME NAME...
"LOUISE ANTOINETTE ROLLE" IS THE NAME OF A MARRIED WOMAN LOVED BY A FAMOUS FRENCH NOVELIST.

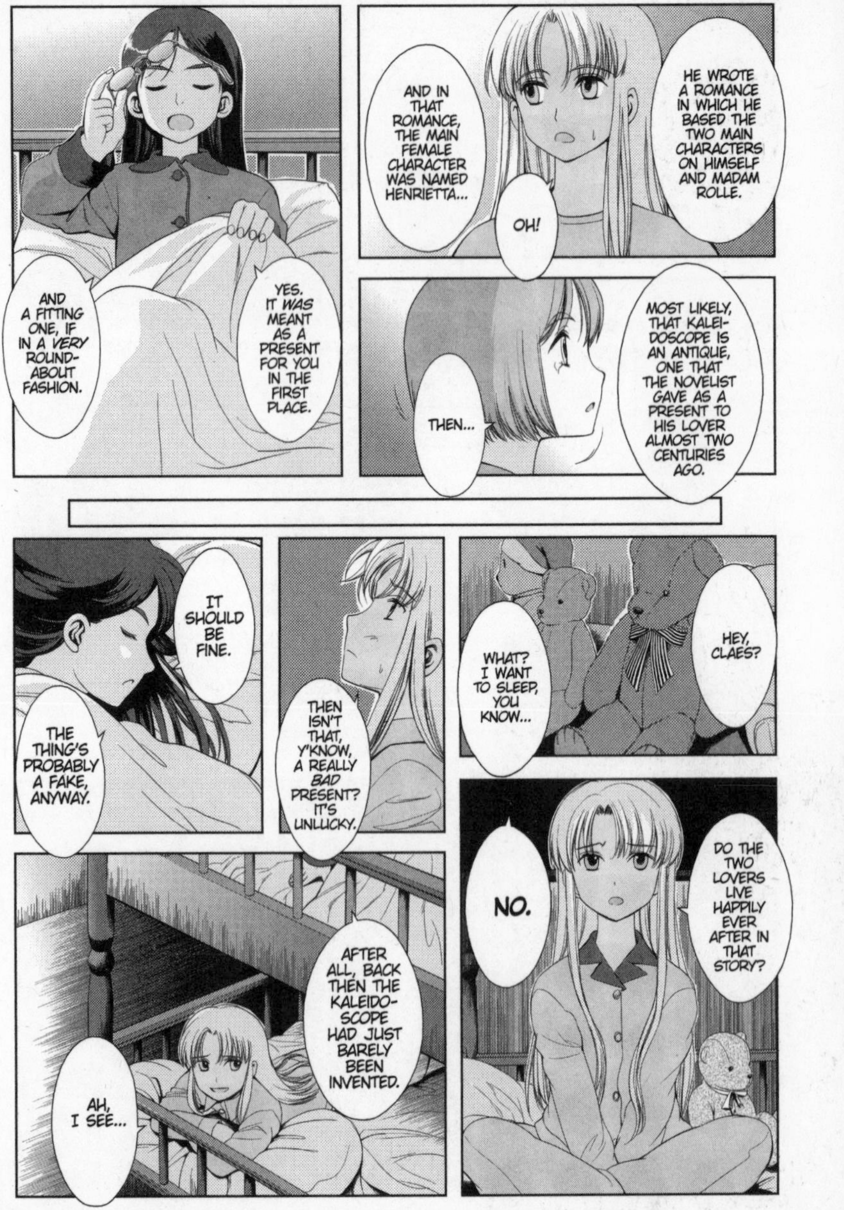
HE WROTE A ROMANCE IN WHICH HE BASED THE TWO MAIN CHARACTERS ON HIMSELF AND MADAM ROLLE.
AND IN THAT ROMANCE, THE MAIN FEMALE CHARACTER WAS NAMED HENRIETTA...
OH!
MOST LIKELY, THAT KALEIDOSCOPE IS AN ANTIQUE, ONE THAT THE NOVELIST GAVE AS A PRESENT TO HIS LOVER ALMOST TWO CENTURIES AGO.
THEN...
YES. IT *WAS* MEANT AS A PRESENT FOR YOU IN THE FIRST PLACE.
AND A FITTING ONE, IF IN A *VERY* ROUNDABOUT FASHION.
HEY, CLAES?
WHAT? I WANT TO SLEEP, YOU KNOW...
DO THE TWO LOVERS LIVE HAPPILY EVER AFTER IN THAT STORY?
NO.
THEN ISN'T THAT, Y'KNOW, A REALLY *BAD* PRESENT? IT'S UNLUCKY.
IT SHOULD BE FINE.
THE THING'S PROBABLY A FAKE, ANYWAY.
AFTER ALL, BACK THEN THE KALEIDOSCOPE HAD JUST BARELY BEEN INVENTED.
AH, I SEE...

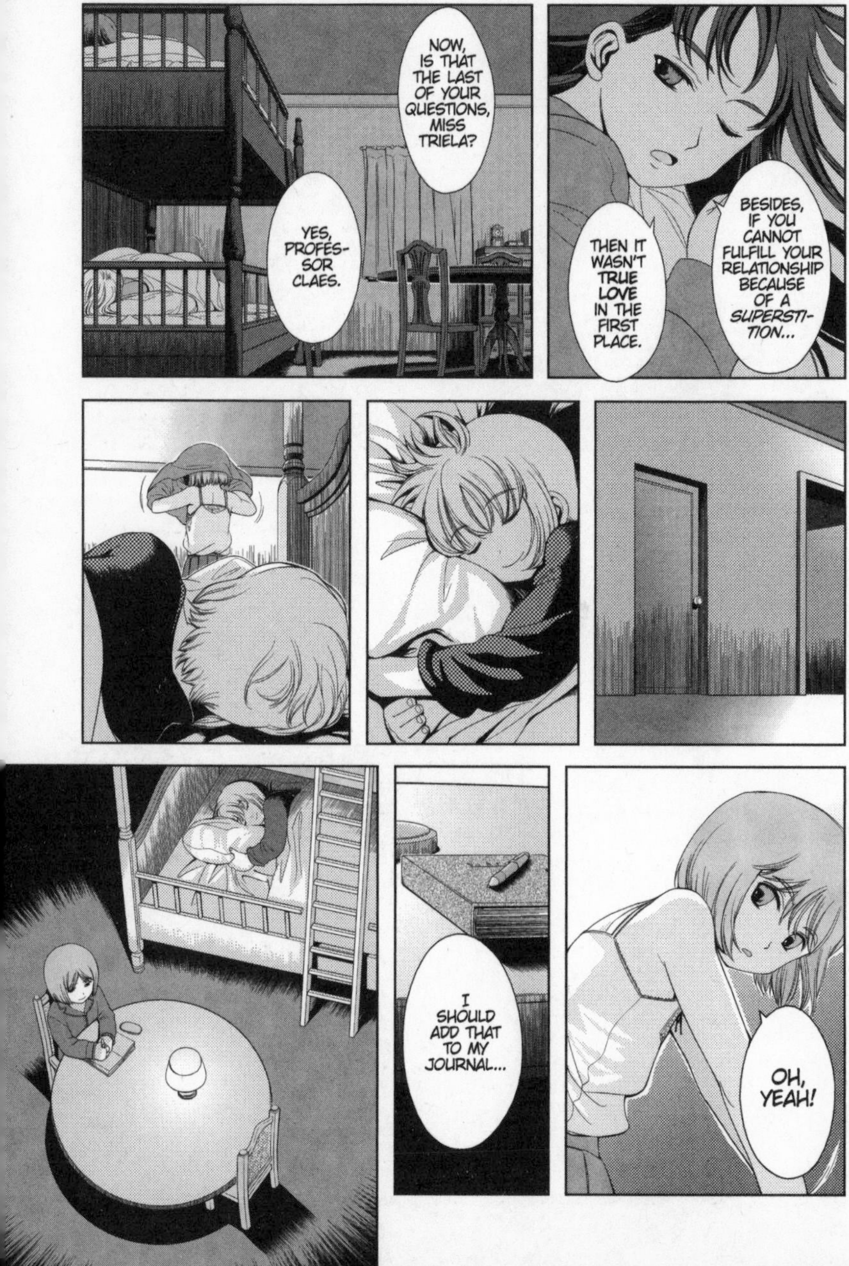
BESIDES, IF YOU CANNOT FULFILL YOUR RELATIONSHIP BECAUSE OF A SUPERSTITION...
THEN IT WASN'T TRUE LOVE IN THE FIRST PLACE.
NOW, IS THAT THE LAST OF YOUR QUESTIONS, MISS TRIELA?
YES, PROFES-SOR CLAES.
OH, YEAH!
I SHOULD ADD THAT TO MY JOURNAL...

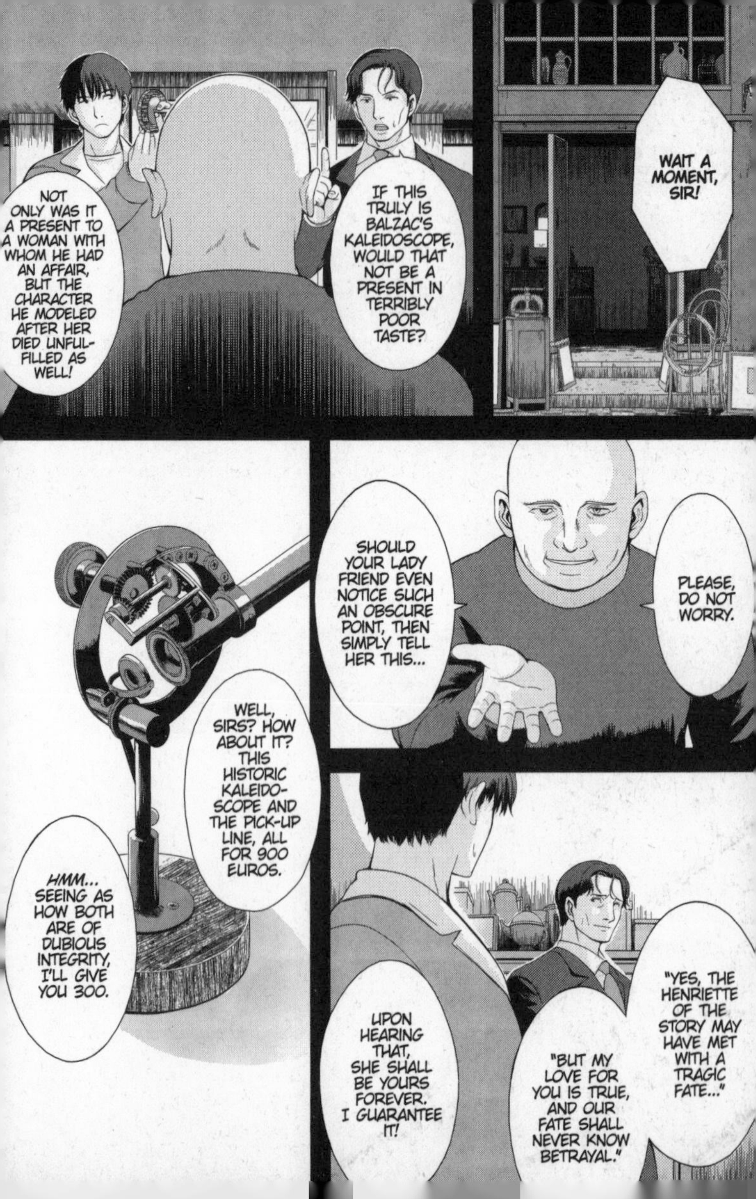
WAIT A MOMENT, SIR!
IF THIS TRULY IS BALZAC'S KALEIDOSCOPE, WOULD THAT NOT BE A PRESENT IN TERRIBLY POOR TASTE?
NOT ONLY WAS IT A PRESENT TO A WOMAN WITH WHOM HE HAD AN AFFAIR, BUT THE CHARACTER HE MODELED AFTER HER DIED UNFUL-FILLED AS WELL!
PLEASE, DO NOT WORRY.
SHOULD YOUR LADY FRIEND EVEN NOTICE SUCH AN OBSCURE POINT, THEN SIMPLY TELL HER THIS...
"YES, THE HENRIETTE OF THE STORY MAY HAVE MET WITH A TRAGIC FATE..."
"BUT MY LOVE FOR YOU IS TRUE, AND OUR FATE SHALL NEVER KNOW BETRAYAL."
UPON HEARING THAT, SHE SHALL BE YOURS FOREVER. I GUARANTEE IT!
WELL, SIRS? HOW ABOUT IT? THIS HISTORIC KALEIDO-SCOPE AND THE PICK-UP LINE, ALL FOR 900 EUROS.
HMM... SEEING AS HOW BOTH ARE OF DUBIOUS INTEGRITY, I'LL GIVE YOU 300.

GUNSLINGER GIRL.

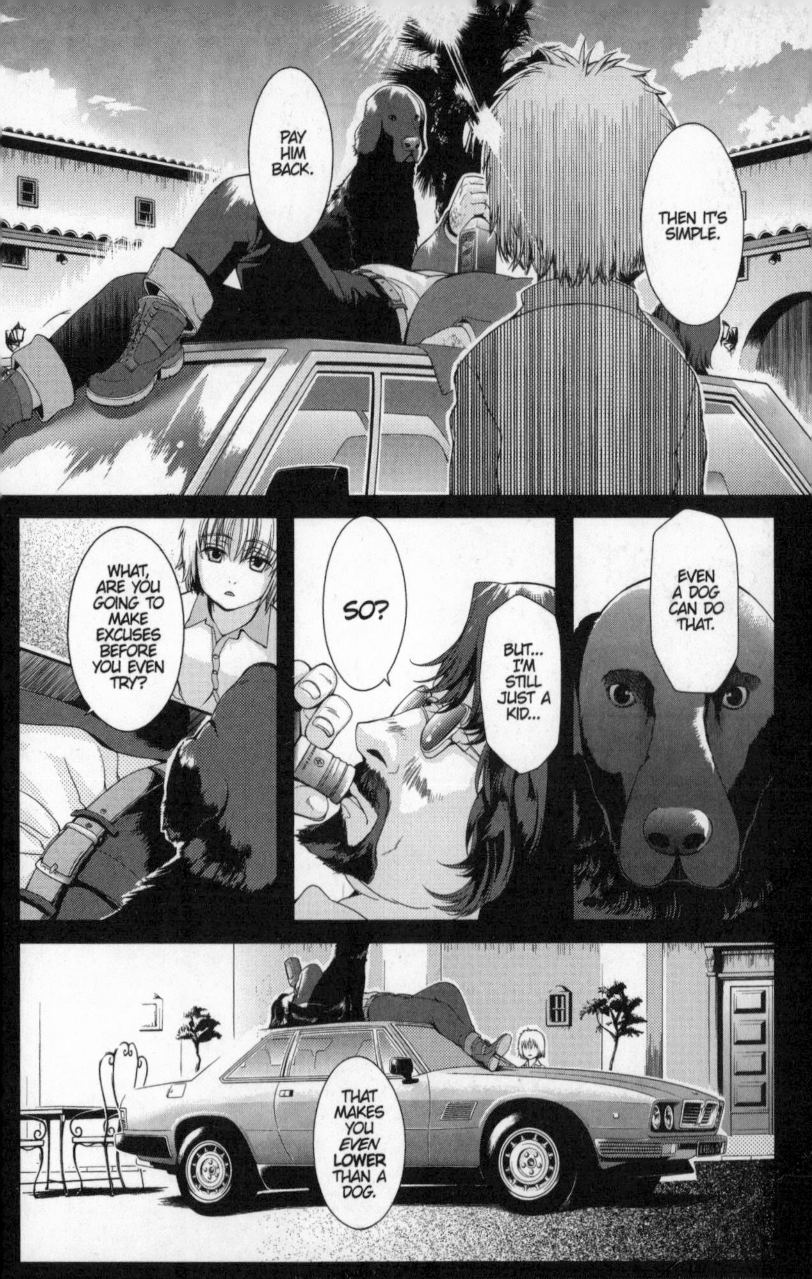
THEN IT'S SIMPLE.
PAY HIM BACK.
EVEN A DOG CAN DO THAT.
BUT... I'M STILL JUST A KID...
SO?
WHAT, ARE YOU GOING TO MAKE EXCUSES BEFORE YOU EVEN TRY?
THAT MAKES YOU EVEN LOWER THAN A DOG.

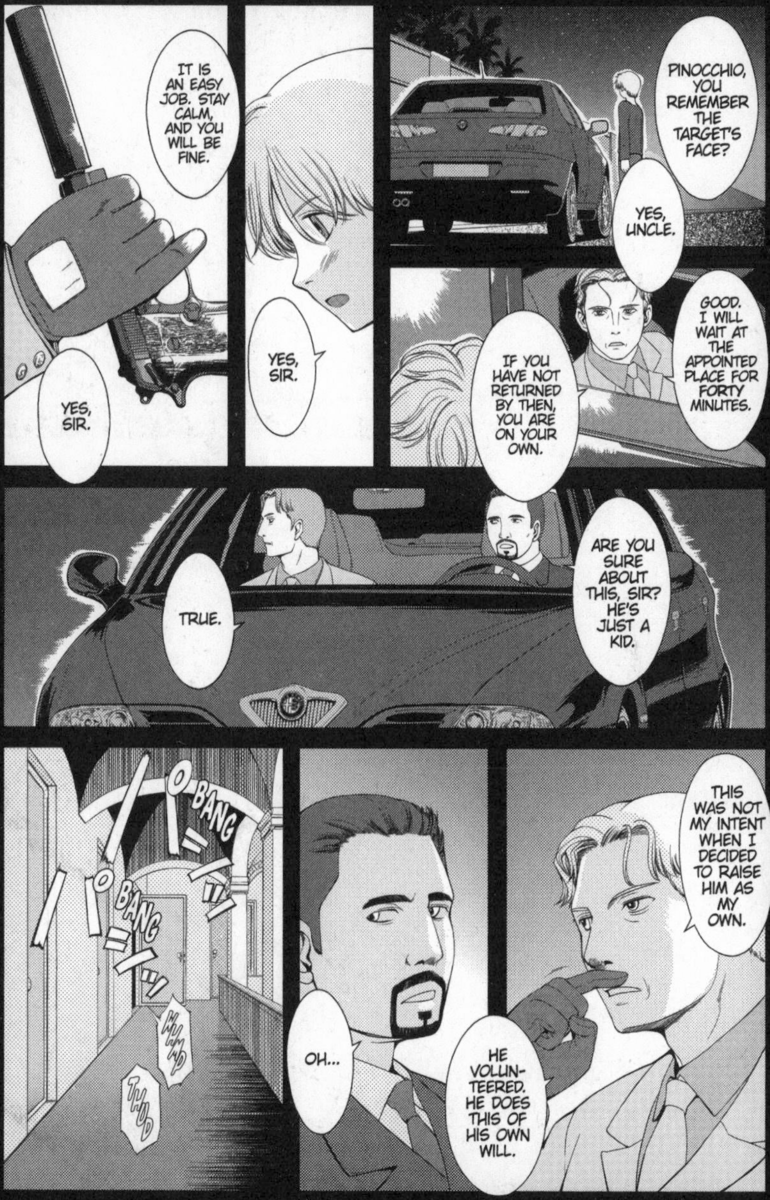
PINOCCHIO, YOU REMEMBER THE TARGET'S FACE?
YES, UNCLE.
GOOD. I WILL WAIT AT THE APPOINTED PLACE FOR FORTY MINUTES.
IF YOU HAVE NOT RETURNED BY THEN, YOU ARE ON YOUR OWN.
YES, SIR.
IT IS AN EASY JOB. STAY CALM, AND YOU WILL BE FINE.
YES, SIR.
ARE YOU SURE ABOUT THIS, SIR? HE'S JUST A KID.
TRUE.
THIS WAS NOT MY INTENT WHEN I DECIDED TO RAISE HIM AS MY OWN.
HE VOLUNTEERED. HE DOES THIS OF HIS OWN WILL.
OH...
BANG
BANG
WHUMP
THUD

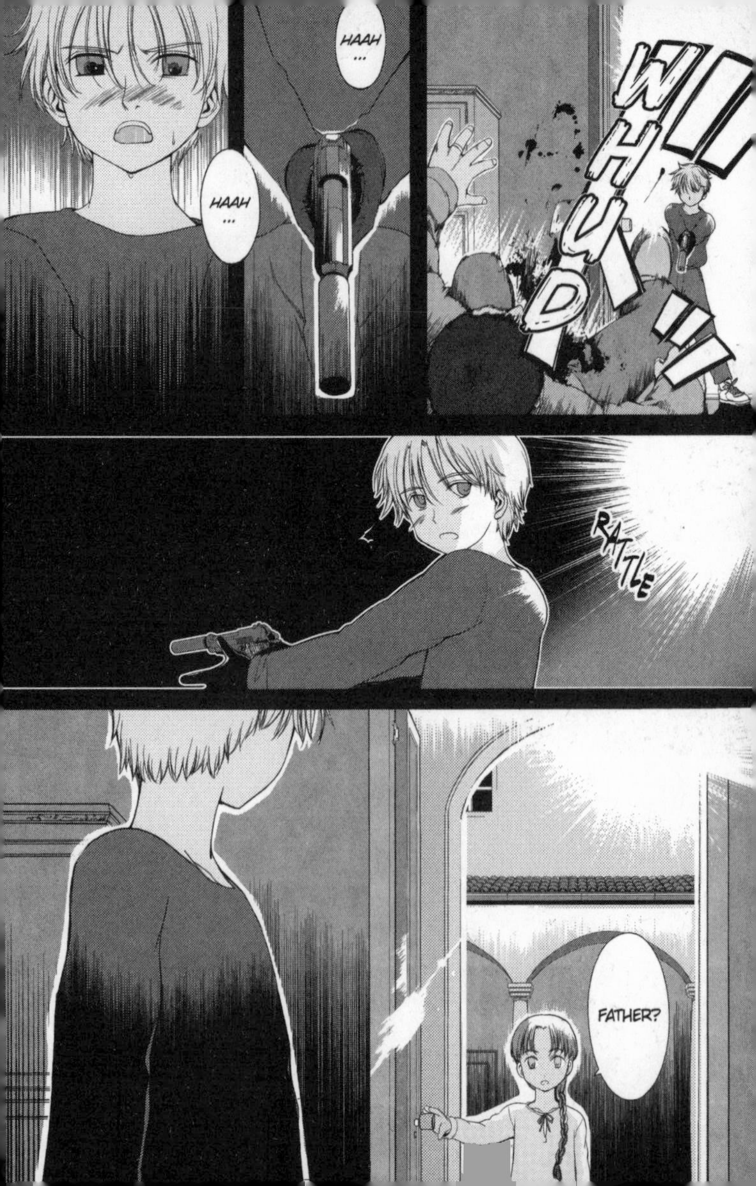
WHUD!!!
HAAH ...
HAAH ...
RATTLE
FATHER?

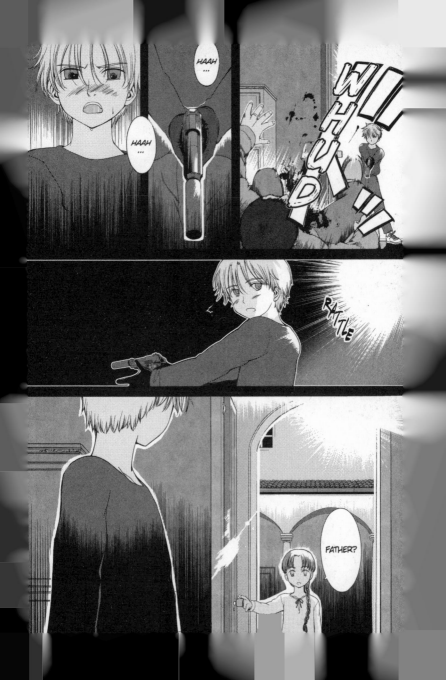

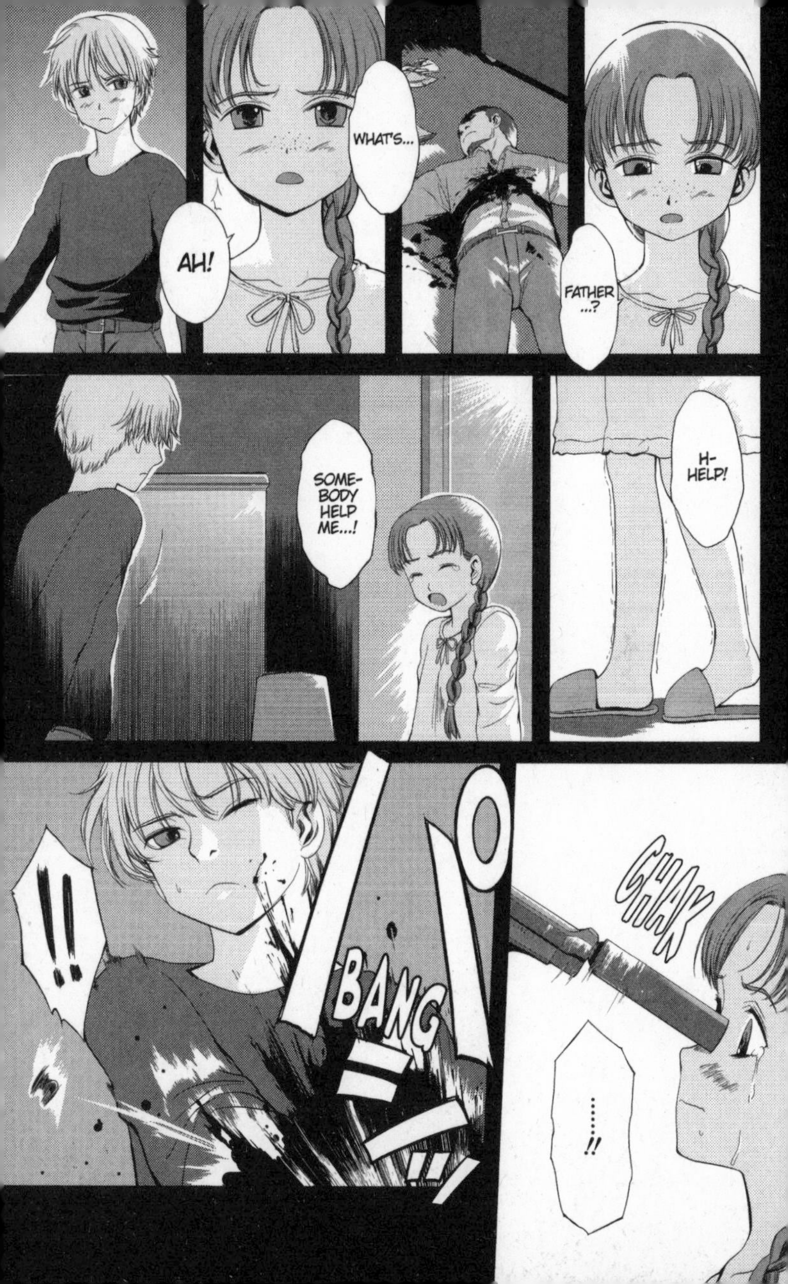
FATHER ...?
WHAT'S...
AH!
H- HELP!
SOME- BODY HELP ME...!
GCHAK
......!!
!!
BANG

WHUMP

CHAPTER 13: PINOCCHIO (1)

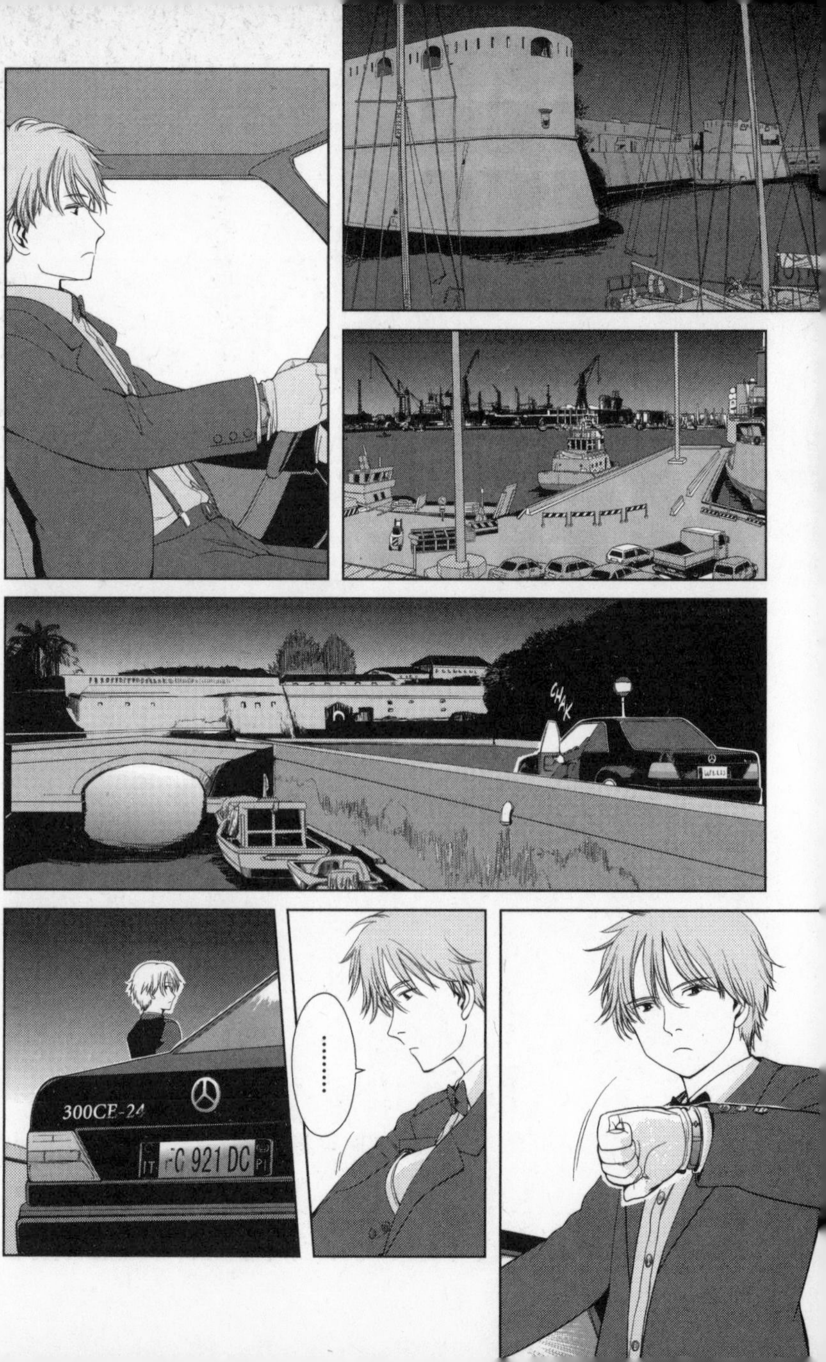
CHAK
......
300CE-24
G 921 DC

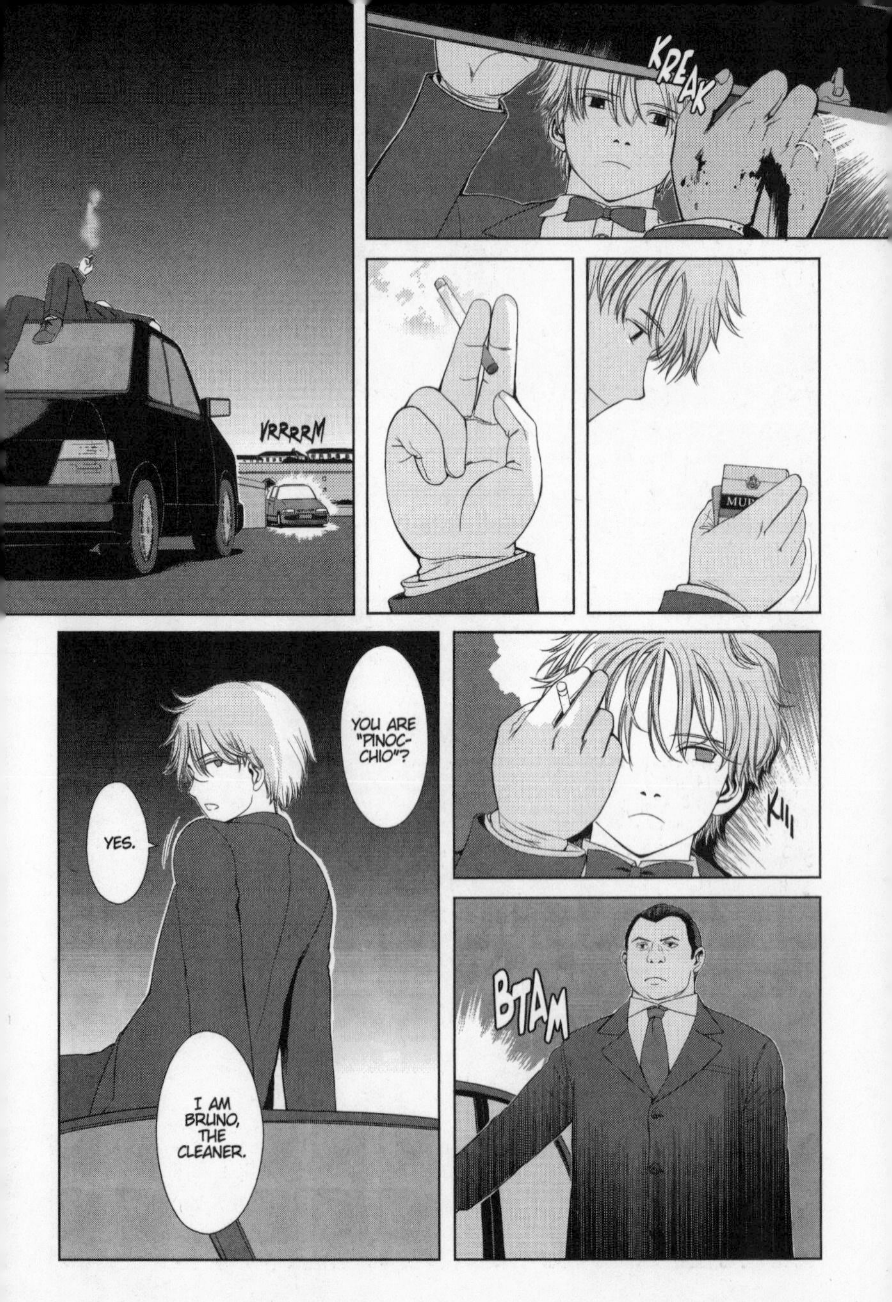
KREAK
VRRRRM
KIII
BTAM
YOU ARE "PINOC-CHIO"?
YES.
I AM BRUNO, THE CLEANER.

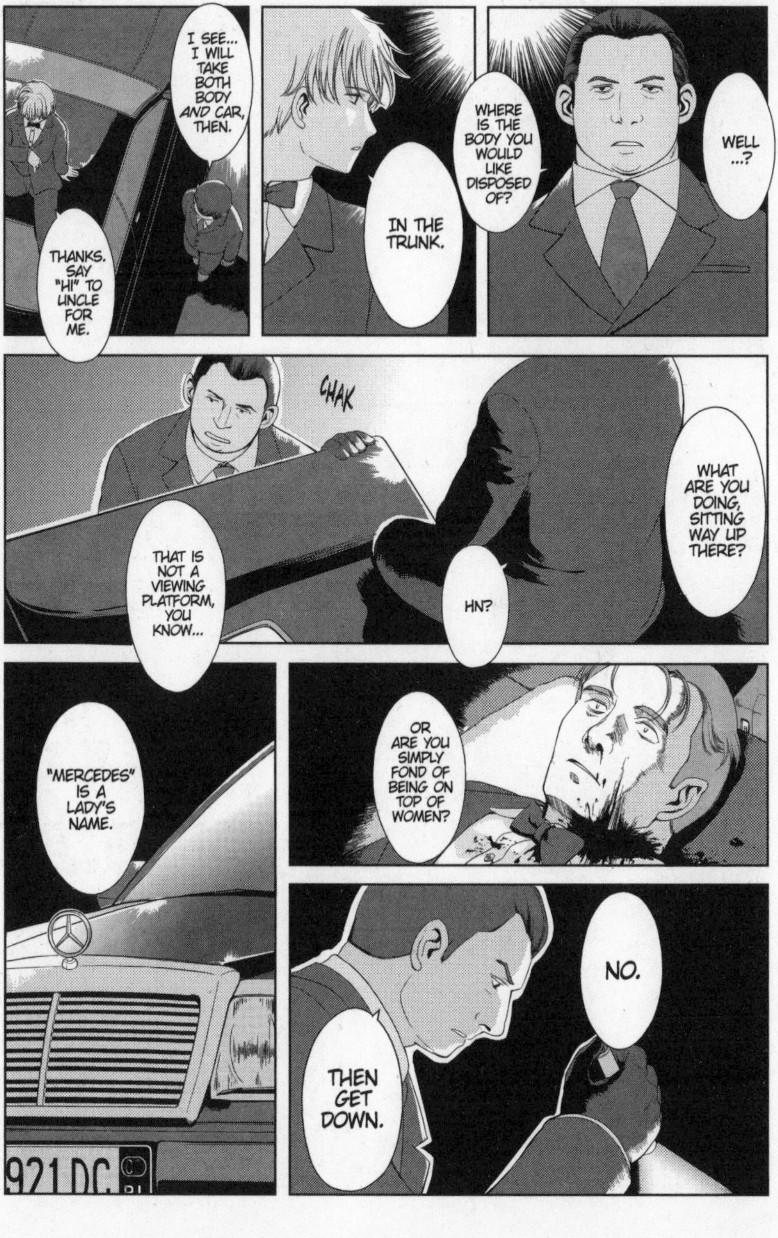
WELL ...?
WHERE IS THE BODY YOU WOULD LIKE DISPOSED OF?
IN THE TRUNK.
I SEE... I WILL TAKE BOTH BODY AND CAR, THEN.
THANKS. SAY "HI" TO UNCLE FOR ME.
CHAK
WHAT ARE YOU DOING, SITTING WAY UP THERE?
HN?
THAT IS NOT A VIEWING PLATFORM, YOU KNOW...
OR ARE YOU SIMPLY FOND OF BEING ON TOP OF WOMEN?
NO.
THEN GET DOWN.
"MERCEDES" IS A LADY'S NAME.
921 DC

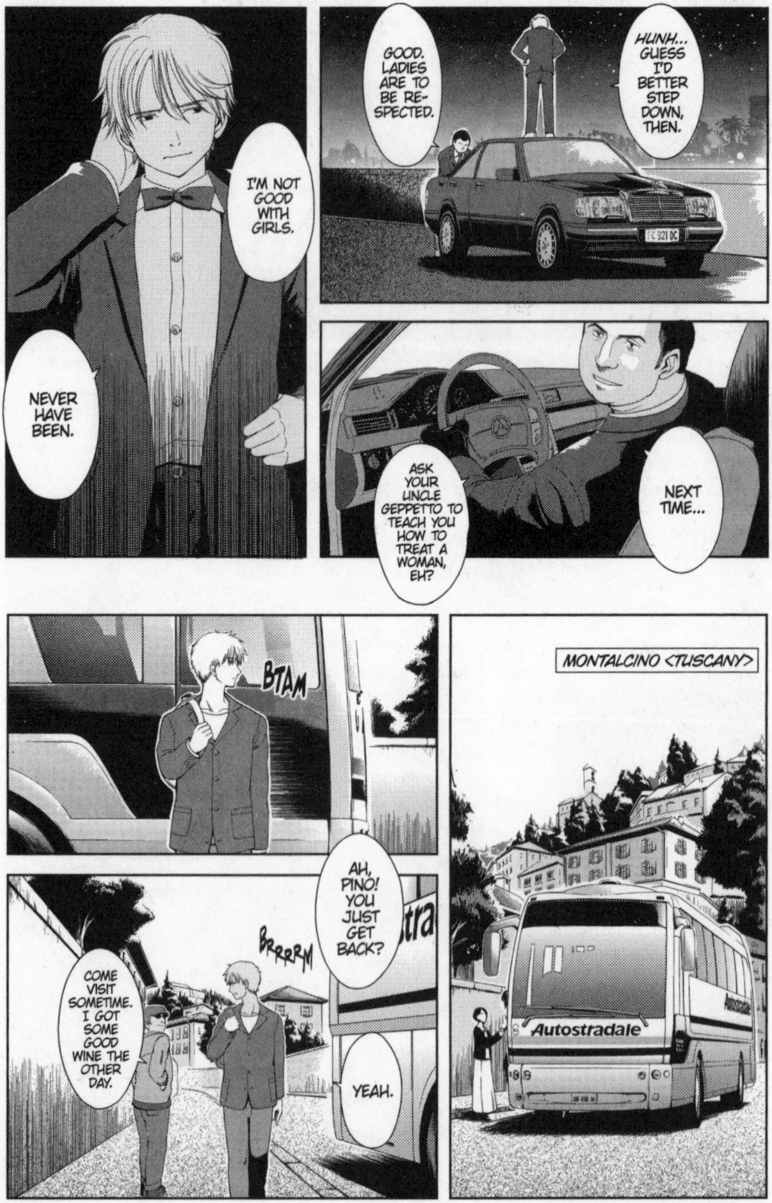
HUNH... GUESS I'D BETTER STEP DOWN, THEN.
GOOD. LADIES ARE TO BE RE-SPECTED.
NEXT TIME...
ASK YOUR UNCLE GEPPETTO TO TEACH YOU HOW TO TREAT A WOMAN, EH?
I'M NOT GOOD WITH GIRLS.
NEVER HAVE BEEN.
MONTALCINO <TUSCANY>
Autostradale
BTAM
AH, PINO! YOU JUST GET BACK?
BRRRRM
COME VISIT SOMETIME. I GOT SOME GOOD WINE THE OTHER DAY.
YEAH.

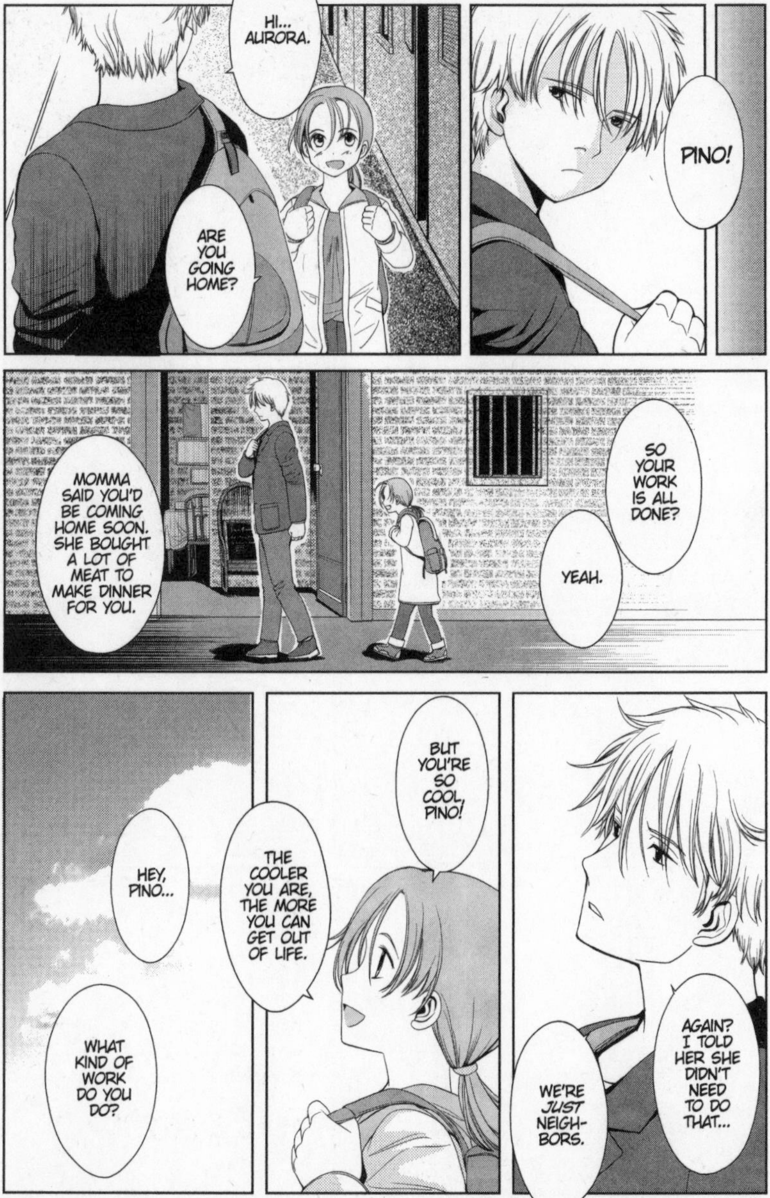
PINO!
HI... AURORA.
ARE YOU GOING HOME?
SO YOUR WORK IS ALL DONE?
YEAH.
MOMMA SAID YOU'D BE COMING HOME SOON. SHE BOUGHT A LOT OF MEAT TO MAKE DINNER FOR YOU.
AGAIN? I TOLD HER SHE DIDN'T NEED TO DO THAT...
WE'RE *JUST* NEIGHBORS.
BUT YOU'RE SO COOL, PINO!
THE COOLER YOU ARE, THE MORE YOU CAN GET OUT OF LIFE.
HEY, PINO...
WHAT KIND OF WORK DO YOU DO?

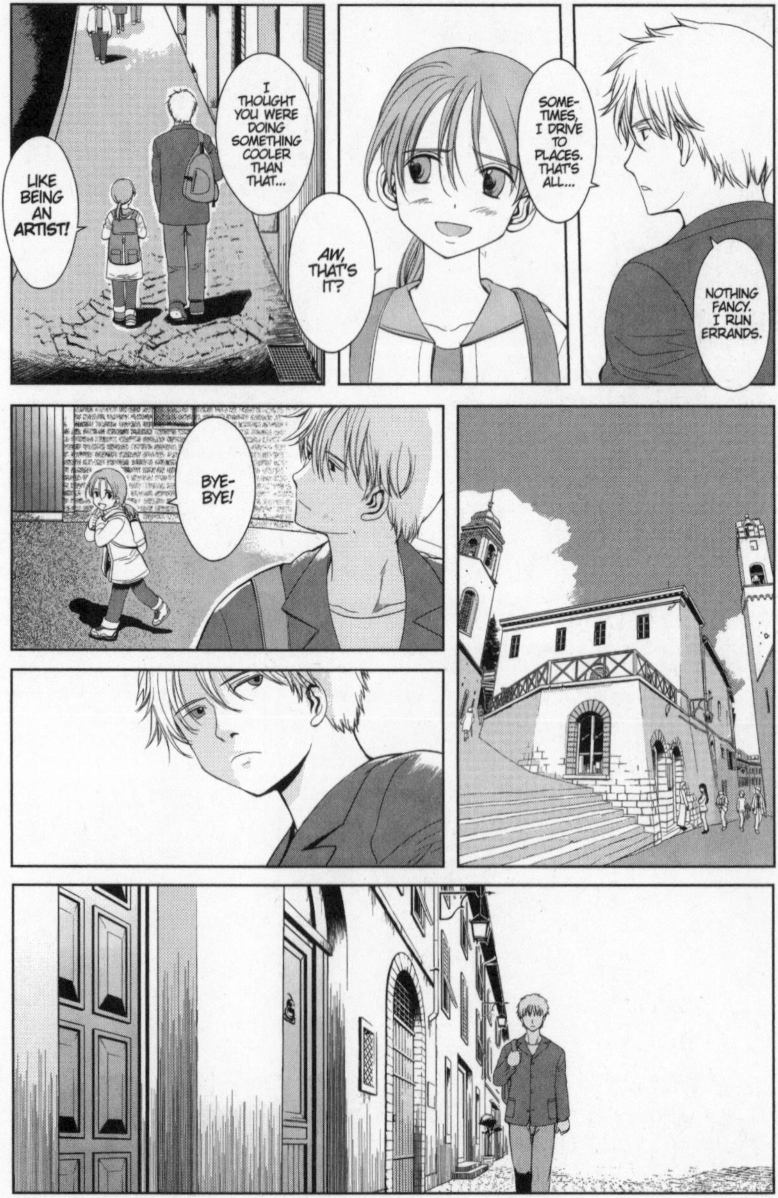
NOTHING FANCY. I RUN ERRANDS.
SOME-TIMES, I DRIVE TO PLACES. THAT'S ALL...
AW, THAT'S IT?
I THOUGHT YOU WERE DOING SOMETHING COOLER THAN THAT...
LIKE BEING AN ARTIST!
BYE-BYE!

TUNK
コト・・
……
SHHK

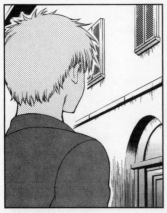

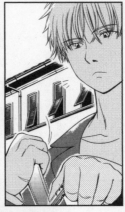

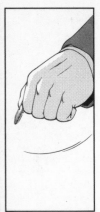

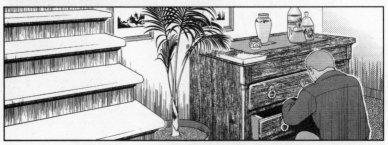

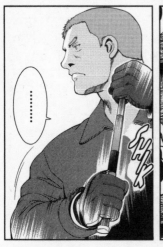

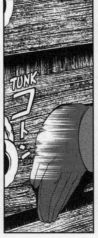

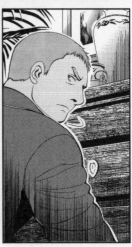

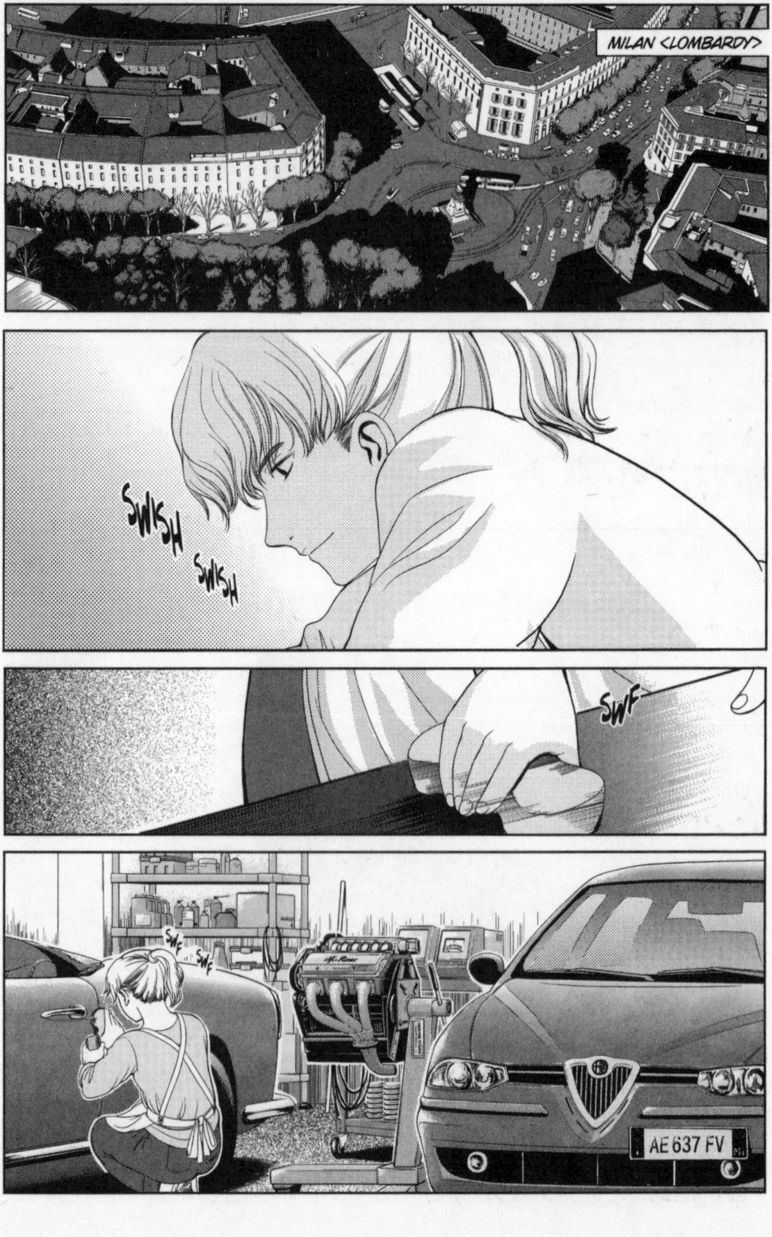
MILAN <LOMBARDY>
SWISH
SWISH
SWF
SWF
SWF

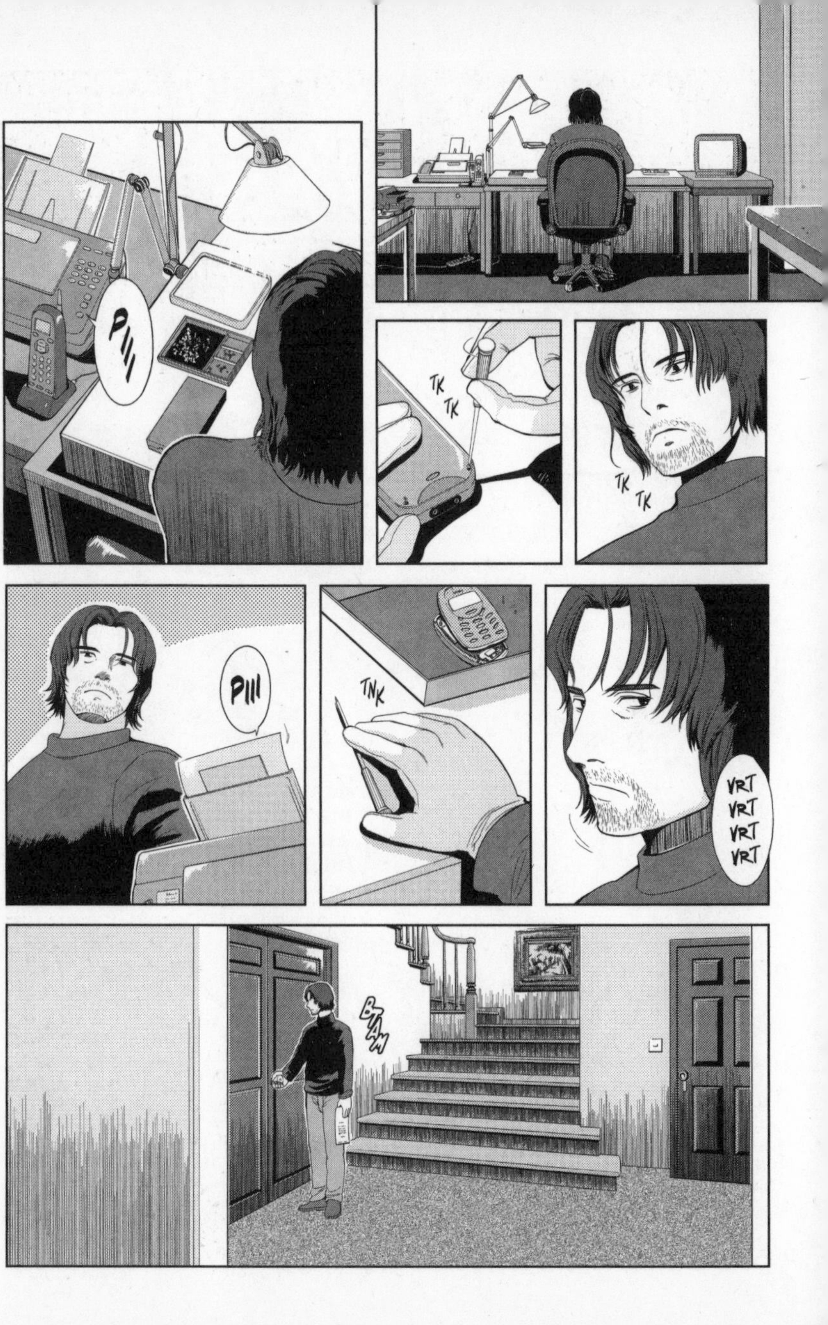
TK TK
TK TK
PIII
VRT VRT VRT VRT
TNK
PIII
BLAM

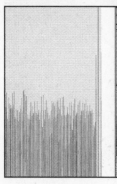

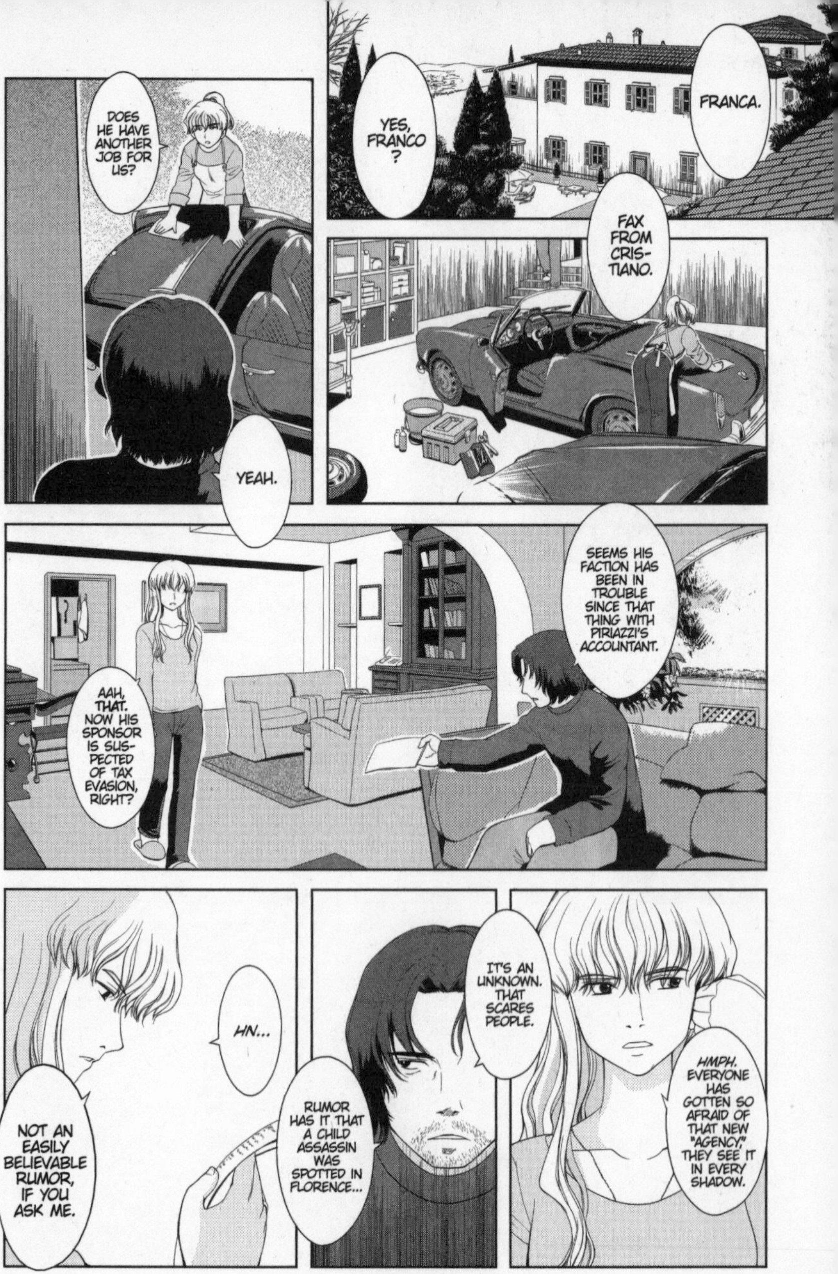
FRANCA.
YES, FRANCO?
FAX FROM CRIS-TIANO.
DOES HE HAVE ANOTHER JOB FOR US?
YEAH.
SEEMS HIS FACTION HAS BEEN IN TROUBLE SINCE THAT THING WITH PIRIAZZI'S ACCOUNTANT.
AAH, THAT. NOW HIS SPONSOR IS SUS-PECTED OF TAX EVASION, RIGHT?
HMPH. EVERYONE HAS GOTTEN SO AFRAID OF THAT NEW "AGENCY," THEY SEE IT IN EVERY SHADOW.
IT'S AN UNKNOWN. THAT SCARES PEOPLE.
RUMOR HAS IT THAT A CHILD ASSASSIN WAS SPOTTED IN FLORENCE...
HN...
NOT AN EASILY BELIEVABLE RUMOR, IF YOU ASK ME.

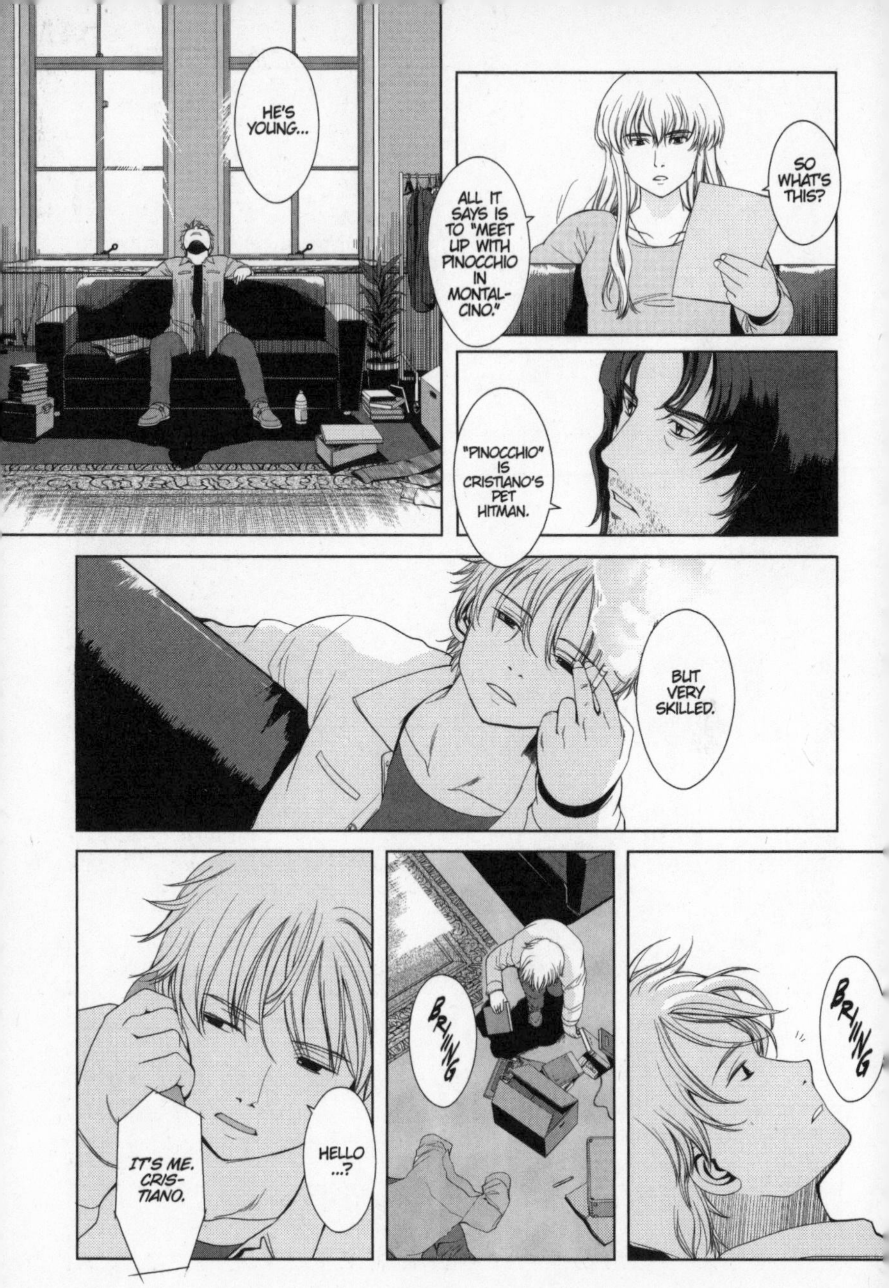
SO WHAT'S THIS?
ALL IT SAYS IS TO "MEET UP WITH PINOCCHIO IN MONTAL-CINO."
"PINOCCHIO" IS CRISTIANO'S PET HITMAN.
HE'S YOUNG...
BUT VERY SKILLED.
BRIIING
BRIIING
HELLO ...?
IT'S ME. CRIS-TIANO.

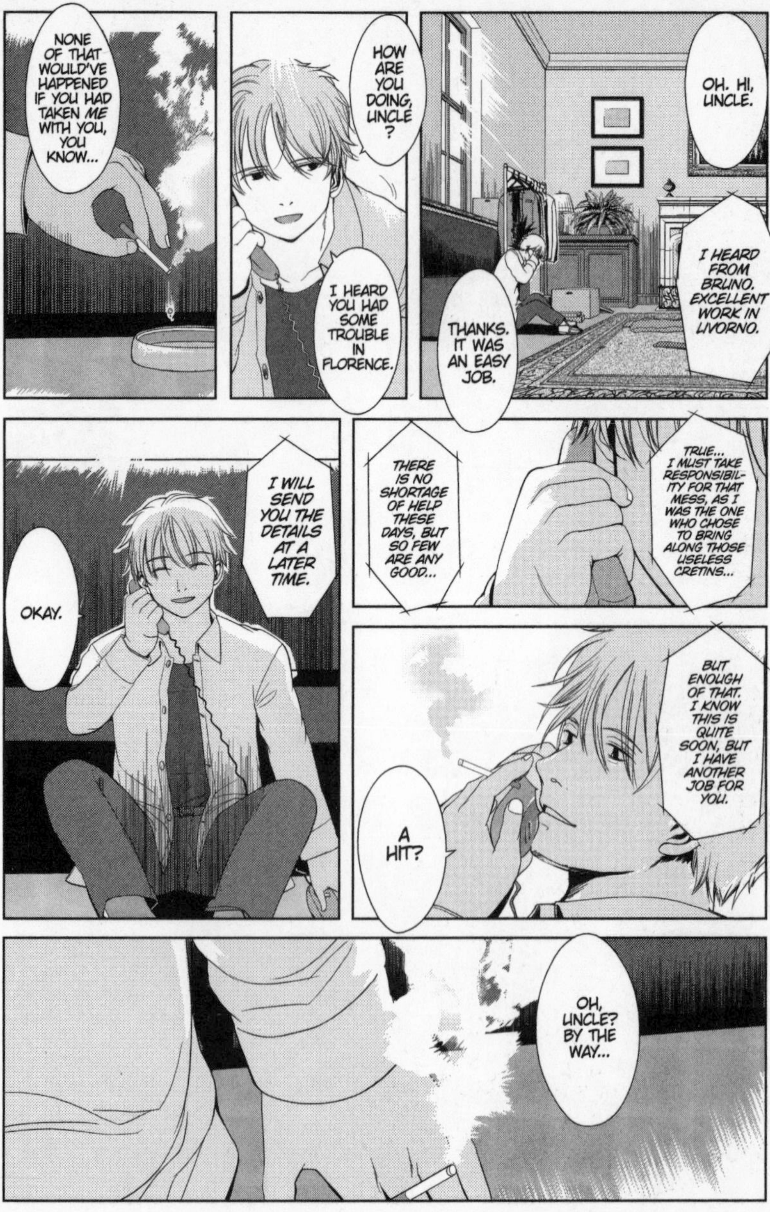
OH. HI, UNCLE.
I HEARD FROM BRUNO. EXCELLENT WORK IN LIVORNO.
THANKS. IT WAS AN EASY JOB.
HOW ARE YOU DOING, UNCLE?
I HEARD YOU HAD SOME TROUBLE IN FLORENCE.
NONE OF THAT WOULD'VE HAPPENED IF YOU HAD TAKEN *ME* WITH YOU, YOU KNOW...
TRUE... I MUST TAKE RESPONSIBILITY FOR THAT MESS, AS I WAS THE ONE WHO CHOSE TO BRING ALONG THOSE USELESS CRETINS...
THERE IS NO SHORTAGE OF HELP THESE DAYS, BUT SO FEW ARE ANY GOOD...
BUT ENOUGH OF THAT. I KNOW THIS IS QUITE SOON, BUT I HAVE ANOTHER JOB FOR YOU.
A HIT?
I WILL SEND YOU THE DETAILS AT A LATER TIME.
OKAY.
OH, UNCLE? BY THE WAY...

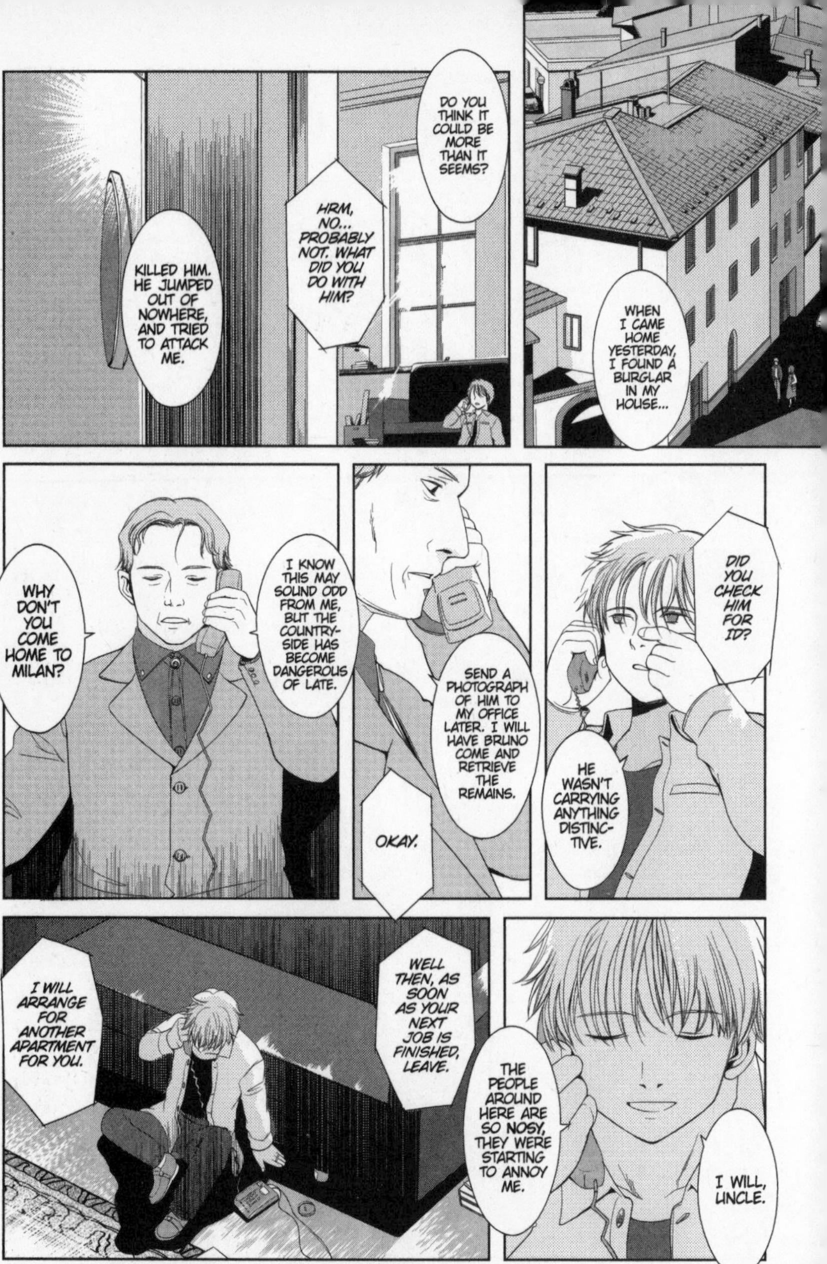
WHEN I CAME HOME YESTERDAY, I FOUND A BURGLAR IN MY HOUSE...
DO YOU THINK IT COULD BE MORE THAN IT SEEMS?
HRM, NO... PROBABLY NOT. WHAT DID YOU DO WITH HIM?
KILLED HIM. HE JUMPED OUT OF NOWHERE, AND TRIED TO ATTACK ME.
DID YOU CHECK HIM FOR ID?
HE WASN'T CARRYING ANYTHING DISTINC-TIVE.
SEND A PHOTOGRAPH OF HIM TO MY OFFICE LATER. I WILL HAVE BRUNO COME AND RETRIEVE THE REMAINS.
OKAY.
I KNOW THIS MAY SOUND ODD FROM ME, BUT THE COUNTRY-SIDE HAS BECOME DANGEROUS OF LATE.
WHY DON'T YOU COME HOME TO MILAN?
WELL THEN, AS SOON AS YOUR NEXT JOB IS FINISHED, LEAVE.
I WILL, UNCLE.
THE PEOPLE AROUND HERE ARE SO NOSY, THEY WERE STARTING TO ANNOY ME.
I WILL ARRANGE FOR ANOTHER APARTMENT FOR YOU.

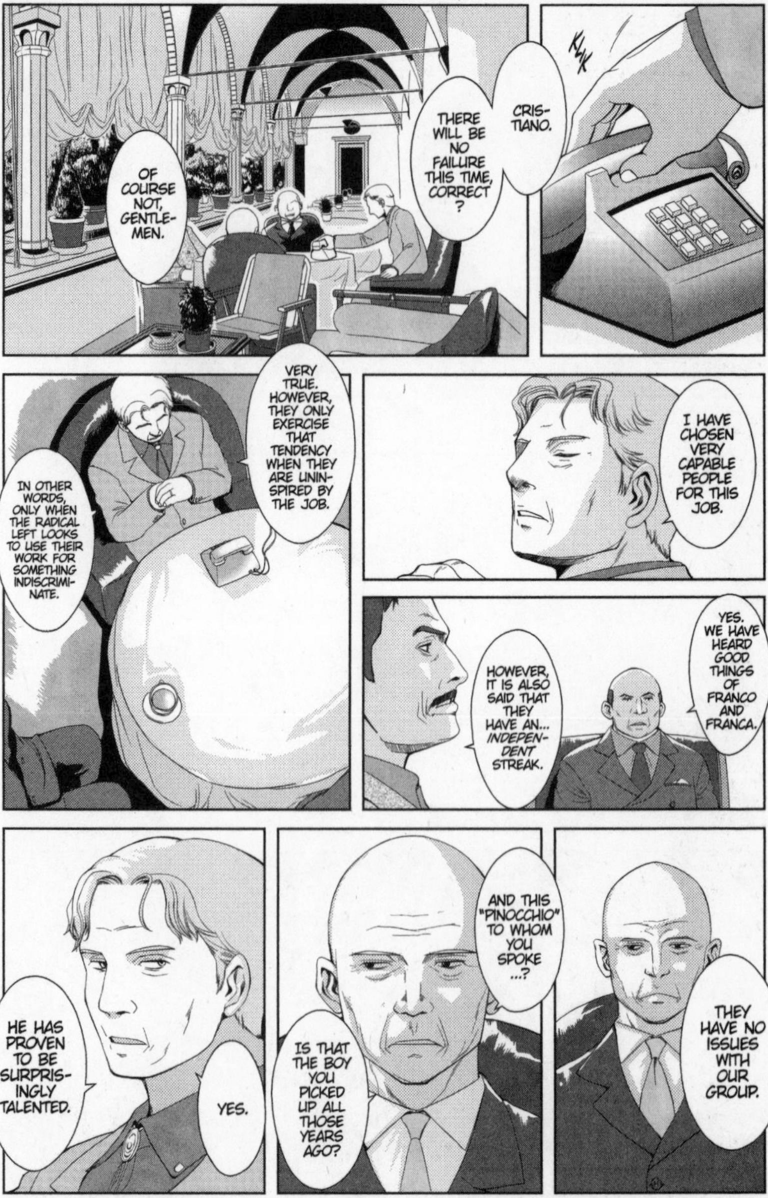
KLIK
CRIS-TIANO.
THERE WILL BE NO FAILURE THIS TIME, CORRECT?
OF COURSE NOT, GENTLEMEN.
I HAVE CHOSEN VERY CAPABLE PEOPLE FOR THIS JOB.
YES. WE HAVE HEARD GOOD THINGS OF FRANCO AND FRANCA.
HOWEVER, IT IS ALSO SAID THAT THEY HAVE AN... *INDEPENDENT* STREAK.
VERY TRUE. HOWEVER, THEY ONLY EXERCISE THAT TENDENCY WHEN THEY ARE UNINSPIRED BY THE JOB.
IN OTHER WORDS, ONLY WHEN THE RADICAL LEFT LOOKS TO USE THEIR WORK FOR SOMETHING INDISCRIMINATE.
THEY HAVE NO ISSUES WITH OUR GROUP.
AND THIS "PINOCCHIO" TO WHOM YOU SPOKE...?
IS THAT THE BOY YOU PICKED UP ALL THOSE YEARS AGO?
YES.
HE HAS PROVEN TO BE SURPRISINGLY TALENTED.

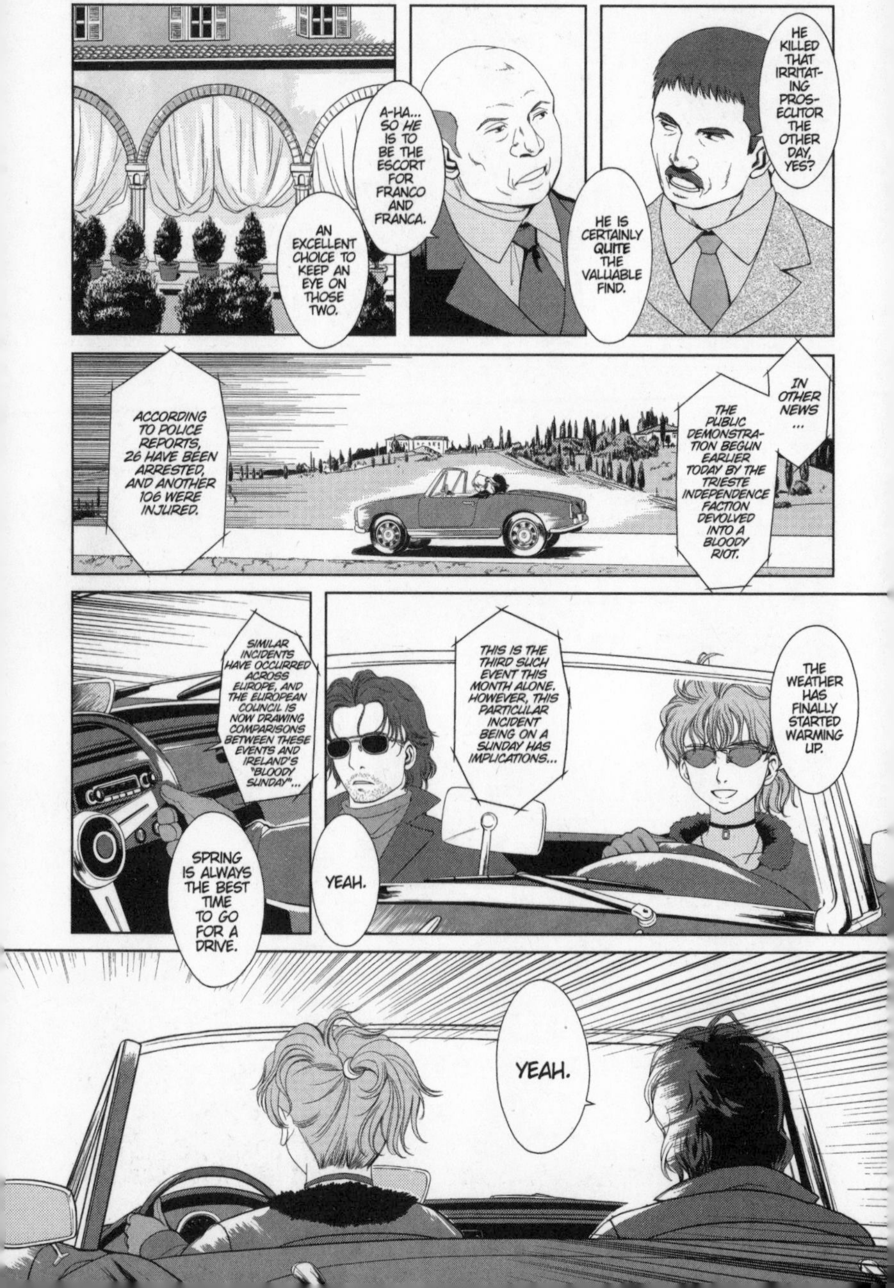
HE KILLED THAT IRRITATING PROSECUTOR THE OTHER DAY, YES?
HE IS CERTAINLY QUITE THE VALUABLE FIND.
A-HA... SO *HE* IS TO BE THE ESCORT FOR FRANCO AND FRANCA.
AN EXCELLENT CHOICE TO KEEP AN EYE ON THOSE TWO.
IN OTHER NEWS...
THE PUBLIC DEMONSTRATION BEGUN EARLIER TODAY BY THE TRIESTE INDEPENDENCE FACTION DEVOLVED INTO A BLOODY RIOT.
ACCORDING TO POLICE REPORTS, 26 HAVE BEEN ARRESTED, AND ANOTHER 106 WERE INJURED.
THE WEATHER HAS FINALLY STARTED WARMING UP.
THIS IS THE THIRD SUCH EVENT THIS MONTH ALONE. HOWEVER, THIS PARTICULAR INCIDENT BEING ON A SUNDAY HAS IMPLICATIONS...
YEAH.
SIMILAR INCIDENTS HAVE OCCURRED ACROSS EUROPE, AND THE EUROPEAN COUNCIL IS NOW DRAWING COMPARISONS BETWEEN THESE EVENTS AND IRELAND'S "BLOODY SUNDAY"...
SPRING IS ALWAYS THE BEST TIME TO GO FOR A DRIVE.
YEAH.

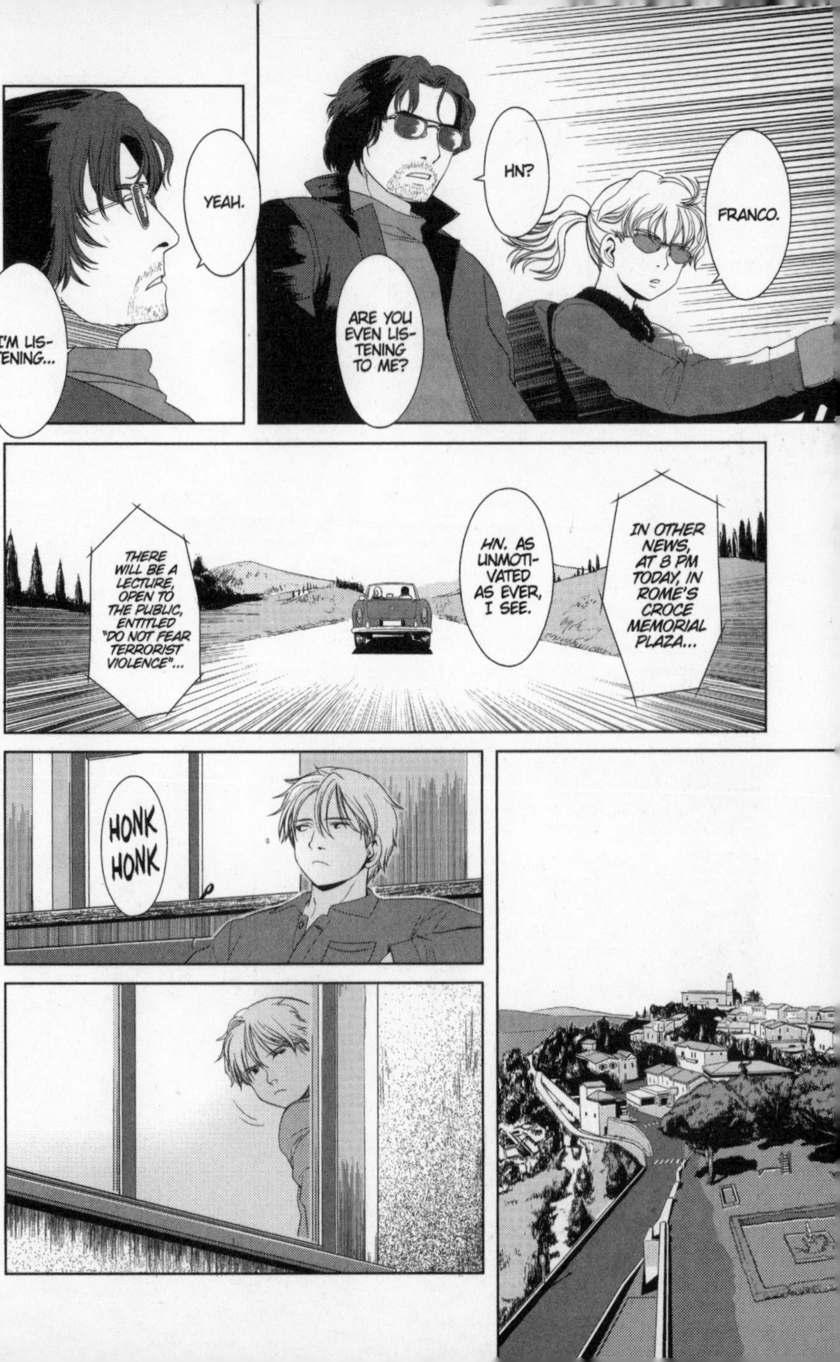
FRANCO.
HN?
ARE YOU EVEN LISTENING TO ME?
YEAH.
I'M LISTENING...
IN OTHER NEWS, AT 8 PM TODAY, IN ROME'S CROCE MEMORIAL PLAZA...
HN. AS UNMOTIVATED AS EVER, I SEE.
THERE WILL BE A LECTURE, OPEN TO THE PUBLIC, ENTITLED "DO NOT FEAR TERRORIST VIOLENCE"...
HONK HONK

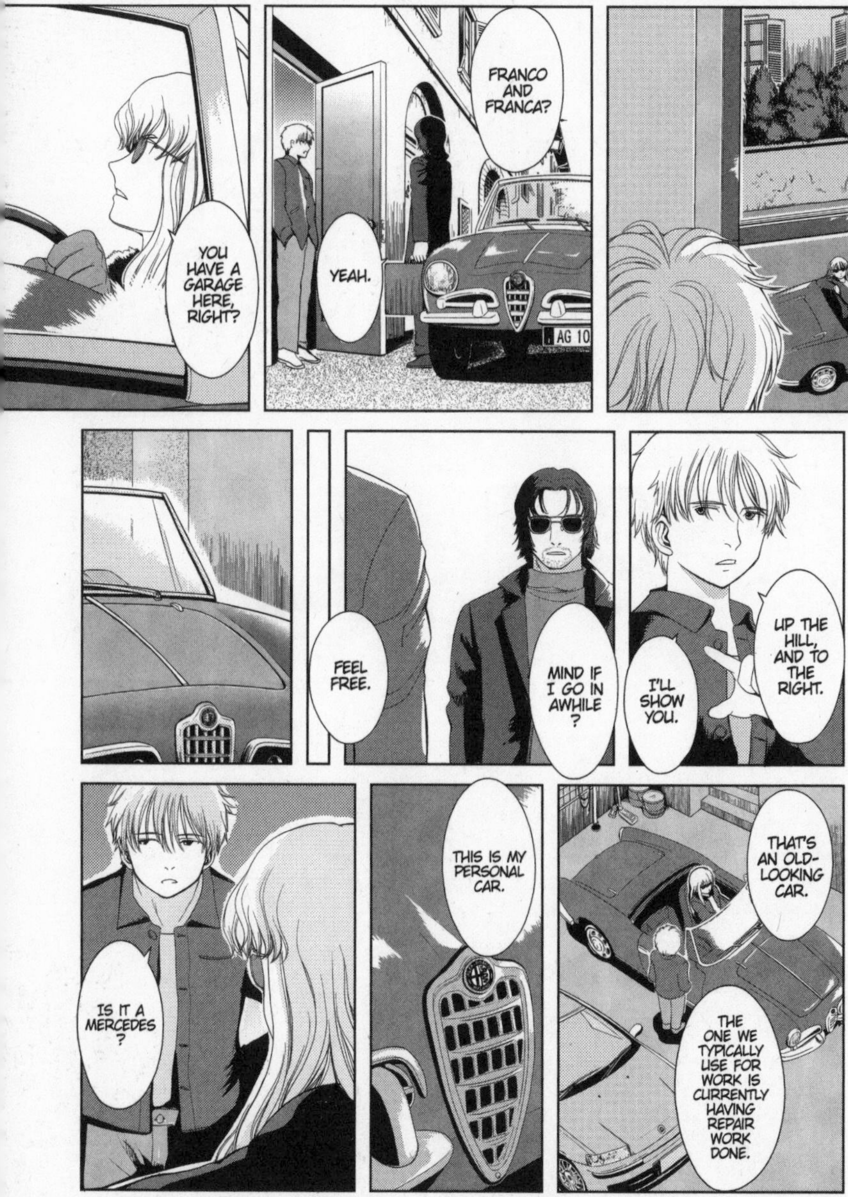
FRANCO AND FRANCA?
YEAH.
YOU HAVE A GARAGE HERE, RIGHT?
UP THE HILL, AND TO THE RIGHT.
I'LL SHOW YOU.
MIND IF I GO IN AWHILE ?
FEEL FREE.
THAT'S AN OLD-LOOKING CAR.
THE ONE WE TYPICALLY USE FOR WORK IS CURRENTLY HAVING REPAIR WORK DONE.
THIS IS MY PERSONAL CAR.
IS IT A MERCEDES ?

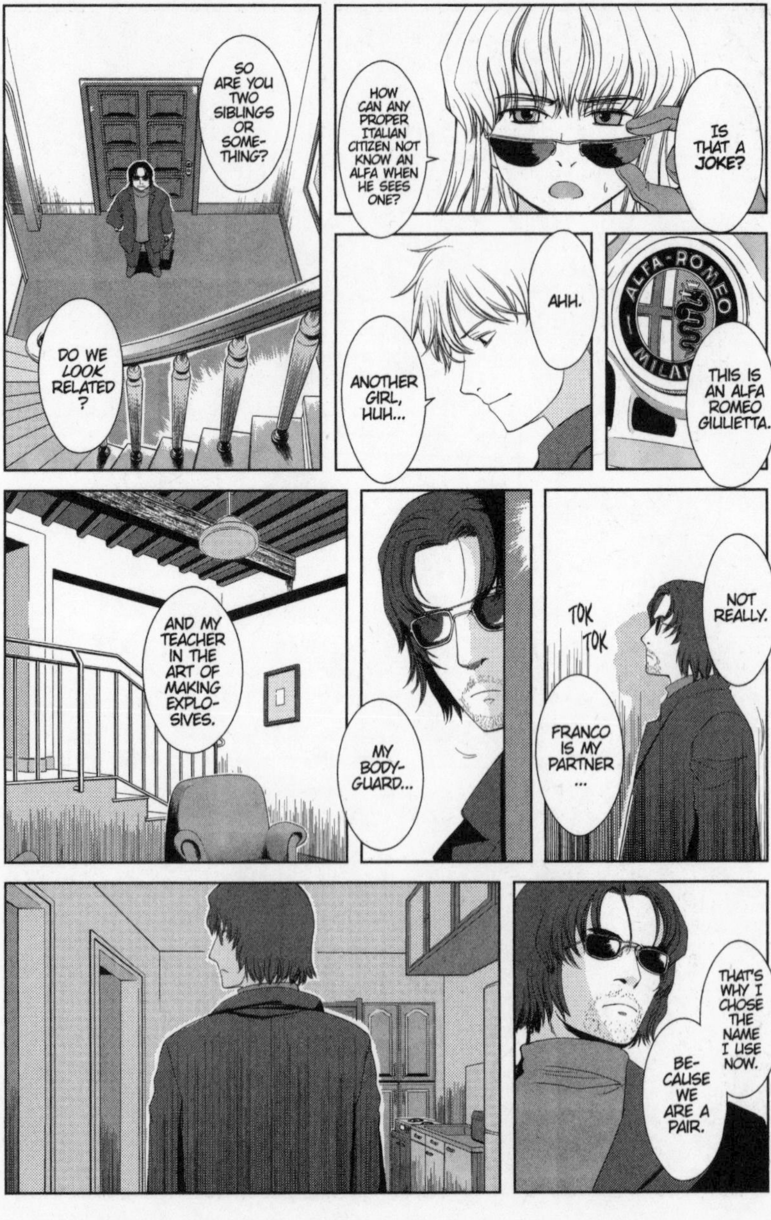
IS THAT A JOKE?
HOW CAN ANY PROPER ITALIAN CITIZEN NOT KNOW AN ALFA WHEN HE SEES ONE?
ALFA-ROMEO
THIS IS AN ALFA ROMEO GIULIETTA.
AHH.
ANOTHER GIRL, HUH...
SO ARE YOU TWO SIBLINGS OR SOME-THING?
DO WE LOOK RELATED?
NOT REALLY.
TOK TOK
FRANCO IS MY PARTNER...
MY BODY-GUARD...
AND MY TEACHER IN THE ART OF MAKING EXPLO-SIVES.
THAT'S WHY I CHOSE THE NAME I USE NOW.
BE-CAUSE WE ARE A PAIR.

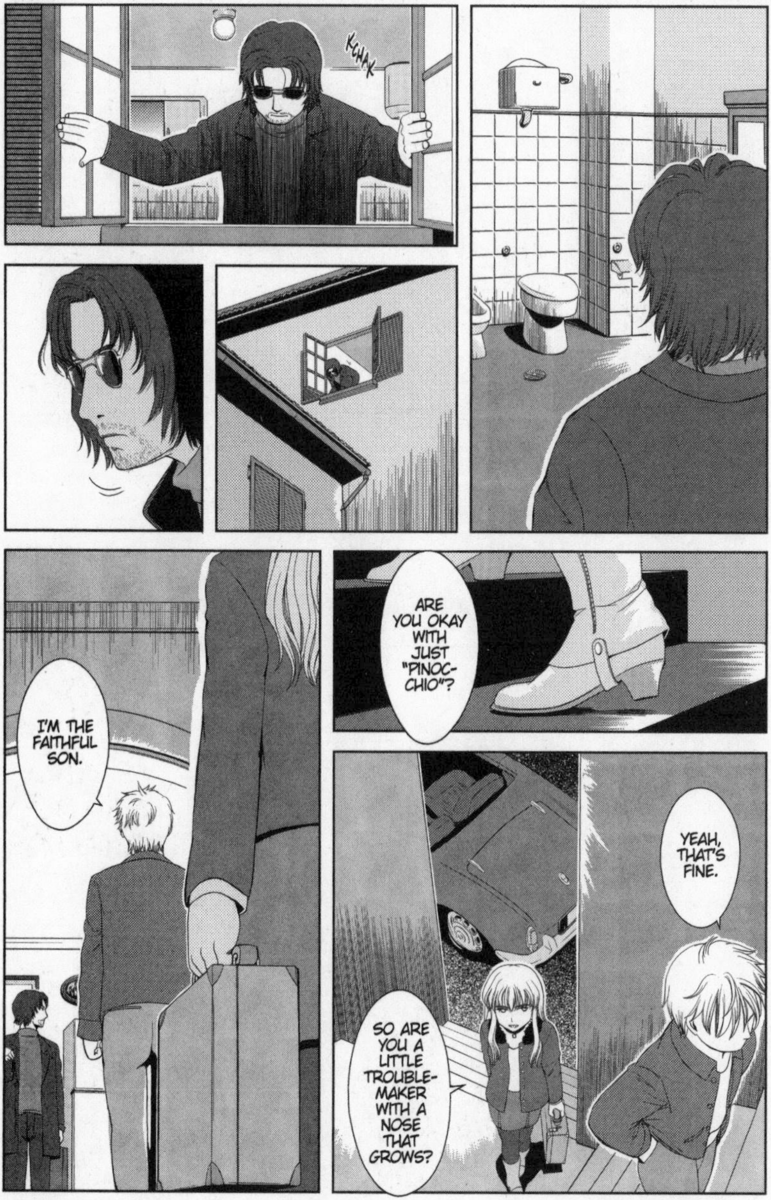
K-CHAK
ARE YOU OKAY WITH JUST "PINOCCHIO"?
YEAH, THAT'S FINE.
SO ARE YOU A LITTLE TROUBLEMAKER WITH A NOSE THAT GROWS?
I'M THE FAITHFUL SON.

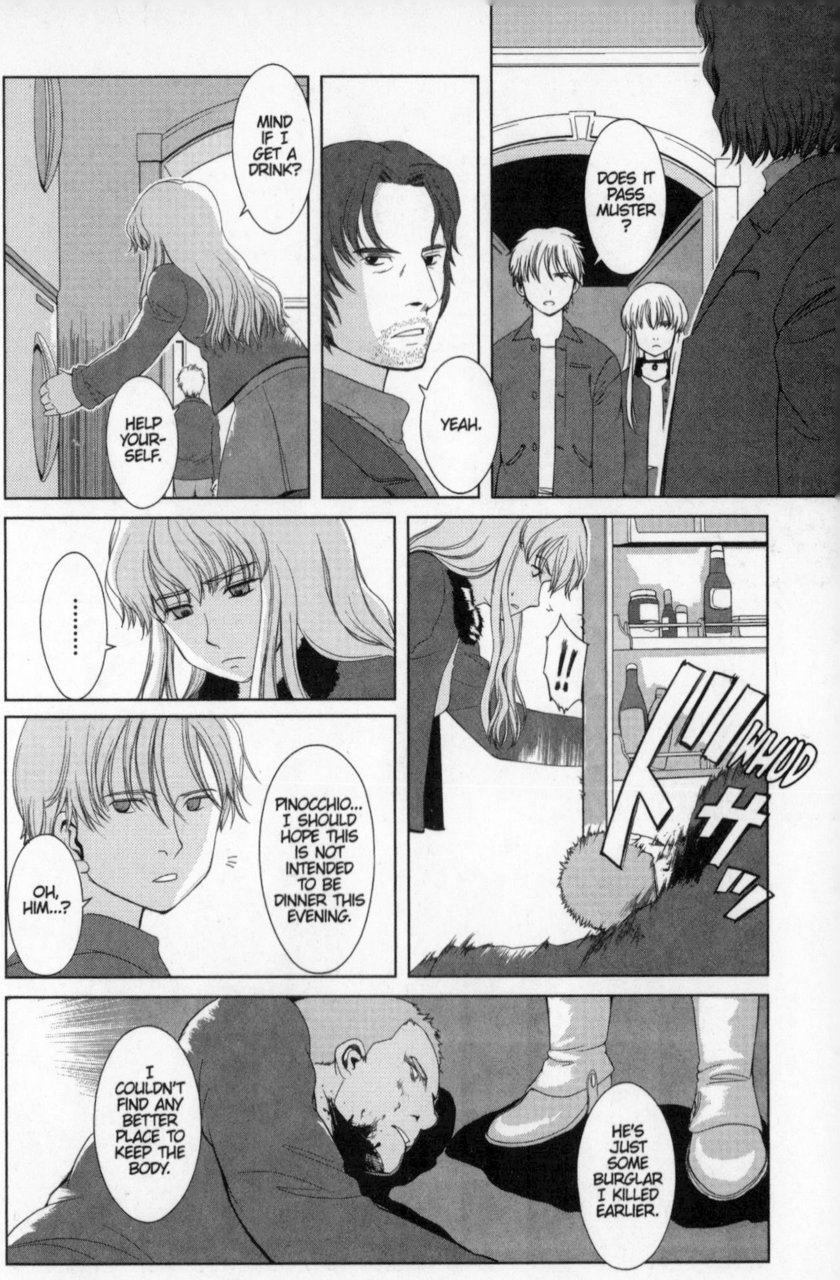
DOES IT PASS MUSTER?
YEAH.
MIND IF I GET A DRINK?
HELP YOURSELF.
!!
ドサッ
WHUD
....
PINOCCHIO... I SHOULD HOPE THIS IS NOT INTENDED TO BE DINNER THIS EVENING.
OH, HIM...?
HE'S JUST SOME BURGLAR I KILLED EARLIER.
I COULDN'T FIND ANY BETTER PLACE TO KEEP THE BODY.

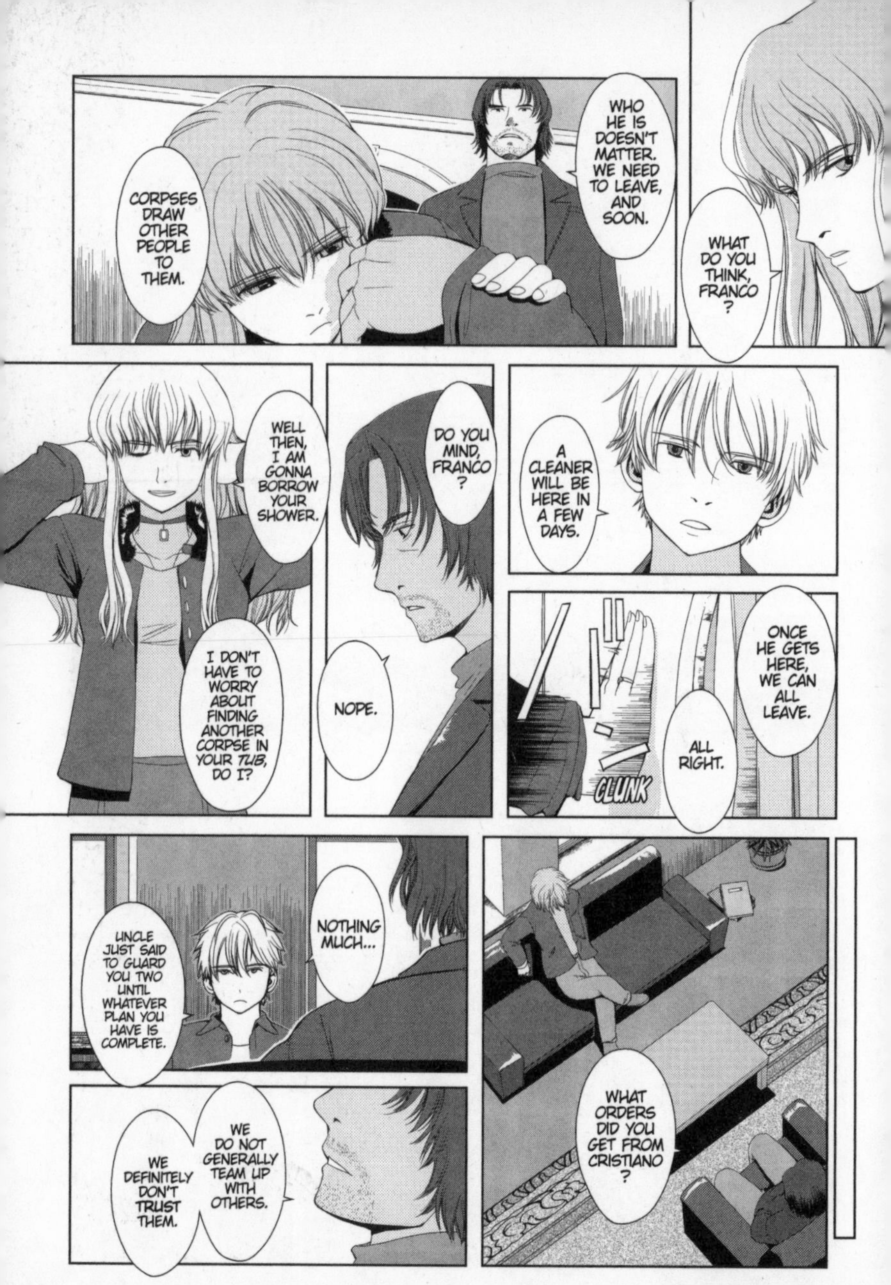
WHAT DO YOU THINK, FRANCO?
WHO HE IS DOESN'T MATTER. WE NEED TO LEAVE, AND SOON.
CORPSES DRAW OTHER PEOPLE TO THEM.
A CLEANER WILL BE HERE IN A FEW DAYS.
ONCE HE GETS HERE, WE CAN ALL LEAVE.
ALL RIGHT.
CLUNK
DO YOU MIND, FRANCO?
NOPE.
WELL THEN, I AM GONNA BORROW YOUR SHOWER.
I DON'T HAVE TO WORRY ABOUT FINDING ANOTHER CORPSE IN YOUR *TUB*, DO I?
WHAT ORDERS DID YOU GET FROM CRISTIANO?
NOTHING MUCH...
UNCLE JUST SAID TO GUARD YOU TWO UNTIL WHATEVER PLAN YOU HAVE IS COMPLETE.
WE DO NOT GENERALLY TEAM UP WITH OTHERS.
WE DEFINITELY DON'T **TRUST** THEM.

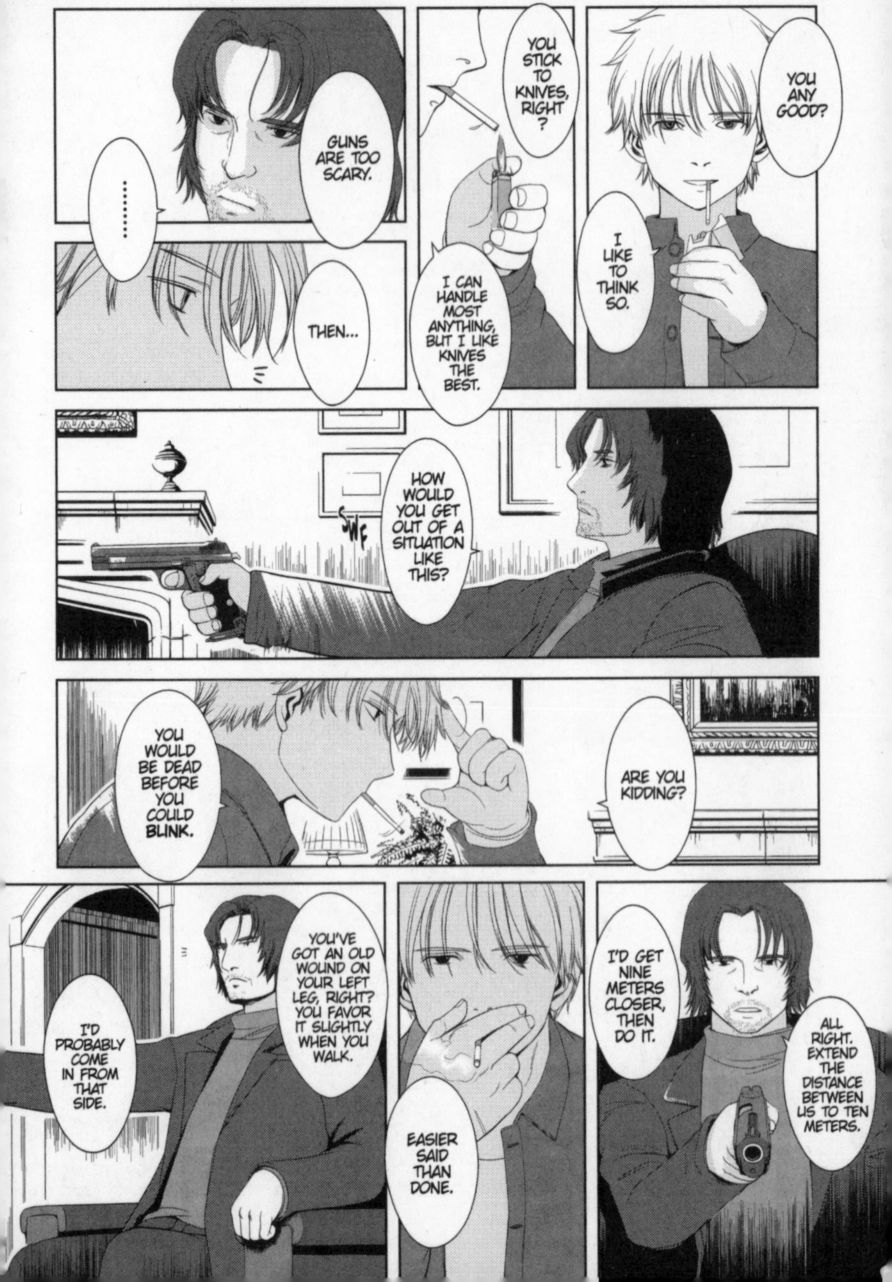

YOU ANY GOOD?
I LIKE TO THINK SO.
YOU STICK TO KNIVES, RIGHT?
I CAN HANDLE MOST ANYTHING, BUT I LIKE KNIVES THE BEST.
GUNS ARE TOO SCARY.
......
THEN...
HOW WOULD YOU GET OUT OF A SITUATION LIKE THIS?
SWF
ARE YOU KIDDING?
YOU WOULD BE DEAD BEFORE YOU COULD BLINK.
ALL RIGHT. EXTEND THE DISTANCE BETWEEN US TO TEN METERS.
I'D GET NINE METERS CLOSER, THEN DO IT.
YOU'VE GOT AN OLD WOUND ON YOUR LEFT LEG, RIGHT? YOU FAVOR IT SLIGHTLY WHEN YOU WALK.
EASIER SAID THAN DONE.
I'D PROBABLY COME IN FROM THAT SIDE.

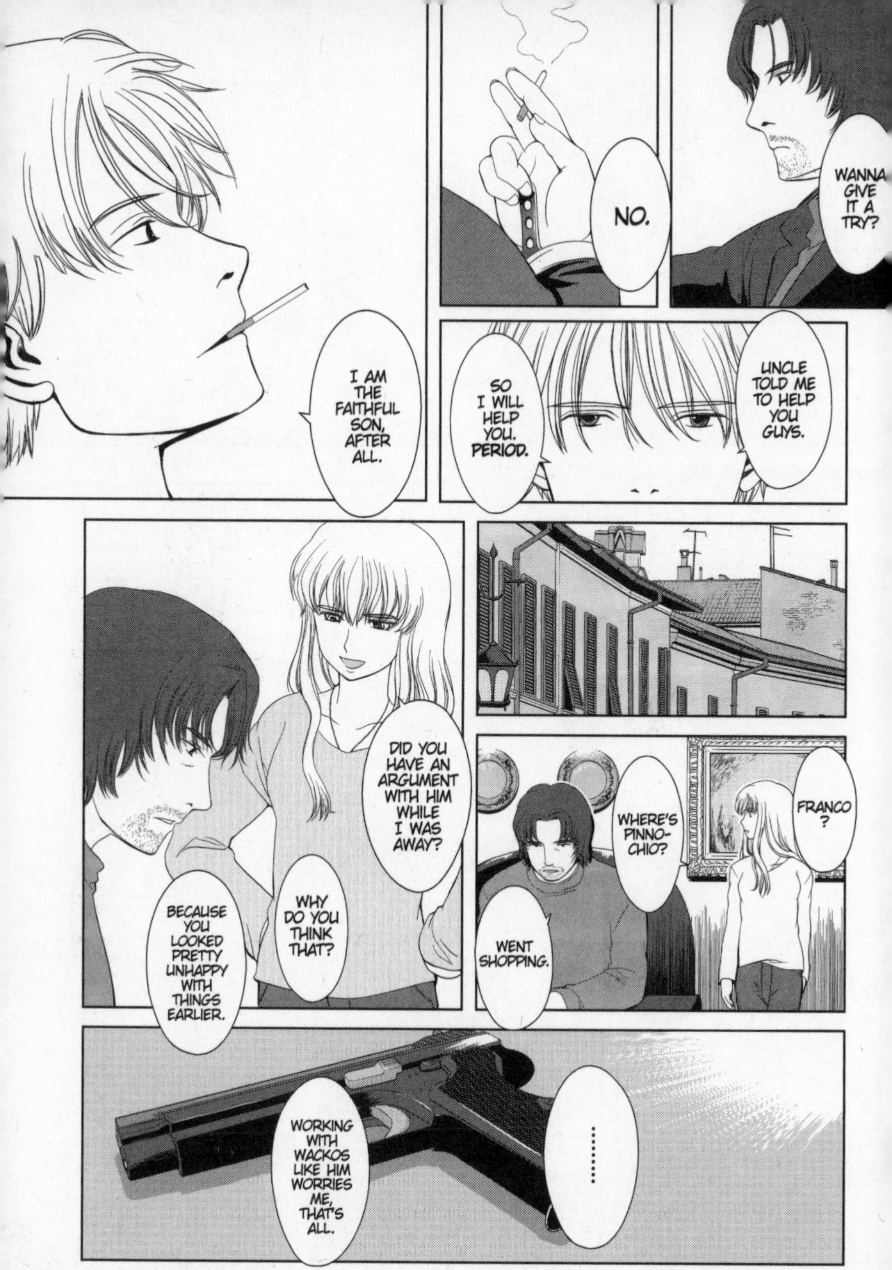
WANNA GIVE IT A TRY?
NO.
UNCLE TOLD ME TO HELP YOU GUYS.
SO I WILL HELP YOU. PERIOD.
I AM THE FAITHFUL SON, AFTER ALL.
FRANCO?
WHERE'S PINNO-CHIO?
WENT SHOPPING.
DID YOU HAVE AN ARGUMENT WITH HIM WHILE I WAS AWAY?
WHY DO YOU THINK THAT?
BECAUSE YOU LOOKED PRETTY UNHAPPY WITH THINGS EARLIER.
....
WORKING WITH WACKOS LIKE HIM WORRIES ME, THAT'S ALL.

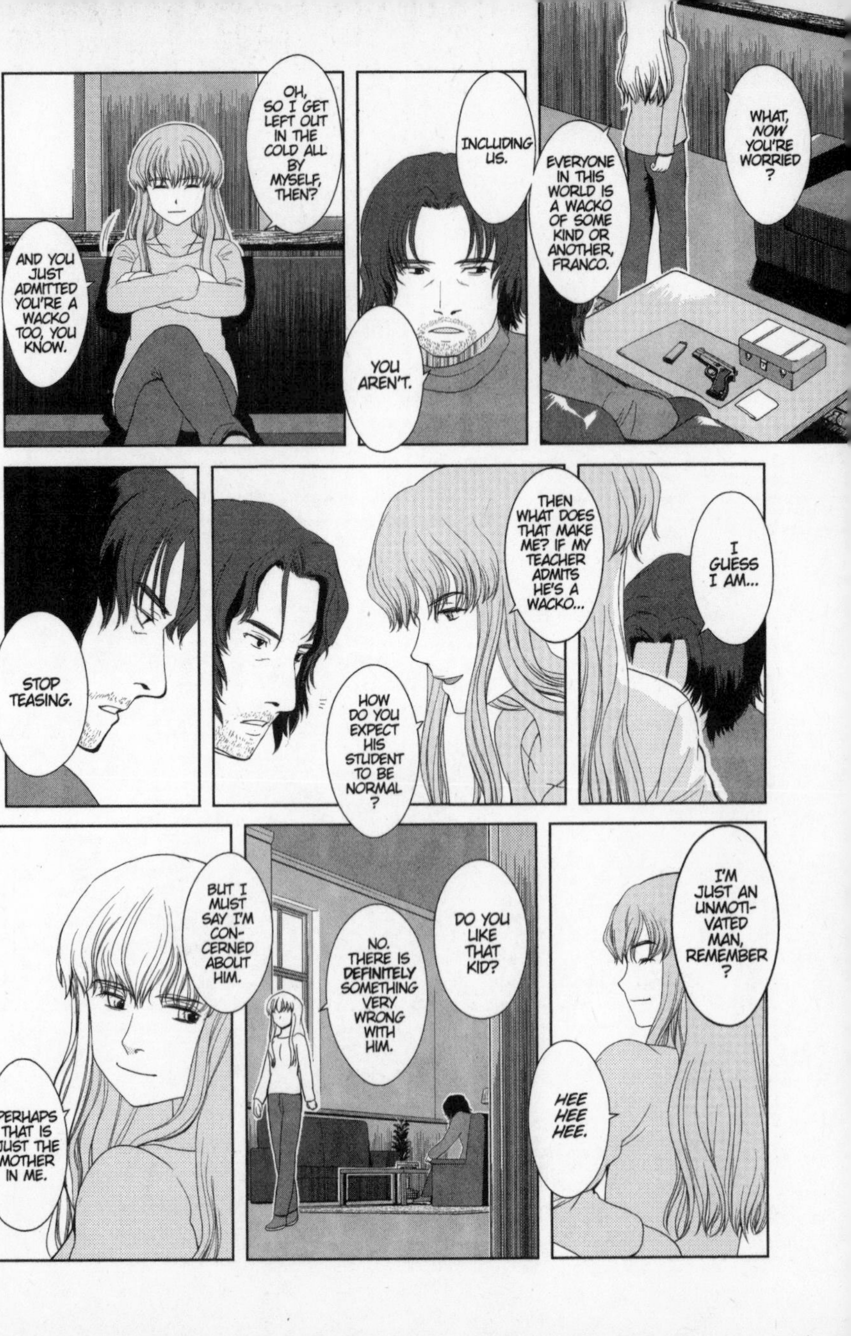
WHAT, NOW YOU'RE WORRIED?
EVERYONE IN THIS WORLD IS A WACKO OF SOME KIND OR ANOTHER, FRANCO.
INCLUDING US.
YOU AREN'T.
OH, SO I GET LEFT OUT IN THE COLD ALL BY MYSELF, THEN?
AND YOU JUST ADMITTED YOU'RE A WACKO TOO, YOU KNOW.
I GUESS I AM...
THEN WHAT DOES THAT MAKE ME? IF MY TEACHER ADMITS HE'S A WACKO...
HOW DO YOU EXPECT HIS STUDENT TO BE NORMAL?
STOP TEASING.
I'M JUST AN UNMOTI-VATED MAN, REMEMBER?
HEE HEE HEE.
DO YOU LIKE THAT KID?
NO. THERE IS DEFINITELY SOMETHING VERY WRONG WITH HIM.
BUT I MUST SAY I'M CON-CERNED ABOUT HIM.
PERHAPS THAT IS JUST THE MOTHER IN ME.

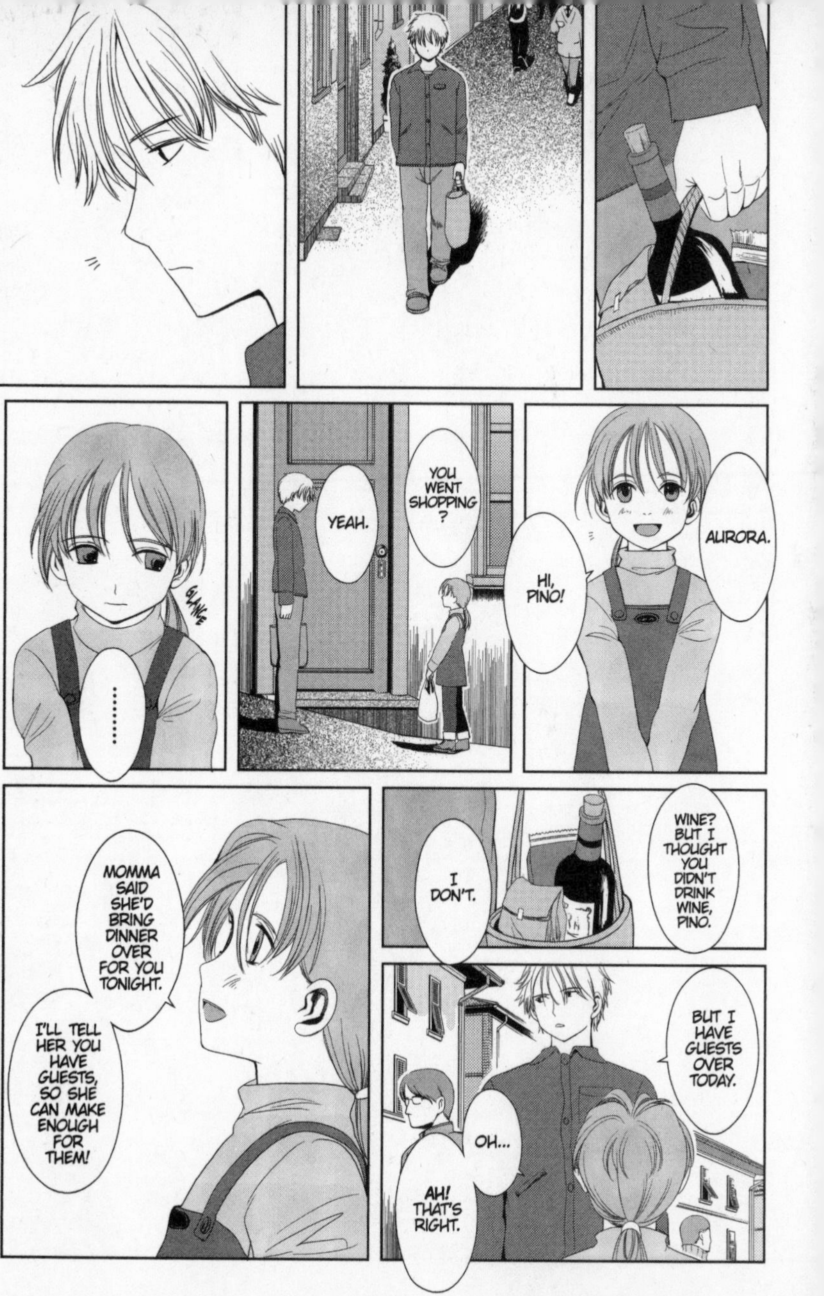
AURORA.
HI, PINO!
YOU WENT SHOPPING?
YEAH.
GLANCE
......
WINE? BUT I THOUGHT YOU DIDN'T DRINK WINE, PINO.
I DON'T.
BUT I HAVE GUESTS OVER TODAY.
OH...
AH! THAT'S RIGHT.
MOMMA SAID SHE'D BRING DINNER OVER FOR YOU TONIGHT.
I'LL TELL HER YOU HAVE GUESTS, SO SHE CAN MAKE ENOUGH FOR THEM!

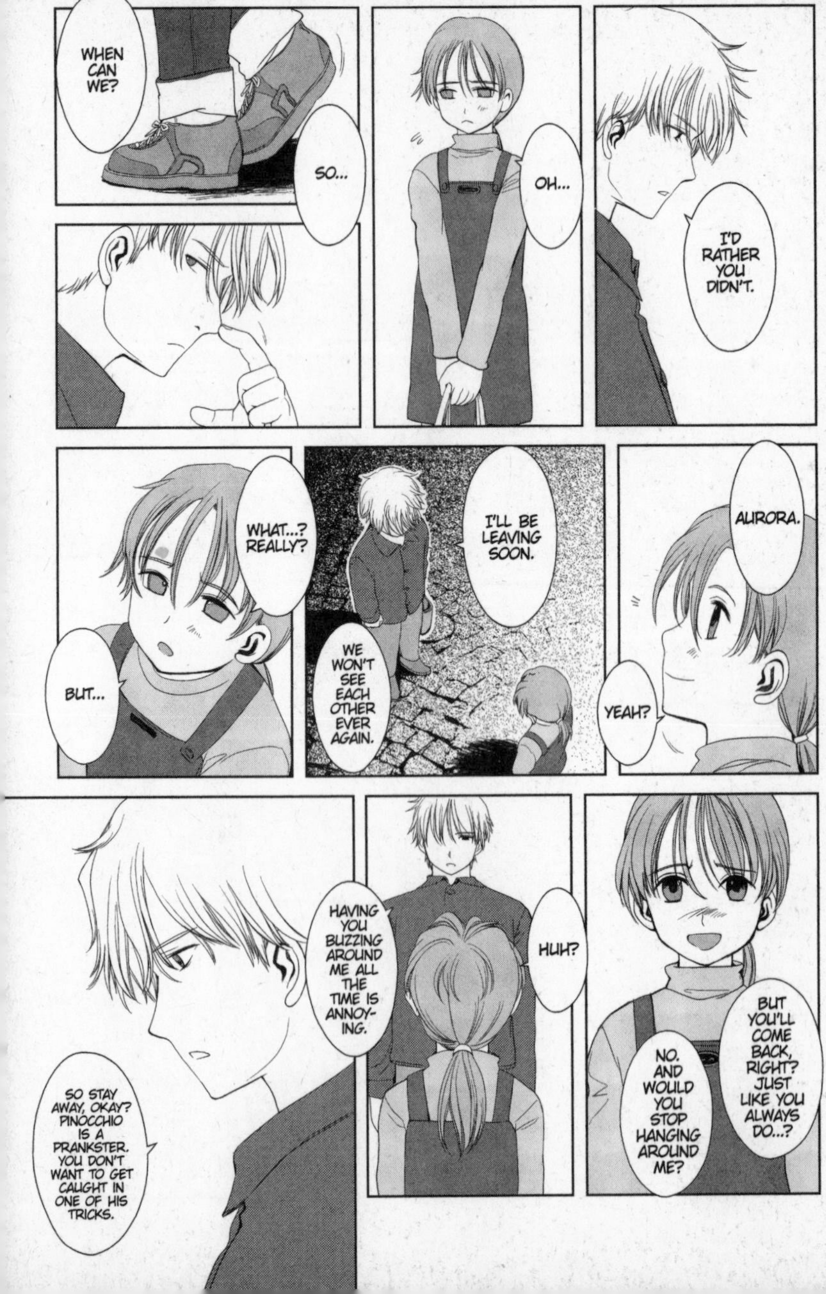
I'D RATHER YOU DIDN'T.
OH...
WHEN CAN WE?
SO...
AURORA.
YEAH?
I'LL BE LEAVING SOON.
WE WON'T SEE EACH OTHER EVER AGAIN.
WHAT...? REALLY?
BUT...
BUT YOU'LL COME BACK, RIGHT? JUST LIKE YOU ALWAYS DO...?
NO. AND WOULD YOU STOP HANGING AROUND ME?
HUH?
HAVING YOU BUZZING AROUND ME ALL THE TIME IS ANNOY-ING.
SO STAY AWAY, OKAY? PINOCCHIO IS A PRANKSTER. YOU DON'T WANT TO GET CAUGHT IN ONE OF HIS TRICKS.

GUNSLINGERGIRL.

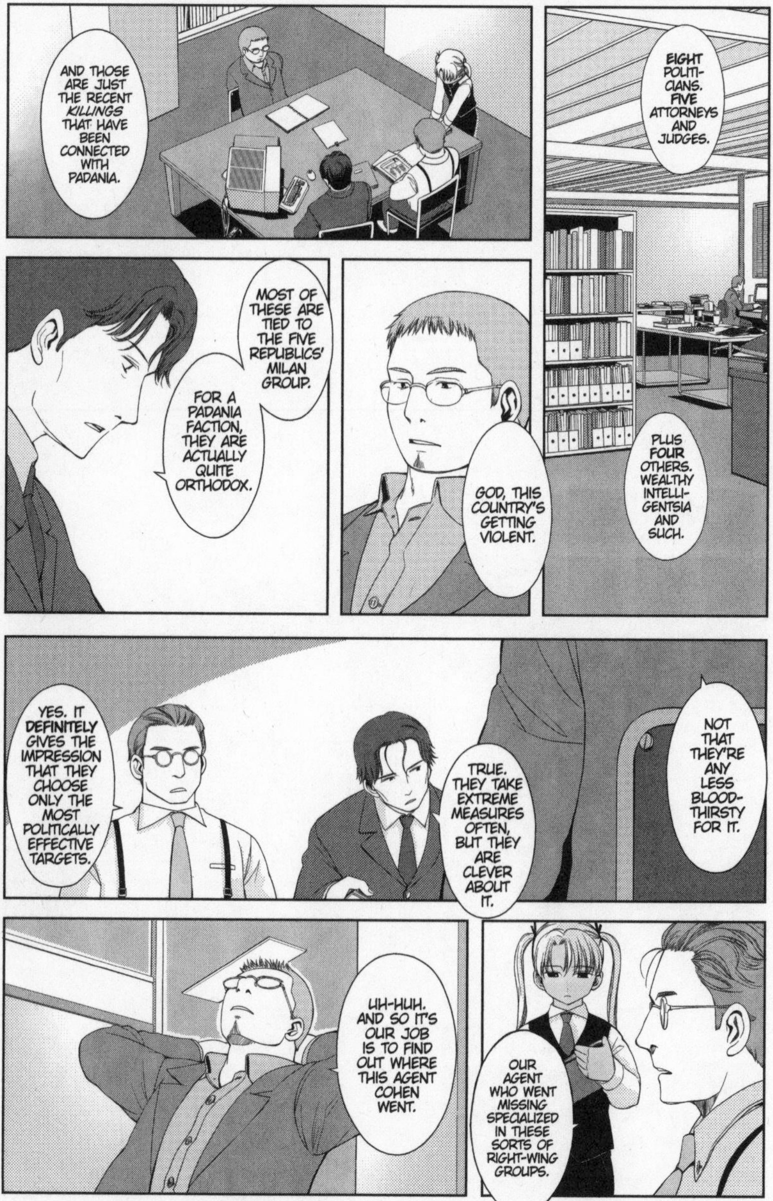
EIGHT POLITICIANS. FIVE ATTORNEYS AND JUDGES.
PLUS FOUR OTHERS. WEALTHY INTELLIGENTSIA AND SUCH.
AND THOSE ARE JUST THE RECENT *KILLINGS* THAT HAVE BEEN CONNECTED WITH PADANIA.
GOD, THIS COUNTRY'S GETTING VIOLENT.
MOST OF THESE ARE TIED TO THE FIVE REPUBLICS' MILAN GROUP.
FOR A PADANIA FACTION, THEY ARE ACTUALLY QUITE ORTHODOX.
YES. IT DEFINITELY GIVES THE IMPRESSION THAT THEY CHOOSE ONLY THE MOST POLITICALLY EFFECTIVE TARGETS.
TRUE. THEY TAKE EXTREME MEASURES OFTEN, BUT THEY ARE CLEVER ABOUT IT.
NOT THAT THEY'RE ANY LESS BLOODTHIRSTY FOR IT.
OUR AGENT WHO WENT MISSING SPECIALIZED IN THESE SORTS OF RIGHT-WING GROUPS.
UH-HUH. AND SO IT'S OUR JOB IS TO FIND OUT WHERE THIS AGENT COHEN WENT.

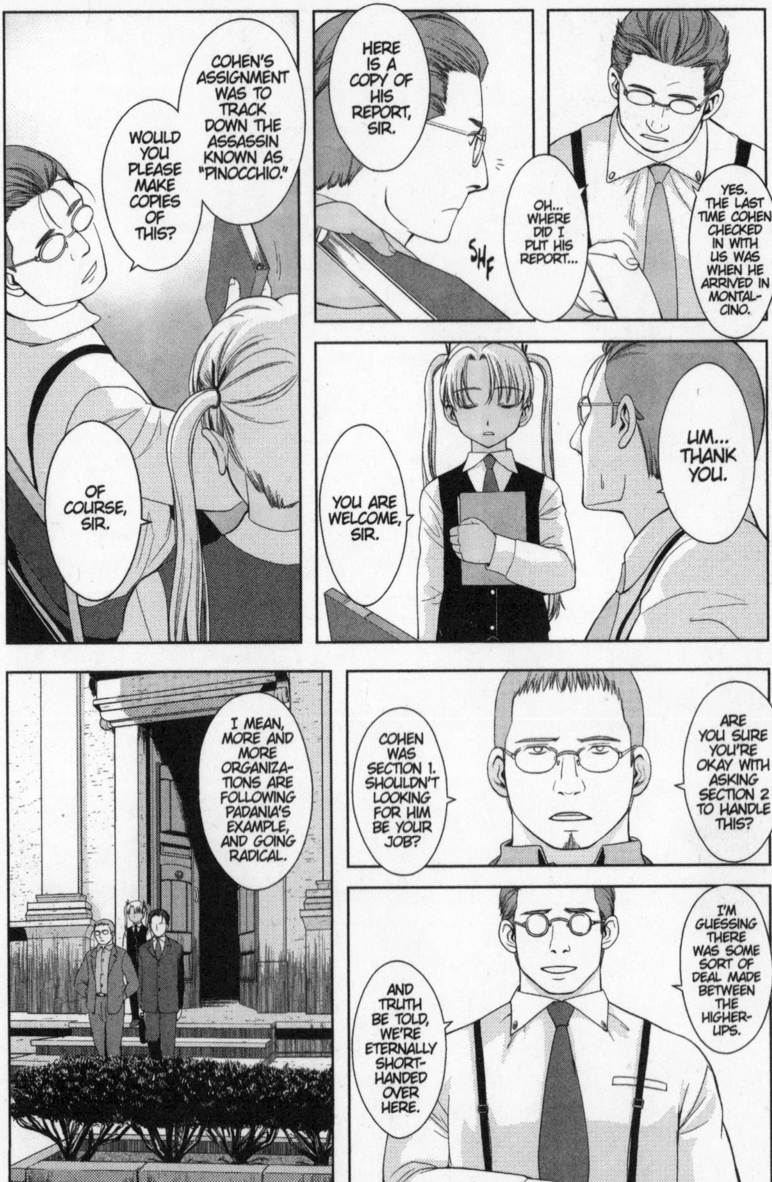
YES. THE LAST TIME COHEN CHECKED IN WITH US WAS WHEN HE ARRIVED IN MONTAL-CINO.
OH... WHERE DID I PUT HIS REPORT...
HERE IS A COPY OF HIS REPORT, SIR.
SHF
UM... THANK YOU.
YOU ARE WELCOME, SIR.
COHEN'S ASSIGNMENT WAS TO TRACK DOWN THE ASSASSIN KNOWN AS "PINOCCHIO."
WOULD YOU PLEASE MAKE COPIES OF THIS?
OF COURSE, SIR.
ARE YOU SURE YOU'RE OKAY WITH ASKING SECTION 2 TO HANDLE THIS?
COHEN WAS SECTION 1. SHOULDN'T LOOKING FOR HIM BE YOUR JOB?
I'M GUESSING THERE WAS SOME SORT OF DEAL MADE BETWEEN THE HIGHER-UPS.
AND TRUTH BE TOLD, WE'RE ETERNALLY SHORT-HANDED OVER HERE.
I MEAN, MORE AND MORE ORGANIZA-TIONS ARE FOLLOWING PADANIA'S EXAMPLE, AND GOING RADICAL.

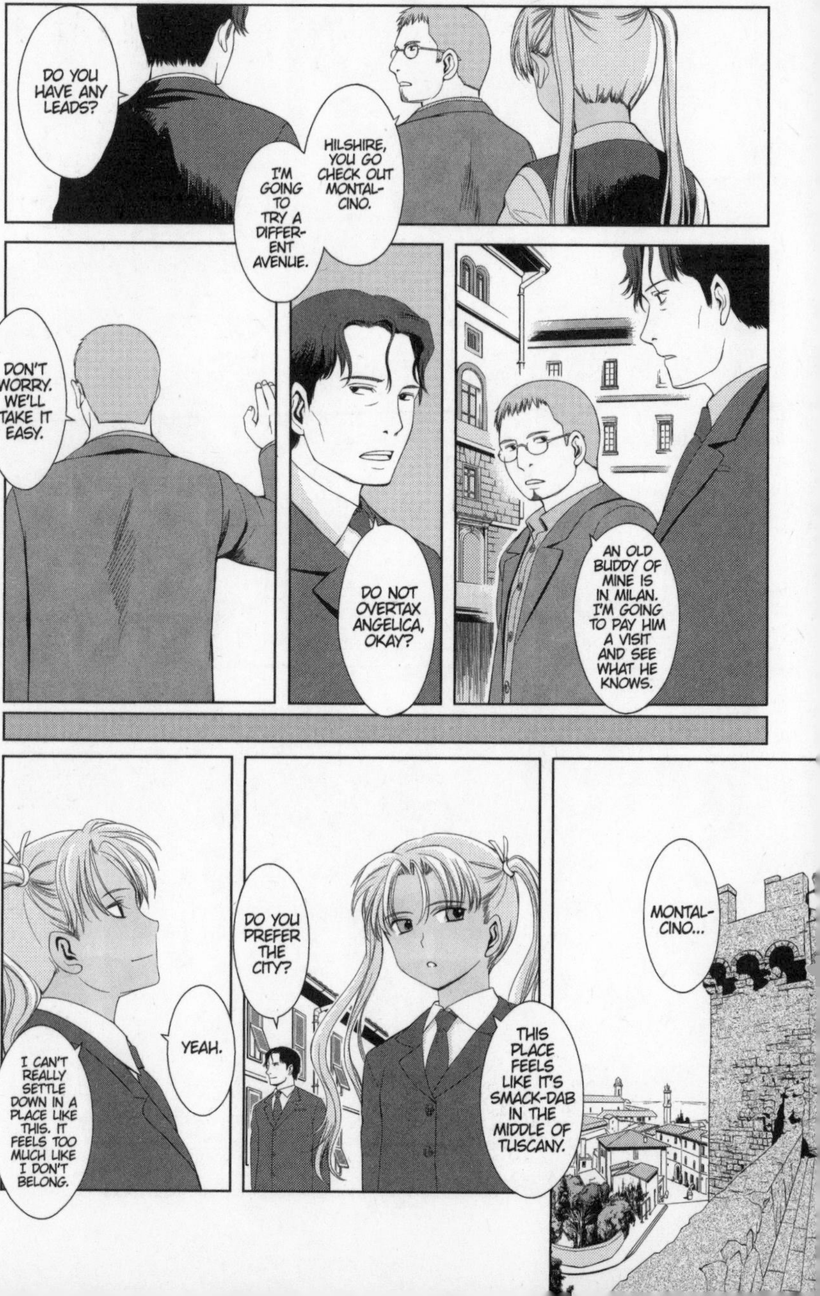
HILSHIRE, YOU GO CHECK OUT MONTALCINO.
I'M GOING TO TRY A DIFFERENT AVENUE.
DO YOU HAVE ANY LEADS?
AN OLD BUDDY OF MINE IS IN MILAN. I'M GOING TO PAY HIM A VISIT AND SEE WHAT HE KNOWS.
DO NOT OVERTAX ANGELICA, OKAY?
DON'T WORRY. WE'LL TAKE IT EASY.
MONTALCINO...
THIS PLACE FEELS LIKE IT'S SMACK-DAB IN THE MIDDLE OF TUSCANY.
DO YOU PREFER THE CITY?
YEAH.
I CAN'T REALLY SETTLE DOWN IN A PLACE LIKE THIS. IT FEELS TOO MUCH LIKE I DON'T BELONG.

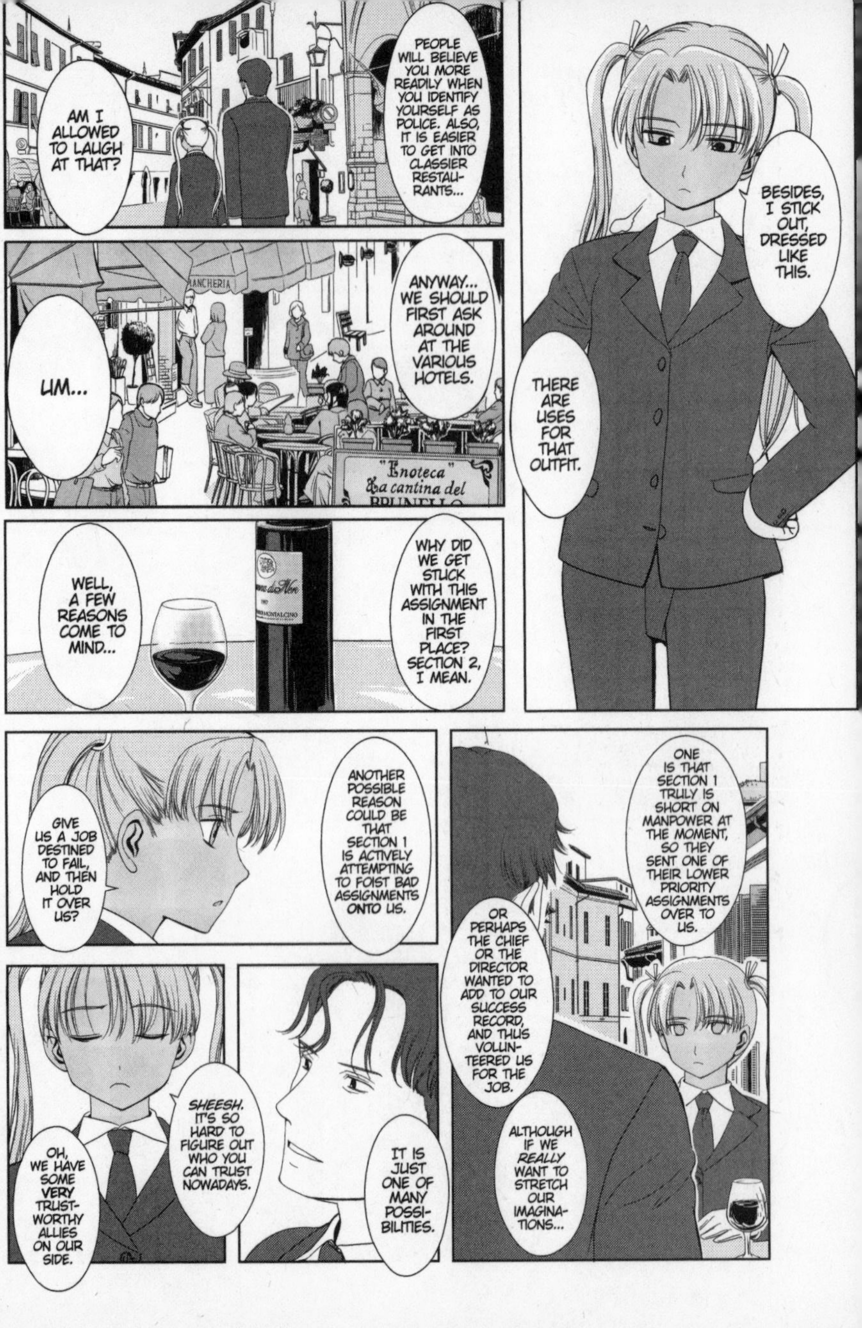

BESIDES, I STICK OUT, DRESSED LIKE THIS.
THERE ARE USES FOR THAT OUTFIT.
PEOPLE WILL BELIEVE YOU MORE READILY WHEN YOU IDENTIFY YOURSELF AS POLICE. ALSO, IT IS EASIER TO GET INTO CLASSIER RESTAU-RANTS...
AM I ALLOWED TO LAUGH AT THAT?
ANYWAY... WE SHOULD FIRST ASK AROUND AT THE VARIOUS HOTELS.
UM...
"Enoteca" La cantina del
WHY DID WE GET STUCK WITH THIS ASSIGNMENT IN THE FIRST PLACE? SECTION 2, I MEAN.
WELL, A FEW REASONS COME TO MIND...
ONE IS THAT SECTION 1 TRULY IS SHORT ON MANPOWER AT THE MOMENT, SO THEY SENT ONE OF THEIR LOWER PRIORITY ASSIGNMENTS OVER TO US.
OR PERHAPS THE CHIEF OR THE DIRECTOR WANTED TO ADD TO OUR SUCCESS RECORD, AND THUS VOLUN-TEERED US FOR THE JOB.
ALTHOUGH IF WE *REALLY* WANT TO STRETCH OUR IMAGINA-TIONS...
ANOTHER POSSIBLE REASON COULD BE THAT SECTION 1 IS ACTIVELY ATTEMPTING TO FOIST BAD ASSIGNMENTS ONTO US.
GIVE US A JOB DESTINED TO FAIL, AND THEN HOLD IT OVER US?
IT IS JUST ONE OF MANY POSSI-BILITIES.
SHEESH. IT'S SO HARD TO FIGURE OUT WHO YOU CAN TRUST NOWADAYS.
OH, WE HAVE SOME **VERY** TRUST-WORTHY ALLIES ON OUR SIDE.

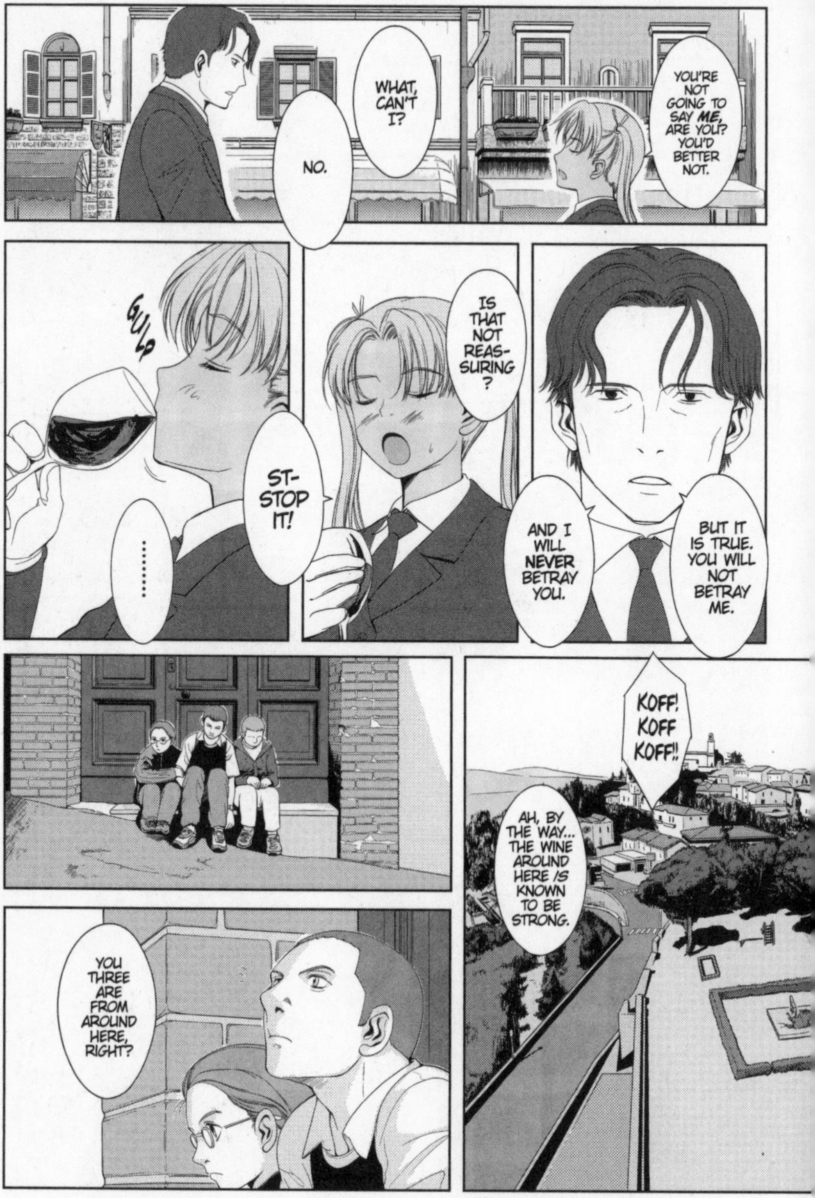
YOU'RE NOT GOING TO SAY *ME*, ARE YOU? YOU'D BETTER NOT.
WHAT, CAN'T I?
NO.
BUT IT IS TRUE. YOU WILL NOT BETRAY ME.
AND I WILL *NEVER* BETRAY YOU.
IS THAT NOT REAS- SURING ?
ST- STOP IT!
GULP
....
KOFF! KOFF KOFF!!
AH, BY THE WAY... THE WINE AROUND HERE *IS* KNOWN TO BE STRONG.
YOU THREE ARE FROM AROUND HERE, RIGHT?

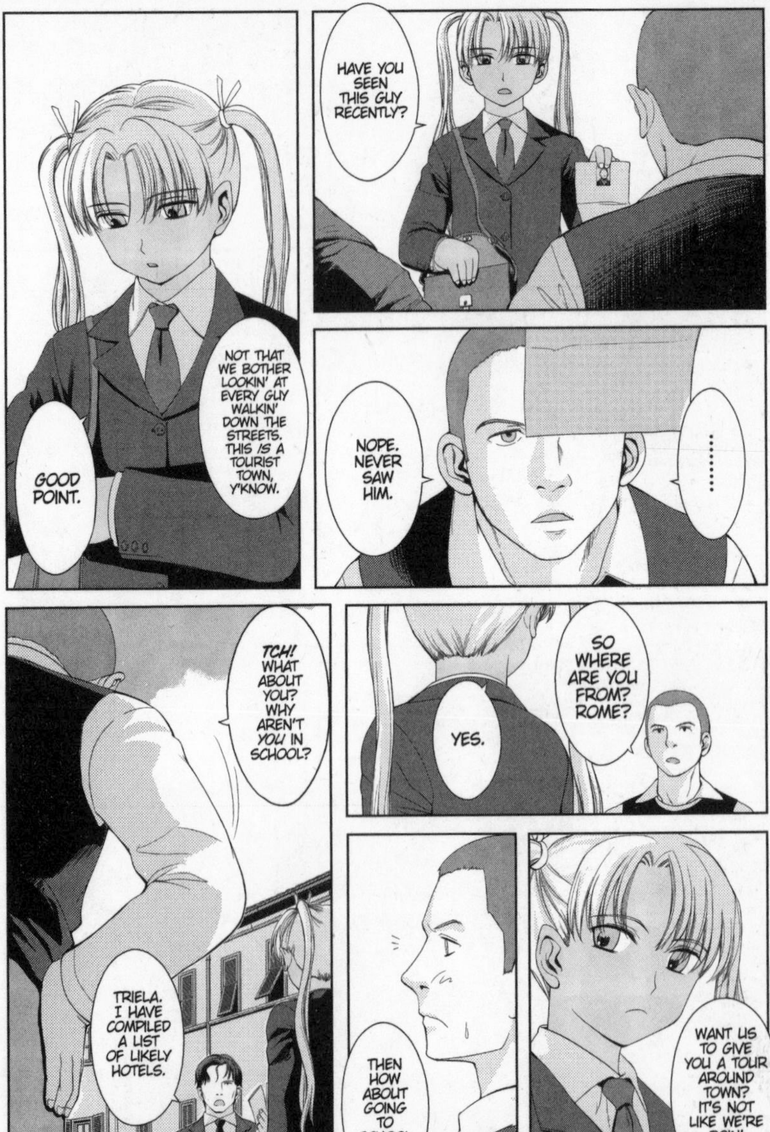
HAVE YOU SEEN THIS GUY RECENTLY?
......
NOPE. NEVER SAW HIM.
NOT THAT WE BOTHER LOOKIN' AT EVERY GUY WALKIN' DOWN THE STREETS. THIS *IS* A TOURIST TOWN, Y'KNOW.
GOOD POINT.
SO WHERE ARE YOU FROM? ROME?
YES.
WANT US TO GIVE YOU A TOUR AROUND TOWN? IT'S NOT LIKE WE'RE DOIN' MUCH ELSE...
THEN HOW ABOUT GOING TO SCHOOL?
TCH! WHAT ABOUT YOU? WHY AREN'T *YOU* IN SCHOOL?
TRIELA. I HAVE COMPILED A LIST OF LIKELY HOTELS.

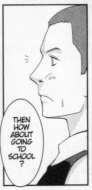

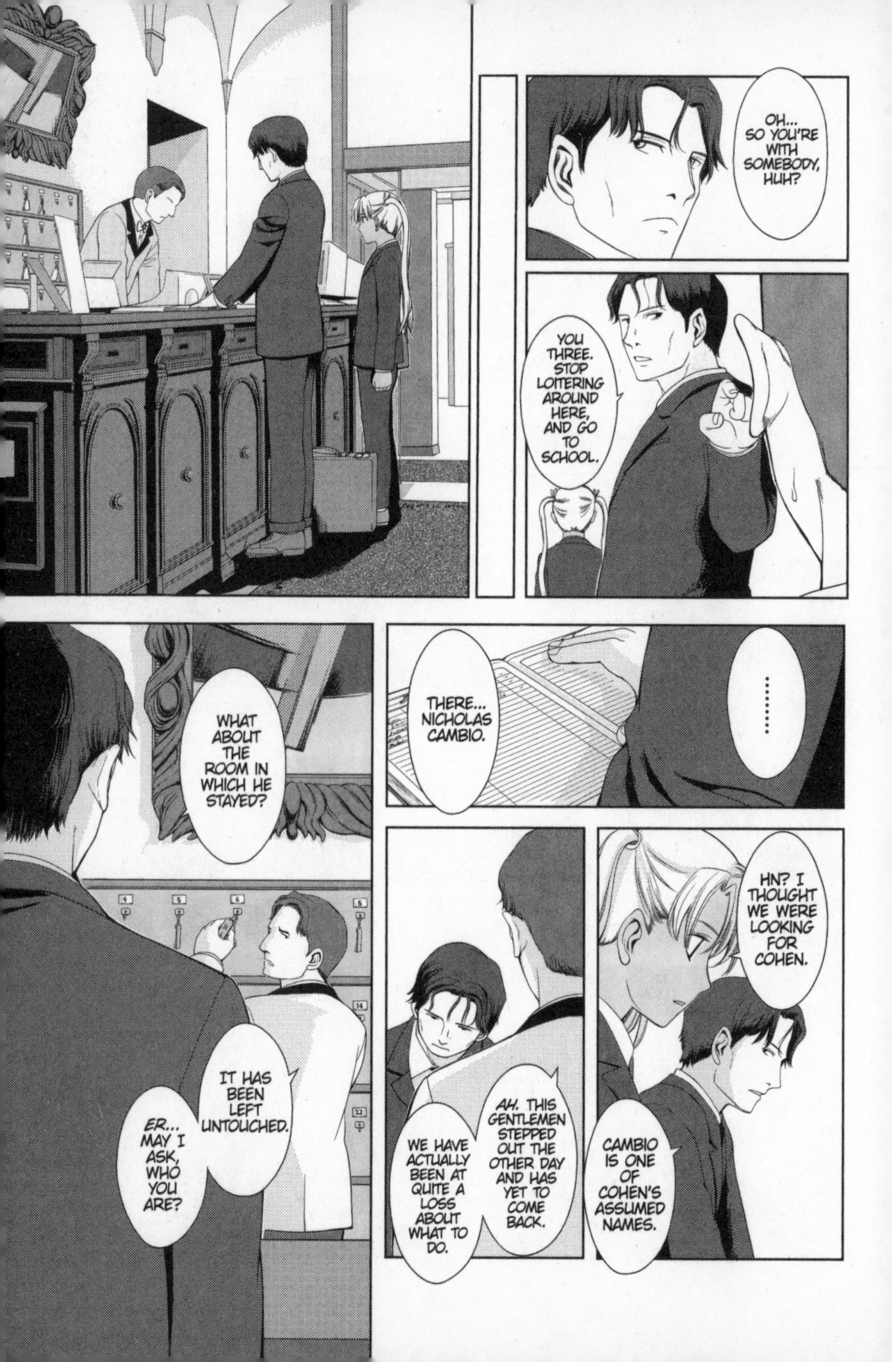

OH... SO YOU'RE WITH SOMEBODY, HUH?
YOU THREE. STOP LOITERING AROUND HERE, AND GO TO SCHOOL.
......
THERE... NICHOLAS CAMBIO.
WHAT ABOUT THE ROOM IN WHICH HE STAYED?
HN? I THOUGHT WE WERE LOOKING FOR COHEN.
CAMBIO IS ONE OF COHEN'S ASSUMED NAMES.
AH. THIS GENTLEMEN STEPPED OUT THE OTHER DAY AND HAS YET TO COME BACK.
WE HAVE ACTUALLY BEEN AT QUITE A LOSS ABOUT WHAT TO DO.
IT HAS BEEN LEFT UNTOUCHED.
ER... MAY I ASK, WHO YOU ARE?

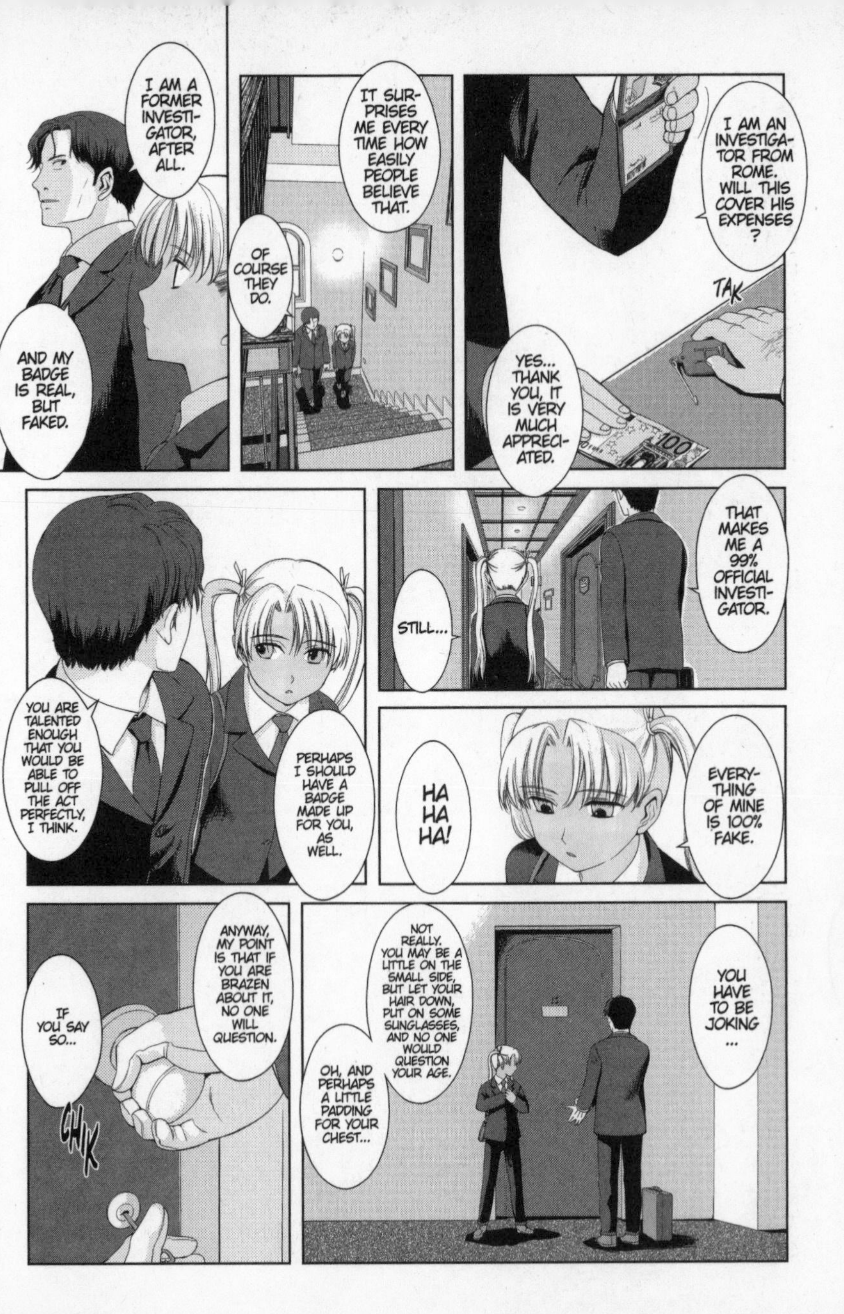
I AM AN INVESTIGATOR FROM ROME. WILL THIS COVER HIS EXPENSES?
TAK
YES... THANK YOU, IT IS VERY MUCH APPRECIATED.
IT SURPRISES ME EVERY TIME HOW EASILY PEOPLE BELIEVE THAT.
OF COURSE THEY DO.
I AM A FORMER INVESTIGATOR, AFTER ALL.
AND MY BADGE IS REAL, BUT FAKED.
THAT MAKES ME A 99% OFFICIAL INVESTIGATOR.
STILL...
EVERYTHING OF MINE IS 100% FAKE.
HA HA HA!
PERHAPS I SHOULD HAVE A BADGE MADE UP FOR YOU, AS WELL.
YOU ARE TALENTED ENOUGH THAT YOU WOULD BE ABLE TO PULL OFF THE ACT PERFECTLY, I THINK.
YOU HAVE TO BE JOKING...
NOT REALLY. YOU MAY BE A LITTLE ON THE SMALL SIDE, BUT LET YOUR HAIR DOWN, PUT ON SOME SUNGLASSES, AND NO ONE WOULD QUESTION YOUR AGE.
OH, AND PERHAPS A LITTLE PADDING FOR YOUR CHEST...
ANYWAY, MY POINT IS THAT IF YOU ARE BRAZEN ABOUT IT, NO ONE WILL QUESTION.
IF YOU SAY SO...
CHIK

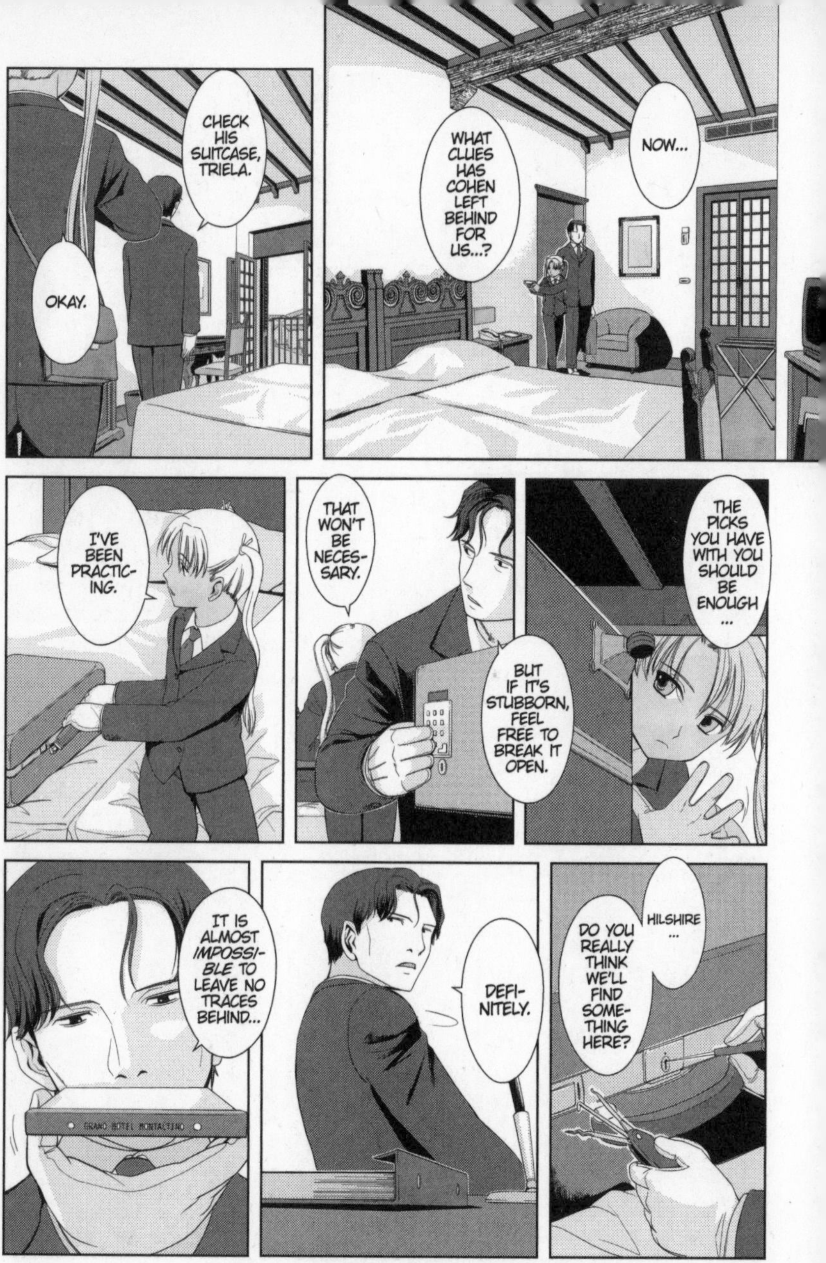
NOW...
WHAT CLUES HAS COHEN LEFT BEHIND FOR US...?
CHECK HIS SUITCASE, TRIELA.
OKAY.
THE PICKS YOU HAVE WITH YOU SHOULD BE ENOUGH...
BUT IF IT'S STUBBORN, FEEL FREE TO BREAK IT OPEN.
THAT WON'T BE NECESSARY.
I'VE BEEN PRACTICING.
HILSHIRE...
DO YOU REALLY THINK WE'LL FIND SOMETHING HERE?
DEFINITELY.
IT IS ALMOST *IMPOSSIBLE* TO LEAVE NO TRACES BEHIND...

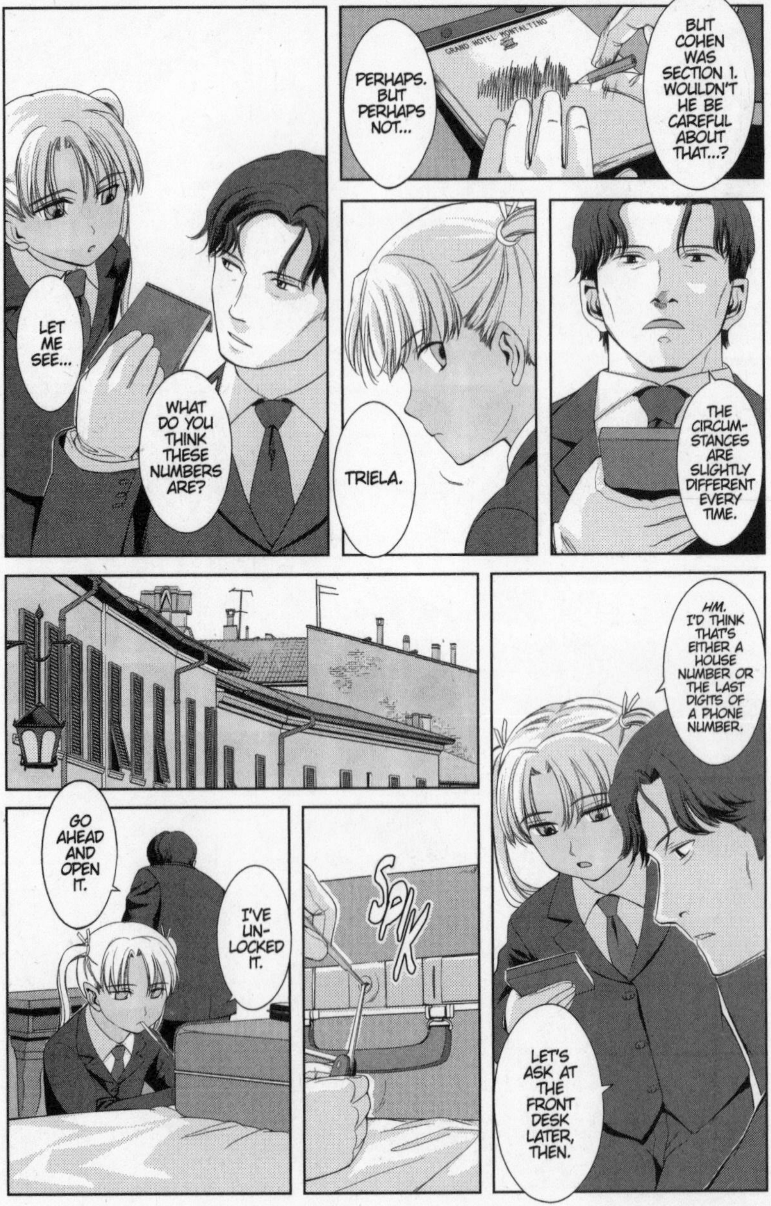
GRAND HOTEL MONTALTINO
BUT COHEN WAS SECTION 1. WOULDN'T HE BE CAREFUL ABOUT THAT...?
PERHAPS. BUT PERHAPS NOT...
THE CIRCUM-STANCES ARE SLIGHTLY DIFFERENT EVERY TIME.
TRIELA.
WHAT DO YOU THINK THESE NUMBERS ARE?
LET ME SEE...
HM. I'D THINK THAT'S EITHER A HOUSE NUMBER OR THE LAST DIGITS OF A PHONE NUMBER.
LET'S ASK AT THE FRONT DESK LATER, THEN.
SPIK
I'VE UN-LOCKED IT.
GO AHEAD AND OPEN IT.

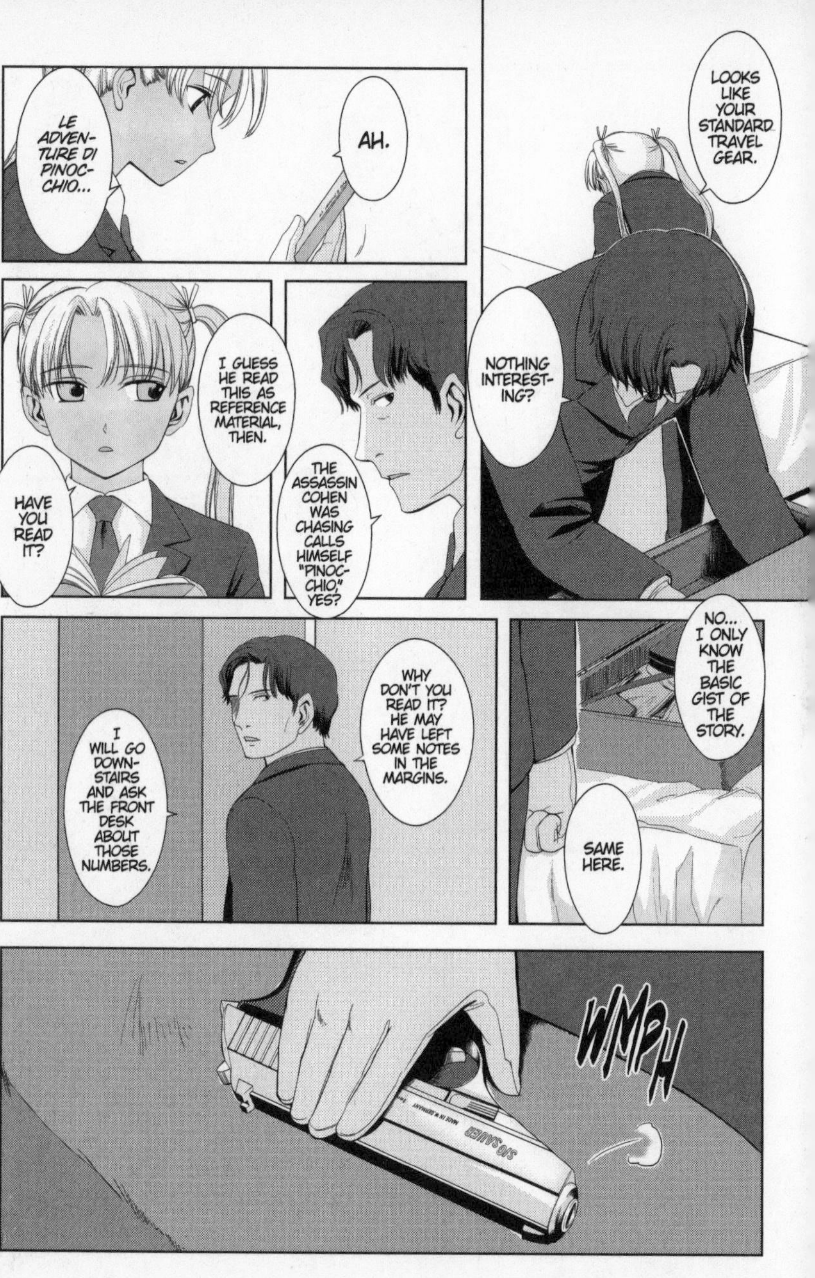
LOOKS LIKE YOUR STANDARD TRAVEL GEAR.
NOTHING INTERESTING?
AH.
LE ADVENTURE DI PINOCCHIO...
THE ASSASSIN COHEN WAS CHASING CALLS HIMSELF "PINOCCHIO," YES?
I GUESS HE READ THIS AS REFERENCE MATERIAL, THEN.
HAVE YOU READ IT?
NO... I ONLY KNOW THE BASIC GIST OF THE STORY.
SAME HERE.
WHY DON'T YOU READ IT? HE MAY HAVE LEFT SOME NOTES IN THE MARGINS.
I WILL GO DOWNSTAIRS AND ASK THE FRONT DESK ABOUT THOSE NUMBERS.
WMPH
SIG SAUER

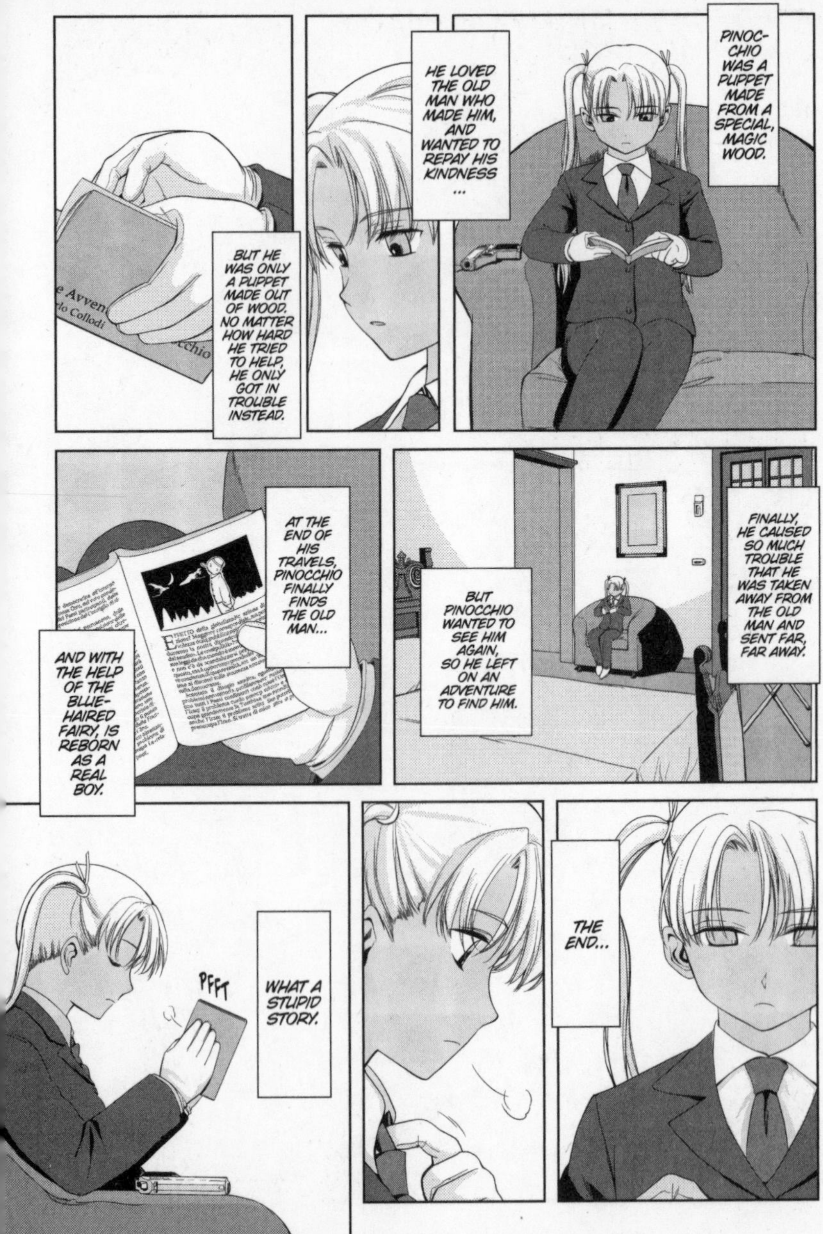
PINOCCHIO WAS A PUPPET MADE FROM A SPECIAL, MAGIC WOOD.
HE LOVED THE OLD MAN WHO MADE HIM, AND WANTED TO REPAY HIS KINDNESS ...
BUT HE WAS ONLY A PUPPET MADE OUT OF WOOD. NO MATTER HOW HARD HE TRIED TO HELP, HE ONLY GOT IN TROUBLE INSTEAD.
FINALLY, HE CAUSED SO MUCH TROUBLE THAT HE WAS TAKEN AWAY FROM THE OLD MAN AND SENT FAR, FAR AWAY.
BUT PINOCCHIO WANTED TO SEE HIM AGAIN, SO HE LEFT ON AN ADVENTURE TO FIND HIM.
AT THE END OF HIS TRAVELS, PINOCCHIO FINALLY FINDS THE OLD MAN...
AND WITH THE HELP OF THE BLUE-HAIRED FAIRY, IS REBORN AS A REAL BOY.
THE END...
PFFT
WHAT A STUPID STORY.

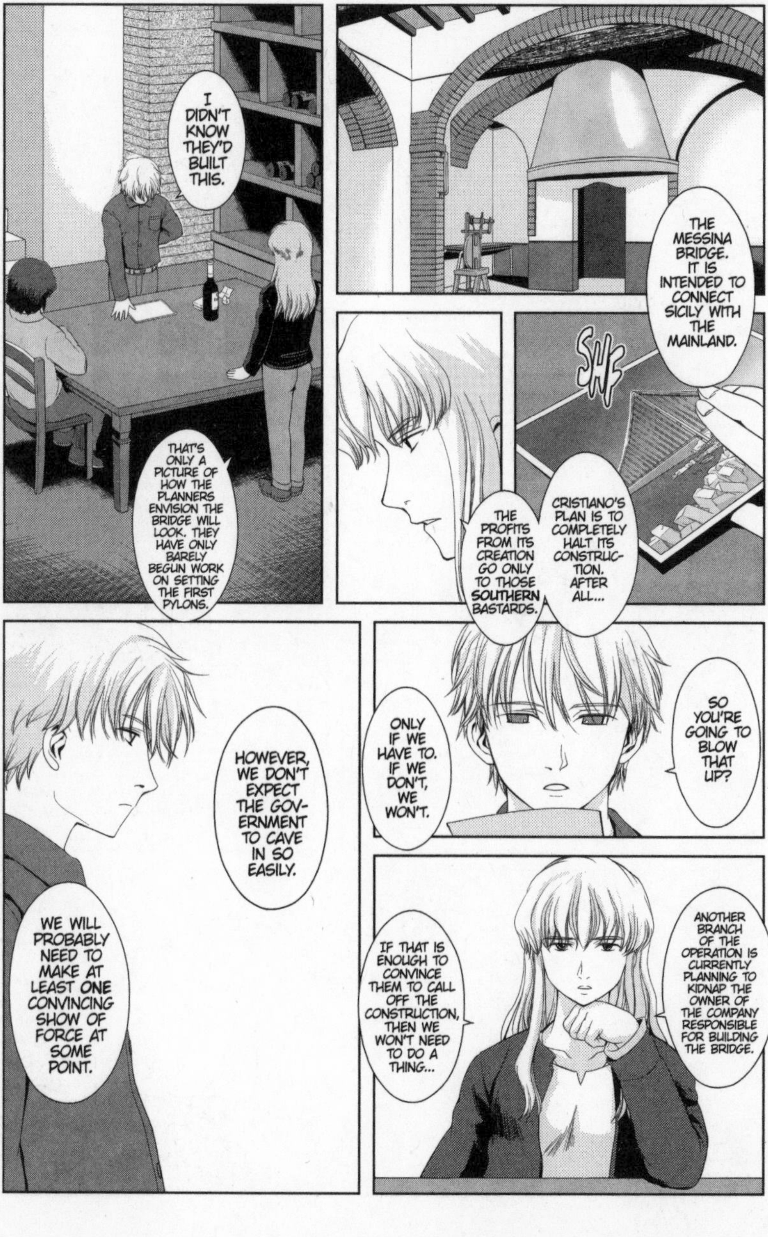
THE MESSINA BRIDGE. IT IS INTENDED TO CONNECT SICILY WITH THE MAINLAND.
SHF
CRISTIANO'S PLAN IS TO COMPLETELY HALT ITS CONSTRUCTION. AFTER ALL...
THE PROFITS FROM ITS CREATION GO ONLY TO THOSE SOUTHERN BASTARDS.
I DIDN'T KNOW THEY'D BUILT THIS.
THAT'S ONLY A PICTURE OF HOW THE PLANNERS ENVISION THE BRIDGE WILL LOOK. THEY HAVE ONLY BARELY BEGUN WORK ON SETTING THE FIRST PYLONS.
SO YOU'RE GOING TO BLOW THAT UP?
ONLY IF WE HAVE TO. IF WE DON'T, WE WON'T.
ANOTHER BRANCH OF THE OPERATION IS CURRENTLY PLANNING TO KIDNAP THE OWNER OF THE COMPANY RESPONSIBLE FOR BUILDING THE BRIDGE.
IF THAT IS ENOUGH TO CONVINCE THEM TO CALL OFF THE CONSTRUCTION, THEN WE WON'T NEED TO DO A THING...
HOWEVER, WE DON'T EXPECT THE GOVERNMENT TO CAVE IN SO EASILY.
WE WILL PROBABLY NEED TO MAKE AT LEAST ONE CONVINCING SHOW OF FORCE AT SOME POINT.

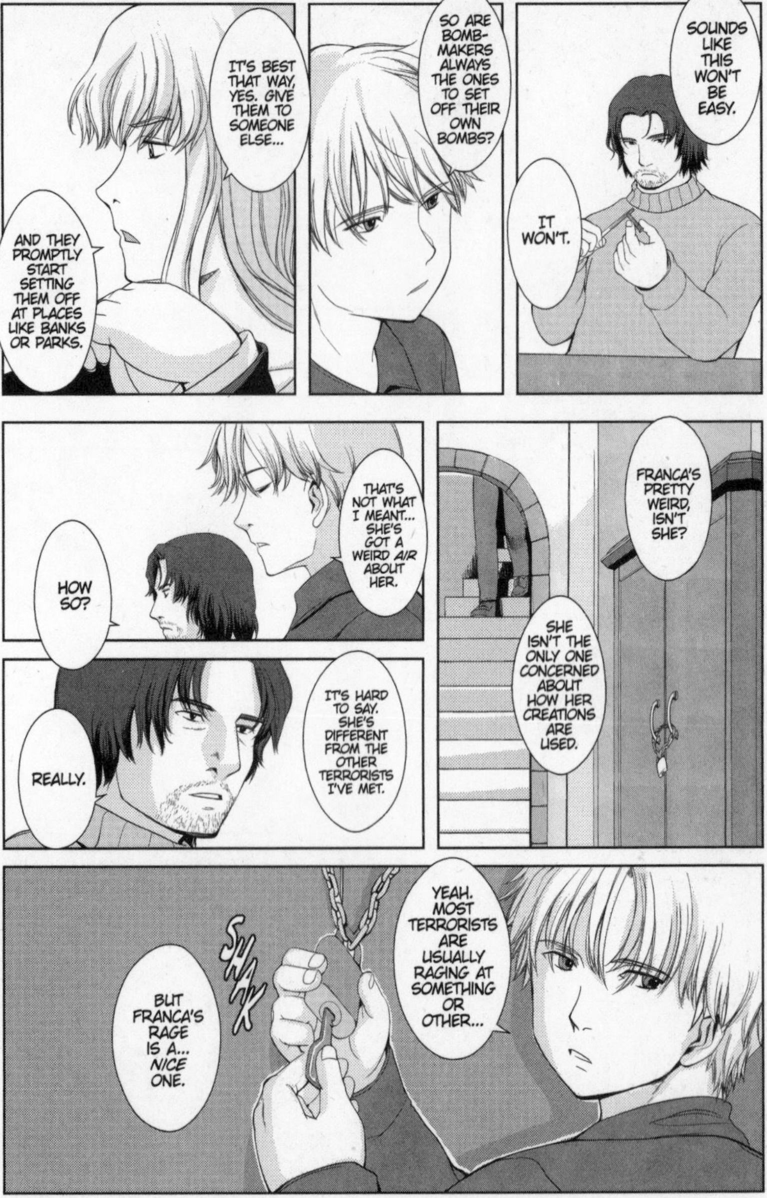
SOUNDS LIKE THIS WON'T BE EASY.
IT WON'T.
SO ARE BOMB-MAKERS ALWAYS THE ONES TO SET OFF THEIR OWN BOMBS?
IT'S BEST THAT WAY, YES. GIVE THEM TO SOMEONE ELSE...
AND THEY PROMPTLY START SETTING THEM OFF AT PLACES LIKE BANKS OR PARKS.
FRANCA'S PRETTY WEIRD, ISN'T SHE?
SHE ISN'T THE ONLY ONE CONCERNED ABOUT HOW HER CREATIONS ARE USED.
THAT'S NOT WHAT I MEANT... SHE'S GOT A WEIRD *AIR* ABOUT HER.
HOW SO?
IT'S HARD TO SAY. SHE'S DIFFERENT FROM THE OTHER TERRORISTS I'VE MET.
REALLY.
YEAH. MOST TERRORISTS ARE USUALLY RAGING AT SOMETHING OR OTHER...
SHAK
BUT FRANCA'S RAGE IS A... *NICE* ONE.

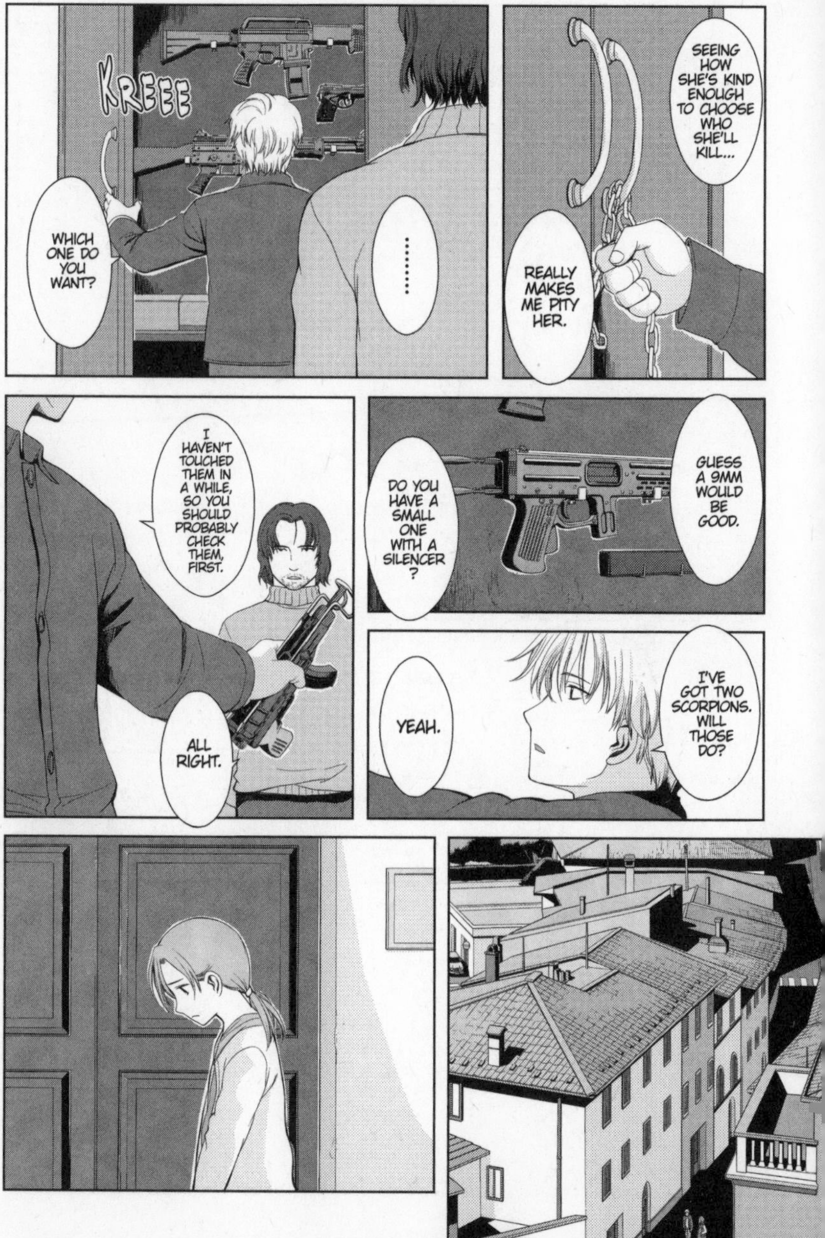
SEEING HOW SHE'S KIND ENOUGH TO CHOOSE WHO SHE'LL KILL...
REALLY MAKES ME PITY HER.
KREEE
WHICH ONE DO YOU WANT?
....
GUESS A 9MM WOULD BE GOOD.
DO YOU HAVE A SMALL ONE WITH A SILENCER?
I'VE GOT TWO SCORPIONS. WILL THOSE DO?
YEAH.
I HAVEN'T TOUCHED THEM IN A WHILE, SO YOU SHOULD PROBABLY CHECK THEM, FIRST.
ALL RIGHT.

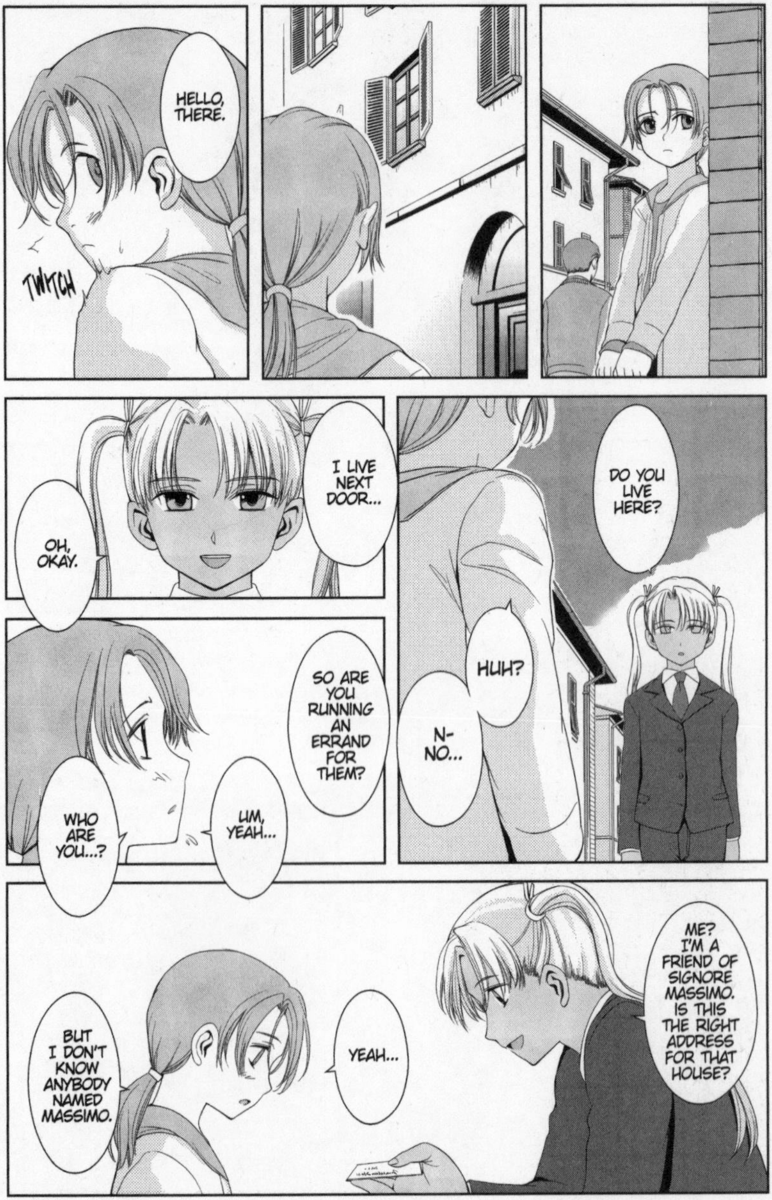
HELLO, THERE.
TWITCH
DO YOU LIVE HERE?
HUH?
N-NO...
I LIVE NEXT DOOR...
OH, OKAY.
SO ARE YOU RUNNING AN ERRAND FOR THEM?
UM, YEAH...
WHO ARE YOU...?
ME? I'M A FRIEND OF SIGNORE MASSIMO. IS THIS THE RIGHT ADDRESS FOR THAT HOUSE?
YEAH...
BUT I DON'T KNOW ANYBODY NAMED MASSIMO.

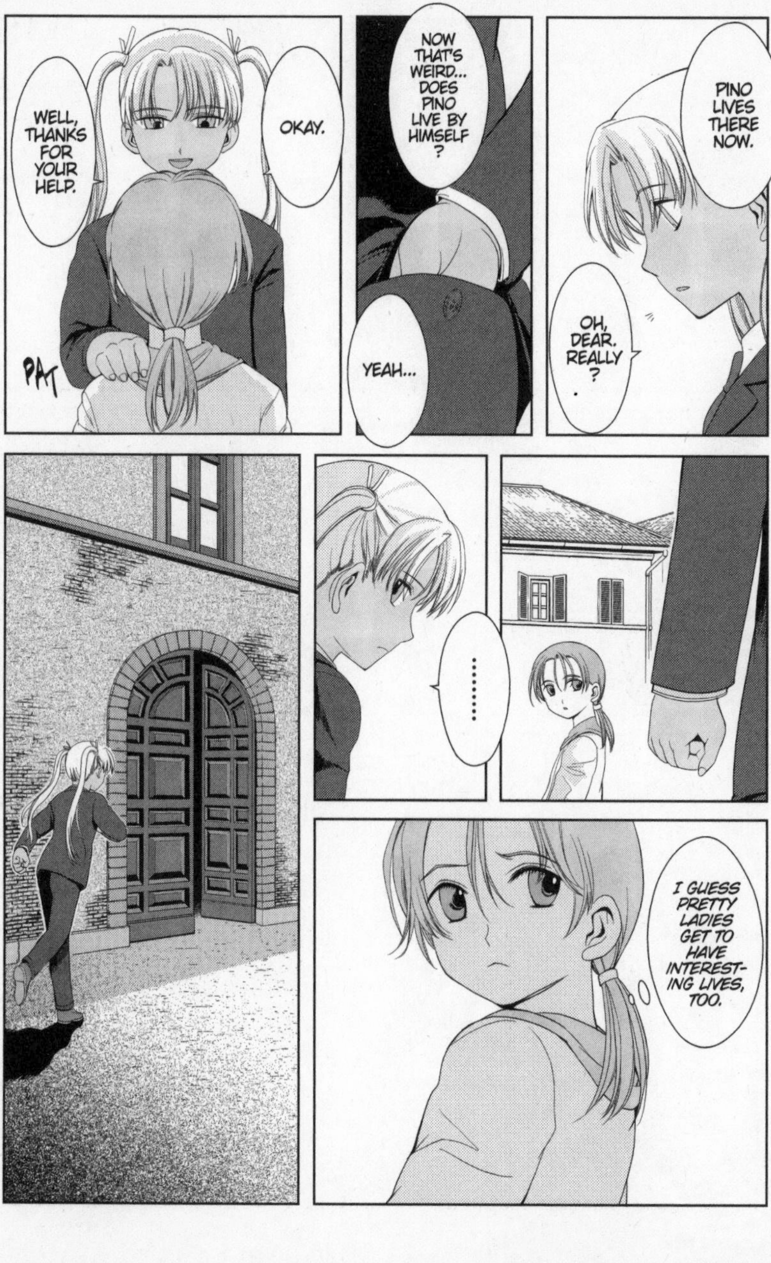
PINO LIVES THERE NOW.
OH, DEAR. REALLY?
NOW THAT'S WEIRD... DOES PINO LIVE BY HIMSELF?
YEAH...
OKAY.
WELL, THANKS FOR YOUR HELP.
PAT
....
I GUESS PRETTY LADIES GET TO HAVE INTERESTING LIVES, TOO.

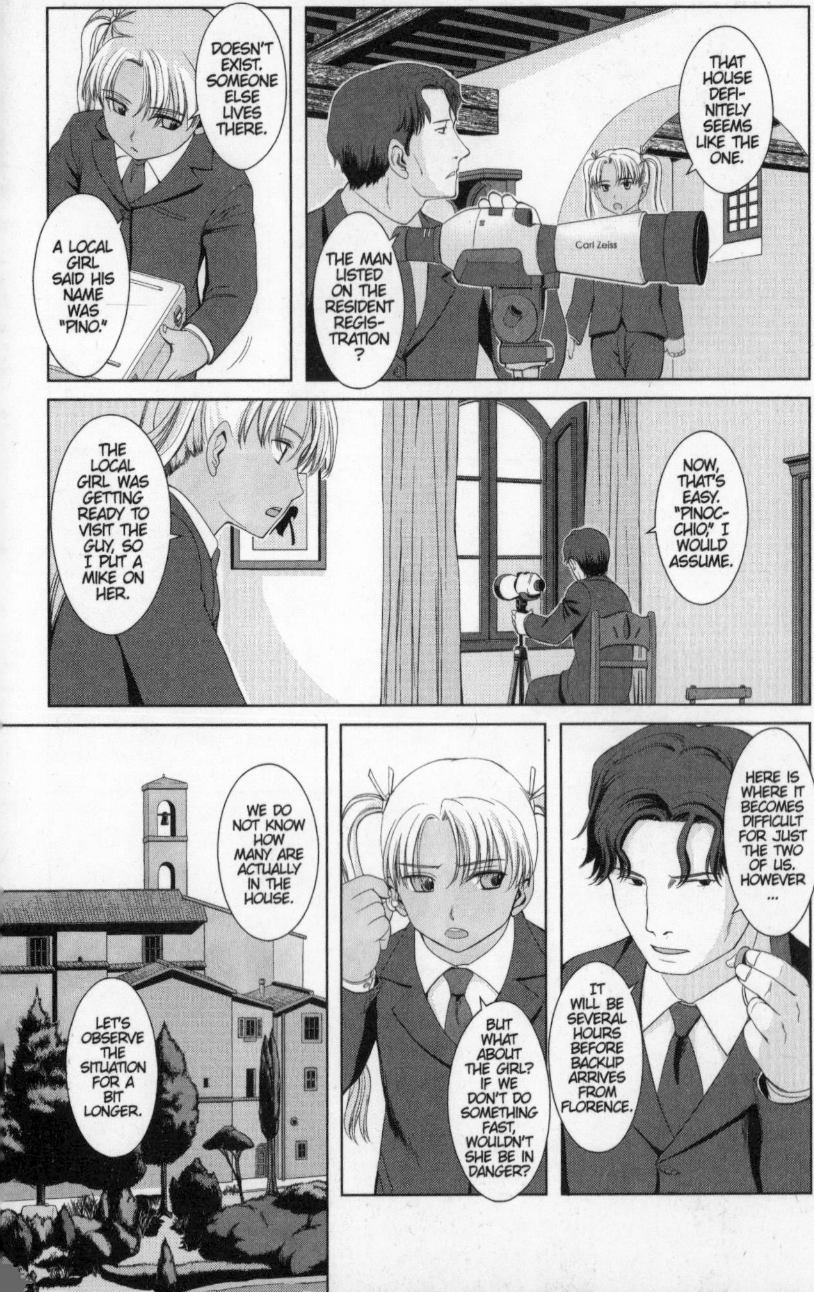
THAT HOUSE DEFINITELY SEEMS LIKE THE ONE.
Carl Zeiss
THE MAN LISTED ON THE RESIDENT REGISTRATION?
DOESN'T EXIST. SOMEONE ELSE LIVES THERE.
A LOCAL GIRL SAID HIS NAME WAS "PINO."
NOW, THAT'S EASY. "PINOCCHIO," I WOULD ASSUME.
THE LOCAL GIRL WAS GETTING READY TO VISIT THE GUY, SO I PUT A MIKE ON HER.
HERE IS WHERE IT BECOMES DIFFICULT FOR JUST THE TWO OF US. HOWEVER...
IT WILL BE SEVERAL HOURS BEFORE BACKUP ARRIVES FROM FLORENCE.
BUT WHAT ABOUT THE GIRL? IF WE DON'T DO SOMETHING FAST, WOULDN'T SHE BE IN DANGER?
WE DO NOT KNOW HOW MANY ARE ACTUALLY IN THE HOUSE.
LET'S OBSERVE THE SITUATION FOR A BIT LONGER.

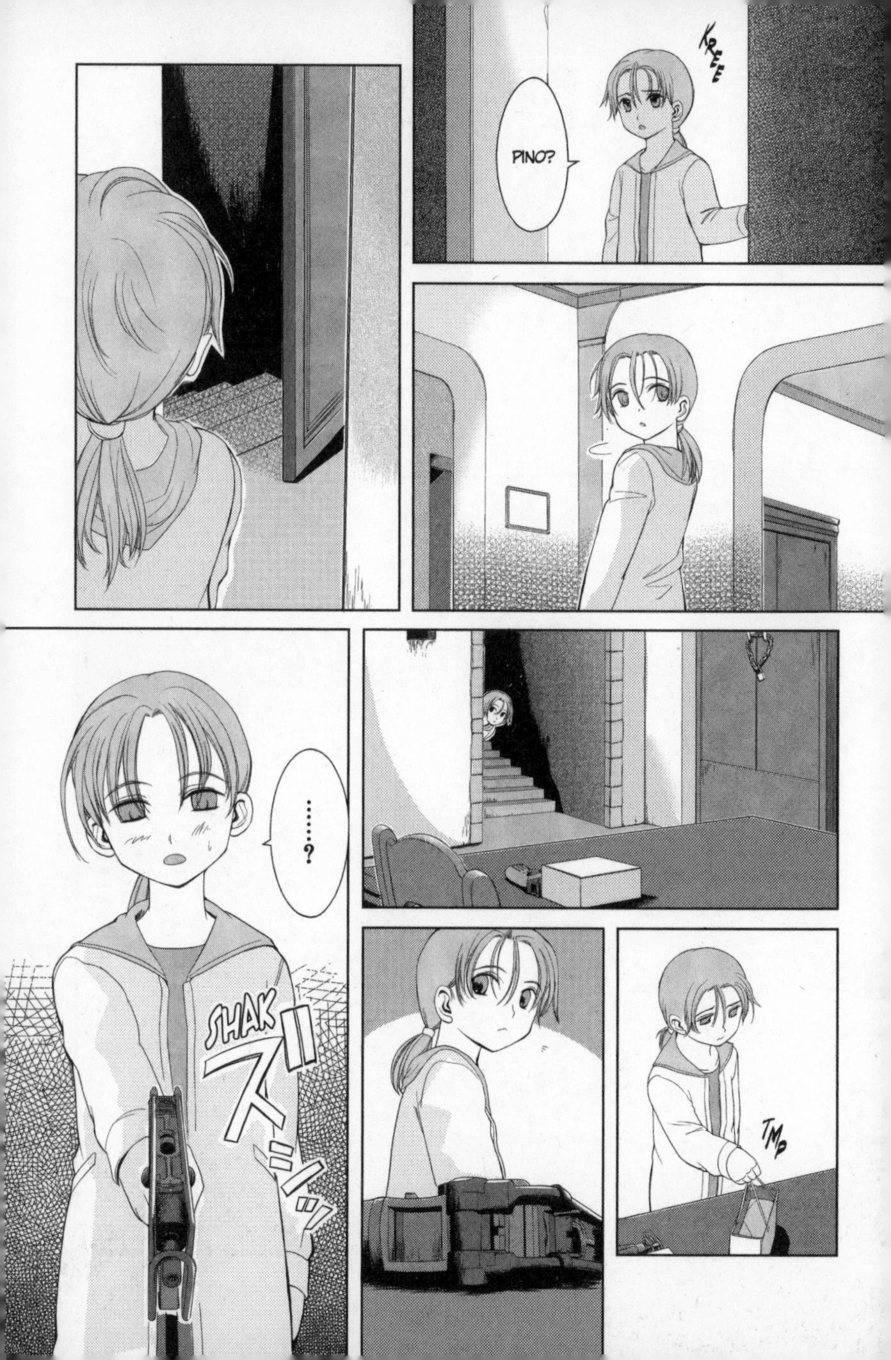
KREEE
PINO?
TMP
......?
SHAK

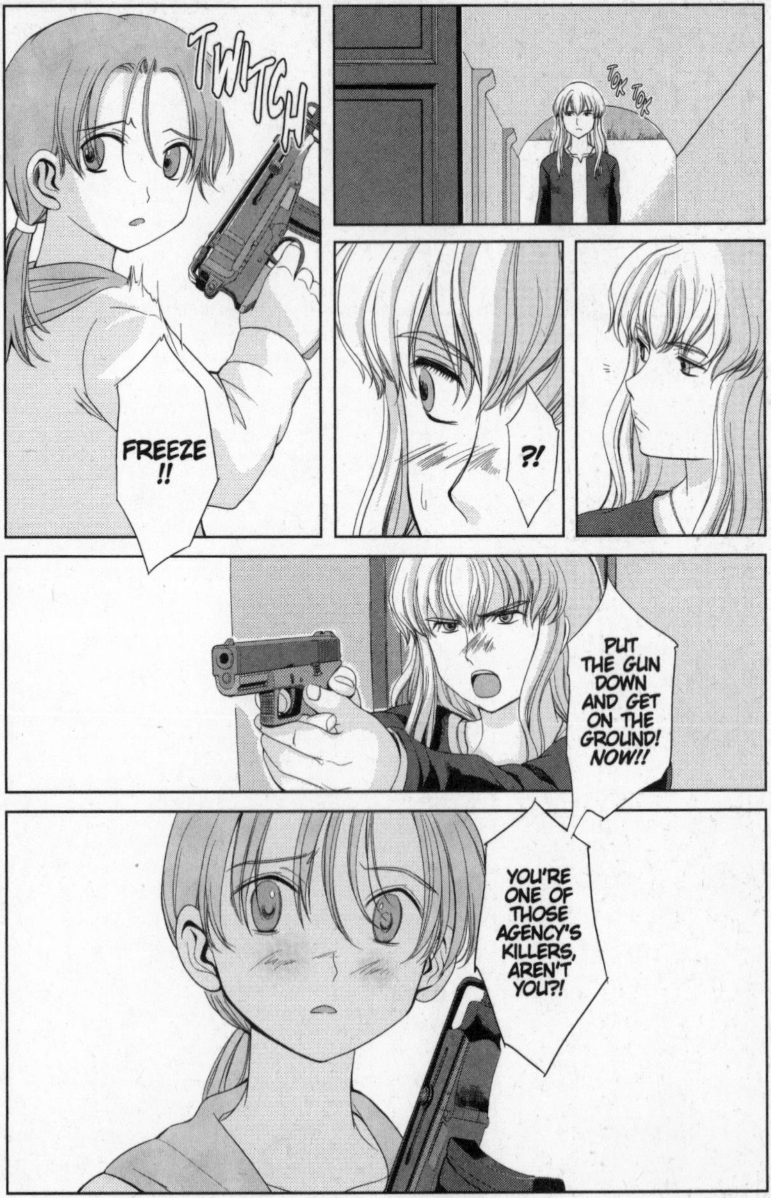
TOK TOK
?!
TWITCH
FREEZE!!
PUT THE GUN DOWN AND GET ON THE GROUND! NOW!!
YOU'RE ONE OF THOSE AGENCY'S KILLERS, AREN'T YOU?!

GUNSLINGERGIRL.

CHAPTER 15: PINOCCHIO (3)

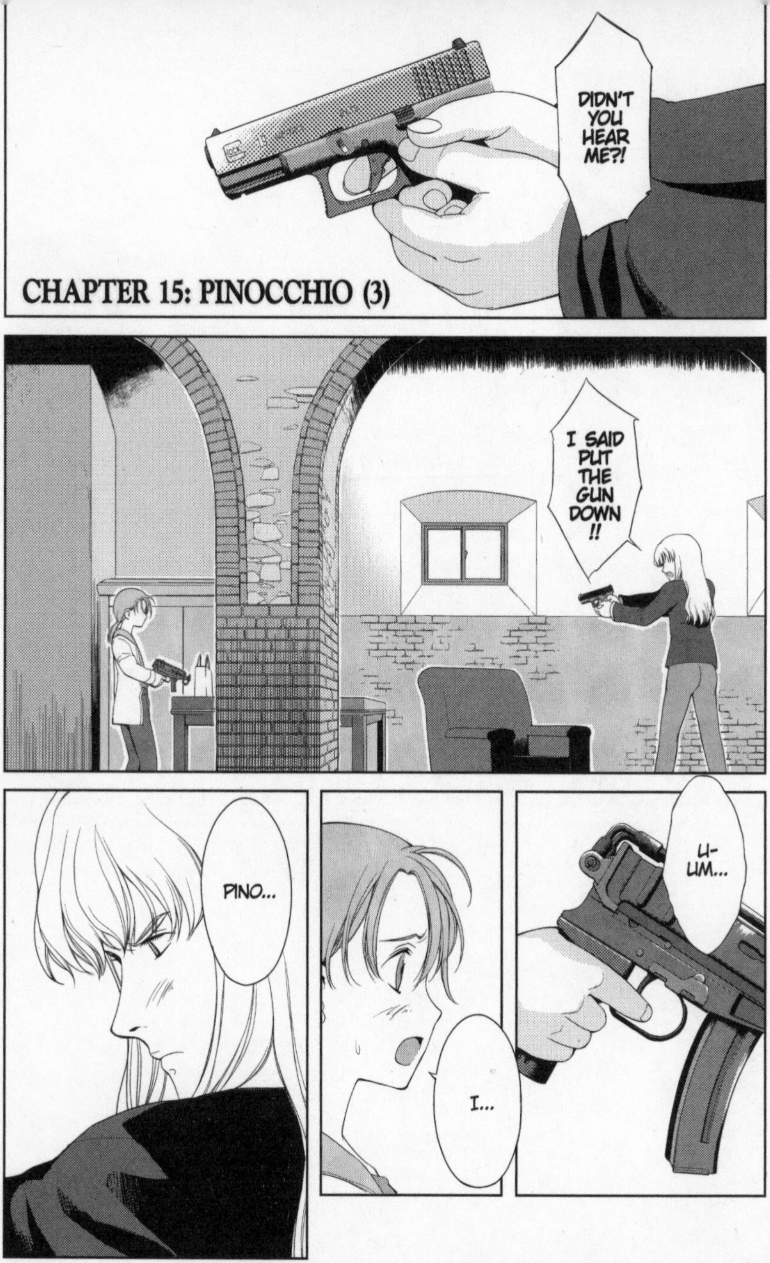
DIDN'T YOU HEAR ME?!
I SAID PUT THE GUN DOWN!!
U-UM...
I...
PINO...

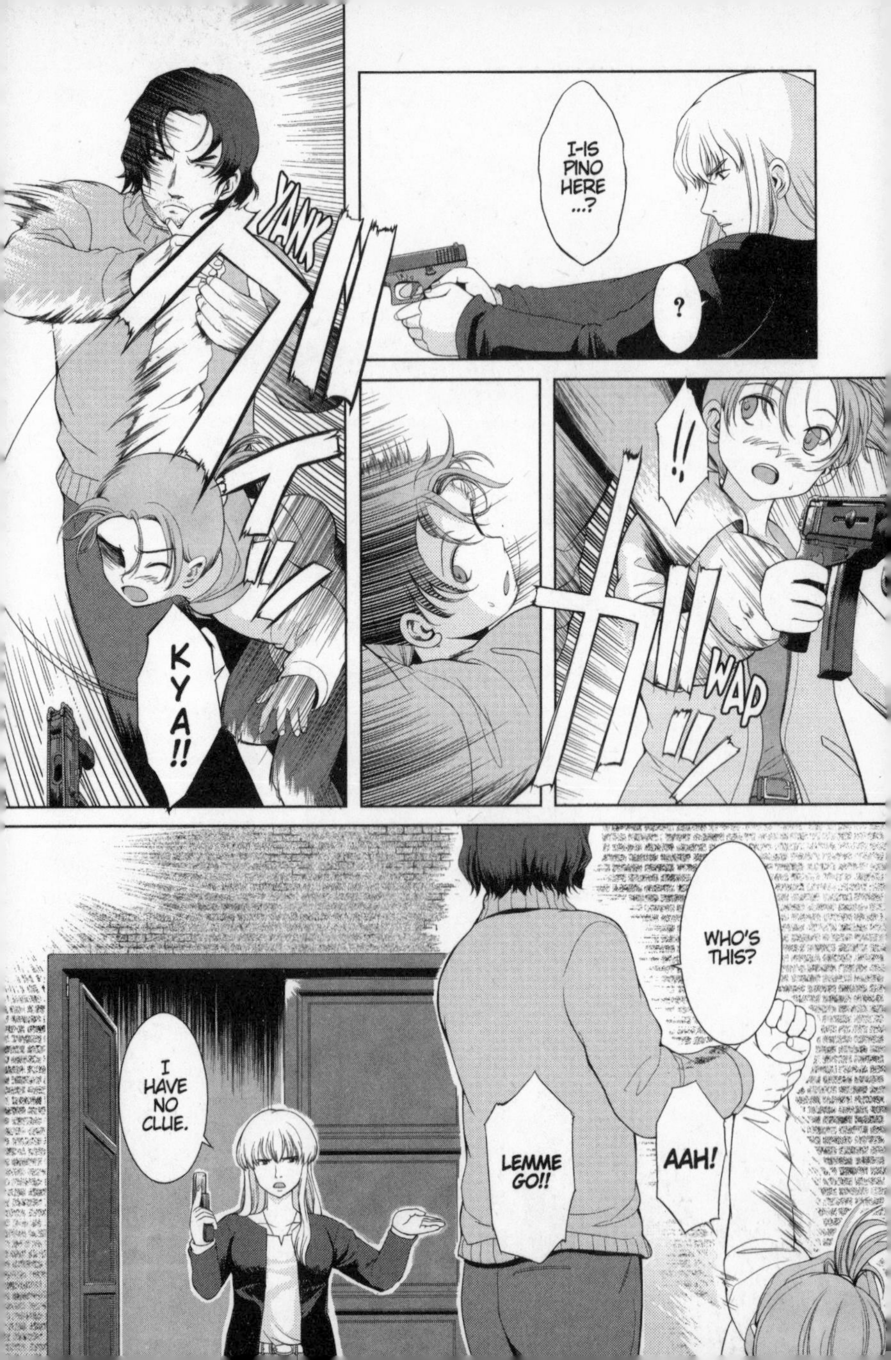
I-IS PINO HERE ...?
?
!!
WAP!!
YANK
KYA!!
WHO'S THIS?
AAH!
LEMME GO!!
I HAVE NO CLUE.

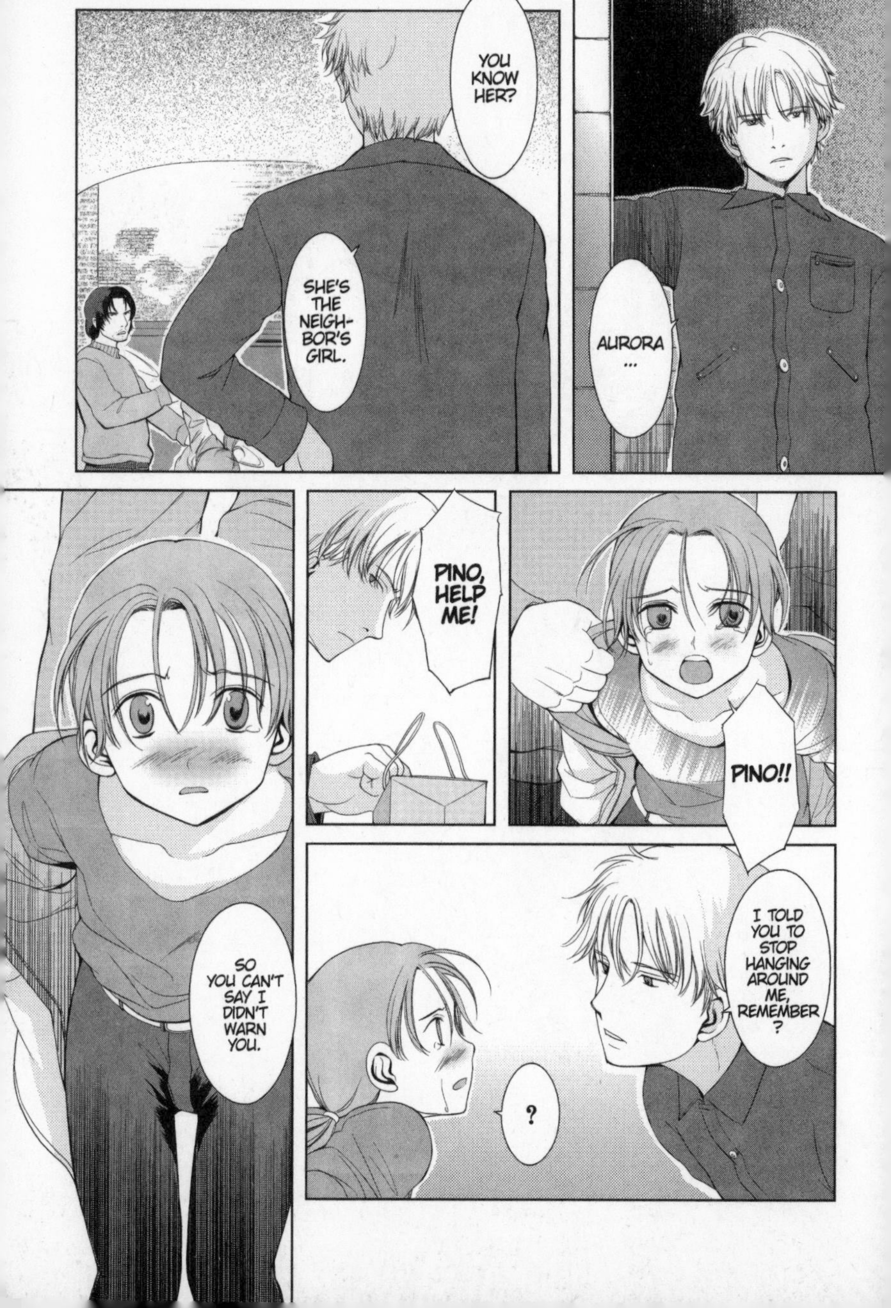
AURORA ...
YOU KNOW HER?
SHE'S THE NEIGHBOR'S GIRL.
PINO!!
PINO, HELP ME!
I TOLD YOU TO STOP HANGING AROUND ME, REMEMBER?
?
SO YOU CAN'T SAY I DIDN'T WARN YOU.

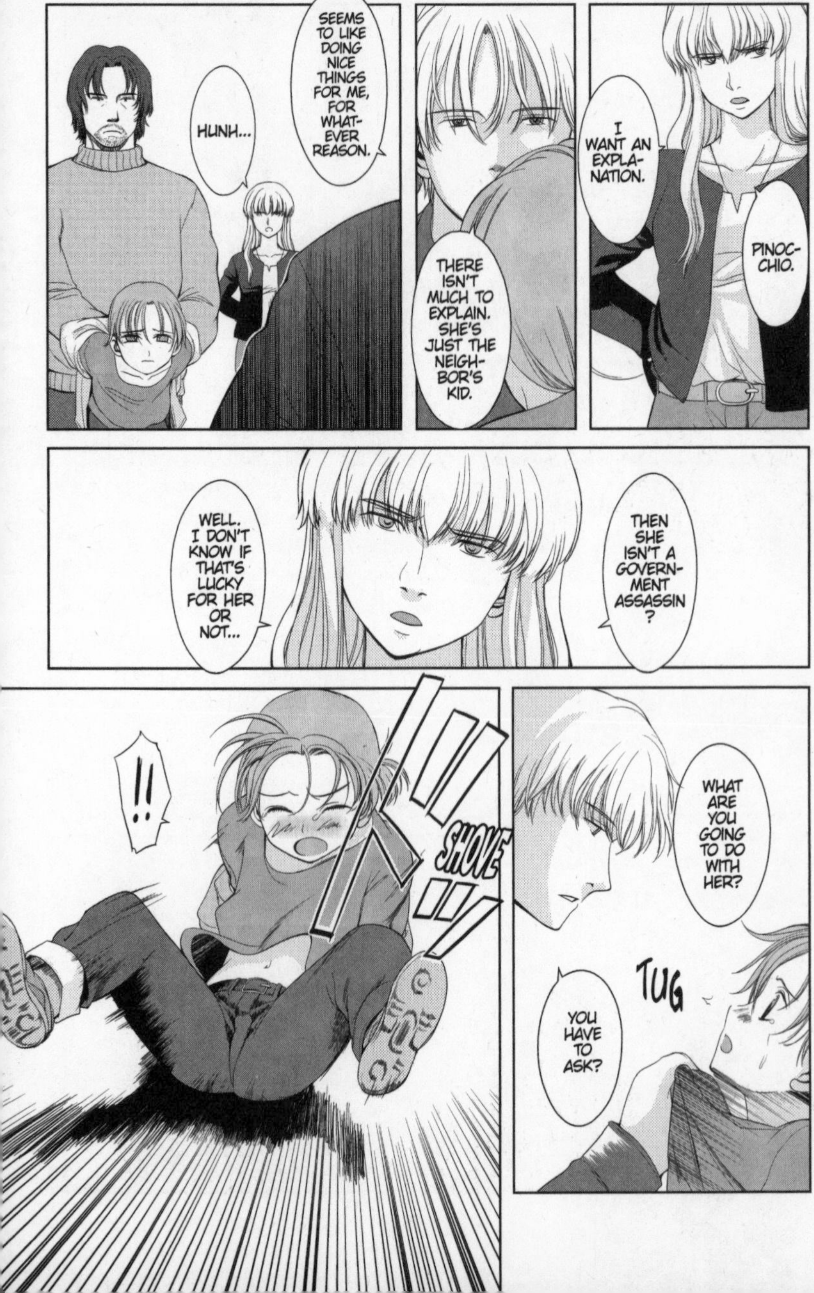
I WANT AN EXPLANATION.
PINOCCHIO.
THERE ISN'T MUCH TO EXPLAIN. SHE'S JUST THE NEIGHBOR'S KID.
SEEMS TO LIKE DOING NICE THINGS FOR ME, FOR WHATEVER REASON.
HUNH...
THEN SHE ISN'T A GOVERNMENT ASSASSIN?
WELL. I DON'T KNOW IF THAT'S LUCKY FOR HER OR NOT...
WHAT ARE YOU GOING TO DO WITH HER?
TUG
YOU HAVE TO ASK?
SHOVE
!!

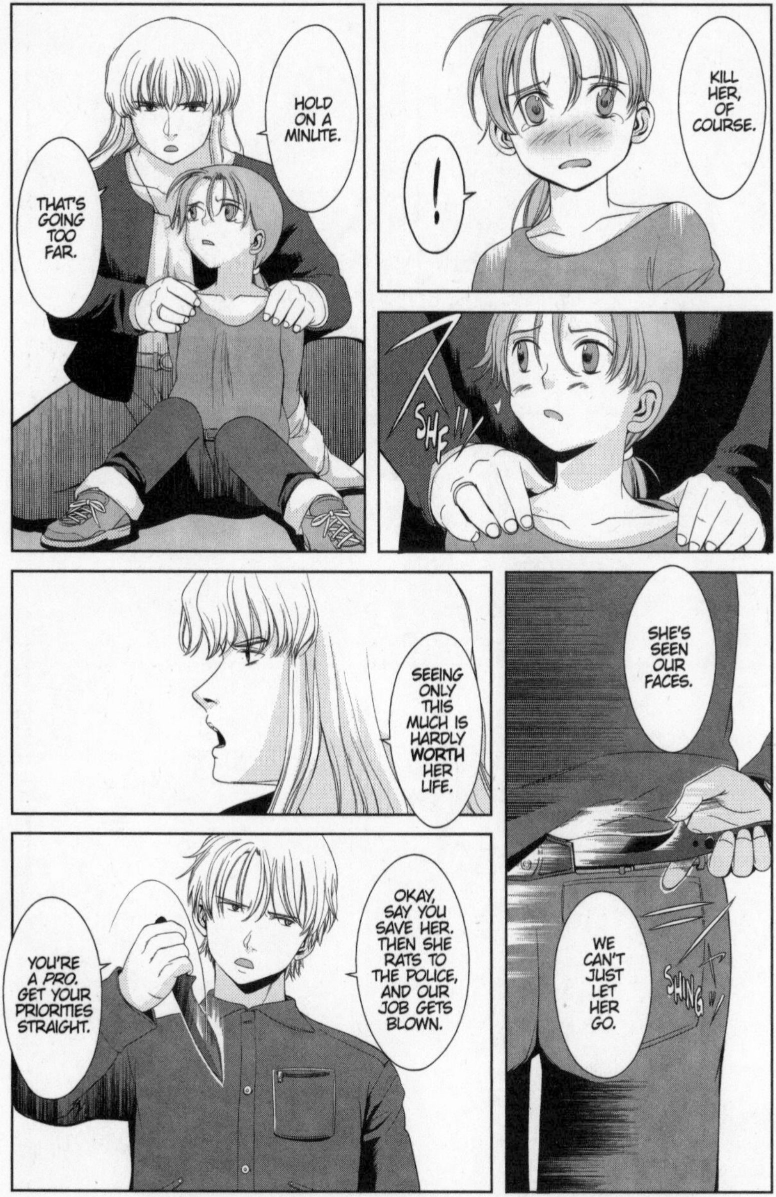
KILL HER, OF COURSE.
!
SHF
HOLD ON A MINUTE.
THAT'S GOING TOO FAR.
SHE'S SEEN OUR FACES.
WE CAN'T JUST LET HER GO.
SHING
SEEING ONLY THIS MUCH IS HARDLY WORTH HER LIFE.
OKAY, SAY YOU SAVE HER. THEN SHE RATS TO THE POLICE, AND OUR JOB GETS BLOWN.
YOU'RE A *PRO.* GET YOUR PRIORITIES STRAIGHT.

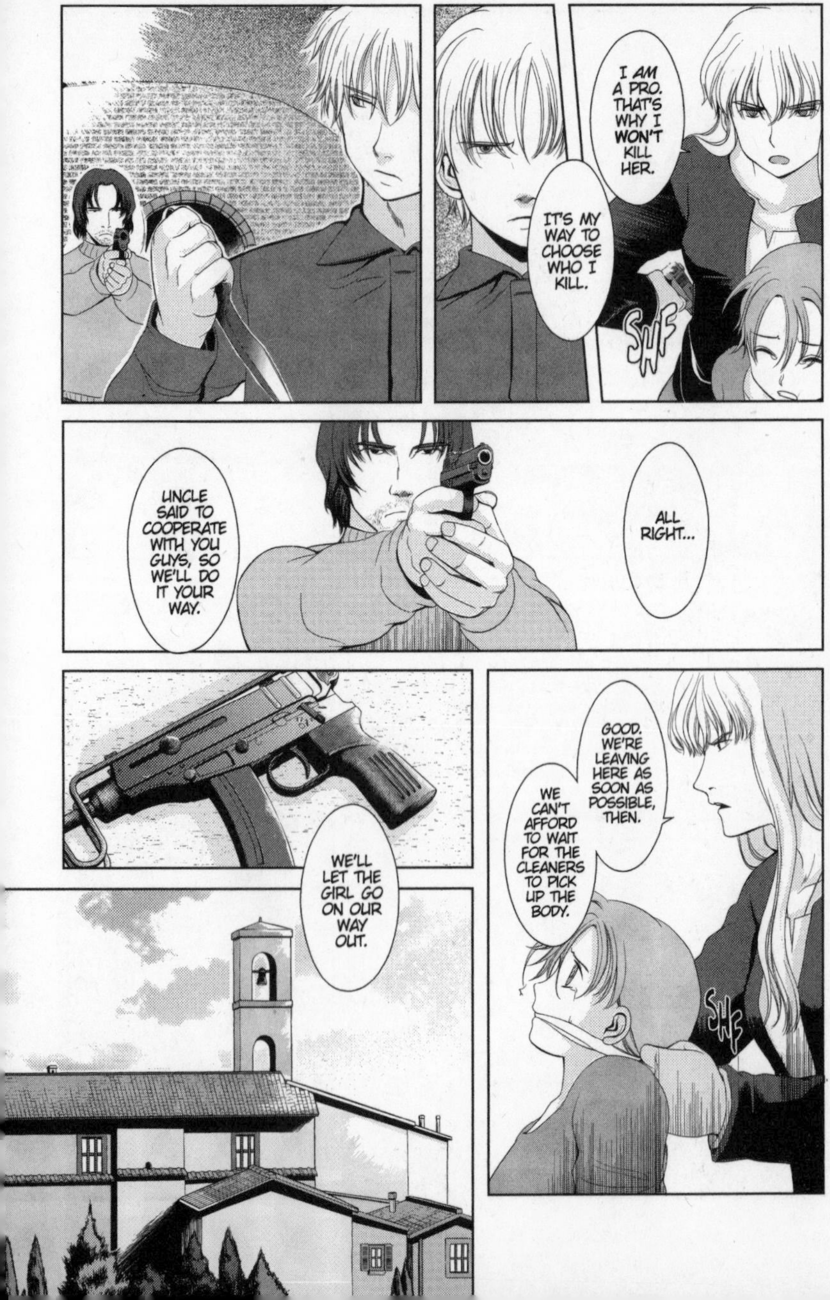
I AM A PRO. THAT'S WHY I WON'T KILL HER.
IT'S MY WAY TO CHOOSE WHO I KILL.
SHF
ALL RIGHT...
UNCLE SAID TO COOPERATE WITH YOU GUYS, SO WE'LL DO IT YOUR WAY.
GOOD. WE'RE LEAVING HERE AS SOON AS POSSIBLE, THEN.
WE CAN'T AFFORD TO WAIT FOR THE CLEANERS TO PICK UP THE BODY.
SHF
WE'LL LET THE GIRL GO ON OUR WAY OUT.

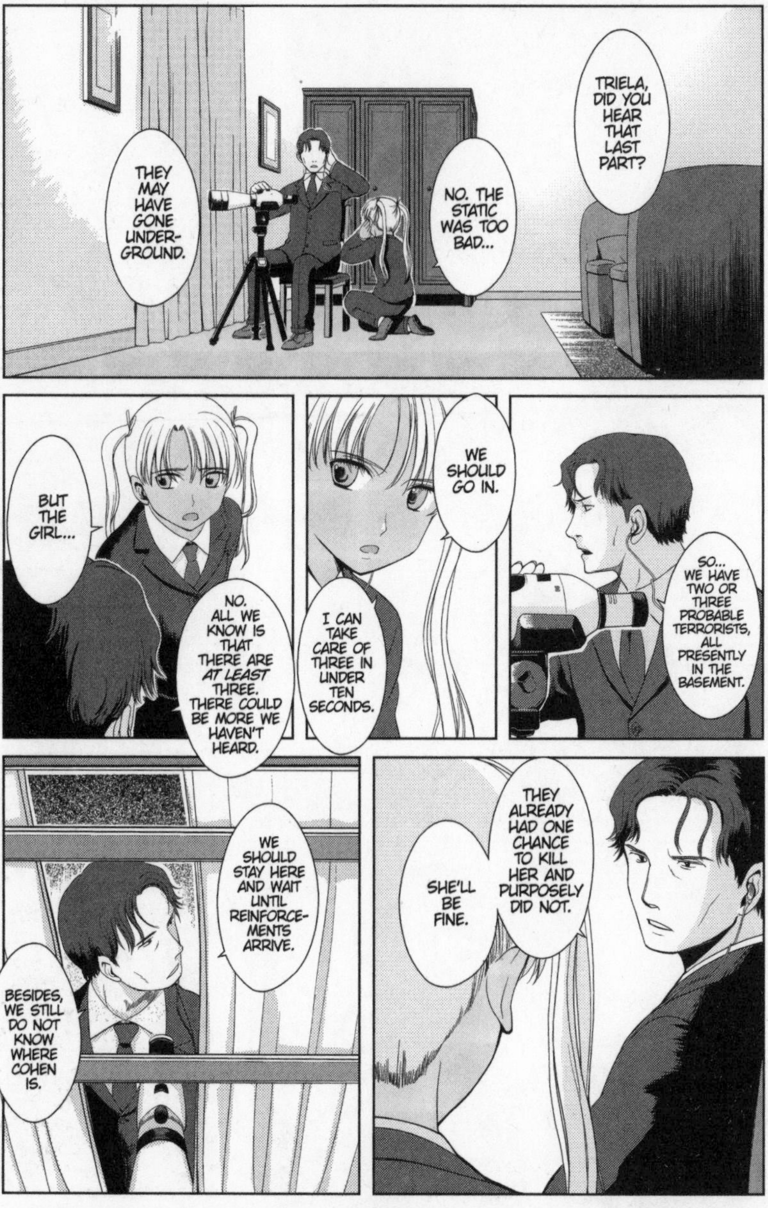
TRIELA, DID YOU HEAR THAT LAST PART?
NO. THE STATIC WAS TOO BAD...
THEY MAY HAVE GONE UNDER-GROUND.
SO... WE HAVE TWO OR THREE PROBABLE TERRORISTS, ALL PRESENTLY IN THE BASEMENT.
WE SHOULD GO IN.
I CAN TAKE CARE OF THREE IN UNDER TEN SECONDS.
NO. ALL WE KNOW IS THAT THERE ARE *AT LEAST* THREE. THERE COULD BE MORE WE HAVEN'T HEARD.
BUT THE GIRL...
THEY ALREADY HAD ONE CHANCE TO KILL HER AND PURPOSELY DID NOT.
SHE'LL BE FINE.
WE SHOULD STAY HERE AND WAIT UNTIL REINFORCE-MENTS ARRIVE.
BESIDES, WE STILL DO NOT KNOW WHERE COHEN IS.

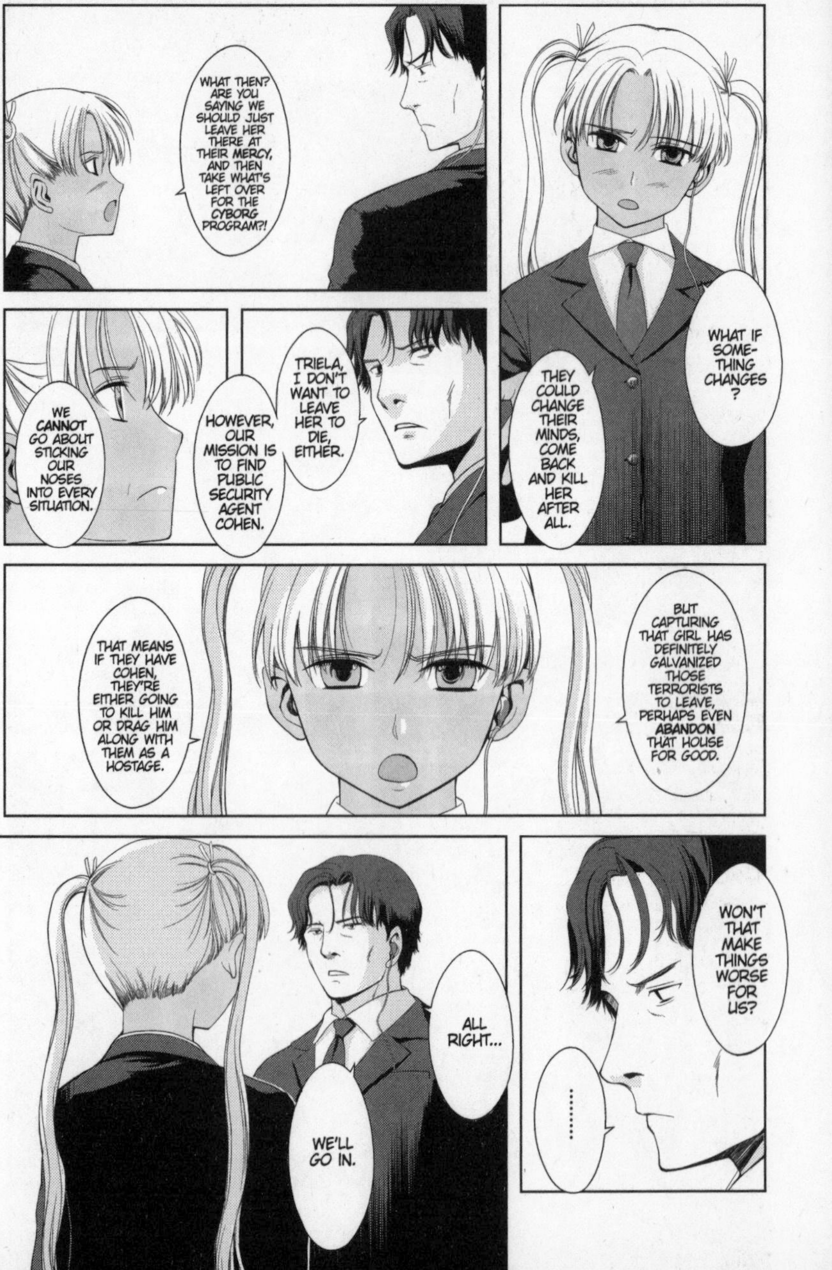
WHAT IF SOMETHING CHANGES?
THEY COULD CHANGE THEIR MINDS, COME BACK AND KILL HER AFTER ALL.
WHAT THEN? ARE YOU SAYING WE SHOULD JUST LEAVE HER THERE AT THEIR MERCY, AND THEN TAKE WHAT'S LEFT OVER FOR THE CYBORG PROGRAM?!
TRIELA, I DON'T WANT TO LEAVE HER TO DIE, EITHER.
HOWEVER, OUR MISSION IS TO FIND PUBLIC SECURITY AGENT COHEN.
WE CANNOT GO ABOUT STICKING OUR NOSES INTO EVERY SITUATION.
BUT CAPTURING THAT GIRL HAS DEFINITELY GALVANIZED THOSE TERRORISTS TO LEAVE, PERHAPS EVEN ABANDON THAT HOUSE FOR GOOD.
THAT MEANS IF THEY HAVE COHEN, THEY'RE EITHER GOING TO KILL HIM OR DRAG HIM ALONG WITH THEM AS A HOSTAGE.
WON'T THAT MAKE THINGS WORSE FOR US?
……
ALL RIGHT...
WE'LL GO IN.

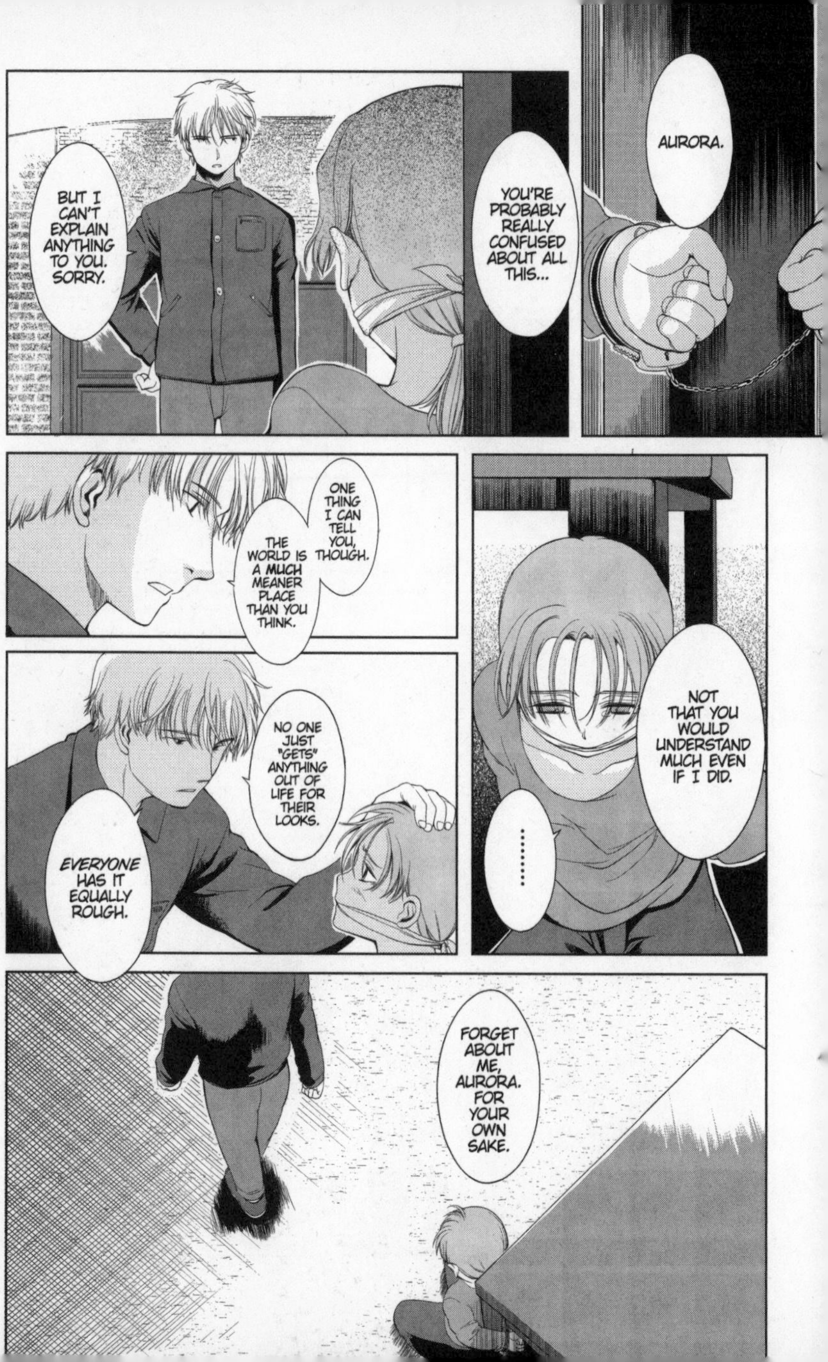
AURORA.
YOU'RE PROBABLY REALLY CONFUSED ABOUT ALL THIS...
BUT I CAN'T EXPLAIN ANYTHING TO YOU. SORRY.
NOT THAT YOU WOULD UNDERSTAND MUCH EVEN IF I DID.
......
ONE THING I CAN TELL YOU, THOUGH.
THE WORLD IS A MUCH MEANER PLACE THAN YOU THINK.
NO ONE JUST "GETS" ANYTHING OUT OF LIFE FOR THEIR LOOKS.
EVERYONE HAS IT EQUALLY ROUGH.
FORGET ABOUT ME, AURORA. FOR YOUR OWN SAKE.

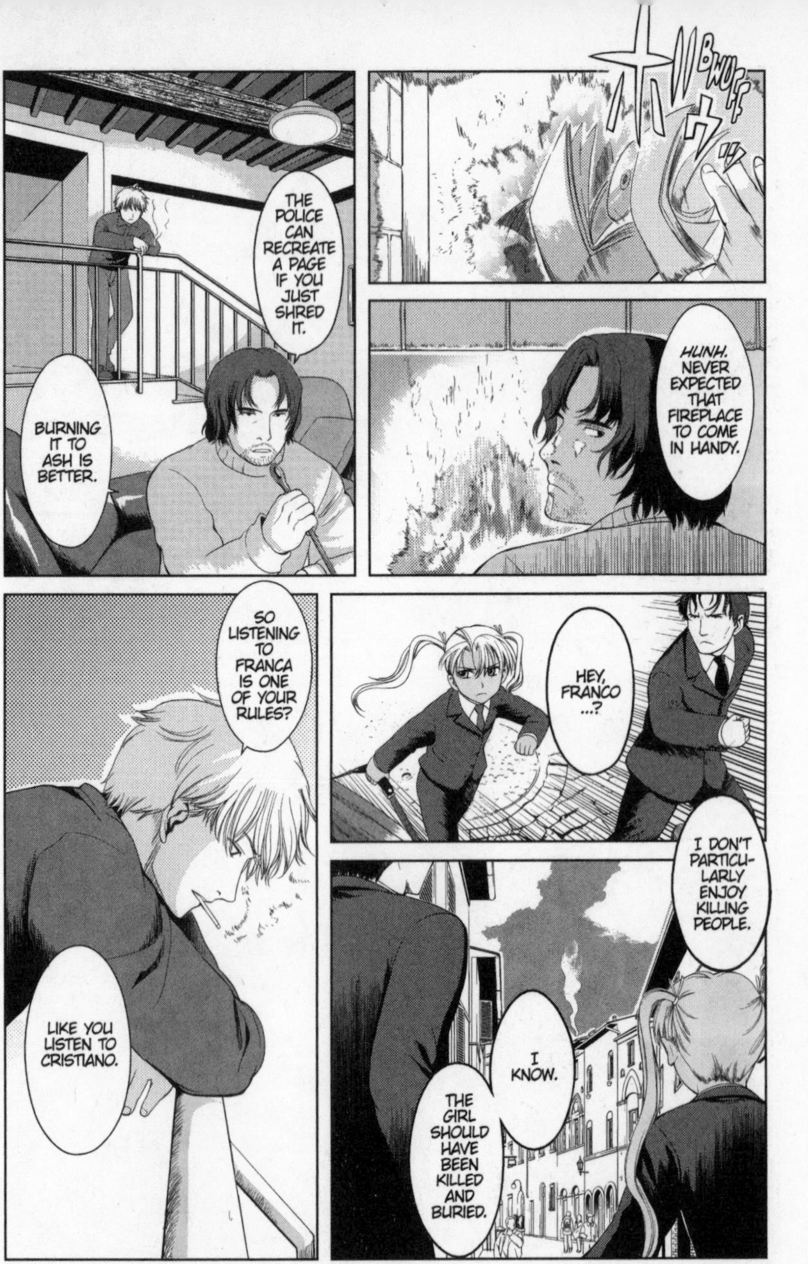
BWUFF
HUNH. NEVER EXPECTED THAT FIREPLACE TO COME IN HANDY.
THE POLICE CAN RECREATE A PAGE IF YOU JUST SHRED IT.
BURNING IT TO ASH IS BETTER.
HEY, FRANCO ...?
I DON'T PARTICU-LARLY ENJOY KILLING PEOPLE.
I KNOW.
THE GIRL SHOULD HAVE BEEN KILLED AND BURIED.
SO LISTENING TO FRANCA IS ONE OF YOUR RULES?
LIKE YOU LISTEN TO CRISTIANO.

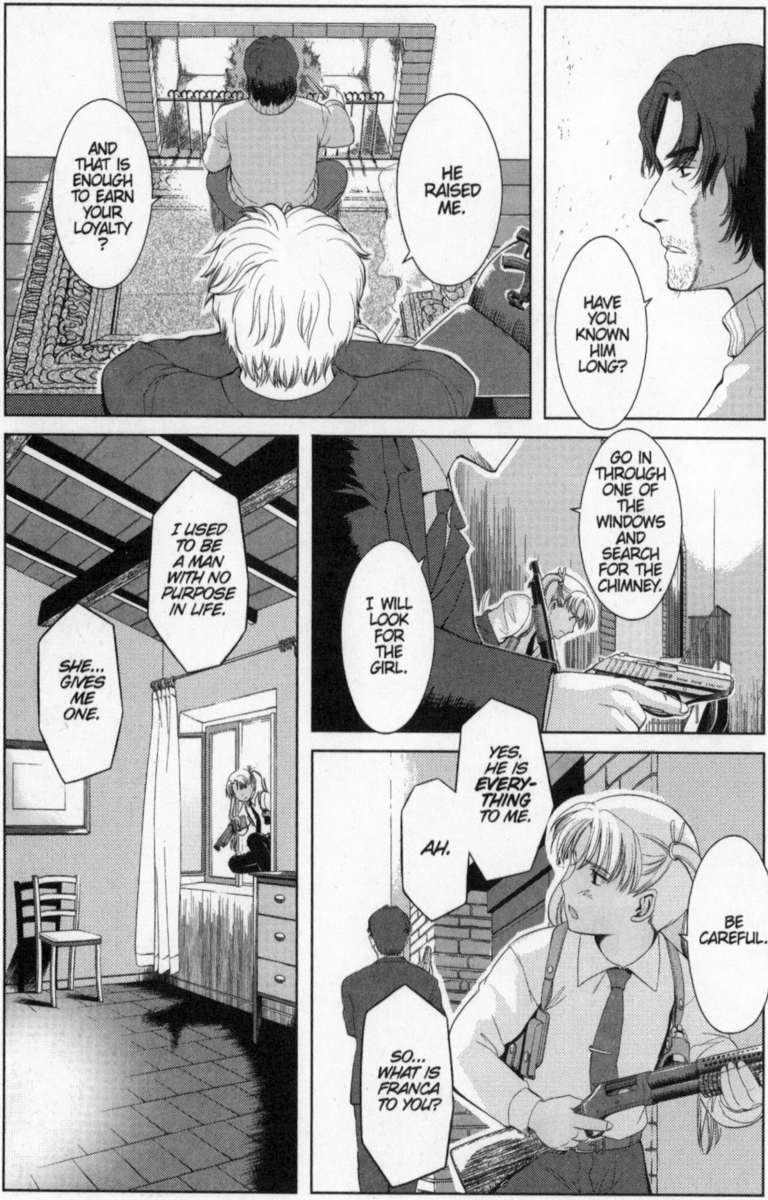
HAVE YOU KNOWN HIM LONG?
HE RAISED ME.
AND THAT IS ENOUGH TO EARN YOUR LOYALTY ?
GO IN THROUGH ONE OF THE WINDOWS AND SEARCH FOR THE CHIMNEY.
I WILL LOOK FOR THE GIRL.
BE CAREFUL.
YES. HE IS EVERYTHING TO ME.
AH.
SO... WHAT IS FRANCA TO YOU?
I USED TO BE A MAN WITH NO PURPOSE IN LIFE.
SHE... GIVES ME ONE.

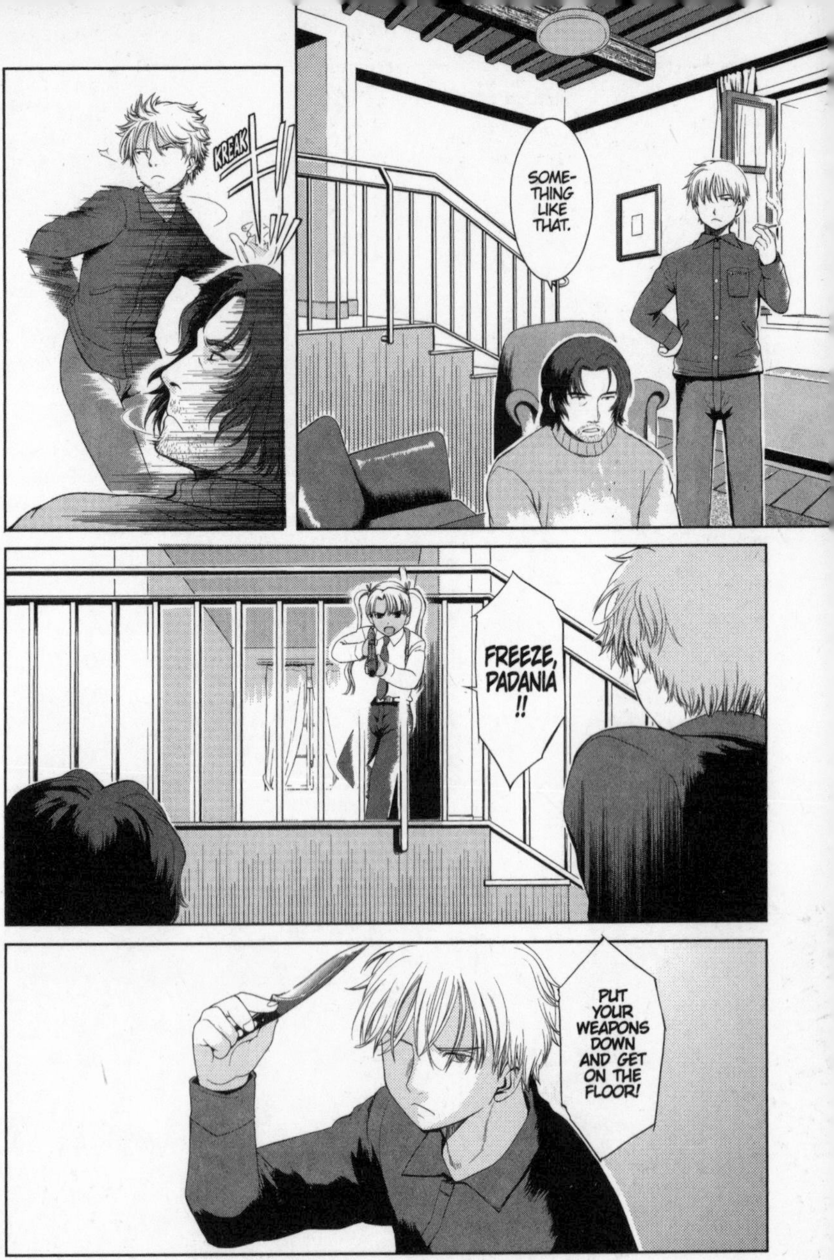
SOMETHING LIKE THAT.
KREAK
FREEZE, PADANIA!!
PUT YOUR WEAPONS DOWN AND GET ON THE FLOOR!

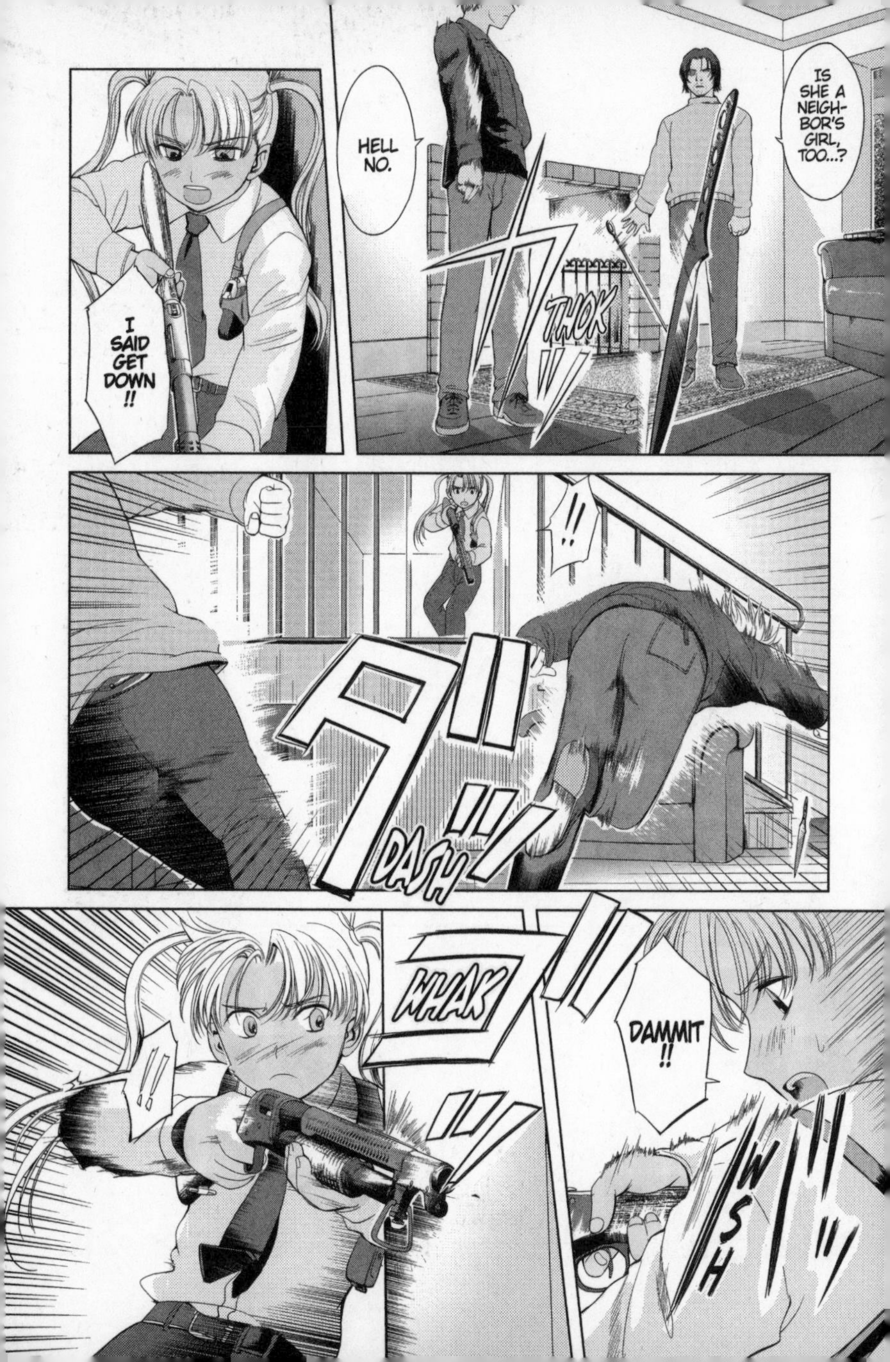
IS SHE A NEIGHBOR'S GIRL, TOO...?
HELL NO.
THOK
I SAID GET DOWN !!
!!
DASH
DAMMIT !!
WSH
WHAK
!!

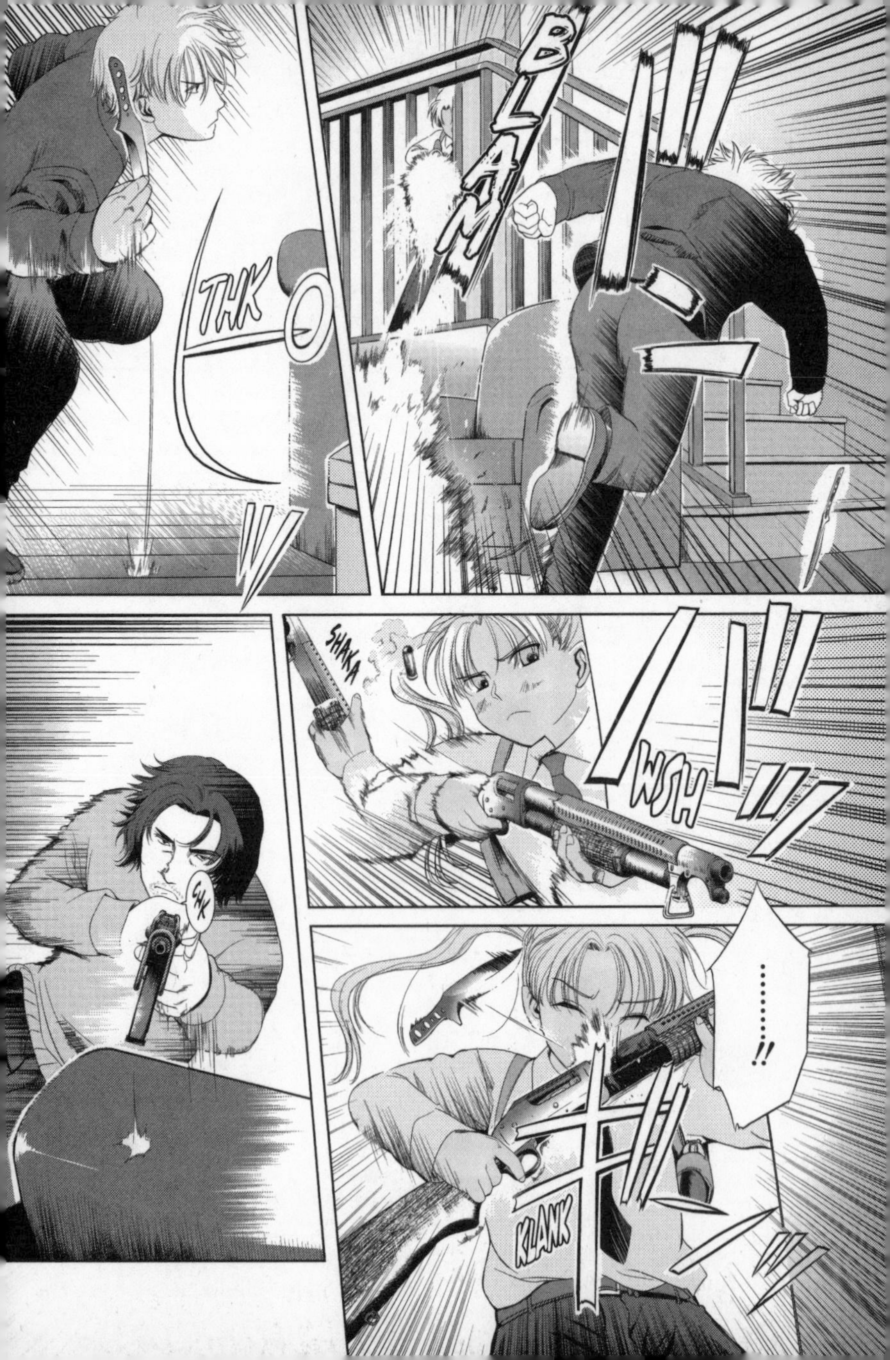
BLAM
THK
SHAKA
WSH
......!!
KLANK
CHK

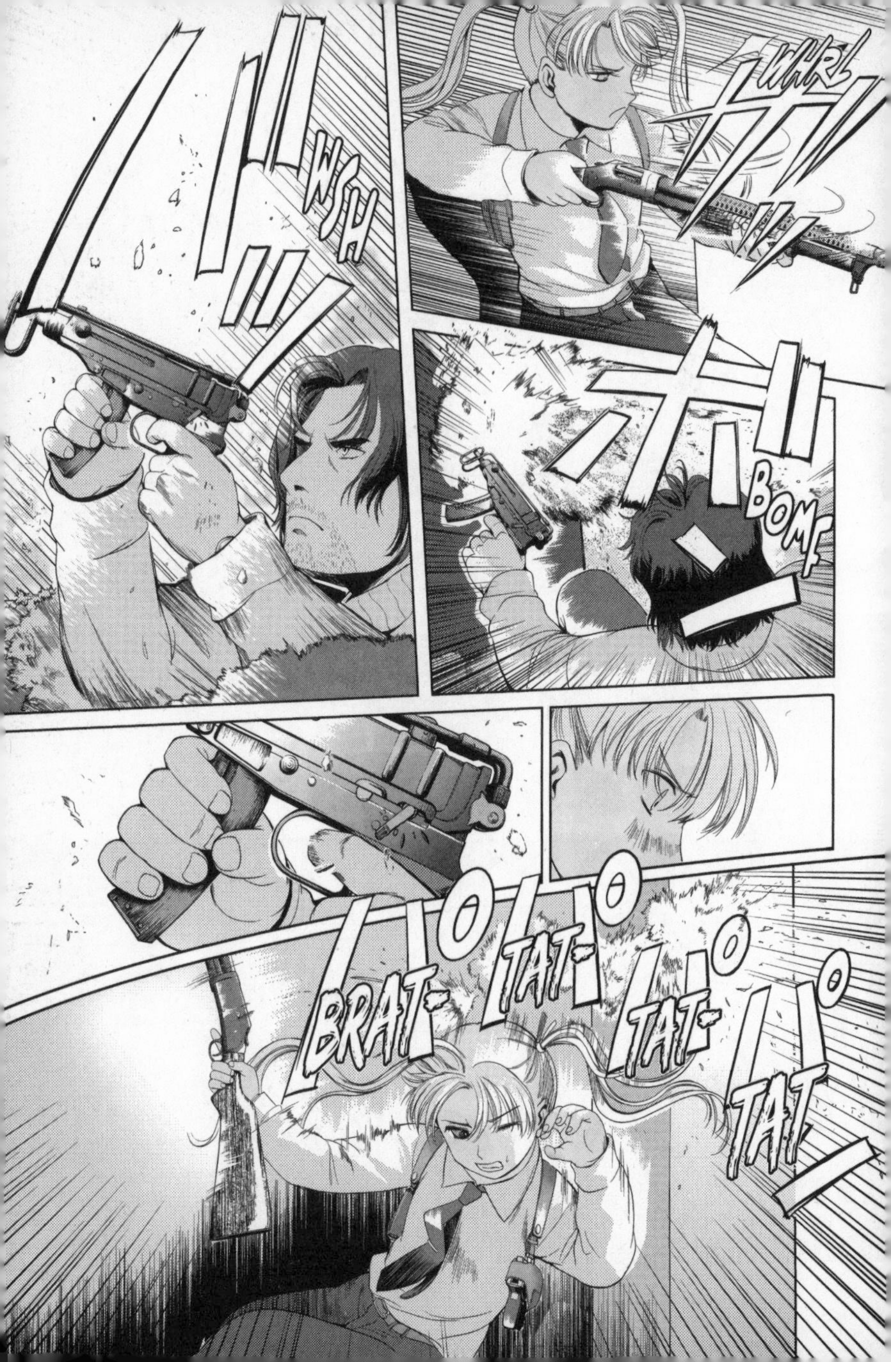
WHIRL
BOMF
WSH
BRAT-TAT-TAT-TAT

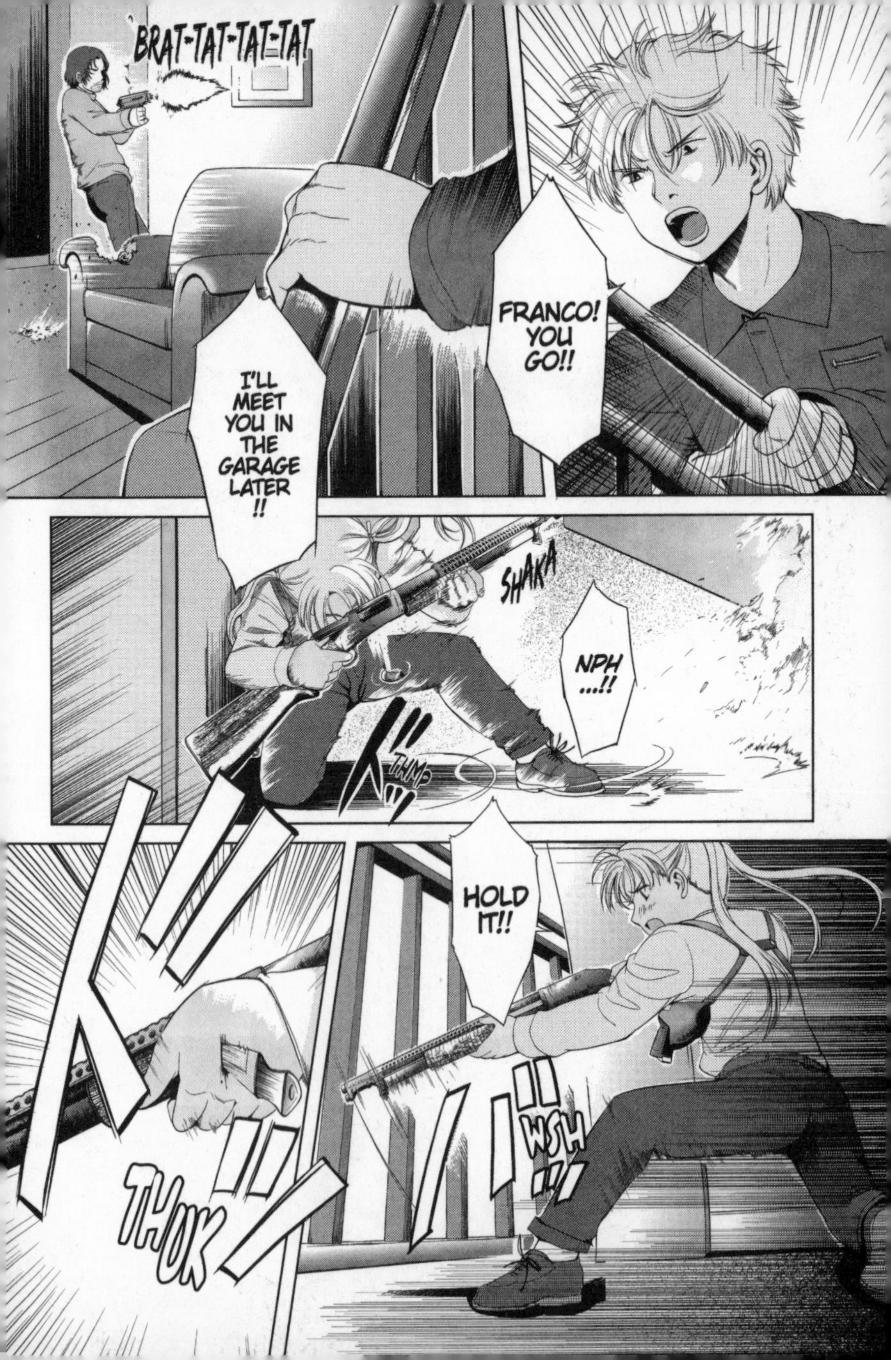
FRANCO! YOU GO!!
I'LL MEET YOU IN THE GARAGE LATER!!
BRAT-TAT-TAT-TAT
SHAKA
NPH ...!!
THMP
HOLD IT!!
WSH
THOK

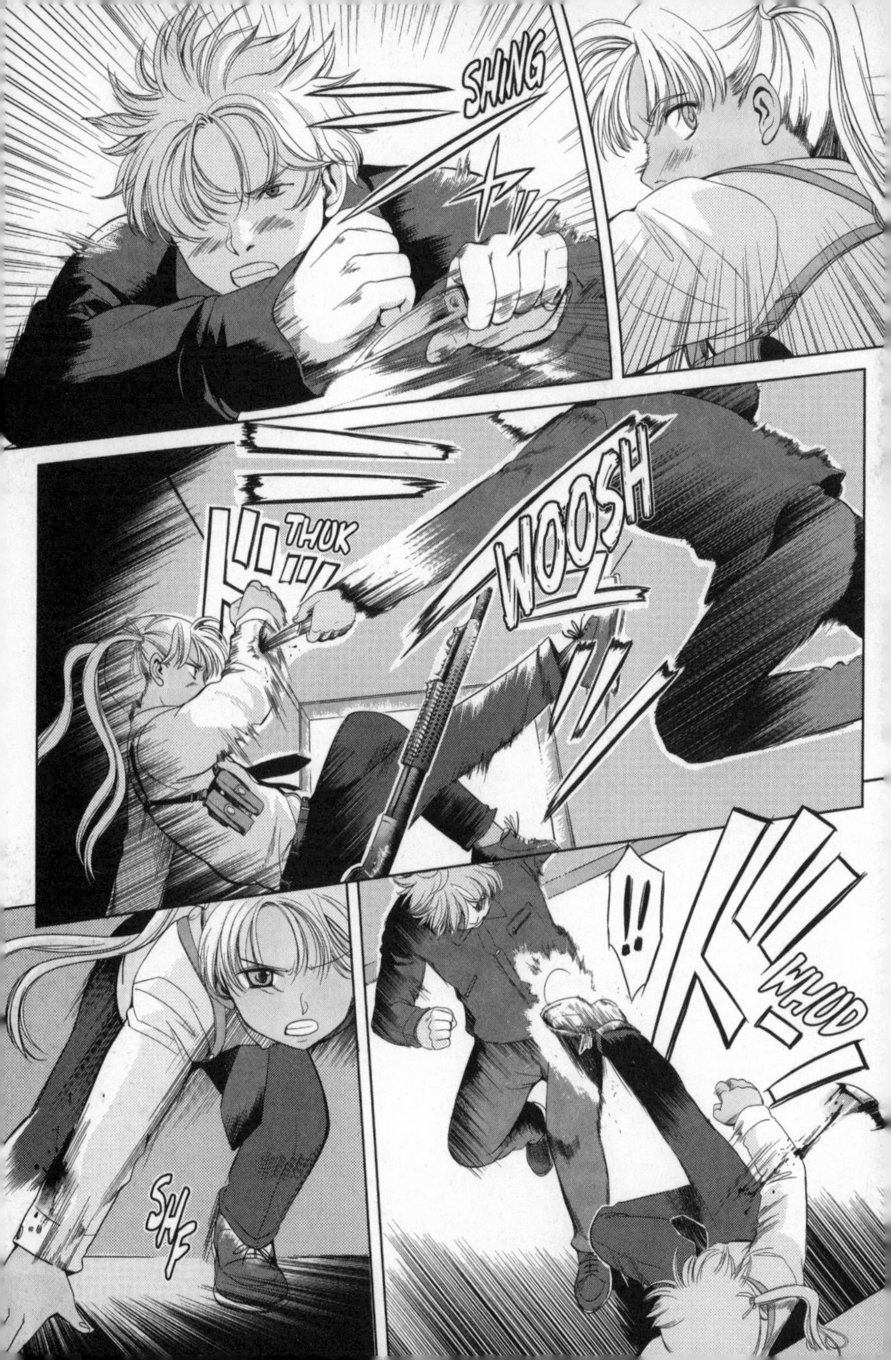
SHING
WOOSH
THUK
!!
WHUD
SHF

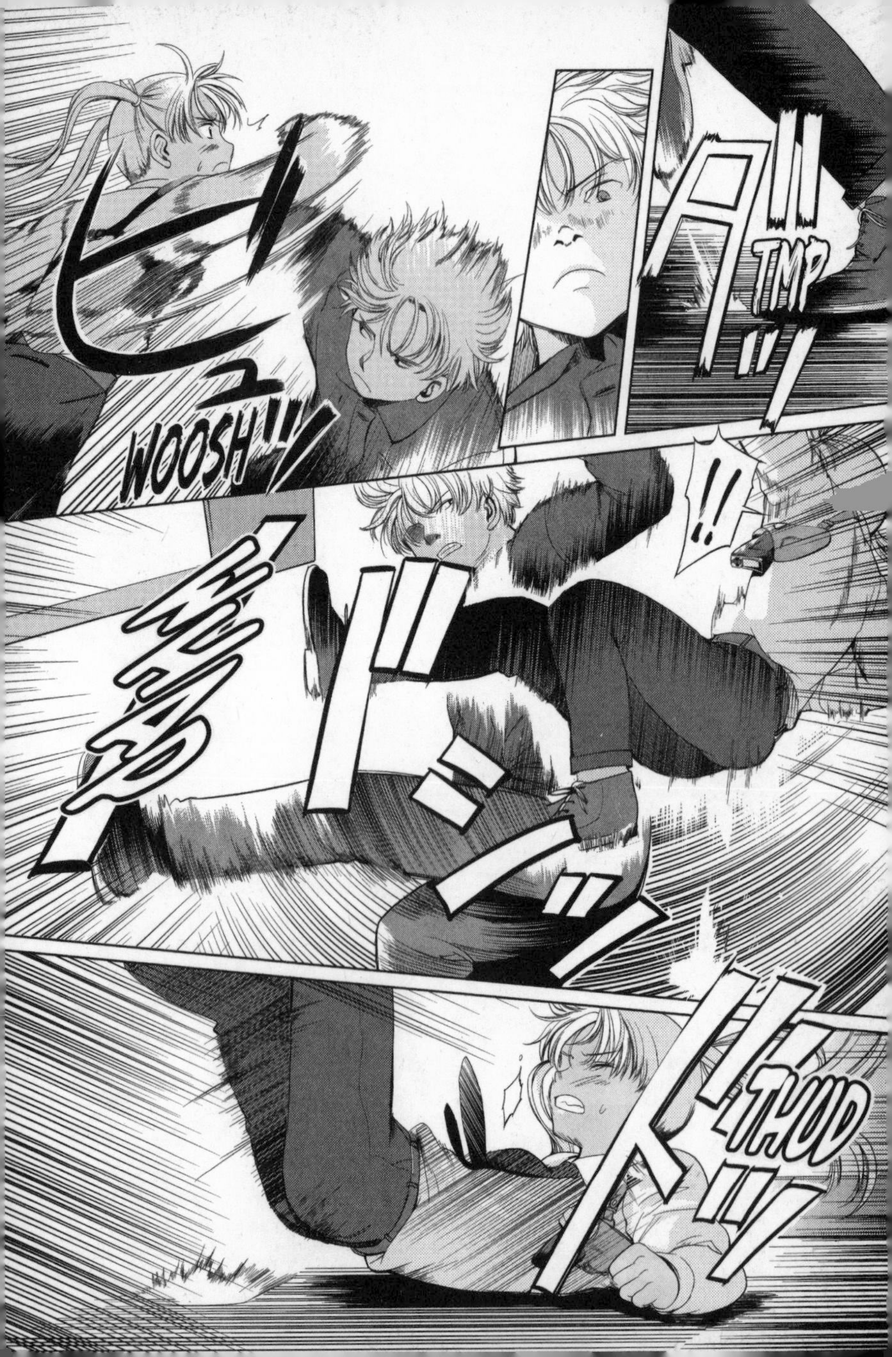
TMP!!
WOOSH!!
!!
THUD!!

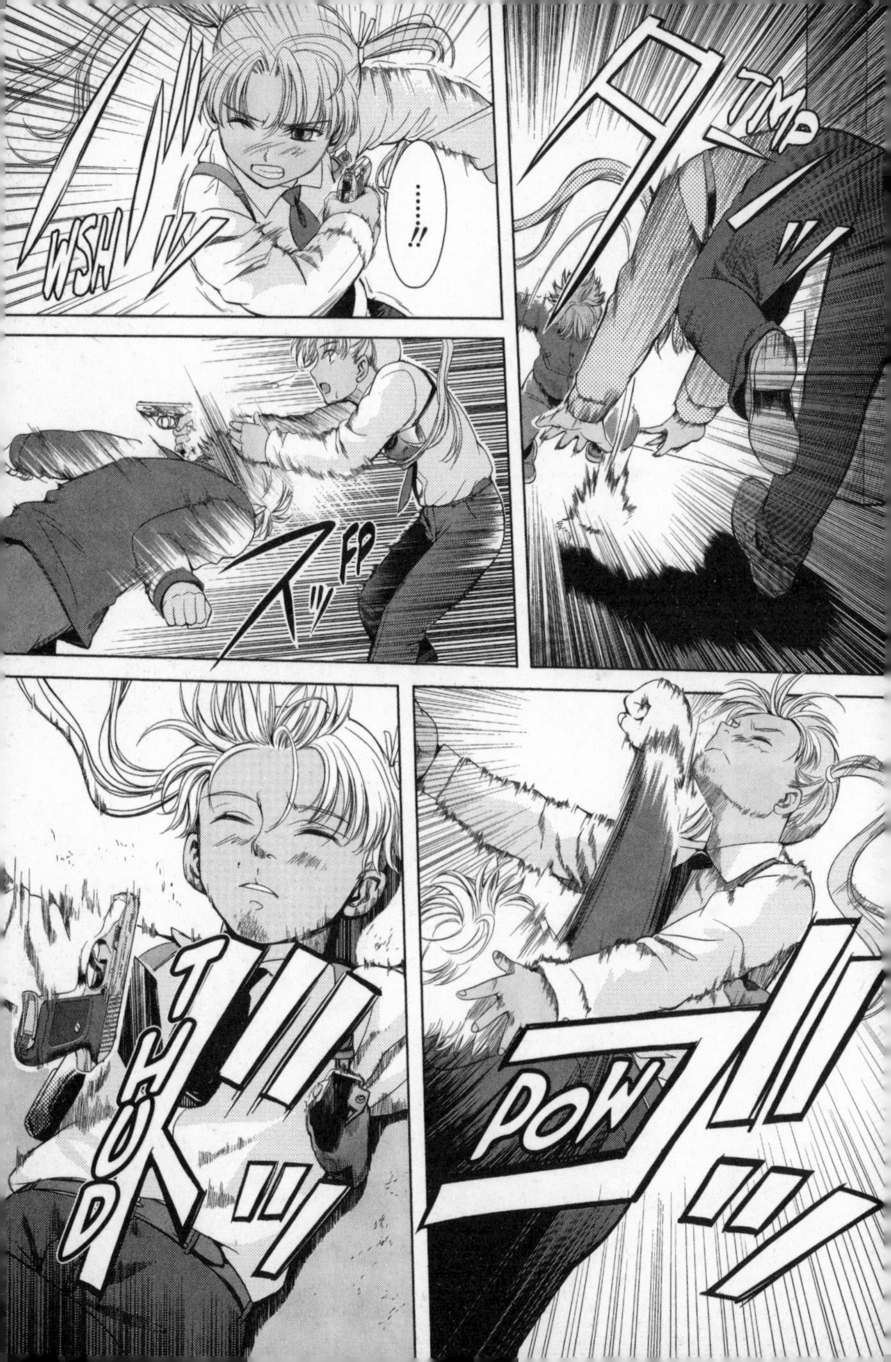

TMP
WSH
......!!
FP
POW
THUD

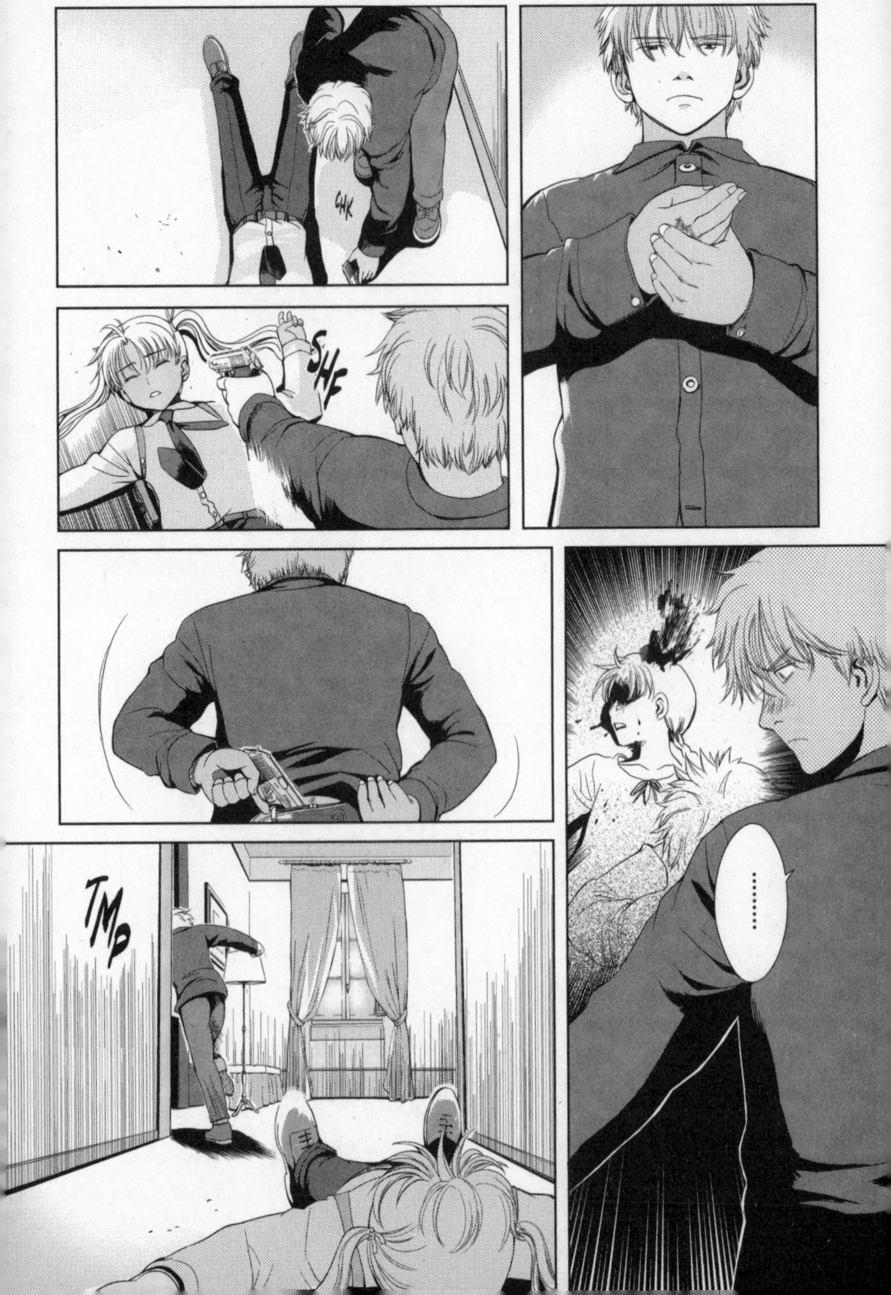
CHK
SHF
....
TMP

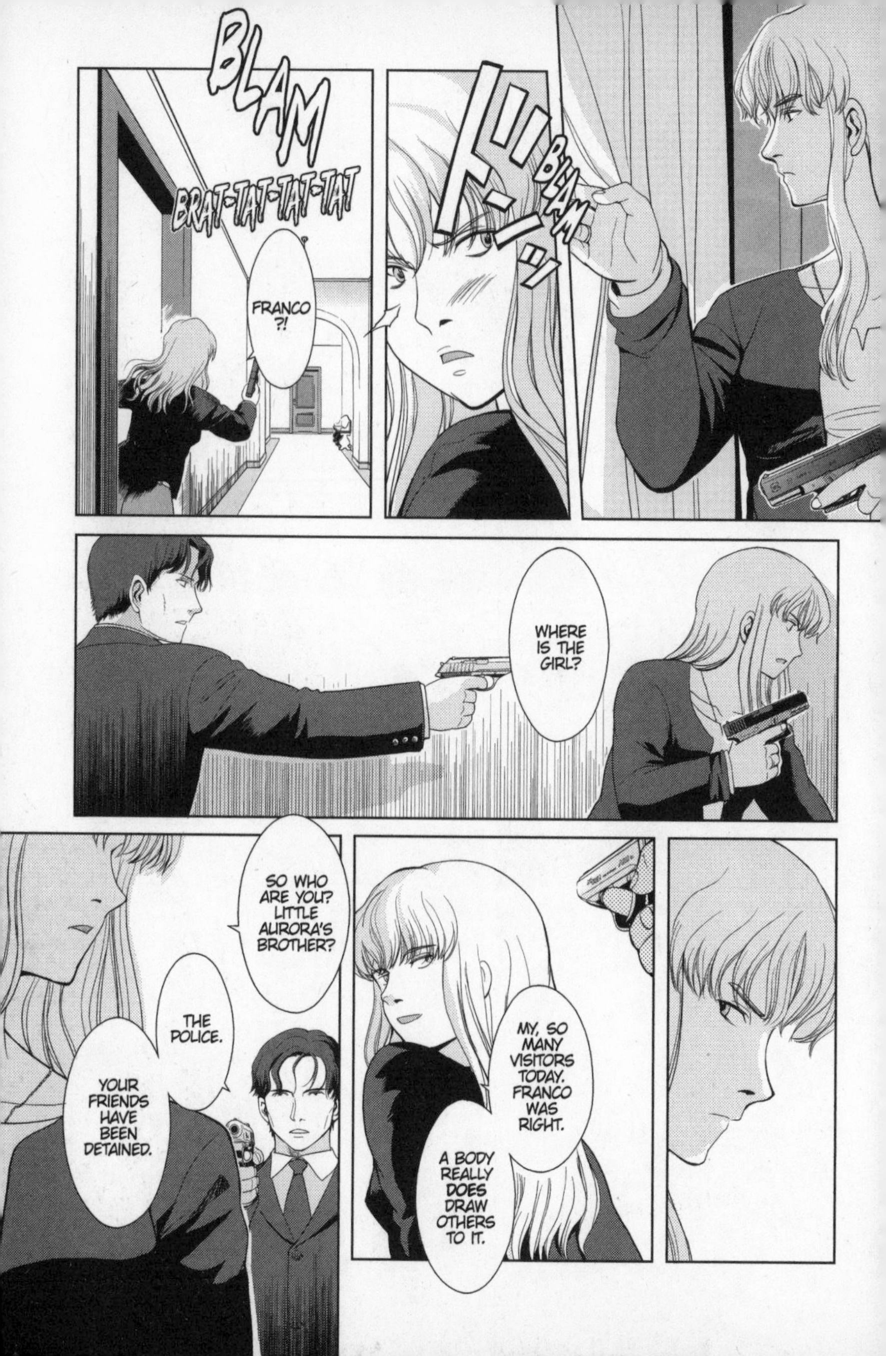
BLAM
BLAM
BRAT-TAT-TAT-TAT
FRANCO ?!
WHERE IS THE GIRL?
MY, SO MANY VISITORS TODAY. FRANCO WAS RIGHT.
A BODY REALLY DOES DRAW OTHERS TO IT.
SO WHO ARE YOU? LITTLE AURORA'S BROTHER?
THE POLICE.
YOUR FRIENDS HAVE BEEN DETAINED.

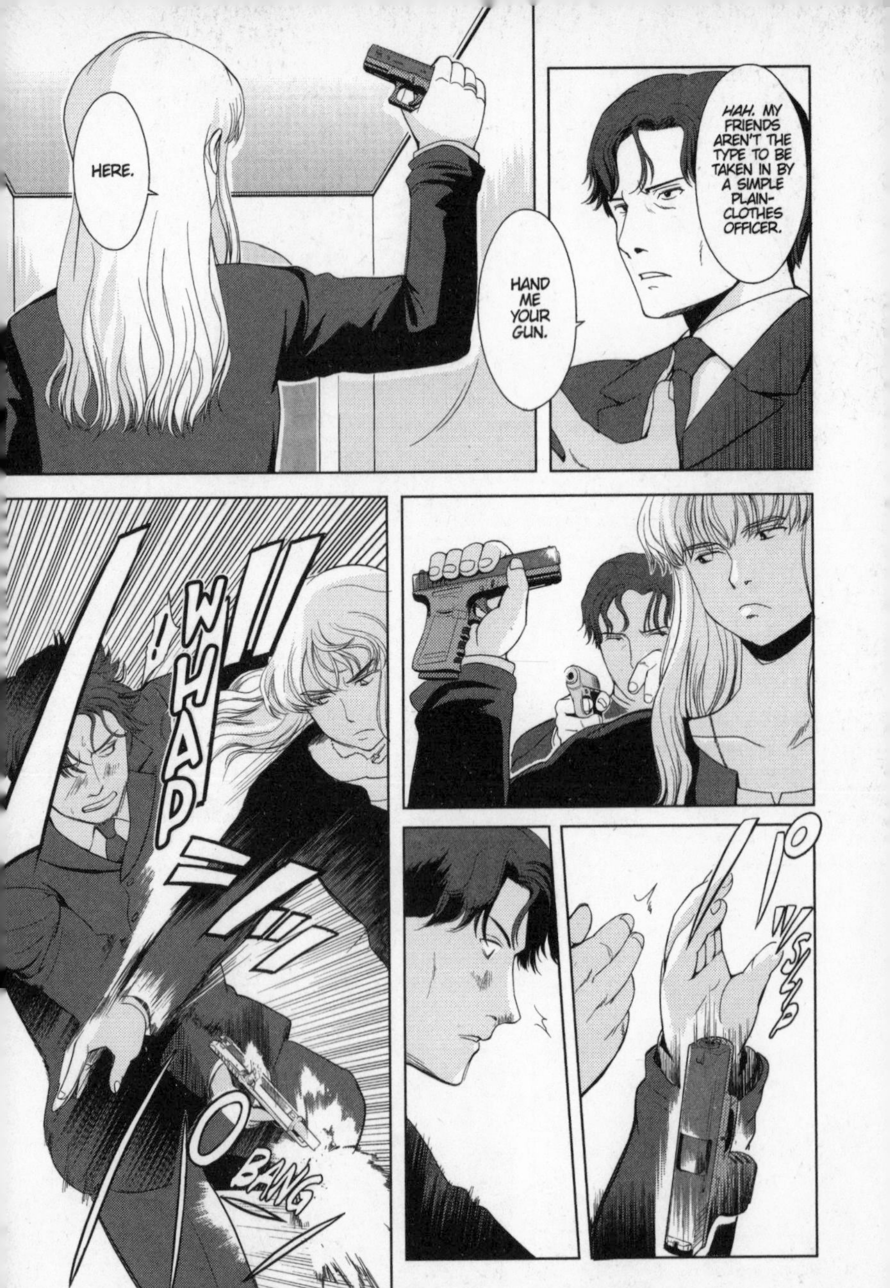
HAH. MY FRIENDS AREN'T THE TYPE TO BE TAKEN IN BY A SIMPLE PLAIN-CLOTHES OFFICER.
HAND ME YOUR GUN.
HERE.
WSHP
WHAP
BANG

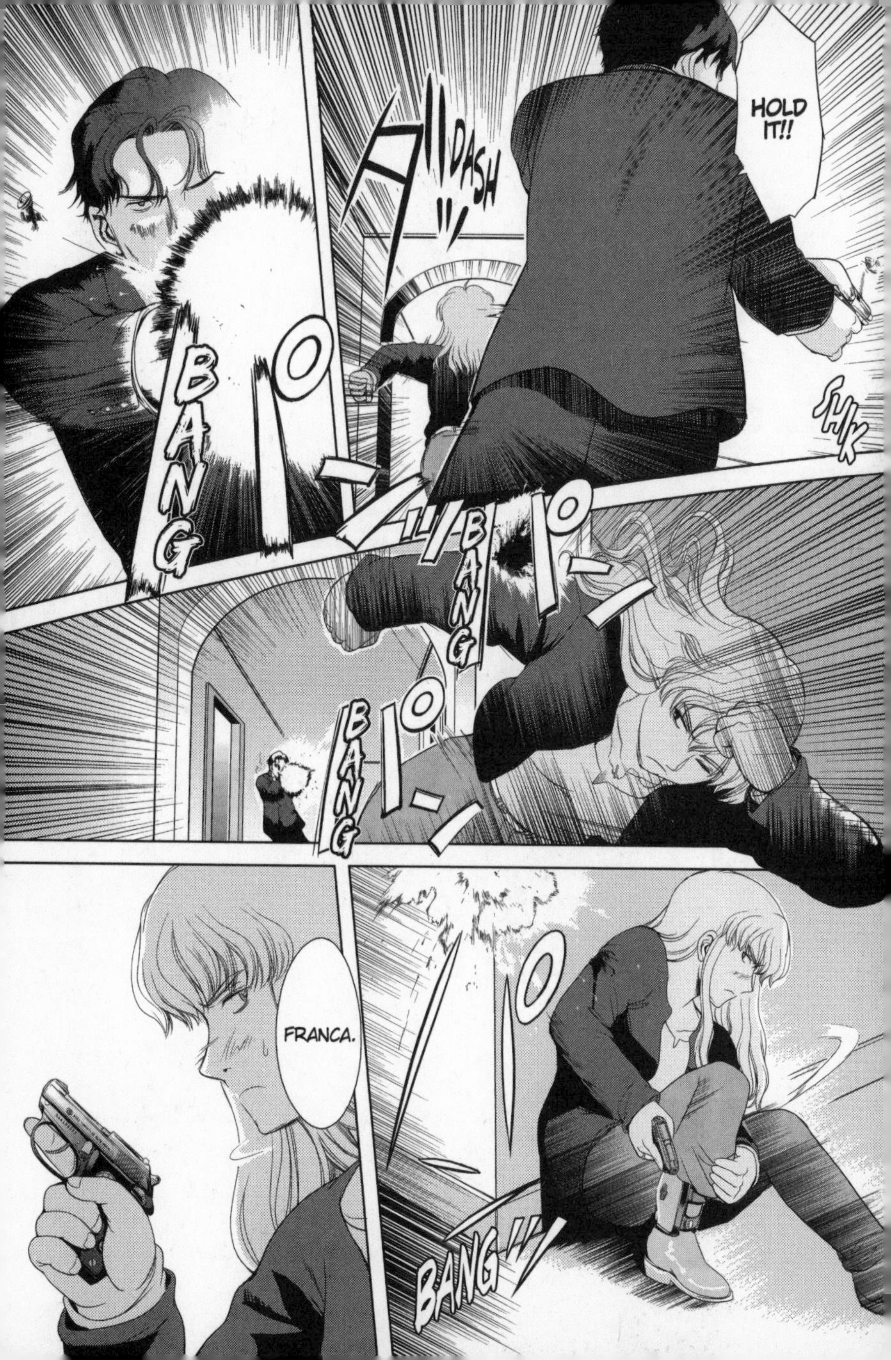
HOLD IT!!
DASH
SHK
BANG
BANG
BANG
BANG!!
FRANCA.

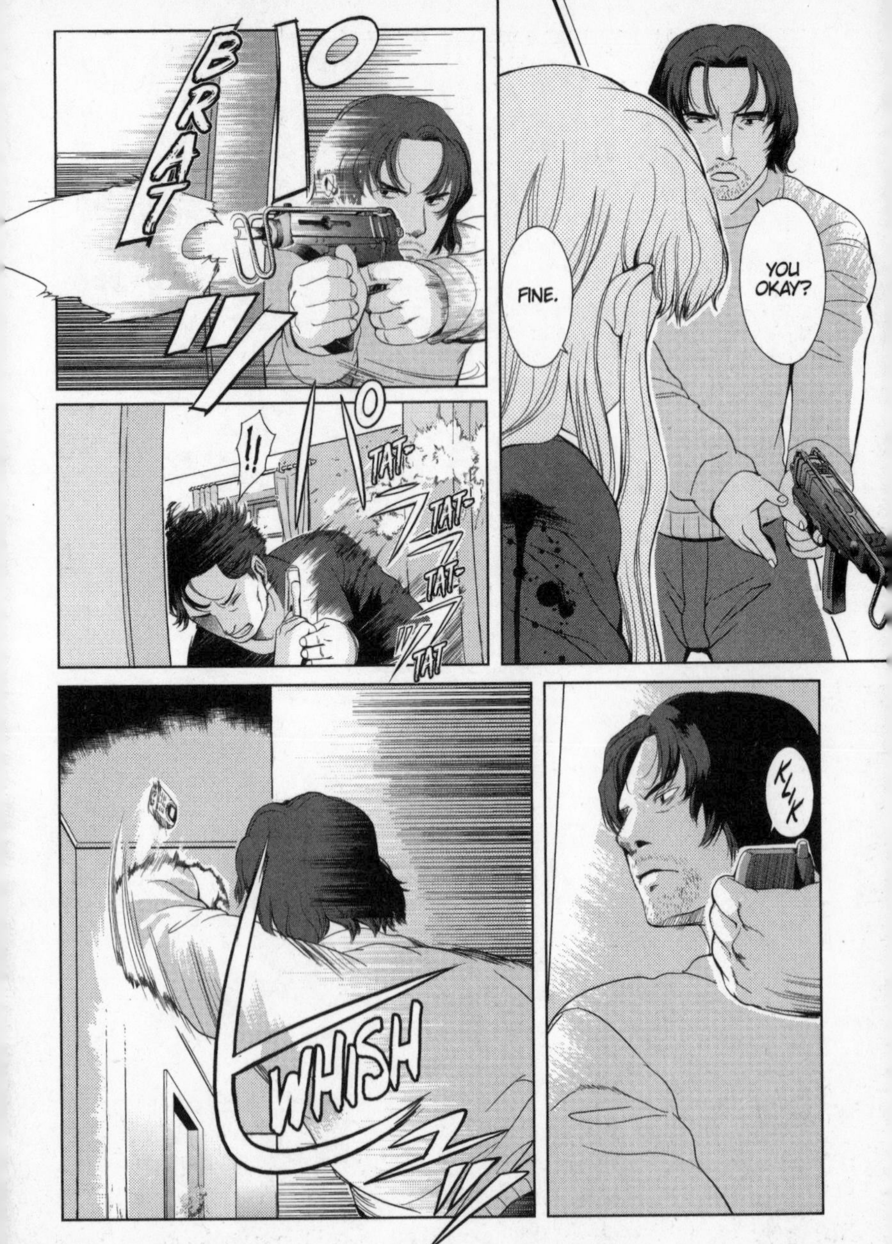
YOU OKAY?
FINE.
BRAT
!!
TAT- TAT- TAT- TAT
KLIK
WHISH

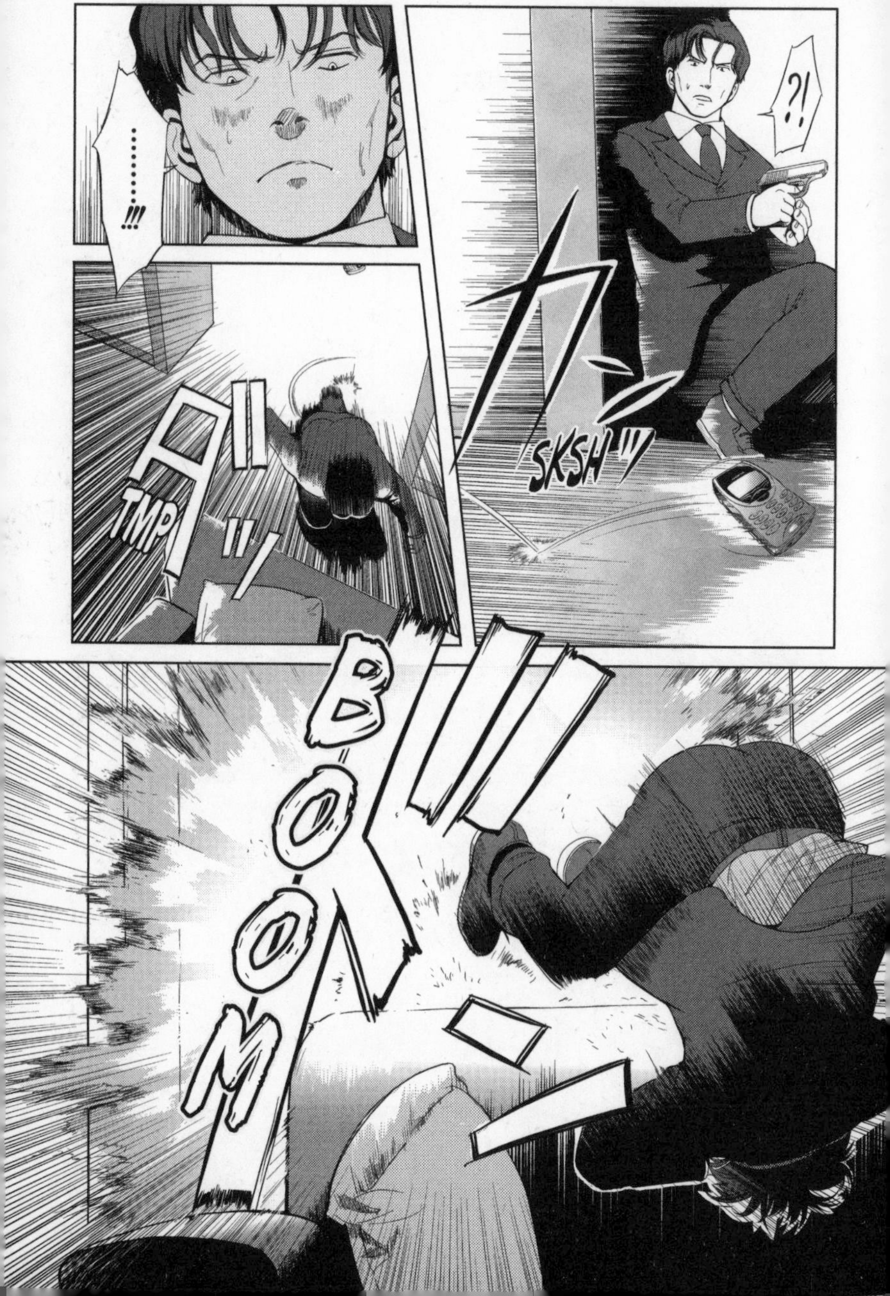
?!
SKSH
......!!!
TMP
BOOM

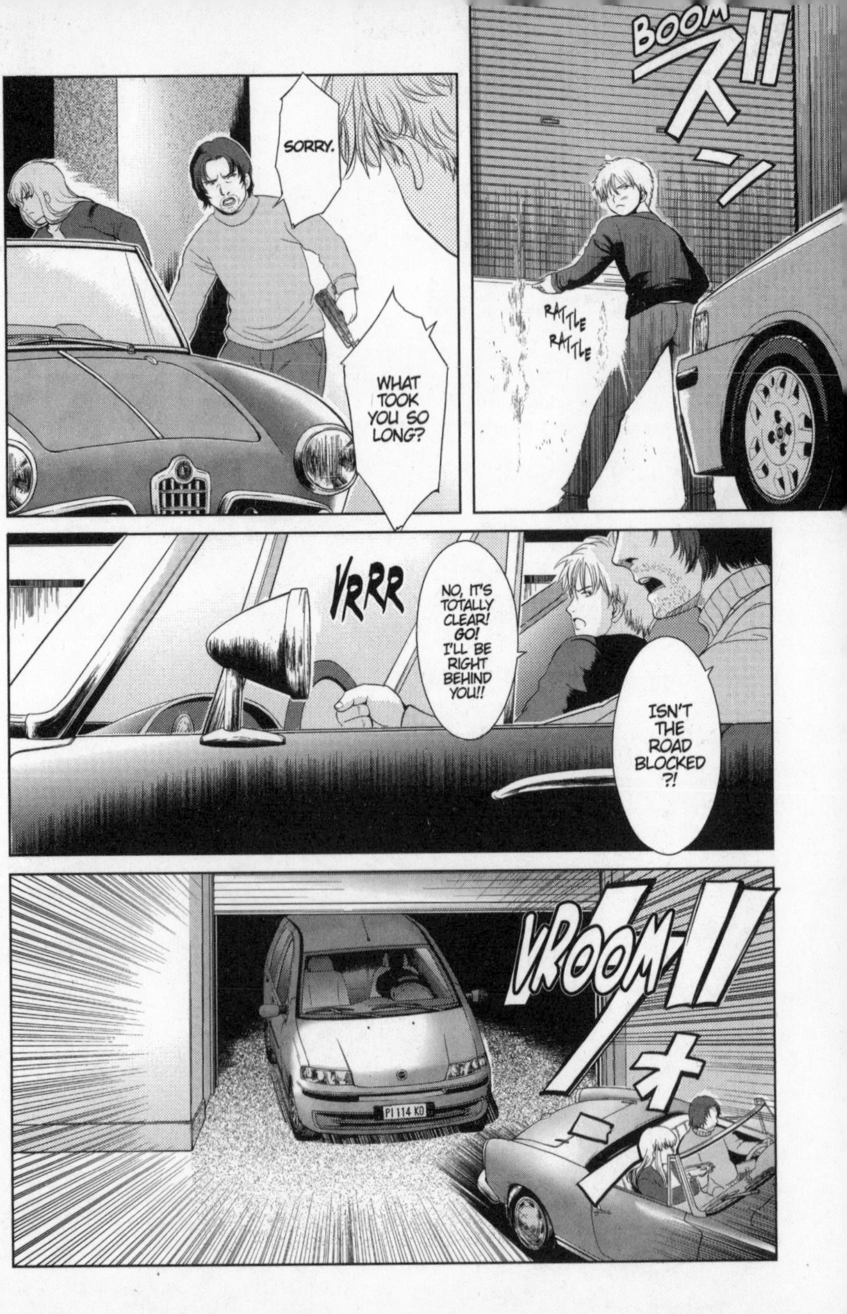
BOOM
RATTLE RATTLE
SORRY.
WHAT TOOK YOU SO LONG?
VRRR
ISN'T THE ROAD BLOCKED?!
NO, IT'S TOTALLY CLEAR! GO! I'LL BE RIGHT BEHIND YOU!!
VROOM
PI 114 KO

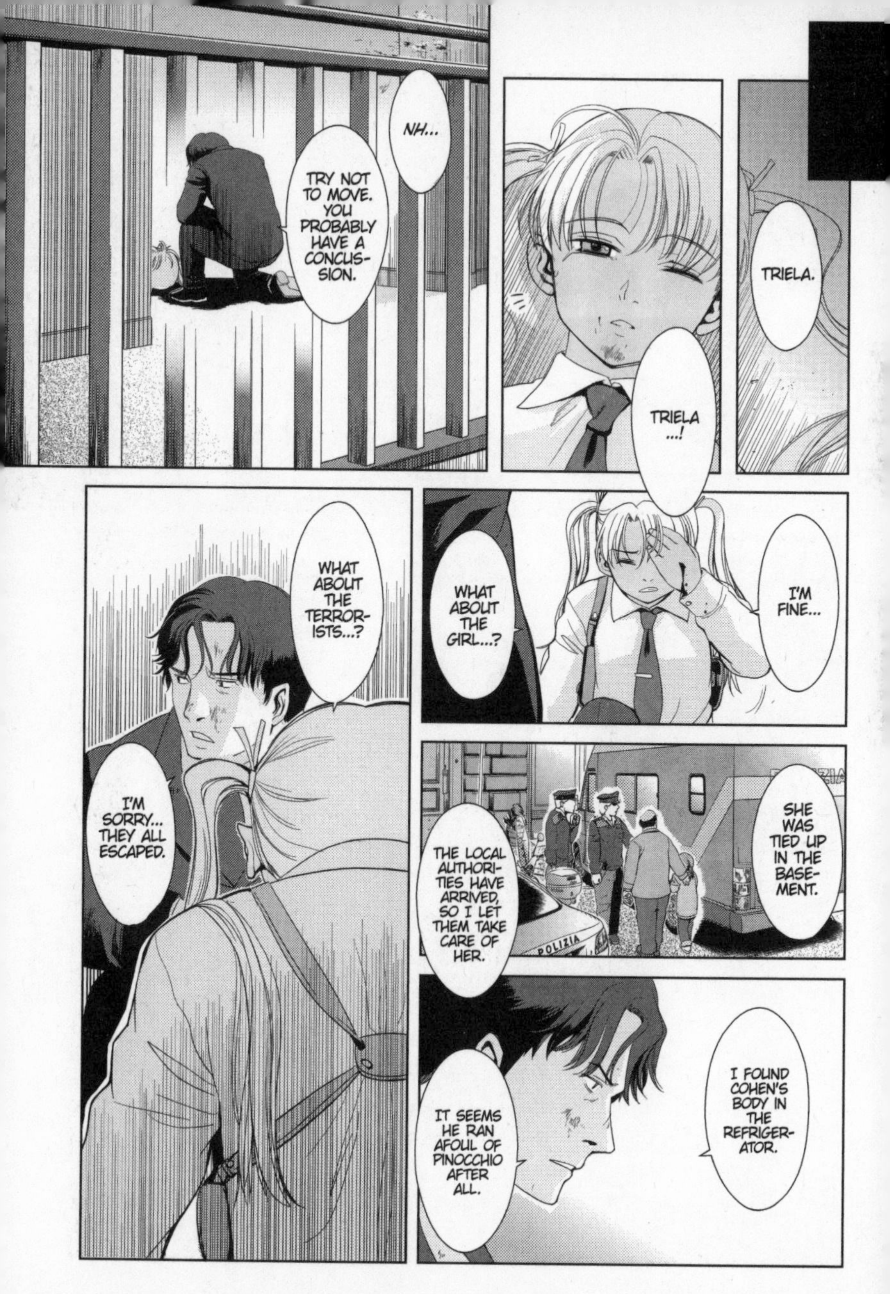
TRIELA.
TRIELA ...!
NH...
TRY NOT TO MOVE. YOU PROBABLY HAVE A CONCUSSION.
I'M FINE...
WHAT ABOUT THE GIRL...?
SHE WAS TIED UP IN THE BASEMENT.
THE LOCAL AUTHORITIES HAVE ARRIVED, SO I LET THEM TAKE CARE OF HER.
I FOUND COHEN'S BODY IN THE REFRIGERATOR.
IT SEEMS HE RAN AFOUL OF PINOCCHIO AFTER ALL.
WHAT ABOUT THE TERRORISTS...?
I'M SORRY... THEY ALL ESCAPED.

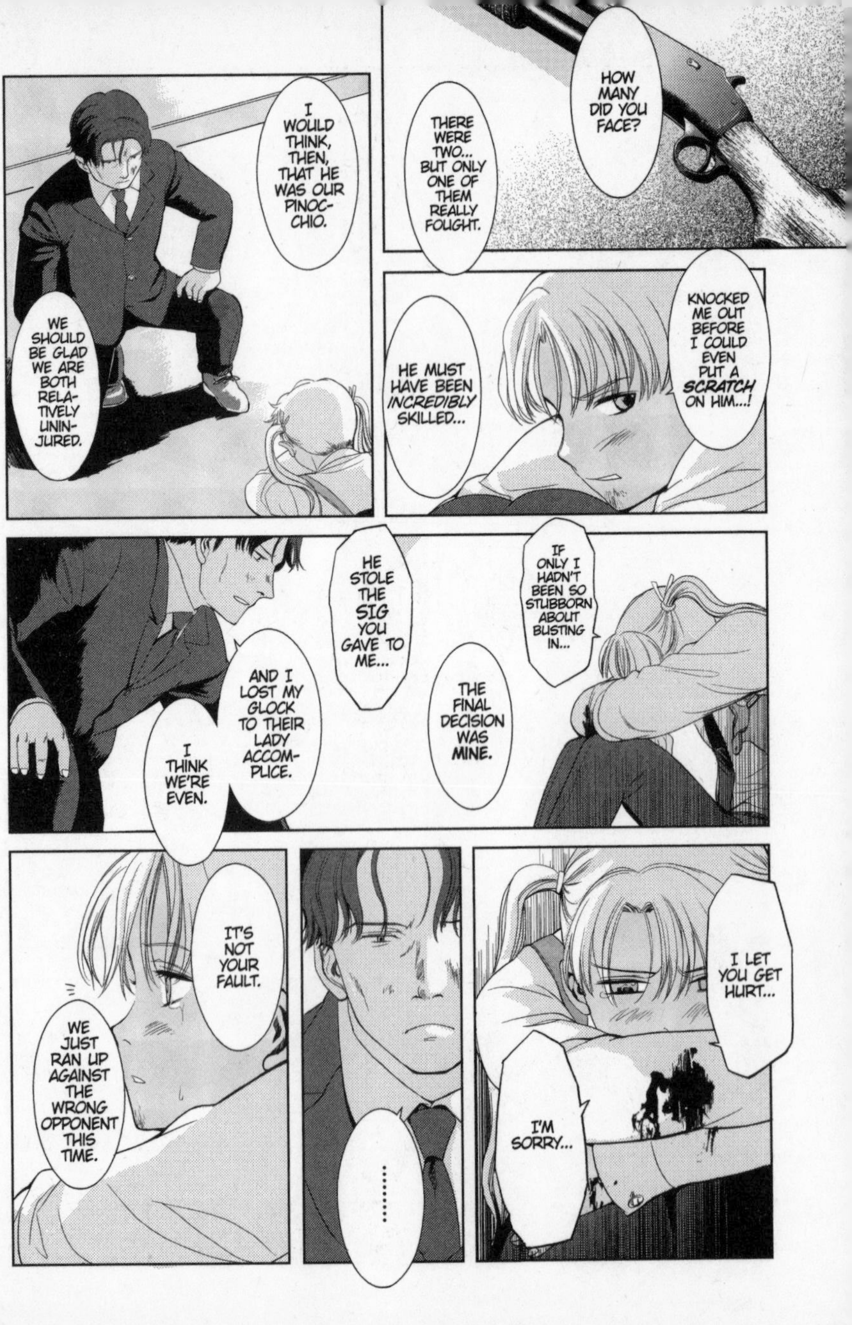
HOW MANY DID YOU FACE?
THERE WERE TWO... BUT ONLY ONE OF THEM REALLY FOUGHT.
KNOCKED ME OUT BEFORE I COULD EVEN PUT A SCRATCH ON HIM...!
HE MUST HAVE BEEN INCREDIBLY SKILLED...
I WOULD THINK, THEN, THAT HE WAS OUR PINOCCHIO.
WE SHOULD BE GLAD WE ARE BOTH RELATIVELY UNINJURED.
IF ONLY I HADN'T BEEN SO STUBBORN ABOUT BUSTING IN...
THE FINAL DECISION WAS MINE.
HE STOLE THE SIG YOU GAVE TO ME...
AND I LOST MY GLOCK TO THEIR LADY ACCOMPLICE.
I THINK WE'RE EVEN.
I LET YOU GET HURT...
I'M SORRY...
......
IT'S NOT YOUR FAULT.
WE JUST RAN UP AGAINST THE WRONG OPPONENT THIS TIME.

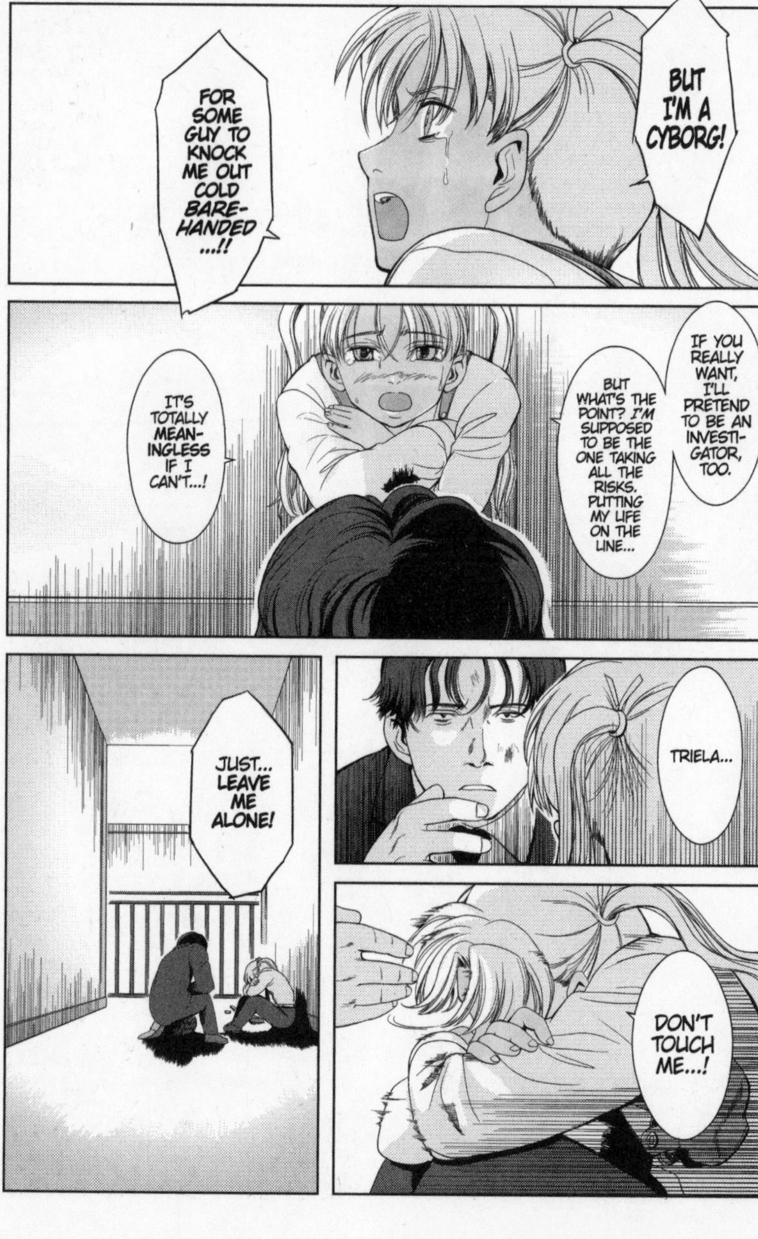
BUT I'M A CYBORG!
FOR SOME GUY TO KNOCK ME OUT COLD BARE-HANDED ...!!
IF YOU REALLY WANT, I'LL PRETEND TO BE AN INVESTIGATOR, TOO.
BUT WHAT'S THE POINT? *I'M* SUPPOSED TO BE THE ONE TAKING ALL THE RISKS, PUTTING MY LIFE ON THE LINE...
IT'S TOTALLY MEANINGLESS IF I CAN'T...!
TRIELA...
DON'T TOUCH ME...!
JUST... LEAVE ME ALONE!

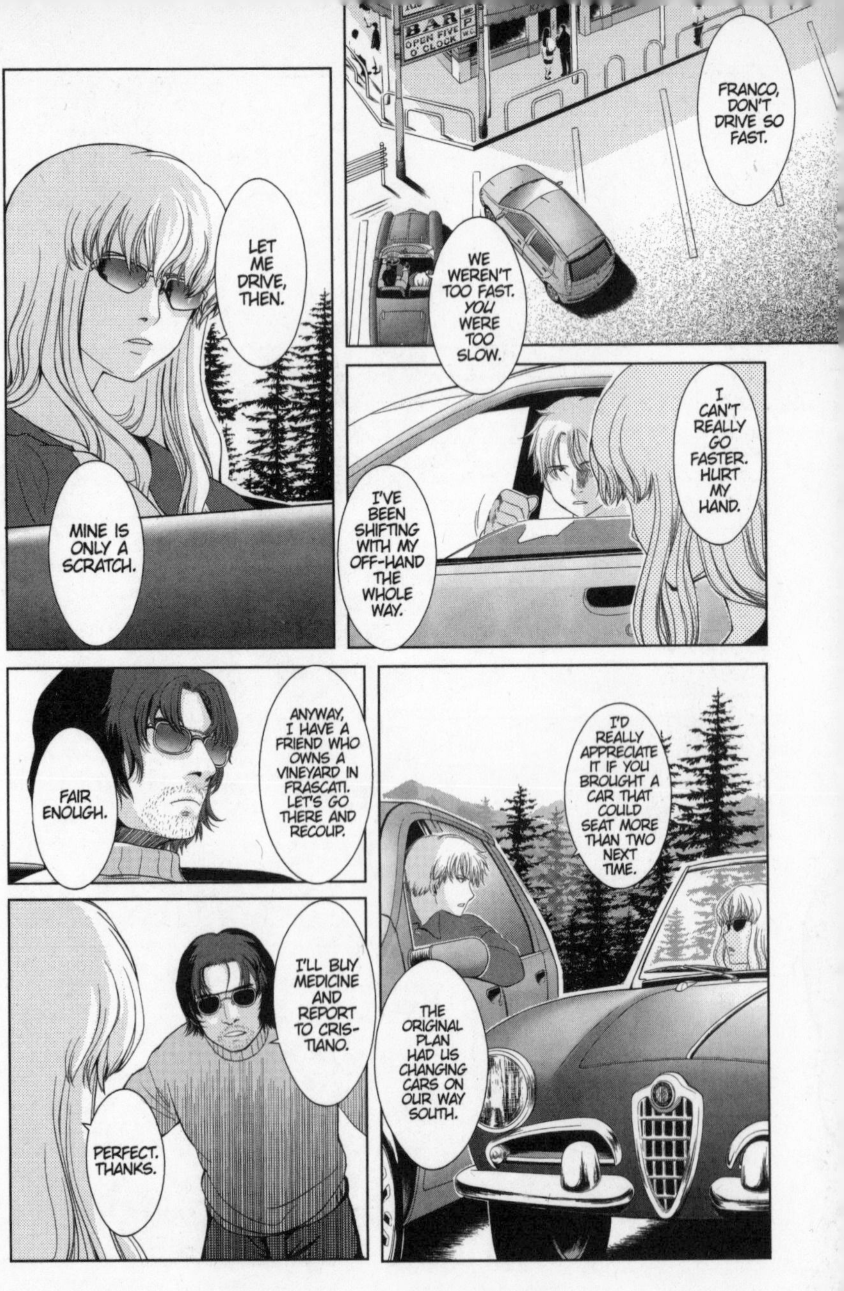
BAR
OPEN FIVE O' CLOCK
FRANCO, DON'T DRIVE SO FAST.
WE WEREN'T TOO FAST. *YOU* WERE TOO SLOW.
I CAN'T REALLY GO FASTER. HURT MY HAND.
I'VE BEEN SHIFTING WITH MY OFF-HAND THE WHOLE WAY.
LET ME DRIVE, THEN.
MINE IS ONLY A SCRATCH.
I'D REALLY APPRECIATE IT IF YOU BROUGHT A CAR THAT COULD SEAT MORE THAN TWO NEXT TIME.
THE ORIGINAL PLAN HAD US CHANGING CARS ON OUR WAY SOUTH.
ANYWAY, I HAVE A FRIEND WHO OWNS A VINEYARD IN FRASCATI. LET'S GO THERE AND RECOUP.
FAIR ENOUGH.
I'LL BUY MEDICINE AND REPORT TO CRIS-TIANO.
PERFECT. THANKS.

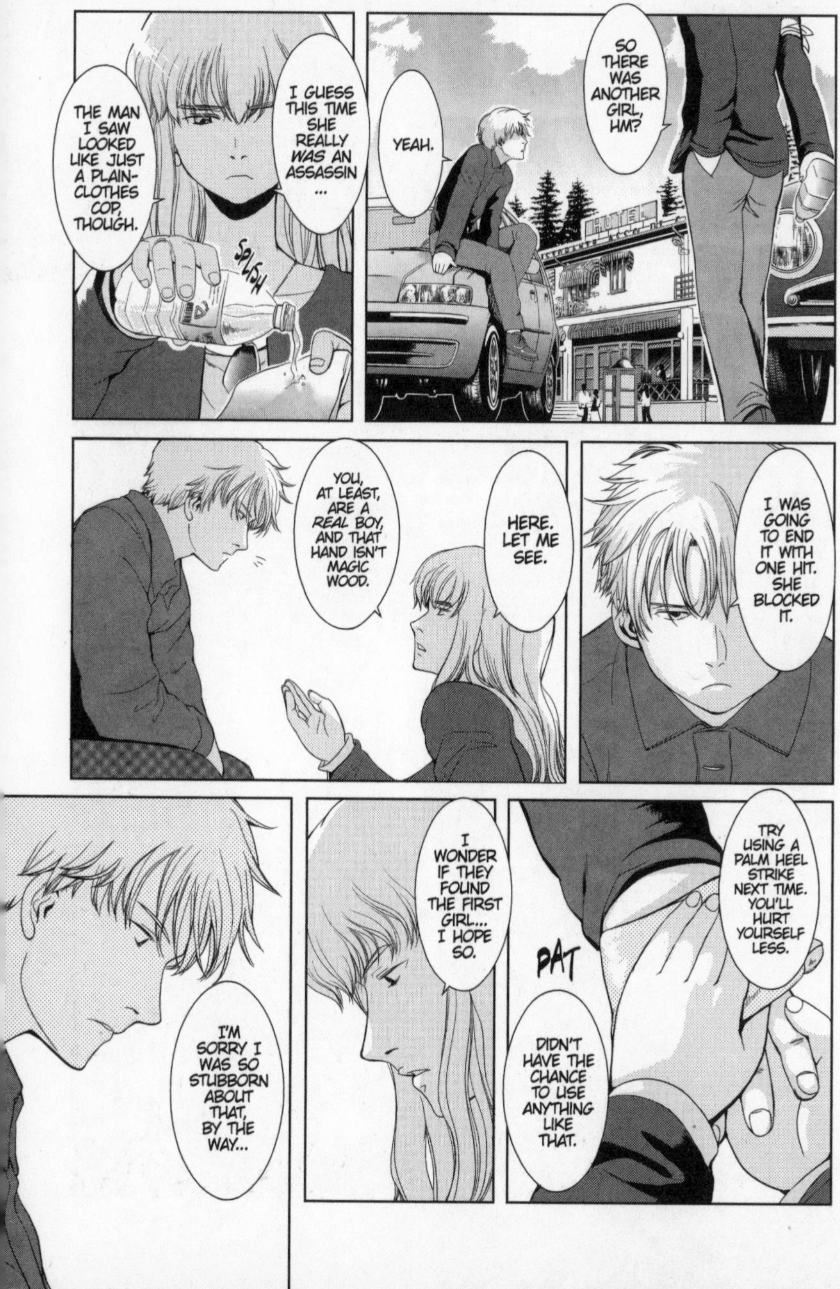
SO THERE WAS ANOTHER GIRL, HM?
YEAH.
I GUESS THIS TIME SHE REALLY *WAS* AN ASSASSIN...
THE MAN I SAW LOOKED LIKE JUST A PLAIN-CLOTHES COP, THOUGH.
SPLISH
I WAS GOING TO END IT WITH ONE HIT. SHE BLOCKED IT.
HERE. LET ME SEE.
YOU, AT LEAST, ARE A *REAL* BOY, AND THAT HAND ISN'T MAGIC WOOD.
TRY USING A PALM HEEL STRIKE NEXT TIME. YOU'LL HURT YOURSELF LESS.
PAT
DIDN'T HAVE THE CHANCE TO USE ANYTHING LIKE THAT.
I WONDER IF THEY FOUND THE FIRST GIRL... I HOPE SO.
I'M SORRY I WAS SO STUBBORN ABOUT THAT, BY THE WAY...

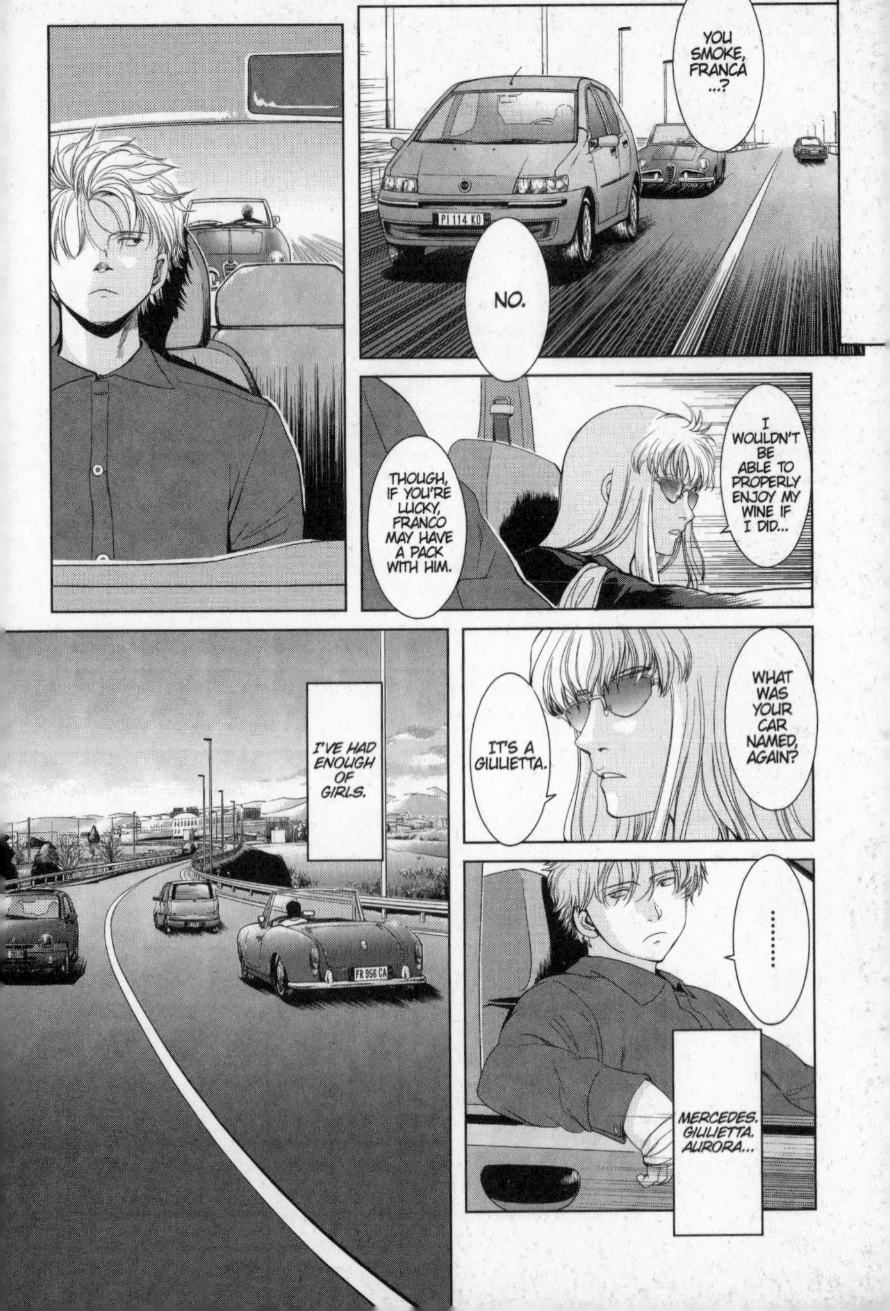
YOU SMOKE, FRANCA...?
NO.
I WOULDN'T BE ABLE TO PROPERLY ENJOY MY WINE IF I DID...
THOUGH, IF YOU'RE LUCKY, FRANCO MAY HAVE A PACK WITH HIM.
WHAT WAS YOUR CAR NAMED, AGAIN?
IT'S A GIULIETTA.
......
MERCEDES. GIULIETTA. AURORA...
I'VE HAD ENOUGH OF GIRLS.

GUNSLINGERGIRL.

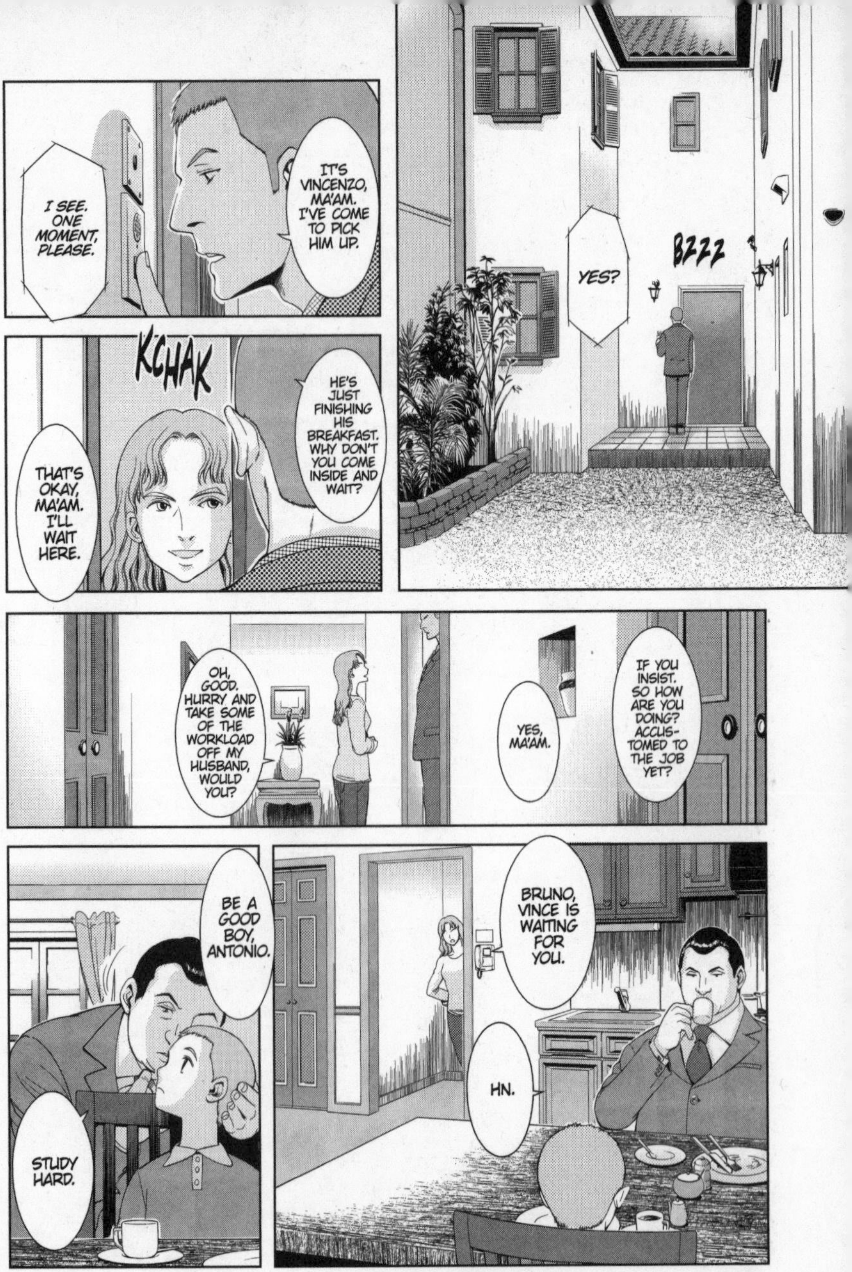
BZZZ
YES?
IT'S VINCENZO, MA'AM. I'VE COME TO PICK HIM UP.
I SEE. ONE MOMENT, PLEASE.
KCHAK
HE'S JUST FINISHING HIS BREAKFAST. WHY DON'T YOU COME INSIDE AND WAIT?
THAT'S OKAY, MA'AM. I'LL WAIT HERE.
IF YOU INSIST. SO HOW ARE YOU DOING? ACCUS-TOMED TO THE JOB YET?
YES, MA'AM.
OH, GOOD. HURRY AND TAKE SOME OF THE WORKLOAD OFF MY HUSBAND, WOULD YOU?
BRUNO, VINCE IS WAITING FOR YOU.
HN.
BE A GOOD BOY, ANTONIO.
STUDY HARD.

Chapter 16: Sever the Chains of Retaliation

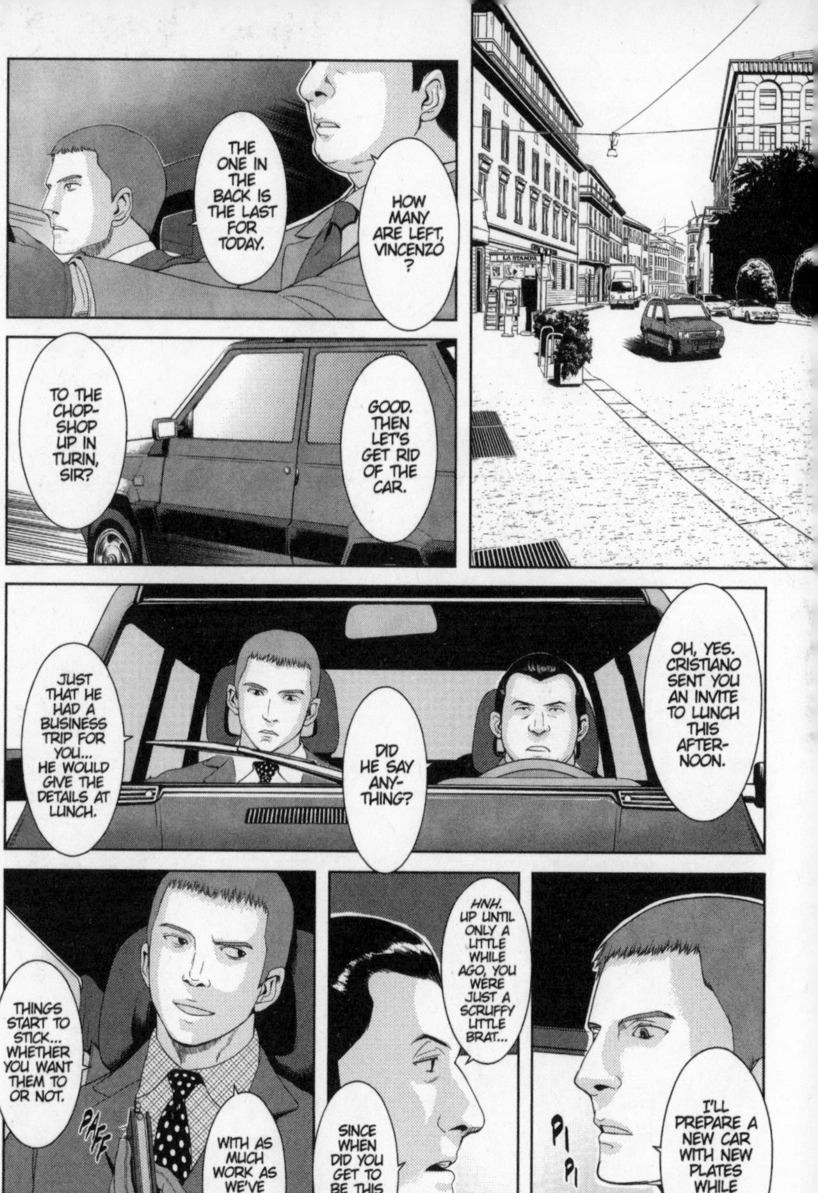
LA STAMPA
HOW MANY ARE LEFT, VINCENZO?
THE ONE IN THE BACK IS THE LAST FOR TODAY.
GOOD. THEN LET'S GET RID OF THE CAR.
TO THE CHOP-SHOP UP IN TURIN, SIR?
OH, YES. CRISTIANO SENT YOU AN INVITE TO LUNCH THIS AFTER-NOON.
DID HE SAY ANY-THING?
JUST THAT HE HAD A BUSINESS TRIP FOR YOU... HE WOULD GIVE THE DETAILS AT LUNCH.
I'LL PREPARE A NEW CAR WITH NEW PLATES WHILE YOU'RE THERE.
PI PI
HNH. UP UNTIL ONLY A LITTLE WHILE AGO, YOU WERE JUST A SCRUFFY LITTLE BRAT...
SINCE WHEN DID YOU GET TO BE THIS USEFUL?
WITH AS MUCH WORK AS WE'VE BEEN GETTING ...
THINGS START TO STICK... WHETHER YOU WANT THEM TO OR NOT.
PAFF

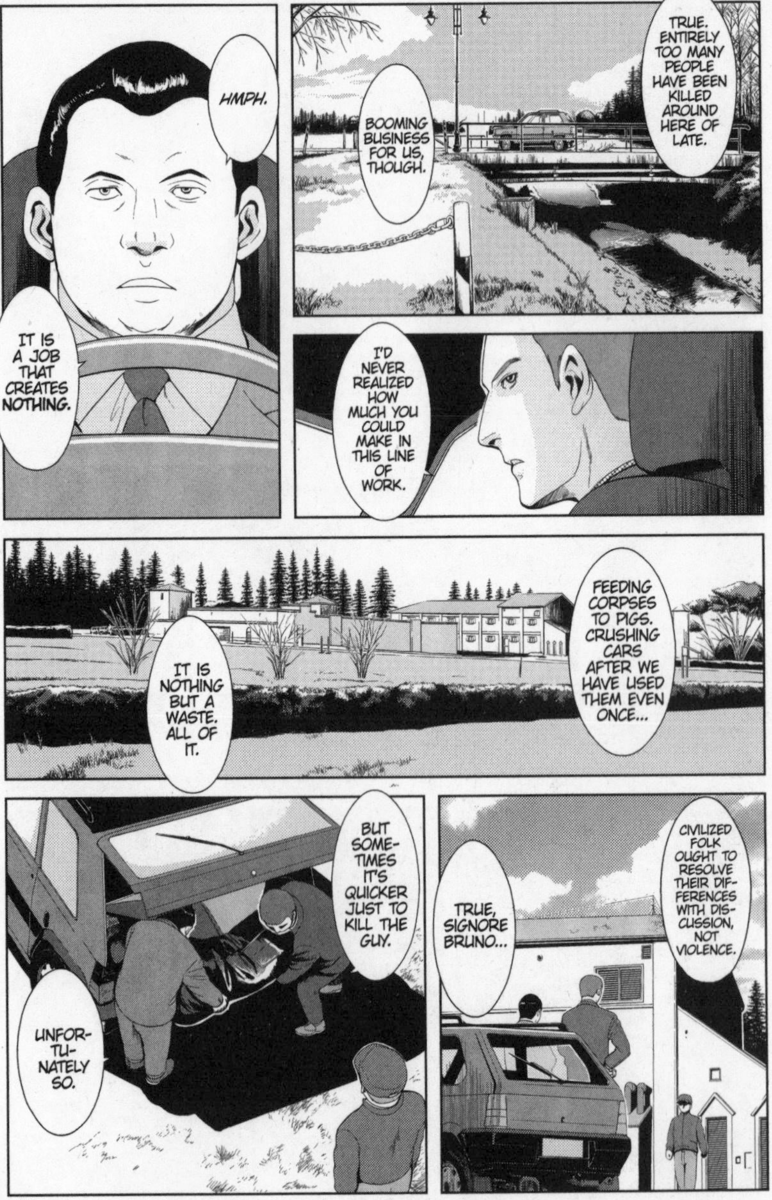

TRUE. ENTIRELY TOO MANY PEOPLE HAVE BEEN KILLED AROUND HERE OF LATE.
BOOMING BUSINESS FOR US, THOUGH.
I'D NEVER REALIZED HOW MUCH YOU COULD MAKE IN THIS LINE OF WORK.
HMPH.
IT IS A JOB THAT CREATES NOTHING.
FEEDING CORPSES TO PIGS. CRUSHING CARS AFTER WE HAVE USED THEM EVEN ONCE...
IT IS NOTHING BUT A WASTE. ALL OF IT.
CIVILIZED FOLK OUGHT TO RESOLVE THEIR DIFFERENCES WITH DISCUSSION, NOT VIOLENCE.
TRUE, SIGNORE BRUNO...
BUT SOMETIMES IT'S QUICKER JUST TO KILL THE GUY.
UNFORTUNATELY SO.

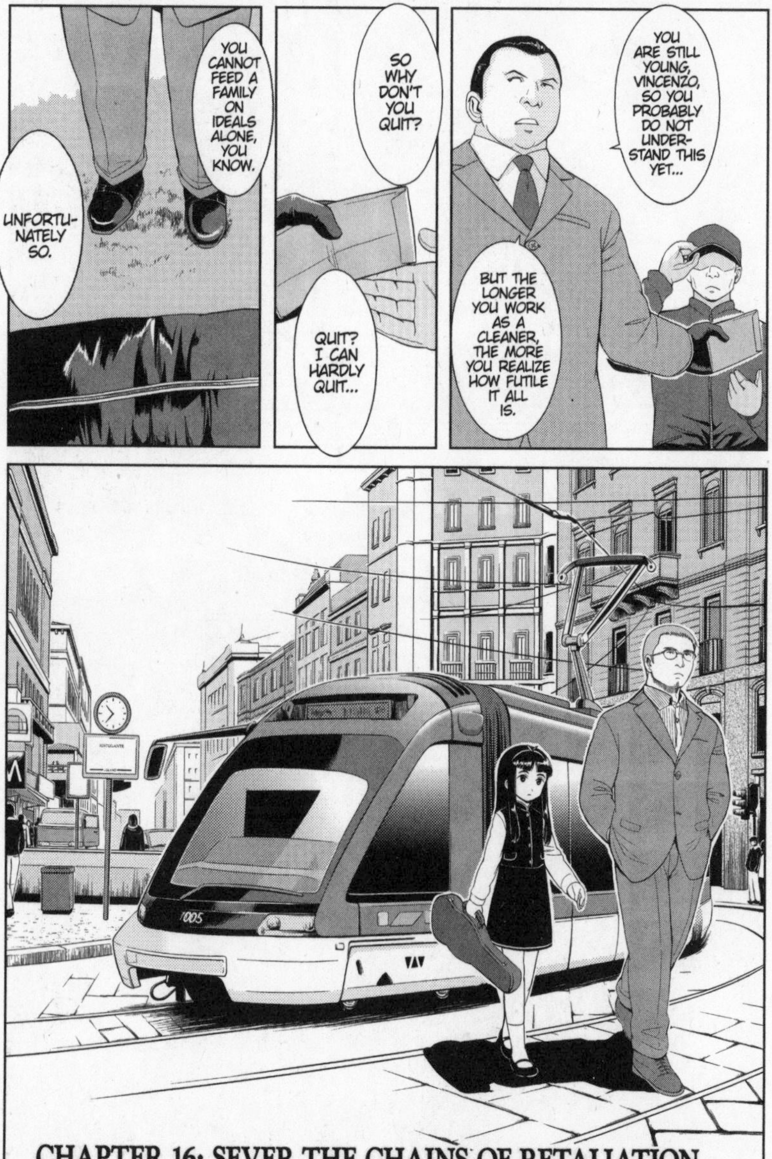
YOU ARE STILL YOUNG, VINCENZO, SO YOU PROBABLY DO NOT UNDER-STAND THIS YET...
BUT THE LONGER YOU WORK AS A CLEANER, THE MORE YOU REALIZE HOW FUTILE IT ALL IS.
SO WHY DON'T YOU QUIT?
QUIT? I CAN HARDLY QUIT...
YOU CANNOT FEED A FAMILY ON IDEALS ALONE, YOU KNOW.
UNFORTU-NATELY SO.
CHAPTER 16: SEVER THE CHAINS OF RETALIATION

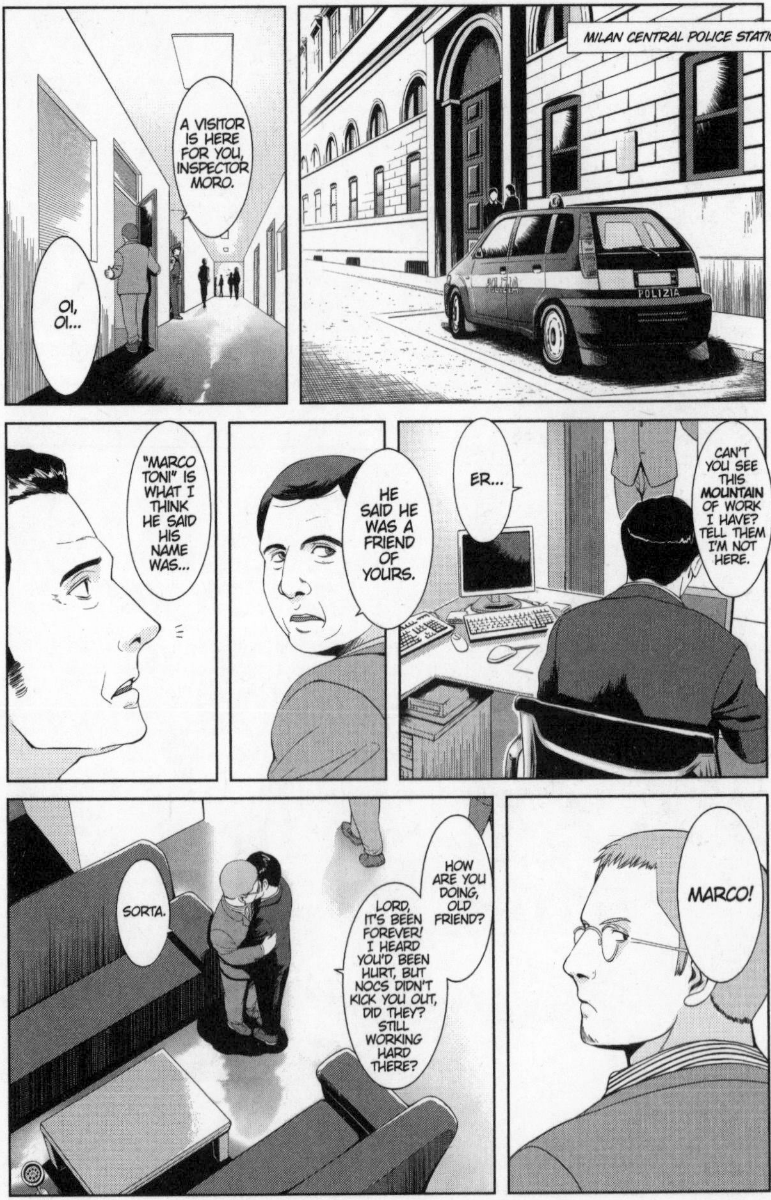
MILAN CENTRAL POLICE STATION
A VISITOR IS HERE FOR YOU, INSPECTOR MORO.
OI, OI...
CAN'T YOU SEE THIS MOUNTAIN OF WORK I HAVE? TELL THEM I'M NOT HERE.
ER...
HE SAID HE WAS A FRIEND OF YOURS.
"MARCO TONI" IS WHAT I THINK HE SAID HIS NAME WAS...
MARCO!
HOW ARE YOU DOING, OLD FRIEND?
LORD, IT'S BEEN FOREVER! I HEARD YOU'D BEEN HURT, BUT NOCS DIDN'T KICK YOU OUT, DID THEY? STILL WORKING HARD THERE?
SORTA.

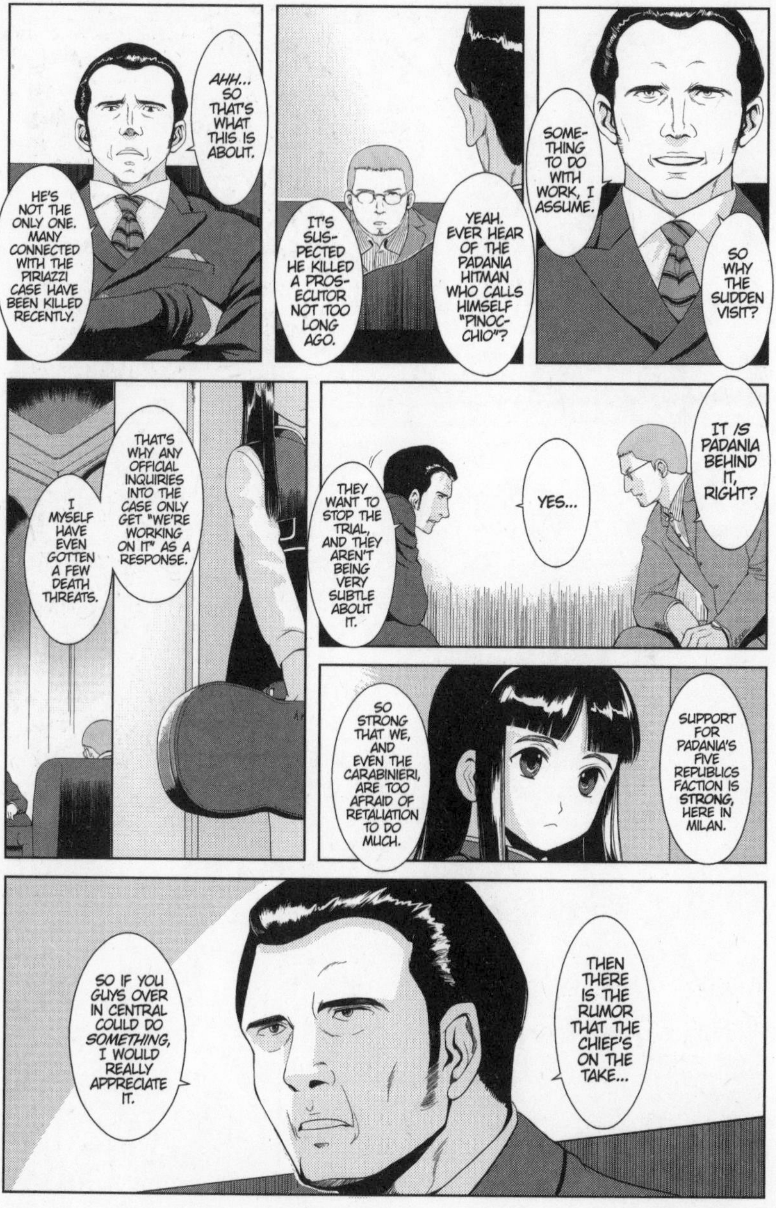
SO WHY THE SUDDEN VISIT?
SOMETHING TO DO WITH WORK, I ASSUME.
YEAH. EVER HEAR OF THE PADANIA HITMAN WHO CALLS HIMSELF "PINOCCHIO"?
IT'S SUSPECTED HE KILLED A PROSECUTOR NOT TOO LONG AGO.
AHH... SO THAT'S WHAT THIS IS ABOUT.
HE'S NOT THE ONLY ONE. MANY CONNECTED WITH THE PIRIAZZI CASE HAVE BEEN KILLED RECENTLY.
IT *IS* PADANIA BEHIND IT, RIGHT?
YES...
THEY WANT TO STOP THE TRIAL, AND THEY AREN'T BEING VERY SUBTLE ABOUT IT.
SUPPORT FOR PADANIA'S FIVE REPUBLICS FACTION IS STRONG, HERE IN MILAN.
SO STRONG THAT WE, AND EVEN THE CARABINIERI, ARE TOO AFRAID OF RETALIATION TO DO MUCH.
THAT'S WHY ANY OFFICIAL INQUIRIES INTO THE CASE ONLY GET "WE'RE WORKING ON IT" AS A RESPONSE.
I MYSELF HAVE EVEN GOTTEN A FEW DEATH THREATS.
THEN THERE IS THE RUMOR THAT THE CHIEF'S ON THE TAKE...
SO IF YOU GUYS OVER IN CENTRAL COULD DO *SOMETHING*, I WOULD REALLY APPRECIATE IT.

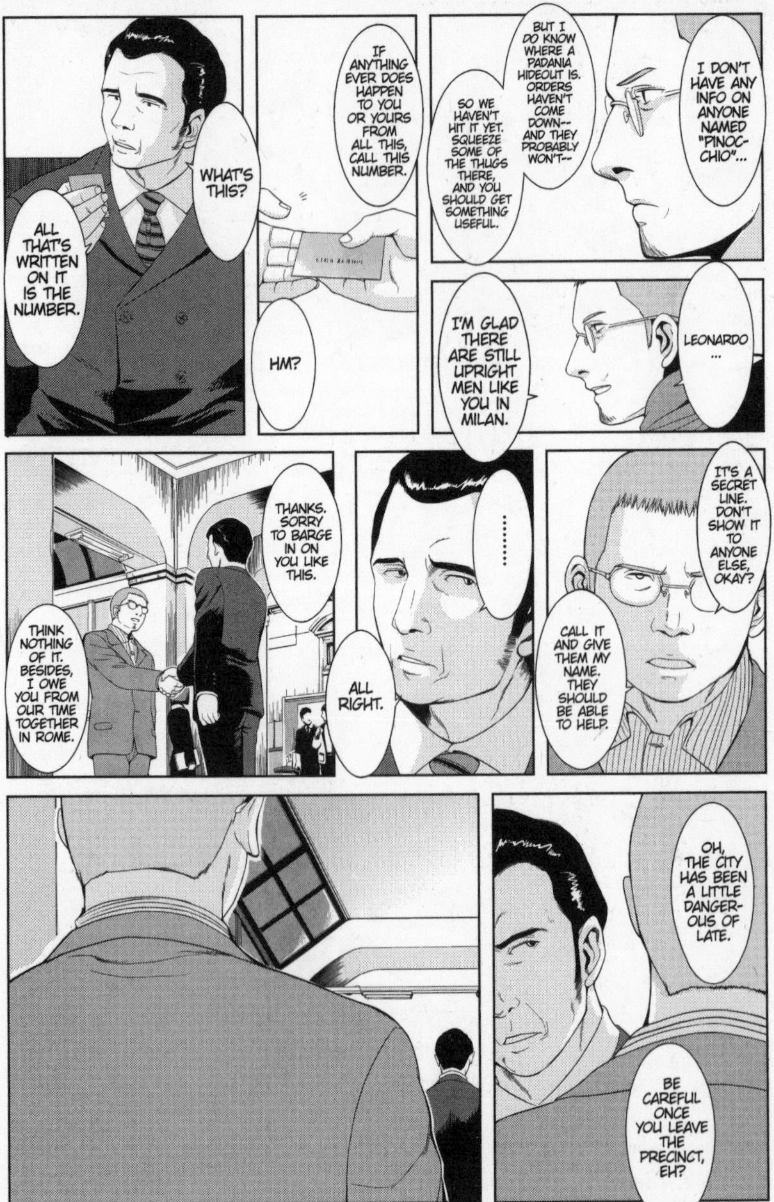
I DON'T HAVE ANY INFO ON ANYONE NAMED "PINOC-CHIO"...
BUT I DO KNOW WHERE A PADANIA HIDEOUT IS. ORDERS HAVEN'T COME DOWN-- AND THEY PROBABLY WON'T--
SO WE HAVEN'T HIT IT YET. SQUEEZE SOME OF THE THUGS THERE, AND YOU SHOULD GET SOMETHING USEFUL.
LEONARDO ...
I'M GLAD THERE ARE STILL UPRIGHT MEN LIKE YOU IN MILAN.
IF ANYTHING EVER DOES HAPPEN TO YOU OR YOURS FROM ALL THIS, CALL THIS NUMBER.
HM?
WHAT'S THIS?
ALL THAT'S WRITTEN ON IT IS THE NUMBER.
IT'S A SECRET LINE. DON'T SHOW IT TO ANYONE ELSE, OKAY?
CALL IT AND GIVE THEM MY NAME. THEY SHOULD BE ABLE TO HELP.
......
ALL RIGHT.
THANKS. SORRY TO BARGE IN ON YOU LIKE THIS.
THINK NOTHING OF IT. BESIDES, I OWE YOU FROM OUR TIME TOGETHER IN ROME.
OH, THE CITY HAS BEEN A LITTLE DANGER-OUS OF LATE.
BE CAREFUL ONCE YOU LEAVE THE PRECINCT, EH?

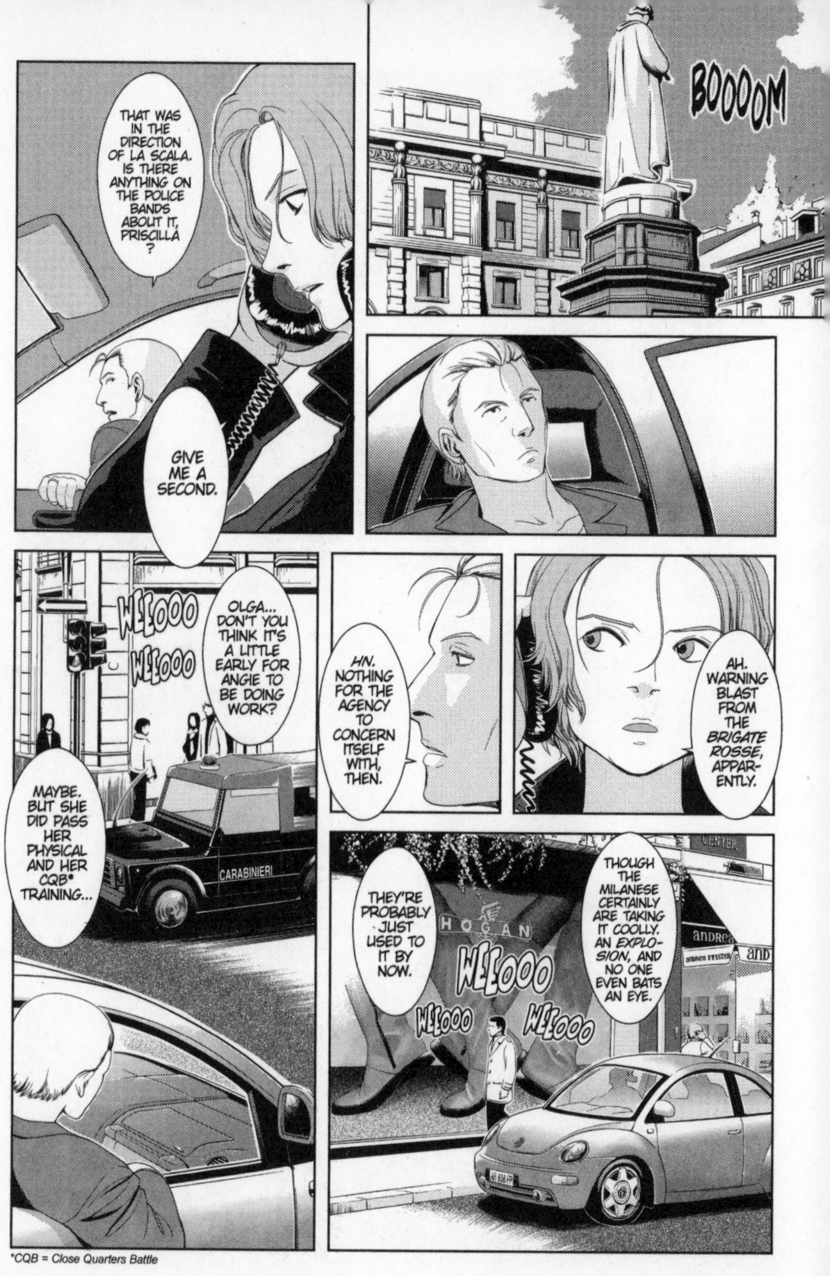

BOOOOM
THAT WAS IN THE DIRECTION OF LA SCALA. IS THERE ANYTHING ON THE POLICE BANDS ABOUT IT, PRISCILLA?
GIVE ME A SECOND.
AH. WARNING BLAST FROM THE *BRIGATE ROSSE*, APPARENTLY.
HN. NOTHING FOR THE AGENCY TO CONCERN ITSELF WITH, THEN.
THOUGH THE MILANESE CERTAINLY ARE TAKING IT COOLLY. AN *EXPLOSION*, AND NO ONE EVEN BATS AN EYE.
THEY'RE PROBABLY JUST USED TO IT BY NOW.
CENTER
HOGAN
andrea pfister
WEEOOO
WEEOOO
WEEOOO
OLGA... DON'T YOU THINK IT'S A LITTLE EARLY FOR ANGIE TO BE DOING WORK?
MAYBE. BUT SHE DID PASS HER PHYSICAL AND HER CQB* TRAINING...
WEEOOO
WEEOOO
CARABINIERI

*CQB = Close Quarters Battle

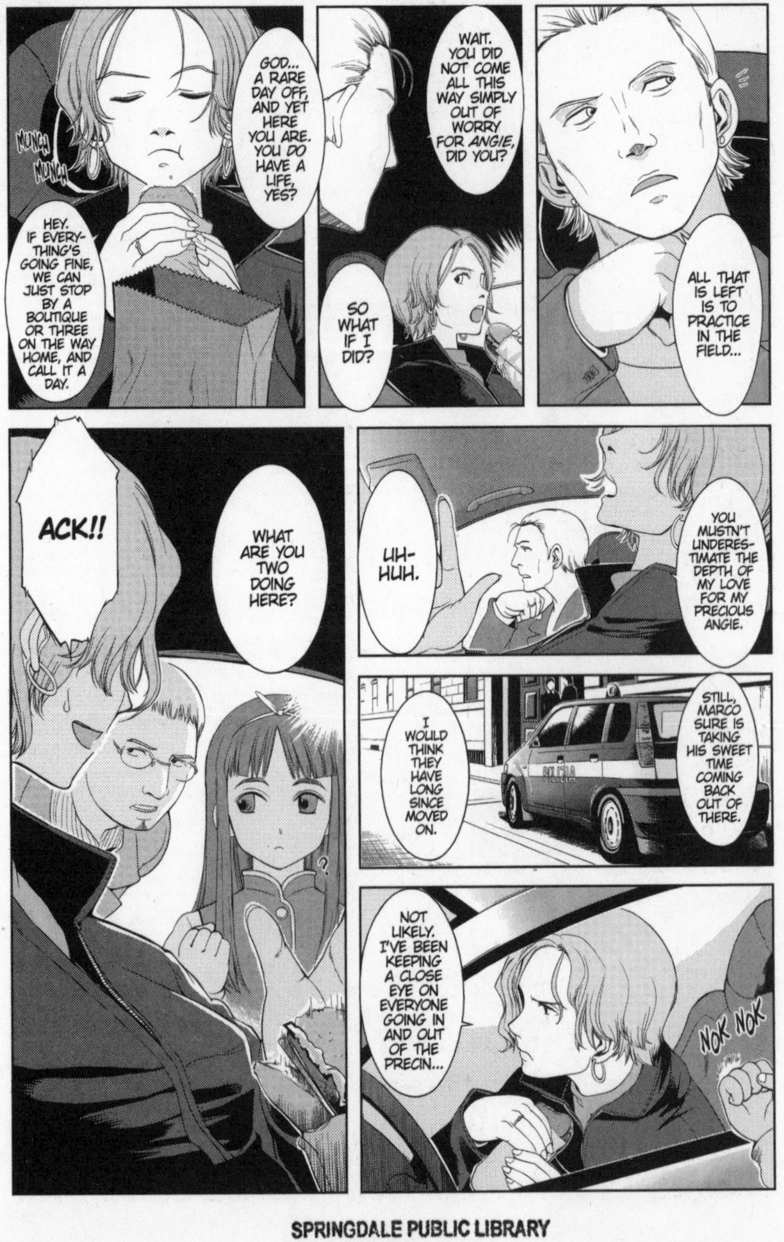
ALL THAT IS LEFT IS TO PRACTICE IN THE FIELD...
WAIT. YOU DID NOT COME ALL THIS WAY SIMPLY OUT OF WORRY FOR *ANGIE*, DID YOU?
SO WHAT IF I DID?
GOD... A RARE DAY OFF, AND YET HERE YOU ARE. YOU *DO* HAVE A LIFE, YES?
MUNCH MUNCH
HEY. IF EVERY-THING'S GOING FINE, WE CAN JUST STOP BY A BOUTIQUE OR THREE ON THE WAY HOME, AND CALL IT A DAY.
YOU MUSTN'T UNDERES-TIMATE THE DEPTH OF MY LOVE FOR MY PRECIOUS ANGIE.
UH-HUH.
STILL, MARCO SURE IS TAKING HIS SWEET TIME COMING BACK OUT OF THERE.
I WOULD THINK THEY HAVE LONG SINCE MOVED ON.
POLIZIA
NOT LIKELY. I'VE BEEN KEEPING A CLOSE EYE ON EVERYONE GOING IN AND OUT OF THE PRECIN...
NOK NOK
WHAT ARE YOU TWO DOING HERE?
ACK!!

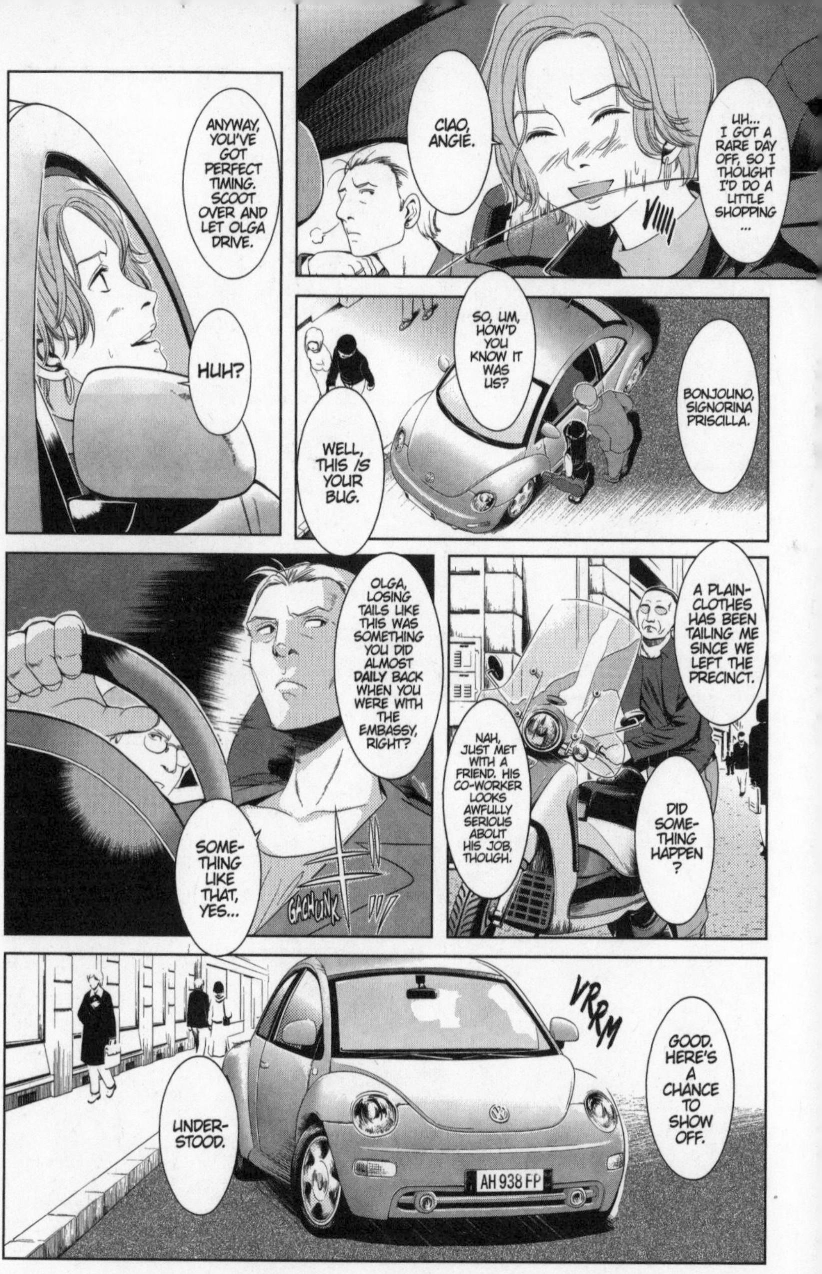
UH... I GOT A RARE DAY OFF, SO I THOUGHT I'D DO A LITTLE SHOPPING ...
CIAO, ANGIE.
BONJOUNO, SIGNORINA PRISCILLA.
SO, UM, HOW'D YOU KNOW IT WAS US?
WELL, THIS IS YOUR BUG.
ANYWAY, YOU'VE GOT PERFECT TIMING. SCOOT OVER AND LET OLGA DRIVE.
HUH?
A PLAIN-CLOTHES HAS BEEN TAILING ME SINCE WE LEFT THE PRECINCT.
DID SOMETHING HAPPEN?
NAH, JUST MET WITH A FRIEND. HIS CO-WORKER LOOKS AWFULLY SERIOUS ABOUT HIS JOB, THOUGH.
OLGA, LOSING TAILS LIKE THIS WAS SOMETHING YOU DID ALMOST DAILY BACK WHEN YOU WERE WITH THE EMBASSY, RIGHT?
SOMETHING LIKE THAT, YES...
GACHUNK
VRRM
GOOD. HERE'S A CHANCE TO SHOW OFF.
UNDER-STOOD.
AH 938 FP

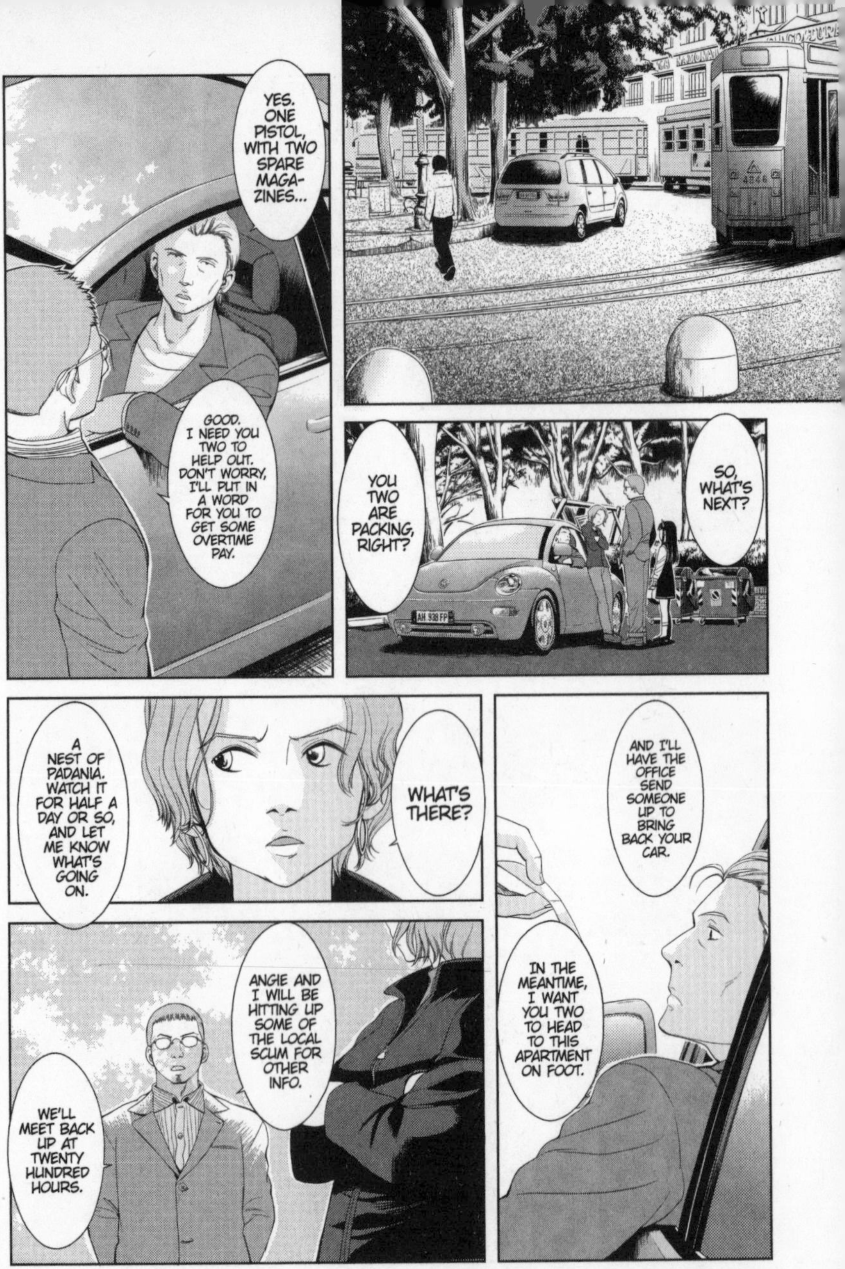
SO, WHAT'S NEXT?
YOU TWO ARE PACKING, RIGHT?
YES. ONE PISTOL, WITH TWO SPARE MAGA-ZINES...
GOOD. I NEED YOU TWO TO HELP OUT. DON'T WORRY, I'LL PUT IN A WORD FOR YOU TO GET SOME OVERTIME PAY.
AND I'LL HAVE THE OFFICE SEND SOMEONE UP TO BRING BACK YOUR CAR.
IN THE MEANTIME, I WANT YOU TWO TO HEAD TO THIS APARTMENT ON FOOT.
WHAT'S THERE?
A NEST OF PADANIA. WATCH IT FOR HALF A DAY OR SO, AND LET ME KNOW WHAT'S GOING ON.
ANGIE AND I WILL BE HITTING UP SOME OF THE LOCAL SCUM FOR OTHER INFO.
WE'LL MEET BACK UP AT TWENTY HUNDRED HOURS.

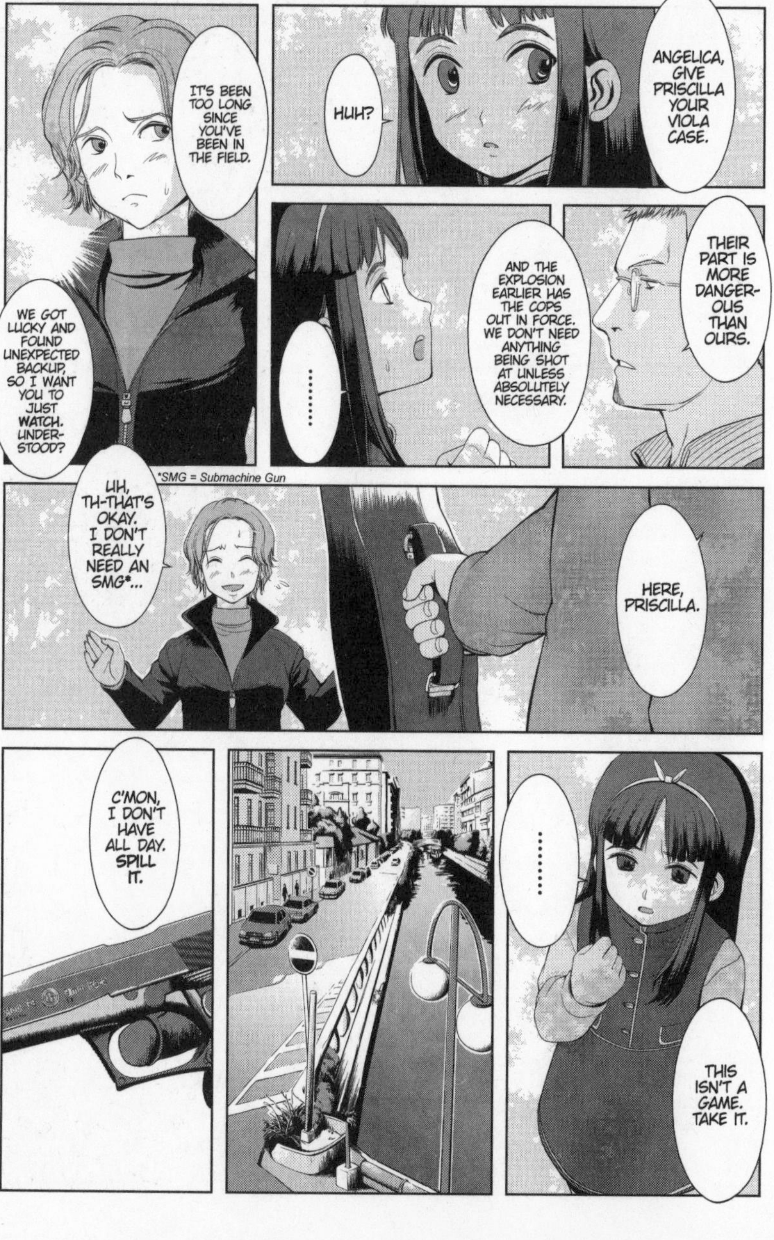
ANGELICA, GIVE PRISCILLA YOUR VIOLA CASE.
HUH?
THEIR PART IS MORE DANGER-OUS THAN OURS.
AND THE EXPLOSION EARLIER HAS THE COPS OUT IN FORCE. WE DON'T NEED ANYTHING BEING SHOT AT UNLESS ABSOLUTELY NECESSARY.
....
IT'S BEEN TOO LONG SINCE YOU'VE BEEN IN THE FIELD.
WE GOT LUCKY AND FOUND UNEXPECTED BACKUP, SO I WANT YOU TO JUST WATCH. UNDER-STOOD?
HERE, PRISCILLA.
UH, TH-THAT'S OKAY. I DON'T REALLY NEED AN SMG*...
*SMG = Submachine Gun
....
THIS ISN'T A GAME. TAKE IT.
C'MON, I DON'T HAVE ALL DAY. SPILL IT.

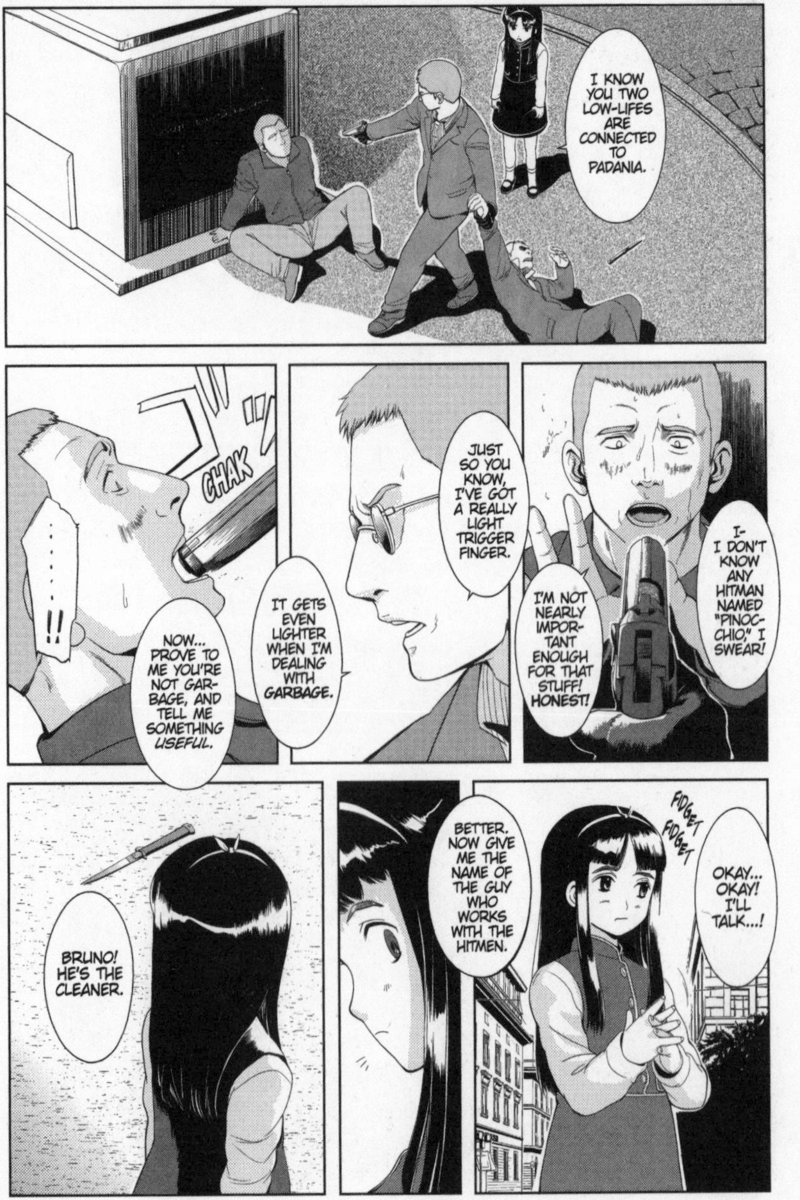

I KNOW YOU TWO LOW-LIFES ARE CONNECTED TO PADANIA.
I- I DON'T KNOW ANY HITMAN NAMED "PINOCCHIO," I SWEAR!
I'M NOT NEARLY IMPORTANT ENOUGH FOR THAT STUFF! HONEST!
JUST SO YOU KNOW, I'VE GOT A REALLY LIGHT TRIGGER FINGER.
IT GETS EVEN LIGHTER WHEN I'M DEALING WITH GARBAGE.
CHAK
......!!
NOW... PROVE TO ME YOU'RE NOT GARBAGE, AND TELL ME SOMETHING USEFUL.
FIDGET FIDGET
OKAY... OKAY! I'LL TALK...!
BETTER. NOW GIVE ME THE NAME OF THE GUY WHO WORKS WITH THE HITMEN.
BRUNO! HE'S THE CLEANER.

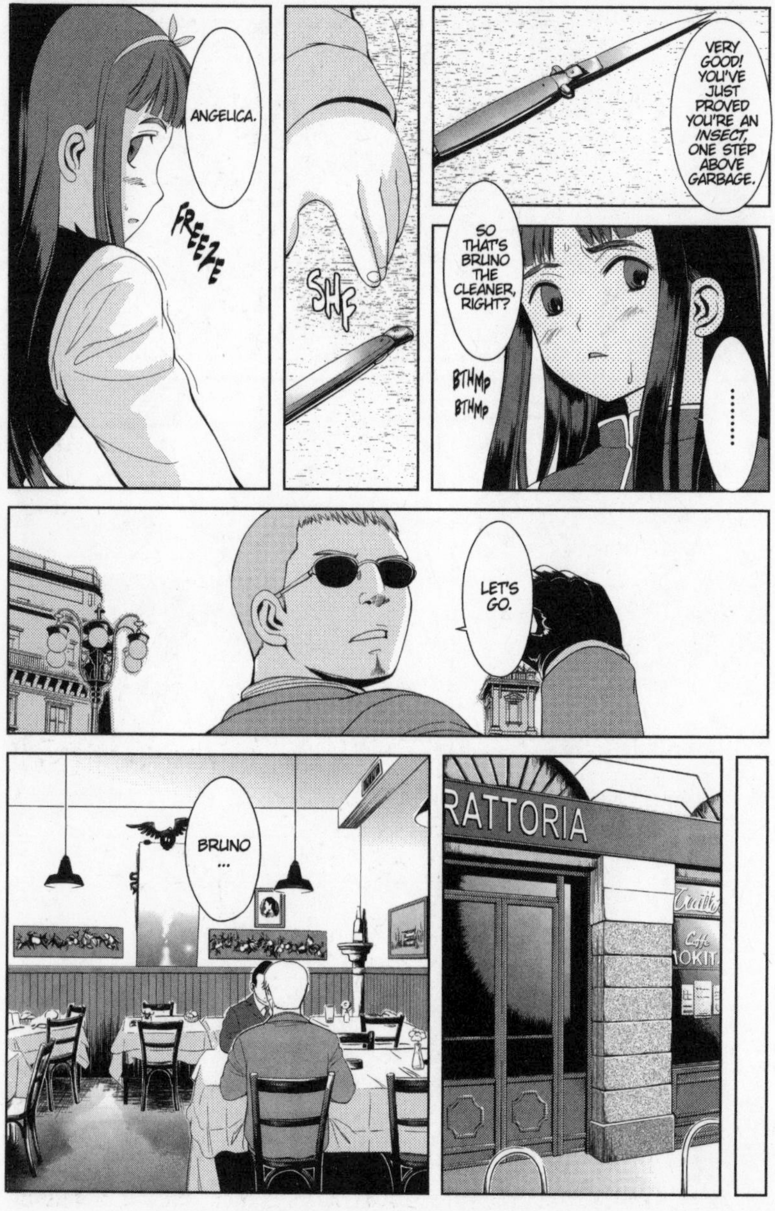
VERY GOOD! YOU'VE JUST PROVED YOU'RE AN *INSECT*, ONE STEP ABOVE GARBAGE.
SO THAT'S BRUNO THE CLEANER, RIGHT?
......
BTHMP
BTHMP
SHF
ANGELICA.
FREEZE
LET'S GO.
RATTORIA
BRUNO
...

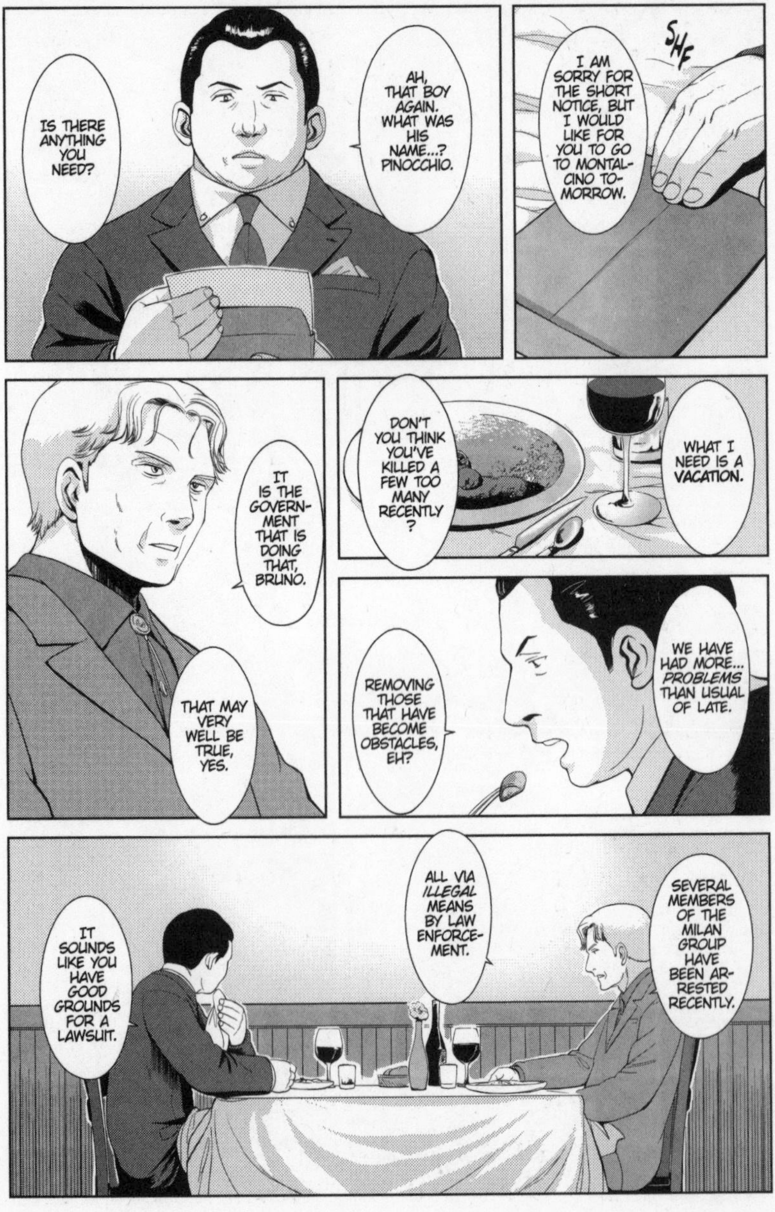
SHF
I AM SORRY FOR THE SHORT NOTICE, BUT I WOULD LIKE FOR YOU TO GO TO MONTALCINO TOMORROW.
AH, THAT BOY AGAIN. WHAT WAS HIS NAME...? PINOCCHIO.
IS THERE ANYTHING YOU NEED?
WHAT I NEED IS A VACATION.
DON'T YOU THINK YOU'VE KILLED A FEW TOO MANY RECENTLY?
WE HAVE HAD MORE... *PROBLEMS* THAN USUAL OF LATE.
REMOVING THOSE THAT HAVE BECOME OBSTACLES, EH?
IT IS THE GOVERNMENT THAT IS DOING THAT, BRUNO.
THAT MAY VERY WELL BE TRUE, YES.
SEVERAL MEMBERS OF THE MILAN GROUP HAVE BEEN ARRESTED RECENTLY.
ALL VIA *ILLEGAL* MEANS BY LAW ENFORCEMENT.
IT SOUNDS LIKE YOU HAVE GOOD GROUNDS FOR A LAWSUIT.

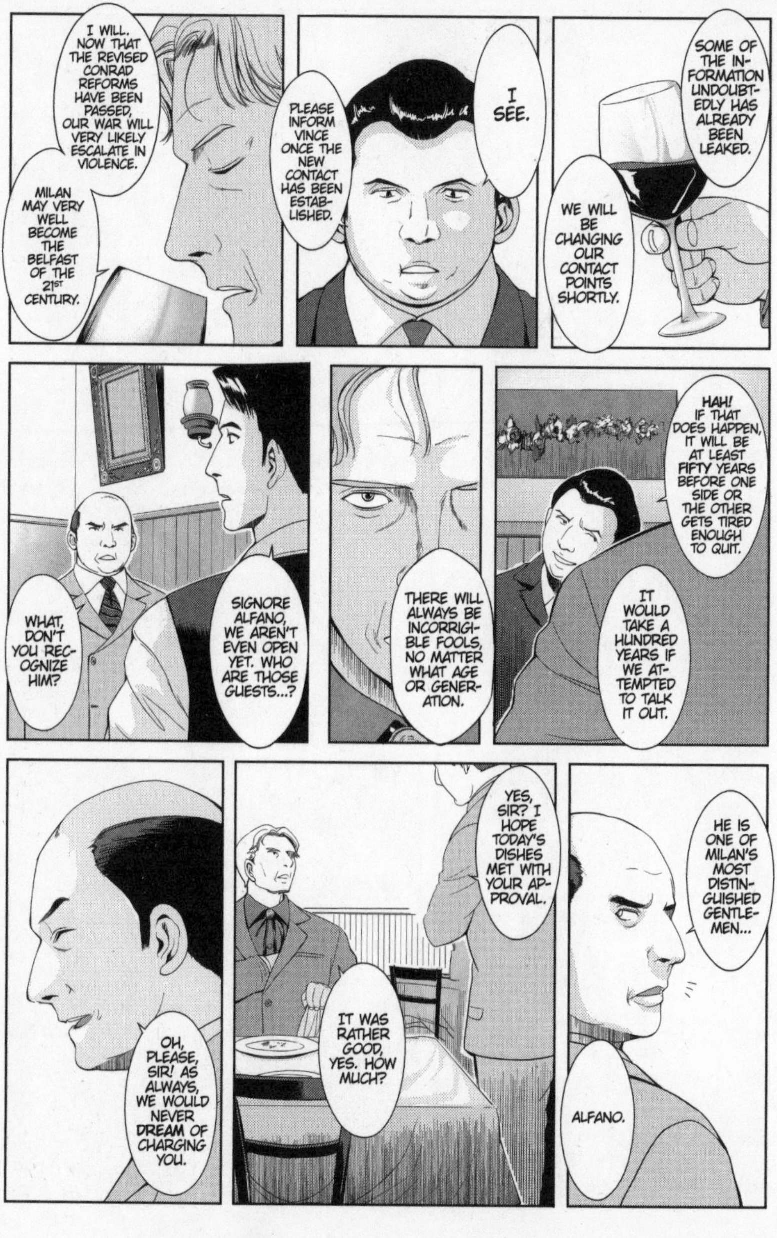
SOME OF THE INFORMATION UNDOUBTEDLY HAS ALREADY BEEN LEAKED.
WE WILL BE CHANGING OUR CONTACT POINTS SHORTLY.
I SEE.
PLEASE INFORM VINCE ONCE THE NEW CONTACT HAS BEEN ESTABLISHED.
I WILL. NOW THAT THE REVISED CONRAD REFORMS HAVE BEEN PASSED, OUR WAR WILL VERY LIKELY ESCALATE IN VIOLENCE.
MILAN MAY VERY WELL BECOME THE BELFAST OF THE 21ST CENTURY.
HAH! IF THAT DOES HAPPEN, IT WILL BE AT LEAST FIFTY YEARS BEFORE ONE SIDE OR THE OTHER GETS TIRED ENOUGH TO QUIT.
IT WOULD TAKE A HUNDRED YEARS IF WE ATTEMPTED TO TALK IT OUT.
THERE WILL ALWAYS BE INCORRIGIBLE FOOLS, NO MATTER WHAT AGE OR GENERATION.
SIGNORE ALFANO, WE AREN'T EVEN OPEN YET. WHO ARE THOSE GUESTS...?
WHAT, DON'T YOU RECOGNIZE HIM?
HE IS ONE OF MILAN'S MOST DISTINGUISHED GENTLEMEN...
ALFANO.
YES, SIR? I HOPE TODAY'S DISHES MET WITH YOUR APPROVAL.
IT WAS RATHER GOOD, YES. HOW MUCH?
OH, PLEASE, SIR! AS ALWAYS, WE WOULD NEVER DREAM OF CHARGING YOU.

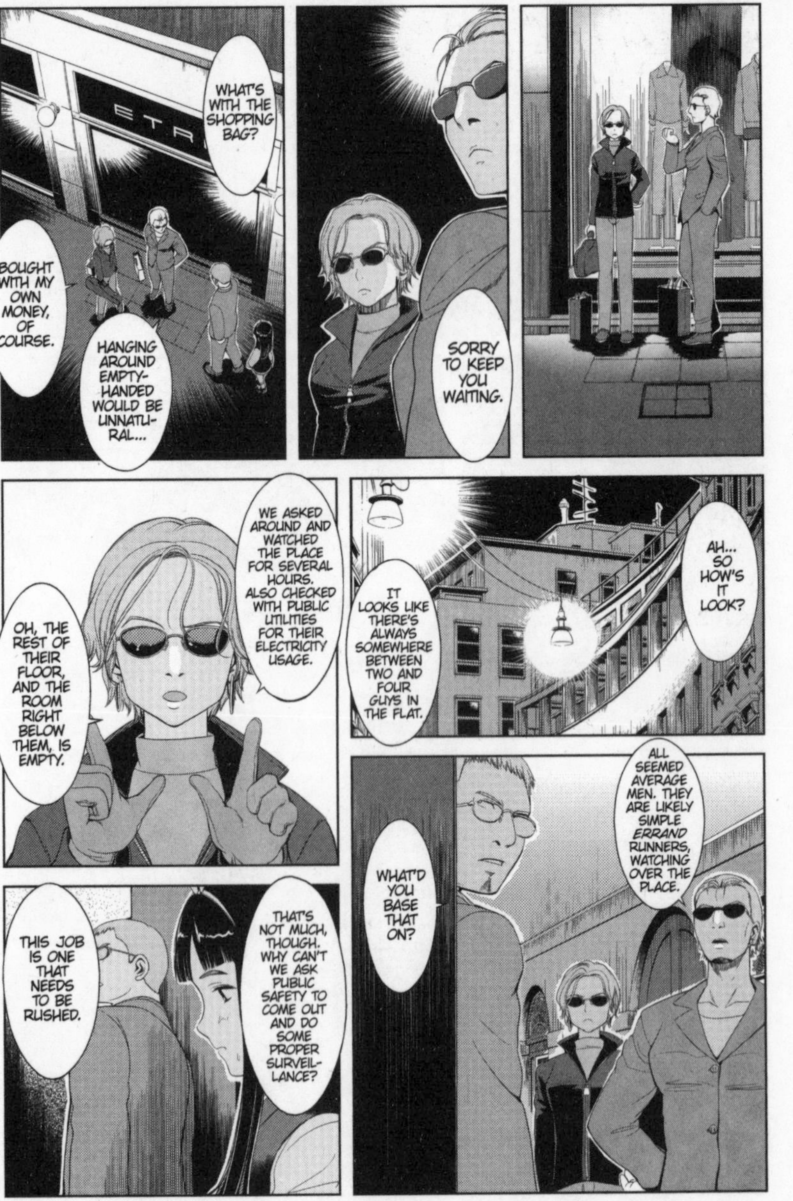
SORRY TO KEEP YOU WAITING.
WHAT'S WITH THE SHOPPING BAG?
BOUGHT WITH MY OWN MONEY, OF COURSE.
HANGING AROUND EMPTY-HANDED WOULD BE UNNATURAL...
AH... SO HOW'S IT LOOK?
IT LOOKS LIKE THERE'S ALWAYS SOMEWHERE BETWEEN TWO AND FOUR GUYS IN THE FLAT.
WE ASKED AROUND AND WATCHED THE PLACE FOR SEVERAL HOURS. ALSO CHECKED WITH PUBLIC UTILITIES FOR THEIR ELECTRICITY USAGE.
OH, THE REST OF THEIR FLOOR, AND THE ROOM RIGHT BELOW THEM, IS EMPTY.
ALL SEEMED AVERAGE MEN. THEY ARE LIKELY SIMPLE *ERRAND* RUNNERS, WATCHING OVER THE PLACE.
WHAT'D YOU BASE THAT ON?
THAT'S NOT MUCH, THOUGH. WHY CAN'T WE ASK PUBLIC SAFETY TO COME OUT AND DO SOME PROPER SURVEILLANCE?
THIS JOB IS ONE THAT NEEDS TO BE RUSHED.

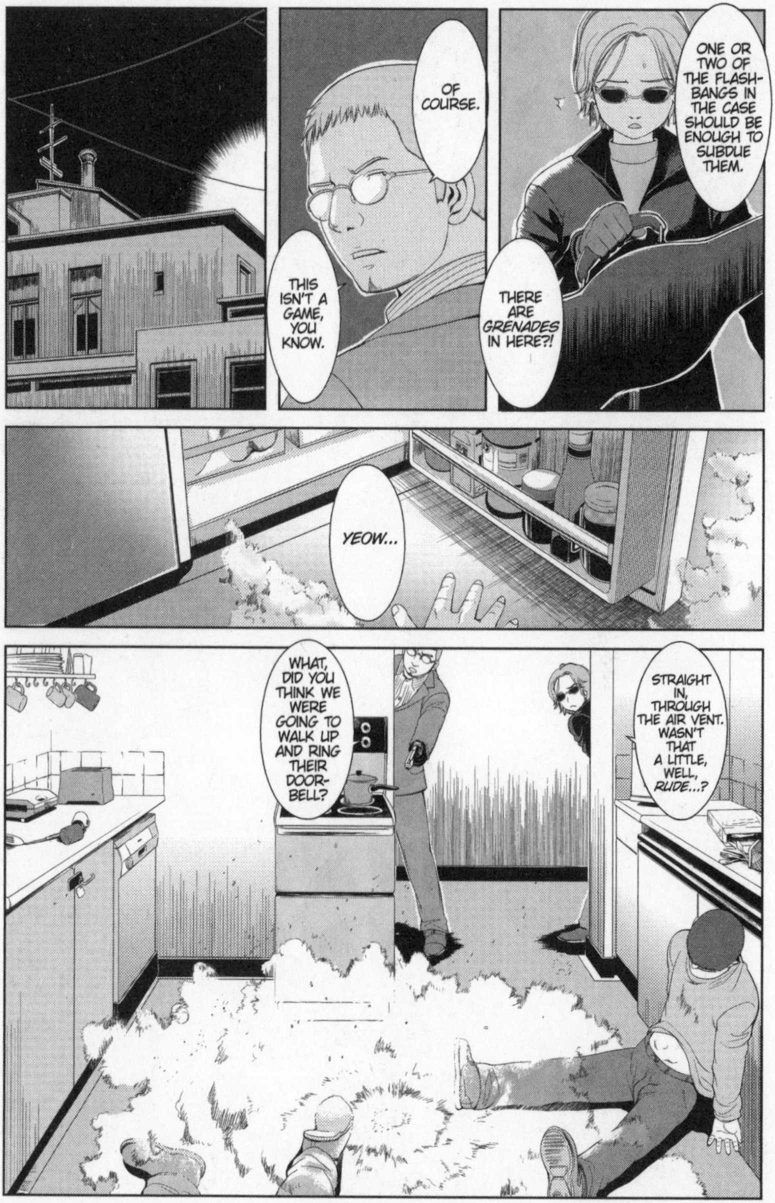
ONE OR TWO OF THE FLASH-BANGS IN THE CASE SHOULD BE ENOUGH TO SUBDUE THEM.
THERE ARE *GRENADES* IN HERE?!
OF COURSE.
THIS ISN'T A GAME, YOU KNOW.
YEOW...
STRAIGHT IN, THROUGH THE AIR VENT. WASN'T THAT A LITTLE, WELL, *RUDE*...?
WHAT, DID YOU THINK WE WERE GOING TO WALK UP AND RING THEIR DOORBELL?

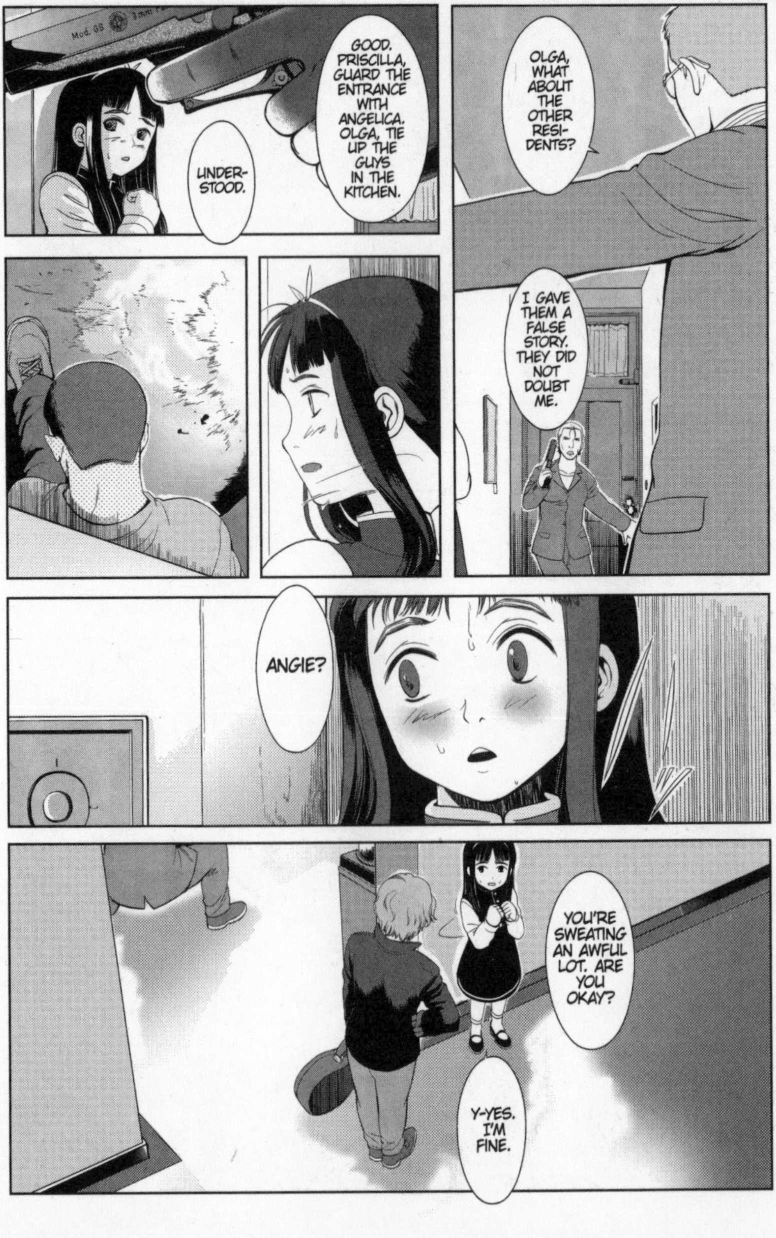
OLGA, WHAT ABOUT THE OTHER RESIDENTS?
I GAVE THEM A FALSE STORY. THEY DID NOT DOUBT ME.
GOOD. PRISCILLA, GUARD THE ENTRANCE WITH ANGELICA. OLGA, TIE UP THE GUYS IN THE KITCHEN.
UNDERSTOOD.
ANGIE?
YOU'RE SWEATING AN AWFUL LOT. ARE YOU OKAY?
Y-YES. I'M FINE.

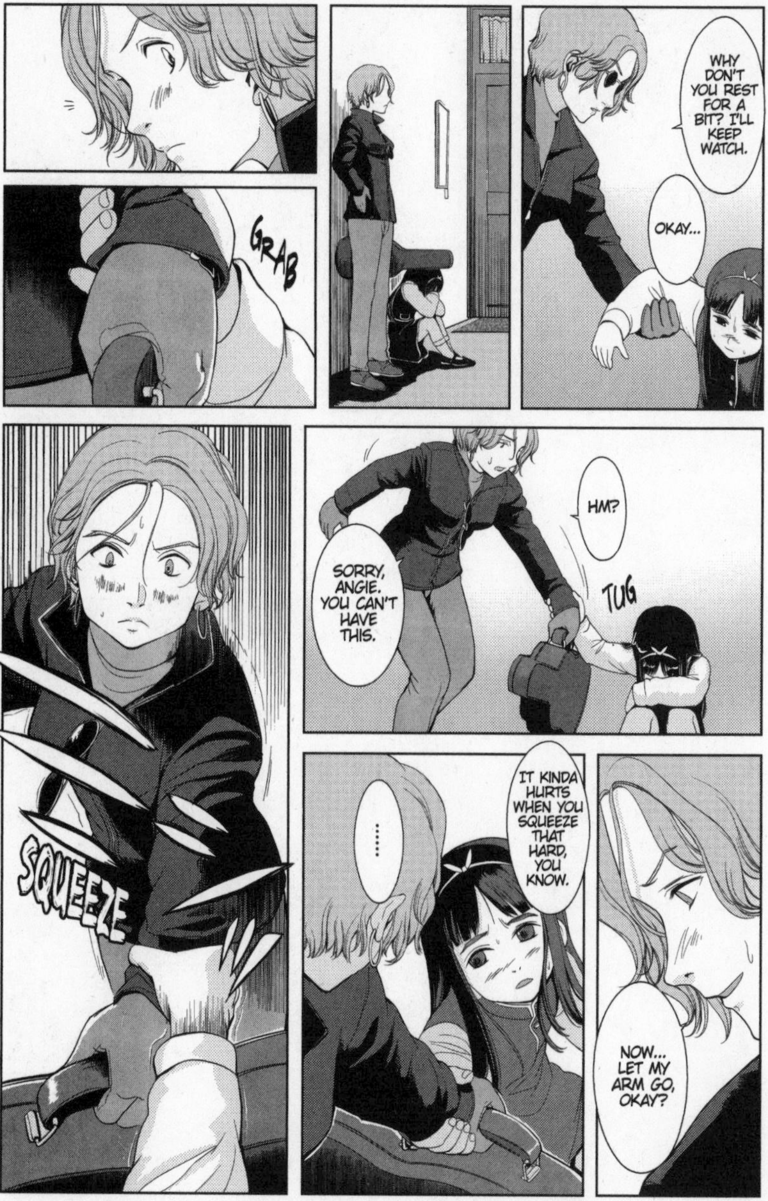
WHY DON'T YOU REST FOR A BIT? I'LL KEEP WATCH.
OKAY...
GRAB
HM?
SORRY, ANGIE. YOU CAN'T HAVE THIS.
TUG
NOW... LET MY ARM GO, OKAY?
IT KINDA HURTS WHEN YOU SQUEEZE THAT HARD, YOU KNOW.
......
SQUEEZE

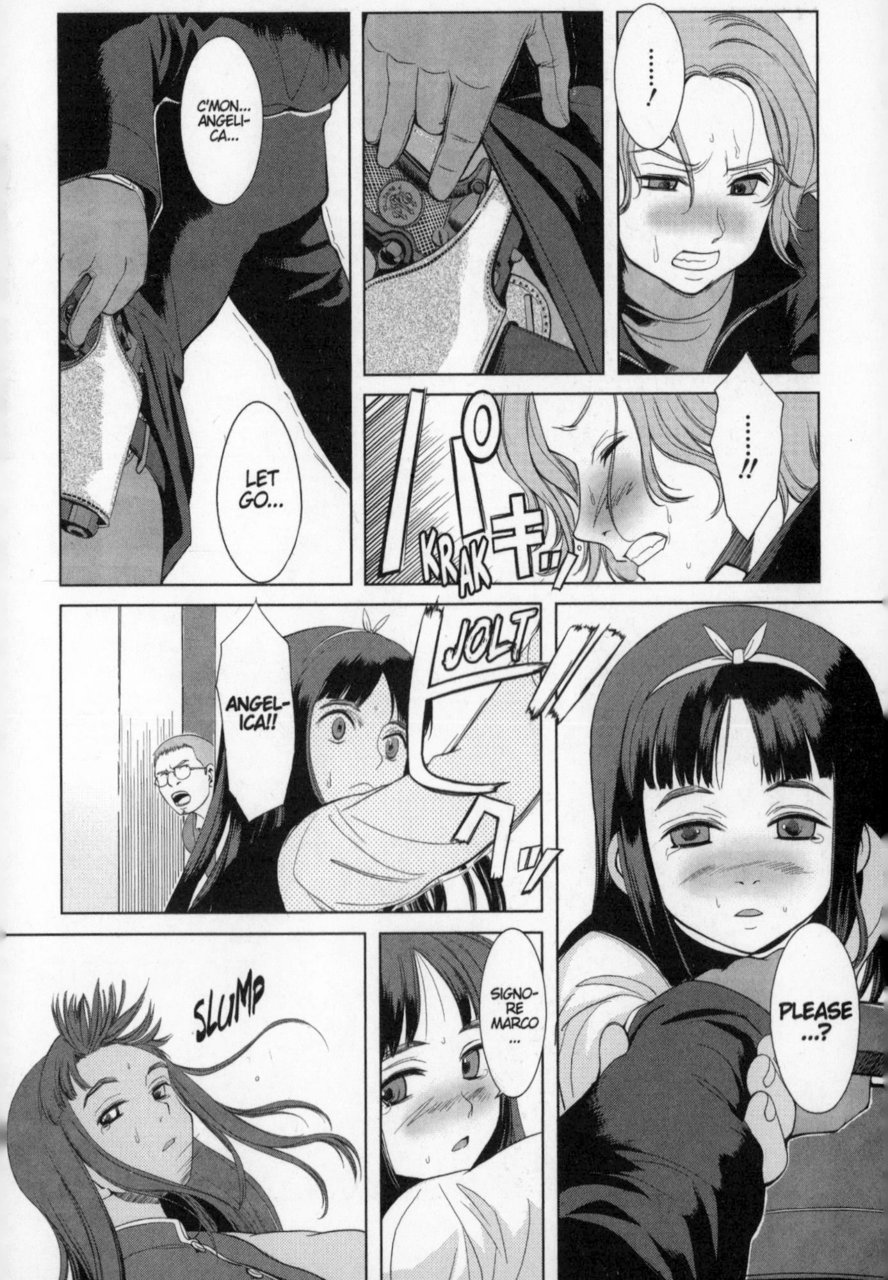
……!
……!!
KRAK
C'MON... ANGELI-CA...
LET GO...
PLEASE ...?
JOLT
ANGEL-ICA!!
SIGNO-RE MARCO ...
SLUMP

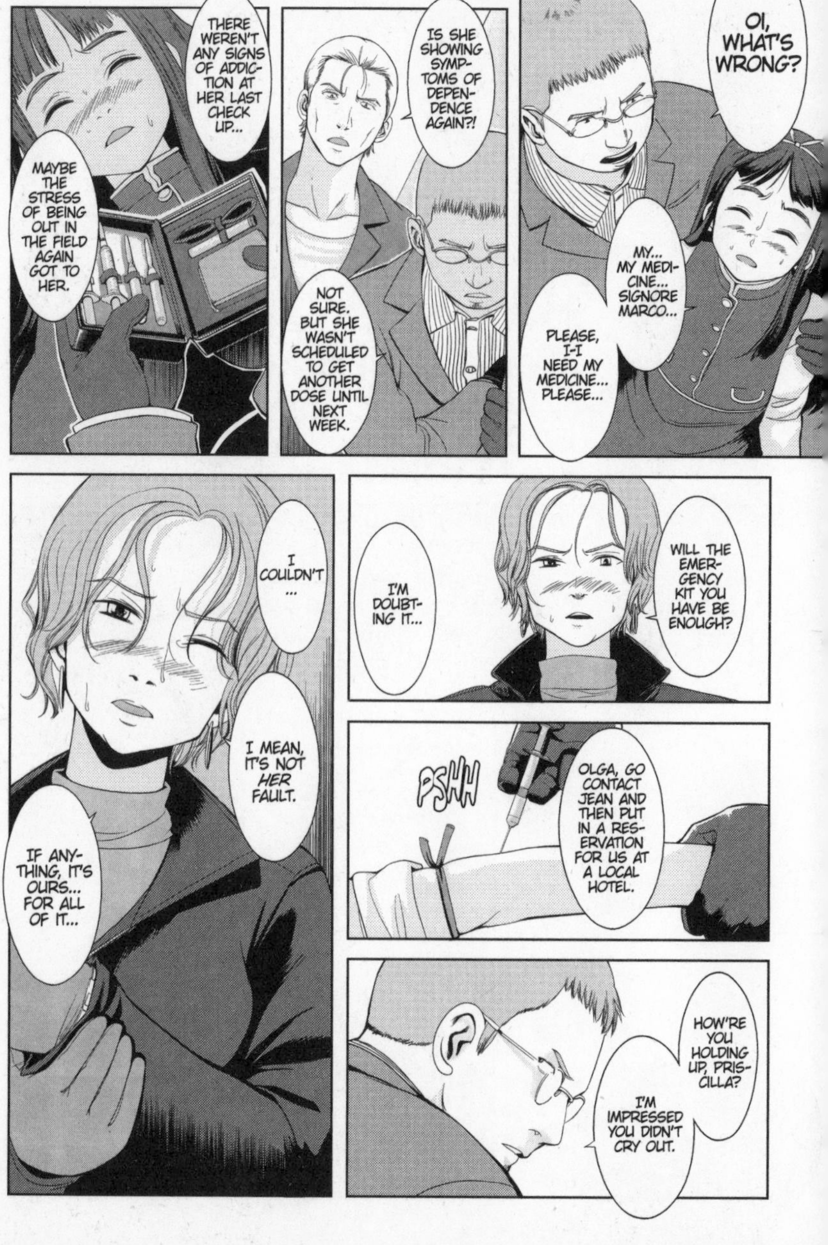
OI, WHAT'S WRONG?
MY... MY MEDICINE... SIGNORE MARCO...
PLEASE, I-I NEED MY MEDICINE... PLEASE...
IS SHE SHOWING SYMPTOMS OF DEPENDENCE AGAIN?!
NOT SURE. BUT SHE WASN'T SCHEDULED TO GET ANOTHER DOSE UNTIL NEXT WEEK.
THERE WEREN'T ANY SIGNS OF ADDICTION AT HER LAST CHECK UP...
MAYBE THE STRESS OF BEING OUT IN THE FIELD AGAIN GOT TO HER.
WILL THE EMERGENCY KIT YOU HAVE BE ENOUGH?
I'M DOUBTING IT...
PSHH
OLGA, GO CONTACT JEAN AND THEN PUT IN A RESERVATION FOR US AT A LOCAL HOTEL.
HOW'RE YOU HOLDING UP, PRISCILLA?
I'M IMPRESSED YOU DIDN'T CRY OUT.
I COULDN'T ...
I MEAN, IT'S NOT *HER* FAULT.
IF ANYTHING, IT'S OURS... FOR ALL OF IT...

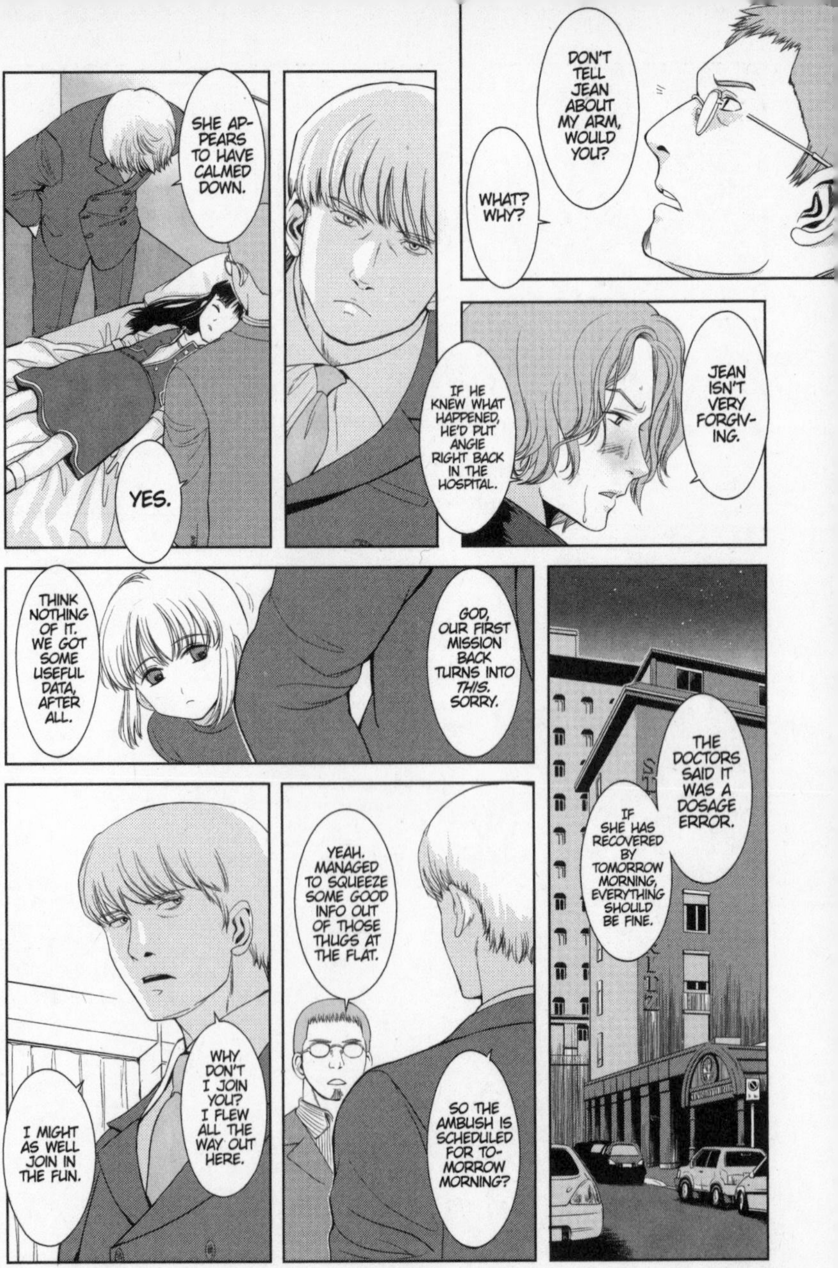
DON'T TELL JEAN ABOUT MY ARM, WOULD YOU?
WHAT? WHY?
JEAN ISN'T VERY FORGIV-ING.
IF HE KNEW WHAT HAPPENED, HE'D PUT ANGIE RIGHT BACK IN THE HOSPITAL.
SHE AP-PEARS TO HAVE CALMED DOWN.
YES.
THE DOCTORS SAID IT WAS A DOSAGE ERROR.
IF SHE HAS RECOVERED BY TOMORROW MORNING, EVERYTHING SHOULD BE FINE.
GOD, OUR FIRST MISSION BACK TURNS INTO *THIS*. SORRY.
THINK NOTHING OF IT. WE GOT SOME USEFUL DATA, AFTER ALL.
SO THE AMBUSH IS SCHEDULED FOR TO-MORROW MORNING?
YEAH. MANAGED TO SQUEEZE SOME GOOD INFO OUT OF THOSE THUGS AT THE FLAT.
WHY DON'T I JOIN YOU? I FLEW ALL THE WAY OUT HERE.
I MIGHT AS WELL JOIN IN THE FUN.

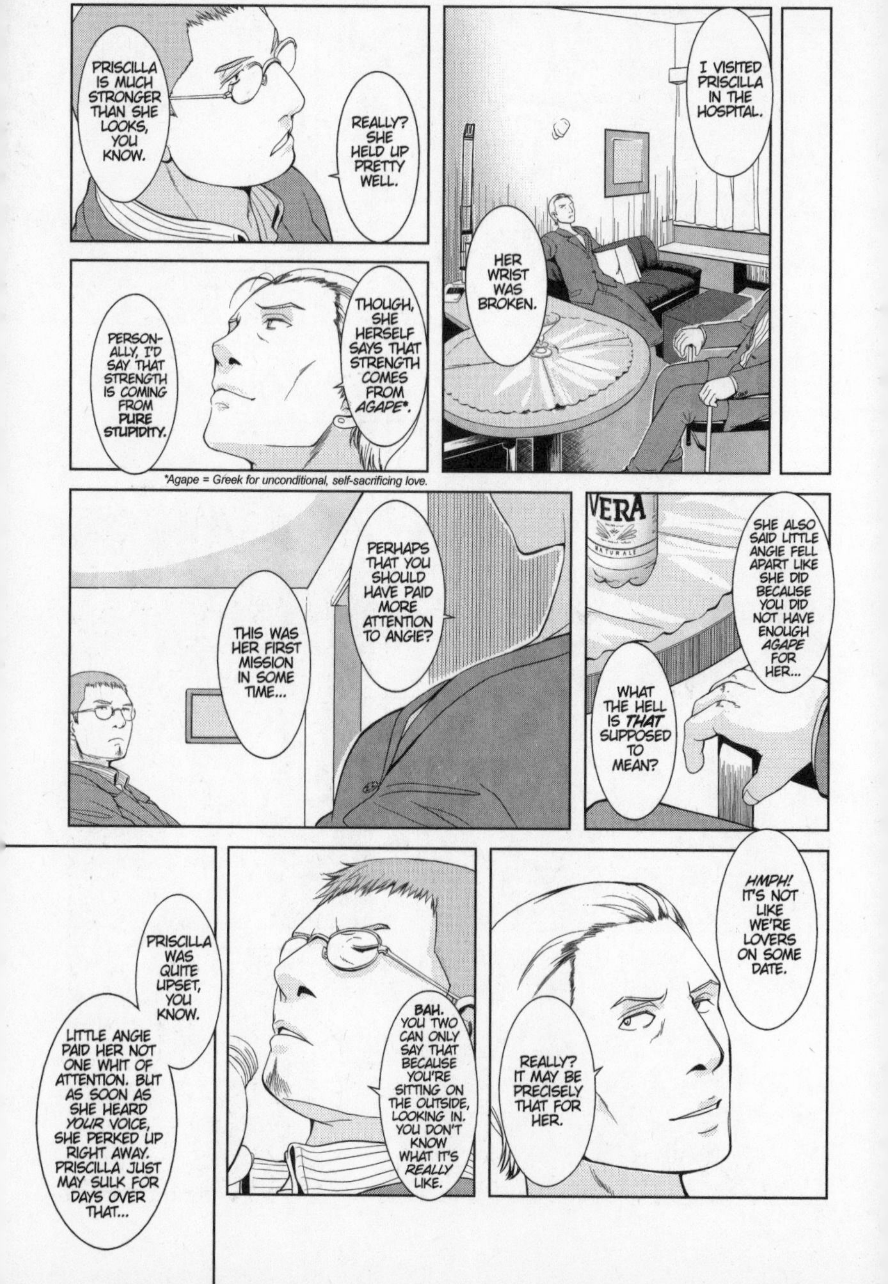
I VISITED PRISCILLA IN THE HOSPITAL.
HER WRIST WAS BROKEN.
REALLY? SHE HELD UP PRETTY WELL.
PRISCILLA IS MUCH STRONGER THAN SHE LOOKS, YOU KNOW.
THOUGH, SHE HERSELF SAYS THAT STRENGTH COMES FROM *AGAPE**.
PERSON-ALLY, I'D SAY THAT STRENGTH IS COMING FROM **PURE STUPIDITY.**
VERA
NATURALE
SHE ALSO SAID LITTLE ANGIE FELL APART LIKE SHE DID BECAUSE YOU DID NOT HAVE ENOUGH *AGAPE* FOR HER...
WHAT THE HELL IS ***THAT*** SUPPOSED TO MEAN?
PERHAPS THAT YOU SHOULD HAVE PAID MORE ATTENTION TO ANGIE?
THIS WAS HER FIRST MISSION IN SOME TIME...
HMPH! IT'S NOT LIKE WE'RE LOVERS ON SOME DATE.
REALLY? IT MAY BE PRECISELY THAT FOR HER.
BAH. YOU TWO CAN ONLY SAY THAT BECAUSE YOU'RE SITTING ON THE OUTSIDE, LOOKING IN. YOU DON'T KNOW WHAT IT'S *REALLY* LIKE.
PRISCILLA WAS QUITE UPSET, YOU KNOW.
LITTLE ANGIE PAID HER NOT ONE WHIT OF ATTENTION. BUT AS SOON AS SHE HEARD *YOUR* VOICE, SHE PERKED UP RIGHT AWAY. PRISCILLA JUST MAY SULK FOR DAYS OVER THAT...

Agape = Greek for unconditional, self-sacrificing love.

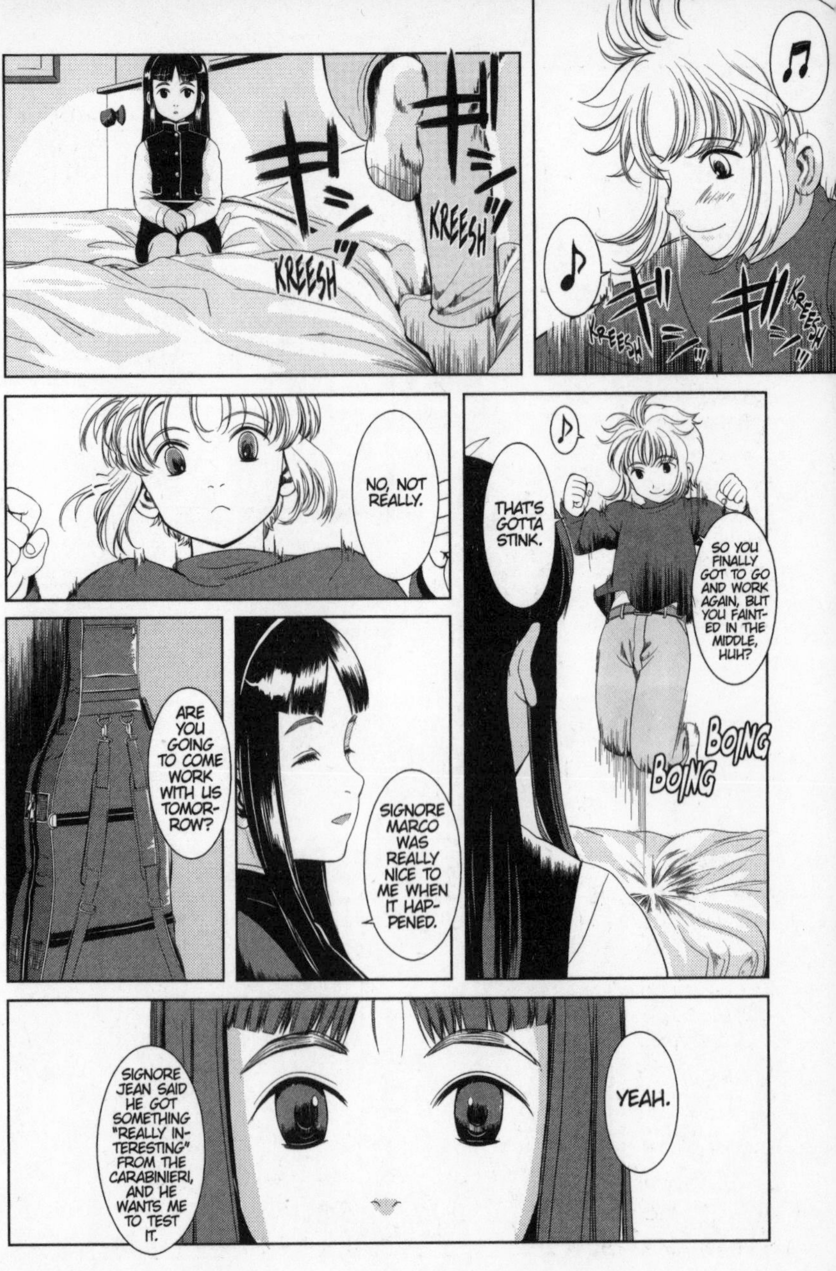

♪
♪
KREESH
KREESH
KREESH
KREESH
SO YOU FINALLY GOT TO GO AND WORK AGAIN, BUT YOU FAINTED IN THE MIDDLE, HUH?
♪
THAT'S GOTTA STINK.
BOING
BOING
NO, NOT REALLY.
SIGNORE MARCO WAS REALLY NICE TO ME WHEN IT HAPPENED.
ARE YOU GOING TO COME WORK WITH US TOMORROW?
YEAH.
SIGNORE JEAN SAID HE GOT SOMETHING "REALLY INTERESTING" FROM THE CARABINIERI, AND HE WANTS ME TO TEST IT.

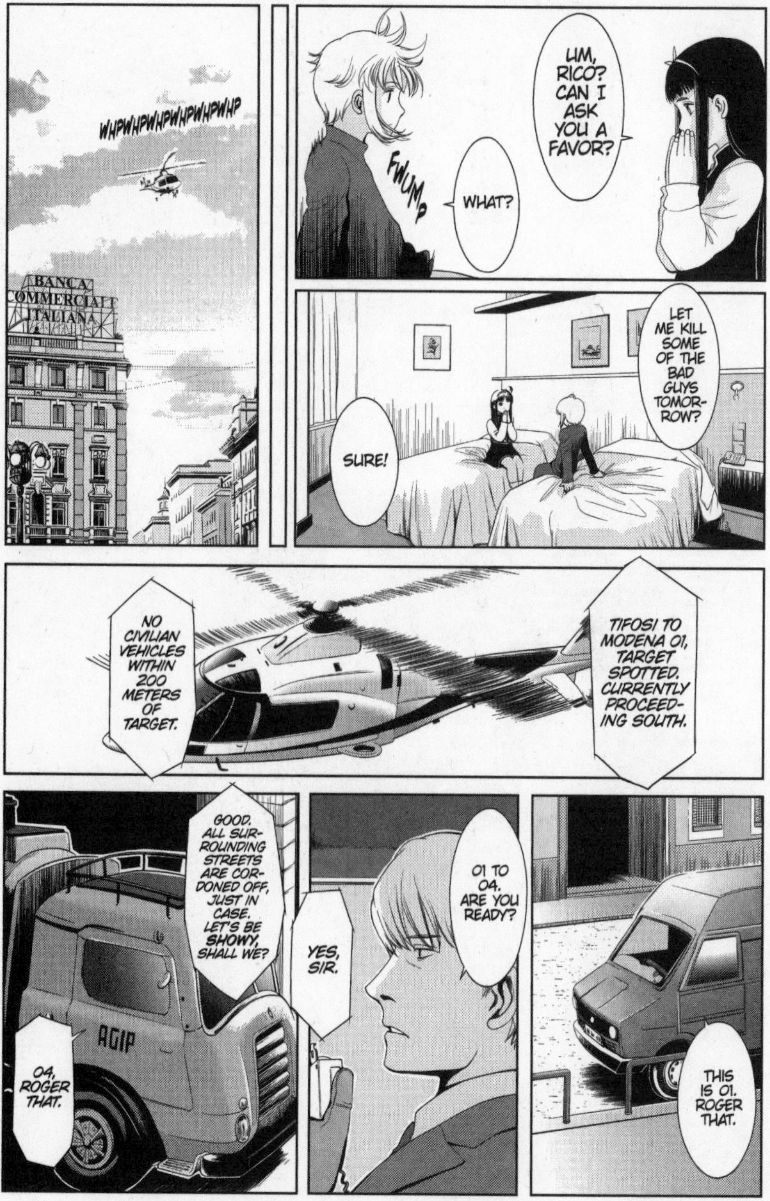

UM, RICO? CAN I ASK YOU A FAVOR?
FWUMP
WHAT?
LET ME KILL SOME OF THE BAD GUYS TOMOR-ROW?
SURE!
WHPWHPWHPWHPWHPWHP
BANCA COMMERCIALE ITALIANA
TIFOSI TO MODENA 01, TARGET SPOTTED. CURRENTLY PROCEED-ING SOUTH.
NO CIVILIAN VEHICLES WITHIN 200 METERS OF TARGET.
THIS IS 01. ROGER THAT.
01 TO 04. ARE YOU READY?
YES, SIR.
GOOD. ALL SUR-ROUNDING STREETS ARE COR-DONED OFF, JUST IN CASE. LET'S BE SHOWY, SHALL WE?
AGIP
04, ROGER THAT.

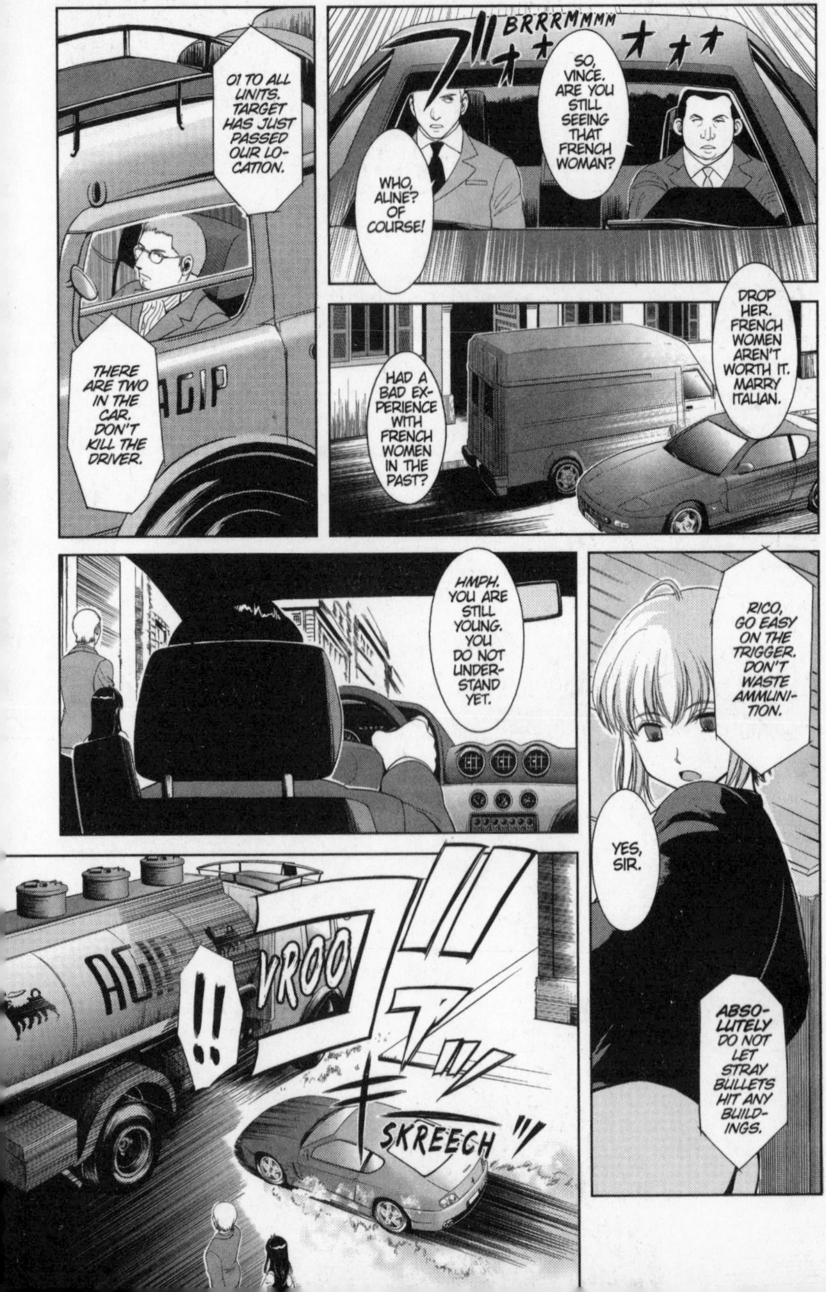
BRRRMMMM
SO, VINCE. ARE YOU STILL SEEING THAT FRENCH WOMAN?
WHO, ALINE? OF COURSE!
DROP HER. FRENCH WOMEN AREN'T WORTH IT. MARRY ITALIAN.
HAD A BAD EXPERIENCE WITH FRENCH WOMEN IN THE PAST?
01 TO ALL UNITS. TARGET HAS JUST PASSED OUR LOCATION.
THERE ARE TWO IN THE CAR. DON'T KILL THE DRIVER.
AGIP
RICO, GO EASY ON THE TRIGGER. DON'T WASTE AMMUNITION.
YES, SIR.
ABSOLUTELY DO NOT LET STRAY BULLETS HIT ANY BUILDINGS.
HMPH. YOU ARE STILL YOUNG. YOU DO NOT UNDERSTAND YET.
!!
VROO
SKREECH

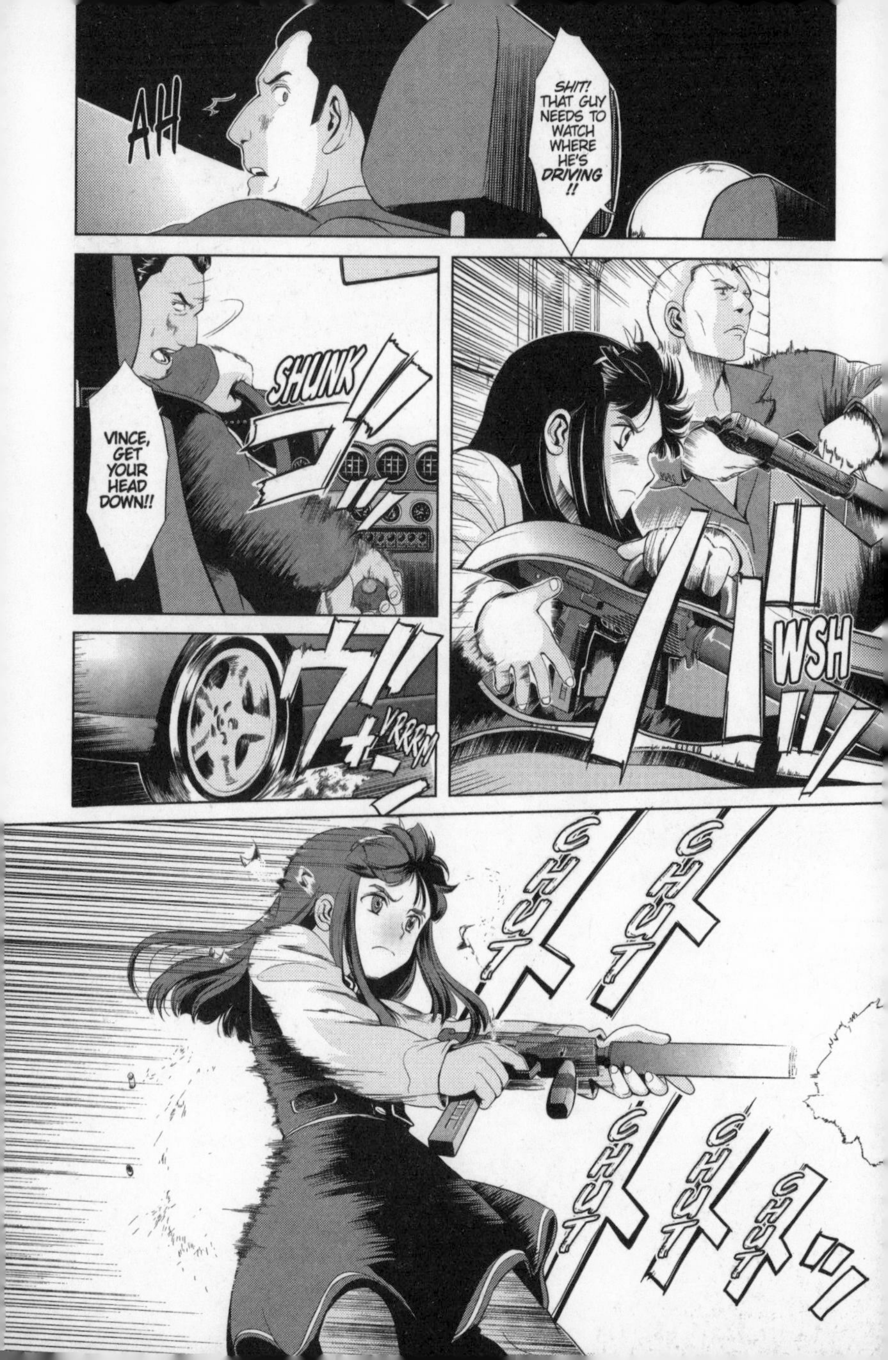
SHIT! THAT GUY NEEDS TO WATCH WHERE HE'S *DRIVING*!!
AH
WSH
SHUNK
VINCE, GET YOUR HEAD DOWN!!
VRRRM
CHUT CHUT
CHUT CHUT CHUT

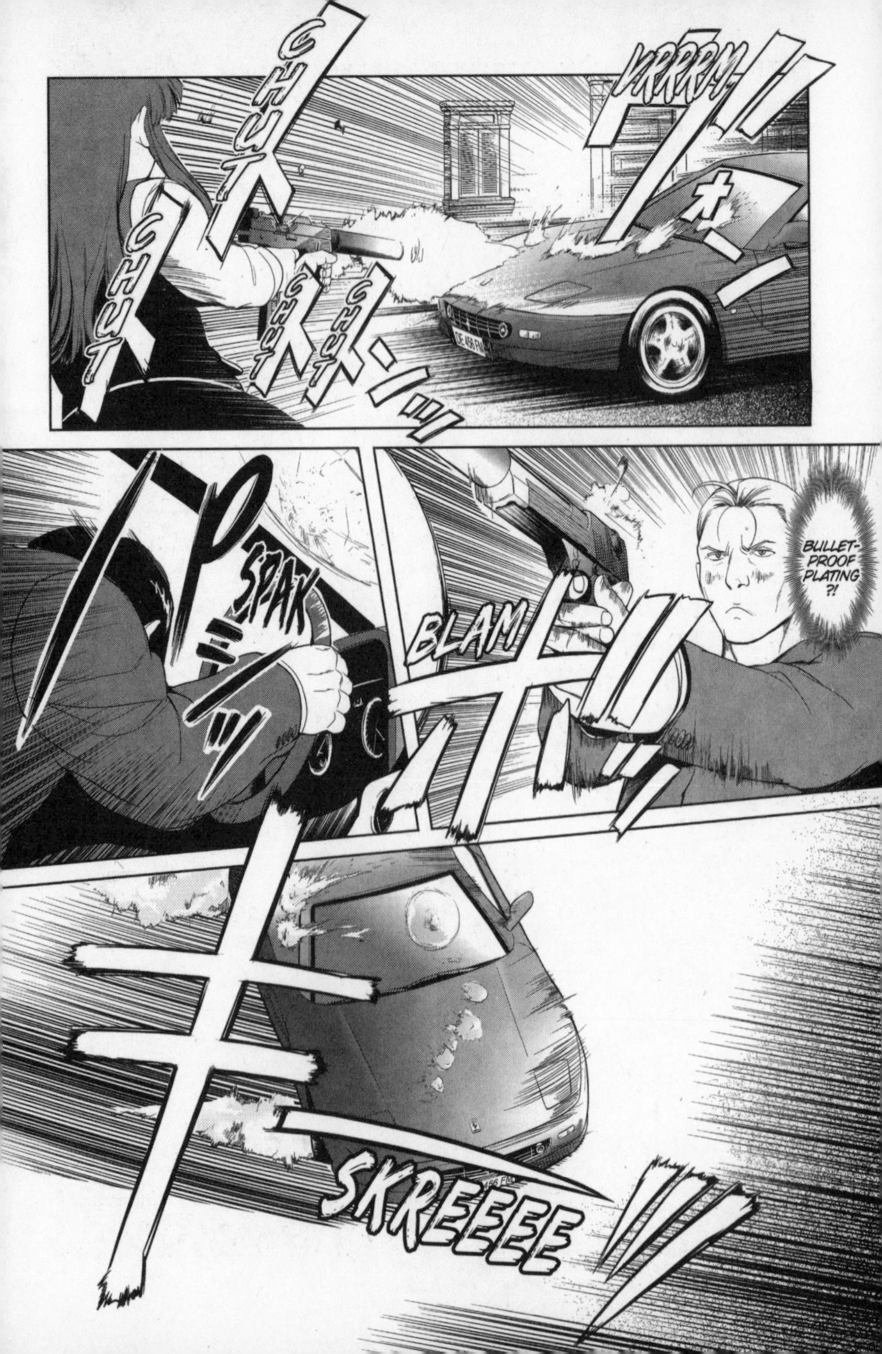
VRRRM
CHUT
CHUT
CHUT
CHUT
CHUT
BULLET-PROOF PLATING ?!
BLAM
SPAK
SKREEEE

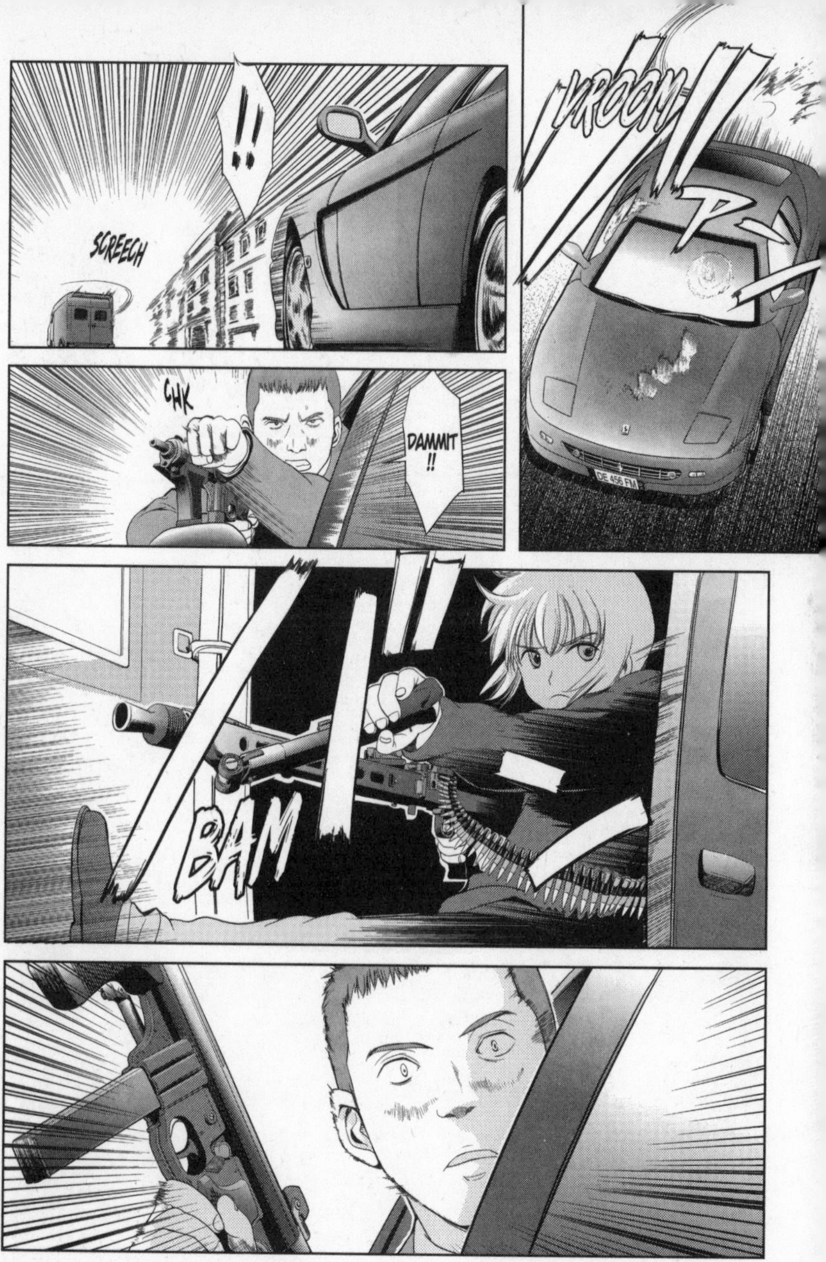
VROOM
DE 456 FM
!!
SCREECH
CHK
DAMMIT !!
BAM

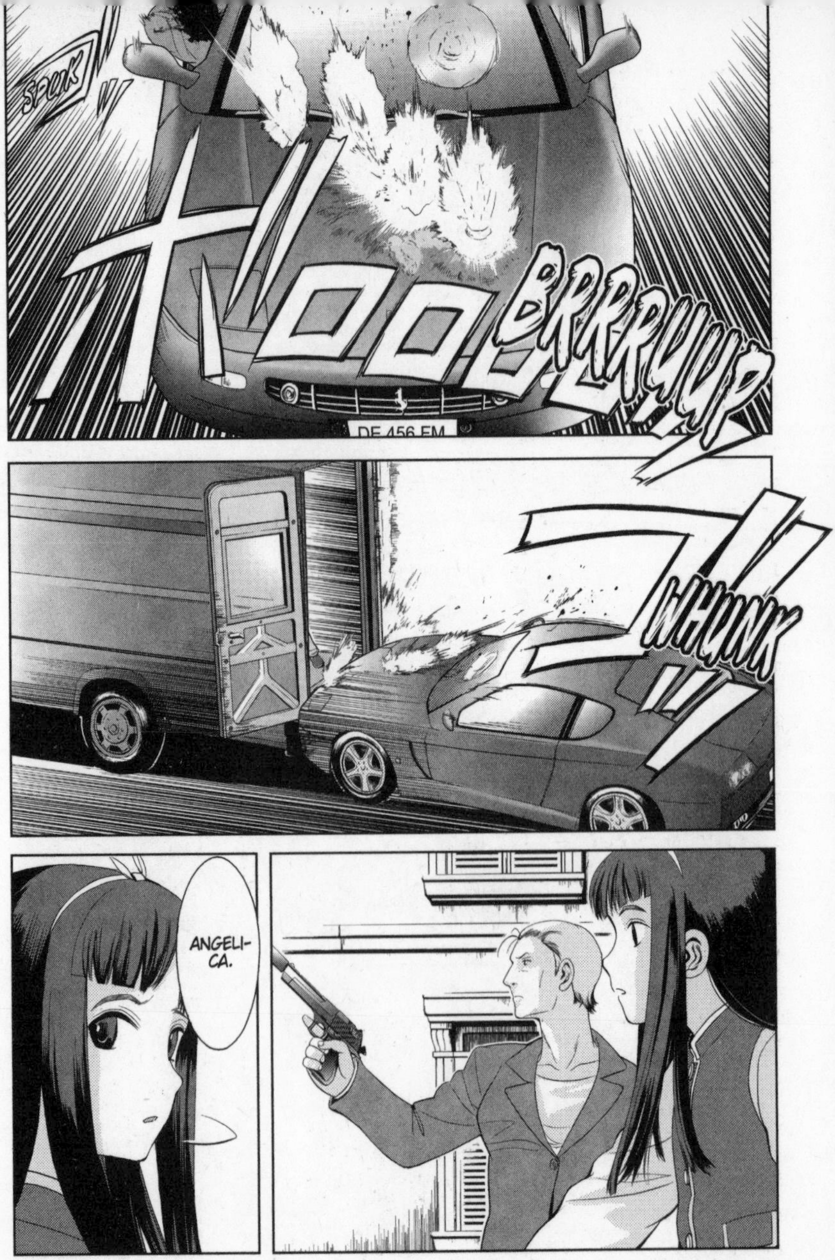
BRRRUUUP
DE 456 EM
WHUNK
ANGELI-
CA.

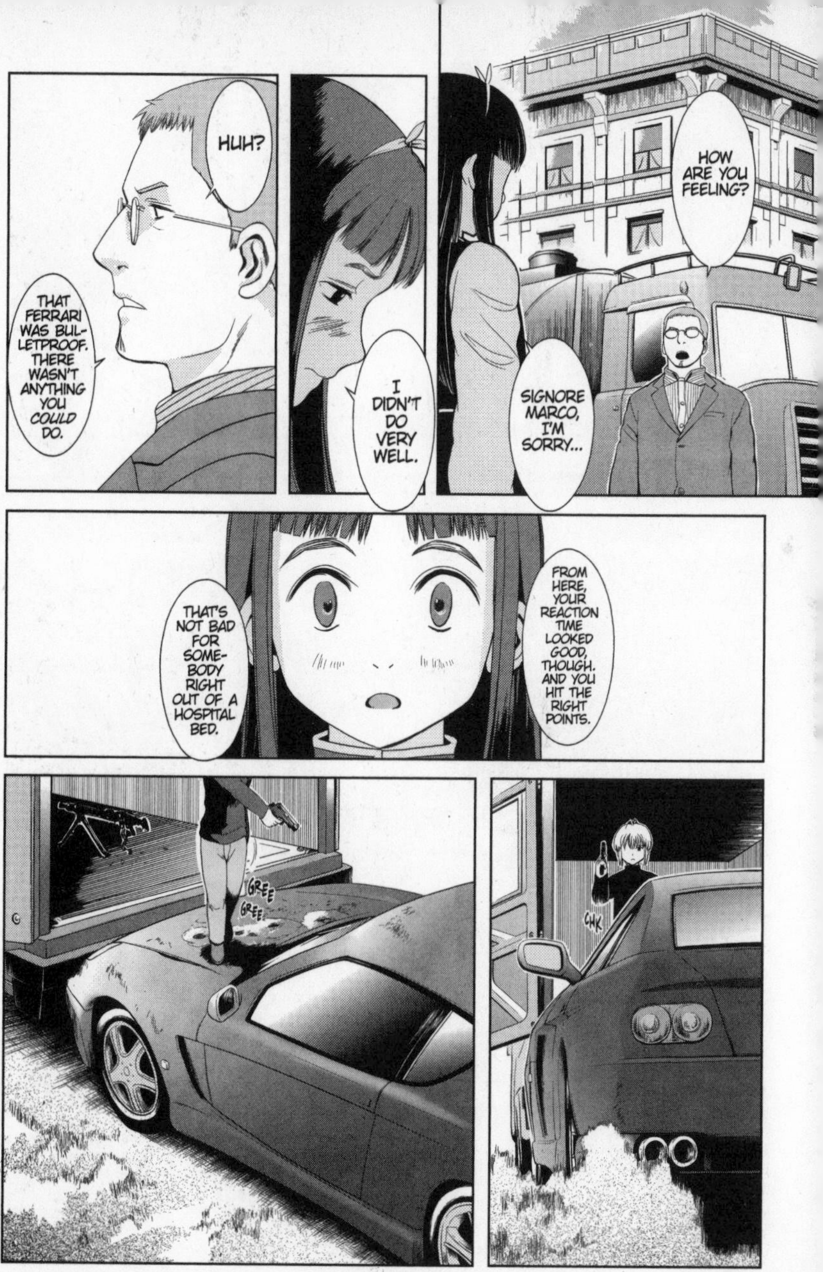
HOW ARE YOU FEELING?
SIGNORE MARCO, I'M SORRY...
I DIDN'T DO VERY WELL.
HUH?
THAT FERRARI WAS BULLETPROOF. THERE WASN'T ANYTHING YOU COULD DO.
FROM HERE, YOUR REACTION TIME LOOKED GOOD, THOUGH. AND YOU HIT THE RIGHT POINTS.
THAT'S NOT BAD FOR SOMEBODY RIGHT OUT OF A HOSPITAL BED.
CHK
GREE
GREE

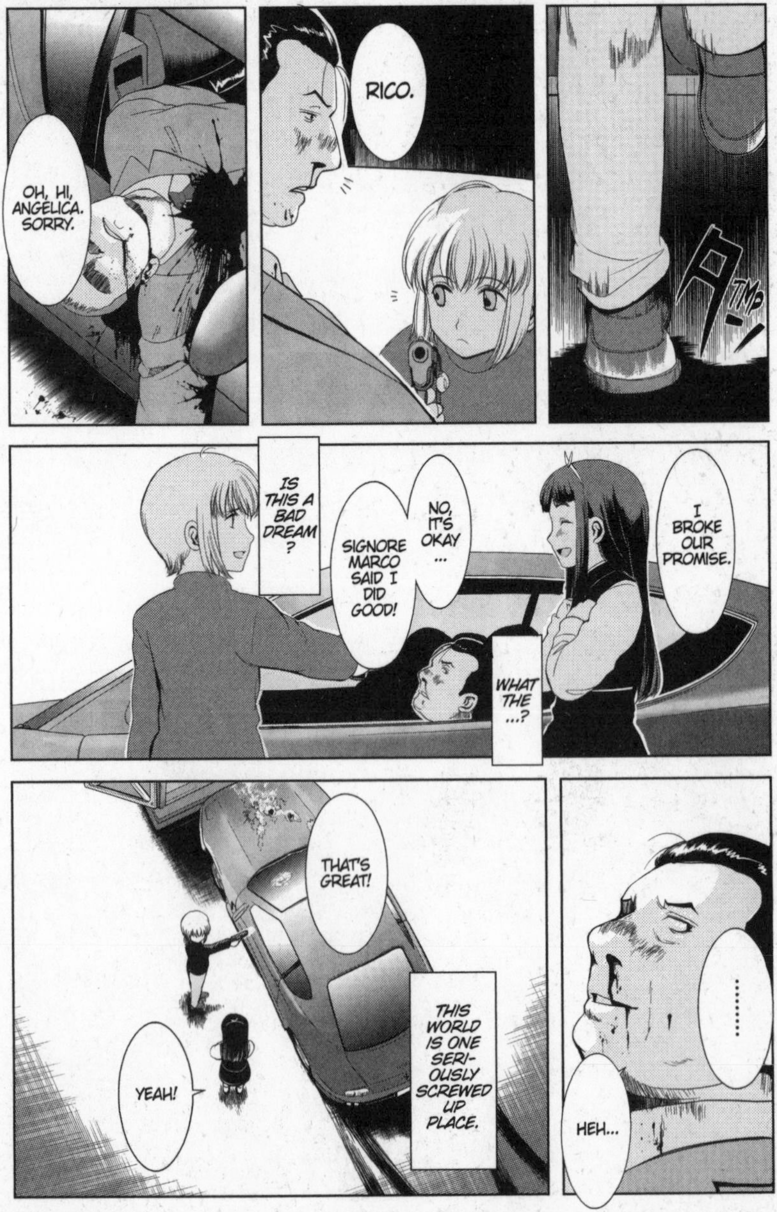
TMP
RICO.
OH, HI, ANGELICA. SORRY.
I BROKE OUR PROMISE.
NO, IT'S OKAY ...
IS THIS A BAD DREAM ?
SIGNORE MARCO SAID I DID GOOD!
WHAT THE ...?
....
HEH...
THAT'S GREAT!
THIS WORLD IS ONE SERI-OUSLY SCREWED UP PLACE.
YEAH!

GUNSLINGERGIRL.

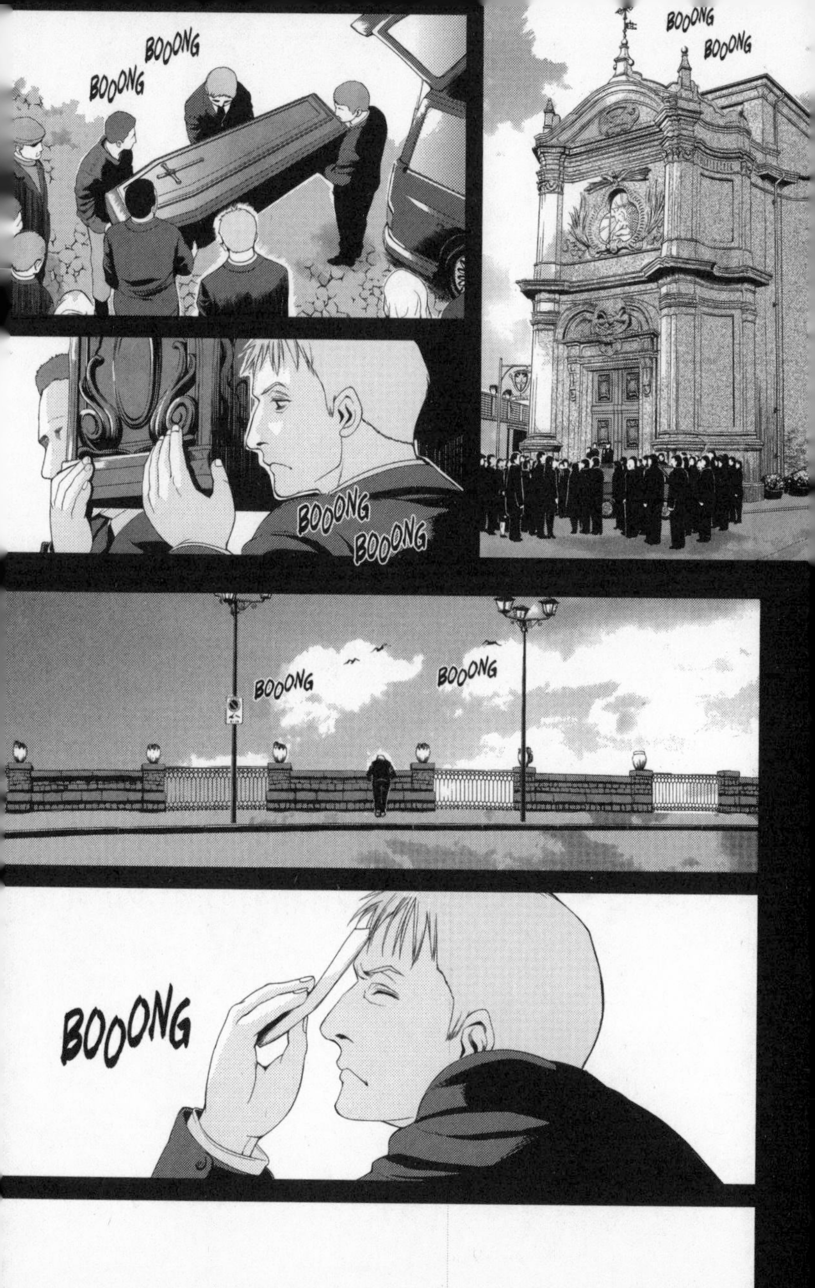
BOOONG
BOOONG
BOOONG
BOOONG
BOOONG
BOOONG
BOOONG
BOOONG
BOOONG

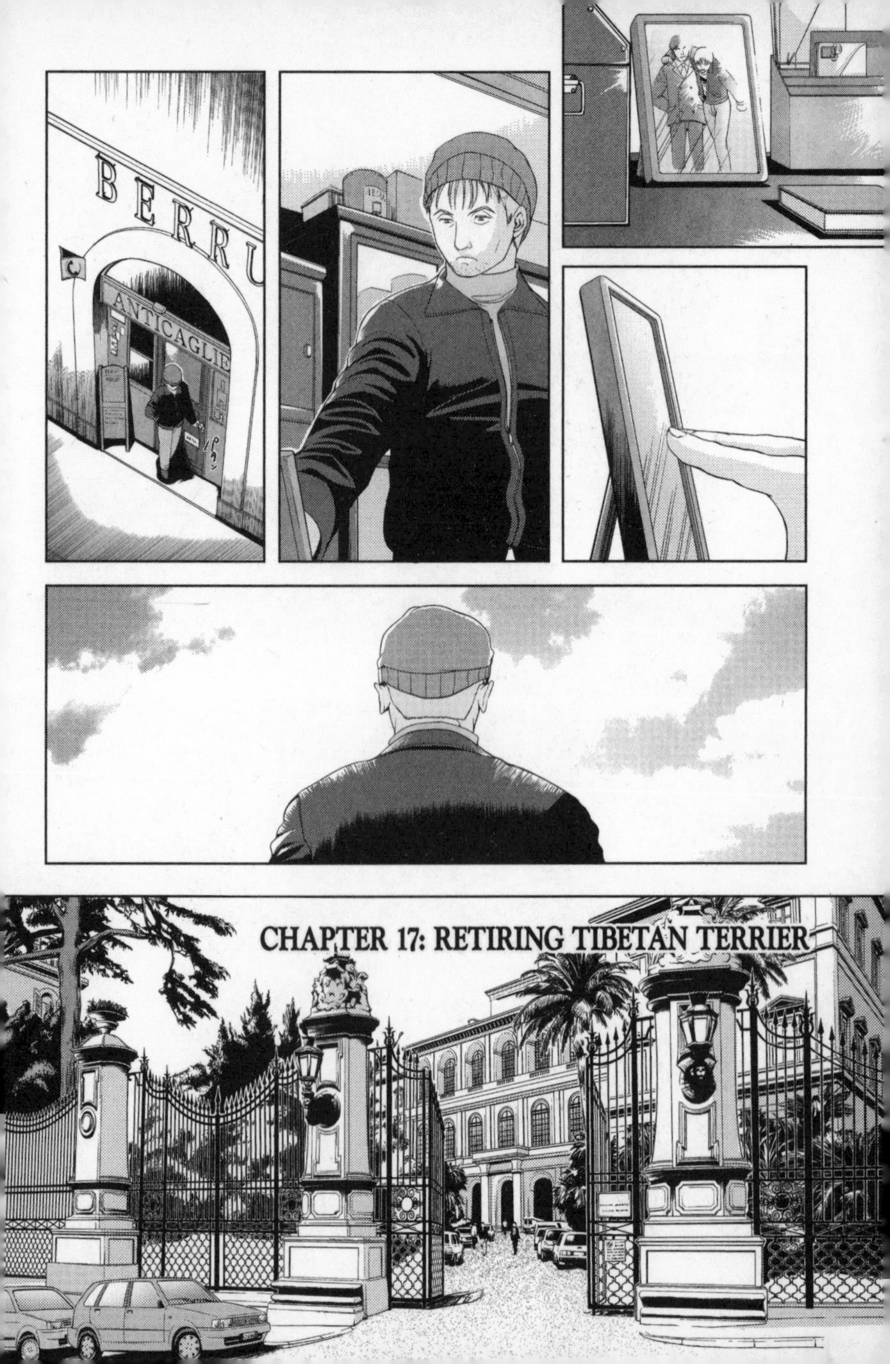
BERRU
ANTICAGLIE
CHAPTER 17: RETIRING TIBETAN TERRIER

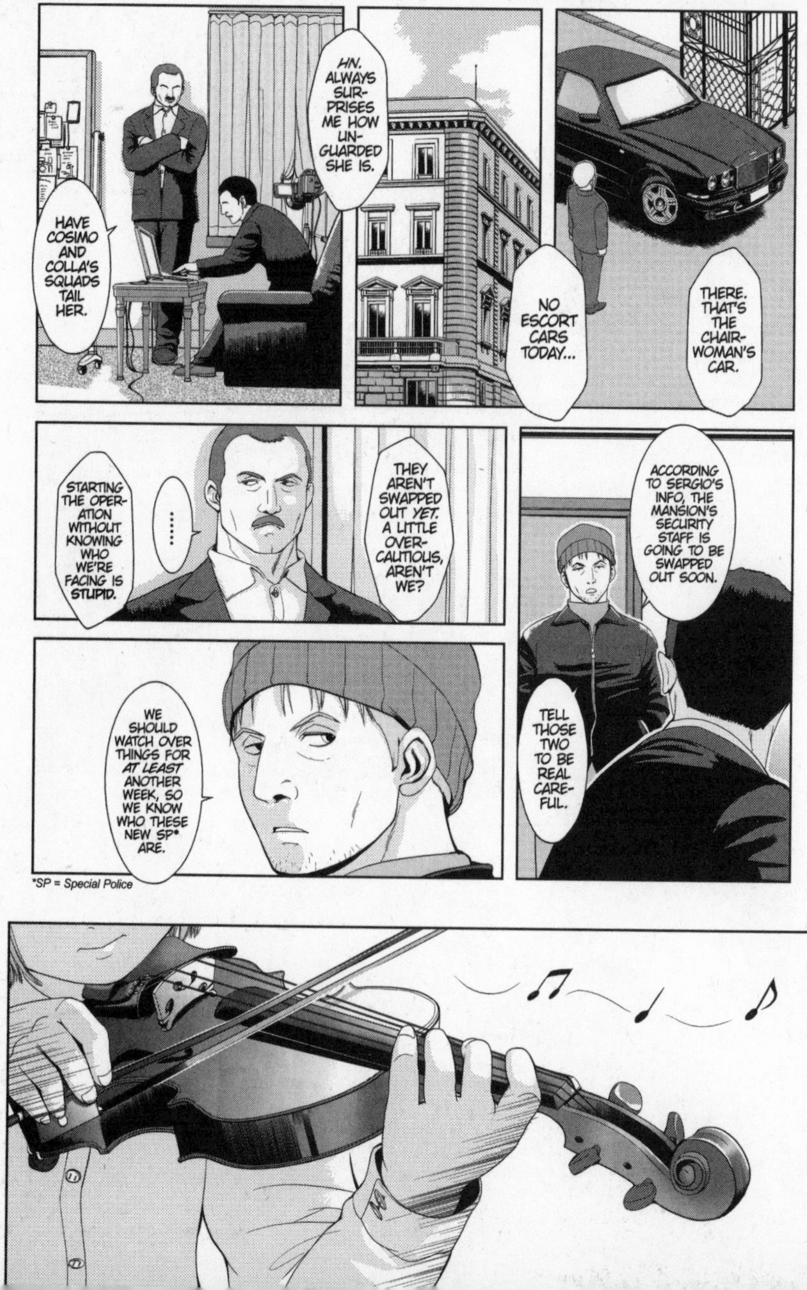
THERE. THAT'S THE CHAIRWOMAN'S CAR.
NO ESCORT CARS TODAY...
HN. ALWAYS SURPRISES ME HOW UNGUARDED SHE IS.
HAVE COSIMO AND COLLA'S SQUADS TAIL HER.
ACCORDING TO SERGIO'S INFO, THE MANSION'S SECURITY STAFF IS GOING TO BE SWAPPED OUT SOON.
TELL THOSE TWO TO BE REAL CAREFUL.
THEY AREN'T SWAPPED OUT *YET*. A LITTLE OVERCAUTIOUS, AREN'T WE?
......
STARTING THE OPERATION WITHOUT KNOWING WHO WE'RE FACING IS **STUPID**.
WE SHOULD WATCH OVER THINGS FOR *AT LEAST* ANOTHER WEEK, SO WE KNOW WHO THESE NEW SP* ARE.

*SP = Special Police

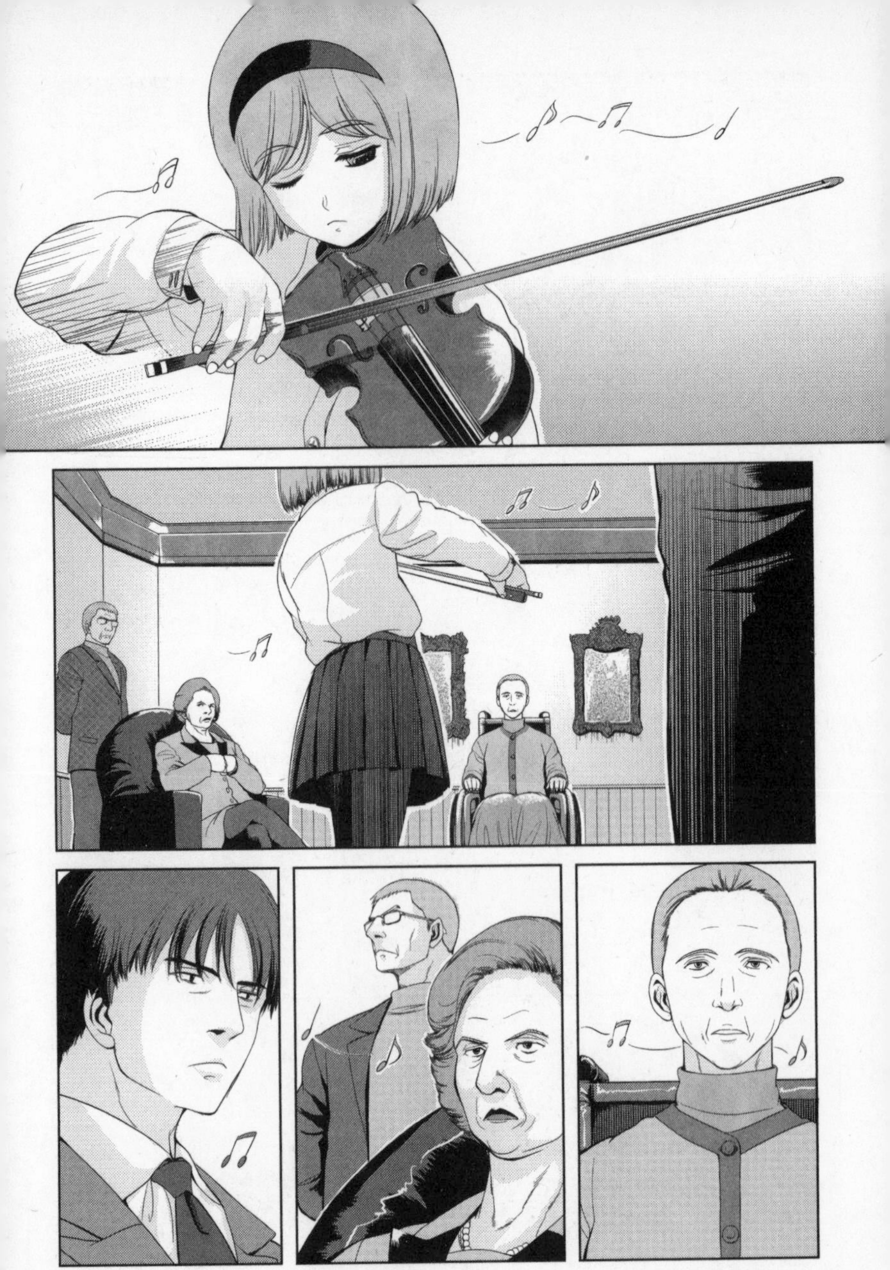

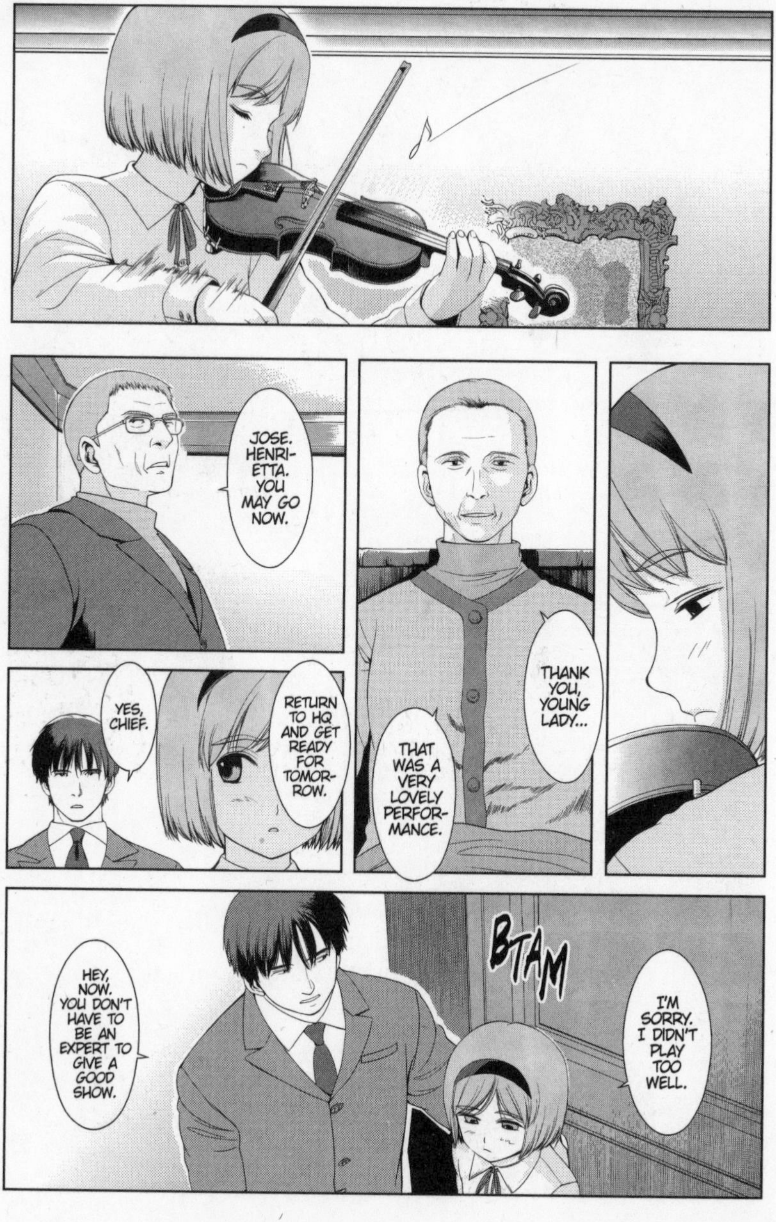
THANK YOU, YOUNG LADY...
THAT WAS A VERY LOVELY PERFORMANCE.
JOSE. HENRIETTA. YOU MAY GO NOW.
RETURN TO HQ AND GET READY FOR TOMORROW.
YES, CHIEF.
BTAM
I'M SORRY. I DIDN'T PLAY TOO WELL.
HEY, NOW. YOU DON'T HAVE TO BE AN EXPERT TO GIVE A GOOD SHOW.

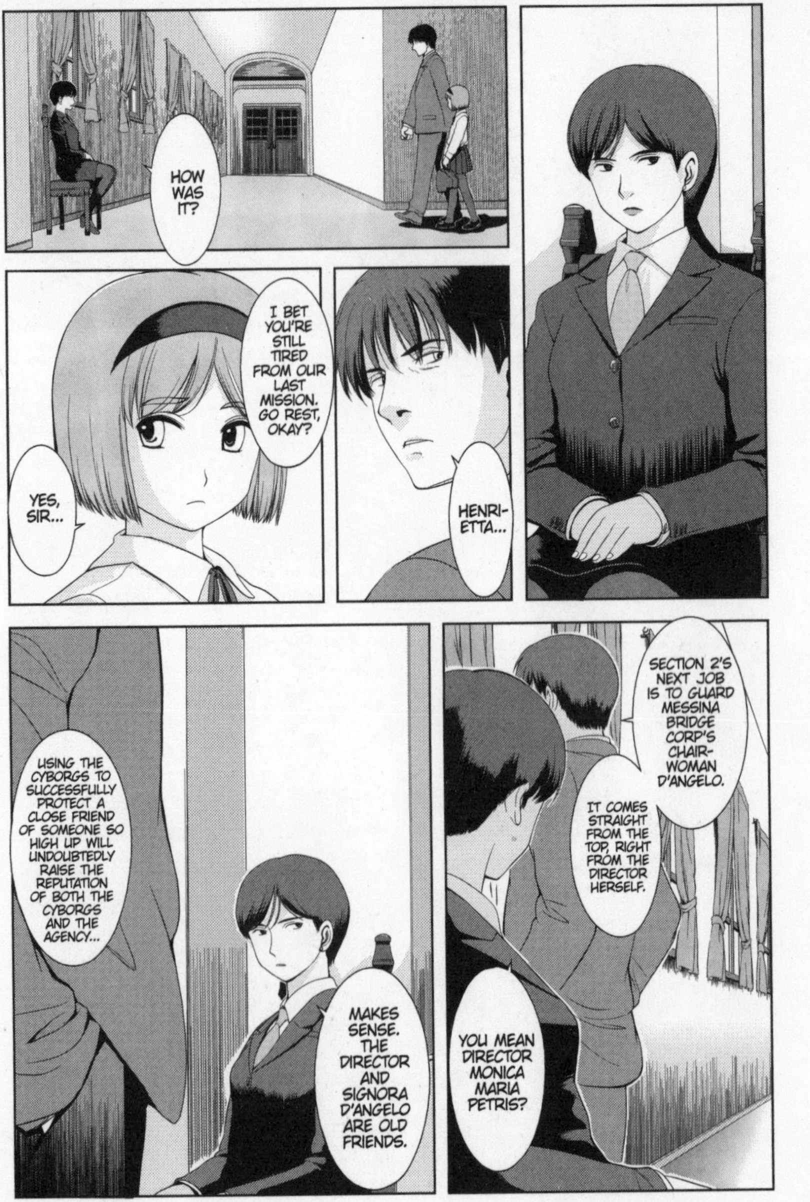
HOW WAS IT?
HENRIETTA...
I BET YOU'RE STILL TIRED FROM OUR LAST MISSION. GO REST, OKAY?
YES, SIR...
SECTION 2'S NEXT JOB IS TO GUARD MESSINA BRIDGE CORP'S CHAIRWOMAN D'ANGELO.
IT COMES STRAIGHT FROM THE TOP, RIGHT FROM THE DIRECTOR HERSELF.
YOU MEAN DIRECTOR MONICA MARIA PETRIS?
MAKES SENSE. THE DIRECTOR AND SIGNORA D'ANGELO ARE OLD FRIENDS.
USING THE CYBORGS TO SUCCESSFULLY PROTECT A CLOSE FRIEND OF SOMEONE SO HIGH UP WILL UNDOUBTEDLY RAISE THE REPUTATION OF BOTH THE CYBORGS AND THE AGENCY...

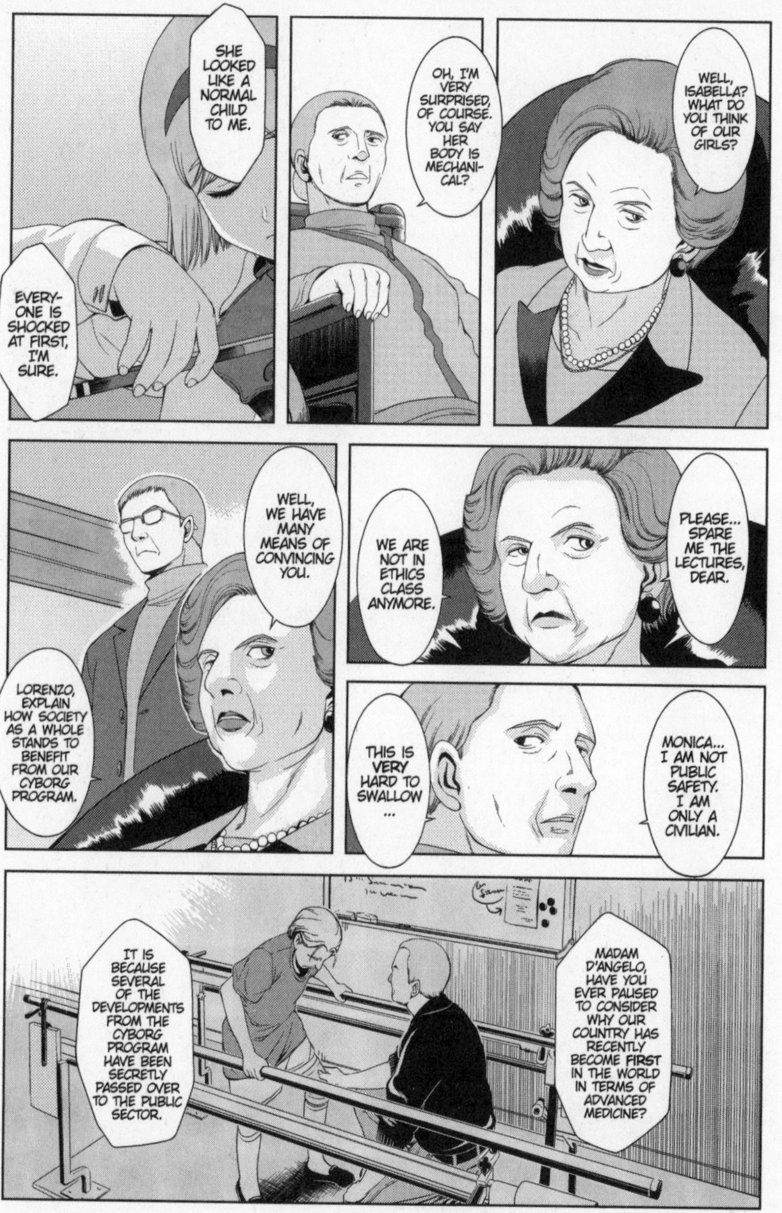
WELL, ISABELLA? WHAT DO YOU THINK OF OUR GIRLS?
OH, I'M VERY SURPRISED, OF COURSE. YOU SAY HER BODY IS MECHANICAL?
SHE LOOKED LIKE A NORMAL CHILD TO ME.
EVERYONE IS SHOCKED AT FIRST, I'M SURE.
PLEASE... SPARE ME THE LECTURES, DEAR.
WE ARE NOT IN ETHICS CLASS ANYMORE.
MONICA... I AM NOT PUBLIC SAFETY. I AM ONLY A CIVILIAN.
THIS IS VERY HARD TO SWALLOW...
WELL, WE HAVE MANY MEANS OF CONVINCING YOU.
LORENZO, EXPLAIN HOW SOCIETY AS A WHOLE STANDS TO BENEFIT FROM OUR CYBORG PROGRAM.
MADAM D'ANGELO, HAVE YOU EVER PAUSED TO CONSIDER WHY OUR COUNTRY HAS RECENTLY BECOME FIRST IN THE WORLD IN TERMS OF ADVANCED MEDICINE?
IT IS BECAUSE SEVERAL OF THE DEVELOPMENTS FROM THE CYBORG PROGRAM HAVE BEEN SECRETLY PASSED OVER TO THE PUBLIC SECTOR.

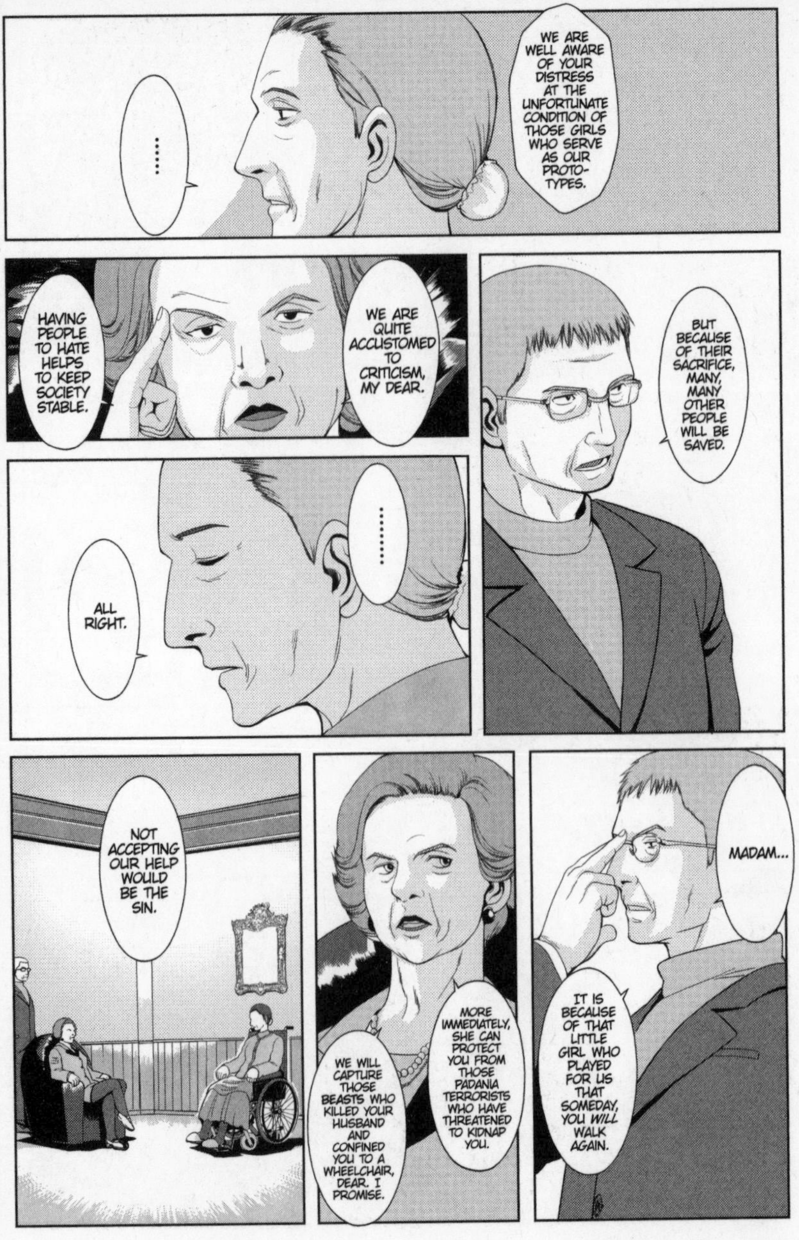
WE ARE WELL AWARE OF YOUR DISTRESS AT THE UNFORTUNATE CONDITION OF THOSE GIRLS WHO SERVE AS OUR PROTO-TYPES.
......
BUT BECAUSE OF THEIR SACRIFICE, MANY, MANY OTHER PEOPLE WILL BE SAVED.
WE ARE QUITE ACCUSTOMED TO CRITICISM, MY DEAR.
HAVING PEOPLE TO HATE HELPS TO KEEP SOCIETY STABLE.
......
ALL RIGHT.
MADAM...
IT IS BECAUSE OF THAT LITTLE GIRL WHO PLAYED FOR US THAT SOMEDAY, YOU *WILL* WALK AGAIN.
MORE IMMEDIATELY, SHE CAN PROTECT YOU FROM THOSE PADANIA TERRORISTS WHO HAVE THREATENED TO KIDNAP YOU.
WE WILL CAPTURE THOSE BEASTS WHO KILLED YOUR HUSBAND AND CONFINED YOU TO A WHEELCHAIR, DEAR. I PROMISE.
NOT ACCEPTING OUR HELP WOULD BE THE SIN.

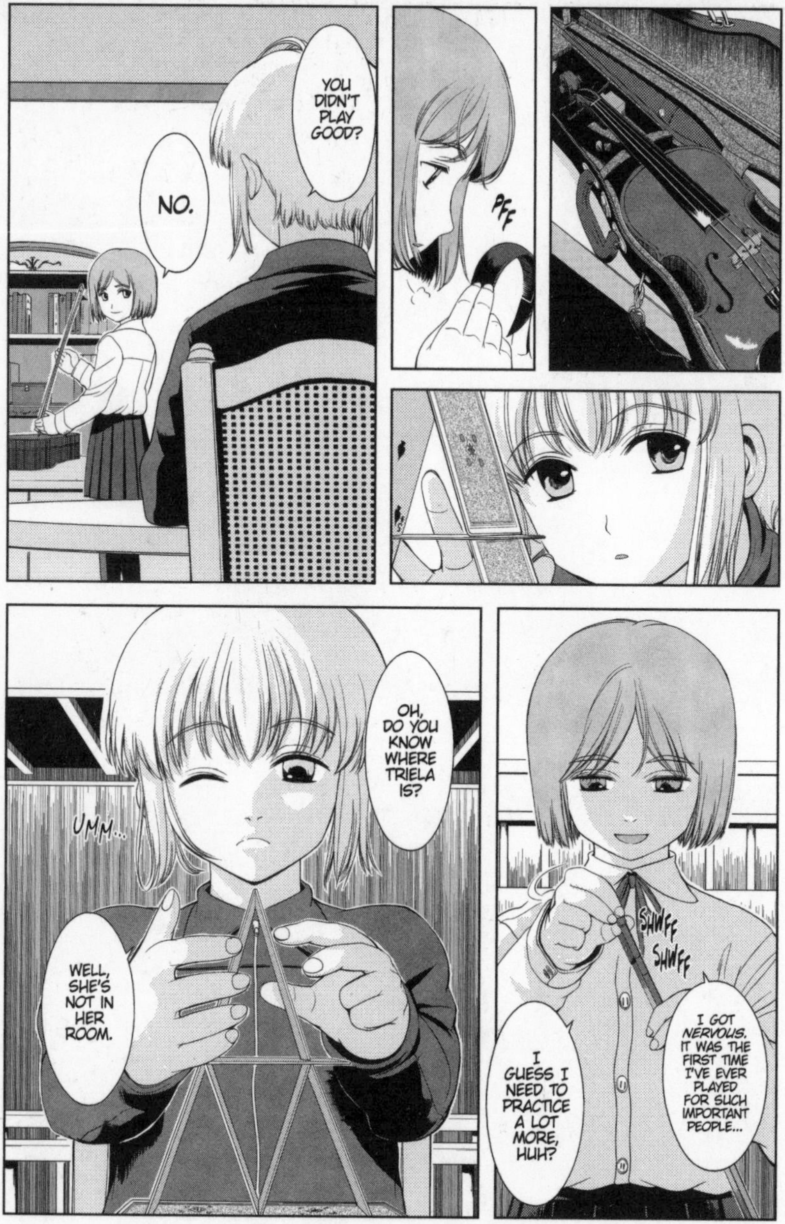
PFF
YOU DIDN'T PLAY GOOD?
NO.
SHWFF SHWFF
I GOT *NERVOUS.* IT WAS THE FIRST TIME I'VE EVER PLAYED FOR SUCH IMPORTANT PEOPLE...
I GUESS I NEED TO PRACTICE A LOT MORE, HUH?
OH, DO YOU KNOW WHERE TRIELA IS?
UMM...
WELL, SHE'S NOT IN HER ROOM.

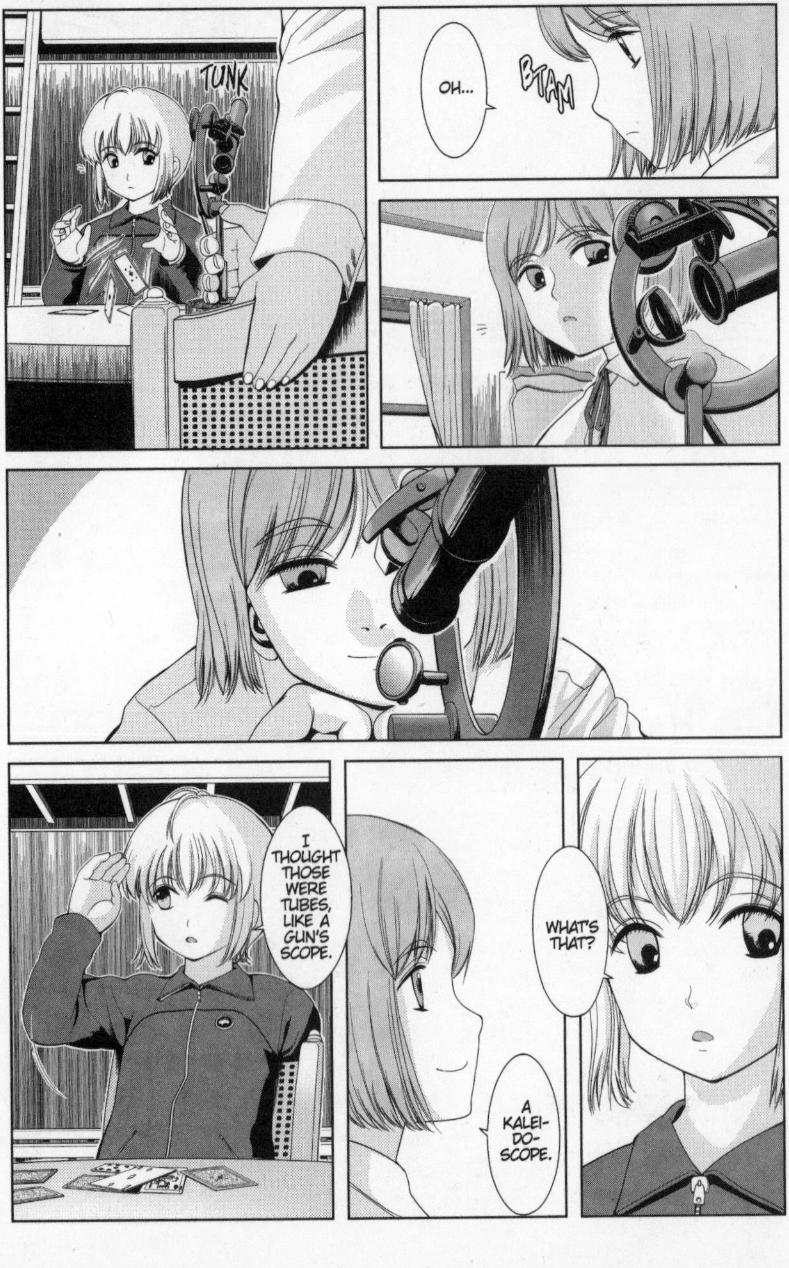
BTAM
OH...
TUNK
WHAT'S THAT?
A KALEI-DO-SCOPE.
I THOUGHT THOSE WERE TUBES, LIKE A GUN'S SCOPE.

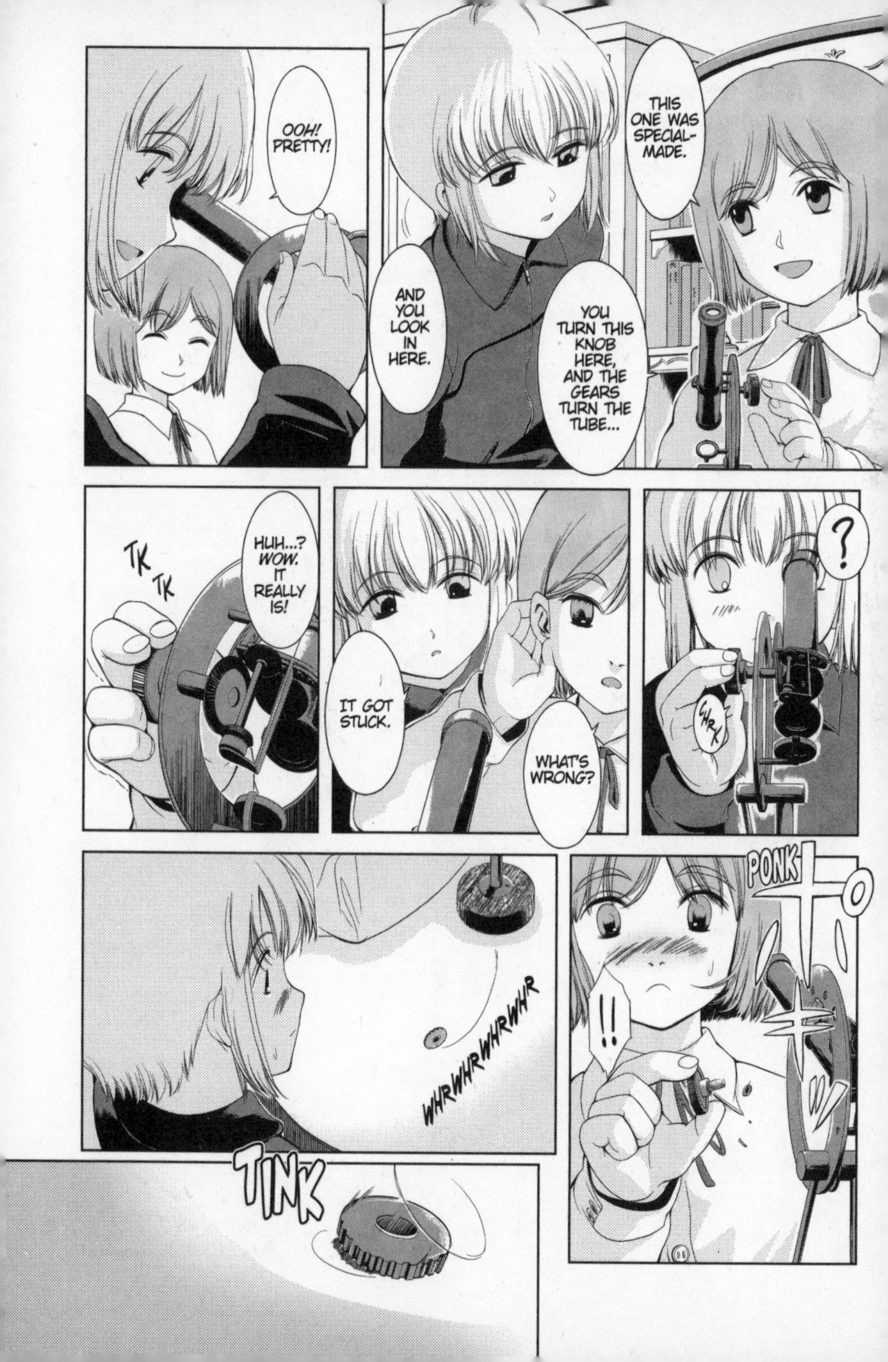
THIS ONE WAS SPECIAL-MADE.
YOU TURN THIS KNOB HERE, AND THE GEARS TURN THE TUBE...
AND YOU LOOK IN HERE.
OOH! PRETTY!
?
CHRK
WHAT'S WRONG?
IT GOT STUCK.
HUH...? WOW. IT REALLY IS!
TK TK
PONK
!!
WHRWHRWHRWHR
TINK

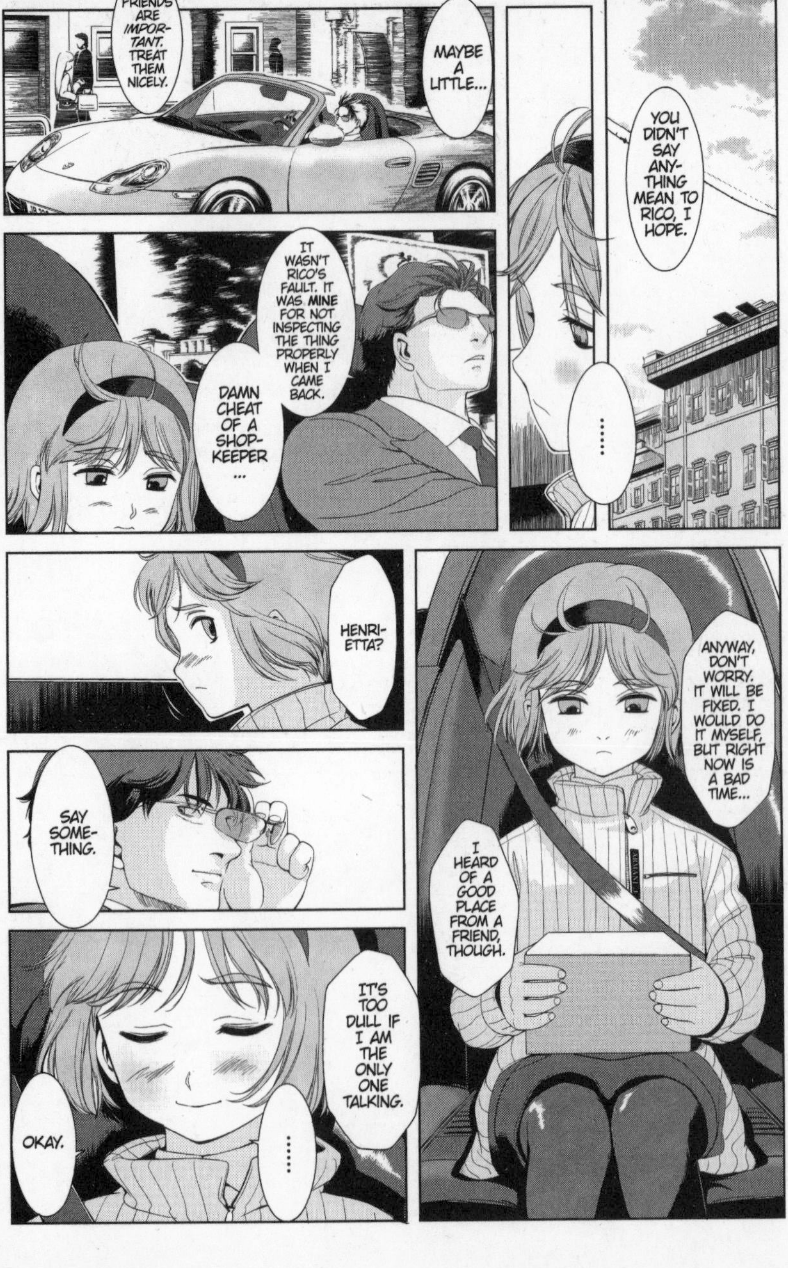
YOU DIDN'T SAY ANYTHING MEAN TO RICO, I HOPE.
......
MAYBE A LITTLE...
FRIENDS ARE IMPORTANT. TREAT THEM NICELY.
IT WASN'T RICO'S FAULT. IT WAS MINE FOR NOT INSPECTING THE THING PROPERLY WHEN I CAME BACK.
DAMN CHEAT OF A SHOPKEEPER...
ANYWAY, DON'T WORRY. IT WILL BE FIXED. I WOULD DO IT MYSELF, BUT RIGHT NOW IS A BAD TIME...
I HEARD OF A GOOD PLACE FROM A FRIEND, THOUGH.
HENRIETTA?
SAY SOMETHING.
IT'S TOO DULL IF I AM THE ONLY ONE TALKING.
......
OKAY.

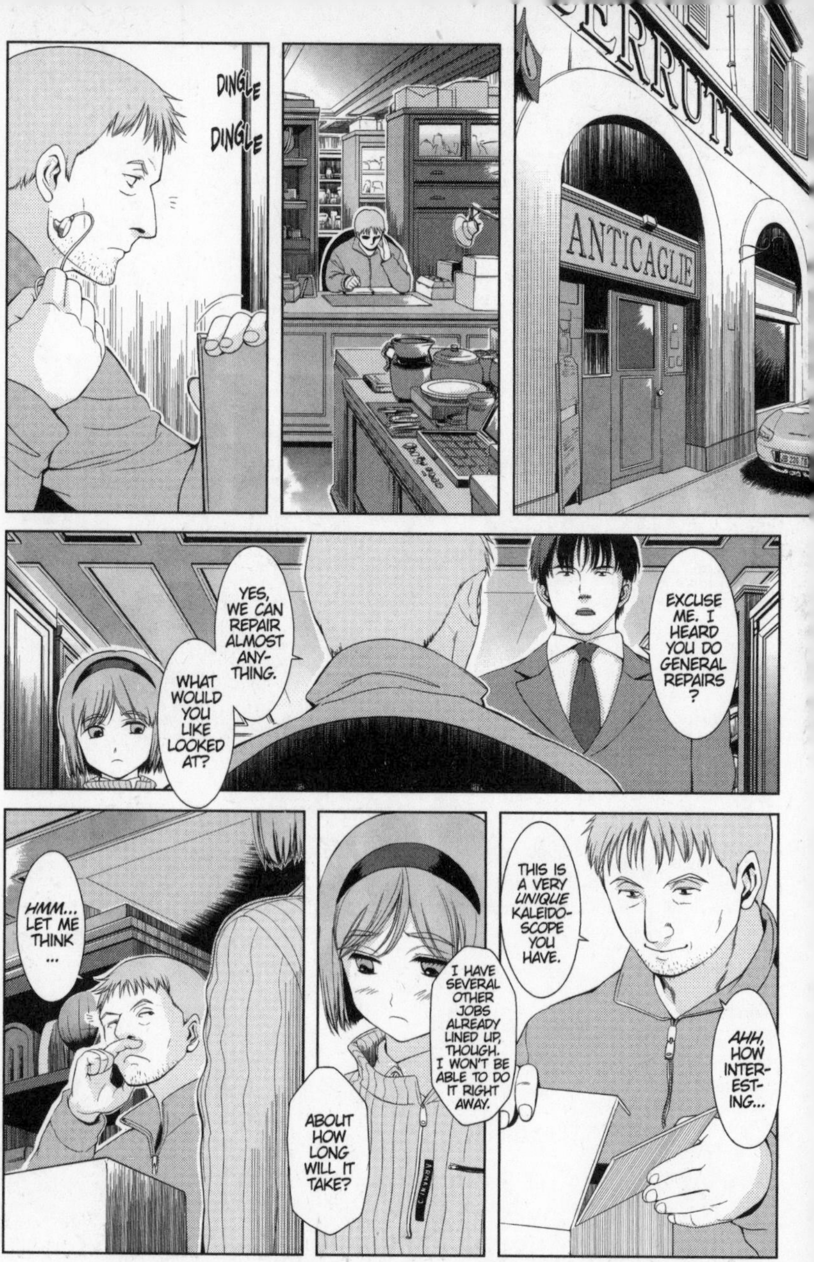
CERRUTI
ANTICAGLIE
DINGLE
DINGLE
EXCUSE ME. I HEARD YOU DO GENERAL REPAIRS?
YES, WE CAN REPAIR ALMOST ANYTHING.
WHAT WOULD YOU LIKE LOOKED AT?
THIS IS A VERY *UNIQUE* KALEIDOSCOPE YOU HAVE.
AHH, HOW INTERESTING...
I HAVE SEVERAL OTHER JOBS ALREADY LINED UP, THOUGH. I WON'T BE ABLE TO DO IT RIGHT AWAY.
ABOUT HOW LONG WILL IT TAKE?
HMM... LET ME THINK ...

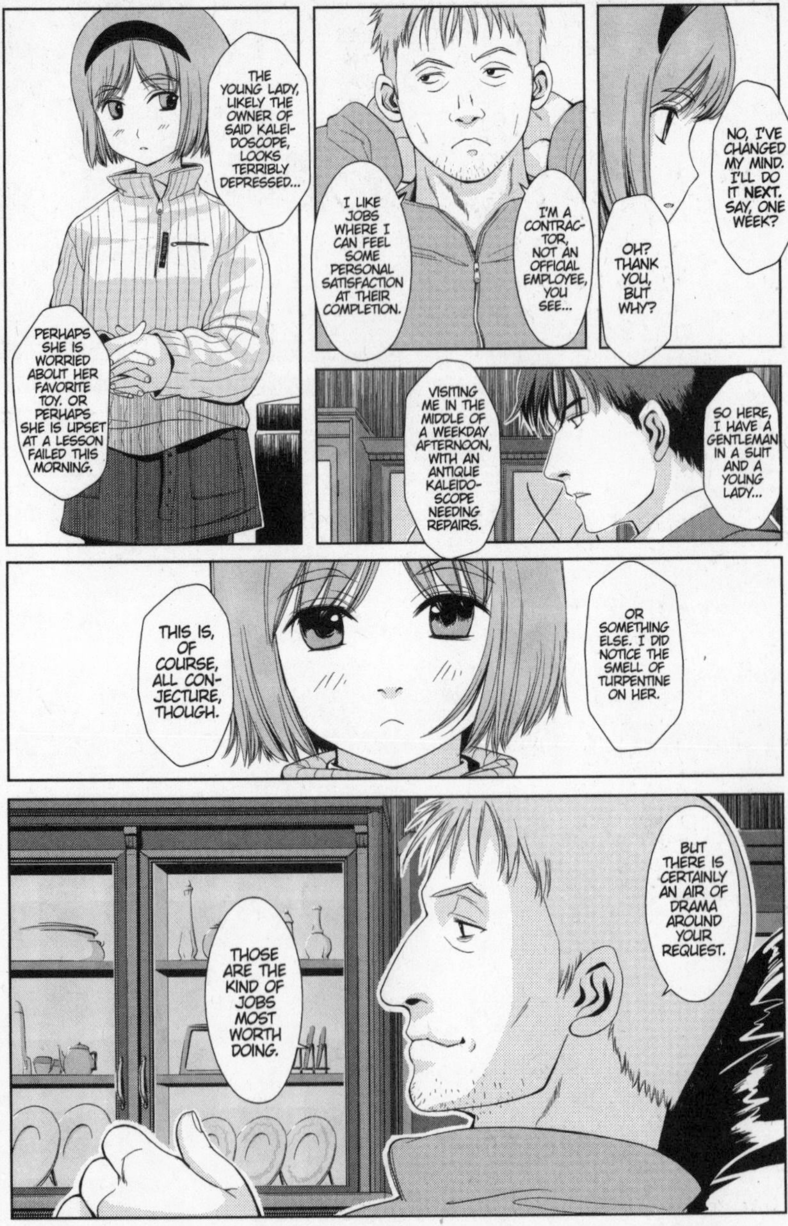

NO, I'VE CHANGED MY MIND. I'LL DO IT NEXT. SAY, ONE WEEK?
OH? THANK YOU, BUT WHY?
I'M A CONTRACTOR, NOT AN OFFICIAL EMPLOYEE, YOU SEE...
I LIKE JOBS WHERE I CAN FEEL SOME PERSONAL SATISFACTION AT THEIR COMPLETION.
SO HERE, I HAVE A GENTLEMAN IN A SUIT AND A YOUNG LADY...
VISITING ME IN THE MIDDLE OF A WEEKDAY AFTERNOON, WITH AN ANTIQUE KALEIDOSCOPE NEEDING REPAIRS.
THE YOUNG LADY, LIKELY THE OWNER OF SAID KALEIDOSCOPE, LOOKS TERRIBLY DEPRESSED...
PERHAPS SHE IS WORRIED ABOUT HER FAVORITE TOY. OR PERHAPS SHE IS UPSET AT A LESSON FAILED THIS MORNING.
OR SOMETHING ELSE. I DID NOTICE THE SMELL OF TURPENTINE ON HER.
THIS IS, OF COURSE, ALL CONJECTURE, THOUGH.
BUT THERE IS CERTAINLY AN AIR OF DRAMA AROUND YOUR REQUEST.
THOSE ARE THE KIND OF JOBS MOST WORTH DOING.

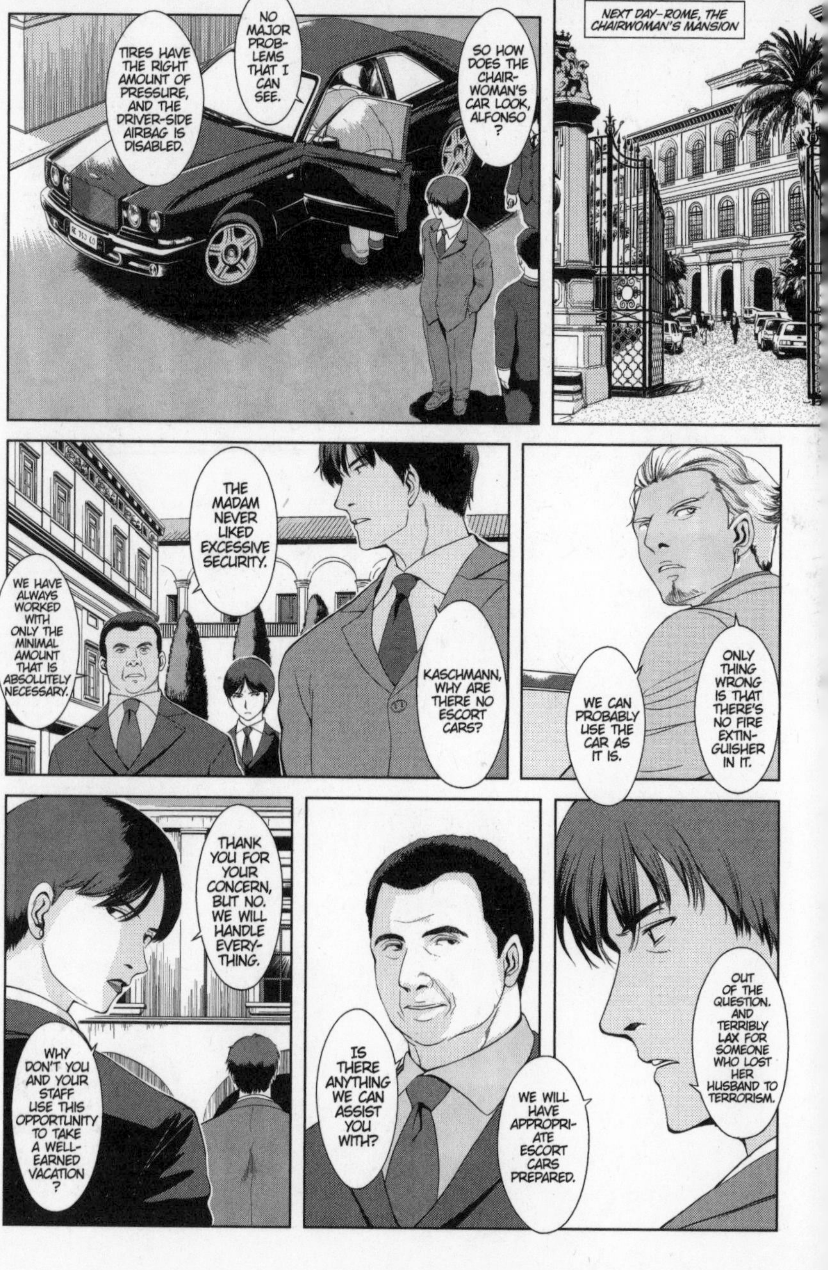
NEXT DAY–ROME, THE CHAIRWOMAN'S MANSION
SO HOW DOES THE CHAIRWOMAN'S CAR LOOK, ALFONSO?
NO MAJOR PROBLEMS THAT I CAN SEE.
TIRES HAVE THE RIGHT AMOUNT OF PRESSURE, AND THE DRIVER-SIDE AIRBAG IS DISABLED.
ONLY THING WRONG IS THAT THERE'S NO FIRE EXTINGUISHER IN IT.
WE CAN PROBABLY USE THE CAR AS IT IS.
KASCHMANN, WHY ARE THERE NO ESCORT CARS?
THE MADAM NEVER LIKED EXCESSIVE SECURITY.
WE HAVE ALWAYS WORKED WITH ONLY THE MINIMAL AMOUNT THAT IS ABSOLUTELY NECESSARY.
OUT OF THE QUESTION. AND TERRIBLY LAX FOR SOMEONE WHO LOST HER HUSBAND TO TERRORISM.
WE WILL HAVE APPROPRIATE ESCORT CARS PREPARED.
IS THERE ANYTHING WE CAN ASSIST YOU WITH?
THANK YOU FOR YOUR CONCERN, BUT NO. WE WILL HANDLE EVERYTHING.
WHY DON'T YOU AND YOUR STAFF USE THIS OPPORTUNITY TO TAKE A WELL-EARNED VACATION?

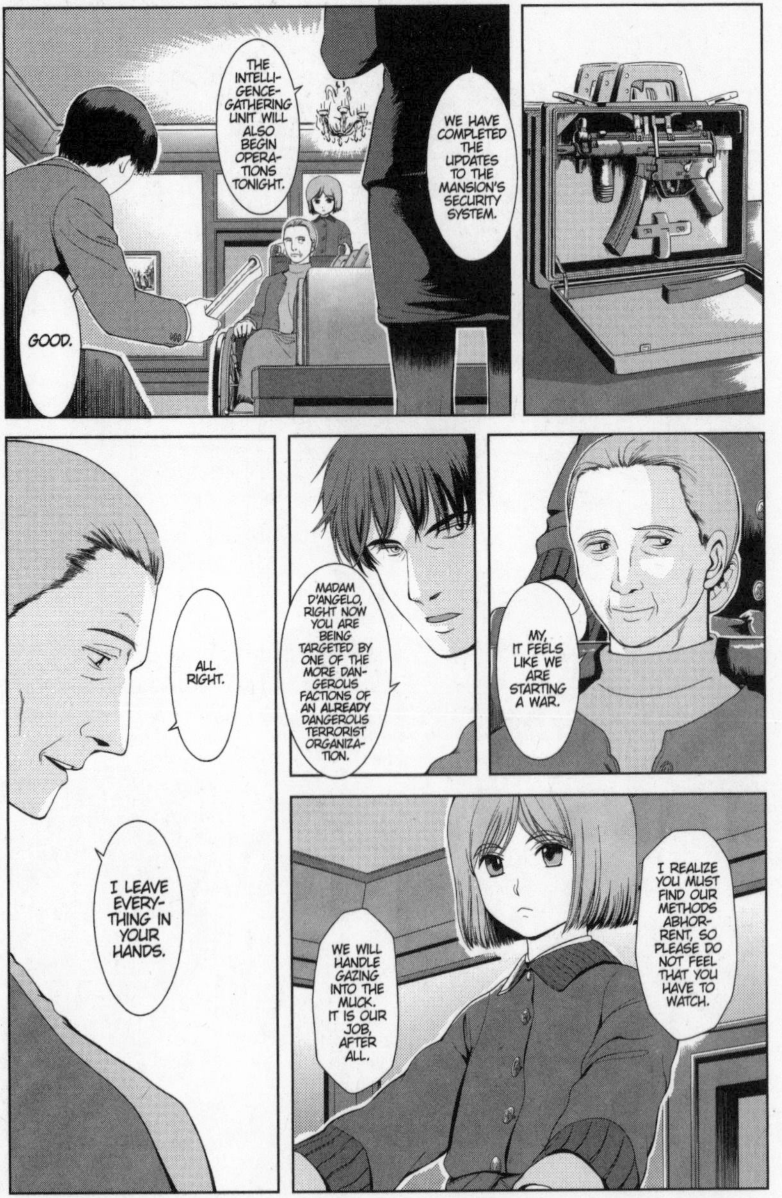
WE HAVE COMPLETED THE UPDATES TO THE MANSION'S SECURITY SYSTEM.
THE INTELLIGENCE-GATHERING UNIT WILL ALSO BEGIN OPERATIONS TONIGHT.
GOOD.
MY, IT FEELS LIKE WE ARE STARTING A WAR.
MADAM D'ANGELO, RIGHT NOW YOU ARE BEING TARGETED BY ONE OF THE MORE DANGEROUS FACTIONS OF AN ALREADY DANGEROUS TERRORIST ORGANIZATION.
I REALIZE YOU MUST FIND OUR METHODS ABHORRENT, SO PLEASE DO NOT FEEL THAT YOU HAVE TO WATCH.
WE WILL HANDLE GAZING INTO THE MUCK. IT IS OUR JOB, AFTER ALL.
ALL RIGHT.
I LEAVE EVERYTHING IN YOUR HANDS.

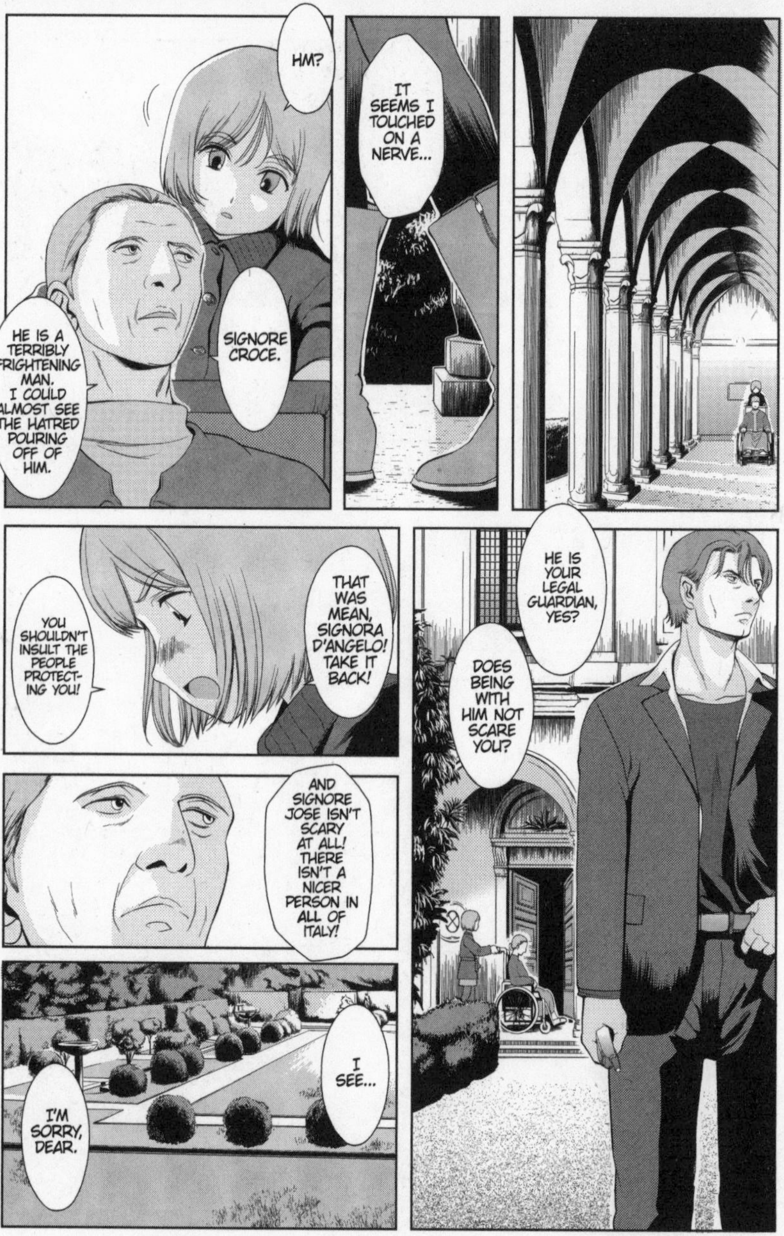
IT SEEMS I TOUCHED ON A NERVE...
HM?
SIGNORE CROCE.
HE IS A TERRIBLY FRIGHTENING MAN. I COULD ALMOST SEE THE HATRED POURING OFF OF HIM.
HE IS YOUR LEGAL GUARDIAN, YES?
DOES BEING WITH HIM NOT SCARE YOU?
THAT WAS MEAN, SIGNORA D'ANGELO! TAKE IT BACK!
YOU SHOULDN'T INSULT THE PEOPLE PROTECTING YOU!
AND SIGNORE JOSE ISN'T SCARY AT ALL! THERE ISN'T A NICER PERSON IN ALL OF ITALY!
I SEE...
I'M SORRY, DEAR.

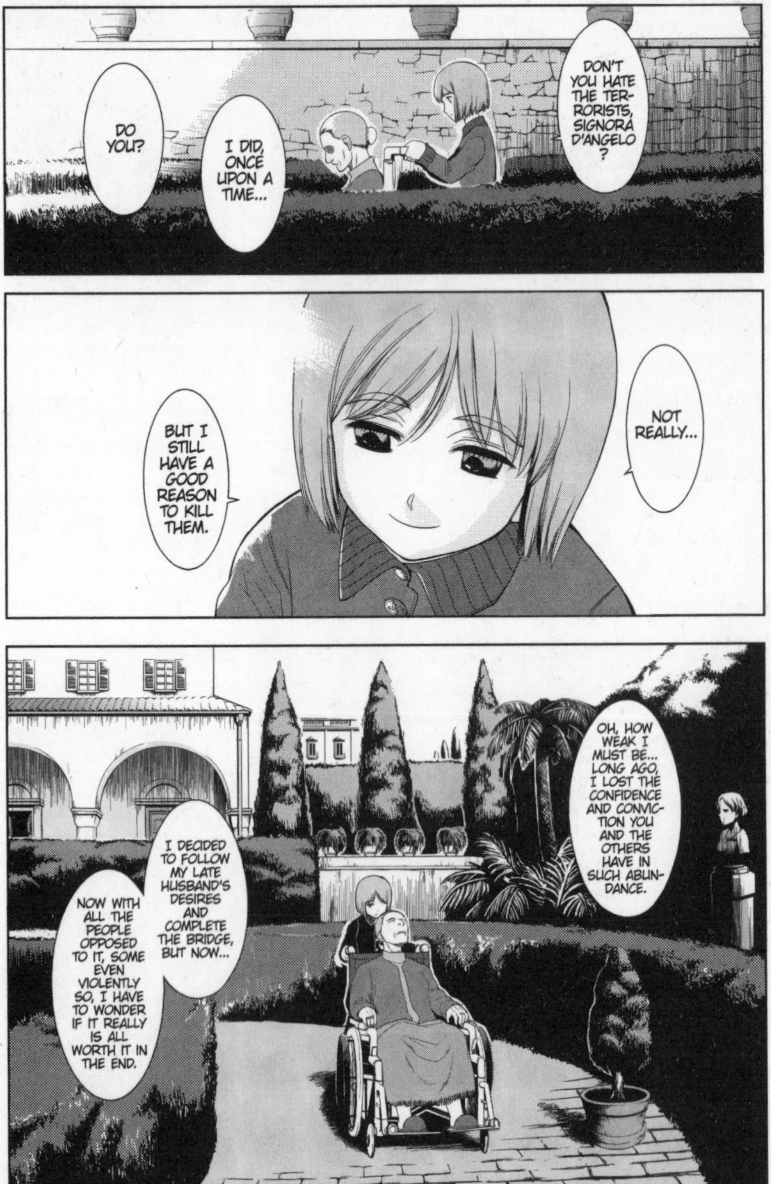
DON'T YOU HATE THE TERRORISTS, SIGNORA D'ANGELO?
I DID, ONCE UPON A TIME...
DO YOU?
NOT REALLY...
BUT I STILL HAVE A GOOD REASON TO KILL THEM.
OH, HOW WEAK I MUST BE... LONG AGO, I LOST THE CONFIDENCE AND CONVICTION YOU AND THE OTHERS HAVE IN SUCH ABUNDANCE.
I DECIDED TO FOLLOW MY LATE HUSBAND'S DESIRES AND COMPLETE THE BRIDGE, BUT NOW...
NOW WITH ALL THE PEOPLE OPPOSED TO IT, SOME EVEN VIOLENTLY SO, I HAVE TO WONDER IF IT REALLY IS ALL WORTH IT IN THE END.

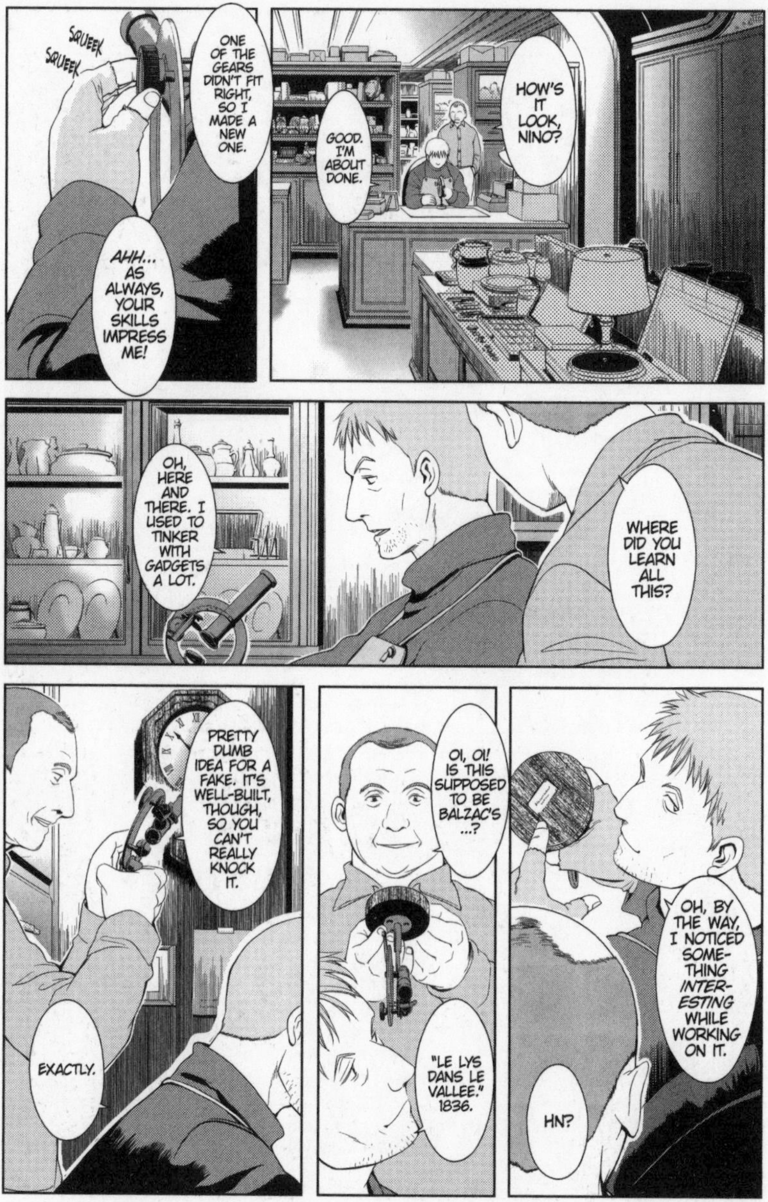
HOW'S IT LOOK, NINO?
GOOD. I'M ABOUT DONE.
ONE OF THE GEARS DIDN'T FIT RIGHT, SO I MADE A NEW ONE.
SQUEEK SQUEEK
AHH... AS ALWAYS, YOUR SKILLS IMPRESS ME!
WHERE DID YOU LEARN ALL THIS?
OH, HERE AND THERE. I USED TO TINKER WITH GADGETS A LOT.
OH, BY THE WAY, I NOTICED SOME-THING *INTER-ESTING* WHILE WORKING ON IT.
HN?
OI, OI! IS THIS SUPPOSED TO BE BALZAC'S ...?
"LE LYS DANS LE VALLEE." 1836.
PRETTY DUMB IDEA FOR A FAKE. IT'S WELL-BUILT, THOUGH, SO YOU CAN'T REALLY KNOCK IT.
EXACTLY.

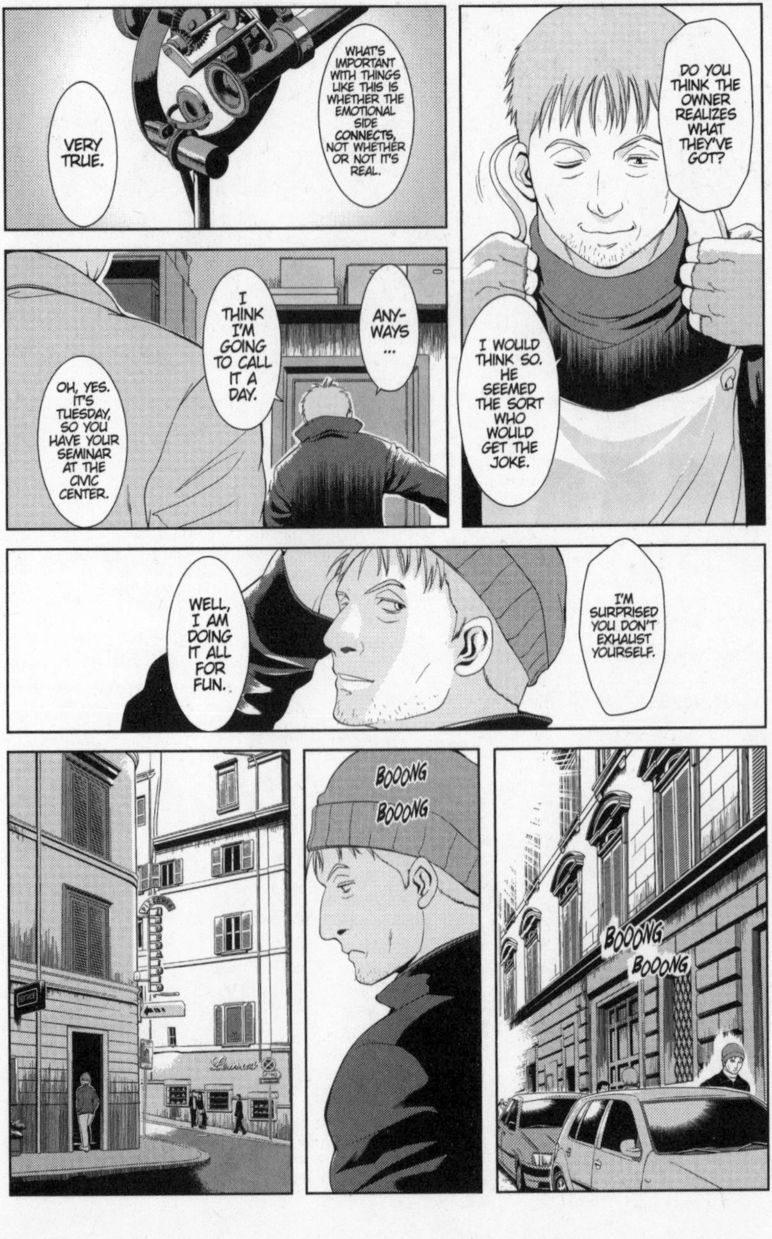
DO YOU THINK THE OWNER REALIZES WHAT THEY'VE GOT?
I WOULD THINK SO. HE SEEMED THE SORT WHO WOULD GET THE JOKE.
WHAT'S IMPORTANT WITH THINGS LIKE THIS IS WHETHER THE EMOTIONAL SIDE CONNECTS, NOT WHETHER OR NOT IT'S REAL.
VERY TRUE.
ANY-WAYS ...
I THINK I'M GOING TO CALL IT A DAY.
OH, YES. IT'S TUESDAY, SO YOU HAVE YOUR SEMINAR AT THE CIVIC CENTER.
I'M SURPRISED YOU DON'T EXHAUST YOURSELF.
WELL, I AM DOING IT ALL FOR FUN.
BOOONG
BOOONG
BOOONG
BOOONG

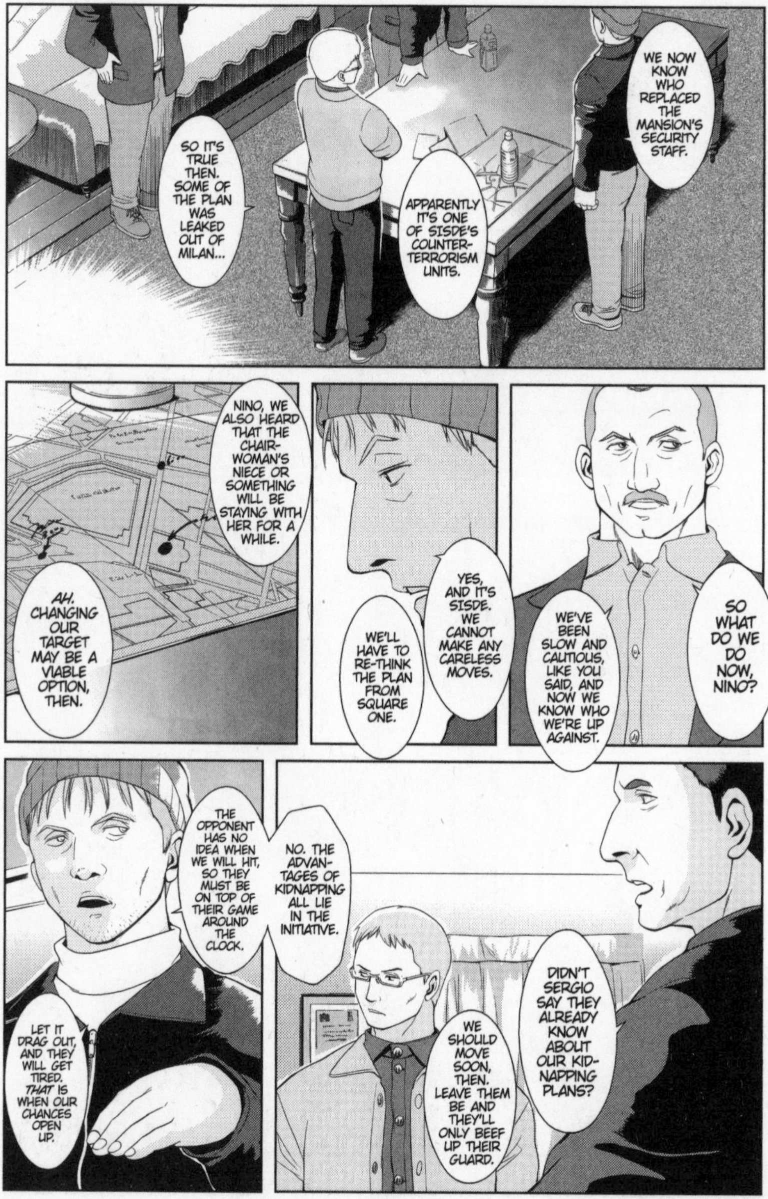
WE NOW KNOW WHO REPLACED THE MANSION'S SECURITY STAFF.
APPARENTLY IT'S ONE OF SISDE'S COUNTER-TERRORISM UNITS.
SO IT'S TRUE THEN. SOME OF THE PLAN WAS LEAKED OUT OF MILAN...
SO WHAT DO WE DO NOW, NINO?
WE'VE BEEN SLOW AND CAUTIOUS, LIKE YOU SAID, AND NOW WE KNOW WHO WE'RE UP AGAINST.
YES, AND IT'S SISDE. WE CANNOT MAKE ANY CARELESS MOVES.
WE'LL HAVE TO RE-THINK THE PLAN FROM SQUARE ONE.
NINO, WE ALSO HEARD THAT THE CHAIR-WOMAN'S NIECE OR SOMETHING WILL BE STAYING WITH HER FOR A WHILE.
AH. CHANGING OUR TARGET MAY BE A VIABLE OPTION, THEN.
DIDN'T SERGIO SAY THEY ALREADY KNOW ABOUT OUR KID-NAPPING PLANS?
WE SHOULD MOVE SOON, THEN. LEAVE THEM BE AND THEY'LL ONLY BEEF UP THEIR GUARD.
NO. THE ADVAN-TAGES OF KIDNAPPING ALL LIE IN THE INITIATIVE.
THE OPPONENT HAS NO IDEA WHEN WE WILL HIT, SO THEY MUST BE ON TOP OF THEIR GAME AROUND THE CLOCK.
LET IT DRAG OUT, AND THEY WILL GET TIRED. *THAT* IS WHEN OUR CHANCES OPEN UP.

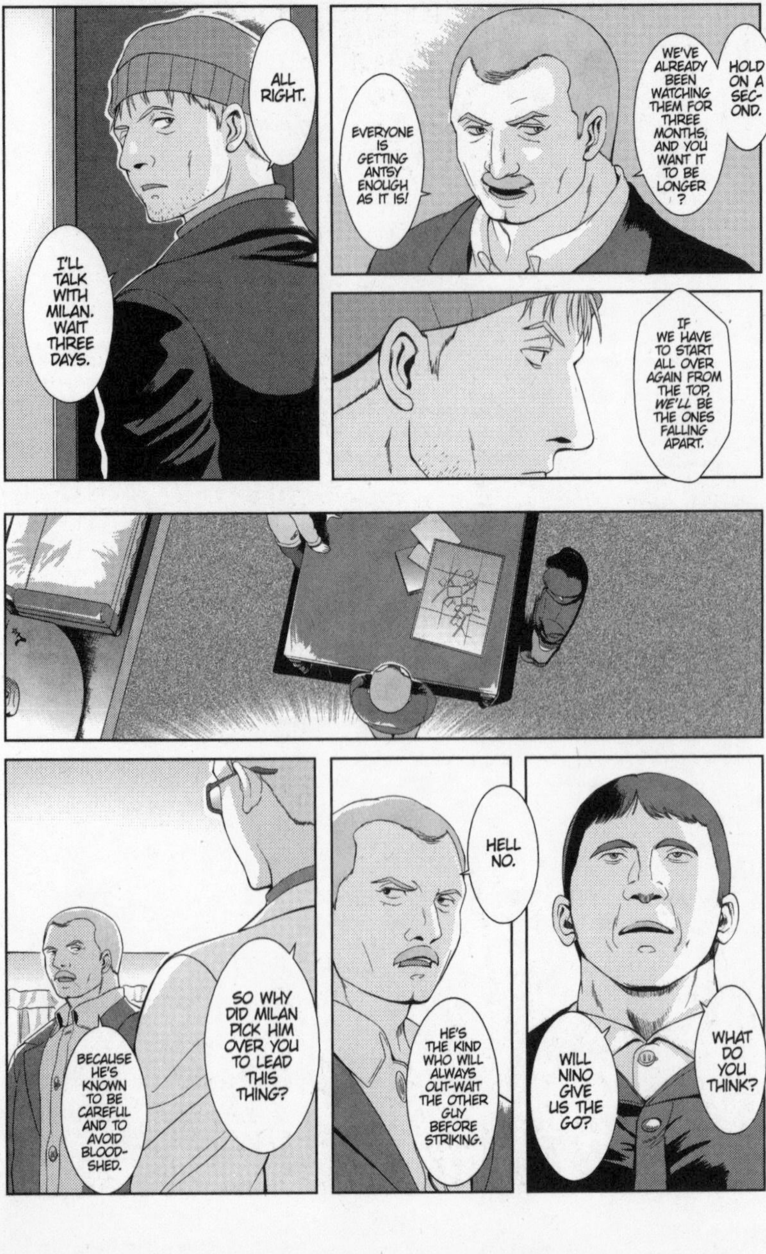
HOLD ON A SECOND.
WE'VE ALREADY BEEN WATCHING THEM FOR THREE MONTHS, AND YOU WANT IT TO BE LONGER?
EVERYONE IS GETTING ANTSY ENOUGH AS IT IS!
IF WE HAVE TO START ALL OVER AGAIN FROM THE TOP, *WE'LL* BE THE ONES FALLING APART.
ALL RIGHT.
I'LL TALK WITH MILAN. WAIT THREE DAYS.
WHAT DO YOU THINK?
WILL NINO GIVE US THE GO?
HELL NO.
HE'S THE KIND WHO WILL ALWAYS OUT-WAIT THE OTHER GUY BEFORE STRIKING.
SO WHY DID MILAN PICK HIM OVER YOU TO LEAD THIS THING?
BECAUSE HE'S KNOWN TO BE CAREFUL AND TO AVOID BLOODSHED.

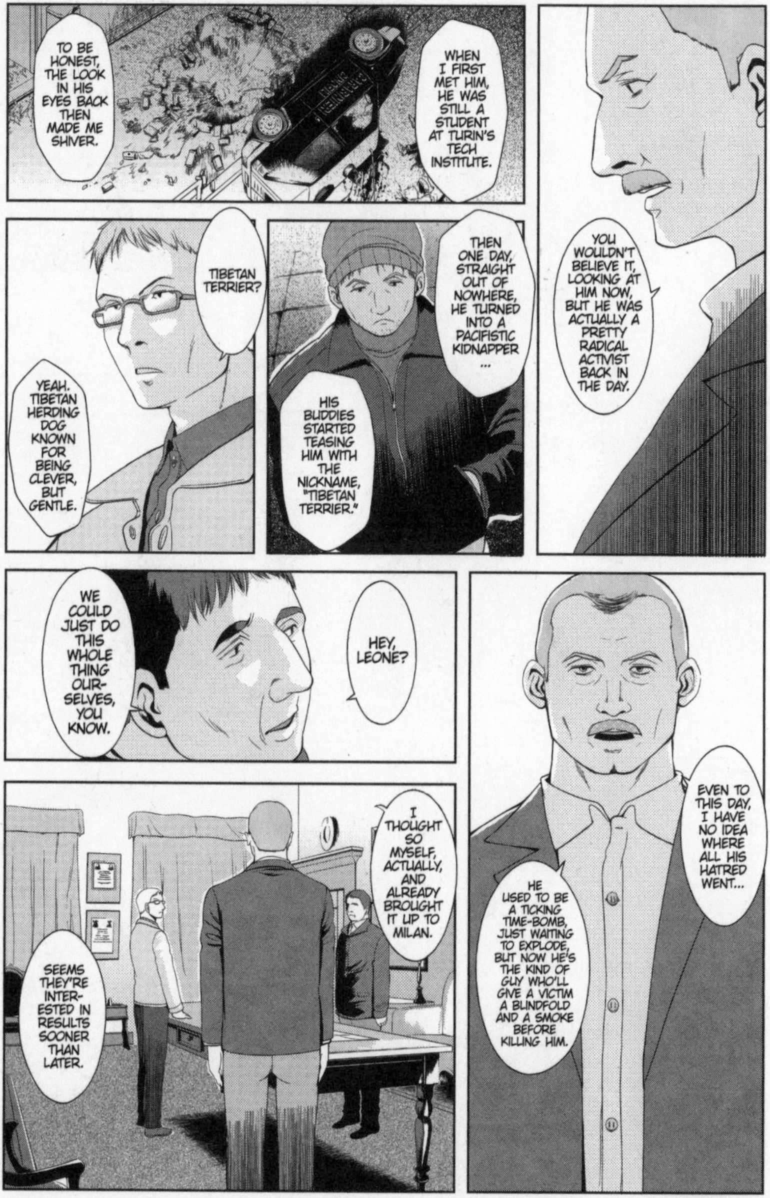
YOU WOULDN'T BELIEVE IT, LOOKING AT HIM NOW, BUT HE WAS ACTUALLY A PRETTY RADICAL ACTIVIST BACK IN THE DAY.
WHEN I FIRST MET HIM, HE WAS STILL A STUDENT AT TURIN'S TECH INSTITUTE.
TO BE HONEST, THE LOOK IN HIS EYES BACK THEN MADE ME SHIVER.
THEN ONE DAY, STRAIGHT OUT OF NOWHERE, HE TURNED INTO A PACIFISTIC KIDNAPPER ...
HIS BUDDIES STARTED TEASING HIM WITH THE NICKNAME, "TIBETAN TERRIER."
TIBETAN TERRIER?
YEAH. TIBETAN HERDING DOG KNOWN FOR BEING CLEVER, BUT GENTLE.
EVEN TO THIS DAY, I HAVE NO IDEA WHERE ALL HIS HATRED WENT...
HE USED TO BE A TICKING TIME-BOMB, JUST WAITING TO EXPLODE, BUT NOW HE'S THE KIND OF GUY WHO'LL GIVE A VICTIM A BLINDFOLD AND A SMOKE BEFORE KILLING HIM.
HEY, LEONE?
WE COULD JUST DO THIS WHOLE THING OUR-SELVES, YOU KNOW.
I THOUGHT SO MYSELF, ACTUALLY, AND ALREADY BROUGHT IT UP TO MILAN.
SEEMS THEY'RE INTER-ESTED IN RESULTS SOONER THAN LATER.

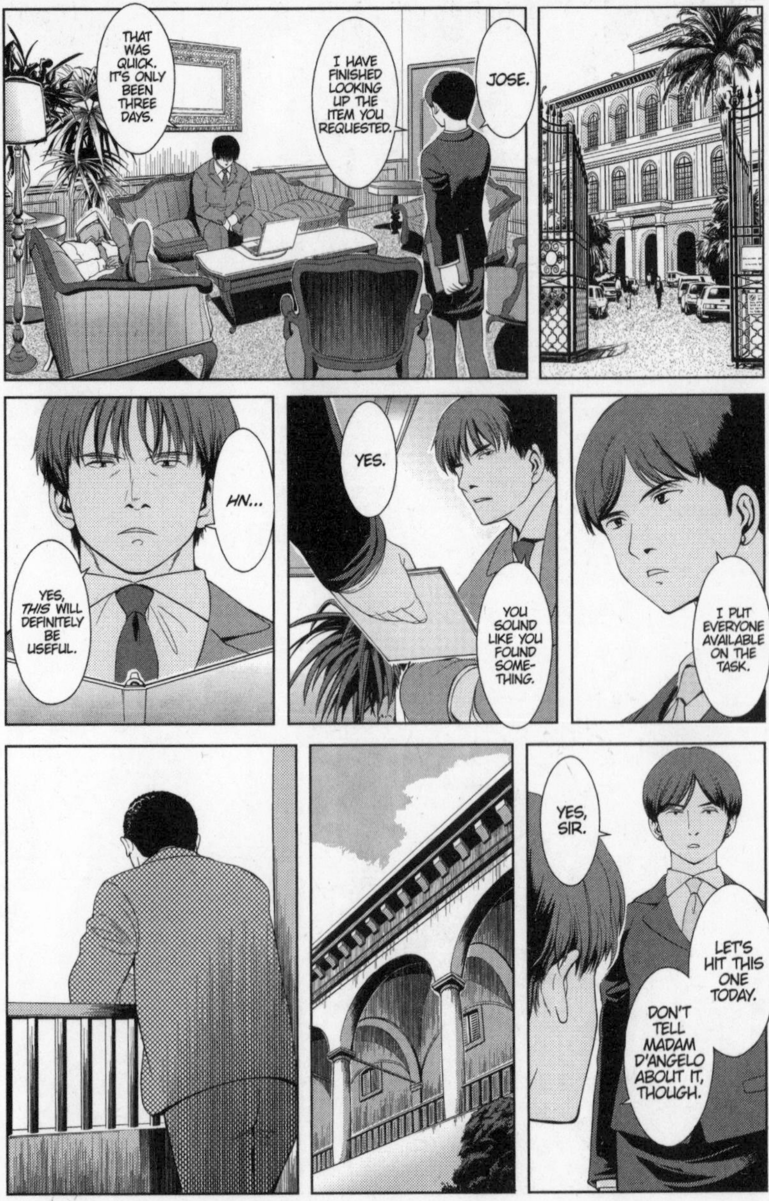
JOSE.
I HAVE FINISHED LOOKING UP THE ITEM YOU REQUESTED.
THAT WAS QUICK. IT'S ONLY BEEN THREE DAYS.
I PUT EVERYONE AVAILABLE ON THE TASK.
YES.
YOU SOUND LIKE YOU FOUND SOMETHING.
HN...
YES, *THIS* WILL DEFINITELY BE USEFUL.
LET'S HIT THIS ONE TODAY.
DON'T TELL MADAM D'ANGELO ABOUT IT, THOUGH.
YES, SIR.

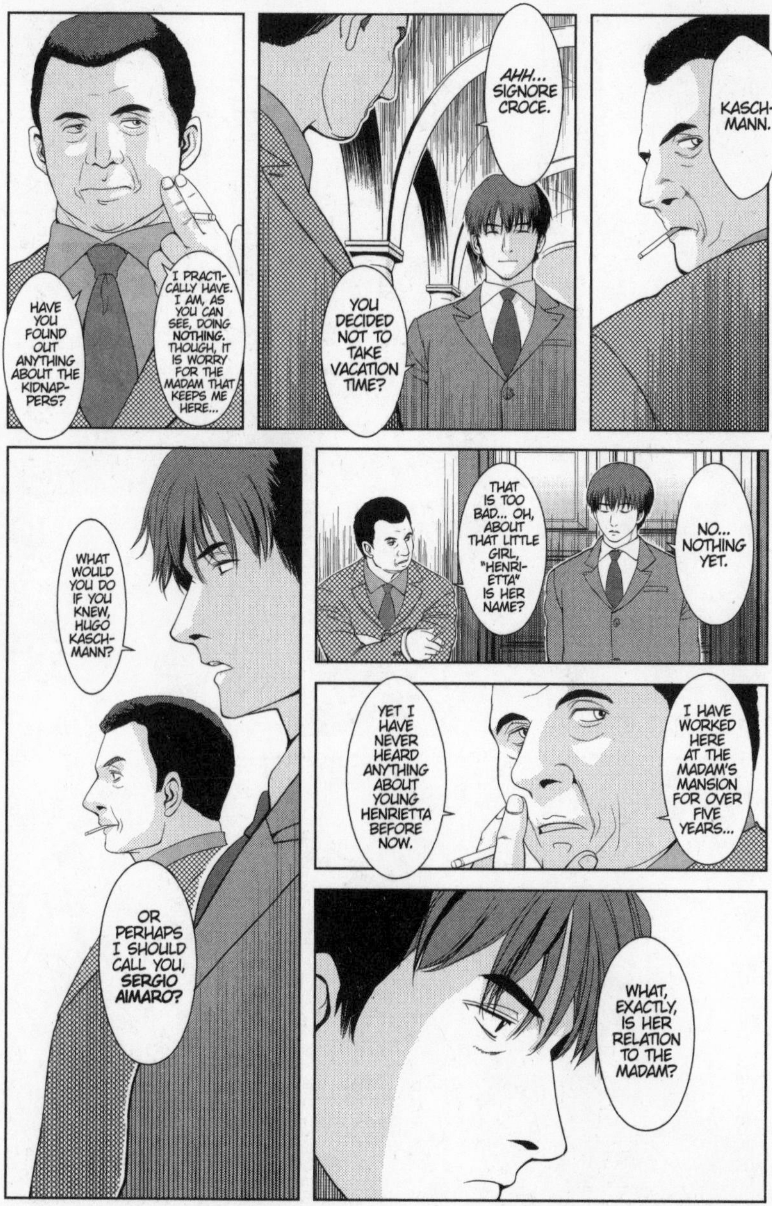
KASCHMANN.
AHH... SIGNORE CROCE.
YOU DECIDED NOT TO TAKE VACATION TIME?
I PRACTICALLY HAVE. I AM, AS YOU CAN SEE, DOING NOTHING. THOUGH, IT IS WORRY FOR THE MADAM THAT KEEPS ME HERE...
HAVE YOU FOUND OUT ANYTHING ABOUT THE KIDNAPPERS?
NO... NOTHING YET.
THAT IS TOO BAD... OH, ABOUT THAT LITTLE GIRL, "HENRIETTA" IS HER NAME?
I HAVE WORKED HERE AT THE MADAM'S MANSION FOR OVER FIVE YEARS...
YET I HAVE NEVER HEARD ANYTHING ABOUT YOUNG HENRIETTA BEFORE NOW.
WHAT, EXACTLY, IS HER RELATION TO THE MADAM?
WHAT WOULD YOU DO IF YOU KNEW, HUGO KASCHMANN?
OR PERHAPS I SHOULD CALL YOU, SERGIO AIMARO?

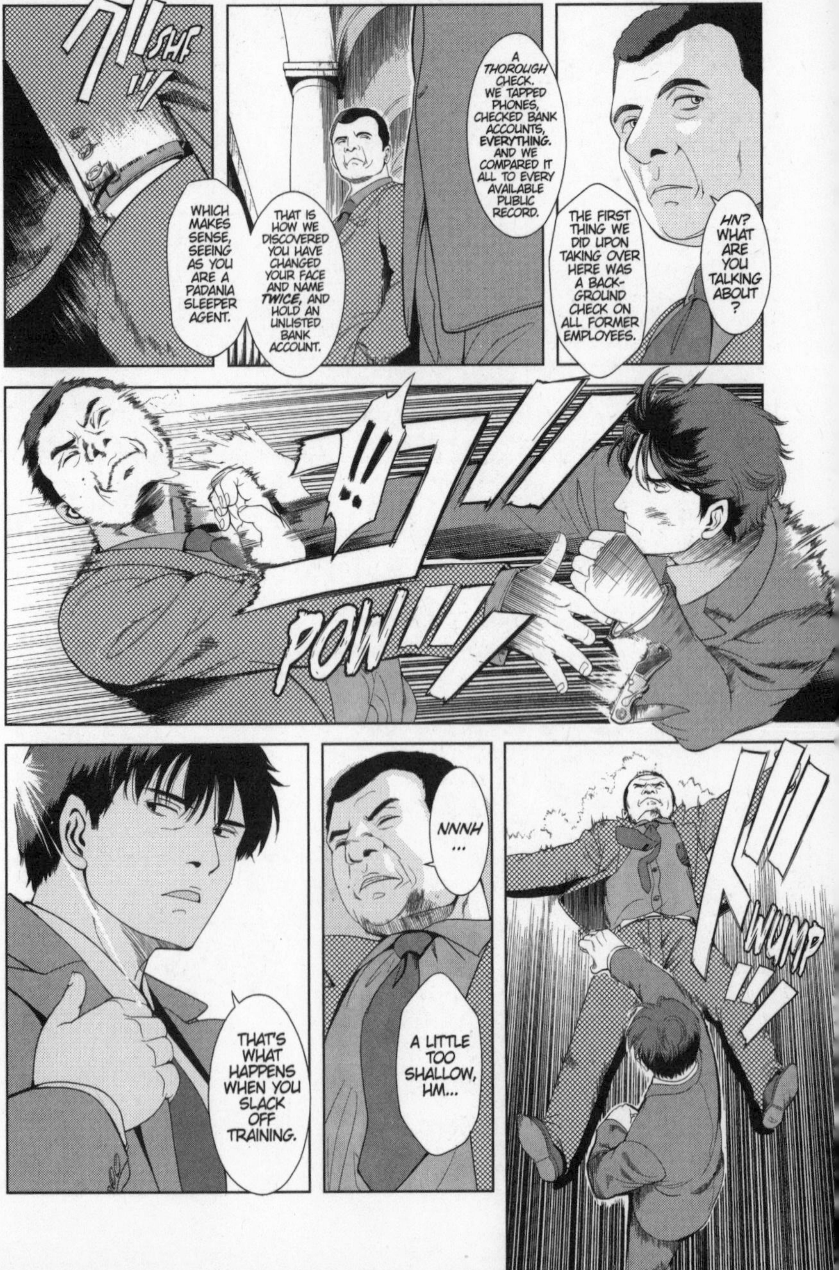
HN? WHAT ARE YOU TALKING ABOUT?
THE FIRST THING WE DID UPON TAKING OVER HERE WAS A BACK-GROUND CHECK ON ALL FORMER EMPLOYEES.
A THOROUGH CHECK. WE TAPPED PHONES, CHECKED BANK ACCOUNTS, EVERYTHING. AND WE COMPARED IT ALL TO EVERY AVAILABLE PUBLIC RECORD.
THAT IS HOW WE DISCOVERED YOU HAVE CHANGED YOUR FACE AND NAME TWICE, AND HOLD AN UNLISTED BANK ACCOUNT.
SHF
WHICH MAKES SENSE, SEEING AS YOU ARE A PADANIA SLEEPER AGENT.
POW!!
WUMP
NNNH ...
A LITTLE TOO SHALLOW, HM...
THAT'S WHAT HAPPENS WHEN YOU SLACK OFF TRAINING.

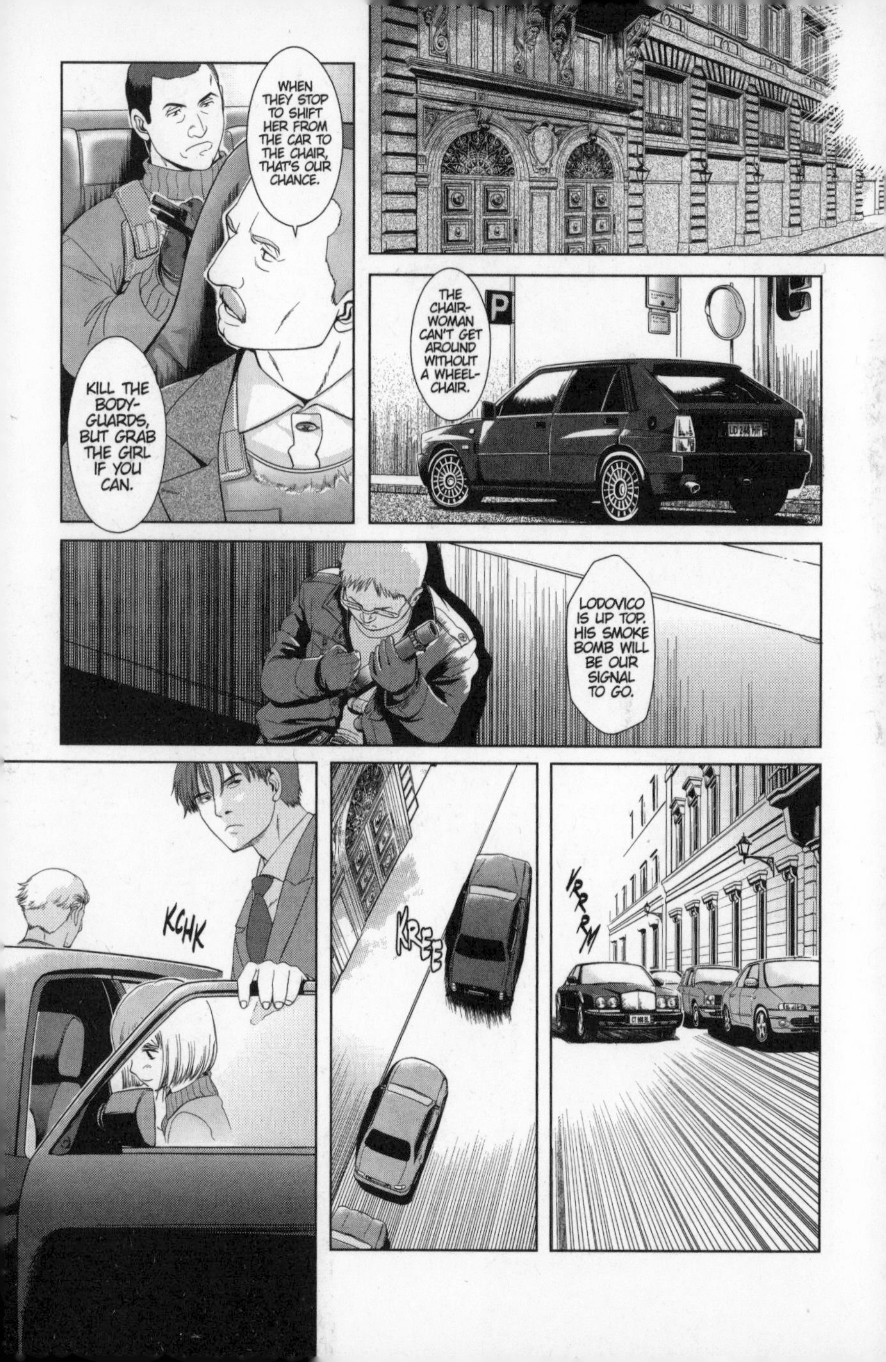
THE CHAIR-WOMAN CAN'T GET AROUND WITHOUT A WHEEL-CHAIR.
WHEN THEY STOP TO SHIFT HER FROM THE CAR TO THE CHAIR, THAT'S OUR CHANCE.
KILL THE BODY-GUARDS, BUT GRAB THE GIRL IF YOU CAN.
LODOVICO IS UP TOP. HIS SMOKE BOMB WILL BE OUR SIGNAL TO GO.
VRRRM
KREE
KCHK

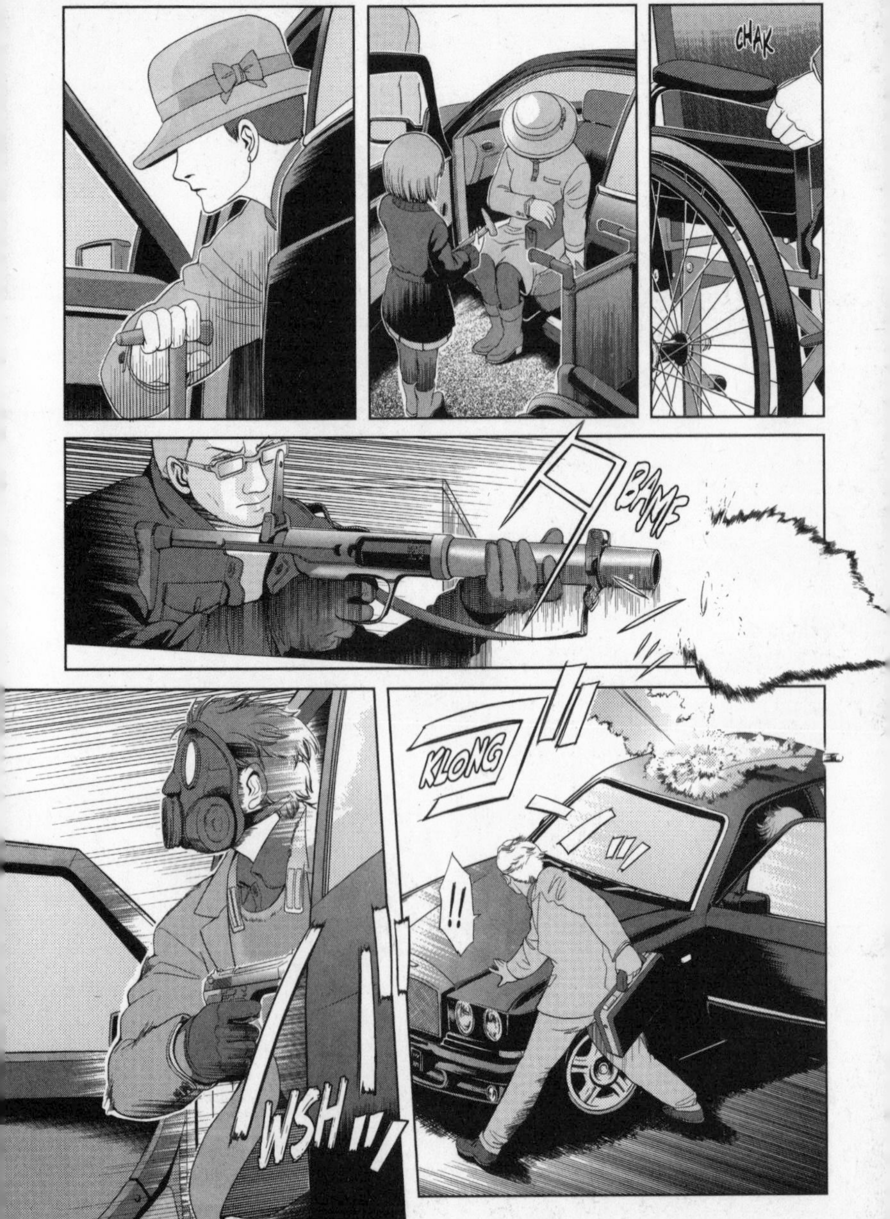
CHAK
BAMF
KLONG
!!
WSH

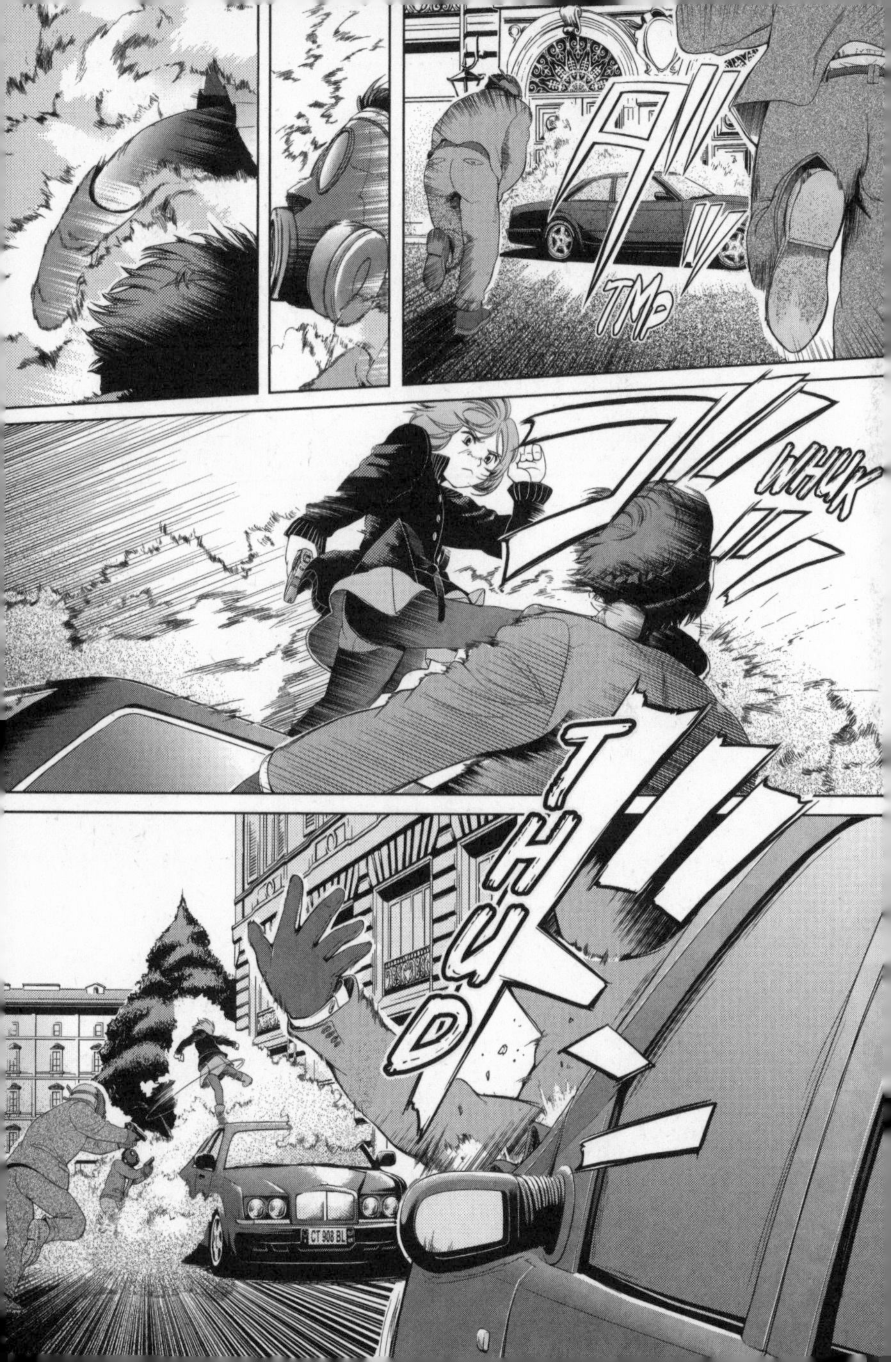
TMP
WHUK
THUD
CT 908 BL

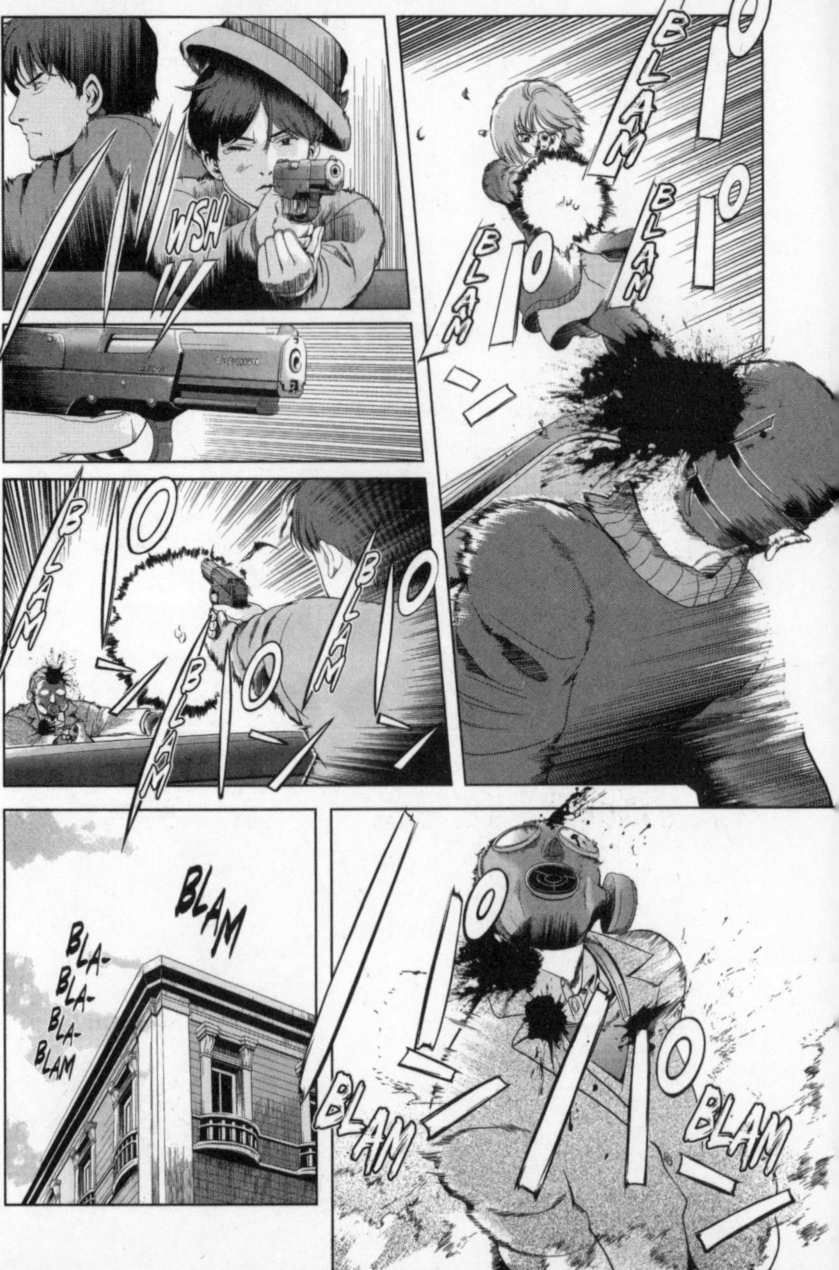
BLAM
BLAM
BLAM
WSH
BLAM
BLAM
BLAM
BLAM
BLAM
BLAM
BLAM
BLA-
BLA-
BLA-
BLAM

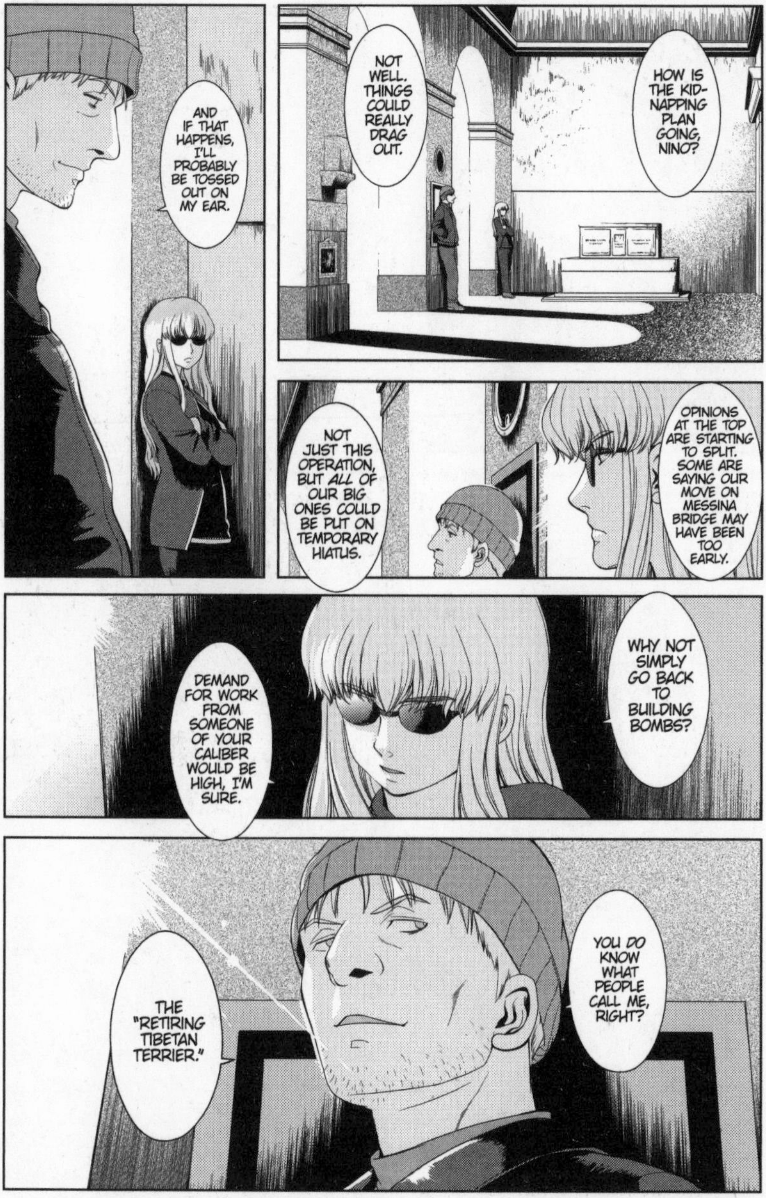
HOW IS THE KID-NAPPING PLAN GOING, NINO?
NOT WELL. THINGS COULD REALLY DRAG OUT.
OPINIONS AT THE TOP ARE STARTING TO SPLIT. SOME ARE SAYING OUR MOVE ON MESSINA BRIDGE MAY HAVE BEEN TOO EARLY.
NOT JUST THIS OPERATION, BUT *ALL* OF OUR BIG ONES COULD BE PUT ON TEMPORARY HIATUS.
AND IF THAT HAPPENS, I'LL PROBABLY BE TOSSED OUT ON MY EAR.
WHY NOT SIMPLY GO BACK TO BUILDING BOMBS?
DEMAND FOR WORK FROM SOMEONE OF YOUR CALIBER WOULD BE HIGH, I'M SURE.
YOU *DO* KNOW WHAT PEOPLE CALL ME, RIGHT?
THE "RETIRING TIBETAN TERRIER."

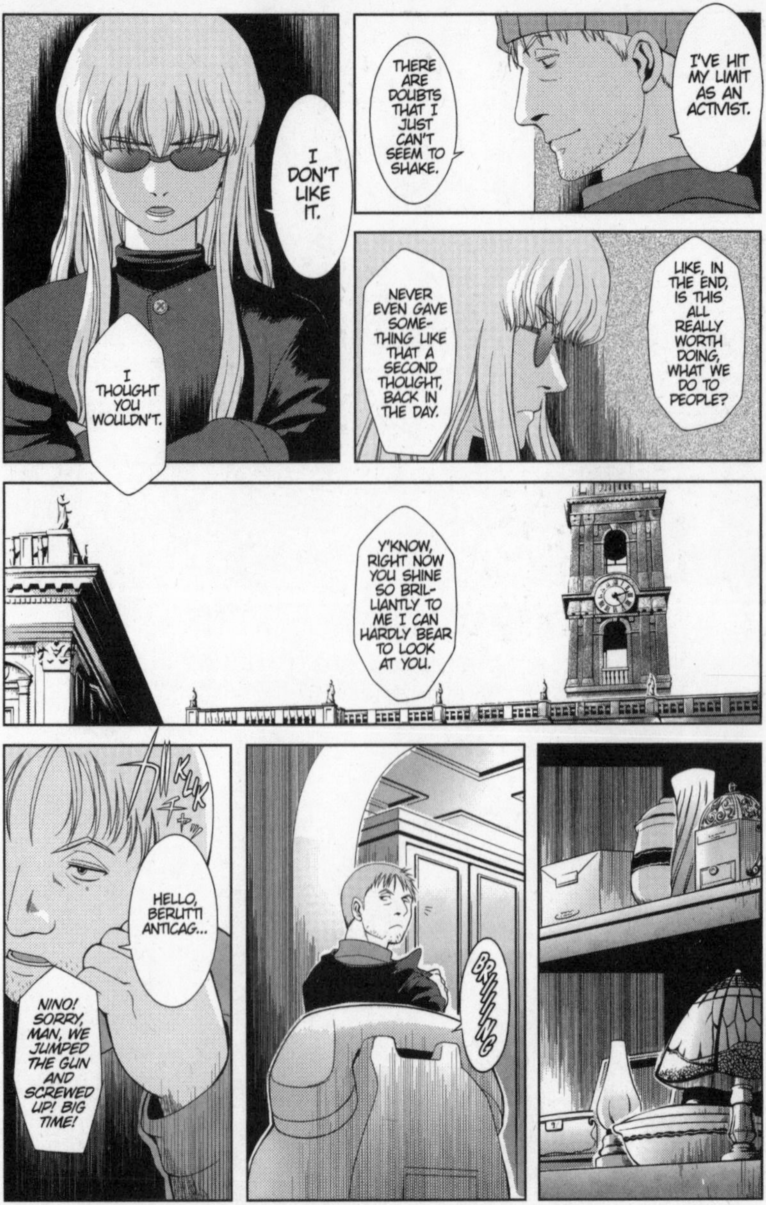
I'VE HIT MY LIMIT AS AN ACTIVIST.
THERE ARE DOUBTS THAT I JUST CAN'T SEEM TO SHAKE.
LIKE, IN THE END, IS THIS ALL REALLY WORTH DOING, WHAT WE DO TO PEOPLE?
NEVER EVEN GAVE SOMETHING LIKE THAT A SECOND THOUGHT, BACK IN THE DAY.
I DON'T LIKE IT.
I THOUGHT YOU WOULDN'T.
Y'KNOW, RIGHT NOW YOU SHINE SO BRILLIANTLY TO ME I CAN HARDLY BEAR TO LOOK AT YOU.
BRIIIING
KLIK
HELLO, BERUTTI ANTICAG...
NINO! SORRY, MAN, WE JUMPED THE GUN AND SCREWED UP! BIG TIME!

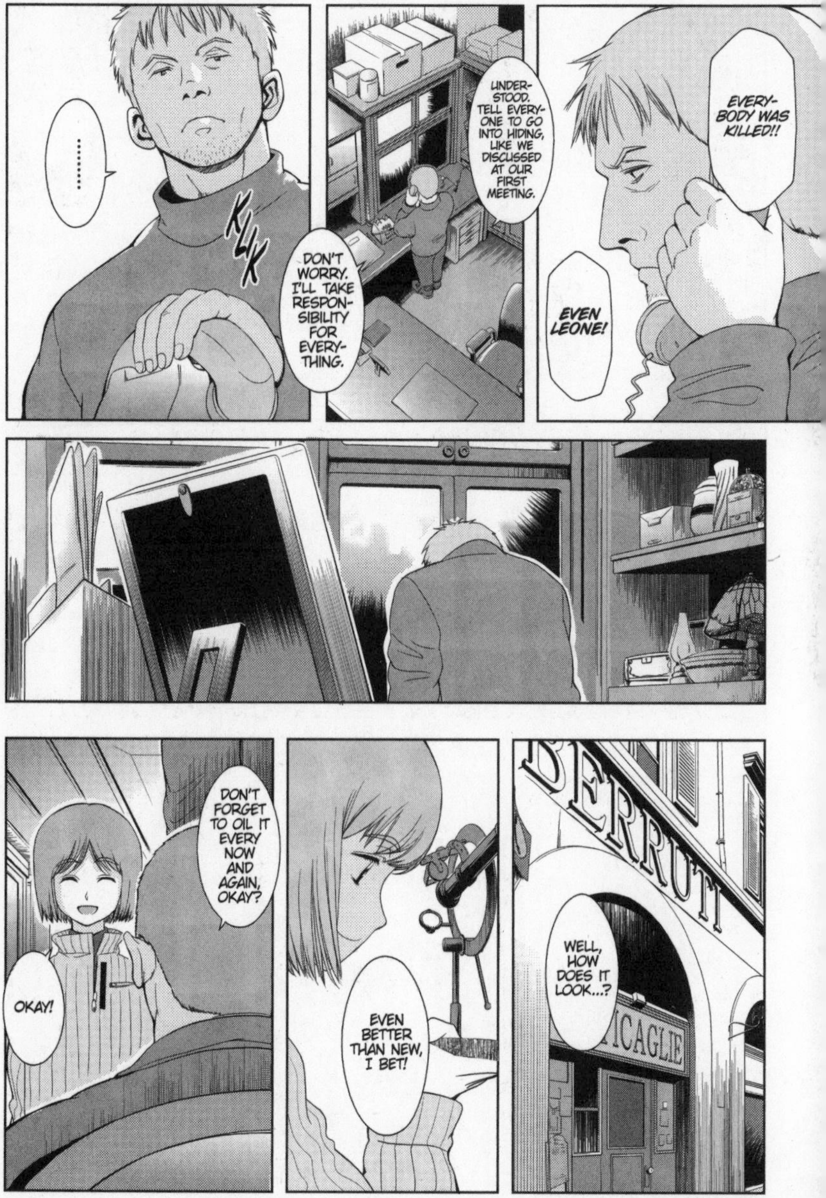
EVERYBODY WAS KILLED!!
EVEN LEONE!
UNDERSTOOD. TELL EVERYONE TO GO INTO HIDING, LIKE WE DISCUSSED AT OUR FIRST MEETING.
DON'T WORRY. I'LL TAKE RESPONSIBILITY FOR EVERYTHING.
......
KLIK
WELL, HOW DOES IT LOOK...?
EVEN BETTER THAN NEW, I BET!
DON'T FORGET TO OIL IT EVERY NOW AND AGAIN, OKAY?
OKAY!

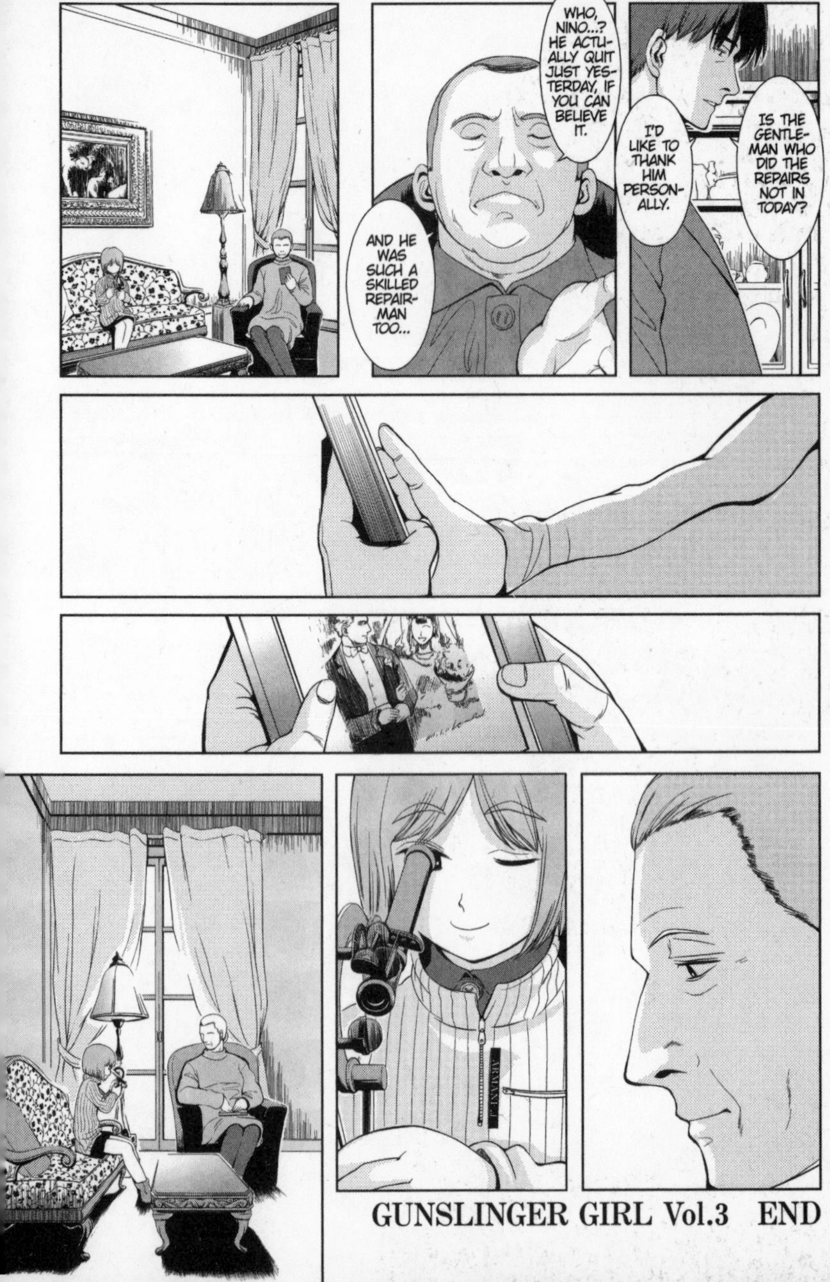
IS THE GENTLEMAN WHO DID THE REPAIRS NOT IN TODAY?
I'D LIKE TO THANK HIM PERSONALLY.
WHO, NINO...? HE ACTUALLY QUIT JUST YESTERDAY, IF YOU CAN BELIEVE IT.
AND HE WAS SUCH A SKILLED REPAIRMAN TOO...
ARMANI J

GUNSLINGER GIRL Vol.3 END

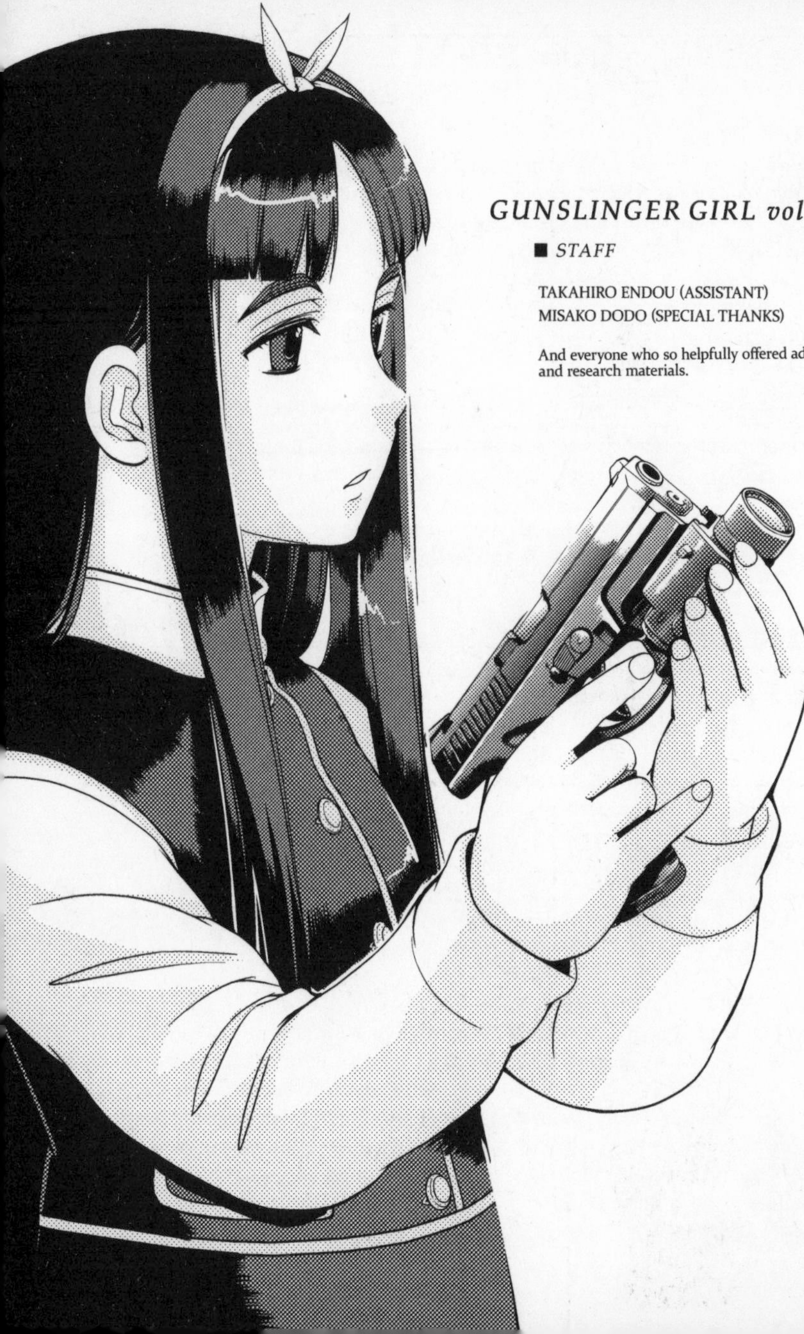

GUNSLINGER GIRL vol.3

■ *STAFF*

TAKAHIRO ENDOU (ASSISTANT)
MISAKO DODO (SPECIAL THANKS)

And everyone who so helpfully offered advice and research materials.

TRANSLATION NOTES

CHAPTER 1

Padania was originally the name of a valley in northern Italy around the River Po. However, the name took on heavy political connotations in the early 1990s with the formation of the *Lega Nord* (lit. "Northern League") political party. Advocates of turning Italy into a federal state, the *Lega Nord* has at times proposed that Northern Italy secede entirely to become an independent nation called "Padania." While the real life Padania party has sometimes expressed a violent rhetoric, it is not nearly to the level depicted here in *Gunslinger Girl*.

CHAPTER 2

A brass catcher is a bag-like attachment that catches the spent shells of a gun, so they won't scatter around the ground of the nearby area.

Ètude is an instrumental musical composition designed for learning and practicing a particular technical skill. By this, Henrietta means that she can barely play a practice piece, much less an actual performance piece of music.

CHAPTER 3

Europol is the European Union's criminal-intelligence agency. Though it was started in 1994, it wasn't fully operational until 1999. Based in the Hague, it has relatively few agents of its own. However, it is in constant liaison with law enforcement agencies throughout Europe, each with their own agents specifically assigned to assist Europol.

CHAPTER 4

SISDE (*Servizio per le Informazioni e la Sicurezza Democratica*) was the Italian domestic intelligence agency, equivalent to the United States' FBI. Operational between 1977 and 2007, government reforms recently replaced SISDE with AISI (*Agenzia Informazioni e Sicurezza Interna*).

CHAPTER 7

The Piazza di Spagna, or "Spanish Square" in English, is part of the scenic and historical Spanish Steps area of Rome. The Steps connect the Piazza, which is at the bottom of a hill, to the French Trinita dei Monte church at the top of the hill. While there doesn't seem to be any intrinsic meaning to eating gelato while there, the Piazza's beautiful architecture does make it one of the more popular places to meet and date in Rome. Likely, those are the lines along which Henrietta was thinking and blushing about.

CHAPTER 9
Military Service – Up until 2004, Italy required all men to serve some time in the military. However, Italian men did retain the right to conscientious objection, the right to choose community service over armed military service. Effective the first day of 2005, the Italian Parliament approved the suspension of mandatory military service.

CHAPTER 10
The Guardia di Finanza is a branch of the Italian Armed Forces that specializes in investigating and preventing financial violations like tax evasion, smuggling and money laundering.

CHAPTER 11
NOCS stands for *Nucleo Operativo Centrale di Sicurezza* (or "Central Security Operations Service," in English). Established in 1975, NOCS is an elite counter-terrorism assault unit along similar lines as the United States S.W.A.T. teams. Originally only a single 35-man unit, today's NOCS has three full tactical-assault teams and a fourth protective division.

The Amalfi Coast is a stretch of Italian coastline about half-way between Rome and the toe of Italy's "boot." It is known for its beautiful scenery and peaceful, picturesque towns.

CHAPTER 12
"Louise Antoinette Rolle" is actually Laure Antoinette de Berny (1784-1838), also known as Laure Junot, Duchesse D'Abrantes. The French author in question is Honore de Balzac. Junot was a patroness of Balzac's writings, including his most famous set of works "La Comedie Humaine," and the two had an affair, even though Junot was over 20 years Balzac's senior. The story Claes is referring to is *Le Lys dans le Vallee*, written in 1835. The main characters, Felix de Vande-nesse and Henriette de Mortsauf, were modeled after Balzac and Junot. Ironi-cally, shortly after Junot read the completed story—in which the character modeled after her dies—she died as well.

CHAPTER 14
The Messina Bridge – The Italian government had long planned to build an actual bridge to span the Messina Strait and connect Sicily to the mainland near the town of Messina. Those plans were completely scrapped in 2006, but revived again by a new administration in 2009. It is currently projected that the bridge will be completed sometime in 2016.

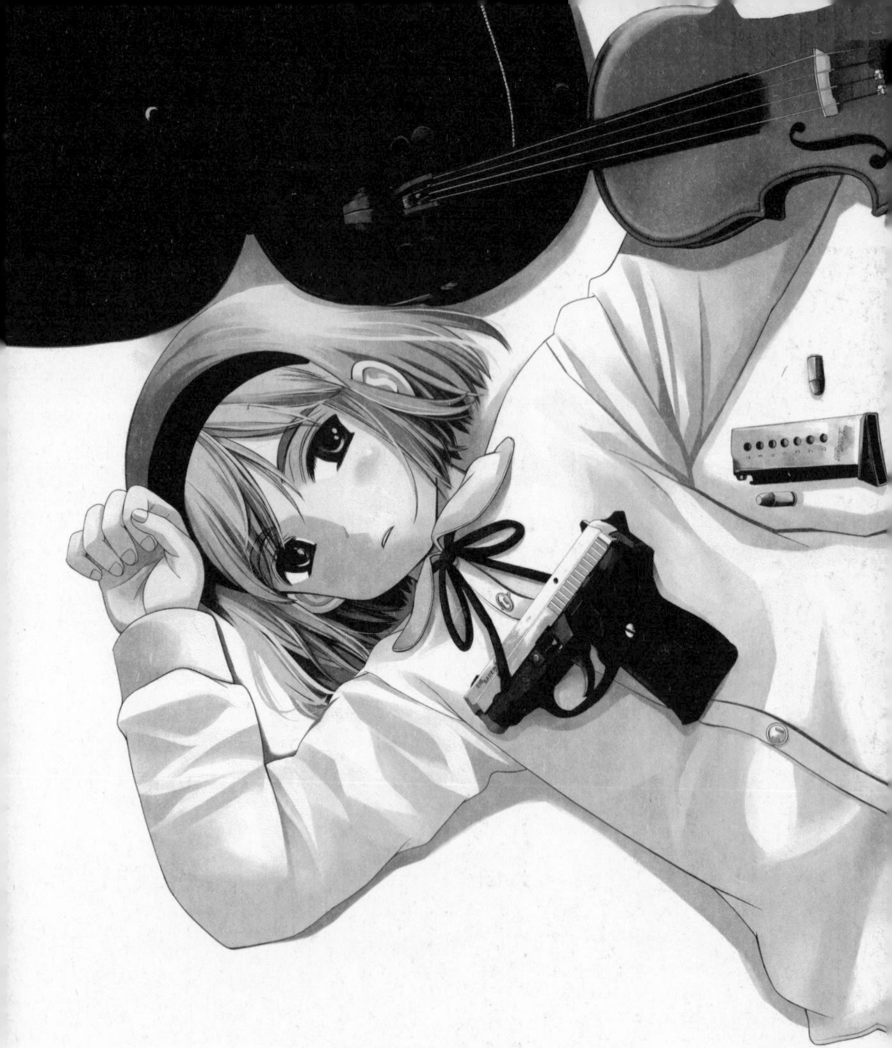

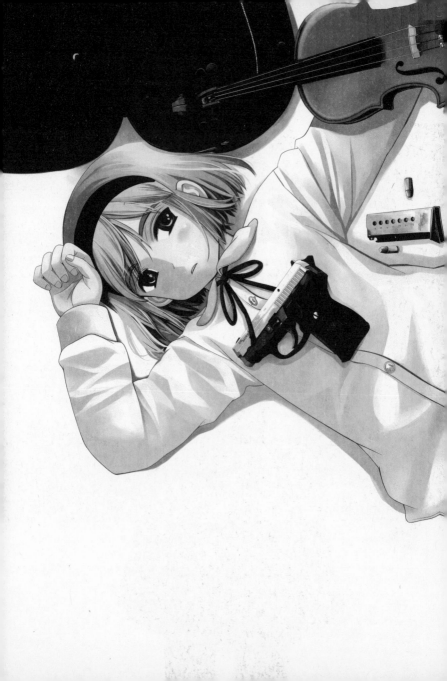

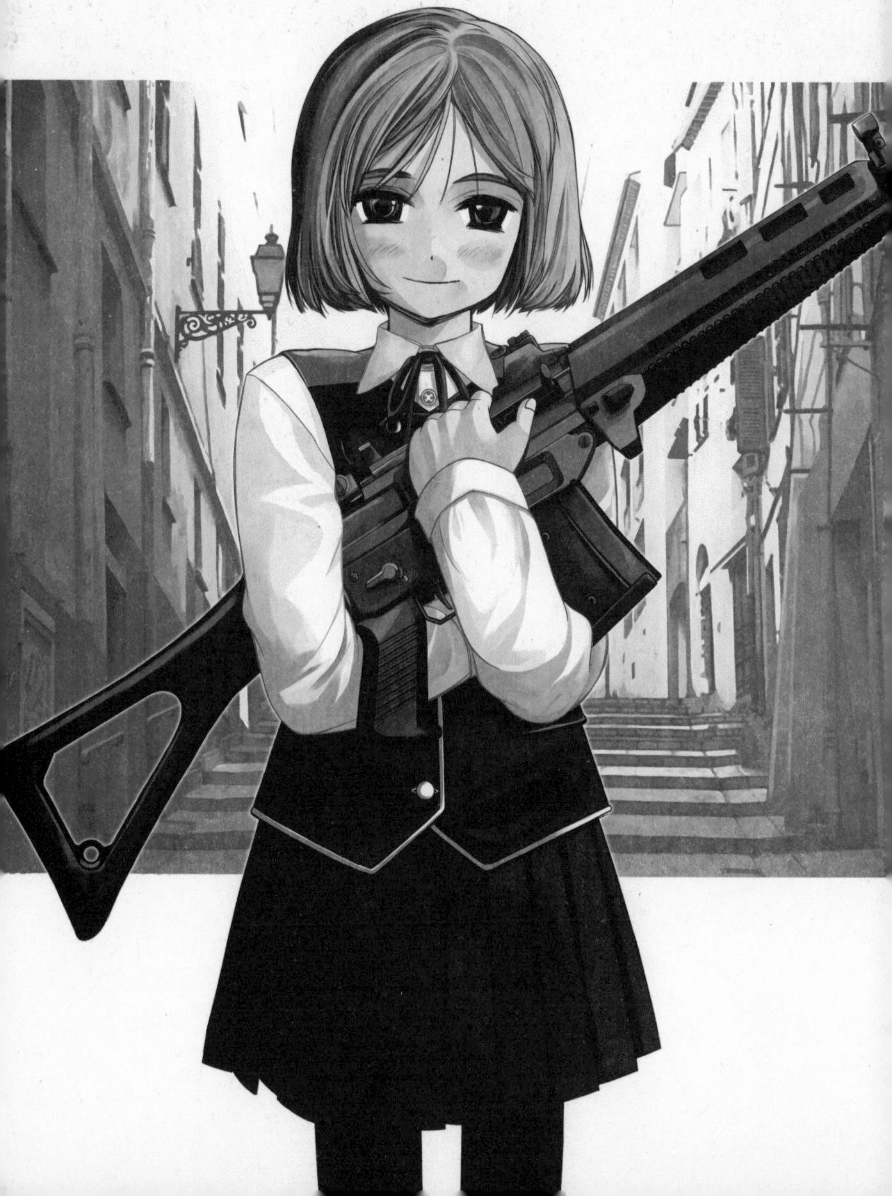

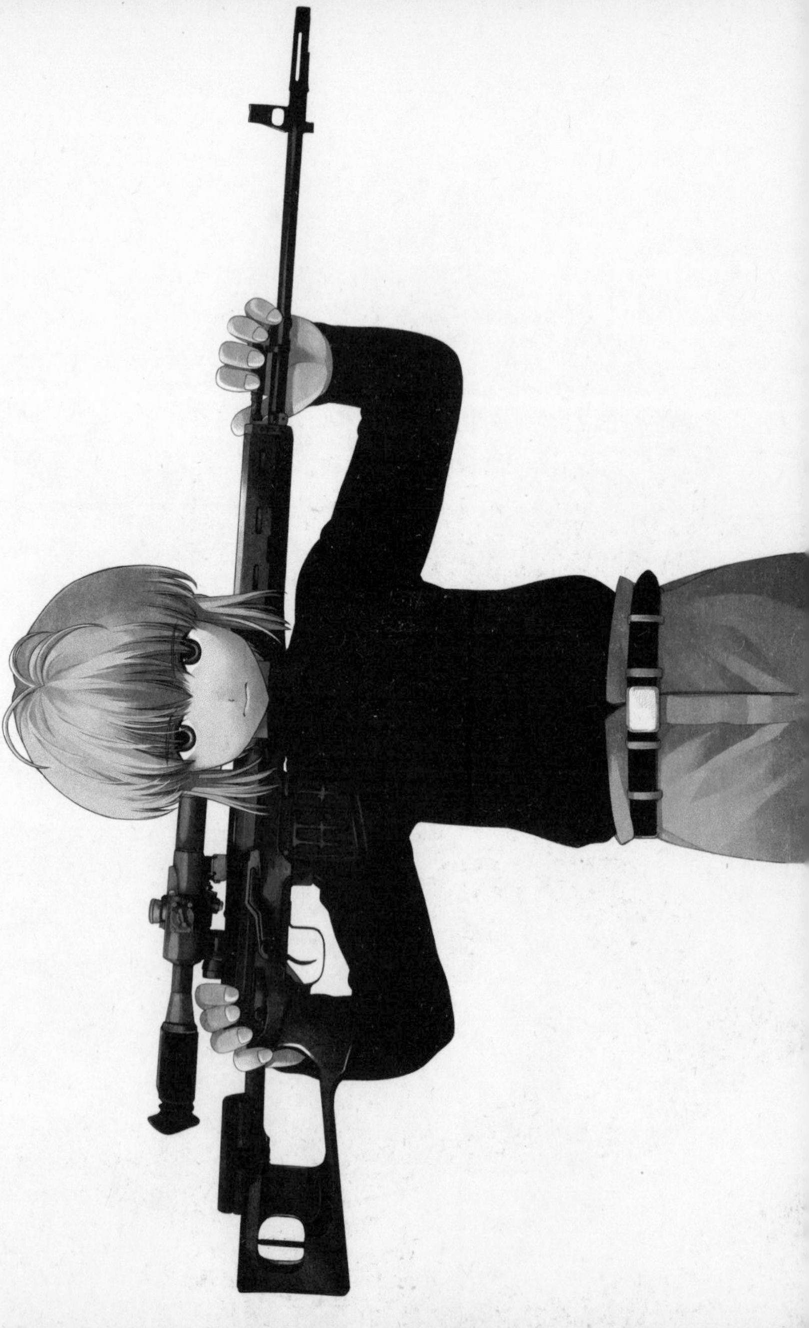

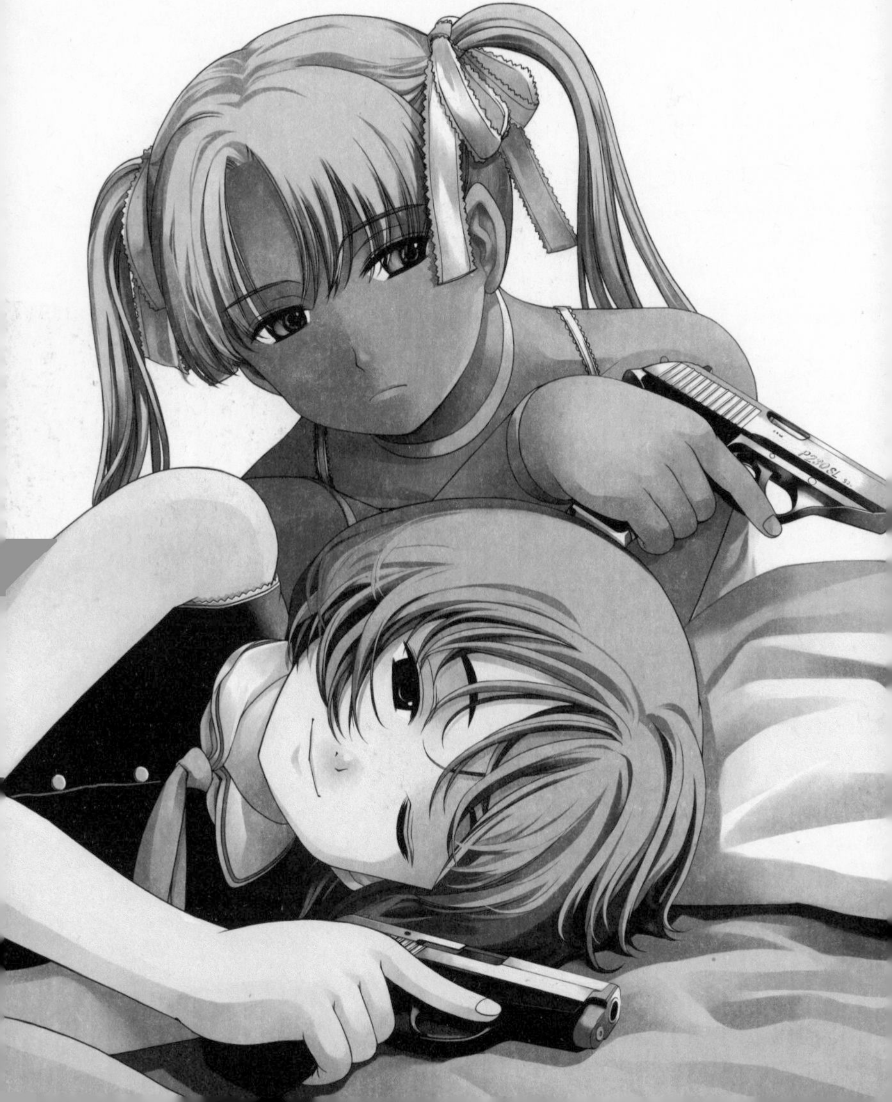
P230 SL

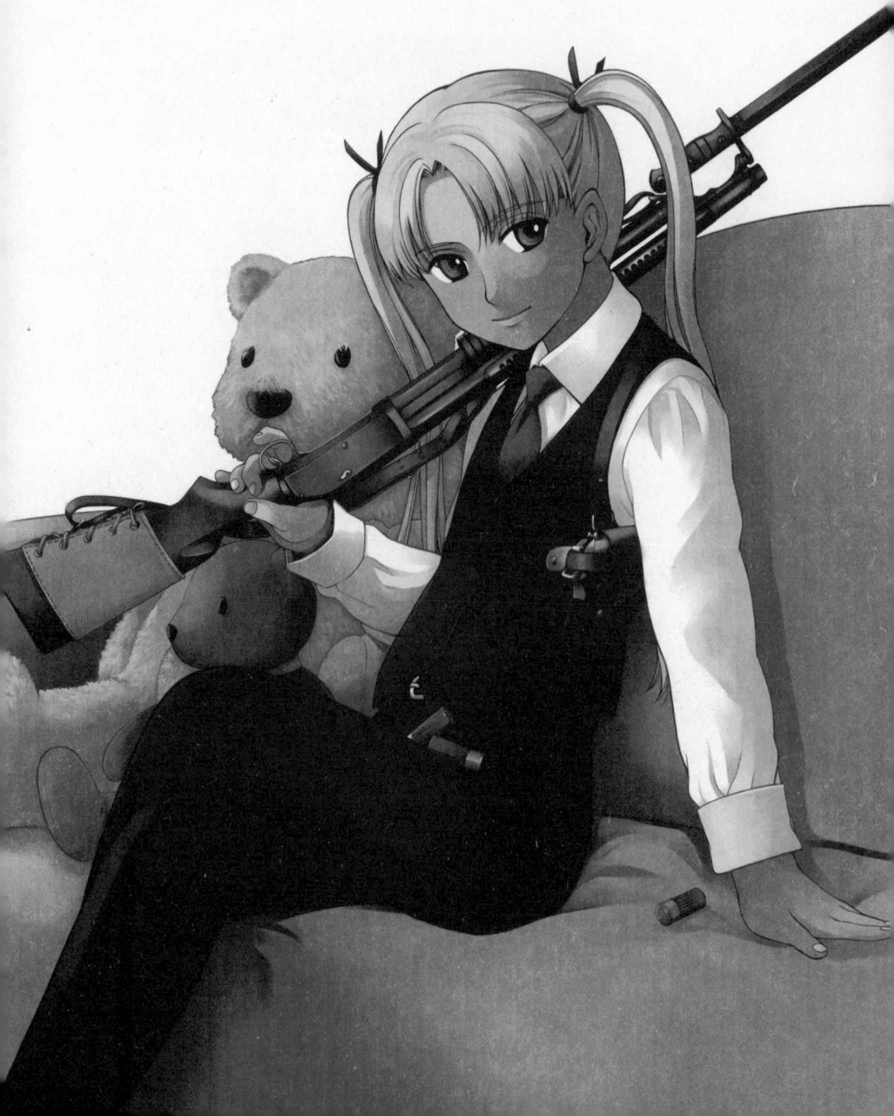

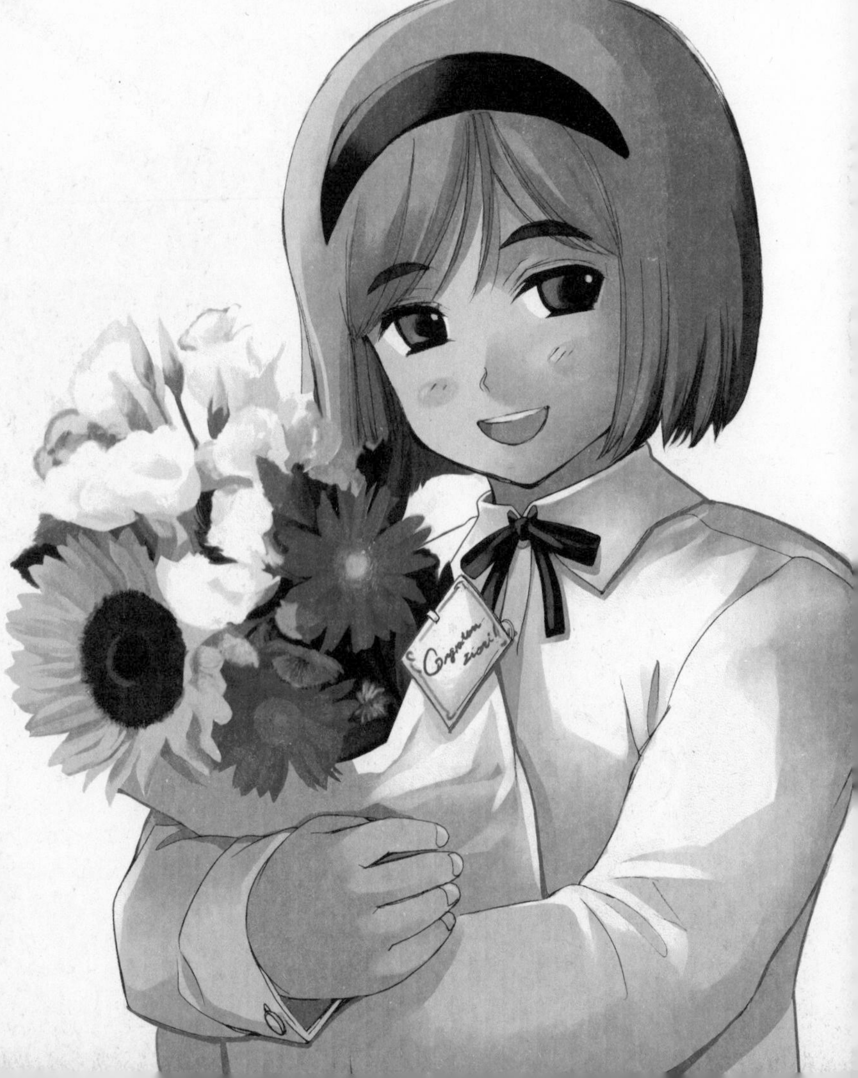

Venus Versus Virus

ヴィーナス ヴァーサス ヴァイアラス

Illustrated by Atsushi Suzumi

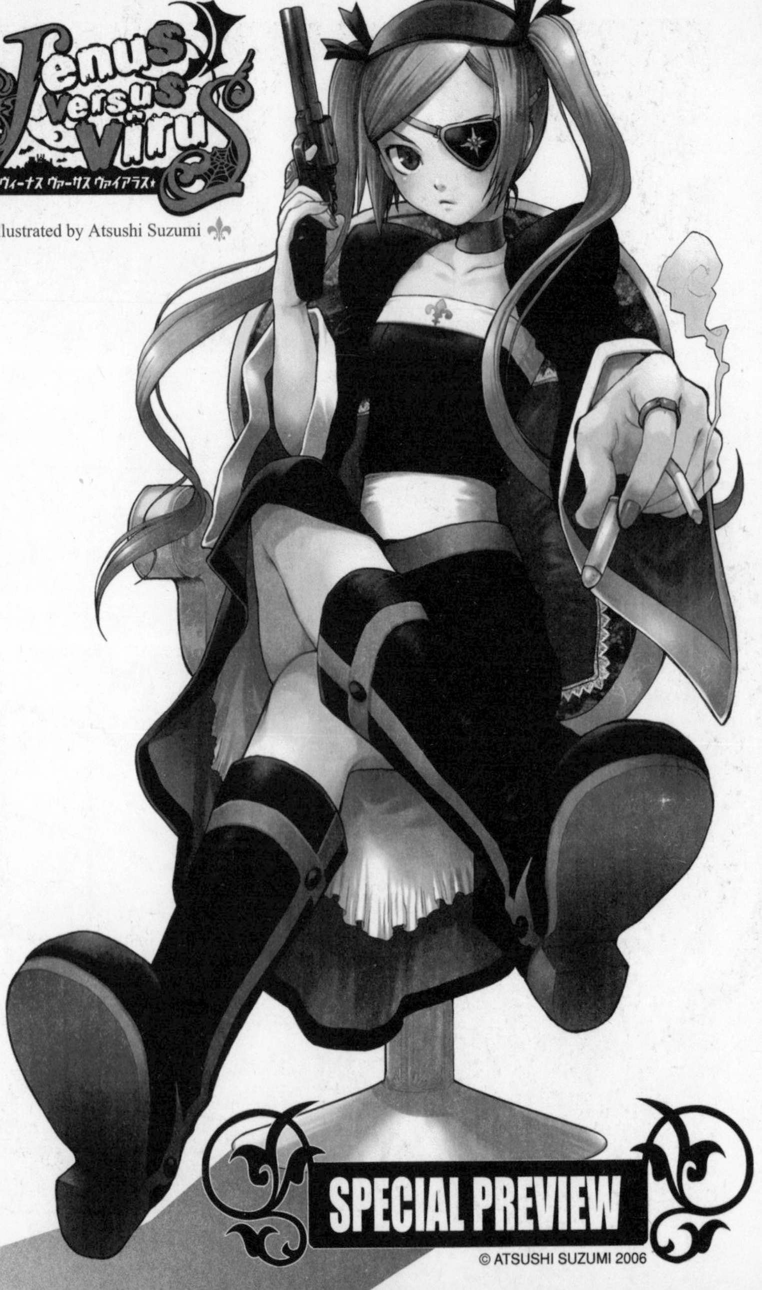

SPECIAL PREVIEW

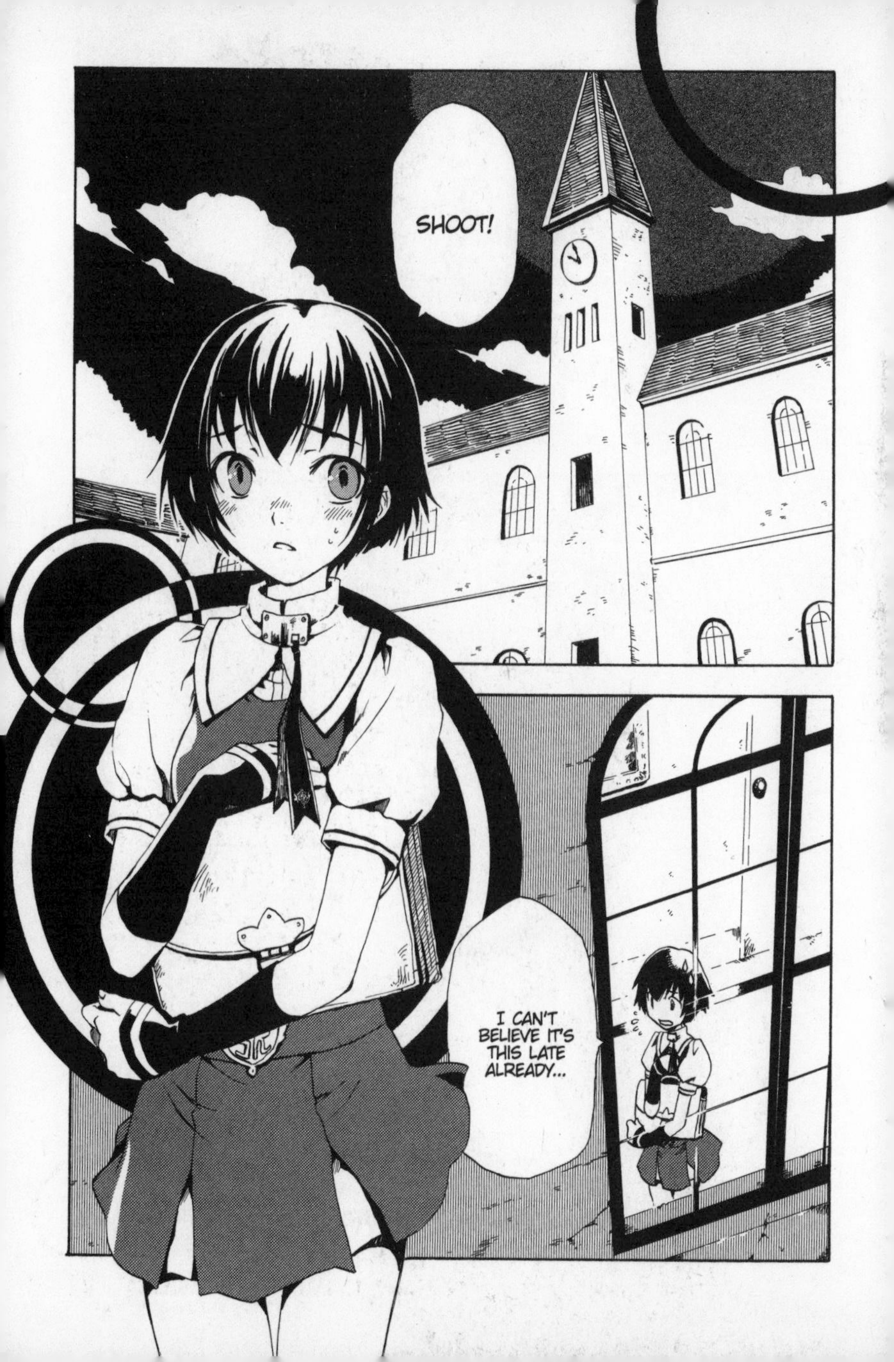
SHOOT!
I CAN'T BELIEVE IT'S THIS LATE ALREADY...

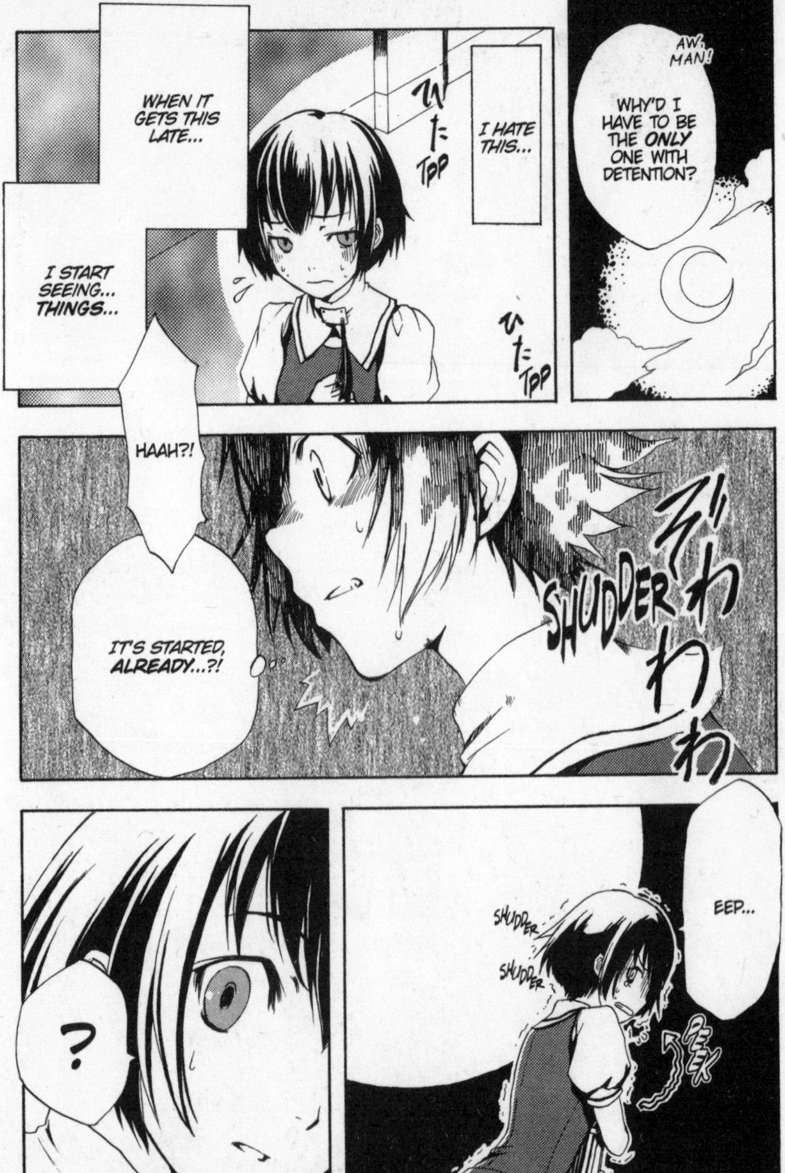
AW, MAN!
WHY'D I HAVE TO BE THE ONLY ONE WITH DETENTION?
ひた TPP
I HATE THIS...
WHEN IT GETS THIS LATE...
ひた TPP
I START SEEING... THINGS...
HAAH?!
ざわわわ SHUDDER
IT'S STARTED, ALREADY...?!
EEP...
SHUDDER
SHUDDER
PEEK
?

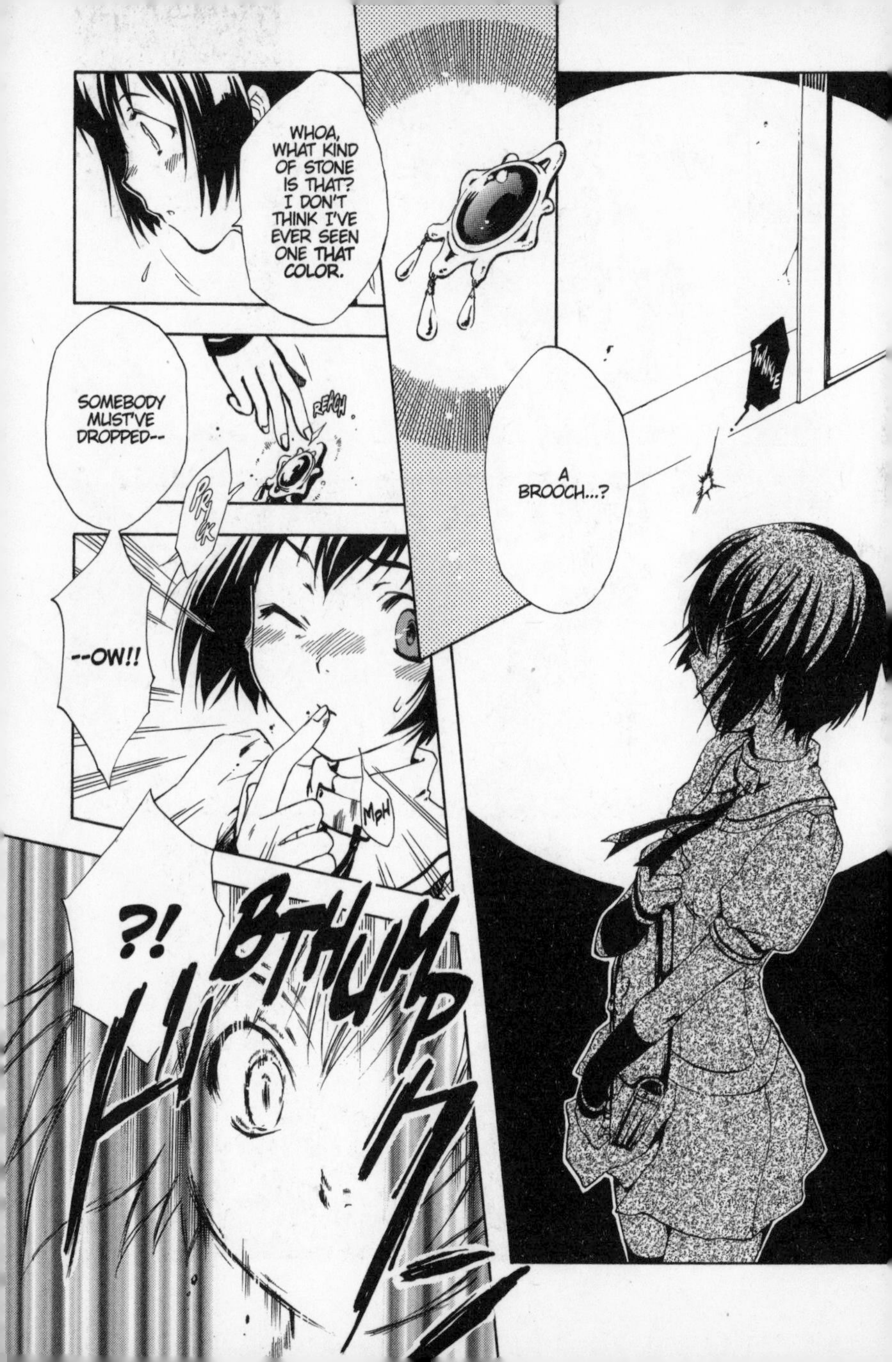
TWINKLE
A BROOCH...?
WHOA, WHAT KIND OF STONE IS THAT? I DON'T THINK I'VE EVER SEEN ONE THAT COLOR.
REACH
SOMEBODY MUST'VE DROPPED--
PRICK
--OW!!
MPH
?!
BTHUMP

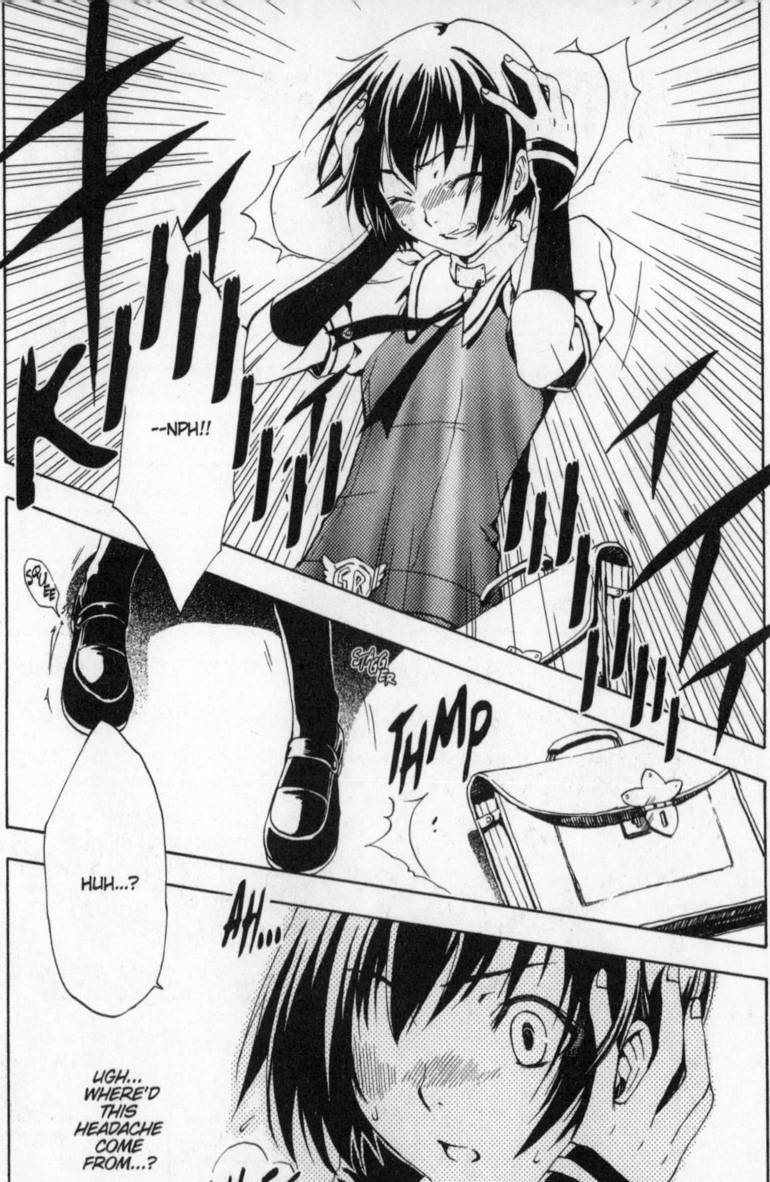
--NPH!!
STAGGER
SQUEE
THMP
HUH...?
AH...
UGH... WHERE'D THIS HEADACHE COME FROM...?
HFF

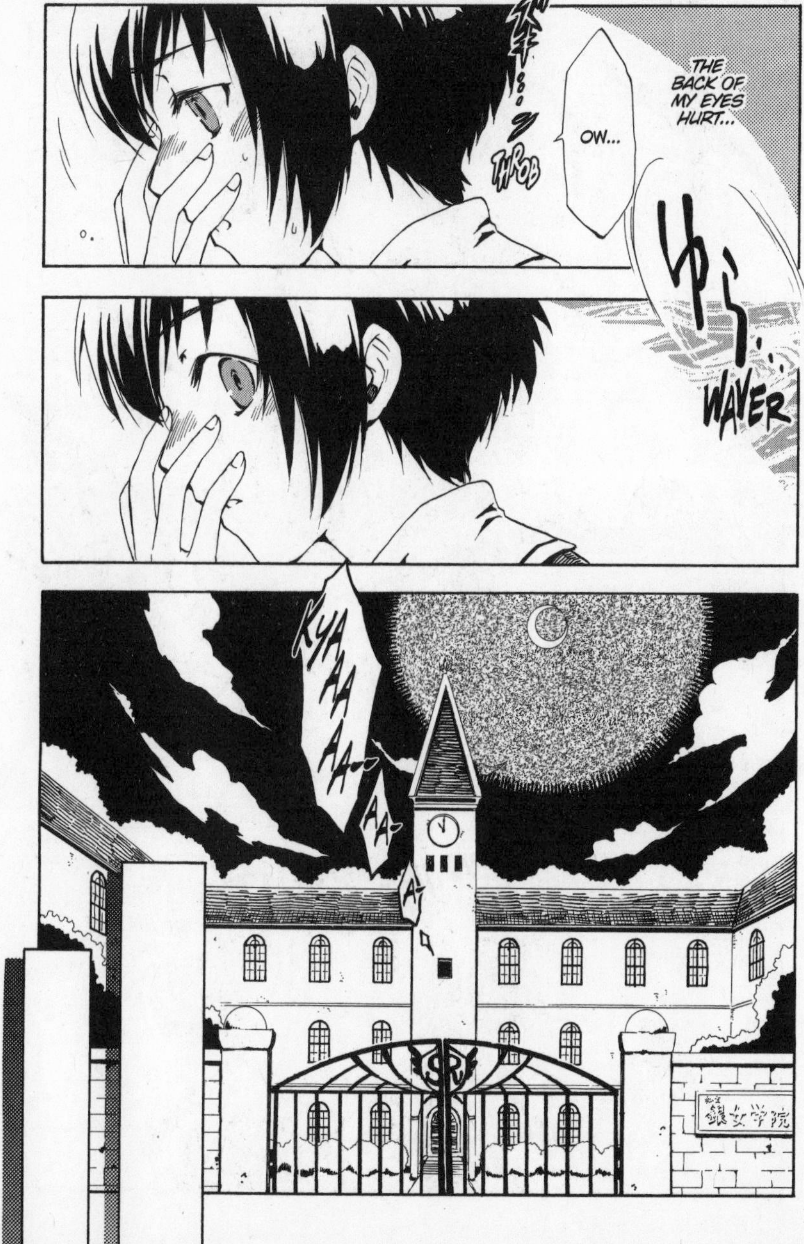
THE BACK OF MY EYES HURT...
OW...
THROB
ゆら
WAVER
KYAAAAAA- AA- A-
銀女学院

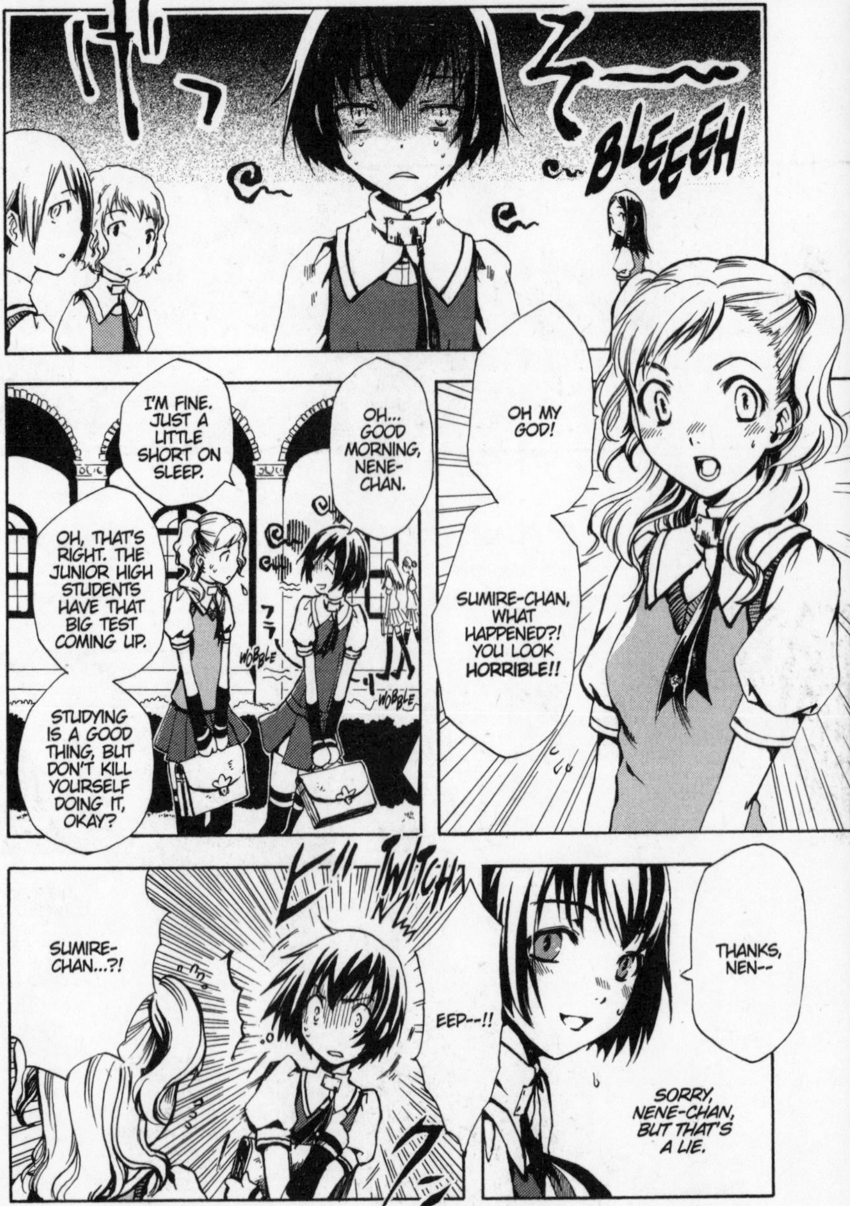
BLEEEH
OH MY GOD!
SUMIRE-CHAN, WHAT HAPPENED?! YOU LOOK HORRIBLE!!
OH... GOOD MORNING, NENE-CHAN.
I'M FINE. JUST A LITTLE SHORT ON SLEEP.
WOBBLE
WOBBLE
OH, THAT'S RIGHT. THE JUNIOR HIGH STUDENTS HAVE THAT BIG TEST COMING UP.
STUDYING IS A GOOD THING, BUT DON'T KILL YOURSELF DOING IT, OKAY?
THANKS, NEN--
SORRY, NENE-CHAN, BUT THAT'S A LIE.
TWITCH
EEP--!!
SUMIRE-CHAN...?!

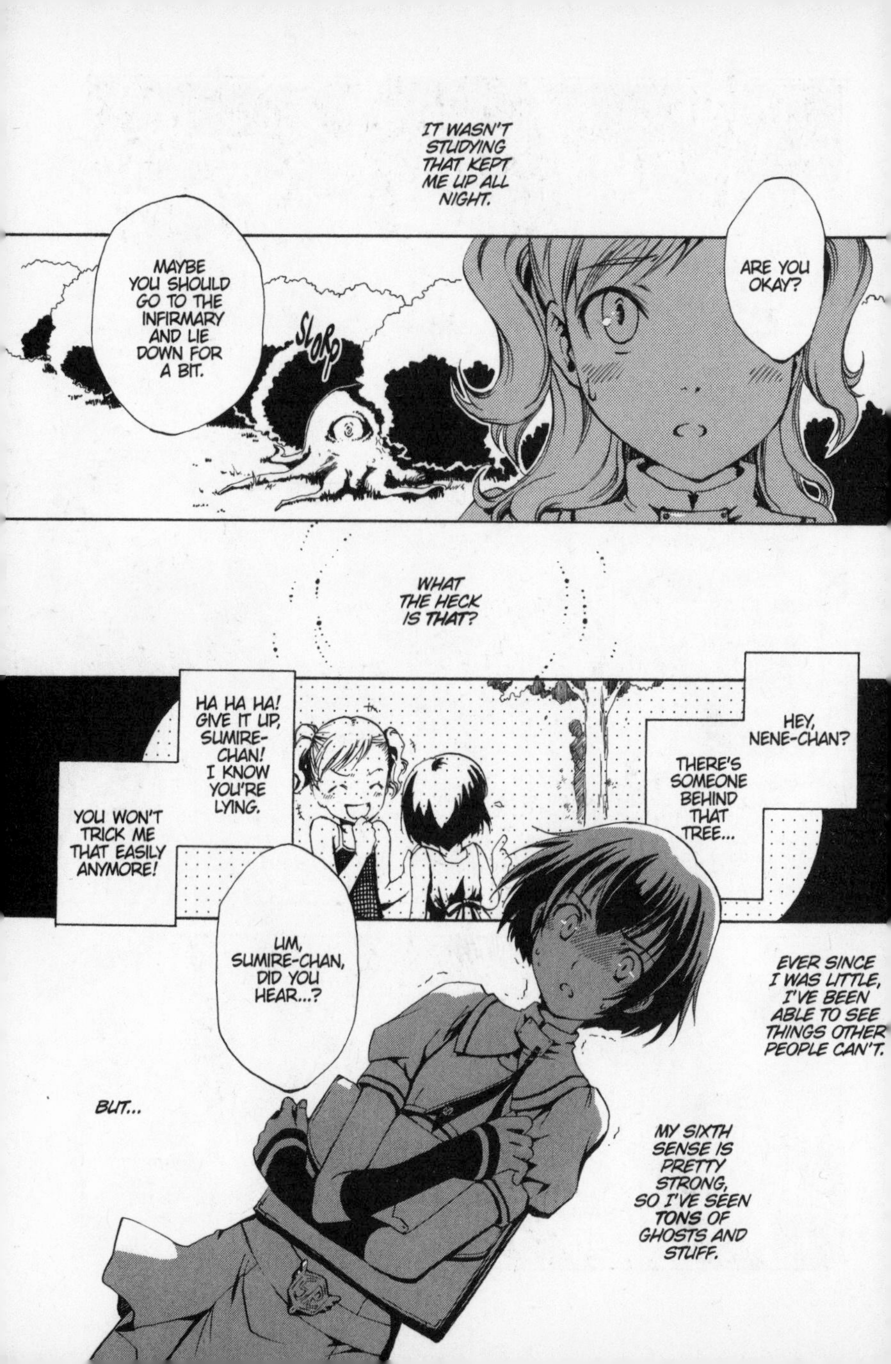
IT WASN'T STUDYING THAT KEPT ME UP ALL NIGHT.
ARE YOU OKAY?
SLORP
MAYBE YOU SHOULD GO TO THE INFIRMARY AND LIE DOWN FOR A BIT.
WHAT THE HECK IS THAT?
HEY, NENE-CHAN?
THERE'S SOMEONE BEHIND THAT TREE...
HA HA HA! GIVE IT UP, SUMIRE-CHAN! I KNOW YOU'RE LYING.
YOU WON'T TRICK ME THAT EASILY ANYMORE!
EVER SINCE I WAS LITTLE, I'VE BEEN ABLE TO SEE THINGS OTHER PEOPLE CAN'T.
MY SIXTH SENSE IS PRETTY STRONG, SO I'VE SEEN TONS OF GHOSTS AND STUFF.
UM, SUMIRE-CHAN, DID YOU HEAR...?
BUT...

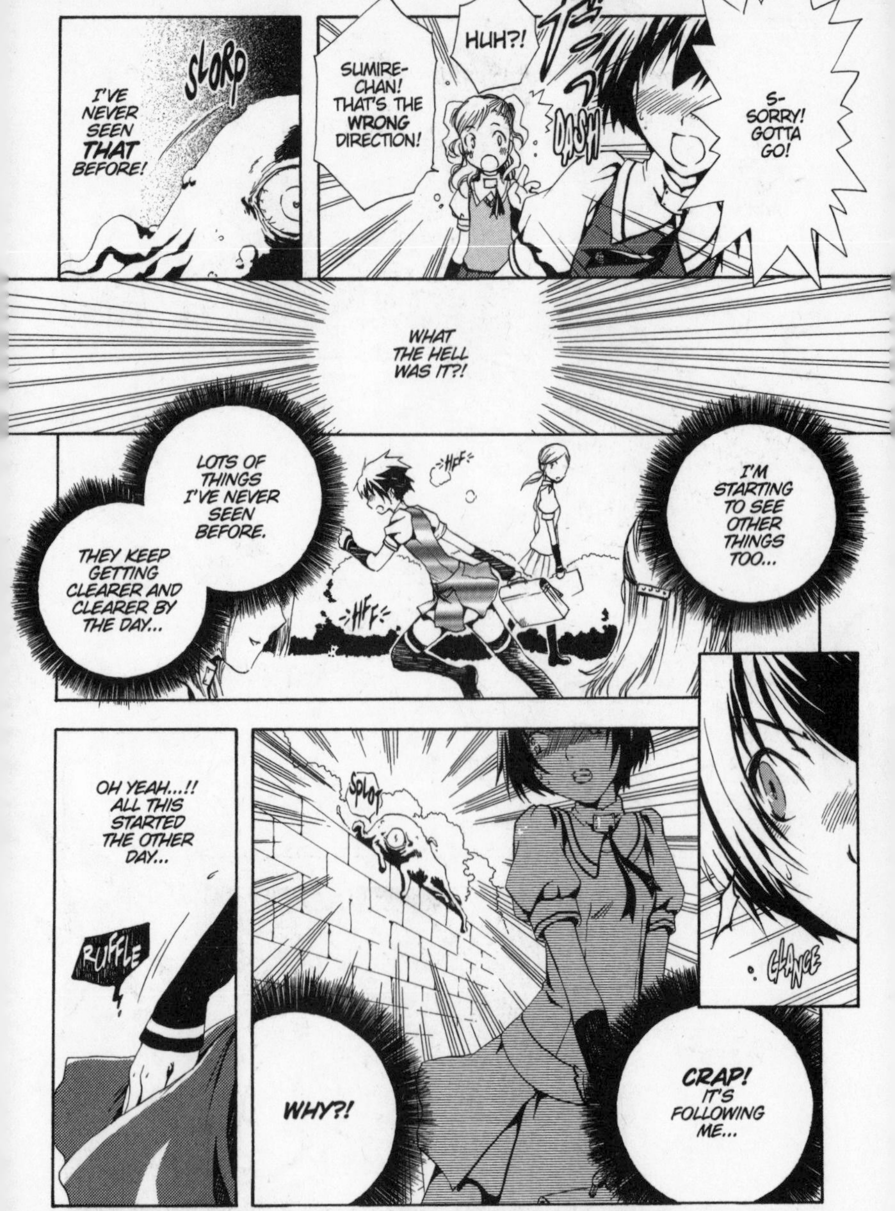
S-SORRY! GOTTA GO!
HUH?!
SUMIRE-CHAN! THAT'S THE WRONG DIRECTION!
DASH
SLORP
I'VE NEVER SEEN THAT BEFORE!
WHAT THE HELL WAS IT?!
I'M STARTING TO SEE OTHER THINGS TOO...
HFF
LOTS OF THINGS I'VE NEVER SEEN BEFORE.
THEY KEEP GETTING CLEARER AND CLEARER BY THE DAY...
HFF
GLANCE
SPLOT
CRAP! IT'S FOLLOWING ME...
WHY?!
OH YEAH...!! ALL THIS STARTED THE OTHER DAY...
RUFFLE

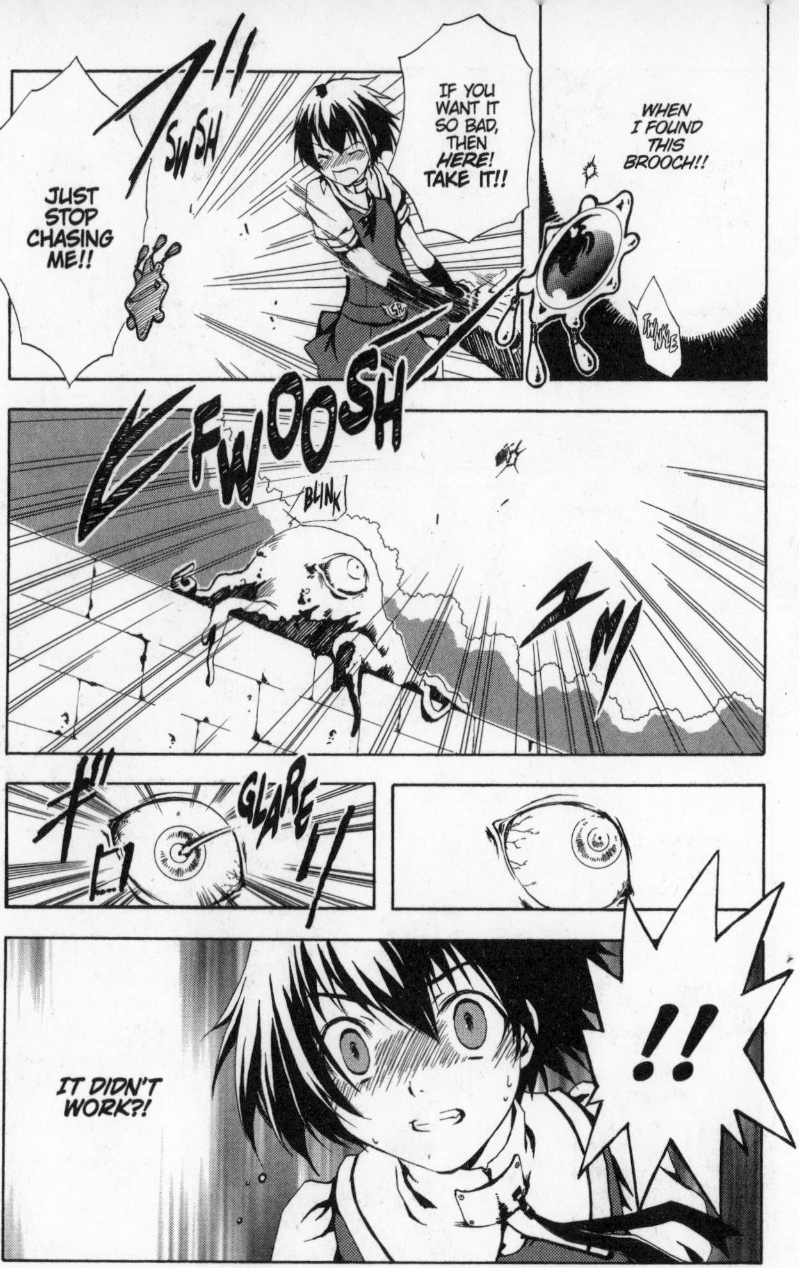
WHEN I FOUND THIS BROOCH!!
TWINKLE
IF YOU WANT IT SO BAD, THEN HERE! TAKE IT!!
SWISH
JUST STOP CHASING ME!!
FWOOSH
BLINK
GLARE!!
!!
IT DIDN'T WORK?!

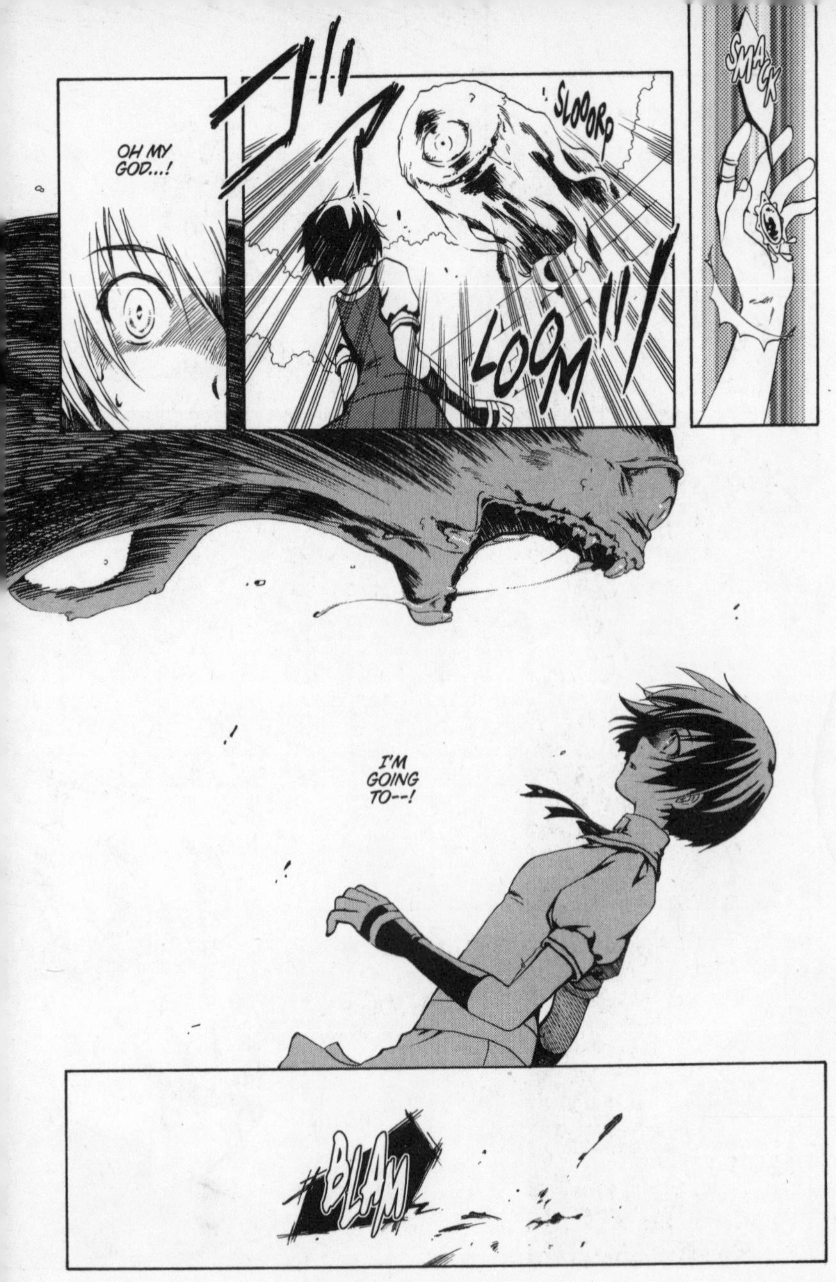
SMACK
SLOOORP
LOOM!!
OH MY GOD...!
I'M GOING TO--!
BLAM

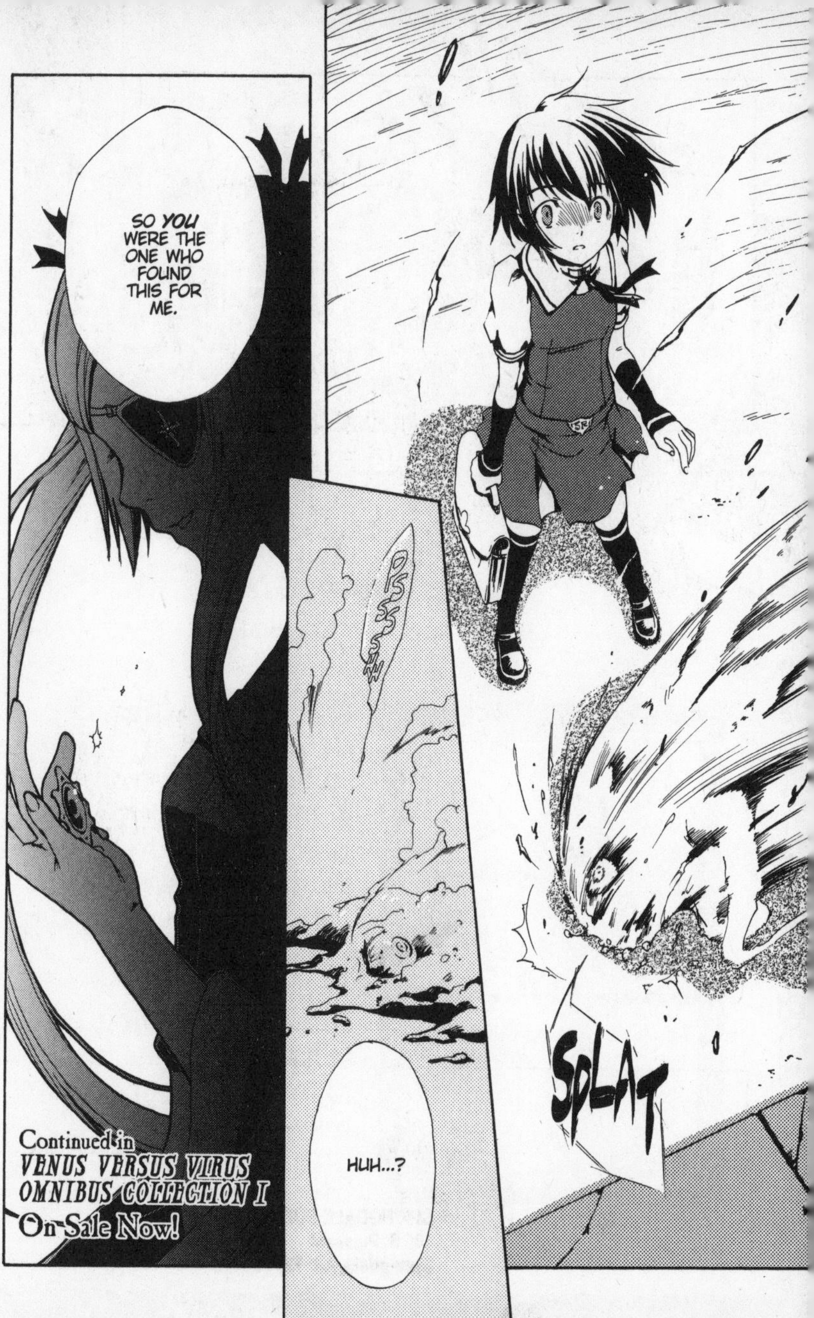
!
SPLAT
PSSSHH
HUH...?
SO YOU WERE THE ONE WHO FOUND THIS FOR ME.

Continued in
VENUS VERSUS VIRUS
OMNIBUS COLLECTION I
On Sale Now!

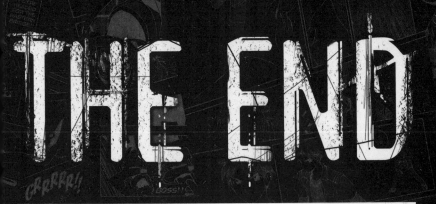

YOU'RE READING THE WRONG WAY

AG 0 1 '16

This is the last page of
Gunslinger Girl
Omnibus Collection 1

This book reads from right to left, Japanese style. To read from the beginning, flip the book over to the other side, start with the top right panel, and take it from there.

If this is your first time reading manga, just follow the diagram. It may seem backwards at first, but you'll get used to it! Have fun!